The Zohar

by
Rav Shimon bar Yochai
From The Book of Avraham

with
The Sulam Commentary

by
Rav Yehuda Ashlag

The First Ever Unabridged
English Translation with Commentary

Published by
The Kabbalah Centre International Inc.
Dean Rav S. P. Berg Shlita

Edited and Compiled by
Rabbi Michael Berg

Published by
The Kabbalah Centre International Inc.

155 E. 48th St., New York, NY 10017
1062 S. Robertson Blvd., Los Angeles, CA 90035

Director Rav Berg

First Printing 2001
Revised Edition 2008

Printed in USA

ISBN: 1-57189-188-9

APPLYING THE POWER OF THE ZOHAR

The Zohar is a book of great mystical power and wisdom. It is Universally recognized as the definitive work on the Kabbalah – and it is also so Much more.

The Zohar is a wellspring of spiritual energy, a fountainhead of metaphysical power that not only reveals and explains, but literally brings blessing, protection, and well-being into the lives of all those who read or peruse its sacred texts. All that is required is worthy desire, the certainty of a trusting heart, and an open and receptive mind. Unlike other books, including the great spiritual texts of other traditions, The Zohar is written in a kind of code, through which metaphors, parables, and cryptic language at first conceal but ultimately reveal the forces of creation.

As electrical current is concealed in wire and cable before disclosing itself as an illuminated light bulb, the spiritual Light of the Creator is wrapped in allegory and symbolism throughout the Aramaic text of the Zohar. And while many books contain information and knowledge, the Zohar both expresses and embodies spiritual Light. The very letters on its pages have the power to bring spiritual wisdom and positive energy into every area of our lives.

As we visually scan the Aramaic texts and study the accompanying insights that appear in English, spiritual power is summoned from above – and worlds tremble as Light is sent forth in response.

It's primary purpose is not only to help us acquire wisdom, but to draw Light from the Upper Worlds and to bring sanctification into our lives. Indeed, the book itself is the most powerful of all tools for cleansing the soul and connecting to the Light of the Creator. As you open these pages, therefore, do not make understanding in the conventional sense your primary goal.

Although you may not have a knowledge of Aramaic, look first at the Aramaic text before reading the English. Do not be discouraged by difficulties with comprehension. Instead, open your heart to the spiritual transformation the Zohar is offering you.

Ultimately, the Zohar is an instrument for refining the individual soul – for removing darkness from the earth – and for bringing well being and blessing to our fellow man.

Its purpose is not only to make us intellectually wise, but to make us spiritually pure.

Torah

Also known as the Five Books of Moses, the Torah is considered to be the physical body of learning, whereas the Zohar is the internal soul. The literal stories of the Torah conceal countless hidden secrets.` The Zohar is the Light that illuminates all of the Torah's sublime mysteries.

Beresheet	Genesis
Shemot	Exodus
Vayikra	Leviticus
Bemidbar	Numbers
Devarim	Deuteronomy

Prophets

Amos	Amos
Chagai	Haggai
Chavakuk	Habakkuk
Hoshea	Hosea
Malachi	Malachi
Melachim	Kings
Michah	Micah
Nachum	Nahum
Ovadyah	Obadiah
Shmuel	Samuel
Shoftim	Judges
Tzefanyah	Zephaniah
Yechezkel	Ezekiel
Yehoshua	Joshua
Yeshayah	Isaiah
Yirmeyah	Jeremiah
Yoel	Joel
Yonah	Jonah
Zecharyah	Zechariah

Writings

Daniel	Daniel
Divrei Hayamim	Chronicles
Eicha	Lamentations
Ester	Esther
Ezra	Ezra
Nechemiah	Nehemiah
Iyov	Job
Kohelet	Ecclesiastes
Mishlei	Proverbs
Rut	Ruth

Sir Hashirim	Songs of Songs
Tehilim	Psalms

The Ten Sfirot – Emanations

To conceal the blinding *Light* of the Upper World, and thus create a tiny point into which our universe would be born, ten *curtains* were fabricated. These ten *curtains* are called Ten Sfirot. Each successive Sfirah further reduces the emanation of *Light*, gradually dimming its brilliance to a level almost devoid of *Light* – our physical world known as *Malchut*. The only remnant of Light remaining in this darkened universe is a *pilot light* which sustains our existence. This Light is the life force of a human being and the force that gives birth to stars, sustains suns and sets everything from swirling galaxies to busy ant hills in motion. Moreover, the Ten Sfirot act like a prism, refracting the Light into many *colors* giving rise to the diversity of life and matter in our world.

The Ten Sfirot are as follows:

Keter	Crown
Chochmah	Wisdom
Binah	Understanding
Da'at	Knowledge
Zeir Anpin	Small Face,
	(includes the next six Sfirot):
Chesed	Mercy (Chassadim - plural)
Gvurah	Judgment (Gvurot - Plural)
Tiferet	Splendor
Netzach	Victory (Eternity)
Hod	Glory
Yesod	Foundation
Malchut	Kingdom

The Partzufim - Spiritual forms

One complete structure of the Ten Sfirot creates a *Partzuf* or Spiritual Form. Together, these forces are the building blocks of all reality. As water and sand combine to create cement, the Ten Sfirot combine to produce a Spiritual Form [*Partzuf*]. Each of the Spiritual Forms below are therefore composed of one set of Ten Sfirot.

These Spiritual Forms are called:

Atik	Ancient
Atik Yomin	Ancient of Days
Atika Kadisha	Holy Ancient
Atik of Atikin	Anceint of Ancients
Aba	Father
Arich Anpin	Long Face
Ima	Mother
Nukva	Female
Tevunah	Intelligence
Yisrael Saba	Israel Grandfather
Zachar	Male

These names are not meant to be understood literally. Each represents a unique spiritual force and building block, producing a substructure and foundation for all the worlds make up reality.

The Five Worlds

All of the above Spiritual Forms [*Partzufim*] create one spiritual world. There are Five Worlds in total that compose all reality, therefore, five sets of the above Spiritual Forms are required.

Our physical world corresponds to the world of: Asiyah – Action

Adam Kadmon	Primordial Man
Atzilut	Emanation
Briyah	Creation
Yetzirah	Formation
Asiyah	Action

The Five Levels of the soul

Nefesh	First, Lowest level of Soul
Ruach	Second level of Soul
Neshamah	Third level of Soul
Chayah	Fourth level of Soul
Yechidah	Highest, fifth level of Soul

Names of God

As a single ray of white sunlight contains the seven colors of the spectrum, the one Light of the Creator embodies many diverse spiritual forces. These different forces are called *Names of God*. Each Name denotes a specific attribute and spiritual power. The Hebrew letters that compose these Names are the interface by which these varied Forces act upon our physical world. The most common Name of God is the Tetragrammaton (the four letters, *Yud Hei Vav Hei* יהוה.) Because of the enormous power that the Tetragrammaton transmits, we do not utter it aloud. When speaking of the Tetragrammaton, we use the term *Hashem* which means, *The Name.*

Adonai, El, Elohim, Hashem, Shadai, Eheyeh, Tzevaot, Yud Hei Vav Hei

People

Er	The son of Noach
Rabbi Elazar	The son of Rabbi Shimon bar Yochai
Rabbi Shimon bar Yochai	Author of the Zohar
Shem, Cham, Yefet	Noach's children
Shet	Seth
Ya'akov	Jacob
Yishai	Jesse (King David's father)
Yitzchak	Isaac
Yosef	Joseph
Yitro	Jethro
Yehuda	Judah

Angels

Angels are distinct energy components, part of a vast communication network running through the upper worlds. Each unique Angel is responsible for transmitting various forces of influence into our physical universe.

Adriel, Ahinael, Dumah (name of Angel in charge of the dead), Gabriel, Kadshiel, Kedumiel, Metatron, Michael, Rachmiel,

Raphael, Tahariel, Uriel

Nations

Nations actually represent the inner attributes and character traits of our individual self. The nation of Amalek refers to the doubt and uncertainty that dwells within us when we face hardship and obstacles. Moab represents the dual nature of man. Nefilim refers to the sparks of Light that we have defiled through our impure actions, and to the negative forces that lurk within the human soul as a result of our own wrongful deeds.

Amalek, Moab, Nefilim

General

Aba	Father
	Refers to the male principle and positive force in our universe. Correlates to the proton in an atom.
Arvit	The Evening prayer
Chayot	Animals
Chupah	Canopy (wedding ceremony)
Et	The
Avadon	Hell
Gehenom	Hell
Sheol	Hell
	The place a soul goes for purification upon leaving this world.
Ima	Mother
	The female principle and minus force in our universe. Correlates to the electron in an atom.
Kiddush	Blessing over the wine
Klipah	Shell (negativity)
Klipot	Shells (Plural)
Kriat Sh'ma	The Reading of the Sh'ma
Mashiach	Messiah
Minchah	The Afternoon prayer
Mishnah	Study
Mochin	Brain, Spiritual levels of Light
Moed	A designated time or holiday
Negev	The south of Israel
Nukva	Female

Partzuf	Face
Shacharit	The Morning prayer
Shamayim	Heavens (sky)
Shechinah	The Divine presence, The female aspect of the Creator
Tefilin	Phylacteries
The Dinur river	The river of fire
Tzadik	Righteous person
Zion	Another name for Jerusalem
Yisrael	The land of Israel
	The nation of Israel or an individual Israelite
Zohar	Splendor

The Hebrew vowels

Chirik **א**, Cholam **אֹ א**, Kamatz **אָ**, Patach **אַ**, Segol **אֶ**, Sh'va **אְ**, Shuruk **אֻ א**, Tzere **אֵ**.

The Twelve Tribes

Asher, Dan, Ephraim, Gad, Issachar, Judah, Levi, Menasheh, Naphtali, Reuben, Shimon, Zebulun

Jewish Holidays

Rosh Hashanah	The Jewish New Year
Yom Kippur	Day of Atonement
Sukkot	Holiday of the Booths
Shmini Atzeret	The day of Convocation
Simchat Torah	Holiday on which we dance with the Torah
Pesach	Passover
Shavout	Holiday of the Weeks

כרך טז

פרשת קדושים, אמור, בהר, בחוקותי

Vol. XVI

Kedoshim, Emor, Behar, Bechukotai

A Prayer from The Ari

To be recited before the study of the Zohar

Ruler of the universe, and Master of all masters, The Father of mercy and forgiveness, we thank You, our God and the God of our fathers, by bowing down and kneeling, that You brought us closer to Your Torah and Your holy work, and You enable us to take part in the secrets of Your holy Torah. How worthy are we that You grant us with such big favor, that is the reason we plead before You, that You will forgive and acquit all our sins, and that they should not bring separation between You and us.

And may it be your will before You, our God and the God of our fathers, that You will awaken and prepare our hearts to love and revere You, and may You listen to our utterances, and open our closed heart to the hidden studies of Your Torah, and may our study be pleasant before Your Place of Honor, as the aroma of sweet incense, and may You emanate to us Light from the source of our soul to all of our being. And, may the sparks of your holy servants, through which you revealed Your wisdom to the world, shine.

May their merit and the merit of their fathers, and the merit of their Torah, and holiness, support us so we shall not stumble through our study. And by their merit enlighten our eyes in our learning as it stated by King David, The Sweet Singer of Israel: "Open my eyes, so that I will see wonders from Your Torah" (Tehilim 119:18). Because from His mouth God gives wisdom and understanding.

"May the utterances of my mouth and the thoughts of my heart find favor before You, God, my Strength and my Redeemer" (Tehilim 19:15).

KEDOSHIM

Names of the articles

1. "You shall be holy"

A Synopsis

Rabbi Elazar begins by saying that on the day of heavenly judgment people will be found defective because they did not pay any attention to the Torah. He adds that it is forbidden to associate with people who lack the Faith. And as for those who are not in a state of holiness at the time of intercourse, they will produce offspring whose souls come from the side of defilement.

א. וַיְדַבֵּר יְיָ׳ אֶל מֹשֶׁה לֵּאמֹר. דַּבֵּר אֶל כָּל עֲדַת בְּנֵי יִשְׂרָאֵל וְאָמַרְתָּ אֲלֵיהֶם קְדוֹשִׁים תִּהְיוּ כִּי קָדוֹשׁ אֲנִי יְיָ׳ אֱלֹהֵיכֶם. ר׳ אֶלְעָזָר פָּתַח, אַל תִּהְיוּ כְּסוּס כְּפֶרֶד אֵין הָבִין וְגוֹ׳. בְּכַמָּה זִמְנִין אוֹרַיְיתָא אַסְהִידַת בְּהוּ בִּבְנֵי נָשָׁא, כַּמָּה זִמְנִין אֲרִימַת קָלִין, לְכָל סִטְרִין לְאִתְעָרָא לְהוּ, וְכֻלְּהוּ דְּמִיכִין בְּשֵׁינָתָא בְּחוֹבֵיהוֹן, לָא מִסְתַּכְּלִין, וְלָא מַשְׁגִּיחִין, בְּהֵיךְ אַנְפִּין יְקוּמוּן לְיוֹמָא דְּדִינָא עִלָּאָה, כַּד יִתְבַּע לוֹן מַלְכָּא עִלָּאָה עֶלְבּוֹנָא דְּאוֹרַיְיתָא, דִּצְוְוחַת לְקֳבְלֵיהוֹן, וְלָא אַהֲדָרוּ אַנְפִּין לְקַבָּלָה, דְּכֻלְּהוּ פְּגִימִין בְּכֹלָּא, דְּלָא יָדְעוּ מְהֵימְנוּתָא דְּמַלְכָּא עִלָּאָה, וַוי לוֹן, וַוי לְנַפְשֵׁיהוֹן.

1. "And Hashem spoke to Moses saying, 'Speak to all the congregation of the children of Yisrael, and say to them: You shall be holy: for I Hashem your Elohim am Holy" (Vayikra 19:1-2). Rabbi Elazar commenced the discussion: "Be not like the horse, or the mule, which have no understanding ..." (Tehilim 32:9). How many times did the Torah attest to people, how many times did she raise her voice in every direction to awaken them, but all lay sleeping, unaware of their sins. They do not look or pay attention to the time when they will rise up to face the day of heavenly Judgment. At this time, the Heavenly King will exact from them the shame of the Torah that cried out against them, and yet they did not even turn their face to her. All are found totally defective since they do not know of the Faith of the Heavenly King. Woe to them, and woe to their souls.

ב. דְּהָא אוֹרַיְיתָא בֵּיהּ אַסְהִידַת, וְאָמְרַת מִי פֶתִי יָסוּר הֵנָּה חֲסַר לֵב אָמְרָה לּוֹ. מַהוּ חֲסַר לֵב. דְּלֵית לֵיהּ מְהֵימְנוּתָא, דְּמַאן דְּלָא אִשְׁתַּדַּל בְּאוֹרַיְיתָא, לָאו בֵּיהּ מְהֵימְנוּתָא, וּפְגִים הוּא מִכֹּלָּא אָמְרָה לּוֹ, אוֹמְרָה

לוֹ מִבְּעֵי לֵיהּ, כד״א אוֹמְרָה לְאֵל סַלְעִי, מַהוּ אָמָרְה. אֶלָּא לְאַכְלְלָא וּלְאִתּוֹסְפָא אוֹרַיְיתָא דְלְעֵילָא, דְּהִיא קַרְיֵיהּ לֵיהּ חֲסַר לֵב, פָּגִים מִמְּהֵימְנוּתָא.

2. For the Torah attests to him and says, "Whoever is simple, let him turn in here: as for he that lacks understanding, she says to him…" (Mishlei 9:4). Who is meant by, "he that lacks understanding"? THIS MEANS one who has no Faith, and is defective in every respect. HE QUESTIONS: Why is it written, "she says to him," when it should read, 'I say to him', as the verse says, "I will say to El my rock…" (Tehilim 42:10). So why does it say here, "she says"? HE ANSWERS: It wishes to include and add the supernal Torah, which also calls him, "he that lacks understanding," MEANING defective in Faith.

3. דְּהָכִי תְּנֵינָן, כָּל מָאן דְּלָא אִשְׁתָּדַל בְּאוֹרַיְיתָא, אָסִיר לְמִקְרַב לְגַבֵּיהּ, לְאִשְׁתַּתְּפָא בַּהֲדֵיהּ, וּלְמֶעְבַּד בֵּיהּ סְחוֹרְתָּא, וְכ״שׁ לְמֵהַךְ עִמֵּיהּ בְּאוֹרְחָא. דְּהָא לֵית בֵּיהּ מְהֵימְנוּתָא. תְּנֵינָן כָּל ב״נ דְּאָזִיל בְּאוֹרְחָא, וְלֵית עִמֵּיהּ מִלֵּי דְאוֹרַיְיתָא, אִתְחַיָּיב בְּנַפְשֵׁיהּ. כ״שׁ מָאן דְּאִזְדַּוָּוג בְּאוֹרְחָא, עִם מָאן דְּלֵית בֵּיהּ מְהֵימְנוּתָא, דְּלָא חָשִׁיב לִיקָרָא דְמָארֵיהּ וְדִידֵיהּ דְּלָא חָס עַל נַפְשֵׁיהּ.

3. We have learned this: it is forbidden to approach all who fail to toil in Torah, and it is forbidden to be partners with him or do business with him, and one must surely not travel with him on the way, since he lacks Faith. We learned that one who walks along the road without mentioning words of Torah endangers his life. This is all the more the case for he who befriends on the road someone who lacks Faith, BECAUSE he himself does not properly honor his Master, nor even his own, as he shows a lack of concern for his own life.

4. רִבִּי יְהוּדָה אוֹמֵר, מָאן דְּלָא חָס עַל נַפְשֵׁיהּ, הֵיךְ יִשְׁלוֹף נַפְשָׁא דְּכַשְׁרָא לִבְרֵיהּ. א״ר אֶלְעָזָר, תַּוְוהֲנָא עַל דָּרָא, וְהָא אִתְּמַר מִלָּה וְכוּ׳. וְעַל דָּא כְּתִיב אַל תִּהְיוּ כְּסוּס כְּפֶרֶד אֵין הָבִין. זַכָּאִין אִינּוּן צַדִּיקַיָּיא,

דְּמִשְׁתַּדְּלֵי בְּאוֹרַיְתָא, וְיַדְעִין אוֹרְחוֹי דְּקוּדְשָׁא בְּרִיךְ הוּא, וּמְקַדְּשֵׁי גַּרְמַיְיהוּ בְּקוּדְשָׁא דְּמַלְכָּא, וְאִשְׁתְּכָחוּ קַדִּישִׁין בְּכֹלָּא, וּבְג"כ מִשְׁלְפֵי רוּחָא דְּקוּדְשָׁא מִלְּעֵילָא, וּבְנַיְיהוּ כֻּלְּהוּ זַכָּאֵי קְשׁוֹט, וְאִקְרוּן בְּנֵי מַלְכָּא בְּנִין קַדִּישִׁין.

4. Rabbi Yehuda said: How will he who shows no concern for his own life, NAMELY, BY ASSOCIATING WITH ONE LACKING FAITH, draw a proper soul to his son? Rabbi Elazar said: I wonder about this generation, and this matter was discussed. About this it is written: "Be not like the horse, or the mule, which have no understanding" (Tehilim 32:9). Happy are the righteous who strive in the Torah and know the ways of the Holy One, blessed be He, and sanctify themselves with the sanctity of the King. They are in a total state of holiness. For this reason they attract a spirit of Holiness from above. Their children are truly righteous and are called 'the children of the King', 'holy children'.

5. וַוי לְהוֹן לְרַשִׁיעַיָּיא, דְּכֻלְּהוּ חֲצִיפִין, וְעוֹבָדַיְיהוּ חֲצִיפִין. בְּגִינֵי כָךְ יַרְתִין בְּנַיְיהוּ נַפְשָׁא חֲצִיפָא, מִסִּטְרָא דִּמְסָאֲבָא. כְּמָה דִּכְתִיב וְנִטְמֵתֶם בָּם, אָתָא לְאִסְתָּאֲבָא, מְסָאֲבִין לֵיהּ. אַל תִּהְיוּ כְּסוּס כְּפֶרֶד, דְּאִינּוּן מָארֵי זְנוּתָא עַל כֹּלָּא. אֵין הָבִין, דְּלָא יִשְׁתַּדְּלוּן בְּנֵי נָשָׁא בְּאָרְחָא דָא, דְּאִי הָכֵי, כְּתִיב הָכָא אֵין הָבִין. וּכְתִיב הָתָם וְהַכְּלָבִים עַזֵּי נֶפֶשׁ לֹא יָדְעוּ שָׂבְעָה וְהֵמָּה רוֹעִים לֹא יָדְעוּ הָבִין. כְּלוֹמַר יֵהוֹן מִזְדַּמְּנִין אִינּוּן דְּאִקְרוּן עַזֵּי נֶפֶשׁ. מַאי טַעֲמָא. מִשּׁוּם דְּלָא יָדְעוּ הָבִין.

5. Woe be to evildoers who are brazen and act with insolence AT TIMES OF INTERCOURSE. For this reason, their offspring acquire a brazen soul from the Side of Defilement, as it is written, "that you should be defiled by them" (Vayikra 11:43). He who seeks to become unclean is made unclean. "Be not like the horse, or the mule," as these animals are very loose in morality, more than all other CREATURES. "…which have no understanding…", for people of this sort do not try TO UNDERSTAND this way. It is written, "which have no understanding," and in another place, "Yea, the dogs are greedy [in soul], they never have enough, and they are shepherds that cannot understand" (Yeshayah 56:11). This means that JUST AS THEY ARE

GREEDY IN THEIR SOUL, ALSO HERE it reveals that they will prepare for themselves CHILDREN who will be called 'greedy in their souls'. For what reason? Because they "cannot understand."

6. וַהֲמָה רוֹעִים, מַאי רוֹעִים, אִלֵּין אִינּוּן מַדְבְּרֵי וּמַנְהִגֵי לב״נ בַּגֵּיהִנָּם, לֹא יָדְעוּ שָׂבְעָה, כד״א לַעֲלוּקָה שְׁתֵּי בָנוֹת הַב הַב, בְּג״כ דְּאִינּוּן הַב הַב, לָא יָדְעוּ שָׂבְעָה. כֻּלָּם לְדַרְכָּם פָּנוּ אִישׁ לְבִצְעוֹ מִקָּצֵהוּ. דְּהָא תַּיָּירֵי דְגֵיהִנָּם אִינּוּן. וְכָל דָּא מַאן גָּרִים לְהוּ. בְּגִין דְּלָא אִתְקַדְּשׁוּ בְּהַהוּא זוּוּגָא כְּמָה דְּאִצְטְרִיךְ. וְעַ״ד כְּתִיב, קְדוֹשִׁים תִּהְיוּ כִּי קָדוֹשׁ אֲנִי יְיָ'. אָמַר קוּדְשָׁא בְּרִיךְ הוּא, מִכָּל שְׁאָר עַמִּין לָא רַעֲיָתִי לְאַדְבְּקָא בִּי, אֶלָּא יִשְׂרָאֵל, דִּכְתִיב, וְאַתֶּם הַדְּבֵקִים בַּיְיָ', אַתּוּן, וְלָא שְׁאָר עַמִּין. בְּג״כ, קְדוֹשִׁים תִּהְיוּ דַּיְיקָא.

6. "And they are shepherds." HE QUESTIONS: Who are these shepherds? AND ANSWERS: These are those who guide and lead people to Gehenom. "They never have enough," JUST AS the verse that says: "The leech," NAMELY GEHENOM, "has two daughters, crying, 'Give, give'" (Mishlei 30:15). Because they SAY "Give, give," then, "they never have enough;" "they all look to their own way, every one for his gain, from his quarter" (Yeshayah 56:11), since they seek out Gehenom. What caused all this? It is because they did not sanctify themselves at mating as much as they should have. Therefore, it is written: "You shall be holy: for I Hashem your Elohim am Holy." The Holy One, blessed be He, says, 'From all nations I wanted only Yisrael to cling to Me,' as it is written: "But you that did cleave of Hashem" (Devarim 4:4); you, not the other nations. For this reason, "You shall be holy," indeed.

2. "O land of buzzing wings"

A Synopsis

Rabbi Yitzchak says that when God created the world He wanted to reveal matters of depth from among concealed matters, and so light came forth from darkness, evil came forth from good, Judgment came from Mercy, all were intermingled and interdependent. Thus when the world is judged, judgment is tempered with mercy, otherwise the world could not survive.

7. קְדוֹשִׁים תִּהְיוּ כִּי קָדוֹשׁ אֲנִי יְיָ. רַבִּי יִצְחָק פָּתַח, הוֹי אֶרֶץ צִלְצַל כְּנָפָיִם וְגוֹ'. וְכִי בְּגִין דְּהִיא אֶרֶץ צִלְצַל כְּנָפַיִם, קִנְטוּרָא בֵּיהּ אִשְׁתְּכַח, דִּכְתִיב הוֹי אֶרֶץ. אֶלָּא אָמַר רַבִּי יִצְחָק, בְּשַׁעֲתָא דְּקוּדְשָׁא בְּרִיךְ הוּא בָּרָא עָלְמָא, וּבָעָא לְגַלָּאָה עֲמִיקְתָא מִגּוֹ מִסְתַּרְתָּא, וּנְהוֹרָא מִגּוֹ חֲשׁוֹכָא, הֲווֹ כְּלִילָן דָּא בְּדָא, וּבְגִין כָּךְ, מִגּוֹ חֲשׁוֹכָא נָפַק נְהוֹרָא, וּמִגּוֹ מִסְתַּרְתָּא נָפַק וְאִתְגַּלְיָיא עֲמִיקָא, וְדָא נָפְקָא מִן דָּא. דְּמִגּוֹ טַב, נָפִיק בִּישׁ. וּמִגּוֹ רַחֲמֵי, נָפִיק דִּינָא. וְכֹלָּא אִתְכְּלִיל דָּא בְּדָא. יֵצֶר טוֹב וְיֵצֶר רָע, יְמִינָא וּשְׂמָאלָא, יִשְׂרָאֵל וּשְׁאָר עַמִּין, חִוָּור וְאוּכָם, וְכֹלָּא חַד בְּחַד תַּלְיָא.

7. "You shall be holy: for I Hashem your Elohim am Holy" (Vayikra 19:2). Rabbi Yitzchak commenced: "O (also: 'Woe') land of buzzing wings..." (Yeshayah 18:1). HE QUESTIONS: Just because it is a land of buzzing wings, is that such a cause for alarm that the verse writes, "Woe land"? HE ANSWERS: As Rabbi Yitzchak explained, at the time the Holy One, blessed be He, created the world and wanted to reveal matters of depth from among concealed matters, and light from darkness, these terms were intermingled. For this reason, from darkness came light, and concealment departed and became known as the depth. And this resulted from it. So from good came evil, from Mercy came Judgment. All intermingled, the Good Inclination with the Evil one, right and left, Yisrael and other nations, white and black. Each thing was dependent on the other.

8. תָּאנָא אָמַר ר' יִצְחָק אָמַר ר' יְהוּדָה, כָּל עָלְמָא כֻּלְּהוּ לָא אִתְחֲזֵי, אֶלָּא בְּחַד עֲטִירָא דְּקוּטְפָא דְּקִיטְרוֹי כַּד אִתְּדָּן עָלְמָא בְּדִינָא כְּלִיל

בְּרַחֲמֵי אִתְּדָן. וְאִי לָאו, לָא יָכִיל עָלְמָא לְקַיְּימָא, אֲפִילוּ רִגְעָא חֲדָא, וְהָא אוֹקִימְנָא מִלֵּי, כְּמָה דִּכְתִיב כִּי כַּאֲשֶׁר מִשְׁפָּטֶיךָ לָאָרֶץ צֶדֶק לָמְדוּ יוֹשְׁבֵי תֵבֵל.

8. We learned that Rabbi Yitzchak said on behalf of Rabbi Yehuda: The whole world appears as if in one composition kept together with its own web, MEANING THE QUALITY OF JUDGMENT AND THE QUALITY OF MERCY, BEING MALCHUT AND BINAH, ARE LINKED AND INTERWOVEN WITH ONE ANOTHER. And so, when the world is judged, it is judged with Judgment tempered with Mercy, WITH MALCHUT INCLUDED IN BINAH. Were it not so, the world could not survive even one moment. We established this matter, as it is written, "for when Your judgments (lit. 'justice') are on the earth," NAMELY MERCY, CALLED 'JUSTICE', "the inhabitants of the world learn righteousness" (Yeshayah 26:9). THEY WERE CAPABLE OF RECEIVING THE JUDGMENT OF RIGHTEOUSNESS, BEING MALCHUT, DUE TO ITS CONNECTION TO THE ATTRIBUTE OF MERCY.

9(1). וְתָאנָא בְּהַהוּא זִמְנָא דְּדִינָא תַּלְיָא בְּעָלְמָא, וְצֶדֶק אִתְעֲטְרָא בְּדִינוֹי, כַּמָּה מָארֵי דְגַדְפִּין מִתְעָרֵי, לְקָבְלֵי מָארֵי דְדִינָא קַשְׁיָא, לְשַׁלְטָאָה בְּעָלְמָא. פַּרְסִין גַּדְפִּין מֵהַאי סִטְרָא, וּמֵהַאי סִטְרָא, לְאַשְׁגָּחָא בְּעָלְמָא. כְּדֵין מִתְעָרִין גַּדְפִּין לְמִפְרַס לוֹן, וּלְאִשְׁתַּאֲבָא בְּדִינָא קַשְׁיָא, וְשָׁאטִין בְּעָלְמָא לְאַבְאָשָׁא. כְּדֵין כְּתִיב, הוֹי אֶרֶץ צִלְצַל כְּנָפָיִם.

9a. We learned at that time when Judgment is suspended over the world, and righteousness, MALCHUT, is crowned with Judgment, many winged ones are stirred against the beings of Harsh Judgment, so as to rule the world. They spread their wings from one side, then from the other, to keep watch over the world. Then they raise their wings to spread and join in the Harsh Judgment, and to fly across the earth to do evil. Then it is written, "Woe land of buzzing wings."

9(2). א"ר יְהוּדָה, חֲמֵינָא בְּנֵי עָלְמָא בְּחַצִּיפוּתָא, בַּר אִינוּן זַכָּאֵי קְשׁוֹט. ובג"כ, כִּבְיָכוֹל, כֹּלָּא הָכִי אִשְׁתָּכַח, אָתָא לְאִתְדַּכָּאָה, מְסַיְּיעִין לֵיהּ. אָתָא לְאִסְתַּאֲבָא, כְּמָה דְאוֹקִימְנָא, וְנִטְמֵתֶם בָּם.

-8-

9b. Rabbi Yehuda said: I see Mankind insolent, except for the truly righteous. For this reason, everything is in such a condition, so to speak. He who comes to purify is helped. He who wishes to defile is as we established, "that you should be defiled by them" (Vayikra 11:43).

3. "You shall be holy"

A Synopsis

Rabbi Yosi and Rabbi Chiya say that the words of Torah are superior to all sacrifices, and even one who has had a judgment decreed against him can have his penalty canceled because of his study of Torah. Healing is found in the Torah, and its function is to purify the unclean, as the Torah itself is constantly in a state of purity. There is also a promise that if one studies Torah one shall become holy. Rabbi Yosi says that as men purify themselves below they are purified on high. We read about the time when mating is appropriate, the moment when one is consecrated. Rabbi Aba also talks about when man is called 'one', and the role of the Tefilin in creating this unity. When a man and woman are clinging to one another in body and soul, then God dwells in their unity and gives them a holy spirit for their child.

10. רַבִּי יוֹסֵי הֲוָה אָזִיל בְּאוֹרְחָא, פָּגַע בֵּיה רַבִּי חִיָּיא, אָמַר לֵיה הַאי דְּאוּקְמוּהָ חַבְרַיָּיא, דִּכְתִּיב בְּעֵלִי, וְלָכֵן נִשְׁבַּעְתִּי לְבֵית עֵלִי אִם יִתְכַּפֵּר עֲוֹן בֵּית עֵלִי בְּזֶבַח וּמִנְחָה עַד עוֹלָם. בְּזֶבַח וּמִנְחָה אֵינוֹ מִתְכַּפֵּר, אֲבָל מִתְכַּפֵּר הוּא בְּדִבְרֵי תוֹרָה. אֲמַאי. בְּגִין דְּדִבְרֵי תוֹרָה, סַלְקִין עַל כָּל קָרְבְּנִין דְּעָלְמָא. כְּמָה דְּאוּקְמוּהָ דִּכְתִּיב, זֹאת הַתּוֹרָה לָעוֹלָה לַמִּנְחָה וְלַחַטָּאת וְלָאָשָׁם וְלַמִּלּוּאִים, שָׁקִיל אוֹרַיְיתָא לָקֳבֵיל כָּל קָרְבְּנִין דְּעָלְמָא. אָ"ל, הָכִי הוּא וַדַּאי, דְּכָל מַאן דְּאִשְׁתְּדַל בְּאוֹרַיְיתָא, אע"ג דְּאִתְגְּזַר עָלֵיהּ עוֹנְשָׁא מִלְּעֵילָא, נִיחָא לֵיהּ מִכָּל קָרְבְּנִין וְעָלָוָון, וְהַהוּא עוֹנְשָׁא אִתְקְרַע.

10. Rabbi Yosi was going on his way when Rabbi Chiya met him. He said to him what the scholars established, about that which is written concerning Eli: "And therefore I have sworn to the house of Eli, that the iniquity of the house of Eli shall not be purged with sacrifice or offering forever" (I Shmuel 3:14), meaning that it is not purged with sacrifice or offering, but atonement comes through the words of Torah. Why? It is because words of Torah are superior to all sacrifices. As has been accepted, it is written, "This is the Torah of the burnt offering, of the meal offering, and of the sin offering, and of the guilt offering" (Vayikra 7:37). THIS INDICATES THAT the Torah is equal to all sacrifices in the world. He replied: This is surely so.

For even if a penalty of Heaven is decreed against he who toils in Torah, the penalty is canceled because the study of the Torah is better for him than all sacrifices and offerings .

11. וְת״ח, לָא אִתְדְּכֵי ב״נ לְעָלְמִין, אֶלָּא בְּמִלִּין דְּאוֹרַיְיתָא. בְּגִינֵי כַּךְ מִלִּין דְּאוֹרַיְיתָא לָא מְקַבְּלִין טוּמְאָה, בְּגִין דְּאִיהִי קַיְּימָא לְדַכְּאָה לְאַלֵּין מְסָאֲבֵי, וְאַסְוּוָתָא בְּאוֹרַיְיתָא אִשְׁתְּכַח. דִּכְתִּיב, רִפְאוּת תְּהִי לְשָׁרֶךָ וְשִׁקּוּי לְעַצְמוֹתֶיךָ. וְדַכְיוּתָא אִשְׁתְּכַח בְּאוֹרַיְיתָא, דִּכְתִּיב, יִרְאַת יְיָ׳ טְהוֹרָה עוֹמֶדֶת לָעַד. מַאי עוֹמֶדֶת לָעַד. דְּקַיְּימָא תְּדִירָא בְּהַהוּא דַּכְיוּתָא, וְלָא אִתְעָדֵי מִנֵּיהּ לְעָלְמִין.

11. Come and behold: man becomes pure solely through words of Torah, For this reason, words of Torah never receive defilement, since THE FUNCTION OF THE TORAH is to purify the unclean. There is healing in the Torah, as it is written: "It shall be health to your navel, and marrow to your bones" (Mishlei 3:8). There is purity in the Torah, as it is written: "The fear to Hashem is clean, enduring forever" (Tehilim 19:10). What is meant by "enduring forever"? IT MEANS that it remains constantly in the state of purity, which is never removed from it.

12. אָ״ל יִרְאַת יְיָ׳ כְּתִיב, וְלָא תּוֹרָה. אָ״ל, הָכִי הוּא וַדַּאי, דְּהָא אוֹרַיְיתָא מִסִּטְרָא דִּגְבוּרָה קָא אַתְיָיא. אָ״ל, וּמֵהָתָם נָפְקָא, מֵהָכָא נָפְקָא, דִּכְתִּיב, רֵאשִׁית חָכְמָה יִרְאַת יְיָ׳, וּכְתִיב יִרְאַת יְיָ׳ טְהוֹרָה.

12. He said to him: Behold, it says, "the fear of Hashem," not 'the Torah'. He replied: This is surely so, THAT IT REFERS TO THE TORAH, as Torah comes from the state of Gvurah, AND HENCE IS CALLED 'FEAR OF HASHEM'. He said to him: You learn THAT IDEA from there, from the verses, "The fear of Hashem is the beginning of wisdom" (Tehilim 111:10), SO WE SEE THAT WISDOM IS CALLED 'FEAR'. And it is written: "fear of Hashem is pure," SO WE SEE THE PURITY IS WITHIN WISDOM, NAMELY IN THE TORAH.

13. וְאוֹרַיְיתָא קְדוּשָׁה אִתְקְרֵי, דִּכְתִּיב כִּי קָדוֹשׁ אֲנִי יְיָ׳, וְדָא אוֹרַיְיתָא,

דְּהִיא שְׁמָא קַדִּישָׁא עִלָּאָה. וְעַ"ד, מַאן דְּאִשְׁתָּדַּל בָּהּ אִתְדְּכֵי, וּלְבָתַר אִתְקַדָּשׁ, דִּכְתִיב קְדוֹשִׁים תִּהְיוּ, קְדוֹשִׁים הֱיוּ לָא כְּתִיב, אֶלָּא תִּהְיוּ. תִּהְיוּ וַדַּאי. אָ"ל הָכִי הוּא, וּמִקְרָא כְּתִיב, וְאַתֶּם תִּהְיוּ לִי מַמְלֶכֶת כֹּהֲנִים וְגוֹי קָדוֹשׁ, וּכְתִיב אֵלֶּה הַדְּבָרִים וְגוֹ'.

13. The Torah is called 'Holiness', as it is written, "for I Hashem your Elohim am Holy" (Vayikra 19:2). And such is the Torah, which is the supernal Holy Name. Therefore, one who toils in it becomes pure, and afterwards he becomes holy, as it is written: "You shall be holy." It does not say, 'be holy,' but it is written, "You shall be"; assuredly you shall, MEANING THAT THIS IS A PROMISE THAT THROUGH TORAH, "YOU SHALL BE HOLY." He replied: This is CERTAINLY correct, as it is written, "and you shall be to Me a kingdom of priests, and a holy nation" (Shemot 19:6), followed by, "These are the words…"

14. תָּאנָא, קְדוּשָׁה דְּאוֹרַיְיתָא, קְדוּשָׁה דְּסַלְּקַת עַל כָּל קְדוּשִׁין. וּקְדוּשָׁה דְּחָכְמְתָא עִלָּאָה סְתִימָא, סַלְּקָא עַל כֹּלָּא. אָמַר לֵיהּ לָאו אוֹרַיְיתָא בְּלָא חָכְמְתָא, וְלָאו חָכְמְתָא בְּלָא אוֹרַיְיתָא, וְכֹלָּא בְּחַד דַּרְגָּא הוּא, וְכֹלָּא חַד, אֶלָּא אוֹרַיְיתָא בְּחָכְמָה עִלָּאָה אִשְׁתְּכַחַת, וּבָהּ קַיְּימָא, וּבָהּ אִתְנְטָעוּ שָׁרְשָׁהָא מִכָּל מִסְטְרִין.

14. We learned that the Holiness of the Torah is a sanctity that surpasses all types of holiness, and the sanctity of the hidden supernal Wisdom exceeds all others. He said: Torah does not exist without wisdom, and wisdom does not exist without Torah. All is on one level; all is one. There is Torah in supernal Wisdom, and it is there through it. And in it, roots are planted on all sides.

15. עַד דַּהֲווֹ אַזְלֵי, אַשְׁכָּחוּ חַד ב"נ, בְּלֶקִינְטָא דְּקוּסְטָא, רָכִיב עַל סוּסְיָא, אַשְׁמִיט יְדוֹי לְחַד עַנְפָּא דְּאִילָנָא. א"ר יוֹסֵי, הַאי הוּא דִּכְתִיב וְהִתְקַדִּשְׁתֶּם וִהְיִיתֶם קְדוֹשִׁים. אָדָם מְקַדֵּשׁ עַצְמוֹ מִלְּמַטָּה, מְקַדְּשִׁין אוֹתוֹ מִלְּמַעְלָה. הה"ד, קְדוֹשִׁים תִּהְיוּ כִּי קָדוֹשׁ אֲנִי יְיָ'.

15. As they were going, they met a person riding on a horse at a place where

the town trash and refuse is kept. AS HE DEPARTED THERE, he put out his hand to a branch of the tree, TO CLEAN HIS HANDS. EVEN THOUGH THERE WAS NO REASON TO FEAR THAT HE HAD TOUCHED THE FILTH AS HE RODE ON A HORSE - NONE THE LESS - HE WAS STRICT WITH HIMSELF ABOUT CLEANSING HIS HANDS SINCE HE FOUND HIMSELF IN A DIRTY ENVIRONMENT. Rabbi Yosi said: This is what is written, "you shall therefore sanctify yourselves, and you shall be holy" (Vayikra 11:44). Man purifies himself below and he is purified on high. This is the essence of the verse, "You shall be holy: for I Hashem your Elohim am Holy."

16. תָּאנֵי רבי אַבָּא, פַּרְשְׁתָּא דָא כְּלָלָא דְאוֹרַיְיתָא הִיא, וְחוֹתָמָא דְקוּשְׁטָא דְגוּשְׁפַּנְקָא הִיא. בְּפַרְשְׁתָּא דָא אִתְחַדְּשׁוּ רָזִין עִלָּאִין דְּאוֹרַיְיתָא, בַּעֲשַׂר אֲמִירָן, וְגִזְרִין וְעוֹנָשִׁין, וּפִקוּדִין עִלָּאִין, דְּכַד מָטָאן חַבְרַיָּיא לְפַרְשְׁתָּא דָא, הֲווֹ חַדָּאן.

16. Rabbi Aba taught that this portion OF KEDOSHIM comprises the entire Torah and is sealed with the ring of Truth. In this portion there are new supernal secrets of Torah, in the Ten Commandments, and decrees, penalties, and heavenly commandments. When the friends reached this chapter, they were overjoyed.

17. אָמַר ר' אַבָּא, מ"ט פַּרְשְׁתָּא דַּעֲרָיוֹת, וּפַרְשְׁתָּא דִקְדוֹשִׁים תְּהְיוּ, סְמוּכִין דָּא לְדָא. אֶלָּא הָכִי תָּאנָא, כָּל מַאן דְּאִסְתָּמַר מֵאַלֵּין עֲרָיָין, בִּקְדוּשָׁה אִתְעֲבֵיד וַדַּאי. וכ"ש אִי אִתְקַדָּשׁ בִּקְדוּשָׁה דְמָארֵיהּ. וְהָא אִתְּעֲרוּ חַבְרַיָּיא.

17. Rabbi Aba said: What is the reason that the portion about incest and the portion of Kedoshim are adjacent? AND ANSWERS: We learned that he who keeps away from incest is definitely produced in holiness, SINCE HIS PARENTS SANCTIFIED THEMSELVES AT TIME OF INTERCOURSE. And this is most certainly so if he also sanctifies himself with the sanctity of his Master, THROUGH WORK ON HIMSELF. This was commented upon by the friends.

18. אֵימָתַי עוֹנָתָן דְּכֹלָּא, לְאִתְקַדָּשׁ ב"נ. ת"ח, מַאן דְּבָעֵי לְאִתְקַדְּשָׁא

בִּרְעוּתָא דְּמָארֵיהּ, לָא לִישַׁמֵּשׁ אֶלָּא מִפַּלְגוּת לֵילְיָא וְאֵילָךְ, אוֹ
בְּפַלְגוּת לֵילְיָא. דְּהָא בְּהַהִיא שַׁעֲתָא, קוּדְשָׁא בְּרִיךְ הוּא אִשְׁתְּכַח
בְּגִנְתָּא דְּעֵדֶן, וּקְדוּשָׁה עִלָּאָה אִתְּעַר, וּכְדֵין שַׁעֲתָא הִיא לְאִתְקַדְּשָׁא.
הַאי לִשְׁאָר בְּנֵי נָשָׁא, תַּלְמִידֵי חֲכָמִים דְּיַדְעִין אוֹרְחוֹי דְּאוֹרַיְיתָא,
בְּפַלְגוּת לֵילְיָא שַׁעֲתָא דִּלְהוֹן לְמֵיקָם לְמִלְעֵי בְּאוֹרַיְיתָא, לְאִזְדַּוְּוגָא
בכ"י, לְשַׁבְּחָא לִשְׁמָא קַדִּישָׁא, לְמַלְכָּא קַדִּישָׁא.

18. When is the time for all men to consecrate in marital duties? Come and behold: he who wishes to consecrate himself with the grace of His master should mate only from midnight on or at midnight, as at that hour, the Holy One, blessed be He, ZEIR ANPIN, is in the Garden of Eden, DENOTING MALCHUT, and the supernal sanctity is awakened. That is the moment to be consecrated. This is fine for all other people. Torah scholars familiar with the ways of Torah know that midnight is the hour to rise and toil in the Torah, join with the Congregation of Yisrael, DENOTING MALCHUT, and praise the Holy Name, DENOTING MALCHUT and the Holy King, DENOTING ZEIR ANPIN.

19. בְּלֵילְיָא דְּשַׁבְּתָא, דִּרְעוּתָא דְּכֹלָּא אִשְׁתְּכַח, זוּוּגָא דִּלְהוֹן בְּהַהִיא
שַׁעֲתָא. לְאַפָּקָא רְעוּתָא דְּקוּדְשָׁא בְּרִיךְ הוּא וכ"י, כְּמָה דְּאִתְּמַר
דִּכְתִיב, בָּנִים אַתֶּם לַיְיָ' אֱלֹהֵיכֶם. וְאִלֵּין אִקְרוּן קַדִּישִׁין, דִּכְתִיב
קְדוֹשִׁים תִּהְיוּ כִּי קָדוֹשׁ אֲנִי יְיָ'. וּכְתִיב וְהָיָה כְּעֵץ שָׁתוּל עַל פַּלְגֵי מַיִם
אֲשֶׁר פִּרְיוֹ יִתֵּן בְּעִתּוֹ וְגוֹ'.

19. Shabbat eve, when there is universal goodwill, is the moment for mating FOR TORAH SCHOLARS, in order to find the grace of the Holy One, blessed be He, and the Congregation of Yisrael, DENOTING BOTH ZEIR ANPIN AND MALCHUT, as we learned from the verse, "You are the children of Hashem your Elohim" (Devarim 14:1). They are called 'holy', as it is written, "You shall be holy: for I Hashem your Elohim am Holy," and it is written, "And he shall be like a tree planted by streams of water, that brings forth its fruit in its season" (Tehilim 1:3).

20. קְדוֹשִׁים תִּהְיוּ, רִבִּי אַבָּא פָּתַח, וּמִי כְעַמְּךָ כְּיִשְׂרָאֵל גּוֹי אֶחָד

בָּאָרֶץ, תָּא חֲזֵי, בְּכָל עַמִּין דְּעָלְמָא, לָא אִתְרְעֵי בְּהוּ קוּדְשָׁא בְּרִיךְ הוּא, בַּר בְּיִשְׂרָאֵל בִּלְחוֹדַיְיהוּ, וְעָבֵד לוֹן עַמָּא יְחִידָאָה בְּעָלְמָא, וְקָרָא לוֹן גּוֹי אֶחָד כִּשְׁמֵיהּ. וְאַעֲטַר לוֹן בְּכַמָּה עִטְרִין, וְכַמָּה פִּקּוּדִין, לְאִתְעַטְּרָא בְּהוּ. וְעַ״ד תְּפִילִין דְּרֵישָׁא וּתְפִילִין דִּדְרוֹעָא, לְאִתְעַטְּרָא בְּהוּ בְּ״נ כְּגַוְונָא דִּלְעֵילָא. וּלְאִשְׁתַּכְּחָא חַד שְׁלִים בְּכֹלָּא.

20. "You shall be holy." Rabbi Aba commenced: "And what one nation in the earth is like Your people, like Yisrael" (II Shmuel 7:23). Come and behold: the Holy One, blessed be He, did not want any of the nations of the world except Yisrael alone. He made them a singular nation in the world. He called them 'one nation', like His Name. He crowned them with numerous adornments, numerous precepts to be adorned, and He gave them the head and hand Tefilin, to adorn them just as is above. THE HEAD TEFILIN ARE MOCHIN OF ZEIR ANPIN. THE HAND TEFILIN ARE MOCHIN ARE MALCHUT. This was so that there would be a consistent perfection in everything, ABOVE AND BELOW.

21. וּבְהַהִיא שַׁעֲתָא דְּאִתְעַטַּר בְּהוּ בְּ״נ, וְאִתְקַדָּשׁ בְּהוּ, אִתְעֲבִיד שְׁלִים, וְאִקְרֵי אֶחָד, דְּאֶחָד לָא אִקְרֵי אֶלָּא כַּד אִיהוּ שְׁלִים. וּמַאן דְּפָגִים, לָא אִקְרֵי אֶחָד. וְעַ״ד קוּדְשָׁא בְּרִיךְ הוּא אִקְרֵי אֶחָד, בִּשְׁלִימוּ דְּכֹלָּא, בִּשְׁלִימוּ דַּאֲבָהָן, בִּשְׁלִימוּ דִּכְנֶסֶת יִשְׂרָאֵל. בְּגִ״כ יִשְׂרָאֵל לְתַתָּא אִקְרוּן אֶחָד. דְּכַד בְּ״נ אֲנַח תְּפִילִין, וְאִתְחֲפֵי בִּכְסוּיָיא דְּמִצְוָה, כְּדֵין אִתְעַטַּר בְּעִטְרִין קַדִּישִׁין כְּגַוְונָא דְּעֵילָא, וְאִקְרֵי אֶחָד.

21. At that time, when man adorns himself with them and sanctifies himself with them, NAMELY TEFILIN, he becomes complete, and is called 'one'. Because he is not called 'one' until he is perfect, one who is defective is not called 'one'. The Holy One, blessed be He, is therefore called 'One' in His total perfection, the perfection of the Patriarchs, CHESED, GVURAH AND TIFERET, and the perfection of the Congregation of Yisrael, DENOTING MALCHUT. For this, Yisrael below is called 'one', as when a man dons Tefilin and is enveloped with a cover according to the commandment, NAMELY THE TALIT, then he is adorned with the holy adornments similar to that on high, and is thus called 'one'.

22. וּבְגִינֵי כָּךְ, לֵיתֵי אֶחָד, וְיִשְׁתַּדַּל בְּאֶחָד. קוּדְשָׁא בְּרִיךְ הוּא דְּאִיהוּ אֶחָד, יִשְׁתַּדַּל בְּאֶחָד. דְּהָא לֵית מַלְכָּא מִשְׁתַּדַּל, אֶלָּא בְּמַאי דְּאִתְחֲזֵי לֵיהּ. וּבְג״כ כְּתִיב, וְהוּא בְּאֶחָד וּמִי יְשִׁיבֶנּוּ, לָא שָׁאֲרֵי קוּדְשָׁא בְּרִיךְ הוּא וְלָא אִשְׁתְּכַח אֶלָּא בְּאֶחָד. בְּאֶחָד, אֶחָד מִבָּעֵי לֵיהּ אֶלָּא בְּמַאן דְּאִתְתְּקַן בִּקְדוּשָׁא עִלָּאָה לְמֶהֱוֵי חַד. כְּדֵין הוּא שַׁרְיָא בְּאֶחָד, וְלָא בַּאֲתַר אָחֳרָא.

22. Because of this, let man come and strive for the One. The Holy One, blessed be He, who is One, deals with one, NAMELY YISRAEL. For the King deals only with what is befitting Him. For this reason, it is written: "But He is unchangeable (lit. 'in one'), and who can turn Him?" (Iyov 23:13) since the Holy One, blessed be He, abides and dwells only in one. HE ASKS: IT SAYS, "He is in one." Should it not read 'one'? HE ANSWERS: YET THE EXPLANATION IS as one established in supernal sanctity to be one, MEANING IN YISRAEL, then He hovers in one, and not in any place else, MEANING IN ANOTHER NATION.

23. וְאֵימָתַי אִקְרֵי ב״נ אֶחָד. בְּשַׁעֲתָא דְּאִשְׁתְּכַח דְּכַר וְנוּקְבָּא, וְאִתְקַדַּשׁ בִּקְדוּשָׁה עִלָּאָה, וְאִתְכַּוָּון לְאִתְקַדְּשָׁא. ות״ח, בְּזִמְנָא דְּאִשְׁתְּכַח בַּר נָשׁ בְּזִוּוּגָא חַד דְּכַר וְנוּקְבָּא, וְאִתְכַּוֵּון לְאִתְקַדְּשָׁא כַּדְקָא יָאוּת. כְּדֵין הוּא שְׁלִים, וְאִקְרֵי אֶחָד בְּלָא פְגִימוּ.

23. When is a person called 'one'? At the time when there is male and female, and he sanctifies himself with supernal holiness and strives to be saintly. Come and behold: when a person is in one union, male and female, and aims to sanctify himself properly, then he is perfect and is considered one without defect.

24. בְּגִינֵי כָּךְ, בָּעֵי בַּר נָשׁ לְמֶחְדֵי לְאִתְתֵּיהּ בְּהַהִיא שַׁעֲתָא, לְזַמְּנָא לָהּ בִּרְעוּתָא חֲדָא עִמֵּיהּ. וְיִתְכַּוְּונוּן תַּרְוַויְיהוּ כְּחַד לְהַהִיא מִלָּה. וְכַד מִשְׁתַּכְּחֵי תַּרְוַויְיהוּ כְּחַד, כְּדֵין כֹּלָּא חַד בְּנַפְשָׁא וּבְגוּפָא: בְּנַפְשָׁא לְאַדְבְּקָא דָּא בְּדָא בִּרְעוּתָא חֲדָא. וּבְגוּפָא: כְּמָה דְּאוֹלִיפְנָא דְּבַר נָשׁ דְּלָא נָסִיב, הוּא כְּמַאן דְּאִתְפְּלִיג, וְכַד מִתְחַבְּרָן דְּכַר וְנוּקְבָּא, כְּדֵין

אִתְעֲבִידוּ חַד גּוּפָא. אִשְׁתְּכַח דְּאִינּוּן חַד נַפְשָׁא, וְחַד גּוּפָא, וְאִקְרֵי בַּר נָשׁ אֶחָד. כְּדֵין קוּדְשָׁא בְּרִיךְ הוּא שָׁארֵי בְּאֶחָד, וְאַפְקִיד רוּחָא דִּקְדוּשָׁה בְּהַהוּא אֶחָד.

24. For this reason, man needs to bring joy to his wife at that time, to prepare her with him with one desire. Both should ready themselves to that matter. And when both are together, then everything is one in body and soul. In soul THEY ARE ONE, to cling to each other in one wish. In body THEY ARE ONE, as we learned that a man who does not marry is like a half BODY; HE IS A HALF BODY AND HIS MATE IS A HALF BODY. When they join male and female, they become one COMPLETE body. Thus, they are one soul, one body, and man is than one. Then the Holy One, blessed be He, dwells in the one and deposits a Holy Spirit in that one, NAMELY IN THAT WHICH IS BORN FROM THEM.

25. וְאִלֵּין אִקְרוּן בְּנִין דְּקוּדְשָׁא בְּרִיךְ הוּא, כְּמָה דְּאִתְּמַר. וּבְגִינֵי כַּךְ קְדוֹשִׁים תִּהְיוּ כִּי קָדוֹשׁ אֲנִי יְיָ׳. זַכָּאִין אִינּוּן יִשְׂרָאֵל דְּלָא אוֹקִים מִלָּה דָּא בַּאֲתַר אַחֲרָא, אֶלָּא בֵּיהּ מַמָּשׁ, דִּכְתִיב כִּי קָדוֹשׁ אֲנִי יְיָ׳. בְּגִין לְאִתְדַּבְּקָא בֵּיהּ, וְלָא בְּאָחֳרָא. וְעַל דָּא קְדוֹשִׁים תִּהְיוּ כִּי קָדוֹשׁ אֲנִי יְיָ׳ אֱלֹהֵיכֶם.

25. These are called 'children of the Holy One, blessed be He', as we learned above, and for this reason, "You shall be holy: for I Hashem your Elohim am Holy." Fortunate are Yisrael for not placing this thing elsewhere, MEANING THEY SOUGHT NO REWARD FOR THEIR HOLINESS, but only TO CLING to Him, as is written, "for I Hashem your Elohim am Holy," MEANING that His children are to cling to Him only, and to no other. Hence, "You shall be holy: for I Hashem your Elohim am Holy."

4. "You shall revere every man his mother, and his father"

A Synopsis

Rabbi Yosi says that whoever fears their mother and father observes the Shabbat. He wonders why the mother is mentioned first, and Rabbi Shimon explains that the mother does not have the power to instill fear that the father does, therefore she is mentioned first. Rabbi Yehuda says that just as heaven and earth were created simultaneously, both parents are equal in fear and honor. Rabbi Shimon tells us about the sanctification below during mating and the supernal mating above.

26. אִישׁ אִמּוֹ וְאָבִיו תִּירָאוּ וְגוֹ'. הָא תָּנֵינָן, דְּפַרְשָׁתָּא דָּא כְּלָלָא דְּאוֹרַיְיתָא. מַקִּישׁ דְּחִילוּ דְּאַבָּא וְאִימָא לְשַׁבְּתוֹתַי. אֶלָּא אָמַר ר' יוֹסֵי, כֹּלָּא חַד, מַאן דְּדָחִיל מֵהַאי, נָטִיר לְהַאי.

26. "You shall fear every man his mother, and his father" (Vayikra 19:3). This chapter contains general principles of the whole Torah. IF THIS IS SO, WE NEED TO EXAMINE WHY one's fear of father and mother is adjacent to "My Shabbatot" (Ibid). AND ANSWERS: Rabbi Yosi said that it is actually all the same. He who has fear of this, NAMELY HIS FATHER AND MOTHER, observes the Shabbat.

27. אִישׁ אִמּוֹ, אַקְדִּים אִמּוֹ לְאָבִיו בִּדְחִילוּ מ"ט. כְּמָה דְּאוּקְמוּהָ. אֲבָל אִימָא דְּלֵית רְשׁוּ בִּידָהָא כָּל כָּךְ כְּאָבִיו אַקְדִּים דְּחִילוּ דִּילָהּ.

27. "You shall revere every man his mother." HE QUESTIONS: Why does mother precede father, AS IT SAYS, "YOU SHALL REVERE EVERY MAN HIS MOTHER, AND HIS FATHER"? What is the reason? AND ANSWERS: As we explained, his mother is powerless TO INSTILL FEAR like his father. Therefore, THE VERSE leads with her fear first.

28. ר' יִצְחָק אָמַר, מַה כְּתִיב לְעֵילָא, קְדוֹשִׁים תִּהְיוּ. אָתֵי ב"נ לְאִתְקַדְּשָׁא בְּאִתְּתֵיהּ כְּחַד. מִמַּאן הוּא שְׁבָחָא יַתִּיר בְּהַהִיא קְדוּשָׁה. הֲוֵי אִימָא מִנּוּקְבָּא. בְּגִין כָּךְ אִישׁ אִמּוֹ וְאָבִיו תִּירָאוּ.

-18-

28. Rabbi Yitzchak said: It is written before, "You shall be holy" (Ibid. 2), MEANING that a man needs to sanctify together with his wife. Whose praise for the sanctity is considered paramount? We say it is the woman's, BECAUSE SHE IS NOT AS KNOWLEDGEABLE IN TORAH AND SANCTITY AS THE MAN. Hence, IT STARTS WITH MOTHER, SAYING, "You shall revere every man his mother, and his father."

29. ר' יְהוּדָה אָמַר, אִישׁ אִמּוֹ וְאָבִיו תִּירָאוּ, כְּהַאי גַּוְונָא, בְּיוֹם עֲשׂוֹת יְיָ' אֱלֹהִים אֶרֶץ וְשָׁמָיִם. וּבְאֲתַר אָחֳרָא, אַקְדִּים שָׁמַיִם לָאָרֶץ. אֶלָּא לְאַחֲזָאָה דְּתַרְוַויְיהוּ כַּחֲדָא אִתְעֲבִידוּ. אוּף הָכָא אַקְדִּים אִימָא לְאַבָּא, וּבְאֲתַר אָחֳרָא אַקְדִּים אַבָּא לְאִימָא, לְאַחֲזָאָה דְּתַרְוַויְיהוּ כַּחֲדָא אִשְׁתָּדָלוּ בֵּיהּ.

29. Rabbi Yehuda said: "You shall revere every man his mother, and his father," PLACING THE MOTHER BEFORE THE FATHER; this is similar to THE VERSE, "in the day that Hashem Elohim made the earth and the heaven" (Beresheet 2:4). In another place, heaven precedes earth. The purpose is to show that both heaven and earth were created simultaneously. This is also the case here. He leads mother before father, and elsewhere he leads father before mother, to show that because both strove for him together, BOTH ARE EQUAL IN FEAR AND HONOR.

30(1). וְאֶת שַׁבְּתֹתַי תִּשְׁמֹרוּ, שָׁקִיל דָּא לְדָא, וְכֹלָּא כַּחֲדָא אִתְקָלוּ בְּמַתְקְלָא חַד. דִּכְתִיב וּשְׁמַרְתֶּם אֶת הַשַּׁבָּת כִּי קֹדֶשׁ הִיא לָכֶם, וּכְתִיב זָכוֹר אֶת יוֹם הַשַּׁבָּת לְקַדְּשׁוֹ. אֶלָּא חַד לְאַבָּא, וְחַד לְאִימָא.

30a. "And keep My Shabbatot" (Vayikra 19:3), INDICATES TWO SHABBATOT, THE DAY OF SHABBAT, DENOTING ZEIR ANPIN, AND SHABBAT EVE, DENOTING MALCHUT. BOTH are equal and their weight is the same. THEREFORE, THE VERSE WROTE THEM AS ONE, as is written: "You shall keep the Shabbat therefore; for it is holy to you" (Shemot 31:14); and, "Remember the Shabbat day, to keep it holy" (Shemot 20:8). ONE PLACE WRITES "KEEP" AND ONE PLACE "REMEMBER." Yet one verse deals with the father, DENOTING ZEIR ANPIN, INDICATED THROUGH

"REMEMBERING." The other verse is from the mother, DENOTING MALCHUT, INDICATED by "KEEPING."

30(2). כְּתִיב הָכָא אִישׁ אִמּוֹ וְאָבִיו תִּירָאוּ וְאֶת שַׁבְּתֹתַי תִּשְׁמֹרוּ. וּכְתִיב הָתָם אֶת שַׁבְּתֹתַי תִּשְׁמֹרוּ וּמִקְדָּשִׁי תִּירָאוּ. מַהוּ מִקְדָּשִׁי. כְּמַשְׁמָעוֹ, תוּ מִקְדָּשִׁי אִלֵּין אִינוּן דִּמְקַדְּשֵׁי גַּרְמַיְיהוּ בְּהַהִיא שַׁעֲתָא. כְּגַוְונָא דָא, וּמִמִּקְדָּשִׁי תָּחֵלּוּ. אַל תִּקְרֵי מִמִּקְדָּשִׁי, אֶלָּא מִמְּקוּדָשַׁי. מַה לְהַלָּן מִמְּקוּדָשַׁי, אַף כָּאן מִמְּקוּדָשַׁי, דְּאִינוּן אַבָּא וְאִימָּא.

30b. It is written here: "You shall revere, every man, his mother and his father, and keep My Shabbatot." It is written elsewhere: "You shall keep My Shabbatot, and revere My sanctuary" (Vayikra 26:2). What is meant by, "My sanctuary"? It is according to the literal meaning, THE TEMPLE. Another way TO EXPLAIN, "My sanctuary" is that it refers to those who sanctify themselves at that time. Similarly, "and begin at My sanctuary" (Yechezkel 9:6), WHICH HAS BEEN EXPLAINED. Do not read it "at My sanctuary," but rather, 'at My sanctified'. And just as there ITS EXPLANATION is 'My sanctified ones,' here also IN THE VERSE, "AND REVERE MY SANCTUARY," ITS MEANING IS 'My sanctified ones', MEANING THE PEOPLE WHO SANCTIFY THEMSELVES, who are the father and mother.

31. אִישׁ אִמּוֹ וְאָבִיו תִּירָאוּ. ר"שׁ אָמַר, כְּתִיב וְאַתֶּם הַדְּבֵקִים בַּיְיָ', וְגוֹ'. זַכָּאִין אִינוּן יִשְׂרָאֵל, דְּמִתְדַּבְּקָן בֵּיהּ בְּקוּדְשָׁא בְּרִיךְ הוּא, וּבְגִין דְּאִינוּן מִתְדַּבְּקָן בֵּיהּ בְּקוּדְשָׁא בְּרִיךְ הוּא, כֹּלָּא אִתְדְּבָקוּ כַּחֲדָא דָא בְּדָא.

31. "You shall revere every man his mother, and his father." Rabbi Shimon said: It is written, "But you that did cleave to Hashem..." (Devarim 4:4). Fortunate are Yisrael that cling to the Holy One, blessed be He. Because they cling to Him, everything clings together, one with the other.

32. ת"ח, בְּשַׁעֲתָא דְּב"נ מְקַדֵּשׁ לְתַתָּא, כְּגוֹן חַבְרַיָּיא דִּמְקַדְּשֵׁי גַּרְמַיְיהוּ מִשַּׁבָּת לְשַׁבָּת, בְּשַׁעֲתָא דְּזוּוּגָא עִלָּאָה אִשְׁתְּכַח, דְּהָא בְּהַהִיא שַׁעֲתָא רַעֲוָא אִשְׁתְּכַח, וּבִרְכָתָא אִזְדַּמְּנַת. כְּדֵין מִתְדַּבְּקָן כֻּלְּהוּ כְּחַד, נַפְשָׁא דְּשַׁבָּת, וְגוּפָא דְּאִזְדְּמַן בְּשַׁבָּת. וְעַל דָּא כְּתִיב, אִישׁ אִמּוֹ וְאָבִיו תִּירָאוּ,

דְּאִינּוּן זַוּוּגָא חַד בְּגוּפָא, בְּהַהִיא שַׁעֲתָא לְאִתְקַדְּשָׁא. וְאֶת שַׁבְּתוֹתַי תִּשְׁמֹרוּ. דָּא שַׁבָּת עִלָּאָה וְשַׁבָּת תַּתָּאָה, דְּאִינּוּן מְזַמְּנֵי לְנַפְשָׁא בְּהַהוּא גּוּפָא, מֵהַהוּא זַוּוּגָא עִלָּאָה. וְעַל דָּא וְאֶת שַׁבְּתוֹתַי תִּשְׁמֹרוּ, תְּרֵי וְכֹלָּא אִתְדְּבַּק דָּא בְּדָא, זַכָּאָה חוּלְקֵיהוֹן דְּיִשְׂרָאֵל.

32. Come and behold: when man sanctifies himself below – such as the friends who sanctify themselves on Shabbat IN THEIR MATING, at the same time when there is supernal mating – grace and blessing are set. Then everything joins together, the soul of Shabbat and the body BORN AND prepared on Shabbat. Hence the verse, "You shall revere every man his mother, and his father." They are one pair in body at that moment that he has been sanctified, MEANING THEY HAVE BROUGHT ABOUT WITH THEIR PAIRING A HOLY BODY. "...and keep My Shabbatot..." refers to the supernal Shabbat, DENOTING ZEIR ANPIN, and the lower Shabbat, DENOTING MALCHUT, who prepare the soul for the body from that supernal pairing, as FROM THE MATING OF ZEIR ANPIN AND MALCHUT THE SOUL IS BORN. Therefore, "and keep My Shabbatot," POINTING TO two. It all cleaves together, the one with the other. Fortunate is the share of Yisrael.

33. ד"א וְאֶת שַׁבְּתוֹתַי תִּשְׁמֹרוּ, לְאַזְהָרָה לְאִינּוּן דִּמְחַכָּן לְזַוּוּגַיְיהוּ מִשַּׁבָּת לְשַׁבָּת, וְהָא אוֹקִימְנָא, כְּמָה דִכְתִיב, לַסָּרִיסִים אֲשֶׁר יִשְׁמְרוּ אֶת שַׁבְּתוֹתַי. מַאן סָרִיסִים. אִלֵּין אִינּוּן חַבְרַיָּיא דִּמְסָרְסָן גַּרְמַיְיהוּ כָּל שְׁאָר יוֹמִין, בְּגִין לְמִלְעֵי בְּאוֹרַיְיתָא. וְאִינּוּן מְחַכָּאן מִשַּׁבָּת לְשַׁבָּת. הַהַ"ד אֲשֶׁר יִשְׁמְרוּ אֶת שַׁבְּתוֹתַי, כד"א וְאָבִיו שָׁמַר אֶת הַדָּבָר. וּבג"כ אֶת שַׁבְּתוֹתַי תִּשְׁמֹרוּ. אִישׁ אִמּוֹ וְאָבִיו תִּירָאוּ, דָּא גּוּפָא. וְאֶת שַׁבְּתוֹתַי תִּשְׁמֹרוּ, דָּא נַפְשָׁא. וְכֹלָּא אִתְדְּבַּק דָּא בְּדָא. זַכָּאָה חוּלְקֵיהוֹן דְּיִשְׂרָאֵל.

33. Another explanation: "and keep My Shabbatot." Is a warning to those who wait to mate from one Shabbat to another Shabbat. We established, as it is written, "to the eunuchs that keep My Shabbatot" (Yeshayah 56:4). Who are these "eunuchs"? These are the scholars that act like eunuchs all other days in order to toil in the Torah. They wait from Shabbat to Shabbat. This is the essence of the writing, "that keep My Shabbatot." The term, "KEEP," MEANS as it says, "but his father kept the matter in mind"

(Beresheet 37:11), MEANING TO WAIT. For this reason, it is written, "and keep My Shabbatot." "You shall revere every man his mother, and his father" refers to THE FATHER AND MOTHER OF the body, "and keep My Shabbatot," refers to THE FATHER AND MOTHER OF the soul. THIS AMOUNTS TO TWO SHABBATOT, ZEIR ANPIN AND MALCHUT. It all comes together, one with the other. Fortunate is the lot of Yisrael.

A Synopsis

The number 32 is emphasized in this section, pertaining to the number of times that Elohim is written in the acts of Creation and the numerical value of *Kavod* (Honor) and the 32 paths of wisdom. Rabbi Shimon speaks to the Faithful Shepherd, Moses, and tells him to be strong because God will appoint him king on high and below. The sages of Mishnah have said that man's father and mother are Zeir Anpin and the Congregation of Yisrael, Malchut. The Torah is the honor of the father. It is for Yisrael to do the commandments of Aba and Ima, Chochmah and Binah, that are the positive precepts. We hear about the difference between those who hear the precepts direct from God and those who hear them from an intermediary and then obey. The former are children of God and the latter are servants of God.

רעיא מהימנא

‫34. אִישׁ אִמּוֹ וְאָבִיו תִּירָאוּ וְאֶת שַׁבְּתֹתַי תִּשְׁמֹרוּ. פְּקוּדָא דָא, שָׁקִיל דָּא לְדָא. שָׁקִיל יְקָרָא דְּאָב וְאֵם, לִיקָרָא דְּשַׁבָּת. לְאַבָּא אַקְדִּים כָּבוֹד, וְהַאי אִיהוּ דְּאָמַר קְרָא, וְאִם אָב אָנִי אַיֵּה כְבוֹדִי וְאִם אֲדוֹנִים אָנִי אַיֵּה מוֹרָאִי. כְּבוֹדִי סָלִיק בְּחוּשְׁבָּן עֶשֶׂר אֲמִירָן, ול"ב אֱלֹהִים דְּעוֹבָדָא דִּבְרֵאשִׁית.‬

Ra'aya Meheimna (the Faithful Shepherd)

34. "You shall revere every man his mother, and his father, and keep My Shabbatot." These precepts are equal to each other, since respect for parents is equivalent to the honor for Shabbat. With regard to his father, it first talks of honor, as the verse said, "if then I am the father, where is My honor (Heb. *kevodi*)? And if I am a master, where is My fear?" (Malachi 1:6) The word *Kevodi* numerically equals 42 and consists of the ten sayings and 32 times Elohim WRITTEN in the acts of Creation.

35. וּבְכָל אֲתַר כָּבוֹד חֲכָמִים יִנְחָלוּ, וְאוֹקְמוּהָ רַבָּנָן, אֵין כָּבוֹד אֶלָּא תוֹרָה. בְּגִין דְּאִינּוּן ל״ב אֱלֹהִים דְּתוֹרָה, יְקָרָא דִּילֵיהּ. וְאִלֵּין אִינּוּן חֲכָמִים דְּאוֹרַיְיתָא, חֲכָמִים בְּחָכְמָה, יַרְתִין הַאי כָּבוֹד וְלָא טִפְּשֵׁי, דַּעֲלַיְיהוּ אִתְּמַר, וּכְסִילִים מְרִים קָלוֹן. וּמְנָלָן דְּמַאן דְּלָא יָדַע בְּאוֹרַיְיתָא אִקְרֵי כְּסִיל, דִּכְתִּיב וּכְסִיל לֹא יָבִין אֶת זֹאת. וְאֵין זֹאת, אֶלָּא תוֹרָה, דִּכְתִּיב וְזֹאת הַתּוֹרָה אֲשֶׁר שָׂם מֹשֶׁה.

35. In every place, "The wise shall inherit honor" (Mishlei 3:35). The sages explained that this "honor" refers to nothing but the Torah, DENOTING ZEIR ANPIN CALLED TORAH, as the 32 expressions of Elohim in the Torah are His honor. THE WORD KAVOD (LIT. 'HONOR' OR 'GLORY') NUMERICALLY EQUALS 32, THE SECRET OF WISDOM, AS EARLIER MENTIONED. These wise men of the Torah, who are the wise in Chochmah, inherit this honor, THE MOCHIN OF 32 ELOHIM. This is not so for the fools about whom it is written, "but fools shall get shame" (Ibid.). How do we know that someone ignorant in Torah is called a 'fool'? As it is written, "nor does a fool understand this" (Tehilim 92:7). The word, "this," refers to Torah, as it is written: "And this is the Torah which Moses set" (Devarim 4:44).

36. רַעְיָא מְהֵימְנָא. בְּגִין דַּחֲלִישׁ תָּא, פָּתַחְנָא לְפָרָשְׁתָּא בְּאִלֵּין פִּקּוּדִין, לְמֶהֱוֵי מְעַט עֵזֶר לָךְ. אִתְתַּקַּף בָּךְ, דְּהָא מַשְׁרְיָין דִּמְתִיבָתָאן אָתָאן לְגַבָּךְ, בְּפִקּוּדָא בָּתַר דָּא, דְּאִיהוּ פִּקּוּדָא לְהַעֲמִיד עָלֶיךָ מֶלֶךְ לְעֵילָּא. וְקוּדְשָׁא בְּרִיךְ הוּא יוֹקִים לָךְ מֶלֶךְ בְּעֶלְאִין וְתַתָּאִין בְּדִיוּקְנֵיהּ. בְּגִין דְּרַבָּנָן דִּמְתִיבָתָא, עֲלַיְיהוּ שְׁכִינְתָּא עֶלָּאָה וְתַתָּאָה. וְקוּדְשָׁא בְּרִיךְ הוּא מֶלֶךְ בְּאֶמְצָעִיתָא, אָחִיד בְּעֶלְאִין וְתַתָּאִין הָכִי אַנְתְּ תְּהֵא בְּדִיוּקְנֵיהּ, בְּרָא דִּילֵיהּ, קוּם בִּיקָרָא דְּמַלְכָּא.

36. THE HOLY LUMINARY, RABBI SHIMON, SAID TO THE FAITHFUL SHEPHERD: Faithful Shepherd, because you are weak, I have begun this portion with these commandments, in order to be somewhat of a support to you. Be strong as the encampments of the Yeshivot come to you with the following commandment, the precept of instituting a king upon you on high. The Holy One, blessed be He, will appoint you king on high and below in

His form, since upon the sages in the Yeshivah rests the supernal Shechinah, BINAH, and also the lower, MALCHUT, THE TWO HEI'S IN THE NAME YUD HEI VAV HEI. And the Holy One, blessed be He, WHO IS THE VAV, is the King in the center OF THE TWO HEI'S, held with the most high and that below, WITH BINAH AND MALCHUT. So you will be in His form, His son. Rise with the glory of the King.

37. קָם רַעְיָא מְהֵימְנָא, וְסָלִיק יְדוֹי לְעֵילָא, וְאָמַר, יְהֵא רַעֲוָא דִילָךְ עִלַּת הָעִלּוֹת, דְּאַנְתְּ מִתְעַלֶּה מֵעִלּוֹי לְעִלּוֹי, עַד דְּלֵית עִלּוֹי. אֶלָּא דְּאַנְתְּ לְעֵילָא מִכָּל עִלּוֹי. לְמֵיהַב לִי חֵילָא, לְמֶעְבַּד רְעוּתָךְ בְּדַרְגִּין דִּילָךְ, דְּאִינּוּן אַבָּא וְאִימָּא, וַאֲנָא בְּרָא דִּלְהוֹן. וּבְיִחוּדָךְ תַּרְוַויְיהוּ אֶחָד. וְאַנְתְּ שָׁקַלְתָּ דְּחִילוּ דְּאַבָּא וְאִימָּא, לִדְחִילוּ דִּילָךְ, בָּתַר דְּאַנְתְּ בְּאֶמְצָעִיתָא חַד, וְלָא תְרֵין, בְּלָא שׁוּתָפוּ, אע"ג דְּאִינּוּן חַד בְּשׁוּתָפוּ דִּילָךְ, אֲבָל אַנְתְּ חַד בְּלָא שׁוּתָפוּ דְּתִנְיָינָא. וּבְגִין דָּא אִתְּמַר בָּךְ, וְאֵין אֱלֹהִים עִמָּדִי.

37. The Faithful Shepherd rose, raised his hands upwards, TO KETER, and said: 'May it be Your will, the cause of all causes, who rises from cause to cause, so there is no cause ABOVE YOU. You are above any cause. MAY IT BE YOUR WILL to give me strength to do Your will within your levels,' being Aba and Ima, MEANING CHOCHMAH AND BINAH. 'And I am their son,' SINCE THE FAITHFUL SHEPHERD IS MOSES, REFERRING TO DA'AT, BEING THE OFFSPRING OF CHOCHMAH AND BINAH. With your unity, the two are one. You have equated the fear of Aba and Ima to the fear of You, in as much as You are in the middle, AS CHOCHMAH AND BINAH ARE RIGHT AND LEFT WITH KETER ABOVE THEM IN THE MIDDLE. They are one, not two, without any sharing. Even though they, ABA AND IMA, are one through your partnership, you are one without any other participant. For this it is written about you, "and there is no Elohim with Me" (Devarim 32:39).

38. הַב לִי חֵילָא, לְאִתְעָרָא בִּיקָרָךְ בְּקַדְמֵיתָא. וּלְבָתַר בִּיקָרָא דְּאָבִי וְאִמִּי דְּבִשְׁמַיָּא, דְּאוּקְמוּהָ עֲלַייְהוּ, גּוֹזֵל אָבִיו וְאִמּוֹ וְאוֹמֵר אֵין פֶּשַׁע חָבֵר הוּא לְאִישׁ מַשְׁחִית. וְאוּקְמוּהָ מָארֵי מַתְנִיתִין, אֵין אָבִיו, אֶלָּא קוּדְשָׁא בְּרִיךְ הוּא. וְאֵין אִמּוֹ, אֶלָּא כ"י. וִיקָרָא דִּילָךְ אַבָּא חָכְמָה,

דְּכָלִיל עֶשֶׂר סְפִירוֹת מִתַּתָּא דִּילֵיהּ לְעֵילָּא, וְתַרְוַויְיהוּ אִינּוּן כּוּרְסְיָיא סַפְסָל תְּחוֹתָךְ לִיקָרָךְ.

38. Give me strength to stir myself first to honor You, and then afterwards in honor of my father and mother in Heaven, AS THEY ARE ZEIR ANPIN AND MALCHUT, regarding whom the verse has been explained, "He who robs his father or his mother, and says, 'It is no transgression;' he is a companion of a destroyer" (Mishlei 28:24). The sages of the Mishnah have established that his father is none other than the Holy One, blessed be He, ZEIR ANPIN, and his mother is none other than the Congregation of Yisrael, BEING MALCHUT. Your honor refers to Aba, NAMELY, CHOCHMAH, included in his ten Sfirot from below upward, AS CHOCHMAH DOES NOT GLOW FROM BELOW UPWARD. And both of them, CHOCHMAH AND BINAH, are the throne and bench beneath you for your glory.

39. וְהָכִי תַּקִּינוּ, לְמֶהֱוֵי קָטָן מְכַבֵּד לַגָּדוֹל דִּלְעֵילָּא מִנֵּיהּ. אַבָּא, אִיהוּ חָכְמָה, הֲלָא אָב אֶחָד לְכֻלָּנוּ, לְמֶהֱוֵי מְשַׁמֵּשׁ תְּחוֹתָךְ, וְאַנְתְּ כֶּתֶר עֶלְיוֹן עַל רֵישֵׁיהּ. וְלֵית כֶּתֶר עֲלָךְ, וְלֵית אֱלָהָא אָחֳרָא. וְאִימָא, לְשַׁמְּשָׁא לְאַבָּא. דְּאִיהוּ תְּחוֹתֵיהּ לְמֶהֱוֵי כֻּרְסָא תְּחוֹתֵיהּ.

39. So they set and proclaimed that the junior respect the senior above him. Aba, being Chochmah, since there is only one father for us all, may serve under You and You shall be a supernal crown over his head. There is no crown above You, nor any other deity. Ima, NAMELY BINAH, NEEDS to serve Aba, as she is beneath him, and is his throne beneath him.

40. וַיֹּאמֶר אִיהוּ, בְּכָל מַאֲמָר, עַד תְּלָתִין וּתְרֵין, יְהִי כֵן, וַיְהִי כֵן. וְאִיהִי, עֲבִידַת מַאֲמָרֵיהּ מִיָּד. וּבְגִין דְּעֲבִידַת מַאֲמָרֵיהּ וְצִוּוּיֵהּ בְּלָא עִכּוּבָא כְּלָל, בל״ב שְׁבִילִין דִּבְהוֹן אִתְבְּרֵי כָּל עוֹבָדָא דִּבְרֵאשִׁית, אִתְקְרִיאַת כָּבוֹד, וּבְהֵיכָלוֹ כֻּלּוֹ אוֹמֵר כָּבוֹד. בָּרוּךְ כְּבוֹד יְיָ מִמְּקוֹמוֹ. אַיֵּה מְקוֹם כְּבוֹדוֹ לְהַעֲרִיצוֹ.

40. "And...said..." (Beresheet 1). ABA appears in every saying, as many as 32 TIMES ELOHIM, WHERE IT SAID, "and it was so." And she, IMA, carried out what He said at once. Because she did His commandments without any delay in the 32 paths OF CHOCHMAH, ILLUMINATING THE 32 ELOHIM IN BINAH, with them were created everything in the acts of Creation. She is called 'glory', AS THE WORD NUMERICALLY EQUALS 32, AS IT IS WRITTEN: "and in His temple everyone speaks of His glory" (Tehilim 29:9). ALSO, "Blessed be the glory of Hashem from His place" (Yechezkel 3:12); also, 'Where is the place of His Glory to adorn Him'. ALL THESE REFER TO BINAH, CALLED 'GLORY'.

41. וְתַרְגּוּם כְּבוֹד אָבִיו, יְקָרָא דַאֲבוּהִי. וְדָא תּוֹרַת יְיָ תְּמִימָה, עֲלָה אִתְּמַר יְקָרָה הִיא מִפְּנִינִים. וְיִשְׂרָאֵל דְּאִתְקְרִיאוּ בָּנִים, בִּכְלַל בֵּן וּבַת, מִסְטְרָא דְּתִפְאֶרֶת וּמַלְכוּת. דְּאִינּוּן בֵּן וּבַת, יְקָרָא דִּאֲבִיו וְאִמּוֹ, לְמֶעְבַּד צַוְוּיֵיהּ, וְצַוּוּיֵי דִּילֵיהּ, אִינּוּן פְּקוּדִין דַּעֲשֵׂה. וְהָא אוּקְמוּהָ מָארֵי מַתְנִיתִין, יֵשׁ מְצֻוֶּה וְעוֹשֶׂה. וּבג״כ אִיהוּ נַעֲשֶׂה וְנִשְׁמָע. וְהַאי אִיהוּ כְּבוֹד דְּאַבָּא וְאִימָא, דִּיצַוֶּה לִבְרֵיהּ דִּיְעָבַד הָכִי וְאִיהוּ עָבִיד מִיַּד, בְּלָא עִכּוּבָא כְּלָל.

41. The Aramaic translation of the honor of his father is 'yakra'. "The Torah of Hashem is perfect" (Tehilim 19:8), about which is written: "She is more precious (Heb. yekarah) than rubies" (Mishlei 3:15). Hence, THE TORAH, BEING THE SECRET OF ZEIR ANPIN, CALLED 'PRECIOUS', IS THE HONOR OF THE FATHER. Yisrael, called 'children', ARE comprised of son and daughter from the aspect of Tiferet and Malchut. It is for these, son and daughter, the precious ones of the father and mother, BEING CHOCHMAH AND BINAH, to do the command OF ABA, and the commandments OF ABA AND IMA are the positive precepts. The sages of the Mishnah have established the concept of being commanded and keeping it. Hence, "will we do and obey" (Shemot 24:7), since that is the honor of Aba and Ima. They command the son to do, and he does at once without any delay.

42. וְעָלַת עַל כֹּלָּא, אֲנָא בָּעֵי לְאִשְׁתַּדְּלָא בִּיקָרָךְ, לְתַקֵּן מִדּוֹת דְּאַבָּא וְאִימָא, לִיקָרָךְ. תְּהֵא בְּעֶזְרִי לְסַדְּרָא כֹּלָּא כַּדְקָא יָאוֹת. וְאַנְתְּ תְּסַדֵּר לִי, וּלְכָל מָארֵי מְתִיבְתָּאן עֵילָּא וְתַתָּא, וּמַשִׁרְיָין דְּמַלְאָכִין עִלָּאִין וְתַתָּאִין, לְמֶהֱוֵי מַתְקְנִין וּמְסַדְּרִין לִיקָרָא דִּילָךְ, וְלִיקָרָא דְּאַבָּא וְאִימָא, לְמֶהֱוֵי

סַפְסָל תְּחוֹת רַגְלוֹי. וּלְמֶעְבַּד צוּוּיֵיהּ בְּכָל פְּקוּדִין דִּילֵיהּ. וּלְמִדְחַל מִנֵּיהּ בְּכָל פְּקוּדִין דְּלָא תַעֲשֶׂה.

42. O Supernal cause OF ALL CAUSES, KETER, I wish to strive for your honor, to establish the attributes of Aba and Ima, BEING CHOCHMAH AND BINAH, for your honor's sake. Help me to arrange everything properly. You will arrange for me and for all masters of the Yeshivot above and below. And the camps on high and the low angels will be arranged and ready for your honor, KETER, and for the honor of Aba and Ima, CHOCHMAH AND BINAH, to serve as a stool under His feet, to do the bidding OF ABA AND IMA in all His precepts, and to fear Him in all the negative precepts.

43. וְהַאי אִיהוּ אִישׁ אִמּוֹ וְאָבִיו תִּירָאוּ, וְסָמִיךְ לֵיהּ וְאֶת שַׁבְּתוֹתַי תִּשְׁמוֹרוּ. וּבְקְרָא אַחֲרִינָא וְאֶת מִצְוֹתַי תַּעֲשׂוּ. מִסִּטְרָא דִּפְקוּדִין דַּעֲשֵׂה דְּאִינּוּן כָּבוֹד, אַקְדִּים אַבָּא לְאִימָּא, וְדָא י"ה. מִסִּטְרָא דְּלָא תַעֲשֶׂה, אַקְדִּים אִימָּא לְאַבָּא, וְדָא ה"י. וְהַיְינוּ כְּבוֹד אֱלֹהִים הַסְתֵּר דָּבָר. לְאִלֵּין דְּלָא מִשְׁתַּדְּלֵי בְּהַאי כָּבוֹד, הַסְתֵּר דָּבָר מִנַּיְיהוּ.

43. This is the meaning of, "You shall revere every man his mother, and his father," adjacent to, "and keep My Shabbatot," and in another verse, "and keep My commandments" (Vayikra 26:3). From the standpoint of the positive precepts such as honor, the father precedes mother. That is *Yud-Hei*, INDICATING ABA FIRST, AS POSITIVE PRECEPTS ARE FROM ABA'S ASPECT. Now from the side of the negative precepts, REPRESENTING FEAR, mother precedes father. This points to *Hei-Yud*, WHERE IMA, *HEI*, PRECEDES ABA, WHO IS *YUD*. This is the essence of, "It is the glory of Elohim to conceal a thing" (Mishlei 25:2). For those who do not strive for this honor, NAMELY, THE PRECEPTS, this thing is to be concealed from them.

44. וְעָלַיְיהוּ אִתְּמַר, וּכְסִילִים מֵרִים קָלוֹן. אִלֵּין אִינּוּן עַמֵּי הָאָרֶץ, בָּתַר דְּלָא מִשְׁתַּדְּלִין בְּהַאי כָּבוֹד דְּאוֹרַיְיתָא, וְאֵיךְ אָמְרִין אָבִינוּ שֶׁבַּשָּׁמַיִם שְׁמַע קוֹלֵנוּ חוּס וְרַחֵם עָלֵינוּ וְקַבֵּל תְּפִלָּתֵנוּ. הָא אִיהוּ לֵימָא לוֹן, וְאִם אָב אָנִי אַיֵּה אַיֵּה כְּבוֹדִי, אַיֵּה אִשְׁתַּדְּלוּתָא דִּלְכוֹן בְּאוֹרַיְיתָא, וּבִפְקוּדִין

דִּילִי, לְמֶעְבַּד צַוֵּוי, דְּמַאן דְּלָא יָדַע בְּצַוְוֵיָּה דְּמָארֵיה, אֵיךְ יַעֲבִיד לֵיה.

44. About them is said: "but fools shall get shame" (Mishlei 3:35). This refers to the unlearned, for they do not work for the glory of Torah. How can they say, 'Our Father, who is in heaven, hear our voice, have pity and compassion upon us, and accept our prayer.' THE HOLY ONE, BLESSED BE HE, replies to them: "if then I am the father, where is My honor?" (Malachi 1:6) THE MEANING IS, 'where are your efforts on behalf of Torah and observance of My precepts?' For if someone does not know the precepts of his Master, how can he worship Him?

45. בַּר מִמַּאן דְּשָׁמַע מֵחַכְמִים וְעָבֵד, וְהַאי אִיהוּ דְּקַבִּיל נַעֲשֶׂה וְנִשְׁמַע. וְעַכֵּ״ד, מַאן דְּלָא קַבִּיל מִמָּארֵיה, אֶלָּא מִשְּׁלוּחֵיה, אִיכָּא אַפְרָשׁוּתָא. וּמַאי אַפְרָשׁוּתָא אִית בֵּין דָּא לְדָא. דְּהָא כְּתִיב, מֹשֶׁה קַבֵּל תּוֹרָה מִסִּינַי, וּלְבָתַר וּמְסָרָה לִיהוֹשֻׁעַ. אֲנָא קַבִּילְנָא, וּלְבָתַר מוֹסַרְנָא לְכֻלְּהוּ. וְהָכִי מַאן דִּמְקַבֵּל מֵאָחֳרָא, כְּקַבָּלַת סִיהֲרָא וְכֹכְבַיָּיא מִשִּׁמְשָׁא, וּבְהַאי קַבּוּל אִתְמְלֵי. וּמַאן דִּמְקַבֵּל יָכִיל לְאִסְתַּלְקָא מִנֵּיה נְבִיעוּ, כְּמָה דַחֲזֵינָא בְּשִׁמְשָׁא וְסִיהֲרָא, דְּאִסְתַּלְקַת נְהוֹרָא דִּלְהוֹן, בְּלֵילְיָא, דְּלָא נָהִיר שִׁמְשָׁא, אֶלָּא בִּימָמָא. וְסִיהֲרָא בְּלֵילְיָא.

45. The exception is one who hears from the scholars and performs, EVEN THOUGH HE DOES NOT UNDERSTAND ON HIS OWN. This is like the verse, "will we do and obey," MEANING HE LISTENS TO THE SCHOLARS AND PERFORMS. Nonetheless, there is a difference for the person that does not receive it from his Master, but only from His messenger. What is the difference between one and the other? It is written that Moses received the Torah from Sinai, and later passed it to Joshua. 'I, THE FAITHFUL SHEPHERD, received and transmitted to them all.' So for he who receives from someone else, IT IS SIMILAR to when the moon and stars receive their light from the sun, and with this reception they are fulfilled. In the case of one who receives, it is possible that this bounty may depart from him, as we see regarding the sun and moon that their light departs at night, since the sun illuminates only by day, and the moon only at night.

46. וְאִי תֵּימָא דְּהַהוּא נְהוֹרָא דְּסִיהֲרָא מִשִּׁמְשָׁא אִיהוּ, דְּאע״ג

דְאִתְכְּנִישׁ, נָהִיר בְּסִיהֲרָא וְכֹכְבַיָּא, הָא חֲזֵינָן מִסִּטְרָא אָחֳרָא בִּלְקוּתָא דְסִיהֲרָא וְשִׁמְשָׁא דְּאִסְתְּלַק נְהוֹרַיְיהוּ, וְאִשְׁתָּאֲרוּ כְּגוּפָא בְּלָא נִשְׁמָתָא, דְּאִית אָדוֹן עֲלֵיהֶם מַחֲשִׁיךְ מְאוֹרֵיהֶם. אֲבָל עִקָּרָא דִּנְהוֹרָא, הַהוּא אֲתַר דְּנָבִיעַ דְּלֵית פְּסָק לִנְהוֹרָא דִּילֵיהּ, וְלָא אִית עָלֵיהּ אֱלָהָא אָחֳרָא לְמִפְסַק מִנֵּיהּ נְהוֹרֵיהּ.

46. You may say that the light of the moon is from the sun; even though ITS LIGHT is gathered, it glows by the moon and stars. HENCE, THE SUN SHINES ALSO AT NIGHT. AND ANSWERS: From another standpoint, we see at an eclipse of the moon and sun that their light has departed and they remain like a body without soul. This is due to the fact that there is a master over them that darkens their light. The essence of the light however, is that place from where it flows, which light never stops. There is no other deity above it that will cut off its light.

47. וְעִלַּת הָעִלּוֹת, בָּתַר דְּאַנְתְּ תַּמָּן, לֵית פְּסָק לִנְבִיעוּ דִּנְהוֹרָא דְּאוֹרַיְיתָא. יְהֵא רַעֲוָא דִּילָךְ דְּלָא תָזוּז מֵאַבָּא וְאִימָּא דִּילִי, וְלָא מִבְּנוֹי. וְהָכִי מַאן דְּאָמֵית גַּרְמֵיהּ עַל אוֹרַיְיתָא, דְּהִיא יְקָרָה, אִתְקַיְּימַת בֵּיהּ, וְלָא מַפְסְקַת מִנֵּיהּ. מַה דְּלָאו הָכִי, מַאן דְּלָא יִשְׁתַּדַּל בָּהּ, אֶלָּא אע״ג דְּעָבֵד צִוּוּי חֲכָמִים, אִיהוּ שַׁמָּשׁ דִּלְהוֹן, עֶבֶד וְלָא בֵּן, אֲבָל אִי אִיהוּ מְהֵימָנָא, מָארֵיהּ אַשְׁלִיט לֵיהּ בְּכָל דִּילֵיהּ.

47. O cause of causes, in as much as you are there, IN TORAH, there is no interruption to the flow of the light of Torah. May it please your never to move away from my father and mother, NAMELY TORAH AND PRECEPTS, ZEIR ANPIN AND MALCHUT, and also not from His children, NAMELY, YISRAEL. And so for he who strains himself for the sake of the Torah, which is precious, THE TORAH will be lasting within him and will not ever be cut off from him. This is not true for he who does not busy himself with it. Even though he observes the precepts of the sages, MEANING THAT HE OBEYS THE SCHOLARS AND OBSERVES AS WE MENTIONED, he serves them. He is then a servant not a son. But if he is a trustful SERVANT, his Master causes him to be in control of all that is His.

48. אֲבָל מַאן דְּלָא אִשְׁתַּדַּל בְּאוֹרַיְיתָא, וְלָא מְשַׁמֵּשׁ חֲכָמִים, לְמִשְׁמַע

מִנַּיְיהוּ פְּקוּדִין, לְקַיֵּם נַעֲשֶׂה וְנִשְׁמָע. אֶלָּא דְּסָרַח וְעָבַר עַל לֹא תַעֲשֶׂה,
אִיהוּ שָׁקִיל לְאוּמִין דְּעָלְמָא עע״ז, בְּנוֹי דְּסָמָאֵ״ל וְנָחָשׁ, דְּאִתְּמַר בְּהוּ,
וּכְסִילִים מֵרִים קָלוֹן, דְּלָא בָּעוּ לְקַבְּלָא אוֹרַיְיתָא, דְּכָל דְּלֵית בֵּיהּ
תּוֹרָה, לֵית בֵּיהּ כָּבוֹד, דְּאִתְּמַר בָּהֶם כָּבוֹד חֲכָמִים יִנְחָלוּ.

48. But one who does not toil in Torah does not serve the sages as to obey them regarding precepts, to fulfill, "will we do and obey." He sins and transgresses the negative precepts. He is considered AND IS LIKENED TO the idolatrous nations of the world, the children of Samael and the serpent, of whom it says, "but fools shall get shame" (Mishlei 3:35) as they refused to receive the Torah. He who does not possess Torah lacks any honor, as it says about them, "the wise shall inherit honor" (Ibid.).

5. "A son honors his father"

A Synopsis

We hear about how a disobedient son can be forced to obey his parents, and what the punishment is if he does not. The mixture of evil inside a son can cause him to disobey, just as the children of Yisrael disobeyed God. The good servant or son stems from Metatron and the bad from Samael. But in the world of Atzilut there is no division, and no sin can come through the soul that is drawn from there.

49. וְעִם כָּל דָּא מָארֵי מְתִיבְתָּא, לָא כָּל כְּבוֹד שָׁוֶה, דְּהָא בֵּן יְכַבֵּד אָב וְעֶבֶד אֲדוֹנָיו. בֵּן יְכַבֵּד, עַל מְנָת דְּלָא לְקַבְּלָא אַגְרָא, אֲבָל מִצְוָּה הוּא בִּכְבוֹד אַבָּא וְאִמָּא. וְאִי לָא בָּעֵי לְמֶעְבַּד צֵוְוּיֵיה, יְכַתַּשׁ לֵיה אַבָּא וְאִמָּא, עַד דְּיַעֲבַד עַל כָּרְחֵיה. וְאִי הֲוֵי בְּרָא רַבְרְבָא, ב״ד כּוֹפִין לֵיה. דְּאִי לָא בָּעֵי לְמֶעְבַּד מַה כְּתִיב בֵּיה, בְּנֵנוּ זֶה סוֹרֵר וּמוֹרֶה אֵינֶנּוּ שׁוֹמֵעַ בְּקוֹלֵנוּ, וְדָנִין לֵיה בִּסְקִילָה. אֲבָל עֶבֶד דִּמְשַׁמֵּשׁ עַל מְנָת לְקַבֵּל פְּרָס, אִי לָא עָבֵיד צֵוְוּיֵיה דְּרַבֵּיה, מָארֵיה אַעֲבָּר לֵיה מִגּוֹ בֵּיתֵיה, וְיִטּוֹל אָחֳרָא. מַה דְּלָא הֲוָה יָכִיל לְמֶעְבַּד הָכִי לִבְרֵיה, אֶלָּא אוֹ יַעֲבֵיד צֵוְוּיֵיה אוֹ יִקְטוֹל לֵיה.

49. With all this, heads of the Yeshivah, not all honor is the same. "A son honors his father, and a servant his master" (Malachi 1:6). A son honors without the object of receiving reward, but nonetheless, he is commanded to honor father and mother. If he does not want to perform this, his parents can punish him until he unwillingly agrees. If he is a grown son, the court of justice can force him. If he does not want to, it is written about him: "This our son is stubborn and rebellious, he will not obey our voice" (Devarim 21:20). He is then sentenced to stoning. But in the case of a servant who serves primarily to receive reward, if he does not comply with the orders of his master, his master can dismiss him from his house and take someone else. He cannot do so with his son; either he complies and performs his command, or he puts him to death.

50. אָ״ל בּוּצִינָא קַדִּישָׁא, מַאן גָּרִים דְּלָא יַעֲבֵיד צֵוְוּיֵיה, הוֹאִיל וּבְרֵיה הוּא. אָמַר רַעְיָא מְהֵימָנָא, וַדַּאי תַּעֲרוֹבֶת דְּרַע, וְרָזָא דָּא גָּרַם לְיִשְׂרָאֵל,

לְמֶחֱטֵי גַבֵּי אֲבוּהוֹן דְּבִשְׁמַיָּא. וְרָזָא דָא, וַיִּתְעָרְבוּ בַגּוֹיִם. וְדָא גָּרַם קְטוּלָא לְיִשְׂרָאֵל, וְחָרִיב בֵּי מַקְדְּשָׁא. וּבְגִין דָּא, אֵין מְקַבְּלִים גֵּרִים לִימוֹת הַמָּשִׁיחַ, אֶלָּא יְיָ' בָּדָד יַנְחֶנּוּ וְאֵין עִמּוֹ אֵל נֵכָר.

50. The holy luminary, NAMELY RABBI SHIMON, said to him: What caused THE SON not to perform his command, even though he is his son? The Faithful Shepherd replied: Surely the mixture of evil WITHIN HIM. This secret caused Yisrael to sin before their Father in heaven. This is the secret of, "but were mingled among the nations" (Tehilim 106:35). This caused the slaying of Yisrael and the destruction of the Temple. For this reason, we do not accept converts in the days of the Messiah, but "so Hashem alone did lead him, and there was no strange El with him" (Devarim 32:12).

51. דְּיִשְׂרָאֵל אִינּוּן מֵאִילָנָא דְּחַיֵּי, עֶבֶד טוֹב וְעֶבֶד רָע, מִסִּטְרָא דִּמְטַטְרוֹ"ן עֶבֶד טוֹב, עֶבֶד נֶאֱמָן לְרַבֵּיהּ. עֶבֶד רָע סָמָאֵ"ל. מַאן דְּאִיהוּ מֵאִילָנָא דְּחַיֵּי, אִיהוּ בֶּן הָעוֹה"ב, בֶּן מִסִּטְרָא דְּבֶן יָ"ה, בִּינָ"ה. וְיָרִית מַלְכוּתָא דְּאִיהִי ה'. וְאֵיךְ יָרִית לָהּ. אִי עָבִיד צַוּוּיֵיהּ דְּאַבָּא וְאִימָא, בְּגִין דְּאִיהוּ מַלְכוּתָא מִצְוַת הַמֶּלֶךְ, וַעֲלֵיהּ אִתְּמַר, מַדּוּעַ אַתָּה עוֹבֵר אֶת מִצְוַת הַמֶּלֶךְ. אִיהִי מִצְוָה, וְצַוּוּיֵיא דְּמַלְכָּא עַל עֲשֵׂה וְלֹא תַעֲשֶׂה.

51. As Yisrael stems from the Tree of Life, AND THERE IS a good and bad servant. From the part of Metatron stems the good servant, SINCE HE IS a loyal servant to his Master. The bad servant stems from Samael. HOWEVER, he who stems from the Tree of Life has part in the World to Come. He is a son from the aspect of the son of *Yud-Hei*, DENOTING ZEIR ANPIN, SINCE Binah (*Bet-Yud-Nun-Hei*) CONSISTS OF THE LETTERS OF 'SON (HEB. *BEN*) OF *YUD-HEI*', and he inherits Malchut, which is *Hei* OF YUD HEI VAV HEI. How does he inherit her? By performing the precepts of Aba and Ima, HE THUS INHERITS HER. For Malchut is the command of the King. About it, it says: "Why are you trespassing the King's commandment?" (Ester 3:3). The commandment and the King's command affect the positive and the negative precepts.

52. מִצְוָה מִדְּאוֹרַיְיתָא, דְּאִיהִי תִּפְאֶרֶת. וְהָכָא לֵית תַּמָּן פְּרוּדָא, קוּדְשָׁא בְּרִיךְ הוּא אֱמֶת, תּוֹרָתוֹ תּוֹרַת אֱמֶת, אִיהוּ תּוֹרָתוֹ וּמִצְוָתוֹ.

כְּגַוְונָא דְּבִינָה, תּוֹרָתוֹ וּמִצְוָתוֹ דְּחָכְמָה. דְּאִית תּוֹרָה דִּבְרִיאָה, וְחָכְמָה
דִּבְרִיאָה, וּבִינָה דִּבְרִיאָה, וְהָכִי בְּכָל מִדּוֹת. בְּהַאי, יָכִיל בֵּן בְּהַאי
אוֹרַיְיתָא, לְמֶהֱוֵי בְּלָא מִצְוָה, וּמִצְוָה בְּלָא תּוֹרָה בְּפֵרוּדָא. וּמֵהָכָא, בֵּן
סוֹרֵר וּמוֹרֶה. אֲבָל מִסִּטְרָא דַּאֲצִילוּת, לֵית אַפְרָשׁוּתָא, תַּמָּן, וְכֵן מִתַּמָּן
אֵין חֵטְא בָּא עַל יָדוֹ וְלֵית בָּה עוֹנֶשׁ וְלָא שָׂכָר וְלָא מִיתָה.

52. The precept is from the Torah, which is Tiferet. Here, there is no division BETWEEN THE TORAH AND THE PRECEPT, SINCE THE TORAH IS GENERAL AND HER PRECEPTS ARE HER PARTICULARS. THUS, THEY ARE ONE. The Holy One, blessed be He, is Truth, His Torah is a Torah of truth. He is His Torah and His Precepts, SINCE THEY ARE ONE. Just as Binah is the Torah and the precept of Chochmah – SINCE THE SUPERNAL TORAH AND PRECEPT ARE THE SECRET OF CHOCHMAH AND BINAH, WHICH ARE ONE AND NEVER PART – there is the Torah of Briyah, MEANING ZEIR ANPIN OF THE WORLD OF BRIYAH, Chochmah of Briyah and Binah of Briyah. And so in all the attributes THERE IS CHOCHMAH AND BINAH, TORAH AND PRECEPT. Here, IN THE WORLD OF BRIYAH, it is possible that the son be in this Torah without the precepts, or the precepts without the Torah, in separation. From here, FROM THE ASPECT OF THE WORLD OF BRIYAH, IS DRAWN the stubborn and rebellious son – SINCE IN THE WORLD OF BRIYAH THERE ARE ALREADY KLIPOT, IN THE SECRET OF THE VERSE, "ELOHIM HAS MADE THE ONE AS WELL AS THE OTHER" (KOHELET 7:14). But in the world of Atzilut, there is no division. Thus, no sin can come through THE SOUL THAT IS DRAWN from there. There is IN IT no penalty, no reward, no death from there, BECAUSE THERE ARE NO KLIPOT THERE AT ALL, IN THE SECRET OF THE VERSE, "NOR SHALL EVIL DWELL WITH YOU" (TEHILIM 5:5).

53. וּבְגִין דָּא, אוֹרַיְיתָא דָּא אִילָנָא דְּחַיֵּי, שְׂכַר הָעוֹלָם הַבָּא, וְאִילָנָא
דָּא, אִילָנָא דְּחַיֵּי אִתְקְרֵי, וְאִתְקְרֵי הָעוֹלָם הַבָּא, וְלָא אִתְקְרֵי בֵּיהּ שָׂכָר.
בְּגִין דְּאִיהוּ בֵּן. מִתַּמָּן, לָא אִשְׁתְּדַּל בְּאוֹרַיְיתָא לְקַבְּלָא אַגְרָא, לָא
בְּמַעֲשֶׂה וְלָא בְּדִיבּוּר וְלָא בְּמַחֲשָׁבָה.

53. Therefore, IN ATZILUT, the Torah is the Tree of Life, CONCEIVING IT TO BE the reward of the World to Come, NAMELY BINAH. This tree is called the Tree of Life, called 'the World to Come' FROM THE ASPECT OF BINAH. No reward pertains to it because the son from there does not toil in Torah in order to receive reward – not in deed, speech, or in thought.

‎54. אָתָא בּוּצִינָא קַדִּישָׁא, לְנַשְּׁקָא לֵיהּ יְדֵיהּ. אָמַר, וַדַּאי אַנְתְּ הוּא בֵּן מִתַּמָּן, בְּדִיּוּקְנָא דִּבְרָא בּוּכְרָא דִּילֵיהּ, תִּפְאֶרֶת בְּרָא דְּאַבָּא וְאִימָא עִלָּאָה, אֲצִילוּת דִּילֵיהּ בְּלָא הַפְסָקָה, לָא קָדְמָךְ בְּרָא אָחֲרָא, לָא בְּמַחֲשָׁבָה, וְלָא בְּדִבּוּר, וְלָא בְּמַעֲשֶׂה. אָמַר רַעְיָא מְהֵימָנָא, וְאַנְתְּ, וְחַבְרַיָּיא, וְרָאשֵׁי מָארֵי מְתִיבְתָּאן, דִּמְזַמְּנִין הָכָא, אַתֵּי, בְּלָא הַפְסָקָה כְּלַל, וּבְלָא תַּעֲרוֹבֶת. נַשְּׁקוּ כֻּלְּהוּ דָּא לְדָא, וְאִשְׁתְּמוֹדְעוּ בְּאַחֲוָה, וּבְכוּ.

54. The holy luminary approached to kiss his hands. He said: Surely you are a son from there, FROM THE WORLD OF ATZILUT, in the form of its first born son, BEING Tiferet. For the son of the supernal Aba and Ima, his Atzilut never ceases. 'No other son preceded you, not in thought, speech nor deed.' The Faithful Shepherd said, 'You and the friends and the heads of the Yeshivot that are present with me are all without any interruption or mixture FROM THE OTHER SIDE, NAMELY OF THE ASPECT OF THE WORLD OF ATZILUT.' They kissed one another, intermingled in brotherhood, and wept.

6. A firstborn son

A Synopsis

Rabbi Shimon says that the brothers of a firstborn son are obligated to honor him because he is the eldest. He talks about being the child of God in the level of all three worlds – Briyah, Yetzirah and Asiyah.

55. פָּתַח ר"ש וְאָמַר, עִם כָּל דָּא, בְּרָא בּוּכְרָא חַיָּיבִין כָּל אֲחוֹי בִּיקָרֵיה, דְּהָא כְּתִיב כַּבֵּד אֶת אָבִיךָ, וְאוּקְמוּהָ רַבָּנָן, אֶת לְרַבּוֹת אָחִיךָ הַגָּדוֹל. וַאֲפִילוּ מִכָּל סִטְרָא אִיהוּ מְפָרֵשׁ עֲלָךְ בְּאוֹרַיְיתָא, בְּשַׁגַּ"ם זֶה הֶבֶל. וְלָא הֲוָה לְאָדָם קַדְמָאָה בְּרָא קַדְמָאָה מִנֵּיה, וְאוּקְמוּהָ רַבָּנָן, בְּשַׁגַּם, זֶה מֹשֶׁה. דְּבְרָא דְּמַלְכָּא בְּכָל אֲתָר, אַנְתְּ בּוּכְרָא מִסִּטְרָא דְּאִילָנָא דְּחַיֵּי דְּטוֹב וָרָע, אַנְתְּ הוּא טוֹב. הה"ד וַיַּרְא אֱלֹהִים אֶת הָאוֹר כִּי טוֹב, וַתֵּרֶא אוֹתוֹ כִּי טוֹב הוּא.

55. Rabbi Shimon commenced, saying: Despite all this, being the firstborn son, ALLUDING TO THE FAITHFUL SHEPHERD, all his brothers are obligated to honor him, as it is written: "Honor your father" (Shemot 20:12). And the sages have established that the particle "Et (lit. 'the')" includes your older brother, WHOM YOU NEED TO HONOR. In every aspect it is explained in the Torah regarding you; "for that (Heb. *beshagam*)" (Beresheet 6:3), namely Abel, INDICATES THAT MOSES WAS THE SOUL OF ABEL. Adam had no son before him, AS CAIN IS FROM THE ASPECT OF THE SERPENT, AND ABEL FROM THE ASPECT OF ADAM. The sages established that "*beshagam*" is Moses, SINCE *BESHAGAM* HAS THE SAME NUMERICAL VALUE AS MOSES, the son to the King in every respect. You are the firstborn from the aspect of the Tree of Life of Good and Evil. You are good, as the verses state: "And Elohim saw the light, that it was good" (Beresheet 1:4); "and when she saw that he was a goodly child" (Shemot 2:2). THIS MEANS THE ANGEL METATRON IS CALLED THE 'TREE OF LIFE OF GOOD AND EVIL', AND MOSES IS THE GOOD ASPECT THEREOF.

56. וּמִתַּמָּן קָרָא יָתָךְ קוּדְשָׁא בְּרִיךְ הוּא עֶבֶד נֶאֱמָן. לְבָתַר סְלִיקַת לְמֶחֱוֵי מַלְכָּא, הה"ד וַיְהִי בִישׁוּרוּן מֶלֶךְ. לְבָתַר בֶּן בַּיִת לְעֵילָא. מֶלֶךְ מִסִּטְרָא דְּמַלְכוּת דִּבְרִיאָה. בֶּן בַּיִת, מִסִּטְרָא דְּבִינָה דִּבְרִיאָה. כְּעַן אַנְתְּ

מֶלֶךְ, מִסִּטְרָא דְּאִילָנָא דְּמַלְכוּת דַּאֲצִילוּת. בֶּן בַּיִת, מִסִּטְרָא דְּבֶ״ן יָ״ה, תִּפְאֶרֶת דַּאֲצִילוּת, זַכָּאָה חוּלָקָךְ. וּמַאן גָּרִים לָךְ דָּא, בְּגִין דְּאִשְׁתַּדָּלוּתָךְ בַּתּוֹרָה וּבְמִצְוָה, לְיַחֲדָא קוּדְשָׁא בְּרִיךְ הוּא וּשְׁכִינְתֵּיה, לְאַעֲלָא מַלְכָּא עַל אַתְרֵיה, וְעַל מַשִׁרְיָיתֵיה לְעֵילָא, וְעַל יִשְׂרָאֵל לְתַתָּא.

56. And from there, the Holy One, blessed be He, called you 'faithful servant', SINCE SERVANT COMES FROM THE ASPECT OF METATRON. Later you were promoted to be king, as the verse states: "And he was a king in Yeshurun" (Devarim 33:5). Then you were a member of the most high household. YOU WERE a king from the aspect of Malchut of Briyah; a member of the household from the aspect of Binah of Briyah. Now you are a king from the aspect of the Tree of Malchut of Atzilut, a member of the household from the aspect of *Yud-Hei*, Tiferet of Atzilut. Fortunate is your lot. What brought this about for you? Your studious involvement in Torah and the precept to unify the Holy One, blessed be He, and His Shechinah, to bring the King to His post over His hosts on high and on Yisrael below.

57. וּבְגִין כַּךְ יָרְתִין כֻּלְּהוּ נִשְׁמָתִין דַּאֲצִילוּת מִנֵּיה, וְאִתְקְרִיאוּ בְּנִין דִּילֵיה, מִשֵּׁם יְדֹוָ״ד דַּאֲצִילוּת, דְּלֵית תַּמָּן פֵּרוּד וְקִצּוּץ. דְּבְקַדְמֵיתָא אִתְּמַר בְּהוּ בְּנִין לְקוּדְשָׁא בְּרִיךְ הוּא וּשְׁכִינְתֵּיה, מִצַּד יְהֹ״ה דִּבְרִיאָה, דְּאִתְּמַר בֵּיה בְּרָאתִיו יְצַרְתִּיו אַף עֲשִׂיתִיו, וּכְעַן בָּנִים לִידֹוָ״ד דַּאֲצִילוּת.

57. Because of this, they all inherit from Him souls of Atzilut, and are thus called 'His children', of the Name Yud Hei Vav Hei of Atzilut where there exists no division or mutilation. At first, it is mentioned about them that they are children of the Holy One, blessed be He, and His Shechinah, from the aspect of Yud Hei Vav Hei of the world of Briyah, as it is written concerning him, "EVERY ONE THAT IS CALLED BY MY NAME: for I have created him FOR MY GLORY, I have formed him; yea, I have made him" (Yeshayah 43:7), MEANING THAT HE CREATED HIM FROM THE ASPECT OF YUD HEI VAV HEI OF BRIYAH, FORMED HIM FROM YETZIRAH, AND ALSO MADE HIM FROM THE ASPECT OF ASIYAH. NOW THEY HAVE BECOME children of Yud Hei Vav Hei of Atzilut.

7. "Then you may appoint a king over you"

A Synopsis

Rabbi Shimon continues speaking to Moses, the Faithful Shepherd, talking about Moses' elevation in the levels of kingship. He says that Moses will be leader of Yisrael and bind them all into one knot with God so that they may all bless and sanctify Him.

58. וּבְךָ אִתְקַיַּים פְּקוּדָא, דְּאִיהִי מִצְוָה עַל יִשְׂרָאֵל, לְהַעֲמִיד עֲלֵיהֶם מֶלֶךָ. הַהִ"ד, שׂוֹם תָּשִׂים עָלֶיךָ מֶלֶךָ. וְאִתְקַיַּים בָּךְ וַיְהִי בִישׁוּרוּן מֶלֶךָ, כַּד בְּקַדְמֵיתָא. וְכֻלְּהוּ מִתְנַהֲגִין אֲבַתְרָךְ, כְּאֵבָרִין דְּמִתְנַהֲגִין כֻּלְּהוּ בִּתְנוּעָה דְּנִשְׁמָתָא, דְּאִתְפַּשְׁטָא עַל כָּל אֵבָר. בְּגִין דְּכֶתֶר עִלָּאָה אַנְתְּ תְּהֵא מְעוּטָר בֵּיהּ, דְּבֵיהּ עִלַּת הָעִלּוֹת אִיהוּ כֶּתֶר עַל כֹּלָּא, טָמִיר וְגָנִיז מִלְּגָיו מִנֵּיהּ. וּמִנֵּיהּ אִתְפְּשָׁט עַל כָּל סְפִירָן, וּמְסַדֵּר לוֹן לְמֶהֱוֵי דָּא רַב, וְדָא זְעֵיר, וְדָא בֵּינוֹנִי, וְאַנְהִיג לוֹן לִרְעוּתֵיהּ, וְנָהִיר בְּהוּ, וּמְקַשֵּׁר לוֹן, וּמְיַחֵד לוֹן.

58. With you was the precept that was given to Yisrael to appoint a king over them fulfilled, as the verse says, "then you may appoint a king over you" (Devarim 17:15). First, it was fulfilled in relation to you, "And he was a king in Yeshurun" (Devarim 33:5), AS HE WAS THE FIRST KING OF YISRAEL. Everyone followed you, like limbs acting all with the strength of the movement of the soul that spreads into each limb. It is due to a supernal crown that you will be adorned with, in which is the cause of all causes. It is Keter over all, hidden and concealed in its innermost being. From it, it spreads to all the Sfirot and organizes them so that CHESED should be prominent, JUDGMENT should be small, and MERCY intermediate. He guides them according to His will, shines within them, binds them, and unifies them.

59. הָכִי אַנְתְּ תְּהֵא מַנְהִיג לְיִשְׂרָאֵל, בְּכָל מִדּוֹת טָבִין דִּילֵיהּ, וּתְסַדֵּר כָּל חַד כִּדְחַזֵי לֵיהּ, הַבְּכוֹר כִּבְכוֹרָתוֹ, וְהַצָּעִיר כִּצְעִירָתוֹ, וּבֵינוֹנִי כְּפוּם דַּרְגֵּיהּ. וּתְקַשֵּׁר לוֹן קֶשֶׁר אֶחָד לְגַבֵּי אֲבוּהוֹן דְּבִשְׁמַיָּא. לְמֶהֱוֵי כֻּלְּהוּ בִּשְׂפָה בְּרוּרָה. לְבָרְכָא לְקוּדְשָׁא בְּרִיךְ הוּא. וּלְקַדְּשֵׁיהּ, וּלְיַיחֲדֵיהּ,

בְּדַרְגָּא דִילָךְ, בְּמַחֲשָׁבָה דִילָךְ, בַּאֲצִילוּת דִילָךְ, דְּאִתְקַיַּים בָּךְ וְאָצַלְתִּי מִן הָרוּחַ אֲשֶׁר עָלֶיךָ וְשַׂמְתִּי עֲלֵיהֶם. קוּם אִתְּעַר בְּפִקּוּדָא, לְהַכְרִית זַרְעוֹ שֶׁל עֲמָלֵק.

59. Similarly, you shall be leader of Yisrael with all its good traits, OF KETER, and arrange each AND EVERY ONE properly, the oldest according to his seniority, the youngest according to his youth, and the intermediate according to his level. You will bind them into one knot to their Father in Heaven, that they may all in clear language bless the Holy One, blessed be He, sanctify Him, and unify Him according to your level, your thoughts, your Atzilut, and there should be fulfilled with you, "and I will take of the spirit which is upon you, and will put it upon them" (Bemidbar 11:17). Arise, awaken yourself to the commandment of erasing the seed of Amalek.

60. אִישׁ אִמּוֹ וְאָבִיו תִּירָאוּ וְגוֹ' פִּקּוּדָא דָא, לְכַבֵּד אָב וְאֵם, דְּאִצְטְרִיךְ בַּ"נ לְמִדְחַל מֵאֲבוֹי וּמֵאִמֵּיה, וּלְאוֹקִיר לוֹן. כְּמָה דְּאִצְטְרִיךְ בַּ"נ לְאוֹקִיר לֵיהּ לְקוּדְשָׁא בְּרִיךְ הוּא. מִסִּטְרָא דְּרוּחָא דְּיָהַב בְּגַוֵּיה. וּלְמִדְחַל מִנֵּיה. הָכִי אִצְטְרִיךְ לֵיהּ לְאוֹקִיר לַאֲבוֹי וּלְאִמֵּיה, מִסִּטְרָא דְּגוּפָא דְּילֵיהּ, וּלְמִדְחַל מִנְּהוֹן, דְּהָא אִינּוּן מִשְׁתַּתְּפִין בְּקוּדְשָׁא בְּרִיךְ הוּא, וְעָבְדֵי לֵיהּ גּוּפָא, וְהוֹאִיל וְאִינּוּן שׁוּתָּפִין בְּעוֹבָדָא, לֶיהֱווּ שׁוּתָּפִין בִּדְחִילוּ וִיקָרָא.

60. "You shall revere every man his mother, and his father." This precept is to honor father and mother, for one needs to fear father and mother and honor them. Just as man needs to honor the Holy One, blessed be He, and fear Him from the aspect of the spirit that He encased within him, so too, he must honor his father and mother from the aspect of his body, and fear them since they participated with the Holy One, blessed be He, to form his body. Since they are partners in the action, they are partners in fear and honor.

8. Adam had nothing of this world

A Synopsis

Rabbi Shimon talks about the three partners in the creation of Adam and man – God, father, and mother. Before Adam sinned he was clothed with light, but when he sinned he became dark and was clothed with skin. We hear how men were created below on earth after Enoch came, and the necessary participation of above and below in their creation.

61. כְּגַוְונָא דָא, ג׳ שׁוּתָּפִין אִשְׁתְּכָחוּ לְעֵילָא בְּרָזָא דְּאָדָם. אָדָם קַדְמָאָה, אע״ג דְּגוּפָא דִּילֵיהּ הֲוָה מֵעַפְרָא, לָאו מֵעַפְרָא דְּהָכָא הֲוָה אֶלָּא מֵעַפְרָא דְּבֵי מַקְדְּשָׁא דִּלְעֵילָּא. אַבָּא וְאִימָּא אִשְׁתְּכָחוּ, וּמַלְכָּא עִלָּאָה אִשְׁתְּתַּף בַּהֲדַיְיהוּ, וְשָׁדַר בֵּיהּ רוּחָא דְּחַיֵּי, וְאִתְבְּרֵי. וּכְגַוְונָא דָא, אִשְׁתְּכַח כֹּלָּא עֵילָּא וְתַתָּא. וְעַ״ד אִצְטְרִיךְ לֵיהּ לב״נ לְמִדְחַל לְקוּדְשָׁא בְּרִיךְ הוּא, וּלְמִדְחַל לַאֲבוּי וּלְאִמֵּיהּ.

61. Similarly, there are three partners above in the secret of Adam. Even though his body was from earth, it was not from earth here OF THIS WORLD, but from the earth of the Temple on high, BEING IN THE STATE OF THE WORLD OF BRIYAH. Aba and Ima are present, NAMELY ZEIR ANPIN AND MALCHUT. And the supernal King, NAMELY BINAH, participated with them and sent the spirit of life, and he was created. Similarly, THREE PARTNERS all exist above and below. Therefore, man needs to fear the Holy One, blessed be He, his father, and his mother.

62. בס״ת, אָדָם קַדְמָאָה לָא הֲוָה לֵיהּ מֵהַאי עָלְמָא כְּלוּם. חַד צַדִּיק עָבֵד שְׁמוּשָׁא בְּנוּקְבֵיהּ, וְאִתְעֲבֵיד מֵהַהוּא שְׁמוּשָׁא גּוּפָא חֲדָא, דְּנְהִירוּ דִּילֵיהּ יַתִּיר מִכָּל אִינּוּן מַלְאָכִין שְׁלִיחָן לְעֵילָּא. וְכַד אִתְבְּרֵי הַהוּא גּוּפָא מַלְכָּא עִלָּאָה, שָׁדַר בְּהַהוּא צַדִּיק כ״ב אַתְוָון, וְאִשְׁתְּתַּף בַּהֲדַיְיהוּ, וְנָפַק לְעָלְמָא.

62. IT IS RECORDED in the secrets of the Torah that Adam had nothing from this world, MEANING, FROM THE STATE OF MALCHUT OF THE QUALITY OF JUDGMENT. The Righteous, BEING THE YESOD OF ZEIR ANPIN, had his

contact with the female, MEANING WITH MALCHUT THAT WAS CLOTHING BINAH. From this contact came one body whose illumination WAS more than all the angels and messenger from above. When that one body was created, the supernal King, BINAH, sent with this Righteous, DENOTING YESOD OF ZEIR ANPIN, 22 letters; BINAH joined with them and then he came into the world.

63. כֵּיוָן דְּנָפַק, חָמוּ לֵיה שִׁמְשָׁא וְסִיהֲרָא, וְאִסְתִּימוּ נְהוֹרַיְיהוּ, דְּתַפּוּחָא דְּרַגְלֵיה אַחְשִׁיךְ נְהוֹרָא דִּלְהוֹן. מַאי טַעְמָא. בְּגִין דְּמֵעוֹבָדָא דְּשִׁמְשָׁא וְסִיהֲרָא עִלָּאָה נָפַק. כֵּיוָן דְּחָטָא, אִתְחֲשָׁךְ, וְאַזְעִיר גַּרְמֵיה, וְאִצְטְרִיךְ לְגוּפָא אָחֳרָא בְּמַשְׁכָא וּבְבִשְׂרָא. דִּכְתִיב, וַיַּעַשׂ יְיָ' אֱלֹהִים לְאָדָם וּלְאִשְׁתּוֹ כָּתְנוֹת עוֹר וַיַּלְבִּשֵׁם. כְּהַהוּא שִׁמּוּשָׁא דְּעֲבַד הַהוּא צַדִּיק בְּנוּקְבֵיה, לָא אִשְׁתְּכַח מִקַּדְמַת דְּנָא, וּלְבָתַר דְּנָא, דְּהָא עַד לָא נָפַק לְצוֹרֶף אוּמָנָא.

63. When he, ADAM, came INTO THE WORLD, the sun and moon saw him and their light was dimmed; the heel of the foot OF ADAM darkened their light. For what reason? Because he is derived from the doings of the supernal sun and moon, NAMELY ZEIR ANPIN AND MALCHUT. However, when he sinned, he became dark and reduced himself and needed another body with skin and flesh, as it is written, "For the man also and for his wife did Hashem Elohim make coats of skins, and clothed them" (Beresheet 3:21). The like of that contact that the righteous had with the female, LEADING TO THE BIRTH OF ADAM AS MENTIONED, there never was before this, NOR afterwards. For the craftsman has not yet come out to refine.

64. עַד דְּאָתָא חֲנוֹךְ, וְנָטִיל לֵיה קוּדְשָׁא בְּרִיךְ הוּא מֵאַרְעָא, וְאַבְרִיר פְּסוֹלֶת וְקַסְטוּרָא מִכַּסְפָּא, וְכֵן בְּכָל אִינּוּן צַדִּיקַיָּיא דִּי בְּאַרְעָא. לְבָתַר אִתְתַּקַּן הַהוּא אֲתַר, וְאִתְעֲבִידוּ רוּחִין וְנִשְׁמָתִין בְּשִׁמּוּשַׁיְיהוּ וְגוּפָא מִתַּתָּא בְּאַרְעָא. וְעַ"ד בְּשׁוּתָּפוּ דִּלְעֵילָּא וְתַתָּא, בַּר נָשׁ אָתֵי לְעָלְמָא, וְאִצְטְרִיךְ לְמִדְחַל לְאִינּוּן שׁוּתָּפִין, וּלְאוֹקִיר לוֹן, כְּמָה דְּאִתְּמַר.

ע"כ רעיא מהימנא

64. When Enoch came, the Holy One, blessed be He, took him from the earth, cleansed him from the refuse and the silver from the tin residue, and so with all the righteous in the land. Afterwards, that place was corrected, MEANING MALCHUT, WHERE MALCHUT OF THE QUALITY OF JUDGMENT WAS CONCEALED AND WAS NO LONGER SEEN. THEN were fashioned from the coupling OF ZEIR ANPIN AND MALCHUT spirits and souls, and the body below on earth. Hence, as a result of the participation of above and below, man comes into the world. And it is incumbent upon him to fear these participants and revere them, as we learned.

End of Ra'aya Mehimna (the Faithful Shepherd)

A Synopsis

Rabbi Shimon says that the precepts men perform, and also their transgressions, ascend and stand before God, and testify for or against him. If the man repents of any transgressions, God removes his sins.

65. אַל תִּפְנוּ אֶל הָאֱלִילִים וֵאלֹהֵי מַסֵּכָה לֹא תַעֲשׂוּ לָכֶם. רִבִּי חִיָּיא פָּתַח, אַל תֵּפֶן אֶל קְשִׁי הָעָם הַזֶּה וְגוֹ'. אַל תֵּפֶן. וְכִי מָאן הוּא דְּיֵּימָא לְמַלְכָּא, אַל תֵּפֶן. וְהָא כְּתִיב כִּי עֵינָיו עַל דַּרְכֵי אִישׁ. וּכְתִיב אִם יִסָּתֵר אִישׁ בַּמִּסְתָּרִים וַאֲנִי לֹא אֶרְאֶנּוּ נְאֻם יְיָ', וְהָא בְּכֹלָּא אַשְׁגַּח קוּדְשָׁא בְּרִיךְ הוּא וְכָל עוֹבָדִין מִסְתַּכָּל, וְעַיֵּיל בְּדִינָא עַל כֻּלְּהוּ, אִם טַב וְאִם בִּישׁ, כד"א, הָאֱלֹהִים יָבִיא בְמִשְׁפָּט עַל כָּל נֶעְלָם אִם טוֹב וְאִם רָע. וּמֹשֶׁה אָמַר אַל תֵּפֶן.

65. "Turn not to idols, nor make to yourselves molten Elohim" (Vayikra 19:4). Rabbi Chiya commenced: "look not to the stubbornness of this people ..." (Devarim 9:27). "…look not…" HE QUESTIONS: Who can tell the King, "look not," seeing that it is written, "For His eyes are upon the ways of man" (Iyov 34:21), and, "'Can any hide himself in secret places, that I shall not see him?' Says Hashem" (Yirmeyah 23:24). The Holy One, blessed be He, watches everything, looks at all deeds, and brings Judgment for all, whether good or bad, as it is written: "For the Elohim shall bring every work into justice, with every secret thing, whether it be good, or whether it be evil" (Kohelet 12:14). Yet Moses says, "look not."

66. אֶלָּא, כַּמָה בָּעֵי בַּר נָשׁ לְאִסְתַּמְּרָא מֵחוֹבוֹי, בְּגִין דְּלָא יֶחֱטֵי קַמֵּי

מַלְכָּא קַדִּישָׁא. תָּא חֲזֵי, בַּר נָשׁ דְּעָבֵיד מִצְוָה, הַהִיא מִצְוָה סַלְקָא, וְקַיְּימָא קַמֵּי קוּדְשָׁא בְּרִיךְ הוּא, וְאָמְרָה אֲנָא מִפְּלַנְיָיא דְּעָבַד לִי. וְקוּדְשָׁא בְּרִיךְ הוּא מָנֵי לָהּ קַמֵּיהּ, לְאַשְׁגָּחָא בָּהּ כָּל יוֹמָא לְאוֹטָבָא לֵיהּ בְּגִינָהּ. עָבַר עַל פִּתְגָּמֵי אוֹרַיְיתָא, הַהִיא עֲבֵירָה סַלְקָא קַמֵּיהּ, וְאָמְרָה אֲנָא מִפְּלַנְיָיא דְּעָבֵד לִי, וְקוּדְשָׁא בְּרִיךְ הוּא מָנֵי לָהּ, וְקַיְּימָא תַּמָּן לְאַשְׁגָּחָא בָּהּ, לְשֵׁיצָאָה לֵיהּ. הה"ד. וַיַּרְא יְיָ' וַיִּנְאָץ מִכַּעַס בָּנָיו וּבְנוֹתָיו. מַהוּ וַיַּרְא. הַהוּא דְּקַיְּימָא קַמֵּיהּ.

66. HE ANSWERS: See how much a person needs to be cautious of sins in order not to transgress before the Holy King. Come and behold: when one performs a precept, this precept ascends and then stands before the Holy One blessed be He, and says, 'I belong to so and so who made me.' The Holy One, blessed be He, places it before him and watches over it daily in order to benefit THE PERSON on its behalf. If A MAN transgresses with a matter of Torah, that transgression appears before Him and says, 'I am a product of the one who made me'. The Holy One, blessed be He, appoints it, and it remains there so that He may see it in order to punish him. This is the essence of the verse, "And when Hashem saw it, He abhorred them, because of the provocation of His sons and daughters" (Devarim 32:19). What is meant by "saw"? IT MEANS THE TRANSGRESSION standing before Him.

67. תָּב בִּתְשׁוּבָה, מַה כְּתִיב. גַּם יְיָ' הֶעֱבִיר חַטָּאתְךָ לֹא תָמוּת. דְּאַעְבַּר הַהוּא חוֹבָא מִקַּמֵּיהּ, בְּגִין דְּלָא יִסְתָּכַּל בֵּיהּ. לְאוֹטָבָא לֵיהּ. וְעַל דָּא אַל תֵּפֶן אֶל קְשִׁי הָעָם הַזֶּה וְאֶל רִשְׁעוֹ וְאֶל חַטָּאתוֹ. אָמַר רִבִּי יוֹסֵי, וְכֵן מֵהָכָא מַשְׁמַע, דִּכְתִיב נִכְתָּם עֲוֺנֵךְ לְפָנַי.

67. He repents. Then it is written, "Hashem also has commuted your sin, you shall not die" (II Shmuel 12:13), meaning that He removed from before Him that sin, in order not to look at it and to benefit him. Therefore, IT IS WRITTEN, "look not to the stubbornness of this people, nor to their wickedness, nor to their sin," MEANING, DO NOT LOOK AT THEM. Rabbi Yosi said: Also from here is derived THIS IDEA, as it is written, "yet the stain of your iniquity is before Me" (Yirmeyah 2:22).

9. "The woman whom You did give to be with me"

A Synopsis

Rabbi Yosi and Rabbi Shimon talk about the creation of Eve, and how she was separated from the attachment that she had to Adam. In this way she became his help mate.

68. רַבִּי יוֹסֵי זְעֵירָא, עָאל קַמֵּיהּ דְּר׳ שִׁמְעוֹן יוֹמָא חַד, אַשְׁכְּחֵיהּ דַּהֲוָה יָתִיב וְקָאֲרֵי, כְּתִיב, וַיֹּאמֶר הָאָדָם הָאִשָּׁה אֲשֶׁר נָתַתָּ עִמָּדִי הִיא נָתְנָה לִי מִן הָעֵץ וָאֹכֵל. מַשְׁמַע דְּאָדָם וְחַוָּה כַּחֲדָא אִתְבְּרִיאוּ, וּבְגוּפָא חֲדָא. דִּכְתִיב אֲשֶׁר נָתַתָּ עִמָּדִי, וְלָא כְּתִיב אֲשֶׁר נָתַתָּ לִי, אָמַר לֵיהּ, אִי הָכִי, וְהִכְתִיב אֲנִי הָאִשָּׁה הַנִּצֶּבֶת עִמְּכָה בָּזֶה. וְלָא כְּתִיב הַנִּצֶּבֶת לְפָנֶיךָ. אָמַר לֵיהּ, אִי כְּתִיב הַנִּתֶּנֶת עִמְּךָ, הֲוָה אֲמֵינָא הָכִי, כְּדִכְתִיב אֲשֶׁר נָתַתָּ עִמָּדִי, אֲבָל הַנִּצֶּבֶת כְּתִיב.

68. Rabbi Yosi the younger entered before Rabbi Shimon one day and found him sitting and reading the verse: "And the man said, 'The woman whom You did give to be with me, she gave me of the tree, and I did eat'" (Beresheet 3:12). THIS HERE means that Adam and Eve were created together, stuck one to the other in one body, as it says, "did give to be with me," and not 'You gave to me'. He replied to him: If so, what of the verse, "I am the woman that stood by you here" (I Shmuel 1:26)? It is not written, 'that stood before you'. He said to him: If the verse read, 'given with you', then I would say it resembles the other verse that says, "whom You did give to be with me." However, as it reads, "stood," THEN THE MEANING IS ONLY STANDING ALONE, BUT NOT ATTACHED TO HIM.

69. אָמַר לֵיהּ, וְהָא כְּתִיב וַיֹּאמֶר יְיָ׳ אֱלֹהִים לֹא טוֹב הֱיוֹת הָאָדָם לְבַדּוֹ אֶעֱשֶׂה לּוֹ עֵזֶר כְּנֶגְדּוֹ. אֶעֱשֶׂה לּוֹ הַשְׁתָּא. אָמַר לֵיהּ הָכִי הוּא וַדַּאי, דְּאָדָם לְבַדּוֹ הֲוָה, דְּלָא הֲוָה לֵיהּ סָמֵךְ מִנּוּקְבֵיהּ, בְּגִין דַּהֲוַת בְּסִטְרוֹי כְּמָה דְּאוֹקִימְנָא. וּמַה דְּאָמַר אֶעֱשֶׂה לּוֹ עֵזֶר, הָכִי הוּא, דְּלָא כְּתִיב אִבְרָא לוֹ עֵזֶר, בְּגִין דִּכְתִיב זָכָר וּנְקֵבָה בְּרָאָם. אֲבָל אֶעֱשֶׂה כְּתִיב. וּמַהוּ אֶעֱשֶׂה. אַתְקָן. מַשְׁמַע דְּקוּדְשָׁא בְּרִיךְ הוּא נָטִיל לָהּ מִסִּטְרוֹי, וְתַקִּין לָהּ בְּתִקּוּנָא, וְאַיְיתֵי לָהּ קַמֵּיהּ. וּכְדֵין אִשְׁתַּמַּשׁ אָדָם בְּאַנְתְּתֵיהּ, וַהֲוָה לֵיהּ סָמֵךְ.

69. He replied: Behold it is written, "And Hashem Elohim said, 'It is not good that the man should be alone; I will make him a help to match [before] him'" (Beresheet 2:18). HENCE, HIS WIFE WAS CREATED ALONE. SHE WAS BEFORE HIM, NOT ATTACHED TO HIM IN ONE BODY. HE ANSWERS: "I will make him," MEANING now I WILL MAKE HER BEFORE HIM, BUT PRIOR TO THIS THEY WERE CREATED ATTACHED IN ONE BODY. He said to him: So it was surely that Adam was alone; he had no help in a female since she was ATTACHED by the rib, as explained. And the meaning of, "I will make him a help" MEANS that it is already so, as it is not written, 'I will create a help', WHICH IS because it is written, "male and female He created them" (Beresheet 5:2) – MEANING THAT SINCE THE TIME OF CREATION, THEY WERE ALREADY A MALE AND FEMALE. But it says, "I will make"; what shall I make? MEANING I will fix, meaning the Holy One, blessed be He, took her from his ribs in order to make this corrective change, brought her before him, and then Adam united with his wife and she was his help mate.

10. It is forbidden for a man to look at a woman's beauty

A Synopsis

Rabbi Shimon says that the souls of Adam and Eve came from such a high place that no one could look at their great light and beauty. Only after they sinned was Adam even able to look at Eve and recognize her for the purpose of mating. We learn that men should not look at women lest they be tempted and acquire bad thoughts that will come to them in the night. It is worse still if a man is mating with his wife and has thoughts about another woman, as this results in the birth of impure children.

70. וְתָנֵינָן, שַׁפִּירוּ דְּאָדָם קַדְמִיתָא דְּקִיטְרָא עִלָּאָה, מִזִּיהֲרָא דְּנַהֲרָא. שַׁפִּירוּ דְּחַוָּה, דְּלָא הֲווֹ יַכְלִין כָּל בִּרְיָין לְאִסְתַּכְּלָא בָּהּ. וַאֲפִילוּ אָדָם לָא הֲוָה אִסְתְּכַּל בָּהּ, עַד הַהוּא זִמְנָא דְּחָאבוּ, וְאַעֲדִיאַת שַׁפִּירוּ דִּלְהוֹן. כְּדֵין אִסְתְּכַּל בָּהּ אָדָם, וְאִשְׁתְּמוֹדַע בָּהּ לְשַׁמְּשָׁא בָּהּ. הֲדָא הוּא דִכְתִיב וַיֵּדַע אָדָם עוֹד אֶת אִשְׁתּוֹ. וַיֵּדַע: בְּכֹלָּא. וַיֵּדַע: בְּתַשְׁמִישׁ. וַיֵּדַע: דְּאִשְׁתְּמוֹדַע בָּהּ וְאִסְתְּכַּל בָּהּ.

70. We learned that the beauty of Adam came from the glow of the supernal knot of the brightness that shines, BEING THE SECRET OF THE GLOW OF ABA, SINCE HE HAD A NESHAMAH OF THE NESHAMAH OF ABA OF ATZILUT. The beauty of Eve was such that no creature could look at her, SINCE HER NESHAMAH OF NESHAMAH OF IMA OF ATZILUT. Even Adam did not look at her until the time they sinned and their beauty was removed. Only then could Adam look at her and recognize her for the purpose of mating. This is the essence of the verse, "And Adam knew his wife again" (Beresheet 4:25). He knew her in everything; he knew her through mating, that is, "knew," in that he recognized her and saw her.

71. וְתָנֵינָן, אָסִיר לֵיהּ לב"נ לְאִסְתַּכְּלָא בְּשַׁפִּירוּ דְּאִנְתְּתָא, בְּגִין דְּלָא יֵיתֵי בְּהִרְהוּרָא בִישָׁא, וְיִתְעַקַּר לְמִלָּה אָחֳרָא. וְכָךְ הֲוָה ר"ש עָבֵיד, כַּד הֲוָה אָזִיל בְּמָתָא, וַהֲווֹ חַבְרַיָּיא אַזְלִין אֲבַתְרֵיהּ, וְחָמָא לְאִינְתּוּ שַׁפִּירָאן, מָאִיךְ עֵינֵיהּ, וַהֲוָה אָמַר לְחַבְרַיָּיא אַל תֵּפֶן.

71. We learned that is it prohibited for a man to look at the beauty of a woman to prevent him from acquiring bad thoughts and being torn into another thing, MEANING THAT A DROP OF SEMEN WILL BE TORN FROM HIM IN VAIN. So did Rabbi Shimon behave when he came to the city. The friends followed him, and when he saw beautiful women, he lowered his eyes and told the friends not to look.

72. וְכָל מַאן דְּיִסְתַּכַּל בְּשַׁפִּירוּ דְּאִנְתְּתָא בִּימָמָא, אָתֵי לְהַרְהוּרֵי בְּלֵילְיָא. וְאִי סָלִיק הַהוּא הִרְהוּרָא בִּישָׁא עֲלֵיהּ, אַעֲבַר מִשּׁוּם וֵאלֹהֵי מַסֵּכָה לֹא תַעֲשׂוּ לָכֶם. תּוּ, אִי שִׁמֵּשׁ בְּאִנְתְּתֵיהּ בְּזִמְנָא דְּסָלִיק בֵּיהּ הַהוּא הִרְהוּרָא בִּישָׁא, אִינּוּן בְּנִין דְּאוֹלִידוּ אֱלֹהֵי מַסֵּכָה אִקְרוּן. וְעַל דָּא כְּתִיב, אַל תִּפְנוּ אֶל הָאֱלִילִים וֵאלֹהֵי מַסֵּכָה לֹא תַעֲשׂוּ לָכֶם. ר' אַבָּא אָמַר, אָסִיר לֵיהּ לב"נ לְאִסְתַּכְּלָא בְּאֱלִילֵי ע"ז, וּבְנָשֵׁי דְּעַמִּין, וְלָא לְאִתְהַנְיָיא מִנַּיְיהוּ, וְלָא לְאִתְרַפְּאָה בְּהוּ, דְּאָסִיר לֵיהּ לב"נ לְאִסְתַּכְּלָא בַּאֲתַר דְּלָא אִצְטְרִיךְ.

72. Whoever look at the beauty of women during the day will have those thoughts coming to him at night. When those evil thoughts come upon him at night, he transgresses, because "nor make to yourselves molten Elohim." FOR THE KLIPOT THAT NURTURE FROM THIS ARE CALLED 'MOLTEN ELOHIM'. Furthermore, if he is mating with his wife when he has these evil thoughts, the children born are called 'molten Elohim' (Leviticus 19:4). Therefore, it is written: "Turn not to idols, nor make to yourselves molten Elohim." Rabbi Aba said: It is prohibited for a person to look at idols and women of the nations, to derive any benefit from them, or to seek a cure from them, as it is forbidden to look at a forbidden place.

11. "Turn away your eyes from me"

A Synopsis

Rabbi Shimon tells Rabbi Aba about another David, a supernal David, who brings mercy from God to the world. His beauty illuminates all the worlds. We then learn about another Garden of Eden, a supernal Garden that exists for God, wherein His love is found. Lastly Rabbi Shimon talks about another land, a supernal land of Yisrael situated beneath the level of Jacob, and which God bequeathed to Yisrael. It is called 'land of life'.

73. ר' אַבָּא פָּתַח, פְּנֵה אֵלַי וְחָנֵּנִי תְּנָה עֻזְּךָ לְעַבְדֶּךָ, פְּנֵה אֵלַי וְחָנֵּנִי, וְכִי לָא הֲוָה לֵיהּ לְקוּדְשָׁא בְּרִיךְ הוּא בְּעָלְמָא שַׁפִּירָא כְּדָוִד, דְּאִיהוּ אָמַר פְּנֵה אֵלַי וְחָנֵּנִי. אֶלָּא הָכִי תָּנֵינָן, דָּוִד אָחֳרָא אִית לֵיהּ לְקוּדְשָׁא בְּרִיךְ הוּא וְהוּא מְמָנָא עַל כַּמָּה אוּכְלוּסִין עִלָּאִין וּמַשִׁרְיָין. וְכַד בָּעֵי קוּדְשָׁא בְּרִיךְ הוּא לְרַחֲמָא עַל עָלְמָא, אִסְתַּכַּל בְּהַאי דָוִד, וְנָהִיר לֵיהּ אַנְפִּין, וְהוּא נָהִיר לְעָלְמִין, וְחַיֵּיס עָלְמָא.

73. Rabbi Aba commenced: "O turn to me, and have mercy upon me; give Your strength to Your servant" (Tehilim 86:16). "O turn to me, and have mercy upon me." HE QUESTIONS: Did the Holy One, blessed be He, have any other person in the world as beautiful as David, so that he needed to say, "O turn to me, and have mercy upon me"? AND ANSWERS: Such we learned, that the Holy One, blessed be He, has another David, NAMELY MALCHUT NAMED 'DAVID', appointed over numerous supernal troops and camps. When the Holy One, blessed be He, wishes to show mercy upon the earth, He looks to this David and shines His radiance upon him. He, in turn, illuminates the worlds and extends Mercy to the world.

74. וּשְׁפִּירוּ דְּהַאי דָוִד, נָהִיר לְעָלְמִין כֻּלְּהוּ רֵישֵׁיהּ גּוּלְגַּלְתָּא דְּדַהֲבָא, אִתְרְקִימַת בְּשִׁבְעָה תַּכְשִׁיטֵי זִינִין דְּדַהֲבָא. וְהָא אוּקְמוּהָ. וַחֲבִיבוּתָא דְּקוּדְשָׁא בְּרִיךְ הוּא לְקָבְלֵיהּ, וּמִסַּגִּיאוּת רְחִימוּתָא דִּילֵיהּ גַּבֵּיהּ, אָמַר לֵיהּ לְקוּדְשָׁא בְּרִיךְ הוּא, דְּיֶהֱדַר עֵינוֹי לְקָבְלֵיהּ, וְיִסְתְּכַּל בֵּיהּ. בְּגִין דְּאִינוּן שַׁפִּירָן בְּכֹלָּא, כד"א, הָסֵבִּי עֵינַיִךְ מִנֶּגְדִּי וְגוֹ'. הָסֵבִּי עֵינַיִךְ מִנֶּגְדִּי דִּבְשַׁעֲתָא דְּאִלֵּין עַיְינִין מִסְתַּכְּלִין בֵּיהּ בְּקוּדְשָׁא בְּרִיךְ הוּא,

כְּדֵין מִתְעָרִין בְּלִבֵּיה קַסְטִין דְּבַלִסְטְרָאֵי, בִּרְחִימוּתָא עִלָּאָה, וּבְסַגִּיאוּת שַׁלְהוֹבִיתָא דִּרְחִימוּ עִלָּאָה לְגַבֵּיה, אָמַר הָסֵבִּי עֵינַיִךְ מִנֶּגְדִּי, אַסְחַר עֵינַיִךְ לִסְטַר אָחֳרָא מִנִּי, דְּאִינּוּן מוֹקְדִין לִי בְּשַׁלְהוֹבֵי רְחִימוּתָא. וְעַל דָּא כְּתִיב בֵּיה בְּדָוִד, וְהוּא אַדְמוֹנִי עִם יְפֵה עֵינַיִם וְטוֹב רֹאִי. וּבְגִין הַהוּא דָוִד עִלָּאָה שַׁפִּירָא, רְחִימְנָא וְתִיאוּבְתָּא דְּקוּדְשָׁא בְּרִיךְ הוּא לְאַדְבְּקָא בֵּיה. אָמַר דָּוִד פְּנֵה אֵלַי וְחָנֵּנִי.

74. The beauty of this David illuminates all worlds. His head, a head of gold, is embroidered with seven ornaments OF SEVEN types of gold, as we have already established. The affection of the Holy One, blessed be He, is directed at him. In his great love for Him, he asked the Holy One, blessed be He, to turn His eyes in his direction and look at him, MEANING HE SAID, "O TURN TO ME, AND HAVE MERCY UPON ME." This is because they are in all aspects the most beautiful, as it says, "Turn away your eyes from Me…" (Shir Hashirim 6:5). The verse MEANS that at the time when these eyes OF MALCHUT look at Him, at the Holy One, blessed be He, then arrows of love from catapults with supernal love are stirred in His heart. And with the great flame of supernal love for him, He said: "Turn away your eyes from me," MEANING turn your eyes from Me, since they burn Me with the flame of love. Therefore, it is written about him, David, "Now he was ruddy, with fine eyes, and good looking" (I Shmuel 16:12). Because this David, the supernal one, is handsome, and the love and yearning of the Holy One, blessed be He, is to cling to him, David said, "O turn to me, and have mercy upon me."

75. כְּגַוְונָא דָא, וַיֹּאמֶר רְאֵה רֵיחַ בְּנִי כְּרֵיחַ שָׂדֶה אֲשֶׁר בֵּרֲכוֹ יְיָ'. מַשְׁמַע דְּעָאל עִמֵּיה עִם יַעֲקֹב גִּנְתָּא דְּעֵדֶן, דְּאִיהוּ שָׂדֶה דְּתַפּוּחִין קַדִּישִׁין. וְכִי הֵיךְ יָכִיל גִּנְתָּא דְּעֵדֶן לְאַעֲלָא עִמֵּיה, דְּהָא גִּנְתָּא דְּעֵדֶן כַּמָה רַב הוּא בְּפוּתְיָא וּבְאָרְכָּא. כַּמָה זִינִין דִּבְיַיתִין עִלָּאִין קַדִּישִׁין, דַּרְגִּין עַל דַּרְגִּין, מָדוֹרִין עַל מָדוֹרִין אִית תַּמָּן.

75. Similar to this, "and said, 'See, the smell of my son is like the smell of the field which Hashem has blessed'" (Beresheet 27:27). We understand from here that with Jacob there entered the Garden of Eden, which is the Field of holy apple trees. HE QUESTIONS: How could the Garden of Eden enter with him when the Garden is so much greater in width and length? Consider how many holy supernal abodes, levels upon levels, dwellings upon dwellings there are there.

76. אֶלָּא גִּנְתָּא אָחֳרָא עִלָּאָה קַדִּישָׁא אִית לֵיהּ לְקוּדְשָׁא בְּרִיךְ הוּא, וְהַהוּא גִּנְתָּא רְחִימוּתָא דִּילֵיהּ, וְאִתְדְּבַק בֵּיהּ, וְלָא אִתְנְטִיר אֶלָּא לְקוּדְשָׁא בְּרִיךְ הוּא בִּלְחוֹדוֹי, דְּהוּא עָיֵיל בֵּיהּ. וְדָא אַחֲסִין קוּדְשָׁא בְּרִיךְ הוּא לְאִשְׁתַּכְּחָא תָּדִיר עִמְּהוֹן דְּצַדִּיקַיָּיא. וכ״ש לְאִשְׁתַּכְּחָא בֵּיהּ בְּיַעֲקֹב, וְדָא זַמִּין לֵיהּ קוּדְשָׁא בְּרִיךְ הוּא לְאַעֲלָאָה עִמֵּיהּ לְסַיְּיעָא לֵיהּ.

76. AND ANSWERS: But another supernal, holy Garden, NAMELY MALCHUT, exists for the Holy One, blessed be He, has. In that garden is found His love. He clings to it, and it is reserved solely for the Holy One, blessed be He, WHERE He enters. This He apportions in order to be always with the righteous, and all the more so with Jacob. The Holy One, blessed be He, prepared it for him, to enter with him to help him.

77. כְּגַוְונָא דָא, אֲנִי יְיָ' אֱלֹהֵי אַבְרָהָם אָבִיךָ וֵאלֹהֵי יִצְחָק הָאָרֶץ וְגוֹ'. תָּנָן, מְלַמֵּד שֶׁנִּתְקַפְּלָה לוֹ אֶרֶץ יִשְׂרָאֵל. וְכִי אֶרֶץ יִשְׂרָאֵל, דְּאִיהִי ד' מֵאוֹת פַּרְסָה עַל ד' מֵאוֹת פַּרְסָה, הֵיךְ אִתְעֲקָרַת מֵאַתְרָהּ, וְיָתְבָא תְּחוֹתוֹי. אֶלָּא אֶרֶץ אָחֳרָא עִלָּאָה קַדִּישָׁא אִית לְקוּדְשָׁא בְּרִיךְ הוּא, וְאֶרֶץ יִשְׂרָאֵל אִקְרֵי. וְהִיא תְּחוֹת דַּרְגָּא דְּיַעֲקֹב דְּקָאֵים עֲלָהּ. וְאַחֲסִין לָהּ קוּדְשָׁא בְּרִיךְ הוּא לְיִשְׂרָאֵל בְּגִין רְחִימוּתָא דִּלְהוֹן, לְדַיְּירָא עִמְּהוֹן, וּלְדַבְּרָא לְהוֹן, וּלְאַגָּנָא לְהוֹן מַלְכָּא, וְאִקְרֵי אֶרֶץ חַיִּים.

77. In the same manner, "I am Hashem, the Elohim of your father Abraham, and the Elohim of Isaac: the land..." (Beresheet 28:13). We learned that the ENTIRE land of Yisrael converged BENEATH HIM, AND SO HE SAID TO HIM, "THE LAND ON WHICH YOU LIE, TO YOU WILL I GIVE IT" (IBID.). AND HE QUESTIONS: The land of Yisrael is four hundred parasangs by four hundred parasangs. How could it have been uprooted from its place and come beneath him? But there is another supernal land which the Holy One, blessed be He, has called 'the land of Yisrael', NAMELY MALCHUT, situated beneath the level of Jacob, who is above it. FOR JACOB IS THE CHARIOT

OF ZEIR ANPIN, AND MALCHUT IS BENEATH ZEIR ANPIN. The Holy One, blessed be He, bequeathed it to Yisrael, due to their love, to live with them, and to lead them and shield them from all. It is called 'land of life'.

12. It is forbidden to man to look at a place which the Holy One, blessed be He, loathes

A Synopsis

Rabbi Shimon tells us that it is forbidden for man to look at a place that God loves, and at a place that He hates. It is forbidden to look at a rainbow because it reflects a supernal image, and to look at the sign of the Covenant because it alludes to the Righteous of the world, and to look at the fingers of the priests when they spread their hands because the glory of the supernal King rests there. Yisrael are warned not to turn to idols, nor to transgress the rest of the Ten Commandments. Rabbi Shimon tells Rabbi Chiya that when Yisrael stood at Mount Sinai they were in one united desire for God.

78. ת"ח, אָסִיר לֵיה לְבַר נָשׁ, לְאִסְתַּכְּלָא בַּאֲתָר דְּקוּדְשָׁא בְּרִיךְ הוּא מָאִיס בֵּיה, וּרְחִיקָא בֵּיה נַפְשֵׁיה. וּמַה בְּמַה דִּרְחִים קוּדְשָׁא בְּרִיךְ הוּא, אָסִיר לְאִסְתַּכְּלָא בֵּיה, בְּמַה דִּרְחִיק עאכ"ו. דת"ח, אָסִיר לֵיה לְבַר נָשׁ לְאִסְתַּכְּלָא בַּקֶּשֶׁת, בְּגִין דְּאִיהוּ חֵיזוּ דְּדִיּוּקְנָא עִלָּאָה. אָסִיר לֵיה לְבַר נָשׁ לְאִסְתַּכְּלָא בְּאָת קַיָּימָא דִּילֵיה, בְּגִין דְּהוּא רָמִיז לְצַדִּיקָא דְּעָלְמָא. אָסִיר לֵיה לְבַר נָשׁ לְאִסְתַּכְּלָא, בְּאֶצְבְּעָן דְּכַהֲנֵי, בְּשַׁעֲתָא דְּפָרְסֵי יְדַיְיהוּ, בְּגִין דְּתַמָּן שַׁרְיָא יְקָרָא דְּמַלְכָּא עִלָּאָה. וּמַה בַּאֲתָר קַדִּישָׁא עִלָּאָה אָסִיר לְאִסְתַּכְּלָא, בַּאֲתָר מְסָאֲבָא רְחִיקָא לָא כָּל שֶׁכֵּן. בְּגִינֵי כַּךְ, אַל תִּפְנוּ אֶל הָאֱלִילִים. ר' יִצְחָק אָמַר, וּמַה לְאִסְתַּכְּלָא בְּהוּ אָסִיר, לְמִפְלַח לְהוּ, אוֹ לְמֶעֱבַּד לְהוּ, עַל אַחַת כַּמָּה וְכַמָּה.

78. Come and behold: it is forbidden to man to look at a place that the Holy One, blessed be He, loathes, and His soul is far from it. Now, if it is prohibited to look at what the Holy One, blessed be He, loves, then that which is far from Him is even more FORBIDDEN. Come and behold: it is forbidden to man to look at a rainbow as it reflects a supernal image, SINCE MALCHUT HAS THE THREE COLORS OF THE RAINBOW, BEING THE SECRET OF HER THREE COLUMNS. ALSO, it is forbidden to man to look at his member of the sign of the Covenant, as it hints about the Righteous of the world. AND ALSO, it is forbidden to look at the fingers of the priests when they spread their hands, since there rests the glory of the Supernal

12. It is forbidden to man to look at a place which the Holy One, blessed be He, loathes

King. So if in a supernal holy place is it forbidden to look, then in a distant, unclean place, it certainly is prohibited to look. For this reason, "Turn not to idols" (Vayikra 19:4). Rabbi Yitzchak said: If looking at them is prohibited, then to worship them or make them is all the more so.

79. וּבְגִינֵי כָּךְ, אַל תִּפְנוּ אֶל הָאֱלִילִים. הָכָא אָתָא לְאַזְהָרָא לְהוּ לְיִשְׂרָאֵל כְּקַדְמֵיתָא. לָקֳבֵיל לֹא יִהְיֶה לְךָ אֱלֹהִים אֲחֵרִים עַל פָּנָי. וֵאלֹהֵי מַסֵּכָה לֹא תַעֲשׂוּ לָכֶם, לָקֳבֵיל לֹא תַעֲשֶׂה לְךָ פֶסֶל אֲנִי יְיָ׳ אֱלֹהֵיכֶם. לָקֳבֵיל אָנֹכִי יְיָ׳ אֱלֹהֶיךָ, אִישׁ אִמּוֹ וְאָבִיו תִּירָאוּ. לָקֳבֵל כַּבֵּד אֶת אָבִיךָ וְאֶת אִמֶּךָ. וְאֶת שַׁבְּתוֹתַי תִּשְׁמוֹרוּ, זָכוֹר אֶת יוֹם הַשַׁבָּת לְקַדְּשׁוֹ. לֹא תִשָּׁבְעוּ בִשְׁמִי לַשָׁקֶר. לֹא תִשָּׂא אֶת שֵׁם יְיָ׳ אֱלֹהֶיךָ לַשָׁוְא. לֹא תִּגְנוֹבוּ, לֹא תִגְנוֹב. וְלֹא תְכַחֲשׁוּ, וְלֹא תְשַׁקְּרוּ אִישׁ בַּעֲמִיתוֹ. לֹא תַעֲנֶה בְרֵעֲךָ עֵד שָׁקֶר. מוֹת יוּמַת הַנּוֹאֵף וְהַנּוֹאָפֶת, לֹא תִנְאָף. לֹא תַעֲמוֹד עַל דַם רֵעֶךָ, לֹא תִרְצָח. וְהָא אוּקְמוּהָ, וְעַ״ד כְּלָלָא דְאוֹרַיְיתָא, בְּפָרְשָׁתָא דָא.

79. For this reason, "Turn not to idols." Here, it comes to warn Yisrael as it did in the beginning, IN THE TEN COMMANDMENTS, FOR, "TURN NOT TO IDOLS," corresponds to, "You shall have no other Elohim beside Me" (Shemot 20:3). The words, "nor make to yourselves molten Elohim," correspond to, "You shall not make for yourself any carved idol" (Ibid.). "I am Hashem your Elohim," corresponds to, "I Hashem your Elohim." "You shall revere every man his mother, and his father," corresponds to, "Honor your father and your mother." The words, "and keep My Shabbatot," CORRESPOND TO, "Remember the Shabbat day, to keep it holy." "And you shall not swear by My Name falsely," CORRESPONDS TO, "You shall not take the Name of Hashem your Elohim in vain." "You shall not steal," CORRESPONDS TO, "You shall not steal." "Neither deal falsely, neither lie one to another," CORRESPONDS TO, "You shall not bear false witness against your neighbor." "The adulterer and adulteress shall surely be put to death" (Vayikra 20:10), CORRESPONDS TO, "You shall not commit adultery." "Neither shall you stand aside when mischief (lit. 'blood') befalls your neighbor," CORRESPONDS TO, "You shall not murder." This has already been established. Hence, this portion contains the whole of the Torah.

80. א"ר חִיָּיא, בְּקַדְמֵיתָא, אָנֹכִי יְיָ' אֱלֹהֶיךָ. זָכוֹר אֶת יוֹם הַשַּׁבָּת. לֹא תִשָּׂא. לֹא תִרְצַח. לֹא תִנְאָף. לֹא תִגְנוֹב. בְּלִישָׁנָא יְחִידָאי. וְהָכָא, אֲנִי יְיָ' אֱלֹהֵיכֶם. אִישׁ אִמּוֹ וְאָבִיו תִּירָאוּ, וְאֶת שַׁבְּתוֹתַי תִּשְׁמֹרוּ. אַל תִּפְנוּ אֶל הָאֱלִילִים. בְּלִישָׁנָא דְסַגִּיאִין. אֶלָּא ת"ח, מִיּוֹמָא דַּהֲווֹ יִשְׂרָאֵל שְׁכִיחִין בְּעָלְמָא, לָא אִשְׁתְּכָחוּ קָמֵי קוּדְשָׁא בְּרִיךְ הוּא, בְּלִבָּא חַד, וּבִרְעוּתָא חֲדָא, כְּמָה דְבְהַהוּא יוֹמָא דְקַיְימוּ בְּטוּרָא דְסִינַי. וְעַ"ד כֹּלָּא אִתְּמַר בְּלִשׁוֹן יְחִידָאי. לְבָתַר בְּלִישָׁנָא דְסַגִּיאִין, דְּהָא לָא אִשְׁתְּכָחוּ כָּל כַּךְ בְּהַהוּא רְעוּתָא.

80. Rabbi Chiya said: At first, IN THE TEN COMMANDMENTS, IT IS WRITTEN: "I am Hashem your Elohim"; "Remember the Shabbat day"; "You shall not take the Name;" "You shall not murder. You shall not commit adultery, You shall not steal." All are written in the singular, but here IT IS WRITTEN: "I am Hashem, your Elohim"; "You shall revere every man his mother, and his father"; "and keep My Shabbatot"; "Turn not to idols." All are written in the plural form. AND HE ANSWERS: Come and behold. Since the first day Yisrael has been on the earth, they were not in such unity in heart and desire before the Holy One, blessed be He, as on the day they stood at Mount Sinai. Therefore, everything there is written in the singular. Afterwards, it is written in the plural because they lacked somewhat that desire, MEANING ONE UNITED DESIRE.

13. "I am Hashem your Elohim from the land of Egypt"

A Synopsis

Rabbi Elazar wonders why it seems that the title verse is saying there was no Elohim before Yisrael were in Egypt, and Rabbi Shimon explains that Yisrael only knew the glory of God from the time they were in Egypt. From that time they saw many miracles and wonders, and His glory was exposed to them when He parted the sea.

81. רִבִּי אֶלְעָזָר הֲוָה אָזִיל לְמֶחֱמֵי לְר' יוֹסֵי בר"ש בֶּן לָקוּנְיָא, חָמוּי
וַהֲווֹ עִמֵּיהּ ר' חִיָּיא וְרִבִּי יוֹסֵי, כַּד מָטוּ חַד בֵּי חַקְל, יָתְבוּ תְּחוֹת אִילָנָא
חֲדָא. א"ר אֶלְעָזָר, כָּל חַד לֵימָא מִלָּה דְּאוֹרַיְיתָא. פָּתַח רִבִּי אֶלְעָזָר
וְאָמַר, וְאָנֹכִי יְיָ' אֱלֹהֶיךָ מֵאֶרֶץ מִצְרָיִם וֵאלֹהִים זוּלָתִי לֹא תֵדָע. לֹא
כְּתִיב אֲשֶׁר הוֹצֵאתִיךָ מֵאֶרֶץ מִצְרָיִם, אֶלָּא אָנֹכִי יְיָ' אֱלֹהֶיךָ מֵאֶרֶץ
מִצְרָיִם, וְכִי מֵאֶרֶץ מִצְרַיִם הֲוָה לְהוּ מַלְכָּא, וְלֹא מִקַּדְמַת דְּנָא, וְהָא
כְּתִיב וַיֹּאמֶר יַעֲקֹב אֶל בָּנָיו הָסִירוּ אֶת אֱלֹהֵי הַנֵּכָר אֲשֶׁר בְּתוֹכְכֶם.
וּכְתִיב וְנָקוּמָה וְנַעֲלֶה בֵּית אֵל, וְאַתְּ אַמְרַת מֵאֶרֶץ מִצְרָיִם.

81. Rabbi Elazar was going to visit Rabbi Yosi, son of Shimon, the son of Lakunya, his father-in-law. With him were Rabbi Chiya and Rabbi Yosi. When they arrived at a field, they sat beneath a tree. Rabbi Elazar commenced to say, each should speak about a passage in the Torah. Rabbi Elazar began, "I am Hashem your Elohim from the land of Egypt, and you know no Elohim but Me" (Hoshea 13:4). It is not written as in another place, "who have brought you out of the land of Egypt" (Shemot 20:2), but, "I am Hashem your Elohim from the land of Egypt." HE QUESTIONS: They had a King only since the time in Egypt and not before? Is it not written: "Then Jacob said to his household... Put away the strange Elohim that are among you...and let us arise, and go up to Bethel" (Beresheet 35:2-3)? Yet you say that it was only since the time of Egypt.

82. אֶלָּא, מִן יוֹמָא דַּהֲווֹ יִשְׂרָאֵל בְּעָלְמָא, לָא אִשְׁתְּמוֹדְעוּ יְקָרָא
דְּקוּדְשָׁא בְּרִיךְ הוּא. בַּר בְּאַרְעָא דְמִצְרַיִם, דַּהֲווֹ בְּהַהוּא פּוּלְחָנָא קַשְׁיָא,
וְצַוְוחוּ לְקַבְּלֵיהּ, וְלָא אִשְׁתְּנוּ מִנִּימוּסָא דִּלְהוֹן לְעָלְמִין. וְתַמָּן אִתְבְּחִינוּ

אַבְהָתָנָא, כִּדְהֲבָא מִגּוֹ שַׁפְכָה. וְעוֹד, דַּהֲווֹ חָמָאן בְּכָל יוֹמָא, כַּמָּה
חַרְשִׁין, כַּמָּה זִינִין בִּישִׁין, לְאַטְעָאָה לוֹן לִבְנֵי נָשָׁא, וְלָא סָטוּ מֵאָרְחָא
לִימִינָא וְלִשְׂמָאלָא. וְאע״ג דְּלָא הֲווֹ יַדְעֵי כָּל כָּךְ בִּיקָרָא דְּקוּדְשָׁא בְּרִיךְ
הוּא, אֶלָּא הֲווֹ אַזְלִין בָּתַר נִימוּסֵי אֲבָהַתְהוֹן.

82. AND HE ANSWERS: From the day Yisrael were in the world, the glory for the Holy One, blessed be He, was never known except in the land of Egypt. When they found themselves in harsh bondage, they cried to Him and did not change from their accustomed practice. There were our ancestors tested as gold taken from the pipe IN THE SMELTING POT. Furthermore, daily they would see numerous sorcerers, many wicked kinds trying to mislead people, but they did not turn right or left from their path, even as they understood little about the glory of the Holy One, blessed be He, but were following the customs of their fathers.

83. וּלְבָתַר, חָמוּ כַּמָּה נִסִּין, וְכַמָּה גְבוּרָאן, וְנָטַל לוֹן קוּדְשָׁא בְּרִיךְ הוּא
לְפוּלְחָנֵיהּ. וּבְגִין דְּכֻלְהוּ חָמוּ כַּמָּה נִסִּין וְאָתִין בְּעֵינֵיהוֹן, וְכָל אִינוּן
אָתִין וּגְבוּרָן. אָמַר וְאָנֹכִי יְיָ׳ אֱלֹהֶיךָ מֵאֶרֶץ מִצְרָיִם. דְּתַמָּן הֲוָה
בְּאִתְגַּלְיָיא יְקָרָא דִילֵיהּ. וְאִתְגְּלֵי עָלַיְיהוּ עַל יַמָּא, וְחָמוּ זִיו יְקָרָא
עִלָּאָה דִילֵיהּ אַפִּין בְּאַפִּין. דְּלָא תֵּימְרוּן אֱלָהָא אָחֳרָא הוּא דְּמַלִּיל
עִמָּנָא, אֶלָּא אֲנָא אֲנָא הוּא דַּחֲמִיתוּן בְּאַרְעָא דְמִצְרַיִם, אֲנָא הוּא דְקַטְלָנָא
סָנְאֵיכוֹן בְּאַרְעָא דְמִצְרַיִם. אֲנָא הוּא דְעָבֵדְנָא כָּל אִינוּן עֶשֶׂר מְחָאן
בְּאַרְעָא דְמִצְרָיִם. וּבְגִינֵי כַּךְ, וֵאלֹהִים זוּלָתִי לֹא תֵדָע, דְּלָא תֵימָא
דְּאָחֳרָא הֲוָא, אֶלָּא אֲנָא אֲנָא הוּא כֹּלָּא.

83. Afterwards, they saw numerous miracles, many mighty deeds, and the Holy One, blessed be He, took them for His service. Since all saw numerous miracles and wonders before their eyes, and all these signs and mighty deeds, He said: "I am Hashem your Elohim from the land of Egypt." For there, His glory was exposed. He was seen by them by the sea. They saw the brilliance of His supernal splendor face to face. Thus, you should not say now that another deity spoke with us. 'But I am He, you saw ME in Egypt. I am He who slew your enemies in the land of Egypt. I am He who performed all ten plagues in Egypt.' For this reason, "you know no Elohim but Me"; you will not say that it was another, but it is I who am in every thing.

14. "The wages of him that is hired shall not abide with you all night"

A Synopsis

We learn that if someone helped the poor, God will extend his life when his time comes to die. If, on the other hand, someone takes the wages of the poor, God will shorten his days, and nor will his soul ascend.

84. תּוּ פָּתַח, לֹא תַעֲשׁוֹק אֶת רֵעֲךָ וְלֹא תִגְזוֹל לֹא תָלִין פְּעוּלַת שָׂכִיר אִתְּךָ עַד בֹּקֶר. לֹא תָלִין פְּעוּלַת שָׂכִיר אֲמַאי. אֶלָּא מִקְרָא אַחֲרָא אַשְׁתְּמַע, דִּכְתִיב בְּיוֹמוֹ תִתֵּן שְׂכָרוֹ וְלֹא תָבֹא עָלָיו הַשֶּׁמֶשׁ כִּי עָנִי הוּא וְאֵלָיו הוּא נוֹשֵׂא אֶת נַפְשׁוֹ. לֹא תָבֹא עָלָיו הַשֶּׁמֶשׁ, אִזְדְּהַר דְּלָא תִתְכְּנֵשׁ בְּגִינוֹי מֵעָלְמָא, עַד לָא יִמְטֵי זִמְנָךְ לְאִתְכַּנְּשָׁא. כְּמָה דְאַתְּ אָמֵר, עַד אֲשֶׁר לֹא תֶחְשַׁךְ הַשֶּׁמֶשׁ וְגוֹ'. מֵהָכָא אוֹלִיפְנָא מִלָּה אַחֲרָא, מַאן דְּאַשְׁלִים לְנַפְשָׁא דְמִסְכְּנָא. אֲפִילוּ דְמָטוּ יוֹמוֹי לְאִסְתַּלְּקָא מֵעָלְמָא, קוּדְשָׁא בְּרִיךְ הוּא אַשְׁלִים לְנַפְשֵׁיהּ, וְיָהִיב לֵיהּ חַיִּין יַתִּיר.

84. Rabbi Elazar continued: "You shall not defraud your neighbor, nor rob him; the wages of him that is hired shall not abide with you all night until the morning" (Vayikra 19:13). HE QUESTIONS: Why, "the wages of him that is hired shall not abide with you all night"? AND ANSWERS: This is understood from another verse, "At his day you shall give him his hire, neither shall the sun go down upon it; for he is poor, and sets his heart upon you" (Devarim 24:15). The words, "neither shall the sun go down upon it" MEAN be warned not to be gathered from this world because of him, before it is your time to be gathered, as the verse says, "before the sun...darkened..." (Kohelet 12: 2). THIS VERSE HINTS AT THE DEMISE OF MAN. From here, I learned another thing: THAT in the case of he who satisfies the poor man's soul, even when the time comes for his demise, the Holy One, blessed be He, satisfies his soul and lengthens his life.

85. לֹא תָלִין פְּעוּלַת שָׂכִיר, ת"ח, מַאן דְּנָטִיל אַגְרָא דְמִסְכְּנָא, כְּאִילּוּ נָטִיל נַפְשֵׁיהּ, וּדְאַנְשֵׁי בֵּיתֵיהּ. הוּא אַזְעַר נַפְשַׁיְיהוּ, קוּדְשָׁא בְּרִיךְ הוּא אַזְעִיר יוֹמוֹי, וְאַזְעַר נַפְשֵׁיהּ, מֵהַהוּא עָלְמָא. דְּהָא כָּל אִינּוּן הֲבָלִים דְּנַפְקֵי מִפּוּמֵיהּ, כָּל הַהוּא יוֹמָא, כֻּלְּהוּ סַלְּקִין קַמֵּיהּ דְּקוּדְשָׁא בְּרִיךְ

הוּא, וְקַיְימִין קַמֵּיה, לְבָתַר סַלְקָא נַפְשֵׁיהּ, וְנַפְשַׁיְיהוּ דְּאֵנָשֵׁי בֵּיתֵיהּ, וְקַיְימִין, בְּאִינּוּן הַבָּלִים דְּפוּמֵיהּ. וּכְדֵין, אֲפִילּוּ אִתְגְּזַר עַל הַהוּא בַּר נָשׁ כַּמָּה יוֹמִין, וְכַמָּה טָבָאן, כֻּלְּהוּ מִתְעַקְּרָאן מִנֵּיהּ, וּמִסְתַּלְּקֵי מִנֵּיהּ.

85. "The wages of him that is hired shall not abide with you all night." Come and behold: taking the wage of the poor is tantamount to taking his life and the life of his household. He shortens his life, and the Holy One, blessed be He, will shorten his days and lessen his life from that world. For all the breaths that emitted from the mouth OF THE POOR MAN that day will ascend before the Holy One, blessed be He, and stand before Him. Later, his soul will ascend and that of his family, maintained with the breath of his mouth, MEANING THAT THEY WILL DEMAND JUSTICE BEFORE THE HOLY ONE, BLESSED BE HE. Then, even if from before there was decreed for this person many years and much good, all will be rooted out and taken away from him.

86. וְלֹא עוֹד, אֶלָּא דְּנַפְשָׁא דִּילֵיהּ לָא סַלְקָא לְעֵילָּא, וְהַיְינוּ דְּאָמַר רִבִּי אַבָּא, רַחֲמָנָא לְשֵׁזְבִינָן מִנַּיְיהוּ, וּמֵעֶלְבּוֹנַיְיהוּ. וְאוֹקִמוּהָ אֲפִילּוּ עָשִׁיר הוּא, וְאֵלָיו הוּא נוֹשֵׂא אֶת נַפְשׁוֹ דַּיְיקָא, אֲפִילּוּ מִכָּל בַּר נָשׁ נָמֵי, וְכ״שׁ מִסְכְּנָא. וְהַיְינוּ דַּהֲוָה רַב הַמְנוּנָא עָבֵיד, כַּד הֲוָה הַהוּא אָגִיר מִסְתְּלַק מֵעֲבִידְתֵּיהּ, הֲוָה יָהִיב לֵיהּ אַגְרֵיהּ, וְאָ״ל, טוֹל נַפְשָׁךְ דְּאַפְקֵידַת בִּידַאי, טוֹל פִּקְדוֹנָךְ.

86. In addition to this, his soul will not ascend. This is what Rabbi Aba said: Merciful One! Save us from them and from their shame. We established that even if he is rich, YOU MUST NOT KEEP HIS WAGE OVERNIGHT. "…and sets his heart (lit. 'soul') upon you…" literally, MEANING, of any man. And more so the poor. This is what Rav Hamnuna did when the workman was departing after work: he would give him his wage and say to him, 'Take back your soul that you deposited with me, take your security.'

87. וַאֲפִילּוּ אָמַר יְהֵא בִּידָךְ, דַּאֲנָא בָּעֵינָא לְסַלְקָא אַגְרִי. לָא הֲוָה בָּעֵי. אָמַר פִּקְדוֹנָא דְּגוּפָךְ, לָא אִתְחֲזֵי לְאַתְפַּקְּדָא בִּידִי, כָּל שֶׁכֵּן פִּקְדוֹנָא דְּנַפְשָׁא. דְּהָא פִּקְדוֹנָא דְּנַפְשָׁא לָא אִתְיְהִיבַת, אֶלָּא לְקוּדְשָׁא בְּרִיךְ

הוּא. דִּכְתִיב בְּיָדְךָ אַפְקִיד רוּחִי, אָמַר ר' חִיָּיא, וּבִידָא דְּאַחֲרָא שָׁרֵי.
אָ"ל, אֲפִילוּ בִּידֵיהּ, בָּתַר דִּיָהִיב.

87. Even if THE WORKER said, 'Let MY WAGE remain in your hand or I do not want to receive my wage,' he would not agree to it. He would say, 'The deposit of your body is not proper to leave with me; all the more so the deposit of your soul. The deposit of the soul is given only to the Holy One, blessed be He,' as it is written: "Into Your hand I command my spirit" (Tehilim 31:6). Rabbi Chiya said: And with someone else, WHO IS NOT HIS EMPLOYER, he may DEPOSIT HIS WAGE? He replied: Even in the hand OF HIS EMPLOYER he may deposit it, but only after he was paid HIS WAGE IN HIS HAND.

88. כְּתִיב לֹא תָלִין פְּעוּלַת שָׂכִיר, וּכְתִיב וְלֹא תָבֹא עָלָיו הַשֶּׁמֶשׁ. אֶלָּא
הָא אוּקְמוּהָ, אֲבָל ת"ח לֵית לָךְ יוֹמָא וְיוֹמָא, דְּלָא שַׁלְטָא בֵּיהּ יוֹמָא
עִלָּאָה אַחֲרָא. וְאִי אִיהוּ לָא יָהִיב לֵיהּ נַפְשָׁא דִּילֵיהּ בְּהַהוּא יוֹמָא,
כְּמַאן דְּפָגִים לְהַהוּא יוֹמָא עִלָּאָה. וּבְגִינֵי כַּךְ בְּיוֹמוֹ תִתֵּן שְׂכָרוֹ, וְלֹא
תָבֹא עָלָיו הַשֶּׁמֶשׁ. וְהָא דְּאִתְּמַר לֹא תָלִין, בְּגִין דְּנַפְשֵׁיהּ לָא סָלִיק,
וְסָלִיק הַהוּא נַפְשָׁא דְּמִסְכְּנָא, וּדְאַנְשֵׁי בֵּיתֵיהּ, כְּמָה דְּאִתְּמַר.

88. HE ASKS: It is written, "the wages of him that is hired shall not abide with you all night," and, "neither shall the sun go down upon it." WE INFER THAT HE IS OBLIGATED TO GIVE HIM HIS WAGE BEFORE THE SETTING OF THE SUN, BUT IN THE PRIOR VERSE HE INDICATES THAT THE PROHIBITION IS FOR HOLDING THE WAGE OVERNIGHT. HE ANSWERS: It is as we established. But come and behold: there is not a day that another supernal day does not govern over, MEANING ONE SFIRAH, BEING ONE DAY OF THE SEVEN SUPERNAL DAYS CALLED CHESED, GVURAH, TIFERET, NETZACH, HOD, YESOD AND MALCHUT. If he did not give him his soul, MEANING HIS WAGE, on that day, it is tantamount to causing a defect to that supernal day. For this reason, "At his day you shall give him his hire, neither shall the sun go down upon it." The words, "shall not abide with you all night," REFERS TO THE PENALTY, since AT NIGHT his soul will not ascend ABOVE, but the soul of the poor man and his household will ascend, as we said.

15. "Nor put a stumbling block before the blind"

A Synopsis

We are told that the title verse is referring to someone who curses a person behind their back; that evil speech ascends and prosecutes the speaker. Every word that people speak ascends and has a consequence. Also, one must not cause another to sin. Anyone who walks in the righteous path of Torah earns a share in the World to Come, since the words of Torah that he speaks ascend very high and are taken higher and higher. We learn the consequences for one who does not study the Torah in a pure way, and of someone who wants to learn Torah but cannot find a good teacher.

89. ר' חִיָּיא פָּתַח וְאָמַר קְרָא אֲבַתְרֵיה, לֹא תְקַלֵּל חֵרֵשׁ וְלִפְנֵי עִוֵּר וְגוֹ', הַאי קְרָא כְּמַשְׁמָעוֹ. אֲבָל פַּרְשָׁתָּא דָא כֹּלָּא, אוֹלִיפְנָא מִינָּה מִלִּין אַחֲרָנִין, וְכֻלְּהוּ תַּלְיָין דָּא בְּדָא. תָּ"ח, מַאן דְּלָיֵיט לְחַבְרֵיה, וְאִיהוּ קַמֵּיה, וְאַכְסִיף לֵיה, כְּאִלּוּ אוֹשִׁיד דָּמֵיה, וְהָא אוֹקִימְנָא. וְהַאי קְרָא, דְּלָאו חַבְרֵיה עִמֵּיה, וְהוּא לָיֵיט לֵיה, הַהִיא מִלָּה סַלְקָא.

89. After him, Rabbi Chiya recited the verse: "You shall not curse the deaf, nor put a stumbling block before the blind" (Vayikra 19:14). This verse has a literal meaning, yet we learned some other SUPERNAL matters connected one to the other from this whole portion. EVERY BRANCH BELOW SHOWS IT HAS A ROOT ON HIGH. Come and behold: one who curses another who stands before him, and shames him, it is considered as if he shed his blood. We established that. This verse IS SPEAKING OF THE TIME the other one is not before him and he curses him. This speech ascends AND PROSECUTES HIM.

90. דְּלֵית לָךְ מִלָּה וּמִלָּה דְּנָפִיק מִפּוּמֵיה, דְּלָא אִית לֵיה קָלָא, הַהוּא קָלָא סָלִיק לְעֵילָּא, וְכַמָּה קַסְטְרִין מִתְחַבְּרָן עִמֵּיה דְּהַהוּא קָלָא, עַד דְּסַלְקָא וְאִתְּעַר אֲתַר דִּתְהוֹמָא רַבָּא, כְּמָה דְּאוּקְמוּהָ וְכַמָּה מִתְעָרִין עֲלֵיה דְּהַהוּא בַּ"נ. וַוי לְמַאן דְּאַפִּיק מִלָּה בִּישָׁא מִפּוּמֵיה, וְהָא אוּקְמוּהָ.

90.

-60-

90. There is not a word that emits from man that has no sound. That sound ascends. Numerous destructive angels are joined with this sound until it ascends and awakens the place of the great abyss, THE SEAT OF THE KLIPOT, as we explained. Many OF THEM are roused against this person TO PUNISH HIM. Woe to one that emits harmful speech from his mouth. That we established.

91. וְלִפְנֵי עִוֵּר לֹא תִתֵּן מִכְשׁוֹל, כְּמַשְׁמָעוֹ. וְאוּקְמוּהָ, בְּמַאן דְּגָרִים לְאָחֳרָא לְמֶחֱטֵי. וְכֵן מַאן דְּמָחֵי לִבְרֵיהּ רַבָּא. וְלִפְנֵי עִוֵּר לֹא תִתֵּן וְגוֹ׳, בְּמַאן דְּלָא מָטָא לְהוֹרָאָה וְאוֹרֵי, דִּכְתִיב כִּי רַבִּים חֲלָלִים הִפִּילָה וַעֲצוּמִים כָּל הֲרוּגֶיהָ. וְהַאי אַעֲבָר, מִשּׁוּם וְלִפְנֵי עִוֵּר לֹא תִתֵּן מִכְשׁוֹל, בְּגִין דְּאַכְשִׁיל לֵיהּ לְחַבְרֵיהּ לְעָלְמָא דְּאָתֵי.

91. "Nor put a stumbling block before the blind," literally. We explained this to mean one who causes another to sin. So too, when one strikes his grown son, ALSO, "nor put a stumbling block before the blind," MEANING one who has not yet reached the level to render Halachic decisions, yet teaches it, as it is written: "For she has cast down many wounded: and many strong men have been slain by her" (Mishlei 7:26). This person transgressed against, "nor put a stumbling block before the blind," because he caused the other to stumble on an obstacle WITH HIS RENDERING THE LAW, before the World to Come.

92. דְּתָנֵינָן מַאן דְּאָזִיל בְּאוֹרַח מֵישָׁר בְּאוֹרַיְיתָא, וּמַאן דְּאִשְׁתְּדַּל בְּאוֹרַיְיתָא כַּדְקָא יָאוּת, אִית לֵיהּ חוּלָקָא טָבָא תָּדִיר לְעָלְמָא דְּאָתֵי. דְּהַהִיא מִלָּה דְּאוֹרַיְיתָא דְּאַפִּיק מִפּוּמֵיהּ, אַזְלָא וְשָׁאֲטָא בְּעָלְמָא, וְסַלְקָא לְעֵילָא. וְכַמָּה עִלָּאִין קַדִּישִׁין מִתְחַבְּרָאן בְּהַהִיא מִלָּה, וְסַלְקָא בְּאוֹרַח מֵישָׁר, וְאִתְעַטַּר בְּעִטְרָא קַדִּישָׁא, וְאִסְתָּחֵי בְּנַהֲרָא דְּעָלְמָא דְּאָתֵי, דְּנָגִיד וְנָפִיק מֵעֵדֶן, וְאִתְקַבַּל בֵּיהּ, וְאִשְׁתְּאַב בְּגַוֵּויהּ, וְאִתְעַנַּג סוֹחֲרָנֵיהּ דְּהַהוּא נַהֲרָא, אִילָנָא עִלָּאָה. וּכְדֵין נָגִיד וְנָפִיק נְהוֹרָא עִלָּאָה וְאִתְעַטַּר בֵּיהּ בְּהַהוּא בַּר נָשׁ כָּל יוֹמָא, כְּמָה דְּאִתְּמַר.

92. We learned that one who walks in the righteous path of Torah and toils in Torah properly earns for himself a permanent good share in the World to

Come, since the word of Torah emanating from his mouth flies in the world and ascends very high. Many holy ANGELS on high join with this word, and it rises in the straight way, adorned with a holy crown. And it washes itself in the river of the World to Come, BINAH, that flows and exits from Eden, DENOTING CHOCHMAH, and is accepted by it, and is drawn within. The supernal tree, NAMELY ZEIR ANPIN, takes pleasure from around that river – MEANING THAT IT CAUSES ZEIR ANPIN TO RECEIVE THE ILLUMINATION OF THE RIVER FROM BINAH. Then the supernal light exits, and it adorns that person all that day, as we learned.

93. וּמַאן דְּלָעֵי בְּאוֹרַיְיתָא, וְלָא אִשְׁתַּדַּל בָּהּ בְּאוֹרַח קְשׁוֹט, וּבְאוֹרַח מֵישָׁר. הַהוּא מִלָּה סַלְקָא, וְסָטֵי אוֹרְחִין, וְלֵית מַאן דְּיִתְחַבַּר בָּהּ, וְכֹלָּא דַּחְיָין לָהּ לְבַר, וְאָזִיל וְשָׁאט בְּעָלְמָא וְלָא יִשְׁכַּח אֲתַר. מַאן גָּרִים לֵיהּ הַאי. הַהוּא דְּסָאטֵי לֵיהּ מֵאוֹרַח מֵישָׁר, הֲדָא הוּא דִכְתִיב וְלִפְנֵי עִוֵּר לֹא תִתֵּן מִכְשׁוֹל. וּבְגִינֵי כָּךְ כְּתִיב, וְיָרֵאתָ מֵאֱלֹהֶיךָ אֲנִי יְיָ׳.

93. When he who toils in Torah does not do so in a pure or righteous way, that word rises and turns off the path. Nothing joins it; all push it out and it flies around the world without finding a haven. Who caused this? That person who turned off from the straight path. As it is written, "nor put a stumbling block before the blind," MEANING DO NOT PLACE AN OBSTACLE BEFORE WORDS OF TORAH THAT EMANATE FROM HIS MOUTH. For this reason, it is written, "but shall fear your Elohim: I am Hashem" (Leviticus 19:4).

94. וּמַאן דְּתִיאוּבְתֵּיהּ לְמִלְעֵי בְּאוֹרַיְיתָא, וְלָא אַשְׁכַּח מַאן דְּיוֹלִיף לֵיהּ, וְהוּא בִּרְחִימוּתָא דְּאוֹרַיְיתָא, לָעֵי בָּהּ, וּמְגַמְגֵם בָּהּ, בְּגִמְגוּמָא דְּלָא יָדַע. כָּל מִלָּה וּמִלָּה סַלְקָא, וְקוּדְשָׁא בְּרִיךְ הוּא חַדֵּי בְּהַהִיא מִלָּה, וְקַבִּיל לָהּ, וְנָטַע לָהּ סָחֲרָנֵיהּ דְּהַהוּא נַחֲלָא, וְאִתְעֲבִידוּ מֵאִלֵּין מִלִּין אִילָנִין רַבְרְבִין, וְאִקְרוּן עַרְבֵי נַחַל, הֲדָא הוּא דִכְתִיב בְּאַהֲבָתָהּ תִּשְׁגֶּה תָמִיד.

94. And there is the situation of one who has the yearning to toil in Torah, but can not find someone to teach him. Yet, with his love of Torah, he speaks of it and stammers with it, as he does not know better. Each word

ascends and the Holy One, blessed be He, rejoices with that word, receives it, plants it around that stream, DENOTING BINAH and from these are made large trees, MEANING GREAT LIGHTS, called 'the willows of the streams'. This is the meaning of the verse, "and be you ravished always with her love..." (Mishlei 5:19).

95. וְדָוִד מַלְכָּא אָמַר, הוֹרֵנִי יְיָ דַּרְכֶּךָ אֲהַלֵּךְ בַּאֲמִתֶּךָ. וּכְתִיב וּנְחֵנִי בְּאֹרַח מִישׁוֹר לְמַעַן שׁוֹרְרָי. זַכָּאִין אִינּוּן דְּיָדְעִין אוֹרְחוֹי דְּאוֹרַיְיתָא, וּמִשְׁתַּדְּלֵי בָּהּ בְּאֹרַח מֵישָׁר, דְּאִינּוּן נַטְעִין אִילָנִין דְּחַיִּין לְעֵילָּא, דְּכֻלְּהוּ אַסְוָותָא. וּבְגִין כַּךְ כְּתִיב, תּוֹרַת אֱמֶת הָיְתָה בְּפִיהוּ. וְכִי אִית תּוֹרָה דְּלָאו אִיהִי אֱמֶת. אֵין כְּגַוְונָא דְּאָמְרָן, דְּאוֹרֵי מַאן דְּלָא יָדַע, וְלָאו אִיהוּ קְשׁוֹט וְהַהוּא דְּאוֹלִיף מִלָּה מִינֵּיהּ, אוֹלִיף מִלָּה דְּלָאו אִיהוּ אֱמֶת. וּבְגִינֵי כַּךְ כְּתִיב, תּוֹרַת אֱמֶת הָיְתָה בְּפִיהוּ.

95. And King David said: "Teach me the way, Hashem; I will walk in Your truth" (Tehilim 86:11), and, "and lead me in an even path, because of my enemies" (Tehilim 27:11). Fortunate are those who know the ways of Torah and toil in it in a straight path, for they plant trees of life above – MEANING THEY DRAW MOCHIN TO ZEIR ANPIN, CALLED 'THE TREE OF LIFE', a healing TO THE SOUL. For this reason, it is written: "The Torah of truth was in his mouth" (Malachi 2:6). HE QUESTIONS: Is there an untruthful Torah? AND ANSWERS: Yes, like we said, if someone, who knows not teaches HALACHIC INSTRUCTIONS, this is untruthful. One who learns from him learns something untruthful. Of this, it is written: "The Torah of truth was in his mouth."

96. וְעַכַּ"ד, מִבָּעֵי לֵיהּ לְבַר נָשׁ לְמֵילַף מִלֵּי דְּאוֹרַיְיתָא מִכָּל בַּ"נ, אֲפִילּוּ מִמַּאן דְּלָא יָדַע. בְּגִין דְּע"ד יִתְעַר בְּאוֹרַיְיתָא, וְיֵיתֵי לְמֵילַף מִמַּאן דְּיָדַע, וּלְבָתַר אִשְׁתְּכַח, דְּאָזִיל בָּהּ בְּאוֹרַיְיתָא בְּאֹרַח קְשׁוֹט. ת"ח, יִשְׁתַּדַּל בַּר נָשׁ בְּעָלְמָא בְּאוֹרַיְיתָא וּפִקּוּדוֹי, אֲפִילּוּ דְּלָא עָבֵיד לִשְׁמָהּ, דְּמִתּוֹךְ שֶׁלֹּא לִשְׁמָהּ בָּא לִשְׁמָהּ.

96. With all this, one needs to learn Torah from all people, even from one who does not know, since through this he will be aroused in Torah and

come to learn from someone who does know. Later, it will turn out that he walked in Torah in a true way. Come and behold: a person should toil in Torah and precepts even if not for its own sake, for studying not for its own sake will lead to studying for its own sake.

16. "In righteousness shall you judge your neighbor"

A Synopsis

This passage speaks about mercy and judgment and justice. When righteousness is triggered, there is no mercy in it, but when justice is triggered there is mercy. Everyone shall be treated equally. We are told that God is found in the place of justice. God judges below as he does above, with righteousness and justice.

97. ר' יוֹסֵי פָּתַח קְרָא אֲבַתְרֵיהּ וְאָמַר, לֹא תַעֲשׂוּ עָוֶל בַּמִּשְׁפָּט וְגוֹ'. לֹא תַעֲשׂוּ עָוֶל בַּמִּשְׁפָּט, כְּמַשְׁמָעוֹ. אֲבָל הָא אִתְּמַר, דְּפַרְשְׁתָּא דָא מִלִּין עִלָּאִין וְיַקִּירִין אִית בָּהּ בְּפִקּוּדֵי אוֹרַיְיתָא. הַאי קְרָא מְסוֹפֵיהּ קָא מַשְׁמַע, דִּכְתִיב בְּצֶדֶק תִּשְׁפּוֹט עֲמִיתֶךָ. ת"ח, תְּרֵי דַרְגִּין אִינוּן הָכָא: מִשְׁפָּט, וְצֶדֶק. מַה בֵּין הַאי לְהַאי. אֶלָּא חַד רַחֲמֵי, וְחַד דִּינָא, וְדָא אִתְבְּסַם בְּדָא.

97. Rabbi Yosi commenced: "You shall do no unrighteousness in judgment (lit. 'justice')..." (Vayikra 19:15). "You shall do no unrighteousness in Judgment," has a literal meaning, but we learned that this portion has within it precious supernal words regarding the precepts of the Torah. This verse is explained at its end, as it is written: "but in righteousness shall you judge your neighbor." Come and behold: two levels are mentioned here, Justice and Righteousness. What is the difference between the two? One is Mercy, MEANING JUSTICE, DENOTING ZEIR ANPIN. One is of Judgment, MEANING RIGHTEOUSNESS, DENOTING MALCHUT. One perfumes the other.

98. כַּד אִתְּעַר צֶדֶק, דָּאִין דִּינָא לְכֹלָּא כַּחֲדָא, דְּלֵית בֵּיהּ רַחֲמֵי, וְלָאו וַותְּרָנוּתָא. כַּד אִתְּעַר מִשְׁפָּט, אִית בֵּיהּ רַחֲמֵי. יָכוֹל יְהֵא כֹּלָּא בְּמִשְׁפָּט. אָתָא קְרָא וְאָמַר, בְּצֶדֶק תִּשְׁפּוֹט עֲמִיתֶךָ. מ"ט. בְּגִין דְּצֶדֶק לָאו דָּאִין לְדָא וְשָׁבִיק לְדָא, אֶלָּא כֻּלְּהוּ כַּחֲדָא בְּשִׁקּוּלָא חֲדָא. כְּגַוְונָא דָא לֹא תִשָּׂא פְנֵי דָל וְלֹא תֶהְדַּר פְּנֵי גָדוֹל, אֶלָּא כֻּלְּהוּ בְּשִׁקּוּלָא חֲדָא, בְּצֶדֶק. יָכוֹל יְהֵא כֹּלָּא דִּינָא בְּצֶדֶק בִּלְחוֹדוֹי. אָתָא קְרָא וְאָמַר תִּשְׁפּוֹט, דְּבָעֵי לְחַבְּרָא לְהוּ כַּחֲדָא, דְּלָא יִשְׁתְּכַח דָּא בְּלָא דָא, וְהַאי שְׁלִימוּ דְּדִינָא.

98. When Righteousness is triggered, it judges everyone collectively since there is no Mercy or forbearance in it. When Justice is triggered, there is mercy. It may be that there is only Justice; then comes the verse that says, "in righteousness shall you judge your neighbor." What is the reason? Righteousness does not judge the one and forgive the other, but all are JUDGED collectively. Similarly, "you shall not respect the person of the poor, nor honor the person of the mighty" (Ibid.), but treat all equally, with righteousness. It may be that all Judgments are in Righteousness alone. Hence, the verse says, "shall you judge your neighbor"; one needs to join them together, for one is not found without the other. This makes up the completeness of Judgment.

99. וכ״כ לָמָה. בְּגִין דְּקוּדְשָׁא בְּרִיךְ הוּא שְׁכִיחַ תַּמָּן. וּבְגִינֵי כָּךְ בָּעֵי לְאַשְׁלְמָא דִינָא. כְּגַוְונָא דְּאִיהוּ עָבֵיד לְתַתָּא, כְּגַוְונָא דִילֵיה מַמָּשׁ עָבֵיד לְעֵילָא. ות״ח, קוּדְשָׁא בְּרִיךְ הוּא שַׁוֵי כּוּרְסַיָּיא דְּדִינָא, בְּשַׁעֲתָא דְּדַיָּינֵי יַתְבִין, הה״ד, כּוֹנֵן לַמִּשְׁפָּט כִּסְאוֹ. וּמֵתַּמָּן אִתְתַּקַן כּוּרְסַיָה דְּקוּדְשָׁא בְּרִיךְ הוּא. וּמַאן אִיהוּ כּוּרְסַיָה. אִלֵּין אִינּוּן צֶדֶק וּמִשְׁפָּט. הה״ד צֶדֶק וּמִשְׁפָּט מְכוֹן כִּסְאֶךָ. וּמַאן דְּדָאִין דִּינָא, בָּעֵי לְמֵיתַב בְּכוּרְסַיֵּה דְּמַלְכָּא. וְאִי פָּגִים חַד מִנַּיְיהוּ, כְּאִלּוּ פָּגִים לְכוּרְסֵיה דְּמַלְכָּא. וּכְדֵין קוּדְשָׁא בְּרִיךְ הוּא אִסְתַּלַּק מִבֵּינַיְיהוּ דְּדַיָּינֵי, וְלָא קָאִים בְּדִינַיְיהוּ. וּמַאי אָמַר. עַתָּה אָקוּם יֹאמַר יְיָ' וְגוֹ'. וְרוּחָא דְּקוּדְשָׁא אָמַר, רוּמָה עַל הַשָּׁמַיִם אֱלֹהִים.

99. What is the reason for all of this? Because the Holy One, blessed be He, is found there, IN THE PLACE OF JUSTICE. For this reason, wholeness of the Judgment is needed. Just as He does below, THE HOLY ONE, BLESSED BE HE, does above. Come and behold: the Holy One, blessed be He, sets up the seat of Judgment at the time the judges are sitting. This is what the verse says, "He has prepared His Throne for Judgment (or: 'Justice')" (Tehilim 9:8). From there is set up the Throne of the Holy One, blessed be He, BINAH. What is His Throne? Righteousness and Justice, as the verse says, "Righteousness and justice are the foundation of Your Throne" (Tehilim 89:15). The judge needs to sit at the seat of the King; if he harms one of them, IT IS SIMILAR TO causing harm to the chair of the King. Then the Holy One, blessed be He, departs from the midst of the judges and does not sustain in their judging. What does He say? "Now will I arise, says Hashem..." (Tehilim 12:6). And the Holy Spirit said, "Be You exalted, Elohim, above the heavens" (Tehilim 57:6).

17. "You shall certainly rebuke your neighbor"

A Synopsis

We learn of the precept to rebuke someone who has sinned and to show him that he is loved, so that he should not be punished but repent. God rebukes people in secret unless they will not repent, in which case he rebukes them publicly. We also learn of the gentle allusions that should be made to someone who is too shy to be rebuked openly. One should never mention another's sin in public since God is concerned about the honor of every person, even the evil-doers.

רעיא מהימנא

100. לֹא תִשְׂנָא אֶת אָחִיךָ בִּלְבָבֶךָ הוֹכֵחַ תּוֹכִיחַ אֶת עֲמִיתֶךָ וְגוֹ'. פִּקּוּדָא דָא, לְאוֹכָחָא לְהַהוּא דְּחָטֵי, לְמֶחֱזֵי לֵיהּ רְחִימוּ סַגִּיא, דְּרָחִים לֵיהּ, בְּגִין דְּלָא יִתְעֲנַשׁ אִיהוּ. דְּהָא בְּקוּדְשָׁא בְּרִיךְ הוּא כְּתִיב, כִּי אֶת אֲשֶׁר יֶאֱהַב יְיָ' יוֹכִיחַ. וּכְמָה דְּקוּדְשָׁא בְּרִיךְ הוּא עָבֵיד וְאוֹכַח לְמַאן דְּרָחִים לֵיהּ, הָכִי יוֹלִיף בַּ"נ מֵהַהוּא אָרְחָא, וְיוֹכַח לְחַבְרֵיהּ. קוּדְשָׁא בְּרִיךְ הוּא בְּמַאי אוֹכַח לְבַ"נ. אוֹכַח לֵיהּ בִּרְחִימוּ בְּסִתְרָא, אִי יְקַבֵּל לֵיהּ יָאוּת. וְאִי לָא, אוֹכַח לֵיהּ בֵּין רְחִימוֹי. אִי יְקַבֵּל לֵיהּ יָאוּת. וְאִי לָא, אוֹכַח לֵיהּ בְּאִתְגַּלְיָיא לְעֵינֵיהוֹן דְּכֹלָּא. אִי יְקַבֵּל יָאוּת. וְאִי לָאו, שָׁרֵי לֵיהּ, וְלָא אוֹכַח לֵיהּ, וְשָׁבִיק לֵיהּ יֵיזִיל וְיַעֲבִיד רְעוּתֵיהּ.

Ra'aya Meheimna (the Faithful Shepherd)

100. "You shall not hate your brother in your heart: you shall certainly rebuke your neighbor..." (Vayikra 19:17). This precept is to rebuke one who sinned and to show him that he loves him, in order that THE REBUKER should not be punished. With regard to the Holy One, blessed be He, it is written, "for Hashem reproves him whom He loves" (Mishlei 3:12). Just as the Holy One, blessed be He, does in rebuking those whom He loves, so should man learn from this practice and rebuke his neighbor WHOM HE LOVES. With what does Holy One, blessed be He, rebuke man? He rebukes him with love, in secret. If he accepts HIS REBUKE, it is well. If not, He rebukes him openly among his friends. If he accepts that, then all is well. If not, He rebukes him publicly, before all. If he accepts, all is well. If not, He deserts him and does not rebuke him ANYMORE; He leaves him to go and do as he pleases.

101. בְּקַדְמֵיתָא אוֹדַע לֵיהּ בְּסִתְרָא, בְּגִין לְאוֹכְחָא לֵיהּ, וּלְאַתְעָרָא לֵיהּ, דְּלָא יִנְדַּע בֵּיהּ ב״נ. וְדָא אִיהוּ בֵּינֵיהּ לְבֵינֵיהּ. אִי מְקַבֵּל יָאוֹת. וְאִי לָאו, אוֹדַע לֵיהּ בֵּין רְחִימוֹי, בְּזִמְנָא דְּכַהֲנָא רַבָּא הֲוָה בְּעָלְמָא, יָהִיב לֵיהּ מַרְעִין בְּעַרְסֵיהּ, וְאָתוּ רְחִימוֹי דְּקוּדְשָׁא בְּרִיךְ הוּא, וְאוֹדְעָן לֵיהּ, אִי אִית בֵּיהּ חוֹבָא דְּיֵיתוּב מִנֵּיהּ, וּלְעַיֵּין בְּמִלֵּיהּ. אִי מְקַבֵּל יָאוֹת, וְאִי לָאו אוֹכַח לֵיהּ בְּאִתְגַּלְיָיא, בְּמָמוֹנֵיהּ, בִּבְנוֹי, דְּכֹלָּא מְלַחֲשָׁן עֲלֵיהּ, וְיֵיתוּן לְגַבֵּיהּ. אִי מְקַבֵּל יָאוֹת. וְאִי לָאו שָׁארִי לֵיהּ מָארֵיהּ לְמֶעְבַּד רְעוּתֵיהּ, וְלָא יַתְקִיף בֵּיהּ לְעָלְמִין. כְּגַוְונָא דָּא אִצְטְרִיךְ לֵיהּ לְאוֹכְחָא לְחַבְרֵיהּ בְּקַדְמֵיתָא בְּסִתְרָא. לְבָתַר בֵּין רְחִימוֹי. לְבָתַר בְּאִתְגַּלְיָיא. מִכָּאן וּלְהָלְאָה יִשְׁבּוֹק לֵיהּ וְיַעֲבִיד רְעוּתֵיהּ.

101. He EXPLAINS HIS WORDS. At first, He informs him privately to rebuke him, to alert him in order that no other person should know about this. This is between them. If he accepts HIS REBUKE, it is good. If not, He informs him among his friends. When there was a High Priest in the world, He would place upon him an illness that confined him to bed. Then the friends of the Holy One, blessed be He, would come, inform him that if he had a sin he should repent, and review his deeds. If he accepted, all would be fine. If not, He would warn him publicly that HE WOULD PUNISH HIM, in his money and his children, so that everyone would whisper about him and come to him TO ENCOURAGE HIM TO REPENT. If he accepts these conditions, all is fine. If not, his Master begins to do as he wishes and does not attack him anymore. Like this one should rebuke his friend: in the beginning, privately, then among his friends, and later publicly. From this point on, leave him be and let him do whatever is his desire.

102. וְעַ״ד כְּתִיב הוֹכֵחַ תּוֹכִיחַ. הוֹכֵחַ: בְּסִתְרָא, דְּלָא יִנְדַּע בֵּיהּ ב״נ. תּוֹכִיחַ: בֵּין חַבְרוֹי וּרְחִימוֹי. אֶת עֲמִיתֶךָ: בְּאִתְגַּלְיָיא. וְעַ״ד לָא כְּתִיב בְּקַדְמֵיתָא תּוֹכִיחַ, אֶלָּא הוֹכֵחַ. תּוּ הוֹכֵחַ, אִי אִיהוּ ב״נ דְּיִכְסוֹף, לָא

יֵימָא לֵיהּ וְלָא יוֹכַח לֵיהּ אֲפִילוּ בְּסִתְרָא, אֶלָּא יֵימָא קַמֵּיהּ, כְּמַאן
דְּמִשְׁתָּעֵי בְּמִלִּין אָחֳרָנִין. בְּגוֹ אִינּוּן מִלִּין, יִדְכַּר מַאן דְּעָבֵד הַהוּא
חוֹבָא הוּא כָּךְ וְכָךְ, בְּגִין דְּאִיהוּ יְדַע בְּגַרְמֵיהּ, וְיִשְׁתְּבִיק מֵהַהוּא חוֹבָא.
וְע"ד הוֹכֵחַ. וְאִם לָאו, תּוֹכִיחַ. וּלְבָתַר אֶת עֲמִיתֶךָ בְּאִתְגַּלְיָיא. מִכָּאן
וּלְהָלְאָה וְלָא תִשָּׂא עָלָיו חֵטְא.

102. Therefore it is written, "you shall certainly rebuke (lit. 'rebuking you shall rebuke')," MEANING that "rebuking" REFERS to this being done privately, so no one knows. "...you shall rebuke..." MEANING between friends and lovers, "your neighbor," NAMELY in public. Therefore, it does not write at the outset, "you shall rebuke," MEANING AMONG FRIENDS, but rather, "rebuking," SECRETLY. Another explanation for, "you shall rebuke" is that if the individual is shy, one should not tell him his fault and should not rebuke him even privately. Instead, one should speak to him as if talking about other things, and in the course of the conversation, mention to him that if someone commits such a sin, he is such and such, in order that he himself will understand what is going on and will desist from such sin. Therefore, "rebuking"; if it is not helping, then, "you shall rebuke"; if that does not help, then publicly "your neighbor," AS MENTIONED BEFORE. From that point on, it says, "and not suffer sin on his account," MEANING, DO NOT REBUKE HIM ANYMORE.

103. ד"א וְלָא תִשָּׂא עָלָיו חֵטְא, דְּהָא כֵּיוָן דְּב"נ אוֹכַח לְחַבְרֵיהּ,
וְאִזְדְּמַן לְאוֹכָחָא לֵיהּ בְּאִתְגַּלְיָא, לָא יִסַּלֵּק קַמֵּיהּ הַהוּא חוֹבָה דַּעֲבֵיד,
דְּאָסִיר לֵיהּ וַדַּאי, אֶלָּא יֵימָא סְתָם, וְלָא יִסַּלֵּק עֲלוֹי הַהוּא חוֹבָא
בְּאִתְגַּלְיָיא, וְלָא יַרְשִׁים עֲלוֹי חוֹבָא, דְּקוּדְשָׁא בְּרִיךְ הוּא חָס עַל יְקָרָא
דְּבַר נָשׁ, אֲפִילוּ בְּחַיָּיבַיָּא.

ע"כ רעיא מהימנא

103. Another explanation for, "and not suffer sin on his account," is that if one man rebukes another, and it so happened that he rebuked the other publicly, he must not mention before him the sin he committed. That is surely prohibited. He must speak in general, and not mention the sin he committed in public, nor ascribe the sin to him, since the Holy One, blessed be He, is concerned about the honor of every person, even the evil-doers.

End of Ra'aya Meheimna (the Faithful Shepherd)

104. פָּתַח וְאָמַר, וַיְהִי קוֹל הַשּׁוֹפָר הוֹלֵךְ וְגוֹ'. וַיְהִי קוֹל הַשּׁוֹפָר, הָכָא אִתְפְּלִיגוּ סִפְרֵי קַדְמָאֵי וְכוּ', עַד דְּאָתוּ רִבִּי אַבָּא וְרִבִּי יְהוּדָה, וְאוֹדוּ לֵיהּ לר' אֲחָא.

104. He commenced: "And then the voice of the Shofar…" (Shemot 19:19) (THIS SEGMENT WAS ALREADY PRINTED IN THE PORTION OF VAYIKRA FROM PARAGRAPH 85 TO PARAGRAPH 109) – UP TO WHERE RABBI ABA AND RABBI YEHUDA ARRIVE AND THANK RABBI ACHA. THE CONCLUSION OF THE ARTICLE, WHICH APPEARS TO HAVE BEEN MISSING THERE, IS PRESENTED HERE.

18. Mixed kinds and garments mixed of linen and wool

A Synopsis
The rabbis discuss the observance of the statutes, and Rabbi Elazar tells them that "You are My witnesses" refers to Yisrael.

105. קָמוּ, עַד דַּהֲווֹ אַזְלֵי, אָמַר ר' אֶלְעָזָר לֹא תֵלֵךְ רָכִיל בְּעַמֶּךָ לֹא תִשְׂנָא אֶת אָחִיךָ לֹא תִקּוֹם וְלֹא תִטּוֹר. הָא אוֹקִימְנָא לוֹן, וְכֻלְּהוּ אִתְעֲרוּ עֲלַיְיהוּ חַבְרַיָּיא, אֲבָל נֵימָא מִלָּה בְּפָרְשָׁתָא דָא, כְּתִיב, אֶת חֻקֹּתַי תִּשְׁמֹרוּ בְּהֶמְתְּךָ לֹא תַרְבִּיעַ כִּלְאַיִם שָׂדְךָ לֹא תִזְרַע כִּלְאָיִם וּבֶגֶד כִּלְאַיִם שַׁעַטְנֵז לֹא יַעֲלֶה עָלֶיךָ.

105. Rabbi Aba, Rabbi Acha, and Rabbi Yehuda rose, and, as they were going, Rabbi Elazar said: "You shall not go up and down as a talebearer among your people...You shall not hate your brother in your heart...You shall not avenge, nor bear any grudge" (Vayikra 19:16-18). We have already dealt with this and all the friends have been attentive to these. But let us say something about this portion. It is written 'You shall keep My statutes. You shall not let your cattle gender with a diverse kind: you shall not sow your field with mingled seed: neither shall a garment mingled of linen and wool come upon you' (Ibid. 19).

106. פָּתַח ר' אֶלְעָזָר וְאָמַר, אַתֶּם עֵדַי נְאֻם יְיָ' וְעַבְדִּי אֲשֶׁר בָּחַרְתִּי לְמַעַן תֵּדְעוּ וְתַאֲמִינוּ וְגו'. אַתֶּם עֵדַי, אִלֵּין אִינּוּן יִשְׂרָאֵל. וְתָנֵינָן, אִלֵּין אִינּוּן שְׁמַיָּא וְאַרְעָא, דִּכְתִיב הַעִידוֹתִי בָכֶם הַיּוֹם אֶת הַשָּׁמַיִם וְאֶת הָאָרֶץ. אֲבָל יִשְׂרָאֵל אִינּוּן סָהֲדִין אִלֵּין עַל אִלֵּין, וּשְׁמַיָּא וְאַרְעָא וְכֹלָּא, סָהֲדִין עֲלַיְיהוּ. וְעַבְדִּי אֲשֶׁר בָּחַרְתִּי, דָּא יַעֲקֹב, דִּכְתִיב וַיֹּאמֶר לִי עַבְדִּי אַתָּה יִשְׂרָאֵל אֲשֶׁר בְּךָ אֶתְפָּאָר, וּכְתִיב, וְאַתָּה אַל תִּירָא עַבְדִּי יַעֲקֹב. וְאִית דְּאַמְרֵי דָּא דָּוִד. וְדָוִד עַבְדִּי אִקְרֵי, דִּכְתִיב, לְמַעֲנִי וּלְמַעַן דָּוִד עַבְדִּי אֲשֶׁר בָּחַרְתִּי, דָּא דָּוִד עִלָּאָה.

106. Rabbi Elazar said: "'You are My witnesses,' says Hashem, 'and My servant whom I have chosen: that you may know and believe Me...'"

(Yeshayah 43:10). "You are My witnesses," refers to Yisrael; we learned, too, that this refers to heaven and earth, as it is written: "I call heaven and earth to witness this day against you" (Devarim 30:19). Yisrael are witnesses one on the other, while heaven and earth, and all are witnesses upon them. "My servant whom I have chosen," this refers to Jacob, as is written, "and said to me, 'You are My servant, Yisrael, in whom I will be glorified" (Yeshayah 49:3), and: "Therefore fear you not, O My servant Jacob" (Yirmeyah 30:10). Some say it refers to David and David is called "My servant" as it is written, "for My own sake, and for My servant David's sake" (Yeshayah 37:35); "whom I have chosen," refers to the heavenly David, MEANING MALCHUT.

19. "I am He"

A Synopsis
Rabbi Elazar explains what it means when God says "I am He" in scripture.

107. לְמַעַן תֵּדְעוּ וְתַאֲמִינוּ לִי וְתָבִינוּ כִּי אֲנִי הוּא. מַאי כִּי אֲנִי הוּא. דְּאִתְרָעֵיתִי בְּהַהוּא דָּוִד, וּבְהַהוּא יַעֲקֹב. אֲנָא, הוּא מַמָּשׁ. לְפָנַי לֹא נוֹצַר אֵל, דְּתָנֵינָן, קְרָא קוּדְשָׁא בְּרִיךְ הוּא לְיַעֲקֹב אֵל, דִּכְתִיב, וַיִּקְרָא לוֹ אֵל אֱלֹהֵי יִשְׂרָאֵל. קוּדְשָׁא בְּרִיךְ הוּא קָרָא לְיַעֲקֹב אֵל. הה"ד, לְפָנַי לֹא נוֹצַר אֵל וְאַחֲרַי לֹא יִהְיֶה. וּבְג"כ, אֲנִי, הוּא, כֹּלָּא. כְּמָה דְּאִתְּמַר. וְאַחֲרַי לֹא יִהְיֶה, דְּהָא דָּוִד הָכִי אִקְרֵי, וְלָאו אִית בַּתְרֵיהּ אָחֳרָא.

107. "That you may know and believe Me, and understand that I am He" (Yeshayah 43:10). HE ASKS: What is meant by, "I am He"? AND ANSWERS: "I AM HE," MEANING I Who chose David and Jacob. "I am He," literally, MEANING I INCLUDE JACOB AND DAVID – JACOB BEING THE SECRET OF ZEIR ANPIN, THE SECRET OF "HE," AND DAVID BEING THE SECRET OF MALCHUT, THE SECRET OF "I". THEY ARE LITERALLY THE HOLY ONE, BLESSED BE HE, AND HIS SHECHINAH. "Before Me there was no El formed" (Ibid.); as we learned, the Holy One, blessed be He, called Jacob 'El', as it is written, "and called it (lit. 'him') El, the Elohim of Yisrael" (Beresheet 33:20). SO WE SEE the Holy One, blessed be He, called Jacob 'El'. This is the meaning of, "before Me there was no El formed, neither shall there be after Me." Hence, "I am He," everything is as we said. "Neither shall there be after Me," because David is called so – SINCE MALCHUT IS ALSO "EL," ZEIR ANPIN AND MALCHUT ARE THE SECRET OF "I", "HE" ARE ONE and there is no other after Him.

20. Mixed kinds and garments mixed of linen and wool (*sha'atnez*)

A Synopsis

We learn that when God created the world he created a supernal force above every single thing, even every blade of grass. All the chieftains that have ever been designated as rulers have always behaved according to one supernal law, and the chieftains themselves are then called 'laws'. As each of them is appointed over a certain aspect of law, the mixture of species below uproots each force from its proper position and causes confusion above. When people behave as they should, they attract a Holy Supernal Spirit to them, but when they perform evil actions they draw a spirit from the side of evil. We are told why it is acceptable and proper to mix wool and linen in the Tzitzit but not elsewhere. Cain was a mixture from the Other Side, and therefore his sacrifice could not be mixed with that of Abel, who was of the same species as Adam and Eve, from the side of Holiness.

108. תָּא חֲזֵי, כַּד בָּרָא קוּדְשָׁא בְּרִיךְ הוּא עָלְמָא, אַתְקִין כָּל מִלָּה וּמִלָּה, כָּל חַד וְחַד בְּסִטְרוֹי. וּמָנֵי עָלַיְיהוּ חֵילִין עִלָּאִין. וְלֵית לָךְ אֲפִילוּ עִשְׂבָּא זְעֵירָא בְּאַרְעָא, דְּלֵית לֵיהּ חֵילָא עִלָּאָה לְעֵילָּא. וְכָל מַה דְּעָבְדִין בְּכָל חַד וְחַד, וְכָל מַה דְּכָל חַד וְחַד עָבִיד, כֹּלָּא הוּא בִּתְקִיפוּ דְּהַהִיא חֵילָא עִלָּאָה, דִּמְמַנָּא עֲלֵיהּ לְעֵילָּא. וְכֻלְּהוּ נִמּוּסִין גְּזִירִין מִדִּינָא, עַל דִּינָא נַטְלִין, וְעַל דִּינָא קַיְּימִין. לֵית מַאן דְּנָפִיק מִן קִיּוּמֵיהּ לְבַר.

108. Come and behold: when the Holy One, blessed be He, created the world, He appointed everything and each one in its position, EITHER RIGHT OR LEFT; He appointed upon them supernal forces. And there is not even a blade of grass in the ground that does not have a supernal force upon it IN THE UPPER WORLDS. Everything that each does or is done to each is under the strength of the supernal force appointed upon it from above. All THEIR practices are based on Judgment, they move through Judgment, and are supported by Judgment. Nothing can move out of its support outside.

109. וְכֻלְּהוּ מְמַנָּן, מִן יוֹמָא דְּאִתְבְּרֵי עָלְמָא, מִתְפַּקְדָן שֻׁלְטוֹנִין עַל כָּל מִלָּה וּמִלָּה. וְכֻלְּהוּ נַטְלִין עַל נִימוּסָא אַחֲרָא עִלָּאָה, דְּנַטְלִין כָּל חַד

וְחַד. כְּמָה דִּכְתִיב, וַתָּקָם בְּעוֹד לַיְלָה וַתִּתֵּן טֶרֶף לְבֵיתָה וְחֹק
לְנַעֲרֹתֶיהָ. כֵּיוָן דְּנַטְלִין הַהוּא חֹק, כֻּלְּהוּ אִקְרוּן חֻקּוֹת, וְהַהוּא חֹק
דְּאִתְיְיהִיב לְהוּ, מִן שְׁמַיָּא קָא אָתֵי, וּכְדֵין אִתְקְרוּן חֻקּוֹת שָׁמַיִם. וּמְנָלָן
דְּמִן שָׁמַיִם קָא אַתְיָין. דִּכְתִיב כִּי חֹק לְיִשְׂרָאֵל הוּא.

109. And all the chieftains, since the day of Creation, were designated rulers over each and every thing. They all behave according to another, supernal law, that is received by each one, as it is written: "She rises also while it is yet night, and gives food to her household, and a portion to her maidens" (Mishlei 31:15). Since they receive this law, all THE APPOINTEES are then called 'laws'. This law given to them comes from heaven, and so they are called 'the statutes of heaven'. How do we know that they stem from heaven? As it is written: "For this is a statute for Yisrael" (Tehilim 81:5), ZEIR ANPIN BEING THE CENTRAL COLUMN, CALLED 'YISRAEL'.

110. וְעַ"ד כְּתִיב, אֶת חֻקֹּתַי תִּשְׁמֹרוּ בְּגִין דְּכָל חַד וְחַד מְמָנָא עַל
מִלָּה יְדִיעָא בְּעָלְמָא, בְּהַהוּא חֹק. בְּגִין כַּךְ אָסִיר לְמִחְלַף זִינִין,
וּלְאַעֲלָא זִינָא בְּזִינָא אָחֳרָא. בְּגִין דְּאָקַר לְכָל חֵילָא וְחֵילָא
מֵאַתְרַיְיהוּ, וְאַכְחִישׁ פּוּמְבֵי דְּמַלְכָּא.

110. Therefore it is written: "You shall keep My statutes" (Vayikra 19:19). This is because each is appointed to a certain aspect of that law. For this reason, it is forbidden to mix species or to bring about one species to another, as this uproots each force from its position and denies the fame of the King.

111. כִּלְאַיִם, מַהוּ כִּלְאַיִם. כְּמָאן דְּיָהִיב אָחֳרָא בְּבֵי מַטְרָא, כד"א אֶל
בֵּית הַכֶּלֶא, בְּגִין דְּלָא לְמֶעְבַּד מִידִי. כִּלְאַיִם: מְנִיעוּתָא, דְּמַנַע לְכָל
אִינּוּן חֵילִין מֵעֲבִידָתָּא דִּלְהוֹן. כִּלְאַיִם: עִרְבּוּבְיָיא, דְּעָבֵיד עִרְבּוּבְיָא
בְּחֵילָא דִּלְעֵילָא, וְאַכְחִישׁ פּוּמְבֵי דְּמַלְכָּא, כְּמָה דְּאִתְּמַר, וּבֶגֶד כִּלְאַיִם
שַׁעַטְנֵז לֹא יַעֲלֶה עָלֶיךָ.

111. HE QUESTIONS: What is mixed kinds (Heb. *kil'ayim*)? AND ANSWERS: ITS EXPLANATION IS like one who puts his friend in jail SO HE

WILL NOT BE ABLE TO DO ANYTHING, as the verse says, "in prison (Heb. *kele*)" (Yirmeyah 37:18), AND KIL'AYIM IS SIMILAR TO KELE IN MEANING. Mixed kinds MEANS prohibition, prohibiting the forces from their performances. Mixed kinds, ITS EXPLANATION is confusing, causing confusion in the supernal forces, and it denies the fame of the King, as it says, "neither shall a garment mingled of linen and wool come upon you" (Vayikra 19:19).

112. ת״ח, כְּתִיב וּמֵעֵץ הַדַּעַת טוֹב וָרָע לֹא תֹאכַל מִמֶּנּוּ כִּי בְּיוֹם אֲכָלְךָ מִמֶּנּוּ מוֹת תָּמוּת. וְהָא אִתְּמַר, דְּשָׁנֵי פִּקוּדוֹי דְּמַלְכָּא, וְאַחְלַף עֵץ חַיִּים, דְּבֵיהּ אִשְׁתְּלִים כֹּלָּא, וּבֵיהּ תַּלְיָא מְהֵימְנוּתָא, וְאִתְדַּבַּק בַּאֲתָר אָחֳרָא. וְהָא תָּנֵינָן, בְּכֹלָּא בָּעֵי ב״נ לְאַחֲזָאָה עוֹבָדָא כְּגַוְונָא דִּלְעֵילָּא, וּלְמֶעְבַּד עוֹבָדָא כְּמָה דְּאִצְטְרִיךְ. וְאִי אִשְׁתָּנֵי בְּמִלָּה אָחֳרָא, הוּא אַנְגִּיד עָלֵיהּ לְשַׁרְיָא בֵּיהּ מִלָּה אָחֳרָא דְּלָא אִצְטְרִיךְ.

112. Come and behold: it is written, "but of the Tree of Knowledge of Good and Evil, you shall not eat of it: for on the day that you eat of it, you shall surely die" (Beresheet 2:17). We learned, IT IS DUE to changing the commands of the King, replacing the Tree of Life, wherein everything is complete, on which Faith depends, and joining another place. We learned that in everything, a person needs to show an action similar to what is above, and perform the action as need be. If THE ACT is changed for something else, he brings down upon him something else that should not rest upon him, NAMELY, THE OTHER SIDE.

113. וְתָא חֲזֵי, בְּשַׁעְתָּא דְּבַר נָשׁ אַחֲזֵי עוֹבָדָא לְתַתָּא בְּאֹרַח מֵישָׁר, כְּמָה דְּאִצְטְרִיךְ, נָגִיד וְנָפִיק וְשַׁרְיָא עֲלוֹי רוּחַ קַדִּישָׁא עִלָּאָה. וּבְשַׁעְתָּא דְּאִיהוּ אַחֲזֵי עוֹבָדָא לְתַתָּא בְּאוֹרְחָא עֲקִימָא, דְּלֵית אִיהוּ אוֹרַח מֵישָׁר, כְּדֵין נָגִיד וְנָפִיק וְשָׁרֵי עֲלוֹי רוּחַ אָחֳרָא, דְּלָא אִצְטְרִיךְ, דְּסָטֵי לֵיהּ לב״נ לְסְטַר בִּישׁ. מַאן מָשִׁיךְ עָלֵיהּ הַהוּא רוּחָא. הֲוֵי אוֹמֵר, הַהוּא עוֹבָדָא דְּאַחֲזֵי בִּסְטַר אָחֳרָא.

113. Come and behold: when a person shows an act below in an appropriate fashion as need be, a holy supernal Spirit is attracted to and rests upon him.

However, when he exhibits an act down here in a crooked fashion that is not appropriate, then another spirit that he does not need, which turns the person to the side of evil, is attracted to him and rests on him. What attracts that spirit upon him? The answer is that act that reflected another side.

114. כְּתִיב דָּרְשָׁה צֶמֶר וּפִשְׁתִּים. דָּרְשָׁה, מַהוּ דָּרְשָׁה. דְּבָעְיָא וְדָרִישׁ עַל צֶמֶר וּפִשְׁתִּים, מַאן דִּמְחַבֵּר לוֹן כַּחֲדָא, וְאִי תֵּימָא בְּצִיצִית אֲמַאי שָׁרֵי. הָא אוּקְמוּהָ. אֲבָל הָתָם הוּא הַהוּא לְבוּשָׁא בְּתִקּוּנוֹי, בְּאַשְׁלְמוּת עוֹבָדָא כַּדְקָא חֲזֵי.

114. HE QUESTIONS: It is written, "She seeks wool and flax" (Mishlei 31:13). What is meant by, "She seeks"? AND HE ANSWERS: THE SHECHINAH, THAT IS CALLED 'A WOMAN OF WORTH', seeks and asks about the wool and linen as to who mingles them, FOR THE PURPOSE OF PUNISHING HIM. One may then question why MIXING WOOL WITH LINEN is permissible in the *Tzitzit* (lit. 'fringes')? AND ANSWERS: We established that clothing is correct, MEANING ACCORDING TO THE COMMANDMENT – perfectly made, MEANING SINCE THE PRECEPT IS SO, IT IS NOT CONSIDERED AN INAPPROPRIATE ACT.

115. תּוּ, דָּרְשָׁה צֶמֶר וּפִשְׁתִּים, לְמֶעְבַּד נוּקְמָא בְּמַאן דִּמְחַבֵּר לוֹן כַּחֲדָא. אֲבָל אֵימָתַי שַׁרְיָא. בְּשַׁעְתָּא דְּאִיהוּ בְּאַשְׁלְמוּתָא, דִּכְתִיב, וַתַּעַשׂ בְּחֵפֶץ כַּפֶּיהָ. וְצִיצִית, הָא אוּקִימְנָא דְּהָתָם בְּהַהוּא כְּלָלָא דִּשְׁלֵימוּתָא אִשְׁתְּכַח, וְלָא עָבִיד מִדִּי. אֲבָל בְּשַׁעְתָּא דְּלָא אִשְׁתְּכַח בִּשְׁלֵימוּתָא, מַאן דְּאָתֵי לְחַבְּרָא לוֹן כַּחֲדָא, אִתְעַר עֲלֵיהּ רוּחָא דְּלָא אִצְטְרִיךְ.

115. More IS THERE TO EXPOUND: "She seeks wool, and flax," to do vengeance against one who mingles them together. But when does HOLINESS hover upon them – MEANING at the time when THE ACT is done with its perfection, as it is written, "and works willingly with her hands" (Ibid.). And with *Tzitzit*, we have established there THE *SHA'ATNEZ* (A MIXTURE OF WOOL AND LINEN) is done with perfection and so does nothing THAT WILL DRAW UPON THE OTHER SIDE. THEREFORE, THIS IS PERMISSIBLE. ABOUT THIS IT IS WRITTEN, "AND WORKS WILLINGLY WITH

HER HANDS." But when THE ACT is not found to be perfect, then he who comes to join WOOL AND FLAX together draws upon himself a spirit he should not have, NAMELY THE OTHER SIDE.

116. מִלָּה דָא מַאן אוֹכַח. קַיִן וְהֶבֶל אוֹכְחָן. דְּדָא אָתֵי מִסִּטְרָא חַד, וְדָא אָתֵי מִסִּטְרָא אָחֳרָא. וּבג״כ לָא לִבְעֵי לָן לְחַבְּרָא לוֹן כַּחֲדָא. וְקָרְבְּנָא דְּקַיִן, אִתְרְחַק מִקַּמֵּי קָרְבְּנָא דְּהֶבֶל.

116. Who proves this matter? Cain and Abel prove THIS, as one came from one direction and the second came from another direction. ABEL CAME FROM THE SIDE OF HOLINESS; CAIN CAME FROM THE SIDE OF THE OTHER SIDE. For this reason, you should not mingle them. WHEN BOTH BROUGHT SACRIFICES, THEY WERE NOT JOINED, since the sacrifices of Cain were made distant from before the sacrifice of Abel.

117. וְעַל דָּא וּבֶגֶד כִּלְאַיִם שַׁעַטְנֵז לֹא יַעֲלֶה עָלֶיךָ. לֹא יַעֲלֶה עָלֶיךָ סְתָם, לֹא יַעֲלֶה עָלֶיךָ רוּחָא אָחֳרָא לְשַׁלְטָאָה בָּךְ. וְאִצְטְרִיךְ לֵיהּ לְבַר נָשׁ לְאַחֲזָאָה עוֹבְדָא דְּכַשְׁרָא כְּמָה דְיָאוּת, וּבְהַהוּא עוֹבְדָא שַׁרְיָא עֲלֵיהּ רוּחַ קַדִּישָׁא, רוּחַ עִלָּאָה, לְאִתְקַדְּשָׁא בֵּיהּ, אָתָא לְאִתְקַדְּשָׁא מְקַדְּשִׁין לֵיהּ, דִּכְתִיב וְהִתְקַדִּשְׁתֶּם וִהְיִיתֶם קְדוֹשִׁים כִּי קָדוֹשׁ אֲנִי יְיָ.

117. Therefore, "neither shall a garment mingled of linen and wool come upon you." The words, "upon you," are unspecified. IT IS TELLING YOU ALSO not to allow another spirit to rule over you. A person needs to show deeds that are proper and appropriate. When doing this act, there will hover over him a Holy Spirit, a supernal Spirit that will sanctify him. He who seeks purity will be sanctified, as it is written: "Sanctify yourselves therefore, and be holy: for I am Hashem" (Vayikra 20:7).

118. כְּתִיב וּמֵעֵץ הַדַּעַת טוֹב וָרָע, וּמַה עַל דָּא גָּרִים אָדָם מִיתָה בְּעָלְמָא, מַאן דְּאַחֲזֵי עוֹבְדָא אָחֳרָא דְּלָא אִצְטְרִיךְ, עַל אַחַת כַּמָּה וְכַמָּה. שׁוֹר וַחֲמוֹר אוֹכְחָן. מִסִּטְרָא דָּא אִקְרֵי שׁוֹרִי, וּמִסִּטְרָא דָּא אִקְרֵי חֲמוֹר, וְעַל דָּא כְּתִיב לֹא תַחֲרֹשׁ בְּשׁוֹר וּבַחֲמוֹר יַחְדָּו. לֹא תַּעֲבִיד

עִרְבּוּבְיָיא כַּחֲדָא, בְּגִין דְּאִתְעַר לְאִתְחַבְּרָא סִטְרָא אָחֳרָא כַּחֲדָא,
לְאַבְאָשָׁא עָלְמָא. וּמַאן דְּפָרִישׁ לוֹן, אַסְגֵּי שְׁלָמָא בְּעָלְמָא. אוּף הָכָא,
מַאן דְּפָרִישׁ לוֹן בְּהַהוּא גַּוְונָא כְּמָה דְּאָמְרוּ, דְּלָא אִשְׁתְּכַח שׁוּע טָווּי
וְנוּז כַּחֲדָא, הַאי בַּר נָשׁ אַסְגֵּי שְׁלָמָא עָלֵיהּ, וְעַל כָּל עָלְמָא.

118. It is written, "but of the Tree of Knowledge of Good and Evil..." If Adam introduced death in this world for this matter, then how much more so is it for the one who exhibits an inappropriate act. An ox and donkey will prove this. On the side OF HOLINESS it is referred to as an ox; from that Side OF DEFILEMENT, it is called donkey. Hence, the verse says, "You shall not plow with an ox and an donkey together" (Devarim 22:10). Do not mix them, because it causes the Other Side to assemble to cause evil in the world. He who parts them increases peace in the world. This is true here also WITH WOOL AND FLAX, for he who parts them in the said manner – as has been said, so that the crosswise (Heb. *shti va'erev*), the spun (Heb. *tavuy*) and the woven (Heb. *nuz*) do not come together, AS THEY FORM THE LETTERS OF *SHA'ATNEZ* – that person multiplies peace for himself and all the world.

119. קָרְבְּנָא דְּקַיִן הֲוָה פִּשְׁתִּים, וְקָרְבְּנָא דְּהֶבֶל הֲוָה צֶמֶר, לָאו דָּא
כְּדָא, וְלָאו דָּא כְּדָא. רָזָא דְּמִלָּה,קַיִן כִּלְאַיִם הֲוָה, עִרְבּוּבְיָא דְּלָא
אִצְטְרִיךְ, סִטְרָא אָחֳרָא, דְּלָא זִינָא דְּחַוָּה וְאָדָם. וְקוּרְבָּנֵיהּ מֵהַהוּא
סִטְרָא קָא אַתְיָא. הֶבֶל מִזִּינָא חֲדָא דְּאָדָם וְחַוָּה. וּבִמְעָהָא דְּחַוָּה
אִתְחַבָּרוּ אִלֵּין תְּרֵין סִטְרִין. וּבְגִין דְּאִתְחַבָּרוּ כַּחֲדָא, לָא אַתְיָא מִנַּיְיהוּ
תּוֹעַלְתָּא לְעָלְמָא, וְאִתְאֲבִידוּ.

119. Cain's sacrifice was flax, DENOTING THE FRUIT OF THE EARTH; the sacrifice of Abel was wool, NAMELY THE FIRSTLINGS OF HIS SHEEP. One sacrifice is not like the other. The secret of this matter is that Cain was a mixture, NAMELY OF ONE SPECIES WITH ANOTHER SPECIES, an inappropriate mix, FOR HE WAS from the Other Side, not the species of Adam and Eve. And his sacrifice came from that side. Abel was of the same species as Adam and Eve, NAMELY FROM HOLINESS. In the bowels of Eve were joined these two opposite aspects, NAMELY TWO DIFFERENT SPECIES, and because they were joined together, no benefit came to the world, and they were lost.

120. וְעַד יוֹמָא דֵין, סִטְרָא דִּלְהוֹן קַיְימָא. וּמַאן דְּאַחְזֵי גַּרְמֵיהּ בְּעוֹבָדָא דְּחַבּוּרָא דָא, אִתְּעַר עָלֵיהּ אִינּוּן סִטְרִין כַּחֲדָא, וְיָכִיל לְאִתְּזְקָא, וְשָׁארֵי עֲלוֹי רוּחָא אָחֳרָא, דְּלָא אִצְטְרִיךְ. וְיִשְׂרָאֵל בָּעָאן לְאִתְּעָרָא עֲלַיְיהוּ רוּחָא קַדִּישָׁא לְמֶהֱוֵי קַדִּישִׁין, לְאִשְׁתַּכְּחָא בִּשְׁלָמָא, בְּעָלְמָא דֵין וּבְעָלְמָא דְּאָתֵי.

120. Until this day, that aspect still exists, NAMELY THE DESTRUCTIVE FORCE OF CAIN AND ABEL. One who exhibits himself performing an act of joining this union awakens these sides together, MEANING THIS MIXTURE OF CAIN AND ABEL. He may get hurt and cause to hover over him an inappropriate spirit. Yisrael need to awaken upon them a saintly spirit in order to be holy, so that they will be in peace in this world and the World to Come.

121. כְּתִיב וְלָבַשׁ הַכֹּהֵן מִדּוֹ בַד וּמִכְנְסֵי בַד יִהְיוּ עַל בְּשָׂרוֹ וּבְאַבְנֵט בַּד יַחְגּוֹר אֲמַאי אִקְרֵי בַד, יְחִידָאי. בְּגִין דְּלָא בָּעֵי לְחַבְּרָא לְהַאי פִּשְׁתִּים בְּאָחֳרָא, וְעַ"ד לָא כְּתִיב מִדּוֹ פִּשְׁתִּים, אֶלָּא בַד יְחִידָאָה.

121. It is written, "And the priest shall put on his linen garment" (Vayikra 6:3), "and he shall have the linen breeches put on his flesh, and shall be girded with a linen (lit. 'cloth') girdle" (Vayikra 16:4). HE ASKS: Why is it called cloth (Heb. bad), MEANING ALONE (HEB. BADAD)? AND ANSWERS: This is because this linen must not be mixed with another. Therefore, the verse is not written, 'AND THE PRIEST SHALL PUT ON his linen garment,' but it says, "cloth," MEANING single.

122. וְכַהֲנָא אֲמַאי אִיהוּ בָּעֵי לְאִתְחֲזָאָה בְּהַאי. אֶלָּא אִלֵּין מָאנֵי בַד, בָּעֵי לְאִתְחֲזָאָה בְּהוּ עַל מִזְבַּח הָעוֹלָה, כַּד הֲוָה מְפַנֵּי קְטָרָא דְּדַשְׁנָא דְּעוֹלָה, דְּהָא עוֹלָה מִסִּטְרָא דְעַ"ז וְהִרְהוּרָא בִּישָׁא קָא אַתְיָא. וּבְג"כ, בָּעֵי לְאִתְחֲזָאָה בְּהוּ בִּלְחוֹדַיְיהוּ, וְלָא בְּעִרְבּוּבְיָא כְּמָה דְּאֲמָרָן, בְּגִין דְּיִתְכַּפֵּר לֵיהּ לִב"נ כָּל אִינּוּן חוֹבִין דְּאַתְיָין מֵהַהוּא סִטְרָא.

122. HE ASKS: Why must the priest be exhibited with this, NAMELY WEARING LINEN, WHICH ALLUDES TO ANOTHER SIDE? AND ANSWERS: These flax garments need to be exhibited when working by the altar of the burnt offering, when he is cleaning the fat pieces of the burnt offering. For the burnt offering is connected with idol worship and evil thoughts – MEANING THAT FOR THOUGHTS ABOUT IDOL WORSHIPPING, ONE MUST BRING A BURNT OFFERING. For this reason, he must appear wearing flax alone, not mingled WITH WOOL, as we said, in order to attain atonement for man for all those sins coming from that side.

123. וְכַד עָיֵיל לְמַקְדְּשָׁא, אֲתַר דִּשְׁלִימוּ אִשְׁתְּכַח, וְכָל אִינּוּן פּוּלְחָנֵי דִּשְׁלֵימוּתָא, אע"ג דְּאִתְחַבְּרוּ, לֵית לָן בָּהּ, כְּמָה דְּאַמָרָן בְּצִיצִית, בְּגִין דְּתַמָּן אִשְׁתְּכָחוּ וְאִתְחַבָּרוּ כָּל אִינּוּן זַיְנִין דִּלְעֵילָּא, וְכָל אִינּוּן מָאנֵי מַקְדְּשָׁא, מִשְׁתַּכְּחִין בֵּיהּ כַּמָה זַיְנִין מְשַׁנְיָין דָּא מִן דָּא, וְכֻלְּהוּ אִתְכְּלִילוּ תַּמָּן כְּגַוְונָא דִּלְעֵילָּא. זַכָּאִין אִינּוּן יִשְׂרָאֵל, דְּקוּדְשָׁא בְּרִיךְ הוּא יָהִיב לְהוּ אוֹרַיְיתָא דִקְשׁוֹט, אוֹרַיְיתָא דִּמְהֵימְנוּתָא, וְרִיחַם לְהוּ מִכָּל שְׁאָר עַמִּין עע"ז, דִּכְתִּיב אָהַבְתִּי אֶתְכֶם אָמַר יְיָ'.

123. When he enters the Temple, the place where there is perfection, where all the services of perfection are, though there is found jointly WOOL AND FLAX, we should not FEAR, this just as we said regarding the *Tzitzit* (lit. 'fringes'). There are found and joined all these species of above, all the vessels of the Temple including many kinds differing from one another. All are included there, similar to those above. Fortunate are the children of Yisrael that the Holy One, blessed be He, gave to them a true Torah, a Torah of Faith, and loved them above the other nations as it is written: "'I have loved you,' says Hashem" (Malachi 1:2).

21. "All its fruit shall be holy for praisegiving to Hashem"

A Synopsis

Rabbi Chiya talks about the concept of fruits that are brought forth only from another force above, and that do not become ripened until three years have passed. In the fourth year, "all its fruit shall be holy for giving praise." The secret meaning of this is that in the fourth year the Congregation of Yisrael is paired with God, and there is praise and joy; the "fourth year" is God Himself and it is also the Congregation of Yisrael. Then the hosts are appointed over the world in their proper place, and everyone is blessed, and the fruits are now in perfection so may now be eaten. Until this point it is forbidden to eat of the fruits.

124. פָּתַח ר' חִיָּיא אֲבַתְרֵיה וְאָמַר, כִּי תָבֹאוּ אֶל הָאָרֶץ וּנְטַעְתֶּם כָּל עֵץ מַאֲכָל וְגוֹ'. וּבַשָּׁנָה הָרְבִיעִית יִהְיֶה כָּל פִּרְיוֹ קֹדֶשׁ הִלּוּלִים לַיְיָ. כִּי תָבֹאוּ אֶל הָאָרֶץ, הָא אוּקְמוּהָ חַבְרַיָּיא, אֲבָל ת"ח, דְּהָא אִילָנָא לָא עָבִיד פֵּירִין, אֶלָּא בְּאַרְעָא. וְאַרְעָא אַפִּיק לְהוֹן, וְאַחֲזֵי הַהוּא אִיבָא לְעָלְמָא. וְאַרְעָא לָא עַבְדָא פֵּירִין אֶלָּא מִגּוֹ חֵילָא אַחֲרָא דְּעָלָּה. כְּמָה דְּנוּקְבָּא לָא עַבְדָא פֵּירִין, אֶלָּא מִגּוֹ חֵילָא דִּדְכוּרָא.

124. Rabbi Chiya commenced to say after him, "And when you shall come to the land, and shall have planted all manner of trees for food... But in the fourth year all its fruit shall be holy for praisegiving to Hashem" (Vayikra 19:23-24). "And when you come to the land"; the friends have established this. But come and behold: a tree, THE SECRET OF ZEIR ANPIN, produces fruits only in the soil, DENOTING MALCHUT. The earth brings them forth, and shows those fruits to the world. The earth produces fruits only from another force above it, MEANING FROM ZEIR ANPIN, just as every female produces fruits only as a result of the force of the male.

125. וְהַהוּא אִיבָא, לָא אִשְׁתְּלִים בְּאַשְׁלְמוּתָא, עַד תְּלַת שְׁנִין. וְחֵילָא לָא אִתְפַּקְדָא עָלֵיהּ לְעֵילָא עַד דְּאִשְׁתְּלִים. בָּתַר דְּאִשְׁתְּלִים אִתְפַּקְדָא עָלֵיהּ חֵילָא וְאַרְעָא אִתְתַּקְנַת בֵּיהּ. דְּהָא עַד תְּלַת שְׁנִין אַרְעָא לָא אִתְתַּקְנַת בֵּיהּ וְלָא אִשְׁתְּלִימַת עַמֵּיהּ. בָּתַר דְּאִשְׁתְּלִים וְאִתְתַּקְנוּ כַּחֲדָא כְּדֵין הוּא שְׁלֵימוּתָא.

125. And that fruit, THAT MALCHUT CALLED 'EARTH', PRODUCES, does not become completed in its fullness until three years, MEANING UNTIL MALCHUT RECEIVES THREE COLUMNS FROM ZEIR ANPIN. The force upon it is appointed above until its completion. After completion, its force is then appointed upon it, and then the earth is established by it. Prior to three years, MEANING BEFORE RECEIVING ALL THREE COLUMNS, the earth is not yet established by it, WITH ZEIR ANPIN, and not completed with him. After MALCHUT is perfected and set together, then there is perfection.

126. תָּא חֲזֵי, נוּקְבָּא, עַד תְּלָת זִמְנִין דְּאִתְעַבְּרָא, אִיבָּא דִּמְעָהָא לָא אִשְׁתְּלִים. בָּתַר ג' עִידוּאָן, נוּקְבָּא אִתְתָּקְנַת בְּהַהוּא אִיבָּא, וְאִסְתְּכְּמוּ כַּחֲדָא. כְּדֵין הַהוּא אִיבָּא שְׁלִימוּ דְּכֹלָּא, וּשְׁפִירוּ דְּכֹלָּא. בָּתַר דְּנָפַק, עַד ג' שְׁנִין לָא אִית לֵיהּ חֵילָא לְעֵילָא, דְּהָא כְּדֵין אִשְׁתְּלִים בְּשׁוּלָא דִּילֵיהּ. לֵוִי אַתְרְעֵי מִכֹּלָּא, תְּלִיתָאָה לְאִמֵּיהּ, דְּאִתְתָּקְנַת בֵּיהּ, וְאִתְבַּסְּמַת בַּהֲדֵיהּ.

126. Come and behold: the Female, NAMELY MALCHUT, before she becomes pregnant three times, the fruit of her stomach, NAMELY THE SOUL, is not complete. FOR IT IS NECESSARY THAT THERE BE IN HER THE THREE COLUMNS, AND IN EACH COLUMN THREE COLUMNS – BECAUSE THREE PREGNANCIES CORRESPOND TO THE THREE COLUMNS, AND IN EACH PREGNANCY TRHERE ARE THREE COLUMNS. After three pregnancies, the Female is established by that fruit and they are reconciled. THIS IS BECAUSE ZEIR ANPIN IS RIGHT, MALCHUT IS LEFT, AND THEY ARE IN AGREEMENT ONLY BY MEANS OF THE CENTRAL COLUMN THAT INCLUDES THREE COLUMNS, SINCE IN EACH COLUMN THERE ARE THREE COLUMNS. Then that fruit, MEANING THE SOUL, is the perfection of it all and the beauty of it all. And after THE FRUIT emerges AND SPROUTS FROM IT, before three years, it has no force from above, BECAUSE THE FRUIT ON ITS OWN ALSO NEEDS THE ILLUMINATIONS OF THE THREE COLUMNS LIKE MALCHUT, THE SECRET OF THREE YEARS. Then its growth is completed. THEREFORE, PRIOR TO THIS THEY ARE THE UNCIRCUMCISED YEARS. And Levi, WITH THREE PREGNANCIES PASSED OVER HIM, was the chosen OF ALL THE TRIBES, as he is third for his mother. By him she was set and with him she was made fragrant.

127. בָּתַר ג׳ שְׁנִין, אִתְפְּקָדַת עָלֵיהּ חֵילָא עִלָּאָה לְעֵילָּא. וּבַשָּׁנָה הָרְבִיעִית, יִהְיֶה כָּל פִּרְיוֹ קֹדֶשׁ הִלּוּלִים. מַאי קֹדֶשׁ הִלּוּלִים. תּוּשְׁבְּחָן, לְשַׁבְּחָא לֵיהּ לְקוּדְשָׁא בְּרִיךְ הוּא. עַד הָכָא, מִכָּאן וְאֵילָךְ רָזָא דְּמִלָּה, דְּבַשָּׁנָה הָרְבִיעִית מִזְדַּוְּוגַת כְּנֶסֶת יִשְׂרָאֵל לְקוּדְשָׁא בְּרִיךְ הוּא, וְהִלּוּלָא חַד אִשְׁתְּכַח. דִּכְתִיב קֹדֶשׁ הִלּוּלִים, הִלּוּלָא וְחֶדְוָה בְּזִמְנָא חֲדָא.

127. After three years, a supernal force from above is appointed upon it, "But in the fourth year all its fruit shall be holy for praisegiving." What is meant by, "holy for praisegiving"? IT'S praises with which to praise the Holy One, blessed be He. Until this point IS THE LITERAL INTERPRETATION. From this point on, LET US EXPLAIN the secret of the matter. In the fourth year, the Congregation of Yisrael, NAMELY, MALCHUT, is paired with the Holy One, blessed be He, DENOTING ZEIR ANPIN, and one joy is prevalent, as it is written: "holy for praisegiving," MEANING giving praise and joy at the same time.

128. מַאי שָׁנָה הָרְבִיעִית דָּא קוּדְשָׁא בְּרִיךְ הוּא. וְתָנֵינָן, שָׁנָה הָרְבִיעִית, דָּא כְּנֶסֶת יִשְׂרָאֵל דְּאִיהִי קַיְימָא רְבִיעָאָה לְכוּרְסְיָיא, וְכֹלָּא חַד, דְּהָא כְּדֵין קוּדְשָׁא בְּרִיךְ הוּא מִזְדַּוַּוג בָּהּ בכ״י, וּכְדֵין הִיא קֹדֶשׁ, וְהִלּוּלָא קַדִּישָׁא אִשְׁתְּכַח, וּכְדֵין אִתְמָנָן עַל עָלְמָא, עַל כָּל מִלָּה וּמִלָּה כַּדְקָא חֲזֵי לֵיהּ מִכָּאן וּלְהַלְאָה מִתְבָּרְכָאן כֻּלְּהוּ, וְשָׁארֵי לְמֵיכַל, דְּהָא כֻּלְּהוּ בִּשְׁלֵימוּתָא דְּכֹלָּא, בִּשְׁלֵימוּתָא דְּעֵילָּא וְתַתָּא.

128. HE QUESTIONS: What is the fourth year? AND ANSWERS: It is the Holy One, blessed be He, DENOTING ZEIR ANPIN. We learned that the fourth year refers to the Congregation of Yisrael, DENOTING MALCHUT, as she is the fourth leg of the Throne. THE THREE COLUMNS, CHESED, GVURAH AND TIFERET OF ZEIR ANPIN, ARE THE THREE LEGS OF THE SUPERNAL THRONE, AND MALCHUT IS THE FOURTH LEG OF THE THRONE. THERE IS NO CONTRADICTION AGAINST WHAT WAS SAID, THAT THE FOURTH YEAR REFERS TO THE HOLY ONE, BLESSED BE HE, as all is one, since the Holy One, blessed be He, pairs Himself with the Congregation of Yisrael. AND SO, YOU CAN CALL HIM ZEIR ANPIN, AND CALL HIM MALCHUT. Then there is Holiness, and holy praisegiving. Then the hosts are appointed over the world upon each thing, as is proper for it. From this point are all blessed and it is permissible to eat THE FRUITS as now everything is in perfection; there is perfection above and below, MEANING PERFECTION OF ZEIR ANPIN AND MALCHUT.

129. וְעַד לָא אִשְׁתְּלִים בְּכֹלָּא מִתַּתָּא וּמֵעֵילָא, אָסִיר לְמֵיכַל מִנֵּיה. וּמַאן דְּאָכִיל מִנֵּיה, כְּמַאן דְּלֵית לֵיה חוּלָקָא בְּקוּדְשָׁא בְּרִיךְ הוּא וּבכ"י, דְּהָא הַהוּא אִיבָּא בְּלָא רְשׁוּתָא עִלָּאָה קַדִּישָׁא קַיְּימָא, דְּלָא שָׁרֵי עֲלֵיה עַד דְּיִשְׁתְּלִים. וּבְלָא רְשׁוּתָא. תַּתָּאָה, דְּהָא לָא אִתְבַּסְּמַת חֵילָא דְּאַרְעָא בֵּיה. וְהַהוּא דְּאָכִיל מִנֵּיה, אַחְזֵי גַּרְמֵיה דְּלֵית לֵיה חוּלָקָא לְעֵילָא וְתַתָּא, וְאִי בָּרִיךְ עֲלֵיה, בְּרָכָה לְבַטָּלָה הוּא. דְּהָא קוּדְשָׁא בְּרִיךְ הוּא עַד כְּעַן לָא שַׁרְיָא עֲלוֹי, וְלֵית בֵּיה חוּלָקָא. רַחֲמָנָא לִישֵׁזְבִינָן מֵאִינּוּן דְּלָא מַשְׁגִּיחִין לִיקָרָא דְּמָארֵיהוֹן.

129. And until everything is completed from above and below, it is forbidden to eat of it. He who does eat of it is considered like one who has no share in the Holy One, blessed be He, and the Congregation of Yisrael since that fruit exists without holy supernal authority, NAMELY ZEIR ANPIN, because this will not hover over it until it is perfected. And it is without authority from below, NAMELY MALCHUT, since the earth force did not ripen with it PRIOR TO THE PASSING OF THE FOURTH YEAR, SINCE THE COUPLING OF ZEIR ANPIN AND MALCHUT HAS NOT YET TAKEN PLACE, AS EARLIER MENTIONED. He who eats of it shows that he has no share of the above and below, ZEIR ANPIN AND MALCHUT. If he made a blessing over it, it is considered a blessing in vain, as up to this point the Holy One, blessed be He, does not hover over him and he has no share in Him. May the Merciful One save us from those who are not mindful of the honor of their Master.

130. זַכָּאִין אִינּוּן צַדִּיקַיָּיא בְּעָלְמָא דֵּין, וּבְעָלְמָא דְּאָתֵי, עָלַיְיהוּ כְּתִיב וְאֹרַח צַדִּיקִים כְּאוֹר נֹגַהּ. בְּגִין דִּבְהַהוּא זִמְנָא, יִסְתְּלַק חִוְיָא דְּשַׁרְיָא בְּנוּקְבָּא בְּקַדְמֵיתָא, וְיֵיתֵי דְּכוּרָא לְמִשְׁרֵי בְּאַתְרֵיה כַּד בְּקַדְמֵיתָא, וְכֹלָּא יְהֵא שְׁלִים. תָּאנָא בְּזִמְנָא דְּזַכָּאָה שָׁרֵי בְּעָלְמָא וְכוּ' עַד צַדִּיק כַּתָּמָר יִפְרָח.

130. Fortunate are the righteous in this world and the next. About them is written: "But the path of just men is like the gleam of sunlight" (Mishlei 4:18). At that time, IN THE FUTURE TO COME, the serpent that dwelt before with the Female will depart, MEANING WHO WAS NURTURING FROM MALCHUT, and instead the Male will come to hover in its place as before – MEANING WITH A UNION THAT WILL NOT CEASE, AS THERE WILL BE NO ONE TO SET APART THIS MATING. And everything will be perfect.

22. "You shall rise up before a hoary head"

A Synopsis

Rabbi Yosi says that the "hoary head" in the title verse is a scroll of Torah for which one must stand up, and that a man should rise up before a scholar because he has the supernal holy image of the supernal priest on him. Rabbi Shimon says that the Torah scroll is the written Torah, and that the Torah scholar is in the state of the oral Torah. Lastly we are told that people should repent before they reach old age; it is more praiseworthy to act rightly when still in one's full strength.

131. רַבִּי יוֹסֵי פָּתַח קְרָא וְאָמַר, לֹא תֹאכְלוּ עַל הַדָּם. הָא בְּכַמָּה אֲתַר אוּקְמוּהָ חַבְרַיָּיא, וְכָל הָנֵי קְרָאֵי אֲבַתְרֵיה. וְכָל חַד וְחַד בְּאִתְגַּלְיָיא. אֲבָל הַאי קְרָא אִית לְאִתְעָרָא בֵּיה, דִּכְתִיב מִפְּנֵי שֵׂיבָה תָּקוּם וְגוֹ'. מִפְּנֵי שֵׂיבָה, שֵׂיבָה דְּאוֹרַיְיתָא סְתָם. תָּקוּם, מִכָּאן דְּבָעֵי בַּר נָשׁ לְמֵיקָם מִקַּמֵּי ס"ת, וְהָכִי רַב הַמְנוּנָא סָבָא, כַּד הֲוָה חָמֵי ס"ת, הֲוָא קָם מִקַּמֵיה, וְאָמַר מִפְּנֵי שֵׂיבָה תָּקוּם. כְּגַוְונָא דָא, בָּעֵי בַּר נָשׁ לְמֵיקָם בְּקִיּוּמֵיה לְקַמֵּיה דת"ח, בְּגִין דְּאִיהוּ קָאֵים בְּדִיּוּקְנָא קַדִּישָׁא עִלָּאָה. וְרָמַז לְכַהֲנָא קַדִּישָׁא עִלָּאָה, דִּכְתִיב וְהָדַרְתָּ פְּנֵי זָקֵן, דְּאִיהוּ בְּעָלְמָא. אר"ש, מִכָּאן רֶמֶז לְתוֹרָה שֶׁבִּכְתָב וְרָמַז לְתוֹרָה שֶׁבְּעַל פֶּה.

131. Rabbi Yosi commenced: "You shall not eat anything with the blood..." (Vayikra 19:26). This verse has been explained by the friends in several places, and also all the verses that follow. Each one EXPLAINED THEM ACCORDING TO THE revealed Torah. However, this verse needs exposition. It is written: "You shall rise up before a the elderly" (Ibid. 32). The words, "before a hoary head," refers generally to a Torah scroll for which you must rise. And so did Rav Hamnuna Saba (the elder). When he saw a Torah scroll, he would rise and say, "You shall rise up before a hoary head" (Vayikra 19:32). Similarly, man should rise fully before a Torah scholar because he has the supernal holy image, which indicates the supernal holy priest, THE SECRET OF SUPERNAL ABA, CALLED 'OLD MAN'. As the verse says, "and honor the face of the old man" (Ibid.), who is in the world, MEANING THE TORAH SCHOLAR WHO IS WITH YOU IN THE WORLD, WHICH ALLUDES TO THE SUPERNAL OLD MAN, SUPERNAL ABA. Rabbi

Shimon said: From here is an allusion to the Written and Oral Torah. THIS MEANS THAT ONE NEEDS TO RISE BEFORE A TORAH SCROLL, CONSIDERED THE WRITTEN TORAH, AND RISE BEFORE A TORAH SCHOLAR, WHO IS CONSIDERED THE ORAL TORAH.

132. וְתוּ תָּנֵינָן, הַאי קְרָא לִדְרְשָׁא הוּא דְּאָתָא, מִפְּנֵי שֵׂיבָה תָּקוּם, כְּמָה דְּאִתְּעָרוּ בֵּיהּ חַבְרַיָּיא, מִפְּנֵי שֵׂיבָה תָּקוּם, אַזְהַר לֵיהּ לְבַר נָשׁ, עַד לָא יִסְתַּלַּק בְּסִיבוּתָא, דְּיִקוּם בְּקִיּוּמָא טָבָא בְּעָלְמָא, בְּגִין דְּדֵין הוּא הַדּוּרָא לֵיהּ, אֲבָל לְסוֹף יוֹמוֹי לֵית שְׁבָחָא לֵיהּ לב"ב, כַּד אִיהוּ סִיב וְלָא יָכִיל לְמֶהֱוֵי בִּישׁ. אֶלָּא שְׁבָחָא דִּילֵיהּ, כַּד אִיהוּ בְּתוּקְפֵּיהּ, וְאִיהוּ טָב. וּשְׁלֹמֹה מַלְכָּא צָוַוח וְאָמַר, גַּם בְּמַעֲלָלָיו יִתְנַכֶּר נָעַר וְגו'. כְּגַוְונָא דָא כְּתִיב, וּזְכֹר אֶת בּוֹרְאֶךָ בִּימֵי בְּחוּרוֹתֶיךָ. א"ר אֶלְעָזָר, וַדַּאי אוֹרְחָא דָא מְתַקְּנָא קַמָּן, וְהַאי אוֹרְחָא דְקוּדְשָׁא בְּרִיךְ הוּא הוּא.

132. We further learned what this verse, "You shall rise up before a hoary head," teaches, as commented on by the friends. "You shall rise up before a hoary head." THE TORAH warns the person that before reaching old age, he should establish himself properly in the world, MEANING HE SHOULD REPENT because this will be better for him. But if HE REPENTS late in life, this is not such a praiseworthy act for him, since he is old and can not do any more wrong. The praiseworthy one is good when he has his full strength. King Solomon exclaimed, "Even a child is known by his doings" (Mishlei 20:11). Similarly, it is written: "Remember now your creator in the days of your youth" (Kohelet 12:1). Rabbi Elazar said: Certainly, this way is ready before us, this being the way of the Holy One, blessed be He.

23. "For Hashem knows the way of the righteous"

A Synopsis

Rabbi Shimon tells us that God knows and looks after the righteous, and that the wicked perish simply because He does not walk with them. He also tells us the difference between "a way" and "a path," saying that a path is a recently opened path that has not been walked upon by many people.

133. פָּתַח וְאָמַר, כִּי יוֹדֵעַ יְיָ' דֶּרֶךְ צַדִּיקִים וְדֶרֶךְ רְשָׁעִים תֹּאבֵד. מַאי כִּי יוֹדֵעַ יְיָ'. אֶלָּא, קוּדְשָׁא בְּרִיךְ הוּא יוֹדֵעַ וְאַשְׁגַּח בְּאָרְחָא דְּצַדִּיקַיָּיא, לְאוֹטָבָא לְהוּ, וּלְאַגָּנָא לְהוּ, וְהוּא אָזִיל קַמַּיְיהוּ לְנַטְרָא לְהוּ. וּבג"כ, מַאן דְּנָפִיק לְאָרְחָא בָּעֵי דְּלֶהֱוֵי הַהִיא אָרְחָא דְּקוּדְשָׁא בְּרִיךְ הוּא, וְיִשְׁתַּתַּף לֵיהּ בַּהֲדַיְיהוּ. ובג"כ כְּתִיב, כִּי יוֹדֵעַ יְיָ' דֶּרֶךְ צַדִּיקִים וְדֶרֶךְ רְשָׁעִים תֹּאבֵד. הִיא מִגַּרְמָהּ, בְּגִין דְּקוּדְשָׁא בְּרִיךְ הוּא לָא אִשְׁתְּמוֹדַע לֵיהּ לְהַהוּא אָרְחָא דִּלְהוֹן, וְלָא אָזִיל בַּהֲדַיְיהוּ.

133. He commenced: "For Hashem knows the way of the righteous; but the way of the wicked shall perish" (Tehilim 1:6). HE QUESTIONS: What is meant by, "Hashem knows"? AND ANSWERS: This is that the Holy One, blessed be He, knows and looks after the way of the righteous to benefit them and defend them, and He walks before them to guard them. Therefore, whoever sets on his way needs to see to it that this way is the way of the Holy One, blessed be He, so that THE HOLY ONE, BLESSED BE HE, will participate with him. For this reason, it is written: "For Hashem knows the way of the righteous: but the way of the wicked shall perish." IT PERISHES on its own, since the Holy One, blessed be He, does not make Himself known to their way, and does not go with them.

134. כְּתִיב דֶּרֶךְ, וּכְתִיב אֹרַח, מַה בֵּין הַאי לְהַאי. אֶלָּא, דֶּרֶךְ: דִּשְׁאָר קַרְסוּלֵי בְּנֵי נָשָׁא אָזְלוּ בָּהּ. אֹרַח: דְּאִיהוּ אִתְפְּתַח מִן זְמָנָא זְעֵירָא וְעַל אָרְחָא דָּא כְּתִיב, וְאֹרַח צַדִּיקִים כְּאוֹר נֹגַהּ הוֹלֵךְ וָאוֹר עַד נְכוֹן הַיּוֹם.

134. HE QUESTIONS: SOMETIMES it is written, "a way," AND SOMETIMES, "a path." What is the difference between them? AND ANSWERS: "A way," implies a way that all the feet of people tread. "A path," is a recently opened

path AND HAS NOT BEEN TRODDEN LONG BY MANY PEOPLE. About this path does the verse say, "But the path of justmen is like the gleam of sunlight, that shines ever more brightly, until the height of noonday" (Misheli 4:18).

אָמֵן כֵּן יְהִי רָצוֹן

Amen, may it be His Will.

EMOR

Names of the articles

1. "The sons of Aaron"

A Synopsis

We learn that when God commanded the people to purify themselves He made the same admonition to the priests, the sons of Aaron. Rabbi Yehuda speaks about the light of God that is stored up for the righteous in the World to Come, but that is hidden from the wicked. We are told about how difficult it is for the soul to leave the body at the time of death and about why the body must not be left unburied for very long. Rabbi Yehuda talks about the possibility of immediate reincarnation and the body of light. He tells us about the flow of holy ointment that is drawn down upon the priest.

‏1. וַיֹּאמֶר יְיָ׳ אֶל מֹשֶׁה אֱמוֹר אֶל הַכֹּהֲנִים בְּנֵי אַהֲרֹן וְאָמַרְתָּ אֲלֵיהֶם לְנֶפֶשׁ לֹא יִטַּמָּא בְּעַמָּיו. א״ר יוֹסֵי, מ״ט דָא לָקֳבֵל דָא, דִּכְתִיב לְעֵילָא, וְאִישׁ אוֹ אִשָּׁה כִּי יִהְיֶה בָהֶם אוֹב אוֹ יִדְּעוֹנִי מוֹת יוּמָתוּ, וְסָמִיךְ לֵיהּ אֱמוֹר אֶל הַכֹּהֲנִים. אֶלָּא כֵּיוָן דְּאַזְהַר לְהוּ לְיִשְׂרָאֵל, לְקַדְּשָׁא לְהוּ בְּכֹלָּא, אַזְהַר לְהוּ לְכַהֲנֵי לְקַדְּשָׁא לוֹן, וְכֵן לַלְוִיִּם. לְכַהֲנֵי מְנַיִן. דִּכְתִיב אֱמוֹר אֶל הַכֹּהֲנִים. לְלֵוָאֵי מְנַיִן. דִּכְתִיב וְאֶל הַלְוִיִּם תְּדַבֵּר וְאָמַרְתָּ אֲלֵיהֶם. בְּגִין דְּיִשְׁתַּכְּחוּן כֻּלְּהוּ זַכָּאִין קַדִּישִׁין דַּכְיָין.‏

1. "And Hashem said to Moses, Speak to the priests the sons of Aaron, and say to them, There shall none be defiled for the dead among his people" (Vayikra 21:1). Rabbi Yosi said, what is the reason that this corresponds with that which is said before, "A man also or woman that is a medium or a wizard, shall surely be put to death" (Vayikra 20:27), so that THE VERSE, "Speak to the priests" is adjacent to it? HE REPLIES: once admonishing Yisrael to sanctify themselves in every manner, it also admonished the priests to sanctify themselves and the Levites as well. How do we know it admonished the priests? From the words, "Speak to the priests." And as for the Levites, it says, "Thus speak to the Levites, and say to them" (Bemidbar 18:26). Thus they will all be righteous, holy and pure.

‏2. אֱמוֹר אֶל הַכֹּהֲנִים בְּנֵי אַהֲרֹן, מ״ט הָכָא בְּנֵי אַהֲרֹן, וְכִי לָא יָדַעֲנָא דִּבְנֵי אַהֲרֹן נִינְהוּ. אֶלָּא בְּנֵי אַהֲרֹן, וְלָא בְּנֵי לֵוִי, דְּאַהֲרֹן דְּהוּא שֵׁירוּתָא דְּכָל כַּהֲנֵי דְעָלְמָא, דְּבֵיהּ אִתְרְעֵי קוּדְשָׁא בְּרִיךְ הוּא מִכֹּלָּא, בְּגִין‏

לְמֶעְבַּד שְׁלָמָא בְּעָלְמָא, וּבְגִין דְּאַהֲרֹן אָרְחוֹי סַלִּיקוּ לֵיהּ לְהַאי, דְּכָל יוֹמוֹי דְּאַהֲרֹן הֲוָה מִשְׁתָּדַּל לְאַסְגָּאָה שְׁלָמָא בְּעָלְמָא. וּבְגִין דְּאוֹרְחוֹי כָּךְ, סָלִיק לֵיהּ קוּדְשָׁא בְּרִיךְ הוּא לְהַאי, לְמֵיעַל שְׁלָמָא בְּפָמַלְיָא דִּלְעֵילָּא, וּבְגִין כָּךְ אֱמוֹר אֶל הַכֹּהֲנִים בְּנֵי אַהֲרֹן.

2. "Speak to the priests the sons of Aaron": HE ASKS, what is the reason it is written here, "the sons of Aaron"? Do I not know they are the sons of Aaron? AND HE ANSWERS, THIS TEACHES US they are "the sons of Aaron" rather than 'the sons of Levi', because Aaron is the first of all the priests. For it is him that the Holy One, blessed be He, had chosen above everyone, so as to make peace in the world, and because Aaron's practices have brought him up to this. For Aaron strove throughout his life to increase peace in the world. Since these were his ways, the Holy One, blessed be He, raised him TO PRIESTHOOD, to introduce peace among the celestial retinue, FOR THROUGH HIS WORSHIP HE BRINGS ABOUT THE UNION OF THE HOLY ONE, BLESSED BE HE AND HIS SHECHINAH, WHICH BRINGS PEACE THROUGHOUT THE WORLDS. Hence, "Speak to the priests the sons of Aaron."

3. אֱמוֹר אֶל הַכֹּהֲנִים בְּנֵי אַהֲרֹן וְאָמַרְתָּ אֲלֵיהֶם. ר' יְהוּדָה פָּתַח, מָה רַב טוּבְךָ אֲשֶׁר צָפַנְתָּ לִירֵאֶיךָ וְגוֹ'. מַה רַב טוּבְךָ, כַּמָּה עִלָּאָה וְיַקִּירָא, הַהוּא נְהוֹרָא עִלָּאָה דְּאִקְרֵי טוֹב, דִּכְתִיב וַיַּרְא אֱלֹהִים אֶת הָאוֹר כִּי טוֹב. וְדָא הוּא אוֹר הַגָּנוּז, דְּבֵיהּ עָבֵיד קוּדְשָׁא בְּרִיךְ הוּא טַב בְּעָלְמָא, וְלָא מָנַע לֵיהּ בְּכָל יוֹמָא, בְּגִין דְּבֵיהּ מִתְקַיֵּים עָלְמָא, וְקָאִים עֲלֵיהּ. אֲשֶׁר צָפַנְתָּ לִירֵאֶיךָ, דִּתְנָן, נְהוֹרָא עִלָּאָה עָבֵד קוּדְשָׁא בְּרִיךְ הוּא כַּד בָּרָא עָלְמָא, וְגָנִיז לֵיהּ לְצַדִּיקַיָּא לְזִמְנָא דְּאָתֵי. הֲה"ד, אֲשֶׁר צָפַנְתָּ לִירֵאֶיךָ.

3. "Speak to the priests the sons of Aaron, and say to them." Rabbi Yehuda opened with the verse, "O how great is Your goodness, which You have laid up for those who fear You…" (Tehilim 31:20). "O how great is Your goodness": how superior and precious is that lofty light that is called good, as written, "And Elohim saw the light, that it was good" (Beresheet 1:4). This is the treasured light with which the Holy One, blessed be He, does good in the world. He does not withhold it any day, and the world is maintained and supported by it. "Which You have laid up for those who fear You": for we have learned that the Holy One, blessed be He, made a lofty light when He created the world, and treasured it for the righteous for the future to come. This is the meaning of, "which You have laid up for those who fear You, which You have performed for those who trust in You."

4. פְּעַלְתָּ לַחוֹסִים בָּךְ. פְּעַלְתָּ, בְּזִמְנָא דְּאִתְבְּרֵי עָלְמָא, הַהוּא נְהוֹרָא הֲוָה קָאִים וְנָהִיר מֵרֵישָׁא דְּעָלְמָא לְסַיְיפֵי דְּעָלְמָא. כַּד אִסְתַּכַּל קוּדְשָׁא בְּרִיךְ הוּא, לְאִינּוּן חַיָּיבִין דְּזְמִינִין לְקַיְימָא בְּעָלְמָא, גָּנִיז לֵיהּ לְהַהוּא נְהוֹרָא, דִּכְתִיב וְיִמָּנַע מֵרְשָׁעִים אוֹרָם. וְזַמִּין לְאַנְהָרָא לְצַדִּיקַיָּיא לְעָלְמָא דְּאָתֵי, וְדָא הוּא אֲשֶׁר צָפַנְתָּ לִירֵאֶיךָ, וּכְתִיב וְזָרְחָה לָכֶם יְרְאֵי שְׁמִי שֶׁמֶשׁ צְדָקָה וּמַרְפֵּא בִּכְנָפֶיהָ.

4. "Performed for those who trust in You" (Ibid.): for when the world was created, this light was shining from the beginning of the world to its end. When the Holy One, blessed be He, saw the wicked that will live in the world, He concealed that light. This is the meaning of, "And from the wicked their light is withheld" (Iyov 38:15). THE HOLY ONE, BLESSED BE HE, will shine it upon the righteous in the World to Come, so, "which You have laid up for those who fear You, WHICH YOU HAVE PERFORMED FOR THOSE WHO TRUST IN YOU." "PERFORMED" ALLUDES TO THE ACTION OF CONCEALMENT. It is also written, "But to you who fear My name the sun of righteousness shall arise with healing in its wings" (Malachi 3:20).

2. When a man is about to go to that world

A synopsis
The Zohar give us description what happens when a peson is about
to leave this world.

5. תָּא חֲזֵי, בְּשַׁעְתָּא דְּבַר נָשׁ קָאִים לְמֵיהַךְ לְהַהוּא עָלְמָא, וְהוּא בְּבֵי
מַרְעֵיהּ, אַתְיָין עָלֵיהּ ג׳ שְׁלוּחִין, וְחָמֵי תַּמָּן, מַה דְּלָא יָכִיל בַּר נָשׁ
לְמֶחֱמֵי כַּד אִיהוּ בְּהַאי עָלְמָא. וְהַהוּא יוֹמָא, יוֹמָא דְּדִינָא עִלָּאָה הוּא,
דְּמַלְכָּא בָּעֵי פִּקְדוֹנָא דִּילֵיהּ. זַכָּאָה הַהוּא בַּר נָשׁ, דְּפִקְדוֹנֵיהּ אָתִיב
לְמַלְכָּא כְּמָה דְּאִתְיְיהִיב לֵיהּ בְּגַוֵּיהּ. אִי הַהוּא פִּקְדוֹנָא אִתְטְנַּף בְּטנּוּפֵי
גוּפָא, מַה יֵּימָא לְמָארֵי פִּקְדוֹנָא.

5. Come and see, when a man is about to go to that world, and is on his
sickbed, three messengers come to him. He sees there what one cannot see
while in this world. That day is Judgment day, when the King asks for His
deposit BACK, NAMELY THE SOUL. Happy is the man who returns the
deposit to the King as it was given him, THAT IS, UNDAMAGED. If that
deposit was soiled with bodily filth, what shall he say to the owner of the
deposit?

6. זָקַף עֵינוֹי, וְחָמֵי לְמַלְאַךְ הַמָּוֶת קָאִים קַמֵּיהּ, וְסַיְיפֵיהּ שְׁלִיפָא
בִּידֵיהּ, קַסְטַר בְּקַטְרִין, בְּקוּטְמָא דְּהַהוּא בַּר נָשׁ. וְלֵית לָהּ לְנַפְשָׁא קַשְׁיוּ
בְּכֹלָּא, כְּפְרִישׁוּ דִּילָהּ מִן גוּפָא. וּבַר נָשׁ לָא מִית, עַד דְּחָמֵי לִשְׁכִינְתָּא,
וּמִגּוֹ סַגִיאוּת תִּיאוּבְתָּא דִּשְׁכִינְתָּא, נַפְשָׁא נָפְקַת לְקַבְּלָא לִשְׁכִינְתָּא.
בָּתַר דְּנָפְקָא, מַאן אִיהִי נַפְשָׁא דְּאִתְדַּבָּק בָּהּ וְתִתְקַבֵּל בְּגַוֵּוהּ וְהָא
אוּקְמוּהָ לְהָנֵי מִלֵּי.

6. He lifts up his eyes and sees the Angel of Death standing before him with
his sword drawn in his hand, the destroying angel in charge of breaking that
man. Nothing is harder for the soul than its separation from the body. The
man does not die until he sees the Shechinah. Through much yearning for
the Shechinah the soul leaves THE BODY to welcome the Shechinah. After
THE SOUL has left THE BODY, what soul CAN cleave to the Shechinah and
be received within Her? These matters have been explained.

7. בָּתַר דְּנָפְקָא נַפְשָׁא מִן גּוּפָא, וְאִשְׁתְּאַר גּוּפָא בְּלָא רוּחָא, אָסִיר לְמִשְׁבַּק לֵיהּ בְּלָא קְבוּרְתָּא, דִּכְתִיב לֹא תָלִין נִבְלָתוֹ עַל הָעֵץ כִּי קָבֹר תִּקְבְּרֶנּוּ בַּיּוֹם הַהוּא. בְּגִין דְּמֵיתָא דְּיִשְׁתְּהֵי כ״ד שָׁעוֹת, דְּאִינוּן יוֹמָם וָלַיְלָה, בְּלָא קְבוּרְתָּא, יָהִיב חַלִּישׁוּתָא בְּשַׁיְיפוֹי דִּרְתִיכָא, וּמְעַכֵּב עֲבִידְתָּא דְּקוּדְשָׁא בְּרִיךְ הוּא מִלְּמֶעְבַּד דְּאֶפְשָׁר דְּקוּדְשָׁא בְּרִיךְ הוּא גָּזַר עֲלֵיהּ, בְּגִין לְמֵיתֵיהּ בְּגִלְגּוּלָא אָחֳרָא, מִיַּד בְּהַהוּא יוֹמָא דְּאִתְפְּטַר, לְאוֹטָבָא לֵיהּ. וְכָל זִמְנָא דְּלָא אִתְקְבַר גּוּפָא, נִשְׁמָתָא לָאו עָאלַת קַמֵּי קוּדְשָׁא בְּרִיךְ הוּא, וְלָא יַכְלָא לְמֶהֱוֵי בְּגוּפָא אָחֳרָא, בְּגִלְגּוּלָא תִנְיָנָא, דְּלָא יָהֲבִין לְנִשְׁמָתָא גּוּפָא אָחֳרָא, עַד דְּיִתְקְבַר קַדְמָאָה. וְדָא דָּמֵי לְבַר נָשׁ דְּמִיתָא אִתְּתֵיהּ, לָא אִתְחֲזֵי לֵיהּ, לְמֵיסַב אִתְּתָא אָחֳרָא, עַד דְּקָבִיר לְקַדְמֵיתָא, וּבְגִין דָּא אָמְרָה אוֹרַיְיתָא, לֹא תָלִין נִבְלָתוֹ עַל הָעֵץ.

7. After the soul has left the body, and it remains spiritless, it is forbidden to leave it unburied, as written, "his body shall not remain all night upon the tree, but you shall surely bury him that day" (Devarim 21:23). For a corpse remaining unburied for 24 hours, a day and a night, causes the parts of the Chariot, WHICH IS ALLUDED TO BY THAT MAN, to weaken, and detains the actions of the Holy One, blessed be He, from being carried out. For the Holy One, blessed be He, may have decreed upon him another incarnation at once, on the very day he died, in order to help him. But as long as the body is not buried, the soul does not come before the Holy One, blessed be He, nor can it be in another body in another incarnation, for a soul is not given another body until the first one is buried. This resembles a man whose wife died. He is not qualified to marry another wife before he buries the first one. Hence the Torah said, "his body shall not remain all night upon the tree."

8. דָּבָר אַחֵר, כַּד אִתְפְּרְשָׁא נִשְׁמָתָא מִן גּוּפָא, וּבַעְיָא לְמֵיזַל לְהַהוּא עָלְמָא, לָא תֵּיעוּל לְהַהוּא עָלְמָא, עַד דְּיָהֲבִין לָהּ גּוּפָא אָחֳרָא מִנְּהוֹרָא, וּלְבָתַר יַכְלָא לְמֵיעַל. וּמֵאֵלַיְיהוּ תִּנְדַּע, דַּהֲווֹ לֵיהּ תְּרֵין גּוּפִין, חַד דְּבֵיהּ אִתְחֲזֵי לְתַתָּא לִבְנֵי נָשָׁא, וְחַד דְּבֵיהּ אִתְחֲזֵי לְעֵילָא, בֵּין מַלְאָכִין עִלָּאִין קַדִּישִׁין. וְכָל כַּמָּה דְּגוּפָא לָא אִתְקְבַר, צַעֲרָא הוּא לְנִשְׁמָתָא, וְרוּחַ מְסָאֲבָא אִזְדְּמַן לְשַׁרְיָיא עֲלוֹי, וּלְסָאֲבָא לְהַהוּא גּוּפָא.

8. Another explanation: when the soul has left the body and wishes to go to that world, it may not enter it until it is given another body of light. Then it can enter. You may derive this from Elijah, who had two bodies, one in which he was seen by people below, and another in which he was seen above among the celestial holy angels. As long as the body is not buried, the soul suffers and the spirit of defilement is there to dwell upon that body and defile it.

9. וּבְגִין דְּהַהוּא רוּחַ מִסְאָבָא, אִזְדְּמַן, לָא לִבְעֵי לֵיהּ לְאֵינִישׁ, לְמֵיבַת הַהוּא גּוּפָא לֵילְיָא חַד, בְּגִין דְּרוּחַ מִסְאָבָא אִשְׁתְּכַח בְּלֵילְיָא, וְאִשְׁתְּטַח בְּכָל אַרְעָא, לְאַשְׁכְּחָא גּוּפָא בְּלָא נַפְשָׁא, לְסָאֲבָא לֵיהּ, וְאִסְתְּאַב יַתִּיר, וְעַל דָּא אַזְהַר לְכַהֲנֵי וְאָמַר, לְנֶפֶשׁ לֹא יִטַּמָּא בְעַמָּיו, בְּגִין דְּאִינוּן קַדִּישִׁין לָא יִשְׁרֵי עֲלַיְיהוּ רוּחַ מִסְאָבָא, וְלָא יִסְתַּאֲבוּן.

9. Since the spirit of defilement is in readiness TO DEFILE THE BODY, one must not keep the body for a night, because the spirit of defilement is present at night and spreads, NAMELY ROAMS, throughout the land to find a soulless body to defile it. THEREFORE AT NIGHT it is defiled even more. Therefore it warned the priests, saying, "There shall none be defiled for the dead among his people" (Vayikra 21:1). Since they are holy, the spirit of defilement will not dwell upon them and they shall not be defiled – FOR THE SPIRIT OF DEFILEMENT CAN DWELL ON A SPIRITLESS BODY.

10. אֱמוֹר אֶל הַכֹּהֲנִים, רִבִּי יִצְחָק אָמַר, אֱמוֹר אֶל הַכֹּהֲנִים, בִּלְחִישׁוּ. כְּמָה דְּכָל עוֹבְדֵיהוֹן דְּכַהֲנֵי בִּלְחִישׁוּ, כָּךְ אֲמִירָה דִּלְהוֹן בִּלְחִישׁוּ. אֱמוֹר וְאָמַרְתָּ: זִמְנָא חַד, וּתְרֵין זִמְנִין, לְאַזְהָרָא לְהוּ עַל קְדוּשַׁיְיהוּ, בְּגִין דְּלָא יִסְתַּאֲבוּן. דְּמַאן דִּמְשַׁמֵּשׁ בַּאֲתַר קַדִּישָׁא, בַּעְיָא דְּיִשְׁתְּכַח קַדִּישָׁא בְּכֹלָּא. לְנֶפֶשׁ לֹא יִטַּמָּא, כְּמָה דְּאוֹקִימְנָא, דְּגוּפָא בְּלָא רוּחַ, מִסְאָבָא הוּא, וְשָׁרֵי עֲלֵיהּ רוּחַ מִסְאָבָא. דְּהָא תִּיאוּבְתָּא דְּרוּחֵי מִסְאֲבֵי לְגַבֵּי גוּפַיְיהוּ דְּיִשְׂרָאֵל אִיהוּ, בְּגִין דְּאִתְפְּרַק מִנַּיְיהוּ רוּחָא קַדִּישָׁא, וּבְמָנָא דְּקוּדְשָׁא, אַתְיָין לְאִתְחַבְּרָא. וְכַהֲנֵי דְּאִינוּן קַדִּישִׁין, קְדוּשָׁתָא עַל קְדוּשָׁתָא, לָא בַּעְיָין לְאִסְתַּאֲבָא כְּלָל, בְּגִין דִּכְתִיב כִּי נֵזֶר אֱלֹהָיו עַל רֹאשׁוֹ. וּכְתִיב כִּי שֶׁמֶן מִשְׁחַת אֱלֹהָיו עָלָיו אֲנִי יְיָ'.

-101-

10. "Speak to the priests." Rabbi Yitzchak said, "Speak to the priests" in a whisper. Just as all the services of the priests are done silently, so are all their words whispered. "Speak...and say" MEANS once and again to remind them of their sanctity so that they shall not be defiled, for whoever serves in a holy place must be holy in every respect. "There shall none be defiled for the dead," as we explained that a spiritless corpse is unholy and the spirit of defilement dwells upon it. For the spirits of defilement long for the bodies of Yisrael, once the spirit of holiness was emptied from them, and they come to join a vessel of holiness, NAMELY A BODY. The priests, who are doubly holy must not be defiled whatsoever, as written, "because the crown of his Elohim is upon his head" (Bemidbar 6:7), and "the anointing oil of his Elohim is upon him" (Vayikra 21:12).

3. Running down upon the head, running down upon the beard

A Synopsis
The Zohar explains the flow from Binah. The work of the Kohanim, and that they have to stay pure.

11. וְהוּא כְּגַוְונָא דִּלְעֵילָּא קָאִים לְתַתָּא, דִּכְתִיב כַּשֶּׁמֶן הַטּוֹב עַל הָרֹאשׁ יוֹרֵד עַל הַזָּקָן זְקַן אַהֲרֹן שֶׁיּוֹרֵד עַל פִּי מִדּוֹתָיו, הַאי קְרָא אוּקְמוּהָ, אֲבָל כַּשֶּׁמֶן הַטּוֹב עַל הָרֹאשׁ, דָּא מְשַׁח רְבוּת קַדִּישָׁא עִלָּאָה, דְּנָגִיד וְנָפִיק מֵאֲתַר דְּנַהֲרָא עֲמִיקָא דְכֹלָּא. ד"א, דְּנָגִיד וְנָפִיק מֵרֵישָׁא דְכָל רֵישִׁין, סְתִימָא דְכָל סְתִימִין. עַל הָרֹאשׁ, עַל הָרֹאשׁ וַדַּאי, רֵישָׁא דְּאָדָם קַדְמָאָה.

11. He, THE PRIEST, like THE PRIEST above, is below, as written, "It is like the precious ointment upon the head, running down upon the beard, the beard of Aaron; running down over the hem of his garments" (Tehilim 133:2). This verse has been explained, yet "the precious ointment upon the head" is the oil of supernal holy ointment, NAMELY THE PLENTY OF MOCHIN, that flows and comes out from the location of the deepest river, BINAH. According to another explanation, it flows and comes out of the head to all heads, the most concealed among the concealed, WHICH IS THE HEAD OF ARICH ANPIN. It is surely "upon the head," the head of Adam Kadmon (Primordial Man), WHICH IS ARICH ANPIN. THE VERSE TEACHES US IT IS LIKE THE PRECIOUS OINTMENT, WHICH IS UPON THE HEAD.

12. יוֹרֵד עַל הַזָּקָן, דָּא דִּיקְנָא יַקִּירָא, כְּמָה דְאוּקְמוּהָ. זְקַן אַהֲרֹן, דָּא כֹּהֵן גָּדוֹל דִּלְעֵילָּא, וְהָא אוּקְמוּהָ. וְהַהוּא שֶׁמֶן, יוֹרֵד עַל פִּי מִדּוֹתָיו, דְּמֵאִינוּן מְשִׁיחָן, נָגִיד וְנָפִיק וְנָחִית לְתַתָּאֵי, וּכְגַוְונָא דָּא נָגִיד וְאִתְעֲטָּר כַּהֲנָא תַּתָּאָה, בִּמְשַׁח רְבוּת לְתַתָּא.

12. It is "running down upon the beard," the precious beard OF ARICH ANPIN, as has been explained. The beard of Aaron refers to the celestial High Priest, NAMELY, THE BEARD OF ZEIR ANPIN, IN THE SECRET OF CHESED OF ZEIR ANPIN. This has already been explained. This ointment, NAMELY THE PLENTY OF ARICH ANPIN, is "running down over the hem of

his garments" OF ZEIR ANPIN. For it flows and comes down to the lower beings over the garments OF ZEIR ANPIN. Similarly THE HIGH PRIEST below drawns and is crowned by the anointing oil below. HE CORRESPONDS TO THE SUPERNAL HIGH PRIEST, CHESED OF ZEIR ANPIN.

13. הַאי קְרָא, לָאו רֵישֵׁיהּ סֵיפֵיהּ, וְלָאו סֵיפֵיהּ רֵישֵׁיהּ. כְּתִיב אֱמוֹר אֶל הַכֹּהֲנִים בְּנֵי אַהֲרֹן וְאָמַרְתָּ אֲלֵיהֶם לְנֶפֶשׁ לֹא יִטַּמָא. לָא יִטַּמְּאוּ מִבָּעֵי לֵיהּ, מַהוּ לֹא יִטַּמָא. אֶלָּא, עַל הַהוּא כֹּהֵן עִלָּאָה מִכֻּלְּהוּ קָאָמַר. אָמַר רִבִּי יְהוּדָה וְהָא כְּתִיב וְהַכֹּהֵן הַגָּדוֹל מֵאֶחָיו. אֶלָּא וַדַּאי הָכִי הוּא כְּמָה דְּאִתְּמַר, וְאָמַר רִבִּי יִצְחָק, כַּהֲנָא דְּקָאֵים לְתַתָּא, כְּגַוְונָא דִּלְעֵילָּא, בִּקְדוּשָׁה אִצְטְרִיךְ לְאִשְׁתַּכְּחָא יַתִּיר מִכֹּלָּא, כְּמָה דְּאִתְּמַר.

13. There is a dissimilarity between the beginning and end of this verse, since it is written, "Speak to the priests the sons of Aaron, and say to them, There shall none be defiled for the dead among his people." THE BEGINNING OF THE VERSE IS IN PLURAL - WHILE THE END IS IN THE SINGULAR. It should have said, 'They shall not be defiled', IN PLURAL, AS AT THE BEGINNING OF THE VERSE. Why "There shall none be defiled" IN THE SINGULAR? HE REPLIES, THE VERSE speaks about the highest priest, NAMELY THE HIGH PRIEST ABOVE. Rabbi Yehuda said, yet it is written, "And he that is the High Priest among his brethren" (Vayikra 21:10). THIS ALLUDES TO THE HIGH PRIEST ABOVE, RATHER THAN THE FIRST VERSE. HE ANSWERS, It is surely so, "THERE SHALL NONE BE DEFILED FOR THE DEAD AMONG HIS PEOPLE" ALLUDES TO THE HIGHEST PRIEST, ZEIR ANPIN, WHILE THE VERSE, "AND HE THAT IS THE HIGH PRIEST AMONG HIS BRETHREN" as we learned, speaks of the High Priest BELOW. As Rabbi Yitzchak said, The priest situated below is in the likeness of above and should be in holiness more than all the others, as we learned. HENCE THE VERSE SPOKE OF HIM SPECIFICALLY THAT HE MUST NOT DEFILE HIMSELF EVEN FOR HIS FATHER OR FOR HIS MOTHER.

4. The secret of the candelabra

A Synopsis

We learn why only the priest is permitted to arrange and light the lamps in the Temple.

רעיא מהימנא

14. פְּקוּדָא דָא, לְסַדְּרָא כַּהֲנָא בְּכָל יוֹמָא בּוּצִינִין בְּבֵי מַקְדְּשָׁא, וְהָא אוּקִימְנָא בְּרָזָא דִּמְנוֹרָא. וְאִיהוּ רָזָא כְּגַוְונָא דִלְעֵילָא, בְּגִין דִּנְהִירוּ עִלָּאָה בְּמִשַׁח רְבוּ, נַחִית עַל רֵישָׁא דְּכַהֲנָא בְּקַדְמֵיתָא לְבָתַר אִיהוּ אַדְלִיק וְאַנְהִיר כָּל בּוּצִינִין. דִּכְתִּיב כַּשֶּׁמֶן הַטּוֹב עַל הָרֹאשׁ וְגוֹ', וּכְתִיב כִּי שֶׁמֶן מִשְׁחַת אֱלֹהָיו עָלָיו וְגוֹ'. וְעַל דָּא אִתְיְיהִיב רְשׁוּ לְכַהֲנָא בִּלְחוֹדוֹי, לְסַדְּרָא בּוּצִינִין, וּלְאַדְלְקָא לְהוֹן בְּכָל יוֹמָא תְּרֵין זִמְנִין, לָקֳבֵל נְהִירוּ דִיחוּדָא תְּרֵין זִמְנִין, קָרְבָּנָא בְּכָל יוֹמָא, תְּרֵין זִמְנִין, וְכֹלָּא אִצְטְרִיךְ.

Ra'aya Meheimna (the Faithful Shepherd)

14. The priest is commanded to daily arrange lamps in the Temple. We have explained this in relation to the candelabra. This secret is in the likeness of above, since the supernal light in the anointing oil first runs over the head of the supernal Priest, WHICH IS THE FIRST THREE SFIROT OF ZEIR ANPIN. Then he kindles the lamps, NAMELY, THE SFIROT OF MALCHUT, THE ILLUMINATIONS OF FIRE, and makes them illuminate, as written, "It is like the precious ointment upon the head" (Tehilim 133:2), and, "the anointing oil of his Elohim is upon him" (Vayikra 21:12). Thus only the priest is permitted to arrange the lamps and light them twice a day, to correspond to the illumination of unity THAT OCCURS twice, and the daily offering which is offered twice daily – all that is needed.

15. וְעַל יְדֵי דְּכַהֲנָא נַהֲרִין בּוּצִינִין בְּכֹלָּא, עֵילָא וְתַתָּא לְמֶחֱדֵי חֵידוּ, וּלְאַשְׁכְּחָא חֵידוּ בְּכָל סִטְרִין. בְּאַדְלְקוּתָא דְּבוּצִינִין, דְּהָא תְּרֵין אִלֵּין עַל יְדֵי דְּכַהֲנָא, לְאַשְׁתַּכְּחָא חֵידוּ בְּכָל סִטְרִין, וְאִלֵּין אִינוּן אַדְלְקוּתָא

דְּבוּצִינִין וּקְטֹרֶת. וְהָא אוֹקִימְנָא שֶׁמֶן וּקְטֹרֶת יְשַׂמַּח לֵב.

ע"כ רעיא מהימנא

15. The candles are shining everywhere by means of the priest, above and below, so there will be rejoicing and so that joy would abound in all directions, NAMELY RIGHT AND LEFT, with the lighting of the lamps. For those two are performed by the priest so that joy would abound in every direction – the kindling of the lamps and incense. We have already explained that "Ointment and perfume (incense) rejoice the heart" (Mishlei 27:9).

End of Ra'aya Meheimna (the Faithful Shepherd)

5. "and for his sister a virgin"

A Synopsis

We are reminded of the destruction of Jerusalem, and of how God
will exact vengeance against the children of Edom who destroyed it.

16. וְלַאֲחוֹתוֹ הַבְּתוּלָה הַקְּרוֹבָה אֵלָיו וְגוֹ'. מַה כְּתִיב לְעֵילָא, כִּי אִם
לִשְׁאֵרוֹ הַקָּרוֹב אֵלָיו וְגוֹ'. רִבִּי אַבָּא פָּתַח, מִי זֶה בָּא מֵאֱדוֹם חֲמוּץ
בְּגָדִים מִבָּצְרָה וְגוֹ', מִי זֶה בָּא מֵאֱדוֹם, זַמִּין קוּדְשָׁא בְּרִיךְ הוּא לְלַבְּשָׁא
לְבוּשֵׁי נוּקְמָא עַל אֱדוֹם, דְּאַחֲרִיבוּ בֵּיתֵיהּ, וְאוֹקִידוּ הֵיכָלֵיהּ, וְגָלוּ
לִכְנֶסֶת יִשְׂרָאֵל בֵּינֵי עַמְמַיָּא. וּלְמֶעְבַּד לְהוֹן נִקְמַת עָלְמִין, עַד
דְּיִשְׁתַּכְּחוּן כָּל טוּרִין מְטוּרֵי עָלְמָא, מַלְיָין מִקְטוֹלֵי עַמִּין, וּלְמִקְרֵי לְכָל
עוֹפָא דִּשְׁמַיָּא עָלַיְיהוּ, וְכָל חֵיוַות בָּרָא יִתְזְנוּן מִנַּיְיהוּ תְּרֵיסַר יַרְחֵי,
וְעוֹפָא דִּשְׁמַיָּא שְׁבַע שְׁנִין, עַד דְּלָא תִּסְבַּל אַרְעָא נִיווּלָא דִּידְהוּ.
הֲה"ד, כִּי זֶבַח לַיְיָ' בְּבָצְרָה וְטֶבַח גָּדוֹל בְּאֶרֶץ אֱדוֹם, עַד דְּאִינּוּן
לְבוּשִׁין יִסְתָּאֲבוּן, הֲה"ד וְכָל מַלְבּוּשַׁי אֶגְאָלְתִּי.

16. "and for his sister a virgin, that is near to him..." (Vayikra 21:3). The
preceding verse says, "but for his kin, that is near to him" (Ibid. 2). Rabbi
Aba opened with the verse, "Who is this that comes from Edom, with
crimsoned garments from Botzrah..." (Yeshayah 63:1). "Who is this that
comes from Edom," MEANS THAT the Holy One, blessed be He, will be
garbed with a garment of vengeance upon Edom, for their ruining His
Temple, and burning His Holy, and exiling the Congregation of Yisrael
among the nations. He will take revenge upon them forever, until all the
mountains in the world will fill with the dead of the nations, and the birds of
the sky will be summoned upon them TO FEED UPON THEIR CADAVERS.
Every wild beast will feed on them for twelve months and the birds of the
sky for seven years until the land will not bear their disgrace. This is the
meaning of, "for Hashem has a sacrifice in Botzrah, and a great slaughter in
the land of Edom" (Yeshayah 34:6), until this raiment OF VENGEANCE will
be defiled BY THOSE KILLED. This is the meaning of, "and I have stained all
my raiment" (Yeshayah 63:3).

17. חֲמוּץ בְּגָדִים מִבָּצְרָה, בְּגִין דְּמִינָּהּ נָפְקוּ אוּכְלוּסִין דְּעָלְמָא,

לְחַיְילָא עַל יְרוּשְׁלֵם, וְאִינּוּן שָׁרוּ לְאוֹקְדָא הֵיכְלָא, וּבְנֵי אֱדוֹם מְפַגְּרִין שׁוּרִין, וְרָמוּ אַבְנֵי יְסוֹדָא, הה"ד זְכוֹר יְיָ' לִבְנֵי אֱדוֹם וְגוֹ', הָאוֹמְרִים עָרוּ עָרוּ עַד הַיְסוֹד בָּהּ.

17. "With crimsoned garments from Batzrah," because legions of the world came out FROM BATZRAH to wage war against Jerusalem. They started to burn the Holy, while the children of Edom were demolishing the walls, and uprooting cornerstones. This is the meaning of, "Remember, O Hashem, against the children of Edom the day of Jerusalem, when they said, Rase it, rase it, to its very foundations" (Tehilim 137:7).

18. זֶה הָדוּר בִּלְבוּשׁוֹ, בְּאִינּוּן לְבוּשֵׁי דְנוּקְמָא דְזַמִּין לְאַלְבְּשָׁא. צוֹעֶה בְּרוֹב כֹּחוֹ, מַהוּ צוֹעֶה. מְתַבַּר. כְּמָה דִכְתִיב עַמִּים תַּחְתֶּיךָ יִפְּלוּ וְגוֹ'. אָמְרוּ יִשְׂרָאֵל לִישַׁעְיָה, מַאן הוּא דֵּין דִּיְעֲבֵיד כָּל כַּךְ. פָּתַח וְאָמַר, אֲנִי מְדַבֵּר בִּצְדָקָה, הַהוּא דְּאִיהוּ רַב לְהוֹשִׁיעַ, הַהוּא דִּכְתִיב בֵּיהּ, אוֹהֵב צְדָקָה וּמִשְׁפָּט. וְאִיהוּ צְדָקָה מַמָּשׁ, וְאִיהוּ רַב לְהוֹשִׁיעַ.

18. "this one that is glorious in His apparel" (Yeshayah 63:1), THAT IS, with the garments of vengeance He will don. "striding in the greatness of His strength" (Ibid.). Striding REFERS TO breaking, as written, "the people fall under you" (Tehilim 45:6). Yisrael said to Isaiah, Who is he that will accomplish so much? He opened with the verse, "I that speak in righteousness" (Yeshayah 63:1), He that is "mighty to save" (Ibid.), He of whom it is written, "He loves righteousness and judgment" (Tehilim 33:5), actual righteousness, NAMELY MALCHUT THAT IS CALLED RIGHTEOUSNESS – and He is "mighty to save."

19. וְכָל כַּךְ לָמָה. בְּגִין דְּגַרְמוּ לכ"י לְמֶהֱוֵי שְׁכִיבַת לְעַפְרָא בְּגָלוּתָא, וּלְמִנְפַּל לְאַרְעָא, כְּמָה דִּכְתִיב נָפְלָה לֹא תוֹסִיף קוּם בְּתוּלַת יִשְׂרָאֵל. ובג"כ, קוּדְשָׁא בְּרִיךְ הוּא יִלְבַּשׁ לְבוּשֵׁי נוּקְמָא עֲלַיְיהוּ, לְסָאֲבָא לוֹן בְּסַגִּיאוּ דְקָטוּלְיָיא, דִּכְתִיב וְכָל מַלְבּוּשַׁי אֶגְאָלְתִּי.

19. Wherefore all that? Because they caused the Congregation of Yisrael to lie in the dust in exile and fall to the ground, as written, "The virgin of

Yisrael is fallen; she shall no more rise" (Amos 5:2). For that the Holy One, blessed be He, will don for them garments of vengeance to defile them with many dead, as written, "and I have stained all My raiment" (Yeshayah 63:3).

20. וְכָל כַּךְ לָמָּה, דִּכְתִיב וְלַאֲחוֹתוֹ הַבְּתוּלָה הַקְּרוֹבָה אֵלָיו אֲשֶׁר לֹא הָיְתָה לְאִישׁ. דְּלָאו חוּלָקֵיה דְּעֵשָׂו, וְלָא הֲוַות בְּעַדְבֵיהּ דְּהַהוּא דִּכְתִיב בֵּיהּ אִישׁ יוֹדֵעַ צַיִד אִישׁ שָׂדֶה, לָהּ יִטַּמָּא, בְּאִינּוּן לְבוּשִׁין דְּנוּקְמָא, דְּזַמִּין לְאִסְתַּאֲבָא בֵּין אִינּוּן אוּכְלוּסִין, דִּכְתִיב בֵּיהּ לָהּ יִטַּמָּא, בְּגִינָהּ, בְּגִין דְּאִיהִי שְׁכִיבַת לְעַפְרָא, וְהוּא בָּעֵי לְאַקָמָא לָהּ, הה"ד קוּמִי אוֹרִי כִּי בָא אוֹרֵךְ.

20. And wherefore all that? SINCE it is written, "and for his sister a virgin, that is near to him, and who has had no husband," WHO IS THE HOLY SHECHINAH, SISTER TO ZEIR ANPIN, who is not the portion of Esau, and was not the lot of him of whom it says, "a cunning hunter, a man of the field" (Beresheet 25:27). "for her he may be defiled" (Vayikra 21:3), FOR HER SAKE, with those garments of vengeance that will be defiled among the multitude OF THE DEAD MENTIONED BEFORE. THEREFORE it is written, "for her he may be defiled," for Her sake, because She is lying IN EXILE in the dust, and he wants to raise Her. This is the meaning of, "Arise, shine, for your light is come" (Yeshayah 60:1).

6. "They shall not make baldness on their head"

A Synopsis
Rabbi Yosi tells us why the priest below must be without any blemish.

21. לֹא יִקְרְחָה קָרְחָה בְּרֹאשָׁם. רְבִּי יוֹסֵי אָמַר, לֹא יִקְרְחָה בְּה"א מַאי טַעֲמָא. אֶלָּא, הַהוּא שֶׁמֶן עִלָּאָה, דְּאִיהוּ מְשַׁח רְבוּת קוּדְשָׁא, דְּאַשְׁלִים לְכָל שִׁבְעָה יוֹמִין כְּמָה דְּאִתְּמַר, דִּכְתִיב כִּי שִׁבְעַת יָמִים יְמַלֵּא אֶת יֶדְכֶם, הַהוּא שֶׁמֶן עִלָּאָה אִתְעֲדֵי מִנֵּיהּ וְאִתְקְרַח, אִי אִיהוּ אַפְגִּים רֵישֵׁיהּ. בְּגִין דְּרֵישָׁא דְּכַהֲנָא עִלָּאָה, הַהוּא שֶׁמֶן עִלָּאָה הֲוֵי, וְעַל דָּא לָא לִיבְעֵי לֵיהּ לְכַהֲנָא דִלְתַתָּא, לְאַחֲזָאָה בֵּיהּ בְּגַרְמֵיהּ פְּגִימוּ כְּלָל, וְהָא אִתְּמַר. וּבְגִין כָּךְ כְּתִיב בְּה"א.

21. "They shall not make baldness (Heb. *yikrechuh*) on their head" (Vayikra 21:5). Rabbi Yosi said, What is the reason '*yikrechuh*' is spelled with Hei AT THE END? HE ANSWERS, That supernal ointment, THE PLENTY OF ABA, is the holy anointing oil that consecrates all seven days, CHESED, GVURAH, TIFERET, NETZACH, HOD, YESOD AND MALCHUT, as we learned from the words, "for seven days shall he consecrate you" (Vayikra 8:33). That supernal oil is removed from him and baldness is made on him, if he blemishes his head. For the head of the High Priest, NAMELY THE FIRST THREE SFIROT OF ZEIR ANPIN, is this supernal oil, THE LIGHTS OF ABA. Hence the priest below must not demonstrate any blemish in himself, as we have already learned, FOR CORRESPONDING TO THE PRIEST ABOVE, HIS OWN DEEDS BLEMISH HIM. Hence, "MAKE BALDNESS" is spelled with Hei.

7. "for seven days shall he consecrate you"

A Synopsis

This section correlates the seventy years of exile with the seven days of consecration and the seven Sfirot. Rabbi Aba says that the High Priest above blemishes the supernal Hei if the High Priest below blemishes the lower Hei.

22. פָּתַח וְאָמַר, בְּשׁוּב יְיָ' אֶת שִׁיבַת צִיּוֹן הָיִינוּ כְּחוֹלְמִים. בְּשׁוּב יְיָ' אֶת שִׁיבַת, דָּא בְּגָלוּת בָּבֶל אִתְּמַר. דְּלָא אִשְׁתְּכָחוּ יַתִּיר בְּגָלוּתָא אֶלָּא שַׁבְעִין שְׁנִין. דִּכְתִיב, כִּי לְפִי מְלֹאת לְבָבֶל שִׁבְעִים שָׁנָה אֶפְקֹד אֶתְכֶם. וּכְתִיב הָיִינוּ כְּחוֹלְמִים, מַאי כְּחוֹלְמִים. אֶלָּא הָא אַתְּעֲרוּ חַבְרַיָּיא, דְּאִיכָּא שַׁבְעִין שְׁנִין בְּחֶלְמָא.

22. He opened with the verse, "When Hashem brought back the captivity of Zion, we were like men in a dream" (Tehilim 126:1). "When Hashem brought back" was said during the exile in Babylon, though they spent only seventy years in that exile, as written, "That after seventy years are accomplished at Babylon I will take heed of you" (Yirmeyah 29:10), and "we were like men in a dream." What is "like men in a dream"? The friends remarked that some dreams last seventy years.

23. וְתָא חֲזֵי, כְּתִיב כִּי שִׁבְעַת יָמִים יְמַלֵּא אֶת יֶדְכֶם. מַאן שִׁבְעַת יָמִים. הָא אִתְּמַר, הַהוּא אֲתַר עִלָּאָה, דְּהוּא כְּלָלָא דְּכָל שִׁיתָא אָחֳרָנִין, אִקְרֵי שִׁבְעַת יָמִים, וְאִקְרֵי תְּשׁוּבָה. תָּנֵינָן, מַאן דְּיָתִיב בְּתַעֲנִיתָא בְּשַׁבְּתָא, קוֹרְעִין לוֹ גְּזַר דִּינוֹ שֶׁל שִׁבְעִים שָׁנָה, וְשַׁבְעִין שָׁנָה אִינוּן שְׁבַע אַנְפֵּי מַלְכָּא, דַּאֲפִילוּ אִסְתְּכְמוּ עֲלֵיהּ כֻּלָּא כְּלָא לְבִישׁ, הַהוּא גְּזַר דִּינָא אִתְקְרַע. מ"ט. בְּגִין דְּאָחִיד בֵּיהּ בְּהַהוּא יוֹמָא, בְּכְלָלָא דְּכֻלְּהוּ, דְּאִקְרֵי שִׁבְעָה, וְאִקְרֵי תְּשׁוּבָה, בְּגִין כָּךְ בְּכֻלְּהוּ אָחִיד, וְאַהֲדָר בִּתְשׁוּבָה, וְאִתְקְרַע גְּזַר דִּינָא בְּכֻלְּהוּ. וְעַל דָּא וַדַּאי שַׁבְעִין שְׁנִין אִיכָּא בְּחֶלְמָא.

23. Come and see, it is written, "for seven days shall he consecrate you" (Vayikra 8:33). What are these seven days? It has been said that the uppermost place that includes all the other six, NAMELY BINAH THAT

INCLUDES IN IT CHESED, GVURAH, TIFERET, NETZACH, HOD AND YESOD, is called seven days and also called repentance. We learned that whoever fasts on Shabbat, his verdict of seventy years standing is torn up. Seventy years are the seven facets of the King, NAMELY THE SEVEN SFIROT, CHESED, GVURAH, TIFERET, NETZACH, HOD, YESOD AND MALCHUT, EACH INCLUDING TEN, THUS AMOUNTING TO SEVENTY. Even though they are unanimously agreed against him, the verdict is torn up. For what reason? Because WHOEVER FASTS is attached to that day, which includes them all, NAMELY BINAH that is called seven and is called repentance. For that reason, WHEN HE IS ATTACHED TO THAT, he is attached to all SEVENTY YEARS when he repents, and any verdict in any of them is THEREFORE torn up. Therefore assuredly there are seventy years in a dream.

24. כְּגַוְונָא דָא, כַּהֲנָא אִתְעַטָּר בְּשֶׁבַע, דְּאִקְרֵי שִׁבְעַת יָמִים, אִי פָּגִים רֵישֵׁיה, הַהוּא שִׁבְעָה דְּאִיהוּ כְּלָלָא דְּכֻלְּהוּ, אַקְרַח מִנֵּיה כָּל הַהוּא קְדוּשָׁא דְּכֻלְּהוּ, דְּשַׁרְיָא עָלֵיה. וְעַ"ד אִזְדְּהָרוּ דְּלָא יִקְרְחָה קָרְחָה בְּרֹאשָׁם, וְיִשְׁתַּכְחוּ פְּגִימִין מִכֹּלָּא. ובג"כ כַּהֲנָא בָּעֵי לְאִשְׁתַּכְּחָא בִּשְׁלִימוּ יַתִּיר מִכֹּלָּא, כ"ש הַהוּא דְּאִיהוּ עִלָּאָה מִכֻּלְּהוּ.

24. Similarly the priest is crowned with seven, WHICH ARE BINAH that is called seven days. If THE PRIEST blemishes his head, that seven, BINAH, the whole of all SEVEN DAYS, CHESED, GVURAH, TIFERET, NETZACH, HOD, YESOD AND MALCHUT, makes him bald from all that overall holiness that dwells on THAT PRIEST. They were therefore careful not to make baldness on their heads, because this will render them defective in all SEVEN SFIROT. Thus the priest needs to abide in perfection more than all the others, and all the more so the most supernal, THE HIGH PRIEST.

25. א"ר אַבָּא, כָּאן בְּהֵ"א תַּתָּאָה, כָּאן בְּהֵ"א עִלָּאָה. כ"ג דְּאִיהוּ עִלָּאָה מִכֻּלְּהוּ, בְּהֵ"א עִלָּאָה. דִּכְתִּיב אֲשֶׁר יוּצַק עַל רֹאשׁוֹ שֶׁמֶן הַמִּשְׁחָה וּמִלֵּא אֶת יָדוֹ וְגוֹ'. וּמִלֵּא יָדוֹ דִּכְתִּיב שִׁבְעַת יָמִים יְמַלֵּא אֶת יֶדְכֶם. כַּהֲנָא אָחֳרָא בְּה' תַּתָּאָה, דִּכְתִּיב, לֹא יִקְרְחָה קָרְחָה בְּרֹאשָׁם, וּכְתִיב בַּתְרֵיה, וְלֹא יְחַלְּלוּ שֵׁם אֱלֹהֵיהֶם. וְהַאי שֵׁם הָא יְדִיעָא אִיהוּ.

וּבְג"כ כְּתִיב, וְהַכֹּהֵן הַגָּדוֹל מֵאֶחָיו אֲשֶׁר יוּצַק עַל רֹאשׁוֹ שֶׁמֶן הַמִּשְׁחָה לְלְבּוֹשׁ אֶת הַבְּגָדִים, כְּמָה דְּאַמְרָן. וּבְגִין דְּאִיהוּ קַדִּישָׁא כְּגַוְונָא דִּלְעֵילָּא, כְּתִיב וּמִן הַמִּקְדָּשׁ לֹא יֵצֵא.

25. Rabbi Aba said, the lower Hei in here and the supernal Hei in there. The High Priest, the highest, BLEMISHES the supernal Hei, WHICH IS BINAH, as written, "upon whose head the anointing oil was poured, and that is consecrated…" (Vayikra 21:10). "And that is consecrated" REFERS TO BINAH as written, "for seven days shall he consecrate you." THE SEVEN DAYS REFER TO BINAH, THE UPPER HEI OF YUD HEI VAV HEI. Any other priest CREATES A BLEMISH in the lower Hei OF YUD HEI VAV HEI, MALCHUT, as written, "They shall not make baldness on their head" (Vayikra 21:5), followed by, "and not profane the name of their Elohim" (Ibid. 6). This name is known AS MALCHUT, THE LOWER HEI. Hence it is written, "And he that is the High Priest among his brethren, upon whose head the anointing oil was poured, and that is consecrated to put on the garments." THIS IS as we said THAT THE ANOINTING OIL INDICATES THE BOUNTY OF ABA THAT HE RECEIVES VIA IMA, THE UPPER HEI. Since he is holy in the likeness of above it is written, "neither shall he go out of the sanctuary" (Ibid. 12), JUST LIKE ABA AND IMA WHOSE UNION IS UNINTERRUPTED.

8. "Hashem, righteousness belongs to You"

A Synopsis

Rabbi Aba says that Yisrael is blessed because God gave them the Torah of Truth. He tells us that Righteousness is truth, overall light, the illumination of the countenance and the joy of all. Confusion, the Other Side, is shame and the departure of truth. The high priest must have a beautiful and welcoming countenance.

26. ר' אַבָּא פָּתַח וְאָמַר, לְךָ יְיָ' הַצְּדָקָה וְלָנוּ בּוֹשֶׁת הַפָּנִים כְּהַיּוֹם הַזֶּה לְאִישׁ יְהוּדָה וּלְיוֹשְׁבֵי יְרוּשָׁלָם. זַכָּאִין אִינּוּן יִשְׂרָאֵל, דְּקוּדְשָׁא בְּרִיךְ הוּא אִתְרְעֵי בְּהוּ, מִכָּל עַמִּין עע"ז, וּמִגּוֹ רְחִימוּתָא דִּלְהוֹן, יָהַב לְהוּ אוֹרַיְיתָא דִּקְשׁוֹט, לְמִנְדַּע אָרְחָא דְּמַלְכָּא קַדִּישָׁא. וְכָל מַאן דְּאִשְׁתְּדַל בְּאוֹרַיְיתָא, כְּאִלּוּ אִשְׁתְּדַל בֵּיהּ בְּקוּדְשָׁא בְּרִיךְ הוּא, דְּאוֹרַיְיתָא כֹּלָּא שְׁמֵיהּ דְּקוּדְשָׁא בְּרִיךְ הוּא הֲוֵי. ובג"כ מַאן דְּאִתְעַסַּק בְּאוֹרַיְיתָא, אִתְעַסַּק בֵּיהּ בִּשְׁמֵיהּ, וּמַאן דְּאִתְרְחַק מֵאוֹרַיְיתָא, רְחִיקָא הוּא מְקוּדְשָׁא בְּרִיךְ הוּא.

26. Rabbi Aba opened with the verse, "Hashem, righteousness belongs to You, but to us confusion of faces, as at this day; to the men of Judah, and to the inhabitants of Jerusalem" (Daniel 9:7). Happy are Yisrael, whom the Holy One, blessed be He, has chosen above all the heathen nations. For the love of them, He gave them the Torah of truth, to know the path of the Holy King. Whoever is occupied with the Torah it is as if he is occupied with the Holy One, blessed be He, for the whole Torah is the name of the Holy One, blessed be He. Therefore, whoever deals in the Torah is occupied with His name, and whoever is away from the Torah is far from the Holy One, blessed be He.

27. תָּא חֲזֵי, לְךָ יְיָ' הַצְּדָקָה, כד"א, לְךָ יְיָ' הַגְּדוּלָה וְהַגְּבוּרָה. מַאן צְדָקָה. אֲתַר דְּכָל אַנְפִּין נְהִירִין אֲחִידָן בֵּיהּ, וְהוּא אָחִיד בְּכֻלְּהוּ, וּבֵיהּ אִשְׁתְּכְחוּ. וְלָנוּ בּוֹשֶׁת הַפָּנִים אֲתַר דְּכָל אַנְפִּין נְהִירִין אִתְרַחֲקָן מִנֵּיהּ. צְדָקָה, אֱמֶת קְשׁוֹט, וּנְהוֹרָא דְּכֹלָּא, וּנְהוֹרָא דְּאַנְפִּין חֵידוּ דְּכֹלָּא. בּוֹשֶׁת, בְּסוֹפָא רְחִיקוּ דִּקְשׁוֹט מַאן דְּאַכְסִיף, בְּגִין דְּאֱמֶת דְּאִיהוּ צְדָקָה,

אִתְרַחַק מִנֵּיהּ. רְחִיקוּ דְּאַנְפִּין נְהִירִין.

27. Come and see, "Hashem, righteousness belongs to You" resembles the words, "Yours, Hashem, is the greatness and the power" (I Divrei Hayamim 29:11), WHICH ARE HIS ATTRIBUTES, CHESED, GVURAH, TIFERET, NETZACH, HOD, YESOD AND MALCHUT. RIGHTEOUSNESS IS ALSO THE ATTRIBUTE OF MALCHUT. What is righteousness? It is a place to which all shining faces are attached, and which is attached to all THE SFIROT OF ZEIR ANPIN which dwell in it, THAT IS, MALCHUT, IN WHICH ARE ALL THE SFIROT OF ZEIR ANPIN. "but to us confusion of faces" is the place which all shining faces shy away from, WHICH IS THE OTHER SIDE. Righteousness, MALCHUT, is truth, overall light, the illumination of the countenance and the joy of all. Confusion, THE OTHER SIDE, is shame and the staying away of truth. For whenever one is ashamed it is because truth, which is righteousness, is gone away from him, which is the shying away of all shining countenances.

28. ת"ח, כַּהֲנָא עִלָּאָה בָּעֵי לְאִתְחֲזָאָה בִּשְׁפִּירוּ דְּאַנְפִּין, בִּנְהִירוּ דְּאַנְפִּין, בְּחֵידוּ יַתִּיר מִכֹּלָּא. וְלָא בָּעֵי לְאִתְחֲזָאָה בֵּיהּ עֲצִיבוּ וְרוּגְזָא, אֶלָּא כֹּלָּא כְּגַוְונָא דִּלְעֵילָא. זַכָּאָה חוּלָקֵיהּ, דְּעָלֵיהּ כְּתִיב, אֲנִי חֶלְקְךָ וְנַחֲלָתְךָ. וּכְתִיב יְיָ' הוּא נַחֲלָתוֹ. וְע"ד בָּעֵי לְאִתְחֲזָאָה שְׁלִים בְּכֹלָּא, בְּגַרְמֵיהּ, בִּלְבוּשׁיהּ, דְּלָא יַפְגִּים גַּרְמֵיהּ כְּלַל, כְּמָה דְּאִתְּמַר.

28. Come and see, the supernal priest, THE HIGH PRIEST, needs to be with a beautiful countenance, with a welcoming countenance, and more joyous than anyone. He must not look sad or angry, but in all in the likeness of above. Happy is his portion, as it is written regarding him, "I am your portion and your inheritance" (Bemidbar 18:20), and "Hashem is their inheritance" (Devarim 18:2). Hence he must look whole in every respect, in his person, in his apparel, so as not to discredit himself whatsoever, as we learned.

9. "And he shall take a wife in her virginity"

A Synopsis

Rabbi Shimon speaks about the verse, "and, lo, he has laid accusing speeches...and they shall fine him a hundred shekels of silver... because he has brought out an evil name upon a virgin of Yisrael."

29. וְהוּא אִשָּׁה בִּבְתוּלֶיהָ יִקָּח. ר' שִׁמְעוֹן פָּתַח, וְהִנֵּה הוּא שָׂם עֲלִילוֹת דְּבָרִים וְגוֹ'. וּכְתִיב וְעָנְשׁוּ אוֹתוֹ מֵאָה כֶּסֶף וְגוֹ', כִּי הוֹצִיא שֵׁם רָע עַל בְּתוּלַת יִשְׂרָאֵל, וְכִי בְּתוּלַת יִשְׂרָאֵל הִיא, בְּתוּלַת אָבִיהָ, אוֹ בְּתוּלַת בַּעְלָהּ הִיא, מַהוּ בְּתוּלַת יִשְׂרָאֵל הָכָא. הֲדָא הוּא דִּכְתִיב, שְׁאַל אָבִיךְ וְיַגֶּדְךָ זְקֵנֶיךָ וְיֹאמְרוּ לָךְ. אוּף הָכָא כַּהֲנָא דְּקָאֵים כְּגַוְונָא דִּלְעֵילָא, כְּתִיב וְהוּא אִשָּׁה בִּבְתוּלֶיהָ יִקָּח, הָכִי נָמֵי בִּבְתוּלֶיהָ, דְּלָא תִּפּוֹק מִבָּבָא דַּחֲצֵרָה מִזִּמְנָא לְבַר, וְהָא אִתְּמַר.

29. "And he shall take a wife in her virginity" (Vayikra 21:13). Rabbi Shimon opened with, "and, lo, he has laid accusing speeches...and they shall fine him a hundred shekels of silver...because he has brought out an evil name upon a virgin of Yisrael" (Devarim 22:17-19). HE ASKS, yet she is the virgin of her father or husband, why does it state here, "the virgin of Yisrael," WHICH MEANS, A VIRGIN THE DAUGHTER OF JACOB CALLED ISRAEL? AND HE ANSWERS, this is the meaning of, "ask your father, and he will recount it to you; your elders, and they will tell you" (Devarim 32:7). THAT REFERS TO ISRAEL YOUR FATHER, WHOSE DAUGHTER DINAH WENT OUT TO SEE THE DAUGHTERS OF THE LAND, AND THAT INCIDENT OCCURRED. SINCE THE VERSE SPEAKS ABOUT SPREADING AN EVIL NAME, IT MENTIONS THE VIRGIN OF YISRAEL, THE SAME CASE AS THAT OF THE DAUGHTER OF ISRAEL, DINAH. Here too, the priest who represents the likeness of above, "shall take a wife in her virginity," NAMELY, who will not go outside from her courtyard from time to time. We have already learned this. HE MAKES AN ANALOGY BETWEEN HER VIRGINITY AND THE VIRGIN OF ISRAEL, SO SHE WILL NOT GO OUT, AS HAPPENED TO THE VIRGIN OF ISRAEL.

10. "He has given food to those who fear Him"

A Synopsis

Rabbi Shimon says that God gives sustenance to the righteous, who are of His household. Anyone who rises at midnight to study Torah is considered to be part of His household, and will inherit the earth.

30. רִבִּי שִׁמְעוֹן הֲוָה אָזִיל בְּאָרְחָא, וַהֲווֹ עִמֵּיהּ ר' יְהוּדָה ר' יוֹסֵי ר' חִזְקִיָּה. פָּתַח ר"ש וְאָמַר, טֶרֶף נָתַן לִירֵאָיו יִזְכּוֹר לְעוֹלָם בְּרִיתוֹ. טֶרֶף נָתַן לִירֵאָיו, אִלֵּין אִינּוּן זַכָּאִין, אִינּוּן דַּחֲלֵי דְּקוּדְשָׁא בְּרִיךְ הוּא, דְּכָל מַאן דְּדָחִיל לֵיהּ, אִתְקְרֵי מֵאִינָשֵׁי דְּבֵיתָא דְּמַלְכָּא, וַעֲלֵיהּ כְּתִיב, אַשְׁרֵי אִישׁ יָרֵא אֶת יְיָ'.

30. Rabbi Shimon was walking along the way with Rabbi Yehuda, Rabbi Yosi and Rabbi Chizkiyah. Rabbi Shimon opened with, "He has given food to those who fear Him; He will ever be mindful of His covenant" (Tehilim 111:5). "He has given food to those who fear Him" refers to the righteous who fear the Holy One, blessed be He, for whoever fears Him is considered of the household of the King, and it is written of him, "Happy is the man who fears Hashem" (Tehilim 112:1).

31. מַהוּ טֶרֶף נָתַן לִירֵאָיו. אֶלָּא כְּמָה דִּכְתִיב, וַתָּקָם בְּעוֹד לַיְלָה וַתִּתֵּן טֶרֶף לְבֵיתָהּ. מֵהָכָא אוֹלִיפְנָא, דְּכָל ב"נ דְּלָעֵי בְּאוֹרַיְיתָא בְּלֵילְיָא, וְקָם בְּפַלְגוּת לֵילְיָא, בְּשַׁעֲתָא דִּכְנֶסֶת יִשְׂרָאֵל אִתְעֲרַת לְאִתְקָנָא בֵּיתָא לְמַלְכָּא, הַאי אִשְׁתְּתַּף בַּהֲדָהּ, וְהַאי אִקְרֵי מִבֵּי מַלְכָּא, וְיָהֲבִין לֵיהּ כָּל יוֹמָא מֵאִינּוּן תִּיקּוּנֵי בֵּיתָא, הה"ד וַתִּתֵּן טֶרֶף לְבֵיתָהּ, וְחֹק לְנַעֲרוֹתֶיהָ. מַאן בֵּיתָהּ. כָּל אִינּוּן דְּמִשְׁתַּתְּפֵי בַּהֲדָהּ בְּלֵילְיָא, אִקְרוּן בֵּיתָהּ. ובג"כ טֶרֶף נָתַן לִירֵאָיו.

31. HE ASKS, what is the meaning of, "He has given food to those who fear Him," AND ANSWERS THAT this resembles the words, "She rises also while it is yet night, and gives food to her household" (Mishlei 31:15). SINCE THE RIGHTEOUS ARE HIS HOUSEHOLD, THEY RECEIVE THIS FOOD. From this

we learned that whoever studies Torah at night and rises at midnight when the Congregation of Yisrael, MALCHUT, awakens to arrange the house for the King, THAT IS, TO DRAW THE ILLUMINATION OF CHOCHMAH FOR HIM, IN ACCORDANCE WITH, "THROUGH WISDOM A HOUSE IS BUILT" (MISHLEI 24:3), such a man takes his part with her, and is considered to be of the household of the King. He is given daily from the allotments of the house. This is the meaning of, "She rises also while it is yet night, and gives food to her household, and a portion to her maidens." "FOOD" REFERS TO THE ILLUMINATION OF CHOCHMAH, WHILE "PORTION" (ALSO: 'LAW') IS THAT THEY WILL NOT DRAW FROM ABOVE DOWNWARDS. Who are her household? Those who join her to study Torah at night are considered her house, her household members. Hence IT IS WRITTEN, "He has given food to those who fear Him."

32. מַהוּ טֶרֶף. טֶרֶף מַמָּשׁ, דְּאִיהִי נַטְלָא מֵאֲתַר רְחִיקָא עִלָּאָה, דִּכְתִיב מִמֶּרְחָק תָּבִיא לַחְמָהּ. וּמַאן זָכֵי לְהַאי טֶרֶף, סוֹפֵיהּ דִּקְרָא אוֹכַח, דִּכְתִיב, יִזְכּוֹר לְעוֹלָם בְּרִיתוֹ. מַאן דְּאִשְׁתְּדַל בְּאוֹרַיְיתָא, לְאִשְׁתַּתְּפָא בַּהֲדָהּ בְּלֵילְיָא. וְלָא עוֹד, אֶלָּא דְצַדִּיק חַד עִלָּאָה אִית לֵיהּ לְקוּדְשָׁא בְּרִיךְ הוּא, וְהוּא אִשְׁתַּתַּף בַּהֲדֵיהּ, וְיַרְתִין תַּרְוַויְיהוּ לִכְנֶסֶת יִשְׂרָאֵל, דִּכְתִיב צַדִּיקִים לְעוֹלָם יִירְשׁוּ אָרֶץ.

32. HE ASKS, What is "food," AND ANSWERS, It is real food (lit. 'prey'), FOR SHE DEVOURS AND TAKES BY FORCE, WHICH ALLUDES TO JUDGMENTS THAT ARE REVEALED WITH CHOCHMAH. For she receives from a lofty faraway place, as written, "she brings her food from afar" (Mishlei 31:14), THAT IS, CHOCHMAH, AS WRITTEN, "I SAID, I WILL BE WISE; BUT IT WAS FAR FROM ME" (KOHELET 7:23). Who obtains this food? This is shown by the end of the verse, "He will ever be mindful of His covenant" (Tehilim 111:5). THIS MEANS whoever strives in the Torah to partake of it at night, AS THE TORAH IS CALLED A COVENANT. Moreover, the Holy One, blessed be He, has another certain supernal Righteous, WHO IS YESOD OF ZEIR ANPIN, and this MAN joins him TO BESTOW UPON MALCHUT, and both inherit the Congregation of Yisrael, as written, "righteous; they shall inherit the land for ever" (Yeshayah 60:21). THIS MEANS THAT THE RIGHTEOUS MAN WHO IS OCCUPIED WITH THE TORAH AT NIGHT AND THE SUPERNAL RIGHTEOUS WILL INHERIT MALCHUT CALLED EARTH.

11. "Neither shall he profane his seed among his people"

A Synopsis

Rabbi Shimon speaks about the precept against ejaculating semen in vain, and says it is even more important for priests to obey because they must be holy in every respect. Rabbi Shimon says that Yisrael are happy because when they went into exile the Shechinah went with them. In the end God will return from exile with Yisrael.

33. תּוּ פָּתַח וְאָמַר, וְלֹא יְחַלֵּל זַרְעוֹ בְּעַמָּיו כִּי אֲנִי יְיָ' מְקַדְּשׁוֹ. תָּ"ח, כָּל מַאן דְּאַפִּיק זֶרַע לְבַטָּלָה, לָא זָכֵי לְמֶחֱמֵי אַפֵּי שְׁכִינְתָּא, וְאִקְרֵי רַע, דִּכְתִיב כִּי לֹא אֵל חָפֵץ רֶשַׁע אָתָּה לֹא יְגוּרְךָ רָע. הַאי מַאן דְּאַפִּיק לֵיהּ בִּידֵיהּ, אוֹ בְּאִנְתּוּ אָחֳרָא דְּלָא כַּשְׁרָא. וְאִי תֵּימָא דְּאַפִּיק לֵיהּ בְּאִנְתּוּ דְּלָא מִתְעַבְּרָא, הָכִי נָמֵי. לָא. אֶלָּא כְּמָה דְּאַמְרָן.

33. He continued with the verse, "Neither shall he profane his seed among his people, for I Hashem do sanctify him"(Vayikra 21:15). Come and see, whoever ejaculates semen in vain is not worthy of beholding the face of the Shechinah, and is considered evil, as written, "For You are not an El that has pleasure in wickedness; nor shall evil dwell with You" (Tehilim 5:5). THIS REFERS TO one who emits it by hand or through another, unworthy woman. You may argue that one who ejaculates it within a woman who does not conceive IS also CONSIDERED TO BE EMITTING SEMEN IN VAIN. This is not so, but only those we mentioned.

34. וְעַל דָּא יִבְעֵי ב"נ מִקוּדְשָׁא בְּרִיךְ הוּא, דְּיִזְדַמִּין לֵיהּ מָאנָא דְכַשְׁרָא, דְּלָא יְפַגִּים זַרְעֵיהּ, מַאן דְּאַפִּיק זַרְעָא בְּמָאנָא דְּלָא כַּשְׁרָא, פָּגִים לֵיהּ לְזַרְעֵיהּ, וַוי לְמַאן דְּפָגִים זַרְעֵיהּ. וּמַה בִּשְׁאָר בְּנֵי נָשָׁא כָּךְ, בְּכַהֲנָא דְּקָאִים לְתַתָּא כְּגַוְּונָא דִּלְעֵילָּא בִּקְדוּשָׁה עִלָּאָה, עַל אַחַת כַּמָּה וְכַמָּה.

34. A man should therefore ask the Holy One, blessed be He, to summon him a worthy vessel, THAT IS A WORTHY WOMAN, so as not to blemish his seed. Whoever ejaculates his seed in an unworthy vessel blemishes his seed. Woe to him who causes damage in his seed. And if this is true for other people, it is much more so to a priest that is below, CORRESPONDING to a likeness of above in utmost holiness. IT IS THEREFORE WRITTEN, "NEITHER SHALL HE PROFANE HIS SEED AMONG HIS PEOPLE."

35. בְּעַמָּיו, מַהוּ בְּעַמָּיו. דְּהָא כְּתִיב לְעֵילָא, אַלְמָנָה וּגְרוּשָׁה וַחֲלָלָה זוֹנָה אֶת אֵלֶּה לֹא יִקָּח, וּכְתִיב וְלֹא יְחַלֵּל זַרְעוֹ בְּעַמָּיו. בָּהֶם מִבָּעֵי לֵיהּ, מַהוּ בְּעַמָּיו. אֶלָּא מִלָּה דָּא קְלָנָא בְּעַמָּיו, פְּגִימוּ בְּעַמָּיו, וְעַל דָּא כְּתִיב, כִּי אִם בְּתוּלָה מֵעַמָּיו יִקַּח אִשָּׁה, מֵעַמָּיו וַדַּאי, כֹּלָּא כְּגַוְונָא דִּלְעֵילָא, כִּי אֲנִי ה' מְקַדְּשׁוֹ, מַהוּ מְקַדְּשׁוֹ. אֶלָּא אֲנָא הוּא הַהוּא, דְּאִיהוּ מְקַדֵּשׁ לֵיהּ בְּכָל יוֹמָא, וּבְגִין כָּךְ לָא יַפְגִּים זַרְעֵיהּ, וְלָא יִשְׁתְּכַח בֵּיהּ פְּגִימוּ. דְּהָא אֲנִי יְיָ' מְקַדְּשׁוֹ דַּאֲנָא בָּעֵינָא לְקַדְּשָׁא לֵיהּ וְיִשְׁתְּכַח קַדִּישָׁא בְּכֹלָּא, דְּקַדִּישָׁא יִשְׁתַּמֵּשׁ עַל יְדָא דְּקַדִּישָׁא.

35. HE ASKS, what is the meaning of "among his people," seeing that it is written before, "A widow, or a divorced woman, or a profaned, or a harlot, these shall he not take" (Vayikra 21:14), and "Neither shall he profane his seed among his people." It should have said, 'among them'. Why "among his people"? HE ANSWERS, this MEANS this would be a disgrace among his people, a blemish among his people. Hence it is written, "but he shall take a virgin of his own people to wife" (Ibid.), "of his own people" assuredly. Everything is in the likeness of above. "for I Hashem do sanctify him." What is "sanctify him"? HE ANSWERS, it is I who daily sanctify him. Hence he must not blemish his seed and no blemish must be in him, "for I, Hashem do sanctify him," as I wish to sanctify him so that he shall be sanctified in every respect, and so that the holy will make use of what is holy.

36. ת"ח, קוּדְשָׁא בְּרִיךְ הוּא יִשְׁתַּמֵּשׁ ע"י דְּכַהֲנָא, וְיִשְׁתְּכַח קַדִּישָׁא כַּד אָתֵי לְשַׁמְּשָׁא, וּבְגִין דְּקוּדְשָׁא בְּרִיךְ הוּא יִשְׁתַּמֵּשׁ עַל יְדָא דְּכַהֲנָא דְּאִיהוּ קַדִּישָׁא, כַּהֲנָא יִשְׁתַּמֵּשׁ ע"י דְּדַכְיָא, דְּאִתְקַדַּשׁ בְּדַכְיוּתֵיהּ, וּמַאי אִיהוּ. לֵיוָאֵי. בַּר נָשׁ אָחֳרָא, יִשְׁתַּמַּשׁ ע"י דְּקַדִּישָׁא אָחֳרָא, בְּגִין דְּיִשְׁתַּכְּחוּן כֹּלָּא בְּקַדוּשָׁא, לְשַׁמְּשָׁא לְקוּדְשָׁא בְּרִיךְ הוּא. זַכָּאִין אִינוּן יִשְׂרָאֵל בְּעָלְמָא דֵּין וּבְעָלְמָא דְּאָתֵי, דַּעֲלַיְיהוּ כְּתִיב, וָאַבְדִּיל אֶתְכֶם מִן הָעַמִּים לִהְיוֹת לִי. כַּמָה פְּרִישָׁן יִשְׂרָאֵל מִכֹּלָּא, בִּקְדוּשָׁה, לְשַׁמְּשָׁא לְקוּדְשָׁא בְּרִיךְ הוּא, הֲה"ד וְהִתְקַדִּשְׁתֶּם וִהְיִיתֶם קְדוֹשִׁים כִּי אֲנִי יְיָ' אֱלֹהֵיכֶם.

36. Come and see, the Holy One, blessed be He, will make use of the priest, who is holy when he comes to serve. Since the Holy One, blessed be He will use the priest who is holy, the latter will be helped by a pure man, who is sanctified by his own purity. These are the Levites. Another MAN, NAMELY THE PRIEST, will be helped by another holy man, THE LEVITE, so they will all be in holiness to serve the Holy One, blessed be He. Happy are Yisrael in this world and in the World to Come, as written of them, "and have separated you from the peoples, that you should be Mine" (Vayikra 20:26). Yisrael are separated by holiness in every respect, so as to serve the Holy One, blessed be He. This is the meaning of, "Sanctify yourselves therefore, and be holy; for I am Hashem your Elohim" (Ibid. 7).

37. תּוּ פָּתַח וְאָמַר, לַייָ' הַיְשׁוּעָה עַל עַמְּךָ בִרְכָתֶךָ סֶּלָה. לַייָ' הַיְשׁוּעָה. הָכִי תָּנֵינָן, זַכָּאִין אִינוּן יִשְׂרָאֵל, דְּבְכָל אֲתַר דְּאִתְגְּלוּ, שְׁכִינְתָּא אִתְגַּלְיָיא בַּהֲדַיְיהוּ. כַּד יִפְקוּן יִשְׂרָאֵל מִגָּלוּתָא, פּוּרְקָנָא לְמַאן, לְיִשְׂרָאֵל, אוֹ לְקוּדְשָׁא בְּרִיךְ הוּא. אֶלָּא הָא אוּקְמוּהָ בְּכַמָּה קְרָאֵי, וְהָכָא, לַייָ' הַיְשׁוּעָה וַדַּאי, אֵימָתַי. עַל עַמְּךָ בִרְכָתֶךָ סֶּלָה. בְּשַׁעֲתָא דְּקוּדְשָׁא בְּרִיךְ הוּא יַשְׁגַּח בְּבִרְכָאן עֲלַיְיהוּ דְּיִשְׂרָאֵל, לְאַפְּקָא לוֹן מִן גָּלוּתָא, וּלְאוֹטָבָא לְהוּ, כְּדֵין לַייָ' הַיְשׁוּעָה וַדַּאי. וְעַל דָּא תָּנֵינָן, דְּקוּדְשָׁא בְּרִיךְ הוּא יֵיתוּב עִמְּהוֹן דְּיִשְׂרָאֵל מִן גָּלוּתָא, הה"ד, וְשָׁב יְיָ' אֱלֹהֶיךָ אֶת שְׁבוּתְךָ וְרִחֲמֶךָ.

37. He opened again and said, "Salvation belongs to Hashem; Your blessings be upon Your people. Selah" (Tehilim 3:9). "Salvation belongs to Hashem": we have so learned, happy are Yisrael, for wherever they were exiled, the Shechinah went into exile with them. When Yisrael will come out of exile, whose salvation shall this be, that of Yisrael or of the Holy One, blessed be He, SEEING THAT THE SHECHINAH AS WELL WILL GO OUT OF EXILE? We have explained it in relation to several verses. Here, "Salvation belongs to Hashem," surely. When will that be? When "Your blessings be upon Your people." When the Holy One, blessed be He, cares for Yisrael with blessings so as to take them out of exile and help them, then "Salvation belongs to Hashem," BECAUSE THE SHECHINAH WILL GO OUT OF EXILE. We therefore learned that the Holy One, blessed be He, will return from exile with Yisrael. This is the meaning of, "then Hashem your

Elohim will turn your captivity, and have compassion upon you" (Devarim 30:3). 'TURN' CAN BE CONSTRUED TO MEAN HE WILL RETURN WITH YISRAEL FROM EXILE.

12. "he shall take a virgin of his own people to wife"

A Synopsis

Moses, the Faithful Shepherd, explains why the High Priest must marry a virgin. Yisrael need to send their gifts to God by the hand of a wholesome man.

רעיא מהימנא

38. כִּי אִם בְּתוּלָה מֵעַמָּיו יִקַּח אִשָּׁה, פָּתַח רַעְיָא מְהֵימָנָא וְאָמַר, פִּקּוּדָא דָא, לְמֵיסַב כַּהֲנָא רַבָּא בְּתוּלְתָּא, הה"ד אַלְמָנָה וּגְרוּשָׁה וַחֲלָלָה זוֹנָה אֶת אֵלֶּה לֹא יִקָּח כִּי אִם בְּתוּלָה מֵעַמָּיו יִקַּח אִשָּׁה. וַאֲמַאי בָּעֵינָן דְּלָא יִסַּב אֶלָּא בְּתוּלְתָּא בְּלָא פְּגִימוּ. אֶלָּא, אִתְּתָא אִיהִי כּוֹס דִּבְרָכָה, טַעֲמוּ פְּגִימוּ. וְכַהֲנָא דְּקָרִיב קָרְבָּנָא יְיָ', בָּעֵי דְּלֶהֱוֵי אִיהוּ שְׁלִים, בְּלָא פְּגִימוּ, שְׁלִים בְּאֵבָרוֹי בְּלָא פְּגִימוּ, דְּמוּמִין פַּסְלִין בְּכַהֲנָיָא. שְׁלִים בְּגוּפֵיהּ, שְׁלִים בְּנוּקְבֵיהּ, לְקַיְּימָא בֵּיהּ, כֻּלָּךְ יָפָה רַעְיָתִי וּמוּם אֵין בָּךְ.

Ra'aya Meheimna (the Faithful Shepherd)

38. "but he shall take a virgin of his own people to wife" (Vayikra 21:14). The Faithful Shepherd opened and said, this commands the High Priest to marry a virgin, as said, "A widow, or a divorced woman, or a profaned, or a harlot, these shall he not take; but he shall take a virgin of his own people to wife." HE ASKS, why is it necessary for him to marry only an unblemished virgin, AND ANSWERS, a woman is a cup of blessing, WHICH IF tasted is blemished, THAT IS, IT ALLUDES TO MALCHUT CALLED A CUP OF BLESSING. A priest who offers a sacrifice before Hashem must be whole and unblemished, whole and unblemished in limbs, because blemishes make priests unfit. He should be wholesome in body, whole in his wife, so as to fulfill in him the verse, "You are all fair, my love; there is no blemish in you" (Shir Hashirim 4:7).

39. דְּקָרְבְּנָא מִנְחָה אִיהוּ, וּצְרִיכִין יִשְׂרָאֵל לְמִשְׁלַח מִנְחָתָא דִּלְהוֹן לְמַלְכָּא, בִּגְבַר שְׁלִים. דְּאִינּוּן בְּהֵפוּכָא דְּסִטְרָא אַחֲרָא, דְּהָא בְּיַד אִישׁ

עֵתֵּי פָּגִים, הֲווֹ שַׁלְחִין לֵיהּ דּוֹרְנָא, דִּכְתִיב גּוֹרָל אֶחָד לַיְיָ' וְגוֹרָל אֶחָד לַעֲזָאזֵל. דֶּאֱלֹהִים אֲחֵרִים כֻּלְּהוּ פְּגִימִין מִסִּטְרָא דְּצָפוֹן וְהָכִי רוּבָּא דְּבָתֵּי ע"ז הֵם פְּגִימִים, בְּנוּקְבָּא דִּלְהוֹן, חוּרְבָּא, לִילִית, פְּגִימוּתָא וְכוּ'.

39. For the sacrifice is a gift. Yisrael need to send their gift to the King by a wholesome man, as they are the opposite of the Other Side, to which they would send a gift by an appointed man who is blemished, as written, "one lot for Hashem, and the other lot for Azazel" (Vayikra 16:8). For other Elohim are all blemished on the northern side, ACCORDING TO THE MEANING OF, "OUT OF THE NORTH THE EVIL SHALL BREAK FORTH" (YIRMEYAH 1:14). In this way most heathen households are defective in respect to their wife, WHO IS a ruin, Lilit, blemished, etc.

40. וְר"מ אִיהוּ ו' מָלֵא וְאִיהוּ בְּסִדּוּרָא דָּא יְה"וּ. ה' בַּתְרָאָה, כּוֹס מָלֵא בְּרְכַּת ה', מִסִּטְרָא דִּימִינָא וּמִסִּטְרָה דִּגְבוּרָה דְּאִיהוּ דִּינָא, שְׁכִינְתָּא אִתְקְרִיאַת הוי"ה, הה"ד, הִנֵּה יַ"ד יְדֹו"ד הוֹיָה בְּמִקְנְךָ אֲשֶׁר בַּשָּׂדֶה. קָם ר"מ, וְאִשְׁתְּטַח קַמֵּיהּ. וְאָמַר זַכָּאָה חוּלָקֵי דְּמָארֵי וּמַטְרוֹנִיתָא אִינְהוּ בְּעֶזְרִי.

ע"כ רעיא מהימנא

40. The Faithful Shepherd is Vav filled WITH YUD HEI, NAMELY, ZEIR ANPIN, THE SECRET OF VAV OF YUD HEI VAV HEI, FULL OF THE BOUNTY OF YUD HEI OF YUD HEI VAV HEI, WHICH ARE CHOCHMAH AND BINAH in the following order: Yud Hei Vav. FOR THIS REASON IT INCLUDES ALL THREE LETTERS, YUD HEI VAV. The last Hei OF YUD HEI VAV HEI, WHICH IS MALCHUT, is a cup filled with the blessing of Hashem from the right side, NAMELY THE CUP OF BLESSING MENTIONED BEFORE. From the side of Gvurah, which is Judgment, the Shechinah is called Hei Vav Yud Hei, SINCE IN THIS COMBINATION, HEI, WHICH IS JUDGMENT, RULES OVER VAV, WHICH IS MERCY, WHILE YUD AND HEI, THE MOCHIN, ARE AT THE END OF THE PERMUTATION, WHICH INDICATES JUDGMENT. This is the meaning of, "behold, the hand of Hashem is (Heb. *hoyah*, Hei Vav Yud Hei) upon your cattle which is in the field" (Shemot 9:3), WHERE MALCHUT, CALLED THE HAND OF HASHEM, IS PERMUTATED INTO HEI

VAV YUD HEI IN ORDER TO EXACT PUNISHMENT OVER THE CATTLE IN EGYPT. The Faithful Shepherd rose and prostrated before him, saying, Happy is my lot, that my Master and the Queen are among my helpers.

End of Ra'aya Meheimna (the Faithful Shepherd)

13. "Whoever he be of your seed in their generations that has any blemish"

A Synopsis

Rabbi Yitzchak tells us that a blemish on a man testifies that he has no faith and is therefore unfit to serve in a holy place. Rabbi Elazar and Rabbi Shimon test a passerby who has a defect in one eye, asking him who is the happiest man in the world. They find that the passerby is not a faithful man because he places all importance on wealth. Rabbi Elazar talks about the written Torah and the oral Torah that can not dwell on a blemished place. When Zeir Anpin and Malchut are united, everything is whole, all is one, and no place is defective; then the Congregation of Yisrael is called 'whole'. The priest must be unblemished and so must the offering. Rabbi Yosi says that when the dead rise from the dust at the resurrection they will rise with the same body they had, and God will heal them. We read of the ceremonial importance of eight days in the timing of some events. Rabbi Chiya says that God first offered the Torah to the children of Esau, and the earth trembled until it was given to Yisrael.

41. אִישׁ מִזַּרְעֲךָ לְדוֹרוֹתָם אֲשֶׁר יִהְיֶה בּוֹ מוּם. רַבִּי יִצְחָק אָמַר, בְּגִין דְּאִיהוּ פָּגִים, וּמַאן דְּאִיהוּ פָּגִים, לָא אִתְחֲזֵי לְשַׁמְּשָׁא בְּקוּדְשָׁא. וְהָא אוּקְמוּהָ, דְּב"נ דְּאִשְׁתְּכַח פָּגִים, לֵית בֵּיהּ מְהֵימְנוּתָא, וְהַהוּא פְּגִימוּ אַסְהִיד עֲלֵיהּ, כ"ש כַּהֲנָא, דְּבָעֲיָא לְאִשְׁתַּכְּחָא שְׁלִים, מָארֵיהּ דִּמְהֵימְנוּתָא, יַתִּיר מִכֹּלָּא, וְהָא אוּקְמוּהָ.

41. "Whoever he be of your seed in their generations that has any blemish" (Vayikra 21:17). Rabbi Yitzchak said THE REASON IS because he is blemished, and whoever is blemished is unfit to serve in the holy place. We explained that a blemished man has no faith, to which that blemish bears testimony. This is truer in a priest, who has to be whole and faithful more than the rest. We have already explained this.

42. ר' אֶלְעָזָר הֲוָה יָתִיב בְּקִסְטְרָא דְּבֵי חָמוּי, וְהוּא הֲוָה אָמַר, זִילְגָּא דְּבְקִסְטְרָא בְּעֵיטָא שְׁכִיחַ. אַדְהָכִי, אַעֲבַר חַד ב"נ, פָּגִים מֵעֵינֵיהּ חַד. אָמַר חָמוּי, נִשְׁאַל לְהַאי. אָמַר, פָּגִים הוּא, וְלָאו מְהֵימְנָא. אָמַר, נִשְׁאַל

בַּהֲדֵיה. אָתוּ שָׁאִילוּ לֵיה. אָ"ל, טוֹפְקָא מַאן הוּא בְּעָלְמָא. אָמַר
עֲתִירָא, אֲבָל דְּיִשְׁלִיף, וַוי עַל דָּא, בַּהֲדֵיה אֲנָא מִכֻּלְּהוּ. אָמַר ר'
אֶלְעָזָר, בְּמִלּוֹי אִשְׁתְּמַע, דְּלָאו מְהֵימְנוּתָא גַּבֵּיה, וְלָאו בַּר מְהֵימְנָא
הוּא. ת"ח, קוּדְשָׁא בְּרִיךְ הוּא אָמַר כָּל אִישׁ אֲשֶׁר בּוֹ מוּם לֹא יִקְרָב,
דְּהָא קְדוּשָׁא דִּלְעֵילָא, לָא שַׁרְיָא בַּאֲתַר פְּגִים.

42. Rabbi Elazar was sitting in his father-in-law's room, saying that a remedy MUST be found for the leak in the room, BECAUSE THE RAIN WAS LEAKING THROUGH THE ROOF. In the meanwhile a man passed who had a defect in one eye. His father-in-law said, let us seek ADVICE from him. RABBI ELAZAR said, he is blemished and therefore not trustworthy. HIS FATHER-IN-LAW SAID, let us test him. They approached to ask him. He asked him, Whoever is the happiest in the world? THAT MAN said, A rich man IS THE HAPPIEST IN THE WORLD, but when taken away FROM HIS WEALTH, woe to him. I WORRY for him most of all, SINCE IF HE LOSES HIS WEALTH, HE IS THE MOST MISERABLE MAN IN THE WORLD. Rabbi Elazar said, From his words I understand he is neither faithful nor trustworthy, SINCE HE THINKS THE RICH MAN, RATHER THAN THE RIGHTEOUS, TO BE THE HAPPIEST. Come and see, the Holy One, blessed be He, said that "whatever man he be that has a blemish, he shall not approach" (Ibid. 18), for supernal holiness does not dwell on a blemished place.

43. פָּתַח וְאָמַר, לַתּוֹרָה וְלַתְעוּדָה אִם לֹא יֹאמְרוּ כַּדָּבָר הַזֶּה. לַתּוֹרָה
וְלַתְעוּדָה. מַאן הוּא תּוֹרָה, וּמַאן הוּא תְּעוּדָה. אֶלָּא תּוֹרָה דָּא תּוֹרָה,
שֶׁבִּכְתָב. תְּעוּדָה דָּא תּוֹרָה שֶׁבְּעַל פֶּה. תּוֹרָה שֶׁבַּעַל פֶּה לָא שַׁרְיָא
בַּאֲתַר פְּגִים, דְּהָא מִתּוֹרָה שֶׁבִּכְתָב אִתְבְּנֵי. כְּתִיב צוֹר תְּעוּדָה חֲתוֹם
תּוֹרָה בְּלִמֻּדָי, צוֹר תְּעוּדָה, דָּא תּוֹרָה שֶׁבְּעַ"פ, בְּגִין דְּתַמָּן אִתְצַר
צְרוֹרָא דְּחַיֵּי, וּבַתְעוּדָה אִתְקַשַּׁר קִשְׁרָא דְּחַיֵּי דִּלְעֵילָא, לְמֶהֱוֵי כֹּלָּא חַד.

43. He opened his discourse saying, "for Torah and for testimony: Surely they will speak according to this word" (Yeshayah 8:20). "for Torah and for testimony": HE ASKS, What is the Torah and what is the testimony, AND ANSWERS that the Torah is the Written Torah, ZEIR ANPIN, while the testimony is the Oral Torah, MALCHUT. The Oral Torah does not dwell on a blemished place, because it is established on the Written Torah, SINCE MALCHUT IS BUILT BY ZEIR ANPIN, WHICH IS WHOLE. It is written, "Bind up the testimony, seal the Torah among My disciples" (Ibid. 16). "Bind up the testimony" refers to the Oral Torah, since there, IN MALCHUT, the bundle of life is bound, and with the testimony the knot of life is tied from above, FROM ZEIR ANPIN so that all will be one.

44. וּמִתַּמָּן לְתַתָּא אִתְפָּרְשָׁן אוֹרְחִין וּשְׁבִילִין, וּמִתַּמָּן מִתְפָּרְשִׁין אוֹרְחִין בְּעָלְמִין כֻּלְּהוּ הה"ד וּמִשָּׁם יִפָּרֵד וְהָיָה לְאַרְבָּעָה רָאשִׁים.

44. From there downwards, THAT IS, UNDERNEATH MALCHUT, routes and paths are separated, and from there the ways diverge throughout the worlds, as written, "and from thence it was parted, and branched into four streams" (Beresheet 2:10).

45. חָתוּם תּוֹרָה, חֲתִימָה דְאוֹרַיְיתָא, דְאִיהִי תּוֹרָה שֶׁבִּכְתָב בְּאָן אֲתַר. בְּלִמּוּדַי, אִלֵּין נְבִיאֵי, כד"א וַיָּקֶם אֶת הָעַמּוּד הַיְמָנִי וַיִּקְרָא שְׁמוֹ יָכִין וַיָּקֶם אֶת הָעַמּוּד הַשְּׂמָאלִי וַיִּקְרָא שְׁמוֹ בוֹעַז. וּמִתַּמָּן אִתְפָּרְשָׁן אוֹרְחֵי לִנְבִיאֵי מְהֵימְנֵי, וְקַיְימֵי אִלֵּין בְּקִיּוּמָא לְגוּפָא, לְשִׁית טְהִירִין, הה"ד שׁוֹקָיו עַמּוּדֵי שֵׁשׁ. וְכֹלָּא לָא קַיְימָא אֶלָּא בִּשְׁלִימוּ, וְלָא שַׁרְיָא קְדוּשָׁה דְכֹלָּא, אֶלָּא בִּשְׁלִימוּ, כַּד מִתְחַבְּרָאן דָּא בְּדָא, כֹּלָּא הוּא שָׁלִים, כֹּלָּא הוּא חַד, לָא אִתְפְּגִים אֲתַר. וְעַל דָּא אִקְרֵי כ"י שָׁלֵם, כד"א וּמַלְכִּי צֶדֶק מֶלֶךְ שָׁלֵם וַיְהִי בְשָׁלֵם סֻכּוֹ.

45. "seal the Torah" refers to the sealing of the Torah, the Written Torah, WHICH IS ZEIR ANPIN. Where does this happen? "among My disciples," the prophets CALLED "TAUGHT OF HASHEM," NETZACH AND HOD, as written, "And he set up the right pillar, and called its name Jachin," WHICH IS NETZACH, "and he set up the left pillar, and called its name Boaz" (I Melachim 7:21), WHICH IS HOD. From there ways extend to the faithful prophets, WHO RECEIVE FROM NETZACH AND HOD, and these support the

body, ZEIR ANPIN with HIS six lights. This is the meaning of, "His legs are pillars of marble" (Shir Hashirim 5:15). HIS LEGS, THE SECRET OF NETZACH AND HOD, ARE PILLARS OF ZEIR ANPIN THAT HAS SIX SFIROT IN HIM. Everything is supported only by MEANS OF perfection, and all their holiness dwells on them only when they are in holiness. For when ZEIR ANPIN AND MALCHUT are united with each other, all is whole, all is one, and no place is rendered defective. Hence the Congregation of Yisrael is called whole, as written, "And Melchizedek king of Shalem (lit. 'whole')" (Beresheet 14:18), AS MELCHIZEDEK IS MALCHUT AND THE KING OF WHOLENESS. AND ALSO, "In Shalem also is His tabernacle" Tehilim 76:3), WHICH REFERS TO MALCHUT.

46. וּבְגִין כַּךְ לָא שַׁרְיָא כֹּלָּא, אֶלָּא בַּאֲתַר שְׁלִים. וְעַל דָּא כָּל אִישׁ אֲשֶׁר בּוֹ מוּם לֹא יִקְרָב. כְּגַוְונָא דָּא קָרְבָּנָא דְּבֵיהּ מוּמָא לָא יִתְקְרִיב. מ"ט. דִּכְתִּיב כִּי לֹא לְרָצוֹן יִהְיֶה לָכֶם. וְאִי תֵּימָא הָא קוּדְשָׁא בְּרִיךְ הוּא לָא שָׁארֵי אֶלָּא בַּאֲתַר תְּבִירָא, בְּמָאנָא תְּבִירָא, דִּכְתִּיב וְאֶת דַּכָּא וּשְׁפַל רוּחַ. הַאי אֲתַר שְׁלִים יַתִּיר הוּא מִכֹּלָּא, בְּגִין דְּמָאִיךְ גַּרְמֵיהּ לְמִשְׁרֵי עָלֵיהּ גָּאוּתָא דְּכֹלָּא, גָּאוּתָא עִלָּאָה, וְדָא הוּא שְׁלִים. אֲבָל לָא כְּתִיב, וְאֶת עִוֵּר וְשָׁבוּר וְחָרוּם וְשָׂרוּעַ. אֶלָּא וְאֶת דַּכָּא וּשְׁפַל רוּחַ, מַאן דְּמָאִיךְ גַּרְמֵיהּ, קוּדְשָׁא בְּרִיךְ הוּא זָקִיף לֵיהּ.

46. Therefore everything dwells only on a wholesome place, and therefore, "whatever man he be that has a blemish, he shall not approach" (Vayikra 21:18). Similarly, a blemished sacrifice shall not be offered, since it is written, "it shall not be acceptable for you" (Vayikra 22:20). You may say that the Holy One, blessed be He, only dwells in a broken place, in a broken vessel, as written, "yet with him also that is of a contrite and humble spirit" (Yeshayah 57:15). HE ANSWERS, such a place is the most wholesome, because one humbles himself so as to allow the loftiest to dwell on him, supernal loftiness. Such a one is whole. But it does not say, "I DWELL ON" (IBID.) "a blind man, or a lame, or he that has a flat nose, or anything superfluous" (Vayikra 21:18), but "with him also that is of a contrite and humble spirit," for the Holy One, blessed be He, raises him who humbles himself.

13. "Whoever he be of your seed in their generations that has any blemish"

47. וּבְגִינֵי כַּךְ, כַּהֲנָא דְקָאֵים לְתַתָּא כְּגַוְונָא דִּלְעֵילָא, בָּעֵי לְמֶהֱוֵי שְׁלִים יַתִּיר מִכֹּלָּא, וְלָא יִתְחֲזֵי פָּגִים, וְעַ״ד אַזְהַר לְהוּ לְכַהֲנֵי, דִּכְתִיב אִישׁ מִזַּרְעֲךָ לְדוֹרוֹתָם אֲשֶׁר יִהְיֶה בּוֹ מוּם.

47. Therefore the priest that is below as the likeness of above needs to be more whole in every respect than anyone else, and show no blemish. The priests are therefore admonished, "Whoever he be of your seed in their generations that has any blemish…"

48. תּוּ פָּתַח וְאָמַר, וְכִי תַגִּישׁוּן עִוֵּר לִזְבֹּחַ אֵין רָע, וְכִי תַגִּישׁוּ פִּסֵּחַ וְחוֹלֶה אֵין רָע, וְכִי קוּדְשָׁא בְּרִיךְ הוּא אָמַר אֵין רָע, אִי הָכִי טוֹב הוּא. אֶלָּא סוֹפֵיהּ דִּקְרָא אוֹכַח, דְּיִשְׂרָאֵל בְּאִינוּן יוֹמִין הֲווֹ מְמָנָן כַּהֲנֵי מָארֵי דְמוּמִין, עַל גַּבֵּי מַדְבְּחָא, וּלְשַׁמְּשָׁא עַל מַקְדְּשָׁא, וְאַמְרֵי מַאי אִכְפַּת לֵיהּ לְקוּדְשָׁא בְּרִיךְ הוּא דָא, אוֹ אַחֲרָא. וְאִינוּן הֲווֹ דְּאַמְרֵי אֵין רָע. וְקוּדְשָׁא בְּרִיךְ הוּא אָתִיב לְהוֹן הַהִיא מִלָּה דַּהֲווֹ אַמְרֵי. אָמַר: יִשְׂרָאֵל אַתּוּן אַמְרֵי כַּד מְקָרְבֵי מָארֵי דְמוּמִין עַל פּוּלְחָנִי אֵין רָע, מַאי אִכְפַּת לֵיהּ לְקוּדְשָׁא בְּרִיךְ הוּא.

48. He continued with, "And if you offer the blind for sacrifice, is it not evil? And if you offer a lame or sick animal, is that not evil?" (Malachi 1:8). HE ASKS, Was it the Holy One, blessed be He, who said it is not evil? Then it is good. AND HE ANSWERS, The end of the verse shows that Yisrael used to appoint blemished priests in those days AND BLEMISHED SACRIFICES on the altar, and to serve in the Temple, and said, What does the Holy One, blessed be He, care whether it is this or another? It is they who used to say, It is not evil, and the Holy One, blessed be He, answered them with the very words they would use, saying, 'Yisrael, you say there is not evil in blemished people sacrificing for My worship'. What does the Holy One, blessed be He, care?

49. סוֹפֵיהּ דִּקְרָא מַה כְּתִיב, הַקְרִיבֵהוּ נָא לְפֶחָתֶךָ הַיִרְצְךָ אוֹ הֲיִשָּׂא פָנֶיךָ. בַּר נָשׁ מִנַּיְיכוּ, אִי בָּעֵיתוּ לְשַׁלּוּמֵי לְמַלְכָּא, וּלְקָרְבָא קַמֵּיהּ

דוֹרוֹנָא, אַתּוּן מְשַׁדְּרִין לֵיהּ בִּפְגִימָא, אוֹ לָא. הֲיִרְצְךָ אוֹ הֲיִשָּׂא פָנֶיךָ
בְּהַהוּא דוֹרוֹנָא, כ״ש וכ״ש דְּאַתּוּן מְקָרְבִין קַמַּאי ב״נ פְּגִים לְקָרְבָא
דוֹרוֹנָא, הָא דוֹרוֹנָא דִּלְכוֹן לְכַלְבָּא אִתְמְסַר, דְּוַדַּאי ב״נ דְּאִיהוּ פָּגִים,
פָּגִים הוּא מִכֹּלָּא, פָּגִים הוּא מְהֵימְנוּתָא. וְעַ״ד כָּל אִישׁ אֲשֶׁר בּוֹ מוּם
לֹא יִקְרָב.

49. The end of the verse says, "offer it now to your governor; will he be
pleased with you, or will he show you favor?" (Ibid.) If a man among you
must make peace with the king and offer him a gift, will you send him a
defective one or not? "will he be pleased with you, or will he show you
favor" with that DEFECTIVE gift? Moreover when you bring before Me a
blemished man to offer Me an offering, that offering of yours shall be given
to the dog. For surely such a blemished man is defective in every respect,
defective in faith. Hence it says, "whatever man he be that has a blemish, he
shall not approach."

50. א״ר יוֹסֵי, זַמִּין קוּדְשָׁא בְּרִיךְ הוּא לְאַשְׁלְמָא לְהוּ לְיִשְׂרָאֵל,
וּלְאַשְׁתַּכְּחָא שְׁלֵימִין בְּכֹלָּא, דְּלָא יְהֵא בְּהוֹן מָארֵי דְמוּמִין כְּלָל, בְּגִין
דִּיהוֹן תִּקּוּנָא דְעָלְמָא, כְּאִלֵּין מָאנֵי וּלְבוּשָׁא דְב״נ דְּאִינּוּן תִּקּוּנָא
דְגוּפָא, הה״ד וַיִּתְיַצְּבוּ כְּמוֹ לְבוּשׁ.

50. Rabbi Yosi said, The Holy One, blessed be He, will make Yisrael whole
so they will be whole in every respect, and there will be none blemished
among them. For the world will reach completion DURING RESURRECTION,
like the vessels and garments of man which are completion for the body.
THIS IS WHY HE WILL PERFECT THEM, as written, "and they stand as a
garment" (Iyov 38:14).

51. תָּא חֲזֵי, כַּד יִתְעָרוּן מֵעַפְרָא, כְּמָה דְעָאלוּ, הָכִי יְקוּמוּן, חִגְּרִין אוֹ
סוּמִין. עָאלוּ חִגְּרִין וְסוּמִין, יְקוּמוּן בְּהַהוּא לְבוּשָׁא, דְּלָא יֵימְרוּן
דְּאָחֳרָא הוּא דְאִתְעַר. וּלְבָתַר, קוּדְשָׁא בְּרִיךְ הוּא יֵיסֵי לוֹן, וְיִשְׁתַּכְּחוּן
שְׁלֵימִין קַמֵּיהּ, וּכְדֵין יְהֵא עָלְמָא שְׁלִים בְּכֹלָּא, כְּדֵין בַּיּוֹם הַהוּא יִהְיֶה
יְיָ אֶחָד וּשְׁמוֹ אֶחָד.

13. "Whoever he be of your seed in their generations that has any blemish"

51. Come and see, when they will awaken from the dust DURING RESURRECTION, they will rise as they came INTO THE GRAVE. If they entered lame or blind, they will rise lame or blind, NAMELY THEY WILL RISE with the same garment, BODY, so that none would say it is another who was revived INTO LIFE. The Holy One, blessed be He, will then heal them so they will be whole before Him, and the world will be whole in everything. Then, "on that day Hashem shall be one, and His Name One" (Zecharyah 14:9).

52. שׁוֹר אוֹ כֶשֶׂב אוֹ עֵז כִּי יִוָּלֵד וְהָיָה שִׁבְעַת יָמִים תַּחַת אִמּוֹ וְגוֹ'. ר' יוֹסֵי פָּתַח, צִדְקָתְךָ כְּהַרְרֵי אֵל מִשְׁפָּטֶיךָ תְּהוֹם רַבָּה אָדָם וּבְהֵמָה תּוֹשִׁיעַ יְיָ. הַאי קְרָא אִית לְאִסְתַּכְּלָא בֵּיהּ, אֲבָל תָּא חֲזֵי, צֶדֶק: כְּתְרָא קַדִּישָׁא עִלָּאָה. כְּהַרְרֵי אֵל: כְּאִינּוּן טוּרִין עִלָּאִין קַדִּישִׁין, דְּאִקְרוּן טוּרֵי דְּאֲפַרְסְמוֹנָא דַּכְיָא. וּבְגִין דְּאִיהִי סַלְקָא לְאִתְקַשְּׁרָא בְּהוּ לְעֵילָּא, כָּל דִּינָהָא בְּשִׁקּוּלָא חֲדָא לְכֹלָּא, דְּלֵית בְּהַהוּא דִּינָא רַחֲמֵי. מִשְׁפָּטֶיךָ תְּהוֹם רַבָּה. מִשְׁפָּט דְּאִיהוּ רַחֲמֵי, נָחִית לְתַתָּא לְהַהוּא דַּרְגָּא לְתַקְּנָא עָלְמִין וְחָיֵיס עַל כֹּלָּא וְעָבֵיד דִּינָא בְּרַחֲמֵי לְבַסְּמָא עָלְמָא.

52. "When a bullock, or a sheep, or a goat, is brought forth, then it shall be seven days under its mother…" (Vayikra 22:27). Rabbi Yosi opened with, "Your righteousness is like the great mountains; Your laws are a great deep. Hashem, You preserve man and beast" (Tehilim 36:7). We have to examine this verse. Yet come and see, righteousness IS a holy supernal Sfirah, NAMELY MALCHUT. "like the great mountains" MEANS like the supernal holy mountains called mountains of pure balsam tree, WHICH ARE BINAH. Since MALCHUT rises to be attached to them above, all her Judgments become equal, since this Judgment contains no Mercy. THEREFORE "Your laws are a great deep." Law, which is Mercy, descends to that grade, MALCHUT, to perfect the world, and have compassion over everything, and executes Judgment with Mercy to mitigate the world.

53. וּבְגִין דְּאִיהוּ רַחֲמֵי, אָדָם וּבְהֵמָה תּוֹשִׁיעַ יְיָ. לְכֹלָּא בְּשִׁקּוּלָא חֲדָא.

אָדָם וּבְהֵמָה, הָא אוּקְמוּהָ, מַאן דְּהוּא אָדָם, וְשַׁוֵּי לְגַרְמֵיהּ כַּבְּהֵמָה. אָדָם וּבְהֵמָה: דִּין אָדָם, וְדִין בְּהֵמָה, חַד הוּא. אָדָם: וּבֶן שְׁמֹנַת יָמִים יִמּוֹל לָכֶם כָּל זָכָר. בְּהֵמָה: וְהָיָה שִׁבְעַת יָמִים תַּחַת אִמּוֹ וּמִיּוֹם הַשְּׁמִינִי וָהָלְאָה יֵרָצֶה לְקָרְבַּן אִשֶּׁה לַיְיָ', בְּגִין דְּיַעֲבַר עֲלַיְיהוּ שַׁבָּת חַד, וְהָא אוּקְמוּהָ.

53. Since it is Mercy, "Hashem, You preserve man and beast," NAMELY equally. In relation to man and beast, it has been explained as referring to a man who behaves like a beast. BUT "man and beast" MEANS the same law applies for men and beasts. For men, "And he that is eight days old shall be circumcised among you" (Beresheet 17:12). For beasts, "it shall be seven days under its mother; and from the eighth day and thenceforth it shall be accepted for an offering made by fire to Hashem" (Vayikra 22:27), SO THAT they will spend at least one Shabbat. This has already been explained.

54. רִבִּי חִיָּיא פָּתַח יְיָ' בְּצֵאתְךָ מִשֵּׂעִיר בְּצַעְדְּךָ מִשְּׂדֵה אֱדוֹם אֶרֶץ רָעָשָׁה גַּם שָׁמַיִם נָטָפוּ. תָּא חֲזֵי, זַכָּאִין אִינּוּן יִשְׂרָאֵל בְּעָלְמָא דֵּין, וּבְעָלְמָא דְּאָתֵי, דְּקוּדְשָׁא בְּרִיךְ הוּא אִתְרְעֵי בְּהוּ, וְאִינּוּן מִתְדַּבְּקִין בֵּיהּ, וְאִקְרוּן קַדִּישִׁין, עַם קָדוֹשׁ. וְכֵן עַד דְּסָלִיק לוֹן לְדַרְגָּא עִלָּאָה דְּאִקְרֵי קֹדֶשׁ, דִּכְתִיב, קֹדֶשׁ יִשְׂרָאֵל לַיְיָ' רֵאשִׁית תְּבוּאָתֹה. כְּמָה דְּאוּקִימְנָא, דְּהָא יִשְׂרָאֵל מִתְמַנְיָא יוֹמִין מִתְדַּבְּקִין בֵּיהּ בִּשְׁמֵיהּ, וּרְשִׁימִין בִּשְׁמֵיהּ, וְאִינּוּן דִּילֵיהּ. כְּמָה דְּאַתְּ אָמַר, וּמִי כְעַמְּךָ כְּיִשְׂרָאֵל גּוֹי אֶחָד בָּאָרֶץ. וְעַמְּמִין לָא מִתְדַּבְּקִין בֵּיהּ, וְלָא אָזְלִין בְּנִימוּסֵיהּ, וּרְשִׁימָא קַדִּישָׁא אַעְדִּיאוּ מִנַּיְיהוּ, עַד דְּאִינּוּן מִתְדַּבְּקָן בְּסִטְרָא אַחֲרָא דְּלָאו קַדִּישָׁא.

54. Rabbi Chiya opened, "Hashem, when You did go out of Seir, when You did march out of the field of Edom, the earth trembled, and the heavens dropped" (Shoftim 5:4). Come and see, happy are Yisrael in this world and in the World to Come, since the Holy One, blessed be He, chose them and they cleave to Him and are called holy, a holy nation, WHICH IS THE ASPECT OF BINAH. Moreover, He even raised them to a supernal grade called holiness, WHICH IS CHOCHMAH, AND THAT WHICH RECEIVES FROM HOLINESS, NAMELY BINAH, IS CONSIDERED HOLY, as is written, "Yisrael is holiness to Hashem, the firstfruits of His increase" (Yirmeyah 2:3). As we explained, that is because Yisrael cleave to Him through His name after eight days, are marked by His name, and are His, as written, "And what one nation in the earth is like Your people, like Yisrael" (II Shmuel 7:23). The nations do not cleave to Him, nor follow His commands and the holy imprint is absent from them, so they cleave to the unholy Other Side.

55. וְתָא חֲזֵי, בְּשַׁעֲתָא דְּבָעָא קוּדְשָׁא בְּרִיךְ הוּא לְמֵיהַב אוֹרַיְיתָא לְיִשְׂרָאֵל, זַמִּין בָּהּ לִבְנֵי עֵשָׂו, אָמַר לוֹן, בָּעָאן אַתּוּן לְקַבְּלָא אוֹרַיְיתָא. בְּהַהִיא שַׁעֲתָא אִתְרְגִיזַת אַרְעָא קַדִּישָׁא, וּבַעַאת לְאַעֲלָא לְנוּקְבָּא דִּתְהוֹמָא רַבָּה. אָמְרָה קַמֵּיהּ, מָארֵי דְעָלְמָא, פַּסְטִירָא דְּחֶדְוָה תְּרֵי אַלְפֵי שְׁנִין עַד לָא אִתְבְּרֵי עָלְמָא, אִזְדְּמַן קַמֵּי עֲרֵלִין דְּלָא רְשִׁימָן בְּקִיּוּמָךְ.

55. Come and see, when the Holy One, blessed be He, wished to give the Torah to Yisrael, He summoned the children of Esau and asked them, 'Do you wish to receive the Torah?' At that moment the earth, MALCHUT, trembled, and wanted to enter a chasm in the great abyss. It said before Him, Master of the Universe, shall the delights of Your joy since 2,000 years prior to the creation of the world, WHICH IS THE TORAH, ACCORDING TO THE MEANING OF, "AND I WAS DAILY HIS DELIGHT" (MISHLEI 8:30), come before the uncircumcised who are not imprinted with Your covenant?

56. אָמַר לָהּ קוּדְשָׁא בְּרִיךְ הוּא, כּוּרְסְיָיא כּוּרְסְיָיא, יֵיבְדוּן אֶלֶף אוּמִין כְּווֹתַיְיהוּ, וְקַיְּימָא דְּאוֹרַיְיתָא לָא יִזְדְּמַן קַמַּיְיהוּ, הַהַ"ד יְיָ' בְּצֵאתְךָ מִשֵּׂעִיר בְּצַעְדְּךָ מִשְּׂדֵה אֱדוֹם אֶרֶץ רָעָשָׁה. וַדַּאי בְּגִין דְּאוֹרַיְיתָא לָא אִתְיְיהִיבַת אֶלָּא לְמַאן דְּאִית בֵּיהּ קַיְּימָא קַדִּישָׁא. וּמַאן דְּיָלִיף אוֹרַיְיתָא לְמַאן דְּלָא אִתְגְּזַר, מְשַׁקֵּר בִּתְרֵי קַיְּימֵי, מְשַׁקֵּר בְּקַיְּימָא דְּאוֹרַיְיתָא, וּמְשַׁקֵּר בְּקַיְּימָא דְּצַדִּיק וּכְנֶסֶת יִשְׂרָאֵל. דְּאוֹרַיְיתָא לְהַאי אֲתַר אִתְיְיהִיבַת, וְלָא לְאַחֲרָא.

56. The Holy One, blessed be He, said to it, 'Throne, throne, NAMELY MALCHUT CALLED THRONE, may a thousand such nations perish, the covenant of the Torah shall not appear before them.' This is the meaning of, "Hashem, when You did go out of Seir, when You did march out of the field of Edom, the earth trembled" surely, for the Torah is given only to him who has the holy covenant in him. Whoever teaches the Torah to the uncircumcised is false to two covenants, the covenant of the Torah, AS THE TORAH IS CALLED COVENANT, AS WRITTEN, "IF I HAVE NOT APPOINTED MY COVENANT…" (YIRMEYAH 33:25), and the covenant of the Righteous and the Congregation of Yisrael. For the Torah was given to that place, THE COVENANT, and to no other, THE FORESKIN.

14. It is forbidden to teach Torah to the uncircumcised

A Synopsis
Rabbi Aba tells us that anyone who teaches the Torah to the uncircumcised is false to the Torah, false to the prophets and false to the Writings. We learn how a circumcised man can attain the light of the Ruach and the Neshamah and the Chayah.

57. רִבִּי אַבָּא אָמַר, מְשַׁקֵּר בִּתְלַת דּוּכְתֵּי עִלָּאֵי, מְשַׁקֵּר בַּתּוֹרָה, מְשַׁקֵּר בַּנְּבִיאִים, מְשַׁקֵּר בַּכְּתוּבִים. מְשַׁקֵּר בַּתּוֹרָה, דִּכְתִּיב וְזֹאת הַתּוֹרָה וְגוֹ׳. מְשַׁקֵּר בַּנְּבִיאִים דִּכְתִּיב וְכָל בָּנַיִךְ לִמּוּדֵי יְיָ׳. אִינּוּן לִמּוּדֵי יְיָ׳, וְלָא אַחֲרָא, וּכְתִיב חֲתוֹם תּוֹרָה בְּלִמּוּדָי, אִינּוּן, וְלָא אָחֳרָא. מְשַׁקֵּר בַּכְּתוּבִים, דִּכְתִּיב וַיָּקֶם עֵדוּת בְּיַעֲקֹב וְתוֹרָה שָׂם בְּיִשְׂרָאֵל, וּכְתִיב אַךְ צַדִּיקִים יוֹדוּ לִשְׁמֶךָ. מַאן צַדִּיקִים. דָּא צַדִּיק וּכְנֶסֶת יִשְׂרָאֵל. דְּמַאן דְּלָא אִתְגְּזַר, וְלָא עָאל בְּקִיּוּמָא דִּלְהוֹן, לָא יוֹדוּן לִשְׁמֵיהּ קַדִּישָׁא, דְּהִיא אוֹרַיְיתָא. אָמַר רִבִּי חִיָּיא כֵּיוָן דְּאִתְגְּלֵי קוּדְשָׁא בְּרִיךְ הוּא עַל טוּרָא דְּסִינַי, לְמֵיהַב אוֹרַיְיתָא לְיִשְׂרָאֵל, שְׁכִיבַת אַרְעָא, וְתָבַת בְּנַיְיחָא, הה"ד אֶרֶץ יָרְאָה וְשָׁקָטָה.

57. Rabbi Aba said, WHOEVER TEACHES THE TORAH TO THE UNCIRCUMCISED is false to three high places. He is false to the Torah, false to the Prophets, false to the Writings. He is false to the Torah, as written, "And this is the Torah which Moses set before the children of Yisrael" (Devarim 4:44), AND NOT BEFORE THE UNCIRCUMCISED. He is false to the Prophets, as written, "And all your children shall be taught of Hashem" (Yeshayah 54:13), not others. It is also written, "seal the Torah among My disciples" (Yeshayah 8:16), among them and not among others. He is false to the Writings, as written, "For He established a testimony in Jacob, and appointed a Torah in Yisrael" (Tehilim 78:5), and, "Surely the righteous shall give thanks to Your name" (Tehilim 140:14). Who are the righteous? They are the Righteous, YESOD OF ZEIR ANPIN, and the Congregation of Yisrael, WHICH IS MALCHUT CALLED RIGHTEOUSNESS. For whoever is not circumcised or has not entered their covenant, will not give thanks to His Holy Name, which it THE STUDY OF the Torah. Rabbi Chiya said, Once the Holy One, blessed be He, was revealed on Mount Sinai to give the

Torah to Yisrael, the land abated FROM ITS TREMBLING, and was quiet. Hence, "the earth feared, and was still" (Tehilim 76:9).

‫58. תָּא חֲזֵי, בַּר נָשׁ דְּאִתְיְלִיד לָא אִתְמָנָא עָלֵיהּ חֵילָא דִּלְעֵילָא, עַד דְּאִתְגְּזַר. כֵּיוָן דְּאִתְגְּזַר, אִתְּעַר עָלֵיהּ אִתְעָרוּתָא דְּרוּחָא דִּלְעֵילָא. זָכֵי לְאִתְעַסְּקָא בְּאוֹרַיְיתָא, אִתְּעַר עָלֵיהּ אִתְעָרוּתָא יַתִּיר. זָכֵי וְעָבֵיד פִּקּוּדֵי אוֹרַיְיתָא, אִתְּעַר עָלֵיהּ אִתְעָרוּתָא יַתִּיר. זָכֵי וְאִתְנְסִיב, זָכֵי וְאוֹלִיד בְּנִין, וְאוֹלִיף לוֹן אוֹרְחוֹי דְּמַלְכָּא קַדִּישָׁא, הָא כְּדֵין הוּא אָדָם שָׁלִים. שָׁלִים בְּכֹלָּא.‬

58. Come and see, when a man is born, no force from above is appointed over him until he is circumcised. Once he is circumcised the awakening of the spirit, NAMELY THE LIGHT OF NEFESH, was roused over him from above. If he merits to be occupied with the Torah, an additional awakening is stirred over him, THE LIGHT OF RUACH. If he merits to perform the commandments of the Torah, an additional awakening is roused over him, WHICH IS THE LIGHT OF NESHAMAH. If he was worthy to be married, begot children and taught them the ways of the Holy King, then he is whole in every respect, BECAUSE HE ATTAINED THE LIGHT OF CHAYAH. THESE FOUR LEVELS ARE FROM THE FOUR WORLDS, ATZILUT, BRIYAH, YETZIRAH AND ASIYAH, AND APPLY TO EACH INDIVIDUAL WORLD.

‫59. אֲבָל בְּהֵמָה דְּאִתְיְלִידַת, בְּהַהִיא שַׁעֲתָא דְּאִתְיְלִידַת, הַהוּא חֵילָא דְּאִית לָהּ בְּסוֹפָהּ, אִית לָהּ בְּהַהִיא שַׁעֲתָא דְּאִתְיְלִידַת, וְאִתְמָנָא עָלֵיהּ. וּבְגִין כָּךְ כְּתִיב, שׁוֹר אוֹ כֶשֶׂב אוֹ עֵז כִּי יִוָּלֵד. עֵגֶל אוֹ טָלֶה, אוֹ שָׂעִיר אוֹ גְּדִי לָא אִתְמַר, אֶלָּא שׁוֹר אוֹ כֶשֶׂב אוֹ עֵז, הַהוּא דְּאִית לֵיהּ לְסוֹפָא, אִית לֵיהּ בְּשַׁעֲתָא דְּאִתְיְלִיד.‬

59. But when an animal is born, whatever force is in it at its end it has at the hour of its birth, which is appointed over it. Hence it is written, "When a bullock, or a sheep, or a goat, is brought forth" (Vayikra 22:27), for whatever it possesses at the end it has when it is born.

15. "then it shall be seven days under its mother"

A Synopsis

We are told that an animal accepted for a burnt offering shall be at least seven days old so that it will have experienced one Shabbat. We learn about why man must undergo one Shabbat before his circumcision. The two bloods spoken of are the blood of the Pascal sacrifice and the blood of circumcision, and the blood of circumcision is itself two bloods, through which one attains the life of the World to Come.

60. וְהָיָה שִׁבְעַת יָמִים תַּחַת אִמּוֹ, בְּגִין לְאִתְיַשְׁבָא בֵּיהּ הַהוּא חֵילָא וְאִתְקַיַּים בֵּיהּ. וּבַמֶּה יִתְקַיַּים בֵּיהּ. כַּד יִשְׁרֵי עֲלֵיהּ שַׁבָּת חַד, וְאִי לָא, לָא יִתְקַיַּים. וּלְבָתַר דְּיִתְקַיַּים בֵּיהּ הַהוּא חֵילָא, כְּתִיב יֵרָצֶה לְקָרְבַּן אִשֶּׁה לַיְיָ', בְּקִיּוּמָא דְּשַׁבָּת חַד, דְּאַעְבָּר עֲלֵיהּ.

60. "then it shall be seven days under its mother" (Vayikra 22:27), in order for that force APPOINTED OVER IT to settle upon it and exist in it. It will exist in it when one Shabbat has rested on it. Otherwise it does not stay, FOR PEOPLE ONLY EXIST THROUGH THE LIGHT OF SHABBAT, AS WRITTEN, "AND BY THE SEVENTH DAY ELOHIM ENDED HIS WORK, WHICH HE HAD DONE" (BERESHEET 2:2). Later, when this force exists in it, it is written, "it shall be accepted for an offering made by fire to Hashem" (Ibid.), through the existence of the one Shabbat it experienced.

61. וּבַר נָשׁ, בְּקִיּוּמָא דְּשַׁבָּת חַד, אִתְקַיַּים בֵּיהּ אִתְעֲרוּתָא דְּהַאי עָלְמָא, וְחֵילָא דִּילֵיהּ. בָּתַר דְּאִתְגְּזַר, אִתְעַר עֲלֵיהּ אִתְעֲרוּתָא דְּרוּחָא עִלָּאָה, וְכַד"י אַעְבָּר עֲלֵיהּ, וְחָמֵאת לֵיהּ, בִּרְשִׁימָא קַדִּישָׁא, וְאִתְעֲרַת עֲלֵיהּ, וְשַׁרְיָא עֲלֵיהּ רוּחָא דְּהַהוּא עָלְמָא קַדִּישָׁא, כְּמָה דְּאַתְּ אָמַר, וָאֶעֱבוֹר עָלַיִךְ וָאֶרְאֵךְ מִתְבּוֹסֶסֶת בְּדָמָיִךְ וְגוֹ'. בְּדָמַיִךְ: בִּתְרֵי.

61. As for man, by undergoing one Shabbat, the awakening of this world and his force, NAMELY THE ANIMAL NEFESH, are established. After he is circumcised, an awakening of the Supernal Spirit, THE SECRET OF THE NEFESH AS MENTIONED, occurs, and the Congregation of Yisrael, MALCHUT,

passes over him and sees him with a holy imprint. Then she is roused towards him and the spirit of that holy world dwells on him. This is written in, "and saw you weltering in your blood, I said to you, In your blood live…" (Yechezkel 16:6), NAMELY two BLOODS.

62. וְאִי תֵּימָא, הָתָם כַּד נָפְקוּ יִשְׂרָאֵל מִמִּצְרַיִם, דִּשְׁכִיחַ בֵּינַיְיהוּ דָם פֶּסַח וְדָם מִילָה, כְּדֵין כְּתִיב בְּדָמַיִךְ חֲיִי, הָכָא מַאי בְּדָמַיִךְ. אֶלָּא תְּרֵין, חַד דְּמִילָה, וְחַד דִּפְרִיעָה. חַד דְּגִזִּירוּ, דִּכְנֶסֶת יִשְׂרָאֵל. וְחַד דִּפְרִיעָה, בְּצַדִּיק יְסוֹד עוֹלָם. וְאִלֵּין תְּרֵין דָּמִין דְּבַר נָשׁ קָאִים בְּגִינַיְיהוּ בְּקִיּוּמָא דְּעָלְמָא דְּאָתֵי, הֲה"ד בְּדָמַיִךְ חֲיִי.

62. You may say that when Yisrael went out of Egypt, there were among them the blood of the Pascal sacrifice and the blood of circumcision. Then it is written, "In your blood live," NAMELY THE TWO BLOODS. BUT what of "In your blood" in this case? THERE IS ONLY THE BLOOD OF CIRCUMCISION? HE ANSWERS, There ARE two, one of circumcision and one of the uncovering of the corona. The blood of circumcision is OF the Congregation of Yisrael, WHICH IS MALCHUT, while that of the uncovering is OF the Righteous, the foundation of the world, NAMELY, YESOD OF ZEIR ANPIN. Through these two bloods one attains the life of the World to Come. This is the meaning of, "In your blood live."

16. Each letter of the name is the perfection of the whole Name

A Synopsis

We learn from Rabbi Shimon how each letter in the Holy Name reflects the perfection of the name, and the inner meaning of the seven days in Vav Hei and the seven days in Yud Hei.

63. רִבִּי שִׁמְעוֹן אָמַר, סוֹד יְיָ' לִירֵאָיו וּבְרִיתוֹ לְהוֹדִיעָם. סוֹד יְיָ' לִירֵאָיו, דָּא כְּנֶסֶת יִשְׂרָאֵל. וּבְרִיתוֹ לְהוֹדִיעָם, דָּא צַדִּיק יְסוֹד עוֹלָם, בְּקִשׁוּרָא חֲדָא.

63. Rabbi Shimon said, "The counsel (or: 'secret') of Hashem is with them that fear Him; and He will reveal to them His covenant" (Tehilim 25:14). "The secret of Hashem is with them that fear Him" refers to the Congregation of Yisrael, NAMELY MALCHUT CALLED THE SECRET OF HASHEM. "and He will reveal to them His covenant" refers to the Righteous, the foundation of the world, NAMELY, YESOD OF ZEIR ANPIN THAT IS CALLED COVENANT. BOTH are joined as one.

64. יוֹ"ד, תְּלַת אַתְוָון, שְׁלֵימוּתָא דְּכֹלָּא. י' רֵאשִׁיתָא דְּכֹלָּא. י' עִלָּאָה דְּכֹלָּא. וָא"ו אֶמְצָעִיתָא, שְׁלֵימוּתָא דְּכָל סִטְרִין. מַעֲבַר לְכָל רוּחִין, בֵּיהּ תַּלְיָא מְהֵימְנוּתָא. דָּלֶ"ת, גִּנְתָּא, צְרוֹרָא דְּחַיֵּי. אָת דָּא זְעֵירָא, שְׁלֵימָא דְּכֹלָּא.

64. Yud HAS IN IT three letters, which are overall perfection. The beginning of everything, NAMELY CHOCHMAH CALLED BEGINNING, IS Yud, which is the most superior, ABOVE ALL THE LETTERS OF YUD HEI VAV HEI, AND ALL THE SFIROT. The Vav WITHIN YUD VAV DALET IS the Central COLUMN, ZEIR ANPIN, which is perfection in every direction, SINCE IT COMPLETES THE RIGHT AND THE LEFT. It completes, NAMELY, IS A ROOT TO all the spirits, and Faith depends on it, WHICH IS MALCHUT, THE DALET IN THE YUD. It is the garden, the bundle of life, NAMELY MALCHUT. This letter Dalet is small, SINCE MALCHUT IS THE SECRET OF SMALL LETTERS, AND IS overall perfection, SINCE MALCHUT COMPLETES ALL THE SFIROT.

65. אָת דָּא סְתִימָא דְּכָל סִטְרִין. כַּד נָפִיק, נָפִיק כְּמַלְכָּא עִם חֵילוֹי. תָּב לְבָתַר, י׳ בִּלְחוֹדוֹי, בֵּיהּ אַסְתִּים מִלָּה, בֵּיהּ נָפִיק, סָגִיר וּפָתַח.

65. The letter Yud is closed on all sides. When it emerges, THAT IS, IS REVEALED, it does so like a king with his soldiers, and then the Yud returns on its own. Matters are concealed within it and come out TO BE REVEALED. It both conceals and discloses.

66. ה"א שְׁלִימוּתָא דְּכֹלָּא, לְעֵילָא וּלְתַתָּא. וְהָא אִתְּמַר, ה׳, הָא יְדִיעָא. א׳ הוּא יו"ד, שְׁלִימוּ דִּתְלַת אַתְוָון, דְּאִינּוּן בְּרֵישָׁא, דְּסְתִימָן בֵּי׳ וְהָא אוּקְמוּהָ, וְכֹלָּא חַד מִלָּה הוּא, שְׁלִימוּ דִּשְׁמָא קַדִּישָׁא, הוּא שְׁלִימוּ דְּעֵילָא וְתַתָּא. בְּגִין כָּךְ, לְזִמְנִין ה"א נָטִיל א׳, בְּזִמְנָא דְּהִיא מִתְעַטְּרָא בְּעִטְרוֹי.

66. Hei OF THE NAME YUD HEI VAV HEI IS overall perfection above and below. We have learned Hei is known TO BE BINAH. The Aleph IN THE FULLY SPELLED HEI is Yud Vav Dalet, SINCE ALEPH IS FORMED WITH VAV IN BETWEEN YUD ABOVE AND DALET BELOW. It completes the three letters at the top that are concealed in Yud OF YUD HEI VAV HEI, WHICH IS FULLY SPELLED AS YUD VAV DALET. This has already been explained and it is the same thing, since the wholeness of the Holy Name is wholeness above and below. This is why Hei takes Aleph FOR ITS FULL SPELLING when it is crowned.

67. תָּא חֲזֵי, כָּל אָת וְאָת דִּשְׁמָא קַדִּישָׁא, אִתְחֲזֵי בֵּיהּ שְׁלִימוּ דְּכָל שְׁמָא. יו"ד הָא אִתְּמַר שְׁלִימוּ דְּכֹלָּא. ה׳ שְׁלִימוּ דְּכֹלָּא וְאע"ג דְּלָאו אִיהוּ בְּאָלֶף, ה׳ בִּלְחוֹדוֹי, הָא אִתְּמַר בְּדִיּוּקְנָא דָּא ה׳. הוּא שְׁלִימוּתָא דְּכֹלָּא. ו׳ בֵּין בְּסִטְרָא דָּא, בֵּין בְּסִטְרָא אַחֲרָא, שְׁלִימוּ הוּא דְּכֹלָּא. ו"ה הוּא שְׁלִימוּ יַתִּיר, לְאַעְטְּרָא לְכֹלָּא הָא דְּכֹלָּא חַד, וְהָא אִתְּעֲרוּ בֵּיהּ חַבְרַיָּיא.

67. Come and see, each letter of the Holy Name reflects the perfection of the whole Name. Yud OF YUD HEI VAV HEI has already been explained to be overall perfection. Hei OF YUD HEI VAV HEI is overall perfection, even

when it is not fully spelled with Aleph, BUT with Hei only, since we learned that there is overall perfection in the shape of Hei, SINCE ITS CHARACTER IS FORMED WITH YUD, VAV AND DALET, WHICH IS OVERALL PERFECTION. Vav OF YUD HEI VAV HEI is overall perfection both ways, EITHER FULLY SPELLED OR AS IT IS. Vav Hei, NAMELY HEI OF YUD HEI VAV HEI CONNECTED WITH VAV OF YUD HEI VAV HEI is GREATER perfection that crowns all THE WORLDS, SINCE VAV HEI ARE THE SECRET OF ZEIR ANPIN AND MALCHUT WHEN UNITED. Thus, it is all one, AS EACH OF THE LETTERS OF YUD HEI VAV HEI INDICATES THE PERFECTION IN YUD HEI VAV HEI. The friends have already explained this.

68. ת״ח, וְהָיָה שִׁבְעַת יָמִים וְגוֹ'. יוּ״ד הֵ״א וָא״ו הֵ״א אִתְגְּלִיפוּ אַתְוָון וְהָיָה. ו' ה', הָא שִׁבְעַת יוֹמִין אִתְכְּלִילוּ בְּחַד. י' ה', שִׁבְעַת יוֹמִין. י' חַד, כְּלָלָא דְּכֹלָּא. ה' תְּלַת, הִיא וּתְרֵין בְּנִין. וּבְרָא חַד תְּרֵין אַבָהָן בֵּיהּ כְּלִילָן, הָא חֲמִשָּׁא. בְּרַתָּא נוּקְבָּא חַד, הָא שִׁיתָא, אִשְׁתְּמַע דְּה' עִלָּאָה כְּלָלָא דְּשִׁיתָא. י״ה הָא שִׁבְעָה. הַיְינוּ דִּכְתִּיב שִׁבְעַת יָמִים וְשִׁבְעַת יָמִים אַרְבָּעָה עָשָׂר יוֹם.

68. Come and see, "then it shall be (Heb. *vehayah*, Vav-Hei-Yud-Hei) seven days under its mother" (Vayikra 22:27). The letters of 'vehayah' were imprinted IN ACCORDANCE WITH THE SECRET OF Yud-Vav-Dalet, Hei-Aleph, Vav- Aleph-Vav, Hei-Aleph, SINCE 'VEYAHAH' IS SPELLED WITH THE SAME LETTERS AS YUD HEI VAV HEI. The seven days were included in Vav Hei together, SINCE VAV HEI, WHICH ARE ZEIR ANPIN AND MALCHUT, ARE THE SEVEN SFIROT, CHESED, GVURAH, TIFERET, NETZACH, HOD, YESOD AND MALCHUT. Yud-Hei are seven days, since Yud is one, including them all, SINCE IT INCLUDES ALL THE LETTERS OF THE NAME. Hei is three, it with its two children, SINCE IT INCLUDES WITHIN ITSELF DALET AND VAV, ZEIR ANPIN AND MALCHUT. And two fathers are included in the one son, NAMELY THE VAV WITHIN THE HEI. THESE ARE THE TWO COLUMNS, CHESED AND GVURAH. Thus they are five, BINAH, ZEIR ANPIN AND MALCHUT, CHESED AND GVURAH, AND MALCHUT WHICH IS INCLUDED WITHIN ZEIR ANPIN. VAV INCLUDES WITHIN IT a female daughter, WHICH IS MALCHUT, WHICH is one. Thus they are six. So the upper Hei OF YUD HEI VAV HEI includes the whole six, NAMELY BINAH, ZEIR ANPIN AND MALCHUT, CHESED AND GVURAH,

AND MALCHUT WHICH IS INCLUDED WITHIN ZEIR ANPIN. WITH Yud-Hei, THAT IS, TOGETHER WITH THE YUD, they are seven. THIS IS THE SECRET OF THE SEVEN SFIROT CALLED YUD-HEI. This is the meaning of the verse, "seven days and seven days, namely fourteen days" (I Melachim 8:65), WHICH IS THE INNER MEANING OF THE SEVEN DAYS IN VAV-HEI AND THE SEVEN DAYS IN YUD-HEI.

69. וְהָיָה שִׁבְעַת יָמִים תַּחַת אִמּוֹ. תַּחַת אִמּוֹ, אִתְעַטְּרוּ שִׁבְעַת יָמִים, דִּכְתִיב לְךָ יְיָ׳ הַגְּדוּלָה וְהַגְּבוּרָה וְגו׳. וְעַל דָּא שִׁבְעַת יָמִים לְתַתָּא, לִיקָרָא דְּאִימָא עִלָּאָה. תַּחַת אִמּוֹ לְתַתָּא. דִּכְתִיב עַד עֲקָרָה יָלְדָה שִׁבְעָה וְרַבַּת בָּנִים אֻמְלָלָה. עִקָּרָא דְּכָל בֵּיתָא, יָלְדָה שִׁבְעָה, אִלֵּין שִׁבְעַת יוֹמִין דְּחַג הַסּוּכּוֹת. וְרַבַּת בָּנִים אֻמְלָלָה, אִלֵּין קָרְבְּנִין דְּחַג, דְּנַחְתִּין בְּכָל יוֹמָא מִן מִנְיָינָא.

69. "then it shall be seven days under its mother," WHICH MEANS THAT under its mother, THAT IS, UNDER YUD-HEI, the seven days OF VAV HEI were adorned, as written, "Yours, Hashem, is the greatness and the power..." (I Divrei Hayamim 29:11), WHICH ARE THE SEVEN SFIROT, CHESED, GVURAH, TIFERET, NETZACH, HOD, YESOD AND MALCHUT OF MALE AND FEMALE. Therefore there are seven days below, IN MALE AND FEMALE, SINCE the glory of supernal Ima, THAT IS, AS A COUNTERPART TO THE SEVEN ASPECTS OF YUD HEI, THERE ARE "under its mother" below SEVEN DAYS. THAT IS the meaning of the words, "while the barren (Heb. *akarah*) has borne seven; and she that has many children has become wretched" (I Shmuel 2:5). THIS MEANS THAT the mainstay (Heb. *ikar*) of the whole house, WHICH IS BINAH, "has borne seven," the seven days of the festival of Sukkot, THE SECRET OF CHESED, GVURAH, TIFERET, NETZACH, HOD, YESOD AND MALCHUT, while "she that has many children has become wretched," which refers to the sacrifices on Sukkot, THE SEVENTY BULLOCKS SACRIFICED ON SUKKOT THAT ARE diminished in number every day. THEY CORRESPOND TO THE SEVENTY NATIONS, WHICH IS THE SECRET OF, "SHE THAT HAS MANY CHILDREN HAS BECOME WRETCHED."

70. ות״ח אִלֵּין סַלְּקִין לְעֵילָא לְעֵילָא, וְאִלֵּין נַחְתִּין לְתַתָּא לְתַתָּא, כד״א אִם תַּגְבִּיהַ כַּנֶּשֶׁר וְאִם בֵּין כֹּכָבִים שִׂים קִנֶּךָ מִשָּׁם אוֹרִידְךָ נְאֻם

וְיִי. וְיִשְׂרָאֵל סַלְקִין מִתַּתָּא לְעֵילָא, דִּכְתִיב וְהָיָה זַרְעֲךָ כַּעֲפַר הָאָרֶץ,
וּכְתִיב וְהִרְבֵּיתִי אֶת זַרְעֲךָ כְּכֹכְבֵי הַשָּׁמַיִם, וּלְבָתַר סַלְקִין עַל כֹּלָּא,
וּמִתְדַּבְּקָן בַּאֲתַר עִלָּאָה עַל כֹּלָּא, הֲדָא הוּא דִּכְתִיב, וְאַתֶּם הַדְּבֵקִים
בַּה' אֱלֹהֵיכֶם וְגוֹ'.

70. Come and see, these SEVEN DAYS OF SUKKOT, THE SECRET OF
CHESED, GVURAH, TIFERET, NETZACH, HOD, YESOD AND MALCHUT,
rise high up, SINCE THE ILLUMINATION OF CHOCHMAH WITHIN THEM
SHINES FROM BELOW UPWARDS, while those SEVENTY BULLOCKS FROM
WHICH THE SEVENTY NATIONS ARE NOURISHED descend lower and lower,
AS THE NATIONS DRAW THEM FROM ABOVE DOWN AS IS THEIR WONT,
THUS SINKING THEM DOWN. This was stated in, "Though you do soar aloft
like the eagle, and though you do set your nest among the stars, from there I
will bring you down, says Hashem" (Ovadyah 1:4). But Yisrael rise from
below upwards, as written, "and your seed shall be as the dust of the earth"
(Beresheet 28:14), and, "and I will multiply your seed as the stars of
heaven" (Beresheet 26:4). IN THIS WAY THEY RISE FROM THE DUST OF
THE EARTH TO THE STARS OF HEAVEN. They then rise above all and
cleave to the loftiest place, as written, "But you that did cleave of Hashem
your Elohim…" (Devarim 4:4).

17. "it and its young"

A Synopsis

The rabbis speak about the proscription against slaughtering the mother animal and its offspring on the same day. We learn that a fast is good for averting a bad dream as long as the fast is on the same day. An action below awakens a similar action above.

71. וְשׁוֹר אוֹ שֶׂה אוֹתוֹ וְאֶת בְּנוֹ. אָמַר רְבִּי יוֹסֵי, כְּתַרְגּוּמוֹ לָהּ וְלִבְרָהּ. דְּעִקָּרָא דְּאִימָא לְמִנְדַּע בְּרָהּ, וְאָזִיל בַּתְרָהּ, וְלָא אָזִיל בָּתַר אֲבוּהָ, וַאֲנַן לָא יַדְעֵינָן מַאן הוּא.

71. "And whether it be cow (lit. 'ox') or ewe, you shall not kill it (lit. 'him') and its young" (Vayikra 22:28). Rabbi Yosi said, THE MEANING follows its Aramaic translation, "her and her young," INSTEAD OF 'HE AND HIS YOUNG', for it is the mother's way to know her young, and HER YOUNG follows her and not the father, and we do not know who HIS FATHER is.

72. לֹא תִשְׁחֲטוּ בְּיוֹם אֶחָד. א״ר יְהוּדָה, מ״ט. אִי תֵּימָא מִשּׁוּם עַגְמַת נֶפֶשׁ דִּבְעִירָא, נֵיכוּס לְהַאי בְּבֵיתָא חַד, וּלְהַאי בְּבֵיתָא אָחֳרָא. אוֹ לְהַאי הַשְׁתָּא, וּלְהַאי לְבָתַר. א״ל, אִית מַאן דְּשָׁרֵי, וְלָאו הָכִי, אֶלָּא בְּיוֹם אֶחָד מַמָּשׁ.

72. "you shall not kill it and its young both in one day." Rabbi Yehuda asks for the reason. If you say it is because it is distressing to the animal, we can slaughter one in one house and the other in another, or at different times. He said to him, some permit that, but it is not so, but SCRIPTURE FORBIDS specifically "in one day."

73. ת״ח תָּנֵינָן יָפָה תַּעֲנִית לַחֲלוֹם, כְּאֵשׁ לַנְעוֹרֶת. וְעִקָּרָא דְּתַעֲנִיתָא בְּהַהוּא יוֹמָא מַמָּשׁ, וְלָאו בְּיוֹמָא אָחֳרָא. מַאי טַעֲמָא. בְּגִין דְּלֵית לָךְ יוֹם לְתַתָּא, דְּלָא שַׁלְטָא בֵּיהּ יוֹמָא אָחֳרָא עִלָּאָה. וְכַד אִיהוּ שָׁארֵי בְּתַעֲנִיתָא דְּחֶלְמָא, אוֹלִיפְנָא דְּהַהוּא יוֹמָא לָא אִתְעֲדֵי, עַד דְּאִתְבְּטַל הַהוּא גְּזֵרָה. וְאִי דָּחֵי לֵיהּ לְיוֹמָא אָחֳרָא, הָא שׁוּלְטָנָא דְּיוֹמָא אָחֳרָא

הוּא, וְלָא עָאל יוֹמָא בְּיוֹמָא אָחֳרָא דְּחַבְרֵיהּ. כְּהַאי גַּוְונָא, לֵית לָךְ יוֹם דְּלָא אִתְמַנָּא עֲלֵיהּ יוֹמָא עִלָּאָה לְעֵילָּא. וּבָעֵי בַּר נָשׁ לְאִסְתַּמְּרָא, דְּלָא יַעֲבִיד פְּגִימוּ בְּהַהוּא יוֹמָא, וְלָא יִתְפְּגִים קַמֵּי שְׁאָר יוֹמִין אָחֳרָנִין.

73. Come and see, We learned that a fast is good for averting a BAD dream as fire for consuming flax, THAT IS, FOR GETTING RID OF IT. The fast is valuable only on the same day and not in any other day. The reason is that every day below has another supernal day ruling over it. We learned that when one is fasting to avert a dream, the decree is annulled before the day is over. If he postpones it to another day, then it is under the jurisdiction of another day, and no day intermingles with its neighbor day. Similarly, there is a supernal day above appointed over every day, and one should be careful not to damage any day, so that it will not remain defective in relation to other days.

74. וְתָנֵינָן, בְּעוֹבָדָא דִּלְתַתָּא אִתְּעַר עוֹבָדָא דִּלְעֵילָּא. אִי בַּר נָשׁ עָבֵיד עוֹבָדָא לְתַתָּא כַּדְקָא יֵאוֹת, הָכִי אִתְּעַר חֵילָא כַּדְקָא יֵאוֹת לְעֵילָּא, עָבֵיד בַּר נָשׁ חֶסֶד בְּעָלְמָא, אִתְּעַר חֶסֶד לְעֵילָּא, וְשָׁארִי בְּהַהוּא יוֹמָא, וְאִתְעַטָּר בֵּיהּ בְּגִינֵיהּ. וְאִי אִתְדַּבַּר בַּר נָשׁ לְרַחֲמֵי לְתַתָּא, אִתְּעַר רַחֲמֵי עַל הַהוּא יוֹמָא, וְאִתְעַטָּר בְּרַחֲמֵי בְּגִינֵיהּ. וּכְדֵין הַהוּא יוֹמָא קָאִים עֲלֵיהּ לְמֶהֱוֵי אַפּוֹטְרוֹפָא בְּגִינֵיהּ, בְּשַׁעֲתָא דְּאִצְטְרִיךְ לֵיהּ.

74. We learned that an action below awakens an action above. If a man performs a worthy action below, the force above also awakens. If a man does kindness in the world, kindness awakens above and dwells on that day, which is crowned with it for his sake. If a man acts mercifully below, he arouses mercy upon that day, which is crowned with mercy for him. That day then stands to protect him in his time of need.

75. כְּגַוְונָא דָּא, בְּהִפּוּכָא דְּדָא. אִי עָבֵיד בַּר נָשׁ עוֹבָדָא דְּאַכְזְרִי, הָכִי אִתְּעַר בְּהַהוּא יוֹמָא, וּפָגִים לֵיהּ, וּלְבָתַר קָאִים עֲלֵיהּ לְאַכְזְרִי לְשֵׁיצָאָה לֵיהּ מֵעָלְמָא. בְּהַהִיא מִדָּה דְּבַר נָשׁ מוֹדֵד, בָּהּ מוֹדְדִין לֵיהּ.

75. The same applies for the opposite case. If a man acts cruelly, he rouses the same in that day and renders THAT DAY defective. Then THAT DAY stands over him to be cruel to him and destroy him. The measure with which man measures will be measured out to him.

76. תְּנָן, דְּיִשְׂרָאֵל אַכְזָרִיּוּת אִתְמְנַע מִנַּיְיהוּ, מִכָּל שְׁאָר עַמִּין, וְלָא יִתְחֲזוּן מִנֵּיה עוֹבָדָא בְּעָלְמָא. דְּהָא כַּמָּה מָארֵי דְּעַיְינִין קַיְימִין עָלֵיה דְּבַר נָשׁ בְּהַהוּא עוֹבָדָא, זַכָּאָה מַאן דְּאַחֲזֵי עוֹבָדָא דְּכַשְׁרָא לְתַתָּא, דְּהָא בְּעוֹבָדָא תַּלְיָיא מִלְתָא בְּכֹלָּא, לְאִתְּעָרָא מִלָּה אָחֳרָא.

76. We learned that cruelty was omitted from Yisrael MORE than the rest of the nations, and no act OF CRUELTY will appear among them, for many eyed ones stand over man TO DENOUNCE HIM for that action. Happy is he who displays a worthy act below, because the awakening of something CORRESPONDING ABOVE wholly depends on that act.

18. "there was corn in Egypt"

A Synopsis

Rabbi Shimon tells us that when there is to be a famine, God decrees it Himself rather than delegating the announcement to one of His messengers. A man who is full must not show it so as not to be seen rejecting the word of God who decreed the famine.

77. רִבִּי שִׁמְעוֹן פָּתַח, וַיַּרְא יַעֲקֹב כִּי יֶשׁ שֶׁבֶר בְּמִצְרָיִם, הַאי קְרָא רָזָא דְּחָכְמְתָא אִית בֵּיהּ, וְאִית לָן לְאִסְתַּכְּלָא בֵּיהּ, דְּלָאו סֵיפֵיהּ רֵישֵׁיהּ, וְלָאו רֵישֵׁיהּ סֵיפֵיהּ.

77. Rabbi Shimon opened with the verse, "Now when Jacob saw that there was corn in Egypt" (Beresheet 42:1). This verse contains the secret of wisdom and we have to examine it, because its beginning and end contradict each other. FOR IN THE BEGINNING IT SAYS, "NOW WHEN JACOB SAW THAT THERE WAS CORN IN EGYPT," AND AT THE END, "JACOB SAID TO HIS SONS, WHY DO YOU LOOK AT ONE ANOTHER." IF THERE IS CORN IN EGYPT, CANNOT THEY LOOK AT EACH OTHER? WHAT IS THE CONNECTION?

78. אֶלָּא ת״ח, בְּשַׁעֲתָא דְּקוּדְשָׁא בְּרִיךְ הוּא בָּעֵי לְמֵידָן עָלְמָא בְּכַפְנָא, לָא יָהִיב מִלָּה דָּא לִידָא דְּכָרוֹזָא, דְּהָא כָּל דִּינִין אַחֲרָנִין דְּעָלְמָא, כָּרוֹזָא כָּרִיז עָלוֹהִי עַד לָא יֵיתוּן לְעָלְמָא, וְדִינָא דָּא לָא אִתְיְיהִיב לְכָרוֹזָא, אֶלָּא קוּדְשָׁא בְּרִיךְ הוּא אַכְרִיז עָלֵיהּ וְקָארֵי. הה״ד, כִּי קָרָא יְיָ׳ לָרָעָב. מֵהַהִיא שַׁעֲתָא אִתְפַּקְּדָן עַל עָלְמָא מְמַנָּן אַחֲרָנִין, בִּפְקִידוּ דְּרָעָב.

78. HE ANSWERS, But come and see, when the Holy One, blessed be He, wanted to sentence the world to famine, He does not deliver this through a crier TO THE ANGELS. For a crier pronounces all other punishments in the world before they enter it, but this one OF FAMINE is not delivered to a crier, but the Holy One, blessed be He, announces it and cries. This is the meaning of, "for Hashem has called for a famine" (II Melachim 8:1). From that time other ministers are appointed over the world, due to the decree of famine.

79. וְאָסִיר לֵיהּ לְבַר נָשׁ דְּאִית לֵיהּ שַׂבְעָא, לְאַחֲזָאָה בְּגַרְמֵיהּ שַׂבְעָא, דְּהָא אַחֲזֵי פְּגִימוּ לְעֵילָא, וְאַכְחִישׁ מִלָּה דְּמַלְכָּא, וּכְבִיָכוֹל כְּאִלּוּ אַעְבַּר מְמָנָן דְּמַלְכָּא מֵאַתְרַיְיהוּ. וְעַ״ד אָמַר יַעֲקֹב לִבְנוֹי, לָמָה תִּתְרָאוּ, לָמָה תַעְבִידוּ פְּגִימוּ לְעֵילָא וּלְתַתָּא, וּלְאַכְחָשָׁא מִלָּה דְּמַלְכָּא, וְכָל אִינוּן מְמָנָן בִּכְרִיזוּ דִּילֵיהּ.

79. A satiated man must not show himself full, because he indicates a blemish above and rejects the word of the King, WHO DECREED FAMINE. It is as if he removed the King's ministers from their position. Hence Jacob said to his sons, "why do you look at (or: 'show') one another," WHICH MEANS, why do you create a defect above and below and deny the King's declaration, and all those appointed by the KING's crier.

80. אֲבָל הִנֵּה שָׁמַעְתִּי כִּי יֶשׁ שֶׁבֶר בְּמִצְרָיִם רְדוּ שָׁמָּה, וְתַמָּן אַחֲזִיאוּ גַרְמַיְיכוּ בְּשַׂבְעָא, וְלָא תַּכְחִישׁוּ פַּמַלְיָא דִּלְעֵילָא הָכָא. ות״ח, יַעֲקֹב כַּמָּה תְּבוּאָה הֲוַת לֵיהּ, וְלָא בָּעֵי לְשַׁבּוֹר אֶלָּא בְּתוֹךְ הַבָּאִים בְּגִין דְּלָא יִשְׁתְּכַח פְּגִימוּ בְּעוֹבָדָא דִּילֵיהּ.

80. But, "Behold, I have heard that there is corn in Egypt. Go down there" (Beresheet 42:2). There you may seem replete, but do not reject the celestial retinue here. Come and see, Jacob had much corn, but he did not want to eat it, except when they came back, so his action would not be considered defective, THAT IS, SO AS NOT TO SEEM FULL.

19. One should raise the right hand over the left

A Synopsis
We learn that the blowing of the Shofar indicates freedom for everyone.

81. תּוּ פָּתַח וְאָמַר, וַיִּשָׂא אַהֲרֹן אֶת יָדָיו אֶל הָעָם וַיְבָרֲכֵם. וְתָנֵינָן יָדוֹ כְּתִיב, דְּבָעֵי לְזַקְפָא יְמִינָא עַל שְׂמָאלָא. וַאֲמַאי. לְאַחֲזָאָה עוֹבָדָא לְתַתָּא, בְּגִין דְּיִתְּעַר עוֹבָדָא לְעֵילָא.

81. He opened again with, "And Aaron lifted up his hands towards the people, and blessed them" (Vayikra 9:22). We learned that 'hands' is spelled without Yud AND IS READ 'HAND', TO TEACH US that one should raise the right over the left. Why? To display an action below so that a CORRESPONDING act will be awakened above.

82. כְּתִיב וְהַעֲבַרְתָּ שׁוֹפָר תְּרוּעָה בַּחֹדֶשׁ הַשְּׁבִיעִי וְגוֹ', שׁוֹפָר תְּרוּעָה אֲמַאי. אֶלָּא שׁוֹפָר, דְּמִתְבַּר שַׁלְשְׁלָאִין, דְּמִתְבַּר שׁוּלְטָנוּתָא מִכָּל עַבְדִּין. וּבָעֵיָא לְאַחֲזָאָה שׁוֹפָר דְּאִיהוּ פָּשִׁיט, וְלָא כָּפִיף, לְאַחֲזָאָה חֵירוּ לְכֹלָּא, דְּהָא יוֹמָא גָּרִים. וּבְכֹלָּא בָּעֵי לְאַחֲזָאָה עוֹבָדָא, וְעַ״ד שׁוֹפָר, וְלָא קֶרֶן, בְּגִין לְאַחֲזָאָה מַאן הוּא אֲתַר דְּאִקְרֵי שׁוֹפָר.

82. It is written, "Then shall you cause the Shofar to sound on the tenth day of the seventh month" (Vayikra 25:9). HE ASKS, Why sound the Shofar, AND ANSWERS, The Shofar breaks the fetters OF THOSE IMPRISONED IN THE CHAINS OF ENSLAVEMENT, which breaks the power on all slaves. FOR 'SOUND' IS DERIVED FROM BREAKING. One should display a simple, THAT IS, STRAIGHT, Shofar, not curved, to indicate freedom to all, which that day has brought about. It behooves one always to demonstrate a deed BELOW TO AWAKEN A CORRESPONDING ONE ABOVE. Hence a Shofar is used rather than a horn, to indicate whence it comes, a place called Shofar, SINCE A SHOFAR IS THE SECRET OF BINAH AND A HORN THE SECRET OF MALCHUT.

83. זַכָּאִין אִינּוּן יִשְׂרָאֵל בְּעָלְמָא דֵּין וּבְעָלְמָא דְּאָתֵי, דְּאִינּוּן יַדְעִין

לְאִתְדַּבְּקָא בְּמַלְכָּא קַדִּישָׁא, וּלְאִתְעֲרָא חֵילָא דִּלְעֵילָא, וּלְאַמְשָׁכָא קְדוּשָׁה דְּמָארֵיהוֹן עֲלַיְיהוּ, בְּג״כ כְּתִיב אַשְׁרֶיךָ יִשְׂרָאֵל מִי כָמוֹךָ וְגוֹ'. וְאַתֶּם הַדְּבֵקִים בַּיְיָ' אֱלֹהֵיכֶם חַיִּים כֻּלְּכֶם הַיּוֹם.

83. Happy are Yisrael in this world and in the World to Come, for they know how to cleave to the Holy King and raise the power from above and draw their Master's holiness upon them. Hence it is written, "Happy are you, O Yisrael. Who is like to you" (Devarim 33:29), and, "But you that did cleave of Hashem your Elohim are alive every one of you this day" (Devarim 4:4).

A Synopsis
We are reminded of the two facets of the commandments in the Torah that are 'remember' and 'keep'. Remembering is 'doing', as the mention below causes the action above.

הַקְדָמַת רַעְיָא מְהֵימְנָא

84. וּשְׁמַרְתֶּם מִצְוֹתַי וַעֲשִׂיתֶם אוֹתָם וְגוֹ'. פִּקּוּדִין דְּמָארֵי עָלְמָא, הָא תָּנֵינָן. דִּכְתִיב וּשְׁמַרְתֶּם מִצְוֹתַי וַעֲשִׂיתֶם אוֹתָם. אִי נְטוּרֵי קָא בָּעֵינָן, עֲבִידָא לָמָּה. תּוּ, כָּל פִּקּוּדֵי אוֹרַיְיתָא אִינוּן בִּתְרֵין גַּוְונִין דְּאִינוּן חַד, זָכוֹר וְשָׁמוֹר, זָכוֹר לִדְכוּרָא, וְשָׁמוֹר לְנוּקְבָא. וְכֻלְּהוּ כְּלָלָא חֲדָא, אִי שָׁמוֹר לְנוּקְבָא אֲמַאי כְּתִיב וּשְׁמַרְתֶּם מִצְוֹתַי.

Introduction by Ra'aya Meheimna (the Faithful Shepherd)

84. "And you shall keep My commandments, and do them" (Vayikra 22:31). We have learned about the commandments of the Master of the universe, as written, "And you shall keep My commandments, and do them." HE ASKS, If they need keeping, WHEN THEN DOES THIS INCLUDE DOING AS WELL, and why DOES IT SAY, "and do them"? Furthermore, HE ASKS, all the commandments in the Torah have two Facets that are one, NAMELY 'remember' and 'keep'; 'remember' is for the Male, NAMELY ZEIR ANPIN, and 'keep' for the Female, MALCHUT, and they are all joined into one. HE ASKS, If 'keep' is for the Female, why is it written, "And you shall keep My commandments," WHICH INDICATES ALL THE PRECEPTS ARE ONLY OF THE ASPECT OF THE FEMALE, NAMELY 'KEEPING'?

85. אֶלָּא כֹּלָּא בְּהַאי קְרָא, וּשְׁמַרְתֶּם: דָּא שָׁמוֹר. וַעֲשִׂיתֶם: דָּא זָכוֹר, דְּכֹלָּא רָזָא חֲדָא. זְכִירָה דָּא אִיהִי עֲשִׂיָּה, דְּהָא מַאן דְּאַדְכַּר מִלָּה לְתַתָּא, אַתְקִין וְאִתְעֲבֵיד הַהוּא רָזָא דִּלְעֵילָא. פִּקּוּדֵי אוֹרַיְיתָא אִלֵּין אִינּוּן שִׁית מֵאָה וּתְלֵיסַר פִּקּוּדִין, דְּאִינּוּן כְּלָלָא דִּדְכַר וְנוּקְבָּא, וְכֹלָּא רָזָא חֲדָא.

85. HE ANSWERS, everything is within this verse. "And you shall keep" refers to 'keep', while, "and do them" refers to 'remember'. It all pertains to the same secret. Remembering is doing. Whoever mentions something below causes the doing of that secret above. There are 613 commandments in the Torah, which are the whole of Male and Female, NAMELY 'REMEMBER' AND 'KEEP', ZEIR ANPIN AND MALCHUT, all pertaining to the same secret.

20. "I will be hallowed" above and below in three grades

A Synopsis
Rabbi Shimon is talking here about the purpose of sanctity on all levels and grades above and below.

86. וְלֹא תְחַלְּלוּ אֶת שֵׁם קָדְשִׁי וְנִקְדַּשְׁתִּי בְּתוֹךְ בְּנֵי יִשְׂרָאֵל וְגוֹ'. פְּקוּדָא דָּא, לְקַדְּשָׁא לֵיהּ בְּכָל יוֹמָא, לְסַלְּקָא קְדוּשָׁתֵיהּ מִתַּתָּא לְעֵילָּא, כְּמָה דְּאִיהוּ קַדִּישָׁא לְעֵילָּא, עַד דְּסָלִיק קְדוּשָׁתֵיהּ לַאֲבָהָן וּבְנִין. וְרָזָא דָּא, וְנִקְדַּשְׁתִּי בְּתוֹךְ בְּנֵי יִשְׂרָאֵל, עֵילָּא וְתַתָּא. עֵילָּא בִּג' דַּרְגִּין. לְתַתָּא בִּג' דַּרְגִּין.

86. "Neither shall you profane My holy name; but I will be hallowed among the children of Yisrael..." (Vayikra 22:32). This commandment is to sanctify Him daily and raise His sanctity from below upwards, NAMELY, TO RAISE MAYIN NUKVIN FROM BELOW SO AS TO AWAKEN HIS SANCTITY ABOVE, just as He is holy above. Thus His sanctity will rise to the fathers, WHO ARE CHESED, GVURAH AND TIFERET OF ZEIR ANPIN, and the children, NETZACH, HOD AND YESOD OF ZEIR ANPIN, CALLED THE CHILDREN OF YISRAEL. This is the secret of, "but I will be hallowed among the children of Yisrael" above THE CHEST and below THE CHEST. FOR "I WILL BE HALLOWED" REFERS TO CHESED, GVURAH AND TIFERET OF ZEIR ANPIN, CALLED FATHERS, WHO ARE ABOVE THE CHEST, AND "AMONG THE CHILDREN OF YISRAEL" REFERS TO NETZACH, HOD AND YESOD OF ZEIR ANPIN, CALLED THE CHILDREN OF YISRAEL, WHO ARE BELOW THE CHEST OF ZEIR ANPIN. Above in three grades, CHESED, GVURAH AND TIFERET OF ZEIR ANPIN; below in three grades, NETZACH, HOD AND YESOD OF ZEIR ANPIN.

87. קְדוּשָׁה הָא, אוֹקִימְנָא בְּכַמָּה דּוּכְתֵּי, אֲבָל כְּמָה דְּאִית קְדוּשָׁה לְעֵילָּא עַל כֹּלָּא, הָכִי אִית קְדוּשָׁה בְּאֶמְצָעִיתָא, קְדוּשָׁה לְתַתָּא. וְכֹלָּא בְּרָזָא דִּלְתַתָּא, קְדוּשָׁה דִּלְעֵילָּא לְעֵילָּא, בְּרָזָא חֲדָא. קְדוּשָׁה בְּאֶמְצָעִיתָא וּלְתַתָּא תְּלַת דַּרְגִּין דְּאִינּוּן חַד.

87. We have explained ABOUT THE PURPOSE OF sanctity in several places. But as there is sanctity in the highest, WHICH IS SUPERNAL ABA AND IMA,

WHO ARE CALLED HOLINESS, so there is sanctity in the middle, WHICH IS ZEIR ANPIN, and sanctity below IN MALCHUT. Everything follows the lower, WHICH MEANS THE ESSENCE IS TO DRAW SANCTITY DOWN TO MALCHUT. The highest sanctity, ABA AND IMA, pertains to one secret, WHICH MEANS THEY ARE HOLINESS THEMSELVES AND ALL THAT PERTAINS TO THEM IS HOLY - the sanctity in the middle and below, ZEIR ANPIN AND MALCHUT, IS DIVIDED into three grades that are one. THIS MEANS SANCTITY IS DRAWN THROUGH THREE COLUMNS. SANCTITY IS IN THE RIGHT COLUMN, WHENCE IT IS DRAWN TO ALL COLUMNS – CHESED, GVURAH AND TIFERET IN ZEIR ANPIN, AND NETZACH, HOD AND YESOD IN MALCHUT.

88. קָדוֹש, אִיהוּ סְטַר עִלָּאָה, דְּאִשְׁתְּכַח רֵאשִׁיתָא לְכָל דַּרְגִּין. וְאע"ג דְּאִיהוּ סְטַר טְמִירָא, וְאִקְרֵי קֹדֶשׁ. מִתַּמָּן אִתְפְּשָׁט פְּשִׁיטוּ, דְּנָהִיר בְּחַד שְׁבִילָא דְּקִיקָא טְמִירָא, גּוֹ אֶמְצָעִיתָא. כֵּיוָן דְּאִתְנְהִיר גּוֹ אֶמְצָעִיתָא, כְּדֵין אִתְרְשִׁים חַד ו', דְּנָהִיר גּוֹ הַאי קֹדֶשׁ, וְאִקְרֵי קָדוֹש. מֵהַאי נְהִירוּ אִתְפְּשָׁט פְּשִׁיטוּ, לְתַתָּא, סוֹפָא דְּכָל דַּרְגִּין. כֵּיוָן דְּאִתְנְהִיר בְּסוֹפָא, כְּדֵין אִתְרְשִׁים בִּנְהִירוּ, חַד ה', וְאִקְרֵי קְדוּשָׁה, וְהָא אוֹקִימְנָא.

88. HE EXPLAINS HIS WORDS: holy is the highest aspect found at the beginning of all grades, NAMELY ABA AND IMA, WHICH ARE CHOCHMAH, THE TOP OF THE GRADES. IT IS THE SECRET OF YUD OF YUD HEI VAV HEI, AND THOUGH IT IS A HIDDEN ASPECT THAT IS CALLED 'HOLINESS', WHICH IS NOT DRAWN DOWN, AS YUD HAS NO LEG, THAT IS, EXPANSION, NEVERTHELESS an expansion emerges, shining through a thin hidden path, YESOD OF ABA AND IMA to the middle GRADE, WHICH IS ZEIR ANPIN. Once it shone upon the middle GRADE, a certain Vav is imprinted WITH THE BOUNTY OF HOLINESS, which shines into the holiness IT RECEIVED, and it is considered holy WITH VAV. From this light an expansion flows down TO MALCHUT, which is the last of the grades, NAMELY THE LAST HEI OF YUD HEI VAV HEI. Once it shone upon the end, a certain Hei OF MALCHUT is imprinted within the light, which is called sanctity WITH AN ADDITIONAL HEI. This has already been explained. THUS, WHEN THE BOUNTY OF SANCTITY ORIGINATES IN SUPERNAL ABA AND IMA, IT IS CALLED HOLINESS (HEB. *KODESH*). WHEN IT FLOWS TO ZEIR ANPIN, A VAV IS ADDED AND IT IS CALLED HOLY (HEB. *KADOSH*) WITH VAV. WHEN IT

FLOWS TO MALCHUT A HEI IS ADDED AND IT IS CALLED SANCTITY (HEB. *KEDUSHAH*) WITH HEI.

89. וּמַה דְּאִקְרֵי קָדוֹשׁ קָדוֹשׁ קָדוֹשׁ, דְּהָא קֹדֶשׁ מִבָּעֵי לֵיהּ, רָזָא דְּרֵאשִׁיתָא דְּכֹלָּא, הוֹאִיל וּמִתַּמָּן אִשְׁתְּכַח, וְאִי הָכִי אֲמַאי אִקְרֵי לְעֵילָּא קָדוֹשׁ, דְּהָא תַּמָּן ו' לָא אִשְׁתְּכַח.

89. That which is called 'Holy, holy, holy' should have said 'holiness' AT FIRST, because the secret OF THE FIRST 'HOLY' MEANS THE BEGINNING of everything, NAMELY SUPERNAL ABA AND IMA, WHICH ARE CALLED 'HOLINESS', since HOLINESS comes from there, AS MENTIONED IN THE PREVIOUS PARAGRAPH THAT HOLINESS IS THE ROOT OF SANCTITY. In that case, why is it called holy above, if there is no Vav there, WHICH INDICATES EXPANSION, BUT YUD THAT DOES NOT EXPAND?

90. אֶלָּא רָזָא הָכִי הוּא וַדַּאי, וְיִשְׂרָאֵל מְקַדְּשֵׁי לְתַתָּא, כְּגַוְונָא דְּמַלְאֲכֵי עִלָּאֵי לְעֵילָּא, דִּכְתִיב בְּהוֹ, וְקָרָא זֶה אֶל זֶה וְאָמַר קָדוֹשׁ. וְכֵיוָן דְּיִשְׂרָאֵל קָא מְקַדְּשֵׁי, סַלְקֵי מִתַּתָּא לְעֵילָּא יְקָרָא עִלָּאָה, עַד דְּאִסְתְּלַק ו' רָזָא דִּשְׁמַיִם עִלָּאִין לְעֵילָּא. כֵּיוָן דְּאִינּוּן שָׁמַיִם אִסְתְּלָקוּ לְעֵילָּא, נָהִיר הַהוּא קֹדֶשׁ בְּהוֹ, וּכְדֵין אִקְרֵי לְעֵילָּא קָדוֹשׁ. וּלְבָתַר נָהִיר הַהוּא נְהִירוּ עִלָּאָה, עַל כּוּרְסַיָּיא דְּאִיהוּ שָׁמַיִם. וְאִינּוּן שָׁמַיִם תַּיְיבִין לְדוּכְתַּיְיהוּ, וּמִתְיַישְּׁבוּ בֵּיהּ בְּהַהוּא נְהִירוּ, וּכְדֵין אִקְרֵי קָדוֹשׁ. לְבָתַר נָחִית הַהוּא נְהִירוּ, עַד דְּנָטִיל כֹּלָּא חַד צַדִּיק עִלָּאָה, דַּרְגָּא יַקִּירָא לְקַדְּשָׁא כֹּלָּא לְתַתָּא. כֵּיוָן דְּאִיהוּ נָטִיל כֹּלָּא, כְּדֵין אִקְרֵי קָדוֹשׁ. וְדָא אִיהוּ רָזָא דְּכֹלָּא.

90. HE ANSWERS, The meaning is as follows: assuredly Yisrael sanctify below, as the celestial angels do above, of whom it is written, "And one cried to another, and said, Holy" (Yeshayah 6:3). When Yisrael sanctify, they raise from below upwards the supernal glory, ZEIR ANPIN, until Vav, the secret of the highest heavens, rises up TO SUPERNAL ABA AND IMA. When the heavens rise up, that holiness shines on them, WHICH IS SUPERNAL ABA AND IMA. Then ZEIR ANPIN THAT ROSE up is called holy.

THUS THE FIRST 'HOLY' REFERS TO ZEIR ANPIN, OR SPECIFICALLY, TO ZEIR ANPIN THAT ROSE TO SUPERNAL ABA AND IMA. Later that supernal light shines FROM SUPERNAL ABA AND IMA to the throne that is CALLED heavens, which is the heavens, NAMELY ZEIR ANPIN, that returned to their place, THAT IS, AFTER THE HEAVENS, ZEIR ANPIN, DESCENDED FROM SUPERNAL ABA AND IMA WITH THE SANCTITY THEY RECEIVED AND CAME TO THEIR PLACE BELOW, WHICH TURNED INTO A THRONE TO ABA AND IMA. They are settled in that light, and it is then called holy, NAMELY THE SECOND 'HOLY'. The light then descends WITHIN ZEIR ANPIN until a certain celestial Righteous receives all, who is a precious grade that sanctifies everything below. THIS IS YESOD OF ZEIR ANPIN THAT POURS BOUNTY DOWN TO MALCHUT. Once it receives everything it is called holy. This is the overall meaning. THUS, THE FIRST 'HOLY' IS ZEIR ANPIN THAT ABIDES IN THE PLACE OF ABA AND IMA AND RECEIVES FROM THEM. THE SECOND 'HOLY' IS ALSO ZEIR ANPIN, AFTER DESCENDING FROM ABA AND IMA INTO HIS PLACE. THE THIRD 'HOLY' IS YESOD OF ZEIR ANPIN THAT POURS UPON MALCHUT.

91. וּמָאן דְּשַׁוֵּי רְעוּתֵיהּ בְּהַאי, שַׁפִּיר קָא עָבֵיד. וּמָאן דְּשַׁוֵּי רְעוּתֵיהּ, בִּתְלַת דַּרְגִּין דַּאֲבָהָן בִּכְלָלָא חֲדָא, לְיַחֲדָא לוֹן גּוֹ קְדוּשְׁתָּא דָּא, אִי לָא יָכִיל לְשַׁוָּואָה רְעוּתֵיהּ יַתִּיר, שַׁפִּיר קָא עָבֵיד. וְכֹלָּא לְנַחְתָּא מִגּוֹ קְדוּשְׁתָּא דִּלְעֵילָּא לְתַתָּא, לְקַדְּשָׁא כָּל חַד גַּרְמֵיהּ בְּהַאי קְדוּשָׁה, וּלְנַטְרָא לֵיהּ, לְמִפְרַשׁ פְּרִישׁוּ דִּקְדוּשְׁתָּא עַל גַּבֵּיהּ. וְרָזָא דָּא, וְנִקְדַּשְׁתִּי בְּתוֹךְ בְּנֵי יִשְׂרָאֵל בְּקַדְמֵיתָא, וּלְבָתַר אֲנִי יְיָ' מְקַדִּשְׁכֶם.

91. Whoever is mindful TO MEDITATE ON THE THREE TIMES 'HOLY', AS SAID ABOVE, ON ABA AND IMA, ZEIR ANPIN AND YESOD, does well. Whoever is mindful TO MEDITATE ON THEM, in the three grades of the fathers, THAT IS, THE THREE COLUMNS OF ZEIR ANPIN, as one whole, to join them through this sanctification, even if he cannot be mindful of more than that, he does well. The purpose of all that is to bring down from the highest sanctity down TO MALCHUT, so that each person OF YISRAEL will RECEIVE FROM IT AND hallow himself with that sanctity and keep it, and spread the expansion of sanctity on himself. This is the secret of, "but I will be hallowed among the children of Yisrael" (Vayikra 22:32), THAT IS, THE CHILDREN OF YISRAEL WILL RAISE MAYIN NUKVIN TO AWAKEN THE

THREE TYPES OF SANCTITY ABOVE. Then, "I am Hashem who makes you holy" (Ibid.), AS YISRAEL RECEIVE SUPERNAL SANCTITY.

92. בְּאָן אֲתַר יְקַדֵּשׁ בַּר נָשׁ גַּרְמֵיהּ גּוֹ קְדוּשָׁתָא דָא, לְאַכְלָלָא גַּרְמֵיהּ בָּהּ. כַּד מָטֵי בַּר נָשׁ, לִשְׁמָא קַדִּישָׁא יְיָ' צְבָאוֹת. וְרָזָא דָא אֲנִי יְיָ' מְקַדִּשְׁכֶם. דָּא אַשְׁכַּחְנָא בְּרָזָא דְסִפְרֵי קַדְמָאֵי. וַאֲנַן לָא עַבְדִּינָן הָכִי, אֶלָּא לְבָתַר יְיָ' צְבָאוֹת בִּלְחוֹדוֹי. וּלְבָתַר כַּד מָטֵי בַּר נָשׁ לְמַלֵּא כָל הָאָרֶץ כְּבוֹדוֹ, כְּדֵין יִכְלֹל גַּרְמֵיהּ בְּהַהוּא קְדוּשָׁה, לְאִתְקַדְּשָׁא לְתַתָּא, גּוֹ הַהוּא כָּבוֹד דִּלְתַתָּא, וְרָזָא דָא וְנִקְדַּשׁ בִּכְבוֹדִי. וּלְבָתַר יַעֲבִיד אוֹרַח פְּרָט, לְאִתְקַדְּשָׁא כֹּלָּא. כְּמָה דַאֲנַן עַבְדִּין לְעֻמָּתָם דְּמַלְאֲכֵי עִלָּאֵי, דְּאָמְרֵי בָּרוּךְ כְּבוֹד יְיָ' מִמְּקוֹמוֹ, דָּא כָּבוֹד עִלָּאָה. וּלְבָתַר יִמְלֹךְ יְיָ' לְעוֹלָם וְכוּ'. דָּא כָּבוֹד דִּלְתַתָּא.

92. When should one hallow himself with this sanctity to include himself within it? When one reaches the holy name, Hashem Tzva'ot MENTIONED AFTER THE THIRD 'HOLY', THE SECRET OF NETZACH AND HOD. There lies the secret of, "I am Hashem who makes you holy." I found this as a secret in ancient books. But we do not do it this way; rather, after THE THREE TIMES 'HOLY', WE SAY "Hashem Tzva'ot" only, THAT IS, WE STILL DO NOT INCLUDE OURSELVES THERE. Then, when one reaches "the whole earth is full of His glory" (Yeshayah 6:3), WHEN SANCTITY IS DRAWN TO MALCHUT, one should include himself in that sanctity to be hallowed below in that lower glory, MALCHUT. This is the secret meaning of, "and it shall be sanctified by My glory" (Shemot 29:43). Then shall he do it specifically. AT FIRST, HE SHOULD INCLUDE HIMSELF IN MALCHUT, THE SECRET OF THE LOWER GLORY IN THE VERSE, "THE WHOLE EARTH IS FULL OF HIS GLORY," WHICH INCLUDES THE WHOLE EARTH AND ALL THE NATIONS. THEN HE SHOULD DRAW SANCTITY SPECIFICALLY, TO YISRAEL ALONE. In this way everything will be sanctified, AND SANCTITY WILL EXTEND FROM YISRAEL TO THE WHOLE WORLD. Whatever we do corresponds to the supernal angels, who say, 'Blessed is the glory of Hashem from His place', which is the supernal glory, ZEIR ANPIN. Then we say, 'May Hashem reign for ever...', which is the lower glory, MALCHUT. WE ALSO INCLUDE OURSELVES IN "THE WHOLE EARTH IS FULL OF HIS GLORY," WHICH IS THE LOWER GLORY, RATHER THAN IN HASHEM TZVA'OT, WHICH IS

NETZACH AND HOD OF ZEIR ANPIN, AND OF THE ASPECT OF THE HIGHER GLORY, AS THE ANCIENT SAGES DID.

93. וּבְסִפְרָא דְּרַב יֵיסָא סָבָא, קָדוֹשׁ קָדוֹשׁ קָדוֹשׁ וְכוּ', דָּא אִיהִי קְדוּשָׁה לְאִתְקַדְּשָׁא תּוֹרָה שֶׁבִּכְתָב בְּכְלָלָא חֲדָא. וּלְבָתַר לְעָמָתָם בָּרוּךְ כְּבוֹד יְיָ', אִלֵּין נְבִיאִים. וּלְבָתַר יִמְלוֹךְ יְיָ' לְעוֹלָם. רָזָא דָּא, אֲנָן צְרִיכִין בִּקְדוּשָׁתָא דָּא, לְאִשְׁתַּכְּחָא תַּמָּן קְדוּשָׁה וּבְרָכָה וּמַלְכוּת, לְאִשְׁתַּכְּחָא כֹּלָּא כַּחֲדָא. קְדוּשָׁה, כְּמָה דְּאִתְּמַר קָדוֹשׁ. בְּרָכָה, בָּרוּךְ כְּבוֹד יְיָ' מִמְּקוֹמוֹ. מַלְכוּת, יִמְלוֹךְ יְיָ' לְעוֹלָם. וְעַל דָּא אֲנָן צְרִיכִין לְאַשְׁלְמָא, וְעַל דָּא יְכַוֵּון בַּר נָשׁ, וִישַׁוֵּי רְעוּתֵיהּ בְּכָל יוֹמָא.

עד כאן רעיא מהימנא

93. In his book, Rav Yesa Saba SAYS, 'Holy, holy, holy' refers to the sanctity with which the Written Torah, ZEIR ANPIN, is hallowed, into one, THAT IS, IN HIS THREE COLUMNS, CHESED, GVURAH AND TIFERET. Then, facing them they give praise saying: 'Blessed is His glory of Hashem', referring to the prophets, NAMELY NETZACH AND HOD OF ZEIR ANPIN. 'May Hashem reign for ever' follows, WHICH IS MALCHUT. The meaning of this is that we need sanctity, a blessing and Malchut to be present in this sanctification, so they will all be together. 'Sanctity' is as it says; 'Holy...' blessing MEANS 'Blessed is the glory of Hashem from His place'; Malchut IS IN 'May Hashem reign for ever'. We should therefore bring everything into completion. For that reason, one should meditate and be mindful of it every day.

End of Ra'aya Meheimna (the Faithful Shepherd)

21. "The feasts of Hashem"

A Synopsis

Rabbi Yitzchak says that when God saw the evil that would prevail in the world He hid the light for the righteous in the World to Come. He tells us about the unity that only exists when night and day are united, when light and darkness are united. Since the Congregation of Yisrael is in exile it is not presently considered to be 'one', and only when it goes out of exile can it be united with God.

94. דַּבֵּר אֶל בְּנֵי יִשְׂרָאֵל וְאָמַרְתָּ אֲלֵיהֶם מוֹעֲדֵי יְיָ' אֲשֶׁר תִּקְרְאוּ אוֹתָם מִקְרָאֵי קֹדֶשׁ אֵלֶּה הֵם מוֹעֲדָי. רִבִּי יִצְחָק פָּתַח, וַיִּקְרָא אֱלֹהִים לָאוֹר יוֹם וְגוֹ'. תָּנֵינָן, אוֹר דַּהֲוָה בְּקַדְמֵיתָא, הֲוָה נָהִיר מִסְּיָיפֵי עָלְמָא לְסַיְיפֵי עָלְמָא, כַּד אִסְתָּכַּל קוּדְשָׁא בְּרִיךְ הוּא לְחַיָּיבִין דִּזְמִינִין לְמֵיקַם בְּעָלְמָא, גָּנִיז לֵיהּ לְצַדִּיקַיָּיא לְעָלְמָא דְּאָתֵי, הֲדָא הוּא דִכְתִיב וְיִמָּנַע מֵרְשָׁעִים אוֹרָם. וּכְתִיב אוֹר זָרוּעַ לַצַּדִּיק.

94. "Speak to the children of Yisrael, and say to them, The feasts of Hashem, which you shall proclaim to be holy gatherings, these are My feasts" (Vayikra 23:2). Rabbi Yitzchak opened with the verse, "And Elohim called the light day" (Beresheet 1:5). We learned that the light that was present in the beginning used to shine from one end of the world to the other. When the Holy One, blessed be He, saw the evil that will live in the world, He hid it for the righteous for the World to Come. This is the meaning of, "And from the wicked their light is withheld" (Iyov 38:15), and, "Light is sown for the righteous" (Tehilim 97:11).

95. ת"ח, וַיִּקְרָא אֱלֹהִים לָאוֹר יוֹם וְלַחֹשֶׁךְ קָרָא לָיְלָה, הָא תָּנֵינָן, יְהִי אוֹר, אוֹר דִּכְבָר הֲוָה. וְהָכָא, אִי תֵּימָא אוֹר דְּאִיהוּ יוֹם בִּלְחוֹדוֹי, הֲדַר וְאָמַר וְלַחֹשֶׁךְ קָרָא לָיְלָה. אִי תֵּימָא כָּל חַד בִּלְחוֹדוֹי, הֲדַר וְאָמַר וַיְהִי עֶרֶב וַיְהִי בֹקֶר יוֹם אֶחָד. דְּלַיְלָה לֵית בְּלָא יוֹם, וְלֵית יוֹם בְּלָא לָיְלָה, וְלָא אִקְרֵי אֶחָד, אֶלָּא בְּזִוּוּגָא חַד, וְקוּדְשָׁא בְּרִיךְ הוּא וּכְנֶסֶת יִשְׂרָאֵל אִקְרֵי אֶחָד, וְדָא בְּלָא דָא לָא אִקְרֵי אֶחָד.

95. Come and see, "And Elohim called the light day, and the darkness He called night." Yet we learned that "Let there be light" (Beresheet 1:3) REFERS TO light that already existed. Here, if you say THAT light MEANS day only, THAT IS, ZEIR ANPIN ALONE, it continues, "and the darkness He called night," WHICH IS MALCHUT THAT IS CALLED NIGHT. ZEIR ANPIN IS CALLED LIGHT ONLY WHEN WITH MALCHUT THAT IS CALLED NIGHT. You may argue that they are separate, NOT UNITED WITH EACH OTHER, so it continues, "And there was evening, and there was morning, one day" (Ibid. 5). THIS MEANS ZEIR ANPIN IS NOT WHOLE SAVE WHEN UNITED WITH MALCHUT, AND MALCHUT IS NOT WHOLE SAVE WHEN UNITED WITH ZEIR ANPIN. They are called one only when they are joined as one. The Holy One, blessed be He, and the Congregation of Yisrael, WHO ARE ZEIR ANPIN AND MALCHUT, are called one, but without each other they are not called one.

96. תָּא חֲזֵי, בְּגִין דִּכְנֶסֶת יִשְׂרָאֵל הַשְׁתָּא בְּגָלוּתָא, כִּבְיָכוֹל לָא אִקְרֵי אֶחָד. וְאֵימָתַי אִקְרֵי אֶחָד. בְּשַׁעֲתָא דְּיִפְּקוּן יִשְׂרָאֵל מִן גָּלוּתָא, וּכְנֶסֶת יִשְׂרָאֵל אַהֲדָרַת לְאַתְרָהָא, לְאִזְדַּוְוּגָא בֵּיהּ בְּקוּדְשָׁא בְּרִיךְ הוּא, הה״ד בַּיּוֹם הַהוּא יִהְיֶה יְיָ׳ אֶחָד וּשְׁמוֹ אֶחָד. וְדָא בְּלָא דָא לָא אִקְרֵי אֶחָד.

96. Come and see, since the Congregation of Yisrael is now in exile, she is not considered one, so to speak. When is she called one? When Yisrael will go out of exile and the Congregation of Yisrael will return to her place to unite with the Holy One, blessed be He. This is the meaning of, "on that day Hashem shall be one, and His Name One" (Zecharyah 14:9). Without each other they are not called one.

97. ת״ח, מוֹעֲדֵי יְיָ׳ אֲשֶׁר תִּקְרְאוּ וְגו׳. לְזַמְּנָא כֹּלָּא לַאֲתַר חַד, וּלְאִשְׁתַּכְּחָא כֹּלָּא בִּשְׁלִימוּ, בְּרָזָא דְּאֶחָד. וּלְמֶהֱוֵי יִשְׂרָאֵל לְתַתָּא גּוֹי אֶחָד בָּאָרֶץ. תֵּינַח קוּדְשָׁא בְּרִיךְ הוּא בִּכְנֶסֶת יִשְׂרָאֵל דְּאִקְרֵי אֶחָד, יִשְׂרָאֵל לְתַתָּא דְּאִינּוּן זְמִינִין כְּגַוְוֹנָא דִּלְעֵילָּא, בְּמָה יִקְרוּן אֶחָד.

97. Come and see, "The feasts of Hashem, which you shall proclaim (or: 'summon')," NAMELY, to summon everything into one place. FOR THE FEASTS OF HASHEM ARE THE SECRET OF CHESED, GVURAH AND

TIFERET OF ZEIR ANPIN THAT NEED TO BE SUMMONED SO THEY WILL
BESTOW UPON ONE PLACE, MALCHUT. Thus everything will be complete
by the secret of one. FOR WHEN CHESED, GVURAH AND TIFERET OF
ZEIR ANPIN ARE UNITED WITH MALCHUT, THEY ARE CALLED ONE, and
when Yisrael will be below "one nation in the earth" (II Shmuel 7:23). HE
ASKS, It is true that the Holy One, blessed be He UNITED with the
Congregation of Yisrael, MALCHUT, is called one, yet Yisrael below, when
established as the likeness of above, how shall they be called one, LIKE
ZEIR ANPIN AND MALCHUT ABOVE?

98. אֶלָּא, בִּירוּשְׁלֵם דִּלְתַתָּא, יִקְרוּן יִשְׂרָאֵל אֶחָד. מְנָא לָן. דִּכְתִּיב גּוֹי
אֶחָד בָּאָרֶץ. וַדַּאי, בָּאָרֶץ הֵם גּוֹי אֶחָד, עִמָּהּ אִקְרוּן אֶחָד, וְלָא אִינּוּן
בִּלְחוֹדַיְיהוּ. דְּהָא וּמִי כְעַמְּךָ יִשְׂרָאֵל גּוֹי אֶחָד סַגִּי לֵיהּ, אֲבָל לָא אִקְרוּן
אֶחָד, אֶלָּא בָּאָרֶץ, בְּזִוּוּגָא דְּהַאי אֶרֶץ כְּגַוְונָא דִּלְעֵילָּא. וּבְגִין כַּךְ, כֹּלָּא
קַשִׁיר דָּא בְּדָא בְּזִוּוּגָא חֲדָא, זַכָּא חוּלְקֵיהוֹן דְּיִשְׂרָאֵל. שֵׁשֶׁת יָמִים
תֵּעָשֶׂה מְלָאכָה אִתְּמַר, וְהָא אוּקְמוּהָ.

98. AND HE ANSWERS, In terrestrial Jerusalem, Yisrael are called one,
WHEN THEY DWELL IN IT. Whence do we know that? From the words, "one
nation in the earth." Assuredly in the earth, BOTH IN THE LAND OF YISRAEL
AND IN JERUSALEM, they are one nation. With it they are called one, but
not on their own. "And what one nation…is like Your people, like Yisrael"
(Ibid.) should have sufficed; WHY THEN IS IT WRITTEN, "AND WHAT ONE
NATION IN THE EARTH IS LIKE YOUR PEOPLE, LIKE YISRAEL"? This is
because they are called one only in the earth, united with this land as the
likeness of above, FOR ZEIR ANPIN IS CALLED ONE ONLY WHEN UNITED
WITH MALCHUT CALLED EARTH. For that reason everything is
interconnected into one union BOTH ABOVE AND BELOW. Happy is the lot
of Yisrael. "Six days shall work be done" (Vayikra 23:3). This has already
been learned and explained.

99. רִבִּי יוֹסֵי וְרִבִּי חִיָּיא אַזְלֵי בְּאָרְחָא וְכוּ'. עַד הוֹשִׁיעָה יְמִינְךָ וַעֲנֵנִי.
אָ"ל אַתְּ חָמֵי וַאֲנָא חֲמֵינָא מִפּוּמֵיהּ דְּרִבִּי שִׁמְעוֹן שְׁמַעְנָא מִלָּה
וּבְכֵינָא. אָ"ל מַאי הַאי.

99. Rabbi Yosi and Rabbi Chiya... THIS ARTICLE WAS PRINTED IN VAERA, 198-206.

22. Holiness and those summoned from holiness

A Synopsis

Rabbi Yitzchak speaks about seeking the face of Hashem. This leads into a discussion of the festivals and holidays, and of the psalms and poetry of David, who spoke the words of Yisrael to Zeir Anpin. The celebrations draw holiness from above. Rabbi Yosi talks about the six days of work; Rabbi Chiya says that the six days are not considered holiness because it is permitted to work on them. Rabbi Yehuda tells us about the great holiness of Shabbat; on that day even the wicked in Gehenom are given respite from their punishments. He says that the day of Shabbat is a delight.

100. אֵלֶּה מוֹעֲדֵי יְיָ׳ מִקְרָאֵי קֹדֶשׁ אֲשֶׁר תִּקְרְאוּ אוֹתָם בְּמוֹעֲדָם. רִבִּי יִצְחָק פָּתַח, לְךָ אָמַר לִבִּי בַּקְּשׁוּ פָנָי אֶת פָּנֶיךָ יְיָ׳ אֲבַקֵּשׁ. הַאי קְרָא אוּקְמוּהָ חַבְרַיָּיא בְּכַמָּה אֲתַר, אֲבָל הַאי קְרָא הָכִי אִתְּמַר, לְךָ אָמַר לִבִּי, דָּוִד מַלְכָּא אָמַר דָּא בְּגִין כְּנֶסֶת יִשְׂרָאֵל, לָקֳבֵל מַלְכָּא קַדִּישָׁא. וּמַאי אָמַר. לְךָ אָמַר לִבִּי, בְּגִינָךְ אָמַר לִבִּי לִבְנֵי עָלְמָא, וְאַזְהַר לוֹן לִבִּי. דְּאִיהוּ אָחִיד בֵּיהּ, דְּדָא בְּגִין מַלְכָּא עִלָּאָה אָמַר. בַּקְּשׁוּ פָנָי, אֵלֵּין עִטְרֵי מַלְכָּא, דְּאִיהוּ אָחִיד בְּהוּ, וְאִינוּן בֵּיהּ. אִינוּן שְׁמֵיהּ, וְאִיהוּ וּשְׁמֵיהּ, מִלָּה חֲדָא הוּא. בְּגִין כָּךְ אָמַר דָּוִד אֶת פָּנֶיךָ יְיָ׳ אֲבַקֵּשׁ, כד״א, דִּרְשׁוּ יְיָ׳ וְעֻזּוֹ בַּקְּשׁוּ פָנָיו תָּמִיד.

100. "These are the feasts of Hashem, holy gatherings, which you shall proclaim in their seasons" (Vayikra 23:4). Rabbi Yitzchak opened with, "Of You my heart has said, Seek My face, Your face, Hashem, I seek" (Tehilim 27:8). This verse has been explained in several places, yet we learned THE MEANING OF this verse this way: David said, "Of You my heart has said" for the Congregation of Yisrael, MALCHUT, before the Holy King, ZEIR ANPIN. What did it say, NAMELY, "Of You my heart has said" – for Your sake, ZEIR ANPIN, my heart said to the people in the world and my heart, which is attached TO MALCHUT, admonished them. It said, "Seek My face" for the supernal King, THAT IS, SEEK THE FACE OF ZEIR ANPIN, which refers to the King's crowns, MOCHIN OF ZEIR ANPIN, to which He is attached, and they to Him. They are His name, FOR THEY ARE ALSO THE

MOCHIN OF MALCHUT CALLED HIS NAME, and He, ZEIR ANPIN, and His name, MALCHUT, are the same. Hence David said, "Your face, Hashem, I seek," as, "Seek Hashem, and His strength. Seek His face continually" (Tehilim 105:4).

101. ת״ח, יָאוּת הֲוָה דָּוִד מַלְכָּא לְמֵימַר שִׁירָתָא בְּגִין כְּנֶסֶת יִשְׂרָאֵל, יַתִּיר מִכָּל בְּנֵי עָלְמָא, וּלְמֵימָר מִלֵּי דִכְנֶסֶת יִשְׂרָאֵל לְמַלְכָּא, בְּגִין דְּאִיהוּ אָחִיד בָּהּ.

101. Come and see, it is proper for David to recite poetry for the Congregation of Yisrael, MALCHUT, more than anyone in the world, and to convey the words of the Congregation of Yisrael to the King, ZEIR ANPIN, because he is attached to her, SINCE DAVID IS A CHARIOT TO MALCHUT.

102. ד״א לְךָ אָמַר לִבִּי בַּקְּשׁוּ פָנָי. בְּגִינָךְ אָמַר לִבִּי לִבְנֵי עָלְמָא, בַּקְּשׁוּ פָנַי אִלֵּין זִמְנַיָּא וְחַגַּיָּיא דְּכֻלְּהוּ זַמִּין לְהוֹן לַאֲתַר דְּאִקְרֵי קֹדֶשׁ, בְּגִין לְעַטְּרָא לוֹן, כָּל חַד וְחַד בְּיוֹמֵיהּ, כָּל חַד וְחַד בְּזִמְנֵיהּ, וְיִשְׁאֲבוּן כֻּלְּהוּ מֵהַהוּא עֲמִיקָא דַעֲמִיקְתָּא, דְּנַחֲלִין וּמַבּוּעִין נָפְקִין מִנֵּיהּ, בְּגִין כָּךְ כְּתִיב מִקְרָאֵי קֹדֶשׁ, זְמִינִין אִינּוּן לְהַהוּא אֲתַר דְּאִקְרֵי קֹדֶשׁ, לְאִתְעַטְּרָא בֵּיהּ, וּלְאִשְׁתַּאֲבָא בֵּיהּ, בְּגִין דְּיִתְקַדְּשׁוּן כֻּלְּהוֹן כַּחֲדָא, וְיִשְׁתְּכַח בְּהוּ חֶדְוָותָא.

102. Another explanation for "Of You my heart has said, Seek my face." IT MEANS for Your sake my heart has said to people in the world, "seek my face." This refers to the festivals and holidays, WHICH ARE CHESED, GVURAH AND TIFERET OF ZEIR ANPIN, WHICH ARE THE FIRST THREE SFIROT OF MALCHUT AND HER FACE. "YOUR FACE, HASHEM, I SEEK" MEANS DAVID summoned all OF CHESED, GVURAH AND TIFERET TO RISE to the place called holiness, WHICH IS SUPERNAL ABA AND IMA, CALLED THE FACE OF YUD HEI VAV HEI, ZEIR ANPIN. FOR ZEIR ANPIN RECEIVES THE MOCHIN OF ABA AND IMA, WHICH IS HOLINESS, WHEN HE ASCENDS TO THEM, in order to crown each one OF CHESED, GVURAH AND TIFERET WITH MOCHIN OF ABA AND IMA, each in its own day, each in its season, so they will all draw from the deepest of the deep, from which all springs and streams emerge, NAMELY FROM SUPERNAL ABA AND IMA. Hence it is written, "holy (lit. 'holiness') gatherings"; GATHERINGS MEAN SUMMONED, for they are summoned TO RISE to that place called holiness, WHICH IS SUPERNAL ABA AND IMA, to be adorned by it and draw from it, so that all will be sanctified together and joy will abound in them.

103. רַבִּי אַבָּא אָמַר, מִקְרָאֵי קֹדֶשׁ: זְמִינִין דְּקֹדֶשׁ. וְכַד מֵהַאי זְמִינִין, זְמִינִין מִן נַחֲלָא דְּנַגִּיד וְנָפִיק. לְמַלְכָּא דְּזַמִּין בְּנֵי נָשָׁא לִסְעוּדָתֵיהּ, אַעְטַר קַמַיְיהוּ מִכָּל זִינֵי מֵיכְלָא דְּעָלְמָא, אֲפָתַח לְהוּ גַּרְבֵי חַמְרָא, שַׁפִּיר בְּרֵיחָא, שַׁפִּיר לְמִשְׁתְּיָא. דְּהָכִי אִתְחֲזֵי, מַאן דִּמְזַמִּין לְמֵיכְלָא וּלְמִשְׁתְּיָא זַמִּין. כָּךְ מִקְרָאֵי קֹדֶשׁ, כֵּיוָן דְּאִינּוּן זְמִינִין לִסְעוּדָתָא דְּמַלְכָּא, זְמִינִין אִינּוּן לְחַמְרָא טַב וְשַׁפִּיר דְּמִנְטְרָא. וְעַל דָּא מִקְרָאֵי קֹדֶשׁ כְּתִיב.

103. Rabbi Aba said, "holiness gatherings" MEANS summoning of holiness, WHICH IS SUPERNAL ABA AND IMA, WHICH ARE CHOCHMAH. When they are summoned TO THAT PLACE CALLED HOLINESS, it is done from the flowing river, BINAH. THIS IS LIKENED to a king, who summoned people to his feast, and bestowed on them different victuals, and opened before them skins of scented wine that is good to drink. For so it ought to be, that whoever summons, does so to eat and drink. So "summoned from holiness" means that since they are invited to the king's feast, they are also invited to the goodly and worthy preserved wine. Hence it is written, "summoned from holiness, which you shall proclaim in their seasons."

104. אֲשֶׁר תִּקְרְאוּ אוֹתָם בְּמוֹעֲדָם, כְּתִיב וְאַנְשֵׁי קֹדֶשׁ תִּהְיוּן לִי, יִשְׂרָאֵל לְתַתָּא אִקְרוּן אַנְשֵׁי קֹדֶשׁ. כֵּיוָן דִּזְמִינִין אִינּוּן מִקְדֵּשׁ דִּלְעֵילָא אַתּוּן אַנְשֵׁי קֹדֶשׁ לְתַתָּא זְמִינָא לְהוּ, כְּדֵין אַתְקִינוּ סְעוּדָתָא, וְחַדּוּ, דְּהָא לְכוּ אִתְחֲזֵי, בְּגִין דְּאַתּוּן אִתְקְרוּן אַנְשֵׁי קֹדֶשׁ, וִיהוֹן כֻּלְּהוּ זְמִינִין בְּכָל סִטְרִין דְּקֹדֶשׁ לְעֵילָא וְתַתָּא.

104. "which you shall proclaim in their seasons." It is written, "And you shall be holy men (lit. 'men of holiness') to Me" (Shemot 22:30). Yisrael below are called men of holiness, because they are invited from holiness

above, THAT IS, THEY ARE INVITED TO RECEIVE FROM THE PLENTY OF ABA AND IMA CALLED HOLINESS THAT IS RECEIVED IN MALCHUT. THE MEANING OF THE VERSE, "WHICH YOU SHALL PROCLAIM IN THEIR SEASONS" IS you men of holiness below invite those FESTIVALS, WHICH ARE CHESED, GVURAH AND TIFERET, IN THEIR SEASON. You should then prepare a meal and rejoice, because it befits you, since you are called men of holiness. Everyone will be invited from all aspects from holiness above, ABA AND IMA, and from below, FROM MALCHUT, BY YISRAEL WHO RECEIVE FROM MALCHUT.

105. ד"א אֵלֶּה מוֹעֲדֵי יְיָ. מַהוּ מוֹעֲדֵי יְיָ. ר"ש אָמַר, מְיְיָ' אִינּוּן. דִּבֵיהּ אִתְקְשָׁרוּ מְתַתָּא לְעֵילָא, וּמֵעֵילָא לְתַתָּא, כָּלְהוּ בֵּיהּ מִתְקַשְּׁרָן, וּמִתְעַטְּרָן כָּלְהוּ, לְאִתְקַשְּׁרָא קִשּׁוּרָא חַד בְּקִשּׁוּרָא דְּמַלְכָּא. מַאי טַעֲמָא. כְּמָה דְּמַלְכָּא יָרִית לְאַבָּא וּלְאִימָּא, וְאָחִיד בְּהַהוּא קֹדֶשׁ, וְאִתְעַטָּר בְּהוּ. כָּךְ כָּל אִינּוּן דַּאֲחִידָן בֵּיהּ בְּמַלְכָּא, בַּעְיָין לְאִזְדַּמְּנָא בְּהַהוּא אֲתַר עִלָּאָה דְּאִקְרֵי קֹדֶשׁ, בְּגִין דְּיִתְאַחֲדוּ כֻּלְּהוּ כַּחֲדָא. וְעַל דָּא מוֹעֲדֵי יְיָ' אִקְרֵי וּלְבָתַר מִקְרָאֵי קֹדֶשׁ, דְּהָא בְּהוּ אִתְעַטָּר בְּמַלְכָּא.

105. Another explanation of "These are the feasts of Hashem." What are the feasts of Hashem? Rabbi Shimon said, THE FESTIVALS ARE from Hashem, NAMELY FROM ZEIR ANPIN, to whom there is attachment both from below upwards and from above downwards. All are attached to Him, and all are adorned so as to be attached together to the King's bond. The reason is that just as the King, ZEIR ANPIN, inherits Aba and Ima, is united with that holiness, and is crowned with them, so are all those who are attached to the King – NAMELY, THE FESTIVALS THAT ARE ATTACHED TO CHESED, GVURAH AND TIFERET OF ZEIR ANPIN, have to reach that supernal place called holiness, ABA AND IMA, so that all will be joined as one. Therefore they are called "the feasts of Hashem," and then "holy gatherings (lit. 'summoned from holiness')," through which they can be crowned by the King.

106. אֲשֶׁר תִּקְרְאוּ אוֹתָם בְּמוֹעֲדָם, תְּרֵין חוּלָקִין אִית לְיִשְׂרָאֵל בְּהוּ אִי מִסִּטְרָא דְּמַלְכָּא, חוּלָקָא עִלָּאָה אִית לְיִשְׂרָאֵל בֵּיהּ, דִּכְתִיב וְאַתֶּם הַדְּבֵקִים בַּיְיָ' אֱלֹהֵיכֶם וְגוֹ', כִּי חֵלֶק יְיָ' עַמּוֹ. וְאִי מִסִּטְרָא עִלָּאָה דִּקֹדֶשׁ,

חוּלָקָא עִלָּאָה אִית לְיִשְׂרָאֵל בֵּיהּ, דִּכְתִיב וְאַנְשֵׁי קֹדֶשׁ תִּהְיוּן לִי, וּכְתִיב קֹדֶשׁ יִשְׂרָאֵל לַיְיָ'. וְעַ"ד לְכוּ אִתְחֲזֵי לְזַמְּנָא לְהוּ, וּלְתַקְּנָא קַמַּיְיהוּ חֶדְוָותָא וּסְעוּדָתָא וּלְמֶחֱדֵי בְּהוּ.

106. "which you shall proclaim": Yisrael have two portions. From the side of the King, ZEIR ANPIN, FROM THE ILLUMINATION OF CHOCHMAH IN HIM, they have a supernal share in Him, as written, "But you that did cleave to Hashem your Elohim are alive every one of you this day" (Devarim 4:4), and, "For Hashem's portion is His people" (Devarim 32:9). From the supernal side of holiness, Yisrael have a supernal share in it, as written, "And you shall be men of holiness to Me," and, "Yisrael is holiness to Hashem" (Yirmeyah 2:3). HASHEM therefore SAID, 'You are worthy of summoning them, THE HOLIDAYS, and arrange before them joy and a feast and rejoice in them'.

107. וּמַאן דִּמְזַמֵּן לְאָחֳרָא, בָּעֵי לְאַחֲזָאָה לֵיהּ חֵידוּ, וְאַנְפִּין נְהִירִין לְעַטְּרָא אוֹרְחֵיהּ דְּהַהוּא אוּשְׁפִּיזָא. לְמַלְכָּא דְּזַמִּין אוּשְׁפִּיזָא יַקִּירָא, אָמַר לִבְנֵי הֵיכָלֵיהּ, כָּל שְׁאַר יוֹמִין הֲוֵיתוּן כָּל חַד וְחַד בְּבֵיתֵיהּ, דָּא עָבֵיד עֲבִידְתֵּיהּ, וְדָא אָזִיל בִּסְחוֹרָתֵיהּ, וְדָא אָזִיל בְּחַקְלֵיהּ. בַּר הַהוּא יוֹמָא דִּילִי, דְּכֻלְּכוֹן מִתְעַתְּדֵי בְּחֶדְוָותָא דִּילִי, הַשָּׁתָּא זְמִינִית אוּשְׁפִּיזָא עִלָּאָה וְיַקִּירָא, לָא בָּעֵינָא דְּתִשְׁתַּדְּלוּן בַּעֲבִידְתָּא, וְלָא בִּסְחוֹרְתָּא, וְלָא בְּמִדְבְּרֵי אֶלָּא כֻּלְּכוּ אִזְדַּמְּנוּ, כְּגַוְונָא דְּהַהוּא יוֹמָא דִּילִי, וְאַתְקִינוּ גַּרְמַיְיכוּ לְקַבְּלָא לְהַהוּא אוּשְׁפִּיזָא, בְּאַנְפִּין נְהִירִין, בְּחֶדְוָותָא בְּתוּשְׁבְּחָתָּא. אַתְקִינוּ לֵיהּ סְעוּדָתָא יַקִּירָא, בְּגִין דְּיֶהֱא זְמִינֵי דִּילִי בְּכָל סִטְרִין.

107. Whoever invites someone to him should display joy and welcoming countenance, and decorate the path of the guest, LIKE a king who invited a precious guest. He told his household people, every other day you were each at home, one doing his craft, one traveling with his merchandise and another walking to his field. This day of mine is an exception; you are all invited to my joy, for I have just invited a lofty precious guest. I do not want you to do your work, handle merchandise, or be in your field. But all of you come TO REJOICE as in my day. Prepare yourself to receive that guest with welcoming countenance, joy and singing, and prepare for him a delectable feast, so he will be invited by me in every respect, THAT IS, SO HE WILL ENJOY ON MY SIDE AND ON YOURS.

108. כָּךְ אָמַר קוּדְשָׁא בְּרִיךְ הוּא לְיִשְׂרָאֵל, בְּנֵי, כָּל שְׁאָר יוֹמִין אַתּוּן מִשְׁתַּדְלֵי בַּעֲבִידְתָּא בִּסְחוֹרָתָא, בַּר הַהוּא יוֹמָא דִילִי. הַשְׁתָּא אוּשְׁפִּיזָא עִלָּאָה וִיקִירָא זְמִינִית, אַתּוּן קַבִּילוּ לֵיהּ, בְּאַנְפִּין נְהִירִין, זַמִּינוּ לֵיהּ, אַתְקִינוּ לֵיהּ סְעוּדָתֵי עִלָּאֵי, פָּתוֹרֵי מְסַדְּרָן, כְּגַוְונָא דְּהַהוּא יוֹמָא דִילִי. בְּג"כ תִּקְרְאוּ אוֹתָם בְּמוֹעֲדָם.

108. So did the Holy One, blessed be He, say to Yisrael, 'My children, every other day you are dealing with your work and with merchandise, except in My day. I have invited now a high and precious guest. Invite him, prepare for him superior meals, and set tables, as befits this day of Mine'. Therefore SCRIPTURE SAYS, "which you shall proclaim (or: 'call') in their seasons."

109. ת"ח, בְּשַׁעֲתָא דְּיִשְׂרָאֵל לְתַתָּא חַדָּאן בְּהָנֵי מוֹעֲדַיָּא, וּמְשַׁבְּחִין שְׁבָחָא לְקוּדְשָׁא בְּרִיךְ הוּא, מְסַדְּרִין פָּתוֹרֵי, מַתְקְנֵי גַּרְמַיְיהוּ בְּמָאנֵי יְקָר, מַלְאֲכֵי עִלָּאֵי אַמְרִין, מַה טִיבָן דְּיִשְׂרָאֵל בְּכָךְ. קוּדְשָׁא בְּרִיךְ הוּא אָמַר, אוּשְׁפִּיזָא עִלָּאָה אִית לוֹן יוֹמָא דָא. אַמְרֵי וְלָאו דִילָךְ הוּא, מֵהַהוּא אֲתַר דְּאִקְרֵי קֹדֶשׁ. אָמַר לוֹן וְכִי יִשְׂרָאֵל לָאו קֹדֶשׁ נִינְהוּ, וְאִקְרוּן קֹדֶשׁ, לוֹן אִתְחֲזֵי לְזַמְּנָא אוּשְׁפִּיזָא דִילִי, חַד מִסִּטְרָא דִילִי, דְּהָא אִינּוּן דְּבֵקִים בִּי. וְחַד מִסִּטְרָא דְּקֹדֶשׁ, דִּכְתִיב קֹדֶשׁ יִשְׂרָאֵל לַיְיָ', הוֹאִיל וְיִשְׂרָאֵל אִקְרוּן קֹדֶשׁ, אוּשְׁפִּיזָא דִּלְהוֹן הוּא וַדַּאי, בְּגִין דְּזַמִּינוּ דְּהַאי אוּשְׁפִּיזָא מִקְדֶּשׁ הוּא, דִּכְתִיב מִקְרָאֵי קֹדֶשׁ. פָּתְחוּ כֻּלְּהוּ וְאָמְרוּ, אַשְׁרֵי הָעָם שֶׁכָּכָה לוֹ.

109. Come and see, when Yisrael below rejoice in those festivals, praise the Holy One, blessed be He, set tables and ready themselves with glorious garments, the supernal angels say, Why do Yisrael do this? The Holy One, blessed be He, said, 'I have a precious guest, this day'. THE ANGELS say, Is

it not Yours, from the place called holiness? He said to them, 'Are not Yisrael holiness? They are called holiness. They are worthy of inviting My guest, once from My aspect, since they are devoted to Me, and once from the side of holiness, as written, "Yisrael is holiness to Hashem"'. Since Yisrael are called holiness, then it is their guest surely, because the guest is summoned from holiness, as written, "holy gatherings (lit. 'summoned from holiness')." They all started saying, "Happy is that people, that is in such a case" (Tehilim 144:15).

110. תְּלָתָא אִינּוּן זְמִינִין מִקֹּדֶשׁ, וְלָא יוֹתֵר. חַג הַמַּצוֹת. וְחַג הַשָּׁבוּעוֹת. וְחַג הַסּוּכּוֹת. אָ"ל רִבִּי אַבָּא, וְכִי שַׁבָּת לָאו מִקֹּדֶשׁ הוּא זְמִין. אָ"ל לָאו, בִּתְרֵי סִטְרִין, חַד, דְּהוּא וַדַּאי קֹדֶשׁ אִקְרֵי, דִּכְתִיב וּשְׁמַרְתֶּם אֶת הַשַּׁבָּת כִּי קֹדֶשׁ הִיא לָכֶם. וְחַד, דְּשַׁבָּת לָאו זְמִין הוּא, דְּהָא יְרוּתָא דִּילֵיהּ הוּא וַדַּאי. יְרוּתָא דְּקֹדֶשׁ הוּא יָרִית, וְלָאו זְמִינִי. וְעַל דָּא כֻּלְּהוֹן זְמִינִין בַּקֹּדֶשׁ, וּמִתְקַשְּׁרָן בְּשַׁבָּת, וּמִתְעַטְּרָן בֵּיהּ. בְּהַאי, יוֹמָא שְׁבִיעָאָה אִתְעַטַּר בֵּיהּ, וְע"ד שַׁבָּת לָאו זְמִין הוּא.

110. Three and no more are summoned from holiness. THESE ARE the feast of unleavened bread, the holiday of Shavuot and the holiday of Sukkot. Rabbi Aba said to him, Is not Shabbat called from holiness? He said to him, No, for two reasons. The one is that it is surely considered to be holiness NO LESS THAN THE FESTIVALS, AS WRITTEN, "You shall keep the Shabbat therefore; for it is holiness to you" (Shemot 31:14). The other is that Shabbat is not called FROM HOLINESS, because SHABBAT receives the inheritance OF HOLINESS and is not called. Hence all are called from holiness, are attached to Shabbat and adorn themselves with it. Through this HOLINESS, the seventh day is adorned. Shabbat therefore is not called FROM HOLINESS.

111. לִבְרָא דְּעָאל לְבֵיתָא דַּאֲבוֹי וְאִמֵּיהּ, וְאָכַל וְשָׁתֵי, בְּשַׁעֲתָא דְּהוּא בָּעֵי. לְמַלְכָּא דַּהֲוָה לֵיהּ בְּרָא יְחִידָאי, חֲבִיבָא דְּנַפְשֵׁיהּ, יָהַב לֵיהּ שׁוּשְׁבִינָא לְנַטְרָא לֵיהּ, וּלְאִתְחַבְּרָא בְּהוּ. אָמַר מַלְכָּא, יָאוּת הוּא לְזַמְּנָא לְאִלֵּין שׁוּשְׁבִינִין דִּבְרִי, וּלְאַחֲזָאָה יְקָרָא וַחֲבִיבוּתָא דִּילִי בְּהוּ, זַמִּין לוֹן לְהָנֵי שׁוּשְׁבִינִין. בְּרָא לָא אִתְחֲזֵי לְזַמְּנָא, אֶלָּא לְמֵיעַל

וּלְמֵיכַל וּלְמִשְׁתֵּי בְּבֵיתָא דַּאֲבוֹי, בְּשַׁעְתָא דְּאִיהוּ בָּעֵי. הֲדָא הוּא
דִּכְתִּיב, מִי כָמוֹכָה בָּאֵלִים יְיָ' מִי כָּמוֹךָ נֶאְדָּר בַּקֹּדֶשׁ, נֶאְדָּר בַּקֹּדֶשׁ
וַדַּאי, כְּבָר דְּאִתְתָקַן בַּאֲבוֹי, נֶאְדָּר בַּקֹּדֶשׁ, וְלָאו זַמִּין מִקֹּדֶשׁ.

111. SHABBAT RESEMBLES the son who comes to the house of his father and mother and eats and drinks whenever he wants to. ABA AND IMA DO NOT HAVE TO INVITE HIM. THIS IS LIKENED to a king who had an only son, beloved by him. He gave him a companion who would protect him and keep him company. The king said, It will be well to invite my son's friends and show them my love and honor, so he invited those friends. But there is no need to invite my son, but he comes in to eat and drink in his father's house whenever he wants to. This is the meaning of, "Who is like You, Hashem, among the Elim. Who is like You, glorious in holiness" (Shemot 15:11). "Glorious in holiness" surely MEANS as a son helped by his fathers, THAT IS, ZEIR ANPIN ALREADY ROSE TO ABA AND IMA AND BECAME LIKE HIM, AS IN SHABBAT. HE IS THEN "GLORIOUS IN HOLINESS" instead of summoned from holiness.

112. שֵׁשֶׁת יָמִים תֵּעָשֶׂה מְלָאכָה, שֵׁשֶׁת יָמִים מַאי עֲבִידְתַּיְיהוּ. א"ר
יוֹסֵי, כְּתִיב כִּי שֵׁשֶׁת יָמִים עָשָׂה יְיָ' אֶת הַשָּׁמַיִם וְאֶת הָאָרֶץ, וְלָא כְּתִיב
בְּשֵׁשֶׁת. וְהָא אוּקְמוּהָ, וְכָל יוֹמָא וְיוֹמָא עָבֵיד עֲבִידְתֵּיהּ, וְאִקְרוֹן יוֹמֵי
מְלָאכָה.

112. "Six days shall work be done" (Vayikra 23:3). He asks: What are these six days? Rabbi Yosi said, It is written, "for six days Hashem made heaven and earth" (Shemot 20:11), and not 'in six DAYS'. We have explained that each day did its work, FOR WHICH REASON they are called days of work. THEY ARE THE SIX SUPERNAL DAYS, CHESED, GVURAH, TIFERET, NETZACH, HOD AND YESOD, FROM WHICH ALL THE WORKS OF CREATION WERE PERFORMED, EACH ONE IN ITS OWN DAY, CHESED IN THE FIRST, GVURAH IN THE SECOND, ETC.

113. א"ר יִצְחָק אִי הָכִי אֲמַאי אִקְרוֹן שֵׁשֶׁת יְמֵי חוֹל, אֲמַאי חוֹל. א"ר
יוֹסֵי, הַשְׁתָּא אִתְנְהִיג עָלְמָא עַל יְדָא דִּשְׁלוּחַיְיהוּ, בְּג"כ יוֹמֵי חוֹל אִקְרוֹן.

113. Rabbi Yitzchak said, If it is so, AND THEY ARE THE SECRET OF THE SIX SFIROT, CHESED, GVURAH, TIFERET, NETZACH, HOD AND YESOD, why are they called weekdays (lit. 'secular days'), IF THEY ARE THE HOLY SFIROT OF ZEIR ANPIN? Rabbi Yosi said, The world is led by their messengers, NAMELY, BY THE SIX SFIROT, CHESED, GVURAH, TIFERET, NETZACH, HOD AND YESOD OF METATRON THE ANGEL. Hence they are called secular, BECAUSE METATRON IS SECULAR.

114. ר' חִיָּיא אָמַר, בְּגִין דְּשָׁרֵי לְמֶעְבַּד בְּהוֹן עֲבִידְתָּא, וּבְגִ"ד לָא אִקְרוּן קֹדֶשׁ. וּמַאן דְּלָאו אִקְרוּן קֹדֶשׁ, חוֹל אִקְרוּן. וְעַל דָּא אַתְקִינוּ חַבְרַיָּיא בְּהַבְדָּלָה, בֵּין קֹדֶשׁ לְחוֹל. מַאי הַבְדָּלָה הָכָא. אֶלָּא קֹדֶשׁ מִלָּה בְּגַרְמֵיהּ הוּא, וּשְׁאַרָא מִנֵּיהּ אַתְיָין. וְעַל דָּא אִלֵּין לְעוֹבָדָא, וְאִלֵּין לְנַטְרָא. וְאֵימָתַי אִשְׁתְּכַח נְטִירוּ בְּהוּ. כַּד זְמִינִין מִקְּדֶשׁ.

114. Rabbi Chiya said, Since it is permitted to work on them, they are not considered holiness, EVEN THOUGH THEY ARE THE SECRET OF CHESED, GVURAH, TIFERET, NETZACH, HOD AND YESOD OF ZEIR ANPIN. For those who are not considered holiness are considered secular. The friends have composed the Havdalah (lit. 'separation') between the holy and the secular. HE ASKS, What does Havdalah have to do with it, WERE THEY EVER INTERMINGLED? AND HE ANSWERS, Holiness is on its own, NOT MIXED WITH ANYTHING, BEING OF SUPERNAL ABA AND IMA, whence all the rest OF THE GRADES come. Therefore, THE SEPARATION IS since those SECULAR DAYS are meant for work while these DAYS OF HOLINESS are for keeping. When are THE WEEKDAYS kept? When they are summoned from holiness, RECEIVING FROM ABA AND IMA DURING THE HOLIDAYS.

115. א"ר יְהוּדָה, חֶדְוָותָא וּנְטִירוּתָא דְּיוֹמָא דְּשַׁבַּתָּא עַל כֹּלָּא הוּא, וּבְגִין דְּהָא יוֹמָא אִתְעֲטַר בְּאַבָּא וְאִמָּא, וְאִתּוֹסַף קְדוּשָׁה עַל קְדוּשָׁתֵיהּ, מַה דְּלָא אִשְׁתְּכַח הָכִי בִּשְׁאָר יוֹמֵי, דְּהָא הוּא קֹדֶשׁ, וְאִתְעֲטַר בְּקֹדֶשׁ, וְאוֹסִיף קְדוּשָׁה עַל קְדוּשָׁתֵיהּ. בְּגִין כַּךְ הַאי יוֹמָא חֶדְוָותָא דְּעֶלָּאֵי וְתַתָּאֵי, כֹּלָּא חַדָּאן בֵּיהּ. מַלֵּי בִּרְכָאן בְּכֻלְּהוּ עָלְמִין. כֻּלְּהוּ מִנֵּיהּ אִתְקָנוּ, בְּהַאי יוֹמָא נַיְיחָא דְּעֶלָּאֵי וְתַתָּאֵי. בְּהַאי יוֹמָא נַיְיחָא דְּחַיָּיבַיָּא דְּגֵיהִנָּם.

115. Rabbi Yehuda said, Joy and keeping on the day of Shabbat is HIGH above anything, and since this day is adorned with Aba and Ima, AS ZEIR ANPIN AND MALCHUT RISE AND CLOTHE SUPERNAL ABA AND IMA, more holiness is added to their own holiness, unlike on other days. For ZEIR ANPIN is holiness, and is crowned with holiness BY CLOTHING HOLINESS, SUPERNAL ABA AND IMA, and adds holiness to its holiness. For that reason that day is the joy of the upper and lower beings. Everybody rejoices in it, and since it fills all worlds with blessings all the worlds are improved BY IT on this day, repose for higher and lower beings. On this day there is respite for the wicked in Gehenom.

116. לְמַלְכָּא דְּעָבֵד הִלּוּלָא לִבְרֵיהּ יְחִידָאי, אַעְטַר לֵיהּ בְּעִטְרָא עִלָּאָה, מַנֵּי לֵיהּ מַלְכָּא עַל כֹּלָּא. בְּהַאי יוֹמָא חֶדְוָותָא לְכֹלָּא. חַד סַנְטִירָא דְּאִתְפְּקַד עַל דִּינָא דִּבְנֵי נָשָׁא, הֲווֹ בִּידֵיהּ גּוּבְרִין דְּבַעְיָין קְטוּלָא, גּוּבְרִין דְּבַעְיָין לְאַלְקָאָה. בְּגִין יְקָרָא דְּהַאי יוֹמָא דְּחֶדְוָותָא דְּמַלְכָּא, שָׁבִיק דִּינוֹי, וְנָטַר לְחֶדְוָותָא דְּמַלְכָּא.

116. THIS IS LIKENED to a king who had a feast for his only son, and put a superior crown on him. The king put him in command over everything. That day there is joy to all THE PEOPLE OF THE LAND. A certain officer in charge of punishing people had in his care people who should be put to death and people who should be flogged, but for the glory of the king's joy, he disregarded his punishments and kept the king's joy SO AS NOT TO INFLICT PAIN ON ANYONE.

117. כָּךְ הַהוּא יוֹמָא, הִלּוּלָא דְּמַלְכָּא בְּמַטְרוֹנִיתָא, חֶדְוָותָא דְּאַבָּא וְאִימָּא עֲלֵיהּ, חֶדְוָותָא דְּעֶלְאִין וְתַתָּאִין. בְּחֶדְוָותָא דְּמַלְכָּא, כֻּלְּהוּ חַדָּאן, וְלָא יִצְטַעֲרוּן בֵּיהּ. עַל דָּא כְּתִיב וְקָרָאתָ לַשַּׁבָּת עֹנֶג. מַאי עֹנֶג. עֹנֶג לָא אִשְׁתְּכַח אֶלָּא לְעֵילָּא בַּאֲתַר דְּקֹדֶשׁ עִלָּאָה שָׁרֵי. כד"א, אָז תִּתְעַנַּג עַל יְיָ'. דְּהַאי עֹנֶג עַל יְיָ' הוּא. וְהַאי יוֹמָא דְּהוּא הִלּוּלָא דְּמַלְכָּא, אִתְעַטַּר בְּהַהוּא עִטְרָא דְּעֹנֶג הה"ד וְקָרָאתָ לַשַּׁבָּת עֹנֶג. מַה דְּלָא אִשְׁתְּכַח הָכִי בִּשְׁאָר יוֹמִין.

117. So is that day, SHABBAT, the feast of joy of the King with the Queen, WHO ARE ZEIR ANPIN AND MALCHUT, and the joy of Aba and Ima. The higher and lower beings rejoice in it. Everyone has joy and have no pain in it. It is therefore written, "and call the Shabbat a delight" (Yeshayah 58:13). What is a delight? HE ANSWERS, Delight only exists above, where supernal holiness dwells, NAMELY IN SUPERNAL ABA AND IMA, as written, "then shall you delight yourself in (lit. 'above') Hashem" (Ibid. 14), NAMELY, ABOVE ZEIR ANPIN. For that delight is above Hashem, NAMELY IN ABA AND IMA THAT ARE ABOVE ZEIR ANPIN. That day, SHABBAT, which is the feast of joy of the King, is adorned with that crown of delight FROM SUPERNAL ABA AND IMA. This is the meaning of, "and call the Shabbat a delight," which is not the case in other days.

23. The third meal of Shabbat on a holiday's eve

A Synopsis

The rabbis discuss the importance of the meals on Shabbat and on holidays, and what to do when they fall together. We are reminded that one must not talk about business or unimportant matters on Shabbat. Rabbi Yitzchak says that one must remember the Shabbat through wine, that equates to the wine of Torah.

118. בְּהַאי יוֹמָא, תְּלַת סְעוּדָתָאן בַּעְיָין בְּנֵי מַלְכָּא, לְזַמְּנָא, וּלְסַדְּרָא פָּתוֹרֵי. בְּגִין יְקָרָא דְּמַלְכָּא, כְּמָה דְּאוֹקִימְנָא. וְכַד אִזְדְּמַן בֵּיה חַגָּא, אוֹ זִמְנָא, לָא יְסַדֵּר ב״נ תְּרֵי פָּתוֹרֵי בְּכָל סְעוּדָתָא, חַד לְשַׁבָּת, וְחַד לְאוּשְׁפִּיזָא, בְּגִין דִּכְתִיב עַל שֻׁלְחַן הַמֶּלֶךְ תָּמִיד הוּא אוֹכֵל, סְפוּקָא הוּא בְּפָתוֹרָא דְּמַלְכָּא, לְהַהוּא אוּשְׁפִּיזָא דְּאַתְיָא לֵיה. וְעַל דָּא בָּעֵי בַּר נָשׁ לְסַדּוּרֵי פָּתוֹרָא שְׁלֵימָא לְמַלְכָּא, וְהוּא יָהִיב מִינֵּיה לְאוּשְׁפִּיזָא.

118. On that day it behooves the King's children to prepare three meals and set the table in honor of the King, as we explained. When a feast happens on it OF THE THREE FESTIVALS, or a holiday, ROSH HASHANAH, one must not set two tables each meal, one for Shabbat and one for the guest, THE HOLIDAY, since it is written, "for he did eat continually at the king's table" (II Shmuel 9:13). For the King's table suffices to the coming guest. Hence one should set a whole table for the King, from which he gives to the guest.

119. אָמַר רַבִּי אֶלְעָזָר, סְעוּדָתָא תְּלִיתָאָה דְּשַׁבָּת, כַּד אִעְרַע בֵּיה אוּשְׁפִּיזָא, שַׁבְקִין לֵיה אוֹ לָא שַׁבְקִין לֵיה, אִי לָא שַׁבְקִין לֵיה, אִשְׁתְּכַח אוּשְׁפִּיזָא דְּחַיָּיא מִפָּתוֹרָא דְּמַלְכָּא, אִי שַׁבְקִין לֵיה, אִשְׁתְּכַח פְּגִימוּ בִּסְעוּדָתָא דְּמַלְכָּא.

119. Rabbi Elazar said, When a guest, A HOLIDAY, happens at Shabbat's third meal, it can be omitted or not omitted. If THE THIRD MEAL is not omitted, BUT EATEN, the guest, THAT IS, THE MEAL ON THE SECOND EVENING OF THE HOLIDAY, is rejected from the King's table, BECAUSE DUE TO THE THIRD MEAL ONE DOES NOT HAVE AN APPETITE FOR THE SECOND EVENING'S MEAL. If it is neglected, AND THE THIRD MEAL IS NOT

EATEN, there is something wrong with the King's meals, SINCE THE KING, SHABBAT, MISSES ONE MEAL.

120. אָמַר לֵיהּ רִבִּי שִׁמְעוֹן אֲבוֹי, לְמַלְכָּא דְּאִיעָרַע בֵּיהּ אוּשְׁפִּיזָא, וְנָטִיל מֵיכְלָא מִקָּמֵיהּ, וְסַלְקָא לְאוּשְׁפִּיזֵיהּ, אִשְׁתְּכַח אַף עַל גַּב דְּמַלְכָּא לָא אָכַל עִמֵּיהּ, מִמֵּיכְלָא דְּמַלְכָּא קָא אָכִיל, וּמַלְכָּא יָהִיב לֵיהּ לְמֵיכַל. וְכָל דָּא, בְּגִין דְּהַהוּא אוּשְׁפִּיזֵיהּ דְּמַלְכָּא. וּבְבֵי רַב הַמְנוּנָא סָבָא, לָא חַיְישֵׁי לְאוּשְׁפִּיזָא בְּשַׁעֲתָא דָּא, וּלְבָתַר מְסַדְּרֵי פָּתוֹרָא לְאוּשְׁפִּיזָא.

120. Rabbi Shimon his father said to him, THIS IS LIKE a king a guest came to visit. He took his own food and gave to the guest. Thus, though the king does not eat with him, the latter eats of the king's victuals, and the king gives him food. HERE TOO, SHABBAT ANNULS THE THIRD MEAL SO THE GUEST, WHO IS THE MEAL ON THE SECOND EVENING OF THE HOLIDAY, WOULD EAT HEARTILY. SO THE HOLIDAY'S SECOND EVE'S MEAL IS THE KING'S, SHABBAT'S, FOOD, BECAUSE SHABBAT POSTPONES ITS MEAL FOR ITS SAKE. All that is because it is the King's guest, THAT IS, BECAUSE THE FIRST DAY OF THE HOLIDAY OCCURS ON SHABBAT AND IS THEREFORE THE GUEST OF SHABBAT. BUT ON SHABBAT ON A HOLIDAY'S EVE, THE THIRD MEAL IS NOT OMITTED FOR THE HOLIDAY'S EVE'S MEAL. WE MUST NOT RAISE A DIFFICULTY THAT RABBI SHIMON AND RABBI ELAZAR HIS SON LIVED IN THE LAND OF YISRAEL, WHERE THERE ARE NO SECOND DAYS TO THE HOLIDAY, BECAUSE IT APPLIES TO THE SECOND DAY OF ROSH HASHANAH THAT IS CELEBRATED IN YISRAEL AS WELL, OR THEY ADDRESS THOSE LIVING ABROAD. In the house of Rav Hamnuna Saba they were not concerned about the guest at that time, BUT ATE THE THIRD MEAL. Later, ON THE EVE OF THE SECOND HOLIDAY, they would prepare a meal for the guest.

121. בְּהַאי יוֹמָא מְלוּלָא אָסִיר, הה"ד מִמְּצוֹא חֶפְצְךָ וְדַבֵּר דָּבָר, וּתְנָן חֶפְצְךָ כְּתִיב, בְּגִין דְּהַאי יוֹמָא כָּל מְהֵימְנוּתָא אִתְקְשַׁר בֵּיהּ.

121. On that day speech is restricted, as in, "nor pursuing your own business, nor speaking of vain matters" (Yeshayah 58:13), AS YOUR SPEECH ON SHABBAT WILL NOT RESEMBLE THAT ON WEEKDAYS. We learned that

it is written, "your own business," FOR YOU MUST NOT SPEAK OF YOUR OWN BUSINESS, since the whole Faith is attached to that day.

א״ל רבִּי אֶלְעָזָר, וְהֵיךְ עֲבִידְנָא דְּלָא לְסַדְּרָא סְעוּדָתָא דְּמַלְכָּא. 122 לְאוֹשְׁפִּיזָא, דְּהָא אַרְבֵּיסַר דְּחַל לִהֱיוֹת בְּשַׁבָּת, סַלְקָא סְעוּדָתָא דְּמַלְכָּא לְפִסְחָא, אַף עַל גַּב דְּלָאו אִיהוּ אוּשְׁפִּיזֵיהּ.

122. Rabbi Elazar said to his father, YOU SAY THAT THE THIRD MEAL IS NOT OMITTED ON A HOLIDAY'S EVE, yet what do we do so as not to hand the King's meal to the guest, NOT TO OMIT THE THIRD MEAL BEFORE THE MEAL OF THE HOLIDAY'S EVE'S THAT IS ON SHABBAT'S EVE? When the fourteenth OF NISSAN occurs on Shabbat, WE OMIT AND postpone the King's meal, THE THIRD MEAL, for the guest, WHICH IS THE PESACH'S (PASSOVER) DINNER, even though THE HOLIDAY is not the guest of Shabbat, BUT FALLS ON SUNDAY.

א״ל הָכִי אֲמֵינָא דְּאִי הוּא אוּשְׁפִּיזֵיהּ, יַכְלָא לְסַלְּקָא לֵיהּ, וְאִי. 123 לָאו לָאו סַלְקָא לֵיהּ. וְאִי נֵימָא די״ד דְּחַל לִהֱיוֹת בְּשַׁבָּת, אִתְדַּחְיָיא סְעוּדָתָא דְּמַלְכָּא מִקַּמֵּי סְעוּדָתָא דְּפִסְחָא. שָׁאנֵי פֶּסַח, דִּסְעוּדָתָא דְּשַׁבָּת אִתְדַּחְיָיא בְּכַמָּה גַּוְונִין. חַד, בְּגִין מַצּוֹת וּמְרוֹרִים, דְּבָעֵי בַּר נָשׁ דְּיִשְׁתְּכַח תָּאִיבָא. וְחַד, בְּגִין פֶּסַח וְהָא נַהֲמָא לָא אִשְׁתְּכַח מו׳ שָׁעוֹת וּלְמַעְלָה, דְּסִדּוּרָא דְּפָתוֹרָא בְּלָא נַהֲמָא, לָאו הוּא סִדּוּרָא.

123. RABBI SHIMON said to him, I say that if THE HOLIDAY is the guest OF SHABBAT, WHEN IT FALLS ON SHABBAT, one can OMIT THE THIRD MEAL AND postpone IT TO THE HOLIDAY'S EVE'S MEAL. But otherwise, WHEN IT DOES NOT FALL ON SHABBAT, BUT BEGINS ON SUNDAY, one does not OMIT IT AND postpone THE THIRD MEAL FOR THE SAKE OF THE HOLIDAY'S EVE'S MEAL SO ONE WOULD EAT HEARTILY. You may argue that on the fourteenth OF NISSAN that falls on Shabbat, the King's meal, THE THIRD MEAL, is postponed because of the Pesach EVE'S meal. Pesach is different in that the third meal of Shabbat is postponed because of a few reasons. The first is that one should have an appetite to eat Matzot and bitter herbs, and another is BECAUSE OF CHAMETZ on Pesach, since there must not be

LEAVENED bread since the sixth hour on, and setting the table without bread is not SETTING a meal.

124. וְאִי תֵּימָא בְּחַמְרָא, חַמְרָא שָׁרֵי, בְּגִין דְּתָאִיב לִבָּא. אֲבָל מִיּוֹמִי אִשְׁתַּדַּלְנָא דְּלָא בָּטִילְנָא סְעוּדָתָא דְּשַׁבָּת, אֲפִילוּ אִינּוּן יוֹמֵי, דְּאִשְׁתְּכַח בֵּיהּ. בְּהַאי יוֹמָא חֲקַל דְּתַפּוּחִין קַדִּישִׁין אִתְבְּרַךְ, וּמִתְבָּרְכָן עִלָּאִין וְתַתָּאִין, וְהַאי יוֹמָא קִשּׁוּרָא הוּא דְּאוֹרַיְיתָא.

124. You may say THAT ONE MAY COMPLY WITH THE REQUIREMENTS OF THE THIRD MEAL by wine. IT IS SO, and it may be done with wine, because it makes the heart hungry, AND DOES NOT SPOIL THE APPETITE. But all my life I made an effort not to annul the meal of Shabbat, THE THIRD MEAL, even on those SHABBAT days that A HOLIDAY falls on. For on that day the field of holy apple trees, MALCHUT, is blessed, and the upper and lower beings are blessed. This day is the bond of the Torah.

125. א"ר אַבָּא, הָכִי הֲוָה עָבִיד ר' שִׁמְעוֹן, בְּזִמְנָא דְּאִסְתְּלַק סְעוּדָתָא דְּשַׁבָּת, מְסַדֵּר פָּתוֹרֵיהּ וְאִשְׁתַּדַּל בְּמַעֲשֵׂה מֶרְכָּבָה, וַהֲוָה אָמַר הָא סְעוּדָתָא דְּמַלְכָּא דְּיֵיתֵי לְמֵיכַל גַּבָּאי. בְּגִינֵי כַּךְ, שַׁבָּת, אִשְׁתְּכַח בְּכֹלָּא עָדִיף מִכָּל זִמְנִין וְחַגִּין, וְאִקְרֵי קֹדֶשׁ וְלָא מִקְרָא קֹדֶשׁ.

125. Rabbi Aba said, Rabbi Shimon would act thus: when the time came to eat the third meal on Shabbat, he would set his table and study the mystic speculations of the divine Chariot. He used to say, This is the meal of the King that will come to eat with me. Hence, Shabbat is valuable in all MATTERS more than any other time and holiday. It is called holiness, rather than summoned from holiness.

126. אָמַר רִבִּי יְהוּדָה, כֻּלְּהוּ מוֹעֲדִים מִקְרָאֵי קֹדֶשׁ קָרֵינָן בְּהוּ. אֲבָל נָפְקֵי ר"ה וְיוֹמָא דְּכִפּוּרָא דְּלָא אִשְׁתְּכַח בְּהוּ חֶדְוָותָא, דְּהָא אִינּוּן דִּינָא הֲווֹ, אֲבָל אִלֵּין תְּלָתָא, זְמִינִין מִקְדָּשׁ, לְחֶדְוָותָא לְכֹלָּא, לְאִשְׁתַּעְשְׁעָא בְּהוּ בְּקוּדְשָׁא בְּרִיךְ הוּא, הה"ד וּשְׂמַחְתֶּם לִפְנֵי יְיָ' אֱלֹהֵיכֶם, וּכְתִיב וְשָׂמַחְתָּ לִפְנֵי יְיָ' אֱלֹהֶיךָ. בְּהַאי יוֹמָא דְּשַׁבַּתָּא, אִתְנְשֵׁי כָּל צַעֲרָא וְכָל

רוּגְזָא וְכָל דּוֹחֲקָא מִכָּל עָלְמָא, בְּגִין דְּאִיהוּ יוֹמָא דְּהִלּוּלָא דְּמַלְכָּא,
דְּנִשְׁמָתִין אִתּוֹסְפָן, כְּגַוְונָא דְּעָלְמָא דְּאָתֵי.

126. Rabbi Yehuda said, We call all the holidays "holy gatherings ('summoned from holiness')," but the exceptions TO THIS RULE are Rosh Hashanah and Yom Kippur, where there is no joy, since they are of Judgments. But these three, PESACH (PASSOVER), SHAVUOT AND SUKKOT, are summoned from holiness to everyone's delight, before the Holy One, blessed be He. This is the meaning of, "and you shall rejoice before Hashem your Elohim" (Devarim 12:12), and, "and rejoice before Hashem your Elohim" (Devarim 27:7). On that day of Shabbat, every sorrow and vexation and distress are removed from the whole world, since it is the day of the King's rejoicing, when souls are added IN IT TO YISRAEL, in the likeness of the World to Come.

127. א"ר יִצְחָק לְרִבִּי יְהוּדָה, כְּתִיב זָכוֹר אֶת יוֹם הַשַּׁבָּת לְקַדְּשׁוֹ,
וְתָנֵינָן זָכְרֵהוּ עַל הַיַּיִן, אֲמַאי עַל הַיַּיִן. א"ל, בְּגִין דְּיַיִן חֶדְוָותָא
דְּאוֹרַיְיתָא, וְיֵינָא דְּאוֹרַיְיתָא, חֶדְוָותָא הוּא דְּכֹלָּא. וְהַאי יַיִן חַדֵּי
לְמַלְכָּא, וְהַאי יַיִן מְעַטְּרָא לְמַלְכָּא בְּעִטְרוֹי, הה"ד צְאֶינָה וּרְאֶינָה בְּנוֹת
צִיּוֹן בַּמֶּלֶךְ שְׁלֹמֹה בַּעֲטָרָה שֶׁעִטְרָה לּוֹ אִמּוֹ. וְתָנֵינָן בְּכֹלָּא בַּעְיָיא
לְאַחֲזָאָה ב"נ עוֹבָדָא. דְּלָא אִשְׁתְּכַח קְדוּשָׁה אֶלָּא בְּיַיִן, כד"א כִּי
טוֹבִים דּוֹדֶיךָ מִיַּיִן, מִיַּיִן אִינּוּן טָבָאן, נַזְכִּירָה דֹּדֶיךָ מִיַּיִן. וְע"ד קְדוּשָׁה
דְּשַׁבָּת בְּיַיִן, וְהָא אוּקְמוּהָ, וְהָא אִתְּמַר.

127. Rabbi Yitzchak said to Rabbi Yehuda, It is written, "Remember the Shabbat day, to keep it holy" (Shemot 20:8). We learned one should remember it through wine. HE ASKS, Why through wine? He said to him, Because wine is the joy of the Torah, BEING THE MOCHIN OF THE ILLUMINATION OF CHOCHMAH THAT IS CALLED WINE, THAT SHINES UPON ZEIR ANPIN THAT IS CALLED TORAH. The wine of the Torah, which is THE MOCHIN OF ZEIR ANPIN IS everyone's joy. This wine gladdens the King, ZEIR ANPIN, with His crowns, THE MOCHIN OF THE FIRST THREE SFIROT. This is the meaning of, "Go forth, O daughters of Zion, and behold King Solomon with the crown with which his mother crowned him" (Shir Hashirim 3:11). We learned that in all THINGS one should demonstrate a deed BELOW TO AROUSE ITS CORRESPONDING ROOT ABOVE, for holiness abounds only in wine, as written, "for your love is better than wine" (Shir Hashirim 1:2), WHICH MEANS it is good because it is wine. ALSO "we will praise (lit. 'remind') your love more than (through) wine" (Ibid. 4). Hence Kiddush on Shabbat is performed over wine, as we already explained and taught.

24. The two bloods, of Pesach and of circumcision

A Synopsis

Rabbi Chiya examines the verse from Shir Hashirim that begins, "I sleep, but my heart wakes...," and talks about the exile of Yisrael, and about the opening one must find to come into God. That opening is the gates of righteousness. Rabbi Chiya talks about the blood marked on the doorposts that was Yisrael's display of Faith at the time that God killed all the firstborn in Egypt. We read about the time of the full moon, when the Klipot are hidden away and the holy union is present. Rabbi Aba explains about the four cups that correspond to the four redemptions, and about the four grades or Sfirot that bond together. He tells Rabbi Yehuda why the Halel is not recited during the seven days of Pesach.

128. וּבַחֹדֶשׁ הָרִאשׁוֹן בְּאַרְבָּעָה עָשָׂר יוֹם לַחֹדֶשׁ וְגוֹ'. רִבִּי חִיָּיא פָּתַח, אֲנִי יְשֵׁנָה וְלִבִּי עֵר קוֹל דּוֹדִי דוֹפֵק וְגוֹ'. אָמְרָה כְּנֶסֶת יִשְׂרָאֵל, אֲנִי יְשֵׁנָה בְּגָלוּתָא דְמִצְרַיִם, דַּהֲווֹ בָּנַי בְּשִׁעְבּוּדָא דְקַשְׁיוּ. וְלִבִּי עֵר, לְנַטְרָא לְהוּ דְּלָא יִשְׁתֵּיצוּן בְּגָלוּתָא. קוֹל דּוֹדִי דוֹפֵק, דָּא קוּדְשָׁא בְּרִיךְ הוּא, דְּאָמַר וָאֶזְכּוֹר אֶת בְּרִיתִי.

128. "On the fourteenth day of the first month..." (Vayikra 23:5). Rabbi Chiya opened with, "I sleep, but my heart wakes. Hark, my beloved is knocking..." (Shir Hashirim 5:2). The Congregation of Yisrael said, I sleep in exile in Egypt, SINCE EXILE COMES FROM THE POWER THE LEFT EXERCISES OVER THE RIGHT AND WITH THE JUDGMENTS OF THE LEFT, THE MOCHIN OF MALCHUT ARE GONE, WHICH IS CONSIDERED SLEEP. My children were there under harsh enslavement, "but my heart wakes" to keep them so they will not be destroyed in exile. "Hark, my beloved is knocking" refers to the Holy One, blessed be He, who said, "and I have remembered My covenant" (Shemot 6:5).

129. פִּתְחִי לִי פִּתְחָא כְּחֲדוּדָא דְמַחֲטָא, וַאֲנָא אֶפְתַּח לָךְ תַּרְעִין עִלָּאִין. פִּתְחִי לִי אֲחוֹתִי, דְּהָא פִּתְחָא לְאַעֲלָא לִי, בָּךְ הוּא, דְּלָא יֵיעֲלוּן לְגַבָּאי בָּנַי אֶלָּא בָּךְ, אַנְתְּ הוּא פִּתְחָא לְאַעֲלָא לִי בָּךְ, אִי אַנְתְּ לָא תִּפְתַּח פִּתְחָךְ, הָא אֲנָא סָגִיר. דְּלָא יִשְׁתַּכְּחוּן לִי. בְּגִין כָּךְ, פִּתְחִי לִי. פִּתְחִי לִי

וְדַאי. וְעַל דָּא אָמַר דָּוִד, כַּד בָּעָא לְאַעֲלָא לְמַלְכָּא, אָמַר פִּתְחוּ לִי
שַׁעֲרֵי צֶדֶק, אָבֹא בָם אוֹדֶה יָה׳. זֶה הַשַּׁעַר לַיְיָ׳, דָּא הוּא פִּתְחָא וְדַאי
לְאַעֲלָא לְמַלְכָּא. זֶה הַשַּׁעַר לַיְיָ׳, לְאַשְׁכְּחָא לֵיהּ, וּלְאִתְדַּבְּקָא בֵּיהּ, וְעַל
דָּא פִּתְחִי לִי אֲחוֹתִי רַעְיָתִי שֶׁרֹאשִׁי וְגו׳. בְּגִין לְאִזְדַּוְּוגָא עִמָּךְ, וּלְמֶהֱוֵי
עִמָּךְ בִּשְׁלָם דְּעָלְמִין.

129. "Open to me" (Shir Hashirim 5:2) MEANS OPEN TO ME an opening as thin as a needle, and I shall open to you the celestial gates. "Open to me, my sister," since the opening to come in to Me is within you, so My children shall enter only through you. Unless you open your opening, I am closed off and cannot be found. Hence, "Open to me." "Open to me" assuredly. Therefore, when David wished to come in to the King, he would say, "Open to me the gates of righteousness. I will go in to them, and I will praise Yah. This is the gate of Hashem" (Tehilim 118:19-20). This, THE GATES OF RIGHTEOUSNESS, WHICH IS MALCHUT, is an opening through which to come in to the King. "This is the gate of Hashem" to find Him and cleave to Him. Hence, "Open to me, my sister, my love…for my head is filled with dew," to unite with you and be at peace with you forever.

130. ת״ח, בְּשַׁעֲתָא דְּקוּדְשָׁא בְּרִיךְ הוּא הֲוָה קָטִיל לְבוּכְרֵי דְּמִצְרָאֵי,
כָּל אִינוּן דְּקָטַל בְּפַלְגוּת לֵילְיָא, וְאָחִית דַּרְגִּין מֵעֵילָּא לְתַתָּא. בֵּיהּ
שַׁעֲתָא עָאלוּ יִשְׂרָאֵל בְּקִיּוּמָא דְּאָת קַדִּישָׁא, אִתְגְּזָרוּ וְאִשְׁתַּתָּפוּ בִּכְנֶסֶת
יִשְׂרָאֵל, וְאִתְאַחֲדוּ בָּהּ. כְּדֵין הַהוּא דָּמָא אַחֲזִיאוּ לֵיהּ עַל פִּתְחָא. וּתְרֵין
דָּמֵי הֲווֹ, חַד דְּפִסְחָא, וְחַד דָּמָא דְּאִתְגְּזָרוּ. וַהֲוָה רָשִׁים עַל פִּתְחָא,
רְשִׁימָא דִּמְהֵימְנוּתָא, חַד הָכָא וְחַד הָכָא וְחַד בֵּינַיְיהוּ, וְהָא אִתְּמַר,
וְנָתְנוּ עַל שְׁתֵּי הַמְּזוּזוֹת וְעַל הַמַּשְׁקוֹף, בְּגִין לְאַחֲזָאָה מְהֵימְנוּתָא.

130. Come and see, when the Holy One, blessed be He, was killing the firstborns Egyptian, NAMELY all those He killed at midnight, and brought the upper grades down, at that very time Yisrael entered the covenant of the holy sign by circumcising and uniting with the Congregation of Yisrael and joining her. They then displayed that blood on the lintel. So there were two kinds of blood, the one of the Pascal sacrifice and the other that of circumcision, and the mark of Faith was imprinted on the lintel, one on one side, the other on the other, and one in between. THESE ARE THE THREE COLUMNS, RIGHT, LEFT AND CENTRAL. It is also said, "and put it on the two side posts and on the upper door post" (Shemot 12:7), to display Faith.

131. וּבְאַרְבָּעָה עֶשֶׂר, הָא אִתְּמַר, דְּהָא כְּדֵין מְבַטְּלִין חָמֵץ וּשְׂאוֹר, וְאִסְתַּלָּקוּ יִשְׂרָאֵל מֵרְשׁוּתָא אָחֳרָא, וְאִתְעֲקָרוּ מִנֵּיהּ, וְאִתְאַחֲדוּ בְּמַצָּה, קְשׁוּרָא קַדִּישָׁא. בָּתַר דְּאִתְגְּזָרוּ, עָאלוּ בָּהּ, עַד דְּאִתְפָּרָעוּ, וְאִתְגַּלְּיָיא רְשִׁימָא דִּלְהוֹן, וּכְדֵין יָהַב לְהוֹן קְשׁוּרָא, בַּאֲתַר עִלָּאָה, בְּקִשׁוּרָא דִּמְהֵימְנוּתָא, בַּאֲתַר דִּכְתִיב הִנְנִי מַמְטִיר לָכֶם לֶחֶם מִן הַשָּׁמַיִם, מִן הַשָּׁמַיִם דַּיְיקָא, וְהָא אוּקְמוּהָ.

131. "On the fourteenth," we learned that then leavened bread and leaven are renounced, and Yisrael are gone from another dominion and are uprooted from it, and join the leavened bread in a holy bond. After they are circumcised they come into it BY MEANS OF THE MATZAH until AFTER THE GIVING OF THE TORAH, WHEN they uncovered the corona and their imprint was revealed. Then He gave them the bond in a high place in the bond of Faith, the place where it is written, "Behold, I will rain bread from heaven for you" (Shemot 16:4), exactly from heaven, NAMELY FROM ZEIR ANPIN CALLED HEAVEN. This has already been explained.

132. ת"ח, בְּאַרְבֵּיסַר בְּשַׁעֲתָא דְּזִוּוּגָא דְּסִיהֲרָא דְּאִשְׁתְּכַח בִּשְׁלִימוּ עִם שִׁמְשָׁא, וְכִתְרִין תַּתָּאִין לָא מִשְׁתַּכְּחִין כָּל כַּךְ בְּעָלְמָא, דְּהָא בְּחִדְתּוּתֵי דְּסִיהֲרָא, זִינִין בִּישִׁין מִשְׁתַּכְּחִין, וּמִתְעָרֵי לְאִתְפַּשְּׁטָא בְּעָלְמָא. וּבְשַׁעֲתָא דְּזִוּוּגָא דְּסִיהֲרָא דְּאִשְׁתְּכַח בִּנְהִירוּ דְּשִׁמְשָׁא בִּשְׁלִימוּ, מִתְכַּנְּשֵׁי כֻּלְּהוּ לַאֲתַר חַד, וְקִדּוּשֵׁי מַלְכָּא אִתְעָרוּ. כְּדֵין כְּתִיב לֵיל שִׁמּוּרִים הוּא לַיְיָ', דְּהָא זִוּוּגָא קַדִּישָׁא אִשְׁתְּכַח, וְהוּא שִׁמּוּרִים בְּכֹלָּא.

132. Come and see, on the fourteenth day AT NIGHT, when the union of the moon, MALCHUT, is in perfection with the sun, ZEIR ANPIN, the lower Sfirot OF THE KLIPOT do not endure so much in the world. For at the time of the renewal of the moon, evil species abound and are roused to expand in the world. BUT when the union of the moon is wholly in the light of the sun, all THE KLIPOT are gathered into one place AND HIDE, while the holy things

of the King are roused. Then, "It is a night of watchfulness to Hashem" (Shemot 12:42), since the holy union is present, which is watchful in every respect.

133. ר' אַחָא אָמַר, בְּגִין כַּךְ תְּקוּנָא דְּכַלָּה בְּהַהוּא יוֹמָא, וּבְלֵילְיָא אִשְׁתְּכַח יְשׁוּבָא דְּבֵיתָא, וַוי לְאִינּוּן דְּלָאו מִבְּנֵי בֵּיתָא נִינְהוּ, כַּד אַתְאָן לְאִזְדַּוְוגָא אוֹרַיְיתָא כַּחֲדָא, וַוי לְאִינּוּן דְּלָא אִשְׁתְּמוֹדְעָן גַּבַּיְיהוּ. בְּגִין כַּךְ יִשְׂרָאֵל קַדִּישִׁין מְתַקְּנִין לוֹן בֵּיתָא, כָּל הַהוּא יוֹמָא, וְעַל יְדַיְיהוּ, עָיְילֵי מַאן דְּעָיְילֵי, וְאִינּוּן חַדָּאן וְזַמְרָן תַּרְוַוייְהוּ זַכָּאִין אִינּוּן יִשְׂרָאֵל בְּעָלְמָא דֵין וּבְעָלְמָא דְּאָתֵי.

133. Rabbi Acha said, For that reason the bride, MALCHUT, is made ready on that day, THE FOURTEENTH, and on the night OF THE FIFTEENTH DAY, the house is settled, NAMELY MALE AND FEMALE ARE UNITED. Woe to those who are not of the household, WHO DO NOT CLEAVE TO MALCHUT, when the two Torahs come to unite – THE WRITTEN TORAH, ZEIR ANPIN, AND THE ORAL TORAH, MALCHUT. Woe to those who are not recognized by them. For that reason, holy Yisrael prepare MALE AND FEMALE a home, THAT IS, A UNION, all that FOURTEENTH day, and through them those who need to, enter, THAT IS, THE MOCHIN NECESSARY FOR THE UNION OF MALE AND FEMALE. And they, MALE AND FEMALE, are glad and both sing. Happy are Yisrael in this world and in the World to Come.

134. אָמַר ר' יוֹסֵי לָמָּה לָן לְאַטְרְחָא כּוּלֵי הַאי, קְרָא שְׁלִים הוּא, דְּהָא בְּהַאי לֵילְיָא, זוּוּגָא עִלָּאָה קַדִּישָׁא אִתְּעַר וְאִשְׁתְּכַח, הה"ד, הוּא הַלַּיְלָה הַזֶּה לַיְיָ' שִׁמּוּרִים, מַאי שִׁמּוּרִים. תְּרֵי, זוּוּגָא דְּסִיהֲרָא בְּשִׁמְשָׁא. לְכָל בְּנֵי יִשְׂרָאֵל לְדֹרֹתָם, דְּהָא מִכָּאן וּלְהָלְאָה, אִתְאַחֲדוּ וְאִתְקְשָׁרוּ בְּקִשּׁוּרָא דִּשְׁמָא קַדִּישָׁא, וְנָפְקוּ מֵרְשׁוּתָא אַחֲרָא. בְּגִינֵי כַּךְ בְּאַרְבָּעָה עֲשַׂר, מְתַקְּנֵי גַּרְמַיְיהוּ, וּמְבַעֲרֵי חָמֵץ מִבֵּינַיְיהוּ, וְעָיְילֵי בִּרְשׁוּתָא קַדִּישָׁא, וּכְדֵין מִתְעַטְּרֵי חָתָן וְכַלָּה, בְּעַטְרוֹי דְּאִימָּא עִלָּאָה, וּבָעֵי בַּר נָשׁ לְאַחֲזָאָה גַּרְמֵיהּ דְּאִיהוּ בַּר חוֹרִין.

134. Rabbi Yosi said, Why should we bother so much? There is a whole verse to the effect that that night the supernal holy union is awakened and is

present. This is the meaning of, "It is a night of watchfulness to Hashem." Why is watchfulness WITH A PLURAL SUFFIX? HE ANSWERS THAT IT ALLUDES TO two, which are the union of the moon with the sun, MALCHUT AND ZEIR ANPIN. "for all the children of Yisrael in their generations" (Ibid.) MEANS THAT from now on YISRAEL are united and connected with the bond of the Holy Name, and have come out from another dominion. For that reason, they prepare themselves on the fourteenth and burn all the leaven among them and enter into a holy dominion. Then the groom and bride, ZEIR ANPIN AND MALCHUT, are crowned with the crowns of supernal Ima, BINAH, and man should show himself free, SINCE THE MOCHIN OF SUPERNAL IMA ARE CALLED FREEDOM.

135. א"ר יוֹסֵי, הָנֵי אַרְבַּע כַּסֵי דְּהַהוּא לֵילְיָא אֲמַאי. א"ר אַבָּא, הָא אוּקְמוּהָ חַבְרַיָּיא, לָקֳבֵיל ד' גְּאוּלוֹת. אֲבָל שַׁפִּיר הוּא בְּסִפְרָא דְרַב יֵיסָא סָבָא, דְּקָאָמַר הוֹאִיל וְזִוּוּגָא קַדִּישָׁא אִשְׁתְּכַח בְּהַאי לֵילְיָא בְּכָל סִטְרִין, וְזִוּוּגָא הוּא בְּאַרְבַּע קִשְׁרִין, דְּאִינּוּן ד' דַּרְגִּין, וְלָא מִתְפָּרְשֵׁי דָּא מִן דָּא, כַּד זִוּוּגָא דָּא אִשְׁתְּכַח, וַאֲנָן בְּחֶדְוָותָא דִּלְהוֹן אִתְעֲרָנָא, בְּגִין דְּהָא זָכֵינָא בְּהוּ, דְּמַאן דְּאָחִיד בְּדָא, זָכֵי בְּכֹלָּא. וְעַ"ד אִשְׁתַּנֵּי לֵילְיָא דָּא מִכָּל שְׁאָר לֵילָוָון, וּבָעֵינָן לְמֶעְבַּד שְׁמָא בְּכֹלָּא, וּלְמֶחְדֵּי בְּהַאי לֵילְיָא, בְּגִין דְּחֶדְוָותָא הוּא לְעֵילָא וְתַתָּא.

135. Rabbi Yosi said, What is the purpose of the four cups on that night? Rabbi Aba said, The friends explained they correspond to the four redemptions, "AND I WILL BRING...AND I WILL DELIVER... AND I WILL REDEEM...AND I WILL TAKE" (SHEMOT 6:6-7). This is well EXPLAINED in the book of Rav Yesa Saba, who said that since the holy union abounds that night in all directions, BOTH IN CHOCHMAH AND CHASSADIM, the union is formed with four bonds, or four grades that are inseparable when this union is present, WHICH ARE CHOCHMAH AND BINAH, TIFERET AND MALCHUT. And we are awakened by their joy, AND DRINK FOUR CORRESPONDING CUPS, because we attained them, since whoever is attached to it, TO THE ILLUMINATION OF THE UNION, attains all FOUR GRADES, CHOCHMAH AND BINAH, TIFERET AND MALCHUT. For that reason this night is different than all other nights, and it behooves us to make AND UNIFY this name in every way, and rejoice that night since it is joy above and below.

136. וְעוֹד אָמַר, דְּאַרְבַּע אִלֵּין אַרְבַּע גְּאֻלוֹת קְרֵינָן לְהוּ. מ"ט. בְּגִין
דְּהַאי דַּרְגָּא בַּתְרָאָה, גּוֹאֵל אִתְקְרֵי, הַמַּלְאָךְ הַגּוֹאֵל, וְלָא אִקְרֵי גּוֹאֵל,
אֶלָּא עַל יְדָא דְּדַרְגָּא אָחֳרָא עִלָּאָה, דְּקַיְימָא עֲלֵיהּ וְנָהִיר לָהּ. וְדָא לָא
אַפִּיק לָהּ נְהוֹרָא, אֶלָּא בְּאִלֵּין תְּרֵין דַּרְגִּין דְּעֲלֵיהּ. אִשְׁתְּכַח, דְּד' אִלֵּין
אַרְבַּע גְּאֻלוֹת נִינְהוּ.

136. He further said that these four, CHOCHMAH AND BINAH, TIFERET AND MALCHUT, are called four redemptions. The reason is that the last grade, MALCHUT, is called 'redeemer', NAMELY the redeeming angel. It is only called redeemer through a higher superior grade, TIFERET, that is situated over it and shines upon it. It, TIFERET, only brings light upon it by means of the two grades above it, CHOCHMAH AND BINAH, FROM WHICH TIFERET RECEIVES. Thus these four, CHOCHMAH AND BINAH, TIFERET AND MALCHUT, are the four redemptions, SINCE THEY ARE CONNECTED TO MALCHUT CALLED REDEEMER.

137. ר' יְהוּדָה שָׁאַל לְר' אַבָּא, הָא כְּתִיב שִׁבְעַת יָמִים שְׂאוֹר לֹא יִמָּצֵא
בְּבָתֵּיכֶם, וְחֶדְוָותָא הוּא כָּל שַׁבְעָה, אֲמַאי לָא אִשְׁתְּלִים הַלֵּל כָּל ז'
יוֹמִין, כְּמוֹ בְּסֻכּוֹת, דְּאִשְׁתְּכַח ח' יוֹמִין הַלֵּילָא, בִּשְׁלִימוּ דְּחֶדְוָותָא כָּל
יוֹמָא וְיוֹמָא.

137. Rabbi Yehuda asked Rabbi Aba: It says, "Seven days shall there be no leaven found in your houses" (Shemot 12:19), and there is joy all those seven. Why is no complete Hallel (Prayer of Thanksgiving) recited throughout the seven days OF PESACH as in Sukkot, where we daily recite Hallel with complete joy?

138. א"ל שַׁפִּיר קָאֲמַרְתְּ, אֲבָל יְדִיעָא הוּא, דְּהָא הָכָא לָא אִתְקַשְּׁרוּ
יִשְׂרָאֵל כָּל כָּךְ בְּכֹלָּא, כְּמָה דְּאִתְקַשְּׁרוּ לְבָתַר. בְּגִין כָּךְ בְּהַאי לֵילְיָא,
דְּזֻוּוּגָא אִשְׁתְּכַח וְחֶדְוָותָא דְּכֹלָּא אִשְׁתְּכַח, וְיִשְׂרָאֵל אִתְקַשְּׁרוּ בְּהַהוּא
חֶדְוָותָא, עֲבִידְנָא שְׁלִימוּ, וְהַלֵּילָא אִשְׁתְּלִים. אֲבָל לְבָתַר אע"ג דְּכֻלְּהוּ
מִשְׁתַּכְּחֵי, עַד כְּעַן יִשְׂרָאֵל לָא אִתְקַשְּׁרוּ בְּהוּ, וְלָא אִתְפָּרְעוּ לְאִתְגַּלְיָיא

רְשִׁימָא קַדִּישָׁא, וְלָא קַבִּילוּ אוֹרַיְיתָא, וְלָא עָאלוּ בְּמָה דְּעָאלוּ לְבָתַר.
בְּגִין כַּךְ בְּסֻכּוֹת שְׁלִימוּ דְּכֹלָא אִשְׁתְּכַח בֵּיהּ, וְחֶדְוָותָא דְכֹלָּא יַתִּיר,
אֲבָל הָכָא עַד כְּעַן לָא זָכוּ, וְלָא אִשְׁתְּכַח שְׁלִימוּ בֵּיהּ כ״כ, אע״ג
דְּאִשְׁתְּכָחוּ כָּל ז', לָאו הוּא בְּאִתְגַּלְיָיא, וְיִשְׂרָאֵל עַד לָא אִתְקְשָׁרוּ בְּהוּ
כַּדְקָא חֲזֵי.

138. He said to him, Well asked. But it is known that here, ON PESACH,
Yisrael are not bonded as wholly as they were later, because on that FIRST
night when the union OF MALE AND FEMALE is present and overall joy, and
Yisrael are bonded with that joy, we bring about perfection and the Hallel is
complete. But later, THROUGHOUT THE DAYS OF PESACH, even though
they are all present, ALL SEVEN GRADES, CHESED, GVURAH, TIFERET,
NETZACH, HOD, YESOD AND MALCHUT THAT SHINE IN THE SEVEN DAYS
OF PESACH, Yisrael have not yet connected to them, nor uncovered the
corona so the holy imprint will be revealed in them. Nor did they receive the
Torah or enter those GRADES, CHESED, GVURAH, TIFERET, NETZACH,
HOD, YESOD AND MALCHUT, as they did later. For that reason on Sukkot
there is overall perfection and overall joy IS IN IT to the utmost. But here ON
PESACH they have not yet attained, and there was not so much perfection in
them. Even though all seven are present, CHESED, GVURAH, TIFERET,
NETZACH, HOD, YESOD AND MALCHUT OF ZEIR ANPIN DURING THE
SEVEN DAYS OF PESACH, they are not revealed, and Yisrael were not well
connected with them yet, UNTIL AFTER THE GIVING OF THE TORAH.

139. וְעַ״ד חֶדְוָותָא דְּכֹלָּא וּשְׁלִימוּ דְּהַלֵּילָא בְּהַאי לֵילְיָא, בְּגִין הַהוּא
חוּלָקָא דְּאִתְקְשָׁרוּ בֵּיהּ. מַאי טַעֲמָא. דְּכֵיוָן דִּבְהַהוּא לֵילְיָא זוּוּגָא
אִשְׁתְּכַח, כָּל קִשּׁוּרָא דְּכֹלָּא אִשְׁתְּכַח בְּסִטְרָא דְּזוּוּגָא, וְלָא בְּסִטְרָא
דְּיִשְׂרָאֵל, דְּכַד זוּוּגָא אִשְׁתְּכַח בָּהּ מִשְׁתַּכְּחֵי אִלֵּין תְּרֵין דַּרְגִּין דְּקַיְימִין
עֲלָהּ. וְכַד אִלֵּין מִשְׁתַּכְּחֵי, הָא כָּל גּוּפָא אִשְׁתְּכַח בְּהוּ, וּכְדֵין שְׁלִימוּ
דְּכֹלָּא, וְחֶדְוָותָא מִכֹּלָּא, וְהַלֵּילָא אִשְׁתְּלִים, דְּהָא כְּדֵין אִתְעַטְּרַת
סִיהֲרָא בְּכֹלָּא. אֲבָל לָא לְבָתַר, דְּכָל יוֹמָא וְיוֹמָא אִשְׁתְּכָחֵי, וְיִשְׂרָאֵל
עַד לָא זָכוּ בְּהוּ, הָא לָא הַלֵּילָא שְׁלֵימָא, כְּמוֹ בִּזְמַנִּין אַחֲרָנִין.

139. Therefore there is overall joy and the Hallel is recited in full that FIRST night OF PESACH, because of that portion Yisrael are attached to. The reason is that union is there that night, and all the bond OF ALL THE GRADES is present from the side of union, FROM THE ASPECT OF AWAKENING ABOVE, but not from the side of Yisrael. When the union OF ZEIR ANPIN is in her, IN MALCHUT, the two grades CHOCHMAH AND BINAH were situated over her AS WELL. When these are present, the whole body, THE WHOLE STATURE OF ZEIR ANPIN, is with them. Then everything is perfected and joyous, and the Hallel is recited in full, for then the moon, MALCHUT, is adorned with everything. But this is not so after THE FIRST NIGHT, since every day OF THE SEVEN DAYS GRADES, CHESED, GVURAH, TIFERET, NETZACH, HOD, YESOD AND MALCHUT, is there yet Yisrael have not yet attained them. Thus the Hallel is not complete as in other times.

25. Why there are not seven days to Shavuot

A Synopsis

We learn why the day of Shavuot is the bond of Faith that bonds everything together, and why that day is not extended to seven days.

140. אָ"ל ר' יְהוּדָה, שַׁפִּיר הוּא, וְהָכִי הוּא וַדַּאי. וְהַאי זִמְנָא אָחֳרָא שְׁמַעֲנָא לֵיהּ בְּהַאי גַּוְונָא, וְאַנְשִׁינָא מִלֵּי. הַשְׁתָּא מִלָּה אָחֳרָא בָּעֵינָא לְמִנְדַּע, הָא חֲזֵינָא בְּפֶסַח ז', וּבְסֻכּוֹת ז', וּשְׁלִימוּ דְּחֶדְוָותָא בְּיוֹמָא אָחֳרָא. בְּשָׁבוּעוֹת, אֲמַאי לָא אִשְׁתְּכָחוּ בֵּיהּ ז' יָמִים, וְהָא הָכָא אִתְחֲזוּן יַתִּיר מִכֹּלָּא.

140. Rabbi Yehuda said, This is well and assuredly it is so. I have already heard this another time this way but I forgot. Now I wish to know something else. We see that on Pesach THERE ARE SEVEN DAYS, and on Sukkot THERE ARE SEVEN DAYS, with the wholeness of joy OF SUKKOT on another day, SHMINI ATZERET. But why are there not seven days to Shavuot? It is worthy TO EXTEND SEVEN DAYS more than all others.

141. פָּתַח וְאָמַר, וּמִי כְעַמְּךָ כְּיִשְׂרָאֵל גּוֹי אֶחָד בָּאָרֶץ. וְכִי מַאי שְׁנָא הָכָא דְּאִקְרוּן יִשְׂרָאֵל אֶחָד, יַתִּיר מֵאֲתַר אָחֳרָא. אֶלָּא, כֵּיוָן דְּשִׁבְחָא דְּיִשְׂרָאֵל, אַתְיָיא לְפָרְשָׁא, קָרָא לוֹן אֶחָד, דְּהָא בְּכָל אֲתַר שִׁבְחָא דְּיִשְׂרָאֵל אֶחָד הוּא. מ"ט. בְּגִין דְּכָל קְשִׁירוּ דְּעִלָּאֵי וְתַתָּאֵי, בְּהַאי אֲתַר דְּאִקְרֵי יִשְׂרָאֵל אִשְׁתְּכַח. דְּאִתְקְשַׁר בְּמָה דִּלְעֵילָא, וְאִתְקְשַׁר בְּמָה דִּלְתַתָּא, וְאִתְקְשַׁר בכ"י. וְע"ד אִקְרֵי כֹּלָּא אֶחָד. וּבַאֲתַר דָּא אִשְׁתְּמוֹדְעָא מְהֵימְנוּתָא, וְקִשּׁוּרָא שְׁלֵימָא, וְיִחוּדָא עִלָּאָה קַדִּישָׁא.

141. He opened by quoting, "And what one nation in the earth is like Your people, like Yisrael" (II Shmuel 7:23). HE ASKS, What is the difference that here Yisrael are called one rather than in other places, AND HE ANSWERS, Since its purpose here is to specify Yisrael's praise, it called them 'one'. For the place of praise of Yisrael is one. The reason is that the whole bond of the upper and lower beings is in the place called Yisrael, NAMELY ZEIR

ANPIN CALLED YISRAEL, since it is connected with that which is above, THAT IS, ABOVE ITS CHEST, WHICH IS CHASSADIM, and is connected to that which is below, THAT IS, NETZACH, HOD AND YESOD BELOW HIS CHEST, WHENCE THE PLENTY OF CHOCHMAH COMES. And it is connected with the Congregation of Yisrael, MALCHUT, WHERE CHOCHMAH IS REVEALED. Therefore, SINCE IT CONNECTS THE THREE PLACES, all is called one. Faith is known in that place, MALCHUT, and the whole bond, NETZACH, HOD AND YESOD, and the supernal holy union IN THE FIRST THREE SFIROT.

142. וְעַ״ד, יוֹמָא דָא, קְשׁוּרָא דִּמְהֵימְנוּתָא הוּא, קְשׁוּרָא דְּכֹלָּא. וּכְתִיב עֵץ חַיִּים הִיא לַמַּחֲזִיקִים בָּהּ אִילָנָא הוּא דְּאִקְרֵי אֶחָד. וְעַ״ד בְּגִין דְּאִינּוּן מִתְקַשְּׁרֵי בַּאֲתַר דָּא, אִקְרֵי הָכִי. וְעֵץ חַיִּים אֶחָד הוּא וַדַּאי אִקְרֵי, בְּגִין דְּכֹלָּא בֵּיהּ אִתְקְשַׁר, וְיוֹמָא דִּילֵיהּ, אֶחָד וַדַּאי, קְשׁוּרָא דְּכֹלָּא, וְאֶמְצָעִיתָא דְּכֹלָּא.

142. This is why this day OF SHAVUOT, THE CENTRAL COLUMN THAT CORRESPONDS TO ZEIR ANPIN THAT IS CALLED YISRAEL, is the bond of Faith that bonds everything. Also, it is written, "She is a Tree of Life to those who lay hold on her" (Mishlei 3:18), SINCE THE TREE OF LIFE, ZEIR ANPIN, is a tree called one. Hence, since YISRAEL BELOW are attached AND HOLD to this place, THE TREE OF LIFE, ZEIR ANPIN, they are called ONE. For the Tree of Life is called one, since everything is attached to it, and its day, SHAVUOT, is assuredly one, bonding everything and being the center of everything, SINCE IT IS THE CENTRAL COLUMN.

143. הה״ד וְעֵץ הַחַיִּים בְּתוֹךְ הַגָּן, בְּתוֹךְ מַמָּשׁ, בְּמְצִיעוּת, וְאָחִיד בְּכָל סִטְרִין, וְאִתְקְשַׁר בֵּיהּ. וְעַ״ד פֶּסַח וְסֻכּוֹת, וְהוּא בְּאֶמְצָעִיתָא. בְּגִין דְּאִיהוּ אֶמְצָעִיתָא דְּכֹלָּא, וְדָא הוּא שְׁבָחָא דְּאוֹרַיְיתָא בְּהַאי יוֹמָא, וְלָא יַתִּיר, שְׁבָחָא דִּמְהֵימְנוּתָא, וְקִשּׁוּרָא דְּכֹלָּא. א״ר יְהוּדָה, בְּרִיךְ רַחֲמָנָא דְּשָׁאִילְנָא, וְזָכֵינָא לְהָנֵי מִילֵי.

143. This is the meaning of, "the Tree of Life also in the midst of the Garden" (Beresheet 2:9), AS ZEIR ANPIN CALLED THE TREE OF LIFE is

actually inside, in the center and includes all directions, NAMELY, THE RIGHT AND LEFT COLUMNS, and is attached to them – hence, Pesach and Sukkot, and it, SHAVUOT, between them, SINCE PESACH IS THE RIGHT COLUMN, SUKKOT THE LEFT COLUMN, AND SHAVUOT THE CENTRAL COLUMN. For it is central to everything, which is why that day is to the praise of the Torah, BECAUSE THIS IS THE TIME OF THE GIVING OF OUR TORAH, and no more. FOR TORAH IS THE SECRET OF ZEIR ANPIN, THE CENTRAL COLUMN, and it is the praise of Faith, MALCHUT, and the bonding of everything, NAMELY THE FIRST THREE SFIROT, FOR ALL THOSE ARE CONNECTED TO THE CENTRAL COLUMN. Rabbi Yehuda said, Blessed is the Merciful One that I have asked and attained these matters.

144. א״ר יִצְחָק, חֶדְוָותָא וְשִׁירָתָא, זְמִינִין יִשְׂרָאֵל לְשַׁבְּחָא לְקוּדְשָׁא בְּרִיךְ הוּא, כְּהַאי שְׁבָחָא דִּמְשַׁבְּחֵי יִשְׂרָאֵל בְּלֵילְיָא דְּפִסְחָא, דִּכְ״י אִתְקְדְּשָׁת בִּקְדוּשָׁה דְמַלְכָּא. הה״ד הַשִּׁיר יִהְיֶה לָכֶם כְּלֵיל הִתְקַדֶּשׁ חָג. כְּלֵיל הִתְקַדֶּשׁ חָג דַּיְיקָא. בָּרוּךְ יְיָ׳. לְעוֹלָם אָמֵן וְאָמֵן.

144. Rabbi Yitzchak said, Yisrael will praise the Holy One, blessed be He, with joy and song, as that praise Yisrael recite on Pesach's eve, when the Congregation of Yisrael, WHICH IS THE SECRET OF NIGHT, is sanctified with the sanctification of the King. This is the meaning of, "You shall have a song, as in the night when a holy solemnity is kept" (Yeshayah 30:29). "The night when a holy solemnity is kept" is precise, such as that UNION ON PESACH'S EVE. Blessed is Hashem for ever and ever. Amen and Amen.

26. The counting of the Omer and the festival of Shavuot

A Synopsis

Rabbi Shimon says that whoever merits the Torah in this world merits it also in the World to Come. He talks about the sacrifice of the Omer and also of barley meal; the latter is a meal offering of jealousy, from "This is the Torah of jealousies," a warning for women not to go to men other than their husbands.

145. וּבְיוֹם הַבִּכּוּרִים בְּהַקְרִיבְכֶם מִנְחָה חֲדָשָׁה לַיְיָ' בְּשָׁבֻעוֹתֵיכֶם מִקְרָא קֹדֶשׁ יִהְיֶה לָכֶם וְגוֹ'. ר"ש פָּתַח, אָז יְרַנְּנוּ עֲצֵי הַיַּעַר מִלִּפְנֵי יְיָ' כִּי בָא לִשְׁפּוֹט אֶת הָאָרֶץ. זַכָּאָה חוּלְקֵיהוֹן דְּאִינּוּן דְּמִשְׁתַּדְּלֵי בְּאוֹרַיְיתָא יְמָמָא וְלֵילֵי, דְּיַדְעִין אָרְחוֹי דְּקוּדְשָׁא בְּרִיךְ הוּא, וְאִתְאַחֲדָן בִּשְׁמֵיהּ. וַוי לְאִינּוּן דְּלָא מִשְׁתַּדְּלֵי בְּאוֹרַיְיתָא, דְּהָא לֵית לוֹן חוּלָקָא בִּשְׁמָא קַדִּישָׁא, וְלָא אִתְאַחֲדָן בֵּיהּ, לָא בְּהַאי עָלְמָא, וְלָא בְּעָלְמָא דְּאָתֵי. מַאן דְּזָכֵי בְּהַאי עָלְמָא, זָכֵי בְּעָלְמָא דְּאָתֵי. דְּהָכִי תָּנֵינָן, דּוֹבֵב שִׂפְתֵי יְשֵׁנִים, אע"ג דְּאִינּוּן בְּהַהוּא עָלְמָא, שִׂפְוָותַיְיהוּ מְרַחֲשָׁן תַּמָּן אוֹרַיְיתָא.

145. "Also on the day of the firstfruits, when you bring a new meal offering to Hashem, in your feast of weeks, you shall have a holy gathering" (Bemidbar 28:26). Rabbi Shimon opened with, "Then shall the trees of the wood sing for joy at the presence of Hashem, because He comes to judge the earth" (I Divrei Hayamim 16:33). Happy is the lot of those who are occupied in the Torah day and night, who know the ways of the Holy One, blessed be He, and join with His name. Woe to those who are not occupied with the Torah, who have no portion in the Holy Name, and do not join it, neither in this world nor in the World to Come. For whoever merits THE TORAH in this world merits IT in the World to Come, as we have so learned that, "causing the sleepers' lips to murmur" (Shir Hashirim 7:10), even when they are in that world, their lips murmur there Torah, FROM THEIR MERIT IN THIS WORLD.

146. ת"ח, עַד הַשְׁתָּא אַקְרִיבוּ יִשְׂרָאֵל תְּבוּאַת הָאָרֶץ, תְּבוּאַת הָאָרֶץ וַדַּאי. וְאִתְעַסְּקוּ בֵּיהּ, וְאִתְקַשְּׁרוּ בְּהַהוּא קְשׁוּרָא. ואע"ג דְּדִינָא

אִשְׁתְּכַח, דִּינָא בִּשְׁלָמָא אִשְׁתְּכַח בֵּיהּ. וְאַקְרִיבוּ שְׂעוֹרִים, בְּגִין דְּאִיהוּ
קַדְמָאָה מִכָּל שְׁאָר תְּבוּאָה, וּמִן קַדְמָאָה מִתְקְרָבָא, וְלָא מֵהַהוּא
דְּמִתְאַחַר, דְּהָא אֲחִידוּ קַדְמָאָה, דְּיִשְׂרָאֵל אִתְאַחֲדוּ בֵּיהּ בְּקוּדְשָׁא בְּרִיךְ
הוּא, הָכָא הוּא. אָמַר קוּדְשָׁא בְּרִיךְ הוּא, אֲנָא יָהֲבִית לְכוּ מָן
בְּמַדְבְּרָא, מֵהַהוּא אֲתָר דְּאִקְרֵי שָׁמַיִם, דִּכְתִיב הִנְנִי מַמְטִיר לָכֶם לֶחֶם
מִן הַשָּׁמַיִם, וְאַתּוּן מְקָרְבִין קַמָּאי שְׂעוֹרִים.

146. Come and see, until now, THAT IS, ON PESACH, Yisrael sacrificed the corn of the earth, NAMELY THE OMER, the corn of the earth indeed, WHICH IS THE ILLUMINATION OF MALCHUT CALLED EARTH. They were occupied with it, and connected to that bond. And even when it is Judgment, Judgment is in it in peace. And they offered barley since it is the first among all kinds of corn, and one should sacrifice the first, and not of those that are late, since the first attachment of Yisrael to the Holy One, blessed be He, lies here. The Holy One, blessed be He, said, 'I give you in the desert out of that place called heaven, ZEIR ANPIN, as written, "Behold, I will rain bread from heaven for you" (Shemot 16:4), while you offer barley before Me, WHICH IS THE ASPECT OF MALCHUT'.

147. וְרָזָא דְּמִלָּה, זֹאת תּוֹרַת הַקְּנָאֹת, חָסֵר. אַזְהֲרוּתָא לִנְשֵׁי עָלְמָא,
דְּלָא יִשְׁטוּן תְּחוֹת בַּעֲלֵיהוֹן. וְאִי לָאו, קֶמַח שְׂעוֹרִים זְמִינָא לְקָרְבָא.
וּמִמִּלָּה חֲדָא, אִשְׁתְּמוֹדַע מִלָּה אָחֳרָא. זַכָּאָה חוּלָקֵיהוֹן דְּיִשְׂרָאֵל, דְּהָא
כְּנֶסֶת יִשְׂרָאֵל לָא שַׁקְרַת בְּמַלְכָּא קַדִּישָׁא לְעָלְמִין. כ״י תַּוְוהַת, אֲשֶׁר
תִּשְׂטֶה אִשָּׁה תַּחַת אִישָׁה, בְּגִין כָּךְ דִּינָא דְּהַאי אִתְּתָא מֵאַתְרָהָא קָא
אַתְיָיא. וּמַאן הוּא אַתְרָהָא הַהוּא דִּכְתִיב בָּהּ אֵשֶׁת חַיִל מִי יִמְצָא
וְרָחוֹק מִפְּנִינִים מִכְרָהּ. אֵשֶׁת חַיִל עֲטֶרֶת בַּעֲלָהּ.

147. The secret of this is, "This is the Torah of jealousies" (Bemidbar 5:29), spelled without Vav. It is a warning for women not to go aside to another instead of their husbands. Otherwise, barley meal is ready to be offered. From one thing we deduce another. Happy is the portion of Yisrael, since the Congregation of Yisrael is never false to the Holy King. The Congregation of Yisrael wonders AND SAYS, COULD IT BE THAT "a wife goes aside to another instead of her husband" (Ibid.), and because of that, the punishment of that woman WHO COMMITTED ADULTERY AGAINST HER HUSBAND comes from her place. Her place is that of which it is written, "who can find a woman of worth? For her price is far above rubies" (Mishlei 31:10), and "A virtuous woman is a crown to her husband" (Mishlei 12:4).

148. וְהַהוּא קֶמַח שְׂעוֹרִים, דְּאַיְיתִית הַהִיא אִתְּתָא, מִנְחַת קְנָאֹת אִתְקְרֵי, חָסֵר, כְּנֶסֶת יִשְׂרָאֵל הָכִי אִקְרֵי. וְעַל דָּא, בְּפִנְחָס כְּתִיב, תַּחַת אֲשֶׁר קִנֵּא לֵאלֹהָיו, דְּקִנְאָה הָכָא אִתְאֲחָד, דְּמַאן דִּמְשַׁקֵּר בְּהַאי בְּרִית, קִנְאָה אִתְּעָרַת עֲלֵיהּ, וְעַל דָּא קַנָּאִין פּוֹגְעִין בּוֹ. תָּא חֲזֵי, קֶמַח שְׂעוֹרִים, הַאי עוֹמֶר, דְּכֵיוָן דַּהֲוָה מָטָא לְרֵיחַיִין דִּגְרוּסוֹת, מַפִּיקִין מִנֵּיהּ עֶשְׂרוֹן מְנוּפֶּה בִּי״ג נָפָה.

148. The barley meal that woman offers is called a meal offering of jealousy, spelled without Vav, since the Congregation of Yisrael, MALCHUT, is so called, AS THE ILLUMINATION OF THE BARLEY MEAL IS IN HER, AND SHE THEREFORE PUNISHES HER. Hence it is written of Pinchas, "because he was zealous for his Elohim" (Bemidbar 25:13), for jealousy, MALCHUT, is attached here, for jealousy, MALCHUT, is aroused to PUNISH whoever is false to the covenant. Hence IT WAS SAID that zealous people have a right to strike him. Come and see, this Omer of barley meal, once at the meal and ground, one tenth is taken away, sifted through thirteen sieves.

27. The festival of Shavuot

A Synopsis

We hear about the rejoicing of all the trees when Malchut is perfected. The entire bond of faith comes from the Tree, Zeir Anpin. We are told that the Congregation of Yisrael, like a bride, is given portions from each of the grades. Rabbi Shimon tells about the union of Zeir Anpin and Malchut. We hear about the tree that is the torso and about all the limbs that are the Sfirot that are attached to it. The feast days of the branches of the Tree were throughout the days of Sukkot, and after that on Shmini Atzeret is the joy of the Tree itself. The Tree atones for the Evil Inclination in man when the leavened bread is brought. The Torah is called "a Tree of Life" because its roots are in the deep river of Binah.

149. וְדָא שֶׁבַע שַׁבָּתוֹת תְּמִימוֹת, לְבָתַר דְּסַלְּקִין שֶׁבַע שַׁבָּתוֹת אִלֵּין, אָתָא מַלְכָּא קַדִּישָׁא לְאִזְדַּוּוּגָא בָּהּ בכ"י, וְאוֹרַיְיתָא אִתְיְיהִיבַת. וּכְדֵין אִתְעֲטַּר מַלְכָּא בְּיִחוּדָא שְׁלִים, וְאִשְׁתְּכַח אֶחָד לְעֵילָּא וְתַתָּא. וְכַד אִתְּעַר מַלְכָּא קַדִּישָׁא, וּמָטָא זִמְנָא דְּאוֹרַיְיתָא. כָּל אִינּוּן אִילָנִין דְּמִבַכְּרֵי אִבַּיְיהוּ, סַלְּקִין שִׁירָתָא. וּמַאי אַמְרֵי בְּשַׁעֲתָא דְּמִלַקְטֵי לְהוֹן, פַּתְחֵי וְאַמְרֵי, יְיָ' בַּשָּׁמַיִם הֵכִין כִּסְאוֹ וּמַלְכוּתוֹ בַּכֹּל מָשָׁלָה. יְיָ' בְּהַשָּׁמַיִם חַסְדֶּךָ. וּכְתִיב, וְכָל עֲצֵי הַשָּׂדֶה יִמְחֲאוּ כָף.

149. This is the meaning of, "seven complete Shabbatot" (Vayikra 23:15), WHICH MEANS THAT after seven Shabbatot have passed, the Holy King comes to unite with the Congregation of Yisrael, and the Torah is given. Then the King, ZEIR ANPIN, is adorned with the complete union, and the time of the Torah has come. All the trees that produce the firstfruits start singing, BECAUSE THEY DO SO BY THE ILLUMINATION OF THE UNION. What do they sing when THE FRUITS are gathered? "Hashem has established His throne in the heavens; and His kingdom rules over all" (Tehilim 103:19), AS THE THRONE, MALCHUT, IS BUILT AND ESTABLISHED IN THE HEAVENS, ZEIR ANPIN. THEN MALCHUT IS PERFECTED IN EVERY RESPECT, and it is written, "Your steadfast love, Hashem, is in the heavens" (Tehilim 36:6), WHICH MEANS THAT CHASSADIM FLOW FROM ZEIR ANPIN TO MALCHUT. And it is also written, "and all the trees of the field shall clap their hands" (Yeshayah 55:12), NAMELY, THE ILLUMINATION

OF MALCHUT CALLED "FIELD" WILL CLAP HANDS. IN RELATION TO THIS UNION, RABBI SHIMON OPENED THE ARTICLE WITH THE VERSE, "THEN SHALL THE TREES OF THE WOOD SING FOR JOY" (I DIVREI HAYAMIM 16:33).

150. תּוּ פָּתַח וְאָמַר, מִזְמוֹר שִׁירוּ לַיְיָ׳ שִׁיר חָדָשׁ כִּי נִפְלָאוֹת עָשָׂה. שִׁיר חָדָשׁ אִקְרֵי. בְּגִין כָּךְ בְּהַקְרִיבְכֶם מִנְחָה חֲדָשָׁה. הָתָם מִנְחַת קְנָאוֹת, הָכָא מִנְחָה חֲדָשָׁה. חֲדָשָׁה דְּחוּדְשָׁא דְּכַלָּה הָכָא. קְשׁוּרָא דְּכַלָּה דְּעֵילָא וְתַתָּא, קְשׁוּרָא דִּמְהֵימְנוּתָא. וְעַ״ד יַעֲקֹב שְׁלֵימָא אִתְעֲטָּר בְּעִטְרוֹי, וְאוֹרַיְיתָא אִתְיְיהִיבַת.

150. He continued with, "A Psalm. O sing to Hashem a new song; for He has done marvelous things" (Tehilim 98:1). It is considered a new song, THE SAME ONE THAT THE TREES RECITE WHEN THE FRUITS ARE GATHERED. For that reason IT IS WRITTEN, "when you bring a new meal offering" (Bemidbar 28:26). There, IN RELATION TO THE OMER, it is a meal offering of jealousies, THAT IS, A BARLEY MEAL OFFERING, while here it is a new offering. IT IS CONSIDERED new because the bride is renewed here, which is the bond of the bride above and below, ABOVE AND BELOW THE CHEST OF ZEIR ANPIN, the bond of Faith. Hence Jacob who is whole, ZEIR ANPIN, is adorned with his crowns and the Torah is given.

151. וְכַד מָטוֹן בִּכּוּרִים לְגַבֵּי כַּהֲנָא, הֲוָה בָּעֵי בַּר נָשׁ לְמֵימַר וּלְפָרְשָׁא מִלִּין, עַל הַהוּא אִילָנָא דְּאַרְעָא, דְּאִשְׁתְּלִים כְּגַוְונָא דִּלְעֵילָא, בִּתְרֵיסַר תְּחוּמִין, בְּשַׁבְעִין עַנְפִּין, וּבָעָא לְאוֹבְדָא לֵיהּ לְבַן אֲרַמָּאָה, דְּאִתְפְּגִים עָלְמָא בְּגִינֵיהּ. וְקוּדְשָׁא בְּרִיךְ הוּא שֵׁזִיב לֵיהּ, וְאִתְעֲטָּר בִּבְנוֹי כְּמָה דְּאוֹקִימְנָא. בְּגִין הַהוּא אִילָנָא, דְּכָל קִשְׁרָא דִּמְהֵימְנוּתָא, בֵּיהּ תַּלְיָיא. וְעַל דָּא מִנְחָה חֲדָשָׁה אִתְקְרֵי. מ״ט. בְּגִין דְּחֶדְוָותָא דְּעֶלָּאֵי וְתַתָּאֵי הוּא, וְחֶדְוָותָא דְּסִיהֲרָא. וּבְכָל זִמְנָא חַדְתּוּתֵי דְּסִיהֲרָא, קִשְׁרָא דִּמְהֵימְנוּתָא הוּא, וְחֶדְוָותָא דִּילָהּ.

151. When the firstfruits arrived at the priest, it behooved one to say and to explain these matters as referring to that tree upon the earth that is perfected

in the likeness of above, ZEIR ANPIN, in twelve regions and seventy branches. When Laban the Aramaean wished to destroy it so the world will be blemished because of it, the Holy One, blessed be He, saved the world and was adorned with His children, NAMELY THE SOULS OF YISRAEL, as we explained. For the entire bond of Faith, WHICH IS MALCHUT, comes from that tree, ZEIR ANPIN; hence MALCHUT is then CALLED a new meal offering. The reason is that the higher and lower beings and the moon, MALCHUT, rejoice in it. Whenever the moon, MALCHUT, is new, it is the bond of Faith WITH ZEIR ANPIN and its joy.

152. לְמַלְכָּא דַּהֲווֹ לֵיהּ בְּנִין, וּבְרַתָּא חֲדָא, אַתְקִין סְעוּדָתָא לְכֻלְּהוּ בְּנִין, לָא אִשְׁתְּכַחַת הַהִיא בְּרַתָּא עַל פָּתוֹרָא. כַּד אָתָאת, אָמְרַת לְמַלְכָּא, מָארִי, לְכָל אַחַי זְמִינַת וְיָהֲבַת לְכָל חַד מָאנִין יְדִיעָן, וְלִי לָא יָהֲבַת חוּלָקָא בֵּינַיְיהוּ. אָ"ל, חַיָּיךְ בְּרַתִּי, מָנָא דִּילָךְ יִשְׁתְּכַּח עַל חַד תְּרֵין. הָא כֻּלָּא יִתְּנוּן לָךְ מֵחוּלָקֵיהוֹן. אִשְׁתְּכַח לְבָתַר בִּידָהָא חוּלָקִין, עַל חַד תְּרֵין מַלְכָּא. כַּךְ כְּנֶסֶת יִשְׂרָאֵל, מִכֹּלָּא נַטְלָא חוּלָקִין, וְעַל דָּא אִתְקְרֵי כַּלָּה, כְּלוּלָא. כְּכַלָּה דְּכֻלְּהוּ מְזַמְּנִין לָהּ מָאנִין וְחוּלָקִין וְתַכְשִׁיטִין, כַּךְ הִיא כ"י, חַדְתּוּתֵי דִּילָהּ בְּכֹלָּא, וְכֹלָּא יָהֲבִין לָהּ חוּלָקִין וּמָאנִין.

152. THIS IS LIKENED to a king who had sons and one daughter. He prepared a meal for all his sons, but the daughter did not sit at the table. When she came, she said to the king, Sir, you have invited all my brothers and have given each one certain portions, but you have not given me a portion among them. He said to her, Upon your life, daughter, you shall have a double portion, for each will give you of their share. Thus she later had a double portion, MORE than anyone. So the Congregation of Yisrael took portions from each OF THE GRADES, BOTH FROM CHOCHMAH AND CHASSADIM. Hence she is called a bride (Heb. *kalah*), SINCE SHE includes (Heb. *kelulah*), EVERYTHING, as a bride, to whom everyone gives garments, portions and jewels. Such is the Congregation of Yisrael. She is renewed in all THE GRADES and everyone gives her portions and garments, NAMELY MOCHIN AND THE GARMENTS OF MOCHIN.

153. תָּא חֲזֵי, בְּשַׁעֲתָא דְּמַלְכָּא קַדִּישָׁא אִשְׁתְּכַח בְּעִטְרוֹי, חֶדְוָותָא

דִּכְנֶסֶת יִשְׂרָאֵל הוּא. וְכַד אוֹרַיְיתָא אִתְיְיהִיבַת, אִתְעַטְּרַת כְּנֶסֶת
יִשְׂרָאֵל בְּעִטְרִין עִלָּאִין, וּבְגִין דְּכָל קָשְׁרָא דִּמְהֵימְנוּתָא, אִתְקְשַׁר בְּהַאי
אִילָנָא, אִקְרֵי יוֹם אֶחָד. דִּכְתִיב, וְהָיָה יוֹם אֶחָד הוּא יִוָּדַע לַיְיָ'. יוֹם
אֶחָד וַדַּאי, דְּכ"י יוֹם אֶחָד, בְּקִשּׁוּרָא דִּלְעֵילָא.

153. Come and see, when the Holy King, ZEIR ANPIN, is adorned WITH THE
MOCHIN OF THE FIRST THREE SFIROT, the Congregation of Yisrael
rejoices BECAUSE SHE TOO IS WITH THOSE MOCHIN. When the Torah was
given, the Congregation of Yisrael was adorned with celestial crowns, and
since the entire bond of Faith, MALCHUT, was attached to this Tree, TO
ZEIR ANPIN, it is considered one day, as written, "but it shall be one
particular day which shall be known as Hashem's" (Zecharyah 14:7).
Assuredly it is one day, since the Congregation of Yisrael is one day
connected above, NAMELY, UNITED WITH ZEIR ANPIN, FOR ZEIR ANPIN IS
CONSIDERED ONE ONLY WHEN UNITED WITH MALCHUT.

154. קִשּׁוּרָא דִּלְעֵילָא, רֵישָׁא וְגוּלְגַּלְתָּא וּמוֹחֵי. קִשּׁוּרָא אָחֳרָא, תְּרֵין
דְּרוֹעִין וְגוּפָא. דַּאֲחִידָן, מֵחֵילָא דְּרֵישָׁא. וְאוֹקְמָא רַב הַמְנוּנָא, בִּתְלַת
קְשִׁירִין דַּאֲבָהָתָא. תְּרֵין קַיְימִין דִּלְתַתָּא דְּאִתְמַשְׁכוּ בְּמֶשַׁח רְבוּת,
בִּתְרֵין דַּרְגִּין, תְּרֵין נַחֲלִין, לְאַכְנְשָׁא זַרְעָא, לְאַפָּקָא בְּדַרְגָּא אָחֳרָא,
בְּפוּם אַמָּה. אִילָנָא דָּא, הוּא גּוּפָא דְּאֶמְצָעִיתָא, דְּאָחִיד לְכָל הָנֵי,
וְכֹלָּא מִתְקַשְּׁרָן בֵּיהּ, וְהוּא בְּהוֹן, וְעַל דָּא כֹּלָּא חַד. וְכַד אִזְדַּוְּוגַת בֵּיהּ
מַטְרוֹנִיתָא, כְּדֵין הוּא אֶחָד, וְהָא אוֹקִימְנָא מִלֵּי.

154. The connection above, IN ZEIR ANPIN, IS the head, WHICH IS the skull
and the brain. THE SKULL IS KETER AND THE PARTS OF THE BRAINS
(MOCHIN) ARE CHOCHMAH, BINAH AND DA'AT. Another connection is the
two arms, CHESED AND GVURAH, and the torso, WHICH IS TIFERET.
CHESED, GVURAH AND TIFERET are attached by means of the head, THAT
IS, THEY COME FROM CHOCHMAH, BINAH AND DA'AT IN THE HEAD. Rav
Hamnuna explained it as the three knots of the patriarchs, NAMELY CHESED,
GVURAH AND TIFERET, the two pillars, NETZACH AND HOD that flow with
the anointing oil in two grades, RIGHT AND LEFT in two rivers, THE SECRET
OF SKIES, to gather the semen IN THEM, NAMELY, THE PLENTY OF

CHESED, GVURAH AND TIFERET, to bring them out in another grade, THE CENTRAL COLUMN at the mouth of the penis, WHICH IS YESOD. The Tree is the torso in the middle, NAMELY TIFERET that is attached to all those, CHOCHMAH, BINAH AND DA'AT, CHESED, GVURAH AND TIFERET, NETZACH, HOD AND YESOD, and they are all attached to it, so that everything is one. And when the Matron, MALCHUT, is united with it, then it is one COMPLETELY. We already explained these matters.

155. תָּא חֲזֵי, כְּתִיב בַּיּוֹם הַשְּׁמִינִי עֲצֶרֶת. מַאן עֲצֶרֶת. אֶלָּא בְּהַהוּא אֲתָר, דְּכֹלָּא מִתְקַשְּׁרָן כַּחֲדָא, אִקְרֵי עֲצֶרֶת, מַאי עֲצֶרֶת, כְּנִישׁוּ. וְאִי תֵּימָא הָכָא דְּאִקְרֵי עֲצֶרֶת, מַאי טַעֲמָא. אֶלָּא בְּכָל אִינּוּן יוֹמִין, יוֹמֵי סְעוּדָתֵי דְּעַנְפֵי אִילָנָא הֲווֹ. וְעַל דָּא, שִׁבְעִים פָּרִים אִינּוּן. לְבָתַר, חֶדְוָותָא דְּאִילָנָא מַמָּשׁ, וְחֶדְוָותָא דְּאוֹרַיְיתָא. וּבְגִינֵיהּ הוּא יוֹמָא חַד עֲצֶרֶת. חֶדְוָותָא דְּאוֹרַיְיתָא, חֶדְוָותָא דְּאִילָנָא, דְּהוּא גּוּפָא.

155. Come and see, it is written, "On the eighth day you shall have a solemn assembly (Heb. *Shmini Atzeret*)" (Bemidbar 29:35). What is the assembly? HE ANSWERS that the place in which everything is connected together is called an assembly, WHICH IS MALCHUT THAT RECEIVES FROM ALL THE SFIROT. For what does "assembly" mean? A gathering. You may ask for the reason that it is called an assembly here. AND HE ANSWERS, Throughout the days OF SUKKOT were the feast days of the branches of the Tree, NAMELY THE SEVENTY MINISTERS THAT COME FROM THE OUTER PART OF ZEIR ANPIN – hence the seventy bullocks SACRIFICED ON THE SEVEN DAYS OF SUKKOT. After that, ON SHMINI ATZERET (THE DAY OF CONVOCATION) comes the joy of the Tree itself, ZEIR ANPIN HIMSELF. For there it is an assembly for one day, which is the joy in the Torah, the joy of the Tree, which is the body, NAMELY ZEIR ANPIN.

156. וְעַל דָּא לֵית לֵיהּ חוּלָקָא בְּהַאי יוֹמָא, אֶלָּא לְקוּדְשָׁא בְּרִיךְ הוּא וכנ"י. בְּג"כ, עֲצֶרֶת תִּהְיֶה לָכֶם, לָכֶם, וְלָא לְאַחֲרָא. דְּהָא בְּשַׁעֲתָא דְּמַלְכָּא אִשְׁתְּכַח, כֹּלָּא אִשְׁתְּכַח בֵּיהּ. וְעַ"ד תָּנֵינָן, בַּעֲצֶרֶת עַל פֵּירוֹת הָאִילָן, וְהָא אוּקְמוּהָ בְּג"כ אֶחָד אִקְרֵי, אֶחָד וַדַּאי, כְּמָה דְּאַמָרָן.

156. Therefore only the Holy One, blessed be He and the Congregation of Yisrael take part in this day, SHMINI ATZERET. For that reason, "you shall

have a solemn assembly," you and no other, for when the King is present, everything is there in Him. We therefore learned in relation to Shmini Atzeret about the fruit of the tree, WHICH ALLUDES TO ZEIR ANPIN THAT IS CALLED TREE, WHOSE DAY IT IS. This was already explained. For that reason He is called one, BEING united with Malchut. Surely one, as we said.

157. ת״ח, מַה כְּתִיב, מִמּוֹשְׁבֹתֵיכֶם תָּבִיאוּ לֶחֶם תְּנוּפָה וְגוֹ', סֹלֶת תִּהְיֶינָה חָמֵץ תֵּאָפֶינָה. מַאי שְׁנָא הָכָא חָמֵץ, אֶלָּא בְּגִין דְּכֹלָּא אֲחִידָן בֵּיהּ בְּאִילָנָא, דְּהָא בְּאִילָנָא אֲחִידָן עַנְפִין, בְּאִילָנָא אֲחִידָן עָלִין, קְלִיפִין, דִּינִין סַגִּיאִין בְּכָל סִטְרִין, כֹּלָּא אִשְׁתְּכַח בֵּיהּ. וּבְגִין דְּהַאי אִילָנָא, מְכַפֵּר עַל יֵצֶר הָרָע, דְּהוּא בְּבֵי מוֹתָבֵיהּ דְּבַר נָשׁ.

157. Come and see, it is written, "You shall bring out of your habitations two wave loaves...they shall be of fine flour; they shall be baked with leaven" (Vayikra 23:17). Why is it different here, that leaven IS BROUGHT? HE ANSWERS, Since everything is attached to the tree, ZEIR ANPIN, WHEN IT IS PERFECTED ON SHAVUOT, since the branches are attached to the Tree, leaves are attached to the Tree, WHICH ARE Klipot and many Judgments on every side, AND IT MITIGATES THEM. Everything is in it, for that Tree atones for the Evil Inclination in its dwelling place in man. FOR THAT REASON LEAVEN IS BROUGHT THAT DAY, WHICH IS AN INDICATION THAT THOUGH KLIPOT ARE ATTACHED TO IT, THEY ARE NEVERTHELESS MITIGATED AND THERE IS NO FEAR OF THEIR ATTACHMENT.

158. אָמַר רִבִּי אֶלְעָזָר, מֵהַאי אִילָנָא אִתְּזָנוּ כָּל שְׁאָר אִילָנִין לְתַתָּא. וְהוּא אִשְׁתְּרְשָׁא עַל חַד נַהֲרָא עֲמִיקָא, דְּנָגִיד וְנָפִיק וְלָא פַּסְקִין מֵימוֹי לְעָלְמִין. עֲלֵיהּ כְּתִיב וְהָיָה כְּעֵץ שָׁתוּל עַל מַיִם וְעַל יוּבַל יְשַׁלַּח שָׁרָשָׁיו, וְעַל דָּא אִקְרֵי אוֹרַיְיתָא, עֵץ חַיִּים הִיא וְגוֹ'. וּמַאי וְתוֹמְכֶיהָ מְאוּשָּׁר. הָא אוּקְמוּהָ, אֲבָל וְתוֹמְכֶיהָ מְאוּשָּׁר, כד״א בְּאָשְׁרִי כִּי אִשְּׁרוּנִי בָּנוֹת.

158. Rabbi Elazar said, From this Tree, ZEIR ANPIN, the other trees below are nourished, WHICH ARE THE GRADES IN MALCHUT AND BRIYAH, YETZIRAH AND ASIYAH. It has its roots in a deep river that flows, which waters never stop flowing, NAMELY BINAH. It is written of it, "For he shall be like a tree planted by the waters, and that spreads out its roots by the river" (Yirmeyah 17:8), THE RIVER BEING BINAH. Hence the Torah, ZEIR ANPIN, is called "She is a Tree of Life…" (Mishlei 3:18), SINCE LIFE IS DRAWN FROM BINAH. What is meant by, "and happy are those who hold her fast" (Ibid.)? We explained it, yet "happy are those who hold her fast" is similar to, "Happy am I (Heb. *oshri*), for the daughters will call me blessed" (Beresheet 30:13), WHICH ALLUDES TO BINAH CALLED ASHER.

28. The sacrifice of the Omer

A Synopsis

This section tells us about the commandment to offer the sacrifice of the Omer in order to unite the Matron and her children, Yisrael. The sacrifice is made of barley and offered so as to bring love between a wife and her husband. The wife of harlotry flees the temple so that she will not perish from the test of the waters of Sotah. We are told that the secret here is that there are two sisters, the woman of valor and the wife of harlotry.

רעיא מהימנא

159. וְהֵנִיף אֶת הָעֹמֶר וְגוֹ'. פִּקּוּדָא דָא, לְקָרְבָא קָרְבָּן הָעֹמֶר, קָרְבָּנָא דָא, כֹּלָּא אִיהוּ בְּדִבְקוּתָא עֵילָּא וְתַתָּא, מַטְרוֹנִיתָא וּבְנָהָא כַּחֲדָא אַזְלִין. עֹמֶר דָא, מְקָרְבִין יִשְׂרָאֵל בְּדַכְיוּתָא דִלְהוֹן, וְהַהוּא קָרְבָּנָא אִיהוּ מִן שְׂעוֹרִים, וְדָא אִתְקְרִיבוּ, לְמֵיעַל רְחִימוּ בֵּין אִתְּתָא וּבַעְלָהּ.

Ra'aya Meheimna (the Faithful Shepherd)

159. "And he shall wave the Omer" (Vayikra 23:11). We are commanded to offer the sacrifice of the Omer. This offering is wholly attached above and below, which means that the Matron and her children, MALCHUT AND YISRAEL BELOW, go together. THIS MEANS THAT THE PURPOSE OF THIS OFFERING IS TO ESTABLISH MALCHUT ABOVE AND YISRAEL BELOW. Yisrael sacrifice this Omer in their state of purity, and this sacrifice is made of barley, offered so as to bring love between a wife and her husband.

160. אֵשֶׁת זְנוּנִים, אִתְרַחֲקַת גַּרְמָהּ מִבֵּינַיְיהוּ, דְּלָא יָכִילַת לְמֵיקָם עַל גַּבָּהּ. אֵשֶׁת חַיִל קְרִיבַת גַּרְמָהּ לְקָרְבָא לְגַבֵּי כַּהֲנָא רַבָּא, וְדַאי טְהוֹרָה הִיא, וְנִקְתָהּ וְנִזְרְעָה זָרַע, וְאוֹסִיפַת חֵילָא וּרְחִימוּ לְגַבֵּי בַּעְלָהּ. אֵשֶׁת זְנוּנִים עַרְקַת מִן מַקְדְּשָׁא, דְּלָא לְמִקְרַב לְגַבֵּיהּ, דְּאִלְמָלֵא בְּהַהוּא זִמְנָא דְּאֵשֶׁת חַיִל אַבְדִּיקַת גַּרְמָהּ, אִיהִי אִתְקְרִיבַת לְגַבָּהּ, אִתְאֲבִידַת מֵעָלְמָא. וְעַ"ד לָא בַּעְיָא לְקָרְבָא לְמַקְדְּשָׁא, וְעַרְקַת מִנֵּיהּ, וְאִשְׁתָּאֲרוּ יִשְׂרָאֵל זַכָּאִין, בְּלָא עִרְבּוּבְיָא אָחֳרָא, לְגַבֵּי רָזָא דִמְהֵימְנוּתָא.

160. The wife of harlotry distances herself from among them, YISRAEL, because she cannot remain BY THE BARLEY OFFERING. The woman of valor, MALCHUT, who approaches to come near the High Priest, ZEIR ANPIN, is assuredly pure, AND OF HER IT SAYS, "then she shall be free, and shall conceive seed" (Bemidbar 5:28), and she adds strength and love to her husband, ZEIR ANPIN. The wife of harlotry flees the Temple so as not to approach it, for if THE WIFE OF HARLOTRY were to approach the woman of valor, when the latter is checking herself WITH THE WATERS OF SOTAH (A WIFE SUSPECTED OF ADULTERY), she would perish. THE CURSE WOULD FALL UPON HER, AND "HER BELLY SHALL SWELL, AND HER THIGH SHALL FALL AWAY" (BEMIDBAR 5:27). She therefore refuses to come near the Temple but runs away, and Yisrael remain worthy, with the secret of Faith, MALCHUT, unmixed, SINCE THE FOREIGN MIXTURE, THE WIFE OF HARLOTRY, HAS ALREADY FLED.

161. רָזָא דִּסְתְרָא דָא, תַּרְתֵּין אַחֲתָן. וְכַד אַרְחַת דָא לְגַבֵּי דָא, בִּבְדִיקוּ דִּילָהּ, צָבְתָה בִטְנָהּ וְנָפְלָה יְרֵכָהּ. דְּהָא בְּדִיקוּ דְּאֵשֶׁת חַיִל, סָמָא דְּמוֹתָא לְאֵשֶׁת זְנוּנִים. וְדָא אִיהוּ עֵיטָא, דְּיָהַב קוּדְשָׁא בְּרִיךְ הוּא לִבְנוֹי, לְקָרְבָא קָרְבָּנָא דָא בְּגִין אֵשֶׁת חַיִל, דְּתִתְעֲרוֹק אֵשֶׁת זְנוּנִים מִנָּהּ. וְאִשְׁתָּאֲרוּ יִשְׂרָאֵל בְּלָא עִרְבּוּבְיָא אָחֳרָא, זַכָּאִין אִינּוּן בְּעָלְמָא דֵּין, וּבְעָלְמָא דְּאָתֵי.

ע״כ רעיא מהימנא

161. The secret behind this mystery is that there are two sisters, THE WOMAN OF VALOR AND WIFE OF HARLOTRY. When the one smells THE MOUTH OF the other, THE WATER OF SOTAH of her examination THAT IS IN HER WOMB, her belly OF THE WIFE OF HARLOTRY swells and her thigh falls away. EVEN THOUGH THE WIFE OF HARLOTRY DID NOT UNDERGO THE TEST, BUT ONLY CAME NEAR THE WOMAN OF VALOR WHO CHECKED HERSELF, WHICH IS THE SECRET OF THE BARLEY OFFERING, ALL THE CURSES FELL UPON HER AS IF SHE DRANK IT HERSELF. For the checking of the woman of valor is a poison of death to the wife of harlotry. This is the counsel the Holy One, blessed be He, gave to His children, to offer this sacrifice OF THE BARLEY OFFERING to the woman of valor, NAMELY THE TEST, SUCH AS THE WATER OF SOTAH, so that the wife of harlotry will flee her and Yisrael will remain unmixed. Happy are they in this world and in the World to Come.

End of Ra'aya Meheimna (the Faithful Shepherd)

29. The counting of the Omer

A Synopsis

Rabbi Aba says that when Yisrael were in Egypt they were attached to impurity until they were circumcised and attained the covenant. He says that seven Shabbatot need to be counted in order to merit Zeir Anpin on the holiday of Shavuot.

162. רִבִּי אַבָּא וְרִבִּי חִיָּיא הֲוֹו אָזְלֵי בְּאוֹרְחָא, אָמַר ר' חִיָּיא, כְּתִיב, וּסְפַרְתֶּם לָכֶם מִמָּחֳרַת הַשַּׁבָּת מִיּוֹם הֲבִיאֲכֶם אֶת עֹמֶר הַתְּנוּפָה. מַאי קָא מַיְירֵי. אָ"ל, הָא אוּקְמוּהָ חַבְרַיָּיא. אֲבָל ת"ח, יִשְׂרָאֵל כַּד הֲוֹו בְּמִצְרַיִם, הֲוֹו בִּרְשׁוּתָא אָחֳרָא, וַהֲווֹ אֲחִידָן בִּמְסָאֲבוּתָא, כְּאִתְּתָא דָא, כַּד הִיא יָתְבָא בְּיוֹמֵי דִמְסָאֲבוּתָא. בָּתַר דְּאִתְגְּזָרוּ, עָאלוּ בְּחוּלָקָא קַדִּישָׁא, דְּאִקְרֵי בְּרִית. כֵּיוָן דְּאִתְאֲחָדוּ בֵּיהּ, פְּסַק מִסָאֲבוּתָא מִנַּיְיהוּ, כְּדָא אִתְּתָא כַּד פָּסְקוּ מִנָּהּ דְּמֵי מְסָאֲבוּתָא. בָּתַר דְּאִתְפְּסָקוּ מִנָּהּ, מַה כְּתִיב. וְסָפְרָה לָהּ שִׁבְעַת יָמִים. אוּף הָכָא, כֵּיוָן דְּעָאלוּ בְּחוּלָקָא קַדִּישָׁא, פָּסְקָא מְסָאֲבוּ מִנַּיְיהוּ, וְאָמַר קוּדְשָׁא בְּרִיךְ הוּא, מִכָּאן וּלְהָלְאָה חוּשְׁבָּנָא לִדְכִיּוּתָא.

162. Rabbi Aba and Rabbi Chiya were walking along the way. Rabbi Chiya said, It is written, "And you shall count for yourselves from the morrow after the Shabbat, from the day that you brought the Omer of the wave offering" (Vayikra 23:15). What does this mean? He said to him, Come and see. When Yisrael were in Egypt, they were under another power, and were attached to impurity as a woman sitting in her days of uncleanness. After they were circumcised, they entered the holy portion called covenant, WHICH IS THE SECRET OF MALCHUT. Once they were attached to her, impurity stopped from among them, as a woman whose blood of uncleanness stopped from her. After THE BLOOD OF UNCLEANNESS stopped in her, it is written, "then she shall number to herself seven days" (Vayikra 15:28). Here too, once they came in the holy portion, THE COVENANT, their impurity stopped and the Holy One, blessed be He, said, 'From now on it is a reckoning for purity'.

163. וּסְפַרְתֶּם לָכֶם, לָכֶם דַּיְיקָא, כד"א וְסָפְרָה לָהּ שִׁבְעַת יָמִים, לָהּ:

לְעַצְמָהּ. אוּף הָכָא לָכֶם: לְעַצְמְכֶם. וְלָמָה. בְּגִין לְאִתְדַּכָּאָה בְּמַיִין עִלָּאִין קַדִּישִׁין, וּלְבָתַר לְמֵיתֵי לְאִתְחַבְּרָא בֵּיהּ בְּמַלְכָּא, וּלְקַבְּלָא אוֹרַיְיתֵיהּ.

163. In "And you shall count for yourselves," "yourselves" is specific, as written, "then she shall number to herself seven days," IN WHICH "to herself" MEANS for her sake. Here too, "for yourselves," MEANS for your own sake. Why is that? In order to be purified in supernal holy waters, NAMELY THE ILLUMINATION OF BINAH, BY MEANS OF THE COUNTING OF THE OMER. After that, IN SHAVUOT, they shall come and join the King, ZEIR ANPIN, and receive His Torah.

164. הָתָם וְסָפְרָה לָהּ שִׁבְעַת יָמִים, הָכָא שֶׁבַע שַׁבָּתוֹת, אֲמַאי שֶׁבַע שַׁבָּתוֹת. בְּגִין לְמִזְכֵּי לְאִתְדַּכָּאָה בְּמַיִין, דְּהַהוּא נָהָר דְּנָגִיד וְנָפִיק. וְאִקְרֵי מַיִם חַיִּים. וְהַהוּא נָהָר, שֶׁבַע שַׁבָּתוֹת נַפְקוּ מִנֵּיהּ. וְע"ד שֶׁבַע שַׁבָּתוֹת וַדַּאי, בְּגִין לְמִזְכֵּי בֵּיהּ, כְּמָה דְאִתְּתָא, דְּכִיו דִּילָהּ בְּלֵילְיָא, לְאִשְׁתַּמְּשָׁא בְּבַעְלָהּ.

164. HE ASKS, There, IN RELATION TO THE MENSTRUATING WOMAN, IT IS WRITTEN, "then she shall number to herself seven days," while here it says, "seven complete Shabbatot" (Vayikra 23:15). Why are seven Shabbatot NEEDED HERE? HE ANSWERS, This is in order to be worthy of being purified by the water from the flowing and emerging river, WHICH IS BINAH, THE LIGHTS of which are called living waters. From that river seven Shabbatot come out, WHICH ARE THE SEVEN SFIROT, CHESED, GVURAH, TIFERET, NETZACH, HOD, YESOD AND MALCHUT, IN EACH OF WHICH ARE SEVEN SFIROT, CHESED, GVURAH, TIFERET, NETZACH, HOD, YESOD AND MALCHUT. THERE ARE THE 49 SFIROT AFTER THE SECRET OF THE 49 GATES OF BINAH. For that reason, seven Shabbatot NEED TO BE COUNTED in order to merit ZEIR ANPIN ON THE HOLIDAY OF SHAVUOT AND RECEIVE THE TORAH like a wife on her night of cleanness mates with her husband.

165. כָּךְ כְּתִיב וּבְרֶדֶת הַטַּל עַל הַמַּחֲנֶה לָיְלָה. עַל הַמַּחֲנֶה כְּתִיב, וְלָא כְּתִיב וּבְרֶדֶת הַטַּל לָיְלָה. אֶלָּא עַל הַמַּחֲנֶה, בְּגִין דְּיוֹרֵד מֵהַהוּא נְקוּדָה,

עַל אִינּוּן יוֹמִין דְּאִתְקְרִיאוּ מַחֲנֶה. וּמִתְחַבְּרַת בְּמַלְכָּא קַדִּישָׁא, וְאֵימָתַי
נָחַת הַאי טַלָּא. כַּד קְרִיבוּ יִשְׂרָאֵל לְטוּרָא דְּסִינַי, כְּדֵין נָחַת הַהוּא טַלָּא
בִּשְׁלִימוּ, וְאַדְכֵּי, וְאִתְפְּסַקַת זוּהֲמַתָן מִנַּיְיהוּ, וְאִתְחַבְּרוּ בֵּיה בְּמַלְכָּא
וּכְנֶסֶת יִשְׂרָאֵל, וְקַבִּילוּ אוֹרַיְיתָא, וְהָא אוֹקִימְנָא. וּבְהַהוּא זִמְנָא, וַדַּאי
כָּל הַנְּחָלִים הוֹלְכִים אֶל הַיָּם, לְאִתְדַּכְּאָה וּלְאִסְתַּחֲאָה, וְכֹלָא אִתְקַשָּׁרוּ
וְאִתְחַבְּרוּ בֵּיה בְּמַלְכָּא קַדִּישָׁא.

165. It is written this way, "And when the dew fell upon the camp in the night" (Bemidbar 11:9). It is written, "upon the camp"; not, 'the dew fell in the night', but, "upon the camp." The reason is THAT DEW, NAMELY, PLENTY, falls down from that point, CHOCHMAH, upon these 49 days IN BINAH called "camp," and BINAH joined THEM through the Holy King, ZEIR ANPIN. When did the dew fall? When Yisrael approached Mount Sinai ON SHAVUOT. The dew then fell completely and purified YISRAEL as the filth was stopped from them, NAMELY THE FILTH OF THE SERPENT THAT HE INJECTED INTO EVE BY THE SIN OF THE TREE OF KNOWLEDGE OF GOOD AND EVIL. They joined the King and the Congregation of Yisrael, and received the Torah. We already explained that. At that time, surely "All the rivers run into the sea" (Kohelet 1:7), to be purified and to wash, and everything is attached and joined with the Holy King, ZEIR ANPIN, THE CENTRAL COLUMN, AS THE HOLIDAY OF SHAVUOT IS AN ASPECT OF HIM.

166. תָּ"ח, כָּל בַּ"נ דְּלָא מָנֵי חוּשְׁבָּנָא דָּא, אִינּוּן שֶׁבַע שַׁבָּתוֹת
תְּמִימוֹת, לְמִזְכֵּי לְדַכְיוּתָא דָּא. לָא אִקְרֵי טָהוֹר, וְלָאו בְּכְלָלָא דְּטָהוֹר
הוּא. וְלָאו הוּא כְּדַאי לְמֶהֱוֵי לֵיה חוּלָקָא בְּאוֹרַיְיתָא, וּמַאן דְּמָטֵי טָהוֹר
לְהַאי יוֹמָא, וְחוּשְׁבָּנָא לָא אִתְאֲבִיד מִנֵּיה, כַּד מָטֵי לְהַאי לֵילְיָא, לִבְעֵי
לֵיה לְמִלְעֵי בְּאוֹרַיְיתָא, וּלְאִתְחַבְּרָא בָּה, וּלְנַטְרָא דַּכְיוּ עִלָּאָה, דְּמָטֵי
עֲלֵיה בְּהַהוּא לֵילְיָא, וְאִתְדְּכֵי.

166. Come and see, whoever did not number this reckoning, these seven complete Shabbatot, to earn this purity is not considered pure and is not among the pure, nor is he worthy of having a portion in the Torah. And whoever arrives pure on that day, SHAVUOT, and did not lose the count, upon reaching that night OF SHAVUOT, he needs to be occupied in the Torah and unite with it, and keep supernal purity that comes to him on that night, so he is purified.

30. Shavuot night

A Synopsis

We learn that one should study the Oral Torah on the night of Shavuot so that everything will be purified, and one should study the Written Torah on the day of Shavuot so that everything will be united. We read of the preparations for that joining.

167. וְאוֹלִיפְנָא, דְּאוֹרַיְיתָא דְּבָעֵי לֵיה לְמִלְעֵי בְּהַאי לֵילְיָא, אוֹרַיְיתָא דבע״פ, בְּגִין דְּיִתְדַּכּוּן כַּחֲדָא, מִמַּבּוּעָא דְּנַחֲלָא עֲמִיקָא. לְבָתַר, בְּהַאי יוֹמָא, לֵיתֵי תּוֹרָה שֶׁבִּכְתָב, וְיִתְחַבֵּר בָּהּ, וְיִשְׁתַּכְחוּן כַּחֲדָא בְּזוּוּגָא חַד לְעֵילָא. כְּדֵין מַכְרִיזֵי עֲלֵיה וְאַמְרֵי, וַאֲנִי זֹאת בְּרִיתִי אוֹתָם אָמַר יְיָ׳ רוּחִי אֲשֶׁר עָלֶיךָ וּדְבָרַי אֲשֶׁר שַׂמְתִּי בְּפִיךָ וְגוֹ׳.

167. We learned that one should study this night OF SHAVUOT the Oral Torah, WHICH IS MALCHUT so that MALCHUT AND YISRAEL HER CHILDREN will be purified together by the flowing of the deep river, NAMELY FROM BINAH. After that, during the day ON SHAVUOT the Written Torah, WHICH IS ZEIR ANPIN, will come and join it, MALCHUT, so they will be together, united as one above. A proclamation then resounds concerning him, saying, "As for Me, this is My covenant with them, says Hashem; My spirit that is upon you, and My words which I have put in your mouth..." (Yeshayah 59:21).

168. וְעַל דָּא, חֲסִידֵי קַדְמָאֵי לָא הֲווֹ נָיְימֵי בְּהַאי לֵילְיָא, וַהֲווֹ לָעָאן בְּאוֹרַיְיתָא, וְאַמְרֵי, נֵיתֵי לְאַחֲסָנָא יְרוּתָא קַדִּישָׁא, לָן, וְלִבְנָן, בִּתְרֵין עָלְמִין. וְהַהוּא לֵילְיָא כְּנֶסֶת יִשְׂרָאֵל אִתְעַטְּרָא עָלַיְיהוּ, וְאַתְיָיא לְאִזְדַּוְּוגָא בֵּיה בְּמַלְכָּא, וְתַרְוַוייְהוּ מִתְעַטְּרֵי עַל רֵישַׁיְיהוּ, דְּאִינּוּן דְּזַכָּאן לְהָכִי.

168. Therefore the pious in ancient times did not sleep that night but were studying the Torah, saying, Let us come and receive this holy inheritance for us and our children in both worlds. That night, the Congregation of Yisrael is an adornment over them, and she comes to unite with the King. Both decorate the heads of those who merit this.

169. ר"ש הָכִי אָמַר, בְּשַׁעֲתָא דְּמִתְכַּנְּשֵׁי חַבְרַיָּיא בְּהַאי לֵילְיָא לְגַבֵּיהּ, נֵיתֵי לְתַקְּנָא תַּכְשִׁיטֵי כַּלָּה, בְּגִין דְּתִשְׁתְּכַח לִמְחָר בְּתַכְשִׁיטָהָא, וְתִקּוּנָהָא, לְגַבֵּי מַלְכָּא כַּדְקָא יָאוּת. זַכָּאָה חוּלָקֵיהוֹן דְּחַבְרַיָּיא, כַּד יִתְבַּע מַלְכָּא לְמַטְרוֹנִיתָא, מַאן תַּקִּין תַּכְשִׁיטָהָא, וְאַנְהִיר עַטְרָהָא, וְשַׁוֵּי תִּקּוּנָהָא. וְלֵית לָךְ בְּעָלְמָא, מַאן דְּיָדַע לְתַקְּנָא תַּכְשִׁיטֵי כַּלָּה, אֶלָּא חַבְרַיָּיא, זַכָּאָה חוּלָקֵיהוֹן בְּעָלְמָא דֵּין וּבְעָלְמָא דְּאָתֵי.

169. Rabbi Shimon said the following when the friends gathered with him that night: Let us come and prepare the jewels of the bride, NAMELY DRAW MOCHIN UPON MALCHUT, so that tomorrow she will be bejeweled, THAT IS, WITH MOCHIN, and properly ready for the King. Happy is the portion of the friends, when the King will ask the Queen who prepared her jewels, illuminated her crowns and put on her adornments. No one in the world knows how to fix the adornments of the bride save the friends. Happy is their portion in this world and in the World to Come.

170. ת"ח, חַבְרַיָּיא מְתַקְּנֵי בְּהַאי לֵילְיָא תַּכְשִׁיטָהָא לְכַלָּה, וּמְעַטְּרֵי לָהּ בְּעִטְרָהָא, לְגַבֵּי מַלְכָּא. וּמַאן מַתְקִין לֵיהּ לְמַלְכָּא, בְּהַאי לֵילְיָא, לְאִשְׁתַּכְּחָא בָּהּ בְּכַלָּה, לְאִזְדַּוְּוגָא בָּהּ בְּמַטְרוֹנִיתָא. נָהֲרָא קַדִּישָׁא עֲמִיקָא דְּכָל נַהֲרִין, אִימָּא עִלָּאָה. הה"ד, צְאֶינָה וּרְאֶינָה בְּנוֹת צִיּוֹן בַּמֶּלֶךְ שְׁלֹמֹה וְגו'. לְבָתַר דְּאַתְקִינַת לֵיהּ לְמַלְכָּא, וְאַעְטְרַת לֵיהּ, אַתְיִית לְדַכְּאָה לָהּ לְמַטְרוֹנִיתָא, וּלְאִינּוּן דְּמִשְׁתַּכְּחֵי גַּבָּהּ.

170. Come and see, the friends prepare that night jewels for the bride, WHO IS MALCHUT, and decorate her with crowns to the King. And who attends the King, ZEIR ANPIN that night so that He will be with the bride, and unite with the Matron, MALCHUT? THAT IS the deep stream, the deepest among the rivers, which is supernal Ima, BINAH, THAT READIES ZEIR ANPIN. This is the secret of, "Go forth, O daughters of Zion, and behold King Solomon with the crown with which his mother crowned him" (Shir Hashirim 3:11). After BINAH readied the King and crowned him, she comes to purify the Matron and those who stand by her, NAMELY THE FRIENDS THAT BUSY THEMSELVES WITH PREPARING HER.

171. לְמַלְכָּא דַּהֲוָה לֵיהּ בַּר יְחִידָאִי, אָתָא לְזַוְוגָא לֵיהּ בְּמַטְרוֹנִיתָא עִלָּאָה, מַאי עַבְדַת אִמֵּיהּ כָּל הַהוּא לֵילְיָא, עָאלַת לְבֵי גְּנִיזָהָא, אַפִּיקַת עִטְרָא עִלָּאָה, בְּשַׁבְעִין יְקַר אַבְנֵי סַחֲרָנָא, וְאַעְטְרַת לֵיהּ. אַפִּיקַת לְבוּשִׁין דְּמֵילַת וְאַלְבִּישַׁת לֵיהּ, וְאַתְקְנַת לֵיהּ בְּתִקּוּנֵי דְמַלְכִין.

171. THIS IS LIKENED to a King who had an only son whom he was about to marry to a lofty Matron. All that night, his mother came to the treasure chambers and brought out a superior crown surrounded by seventy precious stones, and crowned him. She took out silken garments and put them on him, and fixed him with royal embellishments.

172. לְבָתַר עָאלַת לְבֵי כַּלָּה, חָמָאת עוּלֵימָתָהָא, דְּקָא מְתַקְּנֵי עִטְרָהָא, וּלְבוּשָׁהָא, וְתַכְשִׁיטָהָא, לְתַקְּנָא לָהּ. אָמְרָה לוֹן, הָא אַתְקֵינַת בֵּי טְבִילָה, אֲתָר דְּמַיִין נַבְעִין, וְכָל רֵיחִין וּבוּסְמִין סוֹחֲרָנֵי אִינּוּן מַיִין, לְדַכְּאָה לְכַלָּתִי, לֵיתֵי כַּלָּתִי, מַטְרוֹנִיתָא דִּבְרִי, וְעוּלֵימָתָהָא, וְיִתְדְּכוּן בְּהַהוּא אֲתָר דְּאַתְקֵינַת בְּהַהוּא בֵּי טְבִילָה, דְּמַיִין נַבְעִין דְּעִמִּי. לְבָתַר תַּקִּינוּ לָהּ בְּתַכְשִׁיטָהָא, אַלְבִּישׁוּ לָהּ לְבוּשָׁהָא, אַעְטְרוּ לָהּ בְּעִטְרָהָא. לִמְחָר כַּד יֵיתֵי בְּרִי לְאִזְדַּוְּוגָא בְּמַטְרוֹנִיתָא, יַתְקִין הֵיכָלָא לְכֻלְּהוּ, וְיִשְׁתְּכַח מְדוֹרֵיהּ בְּכוּ כַּחֲדָא.

172. HIS MOTHER then entered the bride's home and saw maidens preparing diadems, garments and jewelry to bedeck her. She said to them, Behold, I prepared a house for a ritual bath, a place of fresh water with all scents and spices around it to purify my bride. Let the bride come, my son's Matron, together with her maidens, and let them purify themselves where I prepared a ritual bath that I have of fresh water. Afterwards, bedeck her with her jewels, dress her with her garments and put on her crowns. Tomorrow, when my son shall come to unite with the lady, he shall prepare a palace where he shall live with you.

173. כָּךְ מַלְכָּא קַדִּישָׁא וּמַטְרוֹנִיתָא, וְחַבְרַיָּיא, כְּהַאי גַּוְונָא. וְאִימָא עִלָּאָה דִּמְתַקְּנַת כֹּלָּא. אִשְׁתְּכַח דְּמַלְכָּא עִלָּאָה, וּמַטְרוֹנִיתָא, וְחַבְרַיָּיא,

מְדוֹרֵיהוֹן כַּחֲדָא, וְלָא מִתְפָּרְשִׁין לְעָלְמִין. הה"ד, יְיָ' מִי יָגוּר בְּאָהֳלֶךָ
וְגוֹ', הוֹלֵךְ תָּמִים וּפוֹעֵל צֶדֶק. מַאן הוּא פּוֹעֵל צֶדֶק. אֶלָּא, אִלֵּין אִינּוּן
דִּמְתַקְּנֵי לְמַטְרוֹנִיתָא בְּתַכְשִׁיטָהָא, בִּלְבוּשָׁהָא, בְּעִטְרָהָא. וְכָל חַד,
פּוֹעֵל צֶדֶק אִקְרֵי. א"ר חִיָּיא, אִלְמָלֵא לָא זָכֵינָא בְּעָלְמָא, אֶלָּא
לְמִשְׁמַע מִלִּין אִלֵּין דַּיי. זַכָּאָה חוּלָקֵיהוֹן דְּאִינּוּן דְּמִשְׁתַּדְּלֵי בְּאוֹרַיְיתָא,
וְיַדְעִין אוֹרְחוֹי דְּמַלְכָּא קַדִּישָׁא, דִּרְעוּתָא דִּלְהוֹן בְּאוֹרַיְיתָא, עָלַיְיהוּ
כְּתִיב כִּי בִי חָשַׁק וַאֲפַלְּטֵהוּ. וּכְתִיב אֲחַלְּצֵהוּ וַאֲכַבְּדֵהוּ.

173. So it is with the Holy King, the Matron, MALCHUT, and the friends, and also supernal Ima, BINAH, that prepares everything, so the supernal King, ZEIR ANPIN, the Matron and the friends live together and never separate. This is the meaning behind, "who shall abide in Your tent… He that walks uprightly, and acts justly" (Tehilim 15:1-2). Who acts justly? Those who prepare the Matron with her jewels, dress and crowns. Each one is considered one who acts righteously, SINCE MALCHUT IS CALLED RIGHTEOUSNESS. Rabbi Chiya said, Had I had merit in the world only to hear these words, it would suffice me. Happy is the portion of those who study the Torah and know the ways of the Holy King, whose desire is for the Torah. Of them it is written, "Because he has set his delight upon Me, therefore I will set him on high…I will deliver him, and honor him" (Tehilim 91:14-15).

31. The counting of the Omer and the holiday of Shavuot

A Synopsis

We are told that Yisrael do not recite the Halel in full as in the days of Pesach since they are not yet properly whole and pure. We are told about the fifty days of purification, the purpose of which is to enter the secret of the World to Come, to receive the Torah, and to draw Malchut near Zeir Anpin. 49 of those days are all the aspects of the Torah, while the fiftieth day is the secret of the Torah itself. On the fiftieth day, Shavuot, the hidden is revealed. The two loaves of the offering are the secret of the two Shechinahs, the upper and the lower, that join together. Zeir Anpin receives from above and from below, from Binah and Malchut, because Shabbat is a secret above and below.

רעיא מהימנא

174. וּסְפַרְתֶּם לָכֶם מִמָּחֳרַת הַשַּׁבָּת וְגוֹ'. פִּקּוּדָא דָא, לִסְפּוֹר סְפִירַת הָעֹמֶר, הָא אוֹקִימְנָא, וְרָזָא דָא, יִשְׂרָאֵל, אַף עַל גַּב דְּאִתְדָּכוּ לְמֶעְבַּד פִּסְחָא, וְנָפְקוּ מִמְּסָאֲבוּ, לָא הֲווֹ שְׁלֵמִין וְדַכְיָין כַּדְקָא חֲזֵי. וְעַ"ד, לָאו הַלֵּל גָּמוּר בְּיוֹמֵי דְּפִסְחָא, דְּעַד כְּעַן לָא אִשְׁתְּלִימוּ כַּדְקָא יָאוֹת.

Ra'aya Meheimna (the Faithful Shepherd)

174. "And you shall count for yourselves from the morrow after the Shabbat…" (Vayikra 23:15). We are commanded to perform the counting of the Omer, which we already explained. This is a secret, for Yisrael, even though they were purified so as to perform the Pascal sacrifice and came out of their defilement, were not yet properly whole and pure. Hence the Hallel is not recited in full as in the days of Pesach, since they are not yet properly complete.

175. כְּאִתְּתָא דְּנָפְקָא מִמְּסָאֲבוּ, וְכֵיוָן דְּנָפְקָא, מִתַּמָּן וּלְהָלְאָה, וְסָפְרָה לָהּ. אוּף הָכָא יִשְׂרָאֵל, כַּד נָפְקוּ מִמִּצְרַיִם, נָפְקוּ מִמְּסָאֲבוּ, וְעָבְדוּ פֶּסַח, לְמֵיכַל בְּפָתוֹרָא דַּאֲבוּהוֹן, וּמִתַּמָּן וּלְהָלְאָה יַעַבְדוּן חוּשְׁבָּנָא, לְמִקְרַב אִתְּתָא לְבַעְלָהּ, לְאִתְחַבְּרָא בַּהֲדֵיהּ, וְאִינוּן חַמְשִׁין יוֹמִין דְּדַכְיוּ, לְאַעֲלָא

לְרָזָא דְעָלְמָא דְאָתֵי. וּלְקַבְּלָא אוֹרַיְיתָא, וּלְמִקְרַב אִתְּתָא לְבַעְלָהּ.

175. THIS IS LIKE a woman who comes out of her uncleanness. From the time she comes out, "then she shall number to herself SEVEN DAYS" (Vayikra 15:28). Here too, when Yisrael came out of Egypt, they came out of impurity, and performed the Pesach, eating at their Father's table, NAMELY MALCHUT CALLED TABLE. From that time on, let them do the reckoning to draw a wife near her husband so she would join him. These are the fifty days of purification, the purpose of which is to enter the secret of the World to Come, WHICH IS BINAH THAT HAS FIFTY GATES, to receive the Torah and to draw a wife near her husband, NAMELY TO UNITE MALCHUT WITH ZEIR ANPIN.

176. וּבְגִין דְּאִלֵּין יוֹמִין יוֹמִין, יוֹמִין דְּעָלְמָא דִּדְכוּרָא, לָא אִתְמְסַר חוּשְׁבָּנָא דָּא אֶלָּא לְגַבְרֵי בִּלְחוֹדַיְיהוּ. וְעַ"ד חוּשְׁבָּנָא דָּא, בַּעֲמִידָה אִיהוּ, וּמִלִּין דְּעָלְמָא תַּתָּאָה, בִּישִׁיבָה, וְלָא בַּעֲמִידָה. וְרָזָא דָּא, צְלוֹתָא דַּעֲמִידָה, וּצְלוֹתָא מְיוּשָׁב.

176. Since these days are the days of the male world OF ZEIR ANPIN, only men are commanded to count. Hence the counting is done standing up. BUT that which pertains to the lower world, WHICH IS MALCHUT, is done sitting, not standing. This is the secret of the prayer recited standing up, THE AMIDAH PRAYER, and the prayer recited sitting down, FROM 'WHO FORMS THE LIGHT' TO THE AMIDAH PRAYER.

177. וְאִלֵּין חַמְשִׁין, מ"ט אִינּוּן, כְּלַל אַנְפֵּי אוֹרַיְיתָא, דְּהָא בְּיוֹמָא דְּחַמְשִׁין, אִיהוּ רָזָא דְּאוֹרַיְיתָא מַמָּשׁ. וְאִלֵּין אִינּוּן חַמְשִׁין יוֹמִין, דְּבֵיהּ שְׁמִטָּה וְיוֹבְלָא. וְאִי תֵּימָא, חַמְשִׁין, מ"ט אִינּוּן. חַד טְמִירָא אִיהוּ, וְעָלְמָא אִסְתְּמִיךְ עָלֵיהּ. וּבְהַהוּא יוֹמָא דְּחַמְשִׁין, אִתְגַּלְיָא טְמִירָא, וְאִתְכַּסְיָא בֵּיהּ. כְּמַלְכָּא דְּאָתֵי לְבֵי שׁוֹשְׁבִינֵיהּ, וְאִשְׁתְּכַח תַּמָּן, אוֹף הָכָא יוֹמָא דְּחַמְשִׁין, וְהָא אוֹקִימְנָא רָזָא דָּא.

177. As for those fifty DAYS, 49 DAYS are all the aspects of the Torah, SINCE THERE ARE 49 PURE ASPECTS IN THE TORAH, while the fiftieth day is the secret of the Torah itself. There are a Sabbatical year and a

Jubilee during those fifty days, SEVEN SABBATICAL YEARS AND ONE JUBILEE. You may ask how there are fifty, IF THERE ARE ONLY 49, AS WE DO NOT COUNT THE FIFTIETH. HE ANSWERS, One is hidden, and the world is supported by it. On the fiftieth day, SHAVUOT, the hidden is revealed and concealed in it, as a king coming to his friend's house to stay there. Here too, such is the fiftieth day, which secret we already explained.

178. פְּקוּדָא בָּתַר דָּא, לְמֶעְבַּד חַג שָׁבוּעוֹת, דִּכְתִיב וְעָשִׂיתָ חַג שָׁבוּעוֹת לַיְיָ' אֱלֹהֶיךָ. שָׁבוּעוֹת: עַל דְּעָאלוּ יִשְׂרָאֵל לְרָזָא דְּחַמְשִׁין יוֹמִין, דְּאִינּוּן שִׁבְעָה שָׁבוּעוֹת, וּבְקָרְבְּנָא דְּעֹמֶר, אִתְבַּטַּל יֵצֶר הָרָע, דְּעָרְקַת מֵאֵשֶׁת חַיִל. וְכַד תַּמָּן לָא אִתְקְרִיב, מִתְדַּבְּקִין יִשְׂרָאֵל בְּקוּדְשָׁא בְּרִיךְ הוּא, וְאִתְבַּטַּל מֵעֵילָּא וּמִתַּתָּא.

178. The following precept is to celebrate the holiday of Shavuot, as written, "And you shall keep the feast of weeks to Hashem your Elohim" (Devarim 16:10). IT IS CALLED Shavuot (lit. 'weeks'), since Yisrael have entered the secret of the fiftieth day, which is seven weeks. THAT MEANS THE FIFTIETH DAY ALONE INCLUDES SEVEN WEEKS, BEING THE FIFTIETH GATE. Through the offering of the Omer, THE BARLEY OFFERING, the Evil Inclination, WHICH IS THE WIFE OF HARLOTRY, is voided, fleeing the woman of valor. AND WHEN THE WIFE OF HARLOTRY does not approach THE WOMAN OF VALOR, Yisrael cleave to the Holy One, blessed be He IN THE SECRET OF THE SEVEN WEEKS, and THE EVIL INCLINATION is voided from above and from below, NOT HAVING A GRASP ON ZEIR ANPIN AND MALCHUT.

179. וּבְגִין כַּךְ אִקְרֵי בְּגַוְונָא דָּא עֲצֶרֶת, דְּאִית בֵּיהּ בִּטּוּל יֵצֶר הָרָע. וְעַל דָּא לָא כְּתִיב בֵּיהּ חַטָּאת, כִּשְׁאָר זִמְנִין, דִּכְתִיב בְּהוּ חַטָּאת לַיְיָ'. וּכְדֵין כָּל נְהוֹרִין אִתְכְּנָשׁוּ לְאֵשֶׁת חַיִל, וּבְגִין כַּךְ עֲצֶרֶת.

179. This is why it is named Atzeret (Eng. 'assembly'), for voiding the Evil Inclination. For that reason, no sin offering is mentioned in relation to it, as during other festivals, where sin offering is mentioned. All the lights then gather to the woman of valor – THE LIGHTS OF THE SEVEN WEEKS GATHER TO MALCHUT. For that reason it is called an assembly.

180. שָׁבוּעוֹת, וְלָא כְּתִיב כַּמָּה אִינּוּן. אֶלָּא בְּכָל אֲתָר דְּאִתְּמַר סְתָם, שְׁמָא גָּרִים דְּאִינּוּן מִן שֶׁבַע. וּכְתִיב שִׁבְעָה שָׁבוּעוֹת תִּסְפָּר לָךְ, אֲמַאי כְּתִיב שָׁבוּעוֹת בִּלְחוֹדוֹי. אֶלָּא הָכִי אִצְטְרִיךְ שָׁבוּעוֹת סְתָם, לְאַכְלְלָא עֵילָּא וְתַתָּא, דְּהָא בְּכָל אֲתָר דְּאִלֵּין מִתְעָרֵי, אִלֵּין אוּף הָכִי מִתְעָרֵי עִמְּהוֹן. עַד לָא הֲוָה שְׁלֹמֹה, לָא הֲווֹ אִתְגַּלְיָין, כֵּיוָן דְּאָתָא שְׁלֹמֹה, עֲבַד מִנַּיְיהוּ פְּרָט. דִּכְתִיב, שִׁבְעַת יָמִים וְשִׁבְעַת יָמִים, דָּא אִיהוּ פְּרָט.

180. IT IS WRITTEN Shavuot (Eng. 'weeks'), but not how many WEEKS there are. AND HE ANSWERS, Wherever it plainly says WEEKS, the name implies there are seven WEEKS, as written, "Seven weeks shall you number to you" (Devarim 16:9). Why does it say only, "weeks" WHEN THERE ARE SEVEN? So it should be WRITTEN plainly "weeks," FOR THE PURPOSE OF including THE SEVEN WEEKS above and THE SEVEN WEEKS below, WHICH ARE ALL INCLUDED IN THE FIFTIETH DAY. For whenever these, THE SEVEN WEEKS ABOVE, stir, these, THE SEVEN WEEKS BELOW, stir as well. Until Solomon came AND ATTAINED THE FIFTIETH GATE, AND THE MOON WAS FULL, they were not revealed. Once Solomon came, he individualized them, as written, "seven days, and seven days" (I Melachim 8:65). This is individualization, THAT IS, THE FOURTEEN DAYS REVEALED BY THE FIFTIETH GATE WERE DETAILED.

181. בְּזִמְנָא אָחֳרָא בִּכְלָל, שָׁבוּעוֹת סְתָם. וְלָא אִצְטְרִיךְ לְבַר נָשׁ אָחֳרָא לְמֶעְבַּד מִנְהוֹן פְּרָט, בַּר שְׁלֹמֹה. בְּגִין דְּאִינּוּן שִׁבְעַת יָמִים דִּלְתַתָּא, לָא נְהִירוּ בִּשְׁלִימוּ, עַד דְּאָתָא שְׁלֹמֹה, וּכְדֵין קַיְימָא סִיהֲרָא בְּאַשְׁלְמוּתָא, בְּאִינּוּן שִׁבְעַת יוֹמִין. וְהָכָא חַג שָׁבוּעוֹת סְתָם, בְּגִין דְּאִתְכְּלִילוּ תַּתָּאֵי בְּעִלָּאֵי, וְלָא אַנְהִירוּ כְּיוֹמָא דִּשְׁלֹמֹה.

181. During other times, BESIDES THE DAYS OF SOLOMON, THERE ARE NO INDIVIDUAL FOURTEEN DAYS, BUT only included in weeks in general, for no one else may individualize them except Solomon. For the seven days below did not shine wholly FROM THE SEVEN DAYS ABOVE, until Solomon arrived and the moon remained full during these seven days. But here, it is plainly "feast of weeks," NOT MENTIONED IN DETAIL, because the lower SEVEN DAYS were included in the upper SEVEN DAYS and do not shine THERE as during the days of Solomon.

182. פְּקוּדָא בָּתַר דָּא, לְקָרְבָא שְׁתֵּי הַלֶּחֶם. הָא אוֹקִימְנָא, שְׁתֵּי הַלֶּחֶם:
תַּרְתֵּי שְׁכִינְתֵּי, עֵילָא וְתַתָּא, וְאִתְחַבְּרָן כַּחֲדָא. לְגַבֵּיהוֹן, תְּרֵין נַהֲמֵי
בְּשַׁבָּת, מְזוֹנָא חַד תְּרֵין, דְּעֵילָא וְתַתָּא. וְעַל דָּא כְּתִיב, שְׁנֵי הָעֹמֶר
לָאֶחָד. לְאֶחָד וַדַּאי, לְאִתְיַחֲדָא בַּאֲתַר חַד. לְהַהוּא דְּאִקְרֵי אֶחָד. וּמַאן
אִיהוּ. הַקּוֹל קוֹל יַעֲקֹב, דְּאִיהוּ יָרִית עֵילָא וְתַתָּא, תְּרֵין נַהֲמֵי כַּחֲדָא.
וּבְגִין דְּשַׁבָּת אִיהוּ רָזָא דְּעֵילָא וְתַתָּא, וְכֹלָּא אִיהוּ שַׁבָּת, תְּרֵין נַהֲמֵי.

ע"כ רעיא מהימנא

182. The following commandment is to offer the two loaves, as we explained that the two loaves are the secret of the two Shechinahs, the upper, BINAH, and the lower, MALCHUT, that join together, AND THE LOWER BEINGS RECEIVE FROM MALCHUT JUST AS THEY RECEIVE FROM BINAH, SINCE THEY ARE JOINED. There are two corresponding loaves of bread on Shabbat, THE DOUBLE BREAD, which is double provision from above and from below, FROM BINAH AND FROM MALCHUT. Therefore it is written, "two Omers for one man" (Shemot 16:22), WHICH ALSO ALLUDES TO BINAH AND MALCHUT. Surely they are "for one," because they come together in one place, NAMELY in that which is called one. What is it? It is, "The voice is Jacob's voice" (Beresheet 27:22), NAMELY ZEIR ANPIN, that receives from above and from below, FROM BINAH AND MALCHUT, THAT IS, two loaves together. This is because Shabbat is a secret above and below TOGETHER, and everything TOGETHER is called Shabbat, NAMELY the two loaves.

End of Ra'aya Meheimna (the Faithful Shepherd)

183. פְּקוּדָא בָּתַר דָּא לְהַסְדִּיר לֶחֶם וּלְבוֹנָה, לְהַקְרִיב עֹמֶר. דִּכְתִיב
וַעֲשִׂיתֶם בְּיוֹם הֲנִיפְכֶם אֶת הָעֹמֶר כֶּבֶשׂ תָּמִים לְעוֹלָה. וְכֵן בְּשָׁבוּעוֹת
לְהַקְרִיב שְׁתֵּי הַלֶּחֶם, וְהָכִי בְּכָל יוֹמִין טָבִין, לְהַקְרִיב קָרְבָּן דְּמוּסָפִין.
אֶלָּא וַדַּאי בְּכָל יוֹמָא דְּמוֹעֲדַיָּיא צָרִיךְ לְקָרְבָא קָרְבָּנָא דִּילֵיהּ. צָרִיךְ
לְקָרְבָא עֲלֵיהּ תּוֹסֶפֶת דְּאִית לֵיהּ, כְּגוֹן תּוֹסֶפֶת כְּתוּבְתָּא וּמַתְּנָתָא,
דְּאוֹסִיף חָתָן לְכַלָּה. וְשַׁבָּת מַלְכְּתָא, דְּאִיהִי כַּלָּה, בְּשַׁבָּתוֹת וּבְכָל יוֹמִין

טָבִין, צְרִיכָה תּוֹסֶפֶת, דְּאִינּוּן מוֹסְפִין דְּקָרְבְּנִין, וּמַתְּנָתָא, דְּאִינּוּן מַתְּנוֹת כְּהוּנָה.

183. The following precept is to arrange the bread and the frankincense and to offer the Omer, as written, "And you shall offer that day when you wave the Omer a he lamb without blemish of the first year for a burnt offering TO HASHEM. AND THE MEAL OFFERING THEREOF SHALL BE TWO TENTH MEASURES OF FINE FLOUR MINGLED..." (Vayikra 23:12-13), also to sacrifice on Shavuot the two loaves, and on all holidays to sacrifice an additional sacrifice. For surely on every day during the festivals, its sacrifice should be offered, NAMELY THE DAILY SACRIFICE JUST LIKE DURING WEEKDAYS and also sacrifice the addition, NAMELY THE SECRET OF THE ADDITIONAL LIGHT ON THAT HOLIDAY. This is like an addition on the Ketubah and gifts the groom gives the bride. Also Queen Shabbat, MALCHUT, is a bride during Shabbatot and all holidays, and is in need of an addition, which are the additional sacrifices and the offerings, which are the offering from the priesthood.

184. וּבִשְׁבוּעוֹת דְּאִיהוּ מַתַּן תּוֹרָה, דְּאִתְיְיהִיבוּ תְּרֵין לוּחִין דְּאוֹרַיְיתָא, מִסִּטְרָא דְּאִילָנָא דְּחַיֵּי, צָרִיךְ לְקָרְבָא לְגַבַּיְיהוּ, שְׁתֵּי הַלֶּחֶם דְּאִינּוּן ה"ה דְּהָא אִיהוּ נַהֲמָא דְּאוֹרַיְיתָא, דְּאִתְּמַר בֵּיהּ לְכוּ לַחֲמוּ בְלַחְמִי, ה"ה, מִן הַמּוֹצִיא לֶחֶם מִן הָאָרֶץ.

184. On Shavuot, the giving of the Torah, the two tablets of the Torah were given, BINAH AND MALCHUT, from the aspect of the Tree of Life, WHICH IS ZEIR ANPIN. It behooves us to sacrifice to them the two loaves of bread, the secret of Hei Hei, NAMELY BINAH AND MALCHUT, THE TWO HEIS OF THE YUD HEI VAV HEI. For they are the bread of the Torah, ZEIR ANPIN, of which it says, "Come, eat of my bread" (Mishlei 9:5). THEY ARE Hei Hei of, 'Hamotzi... Ha'aretz (Eng. 'who brings forth bread from the earth')'. THE EARTH IS THE LOWER HEI, MALCHUT. THE HEI OF HAMOTZI IS THE FIRST HEI, BINAH.

185. וְהַאי אִיהוּ מַאֲכַל אָדָם, דְּאִיהוּ יוֹ"ד ה"א וָא"ו ה"א. זֹאת הַתּוֹרָה אָדָם. אָדָם כִּי יַקְרִיב מִכֶּם קָרְבָּן לַיְיָ'. עוֹמֶר שְׂעוֹרִין, מַאֲכַל בְּעִירָן, דְּאִינּוּן חַיּוֹת הַקֹּדֶשׁ, דְּמִנְּהוֹן צָרִיךְ לְקָרְבָא, הה"ד מִן הַבְּהֵמָה. אֵלִים:

מְנַגְּחִים בְּמַתְנִיתִין, בְּאֵלֶּין פַּשְׁטִין. מִן הַבָּקָר: פָּרִים מְנַגְּחִים בְּמַתְנִיתִין, בְּתוּקְפָּא יַתִּיר. וּמִן הַצֹּאן: שְׁאָר עַמָּא, קָרְבָּנָא דִּלְהוֹן צְלוֹתִין, וְעֲלַיְיהוּ אִתְּמַר, וְאַתֶּן צֹאנִי צֹאן מַרְעִיתִי אָדָם אַתֶּם.

185. This, THE TWO LOAVES, is food for man, who is Yud-Vav-Dalet, Hei-Aleph, Vav-Aleph-Vav, Hei-Aleph, WHICH HAS THE SAME NUMERICAL VALUE AS ADAM (ENG. 'MAN'), NAMELY ZEIR ANPIN THAT INCLUDES THE TWO HEIS. THIS IS THE MEANING OF, "This is the Torah: (when) a man" (Bemidbar 19:14). IT INDICATES THAT THE TORAH, WHICH IS THE SECRET OF ZEIR ANPIN, IS THE SECRET OF YUD HEI VAV HEI OF THE NUMERICAL VALUE OF 45, THE NUMERICAL VALUE OF WHICH IS THAT OF MAN. "If any man of you bring an offering to Hashem" (Vayikra 1:2) IS THE SECRET OF FOOD FOR MAN. BUT the Omer of barley is food for animals, which are the holy living creatures, of which one should offer. This is the secret of, "of the cattle" (Ibid.), THE SECRET OF the rams that lock horns AGAINST EACH OTHER in the Mishnah and the literal explanation of the Torah. THESE ARE THE SAGES THAT FIGHT EACH OTHER WHEN EXPLAINING THE MISHNAH. "of the herd" (Ibid.) REFERS TO bullocks that gore each other more forcefully in the Mishnah. "and of the flock" (Ibid.) refers to the rest of the people, whose sacrifice is prayer, of whom it says, "But you My flock, the flock of My pasture, are men" (Yechezkel 34:31). "THE FLOCK OF MY PASTURE" ARE THOSE WHO STUDY THE LITERAL MEANING OF THE TORAH ONLY. "MEN" ARE THE SAGES WHO STUDY KABBALAH, WHO CLEAVE TO ZEIR ANPIN, THE SECRET OF YUD HEI VAV HEI FULLY SPELLED TO THE NUMERICAL VALUE OF 45, ADAM.

A Synopsis

We are given more details about the sacrifices and the offerings. We are told that the Kabbalah masters derive from the aspect of the Tree of Life; the rest of the people are from the side of the Tree of Knowledge of Good and Evil, that are the permissible and the forbidden. Those from the Tree of Life are men whose Torah is the bread of God.

186. דְּמָארֵי קַבָּלָה, וּמָארֵי מִדּוֹת, אִינּוּן מִסְטַר דְּאִילָנָא דְּחַיֵּי. שְׁאָר עַמָּא מִסִּטְרָא דְּאִילָנָא דְּטוֹב וָרָע, אָסוּר וְהֶתֵּר. וּבְגִין דָּא, מִן הַבְּהֵמָה, מַאֲכָל דִּלְהוֹן, עֹמֶר לֶחֶם שְׂעוֹרִים, וַיָּמָד שֵׁשׁ שְׂעוֹרִים. וַיָּשֶׁת עָלֶיהָ,

אוֹרַיְיתָא דִּבְעַל פֶּה, דְּשִׁיַית סִדְרֵי מִשְׁנָה. אֲבָל אִלֵּין דְּאִילָנָא דְּחַיֵּי,
דְּאִינּוּן אָדָם אוֹרַיְיתָא דִּלְהוֹן, נַהֲמָא דְּקוּדְשָׁא בְּרִיךְ הוּא. הה"ד, לְכוּ
לַחֲמוּ בְּלַחְמִי וְהַיְינוּ שְׁתֵּי הַלֶּחֶם. חֲדוּ כֻּלְּהוּ תַּנָּאִין וַאֲמוֹרָאִין, וְאָמְרוּ
מַאן קָאִים קַמֵּי סִינַי.

186. The Kabbalah masters and men of qualities, WHO ARE DEVOTED TO THE QUALITIES OF ZEIR ANPIN, derive from the aspect of the Tree of Life, WHICH IS ZEIR ANPIN, CALLED MAN. The rest of the people are from the side of the Tree of Knowledge of Good and Evil, which are the permissible and the forbidden. THIS IS THE ANGEL METATRON, WHO IS SO CALLED. HE IS A CHARIOT TO MALCHUT CALLED SECOND, AND INCLUDES THE FOUR HOLY LIVING CREATURES. Therefore, those "of the cattle" eat an Omer of barley bread, AS WRITTEN, "he measured six measures of barley, and laid it on her" (Rut 3:15). THIS IS THE SECRET OF the Oral Torah of the six Orders of the Mishnah. But those from the Tree of Life, THE KABBALAH MASTERS, are men, whose Torah is the bread of the Holy One, blessed be He, NAMELY THE FOOD OF ZEIR ANPIN THAT IS CALLED MAN. This is the meaning of, "Come, eat of my bread," namely the two loaves of bread. All the Tannaim and Amoraim rejoiced and said, who can stand before Sinai, NAMELY, BEFORE RA'AYA MEHEIMNA, WHO IS CALLED SINAI.

32. Blowing the Shofar

A Synopsis

Rabbi Yitzchak tells us that God did Yisrael a great kindness by drawing them to Himself from afar. When the higher and lower beings are gathered for Judgment, the blowing of the Shofar causes the attribute of Judgment to turn to Mercy. The sound of the Shofar below causes the supernal Shofar to resound to awaken Mercy. By the sounds below, Yisrael give strength above. We hear about what happens to the wholly wicked, to the wholly righteous, and to the mediocre.

187. בַּחֹדֶשׁ הַשְּׁבִיעִי בְּאֶחָד לַחֹדֶשׁ, ר' יִצְחָק פָּתַח, תִּקְעוּ בַחֹדֶשׁ שׁוֹפָר בַּכֶּסֶה לְיוֹם חַגֵּנוּ. זַכָּאִין אִינּוּן יִשְׂרָאֵל, דְּקוּדְשָׁא בְּרִיךְ הוּא קָרִיב לוֹן לְגַבֵּיה, מִן כָּל אוּמִין עע"ז, וְאִתְרְעֵי בְּהוּ, וּמֵאֲתַר רְחִיקָא קָרִיב לוֹן לְגַבֵּיה, הה"ד, וַיֹּאמֶר יְהוֹשֻׁעַ אֶל כָּל הָעָם כֹּה אָמַר ה' אֱלֹהֵי יִשְׂרָאֵל בְּעֵבֶר הַנָּהָר יָשְׁבוּ אֲבוֹתֵיכֶם מֵעוֹלָם. לְאַחֲזָאָה, דְּהָא מֵאֲתַר רְחִיקָא אִתְרְעֵי בְּהוּ, וְקָרִיב לוֹן לְגַבֵּיה, וּכְתִיב, וָאֶקַּח אֶת אֲבִיכֶם אֶת אַבְרָהָם מֵעֵבֶר הַנָּהָר וְגוֹ'. הָנֵי קְרָאֵי אִית לְאִסְתַּכְּלָא בְּהוּ, וְכִי כָּל יִשְׂרָאֵל לָא הֲווֹ יַדְעֵי דָּא, וְכָל שֶׁכֵּן יְהוֹשֻׁעַ.

187. "In the seventh month, on the first day of the month" (Vayikra 23:24). Rabbi Yitzchak opened with, "Blow a Shofar at the new moon, at the full moon on our feast day" (Tehilim 81:4). Happy are Yisrael whom the Holy One, blessed be He, draw near rather than all the nations in the world, and chose them. From afar He drew them near. This is the meaning of, "And Joshua said to all the people, Thus says Hashem Elohim of Yisrael, Your fathers dwelt on the other side of the river in old time" (Yehoshua 24:2), to indicate that He desired them from a distant place and drew them near Him. It is also written, "And I took your father Abraham from the other side of the river…" (Ibid. 3). We have to examine these verses. Did not the whole of Yisrael know this and Joshua all the more? WHY THE NEED TO SAY, "THUS SAYS HASHEM…"?

188. אֶלָּא אוֹרַיְיתָא כּוּלָּה סָתִים וְגַלְיָא, כְּמָה דִּשְׁמָא קַדִּישָׁא סָתִים וְגַלְיָא, בְּגִין דְּאוֹרַיְיתָא כּוּלָּה שְׁמָא קַדִּישָׁא הִיא, וְעַל דָּא אִיהִי סָתִים

וְגַלְיָא. אִי יִשְׂרָאֵל וִיהוֹשֻׁעַ הֲווֹ יַדְעֵי, אֲמַאי כְּתִיב כֹּה אָמַר יְיָ'. אֶלָּא
וַדַּאי סְתִימָא דְּמִלָּה, טִיבוּ סַגִּי עֲבַד קוּדְשָׁא בְּרִיךְ הוּא בְּיִשְׂרָאֵל, דְּאִתְרְעֵי
בְּהוּ בַּאֲבָהָתָא, וְעָבֵיד לוֹן רְתִיכָא קַדִּישָׁא עִלָּאָה לִיקָרֵיהּ, וְאַפִּיק לוֹן
מִגּוֹ נַהֲרָא עִלָּאָה יַקִּירָא קַדִּישָׁא, בּוֹצִינָא דְּכָל בּוּצִינִין, בְּגִין דְּיִתְעַטַּר
בְּהוּ. הֲדָא הוּא דִכְתִיב, כֹּה אָמַר יְיָ' בְּעֵבֶר הַנָּהָר יָשְׁבוּ אֲבוֹתֵיכֶם
מֵעוֹלָם. הַנָּהָר: הַהוּא נָהָר דְּאִשְׁתְּמוֹדַע, וְאִתְיְידַע.

188. The whole Torah is both hidden and revealed just like the Holy Name, which is hidden and revealed, SPELLED AS YUD HEI VAV HEI BUT PRONOUNCED ADONAI. This is because the whole Torah is the Holy Name, which is why it is hidden and revealed. WE ASKED, If Yisrael and Joshua knew this, why is it written, "Thus says Hashem"? HE ANSWERS, Surely the secret meaning is that the Holy One, blessed be He, did great kindness with Yisrael in choosing the patriarchs, making them into a lofty holy Chariot for His glory. He brought them from the supernal, precious and holy river, the luminary of all luminaries, NAMELY BINAH, in order to be adorned by them. This is the meaning of, "Your fathers dwelt on the other side of the river in old time." The river IS that one specific river, NAMELY BINAH.

189. מֵעוֹלָם, מַאי קָא בָּעֵי הָכָא. אֶלָּא לְאַחֲזָאָה חָכְמְתָא. מֵעֵבֶר הַנָּהָר
מֵעוֹלָם, אֶלָּא הַהוּא נָהָר עוֹלָם אִקְרֵי. וְעַל דָּא, בְּעֵבֶר הַנָּהָר יָשְׁבוּ
אֲבוֹתֵיכֶם מֵעוֹלָם, לְאַחֲזָאָה טִיבוּ וּקְשׁוֹט דְּעָבֵד קוּדְשָׁא בְּרִיךְ הוּא
לְיִשְׂרָאֵל. וָאֶקַּח אֶת אֲבִיכֶם אֶת אַבְרָהָם מֵעֵבֶר הַנָּהָר מַאי קָא מַיְירֵי.
אֶלָּא אַבְרָהָם לָא אִתְדְּבַק בֵּיהּ בְּהַהוּא נָהָר, כְּמוֹ יִצְחָק דְּאִתְדְּבַק בֵּיהּ
בִּסְטָרֵיהּ לְאִתַתְקְּפָא.

189. THE VERSE SAYS, "in old time (also: 'from the world')." HE ASKS, What does this convey, AND ANSWERS, This indicates Chochmah on the other side of the river, NAMELY from the world, since that river is called world. BINAH IS ALSO CALLED WORLD, AND HENCE "FROM THE WORLD" HAS THE SAME MEANING AS ACROSS THE RIVER. Hence IT SAYS, "Your fathers dwelt on the other side of the river from the world," to show the kindness and truth the Holy One, blessed be He did for Yisrael IN THIS, SINCE, "I took your father Abraham from the other side of the river." HE

ASKS, What does THE VERSE teach us IN SAYING, "AND I TOOK YOUR FATHER ABRAHAM FROM THE OTHER SIDE OF THE RIVER," AND NOT SAYING, 'AND I TOOK ISAAC'? HE ANSWERS, Abraham did not cleave to that river like Isaac did, who was attached to his own aspect to draw strength.

190. תָּא חֲזֵי, הַאי נָהָר, אַף עַל גַּב דְּלָאו אִיהוּ דִּינָא, דִּינִין נָפְקֵי מִסְטְרֵיה, וְאִתְתַּקְפוּ בֵּיה. וְכַד יִצְחָק אִתְתַּקַּף בְּדִינוֹי, כְּדֵין עִלָּאִין וְתַתָּאִין מִתְכַּנְּפֵי לְדִינָא, וְכוּרְסְיָיא דְּדִינָא אִתַּתְקַן, וּמַלְכָּא קַדִּישָׁא יָתִיב עַל כּוּרְסְיָיא דְּדִינָא, וְדָאִין עָלְמָא, כְּדֵין, תִּקְעוּ בַחֹדֶשׁ שׁוֹפָר בַּכֶּסֶה לְיוֹם חַגֵּנוּ. זַכָּאִין אִינּוּן יִשְׂרָאֵל, דְּיַדְעִין לְסַלְּקָא כּוּרְסְיָיא דְּדִינָא, וּלְתַקְּנָא כּוּרְסְיָיא דְּרַחֲמֵי. וּבַמָּה. בַּשׁוֹפָר.

190. Come and see, even though this river, BINAH, is not in Judgment, SINCE BINAH IS THE ATTRIBUTE OF MERCY, NEVERTHELESS Judgments come out from its side, AND JUDGMENTS are strengthened in it. When Isaac grows strong in his Judgments FROM THERE, the higher and lower beings are gathered for Judgment, the throne of Judgment, WHICH IS THE ATTRIBUTE OF JUDGMENT IN MALCHUT, is prepared, and the Holy King, ZEIR ANPIN, sits on the throne of Judgment and sentences the world. Then, "Blow a Shofar at the new moon, at the full moon on our feast day." BY THE SHOFAR THE ATTRIBUTE OF JUDGMENT TURNS INTO THE ATTRIBUTE OF MERCY. Happy are Yisrael who know how to remove the throne of Judgment and prepare the throne of mercy. How DO THEY DO IT? By the Shofar.

191. רִבִּי אַבָּא הֲוָה יָתִיב קַמֵּיה דְּרִבִּי שִׁמְעוֹן, אָמַר לֵיה, הָא זִמְנִין סַגִּיאִין שָׁאִילְנָא עַל הַאי שׁוֹפָר, מַאי קָא מַיְירֵי, וְעַד כָּאן לָא אִתְיַשַּׁבְנָא בֵּיה. אָמַר לֵיה, וַדַּאי הַאי הוּא בְּרִירָא דְּמִלָּה, דְּיִשְׂרָאֵל בָּעְיָין בְּיוֹמָא דְּדִינָא, שׁוֹפָר, וְלָא קֶרֶן. בְּגִין דְּקֶרֶן הָא אִתְיְידַע בְּאָן אֲתַר אִיהוּ, וּלְאִתְדַּבְּקָא דִּינָא לָא בָּעֵינָא. אֲבָל הָא תְּנֵינָן, בְּמִלִּין וּבְעוֹבָדָא, בָּעֵינָן לְאַחֲזָאָה וּלְאִתְעֲרָא מִלִּין סְתִימִין.

191. Rabbi Aba was sitting before Rabbi Shimon. He said to him, I have asked many times about the purpose of the Shofar, but never felt settled about it. He said to him, Surely this is its clear meaning. Yisrael need a

Shofar rather than a horn on the day of Judgment, for the place of origin of the horn is known TO INDICATE MALCHUT, THE ATTRIBUTE OF JUDGMENT, and we should not arouse Judgment. IT IS NOT SO WITH THE SHOFAR THAT ALLUDES TO BINAH, WHICH IS MERCY. Indeed we learned that we need to indicate and rouse hidden things by deed, NAMELY, BY THE BLOWING OF THE SHOFAR AND ITS BLESSING.

192. תָּא חֲזֵי, כַּד הַהוּא שׁוֹפָר עִלָּאָה, דִּנְהִירוּ דְּכֹלָּא בֵּיה, אִסְתַּלָּק וְלָא נָהִיר לִבְנִין, כְּדֵין דִּינָא אִתְּעַר, וְכֻרְסָוָון אִתְתַּקָּנוּ לְבֵי דִינָא, וְדָא שׁוֹפָר, אֵילוֹ דְיִצְחָק אִקְרֵי, תּוּקְפֵיה דְּיִצְחָק, תּוּשְׁבַּחְתֵּיה דַּאֲבָהָן, כַּד אִסְתַּלָּק הַהוּא שׁוֹפָר גָּדוֹל, דְּלָא יַנְקָא לִבְנִין, כְּדֵין יִצְחָק אִתְתַּקַּף, וְאִתְתַּקָּן לְדִינָא בְּעָלְמָא.

192. Come and see, if the supernal Shofar, which includes all lights, is gone and does not shine upon the children, ZEIR ANPIN AND MALCHUT, Judgment is roused and thrones are prepared for the courthouse. The Shofar, BINAH, is called Isaac's ram, NAMELY Isaac's strength, SINCE 'RAM' IS DERIVED FROM STRENGTH. It gives importance to the patriarchs, CHESED, GVURAH AND TIFERET THAT RECEIVE ALL THEIR IMPORTANCE FROM THAT SHOFAR, BINAH. When the great Shofar is gone and does not shine on the children, ZEIR ANPIN AND MALCHUT, Isaac grows strong and prepares himself to judge the world.

193. וְכַד אִתְּעַר הַאי שׁוֹפָר וְכַד בְּנֵי נָשָׁא תַּיְיבִין מֵחֲטָאֵיהוֹן, בַּעְיָין לְנַגְּדָא קוֹל שׁוֹפָר מִתַּתָּא, וְהַהוּא קָלָא סָלִיק לְעֵילָּא, כְּדֵין אִתְּעַר שׁוֹפָרָא אָחֳרָא עִלָּאָה, וְאִתְּעַר רַחֲמֵי, וְאִסְתַּלָּק דִּינָא. וּבַעְיָינָן לְאַחֲזָאָה עוֹבָדָא בְּשׁוֹפָר, לְאִתְּעָרָא שׁוֹפָרָא אָחֳרָא, וּלְאַפָּקָא בְּהַאי שׁוֹפָר לְתַתָּא, אִינוּן קָלֵי, לְאַחֲזָאָה דְּכָל אִינוּן קָלִין דִּלְעֵילָּא, דִּכְלִילָן כֻּלְּהוּ בְּהַהוּא שׁוֹפָר עִלָּאָה, יִתְעָרוּן לְנַפְּקָא.

193. When that Shofar is roused and people repent of their sins, the sound of the Shofar should resound from below. The sound arises up and then another, supernal Shofar is roused, WHICH IS BINAH. Mercy is awakened and Judgment is gone. A deed must be displayed by THE BLOWING OF the Shofar, in order to awaken another Shofar, BINAH, and to draw from the

lower Shofar all those sounds, T'KIAH, SHVARIM, T'RUAH, T'KIAH, ETC.,
to show that all the celestial sounds included in the higher Shofar, THE
THREE DETAILED COLUMNS INCLUDED IN BINAH, will be roused to
emerge FROM BINAH TO ZEIR ANPIN AND MALCHUT.

194. וּבְהָנֵי קָלִין דִּלְתַתָּא, יָהֲבִין יִשְׂרָאֵל חֵילָא לְעֵילָא, וְעַל דָּא בָּעֵינָן
לְזַמְּנָא שׁוֹפָר בְּיוֹמָא דָּא, וּלְסַדְּרָא קָלִין, לְכַוְּונָא בֵּיהּ בְּגִין לְאִתְּעָרָא
שׁוֹפָר אַחֲרָא, דְּבֵיהּ כְּלִילָן קַלֵּי לְעֵילָא.

194. By the sounds below Yisrael give strength above. Hence a Shofar
needs to be summoned on that day, to arrange the sounds, NAMELY THE
PATTERNS OF T'KIAH SHVARIM T'RUAH T'KIAH, ETC. to meditate on it so
as to rouse another Shofar, BINAH, in which all the upper sounds, CHESED,
GVURAH AND TIFERET OF ZEIR ANPIN are included.

195. סִדְרָא קַדְמָאָה, קָלָא נָפִיק, וּמִתְעַטַּר לְעֵילָא, סָלִיק רְקִיעִין,
וְאִתְבְּקַע בֵּין טוּרֵי רָמָאֵי, וּמָטֵי לְגַבֵּיהּ דְּאַבְרָהָם, וְשַׁרְיָא בְּרֵישֵׁיהּ,
וְאִתְעַטַּר, וְאִתְּעַר הוּא, וְאַתְקָן לְכוּרְסְיָיא. וּבְסִפְרָא דְּאַגַּדְתָּא תָּנֵינָן,
בְּשַׁעֲתָא דְּהַהוּא קָלָא קַדְמָאָה סָלִיק, אִתְּעַר וְאִתְעַטַּר אַבְרָהָם, וְאַתְקָן
לְכוּרְסְיָיא, פַּקְדִין עֲלֵיהּ אַבָּא.

195. In the first sequence OF THE THREE SEQUENCES, T'KIAH SHVARIM
T'RUAH T'KIAH, ETC., a sound reverberates, adorned above IN BINAH. It
rises through firmaments to be cleft between the high mountains. FROM
THERE comes Abraham, CHESED OF ZEIR ANPIN, to dwell at its top. He is
adorned, is roused and prepares the throne TO BE A THRONE OF MERCY. In
the book of Agadah, we learned that when the first sound rises, Abraham
awakens. He is adorned and prepares the throne. Aba is summoned upon him.

196. אַדְהָכִי, סַלְקָא תִּנְיָינָא, תַּקִּיפָא לְתַבְרָא תּוּקְפֵי רְגִיזִין. וְדָא סִדְרָא
תִּנְיָינָא, הַהוּא קָלָא תְּבִירָא בְּתוּקְפוֹי. וּכְדֵין סַלְקָא, וְכָל דִּינִין דְּאִתְעַרְעַן
קַמֵּיהּ אִתְבָּרוּ, עַד דְּסָלִיק לְאַתְרֵיהּ דְּיִצְחָק. כֵּיוָן דְּיִצְחָק אִתְּעַר, וְחָמֵי
לְאַבְרָהָם מַתְקָן לְכוּרְסְיָיא לְקַיְימָא קַמֵּיהּ, כְּדֵין אִתְכַּפְיָא, וְתָבַר

תּוּקְפָּא קַשְׁיָא. וּבְהַאי, בָּעֵי מַאן דְּתָקַע, לְכַוְּונָא לִבָּא וּרְעוּתָא, בְּגִין לְתַבְּרָא חֵילָא וְתוּקְפָּא דְּדִינָא קַשְׁיָא, הֲדָא הוּא דִּכְתִיב, אַשְׁרֵי הָעָם יוֹדְעֵי תְרוּעָה, יוֹדְעֵי תְרוּעָה וַדַּאי.

196. In the meantime the second sound resonates. It is strong to break harsh Judgments. This is the second sequence OF T'KIAH SHVARIM T'RUAH TEKIAH. The sound breaks with its strength. It rises TO BINAH and all Judgments that meet THERE are broken before it, until they rise to where Isaac is. When Isaac is roused and sees Abraham preparing the throne OF MERCY to stand before it, he is subdued and breaks the harsh Judgment. Whoever blows should meditate in heart and desire upon this, in order to break that power and the strength of the harsh Judgment. This is the meaning of, "Happy is the people that know the joyful note (Heb. *t'ruah*)" (Tehilim 89:16). T'RUAH IS DERIVED FROM BREAKING. Assuredly they know T'ruah.

197. סִדְרָא תְּלִיתָאָה, קָלָא נָפִיק, וְסָלִיק, וּבָקַע כָּל אִינּוּן רְקִיעִין, וְרַחֲמֵי מִתְעָרָן, וּמָטֵי הַהוּא קָלָא לְרֵישֵׁיהּ דְּיַעֲקֹב וְיַעֲקֹב אִתְּעַר, וְחָמֵי לְאַבְרָהָם מִתְתַּקֵן בְּגִיסָא אַחֲרָא, כְּדֵין אֲחִידָן תַּרְוַוייְהוּ בֵּיהּ בְּיִצְחָק, דָּא מֵהַאי סִטְרָא, וְדָא, מֵהַאי סִטְרָא וְלָא יַכְלִין תּוּקְפוֹי לְנָפְקָא לְבַר. וְהָנֵי תְּלָתָא סִדְרִין, כֻּלְּהוּ סִדְרָא חַד.

197. In the third sequence OF T'KIAH SHVARIM T'RUAH T'KIAH, a sound emerges and rises. It cleaves all firmaments and mercy is aroused. ALL THIS OCCURS IN BINAH AND FROM THERE that sound reaches Jacob's head. Jacob wakes up and sees Abraham preparing on the other side. Then both hold Isaac from one side, THE RIGHT, and the other, THE CENTER, and the power OF THE JUDGMENT OF THE LEFT cannot come out. All these three sequences are all one sequence.

198. סִדְרָא אָחֳרָא, קָלָא נָפִיק, וְסָלִיק, וְנָטִיל לְאַבְרָהָם מֵאַתְרֵיהּ, וְנָגִיד לֵיהּ לְתַתָּא, לַאֲתַר דְּתוּקְפֵּיהוֹן דְּיִצְחָק שַׁרְיָין וְקַיְימָן לֵיהּ לְאַבְרָהָם בְּגַוַוייְהוּ.

198. As for the other sequence OF THE THREE TIMES T'KIAH SHVARIM T'KIAH, a sound reverberates, rises, takes Abraham from his place and draws him down to where the powers of Isaac dwell. They maintain Abraham among them.

199. סִדְרָא תִּנְיָינָא, נָפִיק קָלָא תְּבִירָא, לָא תַּקִיפָא כְּקַדְמָאָה, לָא דְּחָלִישׁ הַהוּא קָלָא דְּתָקַע, אֶלָּא דְּהַהוּא קָלָא לָאו אִיהוּ לְגַבֵּי יִצְחָק בְּקַדְמֵיתָא, דְּתַמָּן תּוּקְפָּא תַּקִיפָא שַׁרְיָא, אֶלָּא לְגַבֵּי אִינּוּן בֵּי דִינָא דִלְתַתָּא, דְּאִינּוּן רְפוּיִין יַתִּיר, וְכֻלְּהוּ חָמָאן לְאַבְרָהָם לְגַבַּיְיהוּ, וְאִתְכַּפְיָין קַמֵּיהּ.

199. In the second sequence OF T'KIAH SHVARIM T'KIAH, a broken sound reverberates, not as strong as the first. It is not because the sound he blew is weak, but it is not directed at Isaac as before, where there is great strength. But THIS SOUND is meant for the lower courthouse, WHERE JUDGMENTS are more lax. They all see Abraham by them and are subdued before him.

200. אַדְּהָכִי, סִדְרָא תְּלִיתָאָה, קָלָא נָפִיק, וְסָלִיק, וְאִתְעַטָּר בְּרֵישֵׁיהּ דְּיַעֲקֹב, וְנָגִיד לֵיהּ לְתַתָּא לְהַהוּא אֲתָר דְּאִינּוּן גְּבוּרָאן שַׁרְיָין, וְקָאִים לְקַבְלַיְיהוּ, אַבְרָהָם מֵהַאי סִטְרָא, וְיַעֲקֹב מֵהַאי סִטְרָא, וְאִינּוּן בְּאֶמְצָעִיתָא. כְּדֵין אִתְכַּפְיָין כֻּלְּהוּ, וּמִשְׁתַּכְחִין בְּאַתְרַיְיהוּ. וְהָנֵי כֻּלְּהוּ סִדְרָא אָחֳרָא תִּנְיָינָא.

200. Then comes the third sequence OF T'KIAH SHVARIM T'KIAH. A sound emerges and rises. It is crowned on the head of Jacob and draws him down to where the Judgments of the left dwell. Before it stand Abraham on the one side and Jacob on the other. There are GVUROT inside the two of them, which are then subdued and SHINE where they are. All THREE SEQUENCES are another, INCLUSIVE sequence.

201. סִדְרָא בַּתְרָאָה, דְּבַעְיָיא לְסַלְּקָא לוֹן לְאַתְרַיְיהוּ, וּלְיַישְׁבָא בֵּינַיְיהוּ לְיִצְחָק כְּמִלְּקַדְמִין. בְּגִין דְּהַאי בָּעֵי לְיִשַׁרָא לֵיהּ בְּאַתְרֵיהּ, וְלָא יִפּוּק בְּתוּקְפוֹי לְבַר, כְּדֵין דִּינִין כֻּלְּהוּ אִתְכַּפְיָין, וְרַחֲמִין אִתְּעָרוּ.

201. The last, INCLUSIVE sequence IS THREE TIMES T'KIAH T'RUAH T'KIAH. These need to raise them to their places and settle Isaac among them as before. For that reason, they need to place him in his place IN SUCH A WAY that he will not come out through the power OF HIS GVUROT. All Judgments are subdued then and Mercy awakens.

202. עַל דָּא בָּעֵי לְכַוְּונָא לִבָּא וּרְעוּתָא בְּהָנֵי קָלֵי, וּלְמֶהְדַר בִּתְיוּבְתָּא קַמֵּי מָארֵיהוֹן. כְּדֵין כַּד יִשְׂרָאֵל מִתְקְנֵי וּמְסַדְּרֵי קָלִין בִּרְעוּתָא דְלִבָּא כַּדְקָא יָאוּת, בְּשׁוֹפָרָא דָא, אִהֲדָר הַהוּא שׁוֹפָר עִלָּאָה, וְכַד אַהֲדָר, מְעַטְּרָא לֵיהּ לְיַעֲקֹב, וְאִתְתַּקַן כֹּלָּא. וְכוּרְסְיָיא אָחֳרָא רְמִיו, וּכְדֵין חֵידוּ אִשְׁתְּכַח בְּכֹלָּא, וְקוּדְשָׁא בְּרִיךְ הוּא מְרַחֵם עַל עָלְמָא. זַכָּאָה חוּלָקֵיהוֹן דְּיִשְׂרָאֵל, דְּיַדְעִין לְנַגְדָּא וּלְאַמְשָׁכָא לְמָארֵיהוֹן, מִדִּינָא לְרַחֲמֵי, וּלְתַקְּנָא כֻּלְּהוּ עָלְמִין עַל יְדַיְיהוּ.

202. For that reason it behooves us to meditate and concentrate on these sounds OF THREE TIMES T'KIAH SHVARIM T'RUAH T'KIAH, THREE TIMES T'KIAH SHVARIM T'KIAH AND THREE TIMES T'KIAH T'RUAH T'KIAH. And they need to repent before their Master. Then, when Yisrael ready themselves and arrange these sounds willingly and properly with this LOWER Shofar, BINAH, the upper Shofar SHINES again. When it SHINES again, it adorns Jacob, ZEIR ANPIN, and everything is established. A different throne, THE THRONE OF MERCY, is placed. Joy abounds everywhere and the Holy One, blessed be He has mercy upon the world. Happy is the lot of Yisrael, who know how to direct and draw their Master from Judgment to Mercy, and establish the worlds by their handiwork.

203. ת"ח, לָקֳבֵל דָּא, תְּלָתָא סִפְרִין פְּתִיחִין בְּיוֹמָא דָא, וּכְמָה דְּרַחֲמִין מִתְעָרִין, וְדִינִין קַשְׁיָין אִתְכַּפְיָין וְעָאלִין לְדוּכְתַּיְיהוּ. כַּךְ הוּא לְתַתָּא כְּגַוְונָא דִלְעֵילָּא, דִּינִין קַשְׁיָין אִתְכַּפְיָין וְאִתְעֲבָרוּ מֵעָלְמָא. וּמַאן אִינּוּן. אִלֵּין אִינּוּן רְשָׁעִים גְּמוּרִים, דְּאִינּוּן דִּינִין קַשְׁיָין דְּאִתְכַּפְיָין וְאִתְעֲבָרוּ מֵעָלְמָא. וְעַל דָּא נִכְתָּבִים וְנֶחְתָּמִים וְכו'. א"ר אַבָּא, וַדַּאי דָּא הוּא בְּרִירָא דְמִלָּה, בְּרִיךְ רַחֲמָנָא דְּשָׁאִילְנָא וְרַוְוחָנָא בְּהָנֵי מִילֵי.

203. Come and see, in correspondence to this, THE THREE SEQUENCES OF THE SHOFAR, THE THREE COLUMNS, three books are open on that day. ONE IS FOR THE WHOLLY RIGHTEOUS, THE SECRET OF THE RIGHT COLUMN, ONE FOR THE WHOLLY EVIL, THE SECRET OF THE HARSH JUDGMENT ON THE LEFT COLUMN, AND ONE FOR THE MEDIOCRE, THE SECRET OF THE CENTRAL COLUMN. Just as THROUGH THE BLOWING OF THE SHOFAR Mercy awakens and harsh Judgments are subdued and return to their place, it is below as it is above. The harsh Judgments BELOW are subdued and removed from the world. These are the wholly wicked, who are harsh Judgments. They are subdued, and removed from the world. By that they are written and sentenced to death immediately. THE WHOLLY RIGHTEOUS, A CHARIOT TO THE RIGHT, ARE WRITTEN TO LIFE IMMEDIATELY AND THE MEDIOCRE, WHO ARE A CHARIOT TO THE CENTRAL COLUMN, ARE IN SUSPENSE UNTIL YOM KIPPUR, WHEN IT IS COMPLETED THROUGH THE ILLUMINATION OF CHOCHMAH IN BINAH, THE LIGHT OF LIFE. Rabbi Aba said, Surely this is the clear meaning of the matter. Blessed is the Merciful that I have asked and attained these matters.

204. א"ר יְהוּדָה, כְּתִיב זִכְרוֹן תְּרוּעָה, זִכְּרוֹן עֲבְדֵינָן, לְכַוְּונָא לְבָּא וּרְעוּתָא, יִשְׂרָאֵל עַבְדִּין זִכְּרוֹן לְתַתָּא, בְּמָה. בְּעוֹבָדָא, בְּגִין דְּיִתְּעַר מִלָּה כְּהַהוּא גַּוְונָא לְעֵילָא.

204. Rabbi Yehuda said, It is written, "a memorial of blowing" (Vayikra 23:24), WHICH MEANS we are reminded to direct the heart and wish IN THE MANNER MENTIONED ABOVE. Yisrael perform a memorial below, by the deed OF BLOWING THE SHOFAR so that a similar thing will be roused above.

205. אָמַר ר' אֶלְעָזָר, כְּתִיב בַּכֶּסֶה לְיוֹם חַגֵּנוּ דְּאִתְכַּסְיָא בֵּיהּ סִיהֲרָא. וְהֵיךְ אִתְכַּסְיָא. אֶלָּא, כַּד קַיְימָא עִיבָא, וְשִׁמְשָׁא לָא נָהִיר, כְּדֵין סִיהֲרָא אִתְכַּסְיָא, וְלָא נָהִיר. וְעַל דָּא, מִקַּמֵּי עִיבָא שִׁמְשָׁא לָא נָהִיר, כ"ש סִיהֲרָא דְּאִתְכַּסְיָא וְלָא נְהִירָא. וְעַל דָּא בַּכֶּסֶה לְיוֹם חַגֵּנוּ, בְּהָ"א, דְּאִתְכַּסְיָא סִיהֲרָא. וּבְמָה נָהִיר. כֹּלָּא בִּתְיוּבְתָּא, וּבְקָל שׁוֹפָרָא, דִּכְתִיב אַשְׁרֵי הָעָם יוֹדְעֵי תְרוּעָה כְּדֵין יְיָ' בְּאוֹר פָּנֶיךָ יְהַלֵּכוּן.

205. Rabbi Elazar said, It is written, "at the full moon (also: 'the covering') on our feast day." THIS IS BECAUSE the moon, MALCHUT, was covered on it, FOR ON ROSH HASHANAH THE MOON IS HIDDEN. HE ASKS, How is it covered, AND ANSWERS, When there is a cloud UNDERNEATH THE SUN and the sun, WHICH IS ZEIR ANPIN, does not shine, the moon is covered, WHICH MEANS it does not shine, SINCE THERE IS NO ONE FROM WHICH TO RECEIVE LIGHT, FOR WHATEVER MALCHUT HAS, SHE RECEIVES FROM ZEIR ANPIN. Therefore, if because of the clouds, WHICH INDICATE JUDGMENTS, the sun, ZEIR ANPIN, cannot shine, the moon all the more is hidden and cannot illuminate. Hence, in "at the covering (Heb. *keseh*) on our feast day," *KESEH* IS SPELLED WITH Hei IN FINAL POSITION, TO INDICATE THAT the moon is covered BECAUSE OF JUDGMENTS. How can everything, BOTH ZEIR ANPIN AND MALCHUT, shine? Through repentance and the sound of the Shofar, as written, "Happy is the people that know the joyful note." Then, "they shall walk, Hashem, in the light of Your countenance" (Tehilim 89:16).

33. Rosh Hashanah

A Synopsis

We learn that the day of Rosh Hashanah is a day when the moon is hidden and the world is under Judgment. God allotted the prosecutor a specific day in which to demand all the punishments in the world so that the fear of God would increase. He wants the world to know that there is judgment and there is a judge. Witnesses come on the day of Judgment and testify about all the deeds of everyone in the world; these witnesses are called the eyes of Hashem that see everything. We are told how everything is put down in writing, and how someone's verdict can be torn up if he repents. God prefers people to be saved from punishment; His love for His children overcomes His love of judgment. We hear the explanation of Isaac's blessing of Jacob instead of Esau, and of how this relates to the days between Rosh Hashanah and Yom Kippur.

רעיא מהימנא

206. בַּחֹדֶשׁ הַשְּׁבִיעִי בְּאֶחָד לַחֹדֶשׁ וְגוֹ'. פְּקוּדָא דָּא, לְתִקוֹעַ שׁוֹפָר בְּרֹאשׁ הַשָּׁנָה, דְּהוּא יוֹמָא דְדִינָא לְעָלְמָא, כְּמָה דְּאוּקִימְנָא. וְהָא אוּקְמוּהָ דִּכְתִיב, תִּקְעוּ בַחֹדֶשׁ שׁוֹפָר בַּכֶּסֶה לְיוֹם חַגֵּנוּ. וְהָא אִתְּמַר. דְּהַאי אִיהוּ יוֹמָא דְּסִיהֲרָא אִתְכַּסֵּי בֵּיהּ, וְקָאֵים עָלְמָא בְּדִינָא בְּגִין, דְּהַהוּא מְקַטְרְגָא, חָפֵי וְכַסֵּי וְאַנְעֵל פִּתְחָא עַל מַלְכָּא, אֲתַר דְּדִינָא שָׁרְיָא, לְמִתְבַּע דִּינָא עַל עָלְמָא.

Ra'aya Meheimna (the Faithful Shepherd)

206. "In the seventh month, on the first day of the month" (Vayikra 23:24). This commandment is to blow the Shofar on Rosh Hashanah, which is Judgment day to the world as we explained. We explained the words, "Blow a Shofar at the new moon, at the full moon (or: 'covering') on our feast day" (Tehilim 81:4). We learned that this day is a day when the moon, MALCHUT, is covered and the world is under Judgment. For the prosecutor covers and hides and locks the entrance to the King, WHO IS ZEIR ANPIN, AND THE MOON IS a place where Judgment abides to demand justice from the world.

207. וְאִי תֵּימָא, אֵיךְ אִתְיְיהִיב לֵיהּ רְשׁוּ לְהַהוּא מְקַטְרְגָא לְחַפָּאָה

וּלְמִתְבַּע דִּינָא. אֶלָּא וַדַּאי דְּהַאי בִּידָא דְּהַאי מְקַטְרְגָא, שַׁוֵּי קוּדְשָׁא בְּרִיךְ
הוּא לְמִתְבַּע דִּינָא עַל כָּל עָלְמָא, וְשַׁוֵּי לֵיהּ יוֹמָא יְדִיעָא, לְמִתְבַּע
קַמֵּיהּ כָּל דִּינִין דְּעָלְמָא, דְּהָא קוּדְשָׁא בְּרִיךְ הוּא עָבֵד לֵיהּ וְשַׁוֵּי לֵיהּ
קַמֵּיהּ, לְמֶהֱוֵי דְּחִילוּ דְּקוּדְשָׁא בְּרִיךְ הוּא סַלְקָא, וְשַׁרְיָא עַל כֹּלָּא. וְרָזָא
דָא, וְהָאֱלֹהִים עָשָׂה שֶׁיִּרְאוּ מִלְּפָנָיו. מַאי עָשָׂה. עָשָׂה לְהַאי מְקַטְרְגָא,
וְאַתְקִין לֵיהּ קַמֵּיהּ, לְמֶהֱוֵי סַיְיפָא שְׁנָנָא עַל כָּל עָלְמָא. וְכָל דָּא בְּגִין
דְּיִדְחֲלוּן מִקַּמֵּי קוּדְשָׁא בְּרִיךְ הוּא כֹּלָּא. וְדָא אִיהוּ סַנְטִירָא, דְּתָבַע
חוֹבֵי בְּנֵי נָשָׁא, וְתָבַע דִּינָא, וְתָפִיס בְּנֵי נָשָׁא וְקָטִיל לוֹן וְאַלְקֵי לוֹן,
כֹּלָּא כְּמָה דְּנָפִיק מִן דִּינָא.

207. You may wonder how the prosecutor was given permission to cover THE LIGHT OF MALCHUT and demand punishment. AND HE ANSWERS, Surely the Holy One, blessed be He, allowed the prosecutor to demand justice from the whole world. He allotted him a specific day in which to demand all the punishments in the world, for the Holy One, blessed be He, made him and placed him before Himself, so the fear of the Holy One, blessed be He, will increase and rest on everyone. This is the secret of, "and Elohim does it, so that men should fear before Him" (Kohelet 3:14). What is "does"? He did this prosecutor and made him before Himself to be a sharp sword over the whole world, all for the reason that all will fear the Holy One, blessed be He. He oversees and prosecutes the sins of people, demands punishment and seizes people; kills them and strikes them, all just as it was decided in court.

208. כְּגַוְונָא דְּהַהוּא מְמוּנֶה בֵּית דִּין דִּלְתַתָּא, דְּאִתְיְיהִיב לֵיהּ רְשׁוּ
לְאַדְכְּרָא קַמֵּי בֵּי דִּינָא, פְּלוֹנִי עֲבַד כָּךְ, וּפְלוֹנִי עָבַר עַל כָּךְ, וּלְמִתְבַּע
עֲלַיְיהוּ דִּינָא. וּתְנָן, רְשׁוּ אִתְיְיהִיב לְהַהוּא מְמוּנֶה בֵּית דִּין, לְאַנְעָלָא
עַל בֵּי דִּינָא פִּתְחָא, עַד דִּיגְזְרוּן דִּינָא עַל כָּל מַה דְּאִיהוּ תָבַע, וְלֵית
רְשׁוּ לְבֵית דִּין לְדַחֲיָיא לֵיהּ. בְּגִין כִּי אֲנִי יְיָ׳ אוֹהֵב מִשְׁפָּט. וְאִיהוּ בָּעֵי
דְּעָלְמָא יִתְקַיֵּים בְּדִינָא, וּלְמִנְדַּע דְּאִית דִּין וְאִית דַּיָּין.

208. It is like the minister appointed over the terrestrial court, who was given permission to mention before the court that so and so did this, and so and so transgressed that, and to demand punishment. We learned that the minister appointed over the court was given permission to lock the entrance to the court until verdicts will be meted out to all his persecution. The court is not allowed to decline him, because, "For I Hashem love justice" (Yeshayah 61:8), and He wants the world to be maintained by judgment, so as to make known that there is judgment and there is a judge. ALL THIS APPLIES TO THE TERRESTRIAL COURT.

209. כְּהַאי גַּוְונָא שַׁוֵּי קוּדְשָׁא בְּרִיךְ הוּא קַמֵּיהּ לְהַאי, דְּאִיהוּ תָּבַע דִּינָא קַמֵּי מַלְכָּא, עַל כָּל בְּנֵי עָלְמָא. וּבְהַאי יוֹמָא אִתְיְיהִיב לֵיהּ רְשׁוּ, לְכַסָּאָה פִּתְחָא דְּמַלְכָּא, וְסִיהֲרָא אִתְחַפְיָיא לְגוֹ, עַד דְּיִתְגְזַר דִּינָא עַל כָּל בְּנֵי עָלְמָא. וְאַף עַל גַּב דְּכֹלָּא אִתְגְּלֵי קַמֵּי קוּדְשָׁא בְּרִיךְ הוּא, לָא בָּעֵי אֶלָּא בְּדִינָא.

209. The Holy One, blessed be He, did the same. He placed before Him that PROSECUTOR who demands punishment before the King for all the people in the world. On that day, he is given permission to cover the entrance of the King, ZEIR ANPIN, and the moon, MALCHUT, is hidden inside until punishment is meted out to all the people in the world. Though everything is revealed before the Holy One, blessed be He, He nevertheless desires nothing but according to Judgment.

210. כֹּלָּא כְּגַוְונָא חֲדָא עֵילָא וְתַתָּא, אַתְקִין כּוּרְסְיָא דְּדִינָא בְּהַאי יוֹמָא, וְסַנְטִירָא אָתָא, וְתָבַע דִּינָא עַל כָּל עוֹבְדֵי בְּנֵי עָלְמָא, כָּל חַד וְחַד כְּפוּם אָרְחוֹי, וּכְפוּם מַה דַּעֲבַד. וְסָהֲדִין אַתְיָין וְסָהֲדֵי עַל כָּל עוֹבְדֵי בְּנֵי עָלְמָא. וְאִלֵּין אִינוּן עֵינֵי יְיָ', דְּאִינוּן מְשַׁטְּטֵי בְּכָל עָלְמָא. וְכַמָּה אִינוּן עֵינֵי יְיָ', דְּלֵית לוֹן חוּשְׁבָּנָא, דְּקָא אַזְלֵי וּמְשַׁטְּטֵי בְּכָל עָלְמָא, וְחָמָאן כָּל עוֹבְדֵי בְּנֵי עָלְמָא.

210. Everything operates in the same way above and below. On that day, THE HOLY ONE, BLESSED BE HE, fixes the throne of Judgment, and the administrator comes and demands justice for all the deeds of the people in the world, each according to his ways and deeds. Witnesses come and testify to all the deeds of the people in the world, and these WITNESSES ARE CALLED the eyes of Hashem that roam throughout the whole world and see the deeds of the people in the world.

211. וַוי לְאִינּוּן דְּלָא מַשְׁגִּיחִין וְלָא מִסְתַּכְּלִין בְּעוֹבָדֵיהוֹן, דְּהָא לְגַבַּיְיהוּ קַיְימִין אִלֵּין סַהֲדֵי מַלְכָּא, וּמַשְׁגִּיחִין וְחָמָאן כָּל מַה דְּאִינּוּן עָבְדִין, וְקָאָמְרֵי, דְּהָא אִינּוּן סַלְקֵי וְסַהֲדֵי קַמֵּי מַלְכָּא. וְהַאי סַנְטִירָא קָאֵים קַמֵּי מַלְכָּא, וְתָבַע דִּינָא, פְּלוֹנִי עָבַר דִּינָא, פְּלוֹנִי עֲבַד כָּךְ. וְהָא הָכָא סַהֲדֵי. וְעַד דְּקוּדְשָׁא בְּרִיךְ הוּא לָא שָׁאִיל לוֹן, לֵית לוֹן רְשׁוּ לְסַהֲדָא. כְּדֵין אִינּוּן סַהֲדֵי סַהֲדוּתָא.

211. Woe to those who do not care and do not observe their doings, for the witnesses of the King stand by them, observe and see whatever they do or say. They ascend and testify before the King. The administrator stands before the King and demands punishment: so and so transgressed the law and so and so did that; here are the witnesses. As long as the Holy One, blessed be He, does not ask them, they have no permission to testify. WHEN HE ASKS THEM, they deliver their testimony.

212. וְכֹלָּא אַכְתִּיב קַמֵּי מַלְכָּא בְּפִתְקָא. בְּבֵי מַלְכָּא אִית חַד הֵיכָלָא. הֵיכָלָא דָּא מַלְיָא אֶשָּׁא חִוָּורָא, וְהַאי אֶשָּׁא מִתְגַּלְגְּלָא בְּפַלְקָא, וְלָהִיט שְׁבִיבִין וְהַאי לָא פָּסִיק לְעָלְמִין. לְגוֹ הַאי הֵיכָלָא, אִית הֵיכָלָא אוֹחֲרָא, מַלְיָא אֶשָּׁא אוּכְמָא, דְּלָא פָּסִיק לְעָלְמִין. תְּרֵין סוֹפְרִין קַיְימִין תָּדִיר קַמֵּיהּ מַלְכָּא. בְּשַׁעֲתָא דְּדִינָא, סָהֲדִין כָּל סַהֲדֵי קַמֵּי מַלְכָּא. אִינּוּן סוֹפְרִין נַטְלִין מֵהַהוּא פַּלְקָא דְּאֶשָּׁא חִוָּורָא, וְכַתְבֵי עֲלֵיהּ בְּהַהוּא אֶשָּׁא אוּכְמָא.

212. Everything is put in writing before the King. In the King's house there is a certain chamber, full of white fire. This fire rolls in a circle with burning sparks and never ceases. Inside this chamber there is another chamber, full of black fire, which never ceases. Two scribes stand before the King at all times. During trials, all witnesses testify before the King. The scribes take from the circle of white fire and write THE VERDICT on it with the black circle.

213. וּכְדֵין מַלְכָּא אַחְמִיץ דִּינָא, עַד זִמְנָא יְדִיעָא, דִּלְמָא בֵּין כָּךְ וּבֵין כָּךְ יְהַדְרוּן בִּתְשׁוּבָה. אִי יְהַדְרוּן, פִּתְקִין נִקְרָעִין. וְאִי לָאו, מַלְכָּא יָתִיב,

וְכָל אִינּוּן דְּבֵי זְכוּתָא קַיְימֵי קַמֵּיה, כְּרוֹזָא קָם וְכָרִיז, פְּלוֹנִי עֲבַד כָּךְ, מַאן יוֹלִיף עֲלֵיה זְכוּת, אִי אִית מַאן דְּיוֹלִיף עֲלֵיה זְכוּת, יָאוֹת. וְאִי לָאו הָא אִתְמְסַר לְסַנְטִירָא.

213. The King then holds the verdict for some time, in case they will repent in the meantime. If they returned IN REPENTANCE, the writings are torn up. If not, the King sits and all the defenders stand before Him. The crier stands and announces, so and so did this; who shall defend him? If there is someone to defend him, it is well. Otherwise, he is given to the administrator FOR PUNISHMENT.

214. וְכֹלָּא יָדַע קוּדְשָׁא בְּרִיךְ הוּא, אַמַּאי אִצְטְרִיךְ לְכָל דָּא. אֶלָּא בְּגִין דְּלָא, יְהֵא פִּתְרָא דְּפוּמָא לִבְנֵי עָלְמָא. אֶלָּא לְאַחֲזָאָה דְּכֹלָּא עָבִיד בְּאֹרַח קְשׁוֹט, וְנִיחָא קַמֵּיה מַאן דְּאִשְׁתְּזִיב מִן דִּינֵיה. וְאִי תֵּימָא מְנָלָן. הַאי, אִתְמְסַר לְחַכִּימֵי, וַאֲפִילוּ לְמַאן דְּלָא יַדְעֵי, מַאן דְּבָעֵי לְאִסְתַּכְּלָא, יַשְׁגַּח בְּמָה דְּאִיהוּ בְּאִתְגַּלְיָיא, וְיֵדַע בְּמָה דְּאִיהוּ בְּסִתְרָא, דְּהָא כֹּלָּא בְּגַוְונָא חֲדָא, כָּל מַה דְּפָקִיד קוּדְשָׁא בְּרִיךְ הוּא בְּאַרְעָא, כֹּלָּא אִיהוּ בְּגַוְונָא דִּלְעֵילָא.

214. HE ASKS, Yet the Holy One, blessed be He, knows everything, why does He need all this? AND HE ANSWERS, This is so that people will have no excuse, but rather to show that He does everything truthfully. He prefers it when one is saved from His punishment. You may ask whence we know that. THIS was given to the sages, and even those who do not know, whoever may wish to see, may see what is divulged BELOW IN THIS WORLD, and thus know what is a mystery ABOVE, since everything follows the same pattern. For whatever the Holy One, blessed be He, does in the ways of the world, is in the likeness of above.

215. יוֹמָא דר״ה, אִיהוּ יוֹמָא דְּדִינָא, וּמַלְכָּא יָתִיב בְּכוּרְסַיָּיא דְּדִינָא, סַנְטִירָא קָא אָתֵי וְחָפֵי פִּתְחָא דְּמַלְכָּא, וְתָבַע דִּינָא. וְאַף עַל גַּב דְּקוּדְשָׁא בְּרִיךְ הוּא רָחִים לֵיה לְדִינָא, כְּמָה דְּאַתְּ אָמַר, כִּי אֲנִי יְיָ' אֹהֵב מִשְׁפָּט. נָצַח רְחִימוּ דִּבְנוֹי, לִרְחִימוּ דְּדִינָא. וּבְשַׁעֲתָא דְּסַנְטִירָא

קָם לְמִטְעַן מִלִּין עָלַיְיהוּ, פָּקִיד לְמִתְקַע בַּשׁוֹפָר, בְּגִין לְאִתְּעָרָא רַחֲמֵי מִתַּתָּא לְעֵילָא, בְּהַהוּא שׁוֹפָר.

215. The day of Rosh Hashanah is Judgment day, and the King sits on the throne of Judgment. The administrator comes and covers the entrance to the King and demands punishment. Even though the Holy One, blessed be He, loves judgment, as written, "For I Hashem love justice," the love of His children overcame the love of judgment. When the administrator rises to speak about them, THE HOLY ONE, BLESSED BE HE, commanded to blow the Shofar in order to rouse love from below upward by that Shofar.

216. סַלְקָא הַהוּא קָלָא, כְּלִילָא בְּאֶשָּׁא וְרוּחָא וּמַיָּא, וְאִתְעֲבֵיד מִנַּיְיהוּ קָלָא חֲדָא, וְאִתְּעַר קָלָא אָחֳרָא לְעֵילָא, כַּד הַהוּא קָלָא אִתְּעַר מֵעֵילָא וּמִתַּתָּא, כְּדֵין כָּל טַעֲנוֹת דְּקָא טָעִין הַהוּא מְקַטְרְגָא מִתְעַרְבְּבֵי.

216. The sound rises, included of fire, wind and water, WHICH CORRESPOND TO CHESED, GVURAH AND TIFERET, that merge into one sound. Another sound from above is roused before it, WHICH IS THE CENTRAL COLUMN THAT JOINS LEFT AND RIGHT. When that sound is roused from above and from below, all the charges the prosecutors raise are confused.

217. בְּיוֹמָא דְּרֹאשׁ הַשָּׁנָה, נָפִיק יִצְחָק בִּלְחוֹדוֹי, וְקָרֵי לְעֵשָׂו, לְאַטְעֲמָא לֵיהּ תַּבְשִׁילִין דְּכָל עָלְמָא, כָּל חַד כְּפוּם אוֹרְחוֹי, דְּהָא בְּהַהִיא שַׁעֲתָא וַתִּכְהֶן עֵינָיו מֵרְאוֹת, דְּנָפִיק מִנֵּיהּ מַאן דְּאַחְשִׁיךְ אַפֵּי בִּרְיָין, וְאִתְפְּרַשׁ, וְשָׁכִיב עַל עַרְסֵיהּ דְּדִינָא, וְקָרֵי לְעֵשָׂו, וְאָמַר וְצוּדָה לִי צָיְדָה וַעֲשֵׂה לִי מַטְעַמִּים וְהָבִיאָה לִּי.

217. On the day of Rosh Hashanah, Isaac comes out alone, THAT IS, THE LEFT COLUMN REIGNS WITHOUT THE RIGHT, WITHOUT THE JOINING OF THE CENTRAL COLUMN, WHICH ARE ABRAHAM AND JACOB. He calls Esau, THE OTHER SIDE, to give him dishes to eat of the whole world, according to their deeds, NAMELY, TO DEMAND PUNISHMENT FOR THE ACTIONS OF ALL THE PEOPLE IN THE WORLD. For at that time, "his eyes were dim, so that he could not see" (Beresheet 27:1), because he that darkens people's faces comes out from him – THAT IS, THE PROSECUTOR IS DRAWN FROM THE LEFT, WHEN IT IS WITHOUT THE RIGHT. He is separated FROM THE RIGHT AND CENTRAL COLUMN, lies on the couch of Judgment and calls Esau, WHO IS THE OTHER SIDE AND THE PROSECUTOR. And he said, "catch me some venison; and make me savory food" (Ibid. 3-4) FROM THE EVIL DEEDS OF PEOPLE, "and bring it to me" (Ibid.).

218. וְרִבְקָה אָמְרָה אֶל יַעֲקֹב בְּנָהּ, רְחִימָא דְנַפְשָׁהּ, בְּנָהּ רְחִימָא דְאִתְמְסַר לָהּ מִיוֹמָא דְאִתְבְּרֵי עָלְמָא. וּפְקִידַת לֵיהּ, לְאִתְעֲרָא אִיהוּ בְּאִינוּן מַטְעַמִים דִּילֵיהּ. וְיַעֲקֹב אִתְעַר מִתַּתָּא, וּמִתְלַבַּשׁ בִּצְלוֹתִין וּבָעוּתִין, וְהַקוֹל קוֹל יַעֲקֹב בְּהַהוּא שׁוֹפָר דְּקָא סָלִיק, וְאִתְעַר יַעֲקֹב לְגַבֵּיהּ, וְאִתְקְרִיב בַּהֲדֵיהּ, וַיַּגֶּשׁ לוֹ וַיֹּאכַל, וְאִתְכְּלִיל דָּא בְּדָא. כֵּיוָן דְּאִתְכְּלִיל בַּהֲדֵיהּ, וַיָּבֵא לוֹ יַיִן, דָּא יַיִן דְּמִנְטְרָא, יַיִן דְּהוּא חֶידוּ דְלִבָּא, רָזָא דְעָלְמָא דְאָתֵי, כְּדֵין וַיָּרַח אֶת רֵיחַ בְּגָדָיו, צְלוֹתִין דְּסַלְקִין וּבָעוּתִין. וַיְבָרֲכֵהוּ, נַח רוּגְזָא, וְחָדֵי לִבָּא, וְכֹלָּא אִיהוּ רַחֲמֵי.

218. "And Rivkah spoke to Jacob her son…" (Ibid. 6), her heart's beloved, her beloved son given to her since the world was created. She orders him to rouse himself with his own dishes. Jacob awakens below, dons prayers and petitions, and "The voice is Jacob's voice" (Ibid. 22), with the celestial Shofar. SUPERNAL Jacob awakens, WHO IS THE CENTRAL COLUMN, towards him, ISAAC, and approaches him, BY JOINING HIM WITH ABRAHAM, WHO IS THE RIGHT. "And he brought it near to him, and he did eat" (Ibid. 25), WHICH MEANS they were incorporated within each other, AND THE MOCHIN SHONE, THE SECRET OF EATING. Once THE CENTRAL COLUMN was included in him, "he brought him wine" (Ibid.), the preserved wine, NAMELY, THE ILLUMINATION OF CHOCHMAH THAT SHINES FROM BELOW UPWARDS, FIXED BY THE CENTRAL COLUMN. The wine rejoices the heart, the secret of the World to Come, NAMELY THE ILLUMINATION OF CHOCHMAH THAT IS DRAWN FROM BINAH CALLED THE WORLD TO COME. Then, "he smelt the smell of his garments" (Ibid. 27), THAT IS, the ascending prayers and petitions, "and blessed him" (Ibid.). THAT MEANS anger abated, the heart rejoiced and everything is full of Mercy.

219. כֵּיוָן דְּאִיהוּ אִתְכְּלִיל בְּיַעֲקֹב, כָּל אִינוּן חַיָּילִין וְתוּקְפִין וְרוּגְזִין

דַּהֲווֹ זְמִינִין, אִתְבַּדְרוּ, וְלָא אִשְׁתְּכָחוּ תַּמָּן. וְיִשְׂרָאֵל נָפְקִין מִן דִּינָא, בְּחֶדְוָה וּבְבִרְכָּאן. וַיְהִי אַךְ יָצֹא יָצָא יַעֲקֹב מֵאֵת פְּנֵי יִצְחָק אָבִיו, בְּיוֹמָא דָא, בְּחֶדְוָה, וּבְבִרְכָּאן עִלָּאִין, וְעֵשָׂו אָחִיו בָּא מִצֵּידוֹ, טָעִין טוֹעֲנֵי מֵעוֹבָדֵי דְעָלְמָא, וַיַּעַשׂ גַּם הוּא מַטְעַמִּים, חַדִּיד לִישְׁנֵיהּ לְמִטְעַן טַעֲנוֹת. אַתְקִין סַהֲדֵי, וַיָּבֵא לְאָבִיו וַיֹּאמֶר יָקוּם אָבִי, יִתְּעַר בְּדִינוֹי, וְיֹאכַל כַּמָּה עוֹבָדִין בִּישִׁין דְּכָל עָלְמָא דְּקָא אַשְׁכַּחְנָא.

219. Once he is incorporated in Jacob, all the awaiting powers, harsh Judgments and anger dispersed and were no longer present there. Yisrael emerged from Judgment with happiness and blessings. "and Jacob was yet scarce gone out from the presence of Isaac his father," on that day, with joy and celestial blessings, "that Esau his brother came in from his hunting" (Ibid. 30), loaded with burdens of the deeds of the world TO DENOUNCE THEM. "And he also had made savory food" (Ibid. 31), sharpening his tongue to give charges and prepare testimony, "and brought it to his father, and said to his father, Let my father arise," rousing himself with his Judgment, "and eat" (Ibid.) the many evil deeds DONE in the whole world that I have found.

220. וַיֶּחֱרַד יִצְחָק חֲרָדָה גְּדוֹלָה עַד מְאֹד, דְּהָא לָא יָכִיל לְאִתְפָּרְשָׁא מִכְּלָלָא דְיַעֲקֹב, דְּאִיהוּ בְּחֶדְוָה. וַיֹּאמֶר מִי אֵפוֹא הוּא הַצָּד צַיִד, בְּכַמָּה צְלוֹתִין וּבָעוּתִין, וָאֹכַל מִכֹּל בְּטֶרֶם תָּבֹא וָאֲבָרֲכֵהוּ גַּם בָּרוּךְ יִהְיֶה. כִּשְׁמֹעַ עֵשָׂו אֶת דִּבְרֵי יִצְחָק אָבִיו וַיִּצְעַק צְעָקָה וְגוֹ'. דְּחָמֵי דְּהָא צֵידוֹ לָא הֲוָה כְּלוּם. עַד לְבָתַר דְּאָמַר לֵיהּ, הִנֵּה מִשְׁמַנֵּי הָאָרֶץ וְגוֹ' אִלֵּין תַּקִּיפִין וְאוּכְלוּסִין דִּשְׁאָר עַמִּין וְדָא קַשְׁיָא לֵיהּ מִכֹּלָּא. וַיִּשְׂטֹם עֵשָׂו אֶת יַעֲקֹב, לְמֵיזַל אֲבַתְרֵיהּ, וּלְקַטְרְגָא לֵיהּ תָּדִיר.

220. "And Isaac trembled very much…" (Ibid. 33), for he could not be separated from being incorporated in Jacob, who abides in joy, "and said, Who then is he that has taken venison" by many prayers and petitions, "and I have eaten of all before you came, and have blessed him? Moreover, he shall be blessed. And when Esau heard the words of his father, he cried with a great and exceedingly bitter cry" (Ibid. 33-34), because he saw that his venison was worthless. Eventually he said to him, "Behold, your dwelling shall be of the fatness of the earth..." (Ibid. 39), the mighty men and the multitudes of the other people. This was hardest for him, "And Esau hated Jacob" (Ibid. 41), following him and constantly denouncing him.

‎221. וְיַעֲקֹב אָזִיל בְּאִינּוּן יוֹמִין דְּבֵין ר"ה לְיוֹם הַכִּפּוּרִים, עָרִיק לְאִשְׁתְּזָבָא מִנֵּיהּ. תָּב בְּתִיוּבְתָּא, שַׁוֵּי גַּרְמֵיהּ בְּתַעֲנִיתָא, עַד דְּאָתֵי י"ה, כְּדֵין יַדְעֵי יִשְׂרָאֵל דְּעֵשָׂו בָּא, וְעִמּוֹ אַרְבַּע מֵאוֹת אִישׁ, כֻּלְּהוּ מְקַטְרְגֵי זְמִינִין לְקַטְרְגָא לוֹן, מִיַּד וַיִּירָא יַעֲקֹב מְאֹד וַיֵּצֶר לוֹ וְאַסְגֵּי בִּצְלוֹתִין וּבָעוּתִין. וַיֹּאמֶר יַעֲקֹב אֱלֹהֵי אָבִי אַבְרָהָם וֵאלֹהֵי אָבִי וְגוֹ'. עַד דְּנָטִיל עֵיטָא וְאָמַר, כִּי אָמַר אֲכַפְּרָה פָנָיו בַּמִּנְחָה הַהֹלֶכֶת לְפָנָי וַיִּקַּח מִן הַבָּא בְיָדוֹ מִנְחָה וְגוֹ', עִזִּים מָאתַיִם וּתְיָשִׁים עֶשְׂרִים רְחֵלִים מָאתַיִם וְגוֹ'.

221. Jacob goes the days between Rosh Hashanah and Yom Kippur, and flees so as to be saved from him. He repents and fasts until Yom Kippur. Then Yisrael know that Esau comes with four hundred people, all prosecutors ready to denounce them. Forthwith, "Jacob was greatly afraid and distressed" (Beresheet 32:8), and raised many prayers and petitions, "And Jacob said, O Elohim of my father Abraham, and Elohim of my father..." (Ibid. 10), until he reached a decision, saying, "For he said, I will appease him with the present that goes before me" (Ibid. 21), "and took of that which came to his hand a present...two hundred she goats, and twenty he goats, two hundred ewes..." (Ibid. 14-15).

‎222. גְּמַלִּים וְגוֹ', כָּךְ הוּא סִטְרָא דִּילֵיהּ. גְּמַלִּים הוּא נָחָשׁ, כְּמִין גָּמָל, בְּשַׁעְתָּא דְּפַתֵּי סָמָאֵ"ל לְאָדָם, אַרְכִּיב עַל נָחָשׁ כְּמִין גָּמָל. תָּנֵינָן, מַאן דְּחָמֵי גָּמָל בְּחֶלְמֵיהּ, מִיתָה נִקְנְסָה עֲלֵיהּ מִלְמַעְלָה, וְאִשְׁתְּזִיב מִינָהּ. וְכֹלָּא חַד.

222. "camels..." (Ibid. 16). Such is his side, LIKE CAMELS. Camels are the PRIMORDIAL serpent THAT WAS like a camel. When THE ANGEL Samael tempted Adam TO EAT OF THE TREE OF KNOWLEDGE OF GOOD AND EVIL, he was riding on a camel-like serpent. We learned that whoever sees a camel in his dream was punished by death from above but was saved from it. It is all the same, WHICH MEANS THAT THE CAMEL AND THE SERPENT THAT DELIVERED DEATH TO THE WORLD ARE THE SAME THING.

223. וּכְדֵין, אַהְדָּר עֵשָׂו אַפְּטְרוֹפּוֹסָא דְיַעֲקֹב, וְיַעֲקֹב לָא בָּעָא דּוּבְשֵׁיהּ וְעוּקְצֵיהּ. יַעֲבָר נָא אֲדוֹנִי לִפְנֵי עַבְדּוֹ. כְּדֵין וַיָּשָׁב בַּיּוֹם הַהוּא עֵשָׂו לְדַרְכּוֹ. אֵימָתַי. בְּשַׁעַת נְעִילָה, דְּהָא אִתְפְּרַשׁ מֵעַמָּא קַדִּישָׁא. וְקוּדְשָׁא בְּרִיךְ הוּא שָׁבִיק לְחוֹבֵיהוֹן, וְכַפֵּר עֲלַיְיהוּ. כֵּיוָן דְּהַהוּא מְקַטְרְגָא אָזַל בְּהַהוּא דּוֹרוֹנָא, וְאִתְפְּרַשׁ מִנַּיְיהוּ, בָּעֵי קוּדְשָׁא בְּרִיךְ הוּא לְמֶחֱדֵי בִּבְנוֹי, מַה כְּתִיב, וְיַעֲקֹב נָסַע סֻכֹּתָה וַיִּבֶן לוֹ בָּיִת וְגוֹ'. עַל כֵּן קָרָא שֵׁם הַמָּקוֹם סֻכּוֹת, כֵּיוָן דְּיַתְבֵי בַּסֻּכּוֹת, הָא אִשְׁתְּזִיבוּ מִן מְקַטְרְגָא, וְקוּדְשָׁא בְּרִיךְ הוּא חַדֵי בִּבְנוֹי. זַכָּאָה חוּלָקֵיהוֹן בְּהַאי עָלְמָא וּבְעָלְמָא דְאָתֵי.

ע"כ רעיא מהימנא.

223. Esau then reverted to be Jacob's defender, yet Jacob wanted neither his honey nor his sting, BUT SAID, "Let my master, I pray you, pass over before his servant" (Beresheet 33:14). Then, "Esau returned that day on his way to Seir" (Ibid. 16). When WAS THAT? During the Neilah prayer, since then he parted from the holy nation, and the Holy One, blessed be He, forgives their iniquities and atones for them. Once the prosecutor left with the gift and separated from them, the Holy One, blessed be He, wishes to rejoice with His children. It is then written, "And Jacob journeyed to Sukkot, and built him a house...therefore the name of the place is called Sukkot" (Ibid. 17). Since Yisrael dwelt in Sukkot, they were saved from the prosecutor and the Holy One, blessed be He, rejoiced in His children. Happy is their lot in this world and in the World to Come.

End of Ra'aya Meheimna (the Faithful Shepherd)

34. Yom Kippur

A Synopsis

We are told that on Yom Kippur Malchut is illuminated not from the light of the sun but from supernal light instead. Rabbi Aba learns from Rabbi Shimon that Zeir Anpin does not unite with Malchut except when she shines from supernal Aba, at which time Malchut is called holiness. Rabbi Aba says that Adam stands as an example to all men in that he repented after his sin, and God accepted him and had pity on him.

224. ת״ח, בְּהַאי יוֹמָא אִתְכַּסְיָיא סִיהֲרָא, וְלָא נָהִיר עַד בֶּעָשׂוֹר לַחֹדֶשׁ, דְּיִשְׂרָאֵל תַּיְיבִין כֻּלְּהוּ בְּתִיוּבְתָּא שְׁלֵימָתָא, וְאִימָא עִלָּאָה תָּאבַת וְנָהֲרַת לָה. וְהַאי יוֹמָא נְהִירוּ דְּאִימָא נַטְלָא, וְאִשְׁתְּכַח חֵידוּ בְּכֹלָּא. וְעַל דָּא כְּתִיב, יוֹם הַכִּפּוּרִים הוּא. יוֹם כִּפּוּר מִבָּעֵי לֵיהּ, מַאן יוֹם הַכִּפּוּרִים. אֶלָּא בְּגִין דִּתְרֵי נְהוֹרִין נָהֲרִין בְּחַד. בּוּצִינָא עִלָּאָה, נָהִיר לְבוּצִינָא תַּתָּאָה. וּבְהַאי יוֹמָא מִנְּהוֹרָא עִלָּאָה נָהִיר. וְלָא מִנְּהוֹרָא דְּשִׁמְשָׁא ובג״כ בַּכֶּסֶה לְיוֹם חַגֵּנוּ כְּתִיב.

224. Come and see, on that day OF ROSH HASHANAH the moon is gathered, WHICH IS MALCHUT, and does not shine until the tenth day of the month, when all of Yisrael return in complete repentance and supernal Ima, BINAH, again shines upon it. On that day, YOM KIPPUR, MALCHUT receives the illuminations of Ima, BINAH, and joy abounds everywhere. Hence it is written, "for it is a day of atonement (Heb. *YOM KIPPUR*)" (Vayikra 23:28). It should have said 'Yom Kippur' in the singular; what is the meaning of Yom Kippurim IN THE PLURAL? This is because AT THAT TIME two lights shine together: the supernal luminary, BINAH, shines upon the lower luminary, MALCHUT. On that day, MALCHUT shines with supernal light, WHICH IS BINAH, instead of from the light of the sun, ZEIR ANPIN. Hence it is written, "at the full moon (also: 'the covering') on our feast day" (Tehilim 81:4), BECAUSE MALCHUT DOES NOT SHINE UNTIL YOM KIPPUR.

225. ר' אַבָּא שָׁלַח לֵיהּ לר״ש, אָמַר, אֵימָתַי זִוּוּגָא דִּכְנֶסֶת יִשְׂרָאֵל בְּמַלְכָּא קַדִּישָׁא. שָׁלַח לֵיהּ, וְגַם אָמְנָה אֲחוֹתִי בַת אָבִי הִיא אַךְ לֹא בַת אִמִּי וַתְּהִי לִי לְאִשָּׁה. אִתְרְגִישׁ ר' אַבָּא, אָרִים קָלֵיהּ, בָּכָה וְאָמַר, ר' ר'

בּוּצִינָא קַדִּישָׁא, וַוי, וַוי לְעָלְמָא כַּד תִּפּוּק מִנֵּיהּ, וַוי לְדָרָא דְּיִהוֹן בְּעָלְמָא כַּד תִּסְתְּלַק מִנְּהוֹן וְיִשְׁתַּאֲרוּן יַתְמִין מִנָּךְ. אָ"ל רִבִּי חִיָּיא לְרִבִּי אַבָּא, הַאי דְּשָׁלַח לְקַבְלָךְ. מַאי קָאָמַר.

225. Rabbi Aba sent a question to Rabbi Shimon, saying, When does the union of the Congregation of Yisrael, MALCHUT, with the Holy King, ZEIR ANPIN occur? He sent to him, "And yet indeed she is my sister; she is the daughter of my father, but not the daughter of my mother. And she became my wife" (Beresheet 20:12). Rabbi Aba trembled and raised his voice in crying. He said, Rabbi, Rabbi, holy luminary, woe, woe to the world when you shall depart from it. Woe to that generation, which will be in the world when you shall leave them and they shall be orphaned from you. Rabbi Chiya said to Rabbi Aba, What does this VERSE he sent you mean?

226. אָמַר וַדַּאי לָאו זִוּוּגָא דְּמַלְכָּא בְּמַטְרוֹנִיתָא, אֶלָּא בְּזִמְנָא דְּנָהֲרָא מֵאַבָּא עִלָּאָה, וְכַד אִתְנְהָרָא מִנֵּיהּ, קַרֵינָן לָהּ קֹדֶשׁ דְּהָא מִבֵּי אַבָּא נַטְלָה הַאי. וּכְדֵין מִזְדַּוְּוגֵי כַּחֲדָא, בְּגִין דְּמַלְכָּא קֹדֶשׁ אִקְרֵי, דִּכְתִיב קֹדֶשׁ יִשְׂרָאֵל לַיְיָ', דְּנָטִיל מֵאֲתַר דְּאִקְרֵי קֹדֶשׁ. כְּדֵין אֲחוֹתִי בַּת אָבִי הִיא אַךְ לֹא בַת אִמִּי, דְּהָא מִבֵּי אַבָּא שְׁמָא דָא, וְלָא מִבֵּי אִימָּא, וְעַל דָּא וַתְּהִי לִי לְאִשָּׁה, לְאִזְדַּוְּוגָא כַּחֲדָא, בְּזִמְנָא דָא, וְלָא בְּזִמְנָא אָחֳרָא, בְּזִמְנָא דְּנַטְלָא מִבֵּי אַבָּא, וְלָא בְּזִמְנָא דְּנַטְלָא מִבֵּי אִימָּא. וְיוֹם הַכִּפּוּרִים אוֹכַח, דְּתַשְׁמִישׁ הַמִּטָּה אָסוּר, בְּגִין דְּזִוּוּגָא לָא אִשְׁתְּכַח, דְּהָא מִבֵּי אִימָּא נַטְלָא, וְלָא מִבֵּי אַבָּא. אָמַר רִבִּי חִיָּיא, וַדַּאי זַכָּאָה דָּרָא דר"ש שָׁארֵי בְּגַוֵּיהּ, זַכָּאִין אִינוּן דְּקַיְימִין קַמֵּיהּ כָּל יוֹמָא.

226. RABBI ABA said TO HIM, Surely the King does not unite with the Matron, NAMELY, ZEIR ANPIN WITH MALCHUT, save when she shines from supernal Aba, WHEN CHOCHMAH OF IMA IS CLOTHED IN CHASSADIM OF ABA. When she shines from him, she is called holiness, since she receives it from the abode of SUPERNAL Aba, AS ABA IS THE SECRET OF HOLINESS. Then MALE AND FEMALE mate together. For the King is called holiness, as written, "Yisrael is holiness to Hashem" (Yirmeyah 2:3), receiving from the place called holiness. Then ZEIR ANPIN SAYS, "my sister; she is the daughter of my father, but not the daughter of my mother," because that name, HOLINESS, is from Aba's house, and not from my mother's house, NOT FROM BINAH. Therefore, "And she became my wife," to unite as one during that time but on no other time, THAT IS, when she receives from the house of Aba, but not when she receives from the house of Ima. Yom Kippur proves that, as intercourse is forbidden on it, since then there is no mating OF ZEIR ANPIN AND MALCHUT, as on YOM KIPPUR she receives from the house of Ima and not from the house of Aba. Rabbi Chiya said, Indeed. Happy is the generation amongst whom dwells Rabbi Shimon. Happy are those who daily stand before him.

227(1). אָמַר רִבִּי אַבָּא, בְּרֹאשׁ הַשָּׁנָה נִבְרָא אָדָם, וְקָאֵים בְּדִינָא קַמֵּי מָארֵיה, וְתָב בְּתִיוּבְתָּא, וְקַבִּיל לֵיה קוּדְשָׁא בְּרִיךְ הוּא. א״ל, אָדָם, אַנְתְּ תְּהֵא סִימָנָא לִבְנָיךְ לְדָרֵי דָרִין, בְּהַאי יוֹמָא קַיְימִין בְּדִינָא, וְאִי יְתוּבוּן אֲנָא אֲקַבֵּל לוֹן, וְאֵיקוּם מִכּוּרְסְיָיא דְּדִינָא, וְאֶתְקַיֵּים עַל כּוּרְסְיָיא דְּרַחֲמֵי, וַאֲרַחֵם עֲלַיְיהוּ. וְדָוִד אָמַר, אָהַבְתִּי כִּי יִשְׁמַע יְיָ' אֶת קוֹלִי תַּחֲנוּנָי. וְעַל דָּא כְּתִיב, כִּי עִמְּךָ הַסְּלִיחָה לְמַעַן תִּוָּרֵא. וּכְתִיב, כִּי עִמְּךָ מְקוֹר חַיִּים בְּאוֹרְךָ נִרְאֶה אוֹר.

227a. Rabbi Aba said, Adam was created on Rosh Hashanah and stood on trial before his Master FOR EATING OF THE TREE OF KNOWLEDGE OF GOOD AND EVIL. He repented and the Holy One, blessed be He, accepted him. He said to him, 'Adam, you shall serve as a symbol for your descendants for generations, who are sentenced on that day. If they shall repent, I shall accept them, rise from the throne of Judgment and sit on the throne of Mercy and have pity on them'. David used to say, "I love Hashem who hears my voice and my supplications" (Tehilim 116:1). Hence it is written, "But there is forgiveness with You, that You may be feared" (Tehilim 130:4), and, "For with You is the fountain of life. In Your light we see light" (Tehilim 36:10).

A Synopsis

We learn that it is a commandment to be afflicted on Yom Kippur, to subjugate body and soul.

רעיא מהימנא

227(2). פִּקוּדָא דָא, לְאִתְעַנָּאָה בְּיוֹמָא דְּכִפּוּרֵי, לְאַכְנָעָא גּוּפָא וְנַפְשָׁא,

בְּרָזָא דְּחַמְשָׁה עֲנוּיָין, דְּחֲמִשָּׁה דַּרְגִּין דְּיוֹמָא דְּכִפּוּרֵי. דְּהָא מְקַטְרְגָא
קָא אָתֵי לְאַדְבְּרָא חוֹבַיְיהוּ, כְּמָה דְּאִתְּמַר. וְכֻלְהוּ בְּתִיוּבְתָּא שְׁלֵימָתָא
קַמֵּי אֲבוּהוֹן. כֹּלָּא, כְּמָה דְּאִתְּמַר בְּכַמָּה דוּכְתֵּי.

ע"כ רעיא מהימנא

Ra'aya Meheimna (the Faithful Shepherd)

227b. It is a commandment to be afflicted on Yom Kippur, to subjugate body and soul by means of the five afflictions, the five grades of Yom Kippur, WHICH ARE CHESED, GVURAH, TIFERET, NETZACH AND HOD, for the prosecutor comes to impart their sins as we learned. And they are all, ALL OF YISRAEL, repenting wholly before their Father, as we learned in different places.

End of Ra'aya Meheimna (the Faithful Shepherd)

A Synopsis

Rabbi Chiya tells us about the ten kinds of songs in the book of Tehilim. He speaks about a Maskil, or understanding, that bestows wisdom; from it comes forgiveness and freedom. He says that a man who repents before God has his sins hidden, but if he will not repent then his sins shall be made known before everyone. Rabbi Aba explains what happens to the good deeds that were done by a man who is on balance judged to be evil, and what happens to the sins that were done by a man who is on balance judged to be worthy. He talks about the depths of the sea, where all the sins are found, and about the lot that chooses the goat for Azazel. We are told how God distracted the prosecutor from accusing Yisrael by giving him Job to occupy himself with; this left Yisrael free to cross the sea and escape from the Egyptians. The offering on Yom Kippur is for the same purpose, allowing God to forgive Yisrael without interference from the prosecutor. Rabbi Aba talks about the ritual counting of the priest as he sprinkles the blood of the offering, the purpose of which is to draw and guide the one that is supernal Ima through specific grades and to draw the deep rivers upon the Congregation of Yisrael. Rabbi Yitzchak and Rabbi Aba tell us about the High Priest as he enters the Holy of Holies and hears the wings of the Cherubs singing. Rabbi Shimon says that

Malchut is only able to join with Zeir Anpin when her children Yisrael are judged to be worthy.

228. אַךְ בֶּעָשׂוֹר לַחֹדֶשׁ הַשְּׁבִיעִי הַזֶּה יוֹם הַכִּפּוּרִים הוּא מִקְרָא קֹדֶשׁ יִהְיֶה לָכֶם. ר' חִיָּיא פָּתַח, לְדָוִד מַשְׂכִּיל אַשְׁרֵי נְשׂוּי פֶּשַׁע כְּסוּי חֲטָאָה. לְדָוִד מַשְׂכִּיל, הָא תָּנֵינָן בִּי' זִינֵי זִמְרָא אִתְקְרֵי סֵפֶר תְּהִלִּים, בִּנְצוּחַ, בִּנְגוּן, בְּמַשְׂכִּיל, בְּמִכְתָּם, בְּמִזְמוֹר, בְּשִׁיר, בְּאַשְׁרֵי, בִּתְפִלָּה, בְּהוֹדָאָה, בְּהַלְלוּיָה, וְעִלָּאָה מִכָּלְהוּ הַלְלוּיָה, וְהָא אוּקְמוּהָ.

228. "Also on the tenth day of this seventh month there shall be a day of atonement (Heb. *Yom Kippur*); it shall be a holy gathering to you" (Vayikra 23:27). Rabbi Chiya opened with, "Of David. A maskil. Blessed is he whose transgression is forgiven, whose sin is covered" (Tehilim 32:1). We learned that the book of Tehilim is recited by ten kinds of songs: by the chief musician, by Maskil (Eng. 'understanding'), by Michtam (Eng. 'poem'), by a psalm, by a song, by "Blessed," by prayer, by acknowledgment, by Halleluyah. The highest is Halleluyah, as we already explained.

229. הָכָא מַשְׂכִּיל, אַתְרֵיהּ יְדִיעַ, מַהוּ מַשְׂכִּיל, מַיָּא דְּאַחְכִּימוּ לְאִינּוּן דְּשָׁתוּ לְהוּ, הַהוּא אֲתַר דְּאִקְרֵי מַשְׂכִּיל, כד"א, מַשְׂכִּיל עַל דָּבָר יִמְצָא טוֹב. וּבְגִין דְּאִקְרֵי הָכִי, תַּלְיָא בֵּיהּ סְלִיחָה, חֵירוּ דְּחִירִין. הה"ד אַשְׁרֵי נְשׂוּי פֶּשַׁע כְּסוּי חֲטָאָה.

229. The location of Maskil is known AS YESOD OF BINAH. What is that THAT IS CALLED Maskil? It is that water which makes wise those who drink from it, NAMELY, IT BESTOWS CHOCHMAH. The place called Maskil is as in, "He who considers (Heb. *maskil*) his words shall find good" (Mishlei 16:20). IF MASKIL BESTOWS ON SOMETHING, THERE WILL BE GOOD IN IT, WHICH IS THE ILLUMINATION OF CHOCHMAH CLOTHED IN CHASSADIM. Since it is so called, forgiveness and the greatest freedom come from it, SINCE FORGIVENESS AND FREEDOM ARE BESTOWED FROM CHOCHMAH IN BINAH. This is the secret of, "Blessed is he whose transgression is forgiven, whose sin is covered," SINCE HIS TRANSGRESSION IS FORGIVEN BY THE PLENTY OF CHOCHMAH.

230. מַאי כְּסוּי חֲטָאָה. הָא אוּקְמוּהָ, דְּהוּא כְּסוּי מִבְּנֵי נָשָׁא, הַהוּא

חַטָאָה דְּחָב לְקוּדְשָׁא בְּרִיךְ הוּא, וְאוֹדֵי קַמֵּי קוּדְשָׁא בְּרִיךְ הוּא. אֲבָל תָּ"ח, כַּד בַּר נָשׁ חָטֵי, וְחָב זִמְנָא חֲדָא, וּתְרֵין וּתְלָתָא, וְלָא אַהֲדָר בֵּיהּ, הָא חוֹבוֹי בְּאִתְגַּלְיָא אִינּוּן וּמְפַרְסְמֵי לוֹן לְעֵילָא, וּמְפַרְסְמֵי לוֹן לְתַתָּא. וְכָרוֹזֵי אַזְלִין קַמֵּיהּ וּמַכְרְזֵי, אִסְתְּלָקוּ מִסְּחַרְנֵיהּ דִּפְלַנְיָא, נָזִיף הוּא מִמָּארֵיהּ, נָזִיף הוּא לְעֵילָא, נָזִיף הוּא לְתַתָּא, וַוי לֵיהּ דְּפָגִים דִּיּוּקְנָא דְּמָארֵיהּ, וַוי לֵיהּ דְּלָא חַיְישׁ לִיקָרָא דְּמָארֵיהּ, קוּדְשָׁא בְּרִיךְ הוּא גַּלֵּי חוֹבֵיהּ לְעֵילָא, הֲה"ד, יְגַלּוּ שָׁמַיִם עֲוֹנוֹ וְאֶרֶץ מִתְקוֹמָמָה לוֹ. וְכַד בַּר נָשׁ אָזִיל בְּאוֹרְחָא דְּמָארֵיהּ, וְאִשְׁתָּדַּל בְּפוּלְחָנֵיהּ, וְאִזְדָּמַן לֵיהּ חַטָאָה חַד, כֹּלָּא מְכַסִּין עֲלֵוֵיהּ, עִלָּאִין וְתַתָּאִין, דָּא אִקְרֵי כְּסוּי חַטָאָה.

230. HE ASKS, What is MEANT BY, "whose sin is covered," AND ANSWERS, It was explained that the sin he committed before the Holy One, blessed be He, is covered from people, and he confessed it before the Holy One, blessed be He. Yet come and see, when a man sins, sinning once, twice and thrice, and does not repent, his sins become public, BECAUSE they are made known above and made known below. Criers walk before him and announce, Get away from around so and so. He is chided by his Master, chided above and chided below. Woe to him for blemishing his Master's image. Woe to him, who has no fear for his Master's glory. The Holy One, blessed be He, reveals his iniquity above. This is the meaning of, "The heaven shall reveal his iniquity; and the earth shall rise up against him" (Iyov 20:27). When a man walks the path of his Master and busies himself with His service, and happens to sin, everyone covers it, the higher and lower beings. This is called, "whose sin is covered."

231. א"ל ר' אַבָּא, עַד כְּעַן לָא מָטִית לְעִקָּרָא דְּמִלָּה. וְשַׁפִּיר קָאַמְרְתְּ. וְהַאי דְּקָאַמְרוּ חַבְרַיָּיא שַׁפִּיר. אֲבָל אִי הָכִי, מְכוּסֶה חַטָאָה מִבְעֵי לֵיהּ, מַהוּ כְּסוּי חַטָאָה.

231. Rabbi Aba said to him, You have not yet reached the crux of the matter. You spoke well, and whatever the friends said IS fine. But if this is so, it should have said, 'covered sin'. Why does it say, "whose sin is covered (or: 'covering')"?

232. אֶלָּא תְּרֵי מִלֵּי דְּחָכְמְתָא אִית בֵּיהּ, וְתַרְוַויְיהוּ הָכִי. חַד כְּמָה

דְּתָנֵינָן, דְּעוֹבָדִין טָבִין דְּבַר נָשׁ עָבֵיד בְּהַאי עָלְמָא, עָבְדִין לֵיהּ בְּהַהוּא
עָלְמָא לְבוּשָׁא יַקִּירָא עִלָּאָה, לְאִתְלַבְּשָׁא בְּהוּ. וְכַד בַּ"נ אַתְקִין עוֹבָדִין
טָבִין, וְגָבְרִין עֲלֵיהּ עוֹבָדִין בִּישִׁין, וְאַשְׁגַּח בֵּיהּ קוּדְשָׁא בְּרִיךְ הוּא,
וְעוֹבָדוֹי בִּישִׁין סַגִּיאִין, וְאִיהוּ רָשָׁע, דְּאִשְׁתְּכַח חַטָּאָה קַמֵּי מָארֵיהּ,
וְתוֹהֵא עַל אִינּוּן טָבָאן דַּעֲבַד בְּקַדְמֵיתָא, הָא אִתְאֲבִיד הוּא מִכֹּלָּא,
מֵהַאי עָלְמָא, וּמֵעָלְמָא דְּאָתֵי. מַה עָבֵיד קוּדְשָׁא בְּרִיךְ הוּא מֵאִינּוּן
טָבָאן דַּעֲבֵיד הַאי חַטָּאָה בְּקַדְמֵיתָא.

232. RABBI ABA ANSWERS, There are two matters of wisdom here, IN THE VERSE, "SIN COVERING," as follows. The one, as we learned that from the good deeds man performs in this world a costly garment is made in that world for him to wear. When man does good deeds, yet the evil deeds overpower him, and the Holy One, blessed be He, sees that his evil deeds are more numerous THAN HIS GOOD DEEDS, THEN he is evil, because he is guilty before his Master, SINCE THERE ARE MORE MISDEEDS THAN GOOD DEEDS. He repines and regrets the good deeds he already performed. Then he is entirely lost, from this world and the World to Come. HE ASKS, What does the Holy One, blessed be He, do from the good deeds the sinner accomplished before?

233. אֶלָּא קוּדְשָׁא בְּרִיךְ הוּא, אַף עַ"ג דְּהַהוּא רָשָׁע חַטָּאָה אִתְאֲבִיד.
אִינּוּן טָבָאן וְזַכְיָין לָא אִתְאֲבִידוּ. אִית צַדִּיק דְּאָזִיל בְּאָרְחוֹי דְּמַלְכָּא
עִלָּאָה, וְאַתְקִין לְבוּשׁוֹי מֵעוֹבָדוֹי, וְעַד לָא אַשְׁלִים לְבוּשׁוֹי, אִסְתַּלַּק.
קוּדְשָׁא בְּרִיךְ הוּא אַשְׁלִים לֵיהּ, מֵאִינּוּן עוֹבָדִין דַּעֲבַד הַאי רָשָׁע
חַטָּאָה, וְאַשְׁלִים לְבוּשׁוֹי, לְאִתְתַּקְּנָא בְּהוּ בְּהַהוּא עָלְמָא, הַהָ"ד, יָכִין
וְצַדִּיק יִלְבָּשׁ. הַהוּא חַטָּאָה אַתְקִין, וְצַדִּיק אִתְחֲפֵי מִמָּה דְּאִיהוּ תַּקִּין
הַהָ"ד כְּסוּי חַטָּאָה, וְעַל דָּא לָא כְּתִיב מְכוּסָּה, אֶלָּא כְּסוּי.

233. HE ANSWERS, Even though the wicked man is lost the good deeds and merits he committed are not lost. For there is a righteous man who walks the ways of the supernal King and has made garments from his GOOD deeds, but before completing HIS GARMENTS he departed FROM THE WORLD. The Holy One, blessed be He, completes him HIS GARMENTS from the GOOD deeds the evil sinner has committed and perfects his garment for him to put in that world. This is the meaning of, THE EVIL "may prepare it, but the just shall put it on" (Iyov 27:17). The evil man made it and the righteous man covers himself with what he made. This is the meaning of, "whose sin is a covering"; THE COVERING, NAMELY HIS GARMENT, COMES FROM THE SINNER. Hence it is not written that it is covered, but that is it a covering, BECAUSE IT REFERS TO A GARMENT.

234. וְחַד, דְּאִתְחֲפֵי הַהוּא חַטָּאָה דְּהַאי זַכָּאָה, בְּאִינּוּן דְּאִקְרוּן מְצוּלוֹת יָם, דְּהָא מַאן דְּנָפִיל בִּמְצוּלוֹת יָם, לָא אִשְׁתְּכַח לְעָלְמִין בְּגִין דְּמַיִין חָפִין עָלַיְיהוּ. כְּמָה דְּאַתְּ אָמֵר, וְתַשְׁלִיךְ בִּמְצוּלוֹת יָם כָּל חַטֹּאותָם. מַאן מְצוּלוֹת יָם. אֶלָּא רָזָא יַקִּירָא הוּא, וְהָא אוֹקְמֵיהּ ר׳ שִׁמְעוֹן, וְאָמַר, כָּל אִינּוּן דְּאָתוּ מִסִּטְרָא תַּקִּיפָא, וְאִתְאַחֲדוּ בְּזִינִין בִּישִׁין, בִּכְתָרִין תַּתָּאִין, כְּגוֹן עֲזָאזֵל בְּיוֹמָא דְּכִפּוּרֵי, דָּא אִקְרֵי מְצוּלוֹת יָם. כְּזַפְתָּא דְּכַסְפָּא, כַּד בַּחֲנִין לֵיהּ בְּנוּרָא, הֲדָא הוּא דִּכְתִּיב הָגוֹ סִיגִים מִכָּסֶף.

234. The second MEANING is that the sin that a worthy MAN has committed is covered inside what is called the depths of the sea. For whatever fell into the depths of the sea is never found, since the water covers it. This is the meaning of, "And You will cast all their sins into the depths of the sea" (Michah 7:19). What are the depths of the sea? HE ANSWERS, This is a precious mystery, which Rabbi Shimon explained. He said, All those coming from the harsh side and holding on to evil species and the lower Sfirot, like Azazel on Yom Kippur is considered the depths of the sea. This is called the depths of the sea, like the oars of silver refined by fire. This is meant by, "Take away the dross from the silver" (Mishlei 25:4).

235. כַּךְ הַאי, מֵאִינּוּן מְצוּלוֹת יָם הוּא, וּמְצוּלוֹת יָם אִקְרֵי, מְצוּלוֹת מֵהַהוּא יָם קַדִּישָׁא, מְצוּלוֹת, זוּהֲמָא דְּכַסְפָּא. וְעַל דָּא, כָּל אִינּוּן חַטָּאִין דְּיִשְׂרָאֵל שַׁרְיָין לְגַוֵּיהּ, וְהוּא קַבִּיל לוֹן, וְיִשְׁתַּאֲבוּן בְּגַוֵּיהּ. מַאי טַעֲמָא. בְּגִין דְּאִיהוּ חַטָּאָה אִקְרֵי. מַאי חַטָּאָה. גִּרְעוֹנָא. וְעַל דָּא הוּא גִּרְעוֹנָא דְּכֹלָּא, וְנָטַל גִּרְעוֹנָא דְּגוּפָא וּדְנַפְשָׁא. בְּהַאי יוֹמָא נָחִית הַאי מְצוּלוֹת יָם, זוּהֲמָא דְּנַפְשָׁא, וְנָטִיל זוּהֲמָא דְּגוּפָא. מַאן הוּא זוּהֲמָא דְּגוּפָא. דָּא אִינּוּן חוֹבִין דְּאִתְעֲבִידוּ עַל יְדֵי דְּיֵצֶר הָרָע, דְּאִקְרֵי מְזוֹהָם מְנֻוָּל.

235. Thus, this AZAZEL is from the depths of the sea and is called the depths of the sea, THAT IS, the depths of that holy sea. The depths REFER TO the filth of silver. Hence all the sins of Yisrael rest in it, it receives them and they are drawn into it. The reason is that AZAZEL is called sin. Sin MEANS lessening. Hence it lessens everything, reducing body and soul and receiving the bodily filth, which is the sins done by the Evil Inclination that is called filthy and ugly.

236. אָמַר רִבִּי יוֹסֵי, תְּנָן וְנָתַן אַהֲרֹן עַל שְׁנֵי הַשְּׂעִירִם גּוֹרָלוֹת, אִי הָכִי יִקְרָא הוּא דַּעֲזָאזֵל, חֲמִיתּוּן עַבְדָּא דְּשַׁדֵּי עַדְבִין בְּמָארֵיהּ, אוֹרְחוֹי דְּעָלְמָא דְּעַבְדָּא לָא נָטַל אֶלָּא מַה דְּיָהִיב לֵיהּ מָארֵיהּ. אֲבָל, בְּגִין דְּסָמָא"ל זַמִּין הַאי יוֹמָא בְּדִלְטוֹרָא, וּבְגִין דְּלָא יְהֵא לֵיהּ פִּטְרָא יָהֲבִין לֵיהּ חוּלָקָא בְּהַאי.

236. Rabbi Yosi said, we learned, "And Aaron shall cast lots upon the two goats" (Vayikra 16:8). If this is so, it is an honor to Azazel, for have you ever seen a servant casting lots ON EQUAL FOOTING with his master? According to the custom a servant receives only what his master gives him. AND HE ANSWERS, Since Samael is ready to speak evil OF YISRAEL and in order not to give him any excuse, he is given a portion.

237. וְהַאי עַדְבָא מִגַּרְמֵיהּ הוּא דְּסָלִיק בֵּיהּ, דְּאָמַר רִבִּי יְהוּדָה אָמַר ר' יִצְחָק, מִלָּה עִלָּאָה אַשְׁכַּחְנָא בְּעַדְבָא. עַדְבָא דִּיהוֹשֻׁעַ, כְּתִיב בֵּיהּ, עַל פִּי הַגּוֹרָל, עַל פִּי הַגּוֹרָל וַדַּאי, דְּאִיהוּ אָמַר דָּא חוּלָקָא דִּיהוּדָה, דָּא דְּבִנְיָמִין וְכוּ', וְכֵן כֻּלְּהוּ. אוּף הָכָא, כֵּיוָן דְּכַהֲנָא שַׁוֵּי יְדוֹי, אִינוּן עַדְבִין מְדַלְּגֵי וְסַלְּקִין בִּידָא דְּכַהֲנָא, וְשַׁאֲרָן בְּאַתְרַיְיהוּ. הֲדָא הוּא דִּכְתִיב, וְהַשָּׂעִיר אֲשֶׁר עָלָה עָלָיו הַגּוֹרָל, עָלָה עָלָיו וַדַּאי.

237. The lot reaches it on its own accord, as Rabbi Yehuda said in the name of Rabbi Yitzchak: I found a celestial matter in that lot. It is written of the lot of Joshua, "According to (lit. 'by the mouth of') the lot" (Bemidbar 26:56). Surely the lot said, this is the portion of Judah, this is the portion of Benjamin, etc. Here too, once the priests put his hands, the lots were jumping and climbing the hand of the priest and come to their places. This is the meaning of, "But the goat, on which the lot fell for Azazel" (Vayikra 16:10), surely it "fell for Azazel," ON ITS OWN ACCORD.

238. וְלָא דָא בִּלְחוֹדוֹי, אֶלָּא בְּכָל זִמְנָא דִּדְלָטוֹרָא זַמִּין, וְאִתְיְיהִיב לֵיהּ רְשׁוּתָא, בָּעֵינָן לְשַׁוָּואָה לְקַבְלֵיהּ בְּמָה דְּיִתְעֲסַק, וְשָׁבִיק לוֹן לְיִשְׂרָאֵל. בְּהַאי יוֹמָא דְּלָטוֹרָא זַמִּין לְאַלְלָא אַרְעָא. הֲדָא הוּא דִּכְתִּיב וַיֹּאמֶר יְיָ' אֶל הַשָּׂטָן מֵאַיִן תָּבֹא. וְהָא תָּנֵינָן, מִשּׁוּט בָּאָרֶץ, מַאי הוּא. אֶלָּא הַאי הוּא דִּלָטוֹרָא רַבָּא מְקַטְרְגָא דְּיִשְׂרָאֵל.

238. Not only that, but as long as the prosecutor is ready and has permission, something should be put before him to be occupied with and leave Yisrael. On that day OF YOM KIPPUR, the prosecutor is ready to spy out the land, as written, "And Hashem said to the adversary, From where do you come?" (Iyov 1:7). We learned that "From going to and fro in the earth" (Ibid.), for this is the great prosecutor that denounces Yisrael.

239. וְהָא אַתְּעָרוּ חַבְרַיָּיא, בְּהַהִיא שַׁעֲתָא דַּהֲווֹ זְמִינִין יִשְׂרָאֵל לְמֶעְבַּר יַמָּא, וּלְאִתְפָּרְעָא מִמִּצְרָאֵי, אָמַר, אֲנָא אַעֲבַרְנָא בְּאַרְעָא קַדִּישָׁא, וַחֲמֵינָא דְּלָא אִתְחֲזוּן אִלֵּין לְמֵיעַל, בְּגַוֵּוהּ, אִי אַנְתְּ דָּאִין דִּינָא, דִּינַיְיהוּ הָכָא כְּמִצְרָאֵי, מַה שַׁנְיָין אִלֵּין מֵאִלֵּין, אוֹ יְמוּתוּן כֻּלְּהוּ כַּחֲדָא, אוֹ יְהַדְרוּן כֻּלְּהוּ לְמִצְרָיִם. וְלָאו אַנְתְּ הוּא דְּאָמַרְתְּ, וַעֲבָדוּם וְעִנּוּ אוֹתָם ד' מֵאוֹת שָׁנָה, וְהָא לָא סְלִיקוּ מְחוּשְׁבָּנַיָּיא אֶלָּא רד"ו, וְלָא יַתִּיר.

239. The friends remarked that when Yisrael were ready to cross the sea and take revenge on the Egyptians, THE PROSECUTOR said, I have passed the Holy Land and I see that these are not worthy of entering it. If You mete out punishment, their punishment here IS LIKE the Egyptians. What is the difference between them? Either they will all die together or they will all return to Egypt. Was it not You, who said, "and shall serve them; and they shall afflict them four hundred years" (Beresheet 15:13), but from the reckoning only 210 years have passed, no more.

240. אָמַר קוּדְשָׁא בְּרִיךְ הוּא, מַאי אַעֲבִיד, אִשְׁתַּדְּלוּתָא בַּעְיָא הָכָא, לְאַיְיתָאָה קְרָבָא לָקַבְלֵיהּ, יְהִיבְנָא לֵיהּ בְּמָה דְּיִתְעֲסַק, וְיִשְׁבּוֹק בְּהוּ

לִבְנַי, וְהָא אִשְׁתְּכַח בְּמַאן דְּיִתְעֲסַק, מִיַּד אָמַר לֵיהּ, הֲשַׂמְתָּ לִבְּךָ אֶל
עַבְדִּי אִיּוֹב כִּי אֵין כָּמוֹהוּ בָּאָרֶץ. מִיַּד פָּלִיג לֵיהּ דַּלְטוֹרָא בְּמִלִּין, וַיַּעַן
הַשָּׂטָן אֶת יְיָ' וַיֹּאמַר הַחִנָּם יָרֵא אִיּוֹב אֱלֹהִים.

240. The Holy One, blessed be He, said, 'What shall I do? This calls for occupation. Something is needed to bring here and draw near him. I shall give him something to be occupied with, so he will leave My children. Let us find someone for him to be busy with'. Forthwith He said, "Have you considered My servant Job, that there is none like him on earth?" (Iyov 1:8). He interrupted the prosecutor with words. "Then the adversary answered Hashem, and said, Does Job fear Elohim for naught?" (Ibid. 9).

241. לְרַעְיָא דְּבָעֵי לְאַעְבְּרָא עָאנֵיהּ בְּחַד נַהֲרָא, אַעְבַּר זְאֵבָא לְקַטְרְגָא
לֵיהּ בְּעָאנֵיהּ, רַעְיָא הֲוָה חַכִּים, אָמַר מַאי אַעְבִּיד, דִּבְעוֹד דַּאֲנָא אַעְבַּר
לְטַלְיָיא, יְקַטְרֵג הוּא בְּעָאנֵי. זָקַף עֵינוֹי, וְחָמָא בֵּין עָאנָא, חַד תַּיְישָׁא
מֵאִלֵּין תַּיְישֵׁי בְּרָא, דַּהֲוָה רַב וְתַקִּיף. אָמַר, אַשְׁדֵּי דָּא לְקַבְלֵיהּ, וּבְעוֹד
דִּמְקַטְרְגֵי דָּא בְּדָא, אַעְבַּר לְכָל עָאנָא, וְיִשְׁתֵּזְבוּן מִנֵּיהּ.

241. THIS IS LIKENED to a shepherd who wanted to pass his flock across a river. A wolf passed by and afflicted his flock. The wise shepherd said, What shall I do? He might destroy the flock while I move the lambs across. He raised his eyes and saw a wild goat, big and strong. He said, I shall throw him before the wolf. While they do battle with each other, I shall remove all the flock and they shall be saved from him.

242. כַּךְ קוּדְשָׁא בְּרִיךְ הוּא. אָמַר, וַדַּאי הָא תַּיְישָׁא חַד רַב וְתַקִּיף
וְאַלִּים, אַשְׁדֵּי לְקַבְלֵיהּ, וּבְעוֹד דְּהוּא יִשְׁתְּדַּל בֵּיהּ, יַעַבְרוּן בְּנַי, וְלָא
יִשְׁתְּכַח קַטֵיגוֹרָא לְגַבַּיְיהוּ. מִיַּד, וַיֹּאמֶר יְיָ' אֶל הַשָּׂטָן הֲשַׂמְתָּ לִבְּךָ. עַד
דְּקוּדְשָׁא בְּרִיךְ הוּא זִוֵּוג לְהוּ כַּחֲדָא, דִּכְתִיב הִנּוֹ בְיָדֶךָ. בְּעוֹד דְּהוּא
אִשְׁתְּדַּל בֵּיהּ, שָׁבִיק לוֹן לְיִשְׂרָאֵל, וְלָא אִשְׁתְּכַח קַטֵיגוֹרָא לְגַבַּיְיהוּ.

242. So does the Holy One, blessed be He, do. He said, 'I shall certainly throw a great, powerful and forceful goat in his way, NAMELY JOB. While he will be occupied with it, My children shall cross THE SEA, without a prosecutor over them'. Immediately, "And Hashem said to the adversary, Have you considered." Eventually, the Holy One, blessed be He, joined them together, as written, "Behold, he is in your hand" (Iyov 2:6). While he was busy with him, he left Yisrael alone, and uttered no denouncement on them.

243. אוּף הָכִי בְּהַאי יוֹמָא, דִּלְטוֹרָא זַמִּין לְאַלְלָא אַרְעָא, וּבְעֵינָא לְשַׁדְּרָא לְקַבְלֵיה בְּמָה דְּיִתְעֲסַק, וּבְעוֹד דְּאִיהוּ אִשְׁתַּדַּל בֵּיה, שָׁבִיק לוֹן לְיִשְׂרָאֵל. וּמַתְלָא אַמְרֵי לְזִלְזוּלָא דְּבֵי מַלְכָּא, הַב לֵיה זְעֵיר חַמְרָא, וִישַׁבְּחָךְ קַמֵּי מַלְכָּא. וְאִי לָאו יֵימָא לְמַלְכָּא מִלָּה בִּישָׁא. לְזִמְנִין נַטְלִין לָה לְהַהִיא מִלָּה, עִלָּאֵי דְּבֵי מַלְכָּא, וּמַלְכָּא עֲבִיד דִּינָא בְּגִינֵיה.

243. Similarly, on that day OF YOM KIPPUR, the Satan is ready to spy out the land, and we should send something before him with which to be busy. While he is busy with it, he will leave Yisrael alone. There is an allegory about the lowliest in the king's house – give him a little wine, and he will praise you before the king, otherwise he will speak evil words ABOUT YOU before the king. Sometimes the superiors in the king's house receive THAT EVIL speech and the king punishes that man.

244. רִבִּי יִצְחָק אָמַר, לְשַׁטְיָא דְּקָאֵים קַמֵּי מַלְכָּא, הַב לֵיה חַמְרָא, וּלְבָתַר אֵימָא לֵיה, וְאַחְזֵי לֵיה, כָּל אִינּוּן טַעֲווֹן דְּעַבְדַּת, וְכָל אִינּוּן בִּישִׁין, וְהוּא יֵיתֵי וִישַׁבְּחָךְ, וְיֵימָא דְּלָא יִשְׁתְּכַח בְּעָלְמָא כְּוָותָךְ. אוּף הָכָא, הָא קָאֵים דִּלְטוֹרָא תָּדִיר קַמֵּי מַלְכָּא, יִשְׂרָאֵל יָהֲבִין לֵיה הַאי דּוֹרוֹן, וּבְהַאי דּוֹרוֹן פִּתְקָא, לְכָל בִּישִׁין, וּלְכָל טַעֲווֹן, וּלְכָל חוֹבִין דְּעַבְדוּ יִשְׂרָאֵל, וְהוּא אָתֵי וּמְשַׁבַּח לְהוּ לְיִשְׂרָאֵל, וְאִתְעֲבִיד סַנֵּיגוֹרָא עֲלַיְיהוּ, וְקוּדְשָׁא בְּרִיךְ הוּא אַהֲדָר כֹּלָּא לְרֵישָׁא דְּבִישֵׁי דְּעַמֵּיה, בְּגִין דִּכְתִיב כִּי גֶחָלִים אַתָּה חוֹתֶה עַל רֹאשׁוֹ.

244. Rabbi Yitzchak said, THIS IS LIKENED to a fool who is in the king's presence. Give him a little wine and then tell him and show him all the abominable things you have done and all the evil, yet he will praise you and say there is none in the world like you. Here too, the prosecutor is

constantly in the King's presence. Yisrael give him this offering OF THE GOAT TO AZAZEL. In this offering there is a note WHERE ALL IS WRITTEN DOWN of the evil things, the abominable things and the iniquities Yisrael did. Yet he comes and praises Yisrael and becomes their defender. And the Holy One, blessed be He, returns everything upon the heads of the wicked of his people, since it is written, "for you shall heap coals of fire upon his head" (Mishlei 25:22).

245. א״ר יוֹסֵי, וַוי לוֹן לְעַמָּא דְּעֵשָׂו, בְּשַׁעֲתָּא דְּהַאי שָׂעִיר מְשַׁדְּרֵי לְהַהוּא דִּלְטוֹרָא מְמָנָא דִּעֲלַיְיהוּ, דִּבְגִינֵיה אָתֵי לְשַׁבְּחָא לוֹן לְיִשְׂרָאֵל, וְקוּדְשָׁא בְּרִיךְ הוּא אַהֲדָר כָּל אִינוּן חוֹבִין לְרֵישָׁא דְּעַמֵּיה, בְּגִין דִּכְתִיב דּוֹבֵר שְׁקָרִים לֹא יִכּוֹן לְנֶגֶד עֵינָי. א״ר יְהוּדָה, אִלְמָלֵי הֲוֹו יַדְעֵי אוּמוֹת הָעוֹלָם מֵהַאי שָׂעִיר, לָא שַׁבְקִין לוֹן לְיִשְׂרָאֵל, יוֹמָא חַד בְּעָלְמָא.

245. Rabbi Yosi said, Woe to the people of Esau, when that goat is sent to that slanderer who is appointed over them, NAMELY SAMAEL, THE MINISTER OF ESAU that comes to praise Yisrael for its sake. The Holy One, blessed be He, returns all those iniquities on the head of his people, because, it is written, "he that tells lies shall not remain in my sight" (Tehilim 101:7). Rabbi Yehuda said, If the idolaters knew of the goat, they would not let Yisrael live one day in the world.

246. תָּא חֲזֵי, כָּל הַהוּא יוֹמָא מִשְׁתְּדַּל אִיהוּ בְּהַהוּא שָׂעִיר, ובג״כ קוּדְשָׁא בְּרִיךְ הוּא מְכַפֵּר לְהוּ לְיִשְׂרָאֵל, וְדָכֵי לוֹן מִכֹּלָּא, וְלָא אִשְׁתְּכַח קַטֵיגוֹרְיָא קַמֵּיה. לְבָתַר, הוּא אָתֵי וּמְשַׁבַּח לְהוּ לְיִשְׂרָאֵל. וּכְדֵין שָׁאִיל לֵיה, כד״א, וַיֹּאמֶר יְיָ' אֶל הַשָּׂטָן מֵאַיִן תָּבֹא, אָתִיב בְּתוּשְׁבַּחְתַּיְיהוּ דְּיִשְׂרָאֵל, וְקַטֵיגוֹרָא אִתְעֲבֵיד סַנֵיגוֹרָא וְאָזִיל לֵיה.

246. Come and see, all that day he busies himself with that goat. Then the Holy One, blessed be He, forgives Yisrael and cleanses them in every respect, and there is no prosecutor in His presence. He then comes and praises Yisrael. THE HOLY ONE, BLESSED BE HE, then asks him, as written, "And Hashem said to the adversary, From where do you come?" and he answers by praising Yisrael. The prosecutor turns into a defender and goes his way.

247. כְּדֵין קוּדְשָׁא בְּרִיךְ הוּא אָמַר לְשַׁבְעִין שָׁרִין דְּסָחֲרִין כּוּרְסָיָּא, חֲמִיתּוּן הַאי דִּלְטוֹרָא, הֵיאַךְ קָאִים עַל בְּנֵי תָּדִיר, הָא שְׂעִירָא חֲדָא דְּאִשְׁתְּכַח גַּבֵּיהּ, בְּפִתְקָא דְּכָל חוֹבַיְיהוּ וְכָל טָעֲוָתַיְיהוּ, וְכָל מַה דְּחָטוּ וְחָבוּ קַמַּאי, וְהוּא קַבִּיל לוֹן. כְּדֵין אִסְתְּכְּמוּ כֻּלְּהוּ, דְּיַהַדְרוּן אִינּוּן חוֹבִין עַל עַמֵּיהּ.

247. The Holy One, blessed be He, then says to the seventy ministers that surround HIS throne, THE SECRET OF THE CELESTIAL COURTHOUSE, 'Have you seen this slanderer, how he is always about TO SLANDER My children? Behold, there is a goat by him, with a note with all their iniquities, all their abominable acts and all that they sinned and transgressed before Me. But he accepted them UPON HIMSELF'. They all agree then that these iniquities go back on his people.

248. ר' אַבָּא אָמַר, כָּל אִינּוּן חוֹבִין וְחַטָּאִין מִתְדַּבְּקִין בֵּיהּ, כְּמָה דִּכְתִיב, וְתַשְׁלִיךְ בִּמְצוּלוֹת יָם כָּל חַטֹּאתָם. וּלְבָתַר, כֻּלְּהוּ מִתְהַדְּרָן בְּרֵישֵׁיהוֹן דְּעַמֵּיהּ, הה"ד וְנָשָׂא הַשָּׂעִיר עָלָיו אֶת כָּל עֲוֹנֹתָם אֶל אֶרֶץ גְּזֵרָה. בְּהַאי יוֹמָא מִתְעַטָּר כַּהֲנָא בְּעִטְרִין עִלָּאִין, וְהוּא קָאִים בֵּין עִלָּאֵי וְתַתָּאֵי, וּמְכַפֵּר עָלֵיהּ וְעַל בֵּיתֵיהּ, וְעַל כַּהֲנֵי, וְעַל מַקְדְּשָׁא, וְעַל יִשְׂרָאֵל כֻּלְּהוּ.

248. Rabbi Aba said, All the iniquities and sins FIRST are attached to him, as written, "And You will cast all their sins into the depths of the sea" (Michah 7:19). Then they return upon the heads of his people, as written, "and the goat shall bear upon it all their iniquities to a barren land" (Vayikra 16:22). On that day, the priest is adorned with lofty crowns and is situated between the higher and lower. He atones for him, for his household, for the priests, the Temple and the whole of Yisrael.

249. תָּאנָא, בְּשַׁעֲתָא דְּעָאל בְּדָמָא דְּפַר, מְכַוֵּין בְּרֵישָׁא דִּמְהֵימְנוּתָא וְאָדֵי בְּאֶצְבְּעֵיהּ, כְּמָה דִּכְתִיב, וְהִזָּה אוֹתוֹ עַל הַכַּפֹּרֶת וְלִפְנֵי הַכַּפֹּרֶת וְהֵיךְ עָבִיד. בָּסִים בְּקַפְטָא דְּאֶצְבְּעָא, וְאָדֵי כְּמַצְלִיף, בְּטִיפִין דְּאֶצְבְּעָא, לְסִטְרֵי קַפְתּוּרָא, אָדֵי וְאִתְכַּוְּון, וְשָׁארֵי לְמִמְנֵי אַחַת, אַחַת וְאַחַת. אַחַת

-253-

בִּלְחוֹדָהָא, אַחַת דְּכָלִיל כֹּלָּא, אַחַת שְׁבָחָא דְכֹלָּא, אַחַת דְכֹלָּא אַהֲדְרָן
לְקַבְּלָהּ, אַחַת רֵישָׁא דְכֹלָּא. לְבָתַר אַחַת וְאַחַת, דְּאִינוּן שַׁרְיָין כַּחֲדָא,
בִּרְעוּתָא בְּאַחֲוָותָא, וְלָא מִתְפָּרְשָׁן לְעָלְמִין.

249. We learned that when THE PRIEST entered with the bullock's blood, he meditated on the top of Faith, NAMELY THE FIRST THREE SFIROT, KETER, CHOCHMAH AND BINAH, and sprinkled it with his finger, as written, "and sprinkle it upon the covering, and before the covering" (Vayikra 16:15), THAT IS, ONE ABOVE AND SEVEN BELOW. How did he do that? He dipped the fingertip in blood and sprinkled the drops as if swinging a whip at the side of the Ark covering. HE DID NOT LET THE DROPS FALL ON THE COVERING ITSELF BUT AT ITS SIDE, AND THE DROPS FELL ON THE GROUND. He sprinkled and concentrated and started counting, 'one', which includes everything, one which is the most valuable, one to which everything turns, one that is at the top, NAMELY THE SFIRAH OF KETER. Next is 'one and one', WHICH ARE CHOCHMAH AND BINAH that dwell together willingly, in brotherhood, and never separate FROM EACH OTHER.

250. בָּתַר דְּמָטָא לְהַאי וְאַחַת, דְּהִיא אִימָּא דְכֹלָּא. מִכָּאן שָׁארִי
לְמִמְנֵי בְּזִוּוּגָא, וּמָנֵי וְאָמַר, אַחַת וּשְׁתַּיִם. אַחַת וְשָׁלֹשׁ. אַחַת וְאַרְבַּע.
אַחַת וְחָמֵשׁ. אַחַת וָשֵׁשׁ. אַחַת וָשֶׁבַע. בְּגִין לְאַמְשָׁכָא וּלְנַגְדָא לְהַאי
אַחַת, דְּהִיא אִימָּא עִלָּאָה, בְּדַרְגִּין יְדִיעָן, לְכִתְרָא דְאִימָּא תַּתָּאָה.
וּלְאַמְשָׁכָא נַהֲרִין עֲמִיקִין מֵאַתְרַיְיהוּ לְכִ"י. וְעַ"ד, יוֹמָא דָא תְּרֵין
נְהוֹרִין נַהֲרִין כַּחֲדָא, אִימָּא עִלָּאָה נַהֲרָא לְאִימָּא תַּתָּאָה. וְעַל דָּא
כְּתִיב יה"כ, כְּמָה דְאִתְּמַר.

250. Upon reaching 'and one', which is the mother of everything, NAMELY BINAH, he starts counting from here, FROM BINAH, by joining, counting and saying, 'one and two', NAMELY JOINING BINAH WITH TWO, CHESED AND GVURAH, 'one and three', JOINING BINAH TO CHESED, GVURAH AND TIFERET, 'one and four', JOINING BINAH TO CHESED, GVURAH, TIFERET AND NETZACH, 'one and five', JOINING BINAH TO CHESED, GVURAH, TIFERET, NETZACH AND HOD, 'one and six', JOINING BINAH TO CHESED, GVURAH, TIFERET, NETZACH, HOD AND YESOD, 'one and seven', JOINING BINAH TO CHESED, GVURAH, TIFERET, NETZACH, HOD, YESOD AND

MALCHUT, in order to draw and guide the one, which is supernal Ima, NAMELY BINAH, through specific grades MENTIONED ABOVE, to the Keter of lower Ima, WHICH IS MALCHUT, and draw the deep rivers, THE LIGHTS OF BINAH from their place upon the Congregation of Yisrael, WHICH IS MALCHUT. Therefore, on that day, two lights shine together, WHICH ARE supernal Ima that illuminates lower Ima, BINAH TO MALCHUT. Hence it is written Yom Kippur IN THE PLURAL as we said.

251. א״ר יִצְחָק קְפְטָרָא חֲדָא קְשִׁירָא בְּרַגְלוֹי דְּכַהֲנָא, בְּשַׁעֲתָא דַּהֲוָה עָאל, דְּאִי יָמוּת הָתָם, יַפְּקוּהוּ מִלְּבַר. וּבַמָּה יַדְעֵי. בְּהַהוּא זְהוֹרִיתָא אִתְיָיִדָּע וְאִשְׁתְּמוֹדַע, כַּד לָא יִתְהַפֵּךְ גַּוְונוֹי. בְּהַהִיא שַׁעֲתָא אִשְׁתְּמוֹדַע, דְּכַהֲנָא אִשְׁתְּכַח לְגוֹ בַּחֲטָאָה. וְאִי יִפּוּק בִּשְׁלָם, בִּזְהוֹרִיתָא אִתְיָיַדְע וְאִשְׁתְּמוֹדַע, דְּיֵהֲפֵךְ גַּוְונוֹי לְחִוָּור. כְּדֵין חֶדְוָותָא הִיא בְּעִלָּאֵי וְתַתָּאֵי. וְאִי לָאו כֻּלְּהוּ אִשְׁתְּכָחוּ בְּצַעֲרָא, וַהֲווֹ יַדְעֵי כֹלָּא, דְּלָא אִתְקְבָּלוּ צְלוֹתְהוֹן.

251. Rabbi Yitzchak said, A chain was tied to the feet of the High Priest, when he entered THE HOLY OF HOLIES, so that if he dies there they will take him out, SINCE IT IS FORBIDDEN TO ENTER THERE. How did they know WHETHER HE WAS ALIVE OR NOT? By a crimson colored strap. If its color did not turn WHITE, it was known at that time that the priest was there in sin. And if he came out in peace, it was known and recognized by the crimson strap that turned white. Then there is joy among the higher and lower beings. If not, they were all in sorrow and all knew that their prayer was not accepted.

252. אָמַר רְבִּי יְהוּדָה, כֵּיוָן דַּהֲוָה עָאל, וְטִמְטֵם עֵינוֹי דְּלָא לְאִסְתַּכְּלָא בְּמָה דְּלָא אִצְטְרִיךְ, וַהֲוָה שָׁמַע קַל גַּדְפֵי כְּרוּבַיָּיא מְזַמְּרֵי וּמְשַׁבְּחֵי. הֲוָה יָדַע כַּהֲנָא, דְּכֹלָּא הֲוָה בְּחֶדְוָה, וְיִפּוּק בִּשְׁלָם. וְעִם כָּל דָּא בִּצְלוֹתֵיהּ הֲוָה יָדַע, דְּמִלִּין נָפְקִין בְּחֶדְוָותָא, וּמִתְקַבְּלָן וּמִתְבָּרְכָן כַּדְקָא יָאוּת, וּכְדֵין חֶדְוָותָא הִיא בְּעִלָּאֵי וְתַתָּאֵי.

252. Rabbi Yehuda said, Once he entered, he closed his eyes so as not to look where he shouldn't. When he heard the sound of the wings of the

Cherubs singing and praising, the priest would know that everything is in joy and went out in peace. With all that, through his prayer he would know, since the words came out of his mouth in joy, and were properly accepted and blessed. Then joy abounded among the higher and lower beings.

253. רִבִּי אֶלְעָזָר שָׁאַל לְר"ש אֲבוֹי, א"ל, הַאי יוֹמָא אֲמַאי הוּא בְּהַאי אֲתַר תַּלֵּי, וְלָא בְּדַרְגָּא אָחֳרָא, דְּיָאוֹת הוּא לְמֶהֱוֵי בְּדַרְגָּא דְּמַלְכָּא שָׁארֵי, יַתִּיר מִכֹּלָּא. אָמַר לֵיהּ ר' שִׁמְעוֹן אֶלְעָזָר בְּרִי, הָכִי הוּא וַדַּאי, וְיָאוּת שָׁאֶלְתָּ.

253. Rabbi Elazar asked Rabbi Shimon his father, Why does this day OF YOM KIPPUR originate in that place, BINAH, AS MALCHUT, THE SECRET OF THE LEFT, ASCENDS TO BINAH, instead of from another place? It would have been appropriate for it to be of the grade where the King dwells the most, NAMELY, THAT SHE WOULD UNITE WITH HER HUSBAND ZEIR ANPIN, THE SECRET OF THE RIGHT. Rabbi Shimon said to him, My son Elazar, surely it is so, THAT IT SHOULD COME FROM BINAH, and you have asked well.

254. ת"ח, מַלְכָּא קַדִּישָׁא, שָׁבִיק הֵיכָלֵיהּ וּבֵיתֵיהּ בִּידָא דְּמַטְרוֹנִיתָא, וְשָׁבַק לִבְנוֹי עִמָּהּ, בְּגִין לְדַבְּרָא לוֹן, וּלְאַלְקָאָה לוֹן, וּלְמִשְׁרֵי בְּגַוַּויְיהוּ. דְּאִי זַכָּאן מַטְרוֹנִיתָא עָאלַת בְּחֶדְוָותָא בִּיקָרָא לְגַבֵּי מַלְכָּא. וְאִי לָא זַכָּאן, הִיא וְאִינּוּן, אִתְהַדְרוּ בְּגָלוּתָא. וְהָא אוֹקִימְנָא, כְּמָה דִּכְתִיב, מְשַׁדֶּד אָב יַבְרִיחַ אֵם. וּכְתִיב, וּבְפִשְׁעֵיכֶם שֻׁלְּחָה אִמְּכֶם.

254. HE ANSWERS, Come and see, the Holy King left His temple and house in the hand of the Matron, MALCHUT, and left His children with her, in order for her to guide them, strike them and dwell among them. If they are worthy, the Matron enters joyfully and honorably to the King. If they are not worthy, she and they are returned into exile. We already explained this, as written, "A son of scandalous and shameful ways shall ruin his father, and drive his mother away" (Mishlei 19:26), CHASING HER INTO EXILE, and, "for your transgressions was your mother put away" (Yeshayah 50:1).

255. וְעַל דָּא אִית יוֹמָא חַד בְּשַׁתָּא, לְאַשְׁגָּחָא בְּהוּ, וּלְעַיְּינָא בְּהוּ. וְכַד

אִזְדְּמַן הַאי יוֹמָא, אִימָּא עִלָּאָה דְּכָל חֵירוּ בִּידָהָא, אִזְדְּמַן לְקַבְּלֵיהּ, לְאִסְתַּכְּלָא בְּהוּ בְּיִשְׂרָאֵל. וְיִשְׂרָאֵל אִזְדָּרְזוּ בְּהַאי יוֹמָא, בְּכַמָּה פּוּלְחָנִין, בְּכַמָּה צְלוֹתִין, בְּכַמָּה עֲנוּיִין, כֻּלְּהוּ בְּזָכוּתָא. כְּדֵין אִזְדְּמַן לְהוֹ חֵירוּ, מֵאֲתַר דְּכָל חֵירוּ בִּידָהָא דְּמַטְרוֹנִיתָא. בְּנֵי מַלְכָּא בְּנָהָא, דְּאִתְפַּקְּדָן בִּידָהָא, כֻּלְּהוּ זַכָּאִין, כֻּלְּהוּ בְּלָא חֲטָאָן, בְּלָא חוֹבִין, כְּדֵין אִזְדַּוְוגַת לְגַבֵּי מַלְכָּא, בִּנְהִירוּ, בְּחֶדְוָה, בִּשְׁלִימוּ, בִּרְעוּתָא. דְּהָא רַבִּיאַת בְּנִין לְמַלְכָּא עִלָּאָה כַּדְקָא יָאוֹת.

255. Therefore there is one day in the year, to look at them and observe THEIR DEEDS. When that day comes, supernal Ima, BINAH, has in her hands all kinds of freedom, NAMELY THE MOCHIN OF THE ILLUMINATION OF CHOCHMAH CLOTHED IN CHASSADIM, THE SECRET OF FREEDOM. THEY SUBJUGATE ALL THE KLIPOT AND CAUSE THEM TO FLEE. She comes towards it, THAT DAY, to observe Yisrael, NAMELY TO BESTOW PLENTY UPON THEM, and Yisrael hasten on that day with many kinds of worship and prayers, and many afflictions, all of them meritorious. Then freedom comes upon them from the place where all freedom exists in the hand of the Matron, MALCHUT. THIS MEANS THAT MALCHUT RISES TO BINAH, AND RECEIVES ALL FREEDOM FROM BINAH. The King's children, YISRAEL BELOW, her children, who were trusted in her hands, are all meritorious without sins or iniquities. She then joins the King in light, joy, perfection and goodwill, because she raised proper children to the King, THAT IS, SHE CLEAVES TO THE RIGHT. BEFORE YISRAEL RECEIVE PURITY AND FREEDOM FROM BINAH, MALCHUT CANNOT UNITE WITH ZEIR ANPIN AND RECEIVE THE RIGHT FROM HIM. THIS SETTLES THE QUESTION OF HIS SON RABBI ELAZAR.

256. וְכַד הַאי יוֹמָא לָא אִשְׁתְּכְחוּ כַּדְקָא יָאוֹת, וַוי לוֹן, וַוי לְשָׁלוּחֵיהוֹן, וַוי דְּהָא מַטְרוֹנִיתָא אִתְרַחֲקַת מִן מַלְכָּא, וְאִימָּא עִלָּאָה אִסְתַּלְּקַת, וְלָא נָפִיק מִנָּהּ חֵירוּ לְעָלְמִין. זַכָּאִין אִינוּן יִשְׂרָאֵל, דְּקוּדְשָׁא בְּרִיךְ הוּא אוֹלִיף לוֹן אוֹרְחוֹי, בְּגִין לְאִשְׁתְּזָבָא מִן דִּינָא, וְיִשְׁתַּכְּחוּן זַכָּאִין קַמֵּיהּ. הַהַ"ד, כִּי בַיּוֹם הַזֶּה יְכַפֵּר עֲלֵיכֶם. לְטַהֵר אֶתְכֶם. וּכְתִיב, וְזָרַקְתִּי עֲלֵיכֶם מַיִם טְהוֹרִים וּטְהַרְתֶּם מִכָּל טֻמְאוֹתֵיכֶם וְגוֹ'.

256. When that day is not proper, woe to them, TO YISRAEL, woe to their messenger, THE HIGH PRIEST, woe to the Matron who is distanced from the King; supernal Ima, BINAH, is gone and no freedom comes from her to the worlds. Happy are Yisrael, whom the Holy One, blessed be He, taught His ways so as to be saved from Judgment and to be meritorious before Him. This is the meaning of, "for on that day will He forgive you, to cleanse you" (Vayikra 16:30), and, "Then will I sprinkle clean water upon you, and you shall be clean. From all your uncleannesses..." (Yechezkel 36:25).

35. "The fifteenth day"

A Synopsis

Rabbi Aba tells Rabbi Yosi the meaning of the fifteen days in "The fifteenth day of this seventh month," saying that the first ten belong to the Matron and the next five to the King. On the fifteenth day the moon is full, and the full moon is the secret of Malchut.

257. וּבַחֲמִשָּׁה עָשָׂר יוֹם לַחֹדֶשׁ הַשְּׁבִיעִי וְגוֹ'. ר' יוֹסֵי שָׁאַל לְרָבִּי אַבָּא, אָ"ל, הָנֵי חֲמִשָּׁה עֶשֶׂר יוֹם, מַאי קָא מַיְירֵי. אָ"ל, וַדַּאי רָזָא יַקִּירָא הוּא. ת"ח, בֵּין לְעֵילָא בֵּין לְתַתָּא, כָּל חַד וְחַד, בְּאָרְחֵיהּ נַטְלָא. וּבְאָרְחֵיהּ יָתְבָא, וּבְאָרְחֵיהּ אִתְּעַר וְעָבֵיד מַאי דְעָבֵיד. הַאי עָשׂוֹר מִכְּנֶסֶת יִשְׂרָאֵל אִינּוּן. וְיוֹמָא עֲשִׂירָאָה, בַּעֲשִׂירָאָה קַיְימָא. וְעַל דָּא בֶּעָשׂוֹר לַחֹדֶשׁ הַזֶּה וְיִקְחוּ לָהֶם אִישׁ שֶׂה לְבֵית וְגוֹ'. וְהַאי יוֹמָא, הוּא דִּילָהּ. וַחֲמִשָּׁה יוֹמִין אָחֳרָנִין, דְּמַלְכָּא הוּא. הַהוּא יוֹמָא דְּאָתֵי עֲלָהּ. דְּהָא חֲמִשָּׁאָה, בֵּיהּ יָתִיב מַלְכָּא, בְּכוּרְסָיְיא.

257. "The fifteenth day of this seventh month" (Vayikra 23:34). Rabbi Yosi asked Rabbi Aba. He said to him, What is the meaning of those fifteen days? He said to him, Certainly they are a precious mystery. Come and see, whether above or below, everything journeys in its own way, sits in its own way, and awakens in its own way to do whatever it does. THAT IS, NOTHING RESEMBLES ANYTHING ELSE, BOTH ABOVE AND BELOW. The tenth is from the Congregation of Yisrael, THAT IS, IT ALLUDES TO MALCHUT, since the tenth day is based on the tenth SFIRAH, MALCHUT. Hence IT IS SAID, "On the tenth day of this month they shall take to them every man a lamb, according to the house of their fathers" (Shemot 12:3). FOR THE TENTH IS MALCHUT, AND SINCE THE TEN SFIROT REACHED COMPLETION ON THE TENTH DAY, "THEY SHALL TAKE..." That day, THE TENTH DAY OF THE MONTH, is hers, while the other five days are the King's, ZEIR ANPIN'S. That day comes upon her AND FILLS HER WITH HER LIGHTS. HENCE ON THE FIFTEENTH DAY THE MOON IS FULL, for on the five days, WHEN THE FIVE SFIROT OF ZEIR ANPIN REACH COMPLETION, the King sits on the throne, WHICH IS MALCHUT, THE SECRET OF THE FULL MOON.

258. וּבְכָל אֲתַר בְּעֶשּׂוֹר, דְּמַטְרוֹנִיתָא הוּא. חֲמִשָּׁה עֲלַיְיהוּ, דְּמַלְכָּא הוּא. הַהוּא יוֹמָא דְּאָתֵי עֲלָה. בְּג"כ חֲמִשָּׁה יוֹמִין מִירְחָא, לְאוֹרַיְיתָא. וְאִי תֵּימָא שְׁבִיעָאָה, בְּזִמְנָא דִּתְרֵין אַבָהָן מִשְׁתַּכְּחֵי בֵּיהּ, דְּהָא מַלְכָּא בְּהוּ, וּכְדֵין מִתְעַטֵּר בְּכֹלָּא. וְחַד מִלָּה, שְׁבִיעָאָה וַחֲמִשָּׁאָה.

258. The ten always pertain to the Matron, NAMELY MALCHUT. The five above them are the King's, NAMELY THE FIRST FIVE SFIROT OF ZEIR ANPIN, who is the day that comes upon her, THAT IS ZEIR ANPIN. For that reason, after the five days of the month of Sivan, the Torah IS GIVEN, WHICH INDICATES THE FIVE FIRST SFIROT OF ZEIR ANPIN THAT BESTOWED PLENTY AT THE GIVING OF THE TORAH. You may argue that THE TORAH SHOULD HAVE BEEN GIVEN on the seventh day, NAMELY when the two parents, ABA AND IMA, are CLOTHED in him, IN ZEIR ANPIN. For the King, WHEN HE IS in them, is then adorned with everything AND IS THEN WORTHY TO GIVE THE TORAH. HE ANSWERS, The fifth and the seventh are the same issue.

259. ת"ח, חֲמִשָּׁאָה דִּילֵיהּ הוּא וַדַּאי, כְּמָה דְּאִתְּמַר, וּכְדֵין נָהִיר אַבָּא לְאִימָּא, וְאִתְנְהִירוּ מִנָּהּ חַמְשִׁין תַּרְעִין לְאַנְהֲרָא לַחֲמִשָּׁאָה. וְאִי תֵּימָא שְׁבִיעָאָה, בְּגִין דְּמַלְכָּא בִּשְׁלִימוּ דְּאַבָהָן, וַעֲטָרָה יָרִית מִשְּׁבִיעָאָה, כְּמָה דִּכְתִיב צְאֶינָה וּרְאֶינָה בְּנוֹת צִיּוֹן. וְע"ד בִּשְׁבִיעָאָה הוּא יוֹמָא דִּמְעַטְרָא מַלְכָּא בְּעִטְרוֹי, וּכְדֵין יָרִית מַלְכָּא לְאַבָּא וְאִימָּא, דְּמִזְדַּוְּוגִין כַּחֲדָא. וְע"ד כֹּלָּא בְּחַד תַּלְיָיא.

259. Come and see, the fifth is surely His, as we said. Aba then shine upon Ima, and from her the fifty gates shine upon the fifth. We may argue that it is the seventh. This is because the King abides in the wholeness of the parents that shine ON HIM, AS HIS FIVE TOGETHER WITH ABA AND IMA AMOUNT TO SEVEN. MOREOVER He receives a crown from BINAH THAT IS CALLED the seventh. IF YOU COUNT FROM YESOD, BINAH IS THE SEVENTH SFIRAH. This is as written, "Go forth, O daughters of Zion, and behold KING SOLOMON WITH THE CROWN WITH WHICH HIS MOTHER CROWNED HIM..." (Shir Hashirim 3:11). Hence, the seventh day is the day when BINAH crowns the King, ZEIR ANPIN, WITH HIS CROWNS. The King

ALSO inherits then Aba and Ima that unite AND SHINE INTO HIM together AS WITH HIS OWN FIVE THEY ARE SEVEN. Thus it all depends on the same thing.

36. Manna, the well and the clouds of glory

A Synopsis

Rabbi Yehuda tells us that Moses, Aaron and Miriam, through their merit, gave Yisrael the manna, the clouds of glory and the well, and that all of these celestial gifts are attached above. He emphasizes that there were seven clouds of glory, and that after Aaron died the clouds were gone and Yisrael was no longer protected by them. Rabbi Aba says that whoever excludes himself from the shadow of Faith as represented by those clouds is worthy only of being a servant to servants of servants, yet whoever dwells under the shadow of Faith bequeaths freedom to all his descendants forever.

260(1). וּבַחֲמִשָּׁה עָשָׂר יוֹם, ר' יְהוּדָה פָּתַח, וַיִּשְׁמַע הַכְּנַעֲנִי מֶלֶךְ עֲרָד. תָּנֵינָן, ג' מַתְּנָן עִלָּאִין, אִזְדְּמָנוּ לְהוּ לְיִשְׂרָאֵל, עַ"י תְּלָתָא אָחִין: מֹשֶׁה, אַהֲרֹן, וּמִרְיָם. מָן, בִּזְכוּת מֹשֶׁה. עֲנָנֵי כָבוֹד, בִּזְכוּת אַהֲרֹן. בְּאֵר, בִּזְכוּת מִרְיָם. וְכֻלְּהוּ אֲחִידָן לְעֵילָא. מָן בִּזְכוּת מֹשֶׁה, דִּכְתִיב הִנְנִי מַמְטִיר לָכֶם לֶחֶם מִן הַשָּׁמַיִם מִן הַשָּׁמַיִם, דָּא מֹשֶׁה.

260a. The fifteenth day" (Vayikra 23:34). Rabbi Yehuda opened the discussion with, "And when the Canaanite, the king of Arad" (Bemidbar 21:1). We learned that three celestial gifts were given to Yisrael by the three siblings, Moses, Aaron and Miriam – the manna through the merit of Moses, the clouds of glory through the merit of Aaron and the well through the merit of Miriam. They are all attached above. The manna is by the merit of Moses, as written, "Behold, I will rain bread from heaven for you" (Shemot 16:4). "from heaven" refers to Moses, NAMELY THE CHARIOT TO ZEIR ANPIN CALLED MOSES AND ALSO CALLED HEAVEN.

260(2). עֲנָנֵי כָבוֹד בִּזְכוּת אַהֲרֹן, דִּכְתִיב אֲשֶׁר עַיִן בְּעַיִן נִרְאָה אַתָּה יְיָ' וְגוֹ', וּכְתִיב וְכִסָּה עֲנַן הַקְּטֹרֶת. מַה לְהַלָּן, שִׁבְעָה. אַף כָּאן נָמֵי שִׁבְעָה. דְּהָא בַּקְּטֹרֶת שִׁבְעָה עֲנָנִין מִתְקַשְּׁרָן כַּחֲדָא. וְאַהֲרֹן רֵישָׁא לְכָל שִׁבְעָה עֲנָנִין הוּא וְהוּא קָשִׁיר לְשִׁית אָחֳרָנִין בֵּיהּ בְּכָל יוֹמָא.

260b. The clouds of glory are by merit of Aaron, A CHARIOT TO CHESED, as written, "that You Hashem are seen face to face..." (Bemidbar 14:14), and, "the cloud of the incense may cover" (Vayikra 16:13). As on the other verse, IN RELATION TO INCENSE, there are seven CLOUDS, so in the former, IN, "YOUR CLOUD STANDS OVER THEM" (BEMIDBAR 14:14), there are also seven CLOUDS. For there were seven clouds of incense joined together, and Aaron is the uppermost of the seven clouds. FOR THE SEVEN CLOUDS ARE THE SECRET OF CHESED, GVURAH, TIFERET, NETZACH, HOD, YESOD AND MALCHUT. AARON, WHO IS A CHARIOT TO CHESED, IS THE FIRST SFIRAH, and he is daily connected through it to the six other clouds, GVURAH, TIFERET, NETZACH, HOD, YESOD AND MALCHUT. THE CLOUDS ARE THEREFORE CONSIDERED TO COME BY THE MERIT OF AARON, AS HE IS THE ASPECT OF CHESED, THE TOP CLOUD, WHICH INCLUDES THEM.

261. בְּאֵר בִּזְכוּת מִרְיָם, דְּהָא הִיא וַדַּאי בְּאֵר אִתְקְרֵי. וּבְסִפְרָא דְּאַגַּדְתָּא, וַתֵּתַצַּב אֲחֹתוֹ מֵרָחֹק לְדֵעָה וְגוֹ'. דָּא הוּא בְּאֵר מַיִם חַיִּים, וְכֹלָּא קְשׁוּרָא חַד. מֵתָה מִרְיָם, אִסְתַּלָּק בְּאֵר. דִּכְתִּיב, וְלֹא הָיָה מַיִם לָעֵדָה. וּבְהַהִיא שַׁעֲתָא בָּעָאת בְּאֵר אָחֳרָא לְאִסְתַּלְּקָא, דַּהֲוָה שְׁכִיחַ עִמְּהוֹן דְּיִשְׂרָאֵל. כַּד חָמָאת שִׁיתָא עֲנָנִין דַּהֲווֹ קְשִׁירִין עֲלָהּ, אִתְקַשְּׁרַת הִיא בְּהוּ.

261. The well comes by merit of Miriam, WHO WAS A CHARIOT TO MALCHUT, since she is surely called a well. In the book of Agadah, WE LEARNED, "And his sister stood afar off, to know…" (Shemot 2:4). This is a well of living water, NAMELY MALCHUT, and all was bound into one, SINCE MIRIAM WAS CONNECTED TO MALCHUT. When Miriam died, the well was gone, as written, "And there was no water for the congregation" (Bemidbar 20:2). At that time, another well wished to depart, MALCHUT, that was with Yisrael, BUT when it saw the six clouds, CHESED, GVURAH, TIFERET, NETZACH, HOD AND YESOD, that were connected to it, TO THE CLOUD OF MALCHUT, HER OWN ASPECT, MALCHUT became connected to them.

262. מִית אַהֲרֹן, אִסְתַּלָּקוּ אִינּוּן עֲנָנִין, וְאִסְתַּלָּק עֲנָנָא דְּבֵירָא עִמְּהוֹן. אָתָא מֹשֶׁה, אַהֲדָר לְהוּ. הה"ד, עָלִיתָ לַמָּרוֹם שָׁבִיתָ שֶּׁבִי לָקַחְתָּ מַתָּנוֹת בָּאָדָם. לָקַחְתָּ מַתָּנוֹת וַדַּאי, אִינּוּן מַתָּנוֹת דַּהֲווֹ בְּקַדְמֵיתָא בְּאֵר וַעֲנָנִין.

262. When Aaron died, the clouds of glory were gone, and with them was gone the SEVENTH cloud, TO WHICH the well, MALCHUT, WAS ATTACHED. Moses returned them to them, as written, "You have ascended on high, you have led captivity captive. You have received gifts from men" (Tehilim 68:19). Surely, "You have received gifts from men," the presents that were there before, NAMELY, the well and the clouds.

263. בְּאֵר, דָּא בְּאֵר דְּיִצְחָק. עֲנָנִים, אִלֵּין עֲנָנִים דְּאַהֲרֹן. א"ר יִצְחָק, מִפְּנֵי מַה זָכָה אַהֲרֹן לְדָא, בְּגִין דְּאִיהוּ קָשִׁיר בַּעֲנָנִים. וְהוּא אַקְשִׁיר כָּל יוֹמָא וְיוֹמָא לְכֻלְּהוּ כַּחֲדָא, דְּמִתְבָּרְכָאן כֻּלְּהוּ עַל יְדוֹי.

263. This well is Isaac's well, NAMELY MALCHUT THAT IS CALLED WELL WHEN RECEIVING THE ILLUMINATION OF CHOCHMAH FROM THE LEFT CALLED ISAAC. These clouds are Aaron's clouds, WHICH MEANS THAT CLOUDS ARE CHASSADIM, BECAUSE THEY ARE OF THE ASPECT OF AARON WHO IS CHESED. Rabbi Yitzchak said, What is the reason Aaron was worthy THAT THE CLOUDS OF GLORY WILL COME OVER YISRAEL BY HIS MERIT? This is because he is connected to the clouds, WHICH MEANS HE IS THE ATTRIBUTE OF CHESED LIKE THEM. And he, BEING A CHARIOT TO CHESED OF ZEIR ANPIN, THE TOP CLOUD, used to connect AND UNITE them all into one daily, so they will all be blessed by him.

264. תָּא חֲזֵי, עַל כָּל חֶסֶד דְּעָבֵד קוּדְשָׁא בְּרִיךְ הוּא בְּיִשְׂרָאֵל. קָשִׁיר עִמְּהוֹן ז' עֲנָנֵי יַקִּירָן, וְקָשִׁיר לְהוּ בִּכְנֶסֶת יִשְׂרָאֵל, דְּהָא עֲנָנָא דִּילֵהּ אִתְקְשַׁר בְּשִׁיתָא אָחֳרָנִין. וּבְכֻלְּהוּ שִׁבְעָה, אַזְלוּ יִשְׂרָאֵל בְּמַדְבְּרָא. מַאי טַעֲמָא, בְּגִין דְּכֻלְּהוּ קִשְׁרָא דִּמְהֵימְנוּתָא נִינְהוּ וְעַל דָּא בַּסֻכּוֹת תֵּשְׁבוּ שִׁבְעַת יָמִים. מַאי קָא מַיְירֵי. בְּגִין דִּכְתִיב, בְּצִלּוֹ חִמַּדְתִּי וְיָשַׁבְתִּי וּפִרְיוֹ מָתוֹק לְחִכִּי. וּבָעֵי בַּר נָשׁ לְאַחֲזָאָה גַּרְמֵיהּ, דְּיָתִיב תְּחוֹת צְלָא דִּמְהֵימְנוּתָא.

264. Come and see, whatever kindness (Chesed) the Holy One, blessed be He, did to Yisrael, He attached the seven clouds of glory to it, WHICH CORRESPOND TO CHESED, GVURAH, TIFERET, NETZACH, HOD, YESOD AND MALCHUT. And He connected them to the Congregation of Yisrael,

WHICH IS MALCHUT, since her cloud was connected to the others six, CHESED, GVURAH, TIFERET, NETZACH, HOD AND YESOD. Thus Yisrael walked in the desert with all seven clouds. The reason is that they were all the bonds of Faith, ATTACHED TO MALCHUT THAT IS CALLED FAITH. In relation to that SCRIPTURE SAYS, "You shall dwell in booths seven days" (Vayikra 23:42), THE SECRET OF THE SEVEN CLOUDS OF GLORY THAT WENT WITH YISRAEL IN THE DESERT. What does that teach us? HE ANSWERS, It is written, "I sat down under his shadow with great delight, and his fruit was sweet to my taste" (Shir Hashirim 2:3), THE SECRET OF THE SHADOW OF THE CLOUDS OF GLORY AND THE SECRET OF THE SHADOW OF THE SUKKAH. Man should display himself sitting under the shadow of Faith.

265. ת"ח, כָּל אִינּוּן שְׁנִין דְּקָאִים אַהֲרֹן, הֲווֹ יִשְׂרָאֵל בְּצִלָּא דִּמְהֵימְנוּתָא, תְּחוֹת אִלֵּין עֲנָנִין. בָּתַר דְּמִית אַהֲרֹן, אִסְתַּלָּק עֲנָנָא חַד, דְּהוּא יְמִינָא דְּכֹלָּא. וְכַד הַאי אִסְתַּלָּק, אִסְתַּלָּקוּ כָּל שְׁאָר עִמֵּיהּ וְאִתְחֲזִיאוּ כֻּלְּהוּ בִּגְרִיעוּתָא. וְהָא אוּקְמוּהָ, דִּכְתִיב וַיִּרְאוּ כָּל הָעֵדָה כִּי גָוַע אַהֲרֹן. אַל תִּקְרֵי וַיִּרְאוּ, אֶלָּא וַיֵּרָאוּ. מִיָּד וַיִּשְׁמַע הַכְּנַעֲנִי מֶלֶךְ עֲרָד יֹשֵׁב הַנֶּגֶב כִּי בָא יִשְׂרָאֵל דֶּרֶךְ הָאֲתָרִים. שְׁמַע דְּאִסְתַּלָּקוּ אִינּוּן עֲנָנִים, וּמִית תַּיָּירָא רַבְרְבָא דְּכָל אִינּוּן עֲנָנִים אִתְקַשְׁרוּ בֵּיהּ.

265. Come and see, throughout Aaron's life Yisrael were under the shadow of Faith, under these SEVEN clouds. After Aaron died, one cloud was gone, WHICH IS CHESED OF THE CLOUDS, HIS OWN ATTRIBUTE, the one most to the right. When that was gone, the other clouds were gone with it, THE SIX SFIROT INCLUDED IN IT. Everyone OF YISRAEL were seen lacking. We explained the verse, "And when all the congregation saw that Aaron was dead" (Bemidbar 20:29). Do not pronounce it 'saw (Heb. *vayir'u*)' but 'were seen (Heb. *vayera'u*)', WHICH MEANS THAT THE CLOUDS' SHADOW DISAPPEARED FROM THEM AND THEY WERE EXPOSED. Immediately, "And when the Canaanite, the king of Arad, who dwelt in the Negev, heard that Yisrael came by the way of Atarim" (Bemidbar 21:1), he heard that the clouds of glory were gone and the great guide died, to whom all the clouds were attached.

266. א"ר יִצְחָק, הַכְּנַעֲנִי מֶלֶךְ עֲרָד יֹשֵׁב הַנֶּגֶב וַדַּאי. וְכַד אָתוּ אִינּוּן

מְאַלְלִין דְּשָׁדַר מֹשֶׁה, אָמְרוּ עֲמָלֵק יוֹשֵׁב בְּאֶרֶץ הַנֶּגֶב, בְּגִין לְתַבְּרָא
לְבַיְיהוּ. דְּהָא בַּעֲמָלֵק אִתְּבַּר חֵילֵיהוֹן בְּקַדְמֵיתָא.

266. Rabbi Yitzchak said, Surely it was "the Canaanite, the king of Arad, who dwelt in the Negev." When the spies Moses sent returned, they said, "Amalek dwells in the land of the Negev" (Bemidbar 13:29), in order to break their heart, since their strength was first broken by Amalek.

267. א"ר אַבָּא, וַיִּשְׁמַע הַכְּנַעֲנִי, מַאי קָא מַיְירֵי הָכָא. בָּתַר דְּאִסְתְּלָקוּ
אִינּוּן עֲנָנִים. אֶלָּא כְּנַעַן כְּתִיב בֵּיה, וַיֹּאמֶר אָרוּר כְּנַעַן עֶבֶד עֲבָדִים
יִהְיֶה לְאֶחָיו. הָכָא אוֹלִיפְנָא, מַאן דְּאַפִּיק גַּרְמֵיה מִצִּלָּא דִּמְהֵימְנוּתָא,
אִתְחֲזֵי לְמֶהֱוֵי עֶבֶד לְעַבְדֵּי עַבְדִּין, הה"ד וַיִּלָּחֶם בְּיִשְׂרָאֵל וַיִּשְׁבְּ מִמֶּנּוּ
שֶׁבִי. הוּא נָטַל עַבְדִּין מִיִּשְׂרָאֵל לְגַרְמֵיה.

267. Rabbi Aba said, "the Canaanite…heard." Why is THE CANAANITE MENTIONED here, COMING after the clouds were gone? AND HE ANSWERS, It is written of Canaan, "Cursed be Canaan; a servant of servants shall he be to his brethren" (Beresheet 9:25). We learned here FROM THE VERSE, "THE CANAANITE…HEARD," that whoever excludes himself from the shadow of Faith is worthy of being a servant to servants of servants, NAMELY TO CANAANITES. This is the meaning of, "he fought against Yisrael, and took some of them prisoners" (Bemidbar 21:1), taking himself servants from among Yisrael.

268. וְעַל דָּא כְּתִיב, כָּל הָאֶזְרָח בְּיִשְׂרָאֵל יֵשְׁבוּ בַּסֻּכּוֹת. כָּל מַאן
דְּאִיהוּ מִשָּׁרְשָׁא וְגִזְעָא קַדִּישָׁא דְּיִשְׂרָאֵל, יֵשְׁבוּ בַּסֻּכּוֹת, תְּחוֹת צְלָא
דִּמְהֵימְנוּתָא. וּמַאן דְּלֵיתֵיה מִגִּזְעָא וְשׁוּרְשָׁא קַדִּישָׁא דְּיִשְׂרָאֵל, לָא
יָתִיב בְּהוּ, וְיִפּוּק גַּרְמֵיה מִתְּחוֹת צְלָא דִּמְהֵימְנוּתָא.

268. It is therefore written, "all that are home born in Yisrael shall dwell in booths" (Vayikra 23:42), for whoever is from the root and holy stock of Yisrael shall dwell in booths under the shadow of Faith. Whoever is not from the holy stock and root of Yisrael shall not dwell in them, but excludes himself from under the shadow of Faith.

269. כְּתִיב כְּנַעַן בְּיָדוֹ מֹאזְנֵי מִרְמָה, דָּא אֱלִיעֶזֶר עֶבֶד אַבְרָהָם. וְת"ח, כְּתִיב אָרוּר כְּנַעַן וּבְגִין דְּזָכָה כְּנַעַן דָּא, לְשַׁמְּשָׁא לְאַבְרָהָם, כֵּיוָן דְּשַׁמֵּשׁ לְאַבְרָהָם, יָתִיב תְּחוֹת צְלָא דִּמְהֵימְנוּתָא, זָכָה לְמֵיפַק מֵהַהוּא לָטְיָיא דְּאִתְלַטְיָיא, וְלֹא עוֹד אֶלָּא דִּכְתִיב בֵּיהּ בִּרְכָה. דִּכְתִיב, וַיֹּאמֶר בֹּא בָּרוּךְ יְיָ'. מַאי קָא מַיְירֵי. דְּכָל מַאן דְּיַתִּיב תְּחוֹת צְלָא דִּמְהֵימְנוּתָא, אַחֲסִין חֵירוּ לֵיהּ וְלִבְנוֹי לְעָלְמִין, וְאִתְבָּרַךְ בִּרְכָתָא עִלָּאָה, וּמַאן דְּאַפִּיק גַּרְמֵיהּ מִצְּלָא דִּמְהֵימְנוּתָא, אַחֲסִין גָּלוּתָא לֵיהּ וְלִבְנוֹי, דִּכְתִיב וַיִּלָּחֶם בְּיִשְׂרָאֵל וַיִּשְׁבְּ מִמֶּנּוּ שֶׁבִי.

269. It is written, "As for the merchant (also: 'the Canaanite'), the balances of deceit are in his hand" (Hoshea 12:8). This refers to Eliezer, Abraham's servant. Come and see, it is written, "Cursed be Canaan." Since this Canaan, ELIEZER, merited to serve Abraham and since he did serve Abraham and dwelt under the shadow of Faith, he was worthy of being excluded from the curse he was cursed with. Furthermore, a blessing is written about him, as written, "And he said, Come in, you blessed of Hashem" (Beresheet 24:31). This teaches us that whoever dwells under the shadow of Faith bequeaths freedom for himself and for his descendants for ever, and is blessed with a celestial blessing. Whoever excludes himself from the shadow of Faith bequeaths exile for himself and for his descendants, as written, "he fought against Yisrael, and took some of them prisoners."

270. בַּסֻּכּוֹת תֵּשְׁבוּ חָסֵר, וְדָא עֲנָנָא חַד, דְּכֻלְּהוּ קְשִׁירִין בֵּיהּ. דִּכְתִיב, כִּי עֲנַן יְיָ' עֲלֵיהֶם יוֹמָם. וּכְתִיב, וּבְעַמּוּד עָנָן אַתָּה הֹלֵךְ לִפְנֵיהֶם יוֹמָם. דָּא הוּא עֲנָנָא דְּאַהֲרֹן, דְּאִקְרֵי יוֹמָם, דִּכְתִיב יוֹמָם יְצַוֶּה יְיָ' חַסְדּוֹ. עֲנָנָא חַד, נָטִיל עִמֵּיהּ חָמֵשׁ אָחֳרָנִין, וְאִינּוּן שִׁית. וַעֲנָנָא אָחֳרָא, דִּכְתִיב וּבְעַמּוּד אֵשׁ לַיְלָה, דָּא נָהֲרָא לְהוּ לְיִשְׂרָאֵל, מִנְּהִירוּ דְּאִינּוּן שִׁית.

270. "You shall dwell in booths (Heb. Sukkot)." SUKKOT IS SPELLED WITHOUT VAV, because THIS SUKKOT ALLUDES to one cloud only, WHICH IS CHESED, to which all SIX CLOUDS are attached. HENCE THERE ARE SEVEN DAYS, as written, "And the cloud of Hashem was upon them by day" (Bemidbar 10:34), and, "and that You go before them by day time in a pillar of cloud" (Bemidbar 14:14), which is Aaron's cloud, WHICH IS CHESED

that is called "by day," as written, "Yet Hashem will command His Chesed in the daytime" (Tehilim 42:9). One cloud, WHICH IS CHESED, receives with it five other clouds, WHICH ARE GVURAH, TIFERET, NETZACH, HOD AND YESOD, so they are six. Another cloud, of which is written, "and in a pillar of fire by night" (Bemidbar 14:14), WHICH IS MALCHUT, shines on Yisrael from the illumination of the six CLOUDS.

37. The holiday of Sukkot

A Synopsis

We learn that whoever is in the secret of the Faith dwells in a Sukkah or booth, and that one must offer a daily sacrifice on the seven days of Sukkot. Offerings are made to the other nations because God wants them to be friends with Yisrael.

רעיא מהימנא

271. בְּסֻכּוֹת תֵּשְׁבוּ שִׁבְעַת יָמִים וְגוֹ׳, פְּקוּדָא דָא, לְיַשֵּׁב בַּסוּכָּה. וְהָא אוּקִימְנָא, בְּגִין לְאִתְחֲזָאָה דְיִשְׂרָאֵל יַתְבֵי בְּרָזָא דִמְהֵימְנוּתָא, בְּלָא דְחִילוּ כְּלָל, דְּהָא מְקַטְרְגָא אִתְפְּרַשׁ מִנַּיְיהוּ. וְכָל מַאן דְּאִיהוּ בְּרָזָא דִמְהֵימְנוּתָא, יָתִיב בַּסוּכָּה. כְּמָה דְּאוּקִימְנָא, דִכְתִיב, כָּל הָאֶזְרָח בְּיִשְׂרָאֵל יֵשְׁבוּ בַּסֻכּוֹת. מַאן דְּאִיהוּ בְּרָזָא דִמְהֵימְנוּתָא, וּמִזַּרְעָא וְשָׁרְשָׁא דְיִשְׂרָאֵל, יֵשְׁבוּ בַּסֻכּוֹת. וְרָזָא דָא אִתְּמַר בְּכַמָּה דוּכְתֵּי.

Ra'aya Meheimna (the Faithful Shepherd)

271. "You shall dwell in booths (Heb. *Sukkot*) seven days" (Vayikra 23:42). It is a commandment to dwell in a Sukkah. We explained that its purpose is to show that Yisrael dwell in the secret of Faith, THE SECRET OF THE SHADOW OF THE SUKKAH entirely without fear OF DENOUNCING, since the prosecutor has already separated from them ON YOM KIPPUR THROUGH THE GOAT GIVEN TO AZAZEL. Whoever is in the secret of Faith dwells in a Sukkah, as we explained from the words, "all that are home born in Yisrael shall dwell in booths" (Ibid.), THAT IS, whoever is in the secret of Faith of the seed and root of Yisrael shall dwell in Sukkot. This mystery was brought in several places.

272. פְּקוּדָא בָּתַר דָּא, לְקָרְבָא קָרְבָּנָא בְּכָל יוֹמָא, וְקָרְבָּנָא דָא, לְמֶחֱוֵי חוּלָקָא בְּכֹלָּא, בְּחֶדְוָותָא דִּבְנוֹי. בְּגִין דְּכֻלְּהוּ אֲחִידָן בְּאִילָנָא. עַנְפִין דִלְתַתָּא דִּלְגַבֵּי שָׁרְשָׁא דְאִילָנָא, כֹּלָּא אִתְבָּרְכָן בְּגִין אִילָנָא. אַף עַל גַּב דְּלֵית בְּהוּ תּוֹעַלְתָּא, כֹּלָּא אִתְבָּרְכָאן. וְחֶדְוָותָא דְיִשְׂרָאֵל בַּאֲבוּהוֹן דִּלְעֵילָא, יַהֲבֵי חוּלָקָא דְבִרְכָּאן, לְכָל אִינּוּן שְׁאָר עַמִּין, דְּאִית לוֹן

אֲחִידוּ, וְאִתְאַחֲדוּ בְּהוּ בְּיִשְׂרָאֵל.

272. The following commandment is to offer a daily sacrifice ON THE SEVEN DAYS OF SUKKOT. Everyone should have a part in that sacrifice, in His children's joy, SINCE THE SEVENTY BULLOCKS CORRESPOND TO THE SEVENTY MINISTERS OF THE NATIONS. They are all attached to the tree, ZEIR ANPIN, since the branches below that come from the root of the tree are all blessed because of the tree. Even though they are useless, THEY are all ALSO blessed. Yisrael rejoice in their Father in heaven, NAMELY IN THE ROOT OF THE TREE, and they give a portion of the blessings to the rest of the nations, who can hold and do hold to Yisrael.

273. וְכָל אִלֵּין קָרְבְּנִין, לְמֵיהַב מְזוֹנָא, לְאִינוּן מְמָנָן דִּשְׁאָר עַמִּין, דְּהָא מִגּוֹ רְחִימוּ דְּקָא רָחִים קוּדְשָׁא בְּרִיךְ הוּא לִבְנוֹי, בָּעֵי דְּכֻלָּא יְהוֹן רְחִימִין דִּלְהוֹן. וְרָזָא דָּא, בִּרְצוֹת יְיָ' דַּרְכֵי אִישׁ גַּם אוֹיְבָיו יַשְׁלִים אִתּוֹ. אֲפִילוּ כָּל אִינוּן מְקַטְרְגֵי עִלָּאֵי כֻּלְּהוּ אֲהַדְרָן רְחִימִין לְיִשְׂרָאֵל וְכַד חַיָּילִין דִּלְעֵילָא אֲהַדְרוּ רְחִימִין לְיִשְׂרָאֵל, כָּל אִינוּן דִּלְתַתָּא, עַל אַחַת כַּמָּה וְכַמָּה.

273. All those offerings, THE SEVENTY BULLOCKS, were made to give nourishment to all the ministers appointed over the other nations, since for the love the Holy One, blessed be He, has for His children, He wants all THE MINISTERS to be their friends. This is the meaning behind, "When a man's ways please Hashem, He makes even his enemies to be at peace with him" (Mishlei 16:7). THAT IS, even the highest prosecutors become again friendly with Yisrael. When the celestial forces again become friends to Yisrael, those below do so even more.

274. וְאִי תֵּימָא לְהוֹן הֲווֹ מְקָרְבֵי קָרְבְּנָא, לָאו הָכִי, אֶלָּא כֹּלָּא לְקוּדְשָׁא בְּרִיךְ הוּא סָלִיק וּמִתְקְרַב. וְאִיהוּ פָּרִישׁ מְזוֹנָא לְכֻלְּהוּ אוּכְלוּסִין דִּסְטְרִין אַחֲרָנִין, דְּיִתְהֲנוּן בְּהַהוּא דּוֹרוֹנָא דִּבְנוֹי, וְיִתְהַדְּרוּן רְחִימִין דִּלְהוֹן, דְּיִנְדְּעוּן עֵילָא וְתַתָּא, דְּהָא לֵית עַמָּא כְּעַמָּא דְּיִשְׂרָאֵל, דְּאִינוּן חוּלָקֵיהּ וְעַדְבֵיהּ דְּקוּדְשָׁא בְּרִיךְ הוּא, וְאִסְתַּלָּק יְקָרָא דְּקוּדְשָׁא

בְּרִיךְ הוּא עֵילָא וְתַתָּא כַּדְקָא יָאוּת. וְכָל אוּכְלוּסִין עִלָּאִין פָּתְחֵי וְאַמְרֵי, וּמִי כְעַמְּךָ כְּיִשְׂרָאֵל גּוֹי אֶחָד בָּאָרֶץ.

ע"כ רעיא מהימנא

274. You may say that the sacrifices were offered to them, TO THE SEVENTY MINISTERS. This is not so, but everything was offered and sacrificed to the Holy One, blessed be He, and He divides the nourishment among the multitudes of the other sides, NAMELY THE MINISTERS OF THE SEVENTY NATIONS, so they will enjoy His children's gift and again become their friends. Thus it shall be known above and below that there is no nation like Yisrael, who are the portion and lot of the Holy One, blessed be He. And the glory of the Holy One, blessed be He, rises above and below as it should and all the celestial multitude start by saying, "And what one nation in the earth is like Your people, like Yisrael" (II Shmuel 7:23).

End of Ra'aya Meheimna (the Faithful Shepherd)

A Synopsis
Rabbi Elazar talks about the clouds that went with Yisrael through the wilderness. We hear about the invitation for the guests of Faith to enter the Sukkah, and how important it is to give a portion of the meal to the poor.

275. רִבִּי אֶלְעָזָר פָּתַח, כֹּה אָמַר יְיָ' זָכַרְתִּי לָךְ חֶסֶד נְעוּרַיִךְ וְגוֹ'. הַאי קְרָא עַל כְּנֶסֶת יִשְׂרָאֵל אִתְּמַר, בְּשַׁעֲתָא דַּהֲוַת אַזְלָא בְּמַדְבְּרָא עִמְּהוֹן דְּיִשְׂרָאֵל. זָכַרְתִּי לָךְ חֶסֶד: דָּא עֲנָנָא דְּאַהֲרֹן, דְּנַטְלָא בְּחָמֵשׁ אַחֲרָנִין, דְּאִתְקְשָׁרוּ עֲלָךְ, וּנְהִירוּ עֲלָךְ. אַהֲבַת כְּלוּלוֹתַיִךְ, דְּאִשְׁתְּכְלָלוּ לָךְ, וְאַעְטְּרוּ לָךְ, וְאַתְקִינוּ לָךְ כְּכַלָּה דְּתַעֲדֵי תַכְשִׁיטָהָא. וְכָל כַּךְ לָמָּה. בְּגִין לֶכְתֵּךְ אַחֲרַי בַּמִּדְבָּר בְּאֶרֶץ לֹא זְרוּעָה.

275. Rabbi Elazar opened with, "Thus says Hashem; I remember in your favor, the devotion of your youth…" (Yirmeyah 2:2). This verse was said about the Congregation of Yisrael, WHICH IS MALCHUT, when she was walking with Yisrael in the wilderness. "I remember in your favor (lit. 'Chesed')" refers to Aaron's cloud, WHICH IS CHESED that traveled with five other CLOUDS, GVURAH, TIFERET, NETZACH, HOD AND YESOD that joined over you and shone upon you. "your love as a bride" (Ibid.) AS THOSE CLOUDS that incorporated you, adorned you and bedecked you as a bride wearing her jewelry: why all that? Because, "you did go after Me in the wilderness, in a land not sown" (Ibid.), BECAUSE SHE WALKED WITH YISRAEL IN THE WILDERNESS.

276. תָּא חֲזֵי, בְּשַׁעֲתָא דְּבַר נָשׁ יָתִיב בְּמָדוֹרָא דָּא, צְלָא דִמְהֵימְנוּתָא, שְׁכִינְתָּא פַּרְסָא גַּדְפָהָא עֲלֵיהּ מִלְּעֵילָא, וְאַבְרָהָם וַחֲמִשָׁה צַדִּיקַיָּיא אָחֲרָנִין שַׁוְיָין מָדוֹרֵיהוֹן עִמֵּיהּ. אָמַר רִבִּי אַבָּא, אַבְרָהָם וַחֲמִשָׁה צַדִּיקַיָּיא, וְדָוִד מַלְכָּא, שַׁוְיָין מָדוֹרֵיהוֹן עִמֵּיהּ. הֲדָא הוּא דִכְתִיב, בַּסֻּכֹּת תֵּשְׁבוּ שִׁבְעַת יָמִים. שִׁבְעַת יָמִים כְּתִיב, וְלָא בְּשִׁבְעַת יָמִים. כְּגַוְונָא דָא כְּתִיב כִּי שֵׁשֶׁת יָמִים עָשָׂה יְיָ' אֶת הַשָׁמַיִם וְגוֹ'. וּבָעֵי בַּר נָשׁ לְמֶחֱדֵי בְּכָל יוֹמָא וְיוֹמָא, בְּאַנְפִּין נְהִירִין, בְּאוּשְׁפִּיזִין אִלֵּין דְּשַׁרְיָין עִמֵּיהּ.

276. Come and see, when man sits in this apartment, IN THE SUKKAH, which is the shadow of Faith, the Shechinah spreads her wings over him from above and Abraham, WHO IS CHESED and five other righteous, THE SECRET OF GVURAH, TIFERET, NETZACH, HOD AND YESOD fix their dwelling with him. This is the meaning of, "You shall dwell in booths (Heb. *Sukkot*) seven days" (Vayikra 23:42). It is written, "seven days," WHICH ALLUDES TO CHESED, GVURAH, TIFERET, NETZACH, HOD, YESOD AND MALCHUT, instead of, 'in seven days'. Similarly it is written, "for six days Hashem made heaven and earth" (Shemot 31:17), INSTEAD OF 'IN SIX DAYS'. THEY TOO INDICATE THE SUPERNAL SIX DAYS, CHESED, GVURAH, TIFERET, NETZACH, HOD AND YESOD THAT MADE HEAVEN AND EARTH. One should rejoice every day with a joyful countenance in those guests, CHESED, GVURAH, TIFERET, NETZACH, HOD, YESOD AND MALCHUT that dwell with him.

277. וְאָמַר רִבִּי אַבָּא, כְּתִיב בַּסֻּכֹּת תֵּשְׁבוּ שִׁבְעַת יָמִים, וּלְבָתַר יֵשְׁבוּ בַּסֻּכֹּת. בְּקַדְמֵיתָא תֵּשְׁבוּ, וּלְבָתַר יֵשְׁבוּ. אֶלָּא, קַדְמָאָה לְאוּשְׁפִּיזֵי. תִּנְיָינָא, לִבְנֵי עָלְמָא. קַדְמָאָה לְאוּשְׁפִּיזֵי, כִּי הָא דְּרַב הַמְנוּנָא סָבָא,

כַּד הֲוָה עָיֵיל לַסוּכָּה הֲוָה חַדִּי, וְקָאִים עַל פִּתְחָא לַסוּכָּה מִלְגָאו, וְאָמַר
נְזַמֵּן לְאוּשְׁפִּיזִין. מְסַדֵּר פָּתוֹרָא, וְקָאִים עַל רַגְלוֹהִי, וּמְבָרֵךְ, וְאוֹמַר
בַּסֻכֹּת תֵּשְׁבוּ שִׁבְעַת יָמִים. תִּיבוּ אוּשְׁפִּיזִין עִלָּאִין, תִּיבוּ. תִּיבוּ
אוּשְׁפִּיזֵי מְהֵימְנוּתָא, תִּיבוּ. אָרִים יְדוֹי, וְחַדִּי, וְאָמַר זַכָּאָה חוּלְקָנָא,
זַכָּאָה חוּלְקֵיהוֹן דְּיִשְׂרָאֵל, דִּכְתִּיב, כִּי חֵלֶק יְיָ' עַמּוֹ וְגו', וַהֲוָה יָתִיב.

277. Rabbi Aba said, It is written, "You shall dwell in booths (Heb. *SUKKOT*) seven days," and then, "shall dwell in booths" (Vayikra 23:42). IT first SAYS, "You shall dwell" and then, they "shall dwell." HE ANSWERS, The first one is for the guests, CHESED, GVURAH, TIFERET, NETZACH, HOD, YESOD AND MALCHUT, AND THEREFORE THE TEXT SPEAKS IN THE SECOND PERSON. The second is for people in general, FOR WHICH REASON THE TEXT SAYS IN THE THIRD PERSON, "SHALL DWELL." The first is for the guests. Rav Hamnuna Saba, for example, when he entered the Sukkah, used to stay happily on the inner threshold of the Sukkah, and say, Let us invite the guest. He set the table, stood up and blessed, 'TO DWELL IN THE SUKKAH', then said, "You shall dwell in booths seven days." Sit down, lofty guests, sit you down. Sit down, guests of Faith, sit you down. He joyfully raised his hands and said, 'Happy is our lot, happy the lot of Yisrael, as written, "for Hashem's portion is His people" (Devarim 32:9). Then he would sit down.

278. תִּנְיָינָא, לִבְנֵי עָלְמָא, דְּמַאן דְּאִית לֵיהּ חוּלְקָא בְּעַמָּא וּבְאַרְעָא
קַדִּישָׁא, יָתִיב בְּצִלָּא דִּמְהֵימְנוּתָא, לְקַבְּלָא אוּשְׁפִּיזִין, לְמֶחְדֵּי בְּהַאי
עָלְמָא וּבְעָלְמָא דְּאָתֵי וּבָעֵי לְמֶחְדֵּי לְמִסְכְּנֵי. מַאי טַעְמָא. בְּגִין
דְּחוּלְקָא דְּאִינּוּן אוּשְׁפִּיזִין דְּזַמִּין דְּמִסְכְּנֵי הוּא. וְהַהוּא דְּיָתִיב בְּצִלָּא
דָּא דִּמְהֵימְנוּתָא, וְזַמִּין אוּשְׁפִּיזִין אִלֵּין עִלָּאִין, אוּשְׁפִּיזֵי מְהֵימְנוּתָא,
וְלָא יָהִיב לוֹן חוּלְקֵיהוֹן, כֻּלְּהוּ קַיְימֵי מִנֵּיהּ, וְאָמְרֵי אַל תִּלְחַם אֶת לֶחֶם
רַע עַיִן וְגו', אִשְׁתְּכַח דְּהַהוּא פָּתוֹרָא דְּתַקִּין, דִּילֵיהּ הוּא, וְלָאו
דְּקוּדְשָׁא בְּרִיךְ הוּא, עֲלֵיהּ כְּתִיב וְזֵרִיתִי פֶרֶשׁ עַל פְּנֵיכֶם וְגו', פֶרֶשׁ
חַגֵּיכֶם, וְלָא חַגָּי. וַוי לְהַהוּא בַּר נָשׁ, בְּשַׁעֲתָא דְּאִלֵּין אוּשְׁפִּיזֵי
מְהֵימְנוּתָא קַיְימֵי מִפָּתוֹרֵיהּ.

278. The second MENTION IN THE VERSE, "SHALL DWELL" IN THE THIRD PERSON is for people in general, NAMELY, for whoever has a share in the nation and the holy land; he dwells in the secret of Faith to receive guests and rejoice in this world and in the World to Come. It behooves us to gladden the poor. The reason is that the portion of the guests he invited TO HIS MEAL belongs to the poor. He that sits in the shadow of Faith and invites these lofty guests, the guests of Faith, yet does not give them, NAMELY THE POOR, their share OF THE MEAL, all THE GUESTS stand back from him and say, "Do not eat the bread of him who has an evil eye..." (Mishlei 23:6). Thus the table he set is his, THE ONE WHO HAS AN EVIL EYE, and not of the Holy One, blessed be He. Of him it is written, "and spread dung upon your faces, even the dung of your feasts" (Malachi 2:3). Woe to that man when those guests of Faith stand back from his table.

279. וְאָמַר ר׳ אַבָּא, אַבְרָהָם, כָּל יוֹמוֹי הֲוָה קָאִים בְּפָרָשַׁת אוֹרְחִין, לְזַמְּנָא אוּשְׁפִּיזִין, וּלְתַקְּנָא לוֹן פָּתוֹרֵי, הַשְׁתָּא, דִּמְזַמְּנִין לֵיהּ, וּלְכֻלְּהוּ צַדִּיקַיָּיא, וּלְדָוִד מַלְכָּא, וְלָא יָהֲבִין לוֹן חוּלְקֵיהוֹן, אַבְרָהָם קָאִים מִפָּתוֹרָא, וְקָרֵי, סוּרוּ נָא מֵעַל אָהֳלֵי הָאֲנָשִׁים הָרְשָׁעִים הָאֵלֶּה. וְכֻלְּהוּ סַלְּקִין אֲבַתְרֵיהּ. יִצְחָק אָמַר, וּבֶטֶן רְשָׁעִים תֶּחְסָר. יַעֲקֹב אָמַר, פִּתְּךָ אָכַלְתָּ תְקִיאֶנָּה. וּשְׁאָר כָּל צַדִּיקַיָּיא אָמְרֵי, כִּי כָּל שֻׁלְחָנוֹת מָלְאוּ קִיא צוֹאָה בְּלִי מָקוֹם.

279. Rabbi Aba said, Abraham throughout his life used to stand at the crossroad to invite guests and set the table for them. Now, ON SUKKOT, if one invites him and all the other righteous and King David but does not give them their share, Abraham stands up from the table and cries, "Depart, I pray you, from the tents of these wicked men" (Bemidbar 16:26), and everyone walks away after him. Isaac says, "but the belly of the wicked shall feel want" (Mishlei 13:25), and Jacob says, "The morsel which you have eaten shall you vomit up" (Mishlei 23:8). The rest of the righteous, NAMELY MOSES AND AARON, say, "For all tables are full of vomit and filth, so that there is no place clean" (Yeshayah 28:8).

280. דָּוִד מַלְכָּא אָמַר, וְאַשְׁלִים דִּינוֹי, דִּכְתִיב וַיְהִי כַּעֲשֶׂרֶת הַיָּמִים וַיִּגֹּף יְיָ׳ אֶת נָבָל וַיָּמֹת. מַאי קָא מַיְירֵי. בְּגִין דְּדָוִד שָׁאַל לְנָבָל,

וְאִתְעָבֵיד לֵיהּ אוֹשְׁפִּיזָא, וְלָא בָּעָא. וְדָא זַמִּין לֵיהּ, וְלָא יָהַב לֵיהּ
חוּלָקָא, וּבְאִינּוּן עֲשָׂרָה יוֹמִין דְּדָוִד מַלְכָּא דָּאִין עָלְמָא, אִתְּדָן עָלֵיהּ
הַהוּא בַּר נָשׁ דְּאַשְׁלִים לֵיהּ בִּישׁ יַתִּיר מִנָּבָל.

280. King David said, And He completes the execution of His punishments, as written, "And it came to pass about ten days after, that Hashem smote Nabal, and he died" (I Shmuel 25:38). HE ASKS, What does this mean, AND ANSWERS, This is because David asked Nabal to accept him as a guest, but he declined. Also he WHO SITS AT THE SUKKAH invited him, KING DAVID, yet did not give him his share. THEREFORE KING DAVID RECITED OVER HIM THIS VERSE ABOUT NABAL. During the ten days, when King David, MALCHUT, judges the world, DURING THE TEN DAYS OF REPENTANCE, that man is punished for it, for rewarding him worse than Nabal, BY INVITING HIM YET NOT GIVING HIM HIS SHARE. NABAL AT LEAST DID NOT INVITE HIM.

281. אָמַר רַבִּי אֶלְעָזָר אוֹרַיְיתָא לָא אַטְרַח עָלֵיהּ דְּבַר נָשׁ יַתִּיר, אֶלָּא
כְּמָה דְּיָכִיל, דִּכְתִּיב אִישׁ כְּמַתְּנַת יָדוֹ וְגו'. וְלָא לֵימָא אִינִישׁ אֵכוּל
וְאֶשְׂבַּע וְאַרְוֵוי בְּקַדְמֵיתָא, וּמַה דְּיִשְׁתְּאַר אֶתֵּן לְמִסְכְּנֵי, אֶלָּא רֵישָׁא
דְּכֹלָּא דְּאוֹשְׁפִּיזִין הוּא, וְאִי חַדֵּי לְאוֹשְׁפִּיזִין וְרַוֵּוי לוֹן, קוּדְשָׁא בְּרִיךְ
הוּא חַדֵּי עִמֵּיהּ, וְאַבְרָהָם קָרֵי עָלֵיהּ, אָז תִּתְעַנַּג עַל יְיָ' וְגו'. וְיִצְחָק
קָארֵי עָלֵיהּ, כָּל כְּלִי יוּצַר עָלַיִךְ לֹא יִצְלָח. אָמַר רַבִּי שִׁמְעוֹן, הַאי, דָּוִד
מַלְכָּא אָמַ"ל, בְּגִין דְּכָל זַיְינִין דְּמַלְכָּא, וְקִרְבִין דְּמַלְכָּא, בִּידוֹי דְּדָוִד
אִתְפְּקָדוּ, אֲבָל יִצְחָק קָאָמַר, גִּבּוֹר בָּאָרֶץ יִהְיֶה זַרְעוֹ וְגו', הוֹן וָעוֹשֶׁר
וְגו'.

281. Rabbi Elazar said, The Torah did not trouble man TO GIVE more than what he can afford, as written, "every man shall give as he is able" (Devarim 16:17). One must not say, Let me eat and be full and slake my thirst first, and give the rest to the poor. The first part belongs to the guests. He who gladdens the guests and gives them to drink, the Holy One, blessed be He, is happy with him and Abraham says about him, "then shall you delight yourself in Hashem" (Yeshayah 58:14), and Isaac calls, "No weapon that is formed against you shall prosper" (Yeshayah 54:17). Rabbi Shimon said, King David, WHO IS MALCHUT, recited this VERSE to him, because all the weapons of the King and the King's wars were delivered to David's hands. But Isaac says, "His seed shall be mighty upon earth...Wealth and riches shall be in his house..." (Tehilim 112:2-3).

282(1). יַעֲקֹב אָמַר, אָז יִבָּקַע כַּשַּׁחַר אוֹרֶךָ וְגו', שְׁאָר צַדִּיקַיָּיא אָמְרֵי, וְנָחֲךָ יְיָ' תָּמִיד וְהִשְׂבִּיעַ וְגו', דָּוִד מַלְכָּא אָמַר, כָּל כְּלִי יוּצַר עָלָיִךָ לֹא יִצְלָח, דְּהָא הוּא עַל כָּל זַיְינֵי עָלְמָא אִתְפְּקַד. זַכָּאָה חוּלָקֵיהּ דְּבַר נָשׁ, דְּזָכֵי לְכָל הַאי. זַכָּאָה חוּלָקֵיהוֹן דְּצַדִּיקַיָּיא, בְּעָלְמָא דֵין, וּבְעָלְמָא דְּאָתֵי, עָלַיְיהוּ כְּתִיב וְעַמֵּךָ כֻּלָּם צַדִּיקִים וְגו'.

282a. Jacob said, "Then shall your light break forth (Heb. *Yibaka*) like the morning" (Yeshayah 58:8), BECAUSE *YIBAKA* IS SPELLED WITH THE SAME LETTERS AS JACOB. The other righteous say, "and Hashem shall guide you continually, and satisfy..." (Ibid. 11). King David said, "No weapon that is formed against you shall prosper," because he was appointed over all the weapons in the world. Happy is the lot of the man who merited all this. Happy is the lot of the righteous in this world and in the World to Come. Of them it is written, "Your people also shall be all righteous..." (Yeshayah 60:21).

A Synopsis
We are told that it is a commandment to take a Lulav on the day of Sukkot.

רעיא מהימנא

282(2). פִּקּוּדָא דָּא לִיטוֹל לוּלָב בְּהַהוּא יוֹמָא בְּאִינּוּן זִינִין דִּילֵיהּ וְהַאי רָזָא אוּקִימְנָא וְאוֹקְמוּהָ חַבְרַיָּיא כְּמָה דְּקוּדְשָׁא בְּרִיךְ הוּא נָטִיל לוֹן לְיִשְׂרָאֵל בְּהָנֵי יוֹמִין וְחַדֵי בְּהוֹן. אוּף הָכִי יִשְׂרָאֵל נַטְלֵי לֵיהּ לְקוּדְשָׁא בְּרִיךְ הוּא לְחוּלָקֵיהוֹן וְחַדָּאן בֵּיהּ. וְדָא הוּא רָזָא דְּלוּלָב. וּמִנְיַן דִּבֵּיהּ דְּאִיהוּ רָזָא דְּיוּקְנָא דְּאָדָם וְהָא אִתְּמַר.

ע"כ רעיא מהימנא

Ra'aya Meheimna (the Faithful Shepherd)

282b. It is a commandment to take a Lulav on that day with its kinds. We explained this secret, as did the friends. Just as the Holy One, blessed be He, takes Yisrael during those days and rejoices in them, so do Yisrael take the Holy One, blessed be He, as their portion and rejoice in Him. This is the secret of the Lulav and the kinds in it, the secret of the form of man, NAMELY THE SECRET OF THE SEVEN SFIROT, CHESED, GVURAH, TIFERET, NETZACH, HOD, YESOD AND MALCHUT. THE THREE MYRTLE BRANCHES CORRESPOND TO CHESED, GVURAH AND TIFERET, THE TWO WILLOW BRANCHES TO NETZACH AND HOD, THE LULAV TO YESOD AND THE ETROG TO MALCHUT. We already learned this.

End of Ra'aya Meheimna (the Faithful Shepherd)

38. An image and a likeness

A Synopsis

Rabbi Shimon talks about how Elohim created man in His own image and gave him His name when he produced truth and law in the world, since the word for judges is Elohim. He says that man was created both Male and Female, an image and a likeness. When people mate below, God sends a certain image as the countenance of man that hovers over the union, and by that image man is created. When the man grows in the world he grows through that image that came from above and walks by that image. For holy Yisrael that image comes from the side of holiness, but for the heathen nations the image comes from the Other Side; this is why one must not mix his image with that of the heathen.

283. וּלְקַחְתֶּם לָכֶם בַּיּוֹם הָרִאשׁוֹן וְגוֹ', רַבִּי שִׁמְעוֹן פָּתַח, כֹּל הַנִּקְרָא בִשְׁמִי וְלִכְבוֹדִי בְּרָאתִיו יְצַרְתִּיו אַף עֲשִׂיתִיו. כֹּל הַנִּקְרָא בִשְׁמִי, דָּא אָדָם, דְּקוּדְשָׁא בְּרִיךְ הוּא בָּרָא לֵיהּ בִּשְׁמֵיהּ, דִּכְתִיב וַיִּבְרָא אֱלֹהִים אֶת הָאָדָם בְּצַלְמוֹ. וְקָרָא לֵיהּ בִּשְׁמֵיהּ, בְּשַׁעֲתָא דְּאַפִּיק קְשׁוֹט וְדִינָא בְּעָלְמָא, וְאִקְרֵי אֱלֹהִים, דִּכְתִיב אֱלֹהִים לֹא תְקַלֵּל.

283. "And you shall take for yourselves on the first day…" (Vayikra 23:40). Rabbi Shimon opened with, "every one that is called by My name. For I have created him for My glory; I have formed him; yea, I have made him" (Yeshayah 43:7). "every one that is called by My name" refers to man, whom the Holy One, blessed be He, created by His name, as written, "So Elohim created man in His own image" (Beresheet 1:27), and called him after His name, when he produced truth and law in the world and is called Elohim, as written, "You shall not revile the judges (Heb. *Elohim*)" (Shemot 22:27).

284. קָרָא לֵיהּ בִּשְׁמֵיהּ, דִּכְתִיב וַיִּבְרָא אֱלֹהִים אֶת הָאָדָם בְּצַלְמוֹ וְשַׁפִּיר. הָא אוֹקִימְנָא, דִּכְתִיב נַעֲשֶׂה אָדָם בְּצַלְמֵנוּ כִּדְמוּתֵנוּ, בְּשַׁעֲתָא דְזִוּוּגָא אִתְּמַר. וְכָךְ הוּא בְּזִוּוּגָא דְּתַרְוַויְיהוּ, בְּצֶלֶם וּדְמוּת. וְאָדָם מִדְּכַר וְנוּקְבָּא נָפַק.

284. He called him by His name, as written, "So Elohim created man in His own image." This is well. We explained that the words, "Let Us make man in Our image, after Our likeness" (Ibid. 26) were uttered during the union OF ZEIR ANPIN AND MALCHUT. And so, when the two mate there is an image and a likeness, SINCE THE IMAGE IS FROM ZEIR ANPIN AND THE LIKENESS FROM MALCHUT. Man came out from Male and Female, NAMELY ZEIR ANPIN AND MALCHUT.

285. וַיִּבְרָא אֱלֹהִים אֶת הָאָדָם בְּצַלְמוֹ, בְּסִפְרָא דִּשְׁלֹמֹה מַלְכָּא אַשְׁכַּחְנָא, דִּבְשַׁעֲתָא דְזִווּגָא אִשְׁתְּכַח לְתַתָּא, שָׁדַר קוּדְשָׁא בְּרִיךְ הוּא חַד דִּיּוּקְנָא כְּפַרְצוּפָא דְּב״נ, רְשִׁימָא חֲקִיקָא בְּצוּלְמָא, וְקַיְימָא עַל הַהוּא זִווּגָא. וְאִלְמָלֵא אִתְיְיהִיב רְשׁוּ לְעֵינָא לְמֶחֱזֵי, חָמֵי ב״נ עַל רֵישֵׁיה חַד צוּלְמָא, רְשִׁימָא כְּפַרְצוּפָא דְּב״נ, וּבְהַהוּא צוּלְמָא אִתְבְּרֵי ב״נ, וְעַד לָא קַיְימָא הַהוּא צוּלְמָא דְּשָׁדַר לֵיה מָארֵיה עַל רֵישֵׁיה, וְיִשְׁתְּכַח תַּמָּן, לָא אִתְבְּרֵי ב״נ, הַה״ד, וַיִּבְרָא אֱלֹהִים אֶת הָאָדָם בְּצַלְמוֹ.

285. "So Elohim created man in His own image": I found in the book of King Solomon that when a union is affected below, the Holy One, blessed be He, sends a certain image as the countenance of man, imprinted and engraved with an image. It hovers over that union. If the eye had permission to behold, man would see over his head an image inscribed as a man's face. By that image man is created. Man was not created before that image, which His master sent him, is stationed over his head. This is the meaning of, "So Elohim created man in His own image."

286. הַהוּא צֶלֶם אִזְדָּמַן לְקַבְּלֵיה, עַד דְּנָפִיק לְעָלְמָא. כַּד נָפַק, בְּהַהוּא צֶלֶם אִתְרַבֵּי, בְּהַהוּא צֶלֶם אָזִיל, הַה״ד אַךְ בְּצֶלֶם יִתְהַלֶּךְ אִישׁ. וְהַאי צֶלֶם אִיהוּ מִלְּעֵילָא.

286. That image comes to him before he goes into the world. When he goes out INTO THE WORLD, he grows through the image and walks by that image. This is the meaning of, "Surely every man walks in a vain show (or: 'image')" (Tehilim 39:7). That image comes from above.

287. בְּשַׁעֲתָא דְאִינּוּן רוּחִין נַפְקָן מֵאַתְרַיְיהוּ, כָּל רוּחָא וְרוּחָא אִתְתָּקַן קַמֵּי מַלְכָּא קַדִּישָׁא בְּתִקּוּנֵי יְקַר, בְּפַרְצוּפָא דְקָאִים בְּהַאי עָלְמָא. וּמֵהַהוּא דִיּוּקְנָא תִּקּוּנָא יְקַר, נָפִיק הַאי צֶלֶם. וְדָא תְּלִיתָאָה לְרוּחָא, וְאַקְדִּימַת בְּהַאי עָלְמָא, בְּשַׁעֲתָא דְזִוּוּגָא אִשְׁתְּכַח. וְלֵית לָךְ זִוּוּגָא בְּעָלְמָא, דְּלָא אִשְׁתְּכַח צֶלֶם בְּגַוַּוּיְיהוּ. אֲבָל יִשְׂרָאֵל קַדִּישִׁין, הַאי צֶלֶם קַדִּישָׁא, וּמֵאֲתַר קַדִּישָׁא אִשְׁתְּכַח בְּגַוַּוּיְיהוּ. וְלַעֲכוּ"ם, צֶלֶם מֵאִינּוּן זִינִין בִּישִׁין. מִסִּטְרָא דִמְסָאֲבוּתָא אִשְׁתְּכַח בְּגַוַּוּיְיהוּ. וְעַ"ד, לָא לִיבְעֵי לֵיהּ לְאִינִישׁ, לְאִתְעָרְבָא צוּלְמָא דִילֵיהּ, בְּצוּלְמָא דְעוֹבְדֵי עֲבוֹדָה זָרָה, בְּגִין דְּהַאי קַדִּישָׁא, וְהַאי מְסָאֲבָא. ת"ח מַה בֵּין יִשְׂרָאֵל לְעַכוּ"ם וְכוּ'.

287. When those spirits leave their place, each spirit is bedecked before the Holy King with a precious ornament, the countenance existing in this world. That image comes from that shape and precious ornament. FOR THE IMAGE IS A GARMENT FOR THE SPIRIT OF THAT MAN AND COMES DOWN TOGETHER WITH IT, AS THEY ARE LIKE LIGHT AND VESSEL. It is the third counting from the spirit (Heb. *Ruach*), THAT IS, A THIRD CATEGORY. THE RUACH IS THE FIRST, NEFESH IS THE SECOND AND THE IMAGE IS THE THIRD. It is the first to come into the world during mating. No mating takes place in the world without an image in it, but as for holy Yisrael, that holy image comes to them from a holy place, while the image of the idolatrous comes to them from those evil species on the side of impurity. For that reason, one must not mix his image with that of the heathen, because the one is pure while the other is impure. Come and see the difference between Yisrael and the heathen nations... THE END WAS PRINTED IN VAYECHI, 196-232.

39. Shmini Atzeret

A Synopsis

We read about the eighth day, the assembly that is Sukkot and that is the day of rejoicing. The supernal lamps cause the supernal anointing oil to burn, that draws the blessings to Yisrael. Through the deed of lighting the lamps below the lamps above are lit, because deeds below cause deeds to awaken above.

288. דִּכְתִיב בַּיּוֹם הַשְּׁמִינִי עֲצֶרֶת תִּהְיֶה לָכֶם, דְּהָא יוֹמָא דָא, מִמַּלְכָּא הוּא בִּלְחוֹדוֹי, חֶדְוָותָא דִּילֵיהּ בְּהוּ בְּיִשְׂרָאֵל. מָתָל לְמַלְכָּא דְּזַמִּין אוּשְׁפִּיזִין, אִשְׁתַּדְּלוּ בְּהוּ כָּל בְּנֵי הֵיכָלֵיהּ, לְבָתַר אָמַר מַלְכָּא, ע״כ אֲנָא וְאַתּוּן אִשְׁתַּדְּלָנָא כֻּלְּהוּ בְּאוּשְׁפִּיזִין, וּקְרַבְתּוּן קָרְבְּנִין עַל שְׁאָר עַמִּין בְּכָל יוֹמָא, מִכָּאן וּלְהָלְאָה, אֲנָא וְאַתּוּן נֶחֱדֵי יוֹמָא חַד, הה״ד בַּיּוֹם הַשְּׁמִינִי עֲצֶרֶת תִּהְיֶה לָכֶם. לָכֶם: לְקָרְבָא קָרְבְּנִין עֲלַיְיכוּ. אֲבָל אוּשְׁפִּיזֵי מְהֵימְנוּתָא, בְּמַלְכָּא מִשְׁתַּכְּחֵי תְּדִירָא. וּבְיוֹמָא דְּחֶדְוָותָא דְּמַלְכָּא, כֻּלְּהוּ מִתְכַּנְפֵי עַמֵּיהּ, וּמִשְׁתַּכְּחָן. וְעַל דָּא כְּתִיב, עֲצֶרֶת, תַּרְגּוּמוֹ: כְּנִישׁוּ.

288. As it is written, "On the eighth day (Heb. *shmini*) you shall have a solemn assembly (Heb. *atzeret*)" (Bemidbar 29:35). (THIS IS THE ENDING OF THE ARTICLE FROM VAYECHI 231). For that day is from the King solely, His rejoicing in Yisrael. This is like a king who invited guests. The household people entertained them. At the end the king said TO HIS HOUSEHOLD, Until now I and you all entertained the guests. You offered sacrifices for the other nations every day, THAT IS, THE SEVENTY BULLOCKS. From now on, for one day, let you and Me rejoice. This is the meaning of, "On the eighth day you shall have a solemn assembly": "you" MEANS offering sacrifices for you. But the guests of Faith ON THE SEVEN DAYS OF SUKKOT are always with the King, ON SHMINI ATZERET AS WELL. On the day of the King's joy they all gather to Him, and stay with Him. Hence it is written, "assembly" which is translated into Aramaic as gathering.

289. וְהַאי יוֹמָא, יַעֲקֹב הוּא רֵישָׁא לְחֶדְוָותָא, וְכָל אִינּוּן אוּשְׁפִּיזֵי חַדָּאן עַמֵּיהּ. וְעַ״ד כְּתִיב, אַשְׁרֶיךָ יִשְׂרָאֵל מִי כָמוֹךָ. וּכְתִיב, וַיֹּאמֶר לִי

עַבְדִּי אָתָּה יִשְׂרָאֵל אֲשֶׁר בְּךָ אֶתְפָּאָר.

289. On that day, Jacob, WHO IS TIFERET, is the first to rejoice and all the other guests, ABRAHAM, ISAAC, MOSES, AARON, JOSEPH AND DAVID rejoice with him. Hence it is written, "Happy are you, Yisrael. Who is like you" (Devarim 33:29), and, "You are My servant, Yisrael, in whom I will be glorified" (Yeshayah 49:3).

290. וְיִקְחוּ אֵלֶיךָ שֶׁמֶן זַיִת זַךְ כָּתִית לַמָּאוֹר וְגוֹ', א"ר אֶלְעָזָר, הָא אוּקְמוּהָ. אֲבָל אֲמַאי אַסְמִיךְ קוּדְשָׁא בְּרִיךְ הוּא פָּרָשָׁה דָא, לְפָרָשַׁת מוֹעֲדִים. אֶלָּא, כֻּלְּהוּ בּוֹצִינִין עִלָּאִין, כֻּלְּהוּ בּוֹצִינִין לְאַדְלְקָא מְשַׁח רְבוּת עִלָּאָה, וְהָא אִתְּמַר. וְעַל יְדַיְיהוּ דְיִשְׂרָאֵל, מִתְבָּרְכָאן עִלָּאִין וְתַתָּאִין, וְאַדְלִיקוּ בּוֹצִינִין, כְּמָה דְאוּקְמוּהָ דִּכְתִיב, שֶׁמֶן וּקְטֹרֶת יְשַׂמַּח לֵב, חֶדְוָותָא דְעִלָּאִין וְתַתָּאִין.

290. "that they bring to you pure oil olive pressed for the light…" (Vayikra 24:1). Rabbi Elazar said, This was explained. But why would the Holy One, blessed be He, place this passage next to the passage of the holidays? AND HE ANSWERS, All the supernal lamps, NAMELY THE SFIROT, THE SECRET OF THE HOLIDAYS, are all lamps that cause the supernal anointing oil to burn, THAT IS, DRAW THE PLENTY OF CHOCHMAH CALLED OIL. We already learned that. Through Yisrael, the higher and lower beings are blessed and the lamps are kindled, THAT IS, THEY SHINE UPON THE WORLD. We explained it according to the words, "Ointment and perfume (or: 'incense') rejoice the heart" (Mishlei 27:9), THAT IS, it gladdens the higher and lower beings.

291. רְבִּי אַבָּא פָּתַח, שִׂמְחוּ בַיְיָ' וְגִילוּ צַדִּיקִים, וּכְתִיב, זֶה הַיּוֹם עָשָׂה יְיָ' נָגִילָה וְנִשְׂמְחָה בוֹ. וְאוֹקְמוּהָ, דְּהָא בְּקוּדְשָׁא בְּרִיךְ הוּא בָּעֵי לְמֶחְדֵּי, וּלְאַנְהֲרָא אַנְפִּין, וְיִשְׁתְּכַח ב"נ בְּחֶדְוָוה, בְּגִין דְּהַהוּא חֶדְוָה דְקוּדְשָׁא בְּרִיךְ הוּא הֲוֵי, דִּכְתִיב נָגִילָה וְנִשְׂמְחָה בוֹ בְּיוֹמָא. בּוֹ: בְּקוּדְשָׁא בְּרִיךְ הוּא, וְכֹלָּא חַד מִלָּה.

291. Rabbi Aba opened with, "Be glad in Hashem, and rejoice, O you righteous" (Tehilim 32:11), and, "this is the day which Hashem has made;

we will rejoice and be glad in it" (Tehilim 118:24). It was explained that one should rejoice with and display a joyous face to the Holy One, blessed be He. Man should be in a state of joy on it, because that joy is of the Holy One, blessed be He, as written, "we will rejoice and be glad in it (or: 'Him')." "In it" – NAMELY on that day; "in Him" – NAMELY in the Holy One, blessed be He. It is all the same matter.

292. שִׂמְחוּ בַיְיָ', כַּד דִּינִין אִתְכַּפְיָין, וְרַחֲמֵי אִתְעָרוּ, וְכַד מִתְעָרֵי רַחֲמֵי, כְּדֵין וְגִילוּ צַדִּיקִים, צַדִּיק וְצֶדֶק מִתְבָּרְכָאן כַּחֲדָא, דְּאִקְרוּן צַדִּיקִים, כְּמָה דְּאִתְּמַר, דְּהָא אִלֵּין מִתְבָּרְכָאן לְעָלְמִין, וְחֶדְוָאן לְעָלְמִין כֻּלְּהוּ. וְהַרְנִינוּ כָּל יִשְׁרֵי לֵב, אִלֵּין בְּנֵי מְהֵימְנוּתָא, לְאִתְקַשְּׁרָא בְּהוּ.

292. "Be glad in Hashem," NAMELY when Judgments are subdued and Mercy is roused. When it does, "Be glad in Hashem… O you righteous." The Righteous and Righteousness, WHICH ARE YESOD AND MALCHUT, who are called righteous, are blessed together, as we learned. For they are blessed IN ORDER TO BESTOW PLENTY upon the worlds and cause all the worlds to rejoice. "and shout for joy, all you who are upright in heart" (Tehilim 32:11) refers to people of Faith, to connect to them, TO YESOD AND MALCHUT.

293. וּבְכֹלָּא, בָּעֵי עוֹבָדָא לְתַתָּא, לְאַתְעָרָא לְעֵילָּא. ת"ח, מַאן דְּאָמַר דְּלָא בַּעְיָא עוֹבָדָא בְּכֹלָּא, אוֹ מִלִּין לְאַפָּקָא לוֹן וּלְמֶעְבַּד קָלָא בְּהוּ, תִּיפַּח רוּחֵיהּ. וְהָא הָכָא פָּרְשָׁתָא דָּא אוֹכַח, אַדְלָקוּת בּוּצִינַיָּא, וּקְטֹרֶת בּוּסְמִין, דִּכְתִיב שֶׁמֶן וּקְטֹרֶת יְשַׂמַּח לֵב. וּבְעוֹבָדָא דָּא אִשְׁתְּכַח אַדְלָקוּתָא וְחֶדְוָותָא לְעֵילָּא וְתַתָּא וְאִתְקַשְּׁרוּתָא כַּחֲדָא כַּדְקָא יָאוֹת. אָמַר ר' יְהוּדָה, מִזְבֵּחַ דִּלְתַתָּא, אַתְעַר מִזְבֵּחַ אַחֲרָא. כֹּהֵן דִּלְתַתָּא, אַתְעַר כֹּהֵן אַחֲרָא. בְּעוֹבָדָא דִּלְתַתָּא, אַתְעַר עוֹבָדָא לְעֵילָּא.

293. In everything, one needs a deed below to awaken above. Come and see, whoever says there is no need for an action in every THING or to utter words by means of sound TO CAUSE AWAKENING ABOVE, may he breathe his last. The portion proves it by the kindling of the lamps, and the incense spices, as written, "Ointment and perfume (or: 'incense') rejoice the heart." For

through this deed OF KINDLING THE LAMPS AND THE INCENSE BELOW, there is kindling and joy above and below, and a proper joining together OF CHOCHMAH AND BINAH. FOR OIL AROUSES CHOCHMAH, AND INCENSE BINAH. Rabbi Yehuda said, The altar below arouses another altar, WHICH IS MALCHUT; the priest below arouses another priest, WHO IS CHESED, SINCE by a deed below a deed above is awakened.

40. Vain talk on Shabbat

A Synopsis

Rabbi Yitzchak tells Rabbi Yosi why it is wrong to speak of vain matters on Shabbat, because it awakens non-holiness on the holy day – this causes deficiency. Contemplation without speech is acceptable because it does not activate anything. Holy speech rises up and awakens the holy Sfirot.

294. ר׳ יוֹסֵי וְר׳ יִצְחָק הֲווֹ אַזְלֵי בְּאוֹרְחָא, א״ר יוֹסֵי לר׳ יִצְחָק, כְּתִיב וְקָרָאתָ לַשַּׁבָּת עֹנֶג לִקְדוֹשׁ יְיָ׳ מְכֻבָּד וְגו׳, וְכִבַּדְתּוֹ מֵעֲשׂוֹת דְּרָכֶיךָ שַׁפִּיר. אֲבָל מִמְּצוֹא חֶפְצְךָ וְדַבֵּר דָּבָר מַה הוּא. וּמַאי גְּרִיעוּתָא הוּא לַשַּׁבָּת.

294. Rabbi Yosi and Rabbi Yitzchak were walking along the way. Rabbi Yosi said to Rabbi Yitzchak, It is written, "and call the Shabbat a delight, the holy day of Hashem honorable" (Yeshayah 58:13). "and shall honor it, not doing your own ways" (Ibid.) is fine, but what does, "nor pursuing your own business, nor speaking of vain matters" (Ibid.) mean? And what deficiency is there for the Shabbat IF ONE IS ENGAGED IN SPEAKING OF VAIN MATTERS?

295. א״ל, וַדַּאי גְּרִיעוּתָא הוּא, דְּלֵית לָךְ מִלָּה וּמִלָּה דְּנָפִיק מִפּוּמֵיהּ דְּב״נ, דְּלֵית לָהּ קָלָא, וְסַלְּקָא לְעֵילָא, וְאִתְעַר מִלָּה אָחֳרָא. וּמַאי הוּא. הַהוּא דְּאִקְרֵי חוֹל, מֵאִינּוּן יוֹמִין דְּחוֹל. וְכַד אִתְעַר חוֹל בְּיוֹמָא קַדִּישָׁא, גְּרִיעוּתָא הוּא לְעֵילָא וַדַּאי. וְקוּדְשָׁא בְּרִיךְ הוּא וּכְנֶסֶת יִשְׂרָאֵל שָׁאֲלֵי עֲלֵיהּ, מַאן הוּא דְּבָעֵי לְאַפְרְשָׁא זֵוְוגָא דִּילָן. מַאן הוּא דְּבָעֵי חוֹל הָכָא. עַתִּיקָא קַדִּישָׁא לָא אִתְחֲזֵי, וְלָא שַׁרְיָא עַל חוֹל.

295. He said to him, Assuredly a lack is caused TO THE SHABBAT, because there is not a word coming out of man's mouth that is soundless. The sound rises up and awakens another word. It is that which is called non-holiness, FOR WHATEVER IS NOT HOLY IS NON-HOLY pertaining to the non-holy workdays. When non-holiness is awakened on the holy day it surely causes deficiency. And the Holy One, blessed be He, and the Congregation of

Yisrael ask about him, who is it that desires to interrupt our union? Who is he that needs the non-holy? Atika Kadisha does not appear nor dwell on the non-holy.

296. בְּגִין כָּךְ, הִרְהוּר מוּתָּר. מ"ט. בְּגִין דְּהִרְהוּר לָא עָבֵיד מִדִי וְלָא אִתְעָבֵיד מִנֵּיה קָלָא, וְלָא סָלִיק. אֲבָל לְבָתַר דְּאַפִּיק מִלָּה מִפּוּמֵיה, הַהוּא מִלָּה אִתְעָבֵיד קָלָא, וּבָקַע אֲוִירִין וּרְקִיעִין, וְסַלְקָא לְעֵילָּא, וְאִתְּעַר מִלָּה אָחֳרָא. וְעַ"ד מִמְּצוֹא חֶפְצְךָ וְדַבֵּר דָּבָר כְּתִיב. וּמַאן דְּאַפִּיק מִלָּה קַדִּישָׁא מִפּוּמֵיה, מִלָּה דְּאוֹרַיְיתָא, אִתְעָבֵיד מִנֵּיה קָלָא, וְסָלִיק לְעֵילָּא, וְאִתְּעָרוּ קַדִּישֵׁי מַלְכָּא עִלָּאָה, וּמִתְעַטְּרָן בְּרֵישֵׁיה, וּכְדֵין אִשְׁתְּכַח חֶדְוָותָא לְעֵילָּא וְתַתָּא.

296. For that reason contemplation is permissible. The reason is that contemplation does not activate anything; no sound is formed from it and it does not rise. But after pronouncing words in his mouth, the speech turns into sound. It cleaves the air and firmaments and rises up to awaken another speech OF NON-HOLINESS. Hence it is written, "nor pursuing your own business, nor speaking of vain matters," BUT NOT CONTEMPLATION. If one arouses a holy speech from his mouth, a sound is formed from the words of Torah, rises up and awakens the holy ones of the supernal King, NAMELY THE HOLY SFIROT. They become crowns on his head and joy then abounds above and below.

41. He who fasts on Shabbat

A Synopsis

Rabbi Yosi asks whether someone who fasts on Shabbat creates a lack of some kind, since joy is called for on that day. Rabbi Yitzchak explains what the effect of that sorrow is, and how it can lead to forgiveness. He says that every day has special power resting on it, and talks about those who fast because of a bad dream they had; the fast must take place on the same day because no day has authority over any other day.

297. אָמַר לֵיהּ, וַדַּאי הָכִי הוּא. וְהָא שְׁמַעְנָא מִלָּה. אֲבָל מַאן דִּשְׁאֲרֵי בְּתַעֲנִיתָא בְּשַׁבְּתָא, עָבֵיד גְּרִיעוּתָא לְשַׁבָּת, אוֹ לָא. אִי תֵּימָא דְּלָא עָבֵיד גְּרִיעוּתָא, הָא סְעוּדָתֵי דִּמְהֵימְנוּתָא בָּטִיל מִנֵּיהּ, וְעוֹנְשֵׁיהּ סַגִּי, הָא חֶדְוָותָא דְּשַׁבָּת בָּטִיל מִנֵּיהּ.

297. He said to him, Surely it is so and I heard it. But, HE ASKS, does whoever fasts on Shabbat create a lack on Shabbat or not? If you say he does not, still the meals of Faith were made void and his punishment is great, since the joy of Shabbat fails in him.

298. אָמַר לֵיהּ, מִלָּה הָא שְׁמַעְנָא, דְּדָא הוּא דְּאַשְׁגְּחָן עָלֵיהּ מִלְעֵילָּא, מִכָּל בְּנֵי עָלְמָא. בְּגִין דְּהַאי יוֹמָא, חֶדְוָותָא הוּא לְעֵילָּא וְתַתָּא. חֶדְוָותָא דְּכָל חֶדְוָון. חֶדְוָותָא, דְּכָל מְהֵימְנוּתָא בֵּיהּ אִשְׁתְּכַח. וַאֲפִילּוּ רְשָׁעִים דְּגֵיהִנָּם נַיְיחִין בְּהַאי יוֹמָא. וְהַאי ב״נ לֵית לֵיהּ חֶדְוָה, וְלֵית לֵיהּ נַיְיחָא, וְשַׁנְיָא דָּא מִכָּל עִלָּאִין וְתַתָּאִין. כֻּלְּהוּ שָׁאֲלִין עָלֵיהּ, מַאי שַׁנְיָא דִּפְלַנְיָא הוּא בְּצַעֲרָא.

298. He said to him, I heard this. Attention is paid to this from above MORE THAN to all the people in the world, because that day supplies joy above and below. It is joy above any other joy, joy that contains the whole Faith in it. Even the evil in Gehenom rest on that day. Yet that man has neither joy nor rest, he is at variance with the higher and lower beings. Everyone inquires after him what happens that so and so abides in sorrow.

299. וּבְשַׁעֲתָא דְּעַתִּיקָא קַדִּישָׁא אִתְגְּלֵי בְּהַאי יוֹמָא, וְאִשְׁתְּכַח הַאי

בְּצַעֲרָא, צְלוֹתֵיהּ סַלְקָא וְקַיְּימָא קַמֵּיהּ, כְּדֵין אִתְקְרָעוּ כָּל גִּזְרֵי דִינִין
דְּאִתְגְּזָרוּ עֲלֵיהּ, וַאֲפִילוּ אִסְתַּכְּמוּ בְּבֵי דִינָא דְמַלְכָּא עֲלֵיהּ לְבִישׁ, כֹּלָּא
אִתְקְרַע, בְּגִין דִּבְשַׁעֲתָא דְּעַתִּיקָא אִתְגַּלְיָיא, כָּל חֵירוּ וְכָל חֵידוּ
אִשְׁתְּכַח, בְּגִין דְּאִתְגַּלְיָיא בְּהִלּוּלָא דְמַלְכָּא.

299. When Atika Kadisha appears on that day, ON SHABBAT, yet that man abides in sorrow, his prayer rises and stands before Him. Then all verdicts he was sentenced to are torn up. Even if the King's courthouse agreed upon it, against him everything is torn up, for when Atika Kadisha is revealed, every kind of freedom and joy abides because he is revealed in the feast of joy of the King, ZEIR ANPIN.

300. וְעַ"ד תָּנֵינָן, קוֹרְעִין לוֹ גְּזַר דִּינוֹ שֶׁל ע' שָׁנָה. מַאן שִׁבְעִין שָׁנָה.
אֶלָּא אע"ג דְּאַסְכְּמוּ עֲלֵיהּ כָּל אִינּוּן שַׁבְעִין כִּתְרֵי מַלְכָּא, דְּהוּא אִתְחֲזֵי
בְּהוּ, כֹּלָּא אִתְקְרַע. בְּגִין דְּעַתִּיקָא קַדִּישָׁא נָטִיל לֵיהּ לב"נ, וְהָנֵי מִלֵּי,
כַּד מִתְעֲרֵי עֲלֵיהּ בְּחֶלְמָא בְּלֵילְיָא דְּשַׁבַּתָּא.

300. Hence we learned that his verdict of seventy years is torn up. What are the seventy years? HE ANSWERS, IT MEANS that though all seventy Sfirot of the King, WHICH ARE CHESED, GVURAH, TIFERET, NETZACH, HOD, YESOD AND MALCHUT THAT CONTAIN EACH TEN SFIROT, in which He was seen, agreed upon it, everything is torn up. For Atika Kadisha takes that man, THAT IS, PROTECTS HIM. This refers to the case of rousing him through a dream on Shabbat night, THAT IS, IF HE AFFLICTS HIMSELF WITH FASTING ON ACCOUNT OF A BAD DREAM, BUT NOT FOR A DIFFERENT KIND OF FAST.

301. לְמַלְכָּא דַּעֲבֵיד הִלּוּלָא לִבְרֵיהּ, וְגָזַר חֶדְוָה עַל כֹּלָּא. בְּהַאי יוֹמָא
דְּהִלּוּלָא, כָּל עָלְמָא הֲווֹ חַדָּאן, וּבַר נָשׁ חַד הֲוָה עָצִיב, תָּפִיס בְּקוֹלָרָא.
אֲתָא מַלְכָּא לַחֲדָוִוותָא, חָמָא כָּל עַמָּא כֻּלְּהוֹ חַדָּאן כְּמָה דְּאִיהוּ גָּזַר. זָקַף
עֵינוֹי, חָמָא הַהוּא בַּר נָשׁ תָּפִיס בְּקוֹלָרָא עָצִיב. אָמַר. וּמַה כָּל בְּנֵי
עָלְמָא חַדָּאן בְּהִלּוּלָא דִּבְרִי, וְדָא תָּפִיס בְּקוֹלָרָא. מִיַּד פָּקִיד וְנַפְקֵי לֵיהּ,
וְשָׁארוּ לֵיהּ מִקּוּלְרֵיהּ.

301. THIS IS LIKENED to a king who made a joyful feast for his son and decreed that everybody would be joyful. On that joyful day everyone was glad except one man who was sad, bound by fetters. The king came to the feast and saw everybody glad as he decreed. He lifted his eyes and saw that man in fetters. He said, The whole world rejoices in my son's joy, yet this man is fettered. He immediately gave a command and he was liberated and released from his chains.

302. כַּךְ הַאי דְּשָׁארֵי בְּתַעֲנִיתָא בְּשַׁבַּתָּא, כָּל עָלְמָא חֲדָאן, וְאִיהוּ עָצִיב, וְהַאי אִתְתְּפַס בְּקוּלְרָא. בְּשַׁעֲתָא דְּעַתִּיקָא קַדִּישָׁא אִתְגַּלְיָיא בְּהַאי יוֹמָא, וְאִשְׁתְּכַח הַאי בַּר נָשׁ תָּפִיס בְּקוּלְרָא, אַף עַל גַּב דְּאַסְכִּימוּ עֲלֵיהּ כָּל אִינּוּן שַׁבְעִין שְׁנִין דְּאַמָרָן, כֹּלָּא אִתְקְרַע, וְלָא שָׁארֵי עֲלֵיהּ דִּינָא. בְּיוֹמָא אַחֲרָא אִית בֵּיהּ רְשׁוּ לְמִקְרַע לֵיהּ, בְּהַהוּא יוֹמָא, כ״שׁ שַׁבָּת.

302. It is the same with one who fasts on Shabbat. Everybody is glad yet he is in sorrow, bound by chains. When Atika Kadisha is revealed on that day and this man is bound by fetters, even if the seventy years agreed upon him that we mentioned, THAT IS, THE SEVEN SFIROT OF ZEIR ANPIN, everything is torn up and Judgment does not rest on him. On another day, THAT IS, IF HE FASTS ON A WEEKDAY, there is permission to tear up HIS VERDICT on that day, and all the more so on Shabbat.

303. דְּלֵית לָךְ יוֹם דְּלָא אִשְׁתְּכַח בֵּיהּ חֵילָא, וּמַאן דְּשָׁארֵי בְּתַעֲנִיתָא דְּחֶלְמָא בְּהַהוּא יוֹמָא, לָא סָלִיק הַהוּא יוֹמָא עַד דְּקָרַע דִּינֵיהּ. אֲבָל לָאו דְּשַׁבְעִים שָׁנָה כְּיוֹמָא דְּשַׁבָּת. בְּג״כ, בְּהַהוּא יוֹמָא מַמָּשׁ, וְלָא בְּיוֹמָא אַחֲרָא, דְּלֵית רְשׁוּ לְיוֹמָא עַל יוֹמָא אַחֲרָא. כָּל יוֹמָא, מַה דְּאִירַע בְּיוֹמֵיהּ, עָבֵיד. דְּלָא אִירַע בְּיוֹמֵיהּ, לָא עָבֵיד. וְעַל דָּא לָא לִבְעֵי לֵיהּ לְאֵינָשׁ לְסַלְּקָא לֵיהּ מִיּוֹמָא דָּא לְיוֹמָא אַחֲרָא. וּבְגִין כַּךְ, דְּבַר יוֹם בְּיוֹמוֹ תָּנֵינָן, וְלָא דְּבַר יוֹם לְיוֹמָא אַחֲרָא.

303. Every day has a SPECIAL power RESTING ON IT. Whoever fasts on account of a bad dream the same day HE DREAMT IT, his punishment is torn up before that day passes, but not that of seventy years' standing as on Shabbat, because ONE SHOULD FAST on the very day and on no other day, for no day has an authority over another day. Whatever happens during a certain day, he can act on that day AND REPEAL THE PUNISHMENT. Whatever did not happen on that day he cannot act OR REPEAL THE PUNISHMENT. Hence one must not delay THE FAST from one day to another. For that reason we learned, "everything upon its day" (Vayikra 23:37), and not anything of its day on another day.

304. וְתָא חֲזֵי, לָאו לְמַגָּנָא מִתְעָרֵי עֲלֵיהּ בְּחֶלְמָא, בְּגִין לְמִתְבַּע עֲלֵיהּ רַחֲמֵי. וַוי לְהַהוּא ב״נ דְּלָא מִתְעָרֵי עֲלֵיהּ, וְלָא אוֹדְעוּ לֵיהּ בְּחֶלְמָא, דְּהָא אִקְרֵי רָע. וּבְגִינֵי כָּךְ, לֹא יְגוּרְךָ רָע כְּתִיב. וּכְתִיב בַּל יִפָּקֶד רָע, בַּל יִפָּקֵד, בְּגִין דְּאִיהוּ רָע.

304. Come and see, Not in vain was he roused by means of a BAD dream, BUT in order to beg for mercy on himself. Woe to that man who is not aroused, nor informed in a dream, because he is called evil. Hence, "nor shall evil dwell with You" (Tehilim 5:5), and, "HE THAT HAS IT SHALL ABIDE SATISFIED; he shall not be visited with evil" (Mishlei 19:23), "he shall not be visited" BY A BAD DREAM because he is bad.

305. אָמַר רִבִּי יוֹסֵי, כְּתִיב מִמְּצוֹא חֶפְצְךָ וְדַבֵּר דָּבָר, כֵּיוָן דִּכְתִיב מִמְּצוֹא חֶפְצְךָ, מַהוּ וְדַבֵּר דָּבָר. אֶלָּא, עַד דְּיִגְזַר מִלָּה כַּדְקָא יֵאוֹת, וִימַלֵּל לֵיהּ. וַדַּאי כָּךְ הוּא בְּרִירָא דְמִלָּה, מַשְׁמַע דִּכְתִיב וְדַבֵּר דָּבָר. זַכָּאִין אִינּוּן יִשְׂרָאֵל בְּעָלְמָא דֵין וּבְעָלְמָא דְּאָתֵי, עֲלַיְיהוּ כְּתִיב, וַיֹּאמֶר אַךְ עַמִּי הֵמָּה בָּנִים לֹא יְשַׁקֵּרוּ וַיְהִי לָהֶם לְמוֹשִׁיעַ.

305. Rabbi Yosi said, It is written, "nor pursuing your own business, nor speaking of vain matters" (Yeshayah 58:13). What is "speaking of vain matters"? EVEN SPEAKING ABOUT WHAT ONE NEEDS PERTAINS TO "YOUR OWN BUSINESS." But, HE ANSWERS, IT MEANS until that speech is pronounced and spoken, THAT IS, THE COMMAND TO SPEAK WORDS OF TORAH. Surely this is the meaning of this, which is derived from, "nor speaking of vain matters." Happy are Yisrael in this world and in the World to Come. Of them it is written, "For he said, 'Surely they are My people, children that will not lie'. So He was their deliverer" (Yeshayah 63:8).

42. "And the son of an Yisraeli woman..."

A Synopsis

Rabbi Yehuda says that anyone who comes from polluted seed will eventually expose it before everyone. Rabbi Chiya tells us that a man has no permission to reveal concealed matters that were not disclosed in order to be revealed. Some generations are not worthy of having hidden matters revealed. During Rabbi Shimon's lifetime revelations were made and understood, but after his death they were no longer understood. We read about the consequences of the blasphemy uttered by the Yisraeli woman's son. Rabbi Yehuda says that one is not punished for swearing by his own god, but only if he blasphemes the Holy Name.

306. וַיֵּצֵא בֶּן אִשָּׁה יִשְׂרְאֵלִית וְהוּא בֶּן אִישׁ מִצְרִי וְגוֹ'. וַיֵּצֵא, רַבִּי יְהוּדָה אָמַר, נָפַק מִכְּלָלָא דְּחוּלָקָא דְיִשְׂרָאֵל, דְּנָפַק מִכְּלָלָא דְּכֹלָּא, נָפַק מִכְּלָלָא דִּמְהֵימְנוּתָא. וַיִּנָּצוּ בַּמַּחֲנֶה, מִכָּאן אוֹלִיפְנָא, כָּל מַאן דְּאָתֵי מִזוּהֲמָא דְזַרְעָא, לְסוֹף גַּלְיֵיהּ לֵיהּ קַמֵּי כֹּלָּא. מַאן גָּרִים לֵיהּ, זוּהֲמָא דְחוּלָקָא בִּישָׁא דְאִית בֵּיהּ. דְּלֵית לֵיהּ חוּלָקָא בִּכְלָלָא דְיִשְׂרָאֵל.

306. "And the son of an Yisraeli woman, whose father was an Egyptian man, went out..." (Vayikra 24:10). Rabbi Yehuda said he went out from the portion of Yisrael, went out from being a part of anything, went out from the whole of Faith. "strove together in the camp" (Ibid.): from this we learned that whoever came from polluted seed will eventually expose it before everyone. What brought it upon him? The pollution of the evil part in him, for he has no part among the whole of Yisrael.

307. רַבִּי חִיָּיא פָּתַח, כְּבוֹד אֱלֹהִים הַסְתֵּר דָּבָר וּכְבוֹד מְלָכִים חֲקוֹר דָּבָר. כְּבוֹד אֱלֹהִים הַסְתֵּר דָּבָר, דְּלֵית רְשׁוּ לְבַר נָשׁ לְגַלָּאָה מִלִּין סְתִימִין, דְּלָא אִתְמְסָרוּ לְאִתְגַּלְיָיא. מִלִּין דְּחָפָא לוֹן עַתִּיק יוֹמִין, כד"א, לֶאֱכוֹל לְשָׂבְעָה וְלִמְכַסֶּה עָתִיק. לֶאֱכוֹל לְשָׂבְעָה, עַד הַהוּא אֲתָר דְּאִית לֵיהּ רְשׁוּ וְלָא יַתִּיר. וְעִם כָּל דָּא, וְלִמְכַסֶּה עָתִיק, לִמְכַסֶּה עָתִיק וַדַּאי.

307. Rabbi Chiya opened with, "It is the glory of Elohim to conceal a thing; but the honor of kings is to search out a matter" (Mishlei 25:2). THIS

MEANS a man has no permission to reveal concealed matters that were not disclosed for revelation, things hidden by Atik Yomin, THAT IS, THAT PERTAIN TO THE FIRST THREE SFIROT, as written, "to eat sufficiently, and for stately clothing (or: 'concealing Atik')" (Yeshayah 23:18), NAMELY, REVEALING up to that place one has permission, THAT IS, FROM THE ASPECT OF THE SIX EXTREMITIES, but no more. Hence "concealing Atik" surely, NOT REVEALING WHAT ONE HAS NO PERMISSION TO, NAMELY THE FIRST THREE SFIROT.

308. דָּבָר אַחֵר, לֶאֱכוֹל לְשָׂבְעָה, אִינוּן חַבְרַיָּיא דְיַדְעִין אָרְחִין וּשְׁבִילִין לְמֵיהַךְ בְּאֹרַח מְהֵימְנוּתָא כַּדְקָא יָאוֹת. כְּגוֹן דָּרָא דְרִבִּי שִׁמְעוֹן שָׁארֵי בְּגַוֵּיה. וְלִמְכַסֶּה עָתִיק, מִדָּרִין אַחֲרָנִין דְּהָא כֻּלְהוֹן לָא אִתְחֲזוּן לֶאֱכוֹל וּלְשָׂבְעָה וּלְאִתְגַּלְיָיא מִלִּין בְּגַוַוְיהוּ, אֶלָּא לִמְכַסֶּה עָתִיק, כְּמָה דְאַתְּ אֲמֵר, אַל תִּתֵּן אֶת פִּיךָ לַחֲטִיא אֶת בְּשָׂרֶךָ.

308. Another explanation for, "to eat sufficiently" REFERS TO the friends who know the routes and paths to properly walk the way of Faith, such as the generation when Rabbi Shimon lived. "and concealing Atik" REFERS TO other generations, none of which are worthy of eating to satiation or of having matters revealed among them, but to conceal Atik, as written, "Do not let your mouth cause your flesh to sin" (Kohelet 5:5).

309. בְּיוֹמוֹי דְּרִבִּי שִׁמְעוֹן, הֲוָה בַּר נָשׁ אָמַר לְחַבְרֵיה, פְּתַח פִּיךְ וְיָאִירוּ דְבָרֶיךָ. בָּתַר דְּשָׁכִיב, הֲווֹ אַמְרֵי, אַל תִּתֵּן אֶת פִּיךְ וְגוֹ'. בְּיוֹמוֹי, לֶאֱכוֹל לְשָׂבְעָה. בָּתַר דְּשָׁכִיב, וְלִמְכַסֶּה עָתִיק. דְּחַבְרַיָּיא מְגַמְגְמֵי, וְלָא קַיְּימֵי בְּמִלִּין. ד"א, לֶאֱכוֹל לְשָׂבְעָה: בְּאִינוּן מִלִּין דְּאִתְגַּלְיָין. וְלִמְכַסֶּה עָתִיק: בְּאִינוּן מִילִין דְּאִתְחַפְּיָין.

309. During Rabbi Shimon's life, a man would say to his neighbor, Open your mouth and let your words shine forth. After he died, they used to say, "Do not let your mouth cause your flesh to sin." During his life, "to eat sufficiently," but after his demise, "concealing Atik." The friends would stammer and not understand matters. According to another explanation, "to eat sufficiently," REFERS TO disclosed things, NAMELY EXOTERICA, while, "concealing Atik" REFERS TO undisclosed things, NAMELY, THE SECRET OF THE TORAH.

310. וַיִּקּוֹב בֶּן הָאִשָּׁה הַיִּשְׂרְאֵלִית אֶת הַשֵּׁם, מַהוּ וַיִּקּוֹב. רִבִּי אַבָּא אָמַר, וַיִּקּוֹב וַדַּאי, כְּמָה דְּאַתְּ אָמַר, וַיִּקּוֹב חוֹר בְּדַלְתּוֹ, נָקִיב מַה דַּהֲוָה סָתִים. וְשֵׁם אִמּוֹ שְׁלוֹמִית בַּת דִּבְרִי, עַד כָּאן סָתִים שְׁמָא דְּאִמֵּיהּ, כֵּיוָן דִּכְתִיב וַיִּקּוֹב, נָקִיב שְׁמָא דְּאִמֵּיהּ.

310. "and the Yisraeli woman's son blasphemed the name" (Vayikra 24:11). HE ASKS what is meant by "blasphemed (or: 'bored')." Rabbi Aba said, He surely blasphemed, as in the verse, "and bored a hole in the lid of it" (II Melachim 12:10), piercing that which was covered, WHICH IS NOW AS IF PIERCED. "and his mother's name was Shelomith, the daughter of Dibri" (Vayikra 24:11): up to this point the verse does not disclose his mother's name. Once it says, "blasphemed," he blasphemed his mother's name.

311. אָמַר רִבִּי אַבָּא, אִי לָאו דְּבוּצִינָא קַדִּישָׁא קַיְימָא בְּעָלְמָא, לָא אַרְשֵׁינָא לְגַלָּאָה, דְּהָא לָא אִתְיְיהִיב מִלָּה דָּא לְגַלָּאָה אֶלָּא לְחַבְרַיָּיא, דְּאִינּוּן בֵּין מְחַצְּדֵי חַקְלָא. תִּיפַח רוּחֵיהוֹן דְּאִינּוּן דְּאַתְיָין לְגַלָּאָה, לְאִינּוּן דְּלָא יַדְעֵי.

311. Rabbi Aba said, Had not the holy luminary, RABBI SHIMON, been living in the world, I would not have permission to reveal this. For permission was given to reveal this matter only to the friends among the reapers of the field, THAT IS, THOSE WHO ALREADY ENTERED THE CONCEALED WISDOM AND CAME OUT IN PEACE. May those who wish to reveal to those who do not know breathe their last.

312. תָּא חֲזֵי, כְּתִיב וַיִּנָּצוּ בַּמַּחֲנֶה בֶּן הַיִּשְׂרְאֵלִית וְאִישׁ הַיִּשְׂרְאֵלִי, הַאי קְרָא הָא אוֹקִימְנָא, אֲבָל דָּא בַּר אִינְתּוּ אַחֲרָא דַּאֲבוֹי, בַּעְלָהּ דִּשְׁלוֹמִית הֲוָה. וְכֵיוָן דְּאָתָא הַהוּא מִצְרָאָה עָלָהּ, בְּפַלְגוּת לֵילְיָא, תָּב לְבֵיתָא וְיָדַע מִלָּה, אִתְפְּרַשׁ מִנָּהּ וְלָא אָתָא עָלָהּ. וְנָטַל אִינְתּוּ אַחֲרָא, וְאוֹלִיד לְהַאי, וְאִקְרֵי אִישׁ הַיִּשְׂרְאֵלִי, וְאַחֲרָא בֶּן הַיִּשְׂרְאֵלִית. אִי אִינּוּן אִינְצוּ

הָכָא כַּחֲדָא, מַאי קָא בָּעֵי הָכָא שְׁמָא קַדִּישָׁא. וַאֲמַאי קַלֵּל שְׁמָא
קַדִּישָׁא.

312. Come and see, it is written, "and this son of the Yisraeli woman and a man of Yisrael strove together in the camp." We already explained this verse. Yet THIS MAN OF YISRAEL is the son of his father, Shelomith's husband, from a different wife. When the Egyptian man came in to her, TO SHELOMITH, at midnight, her husband returned home and realized this. He separated from her and no longer came in to her. He married another woman and begot this man, who is called the man of Yisrael. The other man FROM THE EGYPTIAN is called the Yisraeli woman's son. HE ASKS, If they strove here together, why mention the Holy Name here, and why did he curse the Holy Name?

313. אֶלָּא, אִישׁ הַיִּשְׂרְאֵלִי אָמַר מִלָּה מֵאִמֵּיהּ, מִגּוֹ קְטָטָה. מִיַּד וַיִּקֹּב
בֶּן הָאִשָּׁה הַיִּשְׂרְאֵלִית. כְּמָה דְאַתְּ אָמַר, וַיִּקֹּב חוֹר בְּדַלְתּוֹ. רָזָא דְמִלָּה,
נָטַל ה' דִּשְׁמָא קַדִּישָׁא, וְלָיֵיט, לְאַגָּנָא עַל אִמֵּיהּ. וְדָא הוּא נְקִיבָא,
דְּאִיהוּ נָקִיב וּפָרִישׁ שְׁמָא קַדִּישָׁא. וּלְמֶחֱצְדֵי חַקְלָא אִתְּמַר. וְרָזָא
דְמִלָּה, כֵּן דֶּרֶךְ אִשָּׁה מְנָאָפֶת וְגוֹ', זַכָּאָה חוּלָקֵיהוֹן דְּצַדִּיקַיָּיא, דְּיָדְעִין
מִלָּה, וּמְכַסְּיָין לָהּ. וְעַל דָּא אִתְּמַר, רִיבְךָ רִיב אֶת רֵעֶךָ וְסוֹד אַחֵר אַל
תְּגָל.

313. HE ANSWERS, The man of Yisrael said words during the fight about the mother OF THE SON OF THE YISRAELI WOMAN, NAMELY, HE SAID SHE WAS A WHORE. Immediately "the Yisraeli woman's son blasphemed (Heb. *vayikov*) the name," as in "and bored (Heb. *vayikov*) a hole in the lid of it." The meaning behind it is that he took the LAST Hei of the Holy Name, YUD HEI VAV HEI, WHICH IS MALCHUT, and cursed in order to defend his mother. This is the hole he pierced and mentioned the Holy Name explicitly. This was told to the reapers of the field. The secret of it is, "Likewise the way of an adulterous woman…" (Mishlei 30:20). Happy is the lot of the righteous, who know this matter yet keep it hidden. Therefore it is said, "Debate your cause with your neighbor, and do not reveal the secret of another" (Mishlei 25:9). THIS SECRET IS TOO DEEP AND CANNOT BE REVEALED.

314. ה' בַּתְרָאָה, הֲוַת נוּקְבָא דְּיָנְקָא בִּתְרֵין סִטְרִין, בְּגִין כַּךְ נַטְלָא זַיְינִין דְּמַלְכָּא, וְנָקְמַת נִקְמְתָא, דִּכְתִיב הוֹצֵא אֶת הַמְקַלֵּל. עַל דָּא כְּתִיב, אִישׁ אִמּוֹ וְאָבִיו תִּירָאוּ, דְּחִילוּ דְּאִימָּא אַקְדִּים לְאַבָּא. וְזַכָּאִין אִינּוּן יִשְׂרָאֵל בְּעָלְמָא דֵּין וּבְעָלְמָא דְּאָתֵי.

314. The last Hei OF THE NAME YUD HEI VAV HEI was the Nukva nourishing from two sides, MERCY AND JUDGMENT. For that reason, it took the King's weapons and executed its vengeance, as written, "Bring forth him that has cursed" (Vayikra 24:14). For that reason it is written, "You shall fear every man his mother, and his father" (Vayikra 19:3), the fear of one's mother preceding the father's. Happy are Yisrael in this world and in the World to Come.

315. וְאֶל בְּנֵי יִשְׂרָאֵל תְּדַבֵּר לֵאמֹר אִישׁ אִישׁ כִּי יְקַלֵּל אֱלֹהָיו וְנָשָׂא חֶטְאוֹ. רִבִּי יְהוּדָה אָמַר, הָא אוּקְמוּהָ. אֲבָל כִּי יְקַלֵּל אֱלֹהָיו סְתָים. וּבְגִין דְּאָמַר אֱלֹהָיו סְתָם, לְכַךְ וְנָשָׂא חֶטְאוֹ. דְּהָא לָא יַדְעֵינָן מַאן הוּא אֱלֹהָיו, מַאן דַּחֲלָא דִּילֵיהּ, אִי אֶחָד מִן הַשָּׂרִים, אוֹ חַד מִן כֹּכְבַיָּיא, אוֹ חַד מִדַּבְרֵי עָלְמָא.

315. "And you shall speak to the children of Yisrael, saying, Whoever curses his Elohim shall bear his sin" (Vayikra 24:15). Rabbi Yehuda said, This was already explained, yet, "Whoever curses his Elohim" is general. Since it says, "his Elohim" in general, he "shall bear his sin," AND WILL NOT BE PUNISHED, because we do not know who his Elohim is, what he reveres, whether he is one of the appointed angels or one of the stars or one of the leaders of the world.

316. א"ר יוֹסִי, אִי צַדִּיק גָּמוּר הוּא, לָא יִתְעַר חֵילֵיהוֹן, וְכֵיוָן דְּאִתְעַר מִלָּה דָּא, חַיְישִׁינָן מִינוּת אִזְדְּרִיקַת בֵּיהּ, וְלָא יְמוּת עַל דָּא, בְּגִין דְּאִיהוּ מִלָּה סְתָים.

316. Rabbi Yosi said, If he were wholly righteous, he would not have awakened their powers BY CURSING THEM. Since he did so, we fear he is touched by heresy. NONETHELESS he will not die for it, because it is a general word, NOT EXPLAINING WHO HIS ELOHIM IS.

317. ר' יְהוּדָה אָמַר, דְּאִין לֵיהּ לְטָב בְּהָא, דְּאִי אָמַר אֱלֹהַי, יָכִיל לְמִטְעַן אֱלֹהַי דַּהֲוָה עַד הַשְׁתָּא, דְּאִתְמַשְׁכְּנָא אֲבַתְרֵיהּ בְּלִבָּאי, וְהַשְׁתָּא אַהֲדַרְנָא לְקַבְּלָא מְהֵימְנוּתָא עִלָּאָה. אֲבָל אִי אָמַר יְיָ' אֱלֹהִים, אוֹ יְיָ', וְנָקִיב לֵיהּ בִּשְׁמָא, הַאי לֵית לֵיהּ לְמִטְעַן בְּהַאי, בְּגִין דְּדָא הוּא מְהֵימְנוּתָא דְכֹלָּא, וְכָל אָת וְאָת דִּשְׁמָא קַדִּישָׁא דָּא, סַלְקָא לִשְׁמָא שְׁלֵימָא.

317. Rabbi Yehuda said, He is judged favorably that way. Had he said, 'my Elohim' AND CURSED HIM he can argue, This is my Elohim I had until now, after which I was drawn, yet now I return IN REPENTANCE to receive the supernal Faith. But had he said 'Hashem Elohim' or Yud Hei Vav Hei, mentioning it by name, he has no case, for this is everybody's Faith, and each letter of the Holy Name amounts to the whole Name.

318. ד"א וַיִּקֹּב בֶּן הָאִשָּׁה הַיִּשְׂרְאֵלִית אֶת הַשֵּׁם וַיְקַלֵּל. רִבִּי יִצְחָק אָמַר, וַיִּקֹּב בֶּן הָאִשָּׁה, אֲמַאי. אֶלָּא כְּמָה דְאוּקְמוּהָ. אֲבָל הָאִישׁ הַיִּשְׂרְאֵלִי, בַּעְלָהּ דִּשְׁלוֹמִית הֲוָה. רִבִּי יְהוּדָה אָמַר, בְּרֵיהּ דְּבַעְלָהּ דִּשְׁלוֹמִית מֵאִנְתּוּ אָחֳרָא הֲוָה. אָמַר רִבִּי יִצְחָק, נָצוּ כַּחֲדָא, וְאָ"ל מִלָּה מֵאִמֵּיהּ, וְכִי אֲבוֹי הֲוָה דְּאִתְקְטַל בִּשְׁמָא קַדִּישָׁא, כְּמָה דְאוּקְמוּהָ דִּכְתִּיב הַלְהָרְגֵנִי אַתָּה אוֹמֵר, דְּהָא בִּשְׁמָא קַדִּישָׁא, קָטִיל לֵיהּ מֹשֶׁה, וְעַל דָּא אוֹשִׁיט מִלָּה לְקַבְלֵיהּ.

318. According to another explanation for, "and the Yisraeli woman's son blasphemed the name, and cursed," Rabbi Yitzchak said, Why "the Yisraeli woman's son blasphemed"? This is as we explained it. The man of Yisrael was Shelomith's husband. Rabbi Yehuda said, He was Shelomith's husband's son from another woman. Rabbi Yitzchak said they fought together, and he said about his mother THAT SHE WAS A WHORE and that his EGYPTIAN father was killed by means of the Holy Name BY MOSES as we explained the verse, "do you intend (lit. 'speak') to kill me" (Shemot 2:14). He therefore extended this speech to him, THAT IS, LET HIM KNOW WHILE THEY WERE FIGHTING.

319. וְדָא הוּא דִּכְתִיב, וַיִּקֹּב בֶּן הָאִשָּׁה הַיִּשְׂרְאֵלִית אֶת הַשֵּׁם וַיְקַלֵּל

וַיָּבִיאוּ אוֹתוֹ אֶל מֹשֶׁה. אֲמַאי. בְּגִין דְּמָטָא לְגַבֵּיה דְּמֹשֶׁה, עַל דְּקָטִיל
לַאֲבוּהִי בִּשְׁמָא קַדִּישָׁא. בְּגִין כַּךְ וַיָּבִיאוּ אוֹתוֹ אֶל מֹשֶׁה. כֵּיוָן דְּחָמָא
מֹשֶׁה, מִיַּד וַיַּנִּיחֻהוּ בַּמִּשְׁמָר, וְאַבָּא וּבְרָא נָפְלוּ בִּידָא דְּמֹשֶׁה.

319. This is the meaning of, "and the Yisraelite woman's son blasphemed the name, and cursed. And they brought him to Moses." The reason is that he came to Moses COMPLAINING that he killed his father by means of the Holy Name. For that reason, "they brought him to Moses." When Moses saw that, immediately, "they put him in custody" (Vayikra 24:12). Both father and son fell into Moses' hands.

43. "Whoever curses his Elohim"

A Synopsis

Rabbi Yitzchak says that one must not allow the Evil Inclination to enter him, because then a foreign El dwells in him and then he transgresses the Torah. Therefore "whoever curses his Elohim" can claim he was cursing the Evil Inclination that is inside him, but anyone who blasphemes the name of Hashem shall be put to death in this world, and in the World to Come, because all the worlds depend on the Holy Name. While walking through the fields, Rabbi Shimon tells the rabbis that everything in the world serves the world somehow, and that one must not treat anything with contempt. Even things that seem to harm the world are actually good as they serve the world in some way.

320. אִישׁ אִישׁ כִּי יְקַלֵּל אֱלֹהָיו וְנָשָׂא חֶטְאוֹ. רַבִּי יִצְחָק פָּתַח, שְׁמַע עַמִּי וְאָעִידָה בָּךְ יִשְׂרָאֵל אִם תִּשְׁמַע לִי לֹא יִהְיֶה בְךָ אֵל זָר וְלֹא תִשְׁתַּחֲוֶה לְאֵל נֵכָר, כֵּיוָן דִּכְתִיב לֹא יִהְיֶה בְךָ אֵל זָר, מַאי וְלֹא תִשְׁתַּחֲוֶה לְאֵל נֵכָר. אֶלָּא לֹא יִהְיֶה בְךָ אֵל זָר, דְּלָא יֵיעוּל ב"נ לְיֵצֶר הָרָע בְּגַוֵּיהּ, דְּכָל מַאן דְּאָתֵי לְאִתְחַבְּרָא בֵּיהּ, אֵל זָר שַׁרְיָא בְּגַוֵּיהּ, דְּהָא כַּד אִתְחַבַּר ב"נ בֵּיהּ מִיַּד אָתֵי לְאַעְבְּרָא עַל פִּתְגָּמֵי אוֹרַיְתָא. אָתֵי לְאַעְבְּרָא עַל מְהֵימְנוּתָא דִּשְׁמָא קַדִּישָׁא, וְאָתֵי לְבָתַר לְמִסְגַּד לְטַעֲוָון אָחֳרָן, וְעַל דָּא כְּתִיב, לֹא יִהְיֶה בְךָ אֵל זָר, כֵּיוָן דְּלָא יִהְיֶה בְךָ אֵל זָר, לָא תֵּיתֵי לְמִסְגַּד לְטַעֲוָון אָחֳרָן, וּלְמֶעְבַּר עַל מְהֵימְנוּתָא דִּשְׁמָא קַדִּישָׁא. הה"ד, וְלֹא תִשְׁתַּחֲוֶה לְאֵל נֵכָר, וּמְהֵימְנוּתָא בִּישָׁא דְּב"נ דָּא הוּא.

320. "Whoever curses his Elohim shall bear his sin" (Vayikra 24:15). Rabbi Yitzchak opened with, "Hear, O My people, and I will testify against you, O Yisrael, if you will hearken to Me, there shall be no strange El among you, nor shall you worship any foreign El" (Tehilim 81:9-10). HE ASKS, Since it is written, "there shall be no strange El among you," what is meant by, "nor shall you worship any foreign El"? AND HE ANSWERS, "there shall be no strange El among you," MEANS one must not allow the Evil Inclination to enter inside himself, for whoever comes to join it, a foreign El dwells within him. For when man joins it, he promptly comes to transgress the words of

the Torah and transgress the Faith in the Holy Name. Then he comes to bow before a foreign El. It therefore says, "there shall be no strange El among you." If you will have no strange El among you, you shall not come to bow to a foreign El or transgress the Faith in the Holy Name. This is the meaning of, "nor shall you worship any foreign El," which is man's evil Faith.

321. וְעַל דָּא כִּי יְקַלֵּל אֱלֹהָיו, דְּיָכִיל לְמִטְעָן דְּהוּא לָיֵיט לְהַהוּא אֵל זָר, יִצְרָא בִּישָׁא דְּשַׁרְיָא עֲלֵיהּ לְזִמְנִין, וַאֲנַן לָא יַדְעִינָן מִלּוֹי אִי קְשׁוֹט אוֹ לָאו. וְעַל דָּא, וְנָשָׂא חֶטְאוֹ. אֲבָל וְנוֹקֵב שֵׁם יְיָ' מוֹת יוּמָת.

321. Therefore, "Whoever curses his Elohim" can claim he cursed that foreign El, the Evil Inclination that rests over him at times, and we can not know whether his words are true or not. Hence, he "shall bear his sin" ONLY. But, "he that blasphemes the name of Hashem, shall surely be put to death" (Vayikra 24:16).

322. א"ר יְהוּדָה, אִי הָכִי, אֲמַאי וְנָשָׂא חֶטְאוֹ, וְנִסְלַח חֶטְאוֹ מִבָּעֵי לֵיהּ. א"ל, כְּגוֹן דְּאָמַר אֱלֹהַי כְּמָה דְּאוֹקִימְנָא סְתָם, וְלָא פָּרִישׁ. רַבִּי חִיָּיא אָמַר, כִּי יְקַלֵּל אֱלֹהָיו סְתָם, וְלָא פֵּירַשׁ, וְהָא וַדַּאי וְנָשָׂא חֶטְאוֹ. אֲבָל וְנוֹקֵב שֵׁם יְיָ' מוֹת יוּמָת, דְּהָא הָכָא תַּלְיָיא מְהֵימְנוּתָא דְּכֹלָּא, וְלֵית לֵיהּ רְשׁוּ לְמִטְעָן עֲלֵיהּ כְּלָל.

322. Rabbi Yehuda said, If that is so THAT HE SPEAKS ABOUT THE EVIL INCLINATION why IS IT WRITTEN, "shall bear his sin"? It should have said, 'his sin is forgiven.' He said to him, THIS IS like saying 'my Elohim' vaguely, as we said, not specifying WHETHER HE REFERRED TO A FOREIGN EL, WHICH IS THE EVIL INCLINATION. HENCE IT CANNOT BE WRITTEN THAT HIS SIN IS FORGIVEN BECAUSE THE MATTER IS IN DOUBT. Rabbi Chiya said, "Whoever curses his Elohim" is said in general, without specifying. Such a man surely "shall bear his sin" AND NOT BE PUNISHED. But, "he that blasphemes the name of Hashem, shall surely be put to death," for this is the source for everybody's Faith. He is allowed to plead nothing for himself. HE CANNOT CLAIM THAT HE REFERRED TO ANOTHER ELOHIM.

323. אָמַר רַבִּי יוֹסֵי, הָכִי הוּא וַדַּאי, דְּהָא שְׁמָא דָּא מְהֵימְנוּתָא דְּעֶלָּאֵי

וְתַתָּאֵי. וְעַל דָּא קַיְימִין עָלְמִין כֻּלְּהוּ, בְּאָת חַד זְעֵירָא, תַּלְיָין אֶלֶף אַלְפִין וְרִבּוֹא רִבְבָן עָלְמִין דִּכְסוּפִין, וְעַל דָּא תְּנֵינָן, אַתְוָון אִלֵּין, קְשִׁירִין אִלֵּין בְּאִלֵּין, וְכַמָּה אֶלֶף רִבְבָן עָלְמִין, תַּלְיָין בְּכָל אָת וְאָת, וְאִסְתְּלִיקוּ וְאִתְקְשָׁרוּ בִּמְהֵימְנוּתָא וְסָתִים בְּהוּ, מַה דְּלָא אִתְדַּבְּקוּ עִלָּאִין וְתַתָּאִין, אוֹרַיְיתָא בְּהוֹ תַּלְיָיא, עָלְמָא דֵּין וְעָלְמָא דְּאָתֵי, הוּא וּשְׁמֵיהּ חַד. וְעַל דָּא כְּתִיב, אָמַרְתִּי אֶשְׁמְרָה דְרָכַי מֵחֲטוֹא בִלְשׁוֹנִי. וּכְתִיב אַל תִּתֵּן אֶת פִּיךָ לַחֲטִיא אֶת בְּשָׂרֶךָ.

323. Rabbi Yosi said, It is surely so, for this name, YUD HEI VAV HEI, is the Faith of the higher and lower beings. All the worlds are based on it. Thousands and tens of thousands of worlds of yearning suspend from one small letter, WHICH IS YUD, and many thousands and tens of thousands are suspended from each and every letter and rise to be connected to Faith, WHICH IS MALCHUT. All that the higher and lower beings have not comprehended is concealed in them, and the Torah comes out from them, this world and the World to Come, He and His name are One. Hence it is written, "I will take heed to my ways, that I sin not with my tongue" (Tehilim 39:2), and, "Do not let your mouth cause your flesh to sin" (Kohelet 5:5).

324. רִבִּי חִזְקִיָּה פָּתַח, לֹא תִגַּע בּוֹ יָד כִּי כִּי סָקוֹל יִסָּקֵל אוֹ יָרֹה יִיָּרֶה אִם בְּהֵמָה אִם אִישׁ לֹא יִחְיֶה בִּמְשֹׁךְ הַיּוֹבֵל. וּמָה טוּרָא דְסִינַי, דְּאִיהוּ טוּרָא כִּשְׁאָר טוּרֵי עָלְמָא, בְּגִין דְּאִתְחֲזֵי עֲלֵיהּ יְקָרָא דְמַלְכָּא קַדִּישָׁא, כְּתִיב לֹא תִגַּע בּוֹ יָד כִּי כִּי סָקֹל יִסָּקֵל אוֹ יָרֹה יִיָּרֶה, מַאן דְּקָרִיב לְמַלְכָּא לָא כ"ש. וּמָה טוּרָא דְסִינַי דְּיָכִיל ב"נ לְאוֹשִׁיט בֵּיהּ יְדָא אֹרַח יְקָר בִּדְחִילוּ, כְּתִיב לֹא תִגַּע בּוֹ יָד סְתָם, וַאֲפִילוּ בְּאֹרַח יְקָר. מַאן דְּאוֹשִׁיט יְדֵיהּ בְּאֹרַח קְלָנָא לָקֳבֵיל מַלְכָּא, לָא כָּל שֶׁכֵּן.

324. Rabbi Chizkiyah opened with, "no hand shall touch him, but he shall surely be stoned, or shot through; whether it be beast or man, it shall not live. When the horn sounds long..." (Shemot 19:13). And if it is said of Mount Sinai, which is a mountain like any other mountain, once the glory of the Holy King appeared on it, "no hand shall touch him, but he shall surely be stoned, or shot through," it is much more so about whoever approaches the King. And if of Mount Sinai, to which one could extend a hand in a respectful and reverent manner, it is yet said, "no hand shall touch him" in a neutral way, not even in a respectful manner, it would be more emphatic about extending a hand contemptuously towards the King.

325. רִבִּי יֵיסָא פָּתַח וְאָמַר, אַל תִּקְרַב הֲלוֹם שַׁל נְעָלֶיךָ מֵעַל רַגְלֶיךָ כִּי הַמָּקוֹם אֲשֶׁר אַתָּה עוֹמֵד עָלָיו אַדְמַת קֹדֶשׁ הוּא. וּמַה מֹשֶׁה, דְּמִן יוֹמָא דְּאִתְיְלִיד זִיהֲרָא קַדִּישָׁא עִלָּאָה לָא אַעְדֵּי מִנֵּיהּ, כְּתִיב בֵּיהּ אַל תִּקְרַב הֲלוֹם. אָ"ל מֹשֶׁה, ע"כ לָא אַנְתְּ כְּדַאי לְאִשְׁתַּמְּשָׁא בִּיקָרִי, שַׁל נְעָלֶיךָ. וּמַה מֹשֶׁה כָּךְ, דַּהֲוָה קָרִיב בִּדְחִילוּ בִּקְדוּשָׁה כְּתִיב בֵּיהּ הָכִי. מַאן דְּקָרִיב בְּאֹרַח קְלָנָא לְגַבֵּי מַלְכָּא, עַל אַחַת כַּמָּה וְכַמָּה.

325. Rabbi Yesa opened with, "Do not come near. Put off your shoes from off your feet, for the place on which you stand is holy ground" (Shemot 3:5). It says, "Do not come near" of Moses, from whom, since the day he was born, the holy supernal splendor was not removed. THE HOLY ONE, BLESSED BE HE, said to him, 'Moses, until this moment you are not worthy to serve My glory. "Put off your shoes from off your feet"'. If this is written of Moses, EVEN THOUGH he approached in reverence and holiness, it is far more so of whoever approaches the King with contempt.

326. רִבִּי אַבָּא אָמַר, אִישׁ אִישׁ כִּי יְקַלֵּל אֱלֹהָיו וְנָשָׂא חֶטְאוֹ. ת"ח, כַּד הֲווֹ יִשְׂרָאֵל בְּמִצְרַיִם, הֲווֹ יַדְעֵי בְּאִינוּן רַבְרְבֵי עָלְמָא, דִּמְמָנָן עַל שְׁאָר עַמִּין, וְכָל חַד וְחַד הֲוָה לֵיהּ דַּחֲלָא בִּלְחוֹדוֹי מִנַּיְיהוּ. כֵּיוָן דְּאִתְקְשָׁרוּ בְּקִשְׁרָא דִּמְהֵימְנוּתָא, וְקָרִיב לוֹן קוּדְשָׁא בְּרִיךְ הוּא לְפוּלְחָנֵיהּ, אִתְפָּרְשׁוּ מִנַּיְיהוּ וְקָרִיבוּ לְגַבֵּי מְהֵימְנוּתָא עִלָּאָה קַדִּישָׁא. ובג"כ כְּתִיב, אִישׁ אִישׁ כִּי יְקַלֵּל אֱלֹהָיו, ואע"ג דְּפוּלְחָנָא נוּכְרָאָה הוּא, כֵּיוָן דַּאֲנָא פְּקִידַת לוֹן מְמָנָא לְדַבְּרָא עָלְמָא מַאן דְּלָיְיט וּמְבַזֵּי לוֹן, וְנָשָׂא חֶטְאוֹ וַדַּאי, דְּהָא בִּרְשׁוּתִי קַיְימִין וְאָזְלֵי וּמַדְבְּרִין בְּנֵי עָלְמָא. אֲבָל וְנוֹקֵב שֵׁם יְיָ' מוֹת יוּמָת, לָאו וְנָשָׂא חֶטְאוֹ כְּמָה לְאִלֵּין, אֶלָּא מוֹת יוּמָת. מוֹת בְּעָלְמָא דֵין, יוּמָת בְּעָלְמָא דְּאָתֵי. לְאִלֵּין וְנָשָׂא חֶטְאוֹ, בְּגִין דִּמְבַזֵּי

עוֹבָדֵי יְדוֹי, מְבַזֵּי לְשַׁמָּשֵׁי דַּאֲנָא פָּקִידִית, וְאָסִיר הוּא, אֲבָל מִיתָה לָא אִתְחַיִּיב בְּהוּ.

326. Rabbi Aba said, "Whoever curses his Elohim shall bear his sin." Come and see, when Yisrael lived in Egypt, they were familiar with the ministers of the world appointed over the other nations. Each had his own idol. Once they connected to the bond of Faith and the Holy One, blessed be He, drew them toward His service, they left them and drew near the supernal holy Faith. Hence it is written, "Whoever curses his Elohim," NAMELY, ONE OF THE SEVENTY MINISTERS, even though it is idolatry, since I appointed them as ministers to guide the world, whoever curses and desecrates them, "shall bear his sin" surely. For by My power they exist and guide the people in the world. But, "he that blasphemes the name of Hashem, shall surely be put to death" (Vayikra 24:16). It is not WRITTEN, that he "shall bear his sin," as in relation to those SEVENTY MINISTERS, but he "shall surely be put to death." He shall be put to death in this world and surely die in the World to Come. As for those SEVENTY MINISTERS, it is written, that he "shall bear his sin," because he behaves contemptuously towards My handiwork, towards My servant that I appoint, which is forbidden. But he is not punishable by death for that.

327. ר"ש הֲוָה אָזִיל בְּאָרְחָא, וַהֲוָה עִמֵּיהּ ר' אֶלְעָזָר וְר' אַבָּא וְר' חִיָּיא וְר' יוֹסֵי וְר' יְהוּדָה מָטוּ לְחַד טִיקְלֵי דְּמַיָּא, פּוֹסְקְרָא ר' יוֹסֵי בְּקַטְפּוֹי לְגוֹ מַיָּא, אָמַר קוּטְרָא דְּקוּסְטֵי דְּמַיָּא וּלְוַאי לָא שְׁכִיחַ. אֲ"ל ר' שִׁמְעוֹן, אָסִיר לָךְ. שַׁמָּשָׁא דְּעָלְמָא הוּא, וְאָסִיר לְאַנְהָגָא קְלָנָא בְּשַׁמָּשָׁא דְּקוּדְשָׁא בְּרִיךְ הוּא וְכָל שֶׁכֵּן דְּאִינּוּן עוֹבָדֵי קְשׁוֹט, בְּנִימוּסֵי דְּקַסְטִירָא עִלָּאָה שְׁכִיחֵי.

327. Rabbi Shimon was walking along the way together with Rabbi Elazar, Rabbi Aba, Rabbi Chiya, Rabbi Yosi and Rabbi Yehuda. They reached a furrow full of water. Rabbi Yosi walked through the water fully clothed. He said, The furrows and water channels made, WHICH PEOPLE MAKE IN THEIR FIELDS FOR THE WATER TO FLOW, I wish they did not exist. Rabbi Shimon said to him, You are forbidden TO SAY SO. It serves people, and one must not treat with contempt whatever serves the Holy One, blessed be He, EVEN IF IT IS HARMFUL. This is more so if the actions are true, LIKE THOSE

CHANNELS IN THE FIELDS that exist according to the laws of celestial providence; THAT IS, THIS ACTION HAS A ROOT ABOVE.

328. פָּתַח וְאָמַר, וַיַּרְא אֱלֹהִים אֶת כָּל אֲשֶׁר עָשָׂה וְהִנֵּה טוֹב מְאֹד. וַיַּרְא אֱלֹהִים אֶת כָּל אֲשֶׁר עָשָׂה, סְתָם, אֲפִילוּ נְחָשִׁים וְעַקְרַבִּים וְיַתּוּשִׁים, וַאֲפִילוּ אִינוּן דְּאִתְחֲזוּן מְחַבְּלֵי עָלְמָא, בְּכֻלְּהוּ כְּתִיב וְהִנֵּה טוֹב מְאֹד כֻּלְּהוּ שַׁמָּשֵׁי עָלְמָא, מַדְבְּרֵי עָלְמָא, וּבְנֵי נָשָׁא לָא יַדְעֵי.

328. He opened and said, "And Elohim saw everything that He had made, and, behold, it was very good" (Beresheet 1:31). "And Elohim saw everything that He had made" WAS SAID in general, INCLUDING even snakes, scorpions and mosquitoes. Even those that seem to harm the world, it is written of them all, "and, behold, it was very good." They all serve the world and guide the world though people do not know.

329. עַד דַּהֲווֹ אָזְלֵי, חָמוּ חַד חִוְיָא מַדְבַּר קַמַּיְיהוּ, א"ר שִׁמְעוֹן, וַדַּאי דָּא אָזִיל לְאַרְחֲשָׁא לָן נִיסָא, רָהַט הַהוּא חִוְיָא קַמַּיְיהוּ, וְקָטַר בְּחַד אַפְּעֶה בְּקִיטְרָא דְּאוֹרְחָא נָצָן חַד בְּחַד וּמִיתוּ. כַּד מָטוּן, חָמוּ לוֹן לְתַרְוַויְיהוּ שְׁכִיבִין בְּאָרְחָא. אָמַר ר"ש, בְּרִיךְ רַחֲמָנָא דְּרָחִישׁ לָן נִיסָא. דְּהָא כָּל מַאן דְּאִסְתָּכַל בְּהַאי, כַּד אִיהוּ בְּקִיּוּמֵיה, אוֹ אִיהוּ יִסְתָּכַל בב"נ, לָא יִשְׁתְּזִיב וַדַּאי, כ"ש אִי יִקְרַב בַּהֲדֵיה. קָרָא עָלֵיה,לֹא תְאוּנֶּה אֵלֶיךָ רָעָה וְנֶגַע לֹא יִקְרַב בְּאָהֳלֶךָ. וּבְכֹלָּא עָבִיד קוּדְשָׁא בְּרִיךְ הוּא שְׁלִיחוּתָא דִּילֵיה, וְלֵית לָן לְאַנְהָגָא קִלָּנָא בְּכָל מַה דְּאִיהוּ עָבַד. וְעַל דָּא כְּתִיב, טוֹב יְיָ' לַכֹּל וְרַחֲמָיו עַל כָּל מַעֲשָׂיו, וּכְתִיב, יוֹדוּךְ יְיָ' כָּל מַעֲשֶׂיךָ.

329. While they were walking they saw a snake moving before them. Rabbi Shimon, said, It is surely going to perform a miracle for us. The snake moved fast before them and tangled with a viper in the middle of the road. They fought each other and died. When they reached them, they saw the two lying on the road. Rabbi Shimon said, Blessed is the Merciful who made us a miracle. For whoever look at it, THE VIPER, when it is alive, or it looks at a man, he cannot be saved from it, and more so if he comes near it. He

recited over it, "No evil shall befall you, nor shall any plague come near your dwelling" (Tehilim 91:10). The Holy One, blessed be He, makes use of everything for His errands, and we must not treat lightly anything He had made. Hence it is written, "Hashem is good to all, and His tender mercies are over all His works. All Your works shall praise You, Hashem" (Tehilim 145:9-10).

44. The tulip and the lily

A Synopsis

Rabbi Shimon talks about the special relationship that God has with the Congregation of Yisrael. He says that Malchut is the lily of the valleys because she changes, sometimes to the good and sometimes to evil, sometimes to Judgment and at other times to Mercy.

330. רִבִּי שִׁמְעוֹן פָּתַח, אֲנִי חֲבַצֶּלֶת הַשָּׁרוֹן שׁוֹשַׁנַּת הָעֲמָקִים. כַּמָּה חֲבִיבָה כ"י קַמֵּי קוּדְשָׁא בְּרִיךְ הוּא, דְּקוּדְשָׁא בְּרִיךְ הוּא מְשַׁבַּח לֵיהּ, וְהִיא מְשַׁבַּחַת לֵיהּ תָּדִיר. וְכַמָּה שְׁבָחִין וּמְזַמְרִין אַתְקְנַת לֵיהּ לְמַלְכָּא תָּדִיר. זַכָּאָה חוּלָקֵיהוֹן דְּיִשְׂרָאֵל, דַּאֲחִידָן בְּעַדְבָּא דְּחוּלָקָא קַדִּישָׁא, כְּמָה דִכְתִיב כִּי חֵלֶק יְיָ' עַמּוֹ יַעֲקֹב חֶבֶל נַחֲלָתוֹ.

330. Rabbi Shimon opened the discussion with, "I am the tulip of the Sharon; the lily of the valleys" (Shir Hashirim 2:1). How beloved is the Congregation of Yisrael, NAMELY MALCHUT, before the Holy One, blessed be He. The Holy One, blessed be He, praises her and she praises Him constantly. How many hymns and songs did she compose always to the King! Happy is the lot of Yisrael, who are attached to the lot of the holy portion, as written, "For Hashem's portion is His people; Jacob is the lot of His inheritance" (Devarim 32:9).

331. אֲנִי חֲבַצֶּלֶת הַשָּׁרוֹן, דָּא כ"י, דְּאִקְרֵי חֲבַצֶּלֶת, דְּקַיְימָא בְּשַׁפִּירוּ דְּנוֹי בְּגִנְתָּא דְּעֵדֶן לְאִתְנַטְעָא. הַשָּׁרוֹן, דְּהִיא שָׁרָה וּמְשַׁבַּחַת לֵיהּ לְמַלְכָּא עִלָּאָה. ד"א אֲנִי חֲבַצֶּלֶת הַשָּׁרוֹן, דְּבַעְיָא לְאִשְׁתַּקְאָה מְשַׁקְיוּ דְּנַחֲלָא עֲמִיקָא, מַבּוּעָא דְּנַחֲלִין. כד"א הָיָה הַשָּׁרוֹן כָּעֲרָבָה. שׁוֹשַׁנַּת הָעֲמָקִים, דְּקַיְימָא בְּעֲמִיקְתָּא דְכֹלָּא.

331. "I am the tulip of the Sharon" refers to the Congregation of Yisrael, MALCHUT that is called a tulip. She stands with majestic beauty in the Garden of Eden to be planted. Sharon means that she sings (Heb. sharah) and praises the supernal King, ZEIR ANPIN. According to another interpretation, "I am the tulip of the Sharon," as she, MALCHUT, needs to be watered by the flow of the deep river, the source of the streams, BINAH, as

written, "the Sharon is like the Aravah" (Yeshayah 33:9). SHARON MEANS THE PLAIN. THIS MEANS THE TULIP THAT IS IN THE PLAIN IS THIRSTY FOR WATER, BECAUSE THE SUN BURNS IT.

332. שׁוֹשַׁנַּת הָעֲמָקִים. מַאן אִינּוּן עֲמָקִים. כד"א מִמַּעֲמַקִּים קְרָאתִיךָ יְיָ׳. חֲבַצֶּלֶת הַשָּׁרוֹן, מֵהַהוּא אֲתָר דְּשָׁקְיוּ דְּנַחֲלִין עֲמִיקִין נָפְקִין, וְלָא פָסְקִין לְעָלְמִין. שׁוֹשַׁנַּת הָעֲמָקִים, שׁוֹשַׁנָּה דְּהַהוּא אֲתָר דְּאִקְרֵי עֲמִיקָא דְּכֹלָּא, סָתִים מִכָּל סִטְרִין.

332. "The lily of the valleys" means she is situated where it is deepest. What are the deep valleys? They feature in the verse, "Out of the depths I have cried to You, Hashem" (Tehilim 130:1). The lily of the valleys comes from the place where the water of the deep rivers comes FROM and never ceases flowing, THAT IS, WHERE BINAH IS REVEALED. The lily of the valleys IS a lily of that place that is considered the deepest, hidden in every direction, NAMELY, FROM THE HIDDEN PLACE OF BINAH.

333. תָּא חֲזֵי, בְּקַדְמֵיתָא חֲבַצֶּלֶת יְרוֹקָא, בְּטַרְפִּין יְרוֹקִין לְבָתַר שׁוֹשַׁנָּה, בִּתְרֵין גַּוְונִין סוּמָק וְחִוָּור. שׁוֹשַׁנַּת: בְּשִׁית טַרְפִּין. שׁוֹשַׁנַּת: דְּשַׁנִּיאַת גַּוְונָהָא, וְאִשְׁתְּנִיאַת מִגַּוְונָא לְגַוְונָא. שׁוֹשַׁנַּת, בְּקַדְמֵיתָא חֲבַצֶּלֶת, בְּזִמְנָא דְּבַעְיָא לְאִזְדַּוְּוגָא בֵּיהּ בְּמַלְכָּא, אִקְרֵי חֲבַצֶּלֶת. בָּתַר דְּאִתְדַּבְּקַת בֵּיהּ בְּמַלְכָּא, בְּאִינּוּן נְשִׁיקִין, אִקְרֵי שׁוֹשַׁנָּה. בְּגִין דִּכְתִּיב שִׂפְתוֹתָיו שׁוֹשַׁנִּים. שׁוֹשַׁנַּת הָעֲמָקִים. דְּהִיא שַׁנְיָית וּמְשַׁנִּיאַת גַּוְונָהָא, זִמְנִין לְטַב, וְזִמְנִין לְבִישׁ. זִמְנִין לְדִינָא, וְזִמְנִין לְרַחֲמֵי.

333. Come and see, at first MALCHUT IS a green-leafed green tulip; then she is a two-colored lily, red and white. It is a lily (Heb. *shoshanah*) of six (Heb. *shishah*) leaves, a lily that changes (Heb. *meshanah*) its colors and changes from one color to another. A lily first is CALLED a tulip, NAMELY, when she wishes to unite with the King she is called a tulip. After uniting with the King with kisses, she is called a lily, since it is written, "his lips like lilies" (Shir Hashirim 5:13). She is the lily of the valleys because she changes, changing her colors sometimes to the good and sometimes to evil, sometimes to Judgment and at times to Mercy.

45. The sin of the Tree of Knowledge of Good and Evil

A Synopsis

Rabbi Shimon says that when God created Adam He asked him to be always in the bond of Faith, to never change or turn, to be single-hearted in his devotion. But after Adam and Eve sinned they then clung to a place that changes from good to evil and from evil to good. They left their attachment to the highest, that is one and never changing. God then told Adam that they had left life and were now subject to death. All others on earth followed Adam's example, which is why the whole world suffers death. Lastly Rabbi Shimon tells us that in the World to Come God will destroy death forever, and all will cling to the Tree of Life.

334. וַתֵּרֶא הָאִשָּׁה כִּי טוֹב הָעֵץ לְמַאֲכָל וְכִי תַאֲוָה הוּא לָעֵינַיִם וְגוֹ'. ת"ח, דְּהָא בְּנֵי נָשָׁא לָא יַדְעִין, וְלָא מִסְתַּכְּלִין, וְלָא מַשְׁגִּיחִין, בְּשַׁעֲתָא דְּבָרָא קוּדְשָׁא בְּרִיךְ הוּא לְאָדָם, וְאוֹקִיר לֵיהּ בִּיקִירוּ עִלָּאָה, בָּעָא מִנֵּיהּ לְאִתְדַּבְּקָא בֵּיהּ, בְּגִין דְּיִשְׁתְּכַח יְחִידָאי, וּבְלִבָּא יְחִידָאי, וּבַאֲתַר דִּדְבֵיקוּתָא יְחִידָאה, דְּלָא יִשְׁתַּנֵּי וְלָא יִתְהַפֵּךְ לְעָלְמִין, בְּהַהוּא קְשׁוּרָא דִּמְהֵימְנוּתָא יְחִידָאה, דְּכֹלָּא בֵּיהּ אִתְקְשַׁר. הֲדָא הוּא דִּכְתִיב וְעֵץ הַחַיִּים בְּתוֹךְ הַגָּן.

334. "And when the woman saw that the tree was good for food, and that it was a delight to the eyes…" (Beresheet 3:6). Come and see, people do not know, observe or pay attention that when the Holy One, blessed be He, created Adam and honored him with supernal glory, He asked him to cleave to Him, so that he will be unique, of a single heart, in a place of single devotion – that he will never change or turn, but be in that bond of the unique Faith, to which everything is attached. This is the secret of, "the Tree of Life also in the midst of the Garden" (Beresheet 2:9), NAMELY ZEIR ANPIN CALLED THE TREE OF LIFE, SO THAT HE WILL BE ATTACHED TO IT, AS IT HAS NOT THE DUALITY OF GOOD AND EVIL.

335. וּלְבָתַר סָאטוּ מֵאוֹרְחָא דִּמְהֵימְנוּתָא, וְשָׁבְקוּ אִילָנָא יְחִידָאה עִלָּאָה מִכָּל אִילָנִין, וְאָתוּ לְאִתְדַּבְּקָא בַּאֲתַר דְּמִשְׁתַּנֵּי וּמִתְהַפֵּךְ מִגַּוְונָא לְגַוְונָא, וּמִטָּב לְבִישׁ, וּמִבִּישׁ לְטָב, וְנַחְתוּ מֵעֵילָּא לְתַתָּא, וְאִתְדַּבְּקוּ

לְתַתָּא בְּשִׁנּוּיִין סַגִּיאִין, וְשָׁבְקוּ עִלָּאָה דְּכֹלָּא, דְּהוּא חַד, וְלָא אִשְׁתַּנֵּי
לְעָלְמִין. הֲדָא הוּא דִכְתִיב, אֲשֶׁר עָשָׂה הָאֱלֹהִים אֶת הָאָדָם יָשָׁר וְהֵמָּה
בִקְשׁוּ חִשְׁבוֹנוֹת רַבִּים. וְהֵמָּה בִּקְשׁוּ חִשְׁבוֹנוֹת רַבִּים וַדַּאי, כְּדֵין אִתְהַפַּךְ
לִבַּיְיהוּ בְּהַהוּא סִטְרָא מַמָּשׁ, זִמְנִין לְטָב, זִמְנִין לְבִישׁ זִמְנִין לְרַחֲמֵי,
זִמְנִין לְדִינָא. כְּהַהוּא מִלָּה דְּאִתְדְּבָקוּ בָּהּ וַדַּאי. וְהֵמָּה בִּקְשׁוּ חִשְׁבוֹנוֹת
רַבִּים, וְאִתְדְּבָקוּ בְּהוּ.

335. Afterwards, they strayed from the way of Faith and left the peerless supernal tree, elevated above all other trees, WHICH IS THE TREE OF LIFE, NAMELY ZEIR ANPIN. And they came to cleave to a changing place that turns from one manner to another, from good to evil and from evil to good, NAMELY TO THE TREE OF KNOWLEDGE OF GOOD AND EVIL. They descended from above downwards and cleaved below to many changes. They left the highest, which is one and never changing. This is what is meant by, "that Elohim has made man upright; but they have sought out many inventions" (Kohelet 7:29), NAMELY, THE TREE OF KNOWLEDGE OF GOOD AND EVIL THAT CONTAINS MANY CHANGES. Their heart then changed by that very aspect, AS THEY WERE sometimes inclined towards good and sometimes towards evil, sometimes to Mercy and sometimes to Judgment. Surely it resembles that to which they clung; "they have sought out many inventions" and became attached to them.

336. אָ"ל קוּדְשָׁא בְּרִיךְ הוּא, אָדָם, שָׁבְקַת חַיֵּי, וְאִתְדַּבְּקַת בְּמוֹתָא.
חַיֵּי, דִּכְתִיב וְעֵץ הַחַיִּים בְּתוֹךְ הַגָּן, עֵץ דְּאִתְקְרֵי חַיִּים, דְּמַאן דְּאָחִיד
בֵּיהּ, לָא טָעִים טַעֲמָא דְּמוֹתָא לְעָלְמִין. וְאִתְדַּבְּקַת בְּאִילָנָא אַחֲרָא, הָא
וַדַּאי מוֹתָא הוּא לְקָבְלָךְ. הה"ד, רַגְלֶיהָ יוֹרְדוֹת מָוֶת וְגוֹ'. וּכְתִיב וּמוֹצֵא
אֲנִי מַר מִמָּוֶת אֶת הָאִשָּׁה. וַדַּאי. בְּאֲתַר דְּמוֹתָא אִתְדַּבַּק, וְשָׁבַק אֲתַר
דְּחַיֵּי, בְּגִ"כ אִתְגְּזַר עֲלֵיהּ וְעַל כָּל עָלְמָא מוֹתָא.

336. The Holy One, blessed be He, said to him, 'Adam, you have left life and cleaved to death. Life is as in the verse, "the Tree of Life also in the midst of the Garden," NAMELY a tree called life, BECAUSE whoever is attached to it never tastes death. And you cleaved to another tree. Surely death is before you'. This is what is meant by, "Her feet go down to

death…" (Mishlei 5:5), and, "and I find more bitter than death the woman" (Kohelet 7:26). Surely he cleaved to the region of death and left the region of life. For that he and the whole world were sentenced to death.

337. אִי הוּא חָטָא, כָּל עָלְמָא מַאי חָטָאוּ. אִי תֵּימָא דְּכָל בִּרְיָין אָתוּ וְאַכְלוּ מֵאִילָנָא דָּא, וְאִתְרְמֵי מִכֹּלָּא. לָאו הָכִי, אֶלָּא בְּשַׁעֲתָא דְּאָדָם קָאִים עַל רַגְלוֹי, חָמוּ לֵיהּ בִּרְיָין כֻּלְּהוּ, וְדַחֲלוּ מִקַּמֵּיהּ, וַהֲווֹ נַטְלִין בַּתְרֵיהּ, כְּעַבְדִּין קַמֵּי מַלְכָּא. וְהוּא אָמַר לוֹן, אֲנָא וְאַתּוּן, בּוֹאוּ נִשְׁתַּחֲוֶה וְנִכְרָעָה נִבְרְכָה לִפְנֵי יְיָ' עוֹשֵׂנוּ, וְכֻלְּהוּ אָתוּ בַּתְרֵיהּ. כֵּיוָן דְּחָמוּ דְּאָדָם סָגִיד לְהַאי אֲתָר, וְאִתְדַּבַּק בֵּיהּ, כֻּלְּהוּ אִתְמַשְׁכוּ אֲבַתְרֵיהּ, וְגָרִים מוֹתָא לֵיהּ, וּלְכָל עָלְמָא.

337. HE ASKS, If he sinned, what is the sin of the whole world? WHY WAS EVERYBODY SENTENCED TO DEATH? You may say that all creatures came and ate of this tree and it was sampled by all. This is not so. When Adam rose to his feet, all creatures saw him and feared him. They followed him like servants before a king. And he said to him, you and I, "O come, let us worship and bow down, let us kneel before Hashem our maker" (Tehilim 95:6), and they all followed him. When they saw Adam bowing to that place, THE TREE OF KNOWLEDGE OF GOOD AND EVIL, and cleaving to it, they all followed him. For THAT REASON he brought death upon himself and the whole world.

338. כְּדֵין אִשְׁתַּנֵּי אָדָם לְכַמָּה גְּוָונִין, זִמְנִין לְטַב, זִמְנִין לְבִישׁ. זִמְנִין רוּגְזָא, זִמְנִין נַיְיחָא. זִמְנִין דִּינָא, וְזִמְנִין רַחֲמֵי. זִמְנִין חַיֵּי, זִמְנִין מוֹתָא. וְלָא קָאִים בְּקִיּוּמָא תָּדִיר בְּחַד מִנַּיְיהוּ. בְּגִין דְּהַהוּא אֲתָר גַּרְמָא לֵיהּ. וְעַ"ד אִקְרֵי, לַהַט הַחֶרֶב הַמִּתְהַפֶּכֶת, מִן סִטְרָא דָּא, לְסִטְרָא דָּא, מִן טַב לְבִישׁ, מִן רַחֲמֵי לְדִינָא, מִן שָׁלוֹם לִקְרָבָא, אִתְהַפִּיכַת הִיא לְכֹלָּא. וְאִקְרֵי טוֹב וָרָע, דִּכְתִיב וּמֵעֵץ הַדַּעַת טוֹב וָרָע לֹא תֹאכַל מִמֶּנּוּ.

338. Adam then changed in many ways, now to good and now to evil, now to wrath and now to pleasure, now to Judgment and now to Mercy, now to life and now to death. He never remains permanently at any of them. This was brought to him by that place, THE TREE OF KNOWLEDGE OF GOOD

AND EVIL. Hence it is called the blade of the revolving sword from one side to another, from good to evil, from Mercy to Judgment, from war to peace. It revolves in all DIRECTIONS and is called good and evil, as written, "but of the Tree of Knowledge of Good and Evil, you shall not eat of it" (Beresheet 2:17).

339. וּמַלְכָּא עִלָּאָה, רַחֲמָא עַל עוֹבָדֵי יְדוֹי, אוֹכַח לֵיהּ, וְאָמַר לֵיהּ וּמֵעֵץ הַדַּעַת טוֹב וָרָע לֹא תֵּאכֵל מִמֶּנּוּ, וְהוּא לָא קַבִּיל מִנֵּיהּ, וְאִתְמְשַׁךְ בָּתַר אִתְּתֵיהּ, וְאִתְתָּרַךְ לְעָלְמִין. דְּהָא אִתְּתָא לְאַתָר דָּא סַלְקָא, וְלָא יַתִּיר. וְאִתְּתָא גָּרִים מוֹתָא לְכֹלָּא.

339. The supernal King, whose mercy is upon His handiwork, reproved him, saying to him, "but of the Tree of Knowledge of Good and Evil, you shall not eat of it." Yet he did not accept from Him but followed his wife and was banished forever, since the woman rises no higher than that place and the woman brought death unto all.

340. ת״ח, לְעָלְמָא דְּאָתֵי כְּתִיב, כִּי כִּימֵי הָעֵץ יְמֵי עַמִּי. כִּימֵי הָעֵץ: הַהוּא עֵץ דְּאִשְׁתְּמוֹדַע. בֵּיהּ זִמְנָא כְּתִיב, בִּלַּע הַמָּוֶת לָנֶצַח וּמָחָה יְיָ׳ אֱלֹהִים דִּמְעָה מֵעַל כָּל פָּנִים.

340. Come and see, of the World to Come it is written, "for as the days of a tree shall the days of My people be" (Yeshayah 65:22). "the days of a tree" REFERS TO that famous tree, THE TREE OF LIFE. Of that time it is written, "He will destroy death for ever; and Hashem Elohim will wipe away tears from off all faces" (Yeshayah 25:8).

בָּרוּךְ יְיָ׳ לְעוֹלָם אָמֵן וְאָמֵן יִמְלוֹךְ יְיָ׳ לְעוֹלָם אָמֵן וְאָמֵן

Blessed be Hashem for ever and ever, Amen and Amen. May Hashem reign for ever, Amen and Amen.

BEHAR

Names of the articles

1. "Which shall be burning upon the altar all night"

A Synopsis

Rabbi Elazar talks about the nighttime when Judgments are awakened in the world and sorcery is performed. He tells what happens when midnight approaches, and the joy that God finds among the Righteous in the Garden of Eden. In the morning the Judgments and flames are stilled, and Abraham brings rest to all.

וּ. וַיְדַבֵּר יְיָ אֶל מֹשֶׁה בְּהַר סִינַי לֵאמֹר. דַּבֵּר אֶל בְּנֵי יִשְׂרָאֵל וְאָמַרְתָּ אֲלֵיהֶם כִּי תָבֹאוּ אֶל הָאָרֶץ וְגוֹ'. רַבִּי אֶלְעָזָר פָּתַח, זֹאת תּוֹרַת הָעוֹלָה הִיא הָעוֹלָה וְגוֹ'. הַאי קְרָא בִּכְנֶסֶת יִשְׂרָאֵל אוּקִימְנָא, דְּהִיא סַלְקָא וּמִתְחַבְּרָא בְּמַלְכָּא קַדִּישָׁא בְּזוּוּגָא שְׁלִים.

1. "And Hashem spoke to Moses on Mount Sinai, saying, 'Speak to the children of Yisrael, and say to them: When you come to the land...'" (Vayikra 25:1-2). Rabbi Elazar commenced the discussion with the verse: "This is the Torah of the burnt offering (Heb. *olah*). It is the burnt offering..." (Vayikra 6:2). We established this verse address the Congregation of Yisrael, which rises (Heb. *olah*) and joins with the Holy King in a perfect union.

2. הִיא הָעוֹלָה עַל מוֹקְדָה עַל הַמִּזְבֵּחַ כָּל הַלַּיְלָה וְגוֹ'. ת"ח, כֵּיוָן דְּעָאל לֵילְיָא, וְתַרְעִין סְתִימִין, דִּינִין תַּתָּאִין מִתְעָרִין בְּעָלְמָא, וְאַזְלִין וְשָׁאטִין, חֲמָרֵי וַאֲתָנֵי וְכַלְבֵּי. חֲמָרֵי הָא אוּקִימְנָא, וְכַלְבֵּי וַאֲתָנֵי, לָא שָׁאטָן וְלָא אַזְלִין, אֶלָּא בְּהוּ עַבְדֵי חֲרָשַׁיָּא לִבְנֵי נָשָׁא. כְּגוֹן בִּלְעָם, וְאוּקְמוּהָ. כְּדֵין כָּל בְּנֵי עָלְמָא נַיְימִין, וּמִזְבֵּחַ תַּתָּאָה דִּלְבַר אִתּוֹקַד.

2. "It is the burnt offering, which shall be burning upon the altar all night" (Ibid.). Come and behold: when night comes and the gates are shut, Judgments below are awakened in the world, and mules and dogs go and roam about. We established THAT ON THE FIRST WATCH OF THE NIGHT A MULE BRAYS. At this time, dogs and donkeys do not roam about; sorcery is performed with the mules by people such as Bilaam, WHO RODE ON HIS MULE. Then all of mankind is asleep, and the lower outer altar, BEING MALCHUT WHEN FILLED WITH JUDGMENT, burns.

3. בְּפַלְגוּת לֵילְיָא, אִתְּעַר רוּחַ צָפוֹן, וּמֵהַהוּא מִזְבֵּחַ תַּתָּאָה, נָפִיק שַׁלְהוֹבָא דְּאֶשָּׁא, וְתַרְעִין אִתְפְּתָחוּ, וְדִינִין תַּתָּאִין אִתְכְּנָשׁוּ בְּנוּקְבַיְיהוּ, וְהַהוּא שַׁלְהוֹבָא אָזִיל וְשָׁאט, וְתַרְעִין דג"ע אִתְפְּתָחוּ, עַד דְּמָטֵי הַהוּא שַׁלְהוֹבָא, אִתְפְּלַג לְכַמָּה סִטְרִין דְּעָלְמָא, וְעָאל תְּחוֹת גַּדְפוֹי דְּתַרְנְגוֹלָא וְקָארֵי.

3. At midnight, the north wind is stirred, and from that lower altar, FROM MALCHUT, comes a flame of fire. The gates open and the lower Judgments, MEANING THE JUDGMENTS OF THE FEMALE, assemble in their holes. That flame goes and spreads, and the gates of the Garden of Eden open until that flame reaches and then divides to several directions of the world. It then enters beneath the wings of the cock, and it crows.

4. כְּדֵין קוּדְשָׁא בְּרִיךְ הוּא אִשְׁתְּכַח בֵּין צַדִּיקַיָּיא, וכ"י מְשַׁבַּחַת לֵיהּ לְקוּדְשָׁא בְּרִיךְ הוּא, עַד דְּאָתֵי צַפְרָא. כֵּיוָן דְּאָתֵי צַפְרָא, אִשְׁתְּכָחוּ מִשְׁתָּעֵין בְּרָזָא חֲדָא. וְאִית לָהּ נַיְיחָא בְּבַעְלָהּ. הה"ד, עַל מוֹקְדָה עַל הַמִּזְבֵּחַ כָּל הַלַּיְלָה וְגוֹ'. עַד הַבֹּקֶר, דְּהָא בְּצַפְרָא דִּינִין וְשַׁלְהוֹבִין אִשְׁתְּכָכוּ, וּכְדֵין אִתְּעַר אַבְרָהָם בְּעָלְמָא, וְנַיְיחָא הוּא דְּכֹלָּא.

4. Then the Holy One, blessed be He, is found among the righteous, and the Congregation of Yisrael offers praise to the Holy One, blessed be He, until the onset of morning. With the arrival of morning, they are found chatting about one secret, ONE WITH THE OTHER, THE SECRET OF THE THIRD WATCH WHEN THE WIFE CONVERSES WITH HER HUSBAND. She has rest with her husband. This is what is written: "which shall be burning upon the altar all night until the morning." ALL NIGHT SHE BURNS IN HER JUDGMENTS. "Until morning," that is, in the morning, the Judgments and flames are stilled. Then Abraham is stirred, BEING CHESED, with the world, and he brings rest to all.

2. "Then shall the land keep a Shabbat to Hashem"

A Synopsis

We are told that when Yisrael entered the land there were no lower judgments and everything was peaceful. Rabbi Elazar talks about the Sabbatical Year that is total rest for the spirit and body.

ה. ת"ח, כֵּיוָן דְּעָאלוּ יִשְׂרָאֵל לְאַרְעָא, לָא אִשְׁתְּכָחוּ בָהּ דִּינִין תַּתָּאִין, וְכִי הֲוַת בָּהּ בְּנַיְיחָא, עַל כַּנְפֵי דִכְרוּבִים. כְּמָה דְּאִתְּמַר, דִּכְתִּיב, צֶדֶק יָלִין בָּהּ. כְּדֵין הֲוַת לָהּ נַיְיחָא מִכֹּלָּא. דְּהָא יִשְׂרָאֵל לָא נַיְימִין, עַד דִּמְקָרְבֵי קָרְבְּנָא דְּבֵין הָעַרְבַּיִם, וְאִסְתְּלִיקוּ דִינִין. וְעוֹלָה הֲוָה אָתּוֹקַד עַל מַדְבְּחָא, וּכְדֵין הֲוָה לָהּ נַיְיחָא מִכֹּלָּא, וְלָא אִשְׁתְּכַח אֶלָּא אִתְּתָא בְּבַעְלָהּ, הה"ד כִּי תָבֹאוּ וְגוֹ' וְשָׁבְתָה הָאָרֶץ, נַיְיחָא וַדַּאי. וְשָׁבְתָה הָאָרֶץ שַׁבָּת לַיְיָ', שַׁבָּת לַיְיָ' מַמָּשׁ.

5. Come and behold: when Yisrael entered the land, there were no lower Judgments, JUDGMENTS OF THE FEMALE, found in it, and the Congregation of Yisrael, BEING MALCHUT, was resting upon the wings of the Cherubs as they said, "righteousness lodged in it" (Yeshayah 1:21). Then she had respite from all, for Yisrael did not sleep until they offered the twilight sacrifice and the Judgments were dismissed. The burnt offering was consumed upon the altar. Then she had respite from all, and there was only a wife with her husband. This is the essence of, "When you come to the land... then shall the land keep a Shabbat" (Vayikra 25:2). Then the land will rest; true rest WITHOUT JUDGMENTS. "...then shall the land keep a Shabbat to Hashem," MEANING a Shabbat to Hashem literally, WITHOUT ANY JUDGMENTS.

ו. תּוּ פָּתַח רִבִּי אֶלְעָזָר, כִּי תִקְנֶה עֶבֶד עִבְרִי שֵׁשׁ שָׁנִים יַעֲבֹד וְגוֹ'. בְּגִין דְּכָל בַּר יִשְׂרָאֵל דְּאִתְגְּזַר, דְּאִית בֵּיהּ רְשִׁימָא קַדִּישָׁא, אִית לֵיהּ נַיְיחָא בִּשְׁמִטָּה. דְּהָא דִּילֵיהּ הוּא הַהוּא שְׁמִטָּה, לְנַיְיחָא בֵּיהּ. וְדָא אִקְרֵי שַׁבַּת הָאָרֶץ, וַדַּאי חֵירוּ אִית בָּהּ. נַיְיחָא בָּהּ, כְּמָה דְּשַׁבָּת נַיְיחָא הוּא דְכֹלָּא, הָכִי נָמֵי שְׁמִטָּה נַיְיחָא דְכֹלָּא, נַיְיחָא הוּא דְרוּחָא וְגוּפָא.

6. Again, Rabbi Elazar commenced: "If you buy a Hebrew servant, six years he shall serve..." (Shemot 21:2) as every son of Yisrael who is circumcised possesses a holy mark, has rest on the Sabbatical Year. This Sabbatical Year is his, DENOTING MALCHUT; it is his to rest in it. It is referred to as the Shabbat of the land, and surely contains freedom FROM THE KLIPOT. In it, there is rest FROM JUDGMENTS; just as Shabbat is rest for all, so the Sabbatical Year is total rest – rest for the spirit and body. THEREFORE, IT IS WRITTEN, "SIX YEARS HE SHALL SERVE: AND IN THE SEVENTH HE SHALL GO OUT FREE."

7. ת״ח, ה׳ נַייחָא הוּא דְּעֶלָאֵי וְתַתָּאֵי. בְּג״כ, ה׳ עִלָאָה, ה׳ תַּתָּאָה. נַייחָא דְּעֶלָּאִין, נַייחָא דְּתַתָּאִין. ה׳ עִלָאָה, שֶׁבַע שָׁנִים שֶׁבַע פְּעָמִים. ה׳ תַּתָּאָה, שֶׁבַע שָׁנִים בִּלְחוֹדַייהוּ. דָּא שְׁמִטָּה, וְדָא יוֹבְלָא.

7. Come and behold: *Hei* refers to rest of those on high and those lower. Thus, THERE IS the upper *Hei* OF YUD HEI VAV HEI, DENOTING BINAH, and the lower *Hei* OF YUD HEI VAV HEI, REFLECTING MALCHUT. THE UPPER *HEI* POINTS TO rest for the supernal beings, while THE LOWER *HEI* REFERS TO rest for those below. The upper *Hei* IS THE SECRET OF seven years seven times, MEANING 49 GATES OF BINAH; the lower *Hei* is THE SECRET OF merely the seven years. The LOWER IS CALLED 'The Sabbatical Year' and the UPPER is called 'Jubilee'.

8. וְכַד מִסְתַּכְּלִין מִלֵּי כֹּלָּא חַד. בְּג״כ וְשָׁבְתָה הָאָרֶץ, בְּהַהוּא נַייחָא דְּאַרְעָא, אִצְטְרִיכוּ עַבְדִּין נַייחָא. וּבְג״כ, וּבַשְּׁבִיעִית יֵצֵא לַחָפְשִׁי חִנָּם. חִנָּם, מַהוּ חִנָּם. דְּלָא יָהִיב לְמָארֵיה כְּלוּם.

8. When one looks at these things they all the same, BECAUSE THE MOCHIN OF JUBILEE, WHICH IS BINAH, ILLUMINATES WITHIN THE SABBATICAL YEAR, WHICH IS MALCHUT. Therefore, IT IS WRITTEN, "then shall the land keep a Shabbat" (Vayikra 25:1), for when the land is at rest, the servants SHOULD BE at rest. This is why, "in the seventh he shall go out free." What is "free"? It means that he pays his master nothing.

3. The yoke of the Kingdom of Heaven

A Synopsis
Rabbi Elazar tells us that man must accept the yoke of the kingdom of Heaven before he can do any work. This yoke can not rest on anyone who is attached to another, so slaves are exempt from the commandments and from the yoke, as were Yisrael while they were in exile.

9. אֶלָּא דָּא רָזָא, הָכָא אוֹלִיפְנָא, כְּתִיב זָכַרְנוּ אֶת הַדָּגָה אֲשֶׁר נֹאכַל בְּמִצְרַיִם חִנָּם, בְּלָא בְּרָכָה. דְּלָא הֲוָה עֲלָנָא בְּמִצְרַיִם עוֹל דִּלְעֵילָא. ת"ח, עַבְדִּין פְּטוּרִין מֵעוֹל מַלְכוּתָא דִּלְעֵילָא, וְע"ד פְּטוּרִין מִן הַמִּצְוֹת. מַאי עוֹל מַלְכוּת שָׁמַיִם. אֶלָּא, כְּהַאי תּוֹרָא דִּיְהַבִין עָלֵיהּ עוֹל בְּקַדְמֵיתָא, בְּגִין לְאַפָּקָא מִנֵּיה טַב לְעָלְמָא. וְאִי לָא קַבִּיל עָלֵיהּ הַהוּא עוֹל, לָא עָבֵיד מִדִּי. ה"נ אִצְטְרִיךְ לֵיהּ לב"נ לְקַבְּלָא עָלֵיהּ עוֹל בְּקַדְמֵיתָא, וּלְבָתַר דְּיִפְלַח בֵּיהּ בְּכָל מַה דְּאִצְטְרִיךְ. וְאִי לָא קַבִּיל עָלֵיהּ הַאי בְּקַדְמֵיתָא, לָא יֵיכוּל לְמִפְלַח.

9. In truth, this is the secret. We learned that it is written: "We remember the fish, which we did eat in Egypt for nothing" (Bemidbar 11:5), MEANING "FOR NOTHING," without a blessing, as we did not have a heavenly yoke in Egypt. Come and behold: slaves are exempt from the yoke of the Kingdom of Heaven, and so they are exempt from the commandments. What is this the yoke of the Heavenly Kingdom? It is like an ox upon which they first place a yoke in order to work with him and draw benefit from him for the world. If he does not accept that yoke he does no work at all. So man must accept upon himself the yoke OF THE HEAVENLY KINGDOM first, and then he will toil with it all that he needs. However, if he does not accept this yoke upon himself first, he cannot work.

10. הה"ד עִבְדוּ אֶת יְיָ' בְּיִרְאָה. מַהוּ בְּיִרְאָה. כד"א רֵאשִׁית חָכְמָה יִרְאַת יְיָ'. וְדָא מַלְכוּת שָׁמַיִם. וּבְגִין כַּךְ עוֹל מַלְכוּת שָׁמַיִם. וְע"ד הַאי בְּקַדְמֵיתָא הוּא דְכֹלָּא. מַאן אוֹכַח. תְּפִלָּה, בְּקַדְמֵיתָא שֶׁל יַד. בְּגִין דִּבְהַאי עָיֵיל לִשְׁאָר קְדוּשָׁה. וְאִי הַאי לָא אִשְׁתְּכַח לְגַבֵּיה, לָא שַׁרְיָא בֵּיה קְדוּשָׁה לְעֵילָא, בְּג"כ בְּזֹאת יָבֹא אַהֲרֹן אֶל הַקֹּדֶשׁ וְגוֹ' כְּתִיב.

10. It is written: "Serve Hashem with fear" (Tehilim 2:11). What is meant by "fear"? It is as it is written: "The fear of Hashem is the beginning of wisdom" (Tehilim 111:10). This refers to the Kingdom of Heaven, AS MALCHUT IS CALLED 'FEAR,' and for this reason, it becomes the yoke of the Heavenly Kingdom. And so this is where it all starts, SINCE MALCHUT IS THE FIRST SFIRAH GOING FROM BELOW UPWARD. What proves this? THAT WE DON the hand Tfilin first, BEING THE SECRET OF MALCHUT, AND AFTERWARDS THE HEAD TFILIN, WHICH IS THE SECRET OF ZEIR ANPIN. This is because THROUGH MALCHUT, one enters the rest of holiness. If this is not found with him, the celestial holiness cannot rest upon him. For this it writes, "Thus (lit. 'with this') did Aaron come into the holy place" (Vayikra 16:3).

11. וְהַאי עוֹל לָא שַׁרְיָא, בְּמַאן דְּאִיהוּ כָּפִית בְּאָחֳרָא. וְעַ"ד עַבְדִּין פְּטוּרִין מֵעוֹל מַלְכוּת שָׁמַיִם. וְאִי מֵהַאי עוֹל פְּטוּרִין, מִכָּל שְׁאָר פְּטוּרִין. דְּהָא שְׁאָר לָא שַׁרְיָא עָלֵיהּ דְּב"נ, עַד דְּאִשְׁתְּכַח גַּבֵּיהּ בְּהַאי עוֹל. וּבְג"כ הֲווֹ אָכְלֵי יִשְׂרָאֵל בְּמִצְרַיִם חִנָּם. אוֹף הָכָא יֵצֵא לַחָפְשִׁי חִנָּם. דְּהָא עַבְדָּא הֲוָה, וְכָל מַה דְּעָבֵיד, חִנָּם הוּא, בְּלָא עוֹל מַלְכוּת שָׁמַיִם. וְאע"ג דְּחִנָּם הֲווֹ עוֹבָדוֹהִי יֵצֵא לַחָפְשִׁי, וְיֶהֱא לֵיהּ נַיְיחָא.

11. And this yoke can not rest upon one who is attached to another, and so slaves are exempt from the yoke of the Heavenly Kingdom, BECAUSE THEY ARE TIED TO THEIR MASTERS. If they are exempt from this yoke, they are exempt from all other COMMANDMENTS, since other COMMANDMENTS are not placed upon one until this yoke is with him. Therefore, Yisrael in Egypt ate without cost. Here too, "he shall go out free" (Shemot 21:2), since he was a slave and whatever he did was without cost, without the yoke of the Heavenly Kingdom. So even though his deeds were for nothing, "he shall go out," and find rest. THE EXPLANATION OF THE VERSE IS AS IF IT SAID, 'FOR FREE YET HE SHALL GO OUT'.

Behar

4. "And his master shall bore his ear through"

A Synopsis

Rabbi Elazar describes what happens when someone rejects his freedom, preferring to stay attached to his master. The blemish of having his ear bored through remains with him because he refused to listen. Rabbi Elazar says that anyone who shows mercy for the poor contributes peace to the Congregation of Yisrael and multiplies blessings in the world.

12. לְבָתַר דְּאִיהוּ בְּחֵירוּ, וְאִשְׁתְּכַח בֵּיהּ נַיְיחָא, יָהֲבִין עֲלֵיהּ עוֹל, מֵהַהוּא אֲתַר דְּאַפִּיק לֵיהּ לְחֵירוּ. וְאִי ב"נ יְסָרֵב לְמֵיפַּק לְחֵירוּ, כד"א וְאִם אָמֹר יֹאמַר הָעֶבֶד אָהַבְתִּי אֶת אֲדוֹנִי וְגוֹ'. הָא וַדַּאי פָּגִים לֵיהּ לְהַאי אֲתַר, דְּשָׁבִיק עוֹל מַלְכוּתָא דִּלְעֵילָּא, וְנָטִיל עוֹל דְּמָארֵיהּ. וְעַל דָּא מַה כְּתִיב, וְהִגִּישׁוֹ אֲדוֹנָיו אֶל הָאֱלֹהִים וְהִגִּישׁוֹ אֶל הַדֶּלֶת וְגוֹ'. וְהִגִּישׁוֹ אֲדוֹנָיו אֶל הָאֱלֹהִים. אֶל הָאֱלֹהִים סְתָם. לְגַבֵּי הַהוּא אֲתַר דְּפָגִים לֵיהּ דה"נ אֱלֹהִים אִקְרֵי.

12. After gaining freedom and finding himself at rest, a yoke is placed upon him from that place that brought him freedom, MEANING FROM THE SECRET OF THE SEVENTH YEAR, MALCHUT. If someone rejected freedom, as the verse reads, "And if the servant shall say, I love my master..." (Shemot 21:5) he certainly has thwarted that place, NAMELY MALCHUT, since he has rejected the yoke of the Heavenly Kingdom and accepted the yoke of his master. What does it say of this? "Then his master shall bring him to the judges (lit. 'the Elohim'); he shall also bring him to the door..." (Ibid. 6). "Then his master shall bring him to the Elohim"; Elohim IS SAID generally, MEANING HE BROUGHT HIM to that place that he damaged, MALCHUT, also referred to as Elohim.

13. וּלְאָן אֲתַר יִתְקְרִיב לְגַבֵּיהּ. אֶל הַדֶּלֶת אוֹ אֶל הַמְּזוּזָה. בְּגִין דְּהַאי אֲתַר פִּתְחָא הוּא דִּלְעֵילָּא, וּמְזוּזָה אִקְרֵי, וְהָא אִתְּמַר. וְכֵיוָן דְּאִיהוּ אִכְוָון לְאַפְגְּמָא לְהַאי אֲתַר, הַהוּא פְּגִימוּ אִשְׁתְּאַר בַּהֲדֵיהּ בֵּיהּ בְּגוּפֵיהּ הה"ד, וְרָצַע אֲדוֹנָיו אֶת אָזְנוֹ בַּמַּרְצֵעַ וַעֲבָדוֹ לְעוֹלָם. יֶהֱוֵי עַבְדָּא תְּחוֹת רַגְלוֹי דְּמָארֵיהּ, עַד שַׁתָּא דְּיוֹבְלָא.

-319-

13. To what place does he bring him near? "…to the door, or the door post (Heb. *mezuzah*)" (Ibid.), since that place, NAMELY MALCHUT, is the entrance to above, MEANING THE ENTRANCE THROUGH WHICH TO MERIT ZEIR ANPIN, and it is called '*mezuzah*'. And so we learned. Since he intended to blemish that place, MALCHUT, there remained this deficiency in his body. This is what is written: "and his master shall bore his ear through with an awl; and he shall serve him forever" (Ibid.), since the servant will be beneath the feet of his master until Jubilee year.

14. אֶת אָזְנוֹ אֲמַאי. הָא אוֹקְמוּהָ. אֲבָל שְׁמִיעָה תַּלֵּי בְּהַאי אֲתַר, עֲשִׂיָּה לְעֵילָּא. וּבְגִין דְּיִשְׂרָאֵל כַּד קְרִיבוּ לְטוּרָא דְּסִינַי, וַהֲווֹ בִּרְחִימוּ דִּלְבַּיְיהוּ לְאִתְקָרְבָא לְקוּדְשָׁא בְּרִיךְ הוּא, אַקְדִּימוּ עֲשִׂיָּה לַשְּׁמִיעָה, דְּהָא שְׁמִיעָה בְּקַדְמֵיתָא, וּלְבָתַר עֲשִׂיָּה. שְׁמִיעָה בְּהַאי שְׁמִיטָה תַּלְיָא. וְעַ"ד הוּא פָּגִים לְהַאי שְׁמִיעָה, יִתְפְּגִים שְׁמִיעָה דִּילֵיהּ, וְיִשְׁתְּאַר פְּגִימוּ בֵּיהּ. וְלָא יִשְׁתְּאַר הוּא עַבְדָּא לְמָארֵיהּ, עַד דְּיִתְקְרֵב לְהַהוּא אֲתַר דְּפָגִים, וְיִתְפְּגִים הוּא קַמֵּיהּ, וְיִשְׁתְּאַר בֵּיהּ הַהוּא פְּגִימוּ. וּבְגַ"כ, וְהִגִּישׁוֹ אֲדֹנָיו אֶל הָאֱלֹהִים סְתָם, כְּמָה דְּאוֹקִימְנָא. וְעַ"ד, וְשָׁבְתָה הָאָרֶץ שַׁבָּת לַיְיָ'.

14. HE ASKS: Why BORE THROUGH his ear? ANSWER: We already have established this. Hearing is dependent upon this place, NAMELY MALCHUT, acting above UPON BINAH. When the Congregation of Yisrael was approaching Mount Sinai with the love in their hearts to approach the Holy One, blessed be He, they placed doing before hearing. Normally, listening precedes doing. Listening depends on the Sabbatical Year, DENOTING MALCHUT, and so since this servant damaged this listening, his listening was blemished. This blemish remains with him, and he does not remain a servant to his master unless he approaches that place that he blemished and he is blemished before it, and this rebuff remains with him. For this reason, "then his master shall bring him to the Elohim." This is unspecified, POINTING TO MALCHUT, as we established. Hence, "shall the land keep a Shabbat to Hashem" (Vayikra 25:2), SO THAT IT WILL NOT BE RENDERED DEFECTIVE THROUGH SLAVERY. HERE IT IS DIFFERENT FROM MOST INSTANCES WHERE WE SAY THAT LISTENING DENOTES BINAH AND DOING MALCHUT.

15. שֵׁשׁ שָׁנִים תִּזְרַע שָׂדֶךָ וְגוֹ', וּבַשָּׁנָה הַשְּׁבִיעִית שַׁבַּת שַׁבָּתוֹן יִהְיֶה

לְאָרֶץ שַׁבָּת לַיְיָ. וְהָא אוֹקְמוּהָ, דִּכְתִיב וּבַשְּׁבִיעִית תִּשְׁמְטֶנָּה וּנְטַשְׁתָּהּ
וְגוֹ׳. מ״ט. וְאָכְלוּ אֶבְיוֹנֵי עַמֶּךָ. בְּגִין דְּמִסְכְּנֵי בְּהַאי אֲתָר תַּלְיָין, וּבְג״כ
שָׁבִיק לוֹן לְמֵיכַל. וְעַ״ד, מַאן דְּרָחִים לְמִסְכְּנָא, יָהִיב שְׁלָמָא בִּכְנֶסֶת
יִשְׂרָאֵל, וְאוֹסִיף בִּרְכָתָא בְּעָלְמָא, וְיָהִיב חֵידוּ וְחֵילָא לַאֲתָר דְּאִתְקְרֵי
צְדָקָה, לְאַרְקָא בִּרְכָתָא לִכְנֶסֶת יִשְׂרָאֵל, וְאוֹקִימְנָא.

15. "Six years you shall sow your field… but in the seventh year shall be a Shabbat of solemn rest for the land, a Shabbat for Hashem" (Vayikra 25:3-4). We already established, as it is written, "but in the seventh year you shall let it rest and lie fallow" (Shemot 23:11). What is the reason? "That the poor of your people may eat" (Ibid.). For the poor are associated with that place, MALCHUT, DENOTING THE SABBATICAL YEAR; therefore, leave it to them to eat. Consequently, one who shows mercy for the poor contributes peace to the Congregation of Yisrael, AS THE POOR ARE ASSOCIATED WITH IT. He multiplies blessings in the world and gives joy and strength to the place called 'righteousness,' DENOTING MALCHUT, by pouring blessings on the Congregation of Yisrael. This has been explained.

5. The Sabbatical Year and Jubilee

A Synopsis

This section emphasizes the numbers seven and 49 in relation to the seventh year and the seven Sfirot. The numerologys are explained in the counting of the priest. We read about the precepts to count the Jubilee year and to return to one's inheritance on the Jubilee. We are told that there are two houses in the heart, and that they are called differently depending on whether one is a master of the Torah or not; there are also two courts of the House of Hashem, an inner one and an outer one.

רעיא מהימנא

16. וּבַשָּׁנָה הַשְּׁבִיעִית שַׁבַּת שַׁבָּתוֹן וְגוֹ'. פְּקוּדָא דָא לִשְׁבּוֹת בַּשָּׁנָה הַשְּׁבִיעִית וַאֲבַתְרֵיהּ לִשְׁבּוֹת בַּשְּׁבִיעִי. וַאֲבַתְרֵיהּ לְהַשְׁמִיט כְּסָפִים, בַּשְּׁבִיעִית. וַאֲבַתְרֵיהּ לִמְנוֹת שֶׁבַע שָׁנִים שֶׁבַע פְּעָמִים וְהָיוּ לְךָ יְמֵי שֶׁבַע שַׁבָּתוֹת הַשָּׁנִים תֵּשַׁע וְאַרְבָּעִים שָׁנָה. הָכָא רָזָא דְּכָל שְׁבִיעִיּוֹת, מִסִּטְרָא דִּשְׁכִינְתָּא דְּאִתְקְרִיאַת שֶׁבַע מִסִּטְרָא דְּצַדִּיק דְּאִיהוּ שְׁבִיעִי לַבִּינָה, וְאִיהִי בַּת שֶׁבַע, מִסִּטְרָא דְּאִימָא עִלָּאָה, דְּאִתְמַר בָּהּ שֶׁבַע בַּיּוֹם הִלַּלְתִּיךָ.

Ra'aya Meheimna (the Faithful Shepherd)

16. "But in the seventh year shall be a Shabbat of solemn rest..." (Vayikra 25:4). This precept is to rest during the seventh year. The following one is to rest during the seventh day, and the following is to cancel money debts on the seventh and then to count, "seven times seven years; and the space of the seven Shabbatot of years shall be to you 49 years" (Ibid. 8). Here is the secret of the group of sevens as they emanate from the Shechinah, DENOTING MALCHUT, called 'seven' from the standpoint of the Righteous, DENOTING YESOD, which is seventh from Binah. And she, MALCHUT, is the daughter of seven from the side of supernal Ima, DENOTING BINAH THAT ILLUMINATES IT, SINCE BINAH IS THE SEVENTH GOING FROM BELOW UPWARD, of which it is written, "Seven times a day I praise You" (Tehilim 119:164).

17. שֶׁבַע שְׁמָהָן אִינוּן אבג״ית״ץ, וּבְהוֹן מ״ב אַתְוָון, כְּלַל אַתְוָון וְתֵיבִין הֵם תֵּשַׁע וְאַרְבְּעִין, אִימָא עִלָּאָה שְׁנַת הַחֲמִשִּׁים שָׁנָה, דְּבָה וּקְרָאתֶם דְּרוֹר. בָּה תְּהֵא שְׁכִינְתָּא תַּתָּאָה, דְּרוֹר פְּדוּת וּשְׁבִיתָה לְיִשְׂרָאֵל, דְּאִתְּמַר בְּהוֹן וְהָיָה זַרְעֲךָ כַּעֲפַר הָאָרֶץ.

17. There are seven names: *Aleph-Bet-Gimel Yud-Tav-Tzadi; Kuf-Resh-Ayin Sin-Tet-Nun; Nun-Gimel-Dalet Yud-Caf-Shin; Bet-Tet-Resh Tzadi-Tav-Gimel; Chet-Kof-Bet Tet-Nun-Ayin; Yud-Gimel-Lamed Pe-Zayin-Kof; Shin-Kof-Vav Tzadi-Yud-Tav.* They contain 42 letters and the sum of both letters and words is 49, THAT IS, 42 LETTERS AND SEVEN WORDS. Supernal Ima, BINAH, represents the fiftieth year, in which you shall "proclaim liberty" (Vayikra 25:10). For within her, BY RECEIVING HER MOCHIN the lower Shechinah, MALCHUT CALLED 'LAND', shall be liberty, redemption and rest for Yisrael, of whom it is written, "and your seed shall be as the dust of the earth" (Beresheet 28:14), THE EARTH BEING MALCHUT.

18. כָּל סְפִירָה מֵאלֵין שֶׁבַע, שִׁית גַּדְפִּין, דְּאִינוּן שִׁית אַתְוָון לְכָל חַד. וּבְהוֹן קוּדְשָׁא בְּרִיךְ הוּא בְּכָל סְפִירָה מֵאלֵין שֶׁבַע, בִּשְׁתַּיִם יְכַסֶּה פָנָיו וּבִשְׁתַּיִם יְכַסֶּה רַגְלָיו וּבִשְׁתַּיִם יְעוֹפֵף, וּבִינָה אִיהוּ אַחַת, וּשְׁכִינְתָּא תַּתָּאָה שֶׁבַע. וּלְעֵילָּא מִבִּינָה, אַחַת וְאַחַת, הָא עֶשֶׂר סְפִירָן. שְׁתַּיִם, ג׳, וְד׳, וְה׳, וְו׳, וְז׳.

18. Every Sfirah, MEANING EACH NAME from these seven names, POSSESSES six wings, CORRESPONDING TO CHESED, GVURAH, TIFERET, NETZACH, HOD AND YESOD, since there are six letters in every name – *Aleph-Bet-Gimel Yud-Tav-Tzadi* POSSESSES SIX LETTERS, AND AS WELL *Kuf-Resh-Ayin Sin-Tet-Nun,* AND SO IT IS WITH ALL OF THEM. And with them, the Holy One, blessed be He, with each Sfirah from these seven, ILLUMINATES THE ANGELS ABOUT WHOM IT IS WRITTEN, "with two he covered his face, and with two he covered his feet, and with two did he fly" (Yeshayah 6:2). Binah represents one. The lower Shechinah is seven. Above Binah, THE HIGH PRIEST COUNTS one and one. HE WOULD COUNT the ten Sfirot BY MEANS OF SPRINKLING. ONE CORRESPONDS TO KETER; ONE AND ONE EQUALS CHOCHMAH AND BINAH; ONE AND two ARE

CHESED AND GVURAH; ONE and three CORRESPONDS TO TIFERET; ONE and four CORRESPONDS TO NETZACH; ONE and five CORRESPONDS TO HOD; ONE and six CORRESPONDS TO YESOD; ONE and seven CORRESPONDS TO MALCHUT.

19. כָּאן וַיֵּלֶךְ הָלוֹךְ וְגָדֵל. מִסְטְרָא נוּכְרָאָה, וְהַמַּיִם הָיוּ הָלוֹךְ וְחָסוֹר, אֵימָתַי. בְּאֲתַר דִּשְׁכִינְתָּא תַּתָּאָה שַׁרְיָא בְּז'. הה"ד, וַתָּנַח הַתֵּיבָה בַּחֹדֶשׁ הַשְּׁבִיעִי, דָּא שְׁכִינְתָּא תַּתָּאָה. בְּשִׁבְעָה עָשָׂר יוֹם לַחֹדֶשׁ, אִיהִי שְׁבִיעָאָה וַעֲשִׂירָאָה.

19. From here it grows, AS WE PROMOTE TO A HIGHER GRADE OF SANCTITY BY ADDING ONE EACH TIME. From the perspective of the stranger, MEANING THE OTHER SIDE, "the waters decreased continually" (Beresheet 8:5). When WAS THIS? It took place where the lower Shechinah, BEING MALCHUT, dwells with the seven. The verse states, "And the ark rested in the seventh month" (Ibid. 4), corresponding to the lower Shechinah. FROM THEN THE WATER BEGAN TO DECREASE. "...on the seventeenth day of the month..." (Ibid.) DENOTING MALCHUT, REFERRED TO AS seventh, AND REFERRED TO AS tenth. WHEN ONE BEGINS TO COUNT FROM KETER DOWNWARD, MALCHUT IS LOCATED TENTH. FROM CHESED AND DOWN, SHE IS SEVENTH.

20. דְּסַלִּיקַת בְּהוֹן אֶהְיֶה, דְּאִיהִי בֵּינָה, שְׁנַת הַיּוֹבֵל, אִיהִי אֶהְיֶה אֲשֶׁר אֶהְיֶה, תְּרֵין זִמְנִין אֶהְיֶה חוּשְׁבַּן מ"ב, וּתְמַנְיָא אַתְוָון בְּהוֹן חַמְשִׁין. דִּבְהוֹן פִּקּוּדָא לַחֲשׁוֹב שְׁנַת הַיּוֹבֵל. וּבֵיהּ פִּקּוּדָא לַחֲזוֹר לַאֲחַזְתּוֹ בַּיּוֹבֵל, בִּשְׁנַת הַיּוֹבֵל הַזֹּאת תָּשׁוּבוּ וְגוֹ'. כָּל חַד יַחֲזוֹר בֵּיהּ לְדַרְגָּא דִּילֵיהּ, דְּנִשְׁמָתֵיהּ אֲחִיזָא מִתַּמָּן, כְּמָה דְּאוּקְמוּהָ וְהָרוּחַ תָּשׁוּב אֶל הָאֱלֹהִים וְגוֹ'.

20. When THE NAME Eheyeh, denoting Binah, the Jubilee year, rises AND ILLUMINATES upon them, UPON THE 49 YEARS, it, BINAH IS CALLED 'Eheyeh-Asher-Eheyeh'. This means twice Eheyeh, SINCE EACH ONE NUMERICALLY REACHES 21 in the count of 42. With eight letters OF THE TWO NAMES ALEPH-HEI-YUD-HEI, there is now fifty. In them is anchored the precept to count the Jubilee year and the precept to return to one's inheritance on the Jubilee, as it is written: "In the year of the Jubilee you

shall return" (Vayikra 25:13). This MEANS that each will return to the level whence his soul was attached, as we established in, "and the spirit returns to the Elohim..." (Kohelet 12:7), MEANING BINAH, CALLED 'YUD HEI VAV HEI', WITH THE VOWELS OF ELOHIM.

21. שְׁמִיטָה: שְׁכִינְתָּא תַּתָּאָה, דְּאִיהִי מִשְׁבַע שְׁנִין. יוֹבֵל: אִימָא עִלָּאָה, בִּינָה, אִיהִי לְחַמְשִׁין שְׁנִין. וּבָה אִתְיַיחֲסִין יִשְׂרָאֵל בְּמִפְקָנוּתְהוֹן מִן גָּלוּתָא. הה"ד, וְאִישׁ אֶל מִשְׁפַּחְתּוֹ תָּשׁוּבוּ. כְּגַוְונָא דְּמִפְקָנוּ דְּמִצְרַיִם דְּאִינוּן מָאֵרֵי תּוֹרָה בָּה, אִתְּמַר בְּהוֹן וַחֲמוּשִׁים עָלוּ בְּנֵי יִשְׂרָאֵל, וְאוֹקְמוּהָ אֶחָד מֵחֲמִשִּׁים.

21. The Sabbatical Year represents the lower Shechinah, which consists of seven years. Jubilee is Ima supernal, Binah representing the fifteenth year. Yisrael was connected with it when departing Egypt, as it is written: "and you shall return every man to his family" (Vayikra 25:10). This means that just as at the exodus from Egypt there were masters of Torah among them – as it is said of them, "and the children of Yisrael went up armed (Heb. *chamushim*)" (Shemot 13:18), and we established that it meant one out of fifty (Heb. *chamishim*), DENOTING BINAH – SO HERE, "AND YOU SHALL RETURN EVERY MAN TO HIS FAMILY," DENOTES BINAH. AND THIS MEANS "TO HIS FAMILY," AS IN THE EXODUS FROM EGYPT, IN WHICH THEY WERE REDEEMED BY THE FIFTIETH GATE, BINAH.

22. וּשְׁכִינְתָּא תַּתָּאָה, אִיהִי גְּאוּלַת בָּתֵּי עָרֵי חוֹמָה אִתְּמַר בָּה, וּבָתֵּי עָרֵי הַחֲצֵרִים. דְּתְרֵי בָתֵּי אִית בְּלִבָּא, אִם אִינוּן מִמָּאֵרֵי תּוֹרָה, אִתְקְרִיאוּ בָּתֵּי עָרֵי חוֹמָה, כְּגַוְונָא דְּאִתְּמַר בְּמִפְקָנוּ דְּמִצְרַיִם, וְהַמַּיִם לָהֶם חוֹמָה מִימִינָם וּמִשְּׂמֹאלָם. לַאֲחֵרִים, דְּלָאו אִינוּן מָאֵרֵי תּוֹרָה אִתְקְרִיאוּ בָּתֵּי הַחֲצֵרִים.

22. The lower Shechinah corresponds to the redemption of the houses of walled cities, and in relation to it the houses of the villages without walls are mentioned. There are two houses in the heart, CORRESPONDING TO MALCHUT. If they are those of the sages of Torah, they are called 'houses of walled cities,' as it is written when departing Egypt: "And the waters were a wall to them on their right hand and on their left" (Shemot 14:22). Others

who are not Torah masters are called "the houses of the villages which have no wall" (Vayikra 25:31). FOR THE INNER PART OF MALCHUT IS CALLED 'HOUSES OF WALLED CITIES,' AND THE OUTER MALCHUT IS CALLED "THE HOUSES OF THE VILLAGES WHICH HAVE NO WALL."

23. אָמַר רִבִּי שִׁמְעוֹן, וְהָא אַשְׁכַּחְנָא חֲצֵרִים דְּאִתְּמַר בֵּיהּ וַתַּעֲמוֹד בַּחֲצַר בֵּית הַמֶּלֶךְ הַפְּנִימִית נֹכַח בֵּית הַמֶּלֶךְ. וּבְכָל אֲתַר הַמֶּלֶךְ סְתָם, דָּא קוּדְשָׁא בְּרִיךְ הוּא. וַתַּעֲמוֹד, אֵין עֲמִידָה, אֶלָּא צְלוֹתָא. נֹכַח בֵּית הַמֶּלֶךְ: נֹכַח בֵּית הַמִּקְדָּשׁ, דְּכָל יִשְׂרָאֵל צְרִיכִין לְצַלָּאָה צְלוֹתָא דִּלְהוֹן לְתַמָּן, וּלְמֶהֱוֵי נֹכַח בֵּית הַמִּקְדָּשׁ. הָכָא מַאן חֲצַר הַפְּנִימִית. וַדַּאי תְּרֵין אִינוּן חַצְרוֹת בֵּית יְיָ'.

23. Rabbi Shimon said: Of these cities (also: 'courts') it is written: "And stood in the inner court of the king's house, over against the king's house" (Ester 5:1). Everywhere when it is written IN THE SCROLL, 'the King' — without a name — it refers to the Holy One, blessed be He. "And stood": standing means in prayer. "…over against the king's house," MEANING facing the Temple, as all Yisrael are obligated to pray there facing the Temple. And here, what is THE MEANING OF the inner court? Assuredly, there are two courts of the House of Hashem, AN OUTER AND INNER. YET YOU SAY THAT THE HOUSES OF THE COURTYARD WERE OUTER.

24. אָמַר לֵיהּ בּוּצִינָא קַדִּישָׁא, תְּרֵין חֲצֵרִים, אִינוּן חִצוֹנִיִּים דְּלִבָּא, וְאִינוּן תְּרֵין אָזְנִים דְּלִבָּא. וּתְרֵין בָּתִּים פְּנִימִיִּים, תְּרֵין בָּתֵּי דְלִבָּא. וּתְרֵין אִינוּן בָּתֵּי גּוּוָאֵי, וּתְרֵין אִינוּן בָּתֵּי בָרָאֵי. וּבְזִמְנָא דִּיהֵא פּוּרְקָנָא, גְּאוּלָה תְּהֵא לְכֻלְּהוּ לְאִינוּן קְרִיבִין לְלִבָּא, דְּאִיהוּ שְׁכִינְתָּא, וּלְאִלֵּין רְחִיקִין דְּאִתְקְרִיבוּ, הַהִ"ד שָׁלוֹם שָׁלוֹם לָרָחוֹק וְלַקָּרוֹב, וְאוֹקְמוּהָ לָרָחוֹק מֵעֲבֵירָה, וְלַקָּרוֹב מִמִּצְוָה.

24. The holy luminary said to him: The two courtyards refer to the outer part of the heart, MEANING THE OUTER PART OF MALCHUT, representing two handles of the heart. The two inner chambers represent two chambers of the heart, DENOTING THE INNER PART OF MALCHUT. The inner are two and

the outer are two. At the time of the Redemption, the Redemption will be for all of them: those close to the heart, which is the Shechinah, and those from afar who came near, since this is the essence of the verse, "Peace, Peace, both for far and near" (Yeshayah 57:19). And we explained it as far, from the midst of sin, to the near, from the midst of performing a precept.

6. Blowing the Shofar on the Jubilee

A Synopsis

Rabbi Shimon says that at the time of Redemption it will be a precept to blow the Shofar on the Jubilee; then all of Yisrael will assemble from the four points of the earth. He tells how the priests, the Levites and the children of Yisrael all fulfilled their appointed functions. He describes the first 51 precepts in detail.

25. בְּהַהוּא זִמְנָא, פִּקוּדָא לִתְקוֹעַ שׁוֹפַר תְּרוּעָה בְּיוֹבֵל, הה״ד כְּנָשׂא נֵס הָרִים תִּרְאוּ וְכִתְקוֹעַ שׁוֹפָר תִּשְׁמָעוּ. כְּגַוְונָא דְּבִתְקִיעַת שׁוֹפָר דְּיוֹבְלָא, כֻּלְּהוּ עַבְדִּין נָפְקֵי לְחֵירוּת, הָכִי בְּפוּרְקָנָא בַּתְרַיְיתָא, בִּתְקִיעַת שׁוֹפָר, מִתְכַּנְּשִׁין כָּל יִשְׂרָאֵל מֵאַרְבַּע סִטְרֵי עָלְמָא, דְּאִינוּן עַבְדִּין דְּיוֹבְלָא. דְּמָארֵי תּוֹרָה, אִית בְּהוֹן עַבְדִּין עַל מְנָת לְקַבֵּל פְּרָס, וְאִתְקְרִיאוּ עַבְדֵי מַלְכָּא וּמַטְרוֹנִיתָא. אֲבָל בְּנוֹי דְּמַלְכָּא קַדִּישָׁא, וָאֶשָּׂא אֶתְכֶם עַל כַּנְפֵי נְשָׁרִים וָאָבִיא אֶתְכֶם אֵלָי, דְּאִינוּן גַּדְפֵי חֵיוָון דִּמְרְכַּבְתָּא.

25. At that time OF REDEMPTION, it will be a precept to blow the Shofar on the Jubilee. As it is written: "see, when he lifts up a banner on the mountains; and when he blows a Shofar, hear!" (Yeshayah 18:3). For as with the blowing of the Shofar of Jubilee all slaves go free, so is the final Redemption. Through the blowing of the Shofar, all of Yisrael will assemble from the four points of the earth, since they are slaves until the Jubilee, THE SECRET OF THE LIGHT REDEMPTION. Among masters of Torah there are ALSO slaves on the condition of receiving payment, and they are called 'slaves of the King and Queen'. But of the children of the Holy King, it is written: "I bore you on eagles' wings, and brought you to Myself" (Shemot 19:4), MEANING on the wings of the living creatures of the Chariot.

26. פִּקוּדָא בָּתַר דָּא, לָתֵת לַלְוִיִּם עָרִים לָשֶׁבֶת. וּבְגִין דְּאִינוּן לָא אִשְׁתַּתָּפוּ בַּעֵגְלָא, קוּדְשָׁא בְּרִיךְ הוּא חָלַק לוֹן לְגַבֵּיהּ. לְמֶהֱוֵי מְנַגְּנִין לֵיהּ בְּכַמָּה מִינֵי נִגּוּן. דְּכֹהֲנִים בַּעֲבוֹדָתָן, וּלְוִיִּם לְשִׁירָם וּלְזִמְרָם, וְיִשְׂרָאֵל לְנַוֵּיהֶם. כֹּהֲנִים בַּעֲבוֹדָתָם, דְּאִית תַּמָּן כַּמָּה פִקוּדִין.

26. The precept after this is to give the Levites cities of dwelling. Since they did not participate in the sin of the golden calf, the Holy One, blessed be He, set them apart for Himself, to play numerous types of melodies for Him. Thus, the priests fulfilled their function, as did the Levites with song and music, and the children of Yisrael in their dwellings. The priests had numerous commandments.

27. פְּקוּדָא חַד, לַעֲשׂוֹת שֶׁמֶן הַמִּשְׁחָה. ב', לְוִיִּם שׁוֹמְרִין בַּמִּקְדָּשׁ. ג' יִשְׂרָאֵל לִירָא מִן הַמִּקְדָּשׁ. ד', עֲבוֹדַת הַלְוִיִּם בְּבֵית הַמִּקְדָּשׁ. ה', לְהַקְטִיר קְטֹרֶת פַּעֲמַיִם. ו', כֹּהֲנִים תּוֹקְעִים בַּחֲצוֹצְרוֹת בַּמִּקְדָּשׁ. ז', לְקַדֵּשׁ זֶרַע אַהֲרֹן בַּמִּקְדָּשׁ. ח', לִלְבּוֹשׁ בִּגְדֵי כְהוּנָה בַּמִּקְדָּשׁ. ט', רְחִיצַת יָדַיִם וְרַגְלַיִם, לַעֲבוֹד בַּמִּקְדָּשׁ.

27. The first precept is to make the anointing oil. The second is for the Levites to guard in the Temple. The third is for Yisrael to revere the Temple. The fourth concerns the service of the Levites in the Temple. The fifth is to burn incense twice daily. The sixth is for the priests to blow the trumpets in the Temple. The seventh is to sanctify the seed of Aaron in the Temple. The eighth is to wear priestly garments in the Temple. The ninth is the washing of hands and feet for worship in the Temple.

28. י', לִהְיוֹת הַכֹּהֲנִים עוֹשִׂים קָרְבָּנוֹת בַּמִּקְדָּשׁ. י"א, לִפְדּוֹת פְּסוּלֵי הַמֻּקְדָּשִׁין. י"ב, קָרְבַּן הַיּוֹלֶדֶת בַּיּוֹם הַשְּׁמִינִי. י"ג, לִמְלוֹחַ קָרְבָּנוֹת בַּמִּקְדָּשׁ. י"ד, לַעֲשׂוֹת הָעוֹלָה כְּמִשְׁפָּטָהּ. ט"ו, לַעֲשׂוֹת הַחַטָּאת כְּמִשְׁפָּטוֹ. ט"ז, אֲכִילַת קֳדָשִׁים כְּמִשְׁפָּט לַכֹּהֲנִים. י"ז, אֲכִילַת שְׁיָרֵי מְנָחוֹת. ח"י, לַעֲשׂוֹת מְנָחוֹת כְּמִצְוָותָן. י"ט, לְהָבִיא קָרְבָּנוֹת לְבֵית הַמִּקְדָּשׁ. כ', לְהָבִיא נֶדֶר אוֹ נְדָבָה לְבֵית הַמִּקְדָּשׁ. כ"א, לְהָבִיא קָרְבָּנוֹת קֳדָשִׁים תְּמוּרוֹת וּוְלָדוֹת. כ"ב, לְהַקְרִיב שְׁנֵי תְמִידִין כְּהִלְכָתָן. כ"ג, לְהַדְלִיק אֵשׁ תָּמִיד עַל הַמִּזְבֵּחַ.

28. The tenth is for the priests to offer sacrifices in the Temple. The eleventh is to redeem those rejected for offering. The twelfth is the offering of the woman who has given birth on the eighth day. The thirteenth is to strew salt over the sacrifices in the Temple. The fourteenth is to prepare the burnt offering according to its prescribed manner. The fifteenth is to prepare the sin offering according to its prescribed manner. The sixteenth is the eating of the holy things according to the custom of the priests. The seventeenth is the eating of the leftovers of the meal offerings. The eighteenth is to prepare the meal offering according to the prescribed manner. The nineteenth is to bring offerings to the Temple. The twentieth is to bring a vow or a free-will offering. The twenty-first is to bring offerings, holy things, in exchange for the newly born. The twenty-second is to sacrifice two daily offerings according to the prescribed manner. The twenty-third is to burn constant fire on the altar.

29. כ״ד, לַעֲשׂוֹת תְּרוּמַת הַדֶּשֶׁן. כ״ה, לְהַדְלִיק נֵרוֹת הַמְּנוֹרָה. כ״ו, לְהַקְרִיב מִנְחָה בְּכָל יוֹם. כ״ז, לְהַקְרִיב מוּסָף בְּשַׁבָּת. כ״ח, לְהַסְדִּיר לֶחֶם וּלְבוֹנָה. כ״ט, לְהַקְרִיב קָרְבָּן מוּסָף בְּר״ח. ל׳, לְהַקְרִיב בְּז׳ יְמֵי הַפֶּסַח. ל״א, לְהַקְרִיב בְּיוֹם הָעוֹמֶר כֶּבֶשׂ לְעוֹלָה. ל״ב, לְהַקְרִיב הָעוֹמֶר. ל״ג, לְהַקְרִיב קָרְבָּן מוּסָף בְּשָׁבוּעוֹת. ל״ד, לְהַקְרִיב שְׁתֵּי הַלֶּחֶם בְּשָׁבוּעוֹת ל״ה, לְהַקְרִיב מוּסָף בְּר״ה. ל״ו, לְהַקְרִיב מוּסָף בְּיוֹם הַכִּפּוּרִים. ל״ז, לְהַקְרִיב מוּסָף בְּז׳ יְמֵי הֶחָג. ל״ח, לְהַקְרִיב מוּסָף בִּשְׁמִינִי עֲצֶרֶת. ט״ל, לִשְׂרוֹף אֶת הַנּוֹתָר בָּאֵשׁ. מ׳, לִשְׂרוֹף קָדָשִׁים שֶׁנִּטְמְאוּ. מ״א, לַעֲבוֹד כֹּהֵן גָּדוֹל בְּיוֹם הַכִּפּוּרִים.

29. The twenty-fourth is to take of the ashes. The twenty-fifth is to light the candles of the candelabra. The twenty-sixth is to offer a meal offering daily. The twenty-seventh is to offer an additional offering on Shabbat. The twenty-eighth is to arrange bread and frankincense. The twenty-ninth is to offer an additional offering on the new moon. The thirtieth is to sacrifice on the seven days of the Pesach (Passover). The thirty-first is to offer a lamb as burnt offering on the day of the Omer. The thirty-second is to offer the Omer. The thirty-third is to offer an additional offering on Shavuot. The thirty-fourth is to offer two loaves of bread on Shavuot. The thirty-fifth is to offer an additional offering on Rosh Hashanah (the Jewish New Year). The thirty-sixth is to offer an additional offering on Yom Kippur (Day of Atonement). The thirty-seventh is to offer an additional sacrifice on the seven days of Sukkot (the holiday of Booths). The thirty-eighth is to offer an additional offering on Shmini Atzeret. The thirty-ninth is to burn the remains in fire. The fortieth is to burn the holy things that became impure. The forty-first concerns the service of the high priest on Yom Kippur.

לּ. מ"ב, הַמּוֹעֵל בַּהֶקְדֵּשׁ קֶרֶן וָחוֹמֶשׁ. מ"ג, קָרְבָּן חַטָּאת. מ"ד, אָשָׁם תָּלוּי עַל סְפֵקוֹ. מ"ה, קָרְבָּן אָשָׁם וַדַּאי, עַל הַיָּדוּעַ. מ"ו, קָרְבָּן עוֹלֶה וְיוֹרֵד. מ"ז, קָרְבָּן סַנְהֶדְרֵי גְדוֹלָה שֶׁטָּעוּ. מ"ח, לְהַקְרִיב הַזָּב אַחַר שֶׁיִּטְהַר. מ"ט, קָרְבָּן זָבָה אַחַר שֶׁתִּטְהַר. נ', קָרְבָּן יוֹלְדוֹת. נ"א, קָרְבָּן מְצוֹרָעִים, מִתַּמָּן וְאֵילָךְ שְׁאָר פְּקוּדִין.

30. The forty-second concerns he who trespasses against Temple property; his punishment is to repay the cost plus one fifth of the cost of the property concerned. The forty-third is the offering of sin offering. The forty-fourth concerns guilt offering, when there is doubt whether a sin was committed. The forty-fifth concerns an offering for a guilt offering, when guilt is undoubted. The forty-sixth is an offering of higher and lesser value. The forty-seventh is the offering of the members of the Sanhedrin, when they made an error. The forty-eighth is for he who had an issue to offer after he is cleansed of the issue. The forty-ninth is the offering of a woman who had an issue after she is cleansed of it. The fiftieth concerns the offering of a woman who gave birth. The fifty-first concerns the offering of the leprous. From there proceed the other precepts.

7. The joining of the Holy One, blessed be He, and the Shechinah

A Synopsis

Rabbi Shimon speaks to the deans of the Yeshiva, telling them how the Shechinah is the sacrifice for God since she comes near Him with each of His Sfirot and with the total connection of male and female. He says that a man without a wife is like a half body and the Shechinah will not rest on him, and that God is not called 'one' unless united with the Shechinah. From the aspect of Atzilut there is no separation between God and the Shechinah, as the Shechinah is His unity, His blessing and His holiness. But when she is outside of Atzilut then she is not one with Him. Rabbi Shimon says a long praise to the Cause of Causes, the Endless Light. He talks about the commandment of fearing the Temple, that concerns the service of the Levites in the Temple, and the commandment of the daily incense to God. He tells us that not all the sages of Torah are equal, nor are all the prophets equal, as some of their prophecies are superior to those of other prophets. Some prophets prophesy from sight, some from hearing, some from the mouth, some from the breath of the nose, and some from the hand. There are also different grades of meaning in the Torah, different levels of sacrifices. Rabbi Shimon says that people must send their offerings to God via the Shechinah, and she distributes to everyone. One should never sacrifice to the Other Side because all the other Elohim are of the world of separation. Rabbi Shimon goes on to say that every kind of incest is equal to worshipping idols of the Other Side, and God separates those who sacrifice to the Other Side from His Name. He gave Yisrael the Torah from His Name, so they should make themselves partners with Him.

31. מָארֵי מְתִיבְתָּאן, בְּאוֹמָאָה עֲלַיְיכוּ, לָא תַּעַדוּ מִנִּי, עַד דְּאַתְקִין קָרְבָּנִין לְקוּדְשָׁא בְּרִיךְ הוּא. דִּשְׁכִינְתָּא אִיהִי קָרְבָּן לַיְיָ', בְּכָל אֵבָר וְאֵבָר דְּמַלְכָּא, בְּחַבּוּרָא שְׁלִים, בִּדְכַר וְנוּקְבָּא. בְּכָל אֵבְרִים, דְּאִינוּן: מִנְהוֹן בְּרֵישָׁא, עַיְינִין בְּעַיְינִין. אוּדְנִין לְגַבֵּי אוּדְנִין. חוֹטָמָא בְּחוֹטָמָא. אַנְפִּין בְּאַנְפִּין. פּוּמָא בְּפוּמָא. כְּגוֹן וַיָּשֶׂם פִּיו עַל פִּיו וְעֵינָיו עַל עֵינָיו. וּבְדָא הֲוָה מְחַיֶּה הַיֶּלֶד. וְהָכִי יְדִין דְּמַלְכָּא, עִם יְדִין דְּמַטְרוֹנִיתָא, גּוּפָא בְּגוּפָא, בְּכָל אֵבְרִים דִּילֵיהּ. קָרְבָּנָא שְׁלִים.

31. The deans of the Yeshiva, under oath you must not go away from me until I prepare a sacrifice to the Holy One, blessed be He. The Shechinah is

the sacrifice (derived from 'bringing near') for the Holy One, blessed be He, since She comes near to Him with each limb of the King, MEANING WITH EACH OF HIS SFIROT, with the total connection of male and female, with all the limbs which there are. Some are from the head: MEANING eyes to eyes, DENOTING CHOCHMAH; ears to ears, DENOTING BINAH; nose to nose, BEING TIFERET; face to face, BEING CHESED AND GVURAH; mouth to mouth, BEING MALCHUT. This is like, "and put his mouth upon his mouth, and his eyes upon his eyes" (II Melachim 4:34); with this he resurrected the child. And so the hands of the King with the hands of the Queen, BEING CHESED AND GVURAH OF THE SIX ENDS, body to body, MEANING TIFERET OF THE SIX ENDS. And with all His limbs, the sacrifice is complete.

32. דְּב"ן בְּלָא אִתְּתָא, פַּלְגוּ גוּפָא אִיהוּ, וּשְׁכִינְתָּא לָא שַׁרְיָא עֲלֵיהּ. הָכִי קוּדְשָׁא בְּרִיךְ הוּא, לָאו אִיהוּ בְּקָרְבְּנָא עִם שְׁכִינְתָּא, בְּכָל יִשְׂרָאֵל, דְּאִינּוּן אַנְשֵׁי מִדּוֹת, דְּאִינּוּן אֵבָרִים דִּילָהּ. עִלַּת הָעִלּוֹת לָא שַׁרְיָא תַּמָּן, וּכְאִלּוּ לָא הֲוָה קוּדְשָׁא בְּרִיךְ הוּא חַד, בָּתַר דְּלָאו אִיהוּ עִם שְׁכִינְתֵּיהּ. וּבְחוּצָה לָאָרֶץ דִּשְׁכִינְתָּא מְרַחֲקָא מִן בַּעְלָהּ, אִתְּמַר כָּל הַדָּר בחו"ל, דּוֹמֶה כְּמִי שֶׁאֵין לוֹ אֱלוֹהַּ. בְּגִין דְּלֵית תַּמָּן קָרְבְּנִין בח"ל. וּלְזִמְנָא דְּקוּדְשָׁא בְּרִיךְ הוּא מִתְקָרֵב עִם שְׁכִינְתֵּיהּ, אִתְקַיַּים בֵּיהּ הַאי קְרָא, בַּיּוֹם הַהוּא יִהְיֶה יְיָ' אֶחָד וּשְׁמוֹ אֶחָד. וְעִלַּת הָעִלּוֹת שַׁרְיָא עָלַיְיהוּ.

32. A man without a wife is a half body, and the Shechinah does not rest upon him. So is the Holy One, blessed be He, when not in proximity with the Shechinah and with all Yisrael since they are virtuous men, since they are His limbs. Then the cause of all causes, DENOTING KETER, does not rest there, and it is as if the Holy One, blessed be He is not One, as He is not with the Shechinah. THE HOLY ONE, BLESSED BE HE IS NOT CALLED 'ONE' IF NOT UNITED WITH THE SHECHINAH. Outside of the land of Yisrael, where the Shechinah is removed from Her husband, they said: 'He who dwells outside the land of Yisrael is like one who has no Elohim, since there are no sacrifices outside the land of Yisrael,' BEING THE SECRET OF THE UNION OF THE HOLY ONE, BLESSED BE HE WITH THE SHECHINAH, AS MENTIONED. And when the Holy One, blessed be He joins with the Shechinah, this verse is fulfilled: "on that day Hashem shall be One, and His Name One" (Zecharyah 14:9). Then the cause of all causes, KETER, dwells upon them.

33. אע״ג דְּתַקִּינוּ אֲבָהָן, צְלוֹתִין בַּאֲתַר דְּקָרְבְּנִין. הַאי אִיהוּ לְקָרְבָא נַפְשִׁין וְרוּחִין וְנִשְׁמָתִין דְּאִינּוּן שִׂכְלִיִּים לְקוּדְשָׁא בְּרִיךְ הוּא וּשְׁכִינְתֵּיה. כְּאֵבָרִין לְגַבֵּי גוּפָא אֲבָל מִסִּטְרָא דְּכוּרְסְיָּין וּמַלְאָכִין, דְּאִינּוּן גּוּפִין וְאֵבָרִין, דִּלְבַר מִמַּלְכָּא וּמִמַּטְרוֹנִיתָא, לֵית תַּמָּן קָרְבְּנָא. וּבְגִין דָּא אִתְּמַר בְּכוּרְסְיָּיא, וַיֹּאמֶר כִּי יָד עַל כֵּס יָה. כְּסֵא כָּבוֹד מָרוֹם מֵרֹאשׁוֹן מְקוֹם מִקְדָּשֵׁנוּ. וְאֵבָרִין בְּפֵרוּדָא מִן גּוּפָא. אִיהוּ לְגוֹ, וְאִינּוּן לְבַר. הה״ד, הֵן אֶרְאֶלָּם צָעֲקוּ חֻצָה, חוּצָה וַדַּאי.

33. Even though the fathers instituted prayers in place of sacrifices, this was to bring Nefeshot, Ruchot, and Neshamot, which are mental, near to the Holy One, blessed be He, and His Shechinah, like limbs to a body, AS MENTIONED ABOVE. But from the standpoint of the Throne, DEPICTING BRIYAH, and the angels, BEING YETZIRAH, that are bodies and limbs outside of the King and Queen, there is no sacrifice. For this reason, it is said regarding the Throne, "Because Yah has sworn by His Throne (Heb. *kes*)" (Shemot 17:16), MEANING '*KES*' SPELLED WITHOUT THE *ALEPH*. BUT IN REGARDS TO THE TEMPLE, "THRONE" IS SPELLED WITH THE *ALEPH*, AS IT SAYS: "A glorious Throne (Heb. *kise*) exalted from the beginning is the place of our Sanctuary" (Yirmeyah 17:12). THE *ALEPH* WAS MISSING FROM THE THRONE BECAUSE the limbs, WHICH ARE THE ANGELS AND THE THRONE IN BRIYAH, ARE apart from the body, since He, THE HOLY ONE, BLESSED BE HE, is inside, IN ATZILUT, and they are outside, as the verse says, "Behold, the mighty ones shall cry outside" (Yeshayah 33:7); literally outside, MEANING OUTSIDE OF THE HOLY ONE, BLESSED BE HE.

34. יְהֵא רַעֲוָא דִּילָךְ, לְאַחְזְרָא לָן לְבֵי מַקְדְּשָׁא, לְקַיֵּים צְלוֹתָא דְּאוֹקִמוּהָ קַדְמָאֵי, יר״מ יְיָ׳ אֱלֹקֵינוּ וֵאלֹקֵי אֲבוֹתֵינוּ שֶׁתַּעֲלֵנוּ בְּשִׂמְחָה לְאַרְצֵנוּ וְתִטָּעֵנוּ בִּגְבוּלֵנוּ וְשָׁם נַעֲשֶׂה לְפָנֶיךָ אֶת קָרְבְּנוֹת חוֹבוֹתֵינוּ תְּמִידִין כְּסִדְרָן, כָּל חַד בְּסִדּוּרָא דִּילֵיהּ, וּמוּסָפִין כְּהִלְכָתָן. דִּכְעַן לְבַר מֵאַרְעָא דְּיִשְׂרָאֵל, לֵית תַּמָּן קָרְבְּנִין, כְּגוּפִין דִּבְרִיאָה, דְּקוּדְשָׁא בְּרִיךְ הוּא וּשְׁכִינְתֵּיה, מִסִּטְרָא דַּאֲצִילוּת דִּילֵיהּ, לֵית תַּמָּן פֵּרוּדָא וְאִפְרָשׁוּתָא. דִּשְׁכִינְתָּא אִיהִי יְחוּדֵיהּ, וּבִרְכָתֵיהּ, וּקְדוּשָׁתֵיהּ. וְלָא

אִתְקְרִיאַת גּוּפָא, אֶלָּא כַּד אִתְגַּשְׁמוּ בְּכוּרְסַיָּין, וּמַלְאָכִין דִּבְרִיאָה, כְּנִשְׁמָתָא דְּאִתְלַבְּשָׁא בְּגוּפָא שְׁפָלָה. וּבְגִין דָּא, כַּד שְׁכִינְתָּא אִיהִי לְבַר מֵהֵיכָלָא דְּבֵי מַקְדְּשָׁא, וּלְבַר מִכּוּרְסַיָּין דִּילָהּ, כִּבְיָכוֹל כְּאִלּוּ לָא הֲוָה חַד עִמֵּיהּ.

34. 'May it please You to return us to the Temple to fulfill the prayer composed by the ancient ones. May it please You, Hashem our Elohim, and the Elohim of our fathers, to bring us up in joy to our land, and to plant us within its borders. There we offer to You our obligatory sacrifices, the daily burnt offerings according to their order,' each one to its order, THE ONE IN THE MORNING AND THE OTHER IN THE AFTERNOON, '...and the Musaf offerings according to their rule...' Now in the exile there are no sacrifices such as bodies of Briyah, WHICH ARE THE THRONE, AND YETZIRAH, WHICH ARE THE ANGELS, AS MENTIONED – TO WHICH SACRIFICES AND UNION DO NOT PERTAIN. As for the Holy One, blessed be He, and His Shechinah, from His aspect of Atzilut, there is no separation or division, as the Shechinah is His unity, His blessing, and His Holiness. She is called 'body,' only when THE SHECHINAH CLOTHES HERSELF AND manifests Herself in a throne and in the angels of Briyah, she is to them like a soul clothed in a LOWLY humble body. And therefore, when the Shechinah is outside of the chamber of the Temple and outside of Her Thrones, MEANING OUTSIDE OF ATZILUT, MEANING WHEN SHE IS CLOTHED IN A THRONE, AND IN THE ANGELS OF BRIYAH AND YETZIRAH, She is, so to speak, as if She is not One with Him.

35. מִסִּטְרָא דְּכָסֵּא עִלָּוֹן דְּאִיהוּ גּוּפָא לְקוּדְשָׁא בְּרִיךְ הוּא, וּמַלְאָכִין דְּתַלְיָין מִנֵּיהּ, כְּאֶבְרִין דְּתַלְיָין מִן גּוּפָא, דְּאִינּוּן דְּכוּרִין. וְנִשְׁמָתִין דְּאִתְגְּזְרוּ מִנֵּיהּ דְּכוּרִין. כָּסֵּא תִּנְיָינָא, גּוּפָא דִּשְׁכִינְתָּא, וְכָל נִשְׁמָתִין דְּתַלְיָין מִנֵּיהּ, נוּקְבִין. וּמַלְאָכִין דְּתַלְיָין מֵהַהוּא כּוּרְסַיָּיא, נוּקְבִין. וְקָרִיבוּ דִּלְהוֹן בְּקוּדְשָׁא בְּרִיךְ הוּא וּשְׁכִינְתֵּיהּ.

35. From the aspect of the supernal Throne OF BRIYAH – THE SECRET OF TIFERET OF BRIYAH, which is a body AND RAIMENT to the Holy One blessed be He, TIFERET OF ATZILUT – the angels OF YETZIRAH that come down from it are the limbs that protrude from the body, TIFERET OF BRIYAH, which are masculine, and the souls that are formed from it,

TIFERET OF BRIYAH, are masculine. The other Throne, MALCHUT OF BRIYAH, is the body of the Shechinah, MALCHUT OF ATZILUT. All the souls that come from Her are females, and the angels OF YETZIRAH that come from the SECOND Throne are females. Their union, THAT IS, THE JOINING OF THESE MALES AND FEMALES, depends upon the Holy One, blessed be He, and His Shechinah; THAT IS, WHEN THE HOLY ONE, BLESSED BE HE, IS UNITED WITH HIS SHECHINAH, THEY ARE UNITED AS WELL.

36. הָכִי יִחוּד קוּדְשָׁא בְּרִיךְ הוּא וּשְׁכִינְתֵּיה, אע״ג דְּאִינּוּן כְּנִשְׁמָתִין לְגַבֵּי כּוּרְסְיָיא וּמַלְאָכִין, הָכִי אִינּוּן לְגַבָּךְ עִלַּת הָעִלּוֹת, כְּגוּפָא, דְּאַנְתְּ הוּא דִּמְיַיחֵד לוֹן, וּמְקָרֵב לוֹן, וּבְגִין דָּא אֱמוּנָה דִּילָךְ בְּהוֹן, וְאַנְתְּ לֵית עֲלָךְ נִשְׁמָתָא, דְּתֶהֱוֵי אַנְתְּ כְּגוּפָא לְגַבָּהּ, דְּאַנְתְּ הוּא נִשְׁמָה לַנְשָׁמוֹת, וְלֵית נִשְׁמָה עֲלָךְ, וְלָא אֱלָהָא עֲלָךְ, אַנְתְּ לְבַר מִכֹּלָּא, וּלְגָאו מִכֹּלָּא, וּלְכָל סִטְרָא, וּלְעֵילָא מִכֹּלָּא, וּלְתַתָּא מִכֹּלָּא. וְלֵית אֱלָהָא אָחֳרָא, עֵילָא וְתַתָּא, וּמִכֹּל סִטְרָא, וּמִלְגּוֹ דַּעֲשַׂר סְפִירָן, דְּמִנְהוֹן כֹּלָּא, וּבְהוֹן כֹּלָּא תַּלְיָא וְאַנְתְּ בְּכָל סְפִירָה, בְּאָרְכָּה וְרָחְבָּה, עֵילָא וְתַתָּא, וּבֵין כָּל סְפִירָה וּסְפִירָה, וּבְעוֹבִי דְּכָל סְפִירָה וּסְפִירָה.

36. Thus is the union between the Holy One, blessed be He, and His Shechinah. Though they are as souls in relation to the Throne and the angels, they are to You the Cause of Causes, (THE ENDLESS LIGHT,) as a body AND RAIMENT. For it is You who unites them and attracts them, and hence WE ACCEPT our Faith in You, WHEN YOU ARE CLOTHED with them. And there is no soul above You, to which You will be as a body, for You are the Soul of Souls; there is no soul above You, nor any Elohim above You. You are outside everything and inside everything, on every side, above all and below all. There is no other Elohim above, below, in any direction, or inside the ten Sfirot, from which everything comes and upon which everything depends. You are in every Sfirah through its length and width, above and below; You are between the Sfirot and in the thickness of each and every Sfirah.

37. וְאַנְתְּ הוּא דִּמְקָרֵב לְקוּדְשָׁא בְּרִיךְ הוּא וּשְׁכִינְתֵּיה, בְּכָל סְפִירָה וּסְפִירָה, וּבְכָל עַנְפִין דִּנְהוֹרִין דְּתַלְיָין מִנְּהוֹן, כְּגַרְמִין, וְגִידִין, וְעוֹר,

וּבְשַׂר, דְּתַלְיָין מִן גּוּפָא. וְאַנְתְּ לֵית לָךְ גּוּפָא, וְלָא אַבְרִים, וְלֵית לָךְ נוּקְבָּא. אֶלָּא אֶחָד בְּלָא שֵׁנִי. יְהֵא רַעֲוָא דִּילָךְ, דְּתִתְקָרֵב אַנְתְּ שְׁכִינְתָּא לְגַבֵּי קוּדְשָׁא בְּרִיךְ הוּא, בְּכָל דַּרְגִּין דְּאִינּוּן אֲצִילוּת דִּילָהּ, דְּאִינּוּן נִשְׁמָתִין דְּבַעֲלֵי מִדּוֹת. נְשִׂיאֵי יִשְׂרָאֵל. חֲכָמִים. נְבוֹנִים. חֲסִידִים. גִּבּוֹרִים. אַנְשֵׁי אֱמֶת. נְבִיאִים. צַדִּיקִים. מְלָכִים. כֻּלְּהוּ דַּאֲצִילוּת. דְּאִית אָחֳרָנִין דִּבְרִיאָה.

37. It is You who joins AND UNITES the Holy One, blessed be He, and His Shechinah, TIFERET AND MALCHUT, in each and every Sfirah WITHIN THEM, in all the branches of lights that hang from them like bones and sinews, skin and flesh, THE SECRET OF CHOCHMAH AND BINAH, TIFERET AND MALCHUT that come from the body, TIFERET. But You have no body, no limbs, WHICH ARE SFIROT; You have no female, but are one without a second. May it please You to draw the Shechinah near the Holy One, blessed be He, in all the grades that are Her Atzilut, the souls of the virtuous, NAMELY MEN WHO CONCEIVED THE GRADES OF THE TEN SFIROT: the rulers of Yisrael, KETER; the sages, CHOCHMAH; the intelligent, BINAH; the pious, CHESED; the mighty, GVURAH; men of truth, TIFERET; prophets, NETZACH AND HOD; righteous, YESOD; kings, MALCHUT. They all pertain to THE TEN SFIROT OF Atzilut, and there are others OF THE TEN SFIROT of Briyah.

38. דִּשְׁכִינְתָּא אִיהִי קָרְבָּן, שֶׁמֶן הַמִּשְׁחָה. מִימִינָא שֶׁמֶן לַמָּאוֹר, כְּגוֹן אֶת הַמָּאוֹר הַגָּדוֹל. שֶׁמֶן מִשְׁחַת קֹדֶשׁ אִיהוּ מִסִּטְרָא דִּשְׂמָאלָא, דְּאִתְּמַר בָּהּ וְקִדַּשְׁתָּ אֶת הַלְוִיִּם. שֶׁמֶן כָּתִית, אִיהִי מִסִּטְרָא דְּצַדִּיק, דְּאִיהוּ כָּתִישׁ כְּתִישִׁין מֵאַבְרִין דְּאִינּוּן זֵיתִים, לְאַחֲתָא מִשְׁחָא לְגַבֵּי פְּתִילָה. פְּתִילָה תֵּכְלָא. וּגְבוּרָה מִתַּמָּן אִיהִי יִרְאָה, וּלְוִיִּם שׁוֹמְרִין הַמִּקְדָּשׁ.

38. For the Shechinah is an offering, THE SECRET OF the anointing oil. On the right, there is oil for the light, as in "the greater luminary" (Beresheet 1:16), CHESED; the holy anointing oil is on the left side, GVURAH, of which it says that you shall consecrate the Levites. The beaten oil is from the side of the Righteous, YESOD, THE CENTRAL COLUMN, that beats finely the limbs, which are olives, to produce oil to the wick. The wick is blue and signifies THE LOWER Gvurah, NAMELY MALCHUT, whence fear comes. The Levites, THE ASPECT OF GVURAH, guard the Temple.

39. וּמִתַּמָּן פְּקוּדָא לְיִרָא מִן הַמִּקְדָּשׁ, וְאִיהוּ מִצְוַת עֲבוֹדַת הַלְוִיִם בְּמִקְדָּשׁ בְּכ"ד מִשְׁמָרוֹת לְוִיִם דִּבְהוֹן לְוִיִם בְּשִׁירָה וּבְזִמְרָה הֲווֹ מְזַמְּרִין קֳדָמָךְ, לְסַלְּקָא שְׁכִינְתָּא דְּאִיהִי שִׁירָה וְזִמְרָה בְּהוֹן לַיְיָ'. כ"ד עִם שִׁירָה וְזִמְרָה כ"ו, כְּחוּשְׁבָּן יְדֹנָ"ד. וַאֲבַתְרֵיהּ פְּקוּדָא אִיהִי מִצְוַת קְטֹרֶת תָּמִיד לְקוּדְשָׁא בְּרִיךְ הוּא, וּקְטֹרֶת כְּקַרְבְּנָא.

39. This is the origin of the commandment of fearing the Temple. It is the commandment concerning the service of the Levites in the Temple in the 24 watches of the Levites, in which the Levites sang chants and hymns before You, with which to raise the Shechinah, CALLED 'chanting and singing to Hashem'. 24, OF THE TWENTY-FOUR WATCHE, together with chants and hymns amounts to26, as the numerical value of Yud Hei Vav Hei. AND THE COMMANDMENT that follows it is the commandment of the daily incense to the Holy One, blessed be He. And the burning of the incense is like a sacrifice.

40. וְהִפְשִׁיט אֶת הָעוֹלָה וְנִתַּח אוֹתָהּ לִנְתָחֶיהָ. וְאֵמוּרִין וּפְדָרִין דְּאִינּוּן מִתְאַכְּלִין כָּל הַלַּיְלָה, אִינּוּן כַּפָּרָה דְּאֵבָרִין דְּגוּפָא דִּילֵיהּ וְנַפְשֵׁיהּ, דְּלָא יִתּוֹקְדוּן בְּגֵיהִנָּם, וְלָא יִתְמַסְּרוּן בִּידָא דְּמַלְאָךְ הַמָּוֶת, וּבְגִין דְּב"נ חָב בְּיֵצֶר הָרָע, דְּאִיהוּ צָפוֹנִי, הָכִי שְׁחִיטָתוֹ בַּצָּפוֹן לְשֵׁזָבָא לֵיהּ מֵהַהוּא צָפוֹנִי.

40. "And he shall flay the burnt offering, and cut it into its pieces" (Vayikra 1:6). The limbs and the fats that are consumed all night UPON THE ALTAR atone for the limbs of the body OF THE SACRIFICING MAN and his soul, so that they will not burn in Gehenom, nor be delivered into the hand of the Angel of Death. Since man sins by the Evil Inclination, the northern one, OF WHICH IT SAYS, "BUT I WILL REMOVE FAR OFF FROM YOU THE NORTHERN ONE" (YOEL 2:20), it is slaughtered on the north side to save him from that northern one.

41. וּבְקָרְבְּנִין, טוֹל בְּהוּ קַל וָחוֹמֶר מִנְּבִיאִים, דְאע״ג דְּתוֹרָה אִיהוּ שֵׁם יְהֹו״ה, וּנְבוּאָה דְּאִתְּמַר בָּה רוּחַ יְיָ׳ תְּנִיחֶנּוּ. עִם כָּל דָּא, לָאו כָּל מָארֵי תּוֹרָה שְׁקִילִין, וְלָאו כָּל נְבִיאִים שְׁקִילִין, דְּאִית נְבִיאִים, דִּנְבוּאָה דִּלְהוֹן בִּלְבוּשִׁין דְּמַלְכָּא, וְהָכִי הוּא אוֹרַיְיתָא דבע״פ, כַּמָה מָארֵי סְפֵקוֹת וּפֵרוּקִין, בִּלְבוּשָׁא דְמַלְכָּא.

41. It is so for the sacrifices. Thus, how much more so concerning prophets, that though the Torah is the Name of Yud Hei Vav Hei, and it says of prophecy, "the spirit of Hashem gave them rest" (Yeshayah 63:14). For all that, not all the sages of the Torah are equal, nor are all the prophets equal. The prophecies of some prophets pertain to the King's garments, NAMELY IN THE WORLD OF YETZIRAH, CALLED 'GARMENT'. It is the same for the Oral Law; some people raise doubts and explanations from the King's garment, YETZIRAH.

42. וְאִית אָחֳרָנִין דְּסַלְקִין יַתִּיר, בְּאֵבָרִים דְּגוּפָא דְּמַלְכָּא, דְּאִתְּמַר בְּהוֹן וָאֶרְאֶה, וְרָאִיתִי, בַּמַּרְאֶה, בְּעַיְינִין. יְיָ׳ שָׁמַעְתִּי שִׁמְעֲךָ יָרֵאתִי, בִּשְׁמִיעָה. יְחֶזְקֵאל אִסְתַּכְּלוּתֵיהּ וּנְבִיאוּתֵיהּ מֵעַיְינִין. חֲבַקּוּק מֵאוֹדְנִין בִּשְׁמִיעָה. וּבְגִין דָּא, יְחֶזְקֵאל חָזָא כָּל אִלֵּין מַרְאוֹת דְּמֶרְכָּבָה בִּרְאָיָיה, בְּעֵין הַשֵּׂכֶל. חֲבַקּוּק, בִּשְׁמִיעָה. וְאִית נְבִיאָה דִּנְבוּאָתֵיהּ בְּפוּמָא, הה״ד וַיִּגַּע עַל פִּי. נְבוּאָה אָחֳרָא מֵרֵיחָא דְּחוּטְמָא, הה״ד וַתָּבֹא בִי הָרוּחַ. וְאִית דִּנְבוּאָתֵיהּ בְּיָד, הה״ד וּבְיַד הַנְּבִיאִים אֲדַמֶּה. וְאָחֳרָנִין לִפְנִים בְּחַיֵּי הַמֶּלֶךְ, וְאָחֳרָנִין לִפְנַי לִפְנִים.

42. Some PROPHETS are superior IN THEIR PROPHECIES, which are from the limbs of the King's body, NAMELY OF THE GRADES OF THE WORLD OF BRIYAH CALLED 'BODY'. Of them it says, "and I saw," SINCE THEY PROPHECY through eye sight, WHICH IS CHOCHMAH. ALSO, "Hashem, I have heard the report of You, and I was afraid" (Chavakuk 3:2), pertains to hearing, NAMELY BINAH. Ezekiel saw and prophesied from the eyes, and Habakkuk from ears by hearing. Ezekiel therefore saw all the sights of the Divine Chariot in the vision of his mind's eye; Habakkuk by hearing, AS HE SAID, "HASHEM, I HAVE HEARD THE REPORT OF YOU, AND I WAS AFRAID." There is a prophecy coming from the mouth, WHICH IS IN

MALCHUT, as is written: "and he laid it upon my mouth" (Yeshayah 6:7). Another prophecy comes from the breath of the nose, TIFERET, as it says, "And a spirit (also: 'breath') entered into me" (Yechezkel 2:2). There is he who prophecies from the hand, GVURAH, as is written: "and used similes by the hands of the prophets" (Hoshea 12:11). ALL THESE GRADES PERTAIN TO THE WORLD OF BRIYAH. There are some inside the King's life, NAMELY IN THE WORLD OF ATZILUT, and others in the innermost, NAMELY BINAH OF ATZILUT.

43. וְהָכִי בְּאוֹרַיְיתָא, פְּשָׁטֵי״ם, רְאָיוֹ״ת, דְּרָשׁוֹ״ת, סוֹדוֹ״ת דְּסִתְרֵי תוֹרָה, וּלְעֵילָא סִתְרֵי סְתָרִים לַהּ׳ הָכִי בְּקָרְבְּנִין אע״ג דְּקָרְבְּנִין כֻּלְּהוּ לַיהו״ה, אִיהוּ נָטִיל כֹּלָּא, וּפָלִיג קָרְבְּנִין לְמַשִׁירְיָין דִּילֵיהּ. מִנְהוֹן פָּלִיג לְכַלְבִּים, אִינּוּן קָרְבְּנִין פְּסוּלִין, דְּיָהִיב לְהוֹן לְסָמָא״ל כֶּלֶב, וּלְמַשִׁרְיָיתֵיהּ. וּבְגִין דָּא הֲוָה נָחִית הַיּוּקְנָא דְּכַלְבָּא. וּמִנְהוֹן לְשֵׁדִים, דְּאִית בְּהוֹן כִּבְעִירָן, וּמִנְהוֹן כְּמַלְאֲכֵי הַשָׁרֵת, וּמִנְהוֹן כִּבְנֵי נָשָׁא. לְאִינּוּן דְּעוֹבָדֵהוֹן כְּשֵׁדִים, פָּלִיג קָרְבְּנֵיהוֹן לַשֵׁדִים.

43. It is so with the Torah THAT THERE ARE SEVERAL GRADES, plain meanings; THE SECRET OF ASIYAH, evidences; THE SECRET OF YETZIRAH, homiletics; THE SECRET OF BRIYAH, secrets of the mysteries of the Torah; THE SECRET OF ATZILUT, above ATZILUT are the mysteries of mysteries of Hashem. It is the same with sacrifices. Though all the sacrifices are to Hashem, He receives them and distributes the sacrifices among His legions. Some He gives to the dogs – the unfit offerings which He gives to Samael CALLED 'a dog' – and to his legions. A FIRE then descended UPON THE ALTAR in the shape of a dog. Some He gives to the demons, some of which are like beasts, while others are like the ministering angels, and some yet are like men. For those who act like demons, He deals their offerings to the demons.

44. אִלֵּין דְּעוֹבָדֵיהוֹן כְּמַלְאָכִין, פָּלִיג קָרְבְּנִין דִּלְהוֹן לְמַלְאָכִים, הה״ד אֶת קָרְבָּנִי לַחְמִי לְאִשַּׁי. דְּאִינּוּן קָרְבְּנִין דִּלְהוֹן, לָאו תַּלְיָין בִּבְעִירָן. דְּקָרְבְּנִין דִּבְעִירָן, אִינּוּן דְּעַמֵּי הָאָרֶץ. אִינּוּן קָרְבְּנִין דִּבְנֵי נָשָׁא, צְלוֹתִין וְעוֹבָדִין טָבִין. קָרְבְּנִין דת״ח, מָארֵי מִדּוֹת, אִלֵּין מָארֵי רָזֵי דְּאוֹרַיְיתָא,

-340-

וְסִתְרִין גְּנִיזִין דִּבְהוֹן, קוּדְשָׁא בְּרִיךְ הוּא נָחִית הוּא בְּגַרְמֵיהּ, לְקַבְּלָא קָרְבְּנִין דִּלְהוֹן, דְּאִיהִי תּוֹרַת ה' תְּמִימָה, שְׁכִינְתָּא קַדִּישָׁא, מֵי מִדּוֹת.

44. Those whose deeds are like those of the angels, He distributes their sacrifices among the angels. Hence, it says, "My offering, the provision of My sacrifices made by (also: 'to my') fires" (Bemidbar 28:2), NAMELY TO THE ANGELS CALLED 'FIRES,' as their offerings are not of animals, since animal offerings are made by the illiterate. Human offerings are prayers and good deeds, the offerings of students of the Law, men of virtue, those who know secrets of the Torah and the mysteries hidden therein. The Holy One, blessed be He, Himself descends to receive their sacrifices, which are "The Torah of Hashem is perfect" (Tehilim 19:8), the Holy Shechinah, WHICH HAS ten Sfirot.

45. וְתַלְמִידֵי דְרַבָּנָן, אִינּוּן מִלִּין דִּלְהוֹן כַּאֲכִילַת שְׁיָרֵי מִנְחוֹת, וְאִית אָחֳרָנִין דְּמִתְגַּבְּרִין עֲלַיְיהוּ, דְּאוֹרַיְיתָא דִּלְהוֹן כַּאֲכִילַת מִנְחוֹת עַצְמָן, וְלָא שְׁיָרֵי מִנְחוֹת. וְאִית אָחֳרָנִין דְּאוֹרַיְיתָא דִּלְהוֹן אֲכִילַת קָדְשִׁים, מַאֲכָלִים מִכַּמָּה מִינִין לְמַלְכָּא. וְכָל מִנְחוֹת דִּמְאַכְלִין דְּקַרְבְּנִין, מָנֵי קוּדְשָׁא בְּרִיךְ הוּא לְקָרְבָא לֵיהּ כֻּלְּהוּ בְּבֵיתָא דִּילֵיהּ, דְּאִיהִי שְׁכִינְתָּא. וְהַאי אִיהוּ פִּקּוּדָא לְקָרְבָא קָרְבָּנוֹת בְּבֵית הַבְּחִירָה, לְקַיֵּים כִּי אִם בְּזֹאת יִתְהַלֵּל הַמִּתְהַלֵּל וְגוֹ'.

45. The words of the students of the teachers are like the remnants of the meal offerings. Others of greater strength, their Torah study is like the meal offerings proper, not their remnants. There are others whose Torah is eating the holy things and several victuals that are before the King. All the meal offerings and the dishes of offerings the Holy One, blessed be He, commanded to offer in His House, the Shechinah. This is the precept of bringing offering in the Temple, THE SHECHINAH, so that the verse will be fulfilled, "but let him that glories glory in this" (Yirmeyah 9:23), NAMELY IN THE SHECHINAH CALLED 'THIS'.

46. לְמַלְכָּא דַּהֲווֹ עַבְדּוֹי וַאֲפַרְכְּסוֹי וְשׁוּלְטָנֵי מַלְכוּתָא שַׁלְחֵי לֵיהּ כַּמָּה

דּוֹרוֹנֵי, אָמַר, מַאן דְּבָעֵי לְמִשְׁלַח לִי דּוֹרוֹנָא, לָא יְשַׁלַּח אֶלָּא בִּידָא
דְּמַטְרוֹנִיתָא, לְקַיֵּים בָּהּ וּמַלְכוּתוֹ בַּכֹּל מָשָׁלָה. וּבְג״ד אִתְקְרִיאַת
שְׁכִינְתָּא קָרְבָּן לַה׳, עוֹלָה לַה׳, אָשָׁם לַה׳, וַאֲפִילוּ קָרְבָּן נִדּוֹת וְיוֹלְדוֹת
וּמְצוֹרָעִים וְזָבִים וְזָבוֹת, כֹּלָּא צָרִיךְ לְקָרְבָא לַיְיָ׳, וּשְׁכִינְתֵּיהּ, וּלְבָתַר
אִיהִי פְּלִיגַת לְכֹלָּא הה״ד וַתִּתֵּן טֶרֶף לְבֵיתָהּ וְחֹק לְנַעֲרוֹתֶיהָ, וַאֲפִילוּ
מְזוֹנָא דְּחֵיוָון, כְּגוֹן קָרְבָּן שְׂעוֹרִים מַאֲכָל בְּעִירָן, וּמַאֲכַל עֲבָדִים
וּשְׁפָחוֹת דְּבֵי מַלְכָּא, וַאֲפִילוּ דְּכַלְבֵּי וּדְחַמְרֵי וּגְמַלֵּי, לְקַיֵּים בָּהּ
וּמַלְכוּתוֹ בַּכֹּל מָשָׁלָה. וּמְנָלָן דְּעַל יְדָהָא פָּלִיג כֹּלָּא, דִּכְתִיב וַתִּתֵּן טֶרֶף
לְבֵיתָהּ וְחֹק לְנַעֲרוֹתֶיהָ.

46. THIS IS LIKE a king whose servants, ministers, and governors sent him gifts. He said, 'he who wishes to send me a gift shall do so solely through the queen, so that the verse shall be fulfilled by her, "and His kingdom rules over all" (Tehilim 103:19). The Shechinah is therefore called 'an offering to Hashem', 'a burnt offering to Hashem', 'a guilt offering to Hashem', and even 'offerings for an unclean thing'. For mothers, lepers, and men and women who have an issue, everything should be sacrificed to Hashem and His Shechinah. THE SHECHINAH then distributes to everybody, as is written: "and gives food to her household, and a portion to her maidens" (Mishlei 31:15). She even gives the food for the animals, such as an offering of barley, which is food for animals, and the food of slaves and maids of the King's house, and even of dogs, mules, and camels, WHICH ARE KLIPOT. SHE GIVES EVERYTHING, so that it shall be fulfilled by Her, "and His kingdom rules over all." Whence do we know that through Her everything is distributed? As it is written: "and gives food to her household, and a portion to her maidens."

47. בְּגִין דְּקוּדְשָׁא בְּרִיךְ הוּא בֵּן י״ה, ו׳ בֶּן י״ה, כָּלִיל יה״ו. וְשַׁלִּימוּ
דִּילֵיהּ ה׳, אִיהִי עוֹלָה לַידֹנ״ד. קָרְבָּן לַידֹנ״ד. שְׁלָמִים לַיְיָ׳. קָרִיבוּ
דִּילֵיהּ, שְׁלִימוּ דִּילֵיהּ, דְּבֵיהּ אַשְׁלִים יה״ו, לְמֶהֱוֵי יְדֹנ״ד.

47. Since the Holy One, blessed be He, ZEIR ANPIN, is the son of *Yud-Hei*, CHOCHMAH AND BINAH, NAMELY *Vav*, the son of *Yud-Hei*, ZEIR ANPIN, THEN comprises *Yud-Hei-Vav* and is perfected by *Hei*, MALCHUT, SINCE

THEN THE NAME YUD HEI VAV HEI IS COMPLETED. MALCHUT therefore is a burnt offering to Yud Hei Vav Hei; an offering to Yud Hei Vav Hei; peace offerings to Yud Hei Vav Hei. For she is brought near (Heb. *kirvah*) Him, NAMELY AN OFFERING (HEB. *KORBAN*), His perfection (Heb. *shlemut*), NAMELY PEACE OFFERINGS (HEB. *SHLAMIM*), since through her *Yud-Hei-Vav* is completed into Yud Hei Vav Hei.

48. וְכֹלָּא אִתְהֲדָר בֵּיהּ, וּבְגִין דָּא זוֹבֵחַ לָאֱלֹהִים יָחֳרָם, בִּלְתִּי לַיְדֹנָ"ד לְבַדּוֹ, דְּלָא יָהִיב שׁוּלְטָנוּתָא לְסִטְרָא אָחֳרָא בְּקָרְבָּנָא, דְּכָל אֱלֹהִים אֲחֵרִים עָלְמָא דִּפְרוּדָא אִינוּן, וְלֵית לוֹן קְרִיבָא וְיִחוּדָא, וְקוּדְשָׁא בְּרִיךְ הוּא אַפְרִישׁ לוֹן מִשְּׁמֵיהּ, בְּגוֹן דְּאַפְרִישׁ חֹשֶׁךְ מֵאוֹר, הה"ד וַיַּבְדֵּל אֱלֹהִים בֵּין הָאוֹר וּבֵין הַחֹשֶׁךְ. וּמַאן דְּקָרִיב לְקוּדְשָׁא בְּרִיךְ הוּא מַה דְּאַפְרִישׁ, כְּמַאן דְּקָרִיב מְסָאֲבוּ דְּנִדָּה לְבַעְלָהּ, וְהַאי אִיהוּ רָזָא וְאֶל אִשָּׁה בְּנִדַּת טוּמְאָתָהּ לֹא תִקְרַב לְגַלּוֹת עֶרְוָתָהּ.

48. Everything comes back TO YUD HEI VAV HEI, and therefore, "He that sacrifices to any Elohim, save Hashem only, he shall be utterly destroyed" (Shemot 22:19). For he is not to give strength to the Other Side through a sacrifice, as all the other Elohim are of the world of separation and have no closeness and unison, and the Holy One, blessed be He, separated them from His Name. THAT IS, He separated darkness from light, as is written, "and Elohim divided the light from the darkness" (Beresheet 1:4). He who brings close that which the Holy One, blessed be He, separated, is like he who joins a woman impure with her menstrual flow to her husband. This is the secret meaning of "Also you shall not approach a woman in the impurity of her menstrual flow" (Vayikra 18:19).

49. וְהַאי לֹא תְגַלֶּה עֶרְוָתָן, קֵירוּב, דְּכָל עֶרְיָין שְׁקִילִין לע"ז, דְּכָל סִטְרִין אָחֳרָנִין, עֲלַיְיהוּ אִתְּמָר, מֵאֵלֶּה נִפְרְדוּ אִיֵּי הַגּוֹיִם בְּאַרְצוֹתָם. וּכְתִיב לִלְשׁוֹנוֹתָם בְּאַרְצוֹתָם בְּגוֹיֵהֶם. וּכְתִיב כִּי שָׁם בָּלַל יְיָ' שְׂפַת כָּל הָאָרֶץ וּמִשָּׁם הֱפִיצָם יְדֹנָ"ד. וְכָל מַאן דְּקָרִיב שׁוּם קָרְבָּנָא לְסִטְרִין אָחֳרָנִין, קוּדְשָׁא בְּרִיךְ הוּא אַפְרִישׁ לֵיהּ מִשְּׁמֵיהּ, וְלֵית לֵיהּ חוּלָקָא בִּשְׁמֵיהּ. דְּקוּדְשָׁא בְּרִיךְ הוּא בָּחַר לוֹן לְיִשְׂרָאֵל מִכָּל שְׁאָר אוּמִין,

הה"ד וּבְךָ בָּחַר ה'. וּפָלִיג לוֹן מִנַּיְיהוּ לְחוּלָקֵיהּ, הה"ד כִּי חֵלֶק יְיָ' עַמּוֹ.

49. This is the reason for not uncovering their nakedness, WHICH MEANS nearness, as every kind of incest is equal to worshipping idols of all the Other Side, of which it says, "By these were the isles of the nations divided in their lands" (Beresheet 10:5), and, "after their tongues, in their lands, in their nations" (Ibid. 20.) It is also written, "because Hashem did there confound the language of all the earth: and from thence did Hashem scatter them" (Beresheet 11:9). The Holy One, blessed be He, separates whoever brings an offering to Other Sides from His Name, and he has no portion in His Name, since the Holy One, blessed be He, chose Yisrael from the other nations, as written, "and Hashem has chosen you" (Devarim 14:2) and took them from among them as His portion. Hence it says, "For Hashem's portion is His people" (Devarim 32:9).

50. וּבְגִין דָּא יָהִיב לוֹן אוֹרַיְיתָא מִשְּׁמֵיהּ. זֶה שְׁמִי לְעֹלָם וְזֶה זִכְרִי לְדֹר דֹּר, וְהָא אוּקְמוּהָ י"ה עִם שְׁמִי, שס"ה. ו"ה עִם זִכְרִי, רמ"ח. בְּכָל מִצְוָה וּמִצְוָה, קָשִׁיר לוֹן לְיִשְׂרָאֵל בִּשְׁמֵיהּ, לְמֶהֱוֵי כָּל אֵבֶר וְאֵבֶר דִּלְהוֹן, חוּלָק עַדְבֵּיהּ וְאַחֲסָנְתֵּיהּ. וּבְגִין דָּא זוֹבֵחַ לָאֱלֹהִים יָחֳרָם וְגוֹ'.

50. He therefore gave them the Torah from His own Name, AS IS WRITTEN: "this is My Name (Heb. *shmi*) forever, and this is My memorial (Heb. *zichri*) to all generations" (Shemot 3:15). We have explained this. *Yud-Hei*, together with *shmi*, is 365 IN NUMERICAL VALUE, CORRESPONDING TO THE 365 NEGATIVE PRECEPTS OF THE TORAH. *Vav-Hei*, together with *zichri*, is 248 IN NUMERICAL VALUE, CORRESPONDING TO THE 248 POSITIVE PRECEPTS. With each and every precept, He bound Yisrael to His name, so that each of their members would be a part of His lot and portion. Therefore, "He that sacrifices to any Elohim... he shall be utterly destroyed."

51. צְרִיכִין יִשְׂרָאֵל לְשַׁתְּפָא לַיְיָ', בַּהֲלִיכָה דִּלְהוֹן, בְּהָקִיץ דִּלְהוֹן. הֲדָא הוּא דִּכְתִיב, בְּהִתְהַלֶּכְךָ תַּנְחֶה אוֹתָךְ בְּשָׁכְבְּךָ תִּשְׁמוֹר עָלֶיךָ וַהֲקִיצוֹתָ הִיא תְשִׂיחֶךָ. קָם הַהוּא תַּלְמִידָא וְאִשְׁתְּטַח קַמֵּיהּ, וְאָמַר זַכָּאָה אִיהוּ חוּלָקֵיהּ, דְּמַאן דְּזָכֵי לְמִשְׁמַע מִלִּין אִלֵּין, כֻּלְּהוּ שֵׁם יְיָ' בְּכָל סִטְרָא,

וְלָא נָפִיק מִנֵּיה לְבַר בְּכָל סִטְרוֹי.

ע"כ רעיא מהימנא

51. Yisrael should make themselves partners with Hashem, in their walking and in their waking, as is written: "When you walk, it shall lead you; when you lie down, it shall keep you; and when you awake, it shall talk with you" (Mishlei 6:22). The student rose, prostrated before him and said: Happy is the portion of he who is worthy of hearing these words, which are all the Name of Hashem on every side, of which nothing comes outside any of His sides.

End of Ra'aya Meheimna (the Faithful Shepherd)

8. "And if you shall say, What shall we eat in the seventh year"

A Synopsis

Rabbi Yehuda says that one must do good in order to arouse good deeds above, and that if he is perfect with his Master he can come to no harm through the actions of others in the world. He talks about the importance of Faith, and says that Malchut performs according to the wishes and needs of the faithful; if they give charity without sparing themselves, more blessings will come to them. Thus in the sixth year enough abundance will come that there will be no lack during the seventh year when work ceases.

52. וְכִי תֹּאמְרוּ מַה נֹּאכַל וְגוֹ', רִבִּי יְהוּדָה פָּתַח, בְּטַח בַּיְיָ' וַעֲשֵׂה טוֹב שְׁכָן אֶרֶץ וּרְעֵה אֱמוּנָה. לְעוֹלָם בַּר נָשׁ יְהֵא זָהִיר בְּמָארֵיהּ, וְיִדְבַּק לְבֵיהּ בִּמְהֵימְנוּתָא עִלָּאָה, בְּגִין דִּיהֱוֵי שָׁלִים בְּמָארֵיהּ. דְּכַד יֶהֱוֵי שָׁלִים בֵּיהּ, לָא יַכְלִין לְאַבְאָשָׁא לֵיהּ כָּל בְּנֵי עָלְמָא.

52. "And if you shall say, 'What shall we eat'" (Vayikra 25:20). Rabbi Yehuda opened the discussion with, "Trust in Hashem, and do good; dwell in the land, and enjoy security (lit. 'Faith')" (Tehilim 37:3). Man should always be careful with his Master, and cleave with his heart to the supernal Faith, so as to be perfect with his Master. For when he is perfect with his Master, the inhabitants of the world can do him no harm.

53. תָּא חֲזֵי, בְּטַח בַּיְיָ' וַעֲשֵׂה טוֹב, מַאי וַעֲשֵׂה טוֹב. אֶלָּא. הָכִי תַּנִינָן, בְּעוֹבָדָא דִלְתַתָּא, יִתְעַר עוֹבָדָא דִלְעֵילָא. וְהָא אוּקְמוּהָ, וַעֲשִׂיתֶם אוֹתָם, כִּבְיָכוֹל, אַתּוּן תַּעַבְדוּן לְהוֹן, בְּגִין דְּבַהַהוּא אִתְעָרוּתָא דִּלְכוֹן דְּאַתּוּן עַבְדִין לְתַתָּא, אִתְעַר לְעֵילָא וְעַל דָּא וַעֲשֵׂה טוֹב כְּתִיב, וְאֵין טוֹב, אֶלָּא צַדִּיק, דִּכְתִיב אִמְרוּ צַדִּיק כִּי טוֹב. כֵּיוָן דְּאַתּוּן עַבְדִין הַאי, וַדַּאי הַאי טוֹב יִתְעַר, כְּדֵין שְׁכָן אֶרֶץ וּרְעֵה אֱמוּנָה, וְכֹלָּא חַד.

53. Come and behold: "Trust in Hashem, and do good." What is "and do good"? We have learned that by stirring below, a supernal deed is stirred above. It has already been established that, "and do them," means you shall so to speak do them, since by your deed of stirring below, there is stirring above. Therefore, it is written, "and do good," since good is nothing but the

Righteous, YESOD OF ZEIR ANPIN, as is written, "Say of the righteous that it shall be well (lit. 'good')" (Yeshayah 3:10). When you do this, assuredly this goodness will stir ABOVE. Then, "dwell in the land, and enjoy Faith." And everything is one, AS LAND AND FAITH ARE BOTH MALCHUT.

54. שְׁכָן אֶרֶץ, אֶרֶץ עִלָּאָה. דְּהָא לֵית לָךְ בְּעָלְמָא, דְּיָכוֹל לְמִשְׁרֵי בַּהֲדָהּ, עַד דְּיִתְעַר הַאי טוֹב לְגַבָּהּ, כֵּיוָן דְּיִתְעַר לֵיהּ, כִּבְיָכוֹל הוּא עֲבִיד לֵיהּ, וּכְדֵין שְׁכָן אֶרֶץ, שָׁרֵי בְּגַוָּוהּ, אֵיכוּל אֵיבָהּ, אִשְׁתַּעֲשַׁע בַּהֲדָהּ. וּרְעֵה אֱמוּנָה, דָּא אֶרֶץ וְכֹלָּא חַד כְּמָה דְּאַתְּ אָמֵר וֶאֱמוּנָתְךָ בַּלֵּילוֹת. וּרְעֵה אֱמוּנָה, הֱוֵי דָּבַר לָהּ בְּכָל רְעוּתָךְ.

54. HE EXPLAINS HIS WORDS: "dwell in the land," refers to the supernal land, MALCHUT, since there is none in the world that can dwell with her until that good, YESOD OF ZEIR ANPIN, is stirred towards her, AS MALCHUT WITHOUT YESOD IS FILLED WITH SEVERE JUDGMENTS. Once MAN stirs it BY HIS GOOD DEEDS, it is as if he formed it. Then, "dwell in the land"; dwell inside MALCHUT, eat of her fruit and have pleasure with her. "…and enjoy Faith…" This is the land, NAMELY MALCHUT, AS FAITH AND LAND are all one, MALCHUT, as it is written, "and your faithfulness every night" (Tehilim 92:3), NIGHT BEING MALCHUT. "And enjoy (also: 'guide') Faith," MEANS lead her wherever you wish.

55. וְאִי לָא תִּתְעַר לְקַבְלָהּ, הַאי טוֹב אִתְרְחַק מִנָּהּ, וְלָא תִּקְרַב בַּהֲדָהּ, לָא תִּקְרַב לְגוֹ אַתּוּן נוּרָא יְקִידְתָּא, וְאִי תִּקְרַב בַּהֲדָהּ, בִּדְחִילוּ, כְּמַאן דִּדְחִיל מִן מוֹתָא. דְּהָא כְּדֵין נוּרָא דָּלִיק, וְאוֹקִיד, עָלְמָא בְּשַׁלְהוֹבוֹי. וְכֵיוָן דְּאִתְעַר לְקַבְלָהּ הַאי טוֹב, כְּדֵין, שָׁרֵי בְּגַוָּוהּ, וְלָא תִּדְחַל מִנָּהּ אַנְתְּ, כְּדֵין, וַתִּגְזֹר אֹמֶר וְיָקָם לָךְ וְעַל דְּרָכֶיךָ נָגַהּ אוֹר.

55. If one does not stir YESOD towards her, this goodness, YESOD, stays away from her. Do not approach her THEN, do not come near the furnace of burning fire, SINCE WITHOUT YESOD, SHE IS FILLED WITH JUDGMENTS, LIKE A GLOWING FURNACE. If you do come near her, be fearful, as one fearful of death, since then she is a burning fire that consumes the world with its flames. When one stirs this goodness towards her, he then dwells

inside her and is not afraid of her. Then, "You shall also decree a thing, and it shall be established unto you; and the light shall shine upon your ways" (Iyov 22:28).

56. תָּא חֲזֵי, בְּנֵי מְהֵימְנוּתָא מְדַבְּרֵי לְהַאי לִרְעוּתְהוֹן בְּכָל יוֹמָא. מַאן אִינוּן בְּנֵי מְהֵימְנוּתָא. אִינוּן דְּמִתְעָרֵי הַאי טוֹב לְקַבְּלֵיהּ, וְלָא חָס עַל דִּילֵיהּ, וְיָדְעֵי דְּהָא קוּדְשָׁא בְּרִיךְ הוּא יָהִיב לֵיהּ יַתִּיר. כד"א, יֵשׁ מְפַזֵּר וְנוֹסָף עוֹד. מַאי טַעֲמָא. בְּגִין דְּהַאי אִתְּעַר בִּרְכָאן לְקַבְּלֵיהּ, וְלָא יֵימָא אִי אֶתֵּן הַאי הַשְׁתָּא, מַאי אַעֲבִיד לְמָחָר. אֶלָּא קוּדְשָׁא בְּרִיךְ הוּא יָהִיב לֵיהּ בִּרְכָאן עַד בְּלִי דַי, כְּמָה דְּאוּקְמוּהָ.

56. Come and behold: daily, the faithful guide MALCHUT according to their wishes; SHE DOES AS THEY DECREE. Who are the faithful? Those who stir good, YESOD, towards her, BY GIVING CHARITY without sparing their own, knowing that the Holy One, blessed be He, will give them more, as is written: "There is one who gives freely, and yet increases" (Mishlei 11:24). What is the reason for this? That YESOD arouses blessings before him. He must not say, 'what shall I do tomorrow if I give now,' since the Holy One, blessed be He, bestows upon him blessings without end, as explained.

57. וּבְגִין כָּךְ, וְכִי תֹאמְרוּ מַה נֹאכַל בַּשָּׁנָה הַשְּׁבִיעִית וְגוֹ', מַה כְּתִיב. וְצִוִּיתִי אֶת בִּרְכָתִי לָכֶם בַּשָּׁנָה הַשִּׁשִּׁית וְעָשָׂת אֶת הַתְּבוּאָה לִשְׁלֹשׁ הַשָּׁנִים. וְעָשָׂת, וְעָשְׂתָה מִבְּעֵי לֵיהּ, מַאי וְעָשָׂת. אֶלָּא לְאַפָּקָא ה', דְּאִית לָהּ שְׁמִטָּה וְנַיְיחָא, וְלָא עָבִיד עֲבִידְתָּא. כְּתִיב רְאוּ כִּי יְיָ', וְגוֹ' נוֹתֵן לָכֶם בַּיּוֹם הַשִּׁשִּׁי לֶחֶם יוֹמָיִם וְגוֹ', כְּגַוְונָא דָא וְצִוִּיתִי אֶת בִּרְכָתִי לָכֶם בַּשָּׁנָה הַשִּׁשִּׁית וְגוֹ'.

57. Hence, "And if you shall say, 'What shall we eat in the seventh year?'" (Vayikra 25:20) It is written, "then I will command My blessing upon you in the sixth year, and it shall bring forth (Heb. asat) fruit for three years" (Ibid. 21). HE ASKS: Why "asat"? It should have been 'astah'. Why is it written, 'asat,' WITHOUT THE Hei? AND HE ANSWERS: In order to cause the Hei, WHICH IS MALCHUT, to withdraw FROM ACTION, as The Sabbatical Year and rest are its habit and it does no work, as is written, "See

-348-

that Hashem has given you... on the sixth day," WHICH IS YESOD, "the bread of two days" (Shemot 16:29). In a similar manner, "then I will command My blessing upon you in the sixth year," WHICH IS YESOD, "AND IT SHALL BRING FORTH FRUIT FOR THREE YEARS."

9. Charity saves from Death

A Synopsis

We read a story wherein Rabbi Chiya and Rabbi Yosi encounter two men, one of whom gives all of his food to a poor man on the road. The charitable man is saved by a miracle from a snake, and Rabbi Yosi says that he earned the miracle by way of his merit in going hungry. Rabbi Yosi quotes the verse, "Trust in Hashem, and do good; dwell in the land, and enjoy security," which is the whole message of this section.

58. רְבִּי חִיָּיא וְרְבִּי יוֹסֵי הֲווֹ אַזְלֵי בְּאָרְחָא, פָּגְעוּ בְּהַהוּא טוּרָא, אַשְׁכָּחוּ תְּרֵי גּוּבְרֵי דַּהֲווֹ אַזְלֵי, אַדְּהָכִי חָמוּ חַד בַּר נָשׁ דַּהֲוָה אָתֵי, וְאָמַר לוֹן, בְּמָטוּ מִנַּיְיכוּ, הָבוּ לִי מְזוֹנָא פִּתָּא דְּנַהֲמָא, דְּהָנֵי תְּרֵין יוֹמִין דְּתַעֵינָא בְּמַדְבְּרָא, וְלָא אֲכַלְנָא מִדִי. אִשְׁתְּמִיט חַד מֵאִינּוּן תְּרֵי גּוּבְרֵי, וְאַפִּיק מְזוֹנֵיהּ דְּאִיהוּ אַיְיתֵי לְאוֹרְחָא, וְיָהִיב לֵיהּ, וְאָכִיל וְאַשְׁקֵי לֵיהּ. אָמַר לֵיהּ חַבְרֵיהּ, מַה תַּעֲבִיד מִן מְזוֹנָא, דְּהָא אֲנָא דִּידִי אֲכַלְנָא. אָמַר לֵיהּ, וּמָה עֲלֵי דִּידָךְ, אֲנָא אָזִיל, יָתִיב גַּבֵּיהּ הַהוּא מִסְכְּנָא, עַד דְּאָכַל כָּל מַה דַּהֲוָה גַּבֵּיהּ, וְהַהוּא נַהֲמָא דְּאִשְׁתְּאַר, יָהַב לֵיהּ לְאוֹרְחָא, וְאָזַל לֵיהּ.

58. Rabbi Chiya and Rabbi Yosi were walking along the way and chanced upon a mountain. They found two men walking, and at the same time a man coming, who said to them: Please, I pray you, give me a piece of bread. For I have been lost in the desert for two days and have had nothing to eat. One of the men went aside, took out the provision he brought with him for the way and gave it to him; he fed him and gave him drink. His companion said to him: What shall you do when you need food? For as for me, I will eat my own AND SHALL GIVE YOU NOTHING. He said to him: I do not rely upon YOUR FOOD! The poor man sat by him until he had eaten all he had, and he gave the remaining bread to the poor man for the road. And he went away.

59. אָמַר רְבִּי חִיָּיא, לָא בָּעָא קוּדְשָׁא בְּרִיךְ הוּא דְּמִלָּה דָּא יִתְעֲבִיד עַל יְדָן. אָמַר ר' יוֹסֵי דִּילְמָא דִּינָא אִתְגְּזַר עַל הַהוּא ב"נ, וּבָעָא קוּדְשָׁא בְּרִיךְ הוּא לְזַמְּנָא קַמֵּיהּ הַאי, בְּגִין לְשֵׁזָבָא לֵיהּ. עַד דַּהֲווֹ אַזְלֵי, לָאָה

הַהוּא גַּבְרָא בְּאוֹרְחָא, א״ל חַבְרֵיה, וְלָא אֲמֵינָא לָךְ דְּלָא תִּתֵּן נַהֲמָא לְאַחֲרָא. א״ר חִיָּיא לר׳ יוֹסֵי, הָא מְזוֹנָא גַּבָּן נִיהַב לֵיה לְמֵיכַל. א״ר יוֹסֵי תִּבְעֵי לְמֵיפַק מִנֵּיה זְכוּתָא, נֵזִיל וְנֶחֱמֵי, דְּהָא וַדַּאי בְּקַפְטוֹרֵי דְּדָא טִפְסָא דְּמוֹתָא אִתְאֲחִיד, וּבָעָא קוּדְשָׁא בְּרִיךְ הוּא לְזַמְּנָא זְכוּתֵיה, בְּגִין לְשֵׁזָבֵיה.

59. Rabbi Chiya said: The Holy One, blessed be He, did not wish it to be done by us. Rabbi Yosi said: Perhaps there is an impending sentence upon that man, and the Holy One, blessed be He, wanted to put this in his way in order to save him. While they were walking the man became exhausted DUE TO HUNGER. His companion said to him: Did I not tell you not to give your bread to another? Rabbi Chiya said to Rabbi Yosi: We have food with us, let us give him some to eat. Rabbi Yosi said: Do you wish to take away his merit? Let us go and see, for surely death follows in his footsteps – MEANING THAT THE DANGER OF DEATH IS FOLLOWING HIM and the Holy One, blessed be He, wishes to prepare a merit for him in order to save him.

60. אַדְהָכִי, יָתִיב הַהוּא ב״נ, וְנָאִים תְּחוֹת חַד אִילָנָא, וְחַבְרֵיה אִתְרְחִיק מִנֵּיה, וְיָתִיב בְּדֶרֶךְ אַחֲרָא. א״ר יוֹסֵי לְרַבִּי חִיָּיא, הַשְׁתָּא נֵיתִיב וְנֶחֱמֵי, דְּוַדַּאי קוּדְשָׁא בְּרִיךְ הוּא בָּעֵי לְמִרְחַשׁ לֵיה נִיסָא, קָמוּ וְאוֹרִיכוּ. אַדְהָכִי חָמוּ חַד טִפְסָא בְּשָׁלְהוֹבֵי קָאִים גַּבֵּיה. אָמַר רַבִּי חִיָּיא, וַוי עַל הַהוּא בַּר נָשׁ, דְּהַשְׁתָּא יָמוּת. אָמַר רַבִּי יוֹסֵי, זַכָּאָה הַהוּא בַּר נָשׁ, דְּקוּדְשָׁא בְּרִיךְ הוּא יַרְחִישׁ לֵיה נִיסָא. אַדְהָכִי נָחַת מֵאִילָנָא חַד חִוְיָא, וּבָעָא לְמִקְטְלֵיה. קָם הַהוּא טִפְסָא עָלֵיה וְקַטְלֵיה. קַסְטַר בְּרֵישֵׁיה טִפְסָא, וְאָזַל לֵיה.

60. Meanwhile, the man sat to sleep under a tree. His friend went further and sat in a different place. Rabbi Yosi said to Rabbi Chiya: Let us sit down and watch, for surely the Holy One, blessed be He, intends to perform a miracle by him. They stood up and waited. While they were waiting, they saw a fiery rattlesnake standing by him. Rabbi Chiya said: Woe unto that man, for he is about to die. Rabbi Yosi said: This man is worthy of a miracle of the Holy One, blessed be He. A snake then came down the tree with the intention of killing him. The rattlesnake attacked the snake and killed it. Then the rattlesnake turned his head and went on his way.

61. א"ר יוֹסֵי, וְלָא אֲמֵינָא לָךְ דְּקוּדְשָׁא בְּרִיךְ הוּא בָּעָא לְמִרְחַשׁ לֵיהּ נִיסָא, וְלָא תִּיפּוּק זְכוּתֵיהּ מִנֵּיהּ. אַדְהָכִי אִתְעַר הַהוּא ב"נ, וְקָם וְאָזִיל לֵיהּ. אֲחִידוּ בֵּיהּ ר' חִיָּיא וְר' יוֹסֵי, וְיָהֲבוּ לֵיהּ לְמֵיכַל. בָּתַר דְּאָכַל, אַחֲוִיאוּ לֵיהּ נִיסָא דְּרָחִישׁ לֵיהּ קוּדְשָׁא בְּרִיךְ הוּא.

61. Rabbi Yosi said: Have I not told you that the Holy One, blessed be He, wished to perform a miracle for him, and you must not take away his merit, THAT, HE SHOULD NOT GIVE HIM FOOD. In the meanwhile, the man awoke from his sleep and rose to go. Rabbi Chiya and Rabbi Yosi joined him and gave him food. After he ate, they told him of the miracle the Holy One, blessed be He, performed for him.

62. פָּתַח ר' יוֹסֵי וְאָמַר, בְּטַח בַּיְיָ' וַעֲשֵׂה טוֹב שְׁכָן אֶרֶץ וּרְעֵה אֱמוּנָה, זַכָּאָה חוּלְקֵיהּ דְּבַר נָשׁ דְּעָבֵיד טוֹב מִדִּידֵיהּ, דְּהָא אִתְעַר טוֹב בִּכְנֶסֶת יִשְׂרָאֵל. וּבַמֶּה. בִּצְדָקָה. דְּכַד אִתְעַר צְדָקָה, הוּא טוֹב כְּדֵין אִתְעַר לְגַבֵּי כ"י. וְעַ"ד כְּתִיב וּצְדָקָה תַּצִּיל מִמָּוֶת. מ"ט. בְּגִין דִּצְדָקָה אִילָנָא דְּחַיֵּי הוּא, וְאִתְעַר עַל הַהוּא אִילָנָא דְּמוֹתָא, וְנָטִיל אִינּוּן דַּאֲחִידָן בֵּיהּ, וְשֵׁזִיב לוֹן מִן מוֹתָא. מַאן גָּרִים לְהַהוּא אִילָנָא דְּחַיֵּי דְּאִתְעַר לְהַאי, הֲוֵי אֵימָא הַהִיא צְדָקָה דְּאִיהוּ עָבֵיד, כִּבְיָכוֹל הוּא עָבֵיד לֵיהּ לְעֵילָּא, כד"א עוֹשֶׂה צְדָקָה בְּכָל עֵת. וְהָא אִתְּמַר.

62. Rabbi Yosi opened the discussion and said: "Trust in Hashem, and do good; dwell in the land, and enjoy security (also: 'Faith')" (Tehilim 37:3). Happy is the portion of he who does good using what is his, since he stirs good, WHICH IS YESOD, toward the Congregation of Yisrael, WHICH IS MALCHUT. With what DOES HE STIR? With righteousness (Charity), since when Righteousness is stirred, that good stirs toward the Congregation of Yisrael. It is therefore written, "but righteousness delivers from death" (Mishlei 10:2). What is the reason for this? Because Righteousness is the Tree of Life, ZEIR ANPIN. It is aroused against the Tree of Death to take those who are attached to it, and it saves them from death. Who causes the Tree of Life to be stirred to do that? One says: The charity THAT MAN does; it is as if he does it above, IN CAUSING MALCHUT TO BE UNITED WITH THE TREE OF LIFE, as is written: "and do righteousness at all times" (Tehilim 106:3). We have already explained this.

10. "they shall be your bondsmen for ever"

A Synopsis

We are told that it is a commandment to have a Canaanite slave as a bondsman because they come from the side of Ham who uncovered nakedness. Yet Eliezer, the servant of Abraham, was Righteous even though he was the descendant of Ham because God approved of the blessing that Laban gave him.

רעיא מהימנא

63. וְהִתְנַחַלְתֶּם אוֹתָם לִבְנֵיכֶם וְגו', לְעוֹלָם בָּהֶם תַּעֲבֹדוּ וְגו'. פְּקוּדָא דָא לַעֲבוֹד בְּעֶבֶד כְּנַעֲנִי, דִּכְתִּיב, לְעוֹלָם בָּהֶם תַּעֲבֹדוּ וְאִינוּן מִסִּטְרָא דְּחָם דְּגַלֵּי עֶרְיָין דְּאִתְּמַר עֲלֵיה אָרוּר כְּנַעַן עֶבֶד עֲבָדִים יִהְיֶה לְאֶחָיו. אֲמַאי עֶבֶד עֲבָדִים. אֶלָּא עֶבֶד לְהַהוּא עֶבֶד עוֹלָם, דְּאִיהוּ עוֹלָמוֹ שֶׁל יוֹבֵל. וְאִי תֵּימָא דְּהָא אָחוּהָ דְּשֵׁם וְיֶפֶת הֲוָה, אֲמַאי לָא הֲוָה הָכִי כְּוָותַיְיהוּ. וְהָכִי מִזַּרְעָא דְּחָם הֲוָה אֱלִיעֶזֶר עֶבֶד דְּאַבְרָהָם, אֲמַאי לָא הֲוָה כְּוָתֵיה, דְּנָפַק צַדִּיק, וְקוּדְשָׁא בְּרִיךְ הוּא אוֹדֵי בְּבִרְכָתֵיה, כַּד בָּרִיךְ לֵיה לָבָן.

Ra'aya Meheimna (the Faithful Shepherd)

63. "And you shall take them as an inheritance for your children after you... they shall be your bondsmen for ever" (Vayikra 25:46). It is a commandment to have a Canaanite slave as bondsman, as is written: "they shall be your bondsmen for ever." They come from the side of Ham, who uncovered nakedness, of whom it says, "Cursed be Canaan; a servant of servants shall he be to his brethren" (Beresheet 9:25). Why a servant of servants? Because he is a servant to the servant for ever (lit. 'the world'), which is the world of Jubilee. THAT IS, WHEN HE IS A SERVANT TO A SERVANT, YISRAEL'S EAR IS BORED, BUT HE WILL BE SET FREE AT THE WORLD OF JUBILEE. BUT HE WILL NOT BE SET FREE, EVEN AT THE JUBILEE. It may be said that as he is a brother to Shem and Japheth, why should he not be like them? Also, seeing that Eliezer, Abraham's servant, was the descendant of Ham, why was he not like HAM, BUT instead turned out to be righteous? The Holy One, blessed be He, approved of the blessing Laban gave him, AS IT SAYS

OF HIM IN THE TORAH, "YOU BLESSED OF HASHEM" (BERESHEET 24:31). SINCE IT IS WRITTEN IN THE TORAH, THE HOLY ONE, BLESSED BE HE, TESTIFIES IT IS TRUE.

11. Reincarnation

A Synopsis

We are told about the secret of reincarnation, that light can come out of darkness. Darkness comes out of light when drops of semen are mixed in the daughter of a strange El – a man's good should not be mingled with evil. We read how a man can attain a Neshamah through his repentance and study of Torah even if he was reincarnated in a body that consists of good and evil in order to receive punishment. Average people have half their merits below and half their transgressions below; completely evil people have all their transgressions above and their merits below; completely righteous people have all their merits above and their transgressions below.

64. אֶלָּא וַדַּאי הָכָא בְּרָזָא דְּגִלְגּוּלָא, גּוֹלֵל אוֹר מִפְּנֵי חֹשֶׁךְ, עַבְדָּא דְּאַבְרָהָם דְּנָפַק מֵחֹשֶׁךְ, וְדָא זַרְעָא דְּחָם, דַּיּוֹ לְעֶבֶד לִהְיוֹת כְּרַבּוֹ דְּאִיהוּ אַבְרָהָם, דְּנָפַק מִתֶּרַח עוֹבֵד ע"ז. וְחֹשֶׁךְ מִפְּנֵי אוֹר, דָּא יִשְׁמָעֵאל דְּנָפַק מֵאַבְרָהָם, וְעֵשָׂו מִיִּצְחָק.

64. AND HE REPLIES: Surely this pertains to the secret of reincarnation: 'causes the light to vanish before the darkness', NAMELY Abraham's servant who came out of darkness, the issue of Ham. It suffices for the servant to be like his master, Abraham, who came from the idolatrous Terah, the idol worshiper! HE THEREFORE CAME OUT OF THE CURSED AND DARKNESS AND BECAME BLESSED OF HASHEM LIKE ABRAHAM WHO CAME OUT FROM TERAH, ALSO LIGHT FROM DARKNESS. 'And darkness before the light': this is Ishmael who came out from Abraham, and Esau from Isaac.

65. וְרָזָא תַּעֲרוֹבֶת טִפִּין, בַּאֲתַר דְּלָאו דִּילֵיהּ גֵּרִים דָּא. מַאן דְּעָרִיב טִפָּה דִּילֵיהּ, בְּשִׁפְחָה מַחֲלַת בַּת יִשְׁמָעֵאל, אוֹ בְּבַת אֵל נֵכָר, דְּאִינּוּן רַע חֹשֶׁךְ, וְטִפָּה דִּילֵיהּ טוֹב אוֹר, וַיַּרְא אֱלֹהִים אֶת הָאוֹר כִּי טוֹב. מְעָרֵב טוֹב עִם רָע, עָבַר עַל מֵימְרָא דְּמָארֵיהּ, דְּאָמַר וּמֵעֵץ הַדַּעַת טוֹב וָרָע לֹא תֹאכַל מִמֶּנּוּ.

65. The mystery of this is that this is caused by the mixture of drops OF SEMEN in a place it does not belong. This is he who mingles his drop with a

maid, Machalat, the daughter of Ishmael, WHO IS AN EVIL KLIPAH, or a daughter of a strange El, NAMELY THE DAUGHTER OF THE HEATHEN, who are evil and darkness, while his drop is goodness and light, IN THE SECRET OF THE VERSE, "And Elohim saw the light that it was good" (Beresheet 1:4). He who mingles good with evil transgresses the words of His Master, who said, "but of the Tree of Knowledge of Good and Evil, you shall not eat of it" (Beresheet 2:17).

66. קוּדְשָׁא בְּרִיךְ הוּא, בְּהַהוּא דְּעָרַב, אַרְכִּיב לֵיהּ, וְאַיְיתֵי לֵיהּ בְּגִלְגּוּלָא לְקַבְּלָא עוֹנְשֵׁיהּ. חָזַר בִּתְיוּבְתָּא, אִשְׁתַּדַּל בְּאוֹרַיְיתָא, וְאַפְרִישׁ טוֹב מֵרָע, דְּאִינּוּן אָסוּר וְהֶתֵּר, טוּמְאָה וְטַהֲרָה, כָּשֵׁר וּפָסוּל. בְּדָא אִתְפְּרַשׁ רָע מִטּוֹב, דְּאִתְּמַר בֵּיהּ וַיִּיצֶר, יְצִירָה לְטָב, וִיצִירָה לְבִישׁ. בְּאוֹרַיְיתָא אַפְרִישׁ לוֹן, קוּדְשָׁא בְּרִיךְ הוּא יָרִית לֵיהּ נִשְׁמָתָא מִנֵּיהּ, לְמֶהֱוֵי שַׁלְטָא עַל תַּרְוַוייְהוּ, בְּחַד דְּאִיהוּ אוֹר. עָלְמָא דְּאָתֵי. וּבְחַד דְּאִיהוּ חֹשֶׁךְ, עָלְמָא דֵּין. הה"ד וַיִּפַּח בְּאַפָּיו נִשְׁמַת חַיִּים.

66. The Holy One, blessed be He, with that which the man mingled, puts him together and reincarnates him so as to receive punishment, THAT IS, HE BRINGS HIM INSIDE A BODY WHICH CONSISTS OF GOOD AND EVIL. If he repents, studies the Torah, and separates good from evil – FOR BY STUDYING prohibitions and license, defilement and purity, what is fit and unfit, that evil is separated from good, as it says of Him, "AND HASHEM ELOHIM FORMED (HEB. VAYYITZER) MAN" (BERESHEET 2:7). Vayyitzer IS SPELLED WITH TWO YUD'S, TO SHOW THAT MAN IS TWICE CREATED, a creation for good and a creation for evil. And through the Torah he separates them, and the Holy One, blessed be He, bequeaths him a Soul from Him, so he will rule them both, the one which is GOODNESS AND light, the World to Come, and the other, which is EVIL AND darkness, this world. Hence, it is written: "and breathed into his nostrils the breath of life" (Ibid.).

67. וּכְפוּם זַכְוָון וְחוֹבִין. כְּמָה דְּאוּקְמוּהָ, הָעוֹשֶׂה מִצְוָה אַחַת מְטִיבִין לוֹ. בֵּינוֹנִי, זַכְוָון וְחוֹבוֹי שְׁקִילִין, פַּלְגּוּ זַכְוָון לְתַתָּא וּפַלְגּוּ חוֹבוֹי לְתַתָּא, וְרָזָא דָּא מַה שֶּׁאֲלָתֵךְ וְיִנָּתֵן לָךְ וּמַה בַּקָּשָׁתֵךְ עַד חֲצִי הַמַּלְכוּת וְתֵעָשׂ.

צַדִּיק גָּמוּר, כָּל זַכְווֹי לְעֵילָּא, וְחוֹבוֹי לְתַתָּא. רָשָׁע גָּמוּר, חוֹבוֹי לְעֵילָּא,
וְזַכְווֹי לְתַתָּא.

67. MAN IS JUDGED according to his merits and evil actions. As we explained, he who does one good deed is treated well. He who is average, is a person whose merits and transgressions are balanced, the half of merits is below and the half of transgressions below. This is the secret of, "What is your petition, and it shall be granted you: and what is your request? Even to half the kingdom it shall be performed" (Esther 5:6). THAT IS, IF THERE BE A HALF KINGDOM, THE HALF OF MERITS, THEN IT SHALL BE PERFORMED; THE PETITION AND REQUEST IS ACCEPTED. In the case of a completely righteous man, all his merits are above and his transgressions below. For a completely evil man, his transgressions are above and his merits are down below.

68. וב"נ דְּחָב בְּאִתְגַּלְיָיא, בִּתְרֵין דַּרְגִּין אִיהוּ, אִי חָזַר בְּתִיּוּבְתָּא
בְּאִתְגַּלְיָיא, בֵּין צַדִּיקַיָּיא, בְּגִין דְּיַדְעִין דִּינוֹי דְּקוּדְשָׁא בְּרִיךְ הוּא,
וְנַטְרִין גַּרְמַיְיהוּ מִלְּמֶחֱטֵי. וּבְאִתְכַּסְיָיא, בֵּין רַשִׁיעַיָּיא, לְקַיֵּים בְּהוּ וְעֵינֵי
רְשָׁעִים תִּכְלֶינָה.

68. The sin of a man who commits it in public pertains to two grades, NAMELY TWO MANNERS. If he does penance in public, THAT IS, ACCORDING TO THE SIN THAT WAS COMMITTED IN PUBLIC, HE IS SEATED IN THAT WORLD among the righteous, who are familiar with the laws of the Holy One, blessed be He, and refrain from sinning. IF HE REPENTS secretly, HE IS NOT SEATED AMONG THE RIGHTEOUS, BECAUSE HIS SIN IS NOT TOTALLY ANNULLED. RATHER, HE IS SEATED among the wicked men, WHO ENVY HIM HIS REPENTANCE, so that the verse will be fulfilled which says, "But the eyes of the wicked shall fail" (Iyov 11: 20).

12. Change of name, change of place, change of deed

A Synopsis

We learn how Abraham mended the sins of Adam and Terah and how he made God and the Shechinah to rule over the whole world. The section tells of how Adam was reincarnated and how his transgressions were overturned. Through Abraham, Isaac and Jacob Adam obtained a change of name, a change of place and a change of action.

69. וּבְגִין דָּא, חוֹבָא דְּאָדָם עָבַר, עַל וַיְצַו יְיָ' אֱלֹהִים, וְאוּקְמוּהָ, אֵין צַו אֶלָּא ע"ז, אַעֲבַּר עָלֵיהּ, אַרְכִּיב לֵיהּ בְּטִפַּת תֶּרַח, דְּבֵיהּ רָתַח לְקוּדְשָׁא בְּרִיךְ הוּא, דְּעָבַר עַל צַו מע"ז. הָדַר בְּתִיוּבְתָּא, וְתָבַר צוּלְמִין דע"ז, וְכָל מְזוֹנֵי דִּילֵיהּ. הוּא תַּקִּין בְּמַה דְּחָב, וְתָבַר חוֹבָא, וּבִנְיָינָא בִּישָׁא, דְּבָנָה וְאַמְלִיךְ לֵיהּ לְקוּדְשָׁא בְּרִיךְ הוּא וּשְׁכִינְתֵּיהּ. עַל עָלְמָא.

69. Adam's sin was therefore against, "And Hashem Elohim commanded..." (Beresheet 2:16). We explained that "command" refers to idolatry. Since he sinned in idolatry, He formed him, THAT IS, HE CAUSED HIM TO INCARNATE in Terah's drop of semen, in which he vexed (Heb. *ratach*), NAMELY ANGERED, the Holy One, blessed be He, thus transgressing in idolatry, SINCE TERAH WAS IDOLATROUS. FROM A DROP OF HIS SEMEN CAME ABRAHAM, WHO WAS AN INCARNATION OF THE FIRST MAN. ABRAHAM did penance and smashed the images of idols and all the victuals PLACED BEFORE THEM. He mended the sins OF ADAM AND TERAH, and smashed the sin and the evil edifice he built, NAMELY THE EDIFICE OF THE KLIPOT OF ADAM, CAUSED TO BE BUILT BY HIS SIN. And he made the Holy One, blessed be He, and the Shechinah to rule over the whole world.

70. בְּמַאי. בְּגִין דְּקַדִּישׁ שְׁמֵיהּ יַת' בָּרַבִּים, וְעָאל בְּנוּרָא לְאִתּוֹקְדָא גַּרְמֵיהּ. לְקַיֵּים בֵּיהּ פְּסִילֵי אֱלֹהֵיהֶם תִּשְׂרְפוּן בָּאֵשׁ. וְלֹא עוֹד אֶלָּא דְּלְאֲבוֹי תֶּרַח אַהֲדַר בְּתִיוּבְתָּא, וְעָאִיל לֵיהּ וּלְאִמֵּיהּ, וּלְכָל מָארֵי דְּהַהוּא דָּרָא בְּגַן עֵדֶן. וְהָכִי אִתְלַבַּן בְּנוּרָא כְּכַסְפָּא, דְּאִיהִי מוֹנִי"טָא דְּמַלְכָּא, וְשִׁקַּר לָהּ בְּעוֹפֶרֶת, אָעִיל לֵיהּ בְּנוּרָא, וְנַפַּק הָעוֹפֶרֶת לְבַר, יִשְׁמָעֵאל. וּבְגִין דָּא נָפַק, מְצַחֵק בע"ז. וְאִשְׁתְּאַר אָדָם מְלוּבָּן, וְהַאי

אִיהוּ שִׁינּוּי הַשֵּׁם. דְּכַד אִתְגַּלְגַּל אָדָם, בָּעֵי לְמֶעְבַּד לֵיהּ שִׁינּוּי הַשֵּׁם,
שִׁנּוּי מָקוֹם, וְשִׁנּוּי מַעֲשֶׂה.

70. HE ASKS: HOW DID HE MAKE THE HOLY ONE, BLESSED BE HE, AND HIS SHECHINAH RULERS OF THE WORLD? AND HE ANSWERS: By sanctifying His Name in public, and by going into the fire to be burned, so that the words would be fulfilled IN ADAM, that say, "The carvings of their Elohim shall you burn with fire" (Devarim 7:25). THIS MEANS, SINCE ADAM WORSHIPPED IDOLS, HE WAS CONSIDERED AS THE CARVINGS OF THEIR ELOHIM. Furthermore, he caused his father, Terah, to repent and brought him, his mother, and all the rulers of that age to the Garden of Eden. He was thus purified like silver by fire, like the king's SILVER coin that was forged with a mixture of lead. He was therefore put in fire, and the lead came out, which is Ishmael. Ishmael therefore was mocking and worshipped idols, while Adam remained purified by fire. This is the change of name, FOR HIS NAME WAS CHANGED FROM ADAM TO ABRAHAM. For when Adam was incarnated, he had to undergo a change of name, change of place, and change of deed, AS FOLLOWS.

71. לְבָתַר אָתָא יִצְחָק, וְאִתְתְּקַף בֵּיהּ, מְחוֹבָא תִּנְיָינָא, דְּאִתְּמַר בֵּיהּ עַל
הָאָדָם, דְּדָא שְׁפִיכוּת דָּמִים, וְדָא גָּרַם נִסְיוֹנָא דְּיִצְחָק בְּסַכִּינָא. וְאִתְבְּרַר
בֵּיהּ, כְּמַאן דְּבָרִיר אוֹכֶל מִגּוֹ פְּסוֹלֶת, וְנָפִיק פְּסוֹלֶת לְבַר, עֲשׂוּ שׁוֹפֵךְ
דָּמִים.

71. Then came Isaac, and he became stronger through him, THAT IS, ADAM WAS INCARNATED IN HIM AND OVERCAME the second transgression, of which it says, "the man," which refers to bloodshed. THIS IS AN EXPLANATION OF THE VERSE, "AND HASHEM ELOHIM COMMANDED THE MAN SAYING…" (BERESHEET 2:16). "COMMANDED" REFERS TO IDOLATRY, "THE MAN," TO BLOODSHED, AND "SAYING," TO INCEST. HE TRANSGRESSED THEM ALL. This brought the trial of Isaac by knife, NAMELY THE SACRIFICE OF ISAAC, of which it says, "AND TOOK THE KNIFE TO SLAY HIS SON" (BERESHEET 22:10). ADAM was cleansed by him, as food is picked from refuse. And the refuse came out, which is Esau who sheds blood, AND THE FOOD, JACOB, CAME OUT CLEANSED FROM REFUSE. THIS IS WHAT IS WRITTEN: JACOB HAD THE GRACE OF ADAM

BECAUSE IN JACOB, HE CAME OUT CLEANSED AND PURIFIED FROM ALL
REFUSE.

72. לְבָתַר אָתָא יַעֲקֹב, וְאַרְכִּיב לֵיהּ בְּלָבָן, וְאִתְעֲבֵיד עֶבֶד לְגַבֵּיהּ,
הה"ד. אֶעֱבָדְךָ שֶׁבַע שָׁנִים בְּרָחֵל. וּבְהַהִיא סִבָּה דְּאַחְלָף לָהּ בַּאֲחוֹתָא,
עֶבֶד שֶׁבַע שָׁנִים אָחֳרָנִין. לְאַפָּקָא תְּרֵין טִפִּין דְּזָרַק אָדָם בַּאֲתַר
נוּכְרָאָה, וְדָא גִּלּוּי עֲרָיוֹת, וְהַאי אִיהוּ לֵאמֹר. וְאַפִּיק לוֹן מִן לָבָן
הָאֲרַמִּי, נָחָשׁ.

72. Then came Jacob, THE ASPECT OF GOODNESS AND THE FOOD PICKED
FROM THE FIRST MAN, who formed AND ATTACHED it to Laban and
became his servant. Hence it says, "I will serve you seven years for Rachel"
(Beresheet 29:18). Since he exchanged her with her sister, he served an
additional seven years, in order to remove the two drops Adam spilt in a
foreign place – MEANING THE TWO FEMALE SPIRITS THAT MATED WITH
HIM AFTER HE SEPARATED FROM EVE. This is incest, alluded to in the
word "saying" (Beresheet 2:16). He took them out of Laban the Arammian,
WHO IS OF THE ASPECT OF the serpent.

73. וּבִתְלַת אִלֵּין, הֲוָה לְאָדָם שִׁנּוּי הַשֵּׁם, וְשִׁנּוּי מָקוֹם, וְשִׁנּוּי מַעֲשֶׂה.
שִׁנּוּי הַשֵּׁם: בְּאַבְרָהָם. וְשִׁנּוּי מָקוֹם: בְּיִצְחָק. וְשִׁנּוּי מַעֲשֶׂה: בְּיַעֲקֹב. וְאִי
לְהַאי דְּאִתְּמַר בֵּיהּ, אָז רָאָה וַיְסַפְּרָהּ, קַבֵּל בִּתְיוּבְתָּא כָּל שֶׁכֵּן לַאֲחֵרִים.

73. Through these three, ABRAHAM, ISAAC, AND JACOB, Adam obtained a
change of name, a change of place, and a change of action. He obtained a
change of name through Abraham, a change of place through Isaac, and a
change of action through Jacob. And if it was said of him, "then He saw it,
and declared it; HE ESTABLISHED IT, YEA, AND SEARCHED IT OUT. AND
TO MAN (LIT. 'ADAM') HE SAID" (Iyov 28:27-28), that if He accepted his
repentance, all the more so that of others, WHO ARE NOT AS GREAT.

74. וּבְגִין דָּא, עֶבֶד טוֹב אַתְרָא גָּרִים. וְעֶבֶד רַע, אוֹף הָכִי. אֲבָל שְׁאָר
עֲבָדִים, לְעוֹלָם בָּהֶם תַּעֲבֹדוּ. קָמוּ מָארֵי מְתִיבְתָּא, וְאָמְרוּ אַשְׁרֵי הָעָם

שֶׁבְּכָה לוֹ, שֶׁכְּכָ״ה בְּגִימַטְרִיָּא מֹשֶׁה. קָם רַעְיָא מְהֵימָנָא וְאָמַר, אַשְׁרֵי הָעָם שֶׁיְיָ׳ אֱלֹהָיו.

ע״כ רעיא מהימא

74. Therefore, for a good servant, the place brings it about, and for an evil servant, also THE PLACE BRINGS IT ABOUT, but as for other servants, "they shall be your bondsmen for ever" (Vayikra 25:46). The deans of the Yeshivah rose and said, "Happy is that people, that is in such a case (Heb. *shecachah*)" (Tehilim 144:15). The numerical value of *'shecachah'* is as that of Moses, NAMELY THE FAITHFUL SHEPHERD. The Faithful Shepherd rose and said, "happy is that people, whose Elohim is Hashem" (Ibid.).

End of Ra'aya Meheimna (the Faithful Shepherd)

13. "For to Me the children of Yisrael are servants"

A Synopsis

Yisrael are called God's servants because it is a commandment to serve with prayer and with deeds and by observing the precepts of the Torah. Yisrael are also called God's children when they know God in a particular way and when they have permission to look into His mysteries.

75. כִּי לִי בְנֵי יִשְׂרָאֵל עֲבָדִים וְגוֹ'. פְּקוּדָא לַעֲבוֹד בְּכָל מִינֵי עֲבוֹדָה בְּמִקְדָשׁ, וּלְבַר מִמִּקְדָשׁ, בְּכָל אִינוּן פּוּלְחָנִין דְּאִקְרֵי עֲבוֹדָה, בִּצְלוֹתָא, לְאִשְׁתַּדְּלָא בָּתַר פְּקוּדֵי אוֹרַיְיתָא דְּכֹלָא אִקְרֵי עֲבוֹדָה, כְּעֶבֶד דְּאִשְׁתַּדַּל בָּתַר מָארֵיהּ, בְּכָל מַה דְּאִצְטְרִיךְ.

75. "For to Me the children of Yisrael are servants" (Vayikra 25:55). It is commanded to serve by doing many things in the Temple and out of the Temple, by all the deeds that are called 'service,' NAMELY prayer, and to strive to observe the precepts of the Torah, as everything is called 'service,' like a servant laboring to fulfill his master's needs.

76. בְּגִין דְּיִשְׂרָאֵל קָרֵי לוֹן עֲבָדִים, דִּכְתִיב כִּי לִי בְנֵי יִשְׂרָאֵל עֲבָדִים עֲבָדַי הֵם. מַאי טַעֲמָא אִינוּן עֲבָדִים. בְּגִין דִּכְתִיב אֲשֶׁר הוֹצֵאתִי אוֹתָם מֵאֶרֶץ מִצְרָיִם. וּבַג"כ כְּתִיב בַּעֲשֶׂר אֲמִירָן לְבָתַר, דִּכְתִיב אָנֹכִי יְיָ' אֱלֹהֶיךָ אֲשֶׁר הוֹצֵאתִיךָ מֵאֶרֶץ מִצְרַיִם, לְמִפְלַח לֵיהּ כְּעֶבֶד דְּפָלַח לְמָארֵיהּ דְּפָרִיק לֵיהּ מִן מוֹתָא, דְּפָרִיק לֵיהּ מִכָּל בִּישִׁין דְּעָלְמָא.

76. He therefore called Yisrael 'servants,' as is written: "For to Me the children of Yisrael are servants; they are my servants." Why are they servants? Because it is written, "whom I brought forth out of the land of Egypt" (Ibid.). It therefore says later, among the Ten Commandments, "I am Hashem your Elohim, who have brought you out of the land of Egypt" (Shemot 20:2), to serve Him as a servant does his master who saved him from death and redeemed him from all the evil things in the world.

77. בִּתְרֵין זִינִין אִקְרוּן יִשְׂרָאֵל לְקוּדְשָׁא בְּרִיךְ הוּא, עֲבָדִים, דִּכְתִיב

עֲבָדַי הֵם. וְאִקְרוּן בָּנִים, דִּכְתִיב בָּנִים אַתֶּם לַיְיָ' אֱלֹהֵיכֶם. בְּזִמְנָא דְּיָדַע
לֵיהּ ב"נ לְקוּדְשָׁא בְּרִיךְ הוּא בְּאוֹרַח כְּלָל, כְּדֵין אִקְרֵי עֶבֶד דְּעָבֵיד
פִּקּוּדָא דְּמָארֵיהּ, וְלֵית לֵיהּ רְשׁוּ לְחַפְּשָׂא בִּגְנִיזוֹי וּבְרָזִין דְּבֵיתֵיהּ.
בְּזִמְנָא דְּיָדַע לֵיהּ ב"נ בְּאֹרַח פְּרָט, כְּדֵין אִקְרֵי בֵּן רְחִימָא דִּילֵיהּ, כְּבֵן
דְּחָפִישׁ בִּגְנִיזוֹי, בְּכָל רָזִין דְּבֵיתֵיהּ.

77. Yisrael have two names before the Holy One, blessed be He. They are called 'servants,' as is written, "they are My servants," and they are called 'children,' as is written: "You are the children of Hashem your Elohim" (Devarim 14:1). For as long as man knows the Holy One, blessed be He, in a general way, he is called 'a servant' who does as his Master bids him, but has no permission to look into the treasures and the mysteries of His House. When he knows the Holy One, blessed be He, in a particular way, he is called 'His beloved child,' like the child who is looking at the hidden, at all the mysteries of His House.

.78 וְאע"ג דְּאִקְרֵי בֵּן בְּרָא בּוּכְרָא לְקוּדְשָׁא בְּרִיךְ הוּא, כד"א בְּנִי
בְכוֹרִי יִשְׂרָאֵל, לָא יַפּוֹק גַּרְמֵיהּ מִכְּלָלָא דְּעֶבֶד, לְמִפְלַח לַאֲבוּי בְּכָל
פּוּלְחָנִין דְּאִינּוּן יְקָרָא דַּאֲבוֹי. וְהָכִי אִצְטְרִיךְ לְכָל ב"נ לְמֶהֱוֵי לְגַבֵּי
אֲבוֹי בֵּן, לְחַפְּשָׂא בִּגְנִיזוֹי וּלְמִנְדַּע רָזִין דְּבֵיתֵיהּ, וּלְאִשְׁתַּדְּלָא
אֲבַתְרַיְיהוּ. וּלְמֶהֱוֵי לְגַבֵּי אֲבוֹי עֶבֶד.

78. Though he is called 'a son,' the firstborn son of the Holy One, blessed be He, as is written: "Yisrael is My son, My firstborn" (Shemot 4:22), he must not exclude himself from being a servant who serves his Father in everything that glorifies His Father. So should any man be in relation to his father. A child who looks at his secrets and knows the mysteries of his house and strives after them should be a servant to his father.

14. The secret of the servant and the secret of the son

A Synopsis

We learn that one should be in the grade of the servant in order to perform the many kinds of works required; one would then be called, like Malchut, 'master of the whole earth'. The grade of the son is where one strives to know his Father's secrets and all the mysteries of his house, and he then has power over everything; no one can ever stop him from entering his Father's presence at any time. In order to be both a servant and a son, one must undertake the service of prayer – such a one restores the entire secret of the Faith.

79. וְרָזָא דְמִלָּה, תְּרֵין דַּרְגִּין אִינּוּן לְעֵילָּא, דְּאִצְטְרִיךְ בַּר נָשׁ לְאִתְעַטְּרָא בְּהוּ, וְאִינּוּן רָזָא דִמְהֵימְנוּתָא, וְאִינּוּן חַד. חַד, רָזָא דְּעֶבֶד. וְחַד, רָזָא דְּבֵן. וְהַאי עֶבֶד, אִקְרֵי אָדוֹן כָּל הָאָרֶץ. בֵּן, כְּמָה דְּאוֹקִימְנָא בְּנִי בְכוֹרִי יִשְׂרָאֵל. וְכֹלָּא רָזָא חֲדָא דִמְהֵימְנוּתָא. וְאִצְטְרִיךְ ב"נ לְאִתְעַטְּרָא בְּאִלֵּין דַּרְגִּין, לְאִתְכַּלְלָא בְּרָזָא דִמְהֵימְנוּתָא.

79. This is the secret of this matter. There are two grades above in which man should be adorned; they are the secret of Faith, and they are one. The first is the secret of the servant and the other is the secret of the son. THE GRADE OF the servant ABOVE is called 'the master of the whole earth,' WHICH IS THE SECRET OF MALCHUT, AND THE GRADE OF the son ABOVE is as we stated, "Yisrael is My son, My firstborn" (Shemot 4:22), WHICH IS THE SECRET OF ZEIR ANPIN Everything pertains to the one secret of Faith, and it behooves man to be adorned with these grades OF THE SON AND SERVANT ABOVE to be included within the secret of Faith.

80. עֶבֶד, לְמִפְלַח בְּכָל זִינֵי פּוּלְחָנָא, בִּצְלוֹתָא דְּאִקְרֵי עֲבוֹדָה, כְּהַאי עֶבֶד דְּאִיהוּ רָזָא עִלָּאָה, דְּלָא שָׁכִיךְ לְעָלְמִין תָּדִיר. וְקָא מְשַׁבְּחָא וּמְנַגְּנָא תָּדִיר. וְהָא אִתְּמַר בְּפוּלְחָנִין אָחֳרָנִין, דְּכָל פּוּלְחָנִין וּמִלִּין דְּעָלְמִין כֻּלְּהוּ אִיהוּ עָבֵיד וּפָלַח. ובג"ד אִקְרֵי אָדוֹן, בְּגִין דְּאִיהוּ עֶבֶד לְמִפְלַח, אִקְרֵי אָדוֹן כָּל הָאָרֶץ. ב"נ דְּאִתְעַטֵּר בְּרָזָא דָא, לְמֶיהֱוֵי עֶבֶד לְמִפְלַח פּוּלְחָנֵיהּ דְּמָארֵיהּ, אִיהוּ סָלִיק וְאִתְעַטֵּר לְמֶהֱוֵי בְּדַרְגָּא דָא, וְאִקְרֵי אוֹף הָכִי אָדוֹן, דְּהָא אִיהוּ בָּרִיךְ בְּכָל אִינּוּן פּוּלְחָנִין, לְהַאי

עָלְמָא, וְקַיֵּים לֵיהּ. וְעַ״ד אִקְרֵי אָדוֹן.

80. HE EXPLAINS HIS WORDS. ONE SHOULD BE IN THE GRADE OF the servant, in order to perform the many kinds of works in the prayer called 'service,' like the servant, who is the supernal secret, NAMELY THE SECRET OF MALCHUT, that is never silent, but constantly praises and sings TO ZEIR ANPIN. We have learned that it also applies to other services, for all the services and words PERFORMED throughout the worlds, it is MALCHUT that performs and serves them. MALCHUT is therefore CALLED 'a master,' since she is LIKE a servant that works AND DRAWS VITALITY AND PLENTY TO ALL THE WORLDS. She is THEREFORE called 'master of the whole earth'. In the case of man who is adorned with this secret, THE ASPECT OF THE SERVANT WITHIN MALCHUT, and becomes a servant that does his Master's work, he ascends and becomes adorned to be in this grade OF SERVANT and is also called 'master,' since he blesses this world, MALCHUT, through his actions and preserves it. He is therefore called 'master' TOO.

81. זַכָּאָה חוּלָקֵיהּ דְּהַאי בֵּן, דְּזָכֵי לְאִשְׁתַּדְּלָא לְמִנְדַּע בְּגִנְזֵי דַּאֲבוֹי, וּבְכָל רָזִין דְּבֵיתֵיהּ, כִּבְרָא יְחִידָאי דְּאַשְׁלְטֵיהּ אֲבוֹי בְּכָל גִּנְזוֹי, וְדָא אִיהוּ יְקָרָא, דְּשַׁלִּיט עַל כֹּלָּא מַאן דְּיִשְׁתַּדַּל בְּאוֹרַיְיתָא, לְמִנְדַּע לֵיהּ לְקוּדְשָׁא בְּרִיךְ הוּא. וּבְאִינּוּן גְּנִיזִין דִּילֵיהּ, אִקְרֵי בֵּן לְקוּדְשָׁא בְּרִיךְ הוּא, כָּל חֵילֵי שְׁמַיָא, לֵית מַאן דְּיִמְחֵי בִּידֵיהּ, בְּכָל שַׁעֲתָא דְּאִצְטְרִיךְ לְמֵיעַל לְגַבֵּי אֲבוֹי. זַכָּאָה חוּלָקֵיהּ בְּעָלְמִין כֻּלְּהוּ. וּבְגִ״ד, כַּד אִשְׁתַּדַּל לְמִנְדַּע לֵיהּ בְּאֹרַח פְּרָט, בְּרָזָא דְּחָכְמְתָא, כְּדֵין אִקְרֵי בֵּן.

81. HE NOW INTERPRETS THE GRADE OF THE SON, SAYING: Happy is the portion of the son, who deserves to strive to know his Father's secrets and all the mysteries of His house, like an only child whose father gave him authority over all his secrets. It is to the glory OF THE SON to have power over everything. He who strives in the Torah to know the Holy One, blessed be He, and His mysteries is 'the son of the Holy One blessed be He,' and in all the heavenly hosts, there is none that will stop him from entering his Father's presence at any time he needs to. Happy is his portion throughout the worlds. Therefore, he who strives to know his Father in a particular way, within the secret of Chochmah, MEANING THE CHOCHMAH AT THE RIGHT OF ZEIR ANPIN, is called 'a son'.

82. בְּפוּלְחָנָא דְּב"נ פָּלַח לֵיהּ לְקוּדְשָׁא בְּרִיךְ הוּא, אִית פּוּלְחָנָא, דְּאִצְטְרִיךְ ב"נ לְאִתְכַּלְּלָא בְּתַרְוַוְיְיהוּ, לְמֶהֱוֵי עֶבֶד וּבֵן, לְאִתְעַטְּרָא בֵּיהּ בְּקוּדְשָׁא בְּרִיךְ הוּא. וּמָה אִיהוּ. דָּא פּוּלְחָנָא דִּצְלוֹתָא, דְּאִצְטְרִיךְ לְמֶהֱוֵי בָּהּ עֶבֶד וּבֵן, לְאִתְכַּלְּלָא בְּדַרְגִּין עִלָּאִין אִלֵּין. לְמִפְלַח וּלְאַתְקְנָא צְלוֹתָא בְּרָזָא דְּעֶבֶד, לְמִפְלַח פּוּלְחָנָא דְּתִקּוּנָא דְּעָלְמִין. וּלְאִתְדַּבְּקָא רְעוּתֵיה בְּרָזִין דְּחָכְמְתָא, לְאִתְדַּבְּקָא בְּמָארֵיהּ בִּגְנִיזִין עִלָּאִין כַּדְקָא חֲזֵי.

82. Among the deeds it behooves man to do for the Holy One blessed be He, there is a service man needs to do in order to be included in them both and become a servant and a son, adorned by the Holy One, blessed be He. What is it? It is the service of prayer, in which it behooves MAN to be a servant and a son, and to be included within THESE TWO supernal grades, Zeir ANPIN AND MALCHUT. It behooves man to work and restore prayer by the secret of the servant, and to work at restoring the worlds, WHICH PERTAINS TO THE GRADE OF THE SERVANT AND THE SECRET OF MALCHUT, so as to cause his desire to cleave to the secret of Chochmah ON THE RIGHT, and to properly cleave to his Master by the supernal mysteries, WHICH IS THE GRADE OF THE SON, THE SECRET OF ZEIR ANPIN.

83. בֵּן אִתְדְּבַק תָּדִיר בַּאֲבוֹי בְּלָא פֵּרוּדָא כְּלַל, לֵית מַאן דְּיִמְחֵי בִּידֵיהּ. עֶבֶד, עָבֵיד פּוּלְחָנָא דְּמָארֵיהּ, וְאַתְקִין תִּקּוּנֵי עָלְמָא. מַאן דַּהֲוֵי תַּרְוַוְיְיהוּ בִּכְלָלָא חֲדָא, בְּחִבּוּרָא חֲדָא, דָּא אִיהוּ בַּר נָשׁ דְּאַתְקִין רָזָא דְּכָל מְהֵימְנוּתָא בִּכְלָלָא חֲדָא, בְּלָא פֵּרוּדָא כְּלַל, וּמְחַבֵּר כֹּלָא כַּחֲדָא. דָּא אִיהוּ ב"נ, דְּקוּדְשָׁא בְּרִיךְ הוּא אַכְרִיז עֲלוֹי בְּכָל אִלֵּין חַיָּילִין וּמַשְׁרְיָין דְּכָל עָלְמִין, וּבְכָל אִינּוּן רְקִיעִין, אִזְדְּהָרוּ בִּפְלַנְיָא מְהֵימָנָא דְּבֵי מַלְכָּא, דְּכָל גִּנְזֵי דְּמָארֵיהּ בִּידֵיהּ. זַכָּאָה אִיהוּ בְּהַאי עָלְמָא, וְזַכָּאָה אִיהוּ בְּעָלְמָא דְּאָתֵי.

83. HE EXPLAINS FURTHER. A son is always bound to his father without any separation at all, and no one stops him. A servant does his master's work and corrects the constructions of the worlds. Whoever has both, THE SON AND THE SERVANT, united together, joined as one, such is a man who

restores the entire secret of the Faith, WHICH IS MALCHUT, to be wholly WITH ZEIR ANPIN, without any division and joins them all together. This is a man of whom the Holy One, blessed be He, proclaims throughout the hosts and legions of all the worlds and throughout the firmaments, 'Take care of this man, who is trusted of the King, who has all his Master's mysteries in his hands.' Happy is he in this world, and happy is he in the World to Come.

84. מֵהַהוּא יוֹמָא וּלְהָלְאָה, אִשְׁתְּמוֹדַע בַּר נָשׁ, וְאִתְרְשִׁים בְּעָלְמִין כֻּלְּהוּ. בְּשַׁעֲתָא דְּאִצְטְרִיךְ כָּל חֵילִין וּמַשִׁרְיָין כֻּלְּהוּ אִזְדְּהָרָן לְמֶהֱוֵי גַּבֵּיהּ, וְקוּדְשָׁא בְּרִיךְ הוּא לָא בָּעֵי אֶלָּא אִיהוּ בִּלְחוֹדוֹי. וְקָלָא אִתְּעַר, יֵאוֹת הוּא לְיָחִיד לְמֶהֱוֵי גַּבֵּיהּ דְּיָחִיד, וּלְאִתְעַסְּקָא יָחִיד בְּיָחִיד.

84. From that day onward, that man is known and recorded in all those worlds. In his time of need, all the hosts and legions are ordered to be with him. And the Holy One, blessed be He, needs nothing but him alone, THAT IS, ALL THE WORLDS ARE SUPPORTED BY HIM. A voice stirs AND PROCLAIMS, 'It is well for an only one, THAT MAN, to be with an Only One, THE HOLY ONE, BLESSED BE HE, and for the one to be occupied with the One.'

85. וְרָזָא דִּתְרֵין דַּרְגִּין אִלֵּין, אַשְׁכַּחְנָא בְּחַד קְרָא, דִּכְתִּיב וַיֹּאמֶר לִי עַבְדִּי אַתָּה יִשְׂרָאֵל אֲשֶׁר בְּךָ אֶתְפָּאָר. וַיֹּאמֶר לִי עַבְדִּי אַתָּה, הָא עֶבֶד. יִשְׂרָאֵל הָא בֵּן. דְּכַד אִינּוּן כְּלָלָא חֲדָא, כְּדֵין כְּתִיב אֲשֶׁר בְּךָ אֶתְפָּאָר.

עד כאן רעיא מהימנא

85. The secret of these two grades, THE SON AND THE SERVANT, I have found in one verse, in which it is written: "and said to me, 'You are My servant, Yisrael, in whom I will be glorified'" (Yeshayah 49:3). "And said to me, 'You are My servant,'" is the grade of the servant, THE SECRET OF THE LEFT COLUMN AND THE ASPECT OF MALCHUT; "Yisrael" is THE GRADE OF the son, THE SECRET OF THE RIGHT COLUMN AND THE ASPECT OF ZEIR ANPIN. When they are united as one, it is written: "in whom I will be glorified."

End of Ra'aya Meheimna (the Faithful Shepherd)

בָּרוּךְ יְיָ לְעוֹלָם אָמֵן וְאָמֵן יִמְלוֹךְ יְיָ לְעוֹלָם אָמֵן וְאָמֵן

Blessed be Hashem for ever. Amen and amen. May Hashem rule forever. Amen and amen.

BECHUKOTAI

❧❧

Names of the articles

1. "Remember now what Balak king of Moab devised"

A Synopsis

Rabbi Chiya opens by saying how happy are those whose Master reproves them out of His care for them. Rabbi Yosi says even though God told Yisrael to remember Him, when they cry out to him He does not pay attention to them. Rabbi Yehuda disagrees, and contends that if God had not remembered them, Yisrael would not have survived even a single day in exile. He says that when a man wants some action from God he must arouse it through a holy deed or speech below. Similarly, those who want to arouse actions from the Side of Defilement arouse their aspect through action and word of mouth. Rabbi Yehuda draws a distinction between divination and enchantment, and says that Yisrael's deeds are always done in holiness – there is no divination or enchantment in them. God reminds Yisrael of the acts that He has done for them and the protection He gave them while they were attached to Him.

1. אִם בְּחֻקּוֹתַי תֵּלֵכוּ וְגוֹ'. ר' חִיָּיא פָּתַח, עַמִּי זְכָר נָא מַה יָּעַץ בָּלָק מֶלֶךְ מוֹאָב וּמֶה עָנָה אוֹתוֹ בִּלְעָם בֶּן בְּעוֹר וְגוֹ'. עַמִּי זְכָר נָא, זַכָּאָה חוּלָקָא דְעַמָּא דָא, דְּמָארֵיהוֹן אוֹכַח לוֹן הָכִי. עַמִּי זְכָר נָא, אע"ג דְּאַתּוּן סָטָאן מֵאוֹרְחַי, עַמִּי אַתּוּן, דְּלָא בָּעֵינָא לְמֶעְבַּד לְכוּ כְּעוֹבָדַיְיכוּ.

1. "If you walk in My statutes…" (Vayikra 26:3). Rabbi Chiya opened with the verse, "O My people, remember now what Balak king of Moab devised, and how Bilaam, the son of Beor answered him..." (Michah 6:5). "O My people, remember"; happy is the portion of this people, that their Master reproves them so. "O My people, remember," though you have deviated from the way, you are My people, and I do not wish to repay you according to your deeds.

2. ר' יִצְחָק אָמַר, זַכָּאָה חוּלָקָא דְעַמָּא, דְּמָארֵיְיהוּ אָמַר לוֹן, עַמִּי מֶה עָשִׂיתִי לָךְ וּמֶה הֶלְאֵיתִיךָ עֲנֵה בִי. מַה יָּעַץ בָּלָק מֶלֶךְ מוֹאָב. בְּכַמָּה מִלִּין וְעוֹבָדִין אָמַר לְשֵׁיצָאָה לְכוּ מֵעָלְמָא, וְכַמָּה חֲרָשִׁין אִתְּעַר לְקַבְּלַיְיכוּ.

2. Rabbi Yitzchak said: Happy is the portion of the people whose Master

says to them, "O My people, what have I done to you, and wherein have I wearied you? Testify against Me" (Ibid. 3). "What Balak king of Moab devised," THAT IS, how many things did he plan to do to destroy you, and how much wizardry has he incited against you.

3. א"ר יוֹסֵי, אָמַר לוֹן קוּדְשָׁא בְּרִיךְ הוּא לְיִשְׂרָאֵל, זְכוֹר נָא. וַוי דַּאֲנָן צַוְוחִין בְּכָל יוֹמָא, וְגָעֵינָן וּבָכֵינָן, זְכוֹר יְיָ' מֶה הָיָה לָנוּ. זְכוֹר יְיָ' לִבְנֵי אֱדוֹם, וְלָא בָּעֵי לְאַשְׁגָּחָא עֲלָנָא, הוּא אָמַר לָן בִּבְעוּ זְכוֹר נָא, אֵין נָא אֶלָּא לְשׁוֹן בְּעוּתָא, וַאֲנָן לָא אַשְׁגַּחְנָא בֵּיהּ, כְּגַוְונָא דָא אֲנָן צַוְוחִין, זְכוֹר יְיָ' מֶה הָיָה לָנוּ, זְכוֹר יְיָ' לִבְנֵי אֱדוֹם, זְכוֹר עֲדָתְךָ קָנִיתָ קֶּדֶם, זָכְרֵנִי יְיָ' בִּרְצוֹן עַמֶּךָ, וְלָא בָּעֵי לְאַשְׁגָּחָא עֲלָן.

3. Rabbi Yosi said: The Holy One, blessed be He, said to Yisrael, "Remember now." Woe to us that we cry, we sob and weep, "Remember, Hashem, what is come upon us" (Eichah 5:1). "Remember, Hashem, against the children of Edom" (Tehilim 137:7). Yet He does not want to pay attention to us, because when He said to us, "O...remember," in words of entreaty, we did not attend to Him. We therefore shout, with words like: "Remember, Hashem, what is come upon us," "Remember, Hashem, against the children of Edom," "Remember Your congregation, which You have purchased of old" (Tehilim 74:2). "Remember me, Hashem, when You show favor to Your people" (Tehilim 106:4). Yet He does not wish to pay attention to us.

4. רִבִּי יְהוּדָה אָמַר, וַדַּאי קוּדְשָׁא בְּרִיךְ הוּא אַשְׁגַּח עֲלָן תָּדִיר, וְדָכִיר לָן, אִי לָאו דְּאִיהוּ אַשְׁגַּח בְּהוּ בְּיִשְׂרָאֵל, וְדָכִיר לוֹן, לָא יְקוּמוּן חַד יוֹמָא בְּגָלוּתָא, הַהִ"ד וְאַף גַּם זֹאת בִּהְיוֹתָם בְּאֶרֶץ אוֹיְבֵיהֶם וְגוֹ'. קוּדְשָׁא בְּרִיךְ הוּא לָא עָבֵיד לָן כְּעוֹבָדָנָא.

4. Rabbi Yehuda said: Surely the Holy One, blessed be He, constantly pays attention to us and remembers us, for had He not attended to Yisrael and remembered us, they would not have survived in exile a single day. Hence it says, "And yet for all that, when they are in the land of their enemies..." (Vayikra 26:44). For the Holy One, blessed be He, does not reward us in accordance with our deeds.

‫5. ת״ח, בָּלָק חַכִּים הֲוָה, וְרַב חַרְשִׁין בְּעוֹבָדֵי יְדוֹי, יַתִּיר מִן בִּלְעָם.‬
‫וְהָכִי אוֹלִיפְנָא כָּל מַה דְּבָעֵי בַּר נָשׁ בְּהַאי עָלְמָא בְּפוּלְחָנָא דְּקוּדְשָׁא‬
‫בְּרִיךְ הוּא, בָּעֵי לְאִתְּעָרָא בְּעוֹבָדָא לְתַתָּא. דִּבְעוֹבָדָא דִּלְתַתָּא, אִתְּעַר‬
‫עוֹבָדָא לְעֵילָא, וְעוֹבָדָא דָּא בָּעֵי בִּקְדוּשָׁה, וְהָא אוּקְמוּהָ. וּבַאֲתַר דְּלֵית‬
‫עוֹבָדָא, אִית מִלָּה, וּבְמִלָּה דְּפוּמָא, תַּלְיָא עוֹבָדָא, לְאִתְּעָרָא לְעֵילָא.‬
‫כְּמָה דִּבְעֵינָן לְאִתְּעָרָא קְדוּשָׁה עִלָּאָה, בְּעוֹבָדָא וּבְמִלָּה. הָכִי נָמֵי אִינּוּן‬
‫דְּאַתְיָין מִסִּטְרָא דִּמְסָאֲבוּתָא, בַּעְיָין לְאִתְּעָרָא סִטְרָא דִּלְהוֹן, בְּעוֹבָדָא‬
‫וּבְמִלָּה דְּפוּמָא.‬

5. Come and behold: Balak was wise, and the greatest sorcerer in his deeds; even more so than Bilaam. I have learned that when a man wishes for something from the works of the Holy One, blessed be He, it behooves him to arouse it through a deed below, since through the lower deed the upper deed is aroused. The deed below should be done in Holiness, as already explained. Where there is no deed, there is speech, and it depends upon word of mouth to provoke the deed above. As supernal Holiness should be aroused by action and speech, so should all those from the Side of Defilement arouse their aspect through action and word of mouth.

‫6. וְאע״ג דְּבִלְעָם חַרְשָׁא הֲוָה רַב מִכָּל חַרְשִׁין דְּעָלְמָא, חַרְשָׁא עִלָּאָה‬
‫מִנֵּיהּ הֲוָה בָּלָק. בְּקֶסֶם הֲוָה בָּלָק רַב מִכָּל חַכִּימִין. וּבִלְעָם בְּנַחַשׁ. קֶסֶם‬
‫וְנַחַשׁ תְּרֵין דַּרְגִּין אִינּוּן, קֶסֶם תַּלְיָא בְּעוֹבָדָא. נַחַשׁ לָא תַּלְיָא בְּעוֹבָדָא‬
‫אֶלָּא בְּאִסְתַּכְּלוּתָא, וּבְמִלָּה דְּפוּמָא. וּכְדֵין מִתְעָרִין עָלַיְיהוּ רוּחָא‬
‫מְסָאֲבָא, לְאִתְלַבְּשָׁא בְּהוּ, וְעָבֵיד מַה דְּעָבֵיד.‬

6. Though Bilaam was the greatest of all the sorcerers in the world, Balak was a greater sorcerer than he, for Balak was the greatest in divination, while Bilaam WAS GREAT in enchantment. Divination and enchantment are two grades; divination is supported by deeds, while enchantment is supported by sight and speech. The Spirit of Defilement is then roused upon them to be clothed by them, and it does what it does.

‫7. וְיִשְׂרָאֵל קַדִּישִׁין לָאו הָכִי, אֶלָּא כֻּלְּהוּ קַדִּישִׁין, וְכָל עוֹבָדַיְיהוּ‬

לְאִתְעֲרָא עֲלַיְיהוּ רוּחָא קַדִּישָׁא. כד"א, עַד יֵעֲרֶה עָלֵינוּ רוּחַ מִמָּרוֹם. וְעַ"ד כְּתִיב, כִּי לֹא נַחַשׁ בְּיַעֲקֹב וְלֹא קֶסֶם בְּיִשְׂרָאֵל, דְּהָא אִינּוּן בְּסִטְרָא דִּקְדוּשָׁה עִלָּאָה אֲחִידָן. וְעוֹבָדַיְיהוּ בִּקְדוּשָׁה אָתוּ, וּקְדוּשָׁה מִתְעֲרֵי עֲלַיְיהוּ וּמִתְלַבְּשָׁן בָּהּ.

7. It is not so for holy Yisrael, for they are all holy, and all their deeds are done to bring a Holy Spirit upon them, as it is written: "until a spirit be poured upon us from on high" (Yeshayah 32:15). It is therefore written: "Surely there is no enchantment in Jacob, nor is there any divination in Yisrael" (Bemidbar 23:23). For Yisrael are attached to the side of supernal Holiness. Their deeds are done in Holiness; Holiness is brought upon them, and they are clothed with.

ת"ח, בְּקֶסֶם הֲוָה בָּלָק רַב מִכָּל חַכִּימִין, וּבִלְעָם בְּנַחַשׁ. וְעַ"ד בְּשַׁעֲתָא דְּבָעָא בָּלָק לְאִתְחַבְּרָא עִמֵּיהּ, מַה כְּתִיב וַיֵּלְכוּ זִקְנֵי מוֹאָב וְזִקְנֵי מִדְיָן וּקְסָמִים בְּיָדָם. ת"ח, בְּמִלָּה דְּפוּמָא הֲוָה בִּלְעָם רַב מִכָּל חֲרָשִׁין דְּעָלְמָא, וּבְאִסְתַּכְּלוּתָא דְּהַהוּא נַחַשׁ, הֲוָה יָדַע לְכַוְּונָא שַׁעֲתָא. וְעַ"ד בָּעָא בָּלָק לְאַשְׁלְמָא מִלָּה קֶסֶם וְנַחַשׁ.

8. Come and behold: Balak was the greatest sage in divination, and Bilaam in enchantment. Therefore, when Balak wished to join him, it is written: "And the elders of Moab and the elders of Midian departed with the rewards of divination in their hand" (Bemidbar 22:7). Come and behold: according to word of mouth, Bilaam was the greatest sorcerer in the world, and by applying to enchantment he knew how to fix the time OF CURSING. HIS CURSES THEREFORE PREVAILED. Consequently, Balak wished to complete it with divination and enchantment, AND HENCE JOINED HIM.

אָ"ל קוּדְשָׁא בְּרִיךְ הוּא, רָשָׁע, הָא קָדְמוּךְ בָּנַי. עוֹבָדָא אִית בְּגַוַויְיהוּ, דְּכָל סִטְרִין בִּישִׁין וְזִינִין בִּישִׁין וְחֲרָשִׁין דְּעָלְמָא לָא יַכְלִין לְקָרְבָא בַּהֲדַיְיהוּ, דְּכֻלְּהוּ עַרְקִין מִקַמֵּיהּ. וּמַאי אִיהוּ. אֹהֶל מוֹעֵד, וּמָאנֵי קוּדְשָׁא, וְשִׁמּוּשֵׁי מַקְדְּשָׁא, וּקְטֹרֶת בּוּסְמִין, דְּקָא מְבַטֵּל כָּל רַתְחָא וְרוּגְזָא דְּעָלְמָא, דִּלְעֵילָּא וְתַתָּא, וְעֶלְיוֹן וְקָרְבְּנִין בְּכָל יוֹמָא,

וּתְרֵי מִזְבְּחוֹת, לְמֶעְבַּד עוֹבָדָא מִזְבְּחוֹת, וְשֻׁלְחָן וְלֶחֶם הַפָּנִים, וְאֶת הַכִּיּוֹר וְאֶת כַּנּוֹ, וְכַמָּה שְׁמוּשִׁין לְעוֹבָדָא, לְמִלָּה דְּפוּמָא, הָאָרוֹן וּתְרֵי לוּחַיָּיא דְּאוֹרַיְיתָא, וְאַהֲרֹן לְכַפְרָא עַל עַמָּא בִּצְלוֹתָא בְּכָל יוֹמָא. כֵּיוָן דְּאַשְׁגַּח הַהוּא רָשָׁע בְּהַאי, אָמַר כִּי לֹא נַחַשׁ בְּיַעֲקֹב וְלֹא קֶסֶם בְּיִשְׂרָאֵל. מ״ט. יְיָ׳ אֱלֹהָיו עִמּוֹ וּתְרוּעַת מֶלֶךְ בּוֹ.

9. The Holy One, blessed be He, said to him: 'Evil man, My children preceded you. They have something among themselves for which no Evil Sides, no wicked species, nor any magic in the world can approach them; all flee them. What is this? It is the Tent of Meeting, with its vessels of Holiness and articles of service of the Temple: incense of spices that annuls any wrath and fury in the world both above and below, the daily offerings and the burnt offerings, two altars upon which to perform the service of the altar, a table and its shewbread, the laver and its pedestal. There are also its articles of service RELATED TO speech: the ark, the two tablets of the Torah and Aaron who daily atones for the people in prayer.' When that wicked man saw this, he said: "Surely there is no enchantment in Jacob, nor is there any divination in Yisrael." Why? BECAUSE "Hashem his Elohim is with him, and the trumpet blast of a king is in him" (Bemidbar 23: 21)

10. וְעַ״ד עַמִּי זְכָר נָא, בְּבָעוּ מִנַּיְיכוּ, הֲווֹ דְּכִירִין הַהוּא זִמְנָא דְּאִתְחַבְּרוּ בָּלָק וּבִלְעָם לְשֵׁיצָאָה לְכוּ, וְלָא יָכִילוּ, דַּאֲנָא אֲחִידְנָא בְּכוּ, כְּאַבָּא דְּאָחִיד בִּבְרֵיהּ, וְלָא שָׁבִיק לֵיהּ בִּידָא דְּאָחֳרָא. מִן הַשִּׁטִּים וְעַד הַגִּלְגָּל, מַאי דָּא לָקֳבֵיל דָּא. אֶלָּא אָמַר קוּדְשָׁא בְּרִיךְ הוּא לְיִשְׂרָאֵל, בְּבָעוּ מִנַּיְיכוּ, הֲווֹ דְּכִירִין כָּל זִמְנָא דַּהֲוֵיתוּן אֲחִידָן בִּי, וְלָא יָכִיל הַהוּא רָשָׁע בְּחַרְשׁוֹי וְקִסְמוֹי לְשַׁלְטָאָה עֲלַיְיכוּ. כֵּיוָן דְּשַׁבְקִתּוּן יְדַיְיכוּ לְאַחֲדָא בִּי, וַהֲוֵיתוּן בְּשִׁטִּים, מַה כְּתִיב. וַיֹּאכַל הָעָם וַיִּשְׁתַּחֲווּ לֵאלֹהֵיהֶם. בַּגִּלְגָּל, כד״א בַּגִּלְגָּל שְׁוָרִים זִבֵּחוּ, וּכְדֵין שְׁלִיטוּ בְּכוּ שַׂנְאֵיכוֹן. וְכָל דָּא אֲמַאי. לְמַעַן דַּעַת צִדְקוֹת יְיָ׳ כָּל אִינּוּן צִדְקוֹת, דְּעָבְדָּנָא לְכוּ, בְּזִמְנָא דְּאַתּוּן אֲחִידָן בִּי, וְלָא שָׁבִיקְנָא מִלָּה דְּעָלְמָא לְשַׁלְטָאָה בְּכוּ, וְרוּגְזָא דִּלְעֵילָא וְתַתָּא, וְזִינִין בִּישִׁין, לָא יַכְלִין לְקָרְבָא בְּכוּ.

10. THE HOLY ONE, BLESSED BE HE, therefore SAID: "O My people, remember"; pray be mindful of the time when Balak and Bilaam united to destroy you, but could not because I held you as a father holds his child and does not leave his child in the hands of another. "From Shittim to Gilgal" (Michah 6:5). What is THE RELATION between them? HE ANSWERS: The Holy One, blessed be He, said to Yisrael: 'Please remember that as long as you were attached to Me, that evil man did not prevail against you with his magic and wizardry. Once you loosened your hands from holding to Me, and were at Shittim, as it is written: "and the people ate, and bowed down to their Elohim" (Bemidbar 25:2), and at Gilgal, as it is written, "in Gilgal they have sacrificed bullocks" (Hoshea 12:12). Then your enemies overpowered you. What is the reason for all that? "That you may know the righteous acts of Hashem" (Michah 6:5), NAMELY, all the righteous deeds I did for you when you were attached to Me. I let nothing in the world have power over you, and the wrath above and below and the wicked things were not able to come near you.'

2. "And Elohim came to Bilaam at night"

A Synopsis

Rabbi Yehuda talks about the witchcraft that Bilaam made at night by summoning the chieftain of the left side. That Elohim was also summoned by the spells of Laban and Abimelech, as the name Elohim is shared by all – even idolatry is called Elohim, namely Other Elohim, and so are the chieftains of the Other Side.

11. וַיֹּאמֶר אֲלֵיהֶם לִינוּ פֹה הַלַּיְלָה וַהֲשִׁבוֹתִי אֶתְכֶם דָּבָר כַּאֲשֶׁר יְדַבֵּר יְיָ אֵלָי. ת"ח, בְּשַׁעֲתָא דְּעָאל שִׁמְשָׁא, וְתַרְעִין כֻּלְּהוּ אִסְתְּימוּ, וְעָאל לֵילְיָא וְאִתְחֲשַׁךְ, כַּמָּה חֲבִילֵי שָׁרָאן מִשַׁלְשְׁלֵיהוֹן, וְאָזְלִין וְשָׁטָאן בְּעָלְמָא, וְכַמָּה רַבְרְבֵי מְמָנָן עָלַיְיהוּ דִּמְדַבְּרֵי לְהוּ. וְאִית מְמָנָא רַבְרְבָא עַל כֹּלָּא מִסִּטְרָא דִּשְׂמָאלָא וְהַהוּא רָשָׁע הֲוָה שְׁכִיחַ לְגַבֵּי הַהוּא מְמָנָא עִלָּאָה מִכֹּלָּא בְּחַרְשׁוֹי. וְהוּא הֲוָה אָמַר בְּחַרְשׁוֹי בְּלֵילְיָא, בְּזִמְנָא דְּאִיהוּ שַׁלְטָא בְּכָל סִיעָתָא דִּילֵיהּ, וְהוּא הֲוָה אָתֵי לְאִשְׁתַּכְּחָא גַּבֵּיהּ, וְאוֹדַע לֵיהּ מַה דְּאִיהוּ בָּעֵי.

11. "And he said to them, 'Lodge here this night, and I will bring you back word, as Hashem shall speak to me'" (Bemidbar 22:8). Come and behold: when the sun sets, and all the gates are closed, night falls and it becomes dark, many legions are loosed from their chains, and roam about the world with several attendants over them to guide them. On the left side is the greatest chieftain among them all, that highest chieftain whom that evil man, BILAAM, visited by use of his spells. When he was in power with all his companions, he would perform witchcraft by night and THE CHIEFTAIN would come and be with him, and let him know what he wanted.

12. כְּגַוְונָא דָּא וַיָּבֹא אֱלֹהִים אֶל לָבָן הָאֲרַמִּי, הַהוּא דְּשָׁכִיחַ גַּבֵּיהּ. וַיָּבֹא אֱלֹהִים אֶל אֲבִימֶלֶךְ, כֻּלְּהוּ כְּגַוְונָא דָּא. בְּכָל אֲתַר אִקְרוּן לֵיהּ בְּאִינוּן חַרְשִׁין, וְעַל דָּא הֲוָה שְׁכִיחַ בְּלֵילְיָא יַתִּיר מִבִּימָמָא. וְהָא אוּקְמוּהָ. וְכָל הָנֵי חַרְשִׁין וְחַכִּימִין הֲווֹ לַאֲבִימֶלֶךְ, דִּכְתִיב וַיַּשְׁקֵף אֲבִימֶלֶךְ מֶלֶךְ פְּלִשְׁתִּים בְּעַד הַחַלּוֹן. כְּתִיב הָכָא בְּעַד הַחַלּוֹן, וּכְתִיב הָתָם בְּעַד הַחַלּוֹן נִשְׁקְפָה וַתְּיַבֵּב אֵם סִיסְרָא. לָבָן הָא אוּקְמוּהָ, בִּלְעָם כְּדֵין.

12. In the same manner, "Elohim came to Laban the Arammian" (Beresheet 31:24), who was with him, NAMELY WITH THE AFOREMENTIONED CHIEFTAIN. ALSO, "And Elohim came to Abimelech" (Beresheet 20:3). It is all the same; he was universally summoned by the same spells, and was therefore more frequent by night than by day, SINCE THE NIGHT IS HIS TIME OF DOMINION. This has already been explained. Abimelech had many sorcerers and wise men, as is written: "Abimelech, king of the Philistines, looked out at a window" (Beresheet 26:8). It says here, "out at a window," and elsewhere, "The mother of Sisera looked out at the window" (Shoftim 5:28). AS THE FORMER VERSE PERTAINS TO WITCHCRAFT, SO DOES THE LATTER ABOUT ABIMELECH PERTAIN TO WITCHCRAFT. THEREFORE, IT ALSO SAYS, "AND ELOHIM CAME TO ABIMELECH," NAMELY THE CHIEFTAIN THAT IS SUMMONED THROUGH WITCHCRAFT. It was already explained that Laban WAS A SORCERER, as was Bilaam. HENCE, 'ELOHIM,' MENTIONED IN RELATION TO THEM, IS THE CHIEFTAIN.

13. וְעַל דָּא בְּכֻלְּהוּ כְּתִיב אֱלֹהִים, וַיָּבֹא אֱלֹהִים אֶל בִּלְעָם, וַיָּבֹא אֱלֹהִים אֶל לָבָן, וַיָּבֹא אֱלֹהִים אֶל אֲבִימֶלֶךְ, הוּא אָתָא לְגַבַּיְיהוּ, וְלָאו אִינּוּן לְגַבֵּיהּ, דְּהָא לֵית לְהוּ אֲתַר זַמִּין. וְאִי תֵּימָא, הָא כְּתִיב אֱלֹהִים. אֶלָּא, שְׁמָא דָּא אִשְׁתְּתַּף בְּכֹלָּא, וַאֲפִילוּ ע"ז נָמֵי אֱלֹהִים אִקְרֵי, אֱלֹהִים אֲחֵרִים, וּבְכְלָלָא דֶּאֱלֹהִים אֲחֵרִים אִלֵּין מְמָנָן, וּבְכְלָלָא דָּא הֲווֹ, וּבְגִין כָּךְ אִקְרֵי הָכִי. וְהַהוּא רָשָׁע הֲוָה אָמַר בְּחַרְשׁוֹי וְקָרֵי לֵיהּ, וְאָתֵי לְגַבֵּיהּ. וּבְגִין כָּךְ כְּתִיב לִינוּ פֹה הַלַּיְלָה וַהֲשִׁבֹתִי אֶתְכֶם דָּבָר כַּאֲשֶׁר יְדַבֵּר יְיָ' אֵלָי. הַהוּא רָשָׁע קָא מְשַׁבַּח גַּרְמֵיהּ, דְּהָא לָא כְּתִיב בֵּיהּ, אֶלָּא וַיָּבֹא אֱלֹהִים.

13. In relation to them all, it is therefore written, "Elohim," NOT YUD HEI VAV HEI, AS IT IS WRITTEN: "And Elohim came to Bilaam at night" (Bemidbar 22:20). "And Elohim came to Laban the Arammian"; "And Elohim came to Abimelech"; – "ELOHIM" BEING THE SAID CHIEFTAIN. He used to come to them, not they to him, since these CHIEFTAINS have no settled place. You may say it is written, "Elohim"; HOW CAN IT BE SAID IT IS THE OTHER SIDE? HE ANSWERS: The name ELOHIM is shared by all, even idolatry is called Elohim, namely Other Elohim. These chieftains are included amongst Other Elohim, and since they pertain to it, they are called

BY THE NAME ELOHIM. That evil man used witchcraft to summon him, and he came to him. It is therefore written: "Lodge here this night, and I will bring you back word, as Hashem shall speak to me." IT DOES NOT SAY, "ELOHIM," since that evil man boasted AND SAID 'YUD HEI VAV HEI,' though it says of him, "And Elohim came" (Bemidbar 22: 9).

3. "It pleased Hashem to bless Yisrael"

A Synopsis
Rabbi Yehuda says that Bilaam was looking for a way to curse the children of Yisrael but found nothing since there was no great wrath hanging over the world; therefore he discontinued his enchantments.

14. דָּבָר אַחֵר כַּאֲשֶׁר יְדַבֵּר יְיָ׳ אֵלָי, עַל יְדֵי דְּהַהוּא שְׁלִיחָא דְּסִטְרָא אָחֲרָא. וְאִי תֵּימָא הָא בִּימָמָא אִשְׁתְּכַח לְגַבֵּיהּ. אֶלָּא וַדַּאי בְּנַחַשׁ אִסְתַּכְּלוּתָא הֲוָה בֵּיהּ, וּבְהַהוּא זִמְנָא הֲוָה מִסְתַּכֵּל לְכַוּוּנָא שַׁעֲתָא, הה״ד וְלֹא הָלַךְ כְּפַעַם בְּפַעַם לִקְרַאת נְחָשִׁים. וַיַּרְא בִּלְעָם כִּי טוֹב בְּעֵינֵי יְיָ׳ לְבָרֵךְ אֶת יִשְׂרָאֵל. אֶלָּא דְּהַהוּא יוֹמָא אִסְתַּכַּל לְכַוּוּנָא שַׁעֲתָא, וְלָא אִשְׁתְּכַח כִּשְׁאָר יוֹמֵי, וּכְדֵין חָמָא דְּהָא רוּגְזָא רַבָּא לָא אִשְׁתְּכַח בְּעָלְמָא, כְּדֵין יָדַע כִּי טוֹב בְּעֵינֵי יְיָ׳ לְבָרֵךְ אֶת יִשְׂרָאֵל. בְּהַהוּא זִמְנָא שָׁבִיק גַּרְמֵיהּ מִכָּל נְחָשִׁים דְּעָלְמָא, וְלָא אִסְתַּכַּל בְּהוּ, הה״ד וְלֹא הָלַךְ כְּפַעַם בְּפַעַם לִקְרַאת נְחָשִׁים.

14. Another interpretation for, "as Hashem shall speak to me" (Bemidbar 22:8), IS through a messenger of the Other Side; NAMELY THE CHIEFTAIN. One might claim he also visits him by day, AS IT IS WRITTEN: "AND ELOHIM MET BILAAM" (BEMIDBAR 23:16), WHICH HAPPENED BY DAY. AND HE ANSWERS: Surely he was using enchantments, ALSO CALLED 'ELOHIM'. At that time, he was seeking a good opportunity, as is written: "He went not, as at other times, to seek for enchantments" (Bemidbar 24:1). "And Bilaam saw that it pleased Hashem to bless Yisrael" (Ibid.). HOW DID HE SEE? At that time he was searching to find a fitting time TO CURSE YISRAEL but found nothing, unlike in other times. He saw then that there was no great wrath upon the world, and knew that it is good in the eyes of Hashem to bless Yisrael. He discontinued using any of the divinations of the world and did not observe them. Hence, it is written: "he went not, as at other times, to seek for enchantments."

15. תָּא חֲזֵי, בְּהַהִיא שַׁעֲתָא דְּרִתְחָא אִשְׁתְּכַח, כְּדֵין שְׂמָאלָא אִתְּעַר, וַהֲוָה יָדַע הַהוּא רָשָׁע אֲתַר, לְאַחֲדָא בְּסִטְרָא שְׂמָאלָא, לְמֵילַט.

וְאִסְתָּכַּל בְּהַהוּא זִמְנָא, וְלָא אִשְׁתְּכַח. כְּדֵין מַה כְּתִיב, מַה אֶקוֹב לֹא
קַבֹּה אֵל וּמָה אֶזְעוֹם לֹא זָעַם יְיָ'. וּבְגִין כָּךְ, עַמִּי זְכָר נָא מַה יָּעַץ בָּלָק
וְגוֹ'. וּמֶה עָנָה אוֹתוֹ בִּלְעָם בֶּן בְּעוֹר זַכָּאִין אִינּוּן יִשְׂרָאֵל, זַכָּאָה
חוּלָקֵיהוֹן בְּעָלְמָא דֵין וּבְעָלְמָא דְּאָתֵי.

15. Come and behold: during times of wrath, the left ABOVE is roused. That evil man knew a place through which to hold to the left side, in order to curse. At that time he looked but did not find any. Then, it is written: "How shall I curse, whom El has not cursed? How shall I denounce whom Hashem has not denounced?" (Bemidbar 23:8). It therefore says: "O My people, remember now what Balak king of Moab devised, and what Bilaam, the son of Beor answered him" (Michah 6:5). Blessed are Yisrael. Blessed is their portion in this world and in the World to Come.

4. "If you walk in My statutes"

A Synopsis

We read about the statutes, the laws, and the precepts and decrees of the Oral and the Written Torah. Rabbi Yehuda says that transgressing the words of the Torah is the same as rendering the Holy Name defective. One must not only walk in God's statutes and keep His statutes – one must also perform them even as David did so that the blessings from above will be properly restored.

16. אִם בְּחֻקֹּתַי תֵּלֵכוּ. אִם בְּחֻקֹּתַי, דָּא אֲתַר דִּגְזִירִין דְּאוֹרַיְיתָא תַּלְיָין בְּהַהוּא אֲתַר, כד״א אֶת חֻקֹּתַי תִּשְׁמֹרוּ. חוֹק הוּא דְּאִקְרֵי הָכִי, וּגְזִירִין דְּאוֹרַיְיתָא בָּה אִתְכְּלִילָן. וְאֶת מִשְׁפָּטַי תִּשְׁמֹרוּ. מִשְׁפָּטַי, דָּא הוּא אֲתַר אָחֳרָא עִלָּאָה, דְּהַהִיא חֻקָּה אֲחִידַת בֵּיה, וּמִתְחַבְּרָן דָּא בְּדָא דְּעִילָאֵי וְתַתָּאֵי. וְכָל פִּקּוּדֵי אוֹרַיְיתָא, וְכָל גְּזֵרֵי אוֹרַיְיתָא, וְכָל קְדוּשֵׁי אוֹרַיְיתָא, בְּהָנֵי אֲחִידָן. בְּגִין דְּהַאי תּוֹרָה שֶׁבִּכְתָב, וְהַאי תּוֹרָה שֶׁבְּעַל פֶּה.

16. "If you walk in My statutes" (Vayikra 26:3). "My statutes," is the place upon which the decrees of the Torah depend, NAMELY MALCHUT, as is written: "and keep My statutes" (Vayikra 18:4). MALCHUT is called 'a statute', and the decrees of the Torah are comprised in it. "And keep My laws" (Vayikra 25:18). Law is another high place, ZEIR ANPIN, to which the statute, MALCHUT, cleaves, and the upper and lower cleave to each other. All the precepts of the Torah, the decrees of the Torah, and the sanctities of the Torah cleave to ZEIR ANPIN AND MALCHUT, since they are the Written Torah, ZEIR ANPIN, and the Oral Torah, MALCHUT.

17. וְעַל דָּא אִם בְּחֻקֹּתַי, כָּל אִינּוּן גְּזִירִין וְדִינִין וְעוֹנָשִׁין וּפִקּוּדִין, דְּאִינּוּן בְּהַהוּא אֲתַר דְּאִקְרֵי תּוֹרָה שֶׁבְּעַל פֶּה, חֻקָּה. וְאֶת מִשְׁפָּטַי תִּשְׁמֹרוּ, בְּהַהוּא אֲתַר דְּאִקְרֵי תּוֹרָה שֶׁבִּכְתָב, כְּמָה דְּאַתְּ אָמַר מִשְׁפָּט לֵאלֹהֵי יַעֲקֹב. וְדָא אָחִיד בְּדָא וְדָא בְּדָא, וְכֹלָּא חַד. וְדָא הוּא כְּלָלָא דִּשְׁמָא קַדִּישָׁא וּמַאן דְּאַעֲבַר עַל פִּתְגָּמֵי אוֹרַיְיתָא, כְּאִלּוּ פָּגִים שְׁמָא קַדִּישָׁא, בְּגִין דְּחֹק וּמִשְׁפָּט שְׁמָא דְּקוּדְשָׁא בְּרִיךְ הוּא הֲוֵי. וְעַל דָּא, אִם בְּחֻקֹּתַי תֵּלֵכוּ: דָּא תּוֹרָה שֶׁבְּעַל פֶּה. וְאֶת מִשְׁפָּטַי תִּשְׁמֹרוּ: דָּא תּוֹרָה

שֶׁבִּכְתָב. וְדָא הוּא כְּלָלָא דִשְׁמָא קַדִּישָׁא.

17. Hence, "My statutes," are all those decrees and judgments, punishments, and commandments, which pertain to the place called the Oral Torah; NAMELY MALCHUT CALLED 'statute'. "And keep My laws," NAMELY in the place called the Written Torah, ZEIR ANPIN, as is written: "a law of the Elohim of Jacob" (Tehilim 81:5), WHICH IS ZEIR ANPIN CALLED 'JACOB'. They are attached to each other, and all is one, the whole of the Holy Name, NAMELY THE UNION OF ZEIR ANPIN AND MALCHUT. He who transgresses the words of the Torah is as if he renders defective the Holy Name, since a statute and a law is the Name of the Holy One, blessed be He. Therefore, "If you walk in My statutes," is the Oral Torah; and, "and keep my Laws," is the Written Torah. This is the totality of the Holy Name.

18. וַעֲשִׂיתֶם אוֹתָם. מַאי וַעֲשִׂיתֶם אוֹתָם, כֵּיוָן דְּאָמַר תֵּלְכוּ וְתִשְׁמְרוּ, אֲמַאי וַעֲשִׂיתֶם. אֶלָּא, מַאן דְּעָבֵיד פִּקּוּדֵי אוֹרַיְיתָא וְאָזִיל בְּאוֹרְחוֹי, כִּבְיָכוֹל כְּאִלּוּ עֲבִיד לֵיהּ לְעֵילָּא. אָמַר קוּדְשָׁא בְּרִיךְ הוּא, כְּאִלּוּ עֲשָׂאָנִי, וְאוֹקְמוּהָ. וְעַל דָּא וַעֲשִׂיתֶם אוֹתָם. וַעֲשִׂיתֶם אַתֶּם כְּתִיב וַדַּאי, וְהוֹאִיל וּמִתְעָרֵי עֲלַיְיכוּ לְאִתְחַבְּרָא דָּא בְּדָא, לְאִשְׁתַּכְּחָא שְׁמָא קַדִּישָׁא כַּדְקָא יֵאוֹת, וַעֲשִׂיתֶם אַתֶּם וַדַּאי.

18. "And do them" (Vayikra 26:3). HE ASKS: What is the meaning of "and do them"? It already says "walk," and, "keep." Why ADD, "and do them"? HE ANSWERS: He who observes the precepts of the Torah and walks in His paths is as if He made Him above. The Holy One, blessed be He, says, 'as if he made Me.' This has been explained. Therefore, "and do them," THE STATUTE AND THE LAW, ZEIR ANPIN AND MALCHUT. Indeed it says, "and do them," since through being roused by you they join each other, so that the Holy Name will properly prevail. Indeed, you "do them."

19. כְּגַוְונָא דָא אָמַר רַבִּי שִׁמְעוֹן, וַיַּעַשׂ דָּוִד שֵׁם, וְכִי דָוִד עֲבַד לֵיהּ. אֶלָּא בְּגִין דְּאָזִיל בְּאָרְחֵי דְאוֹרַיְיתָא, וְעָבֵיד פִּקּוּדֵי אוֹרַיְיתָא, וְאַנְהִיג מַלְכוּתָא כַּדְקָא יֵאוֹת, כִּבְיָכוֹל, עָשָׂה שֵׁם לְעֵילָּא. וְלָא הֲוָה מַלְכָּא בְּעָלְמָא דְזָכָה לְהַאי כְּדָוִד, דַּהֲוָה קָם בְּפַלְגוּת לֵילְיָא, וַהֲוָה מְשַׁבַּח לֵיהּ

לְקוּדְשָׁא בְּרִיךְ הוּא, עַד דְּסָלִיק שְׁמָא קַדִּישָׁא בְּכוּרְסַיָּיא, בְּשַׁעֲתָא
דְּסָלִיק נְהוֹרָא דִימָמָא. כִּבְיָכוֹל הוּא עָבֵד שֵׁם מַמָּשׁ כד״א, וַיִּקוֹב בֶּן
הָאִשָּׁה הַיִּשְׂרְאֵלִית אֶת הַשֵּׁם וַיְקַלֵּל. ובג״כ וַיַּעַשׂ דָּוִד שֵׁם. וְעַל דָּא
וַעֲשִׂיתֶם אוֹתָם כְּתִיב, וְאִי אַתּוּן תִּשְׁתַּדְּלוּן לְמֶעְבַּד לוֹן, לְאִתְתַּקְנָא
שְׁמָא קַדִּישָׁא כַּדְקָא יָאוֹת, כָּל אִינוּן בִּרְכָאן דִּלְעֵילָא יִשְׁתַּכְּחוּן גַּבַּיְיכוּ
בְּתִקּוּנֵיהוֹן כַּדְקָא יָאוֹת.

19. Rabbi Shimon discussed in the same manner the verse, "And David got himself a name" (II Shmuel 8:13). Did David do that for himself? HE ANSWERS: Since David walked in the ways of the Torah and observed the commandments of the Torah, and led the kingdom well, it is as if he made the name above. There was no king in the world who merited this like David, who used to rise at midnight and praise the Holy One, blessed be He, until the Holy Name, MALCHUT, came up with its Throne when daylight broke. THEREFORE, it is as if he really made a name. HE RAISED IT TO BE UNITED WITH ZEIR ANPIN. It is said OF THE OTHER SIDE, "and the Yisraeli woman's son blasphemed the Name, and cursed" (Vayikra 24:11). Hence, "And David got him a name." It therefore says, "and do them"; NAMELY, if you strive to do them, and properly construct the Holy Name, all the blessings from above will be by you properly set.

5. "Then I will give you rain in due season"

A Synopsis
Rabbi Shimon tells us that anyone who gives charity to the poor constructs the Holy Name.

20. וְנָתַתִּי גִשְׁמֵיכֶם בְּעִתָּם וְגוֹ'. כָּל חַד וְחַד, יִתֵּן חֵילָא דִילֵיהּ עֲלַיְיכוּ. מַאן אִינּוּן. הַהוּא תִּקּוּנָא דַּעֲבַדְתּוּן דְּהַהוּא שְׁמָא קַדִּישָׁא כְּגַוְונָא דָא כְּתִיב, וְשָׁמְרוּ דֶּרֶךְ יְיָ' לַעֲשׂוֹת צְדָקָה וּמִשְׁפָּט. וְכִי כֵּיוָן דִּכְתִיב וְשָׁמְרוּ דֶּרֶךְ יְיָ'. אֲמַאי לַעֲשׂוֹת צְדָקָה וּמִשְׁפָּט. אֶלָּא מַאן דְּנָטִיר אוֹרְחוֹי דְאוֹרַיְיתָא, כְּבִיכוֹל הוּא עוֹשֶׂה צְדָקָה וּמִשְׁפָּט. וּמַאי צְדָקָה וּמִשְׁפָּט. דָּא קוּדְשָׁא בְּרִיךְ הוּא. בָּכָה ר"ש וְאָמַר, וַוי לוֹן לִבְנֵי נָשָׁא, דְּלָא יַדְעִין וְלָא מַשְׁגִּיחִין בִּיקָרָא דְּמָארֵיהוֹן, מַאן עָבֵיד שְׁמָא קַדִּישָׁא בְּכָל יוֹמָא, הֲוֵי אֵימָא מַאן דְּיָהִיב צְדָקָה לְמִסְכְּנֵי.

20. "Then I will give you rain in due season" (Vayikra 26:4). Everyone will bestow of his strength upon you. Who are they? The correction you made, OF THE UNISON of the Holy Name, THE UNISON OF STATUTE AND LAW, ZEIR ANPIN AND MALCHUT, SO THAT THEY WILL BESTOW PLENTY UPON YOU. It is similarly written: "and they shall keep the way of Hashem, to do justice and law" (Beresheet 18:19). If it is written: "and they shall keep the way of Hashem," why SHOULD IT SAY, "to do justice (lit. 'charity') and law?" HE ANSWERS: Whoever keeps the ways of the Torah is as if he does charity and law. What are charity and law? They are the Holy One, blessed be He. Rabbi Shimon wept and said: Woe to the people who do not know or care for the glory of their Master, for he who daily constructs the Holy Name is he who gives charity to the poor.

6. Charity to the poor

A Synopsis

We learn from Rabbi Shimon that giving charity to the poor causes the Holy Name to be made whole since charity is the Tree of Life and it bestows blessings upon righteousness. He says that the awakening above is according to one's actions below. The poor man has nothing of his own except what he is given; the moon has no light except what the sun gives her. Rabbi Shimon says that the poor man is as if dead because he is from the Tree of Knowledge of Good and Evil, but anyone who pities him and gives him charity causes the Tree of Life to rest upon the Tree of Death. He concludes by saying that righteousness is not rectified or perfected except through charity.

21. ת"ח, הָא אוּקְמוּהָ הָכִי הוּא, דְּמִסְכְּנָא אָחִיד בֵּיהּ בְּדִינָא, וְכָל מֵיכְלַיְיהוּ בְּדִינָא הוּא, אֲתַר דְּאִקְרֵי צֶדֶק, כד"א תְּפִלָּה לְעָנִי כִי יַעֲטֹף. תְּפִלָּה, דָּא תְּפִלָּה שֶׁל יַד, וְאוֹקִימְנָא. וּמַאן דְּיָהִיב לֵיהּ צְדָקָה לְמִסְכְּנָא, הוּא עָבֵיד לְעֵילָּא שְׁמָא קַדִּישָׁא שְׁלִים כַּדְקָא יָאוּת. בְּגִין דִּצְדָקָה דָּא אִילָנָא דְּחַיֵּי, וּצְדָקָה יָהִיב לְצֶדֶק. וְכַד יָהִיב לְצֶדֶק, כְּדֵין אִתְחַבַּר דָּא בְּדָא, וּשְׁמָא קַדִּישָׁא אִשְׁתְּכַח שְׁלִים. מַאן דְּעָבֵיד אִתְעֲרוּתָא דָּא דִּלְתַתָּא, וַדַּאי כְּאִלּוּ עָבֵיד שְׁמָא קַדִּישָׁא בִּשְׁלִימוּ. כְּגַוְונָא דְּאִיהוּ עָבֵיד לְתַתָּא, הָכִי אִתְעַר לְעֵילָּא. וְעַל דָּא כְּתִיב, אַשְׁרֵי שׁוֹמְרֵי מִשְׁפָּט עוֹשֵׂה צְדָקָה בְּכָל עֵת. עוֹשֵׂה צְדָקָה, דָּא קוּדְשָׁא בְּרִיךְ הוּא, כִּבְיָכוֹל הוּא עָבֵיד לֵיהּ.

21. Come and behold. It has been explained this way: the poor man is attached to Judgment, and all that he eats is through Judgment, which is the place called 'righteousness,' MALCHUT, as is written, "A prayer (Heb. *tfilah*) of the poor, when he faints" (Tehilim 102:1). This Tfilah is the hand Tefilin, NAMELY MALCHUT, THAT WHEN NOT UNITED WITH ZEIR ANPIN, IS POOR AND IS CALLED 'RIGHTEOUSNESS.' He who gives charity to the poor makes the Holy Name above properly whole. HE JOINS HER WITH ZEIR ANPIN THAT BESTOWS EVERYTHING UPON HER, since charity is the Tree of Life, ZEIR ANPIN, and charity gives and bestows upon righteousness, MALCHUT. When it bestows upon righteousness, they are

united with each other, ZEIR ANPIN WITH MALCHUT, and the Holy Name is whole. He who affects an awakening below, BY GIVING CHARITY, is surely as if he made whole the Holy Name. In a similar manner, according to one's actions below, so is the awakening above. Hence, it is written: "Happy are they who maintain justice, and do righteousness at all times" (Tehilim 106:3). "Do righteousness," refers to the Holy One, blessed be He, whom one made so to speak.

22. תָּא חֲזֵי, מִסְכְּנָא הָא אִתְּמַר מַאן הוּא אַתְרֵיה. מ"ט. בְּגִין דְּמִסְכְּנָא לָא אִית לֵיה מִדִּילֵיה כְּלוּם, אֶלָּא מַה דְּיָהֲבִין לֵיה וְסִיהֲרָא לָא אִית לָה נְהוֹרָא מִדִּילָה, אֶלָּא מַה דְּיָהִיב לָה שִׁמְשָׁא.

22. Come and behold: we learned where the poor man is; THAT IS, MALCHUT, WHEN NOT UNITED WITH ZEIR ANPIN. What is the reason thereof? It is that the poor man has nothing of his own, save that which he is given. The moon, MALCHUT, also has no light of her own, save what the sun, ZEIR ANPIN, gives her.

23. ת"ח, אֲמַאי עָנִי חָשׁוּב כַּמֵּת, מ"ט. בְּגִין דְּהַהוּא אֲתַר גָּרִים לֵיה, דְּהָא בַּאֲתַר דְּמוֹתָא הוּא שְׁכִיחַ, ובג"כ אִקְרֵי מֵת. הַהוּא דְּחַיֵּיס עָלֵיה, הוּא יָהִיב לֵיה צְדָקָה, אִילָנָא דְּחַיֵּי שַׁרְיָא עָלוֹי. כד"א, וּצְדָקָה תַּצִּיל מִמָּוֶת. וּכְגַוְּונָא דְּעָבֵיד ב"נ לְתַתָּא, הָכִי נָמֵי עָבֵיד לְעֵילָּא מַמָּשׁ. זַכָּאָה חוּלְקֵיה דְּזָכֵי לְמֶעְבַּד שְׁמָא קַדִּישָׁא לְעֵילָּא, בג"כ צְדָקָה סָלִיק עַל כֹּלָּא.

23. Come and behold: why is the poor man considered to be as a dead man? Because this is brought about by that place, as he is in a place of death, FOR MALCHUT IS THE SECRET OF THE TREE OF KNOWLEDGE OF GOOD AND EVIL. IF ONE IS WORTHY, IT IS OF GOODNESS AND LIFE, BUT IF HE IS NOT, IT IS OF EVIL AND DEATH. He is therefore called 'a dead man'. He who pities him and gives him charity CAUSES the Tree of Life, CALLED 'CHARITY,' to rest upon THE TREE OF KNOWLEDGE OF GOOD AND EVIL, WHICH IS THE TREE OF DEATH; as it is written, "but righteousness (lit. 'charity') delivers from death" (Mishlei 10:2). Thus, as man does below, IN

RELIEVING THE POOR MAN, CALLED 'A DEAD MAN', so he does exactly above, IN CAUSING THE TREE OF LIFE TO REST UPON THE TREE OF DEATH. Happy is the portion of he who is worthy of making a Holy Name above, NAMELY, TO UNITE IT WITH ZEIR ANPIN. For that reason charity surpasses everything.

24. וְהָנֵי מִלֵּי, צְדָקָה לִשְׁמָהּ. דְּהָא אִתְּעַר צְדָקָה לְצֶדֶק, לְחַבְּרָא לוֹן כַּחֲדָא, וּלְמֶחֱוֵי כֹּלָּא שְׁמָא קַדִּישָׁא כַּדְקָא יָאוֹת. דְּהָא צֶדֶק, לָא אִתְתַּקַּן, וְלָא אִשְׁתְּלִים, אֶלָּא בִּצְדָקָה. דִּכְתִיב, בִּצְדָקָה תִּכּוֹנָנִי, וּלְכְנֶסֶת יִשְׂרָאֵל אִתְּמַר, וּבְג״כ וַעֲשִׂיתֶם אוֹתָם וְגוֹ׳.

24. These words refer to charity for its own sake, as THIS WAY charity arouses righteousness, NAMELY ZEIR ANPIN AROUSES MALCHUT, and causes them to be together, so that everything will turn into a Holy Name properly. For righteousness is not rectified or perfected save through charity, as is written: "In charity shall you be established" (Yeshayah 54:14). This was addressed to the Congregation of Yisrael, MALCHUT, WHICH IS PERFECTED THROUGH CHARITY ALONE. It is therefore WRITTEN, "and do them" (Vayikra 26:3), AS IT IS DONE THROUGH THE AROUSAL BELOW.

7. "And I will give you peace in the land"

A Synopsis

Rabbi Yosi says that a man lying in his bed at night should not speak about the demons that roam around seeking judgment. He tells us that when the children of Yisrael are found to be meritorious God gives them peace in the land. Rabbi Aba talks about the fact that when the leader is good the whole world is saved because of his merit, and yet Josiah was killed even though he was a worthy leader who had done honest deeds. Rabbi Shimon says that was a result of Josiah's disbelief of Jeremiah's warnings and his failure to admonish Yisrael to repent. Rabbi Aba says that the Shechinah went into exile with Yisrael and was God's pledge to them. When He will ask for His pledge back He will come to live with Yisrael. Rabbi Yehuda speaks about Moses taking the Tent and pitching it outside the camp, and Rabbi Shimon explains to him that meant that the Tent of Meeting, that was the Shechinah, should be kept in the hands of a trustee until it was known who should keep it, Yisrael having been false to God with the creation of the Golden Calf. God made Joshua the trusted one who was worthy of guarding the pledge. In spite of the fact that Yisrael sinned, God did not remove His pledge from them and they did not forsake His pledge. Rabbi Yitzchak says that God still watches them and sees them in their synagogues and schools.

25. וְנָתַתִּי שָׁלוֹם בָּאָרֶץ וּשְׁכַבְתֶּם וְאֵין מַחֲרִיד וְגוֹ'. ר' יוֹסֵי פָּתַח, רִגְזוּ וְאַל תֶּחֱטָאוּ וְגוֹ'. רִגְזוּ וְאַל תֶּחֱטָאוּ, הַאי קְרָא אוּקְמוּהָ, דְּבָעֵי בַּר נָשׁ לְאַרְגְּזָא יֵצֶר טוֹב עַל יֵצֶר הָרָע, וְשַׁפִּיר. אֲבָל בְּשַׁעֲתָא דְּרָמַשׁ לֵילְיָא, וּבַר נָשׁ שָׁכִיב עַל עַרְסֵיה, כַּמָה גַּרְדִּינֵי נְמוּסִין מִתְעָרִין בְּעָלְמָא, וְאַזְלִין וְשָׁאטִין, וּבְנֵי נָשָׁא בָּעָאן לְאִתְרַגְּזָא מִקְּמֵיה קוּדְשָׁא בְּרִיךְ הוּא, וּלְדַחֲלָא מִנֵּיה, בְּגִין דְּלָא יִשְׁתְּכַח נַפְשֵׁיה בְּגַוַּויְיהוּ, וְיִשְׁתֵּזִיב מִנַּיְיהוּ. וְיִבְעֵי לֵיה לְב"נ, דְּלָא יַפִּיק מִנַּיְיהוּ מִלָּה בְּפוּמֵיה. בְּגִין דְּלָא יִתְּעַר לְהוּ לְגַבֵּיה, וְלָא יִשְׁתַּכְּחוּן בַּהֲדֵיה. הה"ד אִמְרוּ בִלְבַבְכֶם עַל מִשְׁכַּבְכֶם וְדֹמּוּ סֶלָה. דְּלָא יַפִּיק מִנַּיְיהוּ מִלָּה מִפּוּמֵיה.

25. "And I will give you peace in the land, and you shall lie down, and none shall make you afraid" (Vayikra 26:6). Rabbi Yosi opened the discussion with the verse: "Tremble, and sin not..." (Tehilim 4:5). This verse has been

explained. It behooves man to have his Good Inclination cause his Evil one to tremble. This is well. But when night falls and man lies in his bed, numerous seekers of Judgment, NAMELY DAMAGING DEMONS, stir up in the world and go and roam about. Thus, men should tremble before the Holy One, blessed be He, and fear Him so that their souls will not be among them, but will be saved from them. It behooves one not to utter one word of them, NAMELY, NOT TO SPEAK OF THEM AT ALL, so as not to rouse them against him, and so that they will not be with him. Hence, it says, "commune with your own heart upon your bed, and be still" (Ibid.), WHICH MEANS that one must not talk about them.

26. ת״ח, בְּשַׁעֲתָא דְּאִשְׁתְּכָחוּ יִשְׂרָאֵל זַכָּאִין קַמֵּי קוּדְשָׁא בְּרִיךְ הוּא, מַה כְּתִיב, וְנָתַתִּי שָׁלוֹם בָּאָרֶץ. הַאי לְעֵילָא. דְּאָתֵי קוּדְשָׁא בְּרִיךְ הוּא לְאִתְחַבְּרָא בִּכְנֶסֶת יִשְׂרָאֵל. כְּדֵין וּשְׁכַבְתֶּם וְאֵין מַחֲרִיד. מ״ט. בְּגִין וְהִשְׁבַּתִּי חַיָּה רָעָה מִן הָאָרֶץ. דָּא חַיָּה דְּזִינָא בִּישָׁא לְתַתָּא. וּמַאי אִיהִי. אַגֶּרֶת בַּת מַחֲלַת, הִיא, וְכָל סִיעֲתָא דִּילָהּ. הַאי בְּלֵילְיָא. בִּימָמָא, בְּנֵי נָשָׁא דְּאָתוּ מִסִּטְרָהָא דָּא, הֲהַה״ד וְחֶרֶב לֹא תַעֲבוֹר בְּאַרְצְכֶם.

26. Come and behold: when Yisrael are found meritorious before the Holy One, blessed be He, it is written: "And I will give peace in the land." This is up above, as the Holy One, blessed be He, comes to join the Congregation of Yisrael, AS "PEACE" MEANS YESOD, AND "THE LAND" IS MALCHUT. Then, "you shall lie down, and none shall make you afraid." Why? Because "I will remove evil beasts out of the land." This is an evil kind of beast that is down below. Which? Igeret, the daughter of Machalat, AN EVIL KLIPAH, and all her companions. This is by night. By day, THE VERSE, "AND I WILL REMOVE EVIL BEASTS OUT OF THE LAND," ALLUDES TO men from her side WHO CAUSE DAMAGE IN THE WORLD. This is the meaning of, "neither shall the sword go through your land" (Vayikra 26:6).

27. ר' אַבָּא אָמַר, הָא אוּקְמוּהָ דַּאֲפִילוּ חֶרֶב שֶׁל שָׁלוֹם, כְּגוֹן פַּרְעֹה נְכֹה. אֲבָל וְחֶרֶב לֹא תַעֲבוֹר, דָּא סִיעֲתָא דִּילָהּ. וְהִשְׁבַּתִּי חַיָּה רָעָה, דְּלָא תִשְׁלוֹט בְּאַרְעָא, וַאֲפִילוּ הַעֲבָרָה בְּעָלְמָא לֹא תַעֲבוֹר עָלַיְיכוּ, וַאֲפִילוּ חֶרֶב דִּשְׁאָר עַמִּין, וַאֲפִילוּ ב״נ מִזַּיְינָא, לֹא יַעֲבוֹר עָלַיְיכוּ.

27. Rabbi Aba said: It has been explained that even a sword of peace SHALL NOT "GO THROUGH YOUR LAND," as in the case of Pharaoh Necho, WHO WANTED TO PASS THROUGH THE LAND OF YISRAEL, BUT THE KING JOSIAH DID NOT PERMIT IT. THE MEANING of, "neither shall the sword go through your land," alludes to her companions, WHO COME FROM THE SIDE OF THE SAID KLIPAH. "I will remove evil beasts out of the land," means that THE KLIPAH ITSELF shall not have dominion over the land, nor shall it even go through – not the sword of the other nations, and not even one armed person shall pass you.

28. וְדָא דָרִישׁ יֹאשִׁיָּהוּ מַלְכָּא, וְאוֹקְמוּהָ דְּהוּא אִתְפַּס בְּחוֹבַיְיהוּ דְיִשְׂרָאֵל. כְּמָה דִכְתִּיב, רוּחַ אַפֵּינוּ מְשִׁיחַ יְיָ' נִלְכַּד בִּשְׁחִיתוֹתָם וְגו'. הָכָא אִית לְאִסְתַּכְּלָא, דְּהָא תָּנֵינָן אִי רֵישָׁא דְעַמָּא הוּא טַב, כָּל עַמָּא מִשְׁתְּזְבָן בְּגִינֵיה. וְאִי רֵישָׁא דְעַמָּא לָא אִתְכְּשַׁר, כָּל עַמָּא אִתְפְּסָן בְּחוֹבֵיה. וְהָא יֹאשִׁיָּהוּ רֵישָׁא דְכַשְׁרָא הֲוָה, וְעוֹבָדוֹי מִתְכַּשְׁרָן. אֲמַאי אִתְפַּס בְּחוֹבֵיהוֹן דְיִשְׂרָאֵל.

28. This is what king Josiah asked for WHEN HE DID NOT ALLOW THE SOLDIERS OF PHARAOH NECHO TO GO THROUGH THE LAND. It has been explained that he was caught in the sins of Yisrael AND WAS THEREFORE KILLED, as is written, "The breath of our nostrils, the anointed of Hashem, was taken in their pits" (Eichah 4:20). We must examine this, for we learned that if the leader of the people is good, the whole world is saved due to his merit. If the leader of the people is not honest, the whole people are caught for his sin. Yet why was Josiah, who was a worthy leader of honest deeds, caught in Yisrael's sins?

29. אֶלָּא עַל דְּלָא הַיָּמִין בֵּיהּ בְּיִרְמְיָהוּ, וְלָא כָּפִית לְהוּ לְיִשְׂרָאֵל, דְּחָשִׁיב דְּכֻלְּהוּ זַכָּאִין כְּוָותֵיהּ. וַהֲוָה אָמַר לֵיהּ יִרְמְיָּה, וְלָא הַיָּמִין בֵּיהּ. וּבְגִ"כ אִתְפַּס בְּחוֹבֵיהוֹן. וְעוֹד דְּסִיהֲרָא הֲוָה מָאִיךְ נְהוֹרָא, וּבָעֵיָא לְאִסְתַּמָּא.

29. AND HE ANSWERS: This happened because he did not believe Jeremiah, and did not admonish Yisrael TO REPENT, for he thought they were all as righteous as he was. Yirmeyah told him of this, but he did not believe him and was therefore caught in their sins. Moreover, the moon, MALCHUT, had then the lowest light, and was about to be completely blocked, SINCE IT WAS NEAR THE DESTRUCTION OF THE TEMPLE.

8. "And I will set My Tabernacle among you"

A Synopsis

Rabbi Yosi tells us that God reproves and corrects those He loves but does not do so for those He hates so as not to give them a portion of Himself. Rabbi Yosi also talks about the spirits that wander about and chastise people.

30. וְנָתַתִּי מִשְׁכָּנִי בְּתוֹכְכֶם וְגוֹ'. וְנָתַתִּי מִשְׁכָּנִי, דָּא שְׁכִינְתָּא. מִשְׁכָּנִי: מַשְׁכוֹנָא דִילִי. דַּהֲוָה אִתְמַשְׁכְּנָא בְּחוֹבַיְיהוּ דְיִשְׂרָאֵל. וְנָתַתִּי מִשְׁכָּנִי, מַשְׁכוֹנִי וַדַּאי. מָתָל לב״נ דַּהֲוָה רְחִימָא לְאָחֳרָא, א״ל וַדַּאי בִּרְחִימוּתָא עִלָּאָה דְּאִית לִי גַּבָּךְ, בָּעֵינָא לְדַיְירָא עִמָּךְ. אָמַר הֵיךְ אִנְדַּע דְּתֵידוֹר גַּבַּאי, נָטַל כָּל כְּסוּפָא דְבֵיתֵיהּ, וְאַיְיתֵי לְגַבֵּיהּ, אָמַר הָא מַשְׁכוֹנָא לְגַבָּךְ, דְּלָא אִתְפְּרַשׁ מִנָּךְ לְעָלְמִין.

30. "And I will set My Tabernacle among you" (Vayikra 26:11). The Tabernacle is the Shechinah. "My Tabernacle," means My pledge, as THE SHECHINAH was pledged because of the sins of Yisrael AND WENT INTO EXILE WITH THEM. "And I will set My Tabernacle," My pledge, surely. This is like the fable about a man who loved his neighbor. He said to him: 'I have the highest regard for you and wish to dwell with you.' HIS FRIEND said: 'How can I be sure you shall live with me?' He took all the delightful objects of his house and brought them to him. He said: 'Here is my pledge that I will never part from you.'

31. כַּךְ קוּדְשָׁא בְּרִיךְ הוּא, בָּעָא לְדַיְירָא בְּהוּ בְּיִשְׂרָאֵל, מָה עֲבַד, נָטַל כְּסוּפָא דִילֵיהּ, וְנָחִית לְהוּ לְיִשְׂרָאֵל. אָמַר לוֹן, יִשְׂרָאֵל, הָא מַשְׁכוֹנָא דִילִי גַּבַּיְיכוּ, בְּגִין דְּלָא אֶתְפְּרַשׁ מִנַּיְיכוּ לְעָלְמִין. וְאע״ג דְּקוּדְשָׁא בְּרִיךְ הוּא אִתְרְחִיק מִינָן, מַשְׁכוֹנָא שָׁבִיק בִּידָן, וַאֲנָן נַטְרִין הַהוּא כְּסוּפָא דִילֵיהּ, מַאן דְּיִבְעֵי מַשְׁכוֹנֵיהּ יֵיתֵי לְדַיְירָא גַּבָּן בג״כ וְנָתַתִּי מִשְׁכָּנִי בְּתוֹכְכֶם, מַשְׁכוֹנָא אֶתֵּן בִּידַיְיכוּ, בְּגִין דְּאָדוּר עִמְּכוֹן. וְאע״ג דְּיִשְׂרָאֵל הַשְׁתָּא בְּגָלוּתָא, מַשְׁכוֹנָא דְקוּדְשָׁא בְּרִיךְ הוּא הוּא גַּבַּיְיהוּ. וְלָא שָׁבְקוּ

-394-

לֵיהּ לְעָלְמִין.

31. Likewise, the Holy One, blessed be He, wished to dwell among Yisrael. What did He do? He took His precious delight, THE SHECHINAH, and brought it down to Yisrael. He said to them: 'Here I give you My pledge, so that I will never part from you.' Though the Holy One, blessed be He, has gone away from us, He left the pledge in our hands, AS THE SHECHINAH IS WITH US IN EXILE, and we keep His delight. When He asks for His pledge, He will come to dwell with us. Hence, IT IS WRITTEN: "And I will set My Tabernacle (Heb. *mishkan*) among you," meaning I will give a pledge (Heb. *mashkon*) in your hands that I will dwell with you. And though Yisrael are now in exile, they have the pledge of the Holy One, blessed be He, and they never left Him.

32. וְלֹא תִגְעַל נַפְשִׁי אֶתְכֶם, לְב"ן דְּרָחִים לְחַבְרֵיהּ, וּבָעָא לְדַיְּירָא עִמֵּיהּ, מַה עֲבַד, נָטַל עַרְסָא דִּילֵיהּ וְאַיְיתֵי לְבֵיתֵיהּ. אָמַר דָּא עַרְסָא דִּילִי בְּבֵיתָיךְ, בְּגִין דְּלָא אַרְחִיק מִינָךְ, עַרְסָךְ, וּמָאנָךְ. כַּךְ קוּדְשָׁא בְּרִיךְ הוּא אָמַר, וְנָתַתִּי מִשְׁכָּנִי בְּתוֹכְכֶם וְלֹא תִגְעַל נַפְשִׁי אֶתְכֶם, הָא עַרְסָא דִּילִי בְּבֵיתַיְיכוּ, כֵּיוָן דְּעַרְסָא דִּילִי עִמְּכוֹן, תִּנְדְּעוּן דְּלָא אִתְפְּרַשׁ מִנַּיְיכוּ, ובג"כ וְלֹא תִגְעַל נַפְשִׁי אֶתְכֶם.

32. "...and My Spirit shall not abhor you" (Ibid.). This is likened to a man who loved his friend and wished to dwell with him. What did he do? He took his own bed, brought it to his house and said: 'Here is my bed in your house, so that I shall not go away from you, your bed and your possessions.' So did the Holy One, blessed be He, say: "'And I will set My Tabernacle among you: and My soul shall not abhor you." Behold My bed, THE SHECHINAH, in your house. Now that My bed is with you, know that I shall not be separated from you.' Therefore, "and My soul shall not abhor you;" I WILL NOT GO AWAY FROM YOU.

33. וְהִתְהַלַּכְתִּי בְּתוֹכְכֶם וְהָיִיתִי לָכֶם לֵאלֹהִים, כֵּיוָן דְּמַשְׁכְּנָא דִּילִי גַּבַּיְיהוּ, בְּוַדַּאי תִּנְדְּעוּן דַּאֲנָא אָזִיל עִמְּכוֹן, כד"א כִּי יְיָ' אֱלֹהֶיךָ

מִתְהַלֵּךְ בְּקֶרֶב מַחֲנֶיךָ לְהַצִּילְךָ וְלָתֵת אוֹיְבֶיךָ לְפָנֶיךָ וְהָיָה מַחֲנֶיךָ קָדוֹשׁ.

33. "And I will walk among you, and will be your Elohim" (Ibid. 12). Now that I have given you My pledge, you will surely know that I walk with you, as is written: "for Hashem your Elohim walks in the midst of your camp, to deliver you, and to give up your enemies before you. Therefore shall your camp be Holy" (Devarim 23:15).

9. "And Moses would take the Tent"

‎34. רִבִּי יִצְחָק וְרִבִּי יְהוּדָה, הֲווֹ שְׁכִיחֵי לֵילְיָא חַד בְּכְפַר, קָרִיב לְיַמָּא דְּטְבֶרְיָא, קָמוּ בְּפַלְגוּת לֵילְיָא אָמַר ר' יִצְחָק לְרִבִּי יְהוּדָה נֵימָא בְּמִלֵּי דְּאוֹרַיְיתָא דְאע״ג דַּאֲנָן בְּאַתַר דָּא, לָא בָּעֵינָא לְאִתְפָּרְשָׁא מֵאִילָנָא דְּחַיֵּי.

34. One night, Rabbi Yitzchak and Rabbi Yehuda were in a village near the Sea of Galilee. They arose at midnight. Rabbi Yitzchak said to Rabbi Yehuda: Let us discuss the words of the Torah, for though we are in such a place, we must not be divided from the Tree of Life.

‎35. פָּתַח ר' יְהוּדָה וְאָמַר, וּמֹשֶׁה יִקַּח אֶת הָאֹהֶל וְנָטָה לוֹ מִחוּץ לַמַּחֲנֶה וְגוֹ'. וּמֹשֶׁה יִקַּח אֶת הָאֹהֶל, אֲמַאי. אֶלָּא אָמַר מֹשֶׁה, הוֹאִיל וְיִשְׂרָאֵל קָא מְשַׁקְרֵי בֵּיה בְּקוּדְשָׁא בְּרִיךְ הוּא, וְאַחְלִיפוּ יְקָרָא דִּילֵיה, הָא מַשְׁכּוֹנָא דִּילֵיה, יְהֵא בִּידָא דִּמְהֵימָנָא, עַד דְּנֶחֱמֵי בְּמַאן יִשְׁתְּאַר.

35. Rabbi Yehuda opened the discussion and said: "And Moses would take the Tent, and pitch it outside the camp..." (Shemot 33:7). HE ASKS: "And Moses would take the Tent." Why did he do so? AND ANSWERS: Moses said, 'Since Yisrael are false to the Holy One, blessed be He, and exchanged His glory FOR A GOLDEN CALF, let His pledge – THE SHECHINAH, CALLED 'THE TENT OF MEETING' – be in the hands of a trustee until we know with whom THE PLEDGE shall remain.

‎36. אָמַר לֵיה לִיהוֹשֻׁעַ, אַנְתְּ תְּהֵא מְהֵימָנָא בֵּין קוּדְשָׁא בְּרִיךְ הוּא, וּבֵין יִשְׂרָאֵל, וְיִשְׁתְּאַר מַשְׁכּוֹנָא בִּידָךְ בְּהֵימָנוּתָא, וְנֶחֱמֵי בְּמַאן יִשְׁתְּאַר. מַה כְּתִיב, וְשָׁב אֶל הַמַּחֲנֶה וּמְשָׁרְתוֹ יְהוֹשֻׁעַ בִּן נוּן נַעַר לֹא יָמִישׁ מִתּוֹךְ הָאֹהֶל. מַאי טַעֲמָא לִיהוֹשֻׁעַ בְּגִין דְּאִיהוּ כְּסִיהֲרָא לְגַבֵּי שִׁמְשָׁא, וְאִיהוּ אִתְחֲזֵי לְנַטְרָא מַשְׁכּוֹנָא. וְעַל דָּא, לֹא יָמִישׁ מִתּוֹךְ הָאֹהֶל.

36. He said to Joshua: 'You shall be the trusted one between the Holy One, blessed be He, and Yisrael, and the pledge shall remain in your faithful hands. We shall see with whom it will remain.' It is written: "And he turned back to the camp, but his servant Joshua, the son of Nun, a young man, did not depart out of the Tent" (Ibid. 11). What is the reason HE GAVE IT to Joshua? Because IN RELATION TO MOSES, he was like the moon to the sun, AS THE MOON IS THE SECRET OF MALCHUT, CALLED 'THE TENT OF MEETING'. HENCE, he was worthy of guarding the pledge, WHICH IS OF HIS OWN SIDE. Therefore, he "did not depart out of the Tent."

37. אָ"ל קוּדְשָׁא בְּרִיךְ הוּא לְמֹשֶׁה, מֹשֶׁה, לָא אִתְחֲזֵי הָכִי, דְּהָא מַשְׁכּוֹנָא דִּילִי יָהֲבִית בִּידַיְיהוּ, אַף עַל גַּב דְּאִינּוּן חָאבוּ לְגַבָּאי, מַשְׁכּוֹנָא יְהֵא לְגַבַּיְיהוּ, דְּלָא יִתְפָּרְשׁוּן מִנֵּיהּ. תִּבְעֵי דְּאִתְפְּרַשׁ מִנַּיְיהוּ דְּיִשְׂרָאֵל, וְלָא אֵיתוּב לְגַבַּיְיהוּ, לְעָלְמִין, אֶלָּא אָתִיב מַשְׁכּוֹנָא דִּילִי לְגַבַּיְיהוּ, וּבְגִינֵיהּ לָא אֶשְׁבּוֹק לְהוֹן בְּכָל אֲתַר.

37. The Holy One, blessed be He, said to Moses: 'It is not fit to do it this way, since I gave My pledge into the hands OF THE CHILDREN OF YISRAEL. And though they sinned against Me, they shall have the pledge with them and shall not part with it. Would you wish that I would part from the children of Yisrael and never return to them?' FOR THE SHECHINAH IS THE PLEDGE IN THE HANDS OF THE CHILDREN OF YISRAEL THAT HE SHALL NEVER LEAVE THEM. 'Return My pledge to them, and for its sake I shall never leave them, wherever THEY MAY BE.'

38. אע"ג דְּיִשְׂרָאֵל חָבוּ לְגַבֵּיהּ דְּקוּדְשָׁא בְּרִיךְ הוּא, הַאי מַשְׁכּוֹנָא דִּילֵיהּ לָא שָׁבְקוּ, וְקוּדְשָׁא בְּרִיךְ הוּא לָא נָטִיל לֵיהּ מִבֵּינַיְיהוּ. וְעַל דָּא, בְּכָל אֲתַר דְּגָלֵי יִשְׂרָאֵל, שְׁכִינְתָּא עִמְּהוֹן. וְעַל דָּא כְּתִיב, וְנָתַתִּי מִשְׁכָּנִי בְּתוֹכְכֶם. וְהָא אוּקְמוּהָ.

38. Though Yisrael sinned against the Holy One, blessed be He, they did not forsake His pledge, nor did the Holy One, blessed be He, take it from them. Hence, wherever Yisrael were exiled, the Shechinah was with them. Therefore, it is written: "And I will set My Tabernacle among you." This has already been explained.

10. "My beloved is like a gazelle"

‎39. פָּתַח רַבִּי יִצְחָק וְאָמַר דּוֹמֶה דוֹדִי לִצְבִי אוֹ לְעוֹפֶר הָאַיָּלִים הִנֵּה זֶה
‎וְגו'. זַכָּאִין אִינּוּן יִשְׂרָאֵל, דְּזָכוּ דְּמַשְׁכּוֹנָא דָּא לְמֶהֱוֵי גַּבַּיְיהוּ, מִן מַלְכָּא
‎עִלָּאָה. דְּאַף עַל גַּב דְּאִינּוּן בְּגָלוּתָא, קוּדְשָׁא בְּרִיךְ הוּא אָתֵי בְּכָל רֵישׁ
‎יַרְחֵי וְשַׁבָּתֵי וּזְמַנֵי, לְאַשְׁגָּחָא עָלַיְיהוּ, וּלְאִסְתַּכְּלָא בְּהַהוּא מַשְׁכּוֹנָא
‎דְּאִית לֵיהּ גַּבַּיְיהוּ, דְּאִיהוּ כְּסוּפָא דִּילֵיהּ.

39. Rabbi Yitzchak opened the discussion and said: "My beloved is like a gazelle or a young hart: behold, he..." (Shir Hashirim 2:9). Happy are Yisrael who have merited this pledge of the most High King. And though they are in exile, the Holy One, blessed be He, comes every new moon, every Shabbat, and every holiday, to look in at them and observe His pledge, His delight, that is with them.

‎40. לְמַלְכָּא דְּסָרְחָא מַטְרוֹנִיתָא, אַפְקָהּ מֵהֵיכְלֵיהּ. מָה עֲבָדַת. נַטְלַת
‎בְּרָהּ דִּילֵיהּ כְּסוּפָא דְּמַלְכָּא, רְחִימָא דִּילֵיהּ. וּבְגִין דְּדַעְתָּא דְּמַלְכָּא
‎עֲלָהּ, שַׁבְקֵיהּ בִּידָהָא. בְּשַׁעֲתָא דְּסָלִיק רְעוּתָא דְּמַלְכָּא, עַל מַטְרוֹנִיתָא,
‎וְעַל בְּרָהּ, הֲוָה סָלִיק אַגְרִין, וְנַחְית דַּרְגִּין, וְסָלִיק כּוֹתָלִין, לְאִסְתַּכְּלָא
‎וּלְאַשְׁגָּחָא בֵּין נוּקְבֵי כּוֹתָלָא עָלַיְיהוּ, כֵּיוָן דְּחָמֵי לוֹן, שָׁארֵי בָּכֵי
‎מֵאֲחוֹרֵי קוּסְטֵי כּוֹתָלָא, וּלְבָתַר אָזִיל לֵיהּ.

40. THIS IS like a king against whom his Matron rebelled. He banished her out of his palace. What did she do? She took her son with her, the delight and love of the king. Since the king cared for her, he let him remain in her hands. When the king wished for the Matron and her son, he would ascend the stairs, descend the steps, and climb walls to watch them from between the lattices in the wall. When he saw them, he started to weep from behind the lattices in the wall, and then went away.

‎41. כָּךְ יִשְׂרָאֵל, אַף עַל גַּב דְּאִינּוּן נַפְקוּ מֵהֵיכְלֵיהּ דְּמַלְכָּא, הַהוּא
‎מַשְׁכּוֹנָא לָא שָׁבְקוּ, וּבְגִין דִּרְעוּתָא דְּמַלְכָּא עָלַיְיהוּ, שַׁבְקֵיהּ עִמְּהוֹן.
‎בְּשַׁעֲתָא דְּסָלִיק רְעוּתָא דְּמַלְכָּא קַדִּישָׁא, עַל מַטְרוֹנִיתָא וְעַל יִשְׂרָאֵל.

סָלִיק אַגְרִין, נָחִית דַּרְגִּין, וְסָלִיק כּוֹתָלִין, לְאִסְתַּכְּלָא וּלְאַשְׁגְּחָא בֵּין
קוּסְטֵי כּוֹתָלָא עָלַיְיהוּ. כֵּיוָן דְּחָמֵי לוֹן, שָׁאֵרי וּבָכֵי, הה״ד דּוֹמֶה דוֹדִי
לִצְבִי אוֹ לְעוֹפֶר הָאַיָּלִים לְדַלְגָּא מִכּוֹתָלָא לְאִיגְרָא, וּמֵאִיגְרָא לְכוֹתָלָא.
הִנֵּה זֶה עוֹמֵד אַחַר כָּתְלֵנוּ, בְּבָתֵּי כְנֵסִיּוֹת וּבְבָתֵּי מִדְרָשׁוֹת מַשְׁגִּיחַ מִן
הַחַלּוֹנוֹת, דְּוַדַּאי בֵּי כְּנִישְׁתָּא בַּעְיָא חַלּוֹנוֹת. מֵצִיץ מִן הַחֲרַכִּים,
לְאִסְתַּכְּלָא וּלְאַשְׁגְּחָא עָלַיְיהוּ. וּבְגִין כַּךְ, יִשְׂרָאֵל בָּעוּ לְמֶחְדֵּי בְּהַהוּא
יוֹמָא, דְּאִינְהוּ יַדְעֵי דָא, וְאָמְרֵי. זֶה הַיּוֹם עָשָׂה יְיָ׳ נָגִילָה וְנִשְׂמְחָה בּוֹ.

41. This is true for Yisrael. Though they left the King's palace AND WENT INTO EXILE, they did not forsake the pledge. Since the King cared for them, He left it with them. When the Holy King thought of the Matron and Yisrael, He ascended the stairs, descended the steps, and climbed walls to look at them from between the lattices in the wall. When He saw them, He began to cry. Hence, it is written: "My beloved is like a gazelle or a young hart," jumping from the wall to the roof, and from the roof to the wall. "Behold, He stands behind our wall," NAMELY in the synagogues and schools; "He looks in at the windows," for surely a synagogue must have windows; "He peers through the lattice" (Ibid.), to watch and see them. Yisrael should therefore rejoice on the day they know this and say, "This is the day which Hashem has made; we will rejoice and be glad in it" (Tehilim 118:24).

11. Righteousness together with its Judgments

A Synopsis

Rabbi Yosi tells us that God reproves and corrects those He loves but does not do so for those He hates so as not to give them a portion of Himself. Rabbi Yosi also talks about the spirits that wander about and chastise people.

42. וְאִם בְּחֻקֹּתַי תִּמְאָסוּ וְגוֹ׳. ר׳ יוֹסֵי פָּתַח, מוּסַר יְיָ׳ בְּנִי אַל תִּמְאָס וְאַל תָּקֹץ בְּתוֹכַחְתּוֹ. כַּמָּה חֲבִיבִין יִשְׂרָאֵל קַמֵּי קוּדְשָׁא בְּרִיךְ הוּא, דְּקוּדְשָׁא בְּרִיךְ הוּא בָּעֵי לְאוֹכָחָא לְהוּ, וּלְדַבְּרָא לְהוּ בְּאֹרַח מֵישָׁר, כְּאַבָּא דְּרָחִים לִבְרֵיהּ, וּמִגּוֹ רְחִימוּ דִּילֵיהּ לְגַבֵּיהּ, שַׁרְבִּיטָא בִּידֵיהּ תָּדִיר, לְדַבְּרָא לֵיהּ בְּאֹרַח מֵישָׁר, דְּלָא יִסְטֵי לִימִינָא וְלִשְׂמָאלָא. הה"ד כִּי אֶת אֲשֶׁר יֶאֱהַב יְיָ׳ יוֹכִיחַ וּכְאָב אֶת בֵּן יִרְצֶה. וּמַאן דְּלָא רָחִים לֵיהּ קוּדְשָׁא בְּרִיךְ הוּא, וְסָאנֵי לֵיהּ, סָלִיק מִנֵּיהּ תּוֹכַחְתָּה, סָלִיק מִנֵּיהּ שַׁרְבִּיטָא.

42. "And if you shall despise My statutes" (Vayikra 26:15). Rabbi Yosi opened the discussion with the verse: "My son, do not despise the chastening of Hashem; nor be weary of His correction." (Mishlei 3:11). Yisrael are so beloved to the Holy One, blessed be He, that He wished to chasten them and lead them on the true path, as a father pities his child. In His love for them, His stick is always in His hand, to lead them on the true path so that they will not turn right or left. Hence, it is written: "For Hashem reproves him whom He loves, even as a father the son in whom he delights" (Ibid. 12). The Holy One, blessed be He, refrains from reproving he who He does not love but hates, and He removes the stick away from him.

43. כְּתִיב. אָהַבְתִּי אֶתְכֶם אָמַר יְיָ׳ וְגוֹ׳, מִגּוֹ רְחִימוּתָא דִּילֵיהּ, שַׁרְבִּיטָא בִּידֵיהּ תָּדִיר, לְדַבְּרָא לֵיהּ. וְאֶת עֵשָׂו שָׂנֵאתִי, בְּג"כ סְלִיקִית מִנֵּיהּ שַׁרְבִּיטָא, סְלִיקַת מִנֵּיהּ תּוֹכַחְתָּא, בְּגִין דְּלָא אֶתֵּן לֵיהּ בִּי חוּלָקָא, רְחִיקָא דְּנַפְשַׁאי הוּא. אֲבָל אַתּוּן, אָהַבְתִּי אֶתְכֶם וַדַּאי. ובג"כ, מוּסַר יְיָ׳ בְּנִי אַל תִּמְאָס וְאַל תָּקֹץ בְּתוֹכַחְתּוֹ. מַאי וְאַל תָּקֹץ. לָא תְּקוּצוּן

בֵּיהּ, כְּמַאן דְּעָרַק מִגּוֹ גּוּבִין, דְּאִינּוּן מִילִין כְּגוֹבִין לְגַבֵּיהּ בְּגַרְמֵיהּ.

43. It is written: "'I have loved you', says Hashem" (Malachi 1:2), and in His love the stick is always in His hand to guide us. "'And I hated Esau" (Ibid. 3), and therefore took the stick away from him, removed reproof from him, so as not to give him a portion in Me; My soul despises Him. But as for you, "I have loved you," indeed and therefore, "My son, do not despise the chastening of Hashem; nor be weary of His correction'." What is the meaning of, "do not despise (Heb. *takutzu*)"? IT MEANS do not despise Him, as if fleeing before thorns (Heb. *kotzim*), for the kings WHO ENSLAVE THE CHILDREN OF YISRAEL are like thorns in His body.

44. תָּא חֲזֵי, בְּשַׁעֲתָא דְּאִתְּעַר צֶדֶק בְּדִינוֹי. כַּמָּה סִטְרֵי טְהִירִין, מִתְעָרִין מִימִינָא וּמִשְּׂמָאלָא, כַּמָּה שַׁרְבִיטִין נָפְקִין, מִנְּהוֹן שַׁרְבִיטֵי אֶשָּׁא, שַׁרְבִיטֵי גּוּמְרִין, שַׁרְבִיטֵי שַׁלְהוֹבָא, כֻּלְּהוּ נָפְקִין וּמִתְעָרִין בְּעָלְמָא, וְלָקָאן לִבְנֵי נָשָׁא. תְּחוֹתַיְיהוּ מְמָנָן אָחֳרָנִין, מָארֵי טַפְסִין, מְמָנָן דְּאַרְבְּעִין חָסֵר חַד. שָׁאטִין וְנַחְתִּין, לָקָאן וְסַלְּקִין, וְנַטְלִין רְשׁוּתָא, עָיְילֵי בְּנוּקְבָּא דִּתְהוֹמָא רַבָּא, מִצְבָּעִין טַפְסֵי, וְנוּרָא דְּדָלִיק אִתְחֲבַּר בְּהוּ, נַפְקֵי גּוּמְרִין וְשָׁאטִין וְנַחְתִּין, וְאִשְׁתְּכָחוּ לְקָבְלֵיהוֹן דִּבְנֵי נָשָׁא. וְהַיְינוּ דִּכְתִּיב, וְיָסַפְתִּי לְיַסְּרָה אֶתְכֶם אֵתֵן לְמָארֵיהוֹן דְּדִינָא, תּוֹסֶפֶת עַל דִּינָא דִּלְהוֹן.

44. Come and behold: when Righteousness, MALCHUT ON HER SIDE OF JUDGMENT, is roused together with its Judgments, several aspects of spirits are awakened on the right and on the left, and many sticks come out. Some are sticks of fire, some are sticks of coals and some are sticks of flames. They all come out, roused in the world, and strike people. Under them are other harmful chieftains, forty minus one. They roam about, go down and strike, then come up, obtain permission, and enter into a hole in the great abyss. They paint themselves and climb up, and a burning fire joins them. They go out, as burning coals, and wander and go down to be among men, as is written: "then I will punish you...more" (Vayikra 26:18); I will add more to the Prosecutors' punishment.

12. "Seven times for your sins"

A Synopsis

We learn that God will give the world only as much judgment as it can bear. If He had punished the world according to its sins, the world would never have survived. Rabbi Shimon talks about the 'daughter of seven', the Sabbatical Year and the well of seven. These things allude to a release where judgment is executed and everyone is set free. Rabbi Aba says that God repeatedly warned Yisrael about their sins, but when they did not repent he sent them into exile; nevertheless He did not send them on their own, but sent 'seven', Malchut, with them.

45. כד"א, לֹא אוֹסִיף לְקַלֵּל עוֹד אֶת הָאֲדָמָה בַּעֲבוּר הָאָדָם. מַאי לֹא אוֹסִיף. לֹא אֶתֵּן תּוֹסֶפֶת לְמָארֵי דִינָא לְשֵׁיצָאָה עָלְמָא, אֶלָּא תּוֹסֶפֶת כְּגַוְונָא דְיָכִיל עָלְמָא לְמִסְבַּל. וְע"ד וְיָסַפְתִּי אֶתֵּן תּוֹסֶפֶת וַדַּאי.

45. It says of this, "I will not curse the ground any more for man's sake" (Beresheet 8:21). What is the meaning of, "I will not curse the ground any more"? It means that He will give no more Judgments to the Prosecutors with which to destroy the world, but only as much as the world can bear. It is therefore written: "then I will punish you no more..." (Vayikra 26:8); He will surely give more, AS MUCH AS THE WORLD CAN BEAR.

46. תּוֹסֶפֶת אֲמַאי. בְּגִין לְיַסְּרָה אֶתְכֶם שֶׁבַע עַל חַטֹּאתֵיכֶם. שֶׁבַע, וְהָא קוּדְשָׁא בְּרִיךְ הוּא אִי גָּבֵי הַהוּא דִילֵיהּ לָא יָכִיל עָלְמָא לְמִסְבַּל אֲפִילוּ רִגְעָא חֲדָא, הַהַ"ד, אִם עֲוֹנוֹת תִּשְׁמוֹר יָהּ יְיָ' מִי יַעֲמוֹד, וְאַתְּ אֲמַרְתְּ שֶׁבַע עַל חַטֹּאתֵיכֶם.

46. Why would He give more? To punish you "seven times for your sins" (Ibid.). HE ASKS: Seven times? Had the Holy One, blessed be He, collected His due, THAT IS, PUNISHED IN ACCORDANCE WITH THE SIN, the world would not have been able to bear it for a single moment, as is written: "If You, Yah, should mark iniquities, Hashem, who could stand?" (Tehilim 130:3). Yet you say, "seven times for your sins."

47. אֶלָּא מַה תַּ"ל שֶׁבַע. אֶלָּא הָא שֶׁבַע לָקְבְלַיְיכוּ. וּמַאי אִיהִי. דָּא
שְׁמִטָּה, דְּאִיהִי שֶׁבַע, דְּאִקְרֵי שֶׁבַע, כד"א, מִקֵּץ שֶׁבַע שָׁנִים תַּעֲשֶׂה
שְׁמִטָּה. וְעַל דָּא שֶׁבַע עַל חַטֹּאתֵיכֶם, וְאִקְרֵי שֶׁבַע, וְאִקְרֵי בַּת שֶׁבַע.
מַה בֵּין הַאי לְהַאי. אֶלָּא שֶׁבַע בִּלְחוֹדָהָא, לְמֶעְבַּד שְׁמִטָּה, וּלְמֶעְבַּד
דִּינִין, לְאַפְּקָא חֵירוּ דְּכֹלָּא בָּהּ. בַּת שֶׁבַע אִקְרֵי, דְּאִתְחַבַּר בְּאַחֲרָא
כַּחֲדָא, לְאַנְהָרָא, לְמִשְׁלַט בְּמַלְכוּתָא, לְאוֹדְעָא מַלְכוּתָא בְּאַרְעָא
וּבְכֹלָּא, בַּת שֶׁבַע אִקְרֵי. כְּתִיב, עַל כֵּן שֵׁם הָעִיר בְּאֵר שֶׁבַע עַד הַיּוֹם
הַזֶּה. בְּאֵר שֶׁבַע, בְּאֵרָה דְּיִצְחָק הוּא, וְכֹלָּא חַד מִלָּה הוּא.

47. AND HE ANSWERS: What the verse teaches us IN SAYING, "seven times," is this. Behold seven is before you. Who is she? She is the Sabbatical Year (lit. 'Release Year'), NAMELY MALCHUT SWEETENED BY BINAH, which is seven. For She is called 'seven,' as it says, "At the end of every seven years you shall make a release" (Devarim 15:1). The SCRIPTURE therefore SAYS, "seven times for your sins." MALCHUT is called 'seven' and ALSO 'daughter of seven'. What is the difference between them? In saying seven only, it means to have a release, to execute Judgments, and to set everyone free. She is called 'daughter of seven' when attached to another, ZEIR ANPIN, to illuminate and rule over her kingdom and make known the Kingship throughout the land and to everyone. She is then called 'the daughter of seven'. Hence, it is written: "the name of the city is Beer-Sheva (lit. 'well of seven') to this day" (Beresheet 26:33). The well of seven is Isaac's well. Everything is one.

48. רִבִּי אַבָּא אָמַר, וְיִסַּרְתִּי אֶתְכֶם אַף אֲנִי שֶׁבַע עַל חַטֹּאתֵיכֶם.
וְיִסַּרְתִּי אֶתְכֶם, עַל יְדָא דִּמְמָנָן אַחֲרָנִין, כְּמָה דְּאוּקְמוּהָ. אַף אֲנִי, הָא
אֲנָא אִתְּעַר לָקְבְלַיְיכוּ. הָא שֶׁבַע, לְאִתְעָרָא עֲלַיְיכוּ.

48. Rabbi Aba said: "and I will chastise you, even I, seven times for your sins" (Vayikra 26:28). "And I will chastise you," through other attendants, as already explained. "Even I;" "I" is ZEIR ANPIN, who is roused to save you; "seven" is MALCHUT, which is roused towards you TO SAVE YOU.

THAT IS, ZEIR ANPIN AND MALCHUT SHALL BE WITH THEM IN EXILE.
HENCE, THEY SHALL GET THEM OUT OF EXILE, AS WILL BE EXPLAINED.

49. ת״ח, רְחִימוּתָא עִלָּאָה דְקוּדְשָׁא בְּרִיךְ הוּא בְּיִשְׂרָאֵל, לְמַלְכָּא
דַּהֲוָה לֵיהּ בַּר יְחִידָאי, וַהֲוָה חָטֵי קַמֵּי מַלְכָּא, יוֹמָא חַד סָרַח קַמֵּי
מַלְכָּא, אָמַר מַלְכָּא, כָּל הָנֵי יוֹמִין אַלְקֵינָא לָךְ, וְלָא קַבֵּלְתְּ. מִכָּאן
וְאֵילָךְ חָמֵי מַאי אַעֲבִיד לָךְ, אִי אַתְרִיךְ לָךְ מִן אַרְעָא, וְאַפֵּיק לָךְ
מִמַּלְכוּתָא, דִּילְמָא יְקוּמוּן עֲלָךְ דּוּבֵּי חַקְלָא, אוֹ זְאֵבֵי חַקְלָא, אוֹ
לִסְטִין, וְיַעַבְרוּן לָךְ מֵעָלְמָא. מַה אַעֲבִיד. אֶלָּא אֲנָא וְאַנְתְּ נִיפוּק
מֵאַרְעָא.

49. Come and behold: the Holy One, blessed be He, bears a sublime love for
Yisrael . THIS IS like a king who had an only son who constantly sinned
against him. One day, as he sinned against the king, the king said: 'I have
beaten you previously, but you have not learned. From now on, see what I
shall do to you. If I drive you out of the land, and deport you from the
kingdom, wild bears, wild wolves, or murderers might attack you and kill
you. What shall I do? We shall both leave the country.'

50. כַּךְ אַף אָנִי, אֲנָא וְאַנְתְּ נִיפוּק מֵאַרְעָא. כַּךְ אָמַר קוּדְשָׁא בְּרִיךְ הוּא,
יִשְׂרָאֵל מַה אַעֲבִיד לְכוּ, הָא אַלְקֵינָא לְכוּ, וְלָא אַרְכִּיתוּ אוּדְנַיְיכוּ, הָא
אַיְיתֵינָא עֲלַיְיכוּ מָארֵי תְּרִיסִין, מָארֵי טַפְסִין, לְאַלְקָאָה לְכוֹן, וְלָא
שְׁמַעְתּוּן. אִי אַפֵּיק לְכוּ מֵאַרְעָא לְחוֹדְכוֹן, דָּחִילְנָא עֲלַיְיכוּ מִכַּמָּה
דּוּבִין, מִכַּמָּה זְאֵבִין, דִּיקוּמוּן עֲלַיְיכוּ, וְיַעַבְרוּן לְכוּ מֵעָלְמָא. אֲבָל מַה
אַעֲבִיד לְכוֹן, אֶלָּא אֲנָא וְאַתּוּן נֵפוּק מֵאַרְעָא, וְנֵהַךְ בְּגָלוּתָא. הה״ד
וְיִסַּרְתִּי אֶתְכֶם לָמֶדַךְ בְּגָלוּתָא. וְאִי תֵּימְרוּן דְּאֶשְׁבּוֹק לְכוֹן, אַף אֲנִי
עִמְּכוֹן. שֶׁבַע עַל חַטֹּאתֵיכֶם, דָּא שֶׁבַע דְּיִתְתָּרַךְ עִמְּכוֹן, וַאֲמַאי. עַל
חַטֹּאתֵיכֶם.

50. Similarly, the words "even I," mean that I and you shall leave the land,
NAMELY, GO INTO EXILE. This is what the Holy One, blessed be He, said to
Yisrael: 'I have warned you but you did not lend your ears. I have brought

warriors and angels of destruction upon you to beat you, but you have not hearkened. If I drive you out of the land on your own, I fear that bears and wolves will attack and kill you. What then shall I do to you? You and I shall leave the land and go into exile.' This is the meaning of, "and I will chastise you"; we shall go into exile. 'You may say that I will leave you, but "even I," am with you.' "...seven times for your sins," that is, seven, MALCHUT, will be deported with you. For what reason? "For your sins."

13. "For your transgressions was your mother put away"

A Synopsis

Rabbi Aba says that God is with Yisrael even in their exile, and when their exile is over He will return with them.

51. הה״ד, וּבְפִשְׁעֵיכֶם שֻׁלְחָה אִמְּכֶם. אָמַר קוּדְשָׁא בְּרִיךְ הוּא, אַתּוּן גְּרַמְתּוּן, דַּאֲנָא וְאַתּוּן לָא נֵידוּר בְּאַרְעָא. הָא מַטְרוֹנִיתָא נָפְקַת מֵהֵיכָלָה עִמְּכוֹן, הָא אִתְחַרַב כֹּלָּא, הֵיכָלָא דִּילִי וְדִלְכוֹן אִתְחַרַב. דְּהָא לְמַלְכָּא לָא אִתְחֲזֵי הֵיכָלָא, אֶלָּא כַּד אִיהוּ עָיֵיל עִם מַטְרוֹנִיתָא. וְחֶדְוָה דְּמַלְכָּא לָא אִשְׁתְּכַח, אֶלָּא בְּשַׁעֲתָא דְּעָאל בְּהֵיכָלָא דְּמַטְרוֹנִיתָא, וְאִשְׁתְּכַח בְּרָהָא עִמָּה בְּהֵיכָלָא, חַדְאָן כֻּלְהוּ כַּחֲדָא. הַשְׁתָּא דְּלָא אִשְׁתְּכָחוּ בְּרָא וּמַטְרוֹנִיתָא, הָא הֵיכָלָא חֲרֵיבָא מִכֹּלָּא. אֶלָּא אֲנָא מַה אַעֲבִיד. אַף אֲנָא עִמְּכוֹן. וְהַשְׁתָּא אע״ג דְּיִשְׂרָאֵל אִינְהוּ בְּגָלוּתָא, קוּדְשָׁא בְּרִיךְ הוּא אִשְׁתְּכַח עִמְּהוֹן, וְלָא שָׁבִיק לוֹן, דְּכַד יִפְּקוּן יִשְׂרָאֵל מִן גָּלוּתָא, קוּדְשָׁא בְּרִיךְ הוּא, יָתוּב עִמְּהוֹן. דִּכְתִּיב, וְשָׁב יְיָ' אֱלֹהֶיךָ, וְשָׁב יְיָ' אֱלֹהֶיךָ וַדַּאי. וְהָא אִתְּמַר.

51. This is the meaning of, "for your transgressions was your mother put away" (Yeshayah 50:1). The Holy One, blessed be He, said: 'You brought it about that you and I shall not dwell in the land. Behold the Matron leaving the palace with you. Observe everything in ruin; My palace and yours, in ruins.' For the palace is not fit for a King, save when He enters it together with the Matron, MALCHUT. The King then rejoices only when He enters the Matron's palace, since She is with Her children in the palace. All may then rejoice. 'Now that the son and the Matron are not here, My palace is in ruins. What shall I do? I shall go with you.' And now, though Yisrael are in exile, the Holy One, blessed be He, is with them, and does not leave them. When Yisrael are released from the exile, the Holy One, blessed be He, will return with them, as it is written: "Hashem your Elohim will turn your captivity" (Devarim 30:3). Indeed, "Hashem your Elohim will turn;" THE HOLY ONE, BLESSED BE HE, WILL RETURN. We have already explained this.

14. "These are the words of the Covenant"

A Synopsis

Rabbi Yosi tells Rabbi Chiya that the curses in the Book of Vayikra were said by Gvurah and those in Devarim were said by Moses himself, and yet both were the words of the Covenant because good and evil depend on them. Righteous and Righteousness together are called 'the Covenant'. Thus 'remember' and 'keep' are also bound together, one by day and one by night. Rabbi Chiya agrees and says that Shabbat is called a Covenant. He talks about God's promise to give peace in the land. Rabbi Chiya explains that God promised not to cast Yisrael away nor to abhor them because the Shechinah, the beloved of His soul, is among them. Rabbi Yosi talks about a son's duty to honor his father even after the father's death, and the way to honor him is to walk in Truth and perfect his own actions. This increases the praise of the father both in this world and in the World to Come.

52. רִבִּי חִיָּיא וְר' יוֹסֵי הֲווֹ אָזְלֵי בְּאָרְחָא, אַעְרָעוּ בְּהַהִיא מְעַרְתָּא בְּחַקְלָא. א״ר חִיָּיא לְרִבִּי יוֹסֵי, הַאי דִּכְתִיב אֵלֶּה דִּבְרֵי הַבְּרִית וְגוֹ', מִלְּבַד הַבְּרִית. מַאי דִּבְרֵי הַבְּרִית. דִּבְרֵי גְבוּרָה מִבְּעֵי לֵיהּ. אָמַר לֵיהּ הָא אוּקְמוּהָ, הַלָּלוּ מִפִּי הַגְּבוּרָה, וְהַלָּלוּ מִפִּי עַצְמוֹ שֶׁל מֹשֶׁה, וְהָא אִתְּמַר.

52. Rabbi Chiya and Rabbi Yosi were walking on the road when they chanced upon a cave in the field. Rabbi Chiya questioned Rabbi Yosi concerning the words: "These are the words of the Covenant...besides the Covenant..." (Devarim 28:69). Why does it say, "the words of the Covenant"? It should have said 'the words of Gvurah'. He said to him: It has been explained that these CURSES IN THE BOOK OF VAYIKRA WERE SAID by Gvurah, and that those IN DEVARIM were said by Moses himself, as we have already learned.

53. ת״ח, אַלֵּין וְאַלֵּין דִּבְרֵי הַבְּרִית הֲווֹ, דְּאע״ג דְּמִפִּי הַגְּבוּרָה הֲווֹ מִלִּין. מִלֵּי בְּרִית הֲווֹ, דְּהָא טַב וּבִישׁ בֵּיהּ תַּלְיָין. טַב דְּאָתֵי מִצַּדִּיק. בִּישׁ דְּאָתֵי מִן דִּינָא. דִּינָא, מֵאֲתַר דְּדִינָא, וְהַיְינוּ צֶדֶק. וְצַדִּיק וְצֶדֶק

בְּרִית אִינּוּן, בְּרִית אִקְרוּן. וְעַל דָּא, מִלִּין אִלֵּין, מִלֵּי בְּרִית אִינּוּן. וְקָשִׁיר בְּרִית כַּחֲדָא. וּבְגִינֵי כַּךְ זָכוֹר וְשָׁמוֹר, קָשִׁיר כַּחֲדָא. זָכוֹר בְּיוֹם, שָׁמוֹר בַּלַּיְלָה. הָא בְּרִית כַּחֲדָא, וּבְגִין כַּךְ בְּרִית וַדַּאי, דִּבְרֵי הַבְּרִית נִינְהוּ. וּבְכָל אֲתַר בְּרִית בַּאֲתַר דָּא אִיהוּ.

53. Come and behold: the ones as well as the others are the words of the Covenant, for though they were from Gvurah, yet they are the words of the Covenant, since good and evil depend upon them. Good comes from the Righteous, YESOD; evil comes from Judgment – the place of Judgment, Righteousness – NAMELY MALCHUT. Righteous and Righteousness, YESOD AND MALCHUT, are the Covenant and are called 'the Covenant'. Therefore, these words are the words of the Covenant. The Covenant, WHICH IS YESOD AND MALCHUT, is bound together, and hence 'remember' and 'keep', TIFERET AND MALCHUT, are bound together; 'remember' by day, and 'keep' by night. THEY ARE TOGETHER BY THE SECRET OF THE VERSE, "AND THERE WAS EVENING AND THERE WAS MORNING, ONE DAY" (BERESHEET 1:5). Thus, the Covenant is YESOD AND MALCHUT together, SINCE ZEIR ANPIN IS CONNECTED TO MALCHUT ONLY THROUGH YESOD. It is therefore WRITTEN, "Covenant," since they are indeed the words of the Covenant, THE REPRIMAND IN THE BOOK OF VAYIKRA AND IN THE BOOK OF DEVARIM. Wherever the word "Covenant" is mentioned, it pertains to this place.

54. אָמַר רַבִּי חִיָּיא, וַדַּאי הָכִי הוּא, וּבג״כ שַׁבָּת דְּאִיהוּ זָכוֹר וְשָׁמוֹר, אִקְרֵי בְּרִית. דִּכְתִיב, וְשָׁמְרוּ בְנֵי יִשְׂרָאֵל אֶת הַשַּׁבָּת לַעֲשׂוֹת אֶת הַשַּׁבָּת לְדֹרֹתָם בְּרִית עוֹלָם. וְכֹלָּא מִלָּה חַד, וַאֲתַר דָּא, אִקְרֵי בְּרִית בְּכָל אֲתַר.

54. Rabbi Chiya said: Surely this is so. Hence, Shabbat, which is 'remember' and 'keep', YESOD AND MALCHUT, is called a "Covenant," as is written: "Wherefore the children of Yisrael shall keep the Shabbat, to observe the Shabbat throughout their generations, for a perpetual Covenant" (Shemot 31:16). Everything is one and the same. This place, YESOD AND MALCHUT TOGETHER, is uniformly called 'the Covenant'.

55. ת״ח, כְּתִיב וְנָתַתִּי שָׁלוֹם בָּאָרֶץ, הוּא יְסוֹד, דְּאִיהוּ שְׁלָמָא דְּאַרְעָא,

שְׁלָמָא דְּבֵיתָא, שְׁלָמָא דְּעָלְמָא. וְיִסַּרְתִּי אֶתְכֶם אַף אָנִי שֶׁבַע. מַאי ז'.
דָּא צֶדֶק. הָא וַדַּאי בְּרִית, ובג״כ דִּבְרֵי הַבְּרִית נִינְהוּ.

55. Come and behold: it is written, "And I will give peace in the land" (Vayikra 26:6). "PEACE" is Yesod, which is peace in the land, household peace, and the peace of the world, SINCE MALCHUT IS CALLED 'LAND', 'HOUSE' AND 'WORLD'. "...and I will chastise you, even I, seven" (Vayikra 26:28). What is seven? Surely it is righteousness, MALCHUT ON THE SIDE OF JUDGMENT. Assuredly, this is the Covenant, and therefore these are the words of the Covenant.

15. "I will not cast them away, nor will I abhor them, to destroy them utterly"

56. א"ר יוֹסֵי כְּתִיב. וְאַף גַּם זֹאת בִּהְיוֹתָם בְּאֶרֶץ אוֹיְבֵיהֶם וְגוֹ'. וְאַף גַּם זֹאת, וְאַף, כד"א, אַף אֲנִי. גַּם, לְרַבּוֹת כ"י, דְּאִקְרֵי זֹאת, דְּלָא שַׁבְקַת לוֹן לְעָלְמִין. בִּהְיוֹתָם בְּאֶרֶץ אוֹיְבֵיהֶם, בִּהְיוֹתָם כֹּלָּא כַּחֲדָא. לֹא מְאַסְתִּים וְלֹא גְעַלְתִּים בְּגִין דְּלָא אִתְחַבַּר בְּהוּ. לְהָפֵר בְּרִיתִי אִתָּם, דְּאִי לָא אֶפְרוֹק לְהוּ, הָא בְּרִיתִי פָּלִיג, ובג"כ לְהָפֵר בְּרִיתִי אִתָּם.

56. Rabbi Yosi said: It is written, "And yet for all that (lit. 'and also even this') when they are in the land of their enemies..." (Vayikra 26:44). "And also even this." 'Even,' is as, "even I" (Ibid. 28), WHICH REFERS TO ZEIR ANPIN. 'Also,' includes the Congregation of Yisrael, called 'this' (Heb. *zot*), MALCHUT, that never leaves them. "'When they are in the land of their enemies, I will not cast them away, nor will I abhor them' – though I am not connected to them – "so that I would break My Covenant with them" (Vayikra 26:44), because if I do not redeem them, my Covenant is divided. AND THE UNION BETWEEN YESOD AND MALCHUT IS UNDONE. THE SCRIPTURE therefore SAYS, "to break My Covenant with them."

57. א"ר חִיָּיא, אֲנָא שְׁמַעֲנָא מִלָּה חַדְתָּא, דְּאָמַר רִבִּי אֶלְעָזָר לֹא מְאַסְתִּים וְלֹא גְעַלְתִּים לְכַלּוֹתָם, לֹא הִכֵּיתִים וְלֹא הֲרַגְתִּים לְכַלּוֹתָם מִבָּעֵי לֵיהּ. אֶלָּא לֹא מְאַסְתִּים וְלֹא גְעַלְתִּים, מַאן דְּסָאנֵי לְאָחֳרָא מָאִיס הוּא לְקַבְלֵיהּ, וְגַעֲלָא הוּא בְּגִיעוּלָא קַמֵּיהּ. אֲבָל הָכָא, לֹא מְאַסְתִּים וְלֹא גְעַלְתִּים. מ"ט. בְּגִין דַּחֲבִיבוּתָא דְּנַפְשַׁאי בֵּינַיְיהוּ. וּבְגִינָהּ כֻּלְּהוּ חֲבִיבִין גַּבָּאי, הה"ד לְכַלּוֹתָם. לְכַלּוֹתָם כְּתִיב, חָסֵר וָי"ו, בְּגִינָהּ לֹא מְאַסְתִּים וְלֹא גְעַלְתִּים, בְּגִין דְּאִיהִי רְחִימָתָא דְּנַפְשַׁאי, רְחִימוּתָא דִּילִי גַּבָּהָא.

57. Rabbi Chiya said: I have heard something new that Rabbi Elazar said: "I will not cast them away (also: 'detest them'), nor will I abhor them, to destroy them utterly" (Ibid. 44). It should have been written, 'I will not hit them, nor will I kill them to destroy them utterly'. HE ANSWERS: THE

15. "I will not cast them away, nor will I abhor them, to destroy them utterly"

MEANING OF, "I will not cast them away, nor will I abhor them," is that a man who hates someone is abhorred and detested by Him. But here, "I will not cast them away, nor will I abhor them." Why? Because the beloved of My soul is among them, NAMELY THE SHECHINAH, for whose sake they are all My friends.' Hence, it says, "*lechalotam*" (lit. 'to destroy them utterly'). *Lechalotam* is spelled without the *Vav* AS AN ALLUSION TO THE SHECHINAH, CALLED 'BRIDE' (HEB. *KALAH*). *LECHALOTAM* IS AS 'FOR THE *KALAH*' - 'It is for THE BRIDE that I do not detest or abhor them, because She is the beloved of My soul, and the beloved of My soul is among them.'

58. לבׄ"ן דְּרָחִים אִתְּתָא, וַהֲוַות דַּיְירָא בְּשׁוּקָא דְּבוּרְסְקֵי, אִי לָא הֲוַות הִיא תַּמָּן, לָא עָיֵיל בָּהּ לְעָלְמִין. כֵּיוָן דְּהִיא תַּמָּן, דָּמֵי בְּעֵינוֹי כְּשׁוּקָא דְרוֹכְלֵי, דְּכָל רֵיחִין דְּעָלְמִין טָבִין אִשְׁתְּכָחוּ תַּמָּן.

58. THIS IS like a man who loves a woman who lives in a market of tanners WHO SMELL DISAGREEABLY - were she not there, he would never have entered there. Since she is there, THE TANNERS' MARKET seems to him like a market of spice merchants, where there are all the best odors in the world.

59. אוֹף הָכָא, וְאַף גַּם זֹאת בִּהְיוֹתָם בְּאֶרֶץ אוֹיְבֵיהֶם, דְּאִיהוּ שׁוּקָא דְּבוּרְסְקֵי, לֹא מְאַסְתִּים וְלֹא גְעַלְתִּים. וַאֲמַאי. לְכַלֹּתָם. בְּגִין כַּלָּתָם, דַּאֲנָא רְחִימְנָא לָהּ, דְּאִיהִי רְחִימָתָא דְּנַפְשָׁאי, דְּשַׁרְיָא תַּמָּן, וְדָמֵי עֲלַי כְּכָל רֵיחִין טָבָאן דְּעָלְמָא, בְּגִין הַהִיא כַּלָּה דִּבְגַוַוייהוּ. אׄ"ר יוֹסֵי, אִלּוּ לָא אָתֵינָא הָכָא, אֶלָּא לְמִשְׁמַע מִלָּה דָא דָיי.

59. Here too, "And yet for all that, when they are in the land of their enemies," which is a tanners' market OF EVIL SMELL, "I will not cast them away, nor will I abhor them." Why? "to destroy them utterly (Heb. *lechalotam*)"; 'because their Bride (Heb. *kalatam*), THE SHECHINAH, who abides there, is My love, and the Beloved of My soul. It therefore seems to Me like the best fragrance in the world, due to the Bride that dwells among them.' Rabbi Yosi said: Had I come only to hear this, it would be enough.

16. "A son honors his father"

60. פָּתַח וְאָמַר, בֵּן יְכַבֵּד אָב וְעֶבֶד אֲדֹנָיו. בֵּן יְכַבֵּד אָב, כד"א כַּבֵּד
אֶת אָבִיךְ וְאֶת אִמֶּךְ, וְאוּקְמוּהָ, בְּמֵיכְלָא וּמִשְׁתְּיָא וּבְכֹלָּא. הַאי בְּחַיּוֹי
דְּאִתְחַיָּיב בֵּיהּ. בָּתַר דְּמִית, אִי תֵּימָא הָא פָּטוּר מִנֵּיהּ הוּא, לָאו הָכֵי.
דְּאע"ג דְּמִית, אִתְחַיָּיב בִּיקְרֵיהּ יַתִּיר, דִּכְתִיב כַּבֵּד אֶת אָבִיךְ. דְּאִי
הַהוּא בְּרָא אָזִיל בְּאֹרַח תְּקָלָא, וַדַּאי מְבַזֶּה לַאֲבוּי הוּא, וַדַּאי עָבֵיד
לֵיהּ קְלָנָא. וְאִי הַהוּא בְּרָא אָזִיל בְּאֹרַח מֵישָׁר, וְתַקִּין עוֹבָדוֹי, וַדַּאי דָּא
אוֹקִיר לַאֲבוּי, אוֹקִיר לֵיהּ בְּהַאי עָלְמָא גַּבֵּי בְּנֵי נָשָׁא, אוֹקִיר לֵיהּ
בְּהַהוּא עָלְמָא, גַּבֵּי קוּדְשָׁא בְּרִיךְ הוּא. וְקוּדְשָׁא בְּרִיךְ הוּא חַיֵּיס עֲלֵיהּ,
וְאוֹתִיב לֵיהּ בְּכוּרְסַיָּיא דִּיקָרֵיהּ. וַדַּאי בֵּן יְכַבֵּד אָב.

60. He opened the discussion and said: "A son honors his father, and a servant his master" (Malachi 1:6). "A son honors his father," as it says, "Honor your father and your mother" (Shemot 20:12). It has been explained THAT HONORS ARE SHOWN in food, drink, and in everything during his life. If you think that he is exempt from honoring him after his death, it is not so. Since he is dead, it behooves one to honor him more, as it is written, "Honor your father" – AFTER HIS DEATH AS WELL. If the son treads the crooked way, he surely despises his father and disgraces him. If the son treads the way of Truth and amends his actions, he honors his father. He honors him in this world among men, and honors him in the World to Come by the Holy One, blessed be He. The Holy One, blessed be He, has compassion for him, and puts him on His Throne of Glory. Surely, "A son honors his father."

61. כְּגוֹן רִבִּי אֶלְעָזָר, דְּאִיהוּ אוֹקִיר לֵיהּ לַאֲבוּי בְּהַאי עָלְמָא, וּבְהַהוּא
עָלְמָא הַשְׁתָּא אַסְגֵּי שְׁבָחָא דר"ש בִּתְרֵין עָלְמִין, בְּהַאי עָלְמָא,
וּבְהַהוּא עָלְמָא יַתִּיר מֵחַיּוֹי. דְּזָכָה לִבְנִין קַדִּישִׁין, וּלְגִזְעִין קַדִּישִׁין.
זַכָּאִין אִינּוּן צַדִּיקַיָּיא, דְּזַכָּאן לִבְנִין קַדִּישִׁין, לְגִזְעִין קַדִּישִׁין. עֲלַיְיהוּ
אִתְקְרֵי, כָּל רוֹאֵיהֶם יַכִּירוּם כִּי הֵם זֶרַע בֵּרַךְ יְיָ'.

61. Rabbi Elazar for example, who honored his father in this world and in that world, now increases the praise of Rabbi Shimon in both worlds – in

this world and in the World to Come, more so than during his life, for he merited holy sons and holy scions. Happy are the righteous, who merit holy children and holy scions. It says of them, "all that see them shall acknowledge them, that they are the seed which Hashem has blessed" (Yeshayah 61:9).

בָּרוּךְ יְיָ׳ לְעוֹלָם אָמֵן וְאָמֵן. יִמְלוֹךְ יְיָ׳ לְעוֹלָם אָמֵן וְאָמֵן.

Blessed be Hashem for ever Amen and Amen. Hashem will reign for ever, Amen and Amen.

סְלִיק סֵפֶר וַיִּקְרָא.

End of the book of Vayikra.

NOTES

NOTES

NOTES

NOTES

NOTES

NOTES

32. The nine Corrections of the beard of Zeir Anpin

A Synopsis

Rabbi Shimon says that the beard is not mentioned in scripture because the most precious and concealed of all things are not revealed. The beard is the most valuable part of the entire countenance, its perfection and beauty. When the holy anointing oil drips from the beard of the holy Atika it drips upon the beard of Zeir Anpin, which gets established in nine Corrections, and from which the 22 letters of the Torah emerge. Rabbi Shimon describes all nine Corrections of the black hair of the beard.

247. תָּאנָא, אר״ש, אַסְהַדְנָא עֲלַי שְׁמַיָא, וּלְכָל אִלֵּין דְּעָלָנָא קַיְימִין. דְּחַדָּאן מִלִּין אִלֵּין, בְּכֻלְּהוּ עָלְמִין. וְחַדָּאן בְּלִבָּאי מִלַּי, וּבְגוֹ פְּרוֹכְתָּא עִלָּאָה דְּפָרִיסָא עֲלָנָא, מִתְטַמְּרִין, וְסַלְקִין, וְגָנִיז לְהוּ עַתִּיקָא דְּכֹלָּא, גָּנִיז וְסָתִים מִכֹּלָּא. וְכַד שָׁרֵינָא לְמַלְּלָא, לָא הֲווֹ יַדְעִין חַבְרַיָּא, דְּכָל הָנֵי מִלִּין קַדִּישִׁין מִתְעָרִין הָכָא. זַכָּאָה חוּלָקֵיכוֹן חַבְרַיָּיא דְּהָכָא. וְזַכָּאָה חוּלָקִי עִמְּכוֹן, בְּעָלְמָא דֵין וּבְעָלְמָא דְּאָתֵי.

247. We have learned that Rabbi Shimon said: I invoke as a witness the sky above and all those who are standing above us, MEANING ALL THE CHARIOTS AND ENCAMPMENTS OF THE ANGELS, that these matters rejoice in all the worlds. These matters are rejoicing in my heart and are hiding and ascending in the uppermost curtain that is extended over us. The most Ancient of all, who is concealed and sealed of all, hides them. When I began to speak, the friends did not know that all these holy matters are inspired here. Praised is the lot of the friends that are here. Praised is my lot with you in this world and in the World to Come.

248. פָּתַח ר״ש וְאָמַר, וְאַתֶּם הַדְּבֵקִים בַּיְיָ׳ אֱלֹהֵיכֶם וְגוֹ׳. מַאן עַמָּא קַדִּישָׁא כְּיִשְׂרָאֵל, דִּכְתִיב בְּהוּ אַשְׁרֶיךָ יִשְׂרָאֵל מִי כָמוֹךָ, דִּכְתִיב מִי כָמֹכָה בָּאֵלִם יְיָ׳ מִשּׁוּם דְּאִתְדַּבְּקוּתָא דִּלְהוֹן הוּא בִּשְׁמָא קַדִּישָׁא בְּעָלְמָא דֵין. וּבְעָלְמָא דְּאָתֵי יַתִּיר מֵהָכָא. דְּהָתָם לָא מִתְפָּרְשָׁן מִנֵּיהּ, מֵהַהוּא צְרוֹרָא דִּצְרִירִין בֵּיהּ צַדִּיקַיָּא, הה״ד וְאַתֶּם הַדְּבֵקִים בַּיְיָ׳, וְלָא כְּתִיב הַדְּבֵקִים לַיְיָ׳, אֶלָּא בַּיְיָ׳ מַמָּשׁ.

248. Rabbi Shimon opened the discussion with the verse: "But you that did cleave to Hashem your Elohim... " (Devarim 4:4). Who is a holy nation like Yisrael, that it is written of them: "Happy are you, O Yisrael: who is like to you" (Devarim 33:29), and: "Who is like you, Hashem, among the Elim" (Shemot 15:11). For their adherence is to the Holy Name in this world, and in the World to Come even more than here IN THIS WORLD, since there they are not separated from the bond into which the righteous are tied, MEANING THE BUNDLE OF LIFE, WHICH IS THE SECRET OF MALCHUT THAT IS BOUND IN THE TREE OF LIFE THAT IS ZEIR ANPIN. This is why it is written: "But you that did cleave to Hashem" instead of: 'did cleave towards Hashem', but actually "to Hashem."

249. תָּאנָא, כַּד נָחִית מִן דִּיקְנָא יַקִּירָא עִלָּאָה, דְּעַתִּיקָא קַדִּישָׁא, סָתִים וְטָמִיר מִכֹּלָּא, מְשַׁח דִּרְבוּת קַדִּישָׁא, לְדִיקְנָא דִּזְעֵיר אַפִּין. אִתַּתְקָן דִּיקְנָא דִּילֵיהּ, בְּתִשְׁעָה תִּקּוּנִין. וּבְשַׁעֲתָא דְּנָהִיר דִּיקְנָא יַקִּירָא דְּעַתִּיקָא דְּעַתִּיקִין, בְּהַאי דִּיקְנָא דִּזְעֵיר אַפִּין, נַגְדִּין תְּלֵיסַר מַבּוּעִין דִּמְשַׁח עִלָּאָה, בְּהַאי דִּיקְנָא. וּמִשְׁתַּכְּחִין בֵּיהּ, עֶשְׂרִין וּתְרֵין תִּקּוּנִין. וּמִנֵּיהּ נַגְדִּין, עֶשְׂרִין וּתְרֵין אַתְוָון דְּאוֹרַיְיתָא קַדִּישָׁא.

249. We have learned that when the holy anointing oil descends upon the beard of Zeir Anpin from the precious beard of the uppermost of the holy Atik, who is hidden and concealed from everyone, the beard of Zeir Anpin is established in nine Corrections. During the time that the precious beard of the most Ancient among the ancient illuminates within this beard of Zeir Anpin, thirteen springs flow from the uppermost oil into the beard OF ZEIR ANPIN, and 22 Corrections prevail in it. From it flow the 22 letters of the Torah.

250. וְאָ״ת דִּיקְנָא לָא אִשְׁתְּכַח, וְלֹא אָמַר שְׁלֹמֹה אֶלָּא לְחַיָּיו. אֶלָּא הָכִי תָּאנָא בְּצִנְעִיוּתָא דְּסִפְרָא, כָּל מַה דְּאִטְמַר וְגָנִיז, וְלָא אִדְכַּר וְלָא אִתְגַּלְיָיא. הַהוּא מִלָּה הֲוֵי עִלָּאָה וְיַקִּירָא מִכֹּלָּא, וּבְג״ד הוּא סָתִים וְגָנִיז. וְדִיקְנָא מִשּׁוּם דְּהוּא שְׁבָחָא וּשְׁלִימוּתָא, וְיַקִּירוּתָא מִכָּל פַּרְצוּפָא, גְּנִזֵיהּ קְרָא, וְלָא אִתְגַּלְיָיא. וְתָאנָא, הַאי דִּיקְנָא דְּאִיהוּ שְׁלִימוּתָא דְּפַרְצוּפָא וְשַׁפִּירוּתָא דִּזְעֵיר אַפִּין, נָפִיק מֵאוּדְנוֹי, וְנָחִית

וְסָלִיק וְחָפֵי, בְּתַקְרוֹבָא דְּבוּסְמָא. מַאי תַּקְרוּבָא דְּבוּסְמָא. כד"א לְחָיָיו
כַּעֲרוּגַת הַבּוֹשֶׂם. בְּתִשְׁעָה תִּקּוּנִין, אִתְתָּקַן הַאי דִּיקְנָא דִּזְעֵיר אַנְפִּין.
בְּשַׂעֲרֵי אוּכָמֵי, מִתְתַּקְנָא בְּתִקּוּנָא שַׁפִּיר. כְּגַבָר תַּקִּיף שַׁפִּיר לְמֶחֱזֵי.
דִּכְתִּיב בָּחוּר כָּאֲרָזִים.

250. You might say that the beard is not mentioned anywhere and Solomon mentioned only "his cheeks" (Shir Hashirim 5:13), BUT DOES NOT SAY BEARD. HE REPLIES: So we have learned in the hidden book that everything that is hidden and concealed is neither mentioned nor revealed. This thing, THE BEARD, is uppermost and most precious of all. It is hidden and concealed since the beard is the praise and the most valued feature of the entire countenance; therefore, the scripture concealed it and did not reveal it. We have learned that this beard, which is the perfection of the countenance and the beauty of Zeir Anpin, starts out from his ears and drops and ascends and covers with an offering of fragrance. What is this offering of fragrance? It is as it says: "His cheeks are like a bed of spices" (Ibid.). With nine Corrections, this beard of Zeir Anpin was established with black hair all shaped in a beautiful arrangement like a valiant, beautiful and mighty man, as is written: "Excellent as the cedars" (Ibid. 15).

251. תִּקּוּנָא קַדְמָאָה. מִתְתַּקַן שַׂעֲרָא מִלְּעֵילָּא, וְנָפִיק הַהוּא נִיצוֹצָא
בּוּצִינָא דְּקַרְדִּינוּתָא, וְנָפִיק מִכְּלָלָא דַּאֲוִירָא דַּכְיָא, וּבָטַשׁ בִּתְחוֹת
שַׂעֲרָא דְּרֵישָׁא, מִתְּחוֹת קוֹצִין דְּעַל אוּדְנִין. וְנָחִית מִקַּמֵּי פִּתְחָא
דְּאוּדְנִין נִימֵי עַל נִימֵי, עַד רֵישָׁא דְּפוּמָא.

251. The first Correction: The hairs are arranged from above, FROM THE SIDES OF THE HEAD. That spark goes out, that strong spark, emanates from the pure air and pounds from underneath the head hair, under the HAIR locks above the ears. It descends hair after hair in front of the ear opening to the corner of the mouth.

252. תִּקּוּנָא תִּנְיָינָא. נָפִיק שַׂעֲרָא, וְסָלִיק מֵרֵישָׁא דְּפוּמָא, עַד רֵישָׁא
אַחֲרָא דְּפִתְחָא דְּפוּמָא. וְנָחִית מִתְּחוֹת פּוּמָא, עַד רֵישָׁא אַחֲרָא, נִימִין
עַל נִימִין, בְּתִקּוּנָא שַׁפִּירָא.

252. The second Correction: The hairs exit and ascend from the corner of the mouth, WHICH IS THE UPPER LIP - to the other corner of the mouth opening. They ALSO come down underneath the mouth FROM ONE CORNER to the other corner OF THE LOWER LIP, hair by hair, in a beautiful arrangement.

253. תִּקּוּנָא תְּלִיתָאָה. מֵאֶמְצָעִיתָא דִּתְחוֹת חוֹטָמָא, מִתְּחוֹת תְּרֵין נוּקְבִין, נָפִיק חַד אָרְחָא, וְשַׂעֲרִין זְעִירִין תַּקִּיפִין, מַלְיָין לְהַהוּא אָרְחָא, וּשְׁאָר שַׂעֲרִין מַלְיָין מֵהַאי גִּיסָא, וּמֵהַאי גִּיסָא, סוֹחֲרָנֵיהּ דְּהַהוּא אָרְחָא. וְאָרְחָא לָא אִתְחֲזֵי לְתַתָּא כְּלָל, אֶלָּא הַהוּא אָרְחָא דִּלְעֵילָּא, דְּנָחִית עַד רֵישָׁא דְּשִׂפְוָותָן, וְתַמָּן שְׁקִיעָא הַהוּא אָרְחָא.

253. The third Correction: Under the nose, in the center, under the two nostrils of the nose one path goes out THAT IS FREE OF HAIR, BUT tiny rough hairs fill that path. The rest of the hairs occupy both sides surrounding that path. On the bottom, THE LOWER LIP, there is no path visible at all, THAT IS CLEAR OF HAIR, BUT ONLY the path above IS VISIBLE, OVER THE UPPER LIP, that descends downwards to the beginning where the lips are JOINED. There, the path is submerged. IT DOES NOT CONTINUE UNDER THE LOWER LIP AS BY ARICH ANPIN.

254. תִּקּוּנָא רְבִיעָאָה. נָפִיק שַׂעֲרָא, וְאִתְתָּקַן, וְסָלִיק וְחָפֵי בְּעַלְעוֹי דְּתִקְרוֹבָא דְּבוּסְמָא. תִּקּוּנָא חֲמִשָׁאָה. פָּסִיק שַׂעֲרָא, וְאִתְחֲזִיִין תְּרֵין תַּפּוּחִין, מִכָּאן וּמִכָּאן, סוּמָקָן כְּהַאי וַרְדָא סוּמָקָא. וּמִתְלַהֲטָן בִּמְאָתָן וְשַׁבְעִין עָלְמִין, דְּמִתְלַהֲטִין מִתַּמָּן. תִּקּוּנָא שְׁתִיתָאָה. נָפִק שַׂעֲרָא כְּחַד חוּטָא בְּסַחֲרָנֵיהּ דְּדִיקְנָא, וְתַלְיָין עַד רֵישָׁא דְּמַעוֹי, וְלָא נָחִית עַד טַבּוּרָא. תִּקּוּנָא שְׁבִיעָאָה. דְּלָא תַּלְיָין שַׂעֲרֵי עַל פּוּמָא, וּפוּמָא אִתְפְּנֵי מִכָּל סִטְרוֹי. וְיַתְבִין שַׂעֲרֵי בְּתִקּוּנָא סְחוֹר סְחוֹר לֵיהּ.

254. The fourth Correction: Hairs sprout out and are arranged to ascend and cover His cheeks like a fragrant offering. THAT IS THE SECRET MEANING OF: "HIS CHEEKS ARE LIKE A BED OF SPICES." The fifth Correction: The hairs stop GROWING. The two apples OF THE FACE become visible, CLEAR

OF HAIR, on both sides. They are red like a red rose and glow in 270 worlds that glow from there. The sixth Correction: The hairs sprout out like one string around the beard and hang to the top of His belly, MEANING TO HIS CHEST, and do not go down to the middle. The seventh Correction: The hair does not hang over the mouth and the mouth is free OF HAIR all around. The hairs are set in an arrangement around it.

255. תִּקּוּנָא תְּמִינָאָה. דְּנַחְתִּין שַׂעֲרֵי בִּתְחוֹת דִּיקְנָא, דִּמְחַפְיָין קְדָלָא, דְּלָא אִתְחֲזְיָא. כֻּלְהוּ שַׂעֲרֵי דְּקִיקִין, נִימִין עַל נִימִין. מַלְיָין מִכָּל סִטְרוֹי. תִּקּוּנָא תְּשִׁיעָאָה. דְּמִתְחַבְרָן שַׂעֲרֵי כֻּלְהוּ בְּשִׁקּוּלָא מְעַלְיָיא, עִם אִינוּן שַׂעֲרֵי דְּתַלְיָין. כֻּלְהוּ בְּשִׁקּוּלָא שַׁפִּיר, כְּחַד גִּיבָּר תַּקִּיף, מָארֵי נָצַח קְרָבִין.

255. The eighth Correction: The hairs descend under the beard and cover the back of the neck so it is not seen. All the hairs are thin. Tiny strands upon strands fill every direction. The ninth Correction: The hairs join, altogether evenly, with those hairs that are hanging, all evenly and beautifully like a mighty man who wins battles.

256. בְּתִשְׁעָה תִּקּוּנִין אִלֵּין, נַגְדִּין וְנָפְקִין ט' מַבּוּעִין דִּמְשַׁח רְבוּת דִּלְעֵילָא. וּמֵהַהוּא מְשַׁח רְבוּת, נַגְדִּין לְכָל אִינוּן דִּלְתַתָּא. ט' תִּקּוּנִין אִלֵּין אִשְׁתְּכָחוּ בְּדִיקְנָא דָא. וּבִשְׁלֵימוּת תִּקּוּנָא דְּדִיקְנָא דָא, אִתְקְרֵי גִּיבָּר תַּקִּיף. דְּכָל מַאן דְּחָמֵי דִּיקְנָא קַיְּימָא בְּקִיּוּמֵיה, תַּלְיָיא בֵּיה גְּבוּרָה תַּקִּיפָא. עַד כָּאן תִּקּוּנָא דְּדִיקְנָא עִלָּאָה דִּזְעֵיר אַפִּין.

256. With these nine Corrections nine springs of the anointing oil of above flow and spring forth. From that anointing oil, there is a flow to all those below. These nine Corrections reside in the beard OF ZEIR ANPIN, and with the perfection of the arrangement of the beard, he is considered such a mighty man, that whoever observes this beard prevails, and mighty strength is connected to him. Up until here is the description of the supernal beard of Zeir Anpin.

33. First Correction of the nine Corrections of the beard of Zeir Anpin

A Synopsis

Rabbi Elazar tells us that King David needed these nine Corrections in order to conquer the other kings and nations; he called upon God, who answered him with liberation and took his part. Rabbi Elazar talks about the form of man, including the forms of Lion, Ox and Eagle, and how man is mentioned in the quoted scriptures only in conjunction with the Holy Name. He says that Zeir Anpin will do all that one desires for whoever holds on to the holy beard and honors Him. The essential message of this section is: If God takes my part, I will not fear, for what can man possibly do to me?

257. אָמַר רִבִּי שִׁמְעוֹן לְרִבִּי אֶלְעָזָר בְּרֵיהּ, קוּם בְּרִי, סַלְסֵל תִּקּוּנָא דְּדִיקְנָא קַדִּישָׁא, בְּתִקּוּנוֹי אִלֵּין. קָם ר' אֶלְעָזָר, פָּתַח וְאָמַר, מִן הַמֵּצַר קָרָאתִי יָהּ עָנָנִי בַמֶּרְחָב יָהּ וְגוֹ'. עַד מִבְּטוֹחַ בִּנְדִיבִים. תָּנָא, הָכָא ט' תִּקּוּנִין דִּבְדִיקְנָא דָּא. לְהָנֵי תִּקּוּנִין אִצְטְרִיךְ דָּוִד מַלְכָּא, בְּגִין לְנַצְחָא לִשְׁאַר מַלְכִין, וְלִשְׁאַר עַמִּין.

257. Rabbi Shimon said to his son Rabbi Elazar: Rise my son, and curl the arrangement of the holy beard through these Corrections. Rabbi Elazar stood up and said, "Out of my distress I called upon Yah: Yah answered me with liberation...than to trust in princes" (Tehilim 118:5-9). We have learned here, IN THIS VERSE, of the nine forms that exist in this beard, IN ZEIR ANPIN. King David needed these Corrections in order to conquer the other kings and nations.

258. ת"ח, כֵּיוָן דְּאָמַר הָנֵי ט' תִּקּוּנִין, לְבָתַר אָמַר כָּל גּוֹיִם סְבָבוּנִי בְּשֵׁם יְיָ' כִּי אֲמִילַם. אָמַר, הָנֵי תִּקּוּנִין דַּאֲמֵינָא, לְמַאי אִצְטְרִיכְנָא. מִשּׁוּם דְּכָל גּוֹיִם סְבָבוּנִי. וּבְתִקּוּנָא דְּדִיקְנָא דָּא, ט' תִּקּוּנִין, דְּאִינּוּן שֵׁם יְיָ', אֲשֵׁצִינוּן מִן עָלְמָא, הַהַ"ד בְּשֵׁם יְיָ' כִּי אֲמִילַם.

258. Come and see that as soon as he said those nine Corrections, he concluded with the verse: "All nations compassed me about: but in the name of Hashem I cut them off" (Ibid. 10). He said: All these Corrections that I mentioned, what purpose do they serve me? It is because all nations compassed me about. In the arrangement of this beard are nine Corrections, which are the name of Hashem, AND THROUGH THEM, I will abolish them from the world. This is what is written: "In the name of Hashem I cut them off."

259. וְתָנָא בְּצִנִיעוּתָא דְּסִפְרָא, תִּשְׁעָה תִקּוּנִין אָמַר דָּוִד, הָכָא, שִׁיתָא אִינּוּן בִּשְׁמָא קַדִּישָׁא. דְּשִׁית שְׁמָהָן הֲווֹ, וּתְלַת אָדָם. וְאִי תֵּימָא תְּרֵין אִינּוּן. תְּלָתָא הֲווֹ, דְּהָא נְדִיבִים בִּכְלַל אָדָם הֲווֹ.

259. We have learned in the hidden book that King David has mentioned here nine Corrections IN THE VERSES OF: "OUT OF MY DISTRESS..." Six are in the Holy Name, in that there are IN THESE VERSES six names, and three times man. If you say we only find "MAN" twice, IT IS NOT SO, BUT RATHER there are three, since "princes" are also included in "man." WE CONSIDER THE WORD "PRINCES" AS IF "MAN" IS SAID, SO WE HAVE "MAN" THREE TIMES, AS IS FURTHER EXPLAINED.

260. תָּנָא שִׁיתָא שְׁמָהָן, דִּכְתִּיב: מִן הַמֵּצַר קָרָאתִי יָּה, חַד. עֲנָנִי בַמֶּרְחָב יָּה, תְּרֵין. יְיָ' לִי לֹא אִירָא, תְּלַת. יְיָ' לִי בְּעוֹזְרָי, אַרְבַּע. טוֹב לַחֲסוֹת בַּיְיָ', חֲמִשָׁה. טוֹב לַחֲסוֹת בַּיְיָ', שִׁיתָא. אָדָם תְּלַת, דִּכְתִּיב: יְיָ' לִי לֹא אִירָא מַה יַּעֲשֶׂה לִי אָדָם, חַד. טוֹב לַחֲסוֹת בַּיְיָ' מִבְּטוֹחַ בָּאָדָם, תְּרֵי. טוֹב לַחֲסוֹת בַּיְיָ' מִבְּטוֹחַ בִּנְדִיבִים, תְּלַת.

260. We have learned that there are six names, as is written: 1) "Out of my distress I called upon Yah"; 2) "Yah answered me with liberation"; 3) "Hashem is on my side; I will not fear"; 4) "Hashem takes my part"; 5) "It is better to take refuge in Hashem," and 6) "It is better to take refuge in Hashem," WHICH IS IN THE SECOND VERSE. THUS WE HAVE HERE SIX NAMES. "Man" is there three times, as is written: 1) "Hashem is on my side; I will not fear: what can a man do to me?"; 2) "It is better to take refuge in Hashem than to put confidence in man," and 3) "It is better to take refuge in Hashem than to trust in princes." PRINCES ARE MAN, AS MENTIONED ABOVE, SO WE HAVE "MAN" THREE TIMES.

261. ות"ח רָזָא דְּמִלָּה, דִּבְכָל אֲתָר דְּאִדְכַּר אָדָם הָכָא, לָא אִדְכַּר אֶלָּא

בְּשְׁמָא קַדִּישָׁא. דְּהָכִי אִתְחֲזֵי. מִשׁוּם דְּלָא אִקְרֵי אָדָם, אֶלָּא בְּמָה
דְּאִתְחֲזֵי לֵיהּ. וּמַאי אִתְחֲזֵי לֵיהּ. שְׁמָא קַדִּישָׁא. דִּכְתִּיב וַיִּיצֶר יְיָ'
אֱלֹהִים אֶת הָאָדָם, בְּשֵׁם מָלֵא, דְּהוּא יְיָ' אֱלֹהִים. כְּמָה דְּאִתְחֲזֵי לֵיהּ
וּבג"כ הָכָא לָא אִדְכַּר אָדָם אֶלָּא בִּשְׁמָא קַדִּישָׁא.

261. Come and see the secret of the matter. Everywhere man is mentioned here, it is mentioned only together with the Holy Name, THAT IS TO SAY, IN THE SAME VERSE MAN IS MENTIONED, YUD HEI VAV HEI IS ALSO MENTIONED. This is as it should be, as man is only referred to with that which he deserves. What is THE NAME "MAN" deserving? It is the Holy Name YUD HEI VAV HEI, MEANING TO SAY THAT PRIOR TO THE PERFECTION OF THE HOLY NAME, YUD HEI VAV HEI, THE MOCHIN THAT ARE REFERRED TO AS "MAN" ARE NOT COATED WITH IT, as is written: "Hashem Elohim formed man" (Beresheet 2:7), YUD HEI VAV HEI ELOHIM BEING THE SECRET OF CHOCHMAH AND BINAH, 'THE MAN,' MEANING THE MOCHIN IN THE IMAGE OF ZEIR ANPIN, THAT ARE REFERRED TO AS "MAN," THAT IS, with a full name which is Yud Hei Vav Hei Elohim, as is befitting it, THE NAME MAN. Therefore, man is mentioned only TOGETHER with the Holy Name.

262. וְתָנָא, כְּתִיב מִן הַמֵּצַר קָרָאתִי יָהּ עָנָנִי בַמֶּרְחָב יָהּ, תְּרֵי זִמְנֵי יָ"הּ
יָ"הּ, לָקֳבֵיל תְּרֵי עָלְוֹי, דְּשַׂעֲרֵי אִתְאַחֲדָן בְּהוּ. וּמִדְּחָמָא דְּשַׂעֲרֵי
אִתְמַשְׁכָאן וְתַלְיָין, שָׁארֵי וְאָמַר יְיָ' לִי לֹא אִירָא. יְיָ' לִי בְּעוֹזְרָי. בִּשְׁמָא
דְּלָא חָסֵר. בִּשְׁמָא דְּהוּא קַדִּישָׁא. וּבִשְׁמָא דָּא, אִדְכַּר אָדָם.

262. We have learned that it is written: "Out of my distress I called upon Yah: Yah answered me with liberation"; that is twice Yud-Hei. That is for the two cheeks to which the hairs are attached. When DAVID saw that the hairs flow and hang, he commenced saying, "Hashem is on my side; I will not fear... Hashem takes my part," MEANING WITH THE COMPLETE NAME OF YUD HEI VAV HEI, with a name that is not missing in it VAV-HEI, a name that is holy. Man is mentioned with this FULL name, SINCE MOCHIN RESIDE ONLY WITH A FULL NAME, AS MENTIONED.

263. וּמַה דְּאָמַר מַה יַּעֲשֶׂה לִי אָדָם, הָכִי הוּא. דְּתָנָא כָּל אִינּוּן כְּתָרִין

קַדִּישִׁין דְּמַלְכָּא, כַּד אִתְתַּקָּנָן בְּתִקּוּנוֹי. אִתְקְרוּן אָדָם. דִּיּוּקְנָא דְּכָלִיל
כֹּלָּא. וּמַה דְּמִשְׁתַּלְּפָא בְּהוּ, אִתְקְרֵי שְׁמָא קַדִּישָׁא. וְתַעַרָא וּמַה דְּבֵיהּ,
אִתְקְרֵי ידו״ד, וְאִתְקְרֵי אָדָם בִּכְלָלָא דְּתַעֲרָא, וּמַה דְּבֵיהּ.

263. He said, "What can a man do to me?" This is ITS MEANING. We have learned that all these holy Sfirot of the King that were formed with shapes, THAT IS, THAT THE MOCHIN FLOW THROUGH THEM, are referred to as man, who is the general form including all FORMS. THE THREE FORMS – LION, OX, EAGLE – ARE COMPRISED IN THE FORM OF MAN. THAT IS THE SECRET OF MALCHUT THAT COMPRISES IN IT ALL THE THREE COLUMNS. CONSEQUENTLY, THE UNION OF THE THREE MOCHIN – CHOCHMAH, BINAH AND DA'AT, WHICH CORRESPOND TO LION, OX, EAGLE – ARE ONLY IN THE FORM OF MAN. What emanates FROM THE MOCHIN, THAT IS, WHAT IS CONCEIVABLE TO THE LOWER BEINGS, is referred to as the Holy Name, SINCE NAME MEANS CONCEPTION. The sheath, THAT IS THE SECRET OF MALCHUT REFERRED TO AS SHEATH, and what it contains, WHICH ARE THE MOCHIN, are called Yud Hei Vav Hei and are called man. That is the whole of the sheath together with its content.

264. וְאִלֵּין תִּשְׁעָה תִּקּוּנִין דְּאָמַר דָּוִד הָכָא, לְאַכְנְעָא שַׂנְאוֹי בְּגִין דְּמַאן דְּאָחִיד דִּיקְנָא דְּמַלְכָּא, וְאוֹקִיר לֵיהּ בִּיקָרוּ עִלָּאָה, כָּל מַה דְּבָעֵי מִן מַלְכָּא. מַלְכָּא עָבִיד בְּגִינֵיהּ. מ״ט דִּיקְנָא, וְלָא גוּפָא. אֶלָּא גוּפָא אָזִיל בָּתַר דִּיקְנָא, וְדִיקְנָא לָא אָזִיל בָּתַר גוּפָא.

264. Those nine Corrections that David said here were in order to subdue his enemies. Whoever holds on to the beard of the King and honors him with the utmost honor, the King will oblige and do for him all that he desires from the King. HE ASKS: What is the reason THAT THERE IS A NEED TO HOLD on to the beard and not to his body? HE REPLIES: It is because the body follows the beard, SINCE ALL THE LIGHTS OF THE BODY FLOW FROM THE BEARD, BUT the beard does not follow the body. CONSEQUENTLY, WHEN YOU ARE ATTACHED TO THE BEARD YOU ARE ALSO ATTACHED TO THE BODY, BUT WHEN ONE IS ATTACHED TO THE BODY HE IS NOT YET ATTACHED TO THE BEARD.

265. וּבִתְרֵי גְּוָונֵי אָתֵי הַאי חוּשְׁבָּנָא, חַד כִּדְקָאמְרָן. תְּרֵין: מִן הַמֵּצַר

קָרָאתִי יָהּ, חַד. עָנָנִי בַמֶּרְחָב יָהּ, תְּרֵי. ה' לִי לֹא אִירָא, תְּלַת. מַה
יַּעֲשֶׂה לִי אָדָם, אַרְבַּע. ה' לִי בְּעוֹזְרָי, חָמֵשׁ. וַאֲנִי אֶרְאֶה בְשׂוֹנְאָי,
שִׁיתָא טוֹב לַחֲסוֹת בַּה', שְׁבְעָה. מִבְּטֹחַ בָּאָדָם תְּמַנְיָיא. טוֹב לַחֲסוֹת
בַּיְיָ' מִבְּטֹחַ בִּנְדִיבִים תִּשְׁעָה.

265. There are two ways to count THE NINE CORRECTIONS OF THE BEARD
IN THE VERSES OF: "OUT OF MY DISTRESS." The first is as we already
said, THAT "OUT OF MY DISTRESS I CALLED UPON YAH" IS THE FIRST
AND "YAH ANSWERED ME WITH LIBERATION" IS THE FOURTH
CORRECTION THAT IS REFERRED TO IN OUR PRESENT ACCOUNT AS:
"WHAT CAN A MAN DO TO ME?" The second IS THE ACCOUNT BEFORE
US, OF WHICH "out of my distress I called upon Yah," is the first
CORRECTION. The second is: "Yah answered me with liberation"; the third
is: "Hashem is on my side; I will not fear" and the fourth is: "What can man
do to me?" The fifth is: "Hashem takes my part"; the sixth is: "Therefore I
shall gaze upon those who hate me"; the seventh is: "It is better to take
refuge in Hashem"; the eighth is: "Than to put confidence in man," and the
ninth is: "It is better to take refuge in Hashem than to trust in princes."

266. מִן הַמֵּצַר קָרָאתִי יָ"ה, מַאי קָא מַיְירֵי אֶלָּא דָוִד, כָּל מַה דְּאָמַר
הָכָא, עַל תִּקּוּנָא דְּדִיקְנָא דָּא קָאָמַר. מִן הַמֵּצַר קָרָאתִי יָהּ, מֵאֲתַר
דְּשָׁארֵי דִיקְנָא לְאִתְפַּשְּׁטָא, דְּהוּא אֲתַר דָּחִיק, מִקַּמֵּי פִּתְחָא דְּאוּדְנִין
מֵעֵילָא, תְּחוֹת שַׂעֲרֵי דְּרֵישָׁא. וּבְג"כ אָמַר יָ"ה יָ"ה תְּרֵי זִמְנֵי. וּבַאֲתַר
דְּאִתְפַּשְּׁט דִּיקְנָא, וְנָחִית מֵאוּדְנוֹי, וְשָׁארֵי לְאִתְפַּשְּׁטָא, אָמַר יְיָ' לִי לֹא
אִירָא, דְּהוּא אֲתַר דְּלָא דָחִיק וְכָל הַאי אִצְטְרִיךְ וְכוּ', דָּוִד לְאַכְנָע
תְּחוֹתֵיה מַלְכִין וְעַמִּין, בְּגִין יְקָרָא דְּדִיקְנָא דָּא.

266. HE ASKS: THE FIRST CORRECTION THAT IS REFERRED TO, "Out of
my distress I called upon Yah," what does it say, WHY IS IT CALLED THAT?
HE REPLIES: All that David said here, MEANING THE REST OF THE EIGHT
CORRECTIONS OF THE BEARD, he said about this Correction of the beard,
THE FIRST ONE, "Out of my distress (lit. 'straight') I called upon Yah," that
is, from the place where the beard begins to spread out, which is a narrow
area above and in front of the ear openings below the hair of the head. THIS

MEANS THAT AT THESE POINTS, THE HAIRS ARE SHORT AND THE AREA IS NARROW THAT POINTS OUT THE ASPECT OF JUDGMENT THAT EXISTS IN THE BEARD, WHICH IS THEREFORE REFERRED TO AS: "THE STRAIGHT." This is why he says Yud-Hei Yud-Hei twice, MEANING IN THE FIRST CORRECTION AND THE SECOND, BEFORE THE BEARD STARTS TO WIDEN, SINCE YUD-HEI POINTS OUT THAT THE NAME IS DEVOID OF VAV-HEI. However, in the area where the beard spreads out, where it drops from the ears and begins to widen, MEANING IN THE THIRD CORRECTION, he says, "Hashem is on my side; I will not fear." THAT IS THE COMPLETE NAME – YUD HEI VAV HEI – because that is an area that is not narrow. CONSEQUENTLY, ALL THE CORRECTIONS FOLLOW TO MITIGATE THE JUDGMENT IN THE FIRST CORRECTION, IN WHICH THE NAME IS NOT COMPLETE. David required all these CORRECTIONS in order to subdue kings and nations beneath him, through the glory of this beard.

267. וְתָאנָא בִּצְנִיעוּתָא דְּסִפְרָא, כָּל מַאן דְּחָמֵי בְּחֶלְמֵיהּ דְּדִיקְנָא דְּבַר נָשׁ עִלָּאָה אָחִיד בִּידֵיהּ, אוֹ דְּאוֹשִׁיט יְדֵיהּ לֵיהּ. יִנְדַּע דְּשָׁלִים הוּא עִם עִלָּאֵי, וְאַרְמֵיהּ תְּחוֹתֵיהּ אִינּוּן דִּמְצַעֲרִין לֵיהּ. תָּנָא, מִתַּתְקָן דִּיקְנָא עִלָּאָה בְּתִשְׁעָה תִּקּוּנִין, וְהוּא דִּיקְנָא דִּזְעֵיר אַפִּין, בְּט' תִּקּוּנִין מִתַּתְקָן.

267. We have learned in the hidden book that whoever sees in his dream his hand holding on to the beard of an important person, or extending his hand TO HOLD ON to it, he should be aware that he is in union with higher beings. He will throw under him all those who distress him, SINCE THE BEARD INDICATES THE SUBDUING OF ENEMIES AND WHOLENESS, AS MENTIONED ABOVE. We have learned that the supernal beard is formed with nine Corrections, which is the beard in Zeir Anpin that is formed with nine Corrections SINCE THE BEARD OF ARICH ANPIN IS FORMED WITH THIRTEEN CORRECTIONS.

268. תִּקּוּנָא קַדְמָאָה. מִתַּתְקָן שַׂעֲרָא מֵעֵילָּא, וְנָפִיק מִקַּמֵּי פִּתְחָא דְּאוּדְנִין, מִתְּחוֹת קוֹצֵי דְּתַלְיָין עַל אוּדְנִין, וְנַחְתִּין שַׂעֲרֵי, נִימִין עַל נִימִין, עַד רֵישָׁא דְּפוּמָא. תָּאנָא, כָּל אִלֵּין נִימִין דְּבְדִיקְנָא, תַּקִּיפִין יַתִּיר מִכָּל נִימִין דְּקוֹצִין דְּשַׂעֲרֵי דְּרֵישָׁא, וְשַׂעֲרֵי דְּרֵישָׁא אֲרִיכִין, וְהָנֵי לָאו אֲרִיכִין, וְשַׂעֲרֵי דְּרֵישָׁא, מִנְּהוֹן שְׁעִיעֵי, וּמִנְּהוֹן קְשִׁישִׁין.

268. The first Correction: The hair is arranged from above and grows out in front of the ear openings underneath the locks OF HEAD HAIR that hang over the ears. The hair descends strand by strand to the corner of the mouth. We have learned that all these hairs in the beard are coarsen than all the strands in the locks of head hair. The head hairs are long, while those IN THE BEARD are not long. Of the head hairs, some are smooth and some are rough.

269. וּבְשַׁעֲתָא דְּאִתְמַשְּׁכָן שַׂעֲרֵי חִוָּורֵי דְּעַתִּיק יוֹמִין, לְשַׂעֲרֵי דִּזְעֵיר אַפִּין, כְּתִיב, חָכְמוֹת בַּחוּץ תָּרֹנָּה. מַאי בַּחוּץ. בְּהַאי זְעֵיר אַפִּין. דְּמִתְחַבְּרָן תְּרֵי מוֹחֵי.

269. When the white hairs of Atik Yomin flow to the hair of Zeir Anpin, it is written: "Wisdoms cry aloud in the street (lit. 'outside')" (Mishlei 1:20). What is the meaning of: "outside"? That is in Zeir Anpin, to which two brains join, THE BRAIN OF ARICH ANPIN IN THE BRAINS OF ZEIR ANPIN OUTSIDE ARICH ANPIN, ABOUT WHICH IS SAID "WISDOMS CRY ALOUD OUTSIDE."

270. תְּרֵי מוֹחֵי ס״ד. אֶלָּא אֵימָא אַרְבַּע מוֹחֵי. תְּלַת מוֹחֵי דַּהֲווֹ בִּזְעֵיר אַפִּין, וְאִשְׁתְּכָחוּ בִּתְלַת חַלְּלֵי דְּגוּלְגַּלְתָּא דְּרֵישָׁא. וְחַד מוֹחָא שָׁקִיט עַל בּוּרְיֵיהּ, דְּכָלִיל כָּל תְּלַת מוֹחֵי. דְּאִתְמְשָׁךְ מִנֵּיהּ מְשִׁיכָא כְּלִילָן שְׁקִילָן, בְּשַׂעֲרֵי חִוָּורֵי. לְהַאי זְעֵיר אַפִּין לִתְלַת מוֹחֵי דְּבֵיהּ.

270. HE ASKS: Two brains, how could you imagine this, SINCE IN ZEIR ANPIN ALONE THERE ARE THREE BRAINS? HE REPLIES: Therefore, just say four brains. There are three brains are in Zeir Anpin in the three spherical cavities in the skull and one brain OF ARICH ANPIN rests in its station that includes WITHIN IT all three brains. From it there is a flow FROM ARICH ANPIN, balanced perfectly, continuously, into the white hair IN ARICH ANPIN to the three brains within Zeir Anpin.

271. וּמִשְׁתַּכְּחָן אַרְבַּע מוֹחֵי בְּהַאי זְעֵיר אַפִּין. בְּגִין כָּךְ אִשְׁתְּלִימוּ אַרְבַּע פָּרְשִׁיּוֹת דִּכְתִיבִין בַּתְּפִילִין, דְּאִתְכְּלִיל בְּהוּ שְׁמָא קַדִּישָׁא דְּעַתִּיק יוֹמִין, עַתִּיקָא דְּעַתִּיקִין, וּזְעֵיר אַפִּין. דְּהַאי הוּא שְׁלִימוּתָא דִּשְׁמָא

קַדִּישָׁא. דִּכְתִיב, וְרָאוּ כָּל עַמֵּי הָאָרֶץ כִּי שֵׁם יְיָ' נִקְרָא עָלֶיךָ וְיָרְאוּ מִמֶּךָ. שֵׁם יְיָ'. שֵׁם יְיָ' מַמָּשׁ, דְּאִינּוּן אַרְבַּע רְהִיטֵי בָּתֵּי דִּתְפִילִין.

271. There are four brains in Zeir Anpin, WHICH ARE CHOCHMAH AND BINAH, THE RIGHT OF DA'AT AND THE LEFT OF DA'AT. AS A RESULT OF THE BRAIN ILLUMINATION OF ARICH ANPIN TO HIS THREE BRAINS, HIS THREE BRAINS DIVIDE UP TO FOUR. As a result of these, the four portions, written in Tefilin, are completed, SINCE THE FOUR CHAPTERS IN THE TEFILIN ARE THE SECRET OF THE SURROUNDING LIGHT OF THE THREE BRAINS – CHOCHMAH, BINAH AND DA'AT – IN ZEIR ANPIN. DUE TO THE INCLUSION OF THE BRAIN OF ARICH ANPIN WITHIN THEM, THE BRAIN OF DA'AT IN ZEIR ANPIN IS SPLIT INTO TWO BRAINS, TO THE RIGHT AND TO THE LEFT, AND THAT COMPLETES THE FOUR CHAPTERS – THAT IS, FOUR BRAINS, since the Holy Name of Atik Yomin is included in them, the most ancient among the ancient, WHICH IS THE FIRST BRAIN THAT IS ARICH ANPIN, and that of Zeir Anpin, WHICH CONTAINS THREE BRAINS. This is the perfection of the Holy Name, as is written: "And all people of the earth shall see that you are called by the name of Hashem; and they shall be afraid of you" (Devarim 28:10). The name of Hashem is the actual name of Hashem, which are the boxes of the Tefilin, SINCE THE MOCHIN (LIT. 'BRAINS') ARE THE SECRET OF YUD HEI VAV HEI AND THE COMPARTMENTS OF THE BRAINS ARE THE SECRET OF MALCHUT, REFERRED TO AS THE NAME OF HASHEM.

272. וּבְג"כ, חָכְמוֹת בַּחוּץ תָּרֹנָּה. דְּהָכָא מִשְׁתַּכְּחִין. דְּהָא עַתִּיקָא דְּעַתִּיקִין, סְתִימָא דִּסְתִימִין, לָא אִשְׁתְּכַח, וְלָא זַמִּין חָכְמָתָא דִּילֵיהּ, מִשּׁוּם דְּאִית חָכְמָתָא סְתִימָא דְּכֹלָּא וְלָא אִתְפָּרַשׁ. וּבְגִין דְּאִתְחַבְּרוּ אַרְבְּעָה מוֹחִין בְּהַאי זְעֵיר אַפִּין. אִתְמַשְּׁכָן אַרְבַּע מַבּוּעִין מִנֵּיהּ לְאַרְבַּע עִיבָר, וּמִתְפָּרְשָׁן מֵחַד מַבּוּעָא, דְּנָפִיק מִכֻּלְּהוּ. וּבְג"כ אִינּוּן אַרְבַּע.

272. Therefore, SCRIPTURE SAYS: "Wisdoms cry aloud outside," WHICH ARE CHOCHMAH OF ZEIR ANPIN AND THAT OF ARICH ANPIN. They exist here IN ZEIR ANPIN, WHICH IS OUTSIDE ARICH ANPIN. The wisdom of the Ancient among the ancient, the most concealed of all concealed, is not available and is not prepared TO BE DISCOVERED, since it is wisdom concealed from all and is indescribable. Since the four brains joined in Zeir

Anpin, four springs flow forth from it to every direction, WHICH ARE FOUR BRAINS – CHOCHMAH, BINAH, THE RIGHT OF DA'AT AND THE LEFT OF DA'AT. THESE FOUR are separated by one spring that emanates to them all, THAT IS THE BRAIN OF CHOCHMAH, WHICH GOES OUT AND SPLITS INTO FOUR BRAINS, WHICH IS THE SECRET OF THE 32 PATHS OF WISDOM THAT ARE REVEALED TO THE LOWER GRADES. Therefore, there are four BRAINS IN CHOCHMAH OF ZEIR ANPIN DUE TO THE REASON THAT CHOCHMAH OF ARICH ANPIN IS INCLUDED IN THEM, SO THAT THEY WILL BE BESTOWED BY HIM UPON THE LOWER BEINGS SINCE IN THE CONCEALED BRAIN, FROM ITS LOCATION, NOTHING AT ALL IS REVEALED. THEREFORE, THE VERSE SAYS: "WISDOMS CRY ALOUD OUTSIDE," SINCE ONLY ON THE OUTSIDE IN THE PLACE OF ZEIR ANPIN WILL THEY SING JOYOUSLY – THAT IS, BE REVEALED.

273. וְתָאנָא, הַאי חָכְמְתָא דְּאִתְכְּלִילָא בְּאַרְבַּע, אִתְמַשְׁכָא בְּהָנֵי שַׂעֲרֵי, דְּאִינּוּן תַּלְיָין תָּלִין עַל תָּלִין. וְכֻלְּהוּ קַשְׁיָין וְתַקִּיפִין, וְאִתְמַשְׁכוּ וְנַגְידוּ כָּל חַד לִסְטְרוֹי. וְאֶלֶף אַלְפִין וְרִבּוֹא רִבְבָן תַּלְיָין, מִנַּיְיהוּ דְּלֵיתְהוֹן בְּחוּשְׁבָּנָא. הַה"ד, קְווּצוֹתָיו תַּלְתַּלִּים. תְּלֵי תְלִים. וְכֻלְּהוּ קַשְׁיָין וְתַקִּיפִין לְאִתְחַבְּרָא, כְּהַאי חַלָּמִישׁ תַּקִּיף. וּכְהַאי טִנָרָא דְּאִיהִי תַקִּיפָא. עַד דְּעַבְדִין נוּקְבִין וּמַבּוּעִין מִתְּחוֹת שַׂעֲרָא, וְנַגְדִּין מַבּוּעִין תַּקִּיפִין לְכָל עִיבָר וְעֵיבָר לְכָל סְטָר וּסְטָר. וּבְגִין דְּהָנֵי שַׂעֲרֵי אוּכְמֵי וַחֲשׁוּכָן, כְּתִיב מְגַלֶּה עֲמוּקוֹת מִנִּי חֹשֶׁךְ וַיּוֹצֵא לָאוֹר צַלְמָוֶת.

273. We have learned that this Chochmah that is a combination of four, MEANING THE BRAIN OF CHOCHMAH IN ZEIR ANPIN, is drawn through the hairs OF ZEIR ANPIN that hang wave upon wave. All are rough and coarse and are drawn and go forth, each to its own direction. A thousand of thousands and ten thousand of tens of thousands are hanging, some of them without number. This is what it says, "His locks are wavy" (Shir Hashirim 5:11), wave upon wave. All are too heavy and coarse to join, like a hard flint, and like that stone that is so strong and sturdy, so that they make holes and streams under the hair, and strong currents continue forth in each side and every direction. Since these hairs are black and dark, it is written about them: "He uncovers deep things out of darkness, and brings out to light the shadow of death" (Iyov 12:22).

274. וְתָנָא, הָנֵי שַׂעֲרֵי דְּדִיקְנָא תַּקִּיפִין מִשְּׁאָר שַׂעֲרֵי דְּרֵישָׁא, מִשּׁוּם דְּהָנֵי בִּלְחוֹדַיְיהוּ מִתְפָּרְשָׁן וּמִשְׁתַּכְחָן, וְאִינּוּן תַּקִּיפִין בְּאוֹרְחַיְיהוּ.

274. We have learned that the hairs in the beard are rougher than the head hair because THE BEARD HAIRS alone are available and explainable. CONSEQUENTLY, they are harsher in their ways.

275. אֲמַאי תַּקִּיפִין. אִי תֵּימָא, מִשּׁוּם דְּכֻלְּהוּ דִּינָא, לָאו הָכִי, דְּהָא בְּתִקּוּנִין אִלֵּין אִשְׁתְּכָחוּ רַחֲמֵי. וּבְשַׁעֲתָא דְּנַחְתִּין תְּלֵיסַר מַבּוּעֵי נַהֲרֵי דְּמִשְׁחָא, אִלֵּין כֻּלְּהוּ רַחֲמֵי.

275. HE ASKS: Why are they rough? If you will say because all pertain to Judgment, it is not so, for Mercy ALSO exists in these forms. When the thirteen springs of oil come down, THAT IS THIRTEEN BEARD CORRECTIONS OF ARICH ANPIN THAT DESCEND DOWN TO THE BEARD IN ZEIR ANPIN, they all pertain to Mercy. IF SO, WHY ARE THEY ROUGH?

276. אֶלָּא תָּאנָא, כָּל הָנֵי שַׂעֲרֵי דְּדִיקְנָא, כֻּלְּהוּ תַּקִּיפִין. מ״ט. כָּל אִינּוּן דְּרַחֲמֵי, בַּעְיָין לְמֶהֱוֵי תַּקִּיפִין. לְאַכְפַּיְיא לְדִינָא. וְכָל אִינּוּן דְּאִינְהוּ דִּינָא, הָא תַּקִּיפִין אִינּוּן. וּבֵין כָּךְ וּבֵין כָּךְ בַּעְיָין לְמֶהֱוֵי תַּקִּיפִין, מִתְּרֵין סִטְרִין. כַּד בָּעֵי עָלְמָא רַחֲמִין, רַחֲמֵי תַּקִּיפִין וְנַצְחִין עַל דִּינָא. וְכַד בָּעֵי דִּינָא, דִּינָא תַּקִּיף, וְנָצַח עַל רַחֲמֵי. וּבְג״כ בַּעְיָין לְמֶהֱוֵי תַּקִּיפִין מִתְּרֵין סִטְרִין, דְּכַד בָּעוּ רַחֲמֵי, שַׂעֲרֵי דְּאִינּוּן בְּרַחֲמֵי, קַיְימִין וּמִתְחַזְיָיא דִּיקְנָא בְּאִינּוּן שַׂעֲרֵי, וְכֹלָּא הֲווֹ רַחֲמֵי. וְכַד בַּעְיָיא דִּינָא, אִתְחַזְיָיא דִּיקְנָא בְּאִינּוּן שַׂעֲרֵי. וְכֹלָּא אִתְקַיַּים בְּדִיקְנָא.

276. HE REPLIES: We have learned that all the beard hairs are rough. What is the reason? It is because all these of Mercy – THAT IS, THE ONES THAT DRAW FROM THE CENTRAL COLUMN, WHICH IS MERCY – must be rough in order to subdue THE LEFT COLUMN, WHICH IS Judgment, AND TO JOIN IT WITH THE RIGHT. All these which pertain to Judgment, MEANING THE ONES DRAWN FROM THE LEFT COLUMN, WHICH ARE HARSH JUDGMENTS, are ESSENTIALLY rough. They need to be harsh from the two aspects, BOTH FROM THE COMPASSIONATE SIDE AND FROM THE JUDGMENTAL SIDE. When the world requires Mercy, THOSE HAIRS OF mercy FROM THE CENTRAL COLUMN are strong and overcome judgments, BECAUSE THEY UNITE THE LEFT WITH THE RIGHT COLUMN, WHICH IS CHASSADIM, AND THE BRAINS THAT ARE COMPASSIONATE ARE REVEALED. When the world requires Judgment, DURING THE ILLUMINATION OF CHOCHMAH THAT DOES NOT ILLUMINATE EXCEPT WITH THE EXPOSITION OF JUDGMENT, the Judgment is then strong and overcomes mercy. Therefore, they need to be rough on both sides. When mercy is required, the hairs that are mercy stand up and the beard is seen in these hairs. THE OTHERS ARE NOT VISIBLE and everything happens according to Mercy. When Judgment is needed, the beard is seen ONLY in these hairs OF JUDGMENT AND THE OTHERS ARE NOT VISIBLE. And everything, EITHER MERCY OR JUDGMENT, prevails through the beard.

277. וְכַד אִתְגַּלְיָיא דִּיקְנָא קַדִּישָׁא חִוָּורָא, כָּל הָנֵי וְכָל הָנֵי מִתְנַהֲרִין וּמִסְתַּחְיָין, כְּמַאן דְּאִסְתְּחֵי בְּנַהֲרָא עֲמִיקָא מִמָּה דַּהֲוָה בֵּיהּ. וְאִתְקַיָּימוּ כֻּלְּהוּ בְּרַחֲמֵי, וְלֵית דִּינָא אִשְׁתְּכַח, וְכָל הָנֵי תִּשְׁעָה כַּד נַהֲרִין כַּחֲדָא, כֻּלְּהוּ אִסְתַּחְיָין בְּרַחֲמֵי.

277. When the holy white beard OF ARICH ANPIN is revealed, the ones and the others shine and bathe IN THE CHASSADIM OF THE BEARD IN ARICH ANPIN. This is similar to someone who bathes in a deep river from THE MURKINESS that was in him, MEANING FROM THE JUDGMENTS. Everything exists with Mercy and there is no Judgment. When all these nine BEARD CORRECTIONS illuminate together, they all bathe in mercy.

278. וּבג"כ אָמַר מֹשֶׁה זִמְנָא אַחֲרָא, יְיָ' אֶרֶךְ אַפַּיִם וְרַב חֶסֶד. וְאִלּוּ אֱמֶת לָא קָאָמַר. מִשּׁוּם דְּרָזָא דְּמִלָּה, אִינּוּן תִּשְׁעָה מְכִילָן דְּנַהֲרִין מֵעַתִּיק יוֹמִין לִזְעֵיר אַפִּין. וְכַד אָמַר מֹשֶׁה תִּנְיָינָא, תִּשְׁעָה תִּקּוּנִין אָמַר. וְאִינְהוּ תִּקּוּנֵי דִּיקְנָא דְּמִשְׁתַּכְּחֵי בִּזְעֵיר אַפִּין, וְנַחְתִּין מֵעַתִּיק יוֹמִין וְנַהֲרִין בֵּיהּ. וּבג"כ אֱמֶת תַּלְיָיא בְּעַתִּיקָא, וְהַשְׁתָּא לָא אָמַר מֹשֶׁה וֶאֱמֶת.

278. Therefore, Moses repeated for a second time THE ATTRIBUTES: "Hashem is longsuffering, and great in love" (Bemidbar 14:18), THAT IS IN THE PORTION OF SHELACH. However 'truth' is not mentioned THERE, AS HE SAYS IN THE THIRTEEN ATTRIBUTES IN THE PORTION OF KI TISA. THAT IS because the secret of the matter is those nine attributes, MEANING THE NINE CORRECTIONS OF THE BEARD IN ZEIR ANPIN. They illuminate from Atik Yomin to Zeir Anpin. When Moses said THE ATTRIBUTES the second time, IN THE PORTION OF SHELACH, he said nine Corrections, which are the Corrections of the beard that are in Zeir Anpin, and descend from Atik Yomin and illuminate within him. Therefore, HE DID NOT MENTION IN THEM 'AND TRUTH', SINCE truth depends upon holy Atik, WHO IS THE SECRET OF THE SEVENTH OF THE THIRTEEN CORRECTIONS OF THE BEARD OF ARICH ANPIN, WHICH IS THE SECRET OF THE BRIGHTENING OF THE FACE IN ARICH ANPIN. WHEN HE ONLY RECEIVED NINE CORRECTIONS FROM ATIK, Moses did not say, 'and truth,' SINCE THIS CORRECTION OF ATIK IS NOT SHINING WITHIN HIM AT PRESENT.

279. תָּנָא, שַׂעֲרֵי דְּרֵישָׁא דִּזְעֵיר אַפִּין, כֻּלְּהוּ קְשִׁישֵׁי, תַּלְיִין עַל תַּלְיִין. וְלָא שְׁעִיעִין. דְּהָא חֲמֵינָא דִּתְלַת מוֹחֵי בִּתְלַת חֲלָלֵי מִשְׁתַּכְּחִין בֵּיהּ, וּנְהִרִין מִמּוֹחָא סְתִימָאָה. וּמִשּׁוּם דְּמוֹחָא דְּעַתִּיק יוֹמִין, שָׁקִיט וְשָׁכִיךְ כַּחֲמַר טַב עַל דּוּרְדְּיֵיהּ, שַׂעֲרוֹי כֻּלְּהוּ שְׁעִיעִין, וּמְשִׁיחִין בִּמְשַׁח טַב. וּבְגִ"כ כְּתִיב, רֵאשֵׁהּ כַּעֲמַר נְקֵא.

279. We have learned that the hairs of Zeir Anpin are all rough, wave upon wave, and are not smooth AS THE HAIR OF ARICH ANPIN. I see that there are three brains there in the three spaces and illuminate from the concealed brain OF ARICH ANPIN. The brain of Atik Yomin, THAT IS THE CONCEALED BRAIN, is quiet and resting like fine wine upon its sediments. AS THOSE SEDIMENTS DO NOT SPOIL THE WINE, BUT QUITE THE OPPOSITE, THEY FORTIFY IT, SO TOO THE JUDGMENTS IN THE CONCEALED BRAIN ARE NOT JUDGMENTS THAT WOULD EVEN SLIGHTLY DIMINISH THE CONCEALED BRAIN IN ITS OWN ESSENCE; TO THE CONTRARY, THEY STRENGTHEN IT. THEREFORE, the hairs OF ARICH ANPIN are all smooth and polished in fine oil and it is written: "And the hair of whose head was like the pure wool" (Daniel 17:9).

280. וְהַאי דִּזְעֵיר אַפִּין, קְשִׁישִׁין וְלָא קְשִׁישִׁין. דְּהָא כֻּלְּהוּ תַּלְיִין וְלָא

מִתְקַמְטֵי, ובג״כ חָכְמְתָא נָגִיד וְנָפִיק. אֲבָל לָא חָכְמְתָא דְּחָכְמְתָא,
דְּאִיהִי שְׁכִיכָא וּשְׁקִיטָא. דְּהָא תְּנֵינָא דְּלֵית דְּיָדַע מוֹחֵיה דְּעַתִּיק יוֹמִין,
בַּר אִיהוּ. וְהַאי דִּכְתִיב אֱלֹהִים הֵבִין דַּרְכָּה וְהוּא יָדַע אֶת מְקוֹמָהּ,
בִּזְעֵיר אַפִּין אִתְּמַר. אָמַר רִבִּי שִׁמְעוֹן, בְּרִיךְ בְּרִי לְקוּדְשָׁא בְּרִיךְ הוּא,
בְּעָלְמָא דֵּין וּבְעָלְמָא דְּאָתֵי.

280. Those of Zeir Anpin are rough yet not so rough, since all are hanging and not curly. Therefore, wisdom continues to flow THROUGH THEM. But this is not so for Chochmah of Chochmah, which is silent and quiet, IN THE CONCEALED BRAIN OF ARICH ANPIN. We have learned that there is nobody who could fathom the brain of Atik Yomin, except himself, and it is written: "Elohim understands its way, and he knows its place" (Iyov 28:23). This is said only OF CHOCHMAH of Zeir Anpin THAT IS REVEALED, AND NOT OF CHOCHMAH OF ARICH ANPIN THAT IS CONCEALED AND IS NOT REVEALED AT ALL. Rabbi Shimon said: Blessed is my son to the Holy One, blessed be He, in this world and in the World to Come.

34. The second and third of the nine Corrections of the beard of Zeir Anpin

A Synopsis

Rabbi Aba describes the second Correction as meaning several things: it is like a dominating, great, beautiful and mighty man; it is mercy; it is truth. He talks a good deal about Chesed in various contexts; we learn that the third Correction is "and abundant in Chesed."

281. תִּקּוּנָא תִּנְיָינָא. נָפִיק שַׂעֲרָא, וְסָלִיק מֵרֵישָׁא דְּפוּמָא, עַד רֵישָׁא אַחֲרָא דְּפִתְחָא דְּפוּמָא, וְנָחִית מִתְּחוֹת פּוּמָא, עַד רֵישָׁא אַחֲרָא, נִימִין עַל נִימִין, בְּתִקּוּנָא שַׁפִּיר.

281. The second Correction: The hairs leave and ascend from the corner of the mouth to the other corner of the mouth opening, THAT IS, FROM ONE END TO THE OTHER END ABOVE THE UPPER LIP. They descend under the mouth, BELOW THE LOWER LIP, FROM THE BEGINNING to the other end, AND strands upon strands descend in a beautiful shape.

282. קוּם רַבִּי אַבָּא. קָם ר' אַבָּא, פָּתַח וְאָמַר, כַּד תִּקּוּנָא דְּדִיקְנָא דָּא מִתְתַּקַּן בְּתִקּוּנָא דְּמַלְכָּא, כִּגְבַר תַּקִּיף שַׁפִּיר לְמֶחֱזֵי, רַב וְשַׁלִּיט, הה"ד גָּדוֹל אֲדוֹנֵינוּ וְרַב כֹּחַ. וְכַד אִתְבְּסַם בְּתִקּוּנָא דִּיקְנָא יַקִּירָא קַדִּישָׁא, וְיִשְׁגַּח בֵּיהּ, אִקְרֵי בִּנְהִירוּ דִּילֵיהּ, אֵל רַחוּם וְגו'. וְהַאי תִּקּוּנָא תִּנְיָינָא אִתְתַּקַּן, כַּד נָהִיר בִּנְהִירוּ דְּעַתִּיק יוֹמִין, אִקְרֵי רַב חֶסֶד. וְכַד מִסְתַּכְּלֵי דָּא בְּדָא, אִתְקְרֵי בְּתִקּוּנָא אַחֲרָא וֶאֱמֶת. דְּהָא נְהִירוּ אַנְפֵּיה.

282. RABBI SHIMON SAID TO RABBI ABA: Rise Rabbi Aba. Rabbi Aba stood up, and opened by saying: When this Correction is shaped with the Correction of the King, IT IS like a ruling, great, handsome and mighty man. This is what is written: "Great is our Master, and of great power" (Tehilim 147:5). When he was established with the formation of the precious holy beard OF ARICH ANPIN and looks at it, THIS CORRECTION is called by his light: "El, merciful... " (Shemot 34:6). THAT IS WHEN THE THIRTEEN BEARD CORRECTIONS OF ARICH ANPIN SHINE UPON THE NINE BEARD CORRECTIONS OF ZEIR ANPIN. THEN HIS SECOND CORRECTION IS CALLED BY THE NAME MERCIFUL. This second Correction is established by another of the Corrections OF THE BEARD OF ZEIR ANPIN and it is called: "and truth" (Shemot 34:6), WHICH IS THE SEVENTH CORRECTION OF THESE BEARD CORRECTIONS OF ZEIR ANPIN. His face shines, MEANING THAT IT THEN CONTAINS THE FIRST THREE SFIROT, WHICH ARE THE SECRET OF: "A MAN'S WISDOM MAKES HIS FACE TO SHINE" (KOHELET 8:1).

283. וְתָאנָא, נוֹשֵׂא עָוֹן אִתְקְרֵי דָא תִּקּוּנָא תִּנְיָינָא, כְּגַוְונָא דְּעַתִּיקָא קַדִּישָׁא. אֲבָל מִשּׁוּם הַהוּא אוֹרְחָא דְּנָפִיק, בְּתִקּוּנָא תְּלִיתָאָה תְּחוֹת תְּרֵין נוּקְבִין דְּחוֹטָמָא, וְשַׂעֲרִין תַּקִּיפִין זְעִירִין מַלְיָין לְהַהוּא אוֹרְחָא. לָא אִתְקְרוּן הָכָא נוֹשֵׂא עָוֹן וְעוֹבֵר עַל פֶּשַׁע, וְאִתְקְיָימוּ בְּאֲתָר אַחֲרָא.

283. We have learned that this Correction should have been called "pardons iniquity" (Michah 7:18), similar to THE SECOND CORRECTION OF holy Atik. However, due to the path that departs HERE in the third Correction, under the two nostrils where tiny rough hairs fill in this path, AND IT IS NOT CLEAR OF HAIR, LIKE THE THIRD CORRECTION IN ARICH ANPIN, THEREFORE, it is not called here "pardons iniquity, and forgives the transgression" (Ibid.). It prevails somewhere else; THAT IS, IN THE FOURTH CORRECTION.

284. וְתַנְיָא, תְּלַת מְאָה וְשַׁבְעִין וְחָמֵשׁ חֲסָדִים, כְּלִילָן בְּחֶסֶד דְּעַתִּיק יוֹמִין, וְכֻלְּהוּ אִקְרוּן חַסְדֵּי קַדְמָאֵי. דִּכְתִּיב, אַיֵּה חֲסָדֶיךָ הָרִאשׁוֹנִים. וְכֻלְּהוּ כְּלִילָן בְּחֶסֶד דְּעַתִּיקָא קַדִּישָׁא, סְתִימָא דְּכֹלָּא. וְחֶסֶד דִּזְעֵיר אַפִּין אִקְרֵי חֶסֶד עוֹלָם.

284. We have learned that Shin-Ayin-Hei (= 375) Chassadim are included in Chesed of Atik Yomin, WHICH IS THE MEANING OF: "BUT TO CAIN AND HIS OFFERING HE HAD NO RESPECT (HEB. SHA'AH, SHIN-AYIN-HEI)" (BERESHEET 4:5). FOR HE DID NOT DESERVE THESE CHASSADIM OF ATIK YOMIN and all are referred to as Chassadim of old, as is written: "Where are your former oaths of steadfast love (Heb. Chassadim)" (Tehilim 89:50). All are comprised in Chesed of holy Atik, who is concealed from all. And Chesed of Zeir Anpin is referred to as Chesed of the world (everlasting Chesed).

285. וּבְסִפְרָא דִּצְנִיעוּתָא, קָרֵי בֵּיהּ לְחֶסֶד קַדְמָאָה דְעַתִּיק יוֹמִין רַב חֶסֶד. וּבִזְעֵיר אַפִּין, חֶסֶד סְתָם. וּבְג"כ כְּתִיב הָכָא, וְרַב חֶסֶד. וּכְתִיב, נוֹצֵר חֶסֶד לַאֲלָפִים סְתָם. וְאוֹקִימְנָא, הַאי רַב חֶסֶד, מַטֵּה כְּלַפֵּי חֶסֶד, לְנַהֲרָא לֵיהּ, וּלְאַדְלְקָא בּוֹצִינֵי.

285. In the hidden book, he calls Chesed of old of Atik Yomin: "And abundant in love (Heb. *Chesed*)" (Shemot 34:6). In Zeir Anpin, CHASSADIM ARE simply REFERRED TO AS Chesed. Thus, it is written here IN THE THIRD CORRECTION OF ZEIR ANPIN: "And abundant in Chesed," SINCE THE FIRST CORRECTION IS "LONG" AND THE SECOND CORRECTION IS "SUFFERING." THE THIRD CORRECTION IS: "AND ABUNDANT IN CHESED" AS MENTIONED, SINCE HE RECEIVES HERE FROM THE ORIGINAL CHASSADIM OF ARICH ANPIN AND IS ALSO REFERRED TO AS ABUNDANT IN CHESED. It is written: "Keeping troth (Heb. *Chesed*) to thousands" (Ibid.) simply AND IT IS NOT WRITTEN: 'AND ABUNDANT IN CHESED,' SINCE HE SPEAKS THERE OF CHESED OF ZEIR ANPIN HIMSELF, WHICH IS REFERRED TO AS SIMPLY CHESED. We have explained that "abundant in Chesed" OF ARICH ANPIN leans towards Chesed OF ZEIR ANPIN, to illuminate to him and light the candles, MEANING THE SFIROT OF ZEIR ANPIN.

286. דְּתָנָא הַאי אוֹרְחָא דְּנָחִית תְּחוֹת תְּרֵין נוּקְבִין דְּחוֹטָמָא, וְשַׂעֲרִין זְעִירִין מַלְיָין לְהַהוּא אָרְחָא, לָא אִקְרֵי הַהוּא אָרְחָא עוֹבֵר עַל פֶּשַׁע, דְּלֵית אֲתָר לְאַעְבְּרָא לֵיהּ בִּתְרֵי גְוָונֵי. חַד מִשּׁוּם שַׂעֲרֵי דְּאִשְׁתְּכַח בְּהַהוּא אָרְחָא, הוּא אֲתָר קַשְׁיָא לְאַעְבְּרָא. וְחַד, מִשּׁוּם דְּנָחִית אַעְבְּרָא דְּהַהוּא אוֹרְחָא עַד רֵישָׁא דְּפוּמָא, וְלָא יַתִּיר.

286. We have learned about this path that descends under the two nostrils OF ZEIR ANPIN. Tiny hairs occupy that path, which is not referred to as "forgives (lit. 'passes over') the transgression," since there is no room to pass over THE TRANSGRESSION. This is due to two reasons: Because of the hairs that occupy that path, it is a difficult passage for the passing OF CHOCHMAH THERE and because the passage of that path goes down only to the corners of the mouth and no further.

287. וע"ד כְּתִיב, שִׂפְתוֹתָיו שׁוֹשַׁנִּים, סוּמְקִין כְּוַרְדָא, נוֹטְפוֹת מוֹר
עוֹבֵר, סוּמְקָא תַּקִּיף, וְהַאי אוֹרְחָא דְּהָכָא, בִּתְרֵי גְוָונֵי וְלָא אִתְבְּסַם.
מִכָּאן מַאן דְּבָעֵי לְאַגְזְמָא, תְּרֵי זִמְנֵי בָּטַשׁ בִּידֵיהּ בְּהַאי אוֹרְחָא.

287. Therefore, it is written: "His lips like roses" (Shir Hashirim 5:13), namely, red like roses, "dropping flowing myrrh" (Ibid.), which is deep red, WHICH IS JUDGMENT. This path here, ABOVE THE LIPS, did not get firmly established in two colors, AS MENTIONED. THEREFORE, JUDGMENT IS APPARENT ON THE LIPS, THE MEANING OF THE RED COLOR. From here, whoever wishes to frighten HIS FRIEND IN AN EXTRAORDINARY MANNER strikes twice with his hand on that path.

35. The fourth of the nine Corrections of the beard of Zeir Anpin

A Synopsis

Rabbi Aba says that this Correction is splendor and glory, and from it are suspended the vestments in which Zeir Anpin gets dressed, as He is clothed in glory and majesty. These are the Corrections in which He was dressed and was established in the form of man.

288. תִּקּוּנָא רְבִיעָאָה נָפִיק שַׂעֲרָא, וְאִתְתַּקַּן, וְסָלִיק וְחָפֵי בְּעַלְעוֹי, בְּתִקְרוּבְתָּא דְּבוּסְמָא. הַאי תִּקּוּנָא יָאֶה וְשַׁפִּירָא, לְאִתְחֲזְיָא הוֹד וְהָדָר הוּא. וְתָנֵינָא, הוֹד עִלָּאָה, נָפִיק וְאִתְעַטַּר וְנָגִיד לְאִתְאַחֲדָא בְּעַלְעוֹי, וְאִתְקְרֵי הוֹד זָקָן. וּמֵהַאי הוֹד וְהָדָר, תַּלְיָין אִלֵּין לְבוּשֵׁי, דְּאִתְלָבַּשׁ בְּהוּ, וְאִינּוּן פּוּרְפִּירָא יַקִּירָא דְּמַלְכָּא. דִּכְתִּיב הוֹד וְהָדָר לָבָשְׁתָּ, תִּקּוּנִין דְּאִתְלָבַּשׁ בְּהוּ, וְאִתְתַּקַּן בְּהַאי דִּיּוּקְנָא דְּאָדָם, יַתִּיר מִכָּל דִּיּוּקְנִין.

288. The fourth Correction: The hairs grow and take form, rising and covering over His cheeks with a fragrant offering. This form is beautiful to behold. It is splendor and glory. We have learned the highest glory (Hod) goes out and is decorated and continues to take hold of His cheeks. It is referred to as the glory of the beard. From this glory and splendor are suspended the garments in which ZEIR ANPIN is dressed, which are the precious vestments of the King, as is written: "You are clothed in glory and majesty" (Tehilim 104:1). These are the Corrections in which He was dressed and was established in the form of man, more than in any other form.

289. וְתָאנָא הַאי הוֹד, כַּד אִתְנְהַר בִּנְהִירוּ דְּדִיקְנָא עִלָּאָה, וְאִתְפָּשַׁט בִּשְׁאַר תִּקּוּנִין נְהִירִין. הַאי הוּא נוֹשֵׂא עָוֹן מֵהַאי גִּיסָא, וְעוֹבֵר עַל פֶּשַׁע מֵהַאי גִּיסָא. וּבג"כ, לְחָיָיו כְּתִיב. וּבְצִנְעִיעוּתָא דְּסִפְרָא אִקְרֵי, הוּא וְהָדָר וְתִפְאֶרֶת. דְּהָא תִּפְאֶרֶת הוּא עוֹבֵר עַל פֶּשַׁע, שֶׁנֶּאֱמַר וְתִפְאַרְתּוֹ עֲבוֹר עַל פֶּשַׁע. אֲבָל הַאי תִּפְאֶרֶת לָא אוֹקִימְנָא, אֶלָּא בְּתִקּוּנָא תְּשִׁיעָאָה, כד"א וְתִפְאֶרֶת בַּחוּרִים כֹּחָם. וְתַמָּן אִקְרֵי תִּפְאֶרֶת. וְכַד אִתְתְּקַל, בְּמַתְקְלָא חַד סַלְקִין. אָמַר ר"ש, יָאוֹת אַנְתְּ רִבִּי אַבָּא, לְאִתְבָּרְכָא מֵעַתִּיקָא קַדִּישָׁא, דְּכָל בִּרְכָאן נָפְקִין מִנֵּיהּ.

289. We have learned about the majesty OF THIS BEARD when it shone in the light of the upper beard OF ARICH ANPIN. It spread in the rest of the shining Corrections, MEANING ALSO IN THE FIFTH CORRECTION, which is: "pardons iniquity" (Michah 7:18) on this side and "forgives the transgression" (Ibid.) from that side. Therefore, it is written: "his cheeks" (Shir Hashirim 5:13). FOR IT INCLUDES BOTH THE HAIR ON THE CHEEKS, WHICH ARE THE FOURTH CORRECTION, AND BOTH APPLES THAT ARE CLEAR OF HAIR, WHICH ARE THE FIFTH CORRECTION. In the hidden book, this FOURTH CORRECTION is referred to as majesty, beauty and glory. Glory "forgives the transgression," as it is said: "And it is his glory (Heb. *Tiferet*) to pass over a transgression" (Mishlei 19:11). However, we did not explain this Tiferet until the ninth Correction, as it says, "The glory (Heb. *Tiferet*) of young men is their strength" (Mishlei 20:29). IN THE NINTH CORRECTION, it is called Tiferet. Upon weighing, they are BOTH equal in weight. Rabbi Shimon said: You are worthy, Rabbi Aba, to be blessed by holy Atik, from whom all blessings originate.

36. The fifth Correction of the nine Corrections of the beard of Zeir Anpin

A Synopsis

We learn that all the lights that illuminate from Arich Anpin are referred to as the original Chassadim, and due to these, all the everlasting Chassadim shine that are the Chassadim in Zeir Anpin. Thus His countenance shines upon the world and blesses it.

290. תִּקּוּנָא חֲמִישָׁאָה. פָּסִיק שַׂעֲרָא, וְאִתְחֲזוּן תְּרֵין תַּפּוּחִין מִכָּאן וּמִכָּאן, סוּמָקָן כְּהַאי וַרְדָּא סוּמָקָא. וּמִתְלַהֲטָן בְּמָאתָן וְשַׁבְעִין עָלְמִין, הָנֵי תְּרֵי תַּפּוּחִין, כַּד נְהִירוּ מִנְּהִירוּ דִּתְרֵין תַּפּוּחִין קַדִּישִׁין עִלָּאִין דְּעַתִּיקָא, אִתְמְשַׁךְ סוּמָקָא, וְאָתֵי חִיוָּרָא. בְּהַאי כְּתִיב, יָאֵר יְיָ' פָּנָיו אֵלֶיךָ וִיחֻנֶּךָּ. דְּכַד נְהִירִין מִתְבָּרֵךְ עָלְמָא. וּבְשַׁעֲתָא דְּאִתְעֲבָדוּ סוּמָקָא, כְּתִיב יִשָּׂא יְיָ' פָּנָיו אֵלֶיךָ, כְּלוֹמַר יִסְתָּלַק. וְלָא יִשְׁתְּכַח רוּגְזָא בְּעָלְמָא. תָּאנָא, כֻּלְּהוֹן נְהוֹרִין דְּאִתְנַהֲרָן מֵעַתִּיקָא קַדִּישָׁא, אִתְקְרוּן חַסְדֵּי קַדְמָאֵי. וּבְגִין אִינּוּן, נַהֲרִין כָּל אִינּוּן חַסְדֵּי עוֹלָם.

290. The fifth Correction: The hairs stop and two apples are visible, CLEAR OF HAIR, on either side, red like a red rose. They glow in 270 worlds. When these two apples shine, the light of the two uppermost holy apples of Atik, WHO IS ARICH ANPIN AND THAT ARE HIS SEVENTH CORRECTION, the red color disappears and the white color appears. About this, it is written: "Hashem make his face shine upon you, and be gracious to you" (Bemidbar 6:25). When they are shining, the world is blessed. When it becomes red, it is written: "Hashem lift up his countenance to you" (Ibid. 26), meaning to say that HIS FACE will be gone and there will not be anger in the world. We have learned that all the lights that illuminate from holy Atik, MEANING FROM ARICH ANPIN, are referred to as the original Chassadim. Due to these FIRST CHASSADIM, all these everlasting Chassadim shine, WHICH ARE THE CHASSADIM IN ZEIR ANPIN.

37. The sixth Correction of the beard of Zeir Anpin

A Synopsis
This is called one of the five edges of the beard, that depends on Chesed, and one must not destroy this Chesed by cutting it.

291. תִּקּוּנָא שְׁתִיתָאָה. נָפִיק שַׂעֲרָא, כְּחַד חוּטָא דְּשַׂעֲרֵי בְּסַחֲרָנֵיה דְּדִיקְנָא. פְּאַת הַזָּקָן וְאִיהוּ חַד מֵחָמֵשׁ פֵּאִין, דְּתַלְיָין בְּחֶסֶד, וְלָא אִבְעֵי לְחַבְּלָא הַאי חֶסֶד, כְּמָה דְּאִתְּמַר. וּבְגִין כָּךְ, לֹא תַשְׁחִית אֶת פְּאַת זְקָנֶךָ כְּתִיב.

291. The sixth Correction: The hairs go out like one string of hair around the beard, MEANING THE UPPERMOST AREA OF THE BEARD THAT CONTINUES TO THE CHEST - SIMILAR TO THE EIGHTH CORRECTION OF ARICH ANPIN. That is called one of the five edges of the beard, which depends on Chesed, and one must not destroy this Chesed, as we have learned. Therefore, it is written: "Neither shall you mar the corner of your beard" (Vayikra 19:27).

38. The seventh Correction of the beard of Zeir Anpin

A Synopsis

Here we learn that the mouth is clear because the hairs do not hang over it. Rabbi Yehuda says that the hosts or watchers are invested from the breath that leaves the mouth. Also when the breath spreads out of the mouth many faithful prophets get invested with the breath, and all are called the mouth of Hashem. This Correction dominates over all the six that precede it.

292. תִּקּוּנָא שְׁבִיעָאָה. דְּלָא תַּלְיָין שַׂעֲרָא עַל פּוּמָא, וּפוּמָא אִתְפְּנֵי מִכָּל סִטְרוֹי, וְיַתְבִין שַׂעֲרִין בְּתִקּוּנָא סְחוֹר סְחוֹר לֵיהּ. קוּם רַבִּי יְהוּדָה. קָם רַבִּי יְהוּדָה, פָּתַח וְאָמַר, בִּגְזֵירַת עִירִין פִּתְגָּמָא. כַּמָּה אֶלֶף רִבָּן מִתְיַשְׁבָן וּמִתְקַיְּימָן בְּהַאי פּוּמָא, וְתַלְיָין מִנֵּיהּ, וְכֻלְּהוֹן אִקְרוּן פֶּה. הה"ד וּבְרוּחַ פִּיו כָּל צְבָאָם. וּמֵהַהוּא רוּחָא דְּנָפִיק מִפּוּמָא, מִתְלַבְּשָׁן.

292. The seventh Correction: The hairs do not hang over the mouth and the mouth is clear all around its sides. The hairs are well arranged surrounding it. Rise, Rabbi Yehuda. Rabbi Yehuda rose. He opened the discussion saying, "This matter is by the decree of the watchers" (Daniel 4:14). How many thousands of ten thousands are sustained and exist through this mouth and depend upon it, and all are called mouth. This is what is written: "And all the hosts of them by the breath of his mouth" (Tehilim 33:6). From that breath that leaves the mouth they are invested.

293. כָּל אִינּוּן דִּלְבַר, תַּלְיָין מֵהַאי פּוּמָא. וּמֵהַאי פּוּמָא כַּד אִתְפְּשַׁט הַאי רוּחָא, מִתְלַבְּשָׁן בֵּיהּ כַּמָּה נְבִיאֵי מְהֵימְנָא, וְכֻלְּהוּ פֶּה יְיָ' אִתְקְרוּן. וּבַאֲתַר דְּרוּחָא נָפִיק, לָא אִתְעָרְבָא מִלָּה אַחֲרָא וְכֻלְּהוּ מֵחַכָּאן לְאִתְלַבְּשָׁא בְּהַהוּא רוּחָא דְּנָפִיק. וְהַאי תִּקּוּנָא שַׁלִּיטָא עַל כֻּלְּהוּ שִׁיתָא. מִשּׁוּם דְּהָכָא מִתְקַיְּימָן כֻּלְּהוּ וּמִתְאַחֲדָן. וּבְגִינֵי כַּךְ שַׂעֲרוֹהִי שְׁקִילִין סוֹחֲרָנֵיהּ דְּפוּמָא. וְאִתְפְּנֵי מִכָּל סִטְרוֹי, וְהַאי תִּקּוּנָא שַׁלִּיטָא עַל כֻּלְּהוּ מִשּׁוּם דְּהָכָא מִתְקַיְּימָן כֻּלְּהוּ וּמִתְאַחֲדָן. אָמַר ר"ש, בְּרִיךְ אַנְתְּ לְעַתִּיקָא קַדִּישָׁא.

293. All those that are outside are dependents of this mouth. Many faithful prophets are invested with the breath when it spreads out of this mouth, and all of them are called the mouth of Hashem. On the place where the breath exits, THAT IS THE MOUTH - nothing else is blended with it there. All wait to get invested with that breath that leaves THE MOUTH. This Correction dominates over all the six CORRECTIONS THAT PRECEDE IT, since all prevail here and take hold. Therefore, the hairs are even around the mouth and the mouth itself is cleared FROM HAIR from all its sides. Rabbi Shimon said: Blessed are you to holy Atik.

39. The eighth Correction of the beard of Zeir Anpin

A Synopsis
This Correction refers to the back of the neck, and Rabbi Yehuda says that when Zeir Anpin engages in war the back of the neck is visible to show strength. He talks about the shields of the mighty.

294. תִּקּוּנָא תְּמִינָאָה דְּנַחְתִּין שַׂעֲרֵי בִּתְחוֹת דִּיקְנָא, מְחַפְּיָין קְדָלָא דְּלָא אִתְחֲזֵי. דְּתַנְיָא, אֵין לְמַעֲלָה לֹא עֹרֶף וְלֹא עִפּוּי, וּבְזִמְנָא דְּאַגָּח קְרָבֵי אִתְחֲזֵי. מִשּׁוּם לְאַחֲזָאָה גְּבוּרְתָּא. דְּהָא תָּנֵינָן, אֶלֶף עָלְמִין אִתְאַחֲדִין מִנֵּיהּ, הה"ד, אֶלֶף הַמָּגֵן תָּלוּי עָלָיו כֹּל שִׁלְטֵי הַגִּבּוֹרִים. וְאֶלֶף הַמָּגֵן רָזָא הוּא. בְּצִנִּיעוּתָא דְּסִפְרָא, כֹּל שִׁלְטֵי הַגִּבּוֹרִים דְּאָתוּ מִסְּטַר גְּבוּרָה חַד, מֵאִינּוּן גְּבוּרָאן.

294. The eighth Correction: The hairs go lower below the beard and cover the back of the neck, so it would not be visible. We have learned that above there is no back of the neck and no fatigue. During the time that he engages in war, THE BACK OF THE NECK is visible to show strength, since we have learned that a thousand worlds are attached to it. This is what is written: "On which there hang a thousand bucklers, all shields of mighty men" (Shir Hashirim 4:4). "A thousand bucklers" is a secret. WE FIND in the hidden book all the shields of the mighty, MEANING those who come from the side of one Gvurah of those Gvurot.

40. The ninth Correction of the beard of Zeir Anpin

A Synopsis
We hear that this Correction relates to strength and balance, like a brave man who does mighty deeds. That is Tiferet – power, might, and compassion.

295. תִּקוּנָא תְּשִׁיעָאָה. דְּמִתְחַבְּרָן שַׂעֲרֵי בְּשִׁקוּלָא מַלְיָא, עִם אִינּוּן שַׂעֲרֵי דְּתַלְיָין, כֻּלְּהוּ בְּשִׁקוּלָא שַׁפִּיר, כְּחַד גִּיבָּר תַּקִּיף, מָארֵי נַצְחָן קְרָבַיָּיא. מִשׁוּם דְּכֻלְּהוּ שַׂעֲרֵי אִתְמַשְּׁכָן בָּתַר אִינּוּן דְּתַלְיָין. וּכְלָלָא דְּכֻלְּהוּ בְּאִינּוּן דְּתַלְיָין. וְכֹלָּא אִתְמְשַׁךְ, וְעַל דָּא כְּתִיב, תִּפְאֶרֶת בַּחוּרִים כֹּחָם. כְּתִיב בָּחוּר כָּאֲרָזִים, כְּגִיבָּר עָבֵיד גְּבוּרָאן, וְדָא הוּא תִּפְאֶרֶת, חֵילָא וּגְבוּרְתָּא וְרַחֲמֵי.

295. The ninth Correction: The hairs are joined in full weight with those hanging hairs and all are nicely even like a valiant mighty man who wins battles. Since all the hairs follow after those that hang, they are all generally included in those that hang, and all continue TO THE CHEST. Therefore, it is written: "The glory (Heb. *Tiferet*) of young men is their strength" (Mishlei 20:29). It is also written: "excellent as the cedars" (Shir Hashirim 5:15), meaning like a brave man who does mighty deeds. That is Tiferet, WHICH COMPRISES power, might and compassion.

296. תָּנָא, אר"שׁ כָּל הָנֵי תִּקוּנִין, וְכָל הָנֵי מִלִּין, בָּעֵינָא לְגַלָּאָה לְמָארֵיהוֹן דְּאִתְקָלוּ בְּמַתְקְלָא, וְלָא לְאִינּוּן דְּעָאלוּ, וְלָא נַפְקוּ אֶלָּא לְאָלֵין דְּעָאלוּ וְנַפְקוּ, דְּכָל מָאן דְּעָיֵיל וְלָא נָפִיק, טַב לֵיהּ דְּלָא אִבְרֵי.

296. We have learned that Rabbi Shimon said: All these Corrections and all these matters I wish to reveal to those who were balanced in weight, not to those who entered TO THE ORCHARD OF WISDOM and did not exit FROM IT IN PEACE, but rather to those that entered and left IT IN PEACE, since whoever entered and did not leave, it would have better for him not to have been born.

41. The form of man

A Synopsis

Rabbi Shimon begins by saying that the Atik of Atikin and Zeir Anpin are really all one; time has no meaning in this context. Really there is no change from compassion to justice, for example, it is just that it was established with these Corrections for the sake of the lower ones. The Atika Kadisha established His own Corrections and the Corrections of Zeir Anpin in the image and structure of the form of man. Rabbi Shimon says that when Hashem Elohim formed man he made a form within a form, meaning the highest form called man that is comprised of both male and female. He talks about the breath of life and how the man became a living soul.

297. כְּלָלָא דְּכָל מִלִּין, עַתִּיקָא דְּעַתִּיקִין, וּזְעֵיר אַפִּין, כֹּלָּא חַד. כֹּלָּא הֲוָה. כֹּלָּא הֲוֵי. כֹּלָּא יְהֵא. לָא יִשְׁתַּנֵּי. וְלָא מִשְׁתַּנֵּי. וְלָא שְׁנָא. אִתְתַּקַּן בְּתִקּוּנִין אִלֵּין. אִשְׁתְּלִים הַדִּיּוּקְנָא דְּכָלִיל כָּל דִּיּוּקְנִין. דִּיּוּקְנָא דְּכָלִיל כָּל שְׁמָהָן. דִּיּוּקְנָא דְּאִתְחֲזֵי בְּגַוֵּיהּ כָּל דִּיּוּקְנִין לָאו הַאי דִּיּוּקְנָא הֲוֵי, אֶלָּא כְּעֵין הַאי דִּיּוּקְנָא.

297. The rule of all these matters is that the Atik of Atikin and Zeir Anpin are all one, IN THEIR ESSENCE, ALL IS BEYOND TIME FROM THE ASPECT OF THEIR ESSENCE, AS 'WAS', 'IS', AND 'WILL BE' ARE THE SAME TO THEM. Everything is in the present and everything is in the past and everything is in the future, SINCE THERE DOES NOT EXIST IN DIVINITY A SENSE OF BEFORE AND AFTER. SIMILARLY, THERE DOES NOT EXIST AT ALL ANY CHANGE OF ACTION FROM THEIR ESSENTIAL ASPECT? FOR EXAMPLE, FROM MERCY TO JUDGMENT AND THE LIKE. Since there will be no change IN THE FUTURE and there was no change IN THE PAST, there is no change AT PRESENT. IT IS JUST that it was established with these Corrections FOR THE SAKE OF THE LOWER BEINGS. The form, encompassing all the forms, was completed, THAT IS, ZEIR ANPIN, WHICH IS THE SECRET OF THE HUMAN FORM THAT INCLUDES MALE AND FEMALE. It is the form that includes all the names, SINCE ZEIR ANPIN IS CALLED YUD HEI VAV HEI, WHICH IS A NAME THAT IS COMPRISED OF ALL NAMES, the image in which all images are seen, but not the ACTUAL image, only something similar to this image.

298. כַּד אִתְחַבְּרָן עִטְרִין וְכִתְרִין, כְּדֵין הוּא אַשְׁלָמוּתָא דְּכֹלָּא. בְּגִין, דְּדִיּוּקְנָא דְּאָדָם, הֲוֵי דִּיּוּקְנָא דְּעֶלְאִין וְתַתָּאִין דְּאִתְכְּלָלוּ בֵּיהּ. וּבְגִין דְּהַאי דִּיּוּקְנָא כָּלִיל עֶלְאִין וְתַתָּאִין, אַתְקִין עַתִּיקָא קַדִּישָׁא תִּקּוּנוֹי, וְתִקּוּנָא דִּזְעֵיר אַפִּין, בְּהַאי דִּיּוּקְנָא וְתִקּוּנָא.

298. When the decorations and crowns OF ZEIR ANPIN are joined, THAT IS THE MOCHIN OF THE FIRST THREE SFIROT, it is the perfection of everything, OF ALL THE UPPER AND THE LOWER BEINGS, since the image of man is an image in which the upper and lower beings are all included. This image comprises the higher and the lower beings; holy Atik established his own Corrections and the Corrections of Zeir Anpin in this image and structure.

299. וְאִי תֵּימָא מַה בֵּין הַאי לְהַאי. כֹּלָּא הוּא בְּמַתְקָלָא חֲדָא, אֲבָל מִכָּאן אִתְפָּרְשָׁן אָרְחוֹי. וּמִכָּאן אִשְׁתְּכַח דִּינָא. וּמִסִּטְרָא דִּילָן הֲווֹ שַׁנְיָין דָּא מִן דָּא. וְרָזִין אִלֵּין לָא אִתְמְסָרוּ, בַּר לִמְחַצְּדֵי חַקְלָא קַדִּישָׁא. וּכְתִיב סוֹד יְיָ' לִירֵאָיו.

299. You may wonder what is the difference BETWEEN ATIK AND ZEIR ANPIN. HE REPLIES: It all has the same measure. However, from here on, FROM ATIK, his paths divide up. From here, FROM ZEIR ANPIN, Judgment prevails, AND ONLY from our own perspective are they different from one another. These secrets are not passed on except to the reapers of the holy field, MEANING THOSE THAT DESERVED TO RESTORE MALCHUT THAT IS CALLED THE FIELD AND ARE ALREADY REAPING ITS HARVEST. It is written: "The counsel (lit. 'secret') of Hashem is with them that fear him" (Tehilim 25:14).

300. כְּתִיב וַיִּיצֶר יְיָ' אֱלֹהִים אֶת הָאָדָם, בִּתְרֵין יוֹדִי"ן. אַשְׁלִים תִּקּוּנָא גוֹ תִּקּוּנָא, טַבְרְקָא דְּגוּשְׁפַּנְקָא. וְדָא הוּא וַיִּיצֶר. תְּרֵין יוֹדִין לָמָּה. רָזָא דְּעַתִּיקָא קַדִּישָׁא, וְרָזָא דִּזְעֵיר אַפִּין. וַיִּיצֶר, מַאי צָר. צָר צוּרָה בְּגוֹ צוּרָה. וּמַהוּ צוּרָה בְּגוֹ צוּרָה. תְּרֵין שְׁמָהָן, דְּאִתְקְרֵי שֵׁם מָלֵא, יְיָ' אֱלֹהִים. וְדָא הוּא רָזָא דִּתְרֵין יוֹדִי"ן דְּוַיִּיצֶר, דְּצָר צוּרָה גוֹ צוּרָה. תִּקּוּנָא דִּשְׁמָא שְׁלִים, יְיָ' אֱלֹהִים.

300. It is written: "And Hashem Elohim formed (Heb. *vayyitzer*) the man" (Beresheet 2:7) with two Yud's. He perfected and completed one correction within another, that is the seal of the ring, and that is *vayyitzer* WITH TWO YUD'S. HE EXPLAINS HIMSELF: Why two Yud's? Because they denote the secret of holy Atik and the secret of Zeir Anpin. "Formed": what did He form? HE REPLIES: He formed a form within a form. HE ASKS: What is a form within a form? HE REPLIES: These are two names that are referred to as a full name, which are Yud Hei Vav Hei Elohim. That is the secret of the two Yud's in vayyitzer, indicating that he formed a form within a form, which is the structure of the full name Yud Hei Vav Hei Elohim.

301. וּבַמֶּה אִתְכְּלִילוּ. בְּדִיּוּקְנָא עִלָּאָה דָּא, דְּאִקְרֵי אָדָם. דְּכָלִיל דְּכַר וְנוּקְבָּא. וְעַל דָּא כְּתִיב אֶת הָאָדָם דְּכָלִיל דְּכַר וְנוּקְבָּא. אֶת: לְאַפָּקָא וּלְמִסְגֵּי זִינָא דְּנָפִיק מִנֵּיהּ.

301. HE ASKS: In what were they included, THESE TWO FORMS OF CHOCHMAH MENTIONED ABOVE WHERE HE CREATED A FORM WITHIN A FORM? HE REPLIES: In this highest form called man that is comprised of male and female, WHICH IS ZEIR ANPIN THAT ENCOMPASSES ZEIR ANPIN AND MALCHUT. Therefore, it is written: "the man," which includes male and female. Et (Eng. 'the') AS IN "THE" MAN is meant to include the kind that is produced from him, MEANING MALCHUT, WHICH IS THE FEMALE OF ZEIR ANPIN AND IS DERIVED FROM HIM, CORRESPONDS TO CHOCHMAH OF ARICH ANPIN, WHOSE ILLUMINATION IS VESTED WITHIN IT.

302. עָפָר מִן הָאֲדָמָה: דִּיּוּקְנָא בְּגוֹ דִּיּוּקְנָא. וַיִּפַּח בְּאַפָּיו נִשְׁמַת חַיִּים: טַבְרְקָא דְּגוּשְׁפַנְקָא גּוֹ בְּגוֹ. וְכָל דָּא לְמָה. בְּגִין לְאִשְׁתַּלְּפָא וּלְעַיְּילָא בֵּיהּ סָתִים דְּסָתִימָא עִלָּאָה, עַד סוֹפָא דְּכָל סְתִימִין. נִשְׁמָתָא, דְּכָל חַיֵּי דְּעֵילָא וְתַתָּא תַּלְיָין מֵהַהִיא נִשְׁמָתָא, וּמִתְקַיְּימֵי בָּהּ.

302. "Dust of the ground" (Ibid.): That is an image within an image. "And breathed into his nostrils the breath of life" (Ibid.), NAMELY the seal of the ring in the most inner part. Why is this? In order to produce and bring within it the one concealed with supernal concealment, WHICH IS THE CONCEALED CHOCHMAH OF ARICH ANPIN, to the end of all those concealed. And every life above and below, THAT IS, THE MOCHIN OF

ZEIR ANPIN AND OF THE FEMININE PRINCIPLE THAT COMPRISES THE
LOWER GRADES, depends upon and thrives through this soul.

303. וַיְהִי הָאָדָם לְנֶפֶשׁ חַיָּה, לְאַתְרְקָא, וּלְעַיְּילָא בְּתִקּוּנִין כְּגַוְונָא דָא,
וּלְאַשְׁלְפָא לְהַהִיא נִשְׁמָתָא. מִדַּרְגָּא לְדַרְגָּא עַד סוֹפָא דְּכָל דַּרְגִּין. בְּגִין
דִּיהֵוֵי הַהִיא נִשְׁמָתָא מִשְׁתַּכְּחָא בְּכֹלָּא, וּמִתְפַּשְּׁטָא בְּכֹלָּא. וּלְמֶהֱוֵי כֹּלָּא
בְּיִחוּדָא חַד. וּמַאן דְּפָסִיק הַאי יִחוּדָא מִן עָלְמָא, כְּמַאן דְּפָסִיק
נִשְׁמָתָא דָא, וּמְחֲזֵי דְאִית נִשְׁמָתָא אַחֲרָא, בַּר מֵהַאי. וּבְגִין כָּךְ, יִשְׁתְּצֵי
הוּא וְדוּכְרָנֵיהּ מִן עָלְמָא לְדָרֵי דָרִין.

303. "And the man became a living soul" (Ibid.): The corrections OF THE
SEAL OF THE RING are bestowed upon and entered into the soul of man, and
the soul is taken from the higher levels downward to the last level, THAT IS
FROM THE CONCEALED CHOCHMAH OF ARICH ANPIN, TO MALCHUT,
WHICH IS THE LAST OF THE LEVELS, so that the soul will be present in all
LEVELS and will spread in everything so that everything shall be in a single
union. Whoever interrupts this union from the world, MEANING THAT HE
SEPARATES MALCHUT FROM THE UNION OF THE THREE COLUMNS, it is
as if he severs this soul. THAT IS LIKE SOMEONE THAT VIOLATES THE
MOCHIN OF ZEIR ANPIN and indicates that another soul exists besides this
one, WHICH MEANS THAT HE ADHERES TO THE OTHER SIDE. As a result,
he and his memory will disappear from this world for generations upon
generations.

42. The order of the emanation of the female

A Synopsis

This section tells of the creation of the female from Tiferet of Zeir Anpin; this Tiferet is encompassed in mercy and judgment. Rabbi Shimon lists the five types of impropriety revealed in the female from the side of the five judgments.

304. בְּהַאי דְּיוּקְנָא דְּאָדָם, שָׁארֵי וְתָקִין כְּלָלָא דְּכַר וְנוּקְבָּא. כַּד אִתְתָּקַן הַאי דְּיוּקְנָא בְּתִקּוּנוֹי, שָׁארֵי מֶחָדוֹי, מִבֵּין תְּרֵין דְּרוֹעִין. בְּאֲתָר דְּתַלְיָין שַׂעֲרֵי דְדִיקְנָא, דְּאִתְקְרֵי תִּפְאֶרֶת. וְאִתְפָּשַּׁט הַאי תִּפְאֶרֶת, וְתָקִין תְּרֵין חַדִין, וְאִשְׁתְּלִיף לַאֲחוֹרוֹי, וְעָבַד גּוּלְגַּלְתָּא דְּנוּקְבָּא. כֹּלָא סְתִימָא מִכָּל סִטְרוֹי. בְּשַׂעֲרָא בְּפַרְצוּפָא דְּרֵישָׁא. וּבִכְלָלָא חֲדָא אִתְעֲבִידוּ בְּהַאי תִּפְאֶרֶת, וְאִקְרֵי אָדָם דְּכַר וְנוּקְבָּא. הה"ד כְּתִפְאֶרֶת אָדָם לָשֶׁבֶת בָּיִת.

304. In the image of man, the wholeness of male and female began to be prepared, THAT IS ZEIR ANPIN THAT INCLUDES MALE AND FEMALE. AFTERWARDS, when the form OF MAN was prepared in his Corrections, ZEIR ANPIN began TO SPREAD from his chest, between his two arms, in the area where his beard hairs hang, SINCE THIS AREA is referred to as Tiferet. This Tiferet spread and prepared two chests, and then took to the back and made the skull of the female, WHICH IS MALCHUT. She is totally concealed from all sides, the hair and the facial countenance of the head. These MALE AND FEMALE as one were made by Tiferet, and male and female are referred to as man, as is written: "According to the beauty (Heb. *Tiferet*) of a man; that it may remain in a house" (Yeshayah 44:13).

305. כַּד אִתְבְּרֵי פַּרְצוּפָא דְּרֵישָׁא דְּנוּקְבָּא, תַּלְיָיא חַד קוֹצָא דְּשַׂעֲרֵי מֵאֲחוֹרוֹי דִּזְעֵיר אַפִּין, וְתָלֵי עַד רֵישָׁא דְּנוּקְבָּא. וְאִתְחֲזָרוּ שַׂעֲרֵי בְּרֵישָׁהָא, כֻּלְּהוּ סוּמָקֵי דְּכָלְלָן בְּגוֹ גְּווֹנֵי, הה"ד, וְדַלַּת רֹאשֵׁךְ כָּאַרְגָּמָן. מַהוּ אַרְגָּמָן. גְּווֹנֵי דִּכְלִילָן בְּגוֹ גְּווֹנֵי.

305. When the facial countenance of the female head was created, a lock of hair hung in the back of Zeir Anpin and hung until the head of the female

and her head hairs were roused, all red consisting of all colors. This is what is written: "And the hair of your head like purple" (Shir Hashirim 7:6). What is "purple"? It is colors blended inclusively within hues.

306. תָּאנָא, אִתְפָּשַׁט הַאי תִּפְאֶרֶת מִטַבּוּרָא דְלִבָּא, וְנָקִיב וְאִתְעֲבָר בְּגִיסָא אַחֲרָא, וְתָקִין פַּרְצוּפָא דְנוּקְבָּא עַד טַבּוּרָא. וּמִטַבּוּרָא שָׁארֵי, וּבְטַבּוּרָא שְׁלִים.

306. We have learned that Tiferet spreads from the center of the heart, FROM THE CAVITY OF THE CHEST, permeates and crosses to the other side, MEANING THE BACK, and fixes the countenance of the female to the center. She starts at the center and ends at the center.

307. תּוּ אִתְפְּשַׁט הַאי תִּפְאֶרֶת, וְאַתְקָן מֵעוֹי דִּדְכוּרָא, וְעָיֵיל בְּהַאי אֲתָר כָּל רַחֲמִין, וְכָל סִטְרָא דְרַחֲמֵי. וְתָאנָא, בְּהָנֵי מֵעַיִין אִתְאַחֲדָן, שִׁית מֵאָה אֶלֶף רִבּוֹא מָארֵי דְרַחֲמֵי. וְאִתְקְרוּן בַּעֲלֵי מֵעַיִין. דִּכְתִּיב, עַל כֵּן הָמוּ מֵעַי לוֹ רַחֵם אֲרַחֲמֶנּוּ נְאֻם יְיָ'.

307. Tiferet further expanded and the intestines of the male were prepared. it put into that area all the mercy and every facet of compassion. We have learned that six hundred thousand times ten thousand creatures of compassion are attached to these intestines, and they are referred to as intestinal beings, as is written: "'Therefore My inward parts are moved for him; I will surely have mercy on him', says Hashem" (Yirmeyah 31:19).

308. תָּאנָא, הַאי תִּפְאֶרֶת, כָּלִיל בְּרַחֲמֵי, וְכָלִיל בְּדִינָא, וְאִתְפְּשַׁט רַחֲמֵי בִּדְכוּרָא, וְאִתְעֲבָר וְנָהִיר לְסִטַר אַחֲרָא, וְתָקִין מֵעוֹי דְנוּקְבָּא, וְאִתְתְּקָנוּ מְעָהָא בְּסִטְרָא דְדִינָא.

308. We have learned that Tiferet is encompassed in mercy and encompassed in judgment. Mercy permeates in THE BRAINS OF the male, THAT IS ZEIR ANPIN AS MENTIONED ABOVE, and crosses and illuminates the other side, MEANING THE BACK OF ZEIR ANPIN. It prepares the intestines of the female, MEANING HER MOCHIN, and her intestines are established by the side of judgment.

309. תָּאנָא, אִתְתָּקַן דְּכוּרָא בְּסִטְרֵיה, בְּמָאתָן וְתַמְנְיָא וְאַרְבְּעִין תִּקּוּנִין דִּכְלִילָן בֵּיה, וּמִנְּהוֹן לְגוֹ, וּמִנְּהוֹן לְבַר. מִנְּהוֹן רַחֲמֵי. וּמִנְּהוֹן דִּינָא. כֻּלְּהוּ דְּדִינָא, אִתְאַחֲדוּ בְּדִינָא דַּאֲחוֹרוֹי, דְּנוּקְבָּא אִתְפַּשְׁטַת תַּמָּן, וְאִתְאַחֲדוּ וְאִתְפַּשְׁטוּ בְּסִטְרָהָא.

309. We have learned that the male, WHICH IS ZEIR ANPIN, was prepared on his side, WHICH IS THE RIGHT, in 248 Corrections that are included in him. Some of them are in the innermost OF ZEIR ANPIN and some on his exterior side. Some of them are compassionate and some of them judgmental. All of those that are judgmental were attached to the judgments in the back OF ZEIR ANPIN where the female expands, and they joined together and spread on her side.

310. וְתָאנָא, חֲמִשָּׁה עֲרָיָיתָא אִתְגַּלְיָין בָּה, בְּסִטְרָא דְּדִינִין חֲמִשָּׁה. וְדִינִין ה' אִתְפַּשְּׁטָן, בְּמָאתָן וְאַרְבְּעִין וּתְמַנְיָא אָרְחִין. וְהָכִי תָּאנָא, קוֹל בְּאִשָּׁה עֶרְוָה. שֵׂעָר בְּאִשָּׁה עֶרְוָה. שׁוֹק בְּאִשָּׁה עֶרְוָה. יָד בְּאִשָּׁה עֶרְוָה. רֶגֶל בְּאִשָּׁה עֶרְוָה. דְּאע"ג דִּתְרֵין אִלֵּין לָא שָׁנִיוּהּ חַבְרָנָא, וּתְרֵין אִלֵּין יַתִּיר מֵעֶרְוָה אִינּוּן.

310. We have learned that five types of impropriety were revealed in her from the side of the five judgments. Five judgments were dispersed in 248 paths, as we have learned. Hearing a woman's voice is an impropriety, the sight of a woman's hair is an impropriety, the sight of a woman's thigh is an impropriety, the sight of a woman's hand is an impropriety and the sight of a woman's foot is an impropriety. These two, HAND AND FOOT, our friends did not learn; HOWEVER, these two are even more than an impropriety.

43. A pure covering

A Synopsis

We read about the cubit called Chesed. Rabbi Shimon considers and explains the perfection of Abraham and how it came about. He says that man includes both Chesed and Gvurah, and therefore in all the Sfirot there exist a right and a left, judgment and mercy.

311. וְתָאנָא בְּצְנִיעוּתָא דְסִפְרָא, אִתְפָּשַׁט דְּכוּרָא וְאִתְתָּקַן בְּתִקוּנוֹי. אִתְתָּקַן תִּקוּנָא דִּכְסוּתָא דַּכְיָא. וְהַאי הֲוָה אַמָּה דַכְיָא. אֲרִכֵיהּ דְּהַהוּא אַמָּה, מָאתָן וְאַרְבְּעִין וּתְמַנְיָה עָלְמִין. וְכֻלְּהוּ תַּלְיָין בְּפוּמָא דְאַמָּה, דְּאִתְקְרֵי יוֹ"ד. וְכֵיוָן דְּאִתְגַּלְיָיא יוֹ"ד פוּמֵיהּ דְּאַמָּה, אִתְגְּלֵי חֶסֶד עִלָּאָה. וְהַאי אַמָּה חֶסֶד הוּא דְּאִתְקְרֵי, וְתַלֵי בְּהַאי פוּם אַמָּה. וְלָא אִקְרֵי חֶסֶד, עַד דְּאִתְגַּלְיָיא יוֹ"ד דְּפוּם אַמָּה.

311. We have learned in the hidden book that the male spread and was fixed in his own formations. The shape of a clean covering was prepared and it became a clear cubit. The length of that cubit is 248 worlds. Everything depends on that opening of the cubit called Yud. As soon as that Yud, which is the opening of the cubit, is revealed, supernal Chesed becomes apparent. This cubit is called Chesed and is dependent on the opening of the cubit, but it is not considered Chesed until the Yud of the mouth of the cubit becomes uncovered.

312. וְת"ח, דְּלָא אִתְקְרֵי אַבְרָהָם שָׁלִים בְּהַאי חֶסֶד, עַד דְּאִתְגַּלְיָיא יוֹ"ד דְּאַמָּה. וְכֵיוָן דְּאִתְגְּלֵי אִקְרֵי שָׁלִים, הה"ד הִתְהַלֵּךְ לְפָנַי וֶהְיֵה תָמִים, תָּמִים מַמָּשׁ. וּכְתִיב וְאֶהְיֶה תָמִים לוֹ וָאֶשְׁתַּמְּרָה מֵעֲוֹנִי. מַאי קָא מַיְירֵי, רֵישָׁא וְסֵיפָא. אֶלָּא כָּל דְּגַלֵּי הַאי יוֹ"ד, וְאִסְתְּמַּר דְּלָא עַיֵּילֵיהּ לְיוֹ"ד בִּרְשׁוּתָא אַחֲרָא. לִיהֱוֵי שָׁלִים לְעָלְמָא דְאָתֵי, וְלֶהֱוֵי צָרִיר בִּצְרוֹרָא דְחַיֵּי. מַאי בִּרְשׁוּתָא אַחֲרָא. דִּכְתִיב וּבָעַל בַּת אֵל נֵכָר. וּבְגִין כָּךְ כְּתִיב, וְאֶהְיֶה תָמִים לוֹ, דְּכֵיוָן דְּהוּא תָמִים בְּגִלוּיָיא דְּיוֹ"ד, וָאֶשְׁתַּמְּרָה מֵעֲוֹנִי.

312. Come and see that Abraham was not considered perfect in this Chesed up until the Yud of the cubit was revealed, THAT IS THE CROWN OF YESOD. As soon as it was uncovered, he was considered perfect. This is what is written: "Walk before me, and be perfect" (Beresheet 17:1), actually perfect. It is also written: "I was also upright before him, and have kept myself from my iniquity" (II Shmuel 22:24). HE ASKS: What does it mean, THE RELATIONSHIP OF the beginning of the verse to the conclusion of the verse? HE REPLIES: It is telling about whoever uncovers that Yud, MEANING HE REVEALS THE CHOCHMAH IN THE CROWN OF YESOD, and who is carefully guarding himself so as not to give the Yud to another's jurisdiction, OF THE OTHER SIDE. He will be perfect for the World to Come, and he will be bound in the bundle of life, MEANING THAT HIS SOUL WILL BE INCLUDED IN MALCHUT THAT IS REFERRED TO AS THE BUNDLE OF LIFE, SINCE THE THREE COLUMNS ARE TIED INTO ONE BUNDLE. What is the other's jurisdiction? It refers to what is written: "And has married the daughter of a strange El" (Malachi 2:11). THAT MEANS MALCHUT OF THE OTHER SIDE, WHICH DRAWS CHOCHMAH FROM ABOVE DOWNWARDS. Therefore, it is written: "I was also upright before him," since he is perfect when revealing the Yud, MEANING IN THE ASPECT OF THE CROWN OF YESOD THAT ILLUMINATES FROM BELOW UPWARDS. THEN, "and have kept myself from my iniquity," NOT TO ADHERE TO DAUGHTERS OF A STRANGE EL, AS MENTIONED ABOVE.

313. וְכֵיוָן דְּאִתְפְּשַׁט אַמָּה דָא, אִתְפְּשַׁט סְטַר גְּבוּרָה מֵאִינוּן גְּבוּרָאן בִּשְׂמָאלָא דְנוּקְבָּא, וְאִשְׁתְּקַע בְּנוּקְבָּא בַּאֲתָר חַד, וְאַרְשֵׁם בְּעֶרְיָיתָא, בְּסוּתָה דְּכָל גּוּפָא דְנוּקְבָּא. וּבְהַהוּא אֲתָר אִקְרֵי עֶרְוָה דְכֹלָּא. אֲתָר לְאַצְנָעָא לְהַהוּא אַמָּה, דְּאִקְרֵי חֶסֶד. בְּגִין לְאִתְבַּסְּמָא גְּבוּרָה דָא דְּכָלִיל חָמֵשׁ גְּבוּרָאן, בְּהַאי חֶסֶד דְּכָלִיל בְּחָמֵשׁ חֲסָדִין. חֶסֶד יְמִינָא, גְּבוּרָא שְׂמָאלָא. אִתְבְּסָם דָּא בְּדָא, וְאִקְרֵי אָדָם, כָּלִיל מִתְּרֵין סִטְרִין. וּבְגִין כָּךְ, בְּכֻלְּהוּ כְּתְּרִין אִית יְמִינָא וּשְׂמָאלָא, דִּינָא וְרַחֲמֵי.

313. When this cubit gets extended, the side of Gvurah is extended from the Gvurot of the left of the female. It is submerged in a specific area in the female and the whole covering of the female body is marked by nakedness. In this place, it is considered overall nakedness, which is the area in which to conceal this cubit referred to as Chesed in order to mitigate the Gvurah that is comprised of five Gvurot with the Chesed that comprises five Chassadim. Chesed is right and Gvurah is left. One gets firmly established in the other and is called man, which is inclusive of both sides. Therefore in all the Sfirot, there exists a right and a left, Judgment and Mercy.

44. The seven kings of the Feminine Principle who died

A Synopsis

Rabbi Shimon goes back to the issue of the kings of Edom who perished, and he says that prior to the time the corrections of the king were prepared, Atika of Atikin was constructing worlds and working out corrections for existence. The female did not endure until the uppermost Chesed descended and caused them to endure. The kings of Edom did not endure because they consisted of judgment in judgment without Chesed.

314. תָּאנָא, עַד לָא זַמִּין תִּקּוּנוֹי דְּמַלְכָּא, עַתִּיקָא דְּעַתִּיקִין, בָּנָה עָלְמִין, וְאַתְקִין תִּקּוּנִין לְאִתְקַיְּימָא. הַהוּא נוּקְבָּא לָא אִתְבַּסְּמָא, וְלָא אִתְקַיְּימוּ, עַד דְּנָחִית חֶסֶד עִלָּאָה וְאַתְקַיְּימוּ, וְאִתְבַּסְּמוּ תִּקּוּנֵי נוּקְבָּא, בְּהַאי אַמָּה דְּאִקְרֵי חֶסֶד. הה"ד וְאֵלֶּה הַמְּלָכִים אֲשֶׁר מָלְכוּ בְּאֶרֶץ אֱדוֹם, אֲתָר דְּכָל דִּינִין מִשְׁתַּכְּחִין תַּמָּן וְלָא אִתְבַּסְּמוּ, עַד דְּאַתְקַן כֹּלָּא, וְנָפִיק הַאי חֶסֶד, וְאִתְיְשַׁב בְּפוּמָא דְּאַמָּה. הה"ד, וַיָּמָת וַיָּמָת, דְּלָא אִתְקַיְּימוּ, וְלָא אִתְבַּסְּמוּ, דִּינָא בְּדִינָא.

314. We have learned that prior to the time the corrections of the King were prepared, the most ancient among the ancient, THAT IS THE SUPREME EMANATOR, WAS constructing worlds and working out structures for existence. The female was not firmly established and did not lasr until the uppermost Chesed descended and caused them to last. The constructions of the female were firmly established with Yesod that is considered Chesed. This is what is written: "And these are the kings that reigned in the land of Edom, before there reigned any king..." (Beresheet 36:31), meaning the area where all judgments are, SINCE EDOM IS INDICATIVE OF JUDGMENTS. They were not firmly established until everything was settled. Chesed emerged and was situated at the tip of Yesod, WHICH IS THE CROWN OF YESOD WHERE CHOCHMAH IS REVEALED. This is what is written: "And... died... and... died" (Beresheet 36:32-39), since they did not last and were not firmly established, BECAUSE THEY CONSISTED OF judgment in judgment DEVOID OF CHESED.

315. וְאִי תֵּימָא אִי הָכִי דְּדִינָא כֻּלְּהוּ, וְהָא כְּתִיב וַיִּמְלוֹךְ תַּחְתָּיו שָׁאוּל

מֵרְחוֹבוֹת הַנָּהָר, וְהָא לָא אִתְחֲזֵי דִינָא. דְּתָנֵינָן, רְחוֹבוֹת הַנָּהָר אִיהוּ בִּינָה, דְּמִינָהּ מִתְפַּתְּחִין חַמְשִׁין תַּרְעִין דִּנְהוֹרִין וּבוּצִינִין, לְשִׁית סִטְרֵי עָלְמָא. תָּאנָא, כֻּלְּהוּ דִינָא, בַּר מֵחַד דְּאִתְקַיָּים בַּתְרָאָה, וְהַאי שָׁאוּל מֵרְחוֹבוֹת הַנָּהָר, דָּא הוּא חַד סִטְרָא, דְּאִתְפָּשַׁט וְנָפִיק מֵרְחוֹבוֹת הַנָּהָר.

315. If you will wonder that if all are Judgments, why is it written: "And Saul of Rehoboth by the river reigned in his place" (Ibid. 37). It does not seem THAT THERE WILL BE Judgment, since we have learned that Rehoboth by the river means Binah, from whose source are opened fifty gates of lights and candles to the six corners of the world. THAT IS ZEIR ANPIN REFERRED TO AS WORLD AND, THEREFORE, IT WAS CALLED REHOBOTH, SO WE SEE THAT SAUL OF REHOBOTH BY THE RIVER IS NOT OF JUDGMENT. HE REPLIES: We have learned that they all are Judgments except for one, the last KING that lasted, THAT IS HADAR. This Saul from Rehoboth by the river is only one side, THE LEFT SIDE, that spread and emerged from Rehoboth by the river. THEREFORE, HE TOO IS OF JUDGMENT.

316. וְכֻלְּהוּ לָא אִתְקַיָּימוּ, לָא תֵּימָא דְּאִתְבַּטָּלוּ, אֶלָּא דְּלָא אִתְקַיָּימוּ בְּהַהוּא מַלְכוּ, עַד דְּאִתְּעַר וְאִתְפָּשַׁט הַאי בַּתְרָאָה מִכֻּלְּהוּ, דִּכְתִיב וַיִּמְלֹךְ תַּחְתָּיו הֲדַר. מַאי הֲדַר. חֶסֶד עִלָּאָה. וְשֵׁם עִירוֹ פָּעוּ, מַאי פָּעוּ. בְּהַאי פָּעֵי בַּר נָשׁ דְּזָכֵי לְרוּחָא דְּקוּדְשָׁא וְשֵׁם אִשְׁתּוֹ מְהֵיטַבְאֵל, בְּכָאן אִתְבְּסָמוּ דָּא בְּדָא, וְאִתְקְרֵי אִשְׁתּוֹ, מַה דְּלָא כְּתִיב בְּכֻלְּהוּ.

316. None of them lasted, and yet do not say they ceased to exist. It is simply that they did not endure in that kingdom OF JUDGMENT until this last one of all was roused and awakened and spread out, as is written: "And Hadar reigned in his place" (Ibid. 39). Who is Hadar? It is supernal Chesed. "And the name of his city was Pa'u" (Ibid.). What is Pa'u? It is that through him a man cries (Heb. *po'e*), who merits the Holy Spirit. "*IRO* (ENG. 'HIS CITY')" IS DERIVED FROM *HIT'ORERUT* (ENG. 'REVIVAL'). "And the name of his wife was Mehetabel" (Ibid.): at this point, they were soothed by each other. MALCHUT is called his wife, something that is not written by them all – "THE NAME OF HIS WIFE."

317. מְהֵיטַבְאֵל, אִתְבַּסְּמוּתָא דְּדָא בְּדָא. בַּת מַטְרֵד, תִּקּוּנִין דְּמִסְטַר

גְּבוּרָה. בַּת מֵי זָהָב, אִתְבְּסָמוּ וְאִתְכְּלִילוּ דָּא בְּדָא, מֵי זָהָב: רַחֲמֵי
וְדִינָא. כָּאן אִתְדַּבְּקוּ אִתְּתָא בִּדְכוּרָא.

317. Mehetabel INDICATES improving each other, MALE AND FEMALE. ZEIR ANPIN IS THE SECRET OF YUD HEI VAV HEI FULLY SPELLED WITH ALEPH'S WHICH NUMERICALLY AMOUNT TO 45 AND THE FEMALE, THE SECRET OF YUD HEI VAV HEI, FULLY SPELLED WITH HEI'S, WHICH IS NUMERICALLY 52. AND MEHETABEL NUMERICALLY AMOUNTS TO 45 PLUS 52. "Daughter of Matred" (Ibid.), MEANING THAT DUE TO THE constructions WITHIN HER from the side of Gvurah, MATRED IS DERIVED FROM *TIRDUT* (ENG. 'INCONVENIENCE'). "DAUGHTER OF Mezehab" (lit. 'golden waters') (Ibid.), meaning that golden waters were firmly established and involved one in the other, Mercy and Judgment. SINCE GOLD INDICATES JUDGMENT, THAT IS THE ILLUMINATION OF CHOCHMAH. WATERS IS THE SECRET OF CHASSADIM. THEY ARE INCLUDED TOGETHER. Here the woman was joined and the man, Mehetabel with Hadar.

45. The arms of the male

A Synopsis
Rabbi Shimon describes the arms and legs and the joints tied in the arms. He says that the entire body is connected to all three brains – Chochmah, Binah and Da'at – and they connect to the right arm. This has application to David because he was connected with the patriarchs on the right. He talks about the right hand of God and about the left hand, and about when judgments are tempered with compassion and when they are not.

318. בְּסִטְרוֹי, אִתְפָּרְשָׁן בִּדְרוֹעִין, בַּשׁוֹקִין. דְּרוֹעִין דִּדְכוּרָא, חַד יְמִינָא, חַד שְׂמָאלָא דְּרוֹעָא קַדְמָאָה תְּלַת קִשְׁרִין אִתְקְשָׁרוּ בֵּיהּ, וְאִתְכְּלִילוּ בּ' דְּרוֹעִין. וְאִתְכְּלִילוּ ס"ד. אֶלָּא ג' קִשְׁרִין בִּימִינָא, וְג' קִשְׁרִין בִּשְׂמָאלָא. ג' קִשְׁרִין דִּימִינָא, אִתְכְּלִילָן בְּג' קִשְׁרִין דִּשְׂמָאלָא. וּבְג"כ, דְּרוֹעָא לָא כְּתִיב אֶלָּא חַד. אֲבָל יְמִינָא, לָא כְּתִיב בֵּיהּ זְרוֹעַ, אֶלָּא יְמִינְךָ יְיָ'. יְמִין יְיָ' אִתְקְרֵי, בְּג' קִשְׁרִין דַּאֲבָהָתָא דְּאַחֲסִינוּ לְחוּלָקֵיהוֹן.

318. On his sides, he separates into arms and legs. In the arms of the male, one is right and one is left. Three joints were connected to the one arm, THE RIGHT ONE, and were included in the two arms. HE ASKS: Could you imagine that they were included? IT SHOULD HAVE SAID THAT THEY ARE IN BOTH ARMS. HE REPLIES: It is only that there are three joints in the right ARM and three joints in the left, and the three joints of the right were included in the three joints of the left. This is why it is only written 'one arm.' THIS IS THE LEFT. By the right, it is not written arm but it is merely called "Your right (hand), Hashem" (Shemot 15:6) – "The right (hand) of Hashem" (Tehilim 118:16) WHEN IT CONTAINS the three joints of the patriarchs, that were given them as their portion.

319. וְאִי תֵּימָא הָא בִּתְלַת חַלָּלִין מוֹחָא דְּגוּלְגַּלְתָּא מִשְׁתַּכְּחִין. תָּאנָא, כֻּלְּהוּ ג' מִתְפַּשְׁטִין, וּמִתְקַשְׁרָן בְּכָל גּוּפָא, וְכָל גּוּפָא אִתְקְשַׁר בְּהָנֵי תְּלַת, וּמִתְקַשְׁרָן בִּדְרוֹעָא יְמִינָא. וּבְגִין כַּךְ תָּאִיב דָּוִד וְאָמַר, שֵׁב לִימִינִי. מִשׁוּם דְּהוּא אִתְחַבַּר עִמְּהוֹן דַּאֲבָהָתָא, וְיָתִיב תַּמָּן לְכוּרְסְיָא שְׁלֵימָתָא. וּבְגִין כַּךְ כְּתִיב אֶבֶן מָאֲסוּ הַבּוֹנִים וְגוֹ', מִשׁוּם דְּיָתִיב

לִימִינָא. הַיְינוּ דִּכְתִּיב, וְתָנוּחַ וְתַעֲמוֹד לְגוֹרָלְךָ לְקֵץ הַיָּמִין, כְּלוֹמַר, כְּמַאן דְּזָכֵי לַחֲבִיבוּתָא דְּמַלְכָּא. זַכָּאָה חוּלְקֵיהּ, דְּמַאן דְּפָרִישׁ מַלְכָּא יְמִינֵיהּ. וְקַבִּיל לֵיהּ תְּחוֹת יְמִינֵיהּ. וְהַאי יְמִינָא כַּד יָתִיב, קְשִׁרִין אִתְפַּשְׁטָא.

319. You might ask, Aren't they located in the three cavities of the brain in the skull rather than in the body, SINCE CHOCHMAH, BINAH AND DA'AT ARE ONLY IN THE HEAD? HE REPLIES: We have learned that all three BRAINS – CHOCHMAH, BINAH AND DA'AT – permeate and are connected to the whole body. The entire body is connected to these three, and they connect to the right arm. That is why David wished it and said, "Sit you at my right hand" (Tehilim 110:1), because he was connected with the patriarchs, CHESED, GVURAH AND TIFERET, THAT WERE TRANSFORMED TO CHOCHMAH, BINAH AND DA'AT, AND WERE CONNECTED TO THE RIGHT. DAVID will return there to a perfected throne; THAT IS TO SAY, DAVID IS THE SECRET OF MALCHUT, WHICH IS A LEG OF THE THRONE, SINCE CHESED, GVURAH AND TIFERET IS THE SECRET OF THE THREE LEGS OF THE THRONE. HE IS THE FOURTH, AND COMPLETES THE THRONE. Therefore, it is written: "The stone which the builders rejected has become the head stone of the corner" (Tehilim 118:22), WHICH WAS SAID ABOUT MALCHUT CALLED DAVID, because he sat at the right. This is what is written: "For you shall rest, and stand up for your allotted portion at the end of the days (also: 'right')" (Daniel 12:13). HE REMINDED HIM OF THE RIGHT END; that is to say HE INFORMED HIM THAT HE was like one who gained the King's favor, IN WHICH CASE THE KING RECEIVES HIM TO THE RIGHT. Praised is the lot of the one to whom the King extends His right hand to receive him under His right. When this right sits, its three joints permeate AND ILLUMINATE TO THE LOWER BEINGS.

320. וּדְרוֹעָא לָא אוֹשִׁיט יְדֵיהּ בִּתְלַת קְשִׁירִין דְּאָמְרָן. וְכַד מִתְעָרִין חַיָּיבַיָּא, וּמִתְפַּשְׁטָן בְּעָלְמָא, מִתְעָרִין תְּלַת אַחֲרָנִין, דְּאִינּוּן דִּינָא קַשְׁיָא, וְאוֹשִׁיט דְּרוֹעָא וְכַד אוֹשִׁיט דְּרוֹעָא, יַד יְמִינָא הוּא, אֲבָל אִתְקְרֵי זְרוֹעַ יְיָ', זְרוֹעֲךָ הַנְטוּיָה בִּזְמְנָא דְּג' אִלֵּין אִתְכְּלִילָן בְּג' אַחֲרָנִין, אִקְרֵי כֹּלָּא יְמִינָא, וְעָבֵיד דִּינָא בְּרַחֲמֵי, הֲדָא הוּא דִכְתִּיב, יְמִינְךָ יְיָ' נֶאְדָּרִי בַּכֹּחַ יְמִינְךָ יְיָ' תִּרְעַץ אוֹיֵב, בְּגִין דְּמִתְעָרָן רַחֲמֵי בְּהוּ.

320. The arm does not extend its hand with the three joints that we mentioned, MEANING WITH THE MOCHIN OF CHOCHMAH, BINAH AND DA'AT WHERE THE DOMINATION OF THE RIGHT EXISTS. THEREFORE, IT IS REFERRED TO AS "THE RIGHT OF HASHEM." When the wicked are wakened and increase in the world, the other three JOINTS are reawakened, which are of harsh Judgment, and extend the arm. When he extends the arm, it is the right hand, yet it is called, "O arm of Hashem" (Yeshayah 51:9) and "Your stretched out arm" (Devarim 9:29). During the period that these three joints of the right are included in the three other joints, WHICH ARE HARSH JUDGMENT, all are referred to as the right, and he executes Judgment with Mercy. This is what is written: "Your right hand, Hashem, is glorious in power: Your right hand, Hashem, dashed the enemy in pieces" (Shemot 15:6), since Mercy is awakened IN THE JUDGMENTS.

321. וְתָאנָא, בְּהַאי יְמִינָא מִתְאַחֲדָן תְּלַת מְאָה וְשַׁבְעִין אֶלֶף רִבּוֹא, דְּאִקְרוּן יְמִינָא. וּמְאָה וְתַמְנִין וַחֲמִשָּׁה אֶלֶף רִבּוֹא, מִזְרוֹעַ דְּאִקְרֵי זְרוֹעַ יְיָ'. מֵהַאי וּמֵהַאי תַּלְיָיא זְרוֹעָא, וְהַאי וְהַאי אִקְרֵי תִּפְאֶרֶת, דִּכְתִיב מוֹלִיךְ לִימִין מֹשֶׁה, הָא יְמִינָא. זְרוֹעַ, הָא שְׂמָאלָא. דִּכְתִיב, זְרוֹעַ תִּפְאַרְתּוֹ, דָּא בְּדָא.

321. We have learned that, to this right are attached 3,700,000,000 of those who are called right, WHICH ARE THE NUMBER OF THE ENTIRETY OF MOCHIN, and 1,850,000,000 from the arm that is called "the arm of Hashem." The arm is suspended from the one and the other, FOR THE ARM TOO IS COMPRISED OF THE RIGHT AND THE LEFT. The one and the other are called Tiferet, SINCE TIFERET IS ALSO COMPOSED OF RIGHT AND LEFT, as it is written: "At the right hand of Moses" (Yeshayah 63:12), which is here the right. Arm is the left, as is written: "His glorious arm" (Ibid.). SO WE SEE THAT THEY ARE INCLUDED the one with the other.

322. וְתָאנָא, בִּידָא שְׂמָאלָא, מִתְאַחֲדָן אַרְבַּע מְאָה וְחַמְשִׁין רִבּוֹא מָארֵי תְּרִיסִין, מִתְאַחֲדָן בְּכָל אֶצְבְּעָא וְאֶצְבְּעָא. וּבְכָל אֶצְבְּעָא וְאֶצְבְּעָא עֶשֶׂר אַלְפִין מָארֵי תְּרִיסִין מִשְׁתַּכְּחִין. פּוּק וַחֲשׁוֹב, כַּמָה אִינוּן דְּבִידָא. וְהַהוּא יְמִינָא אִקְרֵי סִיוּעָא קַדִּישָׁא, דְּאָתֵי מִדְּרוֹעָא דִּימִינָא, מִתְּלַת קִשְׁרִין. דִּכְתִיב וְהִנֵּה יָדִי עִמָּךְ. וּמִתְאַחֲדָן מֵהַאי, אֶלֶף וְאַרְבַּע

רִבּוֹא, וּתְמַנְיָא, וְחָמֵשׁ מְאָה אַלְפִּין מָארֵיהוֹן דְּסִיּוּעִין בְּכָל עָלְמָא. וְאִקְרוּן יַד יְיָ' עִלָּאָה. יַד יְיָ' תַּתָּאָה. וְאע״ג דִּבְכָל אֲתָר יַד יְיָ' שְׂמָאלָא. זָכוּ יְמִין יְיָ', אִתְכְּלִל יְדָא בִּזְרוֹעָא, וַהֲוֵי סִיּוּעָא, וְאִקְרֵי יָמִין. וְאִי לָאו, יַד יְיָ' תַּתָּאָה. תָּאנָא, כַּד מִתְעָרִין דִּינִין קַשְׁיָין לְאַחֲתָא בְּעָלְמָא, הָכָא כְּתִיב, סוֹד יְיָ' לִירֵאָיו.

322. We have learned that in the left hand are attached 4,500,000 shielded beings that are suspended from each and every finger. On each and every finger there are ten thousand shielded beings. Go figure out how many there are in the entire hand. The right is called 'holy help' that emerges from the three joints in the right arm, as is written: "And, behold, my hand shall be with you" (II Shmuel 3:12). Attached from this are 41,000 and 580,000 helpers in the whole world. They are called the uppermost hand of Hashem and the lower hand of Hashem. Although the hand of Hashem is always the left one, IF they are worthy, it is the right of Hashem, as the hand is included in the arm and becomes a help and is referred to as right. If not, then it is the lower hand of Hashem, WHICH IS LEFT. We have learned that when harsh Judgments are awakened to descend upon the world, it is written here: "The counsel (lit. 'secret') of Hashem is with them that fear him" (Tehilim 25:14).

46. The sawing

A Synopsis
We learn how Atika of Atikin let sleep fall upon Zeir Anpin and separated the female from Him. Rabbi Shimon talks about the judgments that are from the male and those that are from the female. He tells how the male and female are joined to be perfumed together, and how the upper and lower grades are thus corrected.

323. וְתָאנָא בְּצְנִיעוּתָא דְּסִפְרָא, דְּכָל דִּינִין דְּמִשְׁתַּכְּחִין מִדְּכוּרָא, תַּקִּיפִין בְּרֵישָׁא, וְנַיְיחִין בְּסוֹפָא. וְכָל דִּינִין דְּמִשְׁתַּכְּחִין מִנּוּקְבָּא, נַיְיחִין בְּרֵישָׁא, וְתַקִּיפִין בְּסוֹפָא. וְאִלְמָלֵא דְּאִתְעֲבֵידוּ כַּחֲדָא, לָא יַכְלִין עָלְמָא לְמִסְבַּל. עַד דְּעַתִּיק דְּעַתִּיקֵי סְתִימָא דְּכֹלָא, פָּרִישׁ דָּא מִן דָּא, וְחַבֵּר לוֹן לְאִתְבַּסְּמָא כַּחֲדָא.

323. We have learned in the hidden book that all the judgments that are from the male, ZEIR ANPIN, are harsh in the beginning and soft at the end. All the judgments from the female are soft in the beginning and harsh at the end. Had they not joined to a single union, the world could not have endured until the most ancient among ancient, the most concealed of all, separated them one from each other, AND THEREAFTER joined them to be appeased together.

324. וְכַד פָּרִישׁ לוֹן, אַפִּיל דּוּרְמִיטָא לִזְעֵיר אַפִּין, וּפָרִישׁ לְנוּקְבָּא מֵאֲחוֹרוֹי דְּסִטְרוֹי, וְאַתְקִין לָהּ כָּל תִּקּוּנָהָא, וְאַצְנָעָא לְיוֹמָא דִּילֵיהּ, לְמֵיתָהָא לִדְכוּרָא. הה״ד וַיַּפֵּל יְיָ׳ אֱלֹהִים תַּרְדֵּמָה עַל הָאָדָם וַיִּישָׁן. מַהוּ וַיִּישָׁן. הַאי הוּא דִכְתִיב, עוּרָה לָמָּה תִישָׁן יְיָ׳. וַיִּקַּח אַחַת מִצַּלְעוֹתָיו, מַאי אַחַת. דָּא הִיא נוּקְבָּא. כד״א, אַחַת הִיא יוֹנָתִי תַמָּתִי, וְסַלְקָא, וְאִתְתַּקְּנָא. וּבְאַתְרָהָא שָׁקִיעַ רַחֲמֵי וְחֶסֶד, הה״ד וַיִּסְגּוֹר בָּשָׂר תַּחְתֶּנָּה. וּכְתִיב וַהֲסִירוֹתִי אֶת לֵב הָאֶבֶן מִבְּשַׂרְכֶם וְנָתַתִּי לָכֶם לֵב בָּשָׂר.

324. When He separated them, He let sleep fall upon Zeir Anpin and separated the female from the back of his sides. He prepared her with all her adornments and saved her for his day, FOR SHABBAT, to bring her to the male, TO ZEIR ANPIN. This is what is written: "And Hashem Elohim caused a deep sleep to fall upon the man, and he slept" (Beresheet 2:21). What is meant by: "And he slept." This is what it is written: "Awake, why sleep you, Hashem?" (Tehilim 44:24) and "He took one of his sides" (Beresheet 2:21). What is meant by "one"? That is meant to indicate the female, as it says: "My dove, my undefiled is but one" (Shir Hashirim 6:9). She ascended TO ABA AND IMA and was shaped. In her area are embedded Mercy and Chesed. This is what is written: "And closed up the flesh in its place" (Beresheet 2:21),and: "And I will take away the heart of stone out of your flesh, and I will give you a heart of flesh" (Yechezkel 36:26).

325. וּבְשַׁעֲתָא דְּבָעָא לְמֵיעַל שַׁבְּתָא הֲוָה בָּרֵי רוּחִין וְשֵׁדִין וְעַלְעוּלִין, וְעַד לָא סִיֵּים לוֹן, אָתַת מַטְרוֹנִיתָא בְּתִקּוּנָהָא, וְיָתִיבַת קַמֵּיהּ. בְּשַׁעֲתָא דְּיָתִיבַת קַמֵּיהּ, אֲנַח לוֹן לְאִינוּן בִּרְיָין, וְלָא אִשְׁתְּלִימוּ. כֵּיוָן דְּמַטְרוֹנִיתָא יַתְבַת עִם מַלְכָּא, וְאִתְחַבְּרוּ אַפִּין בְּאַפִּין, מַאן יֵיעוּל בֵּינַיְיהוּ, מַאן הוּא דְּיִקְרַב בַּהֲדַיְיהוּ. וְכַד אִתְחַבְּרוּ, אִתְבְּסְמוּ דָּא בְּדָא. יוֹמָא דְּכֹלָּא אִתְבְּסַם בֵּיהּ. וּבְג״כ, אִתְבְּסְמוּ דִּינִין דָּא בְּדָא, וְאִתְתַּקְנוּ עִלָּאִין וְתַתָּאִין.

325. When the Shabbat wished to enter, THAT IS THE PERIOD BETWEEN SUNDOWN AND NIGHT FALL, 'e was creating spirits, ghosts, and storms, WHICH ARE HARMFUL SPIRITS OF THE WORLD. Before He finished them, the Queen came WITH ALL her adornments FROM THE SHABBAT, and sat down before 'im. IN THIS DAY, SHE ACHIEVES THE FIRST THREE SFIROT OF CHAYAH THAT SUBDUE AND MAKE VOID ALL THE HARMFUL BEINGS AND THE OTHER SIDE, SINCE THEN THERE EXISTS NO DOMINION IN THE WORLD BESIDES HER. During the time she sat in his presence, he put down these creatures and they were not completed, because the Queen sat with the King and they were joined face to face. Who would enter between them and who would dare get close to them? When they joined, they were appeased by each other, SINCE THE SHABBAT IS a day in which everything is soothed. Therefore, the Judgments improved each other, SINCE THE JUDGMENTS OF THE MALE THAT ARE STRONG AT THE BEGINNING ARE SOOTHED AT THE TOP OF THE FEMALE, FOR THE JUDGMENTS THERE ARE SOFT. THE JUDGMENTS OF THE FEMALE THAT ARE ROUGH AT THE END ARE SOOTHED BY THE END OF THE MALE, WHERE THE JUDGMENTS ARE SOFT, and the upper and lower beings are corrected.

47. Cain and Abel

A Synopsis

Rabbi Shimon tells us how the hidden book says that Atika of Atikin wished to see if the judgments were perfumed; when Adam and Eve joined together a harsh judgment emerged from her, and the world could not tolerate it since the snake instilled the impurity of harsh judgment in her so she could not be perfumed. Even though after Cain's birth she was weakened and became perfumed and gave birth to a sweeter soul, Abel, Cain rose above him because he was stronger, having all the judgments adhering to him. God submerged Cain in the hole of the great abyss together with his brother; they formed one body, from which descend the souls of all sinful people who are strong in spirit.

326. וְתָאנָא בְּצִנִיעוּתָא דְסִפְרָא, בָּעָא עַתִּיקָא קַדִישָׁא לְמֶחֱזֵי, אִי אתְבְּסָמוּ דִינִין, וְאִתְדַּבָּקוּ תְּרֵין אִלֵּין דָּא בְּדָא, וְנָפַק מִסִטְרָא דְנוּקְבָּא דִינָא תַּקִיפָא, דִכְתִיב, וְהָאָדָם יָדַע אֶת חַוָּה אִשְׁתּוֹ וַתַּהַר וַתֵּלֶד אֶת קַיִן וַתֹּאמֶר קָנִיתִי וְגוֹ'. וְלָא הֲוָה יָכִיל עָלְמָא לְמִסְבַּל, מִשּׁוּם דְּלָא אתְבַּסְּמַת, וְחִוְיָא תַּקִיפָא אַטִיל בָּה זוּהֲמָא דְדִינָא קַשְׁיָא, ובג"כ לָא הֲוָה יָכִיל לְאתְבַּסְּמָא. וְכַד נָפִיק דָּא קַיִן מִסְטַר דְנוּקְבָּא, נָפַק תַּקִיף קַשְׁיָא, תַּקִיף בְּדִינוֹי, קַשְׁיָא בְּדִינוֹי. כֵּיוָן דְּנָפַק אתְחַלָשַׁת וְאתְבַּסְּמַת. בָּתַר דָּא, אֲפִיקַת אַחֲרָא בְּסִימָא יַתִּיר, וְסָלִיק קַדְמָאָה דַּהֲוָה תַּקִיפָא קַשְׁיָא, וְכָל דִינִין אתְעָרְבוּ עִמֵּיה.

326. We have learned this in the hidden book. The holy Atik wished to see if the Judgments were soothed. ADAM AND EVE were joined to each other, and harsh Judgment emerged from the female side, as is written: "And Adam knew Eve his wife; and she conceived, and bore Cain, saying, I have acquired..." (Beresheet 4:1). The world could not tolerate it, since EVE was not yet appeased and the harsh snake instilled the impurity of harsh Judgment in her, so that she could not be mollified. Therefore, when Cain emerged from the side of the female he exited rough and hard, harsh in judgment and heavy in judgment. As soon AS CAIN emerged FROM HER, she was weakened and was appeased. Following that, she gave birth to another soul that was more sweetened, but the first, CAIN, rose ABOVE HIM, being stronger, in that all the Judgments adhered to him.

327. ת״ח, מַה כְּתִיב, וַיְהִי בִּהְיוֹתָם בַּשָּׂדֶה. בַּשָּׂדֶה: דְּאִשְׁתְּמוֹדָע
לְעֵילָא. בַּשָּׂדֶה דְּאִקְרֵי שָׂדֶה דְּתַפּוּחִים. וְנָצַח הַאי דִּינָא לַאֲחוּה, מִשׁוּם
דַּהֲוָה קַשְׁיָא מִנֵּיה, וְאַכְפְּיֵיה וְאַטְמְרֵיה תְּחוֹתֵיה. עַד דְּאִתְּעַר בְּהַאי
קוּדְשָׁא בְּרִיךְ הוּא, וְאַעֲבְרֵיה מִקַּמֵּיה. וְשַׁקְעֵיה בְּנוּקְבָּא דִּתְהוֹמָא רַבָּא.
וְכָלִיל לַאֲחוּי בְּשִׁקּוּעָא דְּיַמָּא רַבָּא, דִּמְבַסֵּם דִּמְעִין עִלָּאִין. וּמִנְּהוֹן
נָחְתִין נִשְׁמָתִין לְעָלְמָא, אֵינָשׁ לְפוּם אוֹרְחוֹי.

327. Come and see what is written: "And it came to pass, when they were in the field" (Ibid. 8). That is the known field of above, in the field that is called a field of apple trees, MEANING MALCHUT, FROM WHERE THEY WERE BORN. The judgment OF CAIN overcame his brother, because he was harsher than him and he subdued him and hid him under himself until the Holy One, blessed be He, was roused by it and removed CAIN from his presence. He submerged him in the hole of the great abyss and he included his brother in that depression of the great ocean that mitigates the uppermost tears; and from them descend the souls to the world to each man according to his way.

328. וְאע״ג דִּטְמִירִין אִינּוּן. מִתְפַּשְּׁטִין דָּא בְּדָא, וְאִתְעֲבִידוּ גּוּפָא חַד
וּמֵהַאי גּוּפָא, נַחְתִּין נִשְׁמָתְהוֹן דְּרַשִׁיעַיָּיא חַיָּיבַיָּא, תַּקִּיפֵי רוּחָא.
מִתַּרְוַויְיהוּ כַּחֲדָא ס״ד. אֶלָּא דָּא לְסִטְרוֹי, וְדָא לְסִטְרוֹי. זַכָּאִין אִינּוּן
צַדִּיקַיָּיא, דִּמְשַׁלְפֵי נִשְׁמָתְהוֹן מֵהַאי גּוּפָא קַדִּישָׁא דְּאִקְרֵי אָדָם, דְּכָלִיל
כֹּלָּא, אֲתָר דְּעִטְרִין וְכִתְרִין קַדִּישִׁין מִתְחַבְּרָאן תַּמָּן, בְּצִרוּרָא
דְּאֶתְכְּלָּא.

328. Although they were hidden, they prevailed and extended one to the other and formed one body, NAMELY UNDER THE DOMINATION OF CAIN. From that body descend the souls of the wicked, sinful and strong in spirit, BEING UNDER THE DOMINATION OF CAIN. HE ASKS: Is it then from both together THAT THE SOULS DESCEND? ARE THEY NOT TWO OPPOSITES? HE REPLIES: Only the one to his side and the other to his side, MEANING TO SAY THAT FROM CAIN ARE DRAWN THE SOULS OF THE WICKED THAT ADHERE TO THE REFUSE OF THE LEFT AND FROM ABEL ARE DRAWN THE SOULS OF THE WICKED THAT ADHERE TO THE REFUSE OF THE RIGHT -

ALL THIS IS PRIOR TO WHEN THEY WERE COMBINED WITH EACH OTHER IN THE DEPRESSION OF THE GREAT OCEAN THAT APPEASED THE UPPER TEARS OF ABOVE - HOWEVER, AFTER THEY WERE MOLLIFIED, THE SOULS OF THE RIGHTEOUS FLOW FROM THEM THAT ARE NOT SO RIGHTEOUS. Praised are those righteous whose souls are drawn from this holy body called Adam, which includes everyone and is a place that the crowns, THE SECRET OF THE FIRST THREE SFIROT, and the holy Sfirot get joined together in the bundle of the cluster.

329. זַכָּאִין אִינּוּן צַדִּיקַיָּיא, דְּכָל הָנֵי מִלִּין קַדִּישִׁין, דְּאִתְמָרוּ בְּרוּחַ קַדִּישָׁא עִלָּאָה, רוּחַ, דְּכָל קַדִּישִׁין עִלָּאִין אִתְכַּלְלָן בֵּיהּ, אִתְגַּלְיָין לְכוּ. מִלִּין דְּעִלָּאִין וְתַתָּאִין צַיְיתִין לְהוּ, זַכָּאִין אַתּוּן מָארֵיהוֹן דְּמָארִין, מְחַצְדֵּי חַקְלָא, דְּמִלִּין אִלֵּין תִּנְדְּעוּן וְתִסְתַּכְּלוּן בְּהוּ, וְתִנְדְּעוּן לְמָארֵיכוֹן אַפִּין בְּאַפִּין, עֵינָא בְּעֵינָא. וּבְהָנֵי מִלִּין תִּזְכּוּן לְעָלְמָא דְּאָתֵי, הה"ד וְיָדַעְתָּ הַיּוֹם וַהֲשֵׁבֹתָ אֶל לְבָבֶךָ וְגוֹ'. יְיָ': עַתִּיק יוֹמִין הוּא הָאֱלֹהִים. וְכֹלָּא הוּא חַד, בְּרִיךְ שְׁמֵיהּ לְעָלַם וּלְעָלְמֵי עָלְמַיָּא.

329. Praised are the righteous, that all these holy things that are said in the uppermost Holy Spirit, a spirit in which all the most holy were included, was revealed to you, WHICH ARE matters to which those above and those below listen. Praised are you judges, MEANING THOSE WHO SIT IN A COURT OF JUDGES, the reapers of the field, that you will be aware of these things and you will pay attention to them. You shall know your Master face to face, eye to eye. With these matters, you will merit the World to Come. This is what it says: "Know therefore this day, and consider it in your heart, that Hashem (who is Atik Yomin), he is Elohim" (Devarim 4:39) (WHICH IS ZEIR ANPIN). All is One. Blessed is his Name forever and forever more.

48. The upper grades below and the lower grades above

A Synopsis

Rabbi Shimon says that the shape of man is the uppermost correction that comprises everything, and that the righteous man is an everlasting foundation.

330. אָמַר ר״ש, חֲמֵינָא עֶלָאִין לְתַתָּא, וְתַתָּאִין לְעֵילָא. עֶלָאִין לְתַתָּא, דִּיּוּקְנָא דְּאָדָם, דְּהוּא תִּקּוּנֵי עֶלָּאָה, כְּלָלָא דְּכֻלְּהוּ.

330. Rabbi Shimon said: I see the higher beings below and the lower beings above. The upper beings below AND THE LOWER BEINGS ABOVE: that is the shape of man, who is the uppermost correction that comprises everything.

331. תָּאנָא, כְּתִיב וְצַדִּיק יְסוֹד עוֹלָם, דְּכָלִיל שִׁית בְּקַרְטוּפָא כַּחֲדָא. וְהַאי הוּא דִּכְתִיב שׁוֹקָיו עַמּוּדֵי שֵׁשׁ.

331. We have learned that it is written: "But the righteous is an everlasting foundation" (Mishlei 10:25), as he includes six (Heb. *shesh*) in one source. This is what is written: "His legs are pillars of marble (Heb. *shesh*)" (Shir Hashirim 5:15).

49. General and particular, particular and general

A Synopsis
The hidden book says that the highest Sfirot in general and in particular, and the lowest Sfirot in particular and in general, were included in man. Rabbi Shimon explains the meaning of this. Finally he says that the masters of judgment from below get attached in the lowest Sfirot.

332. וְתָאנָא בְּצִנִיעוּתָא דְסִפְרָא, בְּאָדָם אִתְכְּלִילוּ כְּתָרִין עִלָּאִין, בִּכְלָל וּבִפְרָט. וּבְאָדָם אִתְכְּלִילוּ כְּתָרִין תַּתָּאִין, בִּפְרָט וּכְלָל. כְּתָרִין עִלָּאִין בִּכְלָל, כְּמָה דְּאִתְּמַר בְּדִיּוּקָנָא דְכָל הָנֵי דִיוּקְנִין. בִּפְרָט: בְּאֶצְבְּעָן דְּיָדָן, חָמֵשׁ כְּנֶגֶד חָמֵשׁ. כְּתָרִין תַּתָּאִין, בְּאֶצְבְּעִין דְּרַגְלִין דְּאִינּוּן פְּרָט וּכְלָל. דְּהָא גוּפָא לָא אִתְחֲזֵי בַּהֲדַיְיהוּ. דְּאִינּוּן לְבַר מִגּוּפָא. ובג"כ לָא הֲווֹ בְּגוּפָא. דְּגוּפָא אַעְדִּיו מִנַּיְיהוּ.

332. We have learned in the hidden book that in man were included the uppermost Sfirot, FROM THE CHEST UPWARDS, in general and in particular, and in man were included the lower Sfirot, THAT IS FROM THE CHEST DOWNWARDS, in particular and in general. HE EXPLAINS: The uppermost Sfirot are in general, as we have learned, within the image of all the images, THAT IS THE FORM OF MAN. In particular, that is in the fingers of the hand, WHICH ARE five corresponding to five. The lowest Sfirot in the toes of the feet are particular and general, since the body, THAT IS TIFERET, is not seen by them, since they are outside the torso. That is why they are not part of the body, since the body was removed from them.

333. אִי הָכִי, מַאי וְעָמְדוּ רַגְלָיו בַּיּוֹם הַהוּא. אֶלָּא רַגְלָיו דְּגוּפָא, מָארֵיהוֹן דְּדִינִין לְמֶעְבַּד נוּקְמִין וְאִקְרוּן בַּעֲלֵי רַגְלַיִם. וּמִנְּהוֹן תַּקִּיפִין. וּמִתְאַחֲדָן מָארֵיהוֹן דְּדִינִין דִּי לְתַתָּא, בִּכְתָרִין תַּתָּאִין.

333. HE ASKS: If so, what is the meaning of: "And His feet shall stand in that day" (Zechariah 14:4). IT SEEMS THAT THEY ARE NOT OUTSIDE OF THE BODY THAT IS ZEIR ANPIN, SINCE IT IS ASCRIBED TO HIM. HE ANSWERS: It is the legs of the body, MEANING the masters of Judgment

with which, to do revenge ON THE WICKED. They are referred to as those who have legs, since from them are the harsh JUDGMENTS. The masters of Judgment from below are attached in the lower Sfirot THAT ARE CALLED LEGS, AND ABOUT THIS IS WRITTEN: "AND HIS FEET (LIT. 'LEGS') SHALL STAND..."

50. The totality of Man

A Synopsis

Rabbi Shimon tells how all the formations of above that are in the holy body, the whole of man, irrigate and illuminate one another until they enlighten all the world. He talks about the desire of the Klipot for the students of the Torah, since they wish to nourish from the holy body. We learn that even angels are not outside of the principle of the holy body. Rabbi Shimon describes those spirits who left the general holy body and are from the left side, and tells what their actions are. He tells us that the hidden book says that when Seth was born the worlds above and below were perfumed and perfected; this was male and female from the aspect of the holy body, and the worlds were bound together and became one body. Thus as the spirit was drawn and entered that body, everything throughout the universe is seen to be one. Whoever excludes himself from general humanity does not enter into the realm of man when he leaves this world. Within the generality of man there is all the perfection of faith. The hidden book says that whoever keeps a holy body overnight when the spirit has left it makes a flaw in the body of the worlds, so it must not stay overnight. Rabbi Shimon talks about the Nefilim or fallen ones who mated with the daughters of men; the fallen ones are of the aspect of spirits of the left, that do not bond to the body (Zeir Anpin) at all but rather to Malchut referred to as earth. We hear how God repented that He had ever made man on the earth, and how He decided to destroy man below; all the same since one cannot differentiate between man above and man below, the destruction of man below flaws the man above. If the wisdom of Arich Anpin would have illuminated Malchut there would not have been a flood, for wisdom includes everything; this is concealed Chochmah, with which man's correction was established and strengthened. With this, Rabbi Shimon calls upon the most Ancient of all ancient ones to witness that he has not revealed these secrets for his own honor, but only so that the friends should not err in His ways.

334. תָּאנָא, כָּל אִינּוּן תִּקּוּנֵי דִּלְעֵילָא, דִּבְגוּפָא קַדִּישָׁא, כְּלָלָא דְּאָדָם, אִתְמְשִׁיךְ דָּא מִן דָּא, וּמִתְאַחֲדָן דָּא בְּדָא, וְאַשְׁקוּן דָּא לְדָא. כְּמָה דְּאִתְמְשַׁךְ דָּמָא בְּקִטְפִין דְּוַרִידִין לְדָא וּלְדָא, לְהָכָא וּלְהָכָא, מֵאֲתַר דָּא לְאֲתַר אַחֲרָא, וְאִינּוּן מַשְׁקִין דְּגוּפָא. אַשְׁקְיָין דָּא לְדָא, מְנַהֲרִין דָּא לְדָא. עַד דְּאַנְהִירוּ כֻּלְּהוּ עָלְמִין, וּמִתְבָּרְכָאן בְּגִינֵיהוֹן.

334. We have learned that all these formations of above that are in the holy body, which is the whole of man, are derived one from the other and are attached to each other. They irrigate each other like the blood that runs with the flow of the veins in this direction and that direction, from this area to that area, and they irrigate the body. HERE TOO, they irrigate each other and illuminate each other until they enlighten all the worlds, and are blessed for their sake.

335. תָּאנָא, כָּל אִינוּן כִּתְרִין דְּלָא אִתְכְּלָלוּ בְּגוּפָא, כֻּלְּהוּ רְחִיקִין וּמְסָאֲבִין, וּמְסַאֲבָן כָּל מַאן דְּיִקְרַב לְגַבֵּיהוֹן, לְמִנְדַּע מִנְּהוֹן מִלִּין.

335. We have learned that all these Sfirot which were not included in the body, WHICH IS THE CENTRAL COLUMN, BUT ARE DRAWN FROM THE LEFT COLUMN, are all abominable and unclean, and defile everyone that gets near to them, in order to find out things from them.

336. תָּאנָא, מַאי תִּיאוּבְתָּא דִּלְהוֹן לְגַבֵּי תַּלְמִידֵי חֲכָמִים. אֶלָּא מִשּׁוּם דְּחָמָן בְּהוּ גוּפָא קַדִּישָׁא, וּלְאִתְכְּלָלָא בְּהוּ בְּהַהוּא גוּפָא. וְכִי תֵּימָא, אִי הָכִי, הָא מַלְאָכִין קַדִּישִׁין וְלֵיתְהוֹן בִּכְלָלָא דְּגוּפָא. לָא. דְּחַ"וּ אִי לֶיהֱווֹן לְבַר מִכְּלָלָא דְּגוּפָא קַדִּישָׁא, לָא הֲווֹ קַדִּישִׁין וְלָא מִתְקַיְּימֵי. וּכְתִיב וּגְוִיָּיתוֹ כְתַרְשִׁישׁ. וּכְתִיב וְגַבּוֹתָם מְלֵאוֹת עֵינַיִם. וְהָאִישׁ גַּבְרִיאֵל. כֻּלְּהוּ בִּכְלָלָא דְּאָדָם. בַּר מֵהָנֵי דְּלֵיתְהוֹן בִּכְלָלָא דְּגוּפָא, דְּאִינוּן מְסָאֲבִין, וּמְסַאֲבָן כָּל מַאן דְּיִקְרַב בַּהֲדַיְיהוּ.

336. We have learned what the desire OF THESE KLIPOT is for the students of the Torah. HE REPLIES: This is since they observe in them a holy body and they wish to be included, MEANING TO NOURISH from that body. You might say, Yet there are angels, not included in the body. HE ANSWERS: No. If they were, heaven forbid, outside of the wholeness of the holy body, THAT IS THE SECRET OF THE CENTRAL COLUMN, they would not have been holy and they could not have endured, since it is written: "His body also was like the beryl" (Daniel 10:6), and: "And their rims were full of eyes" (Yechezkel 1:18:) and "the man Gabriel" (Daniel 9:21). SO YOU SEE that all are incorporated in the whole of man, IN THE CENTRAL COLUMN,

except those that are not part of the body, BUT ARE FROM THE LEFT
COLUMN, who are unclean and defile all those that will get near to them.

337. וְתָאנָא, כֻּלְּהוּ מֵרוּחָא דִשְׂמָאלָא, דְּלָא אִתְבְּסַם בְּאָדָם מִשְׁתַּכְּחִין,
וְנַפְקוּ מִכְּלָלָא דְּגוּפָא קַדִּישָׁא, וְלָא אִתְדַּבְּקוּ בֵּיהּ. וּבְגִ"כ כֻּלְּהוּ מְסָאֲבִין
וְאַזְלִין וְטָאסִין עָלְמָא, וְעַיְילִין בְּנוּקְבָּא דִּתְהוֹמָא רַבָּא, לְאִתְדַּבְּקָא
בְּהַהוּא דִּינָא קַדְמָאָה דְּאִקְרֵי קַיִן, דְּנָפִיק בִּכְלָל דְּגוּפָא דִלְתַתָּא.
וְשָׁאטִין וְטָאסִין כָּל עָלְמָא, וּפָרְחָן וְלָא מִתְדַּבְּקָאן בִּכְלָלָא דְּגוּפָא,
וּבְגִינֵי כַּךְ אִינּוּן לְבַר, מִכָּל מַשְׁרְיָין דִּלְעֵילָא וְתַתָּא. מְסָאֲבִין אִינּוּן.
בְּהוּ כְּתִיב מִחוּץ לַמַּחֲנֶה מוֹשָׁבוֹ.

337. We have learned that all these are from the spirit of the left side that
was not mitigated in man, WHO IS THE CENTRAL COLUMN, ZEIR ANPIN.
They left the whole holy body and did not adhere to it. Therefore, they are
all unclean. They go wandering in the world and reach the depression of the
great abyss, WHERE CAIN WAS SUBMERGED, to adhere to the primordial
Judgment that is called Cain that was expelled from the general body below
SINCE IT WAS OF THE LEFT WITHOUT A RIGHT. They flutter and wander
throughout the world, and fly and do not get attached to the wholeness of
the body, THAT IS THE CENTRAL COLUMN. Therefore, they are outside of
all the camps above and below and are defiled. About them, it is written:
"Outside of the camp shall his habitation be" (Vayikra 13:46).

338. וּבְרוּחָא דְּאִקְרֵי הֶבֶל, דְּאִתְבְּסַם יַתִּיר בִּכְלָלָא דְּגוּפָא קַדִּישָׁא.
נָפְקִין אַחֲרָנִין דִּמְבַסְּמָן יַתִּיר, וּמִתְדַּבְּקָן בְּגוּפָא, וְלָא מִתְדַּבְּקָן. כֻּלְּהוּ
תַּלְיָין בַּאֲוִירָא וְנָפְקִין מֵהַאי כְּלָלָא דְּאִלֵּין מְסָאֲבִין. וְשַׁמְעִין מַה
דְּשַׁמְעִין מֵעֵילָא, וּמִנַּיְיהוּ יַדְעֵי לְתַתָּא דְּקָאמְרֵי לְהוּ.

338. With the spirit that is called Abel, which is further mollified through
the whole holy body, other SPIRITS emanate that are more mitigated and
they adhere, yet do not adhere to the body. All are suspended in the air and
they emanate from the corpus of defiled spirits, as mentioned above. They
hear whatever they hear above and from them it gets known TO THE SPIRITS
below, because they divulge everything to them.

339. וְתָאנָא בִּצְנִיעוּתָא דְּסִפְרָא, כֵּיוָן דְּאִתְבַּסְּמוּ לְעֵילָּא כְּלָלָא דְּאָדָם, גּוּפָא קַדִּישָׁא, דְּכַר וְנוּקְבָּא. אִתְחַבָּרוּ זִמְנָא תְּלִיתָאָה, וְנָפַק וְאִתְבַּסְּמוּתָא דְּכֹלָּא. וְאִתְבַּסְּמוּ עָלְמִין עִלָּאִין וְתַתָּאִין. וּמִכָּאן אִשְׁתְּכָלַל עָלְמָא דִּלְעֵילָּא וְתַתָּא, מִסִּטְרָא דְּגוּפָא קַדִּישָׁא. וּמִתְחַבְּרָן עָלְמִין, וּמִתְאַחֲדָן דָּא בְּדָא, וְאִתְעֲבֵידוּ חַד גּוּפָא. וּמִשְׁלְפָא רוּחָא, וְעָיֵילָא בְּחַד גּוּפָא. וּבְכֻלְּהוּ לָא אִתְחֲזֵי אֶלָּא חַד. קק"ק יְיָ' צְבָאוֹת מְלֹא כָל הָאָרֶץ כְּבוֹדוֹ. דְּכֹלָּא הוּא חַד גּוּפָא.

339. We have learned in the hidden book that, as soon as the whole of man, the holy body, was appeased above, which is composed of male and female, MEANING ZEIR ANPIN AND ITS FEMININE PRINCIPLE, they were joined for a third time. Overall perfume emerged, THAT IS SETH, and the worlds above and below were improved. From here on, the world of above and below was perfected, WHICH IS MALE AND FEMALE from the aspect of the holy body, WHICH IS THE CENTRAL COLUMN. And the worlds were bound and got attached to each other and became one body, WHICH IS SETH. The spirit got drawn and entered that body; throughout the worlds, only one is seen. "Holy, holy, holy, is Hashem, Tzva'ot: the whole earth is full of his glory" (Yeshayah 6:3), since all is one body, SINCE THREE TIMES HOLY IS THE SECRET OF THE THREE COLUMNS THAT INCORPORATED INTO ONE.

340. תָּאנָא, כֵּיוָן דְּאִתְבַּסְּמוּ דָּא בְּדָא, אִתְקַשָּׁרוּ דִּינָא וְרַחֲמֵי. וְאִתְבַּסְּמַת נוּקְבָּא בִּדְכוּרָא. וּבְגִינֵי כַּךְ לָא סַלְקָא דָּא בְּלָא דָא, כְּהַאי תָּמָר, דְּלָא סַלְקָא דָא בְּלָא דָא. וְעַל הַאי תְּנֵינָן, מַאן דְּאַפִּיק גַּרְמֵיהּ בְּהַאי עָלְמָא מִכְּלָלָא דְּאָדָם, לְבָתַר כַּד נָפִיק מֵהַאי עָלְמָא, לָא עָיֵיל בִּכְלָלָא דְּאָדָם, דְּאִקְרֵי גּוּפָא קַדִּישָׁא. אֶלָּא בְּאִינּוּן דְּלָא אִקְרוּן אָדָם, וְנָפִיק מִכְּלָלָא דְגוּפָא.

340. We have learned that as soon as ZEIR ANPIN AND HIS FEMININE PRINCIPLE appeased each other, Judgment was connected with Mercy and the female was soothed by the male, THAT IS ZEIR ANPIN. Therefore, they could not go on one without the other. This is similar to the palm tree that does not continue AND PRODUCE FRUITS one without the other, FEMALE TREE WITHOUT THE MALE TREE. About this, we have learned that whoever

excludes himself in this world from general humanity, THAT IS THE
CENTRAL COLUMN, thereafter, when he exits from this world, he does not
enter into the realm of man. This is referred to as the holy body, WHICH IS
ZEIR ANPIN AND BRIYAH, YETZIRAH AND ASIYAH OF HOLINESS. Rather
he enters in these that are not called man, THAT IS, BRIYAH, YETZIRAH
AND ASIYAH OF DEFILEMENT, which were expelled from the totality of the
body, THAT IS THE CENTRAL COLUMN.

341. תַּנְיָא, תּוֹרֵי זָהָב נַעֲשֶׂה לָּךְ עִם נְקוּדוֹת הַכָּסֶף, דְּאִתְבְּסָמוּ דִּינָא
בְּרַחֲמֵי. וְלֵית דִּינָא, דְּלָא הֲווֹ בֵּיהּ רַחֲמֵי. וְעַל הַאי כְּתִיב, נָאווּ לְחָיַיךְ
בַּתּוֹרִים צַוָּארֵךְ בַּחֲרוּזִים. בַּתּוֹרִים: כְּמוֹ דִּכְתִּיב, תּוֹרֵי זָהָב נַעֲשֶׂה לָּךְ
וְגוֹ'. בַּחֲרוּזִים: כְּמָה דִּכְתִּיב, עִם נְקוּדוֹת הַכָּסֶף. צַוָּארֵךְ, בִּכְלָלָא
דְּנוּקְבָּא, דָּא מַטְרוֹנִיתָא אִשְׁתְּכַח בֵּי מַקְדְּשָׁא דִּלְעֵילָא, וִירוּשְׁלַם
דִּלְתַתָּא וּמַקְדְּשָׁא. וְכָל דָּא מִדְאִתְבְּסָמַת בִּדְכוּרָא, וְאִתְעֲבֵיד כְּלָלָא
דְּאָדָם, וְדָא הוּא כְּלָלָא דִּמְהֵימְנוּתָא. מַאי מְהֵימְנוּתָא. דִּבְגַוֵּיהּ
אִשְׁתְּכַח כָּל מְהֵימְנוּתָא.

341. We have learned: "We will make you necklets of gold studded with
silver" (Shir Hashirim 1:11), meaning that Judgment CALLED GOLD,
WHICH IS THE ILLUMINATION OF CHOCHMAH OF THE LEFT, was spiced
with Mercy, THAT IS CALLED STUDS OF SILVER, MEANING THAT
CHOCHMAH WAS CLOTHED WITH CHASSADIM, so there is no Judgment
that has no Mercy in it, SINCE THEY ARE INCLUDED IN ONE ANOTHER.
About this, it is written: "Your cheeks would be comely with rows of
jewels, your neck with strings of beads" (Ibid. 10). "Rows of jewels" HAS
THE SAME MEANING AS in the verse, "necklets of gold," WHICH ARE FROM
THE LEFT. "Strings of beads" HAS THE SAME MEANING AS in the verse,
"studded with silver," MEANING RIGHT, CHESED. "Your neck" is of the
totality of the female, which is the Matron, WHICH IS MALCHUT, since THE
NECK contains the celestial Temple, WHICH IS YESOD OF MALCHUT. The
terrestrial Jerusalem and the temple IN IT ARE ALSO CALLED THE NECK. All
this takes place after THE FEMALE is mollified by the male and the
wholeness of man is formed. This is the whole of Faith. Why Faith? It is
because within it, IN THE TOTALITY OF MAN, there is all the perfection of
Faith.

342. וְתָאנָא, מַאן דְּאִקְרֵי אָדָם, וְנִשְׁמָתָא נַפְקַת מִנֵּיהּ, וּמִית. אָסִיר
לְמֵיבַת לֵיהּ בְּבֵיתָא, לְמֶעְבַּד לֵיהּ לִינָה עַל אַרְעָא, מִשׁוּם יְקָרָא דְּהַאי
גּוּפָא, דְּלָא יִתְחֲזֵי בֵּיהּ קְלָנָא, דִּכְתִּיב, אָדָם בִּיקָר בַּל יָלִין, אָדָם דְּהוּא
יְקַר מִכָּל יְקָרָא, בַּל יָלִין. מ״ט. מִשׁוּם דְּאִי יַעַבְדוּן הָכִי, נִמְשַׁל
כַּבְּהֵמוֹת נִדְמוּ. מַה בְּעִירֵי לָא הֲווֹ בִּכְלָלָא דְּאָדָם, וְלָא אִתְחֲזֵי בְּהוּ
רוּחָא קַדִּישָׁא, אוּף הָכָא כִּבְעִירֵי, גּוּפָא בְּלָא רוּחָא, וְהַאי גּוּפָא, דְּהוּא
יְקָרָא דְּכֹלָּא, לָא יִתְחֲזֵי בֵּיהּ קְלָנָא.

342. We have learned that when the soul of whoever is called man left him, and he died, it is not permitted to have him stay in the house and rest overnight on the ground, so as not to put the honor of that body to shame, BEING A BODY WITHOUT A SOUL. It is written: "Nevertheless man abides not in honor" (Tehilim 49:13). Man who is the most honored "abides not" AFTER DEATH. What is the reason? It is because if they do that, "he is like the beasts that perish" (Ibid.). THAT IS, AFTER DEATH HE IS LIKE THE BEASTS. Just like animals were never part of humans, WHICH IS WHY no Holy Spirit is apparent upon them, here too A DEAD MAN is just like an animal, a body without a spirit. Therefore, this body that is most precious of all should not be put to shame.

343 וְתָאנָא בִּצְנִיעוּתָא דְּסִפְרָא, כָּל מַאן דְּעָבֵיד לִינָה לְהַאי גּוּפָא
קַדִּישָׁא, בְּלָא רוּחָא, עָבֵיד פְּגִימוּתָא בְּגוּפָא דְּעָלְמִין. דְּהָא בְּגִין דָּא,
לָא עָבֵיד לִינָה בְּאַתְרָא קַדִּישָׁא, בְּאַרְעָא דְּצֶדֶק יָלִין בָּהּ, מִשׁוּם דְּהַאי
גּוּפָא יְקָרָא, אִתְקְרֵי דְּיוּקְנָא דְּמַלְכָּא. וְאִי עָבֵיד בֵּיהּ לִינָה, הֲוֵי כְּחַד מִן
בְּעִירָא.

343. We have learned in the hidden book that whoever keeps this holy body overnight, when it is devoid of spirit, makes a flaw in the everlasting body, THAT IS THE UPPERMOST MAN. It is therefore not permitted to have it stay overnight in a holy place, in the land where righteousness resides, THAT IS THE LAND OF YISRAEL WHERE IT IS WRITTEN: "HIS BODY SHALL NOT REMAIN ALL NIGHT...THAT YOUR LAND BE NOT DEFILED" (DEVARIM 21:23). This precious body is referred to as the image of the King. If one lets it stay overnight, it WOULD APPEAR TO BE like one of the animals, THAT IS, WITHOUT SPIRIT LIKE A BEAST, AS MENTIONED ABOVE.

344. תָּאנָא, וַיִּרְאוּ בְנֵי הָאֱלֹהִים אֶת בְּנוֹת הָאָדָם. אִינּוּן דְּאִטְמַרוּ,
וְנָפְלוּ בְּנוּקְבָּא דִּתְהוֹמָא רַבָּא. אֶת בְּנוֹת הָאָדָם, הָאָדָם הַיָּדוּעַ. וּכְתִיב
וְיָלְדוּ לָהֶם הֵמָּה הַגִּבּוֹרִים אֲשֶׁר מֵעוֹלָם וְגוֹ'. מֵהַהוּא דְּאִקְרֵי עוֹלָם.
כִּדְתָנֵינָן יְמֵי עוֹלָם. אַנְשֵׁי הַשֵּׁם, מִנְּהוֹן נַפְקוּ רוּחִין וְשֵׁדִין לְעָלְמָא,
לְאִתְדַּבְּקָא בְּרַשִׁיעַיָּיא.

344. We have learned: "The sons of Elohim saw that the daughters of men (lit. 'man') were fair" (Beresheet 6:2). These are the ones that were hidden, MEANING THEY WERE DISTANCED FROM HOLINESS, and fell into a crevice of the great abyss, THAT IS AS MENTIONED ABOVE. 'The daughters of men', that certain man. THIS IS ZEIR ANPIN, THEY BEING AN ASPECT OF ABEL; HE SAYS ABOUT THEM ABOVE THAT THEY ARE MOLLIFIED FURTHER THROUGH THE WHOLE OF THE HOLY BODY, WHICH IS ZEIR ANPIN. It is written: "And they bore children to them; the same were mighty men of old (lit. 'the world')" (Ibid. 4), MEANING TO SAY THAT THEY ARE from the one that was called "the world" as we have learned concerning the days of the world, ZEIR ANPIN, EXCEPT THAT THEY ARE FROM THE OTHER SIDE, THAT SOMETIMES THEY BOND TO ZEIR ANPIN AND SOMETIMES NOT. THEY ADHERE TO THE BODY YET THEY DO NOT ADHERE. ALL ARE SUSPENDED IN THE AIR. "Men of renown (lit. 'name')" (Beresheet 6:4), MEANING OF MALCHUT, THAT IS REFERRED TO AS NAME, AND THEY ARE NOT FROM ZEIR ANPIN REFERRED TO AS WORLD. THESE ARE THE SPIRITS OF THE LEFT THAT DO NOT IMPROVE BY BEING PART OF MAN. THEREFORE, spirits and demons get out into the world from them, to adhere to the wicked.

345. הַנְּפִילִים הָיוּ בָאָרֶץ, לְאַפָּקָא אִלֵּין אַחֲרָנִין. דְּלָא הֲווֹ בָּאָרֶץ.
הַנְּפִילִים: עַזָּ"א וְעֲזָא"ל הֲווֹ בָּאָרֶץ. בְּנֵי הָאֱלֹהִים לָא הֲווֹ בָּאָרֶץ. וְרָזָא
הוּא וְכֹלָא אִתְּמַר.

345. "There were *Nefilim* (lit. 'fallen ones') in the earth" (Ibid.). This excludes the other ones that were not on the earth at that time, THAT ARE NOT OF THE ASPECT OF MALCHUT REFERRED TO AS EARTH. The fallen ones are Aza and Aza'el, who were on the earth. THEY ARE OF THE ASPECT OF SPIRITS OF THE LEFT, WHICH DO NOT BOND TO THE BODY AT ALL,

WHICH IS ZEIR ANPIN BUT TO MALCHUT REFERRED TO AS EARTH, WHICH IS THE LEFT. The sons of Elohim were not on the earth, WHICH IS MALCHUT, BUT THEY WERE ATTACHED, YET NOT ATTACHED, TO THE HOLY BODY THAT IS ZEIR ANPIN, AS MENTIONED ABOVE. This is a secret that we have learned.

346. כְּתִיב וַיִּנָּחֶם יְיָ' כִּי עָשָׂה אֶת הָאָדָם בָּאָרֶץ, לְאַפָּקָא אָדָם דִּלְעֵילָּא, דְּלָא הֲוֵי בָּאָרֶץ. וַיִּנָּחֶם יְיָ' הַאי בִּזְעֵיר אַפִּין אִתְּמַר. וַיִּתְעַצֵּב אֶל לִבּוֹ, וַיֵּעָצֵב לֹא נֶאֱמַר. אֶלָּא וַיִּתְעַצֵּב, אִיהוּ אִתְעַצֵּב, דְּבֵיהּ תַּלְיָיא מִלְּתָא. לְאַפּוֹקֵי מִמַּאן דְּלָא אִתְעַצֵּב. אֶל לִבּוֹ, בְּלִבּוֹ לָא כְּתִיב, אֶלָּא אֶל לִבּוֹ. כְּמַאן דְּאִתְעַצֵּב לְמָארֵיהּ, דְּאַחֲזֵי הַאי לְלִבָּא דְּכָל לִבִּין.

346. It is written: "And Hashem repented that he made man on the earth" (Ibid. 6). THIS excludes the man above that was not on earth, MEANING THAT HE IS NOT FROM THE ASPECT OF MALCHUT CALLED EARTH. THE ENTIRE PUNISHMENT OF THE FLOOD WAS ONLY FROM THE ASPECT OF MALCHUT, WHICH IS THE SECRET OF EARTH, BUT NOT ANYTHING ABOVE IT. "And Hashem repented": That is said of Zeir Anpin. "And it grieved him at his heart" (Ibid.): It does not say that he was grieved, but rather "it grieved Him," since it grieved only him, as this is dependent upon him. THAT IS TO SAY, THE DEEDS OF THE LOWER BEINGS REACH ZEIR ANPIN, to exclude those who are not grieved. BY THE DEEDS OF THE LOWER BEINGS, SINCE THE LOWER BEINGS DO NOT HARM THEM. THAT REFERS TO ABOVE ZEIR ANPIN. "At his heart": It does not say, 'In his heart', but rather "At his heart," as someone that is grieved for his master. This alludes to the heart of all hearts, WHICH IS ARICH ANPIN THAT IS CLOTHED IN THE INNERMOST OF ZEIR ANPIN.

347. וַיֹּאמֶר יְיָ' אֶמְחֶה אֶת הָאָדָם אֲשֶׁר בָּרָאתִי מֵעַל פְּנֵי הָאֲדָמָה וְגוֹ'. לְאַפָּקָא אָדָם דִּלְעֵילָּא. וְאִי תֵימָא אָדָם דִּלְתַתָּא בִּלְחוֹדוֹי. לָאו לְאַפָּקָא כְּלָל. מִשּׁוּם דְּלָא קָאֵים דָּא בְּלָא דָא.

347. "And Hashem said, 'I will destroy man whom I have created from the face of the earth...'" (Ibid. 7). "From the face of the earth" comes to exclude man from above MALCHUT THAT IS CALLED EARTH. You might say only man below exclusively, AND THE MAN ABOVE WAS NOT FLAWED AT ALL

AS A RESULT OF THIS, but you cannot exclude OR DIFFERENTIATE BETWEEN ONE AND THE OTHER at all, since one cannot exist without the other. WHEN THE MAN BELOW IS OBLITERATED, THE MAN ABOVE IS ALSO FLAWED.

348. וְאִלְמָלֵא חָכְמָה סְתִימָא דְּכֹלָּא, כֹּלָּא אִתְתַּקַּן כְּמֵרֵישָׁא. הה"ד אֲנִי חָכְמָה שָׁכַנְתִּי עָרְמָה. אַל תִּקְרֵי שָׁכַנְתִּי, אֶלָּא שִׁכַנְתִּי.

348. If wisdom hidden from all, THAT IS IF CHOCHMAH OF ARICH ANPIN WOULD HAVE ILLUMINATED TO MALCHUT, everything would have been fixed to its original form, AND THERE WOULD NOT HAVE BEEN A FLOOD. It is written: "I, wisdom, dwell with prudence" (Mishlei 8:12). Do not read it as "dwell with," but rather 'cause to dwell'.

349. וְאִלְמָלֵא הַאי תִּקּוּנָא דְּאָדָם, לָא קָאִים עָלְמָא. הֲדָא הוּא דִכְתִיב, יְיָ' בְּחָכְמָה יָסַד אָרֶץ. וּכְתִיב וְנֹחַ מָצָא חֵן בְּעֵינֵי יְיָ'.

349. If not for the correction of man, the world would not have lasted. This is what is written: "Hashem by wisdom founded the earth" (Mishlei 3:19), and: "But Noah found favor in the eyes of Hashem" (Beresheet 6:8).

350. וְתָאנָא, כֻּלְּהוּ מוֹחִין תַּלְיָין בְּהַאי מוֹחָא. וְהַחָכְמָה הוּא כְּלָלָא דְּכֹלָּא הוּא. וְדָא חָכְמָה סְתִימָא, דְּבָה אִתְתַּקִּיף וְאִתְתַּקַּן תִּקּוּנָא דְּאָדָם, לְאִתְיַישְּׁבָא בֹּלָּא עַל תִּקּוּנֵיה, כָּל חַד בְּאַתְרֵיה. הה"ד, הַחָכְמָה תָּעוֹז לֶחָכַם מֵעֲשָׂרָה שַׁלִּיטִים, דְּאִינּוּן תִּקּוּנָא שְׁלֵימָא דְּאָדָם. וְאָדָם הוּא תִּקּוּנָא דִּלְגוֹ, מִנֵּיה קָאִים רוּחָא.

350. We have learned that all the brains flow from that brain, THAT IS IN CONCEALED CHOCHMAH. Chochmah is inclusive of everything. This is concealed Chochmah, with which man's form was established and strengthened, so that everything should be settled in an orderly way, each one in its place. This is what is written: "Wisdom strengthens the wise more than ten rulers" (Kohelet 7:19). THAT IS THE TEN SFIROT that are the perfect establishment of man. The man is their inmost formation, SINCE

-318-

THE BRAINS THAT ARE IN THE INMOST PART ARE REFERRED TO AS MAN, with which the spirit is sustained.

351. וּבְהַאי תִּקּוּנָא דְּאָדָם, אִתְחֲזֵי שְׁלֵימוּתָא מְהֵימְנוּתָא דְּכֹלָּא, דְּקָאֵים עַל כּוּרְסְיָיא. דִּכְתִּיב, וּדְמוּת כְּמַרְאֵה אָדָם עָלָיו מִלְמָעְלָה. וּכְתִיב וַאֲרוּ עִם עֲנָנֵי שְׁמַיָּא כְּבַר אֱנָשׁ אָתֵה הֲוָה וְעַד עַתִּיק יוֹמַיָּא מְטָה וּקְדָמוֹהִי הַקְרְבוּהִי. עַד כָּאן סְתִימָאן מִלִּין. וּבְרִירִין טַעֲמִין. זַכָּאָה חוּלָקֵיהּ דְּמַאן דְּיָדַע וְיַשְׁגַּח בְּהוֹן. וְלָא יִטְעֵי בְּהוֹן. דְּמִלִּין אִלֵּין לָא אִתְיְהִיבוּ, אֶלָּא לְמָארֵי מדין וּמְחַצְדֵי חַקְלָא, דְּעָאלוּ וְנַפְקוּ. דִּכְתִּיב כִּי יְשָׁרִים דַּרְכֵי יְיָ' וְצַדִּיקִים יֵלְכוּ בָם וּפוֹשְׁעִים יִכָּשְׁלוּ בָם.

351. All the perfect Faith of the one who stands on the throne is apparent with this forming of man, as is written: "The likeness as the appearance of a man above upon it" (Yechezkel 1:26) and "One like a son of man came with the clouds of heaven, and came to the ancient of days, and they brought him near before him" (Daniel 7:13). Until here, the matters are vague and the reasons are obvious. Praised is the lot of the one who is aware and observes to understand them, and does not err in them. These matters were given only to those who sat on the seat of justice and the reapers of the field that entered and were able to leave, as is written: "For the ways of Hashem are right, and the just do walk in them: but the transgressors shall stumble in them" (Hoshea 14:10).

352. תָּאנָא, בָּכָה ר"ש, וְאָרִים קָלֵיהּ וְאָמַר, אִי בְּמִלִּין דִּילָן, דְּאִתְגַּלְיָין הָכָא, אִתְגְּנִיזוּ חַבְרַיָּיא בְּאִדְרָא דְּעָלְמָא דְּאָתֵי, וְאִסְתְּלָקוּ מֵהַאי עָלְמָא, יָאוּת וְשַׁפִּיר הֲוָה, בְּגִין דְּלָא אִתְגַּלְיָין לְחַד מִבְּנֵי עָלְמָא. הָדַר וְאָמַר, הַדְרִי בִי, דְּהָא גַּלֵּי קַמֵּיהּ דְּעַתִּיקָא דְּעַתִּיקִין, סְתִימָא דְּכָל סְתִימִין, דְּהָא לָא לִיקָרָא דִּילִי עֲבִידְנָא, וְלָא לִיקָרָא דְּבֵית אַבָּא, וְלָא לִיקָרָא דְּחַבְרַיָּיא אִלֵּין, אֶלָּא בְּגִין דְּלָא יִטְעוּן בְּאוֹרְחוֹי, וְלָא יֵעֲלוּן בְּכְסוּפָא לְתַרְעֵי פַּלְטְרוֹי, וְלָא יִמְחוּן בִּידֵיהוֹן. זַכָּאָה חוּלָקֵי עִמְּהוֹן, לְעָלְמָא דְּאָתֵי.

352. We have learned that Rabbi Shimon cried and raised his voice and said: If only with our words that were revealed here, our friends would have

been hidden in the chamber of the World to Come, and would have passed away from this world, it would have been proper and good, since they would not have been revealed to any one in this world. He then repented and said: I regret what I said, BUT RATHER THEY SHOULD DESERVE TO LIVE LONGER IN THIS WORLD. It is apparent to the most ancient amont the ancient ones, the most concealed of all concealed, that I have not done this for my honor and not for the honor of my family and not for the honor of these friends. It is only that they should not err in his ways and should not enter with shame into the gates of his palace, so they will not be prevented FROM ENTERING. Praised is my lot with them in the World to Come.

51. The passing of the three friends

A Synopsis

We learn that before they could leave the chamber, Rabbi Yosi, Rabbi Chizkiyah and Rabbi Yesa died, and the other friends saw holy angels carrying them away. Rabbi Shimon is beside himself with fear that his revelations have caused this event, until a voice tells him that he deserves praise. The voice says that the souls of the friends passed away through perfection and that they joined with great passionate will and valor at the time of their deaths. The uppermost angels took their souls and raised them above. All the faces of the rabbis were shining brightly. Rabbi Aba was sad for some days until he and Rabbi Shimon saw the angels showing their dead friends the treasures and chambers prepared for their honor, and then he was comforted. From that day on the friends did not leave Rabbi Shimon's house, and no one else was ever present when he revealed secrets to them. He called them 'the seven eyes of Hashem', and Rabbi Yehuda referred to him as Shabbat, from which all six days get their blessing.

353. תָּנָא, עַד לָא נַפְקוּ חַבְרַיָּיא מֵהַהוּא אִדְּרָא, מִיתוּ ר' יוֹסֵי בַּר' יַעֲקֹב, וְר' חִזְקִיָּה, וְר' יֵיסָא. וְחָמוּ חַבְרַיָּיא, דַּהֲווֹ נַטְלִין לוֹן מַלְאָכִין קַדִּישִׁין בְּהַהוּא פַּרְסָא. וְאר״ש מִלָּה, וְאִשְׁתְּכָכוּ. צָוַוח וְאָמַר, שֶׁמָּא ח״ו גְּזֵרָה אִתְגְּזַר עֲלָנָא לְאִתְעַנָּשָׁא, דְּאִתְגְּלֵי עַל יְדָנָא, מַה דְּלָא אִתְגְּלֵי מִיּוֹמָא דְּקָאֵים מֹשֶׁה עַל טוּרָא דְּסִינַי, דִּכְתִּיב וַיְהִי שָׁם עִם יְיָ' אַרְבָּעִים יוֹם וְאַרְבָּעִים לַיְלָה וְגוֹ'. מַה אֲנָא הָכָא. אִי בְּגִין דָּא אִתְעֲנָשׁוּ.

353. We have learned that before these friends came out from that chamber, Rabbi Yosi ben Rabbi Ya'akov, Rabbi Chizkiyah and Rabbi Yesa died. The friends saw that holy angels carried them in that veil. Rabbi Shimon said something and THE FRIENDS calmed down. He cried out and said: Perhaps, heaven forbid, a writ was decreed for us to be punished, since it was revealed through us what has not been revealed since the day Moses stood on Mount Sinai, as it is written: "And he was there with Hashem forty days and forty nights... " (Shemot 34:28). Why am I here if this is the reason for their punishment?

354. שָׁמַע קָלָא, זַכָּאָה אַנְתְּ ר״ש, זַכָּאָה חוּלָקָךְ וְחַבְרַיָּיא, אִלֵּין

דְּקַיְימִין בַּהֲדָךְ, דְּהָא אִתְגְּלֵי לְכוֹן מַה דְּלָא אִתְגְּלֵי לְכָל חֵילָא
דִּלְעֵילָּא, אֲבָל ת"ח, דְּהָא כְּתִיב, בִּבְכוֹרוֹ יְיַסְּדֶנָּה וּבִצְעִירוֹ יַצִּיב
דְּלָתֶיהָ. וכ"ש דְּבִרְעוּ סַגִּי וְתַקִּיף, אִתְדָּבָקוּ נַפְשַׁתְהוֹן בְּשַׁעְתָּא דָא
דְּאִתְנְסִיבוּ. זַכָּאָה חוּלָקֵיהוֹן, דְּהָא בִּשְׁלֵימוּתָא אִסְתָּלָקוּ.

354. He heard a voice say: Rabbi Shimon, you deserve praise. Praised is your lot and the lot of the friends that are with you, since it was revealed to you what has not been revealed to all the legions above. However, come and see that it is written: "He shall lay its foundation with his firstborn, and with his youngest son shall he set up the gates of it" (Yehoshua 6:26). Certainly, the souls OF THE FRIENDS ever devoted with great, strong will and valor at the time they were taken BY THE ANGELS. Praised is their lot that, through perfection, they passed away.

355. תָּאנָא, בְּעוֹד דְּאִתְגַּלְיָין מִלִּין, אִתְרְגִישׁוּ עִלָּאִין וְתַתָּאִין, וְקָלָא
אִתְּעַר בְּמָאתָן וְחַמְשִׁין עָלְמִין דְּהָא מִלִּין עַתִּיקִין לְתַתָּא אִתְגַּלְיָין, וְעַד
דְּאִלֵּין מִתְבַּסְּמָן נִשְׁמָתַיְיהוּ בְּאִינּוּן מִלִּין, נָפְקָא נִשְׁמָתַיְיהוּ בִּנְשִׁיקָה,
וְאִתְקָשַׁר בְּהַהוּא פַּרְסָא, וְנַטְלִין לְהוּ מַלְאֲכֵי עִלָּאֵי, וְסַלְּקִין לוֹן לְעֵילָּא.
וְאֲמַאי אִלֵּין. מִשּׁוּם דְּעָאלָן וְלָא נָפְקוּ זִמְנָא אַחֲרָא מִן קַדְמַת דְּנָא,
וְכֻלְּהוּ אַחֲרִינֵי עָאלוּ וְנָפְקוּ.

355. We have learned that while these matters were revealed, higher and lower beings trembled and a sound was roused AND DECLARED in 250 worlds, that ancient matters were revealed below. While they were still soothing their souls with these matters, their soul left with a kiss and was connected in that veil, and the uppermost angels took them and raised them above.

356. אר"ש, כַּמָּה זַכָּאָה חוּלָקֵיהוֹן דְּהָנֵי תְּלָתָא, וְזַכָּאָה חוּלָקָנָא
לְעָלְמָא דְּאָתֵי, בְּגִין דָּא. נָפַק קָלָא תִּנְיָינוּת וְאָמַר, וְאַתֶּם הַדְּבֵקִים בַּיְיָ'
אֱלֹהֵיכֶם חַיִּים כֻּלְּכֶם הַיּוֹם. קָמוּ וְאַזְלוּ. בְּכָל אֲתָר דַּהֲווֹ מִסְתַּכְּלֵי סָלִיק
רֵיחִין. אר"ש שָׁמַע מִינָּהּ, דְּלְעָלְמָא מִתְבָּרֵךְ בְּגִינָן. וַהֲווֹ נְהִירִין אַנְפּוֹי
דְּכֻלְּהוּ, וְלָא הֲווֹ יַכְלִין בְּנֵי עָלְמָא לְאִסְתַּכְּלָא בְּהוּ.

356. Rabbi Shimon said: How happy is the lot of these three, and praised is our lot in the World to Come for this. A second voice sounded and said, "But you that did cleave to Hashem your Elohim are alive every one of you this day" (Devarim 4:4). They got up and left. Everywhere they looked, fragrances were missing. Rabbi Shimon said: It seems from this that the world is being blessed because of us. All their faces were shining bright and people could not look at them.

357. תָּאנָא, עֲשָׂרָה עָאלוּ, וְשֶׁבַע נָפְקוּ, וַהֲוָה חַדֵּי ר״ש. וְרִבִּי אַבָּא עָצִיב. יוֹמָא חַד הֲוָה יָתִיב ר״ש וְרִבִּי אַבָּא עִמֵּיהּ, אר״ש מִלָּה, וְחָמוּ לְאִלֵּין תְּלָתָא דַּהֲווֹ מַיְיתִין לְהוֹן מַלְאֲכִין עִלָּאִין, וּמְחַזְיָין לְהוּ גְּנִיזִין וְאִדְרִין דִּלְעֵילָּא, בְּגִין יְקָרָא דִּלְהוֹן. וַהֲווֹ עָיְילֵי לוֹן בְּטוּרֵי דַּאֲפַרְסְמוֹנָא דַּכְיָא. נָח דַּעְתֵּיהּ דְּרִבִּי אַבָּא.

357. We have learned that ten entered THE GATHERING and seven left it. Rabbi Shimon was rejoicing but Rabbi Aba was sad. One day, Rabbi Shimon was sitting with Rabbi Aba. Rabbi Shimon said something. They saw the three FRIENDS, whom upper angels were bringing and showing them the treasures and chambers above for their honor. They were introducing them into the mountains of pure balsam. Rabbi Aba's mind was calm and at peace.

358. תָּאנָא, מֵהַהוּא יוֹמָא לָא אַעְדּוּ חַבְרַיָּיא מִבֵּי ר״ש. וְכַד הֲוָה ר״ש מְגַלֶּה רָזִין, לָא מִשְׁתַּכְּחִין תַּמָּן אֶלָּא אִינוּן. וַהֲוָה קָארֵי לְהוּ רִבִּי שִׁמְעוֹן, שִׁבְעָה אֲנָן עֵינֵי יְיָ׳. דִּכְתִיב, שִׁבְעָה אֵלֶּה עֵינֵי יְיָ׳ וְעָלָן אִתְּמַר. א״ר אַבָּא, אֲנָן שִׁיתָא בּוֹצִינֵי, דְּנַהֲרָאן מִשְּׁבִיעָאָה. אַנְתְּ הוּא שְׁבִיעָאָה דְּכֹלָּא. דְּהָא לֵית קְיוּמָא לְשִׁיתָא, בַּר מִשְּׁבִיעָאָה. דְּכֹלָּא תַּלֵי בִּשְׁבִיעָאָה. רִבִּי יְהוּדָה קָארֵי לֵיהּ שַׁבָּת, דְּכֻלְּהוּ שִׁיתָא מִנֵּיהּ מִתְבָּרְכִין, דִּכְתִיב שַׁבָּת לַיְיָ׳, קֹדֶשׁ לַיְיָ׳, מַה שַׁבָּת לַיְיָ׳ קֹדֶשׁ, אוּף ר״ש שַׁבָּת לַיְיָ׳ קֹדֶשׁ.

358. We have learned that from that day on, the friends did not leave the residence of Rabbi Shimon. When Rabbi Shimon was revealing secrets, nobody was present except for them. Rabbi Shimon referred to them as 'We are the seven eyes of Hashem' as is written: "Those seven...the eyes of

Hashem" (Zechariah 4:10), which is applicable to us. Rabbi Aba said: We are six candles illuminating from the seventh, WHICH IS THE SECRET OF BINAH. You are the seventh of all, because the six cannot endure, WHICH ARE CHESED, GVURAH, TIFERET, NETZACH, HOD AND YESOD, save from the seventh, WHICH IS BINAH, since everything is dependent on the seventh. Rabbi Yehuda used to refer to him as Shabbat, from which all six days get their blessing, as is written: "Shabbat to Hashem" (Shemot 20:10) or holy to Hashem. Just as Shabbat is holy to Hashem, so is Rabbi Shimon holy Shabbat to Hashem.

52. Elijah

A Synopsis

Rabbi Shimon is wondering why Elijah was not present in the chamber when the holy matters were revealed. Elijah arrives with three drops of light, and Rabbi Shimon asks him why he was not available during the feast that they had prepared. Elijah explains that he had wanted to be there, but God had sent him on a mission to do miracles for Rabbi Hamnuna Saba (the elder) and his friends. When he returned he found the angels carrying the three friends. He and Rabbi Shimon talk about the crowns that are given to the righteous during the new moon, holidays and Shabbat. Elijah tells him that he will be decorated and sanctified more than all the others, and that Rabbi Shimon bar Yochai is the holy one of Hashem, who is called honorable in this world and in the World to Come.

359. אר״ש, תַּווְהָנָא עַל הַהוּא חֲגִיר חַרְצָן, מָארֵיה דְּשַׁעֲרֵי, אֲמַאי לָא אִשְׁתְּכַח בְּבֵי אִדְרָא דִּילָן, בְּזִמְנָא דְּאִתְגַּלְּיָין מִלִּין אִלֵּין קַדִּישִׁין. אַדְּהָכִי, אָתָא אֵלִיָּהוּ, וּתְלַת קַטְפּוֹרֵי נְהִירִין בְּאַנְפּוֹי. אָ״ל ר״ש, מ״ט לָא שְׁכִיחַ מָר בְּקַרְדוּטָא גְּלִיפָא דְּמָארֵיה, בְּיוֹמָא דְּהִלּוּלָא.

359. Rabbi Shimon said: I wonder about the master of the gates girdled around his waist, THAT IS ELIJAH. Why was he not in our chamber during the time these holy matters were revealed? While he wondered, Elijah arrived with three drops of light, brightening his countenance. Rabbi Shimon said to him: What is the reason that my lord was not present during the wine feast that was being enacted AND PREPARED for his Master on this joyous day?

360. אָ״ל, חַיֶּיךָ רִבִּי שֶׁבַע יוֹמִין אִתְבְּרִירוּ קַמֵּיה קוּדְשָׁא בְּרִיךְ הוּא, כָּל אִינּוּן דְּיֵיתוּן וְיִשְׁתַּכְּחָן עִמֵּיה, עַל לָא עַיֵּילְתּוּן בְּבֵי אִדְרָא דִּלְכוֹן וַאֲנָא הֲוָה זַמִּין תַּמָּן, וּבָעֵינָא קַמֵּיה לְאִשְׁתַּכְּחָא, וּכְדֵין קָטִיר בְּכִתְפוֹי וְלָא יְכִילְנָא, דְּהַהוּא יוֹמָא שָׁדַרְנִי קוּדְשָׁא בְּרִיךְ הוּא, לְמֶעְבַּד נִסִּין לְרַב הַמְנוּנָא סָבָא וְחַבְרוֹי, דְּאִתְמְסָרוּ בְּאַרְמוֹנָא דְּמַלְכָּא, וְאַרְחִישְׁנָא לְהוּ בְּנִסָּא, דְּרָמֵינָא לְהוּ כּוֹתָלָא דְּהֵיכָלָא דְּמַלְכָּא, וְאִתְקְטָרוּ בְּקִטְרוֹי,

דְּמִיתוּ אַרְבָּעִים וַחֲמִשָּׁה פַּרְדַּשְׁכֵּי. וְאַפִּיקְנָא לְרַב הַמְנוּנָא וְחַבְרוֹי
וְרָמֵינָא לוֹן לְבִקְעַת אוֹנוֹ, וְאִשְׁתְּזִיבוּ. וְזַמִּינְנָא קַמַּיְיהוּ נָהֲמָא וּמַיָּיא,
דְּלָא אַכְלוּ תְּלָתָא יוֹמִין. וְכָל הַהוּא יוֹמָא לָא בְּדִילְנָא מִנַּיְיהוּ.

360. He, ELIJAH, said to him: On your life, Rabbi, seven days before you entered your chamber, all those that were to come in and be with you IN THE CHAMBER were being chosen in the presence of the Holy One, blessed be He. I was there and wanted to be in his presence IN THE CHAMBER. They had me yoked, and I was not able TO GO since, on that particular day, the Holy One, blessed be He, sent me on a mission to do miracles for Rav Hamnuna Saba (the elder) and his friends, who had been compromised by an informer to the king's palace. I caused a miracle to happen. For their sake, I collapsed the wall in the king's temple, so that 45 ministers got entangled in the debris of the wall, FELL WITH IT, and died. I removed Rav Hamnuna Saba and his friends and threw them to the valley of Ono, and they were saved. I prepared for them bread and water, because they hadn't eaten for three days. All that day, THAT YOU WERE IN THAT CHAMBER, I did not leave them

361. וְכַד תַּבְנָא, אַשְׁכַּחְנָא פַּרְסָא דְּנַטְלוּ כָּל אִינוּן סַמְכִין, וּתְלַת מִן
חַבְרַיָּיא עֲלָה, וְשָׁאִילְנָא לוֹן. וְאָמְרוּ חוּלָקָא דְּקוּדְשָׁא בְּרִיךְ הוּא,
מֵהִלּוּלָא דר"ש וְחַבְרוֹי. זַכָּאָה אַנְתְּ ר"ש, וְזַכָּאָה חוּלָקָךְ, וְחוּלָקָא
דְּאִינוּן חַבְרַיָּיא דְּיַתְבִין קַמָּךְ. כַּמָּה דַרְגִּין אִתְתָּקְנוּ לְכוֹן לְעָלְמָא דְּאָתֵי.
כַּמָּה בּוֹצִינִין דִּנְהוֹרִין זְמִינִין לְנַהֲרָא לְכוּ.

361. When I returned, I found that three of the friends were on the curtain that these pillars, THAT IS, THE ANGELS, were carrying. I asked THE ANGELS and they told me that this was the portion of the Holy One, blessed be He from Rabbi Shimon's and his friends' festivity. Praised are you, Rabbi Shimon, and praised is your lot and the lot of the friends that reside with you. How many levels were prepared for you in the World to Come and how many bright lights are destined to illuminate for you.

362. ות"ח, יוֹמָא דֵין בְּגִינָךְ אִתְעֲטָרוּ חַמְשִׁין כִּתְרִין לְרַבִּי פִּנְחָס בֶּן
יָאִיר חָמוּךְ. וַאֲנָא אֲזִילְנָא עִמֵּיהּ בְּכָל אִינוּן נַהֲרֵי דְּטוּרֵי דְּאָפַרְסְמוֹנָא

דַּכְיָא, וְהוּא בָּרִיר דּוּכְתֵּיה, וְאִתְתָּקַן. אָ"ל, קְטוּרִין צַדִּיקַיָּיא בְּקַרְטוּפָא
דְּעִטְרִין, בְּרֵישׁ יַרְחֵי וּבְזִמְנֵי וְשַׁבָּתֵי, יַתִּיר מִכָּל שְׁאַר יוֹמִין.

362. Come and see, on this day, Rabbi Pinchas ben Yair, your father-in-law, was adorned with fifty crowns for your sake. I accompanied him in all these rivers of the mountains of pure balsam trees. He picked his place and got ready. RABBI SHIMON said to him: The righteous are connected to the source of the crowns during the new moon, holidays and Shabbat, more than during other days.

363. אָ"ל, וְאַף כָּל אִינּוּן דִּלְבַר, דִּכְתִיב וְהָיָה מִדֵּי חֹדֶשׁ בְּחָדְשׁוֹ וּמִדֵּי
שַׁבָּת בְּשַׁבַּתּוֹ וְגוֹ'. אִי אִלֵּין אַתְיָין, כ"ש צַדִּיקַיָּא. מִדֵּי חֹדֶשׁ בְּחָדְשׁוֹ,
לָמָּה. מִשּׁוּם דְּמִתְעַטְּרֵי אֲבָהָתָא רְתִיכָא קַדִּישָׁא. וּמִדֵּי שַׁבָּת בְּשַׁבַּתּוֹ,
דְּמִתְעַטַּר שְׁבִיעָאָה דְּכָל אִינּוּן שִׁיתָא יוֹמִין, דִּכְתִיב וַיְבָרֶךְ אֱלֹהִים אֶת
יוֹם הַשְּׁבִיעִי וְגוֹ'.

363. ELIJAH told him: Also all those that are outside, THEY ASCEND AS WELL, as is written: "And it shall come to pass, that every new moon, and every Shabbat, shall all flesh come..." (Yeshayah 66:23). THAT IS REFERRING TO THOSE ON THE OUTSIDE, WHO ARE NOT RIGHTEOUS. THEREFORE THE SCRIPTURE REFERS TO THEM AS ALL FLESH. If those come, then most certainly the righteous will come. Why "Every new moon"? Because it is then that the patriarchs, who are the holy Chariots, are decorated. THEN CHESED, GVURAH AND TIFERET OF ZEIR ANPIN, REFERRED TO AS PATRIARCHS, ARE ELEVATED AND BECOME CHOCHMAH, BINAH AND DA'AT. "And every Shabbat": Then, the seventh of the six days is decorated, BECAUSE THEN MALCHUT ACQUIRES THE FIRST THREE SFIROT, as is written: "And Elohim blessed the seventh day" (Beresheet 2:3).

עד כאן האדרא קדישא רבא

364. וְאַנְתְּ הוּא ר"ש, שְׁבִיעָאָה דְּשִׁיתָא, תְּהֵא מִתְעַטַּר וּמִתְקַדָּשׁ יַתִּיר
מִכֹּלָּא. וּתְלַת עֲדוּנִין דְּמִשְׁתַּכְּחִין בִּשְׁבִיעָאָה, זְמִינִין חַבְרַיָּיא אִלֵּין
צַדִּיקַיָּיא לְאִתְעַדְּנָא בְּגִינָךְ לְעָלְמָא דְּאָתֵי. וּכְתִיב וְקָרָאתָ לַשַּׁבָּת עֹנֶג

לִקְדוֹשׁ יְיָ' מְכוּבָּד. מַאן הוא קְדוֹשׁ יְיָ'. דָּא ר' שִׁמְעוֹן בֶּן יוֹחָאי, דְּאִקְרֵי
מְכוּבָּד בְּעָלְמָא דֵּין, וּבְעָלְמָא דְּאָתֵי.

364. You are Rabbi Shimon, the seventh of the six, and you will be crowned and sanctified more than all the others. These righteous friends are will delight in three delights, THAT IS THE THREE MEALS, that are on the seventh, in the World to Come because of you. It is written: "And call the Shabbat a delight, the holy day of Hashem honorable" (Yeshayah 58:13). Who is the holy one of Hashem? That is Rabbi Shimon bar Yochai, who is called honorable in this world and the World to Come.

The end of the Holy Idra Raba

13. Fear, humility and piety

A Synopsis

Rabbi Yitzchak says that whoever fears sin has awe and humility and piety because all of these are included in the fear of heaven. Rabbi Yehuda talks about the angel Michael who is a priest above and about the priest below who called is an angel since he comes from the aspect of Mercy. He says that the priest merited Mercy because of his fear of God. We learn from Rabbi Yehuda that whoever was joined male and female was called Adam; Adam fears heaven so that humility and piety and mercy are with him as well. The world cannot be built without the presence of male and female.

135. דַּבֵּר אֶל אַהֲרֹן וְאֶל בָּנָיו לֵאמֹר כֹּה תְבָרְכוּ וְגוֹ'. רִבִּי יִצְחָק פָּתַח וְאָמַר, וְחֶסֶד יְיָ' מֵעוֹלָם וְעַד עוֹלָם עַל יְרֵאָיו וְצִדְקָתוֹ לִבְנֵי בָנִים. כַּמָּה גְדוֹלָה הַיִּרְאָה לִפְנֵי הַקּוּדְשָׁא בְּרִיךְ הוּא, שֶׁבִּכְלַל הַיִּרְאָה עֲנָוָה, וּבִכְלַל הָעֲנָוָה חֲסִידוּת. נִמְצָא שֶׁכָּל מִי שֶׁיֵּשׁ בּוֹ יִרְאַת חֵטְא, יֶשְׁנוֹ בְּכֻלָּן וּמִי שֶׁאֵינוֹ יְרֵא שָׁמַיִם, אֵין בּוֹ לֹא עֲנָוָה וְלֹא חֲסִידוּת.

135. "Speak to Aaron and to his sons, saying, 'In this way you shall bless'" (Bemidbar 6:22). Rabbi Yitzchak opened the discussion saying, "But the steadfast love of Hashem is from everlasting to everlasting upon those who fear Him, and His righteousness to children's children" (Tehilim 103:17). How great is awe in the presence of the Holy One, blessed be He; that awe includes humility and humility includes piety. Thus whoever has fear of sin has them all. Whoever does not fear heaven has neither humility nor piety.

136. תָּאנָא, מִי שֶׁיָּצָא מִן הַיִּרְאָה, וְנִתְלַבֵּשׁ בַּעֲנָוָה, עֲנָוָה עָדִיף, וְנִכְלַל בְּכֻלְּהוּ. הַהַ"ד, עֵקֶב עֲנָוָה יִרְאַת יְיָ'. כָּל מִי שֶׁיֵּשׁ בּוֹ יִרְאַת שָׁמַיִם, זוֹכֶה לַעֲנָוָה. כָּל מִי שֶׁיֵּשׁ בּוֹ עֲנָוָה, זוֹכֶה לַחֲסִידוּת. וְכָל מִי שֶׁיֵּשׁ בּוֹ יִרְאַת שָׁמַיִם, זוֹכֶה לְכֻלָּם. לַעֲנָוָה, דִּכְתִיב עֵקֶב עֲנָוָה יִרְאַת יְיָ'. לַחֲסִידוּת, דִּכְתִיב וְחֶסֶד יְיָ' מֵעוֹלָם וְעַד עוֹלָם עַל יְרֵאָיו.

136. We have learned that whoever left the realm of awe but acquired humility, humility is better, and he has them all, as it is written: "The reward

of humility and (is) the fear of Hashem" (Mishlei 22:4). All of those who have fear of heaven acquire humility, and everyone who has humility acquires piety. Everyone that has fear of heaven acquires all: humility, as is written: "The reward of humility is the fear of Hashem," and piety (Chesed), as is written: "But the steadfast love (Chesed) of Hashem is from everlasting to everlasting upon those who fear Him."

137. תָּאנָא, כָּל אָדָם שֶׁיֵּשׁ בּוֹ חֲסִידוּת, נִקְרָא מַלְאַךְ יְיָ' צְבָאוֹת. הה"ד, כִּי שִׂפְתֵי כֹהֵן יִשְׁמְרוּ דַעַת וְתוֹרָה יְבַקְשׁוּ מִפִּיהוּ כִּי מַלְאַךְ יְיָ' צְבָאוֹת הוּא. מִפְּנֵי מַה זָכָה כֹּהֵן לְהִקָּרֵא מַלְאַךְ יְיָ' צְבָאוֹת. אָמַר ר' יְהוּדָה, מַה מַלְאַךְ יְיָ' צְבָאוֹת, כֹּהֵן לְמַעְלָה, אַף כֹּהֵן מַלְאַךְ יְיָ' צְבָאוֹת לְמַטָּה.

137. We learned that every man who has piety is referred to as the angel of Hashem, Hashem Tzva'ot. This is what is meant by: "For the priest's lips should keep knowledge, and they should seek Torah at his mouth: for he is a messenger (angel) of Hashem Tzva'ot" (Malachi 2:7). Rabbi Yehuda asked: Why did the priest merit to be referred to as the angel of Hashem Tzva'ot? Just like the angel of Hashem Tzva'ot is a priest above, IN HEAVEN, so too is a priest an angel of Hashem Tzva'ot below.

138. וּמַאן הוּא מַלְאַךְ יְיָ' צְבָאוֹת לְמַעְלָה. זֶה מִיכָאֵ"ל הַשַּׂר הַגָּדוֹל, דְּאָתֵי מֵחֶסֶד שֶׁל מַעֲלָה, וְהוּא כֹּהֵן גָּדוֹל שֶׁל מַעֲלָה, כִּבְיָכוֹל, כֹּהֵן גָּדוֹל דִּלְתַתָּא, אִקְרֵי מַלְאַךְ יְיָ' צְבָאוֹת, מִשּׁוּם דְּאָתֵי מִסִּטְרָא דְּחֶסֶד. מַהוּ חֶסֶד. רַחֲמֵי גּוֹ רַחֲמֵי. וּבְגִין כָּךְ, כֹּהֵן לָא אִשְׁתְּכַח מִסִּטְרָא דְּדִינָא. מ"ט זָכָה כֹּהֵן לְחֶסֶד, בְּגִין הַיִּרְאָה. הה"ד וְחֶסֶד יְיָ' מֵעוֹלָם וְעַד עוֹלָם עַל יְרֵאָיו.

138. Who is the angel of Hashem Tzva'ot above? That is Michael, the great minister who emanates from Chesed above and is the high priest of the above. The high priest below is called an angel of Hashem Tzva'ot, since he is come from the aspect of Chesed. What is Chesed? Mercy within mercy. Therefore, there is no priest coming from the aspect of Judgment. What is the reason that a priest merited Chesed? Because of awe. This is what is meant by: "But the steadfast love (Chesed) of Hashem is from everlasting (lit. 'world') to everlasting (world) upon those who fear Him."

139. עוֹלָם וְעוֹלָם מַהוּ. אָמַר רַבִּי יִצְחָק כְּמָה דְּאִתְתָּקַן בְּאִדְרָא קַדִּישָׁא, עוֹלָם חַד, וְעוֹלָם תְּרֵי. א"ר חִיָּיא אִי הָכִי מִן הָעוֹלָם וְעַד הָעוֹלָם מִבְעֵי לֵיהּ. א"ל, תְּרֵי עָלְמֵי נִינְהוּ. וְאִתְהַדָּרוּ לְחַד. א"ר אֶלְעָזָר לְר' יִצְחָק עַד מָתַי תִּסְתּוֹם דְּבָרֶיךָ. מִן הָעוֹלָם וְעַד הָעוֹלָם, כְּלָלָא דְּרָזָא עִלָּאָה, אָדָם דִּלְעֵילָּא, וְאָדָם דִּלְתַתָּא, וְהַיְינוּ עוֹלָם וְעוֹלָם. וּכְתִיב יְמֵי עוֹלָם, וּכְתִיב שְׁנוֹת עוֹלָם, וְהָא אוּקְמוּהָ בְּאִדְרָא קַדִּישָׁא עִלָּאָה.

139. HE ASKS: Why is it that he says "world" twice IN "FROM WORLD TO WORLD"? Rabbi Yitzchak said: It is like it was established in the holy gathering that "world" is one AND "TO world" is the second. THESE ARE THE TWO WORLDS, ZEIR ANPIN AND MALCHUT. Rabbi Chiya said: If so, it should have said, 'From the world to the world' WITH THE DEFINITE ARTICLE. He said to him: These are two worlds that returned to be one WORLD, MEANING TO SAY THAT THEY UNITE WITH EACH OTHER. THEREFORE, THERE IS NO DEFINITE ARTICLE TO EACH ONE. Rabbi Elazar said to Rabbi Yitzchak: How long will you keep your words so veiled? "From the world to the world" MEANS the inclusion of the uppermost secret, which is man above, WHO IS ZEIR ANPIN, and man below, WHO IS MALCHUT. This is WHAT IS MEANT BY: "world" and "world." It is written: "The days of old (lit. 'world')" (Yeshayah 63:9) and: 'Years of old (world)' It was already explained in the most holy gathering, THAT THEY REFER TO ZEIR ANPIN THAT IS CALLED WORLD.

140. עַל יְרֵאָיו, דְּכָל מַאן דְּאִיהוּ דָּחִיל חַטָּאָה, אִקְרֵי אָדָם. אֵימָתַי. א"ר אֶלְעָזָר, דְּאִית בֵּיהּ יִרְאָה עֲנָוָה חֲסִידוּת, כְּלָלָא דְּכֹלָּא.

140. THAT IS WHAT IS MEANT BY, "BUT THE STEADFAST LOVE OF HASHEM IS FROM WORLD TO WORLD upon those who fear Him." It is to teach that whoever is sin-fearing is called Adam. TWO WORLDS THAT ARE CALLED MAN DWELL ON HIM. When does this happen? Rabbi Elazar said: If he has awe, humility and piety, SINCE AWE is all-inclusive.

141. אָמַר רַבִּי יְהוּדָה, וְהָא תָּנֵינָן אָדָם כְּלָלָא דִּדְכַר וְנוּקְבָא. א"ל וַדַּאי הָכָא הוּא, בִּכְלָלָא דְּאָדָם, דְּמַאן דְּאִתְחַבָּר דְּכַר וְנוּקְבָא, אִקְרֵי

אָדָם, וּכְדֵין דָּחִיל חֵטָאָן. וְלֹא עוֹד אֶלָּא שַׁרְיָא בֵּיהּ עֲנָוָה. וְלֹא עוֹד
אֶלָּא דְּשַׁרְיָא בֵּיהּ חֶסֶד. וּמַאן דְּלָא אִשְׁתְּכַח דְּכַר וְנוּקְבָּא, לָא הֲווֹ בֵּיהּ
לָא יִרְאָה וְלָא עֲנָוָה וְלָא חֲסִידוּת. וּבְגִין כַּךְ אִקְרֵי אָדָם כְּלָלָא דְּכֹלָּא,
וְכֵיוָן דְּאִקְרֵי אָדָם, שַׁרְיָיא בֵּיהּ חֶסֶד, דִּכְתִיב אָמַרְתִּי עוֹלָם חֶסֶד יִבָּנֶה
וְגוֹ'. וְלָא יָכִיל לְאִתְבַּנָּאָה, אִי לָא אִשְׁתְּכַח דְּכַר וְנוּקְבָּא.

141. Rabbi Yehuda said, We learned here that Adam (man) comprises male
and female. He said to him: Certainly it is so, that he was included in Adam,
since whoever was joined male and female was called man, and then he is
heaven-fearing. Not only that, but humility dwells upon him and piety
prevails upon him also. Whoever is not male and female, has no fear, no
humility, no piety. Therefore, Adam is considered all-comprehensive. Since
he is called man, Chesed prevails, as is written: "For I have said, 'The world
is built by love (Chesed)...'" (Tehilim 89:3). THE WORLD cannot be built
without the presence of male and female.

142. וּכְתִיב וְחֶסֶד יְיָ' מֵעוֹלָם וְעַד עוֹלָם עַל יְרֵאָיו. יְרֵאָיו כְּלָלָא דְּאָדָם.
ד"א וְחֶסֶד יְיָ' מֵעוֹלָם וְעַד עוֹלָם, אִלֵּין אִינוּן כַּהֲנֵי דְּאָתוּ מִסִּטְרָא
דְחֶסֶד, וְאַחֲסִינוּ אַחֲסָנָא דָּא דְּנָחִית מֵעוֹלָם דִּלְעֵילָא לְעוֹלָם דִּלְתַתָּא.
עַל יְרֵאָיו, כַּהֲנֵי דִּלְתַתָּא, דִּכְתִיב וְכִפֶּר בַּעֲדוֹ וּבְעַד בֵּיתוֹ לְאִתְכַּלְלָא
בִּכְלָלָא דְּאָדָם. וְצִדְקָתוֹ לִבְנֵי בָנִים, מִשּׁוּם דְּזָכָה לִבְנֵי בָנִים. אָמַר רַבִּי
יְהוּדָה, אִי הָכִי, מַהוּ וְצִדְקָתוֹ, וְחַסְדּוֹ מִבָּעֵי לֵיהּ.

142. It is written: "But the steadfast love of Hashem is from world to world
upon those who fear Him" since those who fear Him are the wholeness of
man, MEANING BOTH MALE AND FEMALE, BECAUSE IF NOT SO, ONE IS
NOT FEARFUL. Another explanation for, "But the steadfast love (Chesed) of
Hashem from world to world": These are the priests that come from the side
of Chesed. They inherit this portion emanating from the upper world, THAT
IS ZEIR ANPIN, to the lower world, WHICH IS MALCHUT. "those who fear
Him," are the priests below THAT ARE INCLUSIVE OF MALE AND FEMALE,
as is written: "And make atonement for himself, and for his house" (Vayikra
16:6), WHICH IS THE FEMALE, in order to be included in the secret of man,
WHO IS BOTH MALE AND FEMALE. "And His righteousness to children's

children," because he merited to have grandchildren. Rabbi Yehuda said: If so, what is "His righteousness"? It needed to say 'His Chesed', SINCE THROUGH CHESED HE MERITED TO HAVE GRANDCHILDREN.

14. An unmarried priest is not allowed to serve

A Synopsis

We are told that a priest who does not have a wife is not permitted to carry out his duties because the Shechinah does not dwell in someone unmarried, and it is imperative for a priest to have the Shechinah dwell in him.

143. אָמַר רִבִּי אֶלְעָזָר, הַיְינוּ רָזָא דִּתְנֵינָן בְּזֹאת, כִּי מֵאִישׁ לֻקֳחָה זֹאת. וּכְתִיב לְזֹאת יִקָּרֵא אִשָּׁה, וְזֹאת אִתְכְּלִילַת בְּאִישׁ, דְּהַיְינוּ חֶסֶד, וְזֹאת נוּקְבָא. חֶסֶד דְּכַר. וּבְגִין כָּךְ דְּאָתֵי מִסִּטְרָא דְּחִוְּורָא דָּא, אִקְרֵי חֶסֶד. וְזֹאת אִתְקְרֵי צֶדֶק, דְּאַתְיָא מִסְטַר סוּמָקָא. וּבְגִין כָּךְ אִקְרֵי אִשָּׁה. וְהַיְינוּ דִּכְתִיב וְצִדְקָתוֹ, מַאי וְצִדְקָתוֹ. צִדְקָתוֹ דְּחֶסֶד, בַּת זוּגוֹ, דְּאִתְבַּסְּמָא דָּא בְּדָא. וּבְגִין כָּךְ תְּנֵינָן, כָּל כֹּהֵן שֶׁאֵין לוֹ בַּת זוּג, אָסוּר בַּעֲבוֹדָה, דִּכְתִיב וְכִפֶּר בַּעֲדוֹ וּבְעַד בֵּיתוֹ.

143. Rabbi Elazar said: This is the secret that we learned of "this (Heb. *zot*)," WHICH REFERS TO MALCHUT, "because she (*zot*) was taken out of man" (Beresheet 2:23). It is also written: "She (*zot*) shall be called woman" (Ibid.) and *zot* is included in man, WHO IS ZEIR ANPIN, which is Chesed, and *zot* is female. Chesed is male. Therefore, the male that comes from the white side, WHICH IS CHESED, is called Chesed and Zot is referred to as righteousness, since she comes from the side of red, THAT IS LEFT AND JUDGMENT. That is why she is called "woman (Heb. *ishah*)," WHICH IS DERIVED FROM FIRE (HEB. *ESH*) AND RIGHTEOUSNESS. That is the reason it is written: "And His righteousness TO CHILDREN'S CHILDREN" (Tehilim 103:17). IT IS NOT WRITTEN: 'AND HIS CHESED'. What is the meaning of "His righteousness"? This is the righteousness of Chesed, its spouse, for they sweeten one another, SINCE HIS RIGHTEOUSNESS INCLUDES ALSO THE MALE THAT IS CHESED. THAT IS WHY IT IS WRITTEN: "HIS RIGHTEOUSNESS." Therefore we have learned that any priest that does not have a wife is not permitted to carry out his duties, since it is written: "and make atonement for himself, and for his house" (Vayikra 16:17).

144. אָמַר ר' יִצְחָק, מִשּׁוּם דְּלֵית שְׁכִינְתָּא שַׁרְיָא, בְּמַאן דְּלָא אַנְסִיב,

וְכַהֲנֵי בַּעֲיָין יַתִּיר מִכָּל שְׁאָר עַמָּא, לְאַשְׁרְיָיא בְּהוֹ שְׁכִינְתָּא. וְכֵיוָן
דְּשַׁרֵת בְּהוֹ שְׁכִינְתָּא, שַׁרְיָא בְּהוֹ חֶסֶד, וְאִקְרוּן חֲסִידִים. וּבַעֲיָין לְבָרְכָא
עַמָּא, הה"ד וַחֲסִידֶיךָ יְבָרְכוּכָה. וּכְתִיב, תֻּמֶּיךָ וְאוּרֶיךָ לְאִישׁ חֲסִידֶךָ.
וּמִשּׁוּם דְּכַהֲנָא אִקְרֵי חָסִיד, בָּעֵי לְבָרְכָא. וּבְגִין כָּךְ כְּתִיב, דַּבֵּר אֶל
אַהֲרֹן וְאֶל בָּנָיו לֵאמֹר כֹּה תְבָרְכוּ. מַאי טַעֲמָא. מִשּׁוּם דְּאִקְרוּן חֲסִידִים,
וּכְתִיב וַחֲסִידֶיךָ יְבָרְכוּכָה.

144. Rabbi Yitzchak said: THEREFORE, A PRIEST IS NOT PERMITTED TO DO HIS DUTIES IF HE HAS NO WIFE, since the Shechinah does not dwell in someone who is not married. It is more imperative for the priests to have the Shechinah dwelling among them than the rest of the nation. When the Shechinah rests on them, Chesed resides among them and they are considered pious men (Heb. *Chassidim*). They are required to bless the nation and this is what is meant by: "And Your pious ones shall bless You" (Tehilim 145:10). It is also written: "Let Your Tummin and Your Urim be with Your pious one" (Devarim 33:8). Since the priest is considered pious, he needs to bless, which is why it is written, "Speak to Aaron and to his sons, saying, In this way you shall bless" (Bemidbar 6:23). The reason is that they are considered pious and it is written, "And Your pious ones shall bless You."

15. "In this way you shall bless"

A Synopsis

Rabbi Yitzchak says that the one who gives the blessing must do so with fear, with humility and with holiness. He talks about righteousness and "a great plague" that awakens judgments. The priest should give his blessings on Malchut with mercy and he should perfume her for the sake of the children of Yisrael so that no judgments will exist in her. Rabbi Yitzchak says that Daniel when he saw the vision was not afraid and he was not a prophet, and yet he was holier than the prophets. We hear Rabbi Yehuda's teaching about what happens when the priest stands up and spreads his hands for the blessing. We are told that every priest who raises his palms needs to become holier through one who is sanctified, the Levite, in order to add holiness to holiness, and that the Levite must first sanctify himself. Everyone should seek knowledge from the priest, who must know the Torah and who is a messenger from God.

145. כֹּה תְבָרְכוּ אֶת בְּנֵי יִשְׂרָאֵל אָמוֹר לָהֶם, כֹּה תְבָרְכוּ, בִּלְשׁוֹן הַקֹּדֶשׁ. כֹּה תְבָרְכוּ, בִּירְאָה. כֹּה תְבָרְכוּ, בַּעֲנָוָה. אָמַר ר' אַבָּא, כֹּה תְבָרְכוּ, תָּאנָא, הַאי צֶדֶ"ק אִתְקְרֵי כֹּ"ה, דְּכָל דִּינִין מִתְעָרִין מִכֹּ"ה, וְהַיְינוּ דְּאָמַר ר' אֶלְעָזָר, מַהוּ מַכָּה רַבָּה. כְּלוֹמַר, מַכָּה מִן כֹּה. וּכְתִיב וְהִנֵּה לֹא שָׁמַעְתָּ עַד כֹּ"ה, כְּמָה דְּאַגְזִים מֹשֶׁה. וּכְתִיב בְּזֹאת תֵּדַע כִּי אֲנִי יְיָ', וְכֹלָּא חַד, וּכְתִיב וְלֹא שָׁת לִבּוֹ גַּם לָזֹאת, דִּזְמִינָא לְחַרְבָּא אַרְעֵיהּ.

145. "In this way you shall bless the children of Yisrael, saying to them" (Bemidbar 6:23). "In this way you shall bless," namely in the holy tongue. "In this way you shall bless," NAMELY with awe. "In this way (Heb. *coh*) you shall bless," NAMELY with humility, SINCE MALCHUT IS CALLED "COH," WHEREIN ARE HOLINESS, AWE AND HUMILITY. Rabbi Aba said: "In this way you shall bless." We learned that this righteousness, WHICH IS MALCHUT, is called Coh, since all the Judgments come from Coh, SINCE COH IS DERIVED FROM *KEHEH* (ENG. 'DARK'), NAMELY WHEN MALCHUT IS IN THE LEFT ASPECT, WHEN SHE IS DIM AND DOESN'T SHINE AND ALL THE JUDGMENTS FLOW FROM HER. That is what Rabbi Elazar said – the meaning of "a great plague (Heb. *makah*)" (Bemidbar 11:33), is a plague of

Coh, as it is written: "till now (Heb. *coh*) you would not hear" (Shemot 7:16), as Moses threatened Pharaoh WITH THE NAME COH. In accordance with this, it is written: "In this (Heb. *zot*) you shall know that I am Hashem" (Ibid. 17). THAT IS, HE WAS THREATENING WITH THE NAME OF ZOT and all is one, SINCE MALCHUT IS CALLED BOTH COH AND ZOT. It is also written: "Neither did he set his heart even to this (*zot*)" (Ibid. 23), which is ready to destroy his country.

146. וּמֵהַאי כֹּ"ה מִתְעָרִין דִּינִין. וּמִדְּאִתְחַבַּר עִמָּהּ חֶסֶד, אִתְבַּסְּמַת. וּבְגִין כַּךְ, אִתְמְסַר דָּא לַכֹּהֵן, דְּאָתֵי מֵחֶסֶד, בְּגִין דְּתִתְבָּרֵךְ וְתִתְבְּסַם כֹּ"ה, הה"ד כֹּה תְבָרֲכוּ, כְּלוֹמַר, אע"ג דְּהַאי כֹּה אִשְׁתְּכַחַת בְּדִינִין, תְּבַסְּמוּן לָהּ, וּתְבָרְכוּן לָהּ, דִּכְתִיב כֹּה תְבָרֲכוּ אֶת בְּנֵי יִשְׂרָאֵל, תְּבָרְכוּ בְּהַאי חֶסֶד לְכֹ"ה, וּתְבַסְּמוּן לָהּ לְקַבְלַיְיהוּ דְּיִשְׂרָאֵל, בְּגִין דְּלָא יִשְׁתַּכְּחוּן בָּהּ דִּינִין.

146. From that Coh, WHICH IS MALCHUT, Judgments are aroused. When Chesed joins with her, she is mollified. Therefore, it is given to a priest who comes from Chesed so that this Coh will be blessed and perfumed. Hence, it is written: "In this way (*coh*) you shall bless the children of Yisrael." THE MEANING IS that you should bless Coh with this Chesed and appease her for the sake of Yisrael, so that there will be no Judgments in her.

147. הה"ד כֹּה תְבָרֲכוּ אֶת בְּנֵי יִשְׂרָאֵל אָמוֹר לָהֶם. אִמְרוּ לֹא כְּתִיב, אֶלָּא אָמוֹר, לְאַפָּקָא מִשֶּׁרַבּוּ הַפְּרִיצִים, דְּלָא מְפַרְסְמִין מִלָּה, דְּהָא לָא אִתְפַּקְּדוּ לְפַרְסְמָא שְׁמָא, מַשְׁמַע דִּכְתִיב אָמוֹר לָהֶם. ד"א אָמוֹר כֵּיוָן דִּכְתִיב כֹּה תְבָרֲכוּ, אֲמַאי לָא כְּתִיב תֹּאמְרוּ. אֶלָּא תָּנֵי ר' יְהוּדָה, אָמוֹר לָהֶם. זָכוּ לָהֶם, לֹא זָכוּ אָמוֹר סְתָם.

147. Hence, it is written: "In this way you shall bless the children of Yisrael, saying to them." "Saying" is not written in plural form, but in singular. This is for reasons of excluding. When transgressors of laws have increased, the matter is not publicized, since it was not commanded to make known the name of Coh. That is derived from the words: "Saying (sing.) to them," "saying" in singular INSTEAD OF 'SAYING TO THEM' IN PLURAL. Another

explanation for "saying (sing.)": Since it is written: "You (pl.) shall bless," why is it not also written: 'saying (pl.) TO THEM'? But Rabbi Yehuda taught, "saying to them": If they are worthy, it is "to them"; THAT IS, THE BLESSINGS REACH YISRAEL. If they are not worthy, it is simply "saying."

148. ר׳ יִצְחָק פָּתַח, וְרָאִיתִי אֲנִי דָנִיֵּאל לְבַדִּי אֶת הַמַּרְאָה וְהָאֲנָשִׁים אֲשֶׁר הָיוּ עִמִּי לֹא רָאוּ אֶת הַמַּרְאָה וְגוֹ׳. וְרָאִיתִי אֲנִי דָנִיֵּאל לְבַדִּי. וְהָא תָּנֵינָן, אִינְהוּ נְבִיאֵי, וְאִיהוּ לָאו נָבִיא, וּמַאן נִינְהוּ. חַגַּי זְכַרְיָה וּמַלְאָכִי. אִי הָכִי, אִתְעֲבֵיד קֹדֶשׁ חֹל, וְהָא כְּתִיב לֹא רָאוּ, אֲמַאי דְּחִילוּ. וּבְדָנִיֵּאל כְּתִיב וְרָאִיתִי אֲנִי, וְלָא דָחִיל. וְאִיהוּ לָאו נָבִיא, הָא חֹל קֹדֶשׁ.

148. Rabbi Yitzchak opened the discussion with the verse: "And I Daniel alone saw the vision: for the men who were with me did not see the vision..." (Daniel 10:7). HE ASKS: "And I Daniel alone saw," yet here we learned that he was not a prophet but there were prophets there – and who are they? They are Chagai, Zechariah and Malachi. If so, the holy becomes non-holy and here it is written: "did not see." Why should they fear then? About Daniel, it is written: "And I Daniel alone saw." Yet he is not fearful though he is not a prophet. Here the non-holy is holy, MEANING TO SAY THAT HE WHO IS NOT A PROPHET IS HOLIER THAN A PROPHET.

149. אֶלָּא הָכִי תָּאנָא, כְּתִיב אִם תַּחֲנֶה עָלַי מַחֲנֶה לֹא יִירָא לִבִּי אִם תָּקוּם עָלַי מִלְחָמָה בְּזֹאת אֲנִי בוֹטֵחַ. בְּזֹאת הָא דְּאָמְרָן זֹאת עַדְבָּא חוּלְקֵיה, לְאִתְחַסְּנָא, וּלְמֶעְבַּד לֵיהּ נוּקְמִין. וְתָנָא, עָבֵיד קוּדְשָׁא בְּרִיךְ הוּא לְדָוִד, רְתִיכָא קַדִּישָׁא עִם אֲבָהָתָא, כִּתְרִין עִלָּאִין קַדִּישִׁין דְּכֹלָּא, דְּאַחְסִינוּ אֲבָהָתָא. וְתָאנָא, מַלְכוּ יָרִית דָּוִד לִבְנוֹי בַּתְרוֹי. וּבַאֲתָר מַלְכוּ דִּלְעֵילָּא, אִתְקַף, וְאַחְסִין הוּא וּבְנוֹי מַלְכוּ דָּא, דְּלָא אַעֲדֵי מִשׁוּלְטָנְהוֹן לְדָרֵי דָרִין.

149. We learned that it is written: "Though a host should camp against me, my heart shall not fear: though war should rise against me, even then I will be confident (lit. 'trust in zot')" (Tehilim 27:3) Here Zot is precisely what we said, THAT IT IS MALCHUT. Zot was his portion and his lot, to become

stronger and execute vengeance. We learned that the Holy One, blessed be He, made David into a holy Chariot with the Patriarchs, AND HE RECEIVED the uppermost of all holy crowns that the patriarchs bequeathed to him. We have further learned that that kingdom was inherited by David and his sons thereafter. In the place of the uppermost Malchut, he was strengthened. He and his sons inherited this kingdom, so that their dominion was not shaken for many generations.

150. וְתָאנָא, בְּשַׁעֲתָא דְּהַאי כִּתְרָא דְּמַלְכוּתָא אִתְּעַר לִבְנוֹי דְּדָוִד, לֵית מַאן דְּקָאִים קַמֵּיהּ. וְרָאִיתִי אֲנִי דָנִיֵּאל לְבַדִּי אֶת הַמַּרְאָה, מִשּׁוּם דְּמִבְּנוֹי דְּדָוִד הֲוָה, דִּכְתִיב וַיְהִי בָהֶם מִבְּנֵי יְהוּדָה דָּנִיֵּאל חֲנַנְיָה וְגוֹ'. וְהוּא חָמָא וְחַדֵּי בְּהַאי דְּהוּא מִסְּטַר אַחְסָנַת חוּלָקָא עַדְבָא דַּאֲבוֹי, וּמִשּׁוּם דַּהֲוָה דִּילֵיהּ הוּא סָבִיל, וְאַחֲרִינֵי לָא סַבְלֵי. דְּאָמַר רַבִּי שִׁמְעוֹן, בְּשַׁעֲתָא דְּהַאי כֹּ"ה אִתְּעַר בְּדִינוֹי, לָא יַכְלִין בְּנֵי עָלְמָא לְמֵיקָם קַמֵּיהּ.

150. We have learned that when the Sfirah of Malchut was roused for the sons of David, no one was able to oppose them. THAT IS WHAT IS MEANT BY: "And I Daniel alone saw the vision," WHICH IS MALCHUT REFERRED TO BY "THE VISION," since he was from the offspring of David, as is written: "Now, among these were the children of Judah: Daniel, Hananiah..." (Daniel 1:6). THEREFORE, he saw and rejoiced in it, since it pertained to the lot and inheritance of his ancestor, DAVID. Since it was his, he was able to bear IT AND WAS NOT FEARFUL, while the others could not endure AND WERE AFRAID. EVEN IF THEY DID NOT SEE, THEY DID PERCEIVE THEIR FORTUNE, as Rabbi Shimon said: When that Coh is roused together with her Judgments, the inhabitants of the world cannot resist it.

151. וּבְשַׁעֲתָא דְּפָרְסִין כַּהֲנֵי יְדַיְיהוּ, דְּאַתְיָין מֵחֶסֶד, אִתְּעַר חֶסֶד דִּלְעֵילָּא, וְאִתְחַבַּר בְּהַאי כֹּה, וּמִתְבַּסְּמָא וּמִתְבָּרְכָא בְּאַנְפִּין נְהִירִין לִבְנֵי יִשְׂרָאֵל, וְאִתְעֲדֵי מִנְּהוֹן דִּינִין, הה"ד כֹּה תְבָרְכוּ אֶת בְּנֵי יִשְׂרָאֵל, וְלָא לִשְׁאַר עַמִּין.

151. BUT when the priests spread their hands that stem from Chesed, upper Chesed awakens and bonds with this Coh, which is appeased and blessed

with the shining faces of the children of Yisrael. The Judgments are removed from them, as is written: "In this way you shall bless the children of Yisrael" and not the rest of the nations.

152. בְּגִין כַּךְ כֹּהֵן, וְלָא אַחֲרָא. כֹּהֵן בְּגִין דְּיִתְעַר הַאי כִּתְרָא דִילֵיהּ חֶסֶ״ד, עַל יְדוֹי, דְּאִקְרֵי חָסִיד, דִּכְתִּיב לְאִישׁ חֲסִידֶךָ. וְהוּא אָתֵי מִסִּטְרָא דְּחֶסֶד. וּכְתִיב וַחֲסִידֶיךָ יְבָרְכוּכָה, אַל תִּקְרֵי יְבָרְכוּכָה, אֶלָּא יְבָרְכוּ כֹּ״ה. כֹּה תְבָרְכוּ, בְּשֵׁם הַמְּפוֹרָשׁ. כֹּה תְבָרְכוּ, בִּלְשׁוֹן הַקֹּדֶשׁ.

152. It is therefore a priest THAT GIVES THE BLESSINGS and nobody else. It is the priest in order to awaken through him his own Sfirah of Chesed, because he is called pious (Heb. *chasid*), as is written: "with your pious one" (Devarim 33:8) and he comes from the side of Chesed. It is written: "And your pious ones shall bless you (Heb. *yevarchuchah*)" (Tehilim 145:10). Do not pronounce it "shall bless you," but rather "shall bless (Heb. *yevarchu*) coh" with the ineffable Name. 'Thus (Heb. *coh*) you shall bless', in the holy tongue.

153. תָּאנָא, אָמַר ר׳ יְהוּדָה, בְּשַׁעֲתָא דְּכַהֲנָא דִלְתַתָּא קָם וּפָרִיס יְדוֹי, כָּל כִּתְרִין קַדִּישִׁין דִּלְעֵילָא מִתְעָרִין, וּמִתְתַּקְּנִין לְאִתְבָּרְכָא, וְנַהֲרִין מֵעוּמְקָא דְּבֵירָא, דְּאִתְמְשַׁךְ לְהוּ מֵהַהוּא עוּמְקָא דְּנָפַק תָּדִיר, וְלָא פָּסִיק בִּרְכָאן דְּנַבְעַן, מַבּוּעִין לְכֻלְּהוּ עָלְמִין וּמִתְבָּרְכָן וּמִתְשַׁקְיָין מִכֻּלְּהוּ.

153. We learned that Rabbi Yehuda said: When the priest below rises and spreads his hands, all the holy Sfirot above are awakening. They are getting ready to be blessed and illuminate from the depth of the well THAT IS BINAH, which flows to them from that depth that flows continuously. The blessings that flow do not cease; THEY BECOME springs to all the worlds, which are blessed and watered from them all.

154. וְתָאנָא, בְּהַהוּא זִמְנָא, לְחִישׁוּתָא וּשְׁתִיקוּתָא הֲוֵי בְּכָל עָלְמִין. לְמֶלֶךְ דְּבָעֵי לְאִזְדַּוְּוגָא בְּמַטְרוֹנִיתָא, וּבָעֵי לְמֵעַאל לָהּ בִּלְחִישׁוּ, וְכָל שַׁמָּשִׁין מִתְעָרִין בְּהַהוּא זִמְנָא וּמִתְלַחֲשִׁין, הָא מַלְכָּא אָתֵי לְאִזְדַּוְּוגָא

בְּמַטְרוֹנִיתָא. מַאן מַטְרוֹנִיתָא. דָּא כְּנֶסֶת יִשְׂרָאֵל. מַאן כ״י. כְּנֶסֶת יִשְׂרָאֵל סְתָם.

154. We also learned that during that time, WHEN THE PRIESTS RAISE THEIR HANDS, secrecy and silence prevail in all the worlds, SIMILAR to a king that wishes to mate with his queen and approaches her secretly. All his servants awaken excitedly during that time and whisper to each other: Behold the king comes to unite with the queen. Who is that queen? That is the Congregation of Yisrael. Who is the Congregation of Yisrael? It is a Congregation of Yisrael; THAT IS MALCHUT.

155. תָּאנָא אָמַר ר׳ יִצְחָק, כֹּהֵן בָּעֵי לְזַקְפָא יְמִינָא עַל שְׂמָאלָא, דִּכְתִיב וַיִּשָּׂא אַהֲרֹן אֶת יָדָיו אֶל הָעָם וַיְבָרְכֵם. יָדוֹ כְּתִיב, וְלָא יָדָיו. מִשּׁוּם דְּשִׁבְחָא דִּימִינָא עַל שְׂמָאלָא. אָמַר רַבִּי אֶלְעָזָר, רָזָא הוּא, מִשּׁוּם דִּכְתִיב וְהוּא יִמְשׁוֹל בָּךְ.

155. We learned that Rabbi Yitzchak said: The priest has to raise his right HAND over the left, as is written: "And Aaron lifted up his hands (Heb. *yadav*) toward the people, and blessed them" (Vayikra 9:22). *Yadav* is spelled without Yud, the mark of plural. That is due to the preference of the right HAND over the left. Rabbi Elazar said: That is a secret, since it is written: "And he shall rule over you" (Beresheet 3:16). THE MALE, WHICH IS RIGHT, SHALL DOMINATE OVER THE FEMALE, WHICH IS THE LEFT.

156. תָּאנָא, כֹּהֵן דְּבָעֵי לְפָרְסָא יְדוֹי, בָּעֵי דְּיִתּוֹסַף קְדוּשָׁה עַל קְדוּשָׁה דִּילֵיהּ, דְּבָעֵי לְקַדְּשָׁא יְדוֹי, עַל יְדָא דְּקַדִּישָׁא. מַאן יְדָא דְּקַדִּישָׁא. דָּא לֵיוָאָה. דְּבָעֵי כַּהֲנָא לִיטוֹל קְדוּשָׁה דְּמַיָּא מִידוֹי, דִּכְתִיב וְקִדַּשְׁתָּ אֶת הַלְוִיִּם, הָא אִינּוּן קַדִּישִׁין. וּכְתִיב בְּהוֹ בַּלְוִיִּם, וְגַם אֶת אַחֶיךָ מַטֵּה לֵוִי וְגוֹ׳. שֵׁבֶט אָבִיךָ כְּלָל. מִכָּאן, דְּכָל כֹּהֵן דְּפָרִיס יְדוֹי, בָּעֵי לְאִתְקַדְּשָׁא ע״י דְּקַדִּישָׁא, לִיתוֹסַף קְדוּשָׁה עַל קְדוּשָׁתֵיהּ. וְעַל דָּא, לָא יְטוֹל קְדוּשָׁה דְּמַיָּא, מִבַּר נָשׁ אַחֲרָא, דְּלָא הֲוֵי קַדִּישָׁא.

156. We learned that a priest who wishes to raise his palms, holiness should be added to his holiness, THAT IS, he should sanctify his hands by a holy hand. What is the holy hand? It is the Levite that the priest needs to accept holiness of water from his hands, as is written that you shall sanctify the Levites. It is written of the Levites: "And your brethren also of the tribe of Levi, THE TRIBE OF YOUR FATHER…" (Bemidbar 18:2), SO THAT THEY ARE included in the tribe of your father. From here we understand that every priest who raises his palms needs to be sanctified through one who is already sanctified, in order to add holiness upon his holiness. Therefore, he must not receive the sanctity of water from another person who is not holy.

157. וּבִצְנִיעוּתָא דְסִפְרָא תָּאנָא, לֵוִי דְּאִתְקַדָּשׁ כַּהֲנָא עַל יְדוֹי, בָּעֵי הוּא לְאִתְקַדָּשָׁא בְּקַדְמֵיתָא. וְאַמַּאי לֵוִי, וְיִתְקַדַּשׁ עַל יְדָא דְּכַהֲנָא אַחֲרָא. תָּאנָא, כַּהֲנָא אַחֲרָא לָא בָּעֵי, דְּהָא כֹהֵן דְּלָא שְׁלִים, לָא בָּעֵי הַאי כַּהֲנָא שְׁלִים, לְאִתְפְּגָם עַל יְדָא דִּפְגִימָא דְּלָא שְׁלִים. אֲבָל לֵוִי דְּאִיהוּ שְׁלִים, וְאִתְחֲזֵי לְסַלְקָא בְּדוּכְנָא, וּלְמִפְלַח מִשְׁכַּן זִמְנָא, הָא שְׁלִים הוּא, וְהָא אִקְרֵי קָדוֹשׁ, דִּכְתִיב וְקִדַּשְׁתָּ אֶת הַלְוִיִּם. א"ר תַּנְחוּם, אַף אִקְרֵי טָהוֹר, דִּכְתִיב וְטִהַרְתָּ אוֹתָם. וּבְגִין כָּךְ בָּעֵי לְאוֹסָפָא כַּהֲנָא קְדוּשָׁה עַל קְדוּשָׁתֵיה.

157. We learned in Safra Detzniuta (the hidden book) – that the Levite, through whom the priest is sanctified, must first sanctify himself. HE ASKS: Why through a Levite, instead of through another priest, AND HE REPLIES: Another priest has no such need TO SANCTIFY HIS FELLOW PRIEST, SINCE HE COULD BE an imperfect priest himself WHO IS NOT PERMITTED TO PERFORM PRIESTLY DUTIES. A perfect priest must not be flawed by a flawed priest who is imperfect. However, a Levite who is perfect, and is worthy to ascend the platform and do the duties of the Tent of Meeting, is considered perfect and is referred to as holy, as is written that you shall sanctify the Levites. Rabbi Tanchum said: He is also called pure, as is written: "And cleanse them" (Bemidbar 8:6). Therefore, a priest needs to add holiness upon his holiness BY BEING INCLUDED OF A LEVITE ALSO, SINCE THE ASPECT OF PURIFICATION APPLIES ONLY TO THE LEVITE.

158. תָּאנָא, כַּהֲנָא דְּפָרִיס יְדוֹי, בָּעֵי דְּלָא יִתְחַבְּרוּן אֶצְבְּעָן דָּא בְּדָא, בְּגִין דְּיִתְבָּרְכוּן כִּתְרִין קַדִּישִׁין, כָּל חַד וְחַד בִּלְחוֹדוֹי, כְּמָה דְאִתְחֲזֵי לֵיהּ. בְּגִין דִּשְׁמָא קַדִּישָׁא בָּעֵי לְאִתְפָּרְשָׁא בְּאַתְוָון רְשִׁימִין דְּלָא

לְאַעְרְבָא הָא בְּדָא. וּלְאִתְכַּוְּונָא בְּאִינוּן מִלִּין.

158. We learned that the priest who raises his palms needs to avoid having his fingers touching one another, so that each of the holy Sfirot shall be blessed individually, as is proper for it. The Holy Name needs to be expressed in letters inscribed so they are not mixed with each other. And he should pay attention to these matters.

159. א״ר יִצְחָק, בָּעֵי קוּדְשָׁא בְּרִיךְ הוּא דְּיִתְבָּרְכוּן עִלָּאֵי, בְּגִין דְּיִתְבָּרְכוּן תַּתָּאֵי, וְיִתְבָּרְכוּן עִלָּאֵי דְּאִינוּן קַדִּישִׁין בִּקְדוּשָׁה עִלָּאָה, עַל יְדָא דְּתַתָּאֵי, דְּאִינוּן קַדִּישִׁין בִּקְדוּשָׁה עִלָּאָה, דְּאִינוּן קַדִּישִׁין מִכָּל קַדִּישִׁין דִּלְתַתָּא, דִּכְתִיב וַחֲסִידֶיךָ יְבָרְכוּכָה.

159. Rabbi Yitzchak said: The Holy One, blessed be He, wished to have the upper grades blessed so the lower grades would be blessed, SINCE AFTER THE UPPER SFIROT ARE FILLED WITH ABUNDANCE OF BLESSINGS, THEY BLESS THE LOWER GRADES. Let the upper grades who are holy with the highest degree of holiness be blessed through the lower grades who are holy with the highest degree of holiness and are holier than any that are holy below, MEANING THE PRIESTS, as it is written: "And your pious ones shall bless you" (Tehilim 145:10).

160. א״ר יְהוּדָה, כָּל כֹּהֵן דְּלָא יָדַע רָזָא דָא, וּלְמַאן מְבָרֵךְ, וּמַאן הִיא בִּרְכְתָּא דִּמְבָרֵךְ, לָאו בִּרְכְתָּא דִּילֵיהּ בִּרְכְתָּא, וְהַיְינוּ דִּכְתִיב, כִּי שִׂפְתֵי כֹהֵן יִשְׁמְרוּ דַעַת וְתוֹרָה יְבַקְשׁוּ מִפִּיהוּ. מַאי דַעַת. דַעַת סְתָם. וְתוֹרָה יְבַקְשׁוּ מִפִּיהוּ, עִלָּאִין, יְבַקְשׁוּ מִפִּיהוּ. וּמַאי יְבַקְשׁוּ מִפִּיהוּ. תּוֹרָה. תּוֹרָה סְתָם, הֵיךְ אֲחִידָא תּוֹרָה דִּלְעֵילָא דְּאִקְרֵי תּוֹרָה סְתָם. דְּתַנְיָא, תּוֹרָה שֶׁבִּכְתָב וְתוֹרָה שבע״פ בְּאִינוּן כִּתְרִין עִלָּאִין דְּאִתְקְרוּן הָכִי. מ״ט. כִּי מַלְאַךְ יְיָ' צְבָאוֹת הוּא. וְתָנֵינָא, דְּבָעֵי כַּהֲנָא לְכַוְּונָא בְּאִינוּן מִלִּין דִּלְעֵילָא, לְיַחֲדָא שְׁמָא קַדִּישָׁא כְּמָה דְּאִצְטְרִיךְ.

160. Rabbi Yehuda said: Every priest that does not know this secret, nor to whom he gives his blessing, nor what the blessing is that he makes, his blessing is not considered a blessing. This is the meaning of: "For the priest's lips should keep knowledge, and they should seek Torah at his mouth" (Malachi 2:7). What is knowledge? It is simply Da'at (Eng. 'knowledge'), MEANING THE SFIRAH OF DA'AT THAT COMBINES CHOCHMAH AND BINAH. "And they should seek Torah at his mouth": The upper beings will seek at his mouth. What will they seek at his mouth? Torah, meaning Torah in general, WHICH IS ZEIR ANPIN THAT THEY WILL INQUIRE OF HIM TO KNOW how the Torah above is unified, which is called Torah in general, since we learned that the Written Torah and the Oral Torah are the supernal crowns that are so called, MEANING IN ZEIR ANPIN CALLED THE WRITTEN TORAH, AND IN MALCHUT CALLED THE ORAL TORAH. What is the reason THAT HE KNOWS ALL THAT? THE VERSE CONCLUDES: "For he is a messenger of Hashem Tzva'ot" (Ibid.). We have learned that the priest must meditate on these matters above to unify the Holy Name as is required.

16. "Saying to them"

A Synopsis

Rabbi Shimon says that the Hidden Book tells us that the Holy Name is both revealed and concealed. Rabbi Yehuda talks about the secret of the name of 22 letters that is referred to in the priestly benediction. Rabbi Elazar explains to Rabbi Yosi that God called Yisrael man and beast; if they are deserving they are a man in the image of the above, and if they are not deserving they are referred to as beasts, and yet they all get blessed simultaneously. No blessings are available below until they are first available above. Rabbi Aba concludes by saying that the blessings are of mercy contained within mercy, as there is no judgment in the 22 letters of the Holy Name.

161. אָמַר ר"ש, תָּאנָא בְּצִנִיעוּתָא דְּסִפְרָא, שְׁמָא קַדִּישָׁא אִתְגַּלְיָיא וְאִתְכַּסְיָיא. דְּאִתְגַּלְיָיא, כְּתִיב בְּיוֹ"ד ה"א וָא"ו ה"א. דְּאִתְכַּסְיָיא כְּתִיב בְּאַתְוָון אַחֲרָנִין, וְהַהוּא דְּאִתְכַּסְיָיא הוּא טְמִירוּ דְּכֹלָּא. א"ר יְהוּדָה, וַאֲפִילּוּ הַהוּא דְּאִתְגַּלְיָיא, אִתְכַּסְיָא בְּאַתְוָון אַחֲרָן, בְּגִין הַהוּא טְמִירָא דִּטְמִירִין בְּגוֹ.

161. Rabbi Shimon said: We learned in Safra Detzniuta (the hidden book) that the Holy Name is both revealed and concealed. The revealed one is spelled Yud-Vav-Dalet, Hei-Aleph, Vav-Aleph-Vav, Hei-Aleph. The concealed one is spelled by other letters, and that which is concealed is the most hidden. Rabbi Yehuda said: Even the one that is revealed is concealed by other letters, due to the most hidden one inside it.

162. דְּהָא הָכָא בָּעֵי כַּהֲנָא לְצָרְפָא שְׁמָא קַדִּישָׁא, וּלְמִיחַת רַחֲמֵי, דְּכֻלְּהוּ כְּלִילָן בְּדִבּוּר דכ"ב אַתְוָון כִּתְרֵי דְּרַחֲמֵי. וּבְהָנֵי אַתְוָון דְּהַאי שְׁמָא, סְתִימָאן כ"ב מְכִילָן דְּרַחֲמֵי, וי"ג דְּעַתִּיקָא סָתִים וְגָנִיז מִכֹּלָּא, וט' דְּאִתְגַּלְיָין מְזִעֵיר אַנְפִּין וּמִתְחַבְּרָן כֻּלְּהוּ בְּצֵרוּפָא דִּשְׁמָא חַד, דַּהֲוָה מְכַוֵּון כַּהֲנָא כַּד פָּרֵיס יְדוֹי בכ"ב אַתְוָון גְּלִיפָן.

162. Here the priest is required to permutate the Holy Name and bring down mercy, since everything is contained in the articulating of the 22 letters, the crowns of Mercy, THE SECRET OF THE NAME OF 22 LETTERS – *ALEPH*

NUN KUF TAV MEM... – THAT IS BROUGHT WITH THE PRIESTLY BENEDICTION. In the letters of this name are concealed the 22 attributes of Mercy, WHICH ARE the thirteen CORRECTIONS OF THE BEARD of Atika, the most concealed and hidden, and the nine CORRECTIONS OF THE BEARD that were revealed from Zeir Anpin, AS NINE AND THIRTEEN EQUAL 22. All THE 22 ATTRIBUTES OF MERCY join in one permutation of the Name, on which the priest used to meditate when he raised his hands, with 22 engraved letters – MEANING THE NAME OF 22, *ALEPH NUN KUF TAV MEM, ETC.*

163. וְתָאנָא, כַּד הֲוָה צְנִיעוּתָא בְּעָלְמָא, הֲוָה מִתְגַּלְיָיא שְׁמָא דָא לְכֹלָּא. מִדְּאַסְגֵּי חֲצִיפוּתָא בְּעָלְמָא, סָתִים בְּאַתְווֹי. דְּכַד הֲוָה מִתְגַּלְיָיא. כַּהֲנָא מְכַוֵּין, וּשְׁמָא מִתְפָּרַשׁ. בְּמַאי מְכַוֵּין. מְכַוֵּין בִּסְתִימָא דְּטָמִיר וְגָנִיז, וּמִתְגַּלְיָיא וּמִתְפָּרַשׁ. מִדְּאַסְגֵּי חֲצִיפוּתָא בְּעָלְמָא, סָתִים כֹּלָּא בְּאַתְווֹן רְשִׁימִין.

163. We learned that when modesty prevailed in the world, this name OF 22 LETTERS was revealed to all, but when impudence became more prevalent in the world, it was concealed along with its letters. During the time the name was revealed, the priest meditated and the name became explicit AND REVEALED. What was he meditating on? He was meditating on the concealed, hidden and covered, AND THE NAME would be revealed and become explicit. When impudence flourished in the world, everything was concealed in engraved letters, MEANING IN THE 22 LETTERS.

164. וְת"ח, דְּכָל הָנֵי כ"ב מְכִילָן דְּרַחֲמֵי, מֹשֶׁה אֲמָרָן בִּתְרֵי זִמְנֵי. זִמְנָא קַדְמָאָה אָמַר, י"ג מְכִילָן דְּעַתִּיקָא דְּעַתִּיקִין סְתִימָא דְּכֹלָּא, לְנַחְתָּא אִלֵּין לַאֲתָר דְּדִינָא אִשְׁתְּכַח, לְאַכְפְּיָא לְהוּ. זִמְנָא תִּנְיָינָא, אָמַר ט' מְכִילָן דְּרַחֲמֵי, דִּכְלִילָן בִּזְעֵיר אַנְפִּין, וּנְהִירִין מֵעַתִּיקָא סְתִימָאָה דְּכֹלָּא. וְכֻלְּהוּ כָּלִיל כַּהֲנָא כַּד פָּרֵיס יְדוֹי לְבָרְכָא עַמָּא, וּמִשְׁתַּכְחָן דְּמִתְבָּרְכָן כֻּלְּהוּ עָלְמִין בְּסִטְרָא דְּרַחֲמֵי, דְּאִתְמַשְּׁכָן מֵעַתִּיקָא טְמִירָא סְתִימָאָה דְּכֹלָּא. וְכָל הָנֵי כ"ב אַתְוָון, מְכִילָן סְתִימָאן.

164. Come and see that Moses twice recited all these 22 attributes of Mercy. In the first instance, he said the thirteen attributes of the most Ancient, who is the most hidden – THAT IS ARICH ANPIN – to lower them to where the Judgment was prevalent – THAT IS ZEIR ANPIN – to subdue the Judgments. THAT IS THE SECRET OF THE THIRTEEN ATTRIBUTES OF MERCY THAT HE SAID IN THE PORTION OF KI TISA: "EL, MERCIFUL AND GRACIOUS" (SHEMOT 34:6). The second time, he said the nine attributes of Mercy, which ARE INCLUDED IN ZEIR ANPIN AND are illuminating from the most concealed ancient one. THEY ARE THE ONES MENTIONED IN THE PORTION OF SHELACH "LONG-SUFFERING, AND GREAT IN LOVE..." (BEMIDBAR 14:18). The priest incorporates all of them when he raises his hands to bless the nation, so that all worlds are blessed by the side of Mercy that flows from the most hidden and concealed ancient one. All 22 letters IN THE NAME THAT COMES OUT FROM THE PRIESTLY BENEDICTION – *ALEPH NUN KUF TAV MEM, ETC.* – are hidden attributes, WHICH ARE THE 22 ATTRIBUTES OF MERCY.

165. יְבָרֶכְךָ יְיָ׳ וְיִשְׁמְרֶךָ, אִלֵּין תְּלַת קְרָאֵי, וְג׳ שְׁמָהָן דְּתְרֵיסַר אַתְוָון כְּלִילָן לְקַבְלֵיהוֹן, וּבְכֹלָּא אִתְכְּוָון כַּהֲנָא. וְכָל עִלָּאֵי וְתַתָּאֵי מִתְבַּסְּמָן בְּכ״ב אַתְוָון, דִּסְתִּימִין בְּהָנֵי ג׳ קְרָאֵי, לָקֳבֵיל כ״ב מְכִילָן דְּרַחֲמֵי דִּכְלִיל כֹּלָּא. וּבְג״כ כְּתִיב אָמוֹר, וְלָא אִמְרוּ, כְּמָה דְּאוֹקִימְנָא. אָמוֹר. דְּבָעֵי לְכַוּונָא בְּכָל הָנֵי סְתִימִין, בְּכָל הָנֵי דַרְגִּין. אָמוֹר: בְּמִלִּין סְתִימִין דִּלְעֵילָּא. אָמוֹר: חוּשְׁבַּן רמ״ח אֵבָרִין דְּבָאָדָם חָסֵר חַד. מ״ט. דְּבַחַד תַּלְיָין כֻּלְּהוּ. וְכֻלְּהוּ מִתְבָּרְכָאן בְּהַאי בִּרְכָתָא, בְּהָנֵי תְּלַת קְרָאֵי, כְּדְאַמְרָן. לָהֶם: לְאִתְכַּלְּלָא בְּהַאי בִּרְכָתָא עִלָּאִין וְתַתָּאִין.

165. IN THE THREE WORDS: "Hashem bless you, and keep you" (Bemidbar 6:24), THERE ARE FIFTEEN LETTERS because of these three verses IN THE PRIESTLY BENEDICTION and the three names. AS IN EACH VERSE, THERE IS ONE NAME OF YUD HEI VAV HEI – WHICH ARE twelve letters, SINCE IN EACH NAME ARE FOUR LETTERS AND THREE TIMES FOUR EQUAL TWELVE. WITH THE THREE VERSES, THEY EQUAL FIFTEEN, which are correspondingly comprised IN THE FIFTEEN LETTERS OF: "HASHEM BLESS YOU, AND KEEP YOU." The priest has to meditate on all those, and all the higher and lower beings are mollified with the 22 letters. THAT IS IN THE NAME OF THE 22 LETTERS that are concealed in these three verses OF

THE PRIESTLY BENEDICTION, which correspond to the all-inclusive 22 attributes of Mercy. Therefore, it is written: "saying TO THEM" in singular instead of the plural, as we have explained. "Saying" means that it is required to meditate on all these concealed secrets in all these levels; "saying" refers to the concealed matters of above and "saying" equals the number of 248 body parts in a person minus one, WHOSE SECRET WAS EXPLAINED ABOVE. What is the reason ONE IS MISSING? Because all 248 come out of the one UPPERMOST, WHICH IS ARICH ANPIN. Everything is blessed with this benediction in the three verses, as we have said. IN THE VERSE "SAYING TO THEM," "to them" is in order to include in this benediction the upper and lower beings.

166. תָּאנָא, א"ר יוֹסֵי, יוֹמָא חַד יָתִיבְנָא קַמֵּיה דר"א ב"ר שִׁמְעוֹן, שְׁאִילְנָא לֵיה, אֲמֵינָא, רַבִּי מַאי קָא חָמָא דָוִד דְּקָאֲמַר אָדָם וּבְהֵמָה תוֹשִׁיעַ יְיָ', אָדָם תִּינַח, בְּהֵמָה לָמָּה. א"ל יָאוּת שָׁאֵלְתָּ, כֹּלָּא בְּמִנְיָינָא הוּא, זָכוּ אָדָם, לֹא זָכוּ בְּהֵמָה.

166. We learned that Rabbi Yosi said: One day I sat before Rabbi Elazar the son of Rabbi Shimon. I asked him, Rabbi, why did David see fit to say: "Hashem, you preserve man and beast" (Tehilim 36:7)? Man befits nicely, but why a beast? He said to me: You asked properly. Everything is taken into account FOR PRESERVATION. If people are worthy, THEY ARE PRSEVED like humans. If they are not worthy, THEY ARE PRESERVED like beasts.

167. אֲמֵינָא, רַבִּי, רָזָא דְּמִלָּה קָא בָּעֵינָא. א"ל כֹּלָּא אִתְּמַר, ות"ח, קָרָא קוּדְשָׁא בְּרִיךְ הוּא לְיִשְׂרָאֵל אָדָם, כְּגַוְונָא דִּלְעֵילָא. וְקָרָא לְהוּ בְּהֵמָה, וְכֹלָּא בְּחַד קְרָא, דִּכְתִיב וְאַתֵּן צֹאנִי צֹאן מַרְעִיתִי וְגוֹ'. וְאַתֵּן צֹאנִי צֹאן מַרְעִיתִי, הָא בְּהֵמָה. אָדָם אַתֶּם, הָא אָדָם. וְיִשְׂרָאֵל אִקְרוּ אָדָם וּבְהֵמָה, ובג"כ אָדָם וּבְהֵמָה תּוֹשִׁיעַ יְיָ'. וְעוֹד רָזָא דְּמִלָּה, זָכוּ אָדָם כְּגַוְונָא דִּלְעֵילָא. לֹא זָכוּ, בְּהֵמָה אִקְרוּן. וְכֻלְּהוּ מִתְבָּרְכָאן בְּשַׁעֲתָא חֲדָא. אָדָם דִּלְעֵילָא. וּבְהֵמָה דִּלְתַתָּא. וכ"ש דְּכֹלָּא אִית בְּהוּ בְּיִשְׂרָאֵל, הה"ד אָדָם וּבְהֵמָה תּוֹשִׁיעַ יְיָ'.

167. I said: My teacher, I wish to know the secret of this matter. He said to me: Everything has been said, BOTH THE ESOTERIC AND THE LITERAL MEANING. Come and see: The Holy One, blessed be He, called Yisrael man, in the likeness of the higher, WHICH IS ZEIR ANPIN, and also called them beast. And it is all in one verse, as is written: "But you, my flock, the flock of my pasture, are men" (Yechezkel 34:31). "But you, my flock, the flock of my pasture": Here HE REFERS TO THEM IN THE NAME OF beast. "Are men": Here HE REFERS TO THEM AS man. For Yisrael are referred to as both man and beast. Therefore, "Hashem, you preserve man and beast." Another secret lies within the matter: if they have merit, they are a man in the image of the above. If they do not have merit, they are referred to as beasts. They are all blessed simultaneously, both man above – THE SECRET OF ZEIR ANPIN, THAT IS CALLED YUD HEI VAV HEI FULLY SPELLED WITH ALEPH'S, WHICH NUMERICALLY AMOUNTS TO "MAN" – and the beast below – THE SECRET OF MALCHUT THAT IS CALLED YUD HEI VAV HEI, FULLY SPELLED WITH HEI'S AND NUMERICALLY EQUALING TO "BEAST." There is everything among Yisrael, SINCE ALSO AMONG YISRAEL THERE ARE THE TWO LEVELS, MAN AND BEAST, MEANING THE SOULS THAT ARE DRAWN FROM ZEIR ANPIN AND THOSE SOULS THAT ARE DRAWN FROM MALCHUT. This is why it says: "Hashem, you preserve man and beast."

168. וְת"ח, לֵית בִּרְכָתָא לְתַתָּא אִשְׁתְּכַח, עַד דְּיִשְׁתְּכַח לְעֵילָא. וּמִדְּאִשְׁתְּכַח לְעֵילָא אוּף לְתַתָּא אִשְׁתְּכַח, וְכֹלָּא הָכִי תַּלְיָא לְטַב וּלְבִישׁ. לְטַב, דִּכְתִיב אֶעֱנֶה אֶת הַשָּׁמַיִם וְהֵם יַעֲנוּ אֶת הָאָרֶץ. לְבִישׁ, דִּכְתִיב יִפְקוֹד יְיָ' עַל צְבָא הַמָּרוֹם בַּמָּרוֹם וְעַל מַלְכֵי הָאֲדָמָה עַל הָאֲדָמָה.

168. Come and see that no blessing is available below until it is available above FIRST. When it is present above, it is also present down below. All this depends upon ABOVE BOTH for good and for bad. For good, as it is written: "I will answer the heavens, and they will answer the earth" (Hoshea 2:23). For bad, as it is written: "That Hashem shall punish the host of the high ones on high, and the kings of the earth upon the earth" (Yeshayah 24:21).

169. א"ר יְהוּדָה, בג"כ כְּתִיב אָמוֹר לָהֶם סְתָם, לְאִתְבָּרְכָא עֶלְאִין

וְתַתָּאִין, כֻּלְּהוּ כַּחֲדָא. דִּכְתִיב כֹּה תְּבָרֲכוּ בַּתְחִלָּה, וְאַחַר כַּךְ אֶת בְּנֵי
יִשְׂרָאֵל אָמוֹר לָהֶם סְתָם, לְאִתְבָּרְכָא כֻּלְּהוּ כַּחֲדָא, יְבָרֶכְךָ יְיָ', לְעֵילָא.
וְיִשְׁמְרֶךָ, לְתַתָּא. יָאֵר יְיָ' פָּנָיו, לְעֵילָא. וִיחֻנֶּךָ, לְתַתָּא. יִשָּׂא יְיָ' פָּנָיו,
לְעֵילָא. וְיָשֵׂם לְךָ שָׁלוֹם לְתַתָּא.

169. Rabbi Yehuda said: Therefore it is simply written: "Saying to them," unspecified, WHICH INDICATES that the higher and lower beings should be blessed all together. It is written at first: "In this way you shall bless" (Bemidbar 6:23), and thereafter "the children of Yisrael, saying to them" (Ibid.), in a general way. IT IS NOT SPECIFICALLY WRITTEN: 'SAYING TO YISRAEL', WHICH MEANS that they should be blessed together, BOTH UPPER AND LOWER GRADES. "Hashem bless you" (Ibid. 24) above, "and keep you" (Ibid.) below, "Hashem make His face shine" (Ibid. 25) above "and be gracious to you" (Ibid.) below, "Hashem lift up His countenance" (Ibid. 26) above, "and give you peace" (Ibid.) below.

170. ר' אַבָּא אָמַר, כֻּלְּהוּ כַּחֲדָא מִתְבָּרְכָאן, בְּכ"ב אַתְוָון גְּלִיפָן דִּשְׁמָא
קַדִּישָׁא דְּאִתְכְּלַל וְסָתִים הָכָא, בְּכ"ב אַתְוָון מִתְבָּרְכָאן כֻּלְּהוּ. וְאִינּוּן
רַחֲמֵי גּוֹ רַחֲמֵי, דְּלָא אִשְׁתְּכַח בְּהוּ דִּינָא. וְלָא, וְהָכְתִיב יִשָּׂא יְיָ' פָּנָיו
אֵלֶיךָ. אָמַר רִבִּי אַבָּא, יִשָּׂא: יְסַלֵּק וְיַעְבָּר בְּגִין דְּלָא יִשְׁתְּכַח דִּינָא כְּלָל.

170. Rabbi Aba said: All are blessed together with 22 engraved letters of the Holy Name that is included and concealed here, IN THE PRIESTLY BENEDICTION. IN THE NAME OF the 22 letters, everything is blessed. They are of Mercy within Mercy, as there is no Judgment in them. HE ASKS: Yet not so, for it is written: "Hashem lift up His countenance to you" AND "LIFT UP" INDICATES JUDGMENT. Rabbi Aba said: "Lift up" MEANS He shall remove and cause to pass away, so there shall be no Judgment at all.

17. When the priest raises his hands

A Synopsis
Rabbi Yosi tells us that people should not look at the hands of the priest when he raises his hands in blessing because, although they can not see the Shechinah that dwells there, they need to be in awe and so they should not be disrespectful of the Shechinah. Compassion prevails in all the worlds during the time of blessing.

171. תָּאנָא, אָמַר רְבִּי יוֹסֵי, בְּשַׁעֲתָא דְּכַהֲנָא פְּרֵיס יְדוֹי, אָסִיר לֵיהּ
לְעַמָּא לְאִסְתַּכְּלָא בֵּיהּ, מִשּׁוּם דִּשְׁכִינְתָּא שַׁרְיָא בִּידוֹי. א"ר יִצְחָק, אִי
הָכִי, כֵּיוָן דְּלָא חָמָאן מַה אִכְפַּת לְהוּ, דְּהָא כְּתִיב כִּי לֹא יִרְאַנִי הָאָדָם
וָחָי, בְּחַיֵּיהוֹן לָא חָמָאן, אֲבָל בְּמִיתַתְהוֹן חָמָאן. א"ל, מִשּׁוּם דִּשְׁמָא
קַדִּישָׁא רְמִיזָא בְּאֶצְבְּעָן דִּידוֹי, וּבָעֵי ב"נ לְדַחֲלָא, אע"ג דְּלָא חָמָאן
שְׁכִינְתָּא, לָא בָּעָאן לְאִסְתַּכְּלָא בִּידַיְיהוּ דְּכַהֲנֵי, בְּגִין דְּלָא יִשְׁתַּכְחוּן
עַמָּא חֲצִיפָאן לְגַבֵּי שְׁכִינְתָּא.

171. We learned that Rabbi Yosi said: when the priest raises his hands, the people must not look at him, since the Shechinah rests on his hands. Rabbi Yitzchak said: Even so, if they cannot see, what harm is there for them? It is because it is written: "For no man shall see me, and live" (Shemot 33:20). It is only during their lifetime that they cannot see. At their death, they do see. He told him: It is because the Holy Name is alluded to in the fingers of their hands, and a person should have awe. Although they cannot see the Shechinah, they should not look at the hands of the priests, so the people should not be impudent towards the Shechinah.

172. תָּאנָא, בְּהַהִיא שַׁעֲתָא דְּכַהֲנָא פְּרֵיס יְדוֹי, צְרִיכִין עַמָּא לְמֵיתַב
בִּדְחִילוּ, בְּאֵימָתָא, וְלִינְדַע דְּהַהִיא שַׁעֲתָא, עִידָן רְעוּתָא אִשְׁתְּכַח
בְּכֻלְּהוּ עָלְמִין, וּמִתְבָּרְכָן עִלָּאִין וְתַתָּאִין, וְלֵית דִּינָא בְּכֻלְּהוּ. וְהוּא
שַׁעֲתָא, דְּאִתְגְּלֵי סְתִימָא עַתִּיקָא דְּעַתִּיקִין בִּזְעֵיר אַנְפִּין וְאִשְׁתְּכַח
שְׁלָמָא בְּכֹלָּא.

172. We learned that when the priest raises his hands, the people must sit in awe and fear, and know that at that time a time of goodwill prevails

throughout the worlds, the upper and lower beings are blessed and there is no Judgment among them all. That is the time when the concealed most ancient among the ancient is revealed in Zeir Anpin and peace prevails in all THE WORLDS.

173(1). אָמַר רִבִּי שִׁמְעוֹן, בְּהָנֵי תְּלַת קְרָאֵי רֵישֵׁיהוֹן יוֹ"ד יוֹ"ד יוֹ"ד, יְ"בָרֶכְךָ יָ"אֵר יִ"שָּׂא. כֻּלְּהוּ לְאַחֲזָאָה מְהֵימְנוּתָא שְׁלֵימָא. וּלְאִתְבָּרְכָא מֵעַתִּיקָא מַאן דְּאִצְטְרִיךְ. יוֹ"ד יוֹ"ד יוֹ"ד, לְאִתְבָּרְכָא זְעֵיר אַנְפִּין מֵעַתִּיקָא דְכֹלָּא. ובג"כ יְבָרֶכְךָ יְיָ' לְעֵילָא, וְיִשְׁמְרֶךָ הֲוָא לְתַתָּא, וְכֵן כֻּלְּהוּ.

173a. Rabbi Shimon said: In the beginning of these three verses, THERE IS Yud, Yud, Yud, meaning the Yud of *Yevarechecha* (Eng. 'bless you'), Yud of *Ya'er* (Eng. 'shine upon') and Yud of *Yisa* (Eng. 'lift up'). They are all SPELLED WITH THIS LETTER to show the perfect Faith, so that whoever needs TO BE BLESSED will be blessed from Atik, WHICH IS THE SECRET OF YUD OF YUD HEI VAV HEI. Yud, Yud, Yud APPEAR THREE TIMES, so that Zeir Anpin shall be blessed from the most ancient AND THE THREE YUD'S CORRESPOND TO THE THREE COLUMNS, AS "BLESS YOU" IS THE RIGHT COLUMN, "SHINE UPON" IS THE LEFT COLUMN AND "LIFT UP" IS THE CENTRAL COLUMN. Therefore, "Hashem bless you" IS ABOVE FOR ZEIR ANPIN, SO IT SHOULD RECEIVE FROM ATIK, "And keep you" is below FOR YISRAEL, and so on all of them.

173(2). וְתָאנֵי תָּנָא קָמֵיה דר"ש, הַאי מַאן דְּמִצְטָעֵר בְּחֶלְמֵיה, לֵיתֵי בְּשַׁעֲתָא דְכָהֲנֵי פָּרְסֵי יְדַיְיהוּ, וְלֵימָא רבש"ע אֲנִי שֶׁלָּךְ וַחֲלוֹמוֹתַי שֶׁלָּךְ וְכוּ'. אֲמַאי. מִשּׁוּם דְּהַהִיא שַׁעֲתָא אִשְׁתְּכָחוּ רַחֲמֵי בְּעָלְמִין כֻּלְּהוּ, וּמַאן דְּיִבְעֵי צְלוֹתֵיה בְּצַעֲרֵיה, אִתְהַפָּךְ לֵיה דִּינָא לְרַחֲמֵי.

173b. The Tanna learned before Rabbi Shimon that whoever is distressed in his dream shall come when the priests spread out their hands, and say: Master of the universe, I am yours and my dreams are yours, etc. What is the reason? It is because Mercy prevails in all the worlds at that time. Whoever will put forth his prayers about his distress, Judgment will turn into Mercy for him.

18. The priestly benediction

A Synopsis
We are told about the inner significance of the spreading of the fingers of the priest during the blessing. The children of Yisrael are blessed from the Holy Name of God.

רעיא מהימנא

174. פְּקוּדָא דָא לְבָרְכָא כַּהֲנָא יַת עַמָּא בְּכָל יוֹמָא, בִּזְקִיפוּ דְאֶצְבְּעָן. וּלְבָרְכָא בִּרְכָתָא בְּכָל יוֹמָא, לְאִשְׁתַּכְּחָא בִּרְכָאן עֵילָא וְתַתָּא. דְּהָא אֶצְבְּעָאן קַיְימָן בְּרָזָא עִלָּאָה, חָמֵשׁ גּוֹ חָמֵשׁ. חָמֵשׁ דִּימִינָא, וְחָמֵשׁ דִּשְׂמָאלָא. חָמֵשׁ דִּימִינָא, אִינּוּן שְׁבָחָא יְתֵירָא עַל אִינּוּן דִּשְׂמָאלָא, בְּגִין, דְּהָא יְמִינָא אִית לֵיהּ שְׁבָחָא יְתֵירָא עַל שְׂמָאלָא. וע״ד בְּבִרְכָתָא דְּקָא בָּרִיךְ כַּהֲנָא יַת עַמָּא, אִצְטְרִיךְ לְזַקְפָא יְמִינָא עַל שְׂמָאלָא. וּלְעַיְינָא בְּעֵינָא טָבָא.

Ra'aya Meheimna (the Faithful Shepherd)

174. It is a commandment that the priest shall bless the people every day by raised fingers and make a daily benediction, so that blessings will prevail above and below, since these fingers are in the uppermost secret, five within five, five of the right and five of the left. The five of the right have more importance than those of the left, since the right is more important than the left. Therefore, during the benediction with which the priest blesses the people, he needs to raise the right hand higher than the left and observe THE BLESSINGS with a good eye.

175. וְכַד פָּרִישׁ יְדוֹי כַּהֲנָא, שְׁכִינְתָּא שַׁרְיָא עַל אִינּוּן אֶצְבְּעָן, דְּהָא קוּדְשָׁא בְּרִיךְ הוּא אִסְתְּכַם עֲמֵיהּ דְּכַהֲנָא בְּאִינּוּן בִּרְכָאן. וְיִשְׂרָאֵל מִתְבָּרְכִין מִתְּרֵין סִטְרִין מֵעֵילָּא וְתַתָּא. מֵעֵילָא, שְׁכִינְתָּא דְּשַׁרְיָא עַל אִינּוּן אֶצְבְּעָן. וְכַהֲנָא דְּקָא מְבָרֵךְ.

175. When the priest spreads his hands, the Shechinah rests on his fingers, since the Holy One, blessed be He, agrees with the priest with these

benedictions. Yisrael are blessed from both sides, from above and from below. From above, it is from the Shechinah that rests on his fingers and FROM BELOW, IT IS from the priest that blesses.

176. ת"ח, מִלִּין דְּקָא עַבְדֵי, מִתְעָרִין מִלִּין לְעֵילָא. כְּגַוְונָא דָּא בִּפְרִישׁוּ דְּאֶצְבְּעָן דְּכַהֲנָא לְתַתָּא, אִתְעָרַת שְׁכִינְתָּא לְמֵיתֵי וּלְשַׁרְיָא עֲלָן. וְכֵן כַּמָּה מִלִּין אִינּוּן בְּעָלְמָא, דְּמִתְעָרִין מִלִּין לְעֵילָא. דְּהָא בְּאִתְעָרוּתָא דִּלְתַתָּא, אִתְּעַר חֵילָא אַחֲרָא לְעֵילָא. וְהָא אוֹקִימְנָא בְּכַמָּה דּוּכְתֵּי. וְהַיְינוּ טַעֲמָא דְּלוּלָב, וְהַיְינוּ טַעֲמָא דְּשׁוֹפָר. וּכְמָה אִינּוּן בְּהַאי גַּוְונָא עֲשַׂר אֶצְבְּעָן, מִתְעָרֵי שְׁכִינְתָּא לְשַׁרְיָא עֲלַיְיהוּ. מִתְעָרֵי עֲשַׂר דַּרְגִּין אַחֲרָנִין לְעֵילָא לְאַנְהָרָא, וְכֹלָּא בְּשַׁעֲתָא חֲדָא.

176. Come and see, the things that are done BELOW awaken CORRESPONDING matters above. Similarly, with the spreading of the fingers of the priest below, the Shechinah awakens to come and rest on them. Also there are various things in the world that inspire matters above, since another power is awakened above with the awakening below. We have already explained this in several places. That is the reason of TAKING the Lulav and the reason of BLOWING the Shofar. Just as in this matter there are ten fingers, the Shechinah is inspired to rest on them and another ten levels are inspired above – WHICH ARE THE TEN SFIROT OF ZEIR ANPIN – to illuminate. And all this is simultaneous.

177. וע"ד, אָסִיר לֵיהּ לְבַר נָשׁ לְזַקְפָּא אֶצְבְּעָן בְּזִקְיפוּ לְמַגָּנָא, אֶלָּא בִּצְלוֹתָא, וּבְבִרְכָּאן, וּבִשְׁמָא דְּקוּדְשָׁא בְּרִיךְ הוּא. וְהָא אוֹקִימְנָא, דְּאִינּוּן אִתְּעֲרוּ דִּשְׁמָא קַדִּישָׁא, וְרָזָא דִּמְהֵימְנוּתָא. זְקִיפוּ דְּאֶצְבְּעָאן, מְמָנָן בְּהַהוּא זְקִיפוּ דִּלְהוֹן, עֲשָׂרָה שַׁלִּיטִין, כְּמָה דְּאוּקְמוּהָ. וְכַהֲנָא בָּעֵי לְבָרְכָא בְּעֵינָא טָבָא, בְּאִסְתַּכְּמוּתָא דִּשְׁכִינְתָּא, כְּמָה דְּאִתְּמַר.

177. Therefore, a person must not raise his fingers in vain, except during prayer and benedictions and at the name of the Holy One, blessed be He. We have already explained that RAISING THE FINGERS IS arousing the Holy Name and the secret of the Faith. The raised fingers appoint by their

uprightness ten rulers. SINCE THE FINGERS ALLUDE TO THE REVELATION OF CHOCHMAH, IT IS WRITTEN: "WISDOM STRENGTHENS THE WISE MAN MORE THAN TEN RULERS" (KOHELET 7:19). We explained this, and the priest has to give his benediction with a proper attitude, with the acknowledging of the Shechinah, as we learned.

178. בְּהַהִיא שַׁעֲתָא דְּבִרְכָתָא דָּא נָפְקָא מִפּוּמֵיה דְּכַהֲנָא, אִינוּן שִׁתִּין אַתְוָון, נָפְקִין וְטָסִין בִּרְקִיעָא, וּמְמַנָּן שִׁתִּין רַבְרְבִין, עַל כָּל אָת וְאָת. וְכֻלְּהוּ אוֹדָן עַל כָּל אָלֵין בִּרְכָאן. מַאי טַעֲמָא שִׁתִּין אַתְוָון בְּבִרְכָן אָלֵין. בְּגִין דְּיִשְׂרָאֵל שִׁתִּין רִבּוֹא אִינוּן, וְרָזָא דְּשִׁתִּין רִבּוֹא קַיְימִין בְּעָלְמָא, וְכָל חַד וְחַד אִיהוּ חַד רִבּוֹא.

178. When the benediction leaves the mouth of the priest, these sixty letters THAT OCCUR IN THE PRIEST'S BENEDICTION go out and fly in the firmament and appoint sixty ministers over each individual letter. They all acknowledge all these blessings. What is the reason that there are sixty letters in these benedictions? It is because Yisrael are six hundred thousand and they always live in the world based on the secret of six hundred thousands. Each and every one OF THE LETTERS IN THE BENEDICTIONS is a ten thousand. THEREFORE, THEY CORRESPOND TO THE SIX HUNDRED THOUSANDS OF YISRAEL.

179. שְׁמָא קַדִּישָׁא דְּנָפְקָא מֵהַאי, סַלְקָא לְעֵילָּא, עַד הַהוּא כֻּרְסַיָּיא דִּלְעֵילָּא. וְכָלָּא שְׁכִינְתָּא עִלָּאָה, וּשְׁכִינְתָּא דִּלְתַתָּא, אוֹדָן בְּכַהֲנָא בְּאִינּוּן בִּרְכָאן, וְכָל אִינּוּן שִׁתִּין מְמַנָּן. וע״ד כְּתִיב, וְשָׂמוּ אֶת שְׁמִי עַל בְּנֵי יִשְׂרָאֵל וַאֲנִי אֲבָרֲכֵם. וּכְדֵין קוּדְשָׁא בְּרִיךְ הוּא מְבָרֵךְ לוֹן לְיִשְׂרָאֵל.

179. The Holy Name that is pronounced BY THE PRIEST'S BENEDICTION rises to that throne above, WHICH IS BINAH. Then the supernal Shechinah, WHICH IS BINAH, and the lower Shechinah, WHICH IS MALCHUT, acknowledge AND AGREE with the priest on these blessings. And all these sixty ministers IN CHARGE OVER EACH AND EVERY LETTER, AS MENTIONED ABOVE, ARE BLESSED. Therefore, it is written: "And they shall put my name upon the children of Yisrael; and I will bless them" (Bemidbar 6:27). Then the Holy One, blessed be He, blesses Yisrael.

180. פְּקוּדָא בָּתַר דָּא, בִּרְכַּת כֹּהֲנִים יְבָרֶכְךָ יְיָ. יָאֵר יְיָ. יִשָּׂא יְיָ. מְקוֹרָא מִתְּלַת שְׁמָהָן אִלֵּין, יוֹ"ד הֵ"י וָא"ו הֵ"י. קְדוּשָׁה, אֶהְיֶ"ה אֶהְיֶ"ה אֶהְיֶ"ה, דִּמְקוֹרָא דִּילֵיהּ, יוֹ"ד הֵ"א וָא"ו הֵ"א. קְשׁוּרָא דְּתַרְוַיְיהוּ, יִחוּד דְּתַרְוַיְיהוּ, אֲדֹנָ"י, דְּבֵיהּ א"י, דְּרְמִיזִין אִיהֲדוֹנָה"י וּרְמִיזִין א"י רְבִיעָאָה, מִתְּרֵי שְׁמָהָן מְפָרְשָׁן, דְּרְשִׁימִין בְּהוֹן.

ע"כ רעיא מהימנא

180. The following commandment is the benediction of the priests. "Hashem bless you...Hashem make his face shine... Hashem lift up": The source of these three names is Yud-Vav-Dalet, Hei-Yud, Vav-Aleph-Vav, Hei-Yud. Sanctification is Eheyeh, Eheyeh, Eheyeh, whose source is Yud Vav-Dalet, Hei-Aleph, Vav-Aleph-Vav, Hei-Aleph. The connection of both, the uniting of both, is Adonai, which contains Aleph-Yud. A fourth Aleph-Yud is alluded to from the two names that are made explicit in them.

End of Ra'aya Meheimna (the Faithful Shepherd)

19. "And they shall put my name"

A Synopsis

Rabbi Yehuda says that any priest who the people do not love should not bless them, for he must love the people and they must love him. The rabbis talk about the evil eye and the good eye, and how important it is to bless with a good eye. Rabbi Yehuda said that God swore He would not enter into celestial Jerusalem until the children of Yisrael entered terrestrial Jerusalem during the redemption.

181. וְשָׂמוּ אֶת שְׁמִי. מַהוּ וְשָׂמוּ אֶת שְׁמִי. א״ר יְהוּדָה, יְתַקְּנוּ. כְּמָה דִּכְתִּיב וְשָׂמוּ אוֹתָם אִישׁ אִישׁ עַל עֲבוֹדָתוֹ וְאֶל מַשָּׂאוֹ. לְאַתְקְנָא בְּבִרְכָתְהוֹן כִּתְרִין דִּימִינָא לִימִינָא, וְכִתְרִין דִּשְׂמָאלָא לִשְׂמָאלָא, כִּדְקָא חֲזֵי. דְּבָעְיָא דְּלָא יִטְעוֹן בְּהוֹן, לְאַתְקְנָא כֹּלָּא, בְּגִין דְּיִתְבָּרְכוּן עִלָּאִין וְתַתָּאִין.

181. HE ASKS, What is the meaning of: "And they shall put my name" (Bemidbar 6:27)? Rabbi Yehuda said THAT THE EXPLANATION IS to establish it, as is written: "And appoint them every one to his service and to his burden" (Bemidbar 4:19), MEANING THAT THE PRIESTS should appoint with their benediction the Sfirot of the right to the right and the Sfirot of the left to the left, as is proper. They must make no mistakes in them and appoint everything so the upper and lower beings will be blessed.

182. וְאִי יַעַבְדוּן הָכִי, מַה כְּתִיב. וַאֲנִי אֲבָרֲכֵם. לְמַאן. לְאִינּוּן כַּהֲנֵי, דִּכְתִּיב וּמְבָרֲכֶיךָ בָּרוּךְ. וּכְתִיב וַאֲבָרְכָה מְבָרֲכֶיךָ. אִינּוּן מְבָרְכִין לְעַמָּא, וַאֲנָא אֲבָרֵךְ לְהוּ. וּלְפִיכָךְ כְּתִיב וְשָׂמוּ, וְלָא כְּתִיב יֹאמְרוּ, אוֹ יִזְכְּרוּ.

182. If they do it that way, it is written: "And I will bless them." Whom? MEANING those priests, as it is written: "And blessed be those that bless you" (Beresheet 27:29). It is written: "And I will bless them that bless you" (Beresheet 12:3). They bless the people and I will bless them, WHO BLESS. Therefore, it is written: "And they shall put" instead of: 'They shall say' or 'they shall remember.'

183. תָּאנָא, כָּל כֹּהֵן דְּלָא רַחֲמִין לֵיהּ עַמָּא, לָא יִפְרוֹס יְדוֹי. וְעוֹבָדָא הֲוָה בְּחַד כֹּהֵן דְּקָם וּפָרִיס יְדוֹי, וְעַד דְּלָא אַשְׁלִים, אִתְעֲבֵיד תָּלָא דְּגַרְמֵי. מ״ט. מִשּׁוּם דְּלָא בְּרִיךְ בַּחֲבִיבוּתָא. וְקָם אַחֵר וּפָרִיס יְדוֹי וּבְרִיךְ, וְאִתְתְּקַן הַהוּא יוֹמָא. כָּל כֹּהֵן דְּהוּא לָא רָחִים לְעַמָּא, אוֹ עַמָּא לָא רַחֲמִין לֵיהּ, לָא יִפְרוֹס יְדוֹי לְבָרְכָא לְעַמָּא, דִּכְתִיב טוֹב עַיִן הוּא יְבוֹרָךְ אַל תִּקְרֵי יְבוֹרָךְ, אֶלָּא יְבָרֵךְ.

183. We have learned that any priest the people do not love should not raise his palms. There was a story about a priest who did stand up and raise his palms. Before he could finish this, he was turned into a pile of bones. What is the reason? That he did not bless lovingly. Another PRIEST stood up and raised his hands and blessed and fixed that day. Any priest that does not love the people, or whom the people do not love, should not raise his hands to bless the people, since it is written: "He that has a generous eye shall be blessed" (Mishlei 22:9). Do not pronounce it "blessed," but rather 'will bless.'

184. תָּאנָא, א״ר יִצְחָק, בֹּא וּרְאֵה מַה כְּתִיב בְּהַהוּא רָשָׁע דְּבִלְעָם, בְּשַׁעֲתָא דְּאִתְּמְסַר לֵיהּ לְבָרְכָא לְיִשְׂרָאֵל, הֲוָה מַשְׁגַּח בְּעֵינָא בִּישָׁא, בְּגִין דְּלָא יִתְקַיָּים בִּרְכָתָא, וַהֲוָה תָּלֵי מִלּוֹי בְּהַהוּא עֵינָא בִּישָׁא, דִּכְתִיב נְאֻם בִּלְעָם בְּנוֹ בְעוֹר. מַאי בְּנוֹ בְעוֹר. מֵהַהוּא דַּהֲוָה סָאנֵי לְהוּ יַתִּיר מִכָּל בְּנֵי עָלְמָא. וּנְאֻם הַגֶּבֶר שְׁתֻם הָעָיִן, דְּסָתִים עֵינָא טָבָא מִנַּיְיהוּ, בְּגִין דְּלָא יִתְבָּרְכוּן, וְלָא יִתְקַיָּים בִּרְכָתָא.

184. We have learned that Rabbi Yitzchak said: Come and see what is written about that wicked Bilaam. When he gave himself to bless the children of Yisrael, he looked with the evil eye so that the blessing would not endure. And he was imbuing his sayings with that evil eye, as is written: "The speech of Bilaam the son of Beor" (Bemidbar 24:3). What is the meaning of "the son of Beor"? It means the one that hated them more than anyone else in the world, SINCE BEOR IS DERIVED FROM HATRED. "And the speech of the man whose eye is open (Heb. *stum*)" (Ibid.), MEANING that he closed (Heb. *satam*) his good eye from them, in order that they would not be blessed and the blessing would not endure.

185. א״ר יְהוּדָה, הָכִי הוּא וַדַּאי, דְּאַשְׁכְּחָן פְּקִיחָא דְּעֵינָא לְבָרְכָא, דִּכְתִיב פְּקַח עֵינֶיךָ, בְּגִין לְבָרְכָא. וּבְרִכָּתָא דְּרַב הַמְנוּנָא סָבָא, הָכִי אָמַר, קוּדְשָׁא בְּרִיךְ הוּא יִפְקַח עֵינוֹי עֲלָךְ. וּבְהַהוּא רָשָׁע כְּתִיב, שְׁתוּם הָעָיִן. בְּגִין דְּלָא יִתְבָּרְכוּן עַל יְדוֹי. וְא״ר יִצְחָק, בְּג״כ כַּהֲנָא דִּבָרִיךְ בְּעֵינָא טָבָא, בִּרְכָתֵיהּ אִתְקָיִים. וּדְלָא מְבָרֵךְ בְּעֵינָא טָבָא, כְּתִיב, אַל תִּלְחַם אֶת לֶחֶם רַע עַיִן וְאַל תִּתְאָו לְמַטְעַמוֹתָיו, כְּלוֹמַר אַל תְּבַעֵי מְנֵיהּ בִּרְכָתָא כְּלָל.

185. Rabbi Yehuda said: It is certainly so that we find the opening of the eye as a prerequisite for giving blessings, as is written: "Open your eyes" (Daniel 9:18), in order to bless. In the blessings of Rav Hamnuna Saba, that is how he used to say: The Holy One, blessed be He, shall open his eyes upon you. About that wicked one, it is written: "Whose eye is open (also: 'closed')." That was in order that they should not be blessed through him. Rabbi Yitzchak said: Therefore, the priest that blesses with a good eye, his blessing endures. Of the one that does not bless with a good eye, it is written: "Do not eat the bread of him who has an evil eye, nor desire his dainties" (Mishlei 23:6), meaning to say, do not wish to have any blessing from him at all.

186. אָמַר ר׳ יוֹסֵי, ת״ח, כְּתִיב וְלֹא אָבָה יְיָ׳ אֱלֹהֶיךָ לִשְׁמוֹעַ אֶל בִּלְעָם וְגוֹ׳. לִשְׁמוֹעַ אֶל בִּלְעָם, אֶל בָּלָק מִבָּעֵי לֵיהּ, דְּהָא עָבֵיד בָּלָק כֹּלָּא, מַהוּ אֶל בִּלְעָם. אֶלָּא מִשּׁוּם דַּהֲוָה סָתִים עֵינוֹי, בְּגִין דְּלָא יִתְבָּרְכוּן יִשְׂרָאֵל. תָּאנָא, א״ר יוֹסֵי, א״ל קוּדְשָׁא בְּרִיךְ הוּא לְבִלְעָם, רָשָׁע, אַתְּ סָתִים עֵינָךְ בְּגִין דְּלָא יִתְבָּרְכוּן בָּנַי. אֲנָא אַפְקַח עֵינַי, וְכָל מִלִּין דְּתֵימָא, אֲהַפֵּךְ לְהוּ לְבִרְכָאן. הה״ד, וַיַּהֲפֹךְ ה׳ אֱלֹהֶיךָ לְךָ אֶת הַקְּלָלָה לִבְרָכָה כִּי אֲהֵבְךָ וְגוֹ׳.

186. Rabbi Yosi said, Come and see that it is written: "But Hashem your Elohim would not hearken to Bilaam..." (Devarim 23:6). HE ASKS: "Hearken to Bilaam"? It should have said, 'to Balak,' since Balak did everything. What then is the meaning of: "to Bilaam"? HE REPLIES: It is only because he was closing his eyes in order that Yisrael should not get the blessings. We learned that Rabbi Yosi said: The Holy One, blessed be He, said to Bilaam, 'Wicked one, you closed your eyes in order that my children should not be blessed. I'll open my eyes and all the things you say, I'll convert to blessings.' This is what is meant by: "But Hashem your Elohim turned the curse into a blessing to you, because Hashem your Elohim loved you..." (Ibid.).

187. וע״ד כְּתִיב, טוֹב עַיִן הוּא יְבֹרָךְ כִּי נָתַן מִלַּחְמוֹ לַדָּל. מַהוּ מִלַּחְמוֹ. כְּמָה דְּאוֹקִימְנָא, דִּכְתִּיב לֶחֶם אֱלֹהָיו מִקָּדְשֵׁי הַקֳּדָשִׁים וְגוֹ'. מַשְׁמַע דְּקָדְשֵׁי הַקֳּדָשִׁים לֶחֶם אֱלֹהָיו נָפַק מִנֵּיהּ. ובג״כ כִּי נָתַן מִלַּחְמוֹ לַדָּל. תַּנְיָא, כַּמָּה חֲבִיבִין יִשְׂרָאֵל קַמֵּי קוּדְשָׁא בְּרִיךְ הוּא, דְּעֶלָּאֵי לָא מִתְבָּרְכֵי אֶלָּא בְּגִינֵיהוֹן דְּיִשְׂרָאֵל.

187. About this, it is written: "He that has a generous eye shall be blessed; for he gives of his bread to the poor" (Mishlei 22:9). What is the meaning of: "of his bread"? It is as we explained that is written: "The bread of his Elohim...of the most holy..." (Vayikra 21:22). It is that the bread of his Elohim emanates from the Holy of Holies "for he gives of his bread to the poor." We learned how beloved Yisrael are before the Holy One, blessed be He, that the higher beings only are blessed for the sake of Yisrael.

188. דְּתָנֵינָן, אָמַר רַבִּי יְהוּדָה, אָמַר רַבִּי חִיָּיא, אָמַר רַבִּי יוֹסֵי, נִשְׁבַּע הַקָּדוֹשׁ בָּרוּךְ הוּא, שֶׁלֹּא יִכָּנֵס בִּירוּשָׁלַם שֶׁל מַעְלָה, עַד שֶׁיִּכָּנְסוּ יִשְׂרָאֵל בִּירוּשָׁלַם שֶׁל מַטָּה, שֶׁנֶּאֱמַר בְּקִרְבְּךָ קָדוֹשׁ וְלֹא אָבֹא בְּעִיר. כְּלוֹמַר, כָּל זִמְנָא דִּשְׁכִינְתָּא הָכָא בְּגָלוּתָא, שְׁמָא דִּלְעֵילָּא לָא אִשְׁתְּלִים. וְכָל תִּקּוּנִין לָא אִתְתַּקְנוּ, כִּבְיָכוֹל אִשְׁתְּאַר שְׁמָא קַדִּישָׁא חַסְרָא.

188. We learned that, in the name of Rabbi Chiya in the name of Rabbi Yosi, Rabbi Yehuda said: The Holy One, blessed be He, swore that He would not enter into celestial Jerusalem, WHICH IS THE SECRET OF THE COMPLETE UNION OF YUD-HEI, until Yisrael entered terrestrial Jerusalem, MEANING UNTIL THE COMPLETE REDEMPTION, as it says: "The Holy One in the midst of you: and I will not come as an enemy (also: 'enter the city')" (Hoshea 11:9). As long as the Shechinah was in exile, the name above was not perfected, and it is as though the Holy Name remains wanting for the entire duration that all the corrections have not been carried out, MEANING, PRIOR TO THE END OF CORRECTION.

189. רִבִּי אַבָּא הֲוָה אָזִיל לְלוֹד, פָּגַע בֵּיהּ ר' זֵירָא בַּר רַב, אָ"ל הָא חֲמֵינָא אַפֵּי שְׁכִינְתָּא, וּמַאן דְּחָמֵי אַפֵּי שְׁכִינְתָּא, בָּעֵי לְמֵיזַל וּלְרַהֲטָא בַּתְרָאָהּ. הֲדָא הוּא דִכְתִיב, וְנֵדְעָה נִרְדְּפָה לָדַעַת אֶת ה'. וּכְתִיב וְהָלְכוּ עַמִּים רַבִּים וְאָמְרוּ לְכוּ וְנַעֲלֶה אֶל הַר יְיָ' וְגו'. כִּי מִצִּיּוֹן תֵּצֵא תוֹרָה וְגו'. וַאֲנָא בָּעֵינָא לְמֵהַךְ בַּתְרָךְ, וּלְמֵילַף מֵאִינּוּן מִלֵּי מְעַלְיָיתָא, דְּאַתּוּן טָעֲמִין כָּל יוֹמָא, מֵאִדְרָא קַדִּישָׁא.

189. Rabbi Aba was going to Lod. Rabbi Zira bar Rav met him. He said to him, Here I saw the presence of the Shechinah, and whoever sees the presence of the Shechinah needs to follow and run after Her. That is what is meant by: "Let us therefore know, let us follow on to know Hashem" (Hoshea 6:3), and: "And many people shall go and say, 'Come, and let us go up to the mountain of Hashem...for out of Zion shall go forth Torah...'" (Yeshayah 2:3). I wish to follow you and learn from the good things that you taste daily from the holy chamber OF RABBI SHIMON BAR YOCHAI.

20. "And he counted it to him for righteousness"

A Synopsis

We learn that God told Abram not to believe in the astrological signs that said he would be childless, for his name would be changed to Abraham and he would produce many offspring; Abram considered Malchut to be of mercy rather than judgment and this allowed him to have children.

190. מַאי דִּכְתִּיב, וְהֶאֱמִין בַּיְיָ' וַיַּחְשְׁבֶהָ לוֹ צְדָקָה, אִי קוּדְשָׁא בְּרִיךְ הוּא חֲשָׁבָה לְאַבְרָהָם, אוֹ אַבְרָהָם לְקוּדְשָׁא בְּרִיךְ הוּא. וַאֲנָא שְׁמַעְנָא, דְּקוּדְשָׁא בְּרִיךְ הוּא חֲשָׁבָה לְאַבְרָהָם, וְלָא אִתְיַשְּׁבָא בְּלִבָּאי. א"ל הָכִי אוֹקִימְנָא, וְלָאו הָכִי הֲוֵי. ת"ח, וַיַּחְשְׁבֶהָ, וַיַּחְשׁוֹב לוֹ לָא כְּתִיב, אֶלָּא וַיַּחְשְׁבֶהָ, אַבְרָהָם וַדַּאי חֲשָׁבָה לְקוּדְשָׁא בְּרִיךְ הוּא. דְּתַנְיָא, כְּתִיב וַיּוֹצֵא אוֹתוֹ הַחוּצָה, א"ל קוּדְשָׁא בְּרִיךְ הוּא, צֵא מֵאִצְטַגְנִינוּת שֶׁלָּךְ, לָאו הַהוּא אוֹרְחָא לְמִנְדַּע שְׁמִי, אֵת חָמֵי, וַאֲנָא חֲמֵינָא, אַבְרָם אֵינוֹ מוֹלִיד, אַבְרָהָם מוֹלִיד. מִכָּאן וּלְהָלְאָה, אִשְׁתְּדַּלוּ בְּאָרְחָא אַחֲרָא, כ"ה יִהְיֶה זַרְעֶךָ. מַאי כ"ה. הִיא כִּתְרָא עֲשִׂירָאָה קַדִּישָׁא דְּמַלְכָּא, לְמִנְדַּע שְׁמֵיהּ, וְהִיא כִּתְרָא דְּדִינִין מִתְעָרִין מִנָּהּ.

190. What is the meaning of the verse: "And he believed in Hashem; and he counted it (her) to him for righteousness" (Beresheet 15:6). Is the meaning that the Holy One, blessed be He, counted it for Abraham for righteousness? Or Abraham to the Holy One, blessed be He? My mind was not quiet about it. He told him: That is the way we explained it yet it was not so. Come and see: It says "counted her." It is not written: 'counted it,' but rather "counted her," WITH A FEMININE SUFFIX, INDICATING that definitely Abraham considered it for the Holy One, blessed be He. Since we have learned that the verse: "And he brought him outside" (Ibid.) was explained that the Holy One, blessed be He, told him, 'Leave your astrology', SINCE ABRAHAM WAS SEEING THROUGH HIS ASTROLOGICAL OBSERVATIONS THAT HE WOULD NOT BEGET A CHILD. 'That is not the way to know my name. You see and I see. Abram will not beget BUT Abraham will beget. From here on, you will make an effort in a different way TO KNOW MY NAME,' since "so (Heb. *coh*) shall your seed be" (Ibid. 5). What is Coh? That is the tenth holy

Sfirah of the King, to know his name. That is the Sfirah from which Judgments spring.

191. וְתָאנָא, כֹּה יִהְיֶה זַרְעֶךָ מַמָּשׁ. בְּהַהִיא שַׁעֲתָא חֲדֵי אַבְרָהָם, לְאִסְתַּכְּלָא וּלְמִנְדַע שְׁמֵיהּ, וּלְאִתְדַּבְּקָא בֵּיהּ, מִשׁוּם דְּאִתְבְּשַׂר בְּכֹ"ה, וְאַע"ג דְּדִינִין מִתְעָרִין מִנָּהּ, חֲשָׁבָה אַבְרָהָם לְהַהוּא כִּתְרָא, אע"ג דְּהִיא דִּינָא, כְּאִלּוּ הִיא רַחֲמֵי. הַה"ד, וַיַּחְשְׁבֶהָ. מַאי וַיַּחְשְׁבֶהָ. לְהַהוּא כִּתְרָא. צְדָקָה רַחֲמֵי. אָמַר רַבִּי יִצְחָק, כֹּ"ה כִּתְרָא עֲשִׂירָאָה הִיא, וְאִתְקְרֵי צֶדֶ"ק, וְדִינִין מִתְעָרִין מִנָּהּ, וְאַבְרָהָם אע"ג דְּיָדַע דְּדִינִין מִתְעָרִין מִנָּהּ מֵהַאי צֶדֶק. הוּא חֲשָׁבָה צְדָקָה, דְּדִינִין לָא מִתְעָרִין מִנָּהּ, בְּגִין דְּהוּא רַחֲמֵי.

191. We have learned that "so (*coh*) shall your seed be" actually, THAT HIS CHILDREN WILL BE FROM THE ACTUAL MALCHUT AND IF IT WERE NOT FOR THE SFIRAH OF MALCHUT HE WOULD NOT HAVE CHILDREN. HEREBY, MALCHUT WAS TURNED INTO MERCY FOR HIM. At that moment, Abraham was happy to observe and to know his name and adhere to him, since he learned about Coh. Although Judgments got awakened from her, Abraham considered her to be a Sfirah, as if she was of Mercy although she was of Judgment – SINCE WITHOUT HER HE WOULD HAVE HAD NO CHILDREN. This is what is meant by: "He counted her" IN FEMININE FORM. What is meant by "he counted her"? It is that Sfirah, MALCHUT, HE COUNTED AS RIGHTEOUSNESS (HEB. *TZEDAKAH*) which is Mercy, SINCE *TZEDEK* (ENG. 'RIGHTEOUSNESS', (MASC.) IS JUDGMENT AND *TZEDAKAH* IS MERCY. Rabbi Yitzchak said: Coh is the last Sfirah, MALCHUT, and is called Tzedek – righteousness – and judgments flow out from her. Though Abraham knew that Judgments are inspired from her, from this Tzedek, he considered her as Tzedakah, from which no Judgments emanate, because she was of Mercy.

21. "And Hashem had blessed Abraham in all things"

A Synopsis

Rabbi Aba explains the deep meaning of God's blessing of Abraham in all things, blessing him with Yesod. In the future the blessing on earth will prevail at all times because the blessing is first established above.

192. תּוּ אָמַר ר' אַבָּא, מַאי דִּכְתִּיב וַיְיָ' בֵּרַךְ אֶת אַבְרָהָם בַּכֹּל, כד"א כִּי כָל בַּשָּׁמַיִם וּבָאָרֶץ. וּכְתִיב כֹּה תְבָרְכוּ, דִּבְגִינַיְיהוּ דְיִשְׂרָאֵל מִתְבָּרֵךְ הַאי כֹּ"ה עַל יְדָא דְּכַהֲנָא, בְּגִין דְּיִתְבָּרְכוּן יִשְׂרָאֵל לְתַתָּא, וְיִשְׁתְּכַּח בִּרְכָתָא בְּכֹלָּא וּלְזִמְנָא דְּאָתֵי כְּתִיב יְבָרֶכְךָ יְיָ' מִצִּיּוֹן וְגוֹ'. בָּרוּךְ יְיָ' מִצִּיּוֹן שׁוֹכֵן יְרוּשָׁלִַם.

192. In addition, Rabbi Aba said that it is written: "And Hashem had blessed Abraham in all things (Heb. *bakol*)" (Beresheet 24:1). It is written: "For all (Heb. *kol*) that is in heaven and on earth" (I Divrei Hayamim 29:11), MEANING THAT HE BLESSED ABRAHAM WITH THE SFIRAH OF YESOD CALLED KOL, WHICH GIVES TO AND BLESSES THE SFIRAH OF MALCHUT. IT IS WRITTEN: "FOR ALL (HEB. *KOL*) THAT IS IN HEAVEN AND ON EARTH." THAT KOL THAT IS YESOD RECEIVES FROM HEAVEN, WHICH IS ZEIR ANPIN, AND SUPPLIES EARTH, WHICH IS MALCHUT. It is also written: "In this way (Heb. *coh*) you shall bless" (Bemidbar 6:23), OF WHICH THE EXPLANATION IS THAT THE PRIESTS SHALL BLESS MALCHUT THAT IS CALLED COH. The reason is that for the sake of Yisrael, this Coh is blessed through the priest, in order that Yisrael below shall get blessed and the blessing shall be prevalent in everything. Of the future to come, it is written: "May Hashem bless you out of Zion..." (Tehilim 134:3) and "blessed be Hashem out of Zion, he who dwells in Jerusalem" (Tehilim 135:21), MEANING THAT MALCHUT WILL HAVE NO NEED TO BE BLESSED FIRST. RATHER, THE BLESSING WILL ALWAYS BE PRESENT IN HER. ZION IS THE INNER PART AND JERUSALEM IS THE SECRET OF THE OUTER PART OF MALCHUT.

22. "Moses had finished"

A Synopsis

Rabbi Yitzchak reminds us that the time sequence is not always preserved in the Torah and that interpretations must be made with this in mind. He talks about Moses entering the tabernacle and about Moses going up on the mountain and separating from his wife, since he had already had his children and it was now time to marry the Shechinah.

193. וַיְהִי בְּיוֹם כַּלּוֹת מֹשֶׁה וְגוֹ'. תָּנָא רַבִּי יוֹסֵי, בְּיוֹם שֶׁנִּכְנְסָה כַּלָּה לַחוּפָּה. בְּמַאי אוֹקִימְנָא בְּיוֹם כַּלּוֹת מֹשֶׁה. אֶלָּא מְלַמֵּד, דְּעַל יְדוֹי דְמֹשֶׁה נִכְנְסָה. אָמַר רַבִּי יְהוּדָה, וְכִי עַד הַשְׁתָּא אִתְעַכְּבַת דְּלָא עַיְילַת לְדוּכְתָּהּ, וְהָכְתִיב וְלָא יָכוֹל מֹשֶׁה לָבֹא אֶל אֹהֶל מוֹעֵד וְגוֹ'. א"ר יִצְחָק אֵין מוּקְדָּם וּמְאוּחָר בַּתּוֹרָה.

193. "And it came to pass on the day that Moses had finished (Heb. kalot)..." (Bemidbar 7:1). Rabbi Yosi learned THAT IT MEANS the day that the bride (Heb. kalah) entered under the bridal canopy, WHO IS THE SHECHINAH. HE ASKS: IF SO, how will we explain "the day that Moses had finished"? IT WOULD HAVE BEEN SUFFICIENT TO SAY, 'THE DAY (HE) FINISHED.' HE REPLIES: It is only to teach us that she entered through Moses. Rabbi Yehuda said: Is it that until now THE SHECHINAH was detained and did not take her place? Why is it written: "And Moses was not able to enter the Tent of Meeting..." (Shemot 40:35)? IT INDICATES THAT THE SHECHINAH WAS ALREADY IN THE TENT OF MEETING PRIOR TO THAT DAY. Rabbi Yitzchak said: Time sequence is not always kept in the Torah, SINCE THE VERSE OF: "AND MOSES WAS NOT ABLE..." WAS ACTUALLY LATER THAN THIS PRESENT VERSE.

194. וַיְהִי בְּיוֹם כַּלּוֹת מֹשֶׁה, כַּלַּת שֶׁל מֹשֶׁה וַדַּאי. דְּתָנֵינָן אָמַר ר"ש, מַאי דִּכְתִיב עָלִיתָ לַמָּרוֹם שָׁבִיתָ שֶּׁבִי וְגוֹ'. אֶלָּא בְּשָׁעָה שֶׁאָמַר לוֹ קוּדְשָׁא בְּרִיךְ הוּא, שַׁל נְעָלֶיךָ מֵעַל רַגְלֶיךָ, אִזְדַּעְזַע הַהָר, אָמַר מִיכָאֵל קַמֵּי קוּדְשָׁא בְּרִיךְ הוּא, רבש"ע תִּבְעֵי לִסְתּוֹר אָדָם. וְהָא כְּתִיב זָכָר וּנְקֵבָה בְּרָאָם וַיְבָרֶךְ אוֹתָם, וְלֵית בִּרְכָתָא אִשְׁתְּכַח, אֶלָּא בְּמַאן דְּאִיהוּ דְּכַר וְנוּקְבָא, וְאַתְּ אָמַרְתְּ לְאִתְפַּרְשָׁא מֵאִתְּתֵיהּ.

-365-

194. "And it came to pass on the day that Moses had finished (Heb. *kalot*)...," MEANING THE SHECHINAH REFERRED TO AS THE BRIDE (HEB. *KALAH*) OF MOSES, who is definitely the bride of Moses. We have learned that Rabbi Shimon said it is written: "You have ascended on high, you have led captivity captive..." (Tehilim 68:19). When the Holy One, blessed be He, told him, "Remove your shoes from your feet" (Shemot 3:5), the mountain was shaken. Michael, THE ANGEL, said before the Holy One, blessed be He: Master of the universe, do you wish to dismantle THE MAKE OF man? Behold, it says: "Male and female he created them; and blessed them" (Beresheet 5:2). A blessing only applies to whoever is of male and female yet you have instructed MOSES to separate from his wife SINCE "REMOVE YOUR SHOES FROM OFF YOUR FEET" MEANS THAT HE SHOULD SEPARATE FROM HIS WIFE, AS THE SCRIPTURE USES A SUBTLE LANGUAGE.

195. אָ"ל הָא קַיֵּים מֹשֶׁה פְּרִיָה וּרְבִיָה, הַשְׁתָּא אֲנָא בָּעֵינָא דְּיִתְנְסַב בִּשְׁכִינְתָּא, וּבְגִינֵיהּ יֵחוּת שְׁכִינְתָּא לְדַיְּירָא עִמֵּיהּ, הה"ד עָלִיתָ לַמָּרוֹם שָׁבִיתָ שֶׁבִי. וּמַאי שֶׁבִי. שְׁכִינְתָּא דְּאִתְנְסִיבַת עִמָּךְ. לָקַחְתָּ מַתָּנוֹת בָּאָדָם. בָּאָדָם לָא כְּתִיב אֶלָּא בָּאָדָם הַיָּדוּעַ לְמַעְלָה. וּבְיוֹמָא דְּנַחְתַּת שְׁכִינְתָּא, הַהוּא יוֹמָא דְּאִתְנַסַּבָא בְּמֹשֶׁה נַחְתָּא, הה"ד כַּלֹּת מֹשֶׁה, כַּלַּת מֹשֶׁה מַמָּשׁ.

195. THE HOLY ONE, BLESSED BE HE, told him, 'Moses has already met his requirement of being fruitful and multiplying. Now I wish that he should marry the Shechinah, and the Shechinah will descend to reside with him.' This is what is meant by: "You have ascended on high, you have led (into) captivity captive." What is captive? It means the Shechinah that was married to you. "You have received gifts from men (lit. 'the man')" (Tehilim 69:19). It is not written here: 'from man', but rather "the man," WHICH INDICATES that particular man above, WHICH IS ZEIR ANPIN, AND THE GIFT IS THE SHECHINAH THAT ZEIR ANPIN GAVE HIM. The day that the Shechinah came down is the day that She was married to Moses. This is what is meant by: "Moses had finished," speaking about the very bride of Moses.

196. וּבִיהוֹשֻׁעַ דְּאַנְפּוֹי כְּאַנְפֵּי סִיהֲרָא כְּתִיב, שַׁל נַעֲלֶךָ, דְּלָא אִתְפְּרַשׁ

אֶלָּא בְּזִמְנִין יְדִיעָן, דְּהָא לָא אִתְנְסִיבַת עִמֵּיהּ שְׁכִינְתָּא כָּל כַּךְ, וְלָא
אִתְחֲזֵי לֵיהּ, דִּכְתִּיב וַיִּפֹּל יְהוֹשֻׁעַ עַל פָּנָיו אַרְצָה. אֲבָל הָכָא כַּלַּת מֹשֶׁה
וַדַּאי. מַתָּנוֹת בָּאָדָם, מַתְּנַת כְּתִיב, זַכָּאָה חוּלָקֵיהּ דְּמֹשֶׁה, דְּמָארֵיהּ
בָּעֵי בִּיקָרֵיהּ, עַל כָּל שְׁאָר בְּנֵי עָלְמָא.

196. About Joshua, whose face was like the face of the moon, it is written: "Put off your shoes" (Yehoshua 5:15), since he did not separate FROM HIS WIFE except for certain times, FOR THE PURPOSE OF PROPHECY. The Shechinah was not married to him too much and he was not worthy of Her, as is written: "And Joshua fell on his face to the earth" (Ibid. 14). But here, She was certainly the bride of Moses. In "Gifts (Heb. *matanot*) from men," Matanot IS SPELLED WITHOUT THE VAV OF THE PLURAL FORM, SINCE IT IS REFERRING TO THE SHECHINAH WHICH IS SINGULAR. Praised is the lot of Moses, whose Master wished his glory other people.

23. "Each prince on his day"

23. "Each prince on his day"

A Synopsis
Rabbi Yehuda tells us of the offerings of the twelve princes, each on his day, and how this upheld the world. Everything was blessed above and below.

197. וַיֹּאמֶר יְיָ' אֶל מֹשֶׁה נָשִׂיא אֶחָד לַיּוֹם נָשִׂיא אֶחָד לַיּוֹם. מַהוּ לַיּוֹם. א"ר יְהוּדָה, יוֹמִין דִּלְעֵילָא, דְּאִתְחַנְּכוּ לְאִתְבָּרְכָא, בְּאִינּוּן תְּרֵיסָר תְּחוּמִין, דְּמִתְפָּרְשָׁא, וְכָל חַד אִתְתַּקָּן וְאִתְחַנַּךְ בְּבִרְכְתָא עַל יְדוֹי דְּאִלֵּין דִּלְתַתָּא. תָּאנָא, כֻּלְּהוּ מִתְבָּרְכָן בְּגִין מַדְבְּחָא דִּלְעֵילָא, וַאֲפִילוּ תַּתָּאָה וַאֲפִילוּ עכו"ם מִתְבָּרְכָן.

197. "And Hashem said to Moses... 'each prince on his day'" (Bemidbar 7:11). HE ASKS: What is the meaning of "on his day"? Rabbi Yehuda said: These are the days above that were prepared to be blessed, which are the twelve boundaries, MEANING CHESED, GVURAH, TIFERET AND MALCHUT, EACH ONE CONTAINING THREE COLUMNS, WHICH IS THE SECRET OF THE TWELVE BOUNDARIES that are divided. Each one is constructed and inaugurated with blessing through these PRINCES below, SINCE EACH PRINCE ESTABLISHED ONE DAY. We have learned that all are blessed for the altar above, WHICH IS BINAH, and even the lower WORLD and even the nations of the world are blessed.

198. דְּתַנְיָא, אָמַר ר' שִׁמְעוֹן, אִלְמָלֵא לָא אַקְרִיבוּ אִלֵּין תְּרֵיסָר נְשִׂיאִין, לָא יָכִיל עָלְמָא לְמֵיקַם קַמֵּי תְּרֵיסָר נְשִׂיאֵי יִשְׁמָעֵאל, דִּכְתִּיב שְׁנֵים עָשָׂר נְשִׂיאִים לְאֻמּוֹתָם. מִדְּאַקְרִיבוּ אִלֵּין דְּיִשְׂרָאֵל, נָסִיבוּ שׁוּלְטָנוּתָא דְּכֻלְּהוּ, בג"כ נָשִׂיא אֶחָד לַיּוֹם.

198. We have learned that Rabbi Shimon said: If these twelve princes would not have brought their offerings, the world could not have prevailed before the twelve princes of Ishmael, as is written: "Twelve princes according to their nations" (Beresheet 25:16). When those TWELVE PRINCES of Yisrael had brought their offerings, the dominion was taken away from all of them. Therefore, it is written: "Each prince on his day."

199. וְכָל מַה דְּאַקְרִיבוּ, כְּגַוְונָא דִּלְעֵילָא אַקְרִיבוּ, בְּגִין דְּיִתְבָּרְכוּן כֻּלְּהוֹן. אֵילָם שִׁשִּׁים, עַתּוּדִים שִׁשִּׁים, כְּמָה דִּכְתִיב שִׁשִּׁים גִּבּוֹרִים סָבִיב לָהּ, דְּבִסְטַר גְּבוּרָה. כַּף אַחַת עֲשָׂרָה זָהָב וְגו', וְהָא אִתְּמַר, זַכָּאָה חוּלָקֵיהוֹן דְּצַדִּיקַיָּיא, דְּקוּדְשָׁא בְּרִיךְ הוּא מֵרִיק עֲלַיְיהוּ בִּרְכָאן, וְצַיָּית צְלוֹתְהוֹן, וַעֲלַיְיהוּ כְּתִיב, פָּנָה אֶל תְּפִלַּת הָעַרְעָר וְלֹא בָזָה אֶת תְּפִלָּתָם וְגו'.

199. Everything that was brought as an offering was offered similar to the above, in order that everything would be blessed. "The rams sixty, the he-goats sixty" (Bemidbar 7:88) resembles the verse: "Sixty valiant men are round about it" (Shir Hashirim 3:7). THAT IS THE SECRET OF CHESED, GVURAH, TIFERET, NETZACH, HOD AND YESOD OF ZEIR ANPIN from the side of Gvurah. EACH ONE COMPRISES TEN, SO THEY ARE SIXTY. "One spoon of ten shekels of gold..." (Bemidbar 7:14) CORRESPONDS TO MALCHUT, as we have already learned. Blessed is the lot of the righteous that the Holy One, blessed be He, pours blessings upon them and listens to their prayers. About them, it is written: "He heeds the prayer of the destitute, and does not despise their prayer..." (Tehilim 102:18).

ברוך יי' לעולם אמן ואמן. ימלוך ה' לעולם אמן ואמן.

Blessed be Hashem forever. Amen and Amen. May Hashem reign forever. Amen and Amen.

BEHA'ALOT'CHA

‰

Names of the articles

1. "Which is like a bridegroom coming out of his chamber"

A Synopsis

Rabbi Yehuda begins by saying that the children of Yisrael are blessed because God granted them the Torah of Truth, a Tree of Life, for all her words are life. He describes how the light of the sun, Zeir Anpin, illuminates and spreads from the top through the trunk, strengthening the right and then the left.

א. וַיְדַבֵּר יְיָ' אֶל מֹשֶׁה לֵּאמֹר. דַּבֵּר אֶל אַהֲרֹן וְאָמַרְתָּ אֵלָיו בְּהַעֲלוֹתְךָ אֶת הַנֵּרוֹת וְגוֹ', רְבִּי יְהוּדָה פָּתַח, וְהוּא כְּחָתָן יוֹצֵא מֵחוּפָּתוֹ וְגוֹ'. זַכָּאָה חוּלָקֵיהוֹן דְּיִשְׂרָאֵל, דְּקוּדְשָׁא בְּרִיךְ הוּא אִתְרְעֵי בְּהוֹן, וְיָהַב לְהוֹן אוֹרַיְיתָא דִּקְשׁוֹט, אִילָנָא דְחַיֵּי, דְּבֵיהּ בַּר נָשׁ יָרִית חַיִּין לְהַאי עָלְמָא, וְחַיִּין לְעָלְמָא דְּאָתֵי. דְּכָל מַאן דְּאִשְׁתְּדַל בְּאוֹרַיְיתָא וְאָחִיד בָּהּ, אִית לֵיהּ חַיִּין. וְכָל מַאן דְּשָׁבִיק מִלֵּי דְאוֹרַיְיתָא, וְאִתְפְּרַשׁ מֵאוֹרַיְיתָא, כְּאִלּוּ מִתְפְּרַשׁ מֵחַיִּין, בְּגִין דְּהִיא חַיִּין, וְכָל מִלּוֹי חַיִּין, הה"ד כִּי חַיִּים הֵם וְגוֹ'. וּכְתִיב רִפְאוּת תְּהִי לְשָׁרֶּךָ וְגוֹ'.

1. "And Hashem spoke to Moses, saying, 'Speak to Aaron, and say to him: When you kindle the lamps...'" (Bemidbar 8:1-2). Rabbi Yehuda opened the discussion saying, "which is like a bridegroom coming out of his chamber..." (Tehilim 19:6). Praised is the lot of Yisrael that the Holy One, blessed be He, favored them and granted them the Torah of Truth, a Tree of Life by which a person inherits life for this world and life for the World to Come. Whoever tries to learn Torah and holds to her has life. Whoever leaves the words of the Torah and separates from the Torah is as if he took leave of life, since she is life and all her words are life, as it is written: "for they are life..." (Mishlei 4:22), and: "I shall be health to your navel..." (Ibid. 3:8).

ב. ת"ח, אִילָנָא דְחַיֵּי, אָחִיד מֵעֵילָּא לְתַתָּא. וְהַאי שִׁמְשָׁא דְּנָהִיר לְכֹלָּא, נְהוֹרָא דִּילֵיהּ שָׁארֵי מֵרֵישָׁא, וְאִתְפָּשַׁט בְּגוּפָא דְּאִילָנָא בְּאֹרַח מֵישָׁר, בּ' סִטְרִין אֲחִידָן בֵּיהּ, חַד לְצָפוֹן, וְחַד לְדָרוֹם. חַד יְמִינָא, וְחַד שְׂמָאלָא. בְּשַׁעֲתָא דְּשִׁמְשָׁא נָהִיר כְּמָה דְּאִתְּמַר, מֵהַהוּא גּוּפָא דְּאִילָנָא, אַתְקִיף לִדְרוֹעָא דִּימִינָא, וְאַנְהִיר בְּתוּקְפֵּיהּ. וּמִתּוּקְפֵּיהּ נָהִיר

שְׂמָאלָא, וְאִתְכְּלִיל בִּנְהוֹרֵיה.

2. Come and behold: the Tree of Life, WHICH IS ZEIR ANPIN, is attached from above downwards. The light of this sun, WHICH IS ZEIR ANPIN, that shines upon all, begins from the top, THAT IS, CHOCHMAH, BINAH AND DA'AT, and spreads to the trunk of the tree, WHICH IS TIFERET, in a straight path. Two sides are attached to it, one to the north and one to the south, one right, WHICH IS CHESED, and one left, WHICH IS GVURAH. When the sun illuminates from the trunk of the tree, as we have learned, it FIRST strengthens the right arm, WHICH IS CHESED, and shines with force. From that force OF THE RIGHT, the left illuminates, WHICH IS GVURAH, and is included in its light.

3. וְהוּא כְּחָתָן יוֹצֵא מֵחֻפָּתוֹ, מַאן אִיהוּ חֻפָּתוֹ. דָּא אִיהוּ עֲטָרָה שֶׁעִטְּרָה לוֹ אִמּוֹ בְּיוֹם חֲתֻנָּתוֹ. יוֹצֵא מֵחֻפָּתוֹ, דָּא אִיהוּ רֵישָׁא דְּכָל נְהוֹרָא כד"א בִּקְרָא דַּאֲבַתְרֵיה, מִקְצֵה הַשָּׁמַיִם מוֹצָאוֹ, דָּא שֵׁירוּתָא דְּכֹלָּא, דְּאִקְרֵי מִקְצֵה הַשָּׁמַיִם. וּכְדֵין, נָפִיק כְּחָתָן מַמָּשׁ, כַּד נָפִיק לְאַרְעָא לְכַלָּתֵיה, רְחִימָתָא דְּנַפְשׁוֹי, וּפָרִישׁ דְּרוֹעוֹי, וּמְקַבֵּל לָה.

3. "which is like a bridegroom coming out of his chamber." HE ASKS: What is his chamber? HE RESPONDS: That is "the crown with which his mother crowned him on the day of his wedding" (Shir Hashirim 3:11). THESE ARE THE MOCHIN – CHOCHMAH, BINAH AND DA'AT – THAT HE RECEIVED FROM HIS MOTHER, WHO IS BINAH. "...coming out of his chamber..." that is the top of all the light, MEANING CHOCHMAH, BINAH AND DA'AT, as you say in the following scripture: "His going forth is from the end of the heaven" (Tehilim 19:7). This is the beginning of everything that is referred to as 'the end of the heaven', MEANING BINAH, FROM WHICH EMERGES AND BEGINS ZEIR ANPIN, REFERRED TO AS 'HEAVENS'. Then he emerges. Like a real bridegroom when he goes out to meet his soul beloved bride, he stretches out his arms, WHICH ARE CHESED AND GVURAH, and receives her.

4. כְּהַאי גַּוְונָא וְהוּא כְּחָתָן יוֹצֵא מֵחֻפָּתוֹ, אַזְלָא שִׁמְשָׁא וְאִתְפָּשַׁט לְגַבֵּי מַעֲרַב, כֵּיוָן דְּמַעֲרַב אִתְקְרִיב, סְטָר צָפוֹן אִתְעַר לְקַבְּלֵיה בְּקַדְמֵיתָא,

וְקָרִיב לְמַעֲרָב, וְזָוֵיג לֵיהּ בְּאַתְרֵיהּ, כְּמָה דְּאִתְּמַר דִּכְתִיב, שְׂמֹאלוֹ תַּחַת לְרֹאשִׁי. וּלְבָתַר סְטַר דָּרוֹם דְּאִיהוּ יְמִינָא, דִּכְתִיב וִימִינוֹ תְּחַבְּקֵנִי. כְּדֵין יָשִׂישׂ כְּגִבּוֹר לָרוּץ אֹרַח, לְאַנְהָרָא סִיהֲרָא וְאוֹקְמוּהָ. ת"ח, בְּהַעֲלוֹתְךָ אֶת הַנֵּרוֹת, אִלֵּין בּוֹצִינִין עִלָּאִין, דְּכֻלְּהוּ נְהִירִין כַּחֲדָא מִן שִׁמְשָׁא.

4. Similar is the verse, "which is like a bridegroom coming out of his chamber." The sun, ZEIR ANPIN, continues to spread to the west, WHICH IS MALCHUT. As soon as the west gets nearer, the north side is the first to be aroused toward it, THAT IS GVURAH, and approaches to the west. It joins it at that place. As we have learned, THE BEGINNING OF ZEIR ANPIN COUPLING IS ON THE LEFT, WHICH IS GVURAH. THAT IS THE SECRET OF RECONCILIATION AND GETTING PERMISSION, as is written: "His left hand is under my head" (Shir Hashirim 2:6). Following that is the south side, which is right, MEANING CHESED, as is written: "And His right hand embraces me" (Ibid.). Then it "rejoices like a strong man to run a race" (Tehilim 19:6), to illuminate the moon FROM THE CENTRAL COLUMN, THAT IS YESOD. And this has been explained. Come and behold: "when you kindle the lamps"; these are the loftiest candles, WHICH ARE THE SFIROT OF MALCHUT, which all shine brightly in unison from the sun, WHICH IS ZEIR ANPIN.

2. "Happy is the people that know the joyful note"

A Synopsis

Rabbi Aba tells how God drew the children of Yisrael near to Him when they left Egypt and how He raised them to unite through His name; only then were they called 'free men'. He killed all the firstborn of those who kept Yisrael in chains, and thus freed them completely, not through an intermediary, but directly. Rabbi Aba gives the reason for marking the blood over the lintel and on both side posts during the killing of the firstborn. He says that on certain occasions offerings are not sufficient; prayers and petitions are also required, and it is necessary to demonstrate deeds with the Shofar as the blowing of the Shofar arouses mercy.

5. ר' אַבָּא פָּתַח, אַשְׁרֵי הָעָם יוֹדְעֵי תְרוּעָה יְיָ' בְּאוֹר פָּנֶיךָ יְהַלֵּכוּן. הַאי קְרָא אוּקְמוּהָ, אֲבָל ת"ח, זַכָּאִין אִינוּן יִשְׂרָאֵל, דְּקוּדְשָׁא בְּרִיךְ הוּא יָהַב לוֹן אוֹרַיְיתָא קַדִּישָׁא, וְאוֹלִיף לוֹן אָרְחוֹי, לְאִתְדַּבְּקָא בֵּיה, וּלְמֶיטַר פְּקוּדֵי דְּאוֹרַיְיתָא, לְמִזְכֵּי בְּהוּ לְעָלְמָא דְּאָתֵי. וְקָרִיב לְהוּ בְּשַׁעֲתָא דְּנָפְקוּ מִמִּצְרַיִם, דְּהָא כְּדֵין אַפִּיק לוֹן מֵרְשׁוּתָא אַחֲרָא, וְסָלִיק לוֹן לְאִתְאַחֲדָא בִּשְׁמֵיה, וּכְדֵין אִקְרוּן בְּנֵי יִשְׂרָאֵל, בְּנֵי חוֹרִין מַמָּשׁ. דְּלָא יָתְבוּ תְּחוֹת רְשׁוּתָא אַחֲרָא, וְסָלִיק לוֹן לְאַחֲדָא בִּשְׁמֵיה, דְּסָלִיק עַל כֹּלָּא, דְּשַׁלִּיט עַל עִלָּאִין וְתַתָּאִין.

5. Rabbi Aba opened the discussion saying, "happy is the people that know the joyful note: they shall walk, O Hashem, in the light of Your countenance" (Tehilim 89:16). This verse has been explained. However, come and behold: praised are Yisrael, to whom the Holy One, blessed be He, gave the holy Torah and taught His ways, to adhere to Him and keep the commandments of the Torah in order to achieve merit through them in the World to Come. And He drew them near when they came out from Egypt, since He withdrew them from another dominion and raised them to unite with His name. Only then Yisrael were called 'free men' in every respect, in that they no longer sojourned under someone else's authority. He raised them to unite with His Name, which is loftier above all and has dominion over the highest and the lowest.

6. וּמִגּוֹ רְחִימוּתָא דִּלְהוֹן, קָרָא לוֹן בְּנִי בְּכוֹרִי יִשְׂרָאֵל, כְּגַוְונָא עִלָּאָה.

וְקָטַל כָּל בְּכוֹר דִּלְעֵילָא וְתַתָּא, וְשָׁרָא קְטִירִין וְאַסִּירִין דְּעֶלָּאִין וְתַתָּאִין, בְּגִין לְאַפָּקָא לוֹן, וְעָבֵד לוֹן בְּנֵי חוֹרִין מִכֹּלָּא. וע"ד לָא בָּעָא קוּדְשָׁא בְּרִיךְ הוּא, לָא מַלְאָךְ, וְלָא שָׂרָף, אֶלָּא אִיהוּ. וְעוֹד, דְּהָא אִיהוּ יָדַע לְאַבְחָנָא וּלְמִנְדַּע כֹּלָּא, וּלְמִשְׁרֵי אֲסִירִין, וְלָאו אִינּוּן בִּרְשׁוּתָא דִּשְׁלִיחָא אַחֲרָא אֶלָּא בִּידֵיהּ.

6. In His love for them, He called them: "Yisrael is My son, My firstborn" (Shemot 4:22), similar to the above, LIKE ZEIR ANPIN THAT IS CALLED 'FIRSTBORN'. He killed all the firstborn above and below, FROM THE OTHER SIDE, and He loosened and untied the knots and shackles, WHICH THE EGYPTIANS TIED SO THAT YISRAEL WOULD NOT BE ABLE TO LEAVE EGYPT, in order to take them out. He made them free of everything. Thus, the Holy One, blessed be He, did not wish TO TAKE THEM OUT THROUGH an angel through a seraph, but only through He Himself. Moreover, only He could distinguish BETWEEN A FIRSTBORN AND A NON-FIRSTBORN, and know everything and release the bond. It is not within the authority of any other emissary, but rather in His hand.

7. תָּא חֲזֵי, בְּהַהוּא לֵילְיָא דְּבָעָא קוּדְשָׁא בְּרִיךְ הוּא לְקַטְלָא כָּל אִינּוּן בְּכוֹרֵי כְּמָה דְּאִתְּמַר, בְּשַׁעֲתָא דְּרָמַשׁ לֵילְיָא, אָתוּ מְזַמְּרִין לְזַמְּרָא קַמֵּיהּ, אָמַר לוֹן, לָאו עִידָן הוּא דְּהָא שִׁירָתָא אַחֲרָא, מְזַמְּרִין בְּנֵי בְּאַרְעָא. בְּשַׁעֲתָא דְּאִתְפְּלִיג לֵילְיָא, אִתְּעַר רוּחַ צָפוֹן, וְקוּדְשָׁא בְּרִיךְ הוּא כְּדֵין עֲבַד נוּקְמִין, וְיִשְׂרָאֵל עַבְדִּין שִׁירָתָא בְּקוֹל רָם, וּכְדֵין עֲבַד לוֹן בְּנֵי חוֹרִין מִכֹּלָּא, וּמַלְאָכִין עִלָּאֵי, וְכָל מַשִׁרְיָין כֻּלְּהוּ, הֲווֹ צַיְּיתִין לְהוֹן לְקַלֵּיהוֹן דְּיִשְׂרָאֵל. בָּתַר דְּאִתְגְּזָרוּ, רְשִׁימוּ לְבָתֵּיהוֹן, מֵהַהוּא דָּמָא, וּמִדָּמָא דְּפִסְחָא, בִּתְלַת רְשִׁימִין. עַל הַמַּשְׁקוֹף וְעַל שְׁתֵּי הַמְּזוּזוֹת.

7. Come and behold: on the night that the Holy One, blessed be He, wanted to slaughter all these firstborn, as we have learned, the singers came to sing for Him when night fell. THE HOLY ONE, BLESSED BE HE, told them that the time was not opportune TO SING ANY SONG, since the inhabitants of the earth were singing another song. At midnight, the north wind was stirring and the Holy One, blessed be He, was wreaking vengeance FOR YISRAEL.

Yisrael were singing their song with loud voices and, at that moment, He made them free from everyone. The supernal angels and all the HIGHEST camps together were listening to the voices of Yisrael after they were circumcised, and marked their houses with that blood and the blood of the Paschal lamb with three marks, "upon the lintel, and on the two side posts" (Shemot 12:23).

8. מ"ט. הָא אוּקְמוּהָ בְּגִין דְּאִיהוּ רְשִׁימָא קַדִּישָׁא, וּמְחַבְּלָא כַּד אִיהוּ נָפִיק, וְחָמֵי הַהוּא דָּמָא דַּהֲוָה רָשִׁים עַל הַהוּא פִּתְחָא, חָיֵיס עֲלַיְיהוּ דְּיִשְׂרָאֵל, הה"ד וּפָסַח יְיָ' עַל הַפֶּתַח וְגוֹ'. הָכָא אִית לְאִסְתַּכְּלָא, אִי קוּדְשָׁא בְּרִיךְ הוּא אָתֵי וְקָטִיל בְּאַרְעָא דְּמִצְרַיִם, וְלֹא שְׁלִיחַ אַחֲרָא, רְשִׁימָא דָּא דְּעַל פִּתְחָא לָמָּה, וְהָא כֹּלָּא גְּלֵי קַמֵּיהּ. וְתוּ, מַהוּ וְלֹא יִתֵּן הַמַּשְׁחִית, וְלֹא יַשְׁחִית מִבָּעֵי לֵיהּ.

8. What is the reason THAT THEY MARKED THE BLOOD OVER THE DOOR LINTEL AND THE TWO SIDE POSTS? It has already been explained. It is because it is a holy mark, and the Angel of Destruction had mercy upon Yisrael when he saw this blood that was marked on the opening. This is what is written: "Hashem will pass over the door..." (Ibid.). We must look closely here. If the Holy One, blessed be He, and no other messenger came and slew in the land of Egypt, what is the purpose of this mark over the door opening, since all is revealed to Him? In addition, what is the meaning of: "and will not allow the Destroyer" (Ibid.), WHICH MEANS IT WAS A MESSENGER? It should have said, 'and will not destroy'.

9. אֶלָּא וַדַּאי הָכִי הוּא, דִּכְתִיב וַיְיָ' הִכָּה כָל בְּכוֹר. וַיְיָ': הוּא וּבֵית דִּינוֹ. וְהַהוּא בֵּי דִּינָא הָכָא אִשְׁתְּכַח. וּבְכֹלָּא בָּעֵי לְאַחֲזָאָה עוֹבָדָא, בְּגִין לְאִשְׁתְּזָבָא. דְּהָא כְּגַוְונָא דָּא עַל גַּבֵּי מַדְבְּחָא, בְּגִין דְּלָא אִשְׁתְּכַח מְחַבְּלָא.

9. It most certainly is so, as it is written: "And Hashem smote all the firstborn" (Ibid. 29). "And Hashem" INDICATES Him, ZEIR ANPIN, and His courthouse, MALCHUT. That courthouse is present here. THEREFORE, IT SAYS, "THE DESTROYER." It is always imperative to show a deed BELOW

in order TO AWAKEN A CORRESPONDING ONE ABOVE to be saved. BECAUSE OF THAT, IT WAS NECESSARY TO PLACE THE BLOOD OVER THE DOOR LINTEL AND THE TWO SIDE POSTS, TO AROUSE MERCY FOR THEM ABOVE. Similar to that are THE OFFERINGS on the altar; this is in order that the Destroyer shall not come there.

10. הַאי בְּעוֹבָדָא, וּבְזִמְנָא דְּלָא אִצְטְרִיךְ הַאי, כְּגוֹן רֹאשׁ הַשָּׁנָה, דְּאִיהוּ יוֹמָא דְּדִינָא, וּמָארֵיהוֹן דְּלִישָׁנָא בִּישָׁא קַיְימִין עֲלַיְיהוּ דְּיִשְׂרָאֵל, בָּעֵינָן מִלִּין, צְלוֹתִין וּבָעוּתִין, וּבָעֵינָן לְאַחֲזָאָה עוֹבָדָא כְּמָה דְּאוֹקִימְנָא. וְהָא אִתְּמַר, וּבְמָה. בַּשׁוֹפָר. לְאִתְּעֲרָא שׁוֹפָרָא אַחֲרָא. וַאֲנָן מַפִּיקִין בְּהַהוּא קָלָא, רַחֲמֵי וְדִינָא כַּחֲדָא, כֹּלָּא כְּדְקָא יָאוּת. כְּמָה דְּהַהוּא שׁוֹפָר עִלָּאָה, אַפִּיק קָלָא דְּאִיהוּ כְּלָלָא כַּחֲדָא. וּלְאִתְּעֲרָא רַחֲמֵי קָאַזְלֵינָן, וּלְתַבְּרָא מָארֵיהוֹן דְּדִינָא, דְּלָא יִשְׁלְטוּן בְּהַאי יוֹמָא. וְכַד רַחֲמֵי מִתְעֲרִין, כֻּלְּהוּ בּוּצִינִין עִלָּאִין נַהֲרִין מֵהַאי גִּיסָא וּמֵהַאי גִּיסָא. כְּדֵין בְּאוֹר פְּנֵי מֶלֶךְ חַיִּים.

10. This is by means of a deed, MEANING OFFERINGS. When it is not needed, for example, on Rosh Hashanah (the Jewish New Year), which is the Day of Judgment, which those of wicked tongues stand ready to DENOUNCE YISRAEL, IT IS NOT SUFFICIENT TO GIVE MERE OFFERINGS. Speech is required; that is, prayers and petitions. It is necessary to demonstrate deeds, as we have explained. And we learned with what these must be demonstrated. It is with the Shofar, in order to invoke another Shofar, WHICH IS BINAH. We produce through the sound OF THIS SHOFAR Mercy and Judgment together, all as is required. This is just like that highest Shofar, WHICH IS BINAH, that emitted a sound, WHICH IS ZEIR ANPIN, which is the inclusion OF CHESED, JUDGMENT AND MERCY together – SINCE TIFERET, WHICH IS ZEIR ANPIN, IS INCLUSIVE OF CHESED, JUDGMENT AND MERCY. To awaken Mercy, we awaken WITH THE BLOWING OF THE SHOFAR and break down the Prosecutors so that they shall have no dominion on that day. When Mercy is awakened, all the upper luminaries, THE SFIROT, illuminate from this side and from that side, MEANING FROM THE RIGHT AND LEFT. Then, "in the light of the King's countenance is life" (Mishlei 16:15).

11. ת"ח, בְּשַׁעֲתָא דְּכַהֲנָא אִתְכְּוָון לְאַדְלְקָא בּוּצִינִין לְתַתָּא, וַהֲוָה

קָרִיב קְטֹרֶת בּוּסְמִין, בְּהַהוּא שַׁעֲתָא כְּדֵין בּוּצִינִין עִלָּאִין נַהֲרִין, וְאִתְקְטַר כֹּלָּא כַּחֲדָא, וְחַדוּ וְחֶדְוָותָא אִשְׁתְּכַח בְּכֻלְּהוּ עָלְמִין, הה"ד שֶׁמֶן וּקְטֹרֶת יְשַׂמַּח לֵב, וע"ד בְּהַעֲלוֹתְךָ אֶת הַנֵּרֹת.

11. Come and behold: the priest intended to light the lamps below and brought the offering of spiced incense. During that moment, the upper candles are shining, THAT IS, THE SFIROT, and everything connects together. Happiness and gladness prevail in all the worlds, and it is written: "ointment and perfume rejoice the heart" (Mishlei 27:9). Therefore, IT IS WRITTEN: "when you kindle the lamps" (Bemidbar 8:2).

3. "And the ark rested in the seventh month"

A Synopsis

Rabbi Elazar tells Rabbi Yosi and Rabbi Yitzchak that every word of the Torah has secrets; even though it may be telling a simple story, the Torah demonstrates the highest matters and the utmost secrets. He uses the story of the landing of the Ark on Mount Ararat as an example, saying that it is to teach us about a universal truth, (the time of judgment). Rabbi Elazar says that God would not have limited Himself to just writing down what various people like Esau and Hagar and Laban and Bilaam said; if He had it would not be called the Torah of Truth, as it is. Every individual word comes to designate the highest things. We learn that "and the Ark rested" refers to the time when judgment hangs upon the world and judgments prevail, the time when God sits on the Throne of Justice to put the world on trial. That throne is only ready during the seventh month, during which is the Day of Judgment. Rabbi Elazar says that Ararat is derived from the Hebrew word for 'cursed', alluding to the Adversaries of Judgment. On that day the children of Yisrael send up their prayers and blow the Shofar so that God reverses justice to mercy; it is therefore required that whoever blows the Shofar should be familiar with the deeper secrets of the matters.

12. רִבִּי אֶלְעָזָר וְר' יוֹסֵי וְר' יִצְחָק, הֲווֹ אָזְלֵי בְּאוֹרְחָא, פָּגְעוּ בְּאִינוּן טוּרֵי קַרְדוּ, עַד דַּהֲווֹ אָזְלֵי, זָקַף עֵינוֹי ר' אֶלְעָזָר, וְחָמֵי אִינוּן טוּרֵי רָמָאֵי, וַהֲווֹ חֲשׁוֹכָן, וְדַחֲלָן בִּדְחִילוּ. א"ר אֶלְעָזָר לְאִינוּן חַבְרַיָּיא, אִלּוּ אַבָּא הָכָא, לָא הֲוָה דָחִילְנָא, אֲבָל כֵּיוָן דַּאֲנַן תְּלָתָא, וּמִלֵּי דְאוֹרַיְיתָא בֵּינָנָא, דִּינָא הָכָא לָא אִשְׁתְּכַח.

12. Rabbi Elazar and Rabbi Yosi and Rabbi Yitzchak were going along their way. They reached those mountains of darkness while traveling. Rabbi Elazar raised his eyes and saw those lofty mountains, and they were dark and awesome and frightful. Rabbi Elazar said to his friends: If my father was here, I would not be frightened. Yet since we are three and are speaking of Torah among us, no Judgment will prevail here.

13. פָּתַח ר' אֶלְעָזָר וְאָמַר, כְּתִיב וַתָּנַח הַתֵּיבָה בַּחֹדֶשׁ הַשְּׁבִיעִי וְגו', עַל הָרֵי אֲרָרָט וְגו', כְּמָה חֲבִיבִין מִלֵּי דְאוֹרַיְיתָא, דִּבְכָל מִלָּה וּמִלָּה, אִית

רָזִין עִלָּאִין, וְאוֹרַיְיתָא כֹּלָּא, עִלָּאָה אִיקְרֵי. וְתָנֵינָן בְּתַלֵיסָר מְכִילָן
דְּאוֹרַיְיתָא, כָּל דָּבָר שֶׁהָיָה בִּכְלָל, וְיָצָא מִן הַכְּלָל, לְלַמֵּד, לֹא לְלַמֵּד
עַל עַצְמוֹ יָצָא, אֶלָּא לְלַמֵּד עַל הַכְּלָל כֻּלּוֹ יָצָא. דְּהָא אוֹרַיְיתָא דְּאִיהִי
כְּלָלָא עִלָּאָה, אע"ג דְּנָפַק מִנָּה, חַד סִפּוּר בְּעָלְמָא. וַדַּאי לָא אָתֵי
לְאַחֲזָאָה עַל הַהוּא סִפּוּר, אֶלָּא לְאַחֲזָאָה מִלִּין עִלָּאִין, וְרָזִין עִלָּאִין.
וְלֹא לְלַמֵּד עַל עַצְמוֹ יָצָא, אֶלָּא לְלַמֵּד עַל הַכְּלָל כֻּלּוֹ יָצָא. בְּגִין
דְּהַהוּא סִפּוּר דְּאוֹרַיְיתָא, אוֹ הַהוּא עוֹבָדָא, אע"ג דְּהוּא נָפְקָא מִכְּלָלָא
דְּאוֹרַיְיתָא, לָאו לְאַחֲזָאָה עַל גַּרְמֵיהּ נָפַק בִּלְבַד, אֶלָּא לְאַחֲזָאָה עַל
הַהוּא כְּלָלָא עִלָּאָה דְּאוֹרַיְיתָא כֹּלָּא נָפַק.

13. Rabbi Elazar opened the discussion with the verse: "and the ark rested in the seventh month...upon the mountains of Ararat..." (Beresheet 8:4). How beloved are the words of Torah that each and every word has lofty secrets and the entire Torah is considered supernal. We learned IN THE BARAITA of the thirteen qualities of the Torah. Whatever is part of the whole, yet it is an exception, it is so in order to teach a general rule, not teach merely about itself. Since the Torah is the highest generality, even though a simple story is an exception to the rule, its function most certainly is not merely to tell us just that story but rather to demonstrate the highest matters and the utmost secrets. It is not considered as an exception so as to teach about itself, but rather to demonstrate a general rule, since that story of the Torah or that occurrence, although it stands to itself outside the Torah, did not come to show this alone but rather came to demonstrate the general law of the entire Torah.

14. כְּגוֹן הַאי דִּכְתִיב, וַתָּנַח הַתֵּיבָה בַּחֹדֶשׁ הַשְּׁבִיעִי בְּשִׁבְעָה עָשָׂר יוֹם
לַחֹדֶשׁ עַל הָרֵי אֲרָרָט. וַדַּאי הַאי קְרָא מִכְּלָלָא דְּאוֹרַיְיתָא נָפַק, וְאָתֵי
בְּסִפּוּר דְּעָלְמָא. מַאי אִכְפַּת לָן, אִי שָׁרֵי בְּהַאי, אוֹ בְּהַאי, דְּהָא בַּאֲתַר
חַד לִישְׁרֵי. אֶלָּא לְלַמֵּד עַל הַכְּלָל כֻּלּוֹ יָצָא. וְזַכָּאִין אִינּוּן יִשְׂרָאֵל,
דְּאִתְיְהִיב לְהוּ אוֹרַיְיתָא עִלָּאָה אוֹרַיְיתָא דִּקְשׁוֹט. וּמַאן דְּאָמַר, דְּהַהוּא
סִפּוּרָא דְּאוֹרַיְיתָא, לְאַחֲזָאָה עַל הַהוּא סִפּוּר בִּלְבַד קָאָתֵי, תִּיפַּח
רוּחֵיהּ. דְּאִי הָכִי, לָאו אִיהִי אוֹרַיְיתָא עִלָּאָה, אוֹרַיְיתָא דִּקְשׁוֹט, אֶלָּא
וַדַּאי אוֹרַיְיתָא קַדִּישָׁא עִלָּאָה, אִיהִי אוֹרַיְיתָא דִּקְשׁוֹט.

14. For example, it is written: "and the ark rested in the seventh month, on the seventeenth day of the month, upon the mountains of Ararat." Most likely, this scriptural verse is an exception to the generality of the Torah and came to relate a simple story. HE ASKS: What do we care if it landed on this mountain or on that mountain? It had to rest somewhere. HE RESPONDS: It is only to instruct us on the general as a whole that it was specified, SINCE IT ALLUDES TO A TIME OF JUDGMENT, AS WE MENTIONED BEFORE. Praised are Yisrael that the loftiest Torah was granted to them, a Torah of truth. Whoever says that this Torah story is mentioned simply to relate only that story alone, may he breathe his last, because then it is not supernal Torah, the Torah of truth. But most certainly, the holy Torah, the loftiest, is a Torah of truth.

15. תָּא חֲזֵי, מֶלֶךְ בָּ"ן, לָאו יְקָרָא דִילֵיהּ הוּא, לְאִשְׁתָּעֵי מִלָּה דְּהֶדְיוֹטָא, כ"ש לְמִכְתַּב לֵיהּ, וְאִי סָלִיק בְּדַעְתָּךְ, דְּמַלְכָּא עִלָּאָה קוּדְשָׁא בְּרִיךְ הוּא, לָא הֲווֹ לֵיהּ מִלִּין קַדִּישִׁין, לְמִכְתַּב וּלְמֶעְבַּד מִנַּיְיהוּ אוֹרַיְיתָא, אֶלָּא דְּאִיהוּ כָּנִישׁ כָּל מִלִּין דְּהֶדְיוֹטִין, כְּגוֹן מִלִּין דְּעֵשָׂו. מִלִּין דְּהָגָר. מִלִּין דְּלָבָן בְּיַעֲקֹב. מִלִּין דְּאָתוֹן. מִלִּין דְּבִלְעָם. מִלִּין דְּבָלָק. מִלִּין דְּזִמְרִי. וְכָנִישׁ לְהוּ, וְכָל שְׁאָר סִפּוּרִין דִּכְתִיבִין, וְעָבֵיד מִנַּיְיהוּ אוֹרַיְיתָא.

15. Come and behold: there is a king of flesh and blood. It is no honor for him to have simple talk and, most certainly, to write these simple things down. Could you imagine if the exalted King, the Holy One, blessed be He, had no holy things to write about with which to produce the Torah, but He merely gathered all the simplest matters, such as: the utterings of Esau; the utterings of Hagar; the utterings of Laban to Jacob; the utterings of the mule; the utterings of Bilaam; the utterings of Balak and the utterings of Zimri. And then He gathered them and all the stories that were written and made a Torah out of them.

16. אִי הָכִי, אֲמַאי אִקְרֵי תּוֹרַת אֱמֶת, תּוֹרַת יְיָ' תְּמִימָה, עֵדוּת יְיָ' נֶאֱמָנָה, פִּקּוּדֵי יְיָ' יְשָׁרִים, מִצְוַת יְיָ' בָּרָה, יִרְאַת יְיָ' טְהוֹרָה, מִשְׁפְּטֵי יְיָ' אֱמֶת, וּכְתִיב הַנֶּחֱמָדִים מִזָּהָב וּמִפָּז רָב. אִלֵּין אִינוּן מִלֵּי דְּאוֹרַיְיתָא. אֶלָּא וַדַּאי אוֹרַיְיתָא קַדִּישָׁא עִלָּאָה, אִיהוּ אוֹרַיְיתָא דִּקְשׁוֹט, תּוֹרַת יְיָ'

תְּמִימָה. וְכָל מִלָּה וּמִלָּה, אַתְיָיא לְאַחֲזָאָה מִלִּין עִלָּאִין, דְּהַהוּא מִלָּה דְּהַהוּא סִפּוּר, לָאו לְאַחֲזָאָה עַל גַּרְמֵיהּ בִּלְבַד קָא אַתְיָא, אֶלָּא לְאַחֲזָאָה עַל הַהוּא כְּלָלָא קָאַתֵי, כְּמָה דְּאוֹקִימְנָא.

16. If so, why is it referred to as "the Torah of Truth" (Malachi 2:6)? "The Torah of Hashem is perfect...the testimony of Hashem is sure... The statutes of Hashem are right...the commandment of Hashem is pure... The fear of Hashem is clean...the Judgments of Hashem are True... More to be desired are they than gold, even much fine gold" (Tehilim 19:8-11); these words refer to Torah matters. Most certainly, the holy loftiest Torah is a Torah of Truth, since "the Torah of Hashem is perfect." Every individual word comes to designate the highest things, since that specific matter which is in a story is not here to teach about itself alone, but rather to imply the overall aspect, as we have explained.

17. תָּא חֲזֵי וַתָּנַח הַתֵּיבָה וְגוֹ'. הַאי קְרָא כָּךְ, כָּל שְׁכֵּן אַחֲרָנִין, בְּשַׁעֲתָא דְּדִינָא תַּלְיָא עַל עָלְמָא, וְדִינִין שַׁרְיָין, וְקוּדְשָׁא בְּרִיךְ הוּא יָתִיב עַל כּוּרְסַיָּיא דְּדִינָא לְמֵידָן עָלְמָא בְּהַהוּא כּוּרְסַיָּא, כַּמָה רְשִׁימִין אִתְרְשִׁימוּ בֵּיהּ, כַּמָה פִּתְקִין גְּנִיזִין בְּגַוֵּויהּ, בְּגוֹ אַחְמְתָא דְּמַלְכָּא, כֻּלְּהוּ סִפְרִים דְּפָתִיחוּ תַּמָּן אִתְגְּנִיזוּ, וּבְגִין כָּךְ לָא אִתְנְשֵׁי מִלָּה מִן מַלְכָּא, וְהַאי כּוּרְסַיָּיא לָא אַתְקַן, וְלָא שַׁרְיָא. אֶלָּא בַּחֹדֶשׁ הַשְּׁבִיעִי, דְּאִיהוּ יוֹמָא דְּדִינָא, יוֹמָא דְּכָל בְּנֵי עָלְמָא אִתְפַּקְּדוּן בֵּיהּ, כֻּלְּהוּ עַבְרִין קַמֵּי הַהוּא כֻּרְסַיָּיא. וע"ד, וַתָּנַח הַתֵּבָה בַּחֹדֶשׁ הַשְּׁבִיעִי, בַּחֹדֶשׁ הַשְּׁבִיעִי וַדַּאי, דְּאִיהוּ דִּינָא דְּעָלְמָא.

17. Come and behold: "and the ark rested." This verse is true, AS WILL BE EXPLAINED, as are others, most certainly. At the moment that Judgment hangs upon the world and Judgments prevail, the Holy One, blessed be He, sits on the Throne of Judgment to put the world on trial. Through that Throne, how many notes are recorded on it, how many verdicts are stored in it, in the bag of the King? All the open books were stored there and, therefore, nothing was forgotten by the King. That Throne is not ready and is not available save during the seventh month. Then is the Day of Judgment, a day in which all the people in the world are counted and everyone passes before that Throne. Hence, "the ark rested." MALCHUT, THAT IS REFERRED TO AS 'ARK', "rested in the seventh month"; most certainly the seventh month, which is when the Judgment of the world comes.

18. עַל הָרֵי אֲרָרָט, אַלֵּין מָארֵיהוֹן דְּדִינִין, מָארֵיהוֹן דִּיבָבָא וִילָלָא, וְכֻלְּהוּ שְׁלִיחִין בְּהַהוּא יוֹמָא קַמֵּי קוּדְשָׁא בְּרִיךְ הוּא וְכַמָּה מָארֵי תְּרִיסִין אִתְּעֲרוּ בְּהַאי יוֹמָא, וְכֻלְּהוּ קַיְימֵי תְּחוֹת הַהוּא כֻּרְסְיָיא, בְּדִינָא דְּעָלְמָא.

18. "...upon the mountains of Ararat..." ARARAT IS DERIVED FROM *ARUR* (ENG. 'CURSED'), INDICATING those Prosecutors, who whine and wail, and all those emissaries THAT ARE PRESENT on that day before the Holy One, blessed be He. How many shielding ones are wakened on that day. And they all stand under that Throne when the world is on trial.

19. וְיִשְׂרָאֵל מְצַלָּאן צְלוֹתָא בְּהַהוּא יוֹמָא, וּבָעָאן וּמִתְחַנְּנָן קַמֵּיה, וְתַקְעִין בַּשּׁוֹפָר, וְקוּדְשָׁא בְּרִיךְ הוּא חָיֵיס עֲלַיְיהוּ, וּמְהַפֵּךְ דִּינָא לְרַחֲמֵי. וְכָל עֵלָּאֵי וְתַתָּאֵי, פָּתְחֵי וְאָמְרֵי, אַשְׁרֵי הָעָם יוֹדְעֵי תְרוּעָה וע״ד בָּעֵינָא בְּהַהוּא יוֹמָא, דְּהַהוּא דְּתָקַע, דְּיָדַע עִקָּרָא דְּמִלָּה, וִיכַוֵּון בֵּיה בִּתְרוּעָה, וְיַעֲבִיד מִלָּה בְּחָכְמְתָא, וע״ד כְּתִיב, אַשְׁרֵי הָעָם יוֹדְעֵי תְרוּעָה, וְלָא כְּתִיב תּוֹקְעֵי תְרוּעָה, וְהָא אִתְּמַר.

19. And Yisrael put forth their prayers on that day and beg and beseech before Him, and blow the Shofar. The Holy One, blessed be He, has mercy for them and reverses Judgment to Mercy. All the upper and lower beings say, "happy is the people that know the joyful note" (Tehilim 89:16). It is therefore required on that day that whoever blows should be familiar with the main SECRETS OF THE matters; he should concentrate on the blowing and expedite the matters with the HIGHEST wisdom. Therefore, it is written: "Happy is the people that know the joyful note," and not: 'that blow the joyful note'. We have already explained this.

4. "When you light the lamps"

A Synopsis

Rabbi Yosi enters a cave where he hears a voice saying what will happen when the seven lamps are lit. When he brings Rabbi Elazar into the cave they encounter two people studying the Torah. The rabbis discuss the kindling of the lamps and the offering of incense. The lighting of the candles is the secret of drawing out the abundance of Chassadim from Chochmah.

20. אָזְלוּ כָּל הַהוּא יוֹמָא, כַּד רָמַשׁ לֵילְיָא, סְלִיקוּ לְחַד אֲתָר, וְאַשְׁכָּחוּ חַד מְעַרְתָּא. א״ר אֶלְעָזָר, לֵיעוּל חַד גּוֹ מְעַרְתָּא, אִי אִשְׁתְּכַח אֲתָר דְּאִיהוּ יַתִּיר מְתַתְּקָן. עָאל ר׳ יוֹסֵי, וְחָמָא מְעַרְתָּא אַחֲרָא בְּגַוַּוִיהּ, נְהוֹרָא דִּשְׁרַגָּא בֵּיהּ, שָׁמַע חַד קָלָא דַּהֲוָה אָמַר, בְּהַעֲלֹתְךָ אֶת הַנֵּרוֹת אֶל מוּל פְּנֵי הַמְּנוֹרָה יָאִירוּ שִׁבְעַת הַנֵּרוֹת. הָכָא נָטְלָא כְּנֶסֶת יִשְׂרָאֵל נְהוֹרָא, וְאִמָּא עִלָּאָה מִתְעַטְּרָא, וְכֻלְהוּ בּוּצִינִין מִינָהּ נַהֲרִין. בָּהּ תְּרֵין טוֹפְסִירִין דְּקִיקִין פַּרְחִין, שׁוּשְׁבִינִין כֻּלְהוּ קַטְרִין לְגַבֵּי עֵלָּאָה, וּמִתַּמָּן לְתַתָּא.

20. They went along all that day and, when nightfall came, they went up to a place and found a cave. Rabbi Elazar said: Let one enter into the cave, for perhaps he will find there a place that is better suited. Rabbi Yosi entered and saw another cave within it and the light of a candle shining in it. He heard a voice that said: "When you light the lamps, the seven lamps shall give light towards the body of the candlestick" (Bemidbar 8:2). Here, the Congregation of Yisrael, THAT IS MALCHUT, received light, as supernal Ima, THAT IS BINAH, is adorned, and all the candles, THAT ARE THE SFIROT OF MALCHUT, illuminate within and from her. THEY SAID ABOUT THEMSELVES: Two refined souls soar from her; THAT IS, THEY UPLIFT MAYIN NUKVIN (ENG. 'FEMALE WATERS') WITH THEIR TORAH STUDY. All the best men – MEANING ALL WHO UPLIFT FEMALE WATERS THROUGH THEIR TORAH THAT ARE REFERRED TO AS 'GROOMSMEN' – connect MALCHUT to the upper one, WHICH IS BINAH. From there, THEY DRAW HER LIGHT downwards.

21. שָׁמַע ר׳ יוֹסֵי וְחַדֵּי, אָתָא לְגַבֵּי ר׳ אֶלְעָזָר, א״ל ר׳ אֶלְעָזָר, נֵיעוּל דְּקוּדְשָׁא בְּרִיךְ הוּא אַקְדִּים לָן הַאי יוֹמָא, לְאִתְרַחֲשָׁא לָן נִסִּין. עָאלוּ,

כֵּיוָן דְּעָאלוּ, חָמוּ תְּרֵין בְּנֵי נָשָׁא, דַּהֲווֹ לָעָאן בְּאוֹרַיְיתָא. א״ר אֶלְעָזָר, מַה יָּקָר חַסְדְּךָ אֱלֹהִים וּבְנֵי אָדָם בְּצֵל כְּנָפֶיךָ יֶחֱסָיוּן. קָמוּ אִלֵּין, וְיָתְבֵי כֻּלְּהוּ, וְחַדוּ כֻּלְּהוּ, אָמַר רַבִּי אֶלְעָזָר, מָה יָּקָר חַסְדְּךָ אֱלֹהִים, דְּאַשְׁכַּחֲנָא לְכוּ. חֶסֶד עָבַד לָן קוּדְשָׁא בְּרִיךְ הוּא בְּאַתְר דָּא, הַשְׁתָּא אַדְלִיקוּ בּוּצִינִין.

21. Rabbi Yosi heard this and was glad. He came to Rabbi Elazar. Rabbi Elazar said to him: Let us enter, since the Holy One, blessed be He, hastened before us on this day to produce miracles for us. They entered. As soon as they entered, they noticed two people who were involved in Torah study. Rabbi Elazar said: "how excellent is Your love, Elohim! Therefore the children of men shelter under the shadow of Your wings" (Tehilim 36:8). They stood up. Then they all sat down and were merry. Rabbi Elazar said: "how excellent is Your love, Elohim!" How excellent that I have found You. The Holy One, blessed be He, has done us grace in this place. Now light the candles – MEANING THAT THEY SHOULD CONVERSE IN MATTERS OF TORAH TO RAISE FEMALE WATERS TO KINDLE THE SFIROT OF MALCHUT FROM IMA, AS WAS SAID ABOVE.

22. פָּתַח רַבִּי יוֹסֵי וְאָמַר. בְּהַעֲלוֹתְךָ אֶת הַנֵּרוֹת, בְּהַעֲלוֹתְךָ מַמָּשׁ, בְּאַדְלְקוּתָךְ. דְּהָא כַּחֲדָא אִתְעֲבֵיד עַל יְדָא דְּכַהֲנָא תְּרֵין פּוּלְחָנִין. דְּאִינוּן קְשׁוּרָא חֲדָא. וּמַאן אִינוּן. שֶׁמֶן וּקְטֹרֶת. כְּדִכְתִּיב, שֶׁמֶן וּקְטֹרֶת יְשַׂמַּח לֵב. דִּכְתִּיב וְהִקְטִיר עָלָיו אַהֲרֹן וְגוֹ'. וּכְתִיב וּבְהַעֲלוֹת אַהֲרֹן אֶת הַנֵּרוֹת בֵּין הָעַרְבַּיִם יַקְטִירֶנָּה. מַאי שְׁנָא הָכָא בְּהֵטִיבוֹ, וּמַאי שְׁנָא הָתָם וּבְהַעֲלוֹת. אָמַר ר׳ יְהוּדָה, כֹּלָּא חַד מִלָּה.

22. Rabbi Yosi opened the discussion saying, "when you kindle the lamps," MEANING when you actually light, that is, while kindling, because two services were done by the priest which are the same connection, and they are oil and incense, THAT IS THE SECRET OF CHOCHMAH AND BINAH, as is written: "ointment and perfume (lit. 'incense') rejoice the heart" (Mishlei 27:9), and: "And Aaron shall burn upon it sweet incense... And when Aaron lights the lamps at evenings, he shall burn incense upon it" (Shemot 7-8). HE ASKS: What is the difference, that here it says, "when he dresses," and

there it says, "lights"? Rabbi Yehuda says: DRESSING AND LIGHTING amount to the same thing, SINCE DRESSING IS LIKE LIGHTING.

‎23. רִבִּי יוֹסֵי אָמַר, בְּהֵטִיבוֹ: כד"א כִּי טוֹבִים דּוֹדֶיךָ מִיָּיִן. טוֹבִים: רֲווֵי חַמְרָא. כד"א, וַנִּשְׂבַּע לֶחֶם וַנִּהְיֶה טוֹבִים. ר' יְהוּדָה אָמַר, הֵטָבָה מַמָּשׁ. כד"א וְטוֹב לֵב מִשְׁתֶּה תָמִיד. וּבְהַעֲלוֹת, דְּהָא בְּזִמְנָא דְּאִתְשַׁקְיָין וְאִתְרַוְויָין מַשְׁקְיוֹ דְּנַחֲלָא, כְּדֵין עָלָּאִין עִלּוּיָא, וּבִרְכָן אִשְׁתַּכְּחוּ בְּכֻלְּהוּ, וְחַדּוּ בְּכֹלָּא. וע"ד וּבְהַעֲלוֹת.

23. Rabbi Yosi said: "when he readies (lit. 'betters')," is as it is written, "for your love is better than wine" (Shir Hashirim 1:2), since those that are saturated with wine are better, or good, as it is written, "for then we had plenty of bread, and were well (also: 'better') off" (Yirmeyah 44:17). THIS MEANS TO SAY THAT WHOEVER IS SATISFIED WITH WINE OR BREAD, THE SECRET OF THE LIGHTS IN THE FIRST THREE SFIROT, THAT ARE CONSIDERED 'GOOD'. CONSEQUENTLY, "WHEN HE READIES THE LAMPS", MEANS THAT HE WILL DRAW ABUNDANTLY THE LIGHTS THAT ARE REFERRED TO AS 'WINE' AND 'BREAD', WHICH IS THE SECRET OF THE ILLUMINATION OF CHOCHMAH AND CHASSADIM. Rabbi Yehuda says: it is a real improvement. HE DISPUTES WHAT RABBI YOSI SAID, THAT THE BETTERING IS A RESULT OF THE ABUNDANT LIGHTS. RATHER, THE LIGHTS OF THE FEAST, WHICH ARE THE SECRET OF ILLUMINATION OF CHOCHMAH, ARE THEMSELVES CONSIDERED BETTERING, as it is written: "but he that is of a merry (lit. 'good') heart has a continual feast" (Mishlei 15:15). "When...lights," MEANS during the time THAT THE SFIROT ARE filled and saturated from the water of the stream, SINCE THE STREAM IS BINAH AND ITS WATER IS FROM CHOCHMAH. The upper grades are then uplifted and blessings prevail in all, and all are glad. CONSEQUENTLY, MAKING GOOD THE LAMPS IS THE ILLUMINATION OF CHOCHMAH THAT FLOWS FROM BINAH, WHICH IS THE SECRET OF WINE, AND THE LIGHTING OF THE CANDLES IS THE SECRET OF DRAWING OUT THE ABUNDANCE OF CHASSADIM THAT NEVER CEASES FROM THAT CHOCHMAH. Therefore, it is written: "when he kindles."

‎24. רִבִּי אֲחָא אָמַר, בְּשַׁעֲתָא דַּעֲמִיקָא דְּכֹלָּא נָהִיר, נָהִיר בְּנַחֲלָא. וְנַחֲלָא, נָגִיד בְּאֹרַח מֵישָׁר לְאַשְׁקָאָה כֹּלָּא. כְּדֵין כְּתִיב, בְּהַעֲלוֹת בְּגִין

דְּהָא מֵעוֹמְקָא דְּכֹלָּא נָפְקֵי, בְּהַעֲלוֹת דְּאָתֵי מִסְּטְרָא עִלָּאָה, דְּעֲמִיקָא
דְּכֹלָּא, דְּאִקְרֵי מַחֲשָׁבָה. וְכֹלָּא חַד מִלָּה, וּכְדֵין כנ"י אִתְבָּרְכָא, וּבִרְכָּאן
אִשְׁתַּכְּחֵי בְּכֻלְּהוּ עָלְמִין.

24. Rabbi Acha said: During the time when the most profound of all – THAT IS, SUPERNAL ABA – shines, it shines upon the stream, THE SUPERNAL IMA ABOVE. The stream flows in a straight way, MEANING THROUGH THE CENTRAL COLUMN, THAT IS ZEIR ANPIN, to irrigate all, MEANING ALL THE GRADES OF MALCHUT. Then it is written: "when lights (lit. 'raises')," since everything exudes from the deepest. "When...raises," MEANS that it comes from the deepest side that is referred to as 'thought', WHICH IS ABA. And all means the same, MEANING THAT IT IS THE SAME AS WHAT RABBI YOSI AND RABBI YEHUDA SAID. Then the Congregation of Yisrael is blessed, and blessings prevail throughout the worlds.

5. Issachar and Zebulun

A Synopsis
Rabbi Yitzchak uses the story of Issachar and Zebulun to illustrate the partnership between those to study the Torah and those who help to support and protect them and learn from them. He and Rabbi Aba talk about the color blue that is judgment.

25. רִבִּי יִצְחָק פָּתַח, כְּתִיב בָּנֹה בָּנִיתִי בֵּית זְבוּל לָךְ מָכוֹן לְשִׁבְתְּךָ עוֹלָמִים. בֵּית זְבוּל, בֵּית זְבוּל וַדַּאי, כַּד אִתְפְּקָדוּ בִּידָהָא, כָּל גִּנְזֵי מַלְכָּא, וְשַׁלְטָא בְּהוּ. כְּדֵין אִקְרֵי בֵּית זְבוּל. וְרָקִיעַ חַד אִית דְּאִקְרֵי זְבוּל, דְּהָא דָּא אַשְׁכַּח לְקַבְּלָא בִּרְכָאן, וּלְסַדְּרָא כֹּלָּא, וְהַאי אִקְרֵי בֵּית זְבוּל.

25. Rabbi Yitzchak opened the discussion with the verse: "I have surely built You a house to dwell in (Heb. *zvul*), a settled place for You to abide in for ever" (I Melachim 8:13). "...a house to dwell in..." most definitely. When all the stored treasures of the King, THAT IS ZEIR ANPIN, were assigned in the hands OF MALCHUT, and she has authority over them, she is called "a house to dwell in." There is one firmament that is called '*Zvul* (Eng. 'temple')', since its function is to receive blessings and put everything in order. That one – MALCHUT, WHEN SHE RULES OVER EVERYTHING – is ALSO called "a house to dwell in."

26. ת״ח, כְּתִיב וְלִזְבוּלֻן אָמַר שְׂמַח זְבוּלֻן בְּצֵאתֶךָ וְיִשָּׂשׁכָר בְּאֹהָלֶךָ, מְלַמֵּד דְּאִשְׁתַּתָּפוּ כַּחֲדָא. דָּא נָפִיק וְאָגַח קְרָבָא, וְדָא יָתִיב וְלָעֵי בְּאוֹרַיְיתָא. וְדָא יָהִיב חוּלָקָא לְדָא, וְדָא יָהִיב חוּלָקָא לְדָא. בְּחוּלָקֵיהּ דִּזְבוּלֻן יַמָּא, וכ״י אִקְרֵי יָם כִּנֶּרֶת. וְהָכִי אִתְחֲזֵי, בְּגִין דְּהָא תְּכֵלֶת נָפִיק מִתַּמָּן, וְאוּקְמוּהָ, דְּהָא לְתַתָּא כְּגַוְונָא דִּלְעֵילָא, יָם כִּנֶּרֶת לְעֵילָא, יָם כִּנֶּרֶת לְתַתָּא. תְּכֵלֶת לְעֵילָא, תְּכֵלֶת לְתַתָּא, וְכֹלָּא בַּאֲתָר חַד.

26. Come and behold: it is written, "and of Zebulun he said, 'Rejoice, Zebulun, in your going out; and Issachar, in your tents'" (Devarim 33:18), to teach us that they participated in a mutual partnership. The one went out and made war and the other sits and is involved in learning Torah. This one gives a part FROM HIS BOUNTY to that one, and that one gives a part OF HIS TORAH STUDY to this one, SINCE ISSACHAR IS THE SECRET OF TIFERET AND ZEBULUN IS THE SECRET OF MALCHUT. In Zebulun's lot was the sea. The Congregation of Yisrael, WHICH IS MALCHUT, is called the 'Sea of Galilee (Heb. *Kineret*)'. It was worthy TO BE CALLED thus because blue comes from there, SINCE BLUE IS THE SECRET OF MALCHUT, AND THE SEA OF GALILEE IS MALCHUT. They have explained that the lower is similar to the higher. There is a Sea of Galilee above, WHICH IS MALCHUT, and a Sea of Galilee below; blue above, WHICH IS MALCHUT, and blue below. Everything pertains to one area, WHICH IS MALCHUT.

27. וע״ד יָרִית זְבוּלוֹן, לְמֵיפַּק לְאַגָּחָא קְרָבָא, וּמְנָלָן דְּהָכִי הוּא. דִּכְתִיב עַמִּים הַר יִקְרָאוּ שָׁם יִזְבְּחוּ זִבְחֵי צֶדֶק. זִבְחֵי צֶדֶק וַדַּאי. מ״ט. כִּי שֶׁפַע יַמִּים יִינָקוּ. וְיִשָׂשכָר חוּלָקֵיה בְּאוֹרַיְיתָא, וְיָהִיב לִזְבוּלוֹן חוּלָקָא דְּאוֹרַיְיתָא וַדַּאי, וע״ד אִשְׁתַּתְּפוּ כַּחֲדָא, לְאִתְבָּרְכָא זְבוּלוֹן מִיִשָׂשכָר, דְּבִרְכָתָא דְּאוֹרַיְיתָא, הִיא בִּרְכָתָא דְּכֹלָּא.

27. Because of this, Zebulun's portion was to go out and wage war, SINCE HE WAS AN ASPECT OF MALCHUT. How do we know that it is so? Because it is written: "they shall call the peoples to the mountain; there they shall offer sacrifices of righteousness" (Ibid. 19). "...sacrifices of righteousness..." most certainly, MEANING OF MALCHUT THAT IS CALLED 'RIGHTEOUSNESS'. What is the reason? "...for they shall suck the abundance of the seas..." (Ibid.) MEANING THE ABUNDANCE THAT COMES THROUGH BATTLES. Issachar's lot is in the Torah, and he surely gives to Zebulun his share in the Torah. Therefore, they were together in a partnership, so that Zebulun should receive blessings from Issachar, since the blessing of the Torah is everyone's blessing.

28. ר' אַבָּא אָמַר, אַחֲסָנְתָּא דְּאוֹרַיְיתָא וַדַּאי הָכִי הוּא, וְדַרְגָּא דָּא שְׁתִיתָאָה יָהִיב אֲגַר אוֹרַיְיתָא, וְאַחֲסִין לָה לכ״י, אַחֲסִין חִוָּורָא לִתְכֶלְתָּא. וע״ד תָּנֵינָן, מְשַׁיֵּיכִיר בֵּין תְּכֵלֶת לְלָבָן, דְּיִשְׁתְּמוֹדְעָן גְּוָונֵי, דְּהָא בְּדֵין אִקְרֵי בֹּק״ר, וְחִוָּורָא אָתֵי לְעָלְמָא, וּתְכֶלְתָּא אִתְעֲבַר. וע״ד כָּל קָרְבִּין דְּמַלְכָּא, וְכָל זַיְינֵי מַלְכָּא בִּידָהָא אִתְמָנָן, וְהָא אוֹקִימְנָא.

28. Rabbi Aba said: The heritage of the Torah is indeed in this way, and this

level is the sixth, WHICH IS YESOD, which gives the reward of the Torah and bequeaths it to the Congregation of Yisrael. It bequeaths the white, WHICH IS CHESED, to the blue, WHICH IS JUDGMENT. Thus, we have learned that when one distinguishes between blue and white FOR THE READING OF THE SH'MA, meaning that the hues shall be distinguishable, then it is considered morning. Then the white comes to the world, and the blue, WHICH IS JUDGMENT, disappears FROM THE WORLD. Therefore, all the wars of the King and all the battle gear of the King were assigned to the hands OF MALCHUT WHEN SHE WAS CONSIDERED, "A HOUSE TO DWELL IN (HEB. ZVUL)," AND ALSO ZEBULUN, AS MENTIONED ABOVE. We have already explained it.

6. "The well that the princes dug out"

A Synopsis

Rabbi Aba says that the title verse refers to the Congregation of Yisrael, to Aba and Ima and to the Patriarchs. Malchut is called both a 'well' when Isaac goes out with weapons from the side of Ima, and a 'sea' when it illuminates from the uppermost river of Aba. From the day that the Congregation of Yisrael entered exile the waters failed, but the righteous, Yesod, fills Malchut with the supernal flow so that the universe inherits all the blessings.

29. בְּאֵר חֲפָרוּהָ שָׂרִים כָּרוּהָ נְדִיבֵי הָעָם, בְּאֵר, דָּא כְּנֶסֶת יִשְׂרָאֵל. חֲפָרוּהָ שָׂרִים, דָּא אַבָּא וְאִמָּא, דְּאוֹלִידוּ לָהּ. כָּרוּהָ נְדִיבֵי הָעָם, אִלֵּין אֲבָהָן. דִּכְתִיב נְדִיבֵי עַמִּים נֶאֱסָפוּ עִם אֱלֹהֵי אַבְרָהָם וְגוֹ'. בְּגִין לְאִתְבָּרְכָא מִנְּהוֹן, ע"י דְּדַרְגָּא חַד, וּמַנּוּ. צַדִּיק דְּקָאֵים עָלָהּ. וע"ד אָמְרֵינָן, כַּד הַאי בְּאֵר נַטְלָא, בְּסִיּוּעָא דַּאֲבָהָן נַטְלָא.

29. "The well that the princes dug out, that the nobles of the people delved..." (Bemidbar 21:18). The well is the Congregation of Yisrael, WHICH IS MALCHUT; "that the princes dug out," is Aba and Ima, that gave birth TO MALCHUT; "that the nobles of the people delved," are the Patriarchs, WHICH ARE CHESED, GVURAH AND TIFERET OF ZEIR ANPIN. It is written: "the nobles of the peoples are gathered together, the people of the Elohim of Abraham" (Tehilim 47:10). THE ELOHIM OF ABRAHAM IS CHESED OF ZEIR ANPIN, FROM WHICH GVURAH AND TIFERET ARE DRAWN. "...THAT THE NOBLES OF THE PEOPLE DELVED..." MEANS THAT THEY CONSTRUCTED it in order that it would be blessed from them through one level that is the Righteous, WHICH IS YESOD OF ZEIR ANPIN, that stands over it AND POURS UPON IT ALL THAT THERE IS IN CHESED, GVURAH AND TIFERET. Therefore, we have this saying: 'When this well travels, it is with the help of the patriarchs that it travels.'

30. וְאִקְרֵי בְּאֵר, וְאִקְרֵי יָם. אִקְרֵי בְּאֵר, בְּשַׁעֲתָא דְּיִצְחָק נָפַק מִזַיְינָא מִסִּטְרָא דְּאִימָא, וְאָתֵי לְאַמְשָׁכָא אֲבַתְרָא דְּדָא, וּמַלֵּי לָהּ, כְּדֵין אִקְרֵי בְּאֵר דְּיִצְחָק. בְּאֵר דְּמַרְיִם. וְהָא אוּקְמוּהָ. יָם כַּד אִתְנַהֲרָא מִנְּהָרָא עִלָּאָה דְּאַבָּא, כְּדֵין אִקְרֵי יָם, דְּנַחֲלִין אַזְלִין לְגַוֵּוהּ, כד"א כָּל הַנְּחָלִים

הוֹלְכִים אֶל הַיָּם וְהַיָּם אֵינֶנּוּ מָלֵא.

30. AT TIMES MALCHUT is called a 'well' AND AT TIMES it is called a 'sea'. It is called a 'well' when Isaac, WHO IS GVURAH OF ZEIR ANPIN, goes out with weapons FROM THE LEFT COLUMN from the side of Ima, and comes to draw THE ILLUMINATION OF CHOCHMAH FROM IMA TO MALCHUT and fill her up, IN ACCORDANCE WITH THE SECRET OF THE VERSE: "HIS LEFT HAND IS UNDER MY HEAD" (SHIR HASHIRIM 2:6). Then She is called 'the well of Isaac' OR 'the well of Miriam', as has already been explained. IT IS CALLED 'sea' when it illuminates from the uppermost river of Aba, SINCE SHE THEN RECEIVES CHOCHMAH AND CHASSADIM, since streams run to her, as it is written: "all the rivers run into the sea; yet the sea is not full" (Kohelet 1:7).

31. וּמִיּוֹמָא דְּגָלְתָה כְּנֶסֶת יִשְׂרָאֵל בְּגָלוּתָא, כְּתִיב אָזְלוּ מַיִם מִנִּי יָם, דָּא כנ״י. וְנָהָר יֶחֱרַב וְיָבֵשׁ, דָּא צַדִּיק, וע״ד כְּתִיב, הַצַּדִּיק אָבָד וְגו׳. דְּהוּא הֲוָה נָהָר עִלָּאָה וְיַקִּירָא, דְּעָיֵיל בְּגַוָּוה, וְהוּא כָּנִישׁ כָּל אִינּוּן נַהֲרִין וּנְחַלִּין, דְּנַגְדִין מִנְּגִידוּ דְּהַהוּא נָהָר קַדִּישָׁא, דְּלָא פַּסְקִין מֵימוֹי לְעָלְמִין, דְּנָגִיד וְנָפִיק מֵעֵדֶן עִלָּאָה, וְהוּא עָיֵיל בְּגַוָּוה וּמַלֵּי אַגְמָהָא, וּמִתַּמָּן יָרְתִין עָלְמִין כֻּלְּהוּ בִּרְכָּן בְּכֹלָּא.

31. From the day that the Congregation of Yisrael, WHICH IS MALCHUT, went into exile, it is written: "the waters fail from the sea" (Iyov 14:11). That refers to the Congregation of Yisrael THAT IS CALLED 'SEA', while, "the river is parched, and dries up" (Ibid.), is the Righteous, WHO IS YESOD. Hence, it is written: "The righteous perishes" (Yeshayah 57:1), since he was the uppermost and precious river that entered her. He gathered all these rivers and streams that are drawn from the flow of that holy river whose waters never cease, THAT IS BINAH, AND that comes out and emerges from the uppermost Eden. It enters within her and fills up her ponds, MEANING THE SFIROT OF MALCHUT, and from there, the universe inherits all the blessings in all PERFECTION.

32. ת״ח, בְּשַׁעֲתָא דְּאִתְבָּרְכָא כְּנֶסֶת יִשְׂרָאֵל, עָלְמִין כֻּלְּהוּ אִתְבָּרְכָן, וְיִשְׂרָאֵל לְתַתָּא, יַנְקִין וּמִתְבָּרְכָן בְּגִינָהּ. וְהָא אוּקִימְנָא דְּהִיא אֲגָנָא

עָלַיְיהוּ, דְּיִשְׂרָאֵל, כְּמָה דְּאִתְּמַר.

32. Come and behold: when the Congregation of Yisrael is blessed, all the worlds are blessed, and Yisrael below suckle and are blessed on her account. We explained that MALCHUT protects Yisrael, as we have learned.

7. The Name of *Ayin-Bet* (72) letters

A Synopsis

Rabbi Aba uses three verses beginning with "and the angel of Elohim, who went before the camp of Yisrael, removed..." to show how the 72 letters in each verse allude to the Name of Ayin-Bet, 72. When the letters are in direct order they point to mercy and when they are in reverse order they point to judgment. The Holy Name of 72 is passed on in these verses in which the Patriarchs are included, and we read about the joining of the left, right and Central Columns in the secret of Faith. The task of the construction of the Holy Name is made known through the uniting of the Patriarchs. The ways to judgment, to mercy, to help, to kindness, to awe, to Torah, to life, to death, to good and to bad are found with this Name of 72.

33. כְּתִיב וַיִּסַּע מַלְאַךְ הָאֱלֹהִים הַהוֹלֵךְ וְגוֹ'. מַלְאַךְ הָאֱלֹהִים דָּא כְּנֶסֶת יִשְׂרָאֵל. וְהָא אוֹקִימְנָא, דְּהַהִיא שַׁעֲתָא, בְּסִיּוּעַ דַּאֲבָהָן נַטְלָא. וְכַד אִינוּן מִשְׁתַּכְּחִין לְגַבָּהּ, כֹּלָּא מִשְׁתַּכְּחֵי. וּבְג"כ אִתְמְסַר בְּאִלֵּין קְרָאֵי שְׁמָא קַדִּישָׁא, דְּכָלִיל בְּהוֹן אֲבָהָתָא, כְּמָה דְּאוֹקִימְנָא. חַד קְרָא כְּסִדְרָא, וְחַד לְמַפְרֵעַ, וְחַד כְּסִדְרָא.

33. It is written: "and the angel of Elohim, who went before the camp of Yisrael, removed..." (Shemot 14:19). The angel of Elohim is the Congregation of Yisrael, who, as we have explained moved with the help of the Patriarchs at that time AS IT SAYS, "AND THE ANGEL...REMOVED," MEANING TO SAY THAT SHE THEN RECEIVED FROM THE THREE COLUMNS – CHESED, GVURAH AND TIFERET – THAT ARE REFERRED TO AS THE 'PATRIARCHS'. When they are by her, everything is, BOTH CHOCHMAH AND CHASSADIM. Due to this, the Holy Name OF 72 is passed on in these verses in which the Patriarchs are incorporated, as we have explained. One verse in forward direction POINTING TO THE RIGHT COLUMN, one verse backward POINTING TO THE LEFT COLUMN, and one verse forward, POINTING TO THE CENTRAL COLUMN.

34. וַיִּסַּע מַלְאַךְ הָאֱלֹהִים הַהוֹלֵךְ וְגוֹ', דָּא כְּסִדְרָא בְּגִין דְּאַבְרָהָם אִשְׁתְּכַח הָכָא, וְכָל אִינוּן דְּאָתוּ מִסִּטְרֵיהּ, וְעַל דָּא אִיהוּ כְּסִדְרָא כְּגַוְונָא דָּא.

34. "And the angel of Elohim, who went before the camp of Yisrael, removed..." This verse is in the regular direction, because Abraham is present here, WHO IS CHESED, THE RIGHT COLUMN, and all those who come from his side. Therefore, THE LETTERS are in this order.

.35 הָכָא אִתְעֲטָר אַבְרָהָם בְּעִטְרוֹי, וְאַעֲטַר לָהּ לִכְנֶסֶת יִשְׂרָאֵל, וְאִלֵּין אַתְוָון כֻּלְּהוּ בְּאֹרַח מֵישָׁר, לְמֵיהַךְ בִּימָמָא. דִּכְתִיב יוֹמָם יְצַוֶּה יְיָ׳ חַסְדּוֹ וּבַלַּיְלָה שִׁירֹה עִמִּי. וְעַ״ד כְּתִיב וַיִּסַּע, אֵימָתֵי נַטְלִין בְּמַטְלָנַיְיהוּ, הֲוֵי אֵימָא בִּימָמָא, כַּד נָהִיר שִׁמְשָׁא. וְדָא חַד קְרָא דְּאִיהוּ בְּשַׁבְעִין וּתְרֵין אַתְוָון.

35. Abraham, WHO IS CHESED, was adorned with his crowns here, and he crowned the Congregation of Yisrael, WHICH IS MALCHUT, in the right way to go by day, MEANING CHESED, as written: "yet Hashem will command His steadfast love (Chesed) in the daytime, and in the night His song shall be with me" (Tehilim 42:9). Therefore, it is written, "removed." When did they move? By day when the sun shines, WHICH IS ZEIR ANPIN, FOR THEN CHESED RULES. This verse (Shemot 14:19) contains 72 letters.

.36 תִּנְיָינָא דְּיִצְחָק, הָכִי נָמֵי דְּאִשְׁתְּכַח בְּע״ב אַתְוָון, לְאִשְׁתַּכְּחָא בְּדִינָא לְגַבֵּי מִצְרָאֵי וּלְגַבֵּי יִשְׂרָאֵל בְּרַחֲמֵי. וְעַ״ד כְּתִיב, וַיָּבֹא בֵּין מַחֲנֵה מִצְרַיִם וּבֵין מַחֲנֵה יִשְׂרָאֵל, לָקֳבֵיל אִלֵּין וְלָקֳבֵיל אִלֵּין. וַיְהִי הֶעָנָן וְהַחֹשֶׁךְ, דְּהָכִי הוּא יוֹמָא דְּיִצְחָק, דְּעֵיבָא הֲוֵי, עֲנָנָא וַחֲשׁוֹכָא מִנֵּיהּ הוּא. וּבְגִין כָּךְ סְדוּרָא דְּאַתְוָון לְמַפְרֵעַ, וְלָא בְּאֹרַח מֵישָׁר, כְּגַוְונָא דָּא.

36. The second verse is of Isaac, WHO IS GVURAH OF ZEIR ANPIN. We find that there are also 72 letters, in which there is Judgment for the Egyptians and Mercy for Yisrael. Therefore, it is written HERE: "and it came between the camp of Egypt and the camp of Yisrael" (Shemot 14:20), that is, toward the ones and toward the others. ISAAC IS THE SECRET OF THE ILLUMINATION OF CHOCHMAH, AND THE ILLUMINATION OF CHOCHMAH FLOWS FORTH ONLY WITH HARSH JUDGMENTS FOR THE WICKED AND GOOD RECOMPENSE FOR THE RIGHTEOUS. THIS IS THE SECRET OF, "AND IT CAME BETWEEN THE CAMP OF EGYPT AND THE CAMP OF

YISRAEL." "And it was a cloud and darkness" (Ibid.), since that is the day of Isaac, A DAY THAT IS cloudy, for the cloud and the darkness originate in it. Therefore, the order of the letters is backward and not straightforward, like this one.

37. וְעַל דָּא אַתְוָון כֻּלְּהוּ לְמַפְרֵעַ, דִּכְתִיב וַיְהִי הֶעָנָן וְהַחֹשֶׁךְ, דְּכֵיוָן דְּעָאל יִצְחָק בְּדִינוֹי, לֹא קָרַב זֶה אֶל זֶה. כְּתִיב זֶה אֶל זֶה, אִינּוּן דְּאָתוּ מִסְּטְרָא דְאַבְרָהָם, לָא קְרִיבוּ דָּא בְּדָא. דְּהָא לָא יַכְלִין, בְּגִין דְּהַאי בְּאֵר אִתְדַּבְּקָא בְּיִצְחָק. כד"א, וַיָּאֶר אֶת הַלַּיְלָה. דְּכַד אִתְמַלְּיָיא לְאִתְחַבְּרָא בְּיִצְחָק, לֹא קָרַב זֶה אֶל זֶה, וְלָא יָכִיל לְקָרְבָא. עַד דְּאָתָא יַעֲקֹב, וְאִתְחַבַּר בְּאַבְרָהָם, וְנָטַל לְיִצְחָק, וְשָׁארִי לֵיה בְּאֶמְצָעִיתָא, כְּדֵין אִתְקְשַׁר מְהֵימְנוּתָא דָּא בְּדָא וְדָא בְּדָא, וְאִשְׁתְּזִיבוּ יִשְׂרָאֵל.

37. Therefore, the letters are all backward, as is written: "and it was a cloud and darkness," WHICH IS JUDGMENT, AND BACKWARD DIRECTION ALLUDES TO JUDGMENT. As soon as Isaac got involved in its Judgments, "the one came not near the other" (Ibid.). It is written: "the one came not near the other," because those that come from the side of Abraham, MEANING FROM THE LIGHT OF CHESED, do not come near the other – MEANING THAT THE RIGHT COLUMN, WHICH IS CHESED, DID NOT GET NEAR TO BESTOW ABUNDANCE ON THE LEFT COLUMN, WHICH IS GVURAH. CONSEQUENTLY, THE LEFT WAS WITH CHOCHMAH WITHOUT CHASSADIM, WHICH IS A HARSH JUDGMENT AND DARK. AND ZEIR ANPIN, THAT IS CHESED, DID NOT APPROACH THE NUKVA TO PRESENT HER WITH CHASSADIM. THE NUKVA WAS RECEIVING FROM THE LEFT COLUMN CHOCHMAH WITHOUT CHASSADIM, WHICH IS DARKNESS. They were unable TO GET NEAR ONE ANOTHER, since this well, WHICH IS MALCHUT, was attached to Isaac, WHO IS THE LEFT COLUMN. It is written: "but it gave light by night" (Ibid.), MEANING THAT THE LEFT COLUMN ILLUMINATED THE NIGHT, WHICH IS MALCHUT. When it was filled up to join with Isaac, "the one came not near the other," and was unable to get near, SINCE THERE WAS NO UNION BETWEEN ZEIR ANPIN AND MALCHUT FROM THE SIDE OF CHESED. They were separated until Jacob, WHO IS THE CENTRAL COLUMN, came and joined to Abraham, WHO IS CHESED, and took Isaac and placed him in the middle – BETWEEN MERCY, WHICH IS THE CENTRAL COLUMN AND CHESED, WHICH IS THE

RIGHT COLUMN. Then the Faith was connected, one with the other, MEANING THAT THE TWO COLUMNS, RIGHT AND LEFT, WERE TIED TOGETHER AND ALSO ZEIR ANPIN AND MALCHUT WERE COUPLED TOGETHER FROM THE SIDE OF CHESED. And Yisrael were saved.

38. וְתָנֵינָן, בַּאֲתָר דַּאֲבָהָתָא אִשְׁתְּכְחֵי, שְׁאָר צַדִּיקַיָּיא מִשְׁתַּכְּחֵי גַּבַּיְיהוּ, וע"ד שְׁמָא דָא, סָלִיק לִסְטְרִין אַחֲרָנִין מִתְפָּרְשָׁן, אע"ג דְּכֻלְּהוּ נָפְקִין לְאָרְחָא חַד.

38. We have learned that in the place where the Patriarchs are, other righteous people are with them, MEANING THAT IN A PLACE WHERE THERE ARE CHESED, GVURAH AND TIFERET – WHICH ARE THE PATRIARCHS – THERE ARE ALSO NETZACH, HOD, YESOD AND MALCHUT – WHO ARE CALLED 'MOSES', 'AARON' AND 'JOSEPH'. Therefore, this name OF AYIN-BET (72) is understood and explained in other ways, MEANING THAT THE NAME OF 72 IS EXPLAINED IN THIS MANNER. THE TWELVE BOUNDARIES – WHICH ARE THE SECRET CHOCHMAH AND BINAH, TIFERET AND MALCHUT, IN EACH OF THE THREE COLUMNS, EQUALING TWELVE – ILLUMINATE IN ALL ENDS OF THE SIX ENDS OF ZEIR ANPIN, AND SIX TIMES TWELVE EQUALS 72. AND SIMILARLY, THERE ARE OTHER MANNERS IN THIS LINE, although all EXPLANATIONS result in one direction.

39. כַּד נַהֲרָא הַאי בְּא"ר מִסִּטְרָא דְּיִצְחָק, וְאִתְקְשַׁר בֵּיה, אִתְעֲבֵיד יַמָּא רַבָּא תַּקִּיפָא, וְגַלְגְּלִין תַּקִּיפִין, סַלְּקִין וְנַחְתִּין בְּזַעַף וְרוּגְזָא בְּתִקְפוּ, נָטִיל לְעֵילָא, סָלִיק, וְנָחִית לְתַתָּא, אַבְרָהָם אָתֵי לְקַבְּלֵיה, וּמִגּוֹ רוּגְזָא וְזַעְפָּא וְחֵימָתָא וּתְקִיפוּ, זֶה אֶל זֶה לָא הֲווֹ מִתְקָרְבִין, עַד דְּאָתָא יַעֲקֹב, וְשָׁכִיךְ רוּגְזָא, וּמָאִיךְ וְתָבַר גַּלְגַּלֵּי יַמָּא, הה"ד וַיֵּט מֹשֶׁה אֶת יָדוֹ עַל הַיָּם וַיּוֹלֶךְ יְיָ' אֶת הַיָּם בְּרוּחַ קָדִים עַזָּה וְגוֹ'. מַאי בְּרוּחַ קָדִים עַזָּה. דָּא רוּחַ יַעֲקֹב, עַזָּה תַּקִּיף לְקַבְּלֵיה, לְתַבְרָא רוּגְזָא דְּהַאי יַמָּא. וַיָּשֶׂם אֶת הַיָּם לֶחָרָבָה וַיִּבָּקְעוּ הַמָּיִם אָרִיק יַמָּא מֵימֵי רוּגְזִין, וְאִתְפְּלִיגוּ מַיָּא לִסְטְרָא דְּאַבְרָהָם וּלְסִטְרָא דְּיַעֲקֹב, הה"ד וַיִּבָּקְעוּ הַמָּיִם לִסְטְרָא דָא וּלְסִטְרָא דָא. וְעַל דָּא אַתְוָון כֻּלְּהוּ בְּאֹרַח מֵישָׁר כַּדְקָא יֵאוֹת.

39. When this well, WHICH IS MALCHUT from the side of Isaac, WHO IS

THE LEFT COLUMN, lights up and is tied to him, the Great Sea is formed, strong AND RAGING. Strong waves go up and go down powerfully, with anger and rage, as they travel up, ascend, and come down. THIS IS THE SECRET OF WHAT IS WRITTEN: "THEY MOUNT UP TO THE SKY, THEY GO DOWN AGAIN TO THE DEPTHS" (TEHILIM 107:26). Abraham comes towards it, WHO IS THE RIGHT COLUMN, MEANING THAT THE RIGHT COLUMN IS OPPOSITE IT. THEREFORE, THIS QUARREL AND NOISE IS PRODUCED. FOR WHEN THE LEFT GAINS STRENGTH, THEN THE WAVES OF THE OCEAN RISE WITH THEIR PEAK TO THE SKY, AND WHEN THE RIGHT GAINS STRENGTH, WHICH IS ABRAHAM, THEN THE WAVES DESCEND TO THE DEPTHS. Because of this anger and rage and wrath, they did not get near to one another, THE TWO COLUMNS, BUT KEPT BATTLING until Jacob came, WHO IS THE CENTRAL COLUMN, and silenced and subdued the anger, MEANING THAT HE REDUCED THE FIRST THREE SFIROT OF THE LEFT. He broke the waves of the sea. This is what is written: "and Moses stretched out his hand over the sea; and Hashem caused the sea to go back by a strong east wind..." (Shemot 14:21). What is "a strong east wind (also: 'spirit')"? That is Jacob's spirit, WHO IS THE CENTRAL COLUMN, WHICH IS strong and powerful against THE LEFT COLUMN, breaking the anger of this sea. THEN, "He made the sea dry land, and the waters were divided" (Ibid.), by emptying the sea of the waters of anger. The waters split to the side of Abraham, WHO IS RIGHT, WHICH IS CHESED, and to the side of Jacob, WHO IS THE CENTRAL COLUMN, WHICH IS MERCY. This is what is written: "and the waters were divided," to this side and to that side. Therefore, all the letters IN THIS VERSE OF THE CENTRAL COLUMN are in the right direction.

40. אֵלֵין אַתְוָון בְּאֹרַח מֵישָׁר, בִּסְטַר דְּיַעֲקֹב, וְכָל אִינוּן דְּאָתוּ מִסִּטְרֵיה, וְכַד אָתָא יַעֲקֹב, אִתְחַבַּר בְּאַבְרָהָם, וְנָטַל לְיִצְחָק, וְשָׁארֵי לֵיהּ בְּאֶמְצָעִיתָא. כְּדֵין אִתְקְשַׁר מְהֵימְנוּתָא דָּא בְּדָא וְדָא בְּדָא. וְעַל דָּא, עוֹבָדָא בְּתִקּוּנָא בִּשְׁמָא קַדִּישָׁא בְּזִוּוּגָא דַּאֲבָהָן אִשְׁתְּמוֹדַע, דְּאִיהוּ קְשׁוּרָא חַד, קְשׁוּרָא מְהֵימְנָא, לְמֶהֱוֵי רְתִיכָא שְׁלֵימָתָא. וּבְזִוּוּגָא דַּאֲבָהָן כַּחֲדָא, אִתְעֲבֵיד כֹּלָּא.

40. These letters are in forward direction on the side of Jacob, WHO IS THE CENTRAL COLUMN, and so are all those who come from his side. When

Jacob arrived, he connected to Abraham, WHO IS THE RIGHT COLUMN, and took Isaac, WHO IS THE LEFT COLUMN, and placed him in the middle, BETWEEN HIM AND THE RIGHT COLUMN. Then the Faith was tied between the one and the other, MEANING THAT THE TWO COLUMNS CONNECTED – THE RIGHT COLUMN AND THE LEFT COLUMN, ONE TO THE OTHER – AND ALL THREE TO MALCHUT, THAT IS CALLED 'FAITH'. Therefore, the task of the construction of the Holy Name is made known through the uniting of the Patriarchs, MEANING THE RIGHT WITH THE LEFT, AND THE LEFT WITH THE RIGHT, AND BOTH WITH THE CENTRAL, which is one knot. ALL THREE COLUMNS BECOME ONE, the knot of Faith, AND ALL THREE COLUMNS ARE CONNECTED IN MALCHUT, THAT IS CALLED 'FAITH', to become a whole Chariot – WHICH ARE THREE COLUMNS AND MALCHUT, THE FOUR LEGS OF THE THRONE, WHICH ARE THE THRONE AND THE CHARIOT TO BINAH. Everything is accomplished with the uniting of the Patriarchs together, AS MENTIONED PREVIOUSLY.

41. וְיַדְעִין חַבְרַיָּיא לְמֵיהַךְ בְּאֹרַח מֵישָׁר, לְאַתְקָנָא עוֹבָדִין כַּדְקָא יֵאוּת, וּבִשְׁמָא דָא קְשׁוּרָא דַּאֲבָהָן, אִשְׁתְּכָחוּ אוֹרְחִין לְדִינָא, וּלְרַחֲמֵי, לְסִיּוּעַ, לְחֶסֶד, לִדְחִילוּ, לְאוֹרַיְיתָא, לְחַיֵּי, לְמוֹתָא, לְטָב, לְבִיש. זַכָּאִין אִנּוּן צַדִּיקַיָּיא, דְּיַדְעִין אוֹרְחוֹי דְּאוֹרַיְיתָא, וְיַדְעִין לְמֵיהַךְ בְּאוֹרְחוֹי דְּמַלְכָּא קַדִּישָׁא, זַכָּאִין אִנּוּן בְּעָלְמָא דֵין וּבְעָלְמָא דְּאָתֵי.

41. The friends know how to proceed in the right way, MEANING IN THE CENTRAL COLUMN, to establish the deeds properly. And with this name OF AYIN-BET (72), that is the knot of the Patriarchs, are found ways to Judgment, to Mercy, to help, to kindness, to awe, to Torah, to life, to death, to good and bad. Praised are those virtuous ones who know the manners of the Torah and know to go in the ways of the Holy King. They are praised in this world and the World to Come.

8. The Name of *Ayin-Bet* (72) names

A Synopsis

We hear about the Patriarchs in their travels, their deeds and their knots or unifications. Wherever the Patriarchs are found, the rest of the Righteous are also found. We are given a detailed description of the seven knots in the 72 names, and are told that during the moment that all the steps of the Name 72 are present, the total Faith is present. The Shechinah always travels with the Patriarchs, and when they travel all other levels travel within them. Finally we hear that while Zebulun inherited the Sea of Kineret that is Malchut, Judah took all Malchut and united it in all its own levels.

42. הָא אֲבָהָן בְּמַטְלָנִין, בְּעוֹבָדִין, בְּקִשּׁוּרִין דְּמִתְקַשְּׁרֵי דָּא בְּדָא. וְכַד מִתְחַבְּרָן כַּחֲדָא, לֵית מַאן דְּיָקוּם קַמַּיְיהוּ. וְתָנֵינָן, בַּאֲתָר דַּאֲבָהָתָא אִשְׁתְּכָחוּ, שְׁאָר צַדִּיקַיָּיא מִשְׁתַּכְּחֵי גַּבַּיְיהוּ. וְעַל דָּא שְׁמָא דָּא סָלִיק לִסְטְרִין אַחֲרָנִין מִתְפָּרְשָׁן, אע״ג דְּכֻלְּהוּ נָפְקִין לְאָרְחָא חַד.

42. Behold the Patriarchs in their travels, in deeds TO RAISE FEMALE WATERS, AND in knots, THAT IS, WITH UNIFICATIONS with which they connect that bind one to the other. IN EACH NAME OF THESE 72 NAMES ALL PATRIARCHS ARE BOUND TOGETHER, SINCE THEY ARE THE THREE COLUMNS. When they join together, there is nobody who can stand up to them. We have learned that wherever the Patriarchs are, we also find with them the rest of the righteous, SUCH AS MOSES, AARON AND JOSEPH. Therefore, THIS NAME OF 72 goes in differently explained ways, although all EXPLANATIONS have a similar outcome.

43. שִׁבְעָה קִשּׁוּרִין אִינּוּן, דְּמִתְקַשְּׁרֵי בְּהוּ ג׳ אֲבָהָן, וד׳ אַחֲרָנִין. רֵישָׁא וְאֶמְצָעִיתָא בְּקִשּׁוּרָא חֲדָא. וְאִלֵּין אִינּוּן דְּחַפְרוּ בֵּירָא דְמַיָּא. תִּנְיָינָא זֶה אֶל זֶה, וְאִינּוּן קִשּׁוּרָא חֲדָא, בִּתְלַת יוֹדִין.

43. There are seven knots IN THE 72 NAMES AND TO EVERY INDIVIDUAL KNOT, the three Patriarchs – THAT ARE CHESED, GVURAH AND TIFERET – are connected along with four others – THAT ARE NETZACH, HOD, YESOD AND MALCHUT. HE GOES ON TO EXPLAIN THAT the head OF THE 72 NAMES, THE THREE SFIROT, CHOCHMAH, BINAH AND DA'AT, THAT ARE

REFERRED TO AS 'HEAD', and the center WITHIN THEM, WHICH IS MALCHUT, are tied into one. FOR CHOCHMAH AND BINAH are the ones that dug the water well, WHICH IS MALCHUT, AS IT IS WRITTEN: "THE WELL THAT THE PRINCES DUG OUT" (BEMIDBAR 21:18), WHO ARE CHOCHMAH AND BINAH. THEREFORE, CHOCHMAH, BINAH, DA'AT AND MALCHUT ARE IN ONE KNOT. The second CONNECTION is, "the one...the other" (Shemot 14:20), MEANING THE TWO COLUMNS OF CHESED AND GVURAH, ABOUT WHICH IS SAID, "THE ONE CAME NOT NEAR THE OTHER." They are one knot THAT STARTS with three *Yud's*.

44. תְּלִיתָאָה, שְׁלִימוּ דְּכָל מְהֵימְנוּתָא. רְבִיעָאָה, תְּרֵין קַיְּימִין, דְּגוּפָא קַיְּימָא עֲלַיְיהוּ. חֲמִישָׁאָה, טַב וּבִישׁ, נַהֲרָא דְּנָפִיק אִילָנָא דְּחַיֵּי וּמוֹתָא, עֲמִיקְתָּא דְּכֹלָּא. שְׁתִיתָאָה, דִּינָא בְּרַחֲמֵי. שְׁבִיעָאָה, בְּקַדְמֵיתָא אִתְּמַר, בְּהַהוּא רֵישָׁא דְּאָמְרָן, בְּגִין דְּאִיהוּ אֶמְצָעִיתָא דְּכֹלָּא. וּבְגִין דְּאִיהוּ אֶמְצָעִיתָא דְּכֹלָּא, אִקְרֵי אֲנִי קִיּוּמָא דְּכָל עַנְפִּין דְּמִתְאַחֲדָן מִסַּחֲרָנֵיהּ.

44. The third KNOT IS TIFERET, WHICH IS THE CENTRAL COLUMN, and that is the total perfection of the whole Faith, FOR IT BESTOWS UPON MALCHUT, THAT IS REFERRED TO AS 'FAITH', AND COMPLEMENTS IT. The fourth KNOT is two pillars upon which the body stands, WHICH ARE NETZACH AND HOD, AND ARE CONSIDERED AS NETZACH. The fifth KNOT IS HOD, within which there is good and evil, a river that flows to the Tree of Life and Death, WHICH IS MALCHUT, SINCE HOD BESTOWS UPON MALCHUT. It is the deepest of all, MEANING THAT IT CONTAINS MORE JUDGMENTS THAN ANY OTHER SFIRAH. The sixth KNOT IS YESOD, within which there is Judgment with Mercy. The seventh KNOT, WHICH IS MALCHUT, was ALREADY mentioned in the beginning, THAT IT IS INCLUDED in that head which we spoke of, since it is the center of everything, AS MENTIONED. Since it is the center of everything, it is called 'Aleph-Nun-Yud', which supports all the branches that are united around it.

45. שִׁבְעָה דַּרְגִּין אִלֵּין, מִדַּרְגָּא חֲדָא לְדַרְגָּא חֲדָא, אִשְׁתְּמוֹדְעָא רְתִיכָא חֲדָא, בְּכָל אִינּוּן דְּמִתְאַחֲדָאן בֵּיהּ. וְכֵן מִדַּרְגָּא לְדַרְגָּא, וְכֻלְּהוּ אִתְנַהֲגָן אֲבַתְרֵיהּ דְּהַהוּא דַּרְגָּא דְּאִתְפַּקְּדָא עֲלַיְיהוּ, וְהָא אוֹקִימְנָא מִלֵּי.

45. These seven steps, THE SEVEN KNOTS MENTIONED ABOVE, are from one level to another level, FROM THE FIRST LEVEL TO THE LAST LEVEL. One Chariot is known in them for all the names that unite in it, and also from one level to another – MEANING THAT SIMILARLY EACH INDIVIDUAL LEVEL IS A COMPLETE CHARIOT ON ITS OWN. ALTHOUGH IN EACH STEP THERE ARE THE SAME SEVEN SFIROT – CHESED, GVURAH, TIFERET, NETZACH, HOD, YESOD AND MALCHUT, THE DIFFERENCE BETWEEN THEM IS THAT IN EACH LEVEL, all follow the level that is assigned to them. We have already explained these matters. FOR EXAMPLE, IN THE LEVEL OF CHESED, THERE ARE SEVEN SFIROT – CHESED, GVURAH, TIFERET, NETZACH, HOD, YESOD AND MALCHUT – BUT ALL FOLLOW THE DOMINANT SFIRAH OF CHESED. SIMILARLY, GVURAH HAS ALL THE SEVEN SFIROT – CHESED, GVURAH, TIFERET, NETZACH, HOD, YESOD AND MALCHUT – ALL CARRY ON ACCORDING TO THE DOMINANT SFIRAH OF GVURAH. AND IT IS THE SAME WITH EVERY LEVEL.

‫46. ת"ח, בְּשַׁעֲתָא דְּאִלֵּין דַּרְגִּין מִשְׁתַּכְחֵי, כָּל מְהֵימְנוּתָא אִשְׁתְּכַח,‬
‫וְאִלֵּין שִׁבְעָה עֲנָנִין דְּאַסְחֲרוּ לְהוּ לְיִשְׂרָאֵל. בְּג"כ כַּד נַטְלָא שְׁכִינְתָּא,‬
‫בַּאֲבָהָתָא נַטְלָא. וְכַד אִלֵּין נַטְלִין, כֻּלְּהוּ דַּרְגִּין אַחֲרָנִין נַטְלִין בְּהוּ,‬
‫וּכְדֵין אִתְעַטְּרַת כ"י כַּדְקָא יָאוּת.‬

46. Come and behold: when all these steps OF THE NAME 72 are present, the total Faith is present, MEANING THE WHOLENESS OF MALCHUT. These SEVEN KNOTS are seven clouds that surrounded Yisrael AND THEY TOTALED TEN, SINCE CHESED INCLUDES THE FIRST THREE SFIROT, AS KNOWN. Therefore, when the Shechinah travels, she travels with the Patriarchs, THAT ARE CHESED, GVURAH AND TIFERET, WHICH ARE THE SECRET OF THE NAME 72. FOR when they travel, all other levels travel within them, AS MENTIONED, and then the Congregation of Yisrael, WHICH IS MALCHUT, is adorned properly.

‫47. ת"ח, זְבוּלֻן דְּקָאַמְרָן יָרִית יָם כִּנֶּרֶת. יָם כִּנֶּרֶת סְתָם, וְהָכִי אִתְחֲזֵי.‬
‫אִי הָכִי יְהוּדָה מַה חוּלְקָא אִית בֵּיהּ, אֶלָּא יְהוּדָה נָטַל מַלְכוּתָא כֹּלָּא,‬
‫וְאִתְאֲחִיד בֵּיהּ בְּכָל סִטְרִין.‬

47. Come and behold: Zebulun, as we spoke, inherited the Sea of Galilee, an unspecified Sea of Galilee, WHICH IS MALCHUT, and so it should be. HE ASKS: If so, Judah, OF WHOM IT WAS SAID THAT HE IS ALWAYS MALCHUT, what part has he got in it, IN MALCHUT THAT ZEBULUN HAS ALREADY TAKEN? HE REPLIES: It is just that Judah took the whole Malchut and united in it all its own levels, BOTH SMALLNESS AND GREATNESS, IN THE SECRET OF *DALET-HEI* OF JUDAH. *DALET* INDICATES THE SMALLNESS BEFORE RECEIVING OVER IT THE MALE, AND THE *HEI* INDICATES THE GREATNESS. THIS IS NOT THE CASE WITH ZEBULUN. HE SIMPLY TOOK THE ASPECT OF MALCHUT WHEN SHE WAS CALLED 'THE SEA OF GALILEE', IN THE SECRET OF THE BATTLES IN IT.

9. The inner altar and the candlestick

A Synopsis

Rabbi Shimon says that the candlestick above, Malchut, and all its lamps, the Sfirot, all shine through Aaron, since he readied the candlestick. He compares the twelve princes of the twelve tribes to the twelve permutations of Yud Hei Vav Hei in Zeir Anpin. The candlestick was assigned with the seven lamps corresponding to the seven Sfirot. It stands through a sign and was produced through a miracle. We learn what the inner altar and the outer altar are, and how abundance flows from the inner to the outer. Incense is the connection of everything.

48. רְבִּי אֶלְעָזָר אָמַר, הַאי פַּרְשָׁתָא, הָא אִתְּמַר עוֹבָדָא, דִּמְנַרְתָּא וְתִקּוּנָהָא, וְכָל מַה דְּבָה, אֲמַאי הָכִי זִמְנָא אַחֲרָא. אֶלָּא כֵּיוָן דִּנְשִׂיאִים קְרִיבוּ קוּרְבְּנָא דְמַדְבְּחָא, וְכָל תִּקּוּנָא דְּאִתְחֲזֵי לֵיהּ, אָתָא קְרָא וְאִשְׁתָּעֵי עוֹבָדָא דִּמְנַרְתָּא, דְּהִיא תִּקּוּנָא עַל יְדָא דְּאַהֲרֹן, דְּהָא לְעֵילָא מְנַרְתָּא, וְכָל בּוֹצִינִין דִּילָהּ, עַל יְדָא דְּאַהֲרֹן נַהֲרִין כֹּלָּא.

48. Rabbi Elazar says in relation to this portion: All the tasks of the candlestick and all the required preparations of it were already mentioned. Why is it REPEATED here a second time? HE RESPONDS: It is just that once the princes have offered their sacrifices on the altar and the necessary services required for it, the Scripture comes to relate the story of the candlestick that was prepared by Aaron, since the candlestick above, WHICH IS MALCHUT, and all its lamps, THAT ARE THE SFIROT, all shine through Aaron.

49. ת"ח, מַדְבְּחָא תְּרֵיסַר נְשִׂיאִין הֲווֹ, לְחַנְּכָא לֵיהּ, וּלְאַתְקְנָא לֵיהּ, וְהָא אוּקְמוּהָ תְּרֵיסַר אִינוּן שְׁבָטִין, לְד׳ סִטְרִין, ד׳ דְּגָלִים, וְכֻלְהוּ תְּרֵיסַר. וְכֹלָּא כְּגַוְונָא דִלְעֵילָא. מְנַרְתָּא אִתְמְנֵי בְּשִׁבְעָה בּוֹצִינִין, לְאַדְלְקָא עַל יְדָא דְּכַהֲנָא, וְכֹלָּא כְּגַוְונָא דִלְעֵילָא. וּמְנַרְתָּא, עַל אָת קַיְּימָא, וּבְנִיסָא אִתְעֲבֵידַת, וְהָא אוּקְמוּהָ בְּעוֹבָדָא דִּמְנַרְתָּא.

49. Come and behold the altar. Twelve princes were there to arrange and prepare it, and it was explained that the twelve represent the tribes to the

four directions with four standards, SINCE THREE TRIBES WERE ASSIGNED TO EACH STANDARD and all TOGETHER were twelve. Everything was similar to above. THE ALTAR ABOVE, WHICH IS MALCHUT, RECEIVES FROM THE TWELVE PERMUTATIONS OF YUD HEI VAV HEI IN ZEIR ANPIN, WHICH ARE THE SECRET OF CHOCHMAH AND BINAH, TIFERET AND MALCHUT, IN EACH OF THE THREE COLUMNS, TOTALING TWELVE. The candlestick was assigned with the seven lamps to be lit by a priest, all similar to above, CORRESPONDING TO ZEIR ANPIN THAT ILLUMINATES CHESED, GVURAH, TIFERET, NETZACH, HOD, YESOD AND MALCHUT OF MALCHUT. The candlestick stands by means of a sign and was produced by a miracle, FOR IT WAS MADE ON ITS OWN. This has been explained in relation to the making of the candlestick.

50. וּמַדְבֵּחַ פְּנִימָאָה, וּמְנַרְתָּא, קַיְימֵי כַּחֲדָא, לְחֶדְוָותָא דְּכֹלָּא. דִּכְתִיב שֶׁמֶן וּקְטֹרֶת יְשַׂמַּח לֵב. וְאוֹקִימְנָא דִּתְרֵי מַדְבְּחָן הֲווֹ, חַד פְּנִימָאָה דְּכֹלָּא, וְהַאי קַיְימָא לְחֶדְוָותָא. וְחַד לְבַר, לְקָרְבָא קָרְבְּנִין. וּמֵהַאי פְּנִימָאָה נָפִיק לְהַאי דִּלְבַר, וּמַאן דְּחָמֵי וְיִסְתַּכַּל, יִנְדַּע חָכְמְתָא עִלָּאָה, רָזָא דְּמִלָּה אֲדֹנָי יְדֹוָד. וְעַל דָּא לָא אִתְקְרַב קְטָרְתָּא, אֶלָּא בְּשַׁעֲתָא דְּשֶׁמֶן אִשְׁתְּכַח.

50. The inner altar and the candlestick are together for everyone's happiness, as is written: "ointment and perfume (or 'incese') rejoice the heart" (Mishlei 27:9). OIL IS THE CANDLESTICK THAT IS MALCHUT THAT RECEIVES FROM CHOCHMAH, AND INCENSE IS THE INNER ALTAR. We have explained that there were two altars. One is innermost, AND THAT IS THE ALTAR FOR INCENSE and it is for happiness, AND CORRESPONDS TO BINAH. The outer one, THAT IS THE EXTERIOR ALTAR, is for sacrificial offerings, WHICH CORRESPONDS TO MALCHUT. Abundance flows from the inner altar, WHICH CORRESPONDS TO BINAH, to the one outside, WHICH IS MALCHUT. Whoever gazes and observes, understands and knows the uppermost Wisdom, that the secret of the matter is Adonai Yud Hei Vav Hei, SINCE THE INNER ALTAR IS YUD HEI VAV HEI, BINAH, AND THE OUTER IS ADONAI, MALCHUT. Therefore, incense is offered only when there was oil. THAT IS THE SECRET OF ONE UNIFICATION OF CHOCHMAH AND BINAH.

51. אַשְׁכַּחְנָא בְּסִפְרָא דִשְׁלֹמֹה מַלְכָּא, קְטֹרֶת הוּא לְחֶדְוָה, וּלְסַלְּקָא מוֹתָנָא. מַאי טַעֲמָא. בְּגִין דְּדִינָא מֵהַאי דִּלְבַר אִשְׁתְּכַח, וְחֶדְוָותָא וְחַדוּ וְקִשׁוּרָא דִּנְהִירוּ, מֵהַהוּא פְּנִימָאָה, דְּכָל חֵידוּ בֵּיהּ קַיְימָא. וְכַד הַאי אִתְעַר, כָּל דִּינָא אִסְתַּלָּק מֵהַאי, וְלָא יָכִיל לְמֶעְבַּד דִּינָא. וּבְג"כ קְטֹרֶת קַיְימָא לְבַטְּלָא מוֹתָנָא, וְעַל דָּא, קְטֹרֶת קְשִׁירוּ הוּא דְּכֹלָּא, וְדָא אִתְקְרִיב בְּהַהוּא פְּנִימָאָה. זַכָּאִין אִינּוּן יִשְׂרָאֵל בְּעָלְמָא דֵין וּבְעָלְמָא דְּאָתֵי, עֲלַיְיהוּ כְּתִיב וַיֹּאמֶר לִי עַבְדִּי אַתָּה יִשְׂרָאֵל וְגוֹ'.

51. I discovered in the book of King Solomon that incense is for happiness and to eradicate death. What is the reason? It is because Judgment is prevalent from the outer ALTAR, WHICH IS MALCHUT. Happiness and gladness and the connection of light come from the inner ALTAR where all rejoicing exists, WHICH IS BINAH. When this is roused, THAT IS THE INNER, all Judgment disappears from here, FROM THE OUTER, and no Judgment can be executed. Therefore, the business of incense, WHICH IS THE SECRET OF THE INNER ONE, is to void death – SINCE WHEN THE INNER, WHICH IS THE SECRET OF BINAH, IS AWAKENED BY INCENSE, THE OUTER, WHICH IS MALCHUT, IS NOT CAPABLE OF CARRYING OUT JUDGMENT. Therefore, incense is the connection of everything and it is offered in the inner ALTAR, WHERE ALL HAPPINESS EXISTS. Praised are Yisrael in this world and the World to Come. About them, it is written: "and said to me, 'You are My servant, Yisrael, in whom I will be glorified'" (Yeshayah 49:3).

10. One who comes from the side of Judgment must not grow hair

A Synopsis

We hear that whoever comes from the side of Judgment, like the Levites, must not grow hair since that increases Judgment in the world. All powers and corrections come from the priests, who are from the right side. And the body that is the Central Column is the essence of everything, connecting left and right.

52. קַח אֶת הַלְוִיִּם וְגוֹ', הָא אוּקְמוּהָ דְּבָעֵי לְדַכְּאָה לוֹן, וּלְאַמְשָׁכָא לוֹן, לְאִתְקַשְּׁרָא בְּאַתְרַיְיהוּ, בְּגִין דְּאִינּוּן דְּרוֹעָא שְׂמָאלָא, וְסִטְרָא דְּדִינָא, וְכָל מַאן דְּאָתֵי מִסִּטְרָא דְּדִינָא, בָּעֵי דְּלָא יַרְבֵּי שַׂעֲרָא, בְּגִין דְּאַסְגֵי דִינָא בְּעָלְמָא. וְעַל דָּא אִתְּתָא כְּהַאי גַּוְונָא, דְּלָא יִתְחֲזֵי שַׂעֲרָא לְבַר, וּבַעְיָיא לְאִתְחַפְּיָיא רֵישָׁה, וּלְכַסֵּי שַׂעֲרָהָא, וְאוֹקִימְנָא, וְהָא אִתְּמַר. וּכְדֵין אִתְבָּרְכָן כָּל אִינּוּן דְּאַתְיָין מִסִּטְרָא דְּדִינָא. וְעַל דָּא בְּלֵיוָאֵי כְּתִיב, וְכֹה תַעֲשֶׂה לָהֶם לְטַהֲרָם וְגוֹ', וְהֶעֱבִירוּ תַעַר וְגוֹ'. וְאִתְּמַר לֵיוָאֵי לָא סַלְּקִין לְאַתְרַיְיהוּ, עַד דְּיָרִים לוֹן כַּהֲנָא, בְּגִין דִּימִינָא מַדְבַּר תָּדִיר לִשְׂמָאלָא.

52. "Take the Levites..." (Bemidbar 8:6). It has already been explained that there is a requirement to cleanse them and draw them to connect at their place, IN THE LEFT COLUMN, since they are from the left arm OF GVURAH OF ZEIR ANPIN and the side of Judgment. Whoever comes from the side of Judgment must not grow hair, since it increases Judgment in the world. Consequently, a woman similarly is required to attend to it that her hair should not be visible outside, and she must cover her head and veil her hair. This has been explained and we have already learned it. All those that come from the side of Judgment are then blessed. Therefore, it is written of the Levites: "and thus shall you do to them, to cleanse them...and let them shave..." (Ibid. 7). We have learned that the Levites cannot reach to their assigned place until the priest uplifts them, because the right always leads the left.

53. ר"שׁ אָמַר, בְּיוֹמָא דְּסַלְּקִין לֵיוָאֵי בְּדוּכְתַּיְיהוּ, בִּתְרֵין פָּרִים. מ"ט פָּרִים. אֶלָּא אִינְהוּ כְּפָרִים, לְקַבְּלָא בִּשְׂמָאלָא לְהַאי פָּרָה דְּאִקְרֵי פָּרָה

אֲדוּמָה. כַּהֲנָא כָּל חֵילָא וְכָל תִּקוּנָא בֵּיה תַּלְיָיא, בְּגִין דְּכָל חֵילָא
דְּגוּפָא בִּדְרוֹעָא יְמִינָא קַיְימָא. וְעַל דָּא כַּהֲנָא דְּרוֹעָא דְּיִשְׂרָאֵל כֻּלְּהוּ
הֲוֵי. וּבֵיה קַיְימָא לְאַתְקְנָא כֹּלָא וּלְאַתְקְנָא עָלְמָא וְעִם כָּל דָּא, לָא
אִשְׁתְּכַח בִּלְחוֹדוֹי, אֶלָּא בְּגוּפָא וּשְׂמָאלָא, וְגוּפָא עִקְרָא הוּא דְכֹלָּא.

53. Rabbi Shimon said: The day that the Levites reached their place, THEY OFFERED FOR SACRIFICE two oxen. Why oxen? HE RESPONDS: They are like oxen, MEANING IN THE LEFT COLUMN, IN THE SECRET OF, "THE FACE OF AN OX ON THE LEFT SIDE" (YECHEZKEL 1:10), to receive with the left this cow that is called a 'red heifer', MEANING MALCHUT OF THE LEFT SIDE. Every power and every correction depends on the priest, WHO IS THE RIGHT COLUMN, since the whole power of the body is in the right arm. Therefore, the priest was the right arm of all Yisrael, by which he was ready to arrange everything and sustain the world. In spite of all this, THE RIGHT COLUMN is not alone, but CONNECTED to the body and to the left, THAT IS, WITH THE TWO COLUMNS – CENTRAL AND LEFT. And the body, THAT IS THE CENTRAL COLUMN, is the essence of everything, SINCE IT UNITES THE TWO COLUMNS AND COMPLETES THEM, AND ALSO INCLUDES THEM.

11. "This is that which belongs to the Levites"

A Synopsis

Rabbi Shimon says that the Levite must serve from age 25 to age fifty, after which his strength is declining and his voice is not as strong. The place to which the Levite is assigned is from strong judgment and must not be flawed by any weakness.

54. זֹאת אֲשֶׁר לַלְוִיִּם וְגוֹ'. ת"ח, לֵיוָאָה בַּר חָמֵשׁ וְעֶשְׂרִין שְׁנִין סָלִיק לְדוּכְתֵּיהּ וְאִתְעֲטַּר. וְחָמֵשׁ וְעֶשְׂרִין יִפְלַח עַד דְּסָלִיק לְדַרְגָּא דְּחַמְשִׁין. כַּד סָלִיק לְהַאי דַּרְגָּא דְּחַמְשִׁין שְׁנִין וּלְהָלְאָה, נָחִית מִן תּוּקְפָּא דְּאֶשָּׁא דְּבֵיהּ, וְכֵיוָן דְּאֶשָּׁא וַחֲמִימוּתָא אִתְקָרַר, הָא פָּגִים לְהַהוּא אֲתָר דְּאִתְקְשַׁר בֵּיהּ.

54. "This is that which belongs to the Levites" (Bemidbar 8:24). Come and behold: the Levite, who is 25 years old, reaches his place and is adorned. He will do service work for 25 years until he reaches the grade of fifty. When he reaches the grade of the fiftieth year and onward, he declines from the strength of fire within him. Since the fire and heat get cooler, he causes damage to the place to which he is connected, WHICH IS THE LEFT.

55. וְעוֹד, דְּקָלָא דִּזְמָרָא לָא אִתְקְשַׁר בַּהֲדֵיהּ כָּל כָּךְ. וְקָלָא בָּעֵי דְּלָא יִתְפְּגַם, אֶלָּא בָּעֵי לְאִתְתַּקְּפָא, דְּהָא בַּאֲתָר דְּדִינָא תַּקִּיף קַיְימָא, וְלָא בְּחַלְשָׁא. וּבְג"כ בָּעֵי דְּלָא יַפְגִים הַהוּא אֲתָר דְּאִתְקְשַׁר בֵּיהּ, דְּאִיהוּ דִּינָא תַּקִּיפָא, וְלָא חַלְשָׁא, וְעַל דָּא לָא בָּעֵי לְאַחֲזָאָה חוּלְשָׁתָא כְּלָל בְּכָל סִטְרִין. זַכָּאָה הוּא ב"נ דְּאִשְׁתַּדַּל בְּאוֹרַיְיתָא, וְיִנְדַּע אוֹרְחוֹי דְּקוּדְשָׁא בְּרִיךְ הוּא, וְלָא סָטֵי לִימִינָא וְלִשְׂמָאלָא, דִּכְתִיב כִּי יְשָׁרִים דַּרְכֵי יְיָ'.

55. In addition, AFTER FIFTY YEARS, the singing voice is no longer that well connected with him, SINCE IT BECOMES A LITTLE WEAKER. It is necessary that this voice should not be flawed, but rather get stronger, since it stands in a place of strong Judgment and not in a weak one. Therefore, it is important not to degrade that place, THAT IS THE LEFT, to which he is

assigned, since it is powerful Judgment and not feeble. It is necessary not to show any feebleness in any direction. Praised is the man that toils in the Torah, knows the ways of the Holy One, blessed be He, and does not deviate to the right or the left. It is written: "for the ways of Hashem are right" (Hoshea 14:10), MEANING ONE WHO FOLLOWS STEADILY IN THE CENTRAL COLUMN.

12. The Pesach at its appointed season and second Pesach

A Synopsis

Rabbi Shimon explains why God spoke to Moses in the wilderness of Sinai about Pesach since He had already told them about it in Egypt. He says that if the Torah had come simply to relate simple tales we could produce a better Torah today; it is obvious that everything in the Torah contains higher secrets. The stories told therein are merely its garment or dress, the same as the body is the garment for the person who comes to earth. He says that the soul that is the splendor of Yisrael that is Zeir Anpin is the actual soul of the Torah at which the sages look.

56. וַיְדַבֵּר יְיָ׳ אֶל מֹשֶׁה בְּמִדְבַּר סִינַי וְגוֹ׳. א״ר אַבָּא, מ״ט אַזְהַר לְהוֹן הָכָא עַל פִּסְחָא, וְהָא אִתְּמַר לְהוֹ בְּמִצְרַיִם. אֶלָּא בַּשָּׁנָה הַשֵּׁנִית הֲוָה, דְּיִשְׂרָאֵל חָשִׁיבוּ דְּהָא פֶּסַח לָאו אִיהוּ אֶלָּא בְּמִצְרַיִם, וְכֵיוָן דְּעַבְדוּ לֵיהּ זִמְנָא חֲדָא בְּמִצְרַיִם, חֲשִׁיבוּ דְּלָא אִצְטְרִיךְ יַתִּיר. אָתָא קוּדְשָׁא בְּרִיךְ הוּא וְאַזְהַר לוֹן עֲלֵיהּ, דְּלָא יַחְשְׁבוּן דְּהָא קָא עָבַר זִמְנֵיהּ בְּמִצְרַיִם, וְאֵל יִצְטְרִיךְ. בְּגִין כַּךְ בְּמִדְבַּר סִינַי בַּשָּׁנָה הַשֵּׁנִית, לְאַתְקָנָא לְהוּ לְדָרֵי דָרִין.

56. "And Hashem spoke to Moses in the wilderness of Sinai..." (Bemidbar 9:1). Rabbi Aba said: What is the reason that He exhorted them here about the Pesach? It was already told to them in Egypt. HE RESPONDS: This is because it was the second year and Yisrael thought that it only applied in Egypt. Since they had already performed it in Egypt once, they assumed that it was no longer necessary. The Holy One, blessed be He, came and cautioned them about this, so that they should not think that its time had passed in Egypt and that it was not needed ANY LONGER. Therefore, HE EXHORTED THEM about it "in the wilderness of Sinai...in...the second year," to institute PESACH for the generations to come.

57. וְאע״ג דְּהָא אַזְהַר לְהוּ בְּמִצְרַיִם, הַשְׁתָּא פָּקִיד לוֹן זִמְנָא אַחֲרָא, בְּהַהוּא אֲתָר דְּכָל פִּקּוּדִין דְּאוֹרַיְיתָא בֵּיהּ אִתְיְהִיבוּ. וע״ד בַּשָּׁנָה הַשֵּׁנִית. מַאי בַּשָּׁנָה הַשֵּׁנִית בַּחֹדֶשׁ הָרִאשׁוֹן. אֶלָּא רָזָא עִלָּאָה הִיא, חַד שָׁנָה. וְחַד חֹדֶשׁ. מַה בֵּין הַאי לְהַאי. חֹדֶשׁ: דָּא סִיהֲרָא. שָׁנָה: דָּא

שִׁמְשָׁא, דְּנָהִיר לְסִיהֲרָא. וּכְדֵין הֲוָה בְּזִמְנָא דְּכָל פִּקּוּדִין דְּאוֹרַיְיתָא אִתְמְסָרוּ בֵּיהּ.

57. ANOTHER EXPLANATION. Although He exhorted them about that in Egypt, He commanded them a second time in the place where all the commandments and laws of the Torah were given. Therefore, "in...the second year..." HE ASKS: What is the meaning of: "in the first month of the second year"? NAMELY, WHAT DOES THIS ALLUDE TO? HE REPLIES: This is a lofty secret. THERE IS that which is referred to as a year, AND THERE IS that which is referred to as a month. What is the difference between them? Month is the moon, MEANING MALCHUT, while a year is the sun, ZEIR ANPIN, which illuminates the moon. "IN THE FIRST MONTH OF THE SECOND YEAR," POINTS TO THE UNION OF ZEIR ANPIN AND MALCHUT, WHICH ARE CALLED 'YEAR' AND 'MONTH', IN THE PLACE OF THE SINAI DESERT. THAT IS THE SECOND UNION AFTER THE EXODUS OF EGYPT. This was during the time that all the commandments of the Torah were passed on to them, SINCE THROUGH THE UNION OF MALE AND FEMALE IN THE DESERT OF SINAI, ALL THE COMMANDMENTS OF THE TORAH WERE GIVEN.

58. ר"ש אָמַר, וַוי לְהַהוּא ב"נ דְּאָמַר, דְּהָא אוֹרַיְיתָא אָתָא לְאַחֲזָאָה סִפּוּרִין בְּעָלְמָא, וּמִלִּין דְּהֶדְיוֹטֵי. דְּאִי הָכִי, אֲפִילוּ בְּזִמְנָא דָּא, אֲנַן יַכְלִין לְמֶעְבַּד אוֹרַיְיתָא, בְּמִלִּין דְּהֶדְיוֹטֵי, וּבְשִׁבְחָא יַתִּיר מִכֻּלְּהוּ. אִי לְאַחֲזָאָה מִלָּה דְּעָלְמָא, אֲפִילוּ אִינּוּן קַפְסִירֵי דְּעָלְמָא, אִית בֵּינַיְיהוּ מִלִּין עִלָּאִין יַתִּיר. אִי הָכִי נֵזִיל אֲבַתְרַיְיהוּ, וְנַעֲבֵיד מִנַּיְיהוּ אוֹרַיְיתָא, כְּהַאי גַּוְונָא. אֶלָּא כָּל מִלִּין דְּאוֹרַיְיתָא, מִלִּין עִלָּאִין אִינּוּן, וְרָזִין עִלָּאִין.

58. Rabbi Shimon says: Woe to the man who says that the Torah came to relate stories, simply and plainly, and simpleton tales ABOUT ESAU AND LABAN AND THE LIKE. If it was so, even at the present day we could produce a Torah from simplistic matters, and perhaps even nicer ones than those. If THE TORAH CAME to exemplify worldly matters, even the rulers of the world have among them things that are superior. If so, let us follow them and produce from them a Torah in the same manner. It must be that all items in the Torah are of a superior nature and are uppermost secrets.

59. ת״ח, עָלְמָא עִלָּאָה וְעָלְמָא תַּתָּאָה בְּחַד מַתְקְלָא אִתְקָלוּ. יִשְׂרָאֵל לְתַתָּא, מַלְאֲכֵי עִלָּאֵי לְעֵילָא. מַלְאֲכֵי עִלָּאֵי כְּתִיב בְּהוּ, עוֹשֶׂה מַלְאָכָיו רוּחוֹת. בְּשַׁעֲתָא דְּנַחְתִּין לְתַתָּא, מִתְלַבְּשֵׁי בִּלְבוּשָׁא דְּהַאי עָלְמָא. וְאִי לָאו מִתְלַבְּשֵׁי בִּלְבוּשָׁא בְּגַוְונָא דְּהַאי עָלְמָא, לָא יַכְלִין לְמֵיקַם בְּהַאי עָלְמָא, וְלָא סָבִיל לוֹן עָלְמָא. וְאִי בְּמַלְאֲכֵי כָּךְ, אוֹרַיְיתָא דְּבָרָא לְהוּ, וּבָרָא עָלְמִין כֻּלְּהוּ, וְקַיְימִין בְּגִינָהּ, עאכ״ו כֵּיוָן דְּנַחְתַּת לְהַאי עָלְמָא, אִי לָאו דְּמִתְלַבְּשָׁא בְּהָנֵי לְבוּשִׁין דְּהַאי עָלְמָא, לָא יָכִיל עָלְמָא לְמִסְבַּל.

59. Come and behold: the world above and the world below are measured with one scale. Yisrael below CORRESPOND TO the lofty angels above. It is written about the lofty angels: "Who makes the winds His messengers" (Tehilim 104:4). When they go down, they don with the vestments of this world. If they had not acquired the dress for this world, they would not be able to exist in this world, and the world would not be able to stand them. And if this is so for the angels, how much more so is it for the Torah that created these MESSENGERS and all the worlds, that exist due to it. Once it came down to this world, if it had not donned all these garments of this world, WHICH ARE THE STORIES AND SIMPLISTIC TALES, the world would not have been able to tolerate it.

60. וע״ד הַאי סִפּוּר דְּאוֹרַיְיתָא, לְבוּשָׁא דְּאוֹרַיְיתָא. אִיהוּ. מַאן דְּחָשִׁיב דְּהַהוּא לְבוּשָׁא אִיהוּ אוֹרַיְיתָא מַמָּשׁ, וְלָא מִלָּה אַחֲרָא, תִּיפַּח רוּחֵיהּ, וְלָא יְהֵא לֵיהּ חוּלָקָא בְּעָלְמָא דְּאָתֵי. בְּגִין כָּךְ אָמַר דָּוִד, גַּל עֵינַי וְאַבִּיטָה נִפְלָאוֹת מִתּוֹרָתֶךָ. מַה דִּתְחוֹת לְבוּשָׁא דְּאוֹרַיְיתָא.

60. Therefore, this story of the Torah is the mantle of the Torah. He who thinks that this mantle is the actual essence of the Torah and that nothing else is in there, let him breathe his last and let him have no portion in the World to Come. Therefore, David said, "open my eyes, that I may behold wondrous things out of Your Torah" (Tehilim 119:18); THAT IS, LOOK what lies under that garment of the Torah.

61. ת״ח, אִית לְבוּשָׁא דְּאִתְחֲזֵי לְכֹלָּא, וְאִינוּן טִפְּשִׁין כַּד חָמָאן לְבַר

נָשׁ בִּלְבוּשָׁא דְּאִתְחֲזֵי לוֹן שַׁפִּירָא, לָא מִסְתַּכְּלִין יַתִּיר. חֲשִׁיבוּ דְּהַהוּא לְבוּשָׁא, גּוּפָא, וַחֲשִׁיבוּ דְּגוּפָא, נִשְׁמְתָא.

61. Come and behold: There is a dress that is visible to everyone. The fools, when they see a person dressed beautifully, WHO APPEARS TO THEM DISTINGUISHED BY HIS CLOTHING, do not observe any further. THEY JUDGE HIM ACCORDING TO HIS DISTINGUISHED APPAREL and consider the dress as the body OF MAN, and the body OF THE PERSON LIKE his soul.

62. כְּהַאי גַּוְונָא אוֹרַיְיתָא, אִית לָהּ גּוּפָא, וְאִינּוּן פְּקוּדֵי אוֹרַיְיתָא, דְּאִקְרוּן גּוּפֵי תּוֹרָה. הַאי גּוּפָא מִתְלַבְּשָׁא בִּלְבוּשִׁין, דְּאִינּוּן סִפּוּרִין דְּהַאי עָלְמָא. טִפְּשִׁין דְּעָלְמָא, לָא מִסְתַּכְּלֵי אֶלָּא בְּהַהוּא לְבוּשָׁא, דְּאִיהוּ סִפּוּר דְּאוֹרַיְיתָא, וְלָא יַדְעֵי יַתִּיר, וְלָא מִסְתַּכְּלֵי בְּמָה דְּאִיהוּ תְּחוֹת הַהוּא לְבוּשָׁא. אִינּוּן דְּיַדְעִין יַתִּיר, לָא מִסְתַּכְּלָן בִּלְבוּשָׁא, אֶלָּא בְּגוּפָא, דְּאִיהוּ תְּחוֹת הַהוּא לְבוּשָׁא. חַכִּימִין עַבְדֵי דְּמַלְכָּא עִלָּאָה, אִינּוּן דְּקַיְימוּ בְּטוּרָא דְּסִינַי, לָא מִסְתַּכְּלֵי אֶלָּא בְּנִשְׁמְתָא, דְּאִיהִי עִקָּרָא דְּכֹלָּא אוֹרַיְיתָא מַמָּשׁ. וּלְזִמְנָא דְּאָתֵי, זְמִינִין לְאִסְתַּכְּלָא בְּנִשְׁמְתָא דְּנִשְׁמְתָא דְּאוֹרַיְיתָא.

62. Similar to this is the Torah. It has a body, which is composed of the commandments of the Torah that are called the 'body of the Torah'. This body is clothed with garments, which are stories of this world. The ignorant look only at that dress, which is the story in the Torah, and are not aware of anything more. They do not look at what lies beneath that dress. Those who know more do not look at the dress, but rather at the body beneath that dress. The wise, the sages, the servants of the Loftiest King, those that stood at Mount Sinai, look only at the soul OF THE TORAH, which is the essence of everything, the real Torah. In the time to come, they will look at the soul, the soul of the Torah.

63. ת"ח, הָכִי נָמֵי לְעֵילָּא, אִית לְבוּשָׁא, וְגוּפָא, וְנִשְׁמְתָא, וְנִשְׁמְתָא לְנִשְׁמְתָא. שְׁמַיָּא וְחֵילֵיהוֹן. אִלֵּין אִינּוּן לְבוּשָׁא. וּכְנֶסֶת יִשְׂרָאֵל, דָּא גּוּפָא, דִּמְקַבְּלָא לְנִשְׁמְתָא, דְּאִיהִי תִּפְאֶרֶת יִשְׂרָאֵל. וע"ד אִיהוּ גּוּפָא

לְנִשְׁמָתָא. נִשְׁמָתָא דְּאֲמָרָן דָּא תִּפְאֶרֶת יִשְׂרָאֵל, דְּאִיהִי אוֹרַיְיתָא
מַמָּשׁ. וְנִשְׁמְתָא לְנִשְׁמָתָא, דָּא אִיהוּ עַתִּיקָא קַדִּישָׁא. וְכֹלָּא אָחִיד דָּא
בְּדָא.

63. Come and behold: it is also like that above. There exists an apparel, a body, a soul, and a soul of the soul. The heavens and their legions are the apparel, and the Congregation of Yisrael, WHICH IS MALCHUT, is the body that receives the soul, which is the splendor of Yisrael, MEANING ZEIR ANPIN. Therefore, MALCHUT is a body for the soul, SINCE ZEIR ANPIN IS DONNED WITH HER, LIKE THE SOUL IN A BODY. The soul that we mentioned, which is the splendor of Yisrael, is the actual Torah, MEANING THE SOUL OF THE TORAH AT WHICH THE SAGES LOOK. It is the soul of the soul that is Atika Kadisha, ON WHOM THEY WILL LOOK IN THE FUTURE TO COME, AS MENTIONED. Everything is interconnected. ATIKA KADISHA IS CLOTHED WITH ZEIR ANPIN, ZEIR ANPIN IS CLOTHED WITH MALCHUT, AND MALCHUT IS CLOTHED WITH THE WORLDS BRIYAH, YETZIRAH, ASIYAH AND ALL THEIR LEGIONS.

64. וַוי לְאִינּוּן חַיָּיבַיָּא, דְּאֲמְרֵי דְּאוֹרַיְיתָא לָאו אִיהִי אֶלָּא סִפּוּרָא
בְּעָלְמָא, וְאִינּוּן מִסְתַּכְּלֵי בִּלְבוּשָׁא דָּא וְלָא יַתִּיר. זַכָּאִין אִינּוּן
צַדִּיקַיָּיא, דְּמִסְתַּכְּלֵי בְּאוֹרַיְיתָא כַּדְקָא יָאוּת. חַמְרָא לָא יָתִיב אֶלָּא
בְּקַנְקָן. כַּךְ אוֹרַיְיתָא לָא יָתִיב אֶלָּא בִּלְבוּשָׁא דָּא. וְע"ד לָא בָּעֵי
לְאִסְתַּכְּלָא, אֶלָּא בְּמָה דְּאִית תְּחוֹת לְבוּשָׁא. וְע"ד כָּל אִינּוּן מִלִּין, וְכָל
אִינּוּן סִפּוּרִין, לְבוּשִׁין אִינּוּן.

64. Woe to the wicked who say that the Torah is merely a story and nothing more, for they look at the dress and no further. Praised are the righteous, who look properly at the Torah. Wine lasts only if it is in a jug. Similarly, the Torah does not endure, except in this mantle. Therefore, there is no need to look except at what is beneath the mantle. That is why all these matters and all these stories are garments.

13. The second Pesach

A Synopsis

We hear about the ordinance to keep Pesach at the correct time and about the inner meaning of what happens if it is kept a month later due to uncleanness or traveling.

‎65. וַיַּעֲשׂוּ בְנֵי יִשְׂרָאֵל אֶת הַפֶּסַח בְּמוֹעֲדוֹ מַאי וַיַּעֲשׂוּ. אָמַר רְבִּי יוֹסֵי, הָא אִתְּמַר, כָּל מַאן דְּאַחְזֵי עוֹבָדָא לְתַתָּא כַּדְקָא יֵאוּת, כְּאִילוּ עָבֵיד לֵיהּ לְעֵילָא. דְּהָא בְּגִינֵיהּ אִתְּעַר הַהוּא מִלָּה, כִּבְיָכוֹל, כְּאִילוּ הוּא עָבֵיד לֵיהּ, וְהָא אִתְּמַר.

65. "Let the children of Yisrael also keep the Pesach at its appointed season" (Bemidbar 9:2). HE ASKS: What is "keep"? IT SHOULD HAVE SAID, 'EAT'. Rabbi Yosi said: Have we not learned that whoever shows a proper worthy action below is as if he made that above. Due to him, this matter is roused ABOVE, and it is as if he actually made it, as we have already learned.

‎66. אִישׁ אִישׁ כִּי יִהְיֶה טָמֵא וְגוֹ'. אִישׁ אִישׁ תְּרֵי זִמְנֵי, אֲמַאי, אֶלָּא אִישׁ דְּהוּא אִישׁ, וְיִתְחֲזֵי לְקַבְּלָא נִשְׁמָתָא עִלָּאָה, וְהוּא פָּגִים גַּרְמֵיהּ. דְּלָא שַׁרְיָיא עֲלוֹי שְׁכִינְתָּא עִלָּאָה. מ"ט. בְּגִין דְּאִיהוּ גָּרִים, וְהוּא מְסָאֵב לֵיהּ לְגַרְמֵיהּ. וע"ד אִישׁ אִישׁ. אִישׁ דְּיִתְחֲזֵי לְמֶהֱוֵי אִישׁ, וְהוּא מְסָאֵב גַּרְמֵיהּ, דְּלָא יִשְׁרֵי עֲלוֹי קְדוּשָׁה דִּלְעֵילָא.

66. "If any man (lit. 'man man') of you or your posterity shall be unclean..." (Ibid. 10). HE ASKS: Why does it say "man" twice? HE ANSWERS: THE EXPLANATION IS that it is a man who is a man and is worthy to receive the lofty soul, yet he flawed himself so the supernal Shechinah does not reside with him. What is the reason? He brought it about by defiling himself. Therefore, IT IS WRITTEN 'man man', WHICH MEANS that he is worthy to be a man, but he caused himself to be defiled so Holiness from above should not be with him.

‎67. אוֹ בְדֶרֶךְ רְחוֹקָה, הָא אִיהוּ חַד מֵעֲשָׂרָה דְּאִינּוּן נְקוּדִים בְּאוֹרַיְיתָא,

וְכֻלְּהוּ אַתְיָין לְאַחֲזָאָה מִלָּה. מַאי בְּדֶרֶךְ רְחוֹקָה. בְּגִין דְּב"ן דְּאִיהוּ
מְסָאִיב גַּרְמֵיהּ, מְסָאֲבִין לֵיהּ לְעֵילָּא. כֵּיוָן דִּמְסָאֲבִין לֵיהּ לְעֵילָּא, הָא
אִיהוּ בְּדֶרֶךְ רְחוֹקָה. מֵהַהוּא אֲתָר וְאָרְחָא דְּזַרְעָא דְּיִשְׂרָאֵל אֲחִידָן בֵּיהּ,
הָא בְּדֶרֶךְ רְחוֹקָה אָחִיד, דְּאִתְרְחַק לְמִקְרַב לְכוֹן, וּלְאִתְקַשְׁרָא בְּכוֹן,
כְּמָה דְּאַתּוּן מִתְקַשְׁרִין.

67. "…or be on a journey afar off" (Ibid.). This is one of the ten PLACES that have dots in the Torah. They all come to demonstrate something. What is "afar off"? THERE IS A POINT ABOVE THE *HEI* OF 'AFAR' (HEB. *RECHOKAH*). It is because a person that defiles himself is made unclean above. As soon as he is made unclean above, he is afar off, far from the place and the road to which the offspring of Yisrael are attached. He is attached to a journey afar off; he removed himself from getting close to you, Yisrael, and to connect with you as you connect. THAT IS WHY IT SAYS, "ON A JOURNEY AFAR OFF," WITH A DOT ON THE *HEI* OF 'AFAR', TO INDICATE THAT THE INTENTION IS ON THE OTHER SIDE THAT IS FAR FROM HOLINESS.

68. א"ר יִצְחָק, וְהָא כְּתִיב כִּי יִהְיֶה טָמֵא לָנֶפֶשׁ אוֹ בְּדֶרֶךְ רְחוֹקָה,
דְּאִתְחֲזֵי תְּרֵין מִלִּין. מַשְׁמַע דִּכְתִיב אוֹ. אָמַר ר' יוֹסֵי, כָּאן, עַד לָא
מְסָאֲבִין לֵיהּ. כָּאן, בָּתַר דִּמְסָאֲבִין לֵיהּ. וּמַשְׁמַע אֲפִילוּ הַאי, אוֹ הַאי,
לָא יִשְׁרֵי עֲלוֹי קְדוּשָׁה דִּלְעֵילָּא, וְלָא יַעַבְדוּן פִּסְחָא בְּזִמְנָא דְּיִשְׂרָאֵל
עָבְדִין לֵיהּ.

68. Rabbi Yitzchak said: Why is it written, "shall be unclean by reason of a dead body, or be on a journey afar off"? That seems to indicate that there are two things here, which is understood from the word "or." AND HOW CAN YOU SAY THAT THEY ARE ONE THING, THAT THE UNCLEANNESS CAUSED HIM TO BE AFAR OFF? Rabbi Yosi said: Here, WHEN IT SAYS "UNCLEAN BY REASON OF A DEAD BODY," IT MEANS prior to having been made unclean FROM ABOVE. Here, WHEN IT SAYS, "ON A JOURNEY AFAR OFF," THE MEANING IS after he was made unclean FROM ABOVE AND HE STUMBLED TO THAT JOURNEY AFAR OFF, WHICH IS THE OTHER SIDE. It seems that neither the one nor the other will have Holiness from above reside with them, and they will not observe the Pesach at the same time that Yisrael observe it.

69. וְאִי תֵּימָא, הָא בְּיַרְחָא תִּנְיָינָא עָבֵיד אִי לָא מְתַקֵן גַּרְמֵיה. לָא, אֶלָּא כֵּיוָן דְּמִתַדְכֵי וּמְתַקֵן גַּרְמֵיה, הָא יַרְחָא תִּנְיָינָא לְמֶעְבַּד פִּסְחָא. מִכָּאן, כָּל ב״נ דִּמְדָּכֵי גַּרְמֵיה, מְדַכָּאן לֵיה.

69. If you wonder whether he observes THE PESACH on the following month, even if he does not correct himself, it is not so. It is only after he has purified and corrected himself, that he has another month to keep the Paschal lamb. From here, we take it that every person that purifies himself is also purified FROM ABOVE.

70. דְּאִי תֵּימָא דִּבְדַרְגָּא עִלָּאָה יַתִּיר קָאֵים בְּיַרְחָא תִּנְיָינָא. לָאו הָכִי, דְּהָא יִשְׂרָאֵל זַרְעָא קַדִּישָׁא דְּעָבְדוּ פִּסְחָא בְּזִמְנֵיה, נַטְלוּ לֵיה לְסִיהֲרָא וּלְשִׁמְשָׁא כְּחַד. וּמַאן דְּנָטִיל יְסוֹדָא בְּקַדְמֵיתָא, נָטִיל בִּנְיָינָא. מַאי יְסוֹדָא. לָא תֵּימָא יְסוֹדָא עִלָּאָה דְּצַדִּיקָא דְּעָלְמָא, אֶלָּא יְסוֹדָא דְּאֶבֶן טָבָא, כד״א אֶבֶן מָאֲסוּ הַבּוֹנִים הָיְתָה לְרֹאשׁ פִּנָּה. וְהַאי הוּא אֶבֶן דִּשָׁארֵי עָלֵיה מַאן דִּשָׁארֵי.

70. If you will venture to say that he will find himself on a higher level that second month, it is not so. This is because Yisrael, the holy offspring that prepare the Paschal lamb at its appointed time, receive the moon and the sun, THAT ARE MALCHUT AND ZEIR ANPIN, together as one. Whoever receives first the foundation receives the building upon it. What is the foundation? Do not say that it is the loftiest foundation of the everlasting Righteous, THAT IS YESOD OF ZEIR ANPIN, but rather the foundation of a precious stone, MALCHUT, as is written: "the stone which the builders have rejected has become the head stone of the corner" (Tehilim 118:22). For this is a stone upon which something lies, THAT IS ZEIR ANPIN.

71. אָמַר רִבִּי יְהוּדָה, וְדַאי כֹּלָּא נָטִיל אֲפִילוּ בְּיַרְחָא תִּנְיָינָא. אֲבָל לָאו אִיהוּ כְּמַאן דְּנָטִיל לֵיה בְּזִמְנֵיה. מַאי טַעֲמָא. דָּא דְּנָטִיל פִּסְחָא בְּזִמְנֵיה, נָטִיל מִתַּתָּא לְעֵילָּא, וְלָא נָחִית. בְּגִין דְּמַעֲלִין בַּקֹדֶשׁ, וְלָא

מוֹרִידִין. וְדָא דְּנָטִיל בָּתַר זִמְנֵיה, נָחִית מֵעֵילָא לְתַתָּא. בְּג"כ שַׁוְיָן
בְּכֹלָּא, וְלָא שַׁוְיָן. דְּדָא סָלִיק וְלָא נָחִית, וְדָא נָחִית וְלָא סָלִיק. בְּגִין כָּךְ
מַאן דִּמְקָרֵב פִּסְחָא בְּזִמְנֵיה, שְׁבָחָא יַתִּיר אִית לֵיה. זַכָּאִין אִינּוּן
יִשְׂרָאֵל, דְּזַכָּאן בְּכֹלָּא, דְּזַכָּאן בְּאוֹרַיְיתָא, וְכָל מַאן דְּזָכֵי בְּאוֹרַיְיתָא,
זָכֵי לֵיה בִּשְׁמָא קַדִּישָׁא. זַכָּאִין אִינּוּן יִשְׂרָאֵל, בְּעָלְמָא דֵּין וּבְעָלְמָא
דְּאָתֵי.

71. Rabbi Yehuda said: Certainly he receives everything, even on the second month. THAT IS, ONE CAN ACQUIRE EVEN IN THE SECOND MONTH MALCHUT AND ZEIR ANPIN TOGETHER, AT ONCE, JUST LIKE IN THE FIRST PASCHAL PREPARATIONS OF THE LAMB. HOWEVER, it is not quite the same as if someone partakes the Paschal lamb on the designated period. What is the reason? It is because the one who partakes of the Paschal lamb at its appointed time receives from below upward and does not regress, since we may promote to a higher grade of sanctity but not degrade. The one who partakes of the Paschal lamb past the designated time descends from higher to lower. Therefore, even if it is the same in everything, it is not equal, since the one rises to a higher degree does descend, and the other descends and does not rise. Therefore, whoever brings the Paschal lamb at its appointed season is more worthy. Praised are Yisrael who are meritorious in every way. They are worthy of the Torah, and whoever is worthy of the Torah merits the Holy Name. Praised are they in this world and the World to Come.

A Synopsis

We are told that once the Congregation of Yisrael is adorned with her crowns in the month of Nissan she does not remove the crowns from herself for thirty days, so it is still possible to have a second Passover in the second month. The commandments for the slaughter of the Paschal lamb and the delay of the celebration for those who are unclean or far away to the second date are laid out for us. The first Passover is from the right and the second is in the left.

רעיא מהימנא

72. פְּקוּדָא לְמֶעְבַּד פֶּסַח שֵׁנִי, עַל אִינּוּן דְּלָא יָכִילוּ, אוֹ דְּאִסְתָּאֲבוּ
בְּמִסְאֲבוּ אַחֲרָא. אִי רָזָא דְּפֶסַח, רָזָא דִּמְהֵימְנוּתָא דְּיִשְׂרָאֵל עָאלִין בָּה,

שַׁלְטָא בְּנִיסָן, וּכְדֵין אִיהוּ זִמְנָא לְחֶדְוָה, אֵיךְ יַכְלִין אִלֵּין דְּלָא יָכִילוּ,
אוֹ דְּאִסְתְּאָבוּ, לְמֶעְבַּד בְּיַרְחָא תִּנְיָינָא, דְּהָא אַעֲבָר זִמְנָא.

Ra'aya Meheimna (the Faithful Shepherd)

72. It is a commandment to make a second Pesach for those that were
unable TO DO THE PASCHAL OFFERING ON ITS DESIGNATED DATE,
BECAUSE THEY WERE TOO FAR AWAY or were defiled by any other
uncleanness. HE ASKS: If the secret of Pesach, which is the secret of the
Faith into which Yisrael entered, dominates in the month of Nissan and then
it is the time for rejoicing, how could those who were unable to prepare it on
time, or were defiled, make up for it in the second month, seeing that its
time had already passed?

73. אֶלָּא כֵּיוָן דכ"י מִתְעַטְּרָא בְּעִטְרָהָא בְּנִיסָן, לָא אִתְעֲדִיאַת כִּתְרָהָא
וְעִטְרָהָא מִנָּה תְּלָתִין יוֹמִין. וְכָל אִינּוּן ל' יוֹמִין מִן יוֹמָא דְּנַפְקוּ יִשְׂרָאֵל
מִפֶּסַח יָתְבָא מַטְרוֹנִיתָא בְּעִטְרָהָא, וְכָל חֵילָאָה בְּחֶדְוָה. מַאן דְּבָעֵי
לְמֶחֱמֵי לְמַטְרוֹנִיתָא, יָכִיל לְמֶחֱמֵי. כָּרוֹזָא כָּרִיז, כָּל מַאן דְּלָא יָכִיל
לְמֶחֱמֵי מַטְרוֹנִיתָא, יֵיתֵי וְיֶחֱמֵי עַד לָא יִנְעֲלוּן תַּרְעֵיה. אֵימָתֵי כָּרוֹזָא
כָּרִיז. בְּאַרְבְּעָה עֲשָׂר לְיַרְחָא תִּנְיָינָא, דְּהָא מִתַּמָּן עַד שִׁבְעָה יוֹמִין,
תַּרְעִין פְּתִיחָן. מִכָּאן וּלְהָלְאָה יִנְעֲלוּן תַּרְעֵי. וְעַל דָּא פֶּסַח שֵׁנִי

73. HE REPLIES: Once the Congregation of Yisrael, WHICH IS MALCHUT,
is adorned with its crowns, MEANING THE MOCHIN OF THE FIRST THREE
SFIROT, in the month of Nissan, she does not remove these crowns and
adornments from herself for thirty days. The Matron sits in her adornments
all these thirty days, beginning with the day of the exodus of Yisrael on
Pesach and all her legions are in a state of happiness. Whoever wishes to see
the Matron may look. And the proclamation calls: Whoever did not get a
chance to see the Matron should come and look before the gates are locked.
When is this proclamation proclaimed? It is on the fourteenth day of the
second month, since the gates remain open from then on for seven days
following. Following that, they lock the gates. Therefore, THEY BRING a
second Pesach.

74. פִּקוּדָא דָּא, שְׁחִיטַת הַפֶּסַח בִּזְמַנּוּ. וַאֲבַתְרֵיהּ פֶּסַח רִאשׁוֹן וּפֶסַח

שֵׁנִי לֶאֱכוֹל אוֹתָן כְּמִשְׁפָּטָן. וּטְמֵאִים לִהְיוֹת נִדְחִים לְפֶסַח שֵׁנִי, דְּאִיהוּ
פְּקוּדָא תְּלִיתָאָה. תַּנָּאִין וַאֲמוֹרָאִין, אִית בְּנֵי נָשָׁא כְּחוּלִין דְּטַהֲרָה,
מִסִּטְרָא דְּמִיכָאֵל. וּכְחוּלִין דְּהֶקְדֵּשׁ, כְּגוֹן בְּשַׂר קֹדֶשׁ, וְאִינּוּן מִסִּטְרָא
דְּגַבְרִיאֵל. כֹּהֵן וְלֵוִי. וְאִית בְּנֵי נָשָׁא דְּאִינּוּן כְּיוֹמִין טָבִין, וְאִינּוּן קֹדֶשׁ
קָדָשִׁים.

74. This commandment entails the slaughter of the Paschal lamb at its appointed time. The following one concerns the first Paschal lamb date and the second Paschal lamb, and cautions us to consume them in accordance with their laws. The unclean should be delayed to the second Paschal lamb date. That is a third commandment. Tannaim and Amoraim: some people are like pure, mundane objects from the aspect of Michael, and some are like mundane objects that pertain to holiness, for example holy meat, from the aspect of Gabriel, SINCE MICHAEL AND GABRIEL ARE the priest and the Levite, THAT IS, CHESED AND GVURAH. And some people are like holidays and they are the Holy of Holies.

75. שְׁכִינְתָּא אִיהִי פֶּסַח רִאשׁוֹן, מִימִינָא. וּפֶסַח שֵׁנִי, מִשְּׂמָאלָא. פֶּסַח
רִאשׁוֹן מִימִינָא, דְּתַמָּן חָכְמָ"ה. פֶּסַח שֵׁנִי מִשְּׂמָאלָא, דְּתַמָּן בִּינָה.
וּבְגִין דְּבִגְבוּרָה מִתְעַבְּרִין כָּל אֶשִׁין נוּכְרָאִין, דְּאִינּוּן כְּקַשׁ וְתֶבֶן לְגַבֵּי
אֵשׁ דִּגְבוּרָה, טְמֵאִים נִדְחִים לְפֶסַח שֵׁנִי.

75. The Shechinah is the first Pesach from the right side, SINCE THE FIRST MONTH IS FROM THE RIGHT COLUMN, and the second Pesach from the left, SINCE THE SECOND MONTH IS THE LEFT COLUMN, AS NISSAN AND IYAR ARE CHESED AND GVURAH. The first Pesach is from the right where Chochmah prevails, SINCE CHOCHMAH IS IN THE RIGHT COLUMN. The second Pesach is in the left where Binah prevails, SINCE BINAH IS IN THE LEFT COLUMN. In Gvurah, WHICH IS IN THE LEFT COLUMN, all foreign fires are removed, which are like straw and chaff in relation to the fire of Gvurah. THEREFORE, the unclean are delayed until the second Pesach.

14. "Everything that comes into the fire...
you shall pass through the fire"

A Synopsis

We learn that the soul is the vessel of God, and that God will not dwell in it until it is purged in the fire of Gvurah. Also, people are cleansed by the Written Torah from the right, that is referred to as 'water'. The completely wicked are purified in Gehenom but those who study the Oral Torah and the Written Torah are purified through the Torah.

76. וְכָל טוּמְאָה נִדָּה, וּמְצוֹרָע, וְזָב וְזָבָה וְיוֹלֶדֶת, בְּאֶשָׁא דְּגְבוּרָה אִיהוּ שׂוֹרֵף. דְּנִשְׁמָתָא אִיהוּ מָאנָא דְּקוּדְשָׁא בְּרִיךְ הוּא, וְאִיהוּ לָא שָׁרֵי בָּהּ, עַד דְּאִתְלַבְּנַת בְּאֶשָׁא דְּגְבוּרָה, דִּכְתִּיב הֲלֹא כֹה דְּבָרִי כָּאֵשׁ נְאָם יְיָ׳. וּבְהַאי אֶשָׁא, אִם בַּרְזֶל הוּא מִתְפּוֹצֵץ, וְאִם אֶבֶן הוּא נְמוֹחַ.

76. Every uncleanness – such as that of a woman in her menstrual flow, a leper, or a man or a woman who has a discharge and a woman who gives birth – the fire of Gvurah consumes THEM - the soul is the vessel of the Holy One, blessed be He, AND THE HOLY ONE, BLESSED BE HE, does not dwell in it until it is purged in the fire of Gvurah, as is written: "'is not My word like a fire?' says Hashem" (Yirmeyah 23:29). In this fire, if THE EVIL INCLINATION is like iron, it explodes; if it is like stone, it melts.

77. וּבִימִינָא דְּתַמָּן תּוֹרָה שֶׁבִּכְתָב, דְּאִיהִי מַיִם, וְטָהֲרָה מִמְּקוֹר דָּמֶיהָ, וְאִתְדַּכֵּי בָּהּ מְצוֹרָע, וְטָמֵא מֵת, וְזָב וְטָמֵא בְּכָל מִינֵי שֶׁרֶץ. הה"ד וְזָרַקְתִּי עֲלֵיכֶם מַיִם טְהוֹרִים וּטְהַרְתֶּם וְגוֹ׳.

77. And of the right, the place of the Written Torah, that is REFERRED TO AS 'water', IT SAYS: "and she shall be cleansed from the flow of her blood" (Vayikra 12:7). Through her are cleansed a leper, one who is unclean through contact with a dead body, one who has a discharge and one who is defiled through contact with any kind of insect. This is what is meant by: "then will I sprinkle clean water upon you, and you shall be clean" (Yechezkel 36:25).

78. בְּעַמּוּדָא דְּאֶמְצָעִיתָא מָאנָא אִתְיַחֲדַת בְּבַעְלָהּ, דְּאִיהִי אִתְּתָא, בָּתַר דְּאִתְקַדְּשַׁת בִּשְׂמָאלָא, וְאִתְדַּכְּאַת בְּמֵי מִקְוֵה בִּימִינָא, וְאוֹמְרִים עַל מָאנֵי דְפִסְחָא, כֵּלִים שֶׁנִּשְׁתַּמְּשׁוּ בָּהֶן בְּצוֹנֵן, מַטְבִּילָן בְּצוֹנֵן, וְהֵן טְהוֹרִים. אִינּוּן נִשְׁמָתִין דְּאִינּוּן מִסִּטְרָא דְרַחֲמֵי, וְאִינּוּן רַחֲמָנִים, מָארֵי חַנָּא וְחַסְדָּא, לָא צְרִיכִין לְאַדְכָּאָה בְּמַיִם פּוֹשְׁרִים כַּבֵּינוֹנִיִּים. כ"ש בְּחַמֵּי חַמִּין, דִּבְהוֹן מִתְדַּכְּכִין רְשָׁעִים גְּמוּרִים, דִּמְחַמְּמִין גַּרְמַיְיהוּ בְּאֶשָּׁא דיצה"ר. וְעָלַיְיהוּ אִתְּמַר, כָּל דָּבָר אֲשֶׁר יָבֹא בָאֵשׁ. בְּגִין דְּזוּהֲמָא דִּלְהוֹן נְפִישָׁא. אֲבָל צַדִּיקִים גְּמוּרִים בְּצוֹנֵן. דְּעָלַיְיהוּ אִתְּמַר, כָּל הַמֵּשִׂים רֶיוַח בֵּין הַדְּבֵקִים, מְצַנְּנִים לֵיהּ גֵּיהִנָּם.

78. In the Central Column, the vessel is united with her husband, THE VESSEL being a woman, MALCHUT. After becoming sanctified in the Left COLUMN and becoming cleansed in the ritual waters in the Right COLUMN, SHE IS UNITED IN THE CENTRAL COLUMN. It is said about Pesach utensils: such utensils that were used to serve cold things, one dips them ritually in cold water and they are cleansed. Since they are the souls that came from the side of Mercy and they are merciful, graceful and kind, they do not require cleansing in lukewarm water like those of average people. Most certainly they are not cleansed in the very hot waters, through which the completely wicked purify themselves, those who heat themselves in the fire of the Evil Inclination. About them, it is written: "everything that comes into the fire...you shall pass through the fire" (Bemidbar 31:23), since the filth on them is great. However, the completely righteous are cleansed with cold water, since it was said about them: whoever puts space between the ones that cleave together – MEANING THAT HE DOES NOT STICK TOGETHER WHILE PRONOUNCING THE LETTERS IN THE RECITAL OF SH'MA – ONE TO THE OTHER, the Gehenom is cooled down for him.

79. וְאִי נִשְׁמָתִין חֲמִירַיִם, דְּאִינּוּן כְּמָאנֵי חֶרֶס, שְׁבִירָתָן זוֹ הִיא טַהֲרָתָן. כד"א נִשְׁבְּרוּ, נִטְהָרוּ. וְרָזָא דְמִלָּה, זִבְחֵי אֱלֹהִים רוּחַ נִשְׁבָּרָה וְגו'. אֲבָל אִינּוּן דְּמִשְׁתַּדְּלִין בְּאוֹרַיְיתָא דִּבְכְתָב וּבְאוֹרַיְיתָא דבע"פ, דְּאִינּוּן אֵשׁ וּמַיִם, וְאִינּוּן דְּמִשְׁתַּדְּלִין בְּרָזֵי דְאוֹרַיְיתָא, דְּאִיהוּ אוֹר, דִּכְתִיב בָּהּ, וְתוֹרָה אוֹר, בְּאוֹרַיְיתָא אִינּוּן מִתְדַּכְּכִין בָּהּ.

14. "Everything that comes into the fire...
you shall pass through the fire"

79. If the souls are materialistic, in that they are like clay utensils, their breakage is their purification. As it is said, if they are broken, they are cleansed. The secret of this is: "the sacrifices of Elohim are a broken spirit" (Tehilim 51:19). However, as for those involved in studying the Written Torah and the Oral Torah, which are fire and water, and those who are striving after the secrets of the Torah, which is light, of which it is written: "and Torah is light" (Mishlei 6:23), they are purified through the Torah AND DO NOT NEED GEHENOM.

80. וְעוֹד בְּפֶרֶק הָרוֹאֶה, הָרוֹאֶה תְּמָרִים בַּחֲלוֹם, תַּמּוּ עֲוֹנוֹתָיו. הה״ד, תַּם עֲוֹנֵךְ בַּת צִיּוֹן. בְּגִין דִּתְמָרִים, בֵּיהּ תַּם, דַּרְגָּא דְּיַעֲקֹב, דְּאִתְּמַר בֵּיהּ, וְיַעֲקֹב אִישׁ תָּם. חוֹבִין מָרִים, וע״ד תְּמָרִים: תַּמָּן תָּ״ם, וְתַמָּן מָ״ר.

80. Furthermore, we find in the chapter about seeing, 'One who sees dates (Heb. *temarim*) in his dream, it means his iniquities have ended (Heb. *tamu*)'. This is what is written: "the punishment of your iniquity is accomplished, O daughter of Zion" (Eichah 4:22), because *temarim* consists of THE LETTERS of *tam* (Eng. 'whole'), which is Jacob's level, about whom it is written: "and Jacob was a plain (Heb. *tam*) man" (Beresheet 25:27). The sins are bitter (Heb. *marim*) and, therefore, dates contain THE LETTERS *tam* and *mar*. THEREFORE, THAT INDICATES THAT HIS SINS ARE OVER.

15. "The waters were made sweet"

A Synopsis

This section talks about the days to come, emphasizing the stress and poverty that will come to the teachers of the Mishnah during the time of testing. The text addresses the Faithful Shepherd, Moses, telling him that through his revelation of the secrets will come the sweetening of the waters. Sufferings are like salt that sweetens the meat.

81. הָכָא רָמִיז, וַיִּמְתְּקוּ הַמָּיִם. הה"ד, וַיּוֹרֵהוּ יְיָ' עֵץ וַיִּמְתְּקוּ הַמָּיִם. מֵהָכָא, מַאן דְּאִשְׁתְּדַּל בְּאוֹרַיְיתָא, דְּאִיהוּ עֵץ. חוֹבִין דִּילֵיהּ, דְּאִתְּמַר בְּהוֹן וַיְמָרְרוּ אֶת חַיֵּיהֶם בַּעֲבוֹדָה קָשָׁה, קוּדְשָׁא בְּרִיךְ הוּא מָחִיל לֵיהּ, וְיִתְחַזְרוּן מְתִיקִין.

81. Here, it is hinted that "the waters were made sweet." This is what is written: "and Hashem showed him a tree...the waters were made sweet" (Shemot 15:25). It is apparent from here that for whoever strives in the Torah, which is the Tree of Life, it is said about his sins: "and they made their lives bitter with hard bondage" (Shemot 1-14). The Holy One, blessed be He, forgives them and they BECOME sweet again, MEANING THAT THE INIQUITIES TURN TO BECOME LIKE MERITS.

82. דְּיוֹמִין יֵיתוּן, דְּיִתְקַיְּים בְּהוּ כְּמַפְקָנוּ דְּמִצְרַיִם, דְּאִתְּמַר בֵּיהּ וַיָּמָת יוֹסֵף וְכָל אֶחָיו וְכֹל הַדּוֹר הַהוּא. וּבְגָלוּתָא בַּתְרָאָה, לֵית מִיתָה אֶלָּא עוֹנִי דְּעָנִי חָשׁוּב כַּמֵּת. לְקַיֵּים בְּהוֹן וְהִשְׁאַרְתִּי בָךְ עַם עָנִי וָדָל וְחָסוּ בְּשֵׁם יְיָ'. לְאִתְקַיְּימָא בְּהוֹן וְאֶת עַם עָנִי תּוֹשִׁיעַ. וְאִלֵּין עֲתִירִים דְּיִשְׁתְּאָרוּן בְּהוֹן יִתְקַיֵּים בְּהוֹן, נִרְפִּים אַתֶּם נִרְפִּים. נִרְפִּים הֵם בְּאוֹרַיְיתָא. נִרְפִּים הֵם, לְמֶעְבַּד טִיבוּ עִם מָארֵי תוֹרָה. וְאַנְשֵׁי חַיִל הַמְסוֹבְבִים מֵעִיר לָעִיר וְלֹא יְחוֹנֵנוּ.

82. Days will come of which will be fulfilled, like in the time of the exodus from Egypt, what is written there: "and Joseph died, and all his brethren, and all that generation" (Ibid. 6). In the last exile, death is nothing but poverty, since a poor person is regarded as dead. The verse will be fulfilled

of them: "and I will leave in the midst of you a poor and lowly people, and they shall trust in the Name of Hashem" (Tzefanyah 3:12). It will also be fulfilled in relation to them: "and the afflicted people You will save" (II Shmuel 22:28). Those rich that will survive among them, this will be fulfilled about them: "you are idle, you are idle" (Shemot 5:17). They are slack in learning Torah, slow to do kindness toward Torah people, and people of virtue that wander from city to city are not received graciously.

83. וְנִרְפִּים הֵם בְּכוֹבֶד הַמַּס, דְּאִי תֵּימָא כְּבֵדִין אִינּוּן בְּכוֹבֶד הַמַּס, וְלָא עַבְדִין טִיבוּ, בְּגִין דָּא תִּכְבַּד הָעֲבוֹדָה עַל הָאֲנָשִׁים וְיַעֲשׂוּ בָּהּ, דְּכוֹבֶד הַמַּס עֲלַיְיהוּ, וְאַל יִשְׁעוּ בְּדִבְרֵי שָׁקֶר, דְּאִינּוּן מְשַׁקְּרִין וְאַמְרִין דְּכוֹבֶד הַמַּס עֲלַיְיהוּ, וּבְגִין דָּא לָא יַעַבְדוּן טִיבוּ. אִינּוּן מְשַׁקְּרָן בְּמִלּוּלַיְיהוּ, וְאַמְרִין דְּמֵהַכּוֹבֶד דְּתִתְכְּבַּד עֲלַיְיהוּ, תֶּבֶן אֵין נִתָּן, מָמוֹנָא דְּשִׁקְרָא, דְּבֵיהּ טוֹעִין לְקוּדְשָׁא בְּרִיךְ הוּא וּבְגִין דְּלָא יִשְׁעוּן בֵּיהּ, וְלָא חָסוּ בְּשֵׁם יְיָ', אֵין נִתָּן לַעֲבָדֶיךָ.

83. They are idle under the heavy burden. You may say that it is because THEY ARE heavily burdened that they do not do kindness. Therefore, "let more work be laid upon the men, that they may labor in it" (Ibid. 9), and cause that their burden will actually be REAL. "And let them not regard vain words" (Ibid.), that they lie and say that the burden is heavy on them, and therefore they refrain from kindness. They TOO are lying by saying that due to the burden that is heavily upon them, "there is no straw given." That is the lie of money, by which they have erred before the Holy One, blessed be He, by paying no attention to Him nor trusting in the Name of Hashem. STRAW, WHICH IS MONEY, is not "given to your servants," AND NOT BECAUSE OF THE HEAVY BURDEN.

84. וְאִלֵּין דְּאִית לוֹן, טָמִיר וְגָנִיז מָמוֹנָא מִלְּגוֹ, דְּאִיהוּ תּוֹכֶן, כְּגוֹן תּוֹךְ הָאוֹצָר וְתֵיבָה, אִתְקַיָּים בְּהוּ וְתוֹכֶן לְבֵנִים תִּתֵּנוּ. וְדָא כְּסָפִים לְבָנִים, דִּיהוֹן בְּהַהוּא דָּרָא.

84. Those that have straw, hide and store their money in it, which is inside (Heb. tochen), like inside the storage or inside the safety-box. It is applicable to them, "yet shall you deliver the quantity (Heb. tochen) of

bricks" (Ibid. 18) which refers to sums of money that are bricks that will exist during that generation.

85. בְּהַהוּא זִמְנָא שָׁם שָׂם לוֹ חֹק וּמִשְׁפָּט, וְאִינּוּן מָארֵי מִשְׁנָה. אוּף הָכָא וַיָּבֹאוּ מָרָתָה, אִתְהַדָּר לוֹן אוֹרַיְיתָא דִּבְעַל פֶּה, מָרָה בְּדַחֲקִין סַגִּיאִין, בַּעֲנִיוּתָא, דְּיִתְקַיַּים בְּהוּ, וַיְמָרְרוּ אֶת חַיֵּיהֶם בַּעֲבוֹדָה קָשָׁה: זוֹ קוּשְׁיָא. בְּחֹמֶר: דָּא ק"ו. וּבִלְבֵנִים: דָּא לִבּוּן הֲלָכָה. וּבְכָל עֲבוֹדָה בַּשָּׂדֶה: דָּא בָּרַיְיתָא. אֶת כָּל עֲבוֹדָתָם אֲשֶׁר עָבְדוּ בָהֶם בְּפָרֶךְ: דָּא תֵּיק"וּ.

85. During that period, "there He made for them a statute and an ordinance, and there He tested him" (Shemot 15:25), referring to the scholars of the Mishnah. They too, "came to Mara (Eng. 'bitter')" (Ibid. 23). The Oral Law will again be bitter to them with great stress and poverty, and it will be fulfilled for them: "and they made their lives bitter with hard bondage" (Shemot 1:14), which refers to hard questions. "...in mortar (Heb. *chomer*) ..." refers to inference from minor to major (Heb. *chomer*). "...and in brick (Heb. *levenah*)" (Ibid.), refers to explaining (Heb. *libun*) law. "...and in all manner of bondage in the field..." (Ibid.), refers to the Baraita, SINCE BARAITA MEANS FIELD. "All their bondage, wherein they made them serve, was with rigor" (Ibid.); that is, the unanswered problems and questions.

86. וְרַעְיָא מְהֵימָנָא, תַּמָּן אִתְקַיַּים בָּךְ, שָׁם שָׂם לוֹ חֹק וּמִשְׁפָּט וְשָׁם נִסָּהוּ. וּבְהַאי עֵץ הַדַּעַת טוֹב וָרָע, דְּאִיהוּ אִסּוּר וְהֶיתֵּר. וּבְאִינּוּן רָזִין דְּאִתְגַּלְיָין עַל יָדָךְ, וַיִּמְתְּקוּ הַמָּיִם. כְּמֶלַח דְּמַמְתְּקַת בִּשְׂרָא, הָכִי יִתְמַתְּקוּן בְּרָזַיָּיא דְּאִתְגַּלְיָין עַל יָדָךְ, כָּל אִינּוּן קוּשְׁיָין וּמַחְלוֹקוֹת, דְּמַיִּין מְרִירָן דְּאוֹרַיְיתָא דִּבְעַל פֶּה, אִתְהַדָּרוּ מְתִיקָן מֵי אוֹרַיְיתָא, וְיִסּוּרִין דִּילָךְ, בְּרָזִין אִלֵּין דְּאִתְגַּלְיָין עַל יָדָךְ, יְהוֹן לָךְ מְתִיקָן, וִיהַדְּרוּן לָךְ כָּל דַּחֲקִין דִּילָךְ, כְּחֶלְמִין דְּעַבְרִין. וַחֲל"ם, בְּהִיפּוּךְ אַתְוָון מַל"ח. דְּמַמְתְּקַת יַת בִּשְׂרָא. אוּף יִסּוּרִין מְמַתְּקִים. כְּמָה דְאוּקְמוּהָ.

86. And you, Faithful Shepherd, it will come true there for you: "there He made for them a statute and an ordinance, and there He tested him." With

this Tree of Knowledge of Good and Evil – that is, prohibition and permission – and through these secrets that will be revealed through you, "the waters were made sweet." Like salt that sweetens the meat, so will they be sweetened through you by the secrets that will be revealed through you. All these difficulties and disagreements of the bitter waters in the Oral Torah will return to be sweet waters of the Torah. These sufferings that you have will again be sweet to you through the secrets that will be revealed through you, and all your pains will seem to you like passing dreams THAT ARE NO MORE. Dream (Heb. *chalom, Chet-Lamed-Mem*) is like salt (Heb. *melach, Mem Lamed Chet*), AND LIKE SALT that sweetens the meat, so too are sufferings, as we have explained.

87. וְלָרְשָׁעִים מִתְהַדְּרָן יְסוּרִין מֶלַח סְדוֹמִית, דְּאִיהִי מְסַמֵּא אֶת הָעֵינַיִם, לְקַיְּימָא בְּהוּ וְעֵינֵי רְשָׁעִים תִּכְלֶינָה. וְאִינּוּן עֵרֶב רַב רַשִׁיעַיָּיא, דְּיִתְקַיֵּים בְּהוּ בְּהַהוּא זִמְנָא, יִתְבָּרְרוּ וְיִתְלַבְּנוּ וְיִצָּרְפוּ רַבִּים וְהִרְשִׁיעוּ רְשָׁעִים. יִתְלַבְּנוּ: אִינּוּן מָארֵי מִשְׁנָה. וְיִצָּרְפוּ: אִינּוּן זַרְעָא קַדִּישָׁא דִּשְׁאַר עַמָּא. הה"ד וּצְרַפְתִּים כִּצְרוֹף אֶת הַכֶּסֶף. וְהִרְשִׁיעוּ רְשָׁעִים, אִינּוּן עֵרֶב רַב.

87. The suffering will again be like salt of Sodom that blinds the eyes to the wicked, to have the verse come true upon them: "but the eyes of the wicked shall fail" (Iyov 11:20). These are the wicked mixed multitudes, upon whom will come true: "many shall purify themselves, and refine themselves, and be tried; but the wicked shall do wickedly" (Daniel 12:10). "...refine themselves..." refers to the students of the Mishnah; "and be refined" (Ibid.), refers to the holy offspring of the rest of the nation, as it says: "and will refine them as the silver is refined" (Zecharyah 13:9). "But the wicked shall do wickedly," refers to the mixed multitudes.

16. The raven and the dove

A Synopsis

We hear that those who toil in the splendor called 'The Zohar' will be wise and shine like the brightness of the firmaments. They must teach every secret and teach others how to be receptive to the light of the Torah and to the light of the Zohar. At that time they will be like the dove that was sent from Noah's ark, not like the raven that betrayed his mission. The prophet saw them become connected in three levels – Keter, Tiferet, Yesod – in the center and thus said that they shall prosper, be exalted, be very high, and be connected to two Messiahs.

88. וְהַמַּשְׂכִּילִים יָבִינוּ, אִינוּן מָארֵי קַבָּלָה, דְּאִתְּמַר בְּהוֹן וְהַמַּשְׂכִּילִים יַזְהִירוּ כְּזֹהַר הָרָקִיע. אַלֵּין אִינוּן דְּקָא מִשְׁתַּדְּלִין בְּזֹהַר דָּא, דְּאִקְרֵי סֵפֶר הַזֹּהַר, דְּאִיהוּ כְּתֵיבַת נֹחַ, דְּמִתְכַּנְּשִׁין בָּהּ שְׁנַיִם מֵעִיר, וְשֶׁבַע מִמַּלְכוּתָא. וּלְזִמְנִין אֶחָד מֵעִיר, וּשְׁנַיִם מִמִּשְׁפָּחָה. דְּבְהוֹן יִתְקַיֵּים כָּל הַבֵּן הַיִּלּוֹד הַיְאוֹרָה תַּשְׁלִיכוּהוּ. וְדָא אוֹרָה דִּסְפָרָא דָא, וְכֹלָּא עַל סִיבָה דִּילָךְ.

88. "But the wise shall understand" (Daniel 12:10). These are the scholars of Kabbalah. It says about them: "and they who are wise shall shine like the brightness of the firmaments" (Ibid. 3). This refers to those that place their effort in the splendor called 'The Zohar', that is like Noah's ark, to which are gathered two from a city, seven from a kingdom and, occasionally, one from a city and two from a family, by whom comes true, "Every son that is born you shall cast into the river" (Shemot 1:22). THE SECRET OF THE TORAH IS CALLED "SON"; "THAT IS BORN," MEANS COMPREHENDED; "THE RIVER," IS THE LIGHT OF THE TORAH. "THROW HIM (HEB. TASHLICHUHU)," IS LIKE 'TEACH HIM (HEB. TASKILUHU)' – EVERY INDIVIDUAL SECRET THAT IS BORN TO YOU, TEACH IT THE LIGHT OF THE TORAH AND ITS SOUL. Teach how to be RECEPTIVE TO THE LIGHT OF THE TORAH AND TO ITS SOUL. This is the light of this book OF ZOHAR, and all is due to you.

89. וּמַאן גָּרִים דָּא. עוֹרֵב דְּאַנְתְּ תְּהֵא בְּהַהוּא זִמְנָא, כְּיוֹנָה. דְּשָׁלִיחַ

אַחֲרָא דְּאִקְרֵי בִּשְׁמָךְ, כְּעוֹרֵב דְּאִשְׁתְּלַח בְּקַדְמֵיתָא, וְלָא אִתְהַדָּר
בִּשְׁלִיחוּתָא, דְּאִשְׁתְּדַּל בַּשְׁקָצִים, דְּאִתְּמַר בְּהוֹן, עַמֵּי הָאָרֶץ שֶׁקֶץ. בְּגִין
מָמוֹנָא דִּלְהוֹן, וְלָא אִשְׁתְּדַּל בִּשְׁלִיחוּתֵיהּ לְאַהֲדְרָא לְצַדִּיקַיָּיא
בְּתִיוּבְתָּא. כְּאִילּוּ לָא עָבֵיד שְׁלִיחוּתָא דְּמָארֵיהּ.

89. Who caused all this? The raven, since at that time you will be like a dove. THIS ALLUDES TO THE RAVEN AND THE DOVE THAT NOAH SENT FROM THE ARK AFTER COMPARING THE ZOHAR TO NOAH'S ARK. There was another messenger named after you, like the raven that was originally sent FROM THE ARK but did not return from his mission and made his effort with forbidden abominations, about which it is said that the ignorant are abominable. AND HE SPENT HIS EFFORTS ON THEM, because of their money, and did not strive in his mission to cause the righteous to repent. It is as if he has not fulfilled the mission of his Master. RABBI MOSES KORDOVERO OF BLESSED MEMORY WROTE THAT IT REFERS TO JEROBOAM, THE SON OF NEBAT, WHO WAS WORTHY TO BE THE REDEEMER OF YISRAEL. HE FALTERED WITH THE GOLDEN CALVES, SINNED, AND CAUSED MANY OTHERS TO SIN. HE IS COMPARED TO THE RAVEN THAT BETRAYED HIS MISSION.

‏90. וּבָךְ יִתְקַיֵּים רָזָא דְּיוֹנָה, דְּעָאל בְּעִמְקִין דִּתְהוֹמֵי יַמָּא, הָכִי תֵּיעוּל
אַנְתְּ בַּעֲמִיקוּ דִּתְהוֹמֵי אוֹרַיְיתָא, הַהָ"ד וַתַּשְׁלִיכֵנִי מְצוּלָה בִּלְבַב יַמִּים.
וְיֵהוֹן חָכְמָה חֶסֶד נֵצַח לַיָּמִין. דִּבְגִינַיְיהוּ אָמַר דָּוִד, יְמִין יְיָ' עוֹשָׂה חָיִל
יְמִין יְיָ' רוֹמֵמָה יְמִין יְיָ' עוֹשָׂה חָיִל. וּתְלַת מִשְּׂמָאלָא יִתְקַשְּׁרוּן כַּחֲדָא,
דְּאִינּוּן בִּינָה גְּבוּרָה הוֹד. וְג' דַּרְגִּין דְּאֶמְצָעִיתָא, כֶּתֶר תִּפְאֶרֶת יְסוֹד,
דַּאֲחִידָן בִּימִינָא וּשְׂמָאלָא.

90. The secret of the dove that entered the depths of the sea shall come true with you, and likewise you will enter the deep chasms of the Torah. This is what is written by the prophet Jonah: "for You did cast me into the deep, into the heart of the seas" (Yonah 2:4), MEANING IN THE SEA OF THE TORAH. THEN there will be Chochmah, Chesed and Netzach to the right. Of those, David said: "the right hand of Hashem does valiantly. The right hand of Hashem is exalted. The right hand of Hashem does valiantly" (Tehilim 118:15-16). The three LEVELS of the left become connected together –

which are Binah, Gvurah and Hod – and the three levels in the center – which are Keter, Tiferet and Yesod – are attached to right and left, SINCE THE CENTRAL COLUMN IS ATTACHED TO RIGHT AND LEFT. IN THIS WAY, THE TEN SFIROT ARE PERFECTED, INCLUDING THE FIRST THREE SFIROT.

91. וּבְגִין דְּחָזָא לָךְ נָבִיא מִתְקַשָּׁר בִּתְלַת דַּרְגִּין דְּאֶמְצָעִיתָא, פָּתַח עֲלָךְ הַאי קְרָא, הִנֵּה יַשְׂכִּיל עַבְדִּי יָרוּם וְנִשָּׂא וְגָבַהּ מְאֹד. וּבְגִין דְּאַנְתְּ תְּהֵא אָחִיד בִּתְרֵין מְשִׁיחִין, אָמַר דָּוִד עַל ג' יְמִינִין דְּמָשִׁיחַ בֶּן דָּוִד, יְמִין יְיָ' תְּלַת זִמְנִין. לָקֳבֵיל ג' שְׂמָאלִין, דְּאָחִיד בְּהוֹן מָשִׁיחַ בֶּן אֶפְרַיִם, אָמַר מִסִּטְרָא דְּחַד שְׂמָאלָא, גְּבוּרָה, לֹא אָמוּת. כִּי אֶחְיֶה, מִסִּטְרָא דִּשְׂמָאלָא דהו"ד דִּילָךְ, דְּאִתְּמַר בֵּיהּ וְנָתַן הַהוֹד לְמֹשֶׁה. אִתְיְיהִיב בָּךְ, מִסִּטְרָא דְּבִינָה.

91. Since the prophet saw you become connected to these three levels – KETER, TIFERET AND YESOD – in the center, he pronounced upon you this verse: "behold, My servant shall prosper," THE SECRET OF YESOD; "he shall be exalted and extolled," THE SECRET OF TIFERET; "and be very high" (Yeshayah 52:13), THE SECRET OF KETER. You will be connected and attached to the two Messiahs. David spoke of the three to the right – of CHOCHMAH, CHESED AND NETZACH – of Messiah, the son of David, and, "the right of Hashem," three times, AS MENTIONED NEARBY. In relation to the three left ones – BINAH, GVURAH AND HOD – to which Messiah, son of Ephraim, is attached, he said of the one aspect of the left, Gvurah, "I shall not die," AND FURTHER SAID, "but live" (Tehilim 118:17), from the SECOND aspect of the left, which is your Hod. About this, it is said that He gave Hod to Moses, MEANING AS IT SAYS: "AND YOU SHALL PUT SOME OF YOUR HONOR (HEB. HOD) UPON HIM" (BEMIDBAR 27:20), MEANING THAT THE HOLY ONE, BLESSED BE HE, GAVE HIM HOD TO BE HIS OWN. It is given to you from the side of Binah, SINCE THE ILLUMINATION OF CHOCHMAH OF THE LEFT OF BINAH IS REVEALED IN HOD.

92. בְּגִין דְּבֵיהּ הֲוֵית אַנְתְּ חָרֵב וְיָבֵשׁ בְּכֹלָּא, בְּגִין מָשִׁיחַ בֶּן אֶפְרַיִם, בְּאוֹרַיְיתָךְ, בִּנְבִיאוּתָךְ עֲלֵיהּ, בְּגוּפָךְ דְּסָבִילַת כַּמָּה מִינֵי יִסּוּרִין, בְּגִין דְּלָא יְמוּת הוּא. וּבְעֵית רַחֲמֵי עֲלֵיהּ. אִתְּמַר בֵּיהּ כִּי אֶחְיֶה, מִסִּטְרָא

דְּבִינָה. וּבְגִין דָּא לָא אָמוּת, מִסִּטְרָא דִּגְבוּרָה. כִּי אֶחְיֶה מִסִּטְרָא דְּבִינָה, אִילָנָא דְּחַיֵּי, דְּאִתְגַּבָּר עָלֵיהּ ק״ש שֶׁל שַׁחֲרִית, וְקָשִׁיר לֵיהּ בְּקִשּׁוּרָא דִּתְפִילִין, בִּימִינָא דְּאַבְרָהָם, דְּאִיהוּ שַׁחֲרִית.

92. Thus, IN GVURAH, you would have been arid and dry in every respect, due to Messiah, the son of Ephraim; DRY in your Torah and your prophecy and in your body, in which you have suffered too many agonies, so that he should not die, MESSIAH, THE SON OF EPHRAIM, and you pleaded for mercy on his behalf. THEREFORE, it says about him, "but live," from the side of Binah, and therefore, "I shall not die," from the side of Gvurah, FROM WHICH COMES IT HARSH JUDGMENT, AS MENTIONED ABOVE. "...but live..." is from the side of Binah, MEANING AFTER MOCHIN WERE REVEALED FROM IT, WHICH ARE THE SECRET OF the Tree of Life, WHICH IS THE CENTRAL COLUMN that overpowers THE LEFT COLUMN, GVURAH, THROUGH the reading of Sh'ma of Shacharit (the morning prayer), WHICH IS THE SECRET OF CHESED. It is connected to it through the knot of the Tefilin to the right of Abraham, which is Shacharit (the morning prayers), NAMELY CHESED.

93. וַאֲסַפֵּר מַעֲשֵׂי יָהּ, מִסִּטְרָא דְּהוֹד. יַסּוֹר יִסְּרַנִּי יָהּ, חָכְמָה וּבִינָה, מִימִינָא וּמִשְּׂמָאלָא, בִּתְלַת יְמִינִין, וּתְלַת שְׂמָאלִין. וְלַמָּוֶת לֹא נְתָנָנִי, עַמּוּדָא דְּאֶמְצָעִיתָא, בְּג׳ דְּכָלִיל כֶּתֶר, וְצַדִּיק, וְאִיהוּ בֶּן יָ״הּ. וּמִיַּד יָקוּם ו׳ לֵהּ בְּיָ״הּ, בִּימִינָא וּשְׂמָאלָא, בְּרַחֲמֵי וְתַחֲנוּנֵי, בְּכַמָּה פִיּוּסִים לָהּ וּלְבִנְהָא, הה״ד בַּיּוֹם הַהוּא אָקִים אֶת סוּכַּת דָּוִד הַנּוֹפֶלֶת. וּבְגִין דָּא אָמַר נָבִיא, בִּבְכִי יָבֹאוּ וּבְתַחֲנוּנִים אוֹבִילֵם.

93. "...and declare the works of Yah..." (Tehilim 118:17) from the side of Hod, SINCE THE ILLUMINATION OF CHOCHMAH THAT IS REVEALED FROM BINAH IS REVEALED ONLY FROM THE CHEST DOWNWARD THAT IS IN HOD. "Yah has chastised me severely" (Ibid. 18), MEANING WITH Chochmah and Binah, WHICH ARE from right and left, SINCE CHOCHMAH COMPRISES three right ones – CHOCHMAH, CHESED AND NETZACH – AND BINAH COMPRISES three left ones – BINAH, GVURAH AND HOD. PRIOR TO THE INTERVENTION OF THE CENTRAL COLUMN, THE RIGHT AND THE LEFT ARE IN CONFLICT WITH EACH OTHER AND JUDGMENTS

FLOW FROM THEM. THEREFORE, IT SAYS: "YAH HAS CHASTISED ME SEVERELY." "But He has not given me up to death" (Ibid. 18). This is the Central Column that comprises the three CENTRAL ONES: Keter, the Righteous, NAMELY YESOD, and ITSELF, NAMELY TIFERET, that is the son of Yah (*Yud-Hei*). Immediately, the *Vav* will then raise *Hei* to *Yud-Hei*, AND THE NAME OF YUD HEI VAV HEI WILL BE PERFECTED in the right and the left with mercy and beseeching with many entreaties to MALCHUT and her descendants. This is what is written: "on that day I will raise up the Tabernacle of David that is fallen" (Amos 9:11); THAT IS, MALCHUT. Therefore, the prophet said, "they shall come with weeping, and with supplications will I lead them" (Yirmeyah 31:8).

94. קָם רַעְיָא מְהֵימָנָא, וְנָשִׁיק לֵיה, וּבָרִיךְ לֵיה, וְאָמַר וַדַּאי שְׁלִיחָא דְּמָארָךְ אַנְתְּ לְגַבָּן. פַּתְחוּ תַּנָּאִין וַאֲמוֹרָאִין וְאָמְרוּ, רַעְיָא מְהֵימָנָא, אַנְתְּ הֲוֵית יָדַע כָּל דָּא, וְעַל יְדָךְ הִיא אִתְגַּלְיָיא, אֲבָל בַּעֲנָוָה דִילָךְ, דְּאִתְּמַר בָּךְ וְהָאִישׁ מֹשֶׁה עָנָו מְאֹד, בְּאִלֵּין אַתְרִין דְּאַנְתְּ מִתְבַּיֵּישׁ לְאַחְזָקָא טִיבוּ לְגַבָּךְ, מַנִּי קוּדְשָׁא בְּרִיךְ הוּא לָן, וּלְבוּצִינָא קַדִּישָׁא, לְמֶהֱוֵי בִּידָךְ וּבְפוּמָךְ בְּאִלֵּין אַתְרִין.

ע"כ רעיא מהימנא

94. The Faithful Shepherd rose, kissed him, and blessed him. He said: You are most likely the messenger of your Master to us. The Tannaim and Amoraim opened the discussion saying: Faithful Shepherd, you knew all this and through you it was revealed. But in your humility, as was said about you, "now the man Moses was very meek" (Bemidbar 12:3); in these areas that you are shy to take credit for yourself, the Holy One, blessed be He, has nominated us to the holy luminary, MEANING RABBI SHIMON BAR YOCHAI, to act as your hand and your mouthpiece in these areas.

End of Ra'aya Meheimna (the Faithful Shepherd)

17. "And on the day that the Tabernacle was erected"

A Synopsis

Rabbi Shimon tells Rabbi Chiya that anyone who gives freely to the poor becomes worthy to be blessed; he increases in both wealth and life. He elaborates by saying that his charity causes him an increase in life above so that it increases his life below. We hear that in this way the Tree of Life is awakened to add life to the Tree of Death. Through a person's charity he causes Zeir Anpin and Malchut to join together and blessings to pour above and below. He is saved in this world and he shall have life in the World to Come.

95. וּבְיוֹם הָקִים אֶת הַמִּשְׁכָּן. ר' חִיָּיא פָּתַח, פִּזַּר נָתַן לָאֶבְיוֹנִים צִדְקָתוֹ עוֹמֶדֶת לָעַד קַרְנוֹ תָּרוּם בְּכָבוֹד. פִּזַּר לָאֶבְיוֹנִים, מַאי פִּזַּר. כד"א יֵשׁ מְפַזֵּר וְנוֹסָף עוֹד. יָכוֹל פִּזּוּר בְּעָלְמָא, קמ"ל פִּזַּר נָתַן לָאֶבְיוֹנִים, כֵּיוָן דְּיָהִיב לְמִסְכְּנֵי, הַאי פִּזּוּרָא יָאוּת. מַאי וְנוֹסָף עוֹד. בְּכֹלָּא. וְנוֹסָף עוֹד בְּעוּתְרָא. וְנוֹסָף עוֹד בְּחַיֵּי.

95. "And on the day that the Tabernacle was erected..." (Bemidbar 9:15). Rabbi Chiya opened the discussion saying, "He has distributed freely, he has given to the poor; his righteousness endures for ever; his horn shall be exalted with honor" (Tehilim 112:9). "He has distributed freely, he has given to the poor." HE INQUIRES: What is the meaning of, "distributed freely"? HE RESPONDS: It is as you say, "there is one who gives freely, and yet increases" (Mishlei 11:24). We can also say that it is true for everyone who distributed freely. Therefore, he lets us know and hear, "he has distributed freely, he has given to the poor." As soon as he gives freely to the poor, he becomes worthy TO BE BLESSED. What is the meaning of: "and yet increases"? It means in everything. He increases in wealth and increases in life.

96. הַאי קְרָא הָכִי מִבָּעֵי לֵיהּ, יֵשׁ מְפַזֵּר וְיוֹסֵף עוֹד, מַאי וְנוֹסָף. אֶלָּא הַהוּא אֲתָר דְּשָׁרֵי בֵּיהּ מִיתָה, הוּא גָּרִים לֵיהּ דְּיִתּוֹסַף מֵחַיִּים דִּלְעֵילָּא לְאוֹסְפָא לֵיהּ. אָמַר רַבִּי יְהוּדָה אָמַר רַבִּי חִיָּיא, קְרָא אַסְהִיד, דְּכָל מַאן דְּיָהִיב לְמִסְכְּנֵי, אִתְּעַר אִילָנָא דְּחַיֵּי, לְאוֹסְפָא לְהַהִיא אִילָנָא דְּמוֹתָא,

וּכְדֵין אִשְׁתְּכַח חַיִּים וְחֶדוּ לְעֵילָא. וּבַר נָשׁ דְּגָרִים דָּא, בְּשַׁעֲתָא דְּאִצְטְרִיךְ לֵיהּ, הַהוּא אִילָנָא דְּחַיֵּי קָאֵים עֲלֵיהּ, וְהַהוּא אִילָנָא דְּמוֹתָא אַגִּין עֲלוֹי. וּבְגִין כַּךְ וְנוֹסָף עוֹד.

96. HE INQUIRES: This verse should have been read this way, 'There is one who gives freely, and yet it will increase'. What is meant by "increases"? HE RESPONDS: It is this place where death resides, MEANING MALCHUT. It causes it an increase in life above AND DRAWS FROM THERE, and increases its LIFE. Rabbi Yehuda said in the name of Rabbi Chiya: The verse gives evidence that for whoever gives CHARITY to the paupers, the Tree of Life is awakened, THAT IS ZEIR ANPIN, to add life to the Tree of Death, WHICH IS MALCHUT. Then there is life and happiness above, IN MALCHUT, and that Tree of Life stands over the person who caused this, BY HIS GIVING OF CHARITY, in a time of need. That Tree of Death shields him and, therefore, it is proper to say, "yet increases."

97. צִדְקָתוֹ עוֹמֶדֶת לָעַד. מַאי עוֹמֶדֶת לָעַד. עוֹמֶדֶת עֲלֵיהּ דְּבַר נָשׁ, לְזַמְנָא לֵיהּ קִיּוּמָא וְחַיִּים, כְּמָה דְּאִיהוּ יָהִיב לֵיהּ חַיִּים, וְאִתְּעַר לְגַבֵּי חַיִּין, ה"נ יַהֲבִין לֵיהּ. וְאִינּוּן תְּרֵי אִילָנִין קַיְימִין עֲלֵיהּ לְשֵׁיזָבָא לֵיהּ, וּלְאוֹסָפָא לֵיהּ חַיִּין.

97. HE ASKS: What is the meaning of, "his righteousness (also 'charity') endures for ever"? HE RESPONDS: CHARITY stands for a person to give him his existence and life, in the same manner that this person gives subsistence TO THE POOR. And the SUPERNAL life awakens toward him, NAMELY BECAUSE OF HIM, AS MENTIONED NEARBY. It gives him life. These two trees, ZEIR ANPIN AND MALCHUT, stand by him to save him and increase his life.

98. קַרְנוֹ תָּרוּם בְּכָבוֹד, ת"ח עָלְמָא דְּאָמְרָן, הַהוּא קֶרֶן תָּרוּם. וּבְמָה. בְּכָבוֹד דִּלְעֵילָא, דְּהַאי ב"נ גָּרִים לְחַבְּרָא לוֹן כַּחֲדָא, וּלְאַרְקָא בִּרְכָאן לְעֵילָא וְתַתָּא.

98. "His horn shall be exalted with honor." Come and behold: observe the world we talked about, THAT IS ZEIR ANPIN. IT SAID TO HIM that the horn, WHICH IS MALCHUT, will be exalted. And how? With the honor of above, WHICH IS BINAH, SINCE MALCHUT IS EXALTED THROUGH THE ILLUMINATION OF BINAH. That person, THROUGH THE CHARITY THAT HE GAVE, caused them to join together, MEANING ZEIR ANPIN AND MALCHUT, and blessings to pour above and below.

99. רִבִּי אַבָּא אָמַר, בְּכָל זִמְנָא דְמַשְׁכְּנָא אִתְּקַם בְּעוֹבָדֵיהוֹן דִּבְנֵי נָשָׁא, כְּדֵין הַהוּא יוֹמָא, יוֹמָא דְּחֶדְוָוה דְּכֹלָּא, וּמָשַׁח רְבוּת קַדִישָׁא אִתְרַק בְּהַנְהוּ בּוֹצִינִין, וְנַהֲרִין כֻּלְּהוּ. מַאן דְּגָרִים דָּא, גָּרִים לֵיה דְּיִשְׁתְּזִיב בְּהַאי עָלְמָא, וִיהֵא לֵיה חַיִּים בְּעָלְמָא דְּאָתֵי, הה"ד וּצְדָקָה תַּצִיל מִמָּוֶת, וּכְתִיב וְאֹרַח צַדִּיקִים כְּאוֹר נֹגַהּ הוֹלֵךְ וָאוֹר עַד נְכוֹן הַיּוֹם.

99. Rabbi Aba said: During the whole time that the Tabernacle was erected, MEANING WHEN MALCHUT UNITES WITH ZEIR ANPIN, through the activities of people, then that was a time of rejoicing for everyone. Holy anointing oil is poured into these candles, THE SFIROT OF MALCHUT, which all give off light. Whoever brings this about, brings himself to be saved in this world, and he shall have life in the World to Come. This is what is written: "but righteousness delivers from death" (Mishlei 11:4), and, "but the path of just men is like the gleam of sunlight, that shines ever more brightly until the height of noonday" (Mishlei 4:18).

18. The standards

A Synopsis
Rabbi Shimon elucidates the vision of Ezekiel as found beginning in Yechezkel 1:19. He describes the standard and the army of the lion, with its dominating angel Michael.

100. עֲשֵׂה לְךָ שְׁתֵּי חֲצוֹצְרוֹת כֶּסֶף וְגוֹ'. רִבִּי שִׁמְעוֹן פָּתַח, וּבְלֶכֶת הַחַיּוֹת יֵלְכוּ הָאוֹפַנִּים אֶצְלָם וּבְהִנָּשֵׂא הַחַיּוֹת מֵעַל הָאָרֶץ יִנָּשְׂאוּ הָאוֹפַנִּים. וּבְלֶכֶת הַחַיּוֹת, בְּקוּזְפִירָא דִּלְעֵילָא הֲווֹ אָזְלֵי. דְּאִי תֵּימָא דְּהַאי לְעֵילָא לְעֵילָא. לָאו, לְתַתָּא. אֶלָּא כְּגַוְונָא הַאי מִקַּמֵּי אַנְפִּין, וְהַאי לְבָתַר אַנְפִּין.

100. "Make for yourself two silver trumpets..." (Bemidbar 10:1). Rabbi Shimon opened the discussion saying: "and when the living creatures moved, the wheels went by them. And when the living creatures were lifted up from the earth, the wheels were lifted up" (Yechezkel 1:19). "And when the living creatures moved"; they moved by means of the higher bounty. One may think that it is higher above. HE RESPONDS: No, down below. Just like, the one is before the FOUR faces and the other after the FOUR faces.

101. זִיקָא מֵאַרְבַּע זִיקִין, בַּד' מָדוֹרִין, וּבַד' סְטָרִין, בְּזִיוָון דְּאִתְבְּרוֹן בְּקוֹלְמִיטִין דְּאַנְפִּין נְהִירִין. בְּגִין כָּךְ כְּמַרְאֵה הַחַיּוֹת, דְּאִינּוּן אַרְבַּע זִוְיָין, דְּגָלִין פְּרִישָׁן, אַרְיֵ"ה, שׁוֹ"ר. נֶשֶׁ"ר. אָדָ"ם. דְּכָלִיל כֻּלְּהוּ ד' מַלְאָכִין דְּשַׁלְטִין וּכְלִילָן בֹּלָא.

101. A wind of the four winds IS ROBED in four compartments and four sides in the brilliance that was created that supports the illuminated faces. Therefore, they are like the appearance of the living creatures, which are the four corners UPON WHICH the standards were unfurled, THAT ARE REFERRED TO AS lion, eagle, ox, man. These comprise the four dominating angels – WHO ARE MICHAEL, GABRIEL, URIEL, RAPHAEL – and include everything, SINCE THESE FOUR ANGELS COMPRISE ALL THE HEAVENLY HOSTS.

102. דְּגִלָא קַדְמָאָה, מַשְׁרְיָא מְזַיְּינָא, אַרְיֵ״ה. מִיכָאֵ״ל, רָשִׁים בִּפְרִישׁוּ דְּגִלָא פְּרִישָׁא לִימִינָא. מִזְרָח שֵׁירוּתָא דְּשִׁמְשָׁא, אָזִיל בְּמַטְלָנוֹי, בִּנְהִירוּ. תְּרֵין מְמָנָן תְּחוֹת יְדֵיהּ, יוֹפִי״אֵל, צַדְקִי״אֵל. חַד לְאוֹרַיְיתָא. וְחַד, לְמֵיהַךְ בְּשׁוּקָא.

102. The first standard is an armed camp THAT IS THE SECRET OF THOSE ABLE TO GO TO WAR FROM THE AGE OF TWENTY AND HIGHER. ITS LIVING CREATURE IS a lion. THE ANGEL IS Michael, recorded in the unfurled standard that is spread to the right side, AND ITS WIND IS the east – that is, the rising of the sun that travels with its light. Yofiel and Tzadkiel are appointed under him, THAT IS, UNDER MICHAEL, one for Torah and one to go to the marketplace.

103. כַּד אִלֵּין נַטְלִין, נַטְלִין כַּמָּה מַשְׁרְיָין מְזַיְּינִין, מִסִּטְרָא דִּימִינָא, וְכֹלָּא חַד. לְסִטְרָא שְׂמָאלָא, שִׁמְשָׁא אָזִיל וְנָהִיר, וּמְעַטֵּר לְהוּ. אֶלֶף וְרִבְּוָון מְמָנָן תְּחוֹתוֹי. וְכֻלְּהוּ בִּדְחִילוּ בְּאֵימָתָא בְּזִיעַ בְּרֶתֶת.

103. When they travel, several armed camps move from the right side, and all are one; THAT IS, THEY ARE UNDER THE LEADERSHIP OF THE THREE ANGELS MENTIONED ABOVE. To the left side, the sun advances to shine and crowns them, THE CAMPS. Thousands and ten thousands are appointed under it and all are in awe and fear, trembling and shaking.

104. אַרְיֵה אוֹשִׁיט יְדֵיהּ יְמִינָא, כָּנִישׁ לְכָל חֵילוֹי לְגַבֵּיהּ, תְּלַת מְאָה וְשַׁבְעִין אֶלֶף אַרְיָוָותָא, סוֹחֲרָנֵיהּ דְּהַהוּא אַרְיֵ״ה, וְאִיהוּ בֵּינַיְיהוּ בְּאֶמְצָעִיתָא.

104. The lion extends his right hand, gathers all the legions to him, and 370,000 lions surround that lion. He is in the center among them.

105. כַּד גָּעֵי הַאי אַרְיֵה, מִזְדַּעְזְעָן רְקִיעִין, וְכָל חַיָּלִין וּמַשְׁרְיָין מִזְדַּעְזְעִין, מִדְּחִילוּ דִּילֵיהּ. מֵהַהוּא קָלָא, נְהַר דִּי נוּר מִתְלַהֲטָא, וְנָחִית

בְּאֶלֶף וַחֲמֵשׁ מְאָה דַּרְגִּין דְּגֵיהִנָּם לְתַתָּא, כְּדֵין כֻּלְּהוּ חַיָּיבִין דְּגֵיהִנָּם מִזְדַּעְזְעָן, וּמְלַהֲטָן אֶשָּׁא, וע״ד כְּתִיב, אַרְיֵה שָׁאַג מִי לֹא יִירָא.

105. When that lion roars, the firmaments shake and all the legions and camps tremble from the fear of him. From that sound, the river Dinur goes up and descends the 1,500 steps to Gehenom below. Consequently, all the wicked in Gehenom shake and burn in the fire. About this, it is written: "the lion has roared, who will not fear?" (Amos 3:8).

106. גָּעֵי תִּנְיָינוּת, תְּלַת מְאָה וְשַׁבְעִין אֶלֶף אַרְיָוָותָא, כֻּלְּהוּ גָּעָאן. אוֹשִׁיט יְדֵיהּ שְׂמָאלָא, כָּל מָארֵיהוֹן דְּדִינָא לְתַתָּא דַּחֲלִין, וְאִתְכַּפְיָין תְּחוֹת הַהוּא יְדָא. וְהַהוּא יְדָא פָּשִׁיט עָלַיְיהוּ, וְכֻלְּהוּ תְּחוֹתֵיהּ. כד״א, יָדְךָ בְּעֹרֶף אֹיְבֶיךָ.

106. He roars a second time and 370,000 lions all roar. THE LION extends his left hand. All the Prosecutors below become fearful and are subdued under that hand. He spreads that hand over them and all are under him, as it says: "your hand shall be on the neck of your enemies" (Beresheet 49:8).

107. אַרְבַּע גַּדְפִּין לְכָל חַד וְחַד, מֵאֶשָּׁא חִוָּורָא. כֻּלְּהוּ מְלַהֲטִין. כָּל אַפִּין דְּחִזּוּר וְשׁוֹשָׁן בְּחִוָּורְתָּא דְּהַהוּא אֶשָּׁא שְׁקִיעָן.

107. There are four wings to each one, all glowing with white fire. All the countenances of a pomegranate and a blossom are impressed in the whiteness of that fire.

108. אַרְבַּע אַנְפִּין לְכָל חַד וְחַד לְאַרְבַּע סִטְרִין, כֻּלְּהוּ נְהִירִין בְּחִוָּורָא דְּשִׁמְשָׁא. חַד לִסְטַר מִזְרָח, נָהִיר בְּחֶדוּ. וְחַד לִסְטַר מַעֲרָב, דָּא כָּנִישׁ נְהוֹרֵיהּ. וְחַד לִסְטַר צָפוֹן, חָשׁוּךְ בְּלָא נְהִירוּ, כְּצִלָּא דְּשִׁמְשָׁא לְגַבֵּי שִׁמְשָׁא. צִלָּא חָשׁוּךְ, שִׁמְשָׁא נָהִיר. בְּגִין דְּשִׁמְשָׁא וְצִלָּא, יְמִינָא וּשְׂמָאלָא, וְאַזְלָא כַּחֲדָא. חֲשׁוֹכָן דְּאַזְלִין עִמֵּיהּ, כָּל אִינּוּן דְּנַטְלִין זַיְינָא.

108. There are four countenances to each individual one, on four sides, all shining in the whiteness of the sun. One to the east side shines with happiness. The one to the west side gathers its light. The one to the north side is dark, without any light, like the shadow of the sun in relation to the sun. The shadow is dark and the sun is bright, since the sun and the shadow are right and left, and go together. All the dark ones go along with it, all carrying weapons of war.

109. וְכֻלְּהוּ מִימִינָא וּמִשְּׂמָאלָא בִּתְלַת רֵישִׁין. רֵישָׁא חֲדָא דִּילֵיהּ, שַׁבְעִין וְאַרְבַּע אֶלֶף, וְשִׁית מְאָה. אִלֵּין אִינּוּן רֵישָׁא חַד. נָפְקֵי חֵילָא בִּימִינָא, דְּאִיהוּ אָרִים עָלַיְיהוּ. בַּר כָּל אִינּוּן מְמָנָן דִּלְתַתָּא, תְּחוֹת אִלֵּין. שֻׁלְטוֹנִין אִלֵּין עַל אִלֵּין, דַּרְגִּין תַּתָּאִין עִם עִלָּאִין, דְּלֵית לוֹן חוּשְׁבָּנָא.

109. All from right and left have three heads, each head containing 74,600. Those legions depart according to the right hand that he raised over them, in addition to all those that are appointed below, which are under those rulers – the ones over the others, innumerable lower levels with higher ones.

110. רֵישָׁא תִּנְיָינָא, דְּאָזִיל בְּרֵישָׁא קַדְמָאָה, חוּשְׁבָּן דִּילֵיהּ חַמְשִׁין וְאַרְבַּע אֶלֶף, וְאַרְבַּע מְאָה. בַּר כָּל אִלֵּין מְמָנָן דִּתְחוֹת לְד׳ סִטְרִין, דְּלֵית לוֹן חוּשְׁבָּנָא. רֵישָׁא תְּלִיתָאָה, דְּאָזִיל בַּתְרַיְיהוּ, חַמְשִׁין וְשִׁבְעָה אֶלֶף, וְאַרְבַּע מְאָה. כְּגַוְונָא דְּנָטִיל יְמִינָא, הָכִי נָמֵי נָטִיל שְׂמָאלָא, הָכִי נָמֵי מִקַּמַּיְיהוּ, הָכִי נָמֵי מִבַּתְרַיְיהוּ.

110. The count of the second head that goes along with the first head contains 54,400, in addition to all those appointed below to the four sides which are countless. The third head that follows them has 57,400. The left travels in a way similar to how the right travels, and likewise the one in front and the one at the back.

111. כֵּיוָן דְּנָטִיל הַאי קַדְמָאָה, וְהוּרַד הַמִּשְׁכָּן. וְכֻלְּהוּ לֵיוָואֵי אַמְרֵי שִׁירָתָא, מָארֵי דְתוּשְׁבְּחָן כֻּלְּהוּ מִסְטְרֵיהּ. כְּדֵין כִּי רוּחַ הַחַיָּה בָּאוֹפַנִּים כְּתִיב.

111. As soon as this first one moves and the Tabernacle is lowered, all the Levites sing their song and all those who praise are at its side. Then, it is written: "for the spirit of the living creatures was in the wheels" (Yechezkel 1:20).

19. The second standard

A Synopsis

Here we read of the standard and the army of the eagle, under the dominating angel Uriel.

112. דְּגְלָא תִּנְיָינָא. מַשִׁרְיָיא מְזַיְינָא, נֶשֶׁ״ר, אוּרִיאֵ״ל, דָּרוֹ״ם. תְּרֵי מְמָנָן עִמֵּיה, שַׁמְשִׁיאֵ״ל חַסְדִּיאֵ״ל. הַאי נֶשֶׁר סָלִיק, וְכָל מָאֲרֵיהוֹן דְּגַדְפִּין מִקַּמֵּיה. כַּמָּה מַשִׁרְיָין סַלְּקִין בְּכָל סִטְרִין. כָּל חַד וְחַד בְּתוּקְפָּא דְשִׁמְשָׁא.

112. The second standard, WHICH IS THE STANDARD OF THE CAMP OF REUBEN, is an armed camp. THAT IS, ACCORDING TO THE SECRET OF THOSE ABLE TO GO TO WAR, OF TWENTY YEARS AND UPWARDS, IN THE ASPECT OF an eagle UNDER THE DOMINATION OF THE ANGEL Uriel, WHO RULES FROM THE PERSPECTIVE OF THE CENTRAL COLUMN. THE DIRECTION OF THE STANDARD'S TRAVEL IS TO the south side, WHICH IS THE RIGHT COLUMN AND CHESED. Two chieftains are WITH URIEL, WHICH ARE Shamshiel and Chasdiel. This eagle ascends, with all the winged creatures before him. Many camps ascend from all directions, each individual with the strength of the sun.

113. רוּחָא דְּרוּחָא פְּנִימָאָה נָפִיק, וְהַהוּא רוּחָא מָטֵי לְהַאי נֶשֶׁר, וְסָלִיק אֶבְרוֹי וּמְכַסְּיָיא לְגוּפָא. כד״א, הֲמִבִּינָתְךָ יַאֲבֶר נֵץ יִפְרוֹשׂ כְּנָפָיו לְתֵימָן. כְּגַוְונָא כְּדוּגְמָא כְּעֵין כְּנֶשֶׁר יָעִיר קִנּוֹ הַאי נֵץ בַּהֲדֵיה יוֹנָה, בַּהֲדֵיה נֵץ, וְכָל מָאֲרֵי דְגַדְפִּין כֻּלְּהוּ מְצַפְצְפָן וְחַדָּאן. חַד מִסִּטְרָא קַמֵּיה, סָלִיק מִתַּתָּא לְעֵילָא. כַּמָּה צִיפָּרִין נַחְתִּין וְעָאלִין, מְצַפְצְפָן וְחַדָּאן, אַזְלִין וְשָׁאטִין.

113. The spirit of the inner spirit emerges. That spirit reaches the eagle and he raises his wings and covers his body, as it says, "does the hawk fly by your wisdom, and stretch her wings toward the south?" (Iyov 39:26). This eagle quarrels with the dove and the hawk, and all the winged birds are chirping and joyful. One from the front goes from below upwards. Several birds go down and enter, chirping and joyful. They go and wander.

114. כַּד נָטִיל, אוֹשִיט גַּדְפָּא יְמִינָא, כָּנִיש לְכָל חֵילוֹי, תְּלַת מְאָה
וְחַמְשִׁין אֶלֶף מָארֵי דְּגַדְפִין, בִּתְרֵי גוּפֵי, נֶשֶ"ר וְאַרְיֵ"ה כַּחֲדָא. אָרִים
קָלָא, כֻּלְּהוּ אַחֲרָנִין סַלְקִין וְנַחְתִּין, מְצַפְצְפָן מִסְטְרַיְיהוּ, מִכַּמָּה דַּרְגִּין.

114. When he, THE EAGLE, travels, he extends his right wing and gathers all his legions, those 350,000 winged ones, in two bodies composed of the eagle and the lion together. When he raises a voice, all the others ascend and descend, whistling from their end from several grades.

115. ג' רֵישִׁין אִינּוּן כַּחֲדָא, בְּמַשְׁרְיָין אִלֵּין. וְכֻלְּהוּ בְּחַד חוּשְׁבָּן.
וְחוּשְׁבָּן דְּאִלֵּין רֵישִׁין, רֵישָׁא חֲדָא, אַרְבְּעִין וְשִׁית אֶלֶף וַחֲמֵשׁ מְאָה.
רֵישָׁא תִּנְיָנָא חַמְשִׁין וְתֵשַׁע אֶלֶף וּתְלַת מְאָה. רֵישָׁא תְּלִיתָאָה, אַרְבְּעִין
וַחֲמֵשׁ אַלְפִין, וְשִׁית מְאָה וְחַמְשִׁין.

115. Three heads are together in these camps, SINCE THREE TRIBES ARE IN THE CAMP OF REUBEN. All are in a special count, and the count of these heads IS AS FOLLOWS. One head is 46,500, THE CENSUS OF THE TRIBE OF REUBEN. The second head is 59,300, THE CENSUS OF THE TRIBE OF SHIMON. The third head is 45,650. THAT IS THE CENSUS OF THE TRIBE OF GAD.

116. מֵאִלֵּין תְּרֵי סִטְרִין, נָפִיק תְּרֵין כָּרוֹזֵי, דְּאָזְלֵי מְקַמֵּי כֻּלְּהוּ מַשְׁרְיָין.
כַּד אִלֵּין תְּרֵי מַכְרִיזֵי, כָּל חֵילִין, וְכָל מַשְׁרְיָין, חֵיוָון זְעִירִין עִם רַבְרְבָן,
כֻּלְּהוּ מִתְכַּנְּשֵׁי. מַאן חָמֵי נְטִילָא דְּכֻלְּהוּ רְקִיעִין, כּוּלְּהוּ נַטְלִין בְּמַטּוּלָא
בְּמַשְׁרְיָין, לְקַמֵּיה דְּהַהוּא מַשְׁכְּנָא.

116. From the two sides, WHICH ARE EAGLE AND LION, MENTIONED ABOVE, two proclamations go forth to all the camps. When these two, THE SECRET OF THE TWO TRUMPETS, AS SHALL BE EXPLAINED, make their proclamation, the legions and camps, living creatures, and large and small animals all gather. Who has beheld the traveling of all the firmaments along with the camps before the Tabernacle, WHICH IS MALCHUT!

117. בְּשַׁעֲתָא דְּחַד מִנַּיְיהוּ, הַהוּא דְּאָתֵי מִסִּטְרָא דְּאַרְיֵה, פָּשִׁיט קָלָא,

בְּגִין דְּלָא יִזְדַּעְזְעוּן כָּל אִינוּן קָלִין. כְּדֵין מִתְכַּנְּשִׁין כָּל אִינוּן מַשִׁרְיָין. בְּשַׁעֲתָא דְּאַחֲרָא קָרֵי, מִתְּבַר קָלָא וְלָא פָּשִׁיט, כָּל אִינוּן מַשִׁרְיָין דְּהַאי נֶשֶׁר, כֻּלְּהוּ מִתְכַּנְּשׁוּ לְנַטְלָא בִּמְטַלְנַיְיהוּ. לָקֳבֵיל אִינּוּן, שְׁתֵּי חֲצוֹצְרוֹת כֶּסֶף, כְּגַוְונָא דָּא כֹּלָּא לְתַתָּא. ת״ח, כַּד אִלֵּין נַטְלִין מַה כְּתִיב, וּבְלֶכֶת הַחַיּוֹת יֵלְכוּ הָאוֹפַנִּים אֶצְלָם, אִינוּן דְּמִתְכַּנְּשׁוּ לְגַבַּיְיהוּ, כְּגַוְונָא דְּרֵישָׁא אִסְתָּכַּל, הָכִי נָמֵי כֻּלְּהוּ.

117. One of them, MEANING the one that comes from the lion's side, spreads his voice, MEANING THAT HE BLOWS WITH THE TRUMPETS A *TEKIA*, WHICH IS A MONOTONE SOUND – in order not to cause tremors in the sounds, HE BLOWS, BUT RATHER SIMPLE SOUNDS WITHOUT TREMOR. Then all these camps assemble, MEANING IN THE SECRET OF: "AND WHEN THEY SHALL BLOW WITH THEM, ALL THE ASSEMBLY SHALL ASSEMBLE THEMSELVES TO YOU" (BEMIDBAR 10:3). During the time the other calls, MEANING THAT HE BLOWS THE TRUMPETS UNDER THE RULE OF THE ONE COMING FROM THE EAGLE'S SIDE, the sound is broken and not simply elongated, MEANING IT IS THE SOUND OF A *TRUAH*. AND THEN all these camps of this eagle congregate to travel on their journeys, MEANING WHAT IS WRITTEN: "WHEN YOU BLOW AN ALARM, THEN THE CAMPS...SHALL GO FORWARD" (IBID. 5). Corresponding to these TWO, WHICH ARE LION AND EAGLE, are two trumpets of silver, since as it APPLIES ABOVE, so it is all down below. Come and behold: when these travel, it is written, "and when the living creatures moved, the wheels went by them" (Yechezkel 1:19). This means those LEGIONS that congregate TO THE APPOINTED ARE REFERRED TO AS THE 'WHEELS', and as the head observes, MEANING THE CHIEFTAIN, so do all OBSERVE, NAMELY THE LEGIONS UNDER THEM.

20. The third standard

A Synopsis

This section describes the standard of the ox, under the dominating angel Gabriel. From here comes judgment of all the sins of the world. We learn that the supernal Torah is written in black fire on white fire, and are told of the four divisions of fire, water and wind.

118. דִּגְלָא תְּלִיתָאָה. שׁוֹר. גַּבְרִיאֵל. צָפוֹן. תְּרֵין מְמָנָן עִמֵּיהּ, קַפְצִיאֵ"ל חִזְקִיאֵ"ל. הַאי שׁוֹר מִסִּטְרָא דִשְׂמָאלָא. קַרְנוֹי סַלְקִין בֵּין תְּרֵין עֵינוֹי. רָגִיז בְּאִסְתַּכְּלוּתָא, עַיְינִין מְלַהֲטָן כְּאֶשָׁא דְּנוּר דָּלִיק. נָגַח וְרַפְסָא בְּרַגְלוֹי וְלָא חָיֵיס.

118. The third standard, WHICH IS THE STANDARD OF DAN'S CAMP, IS THE FACE OF an ox OF THE LIVING CREATURES, THAT IS, LEFT. OF THE FOUR ANGELS, THIS IS Gabriel FROM THE LEFT COLUMN. AND IT TRAVELS ON THE NORTH SIDE OF THE TABERNACLE, WHICH IS LEFT. With GABRIEL, there are two appointed chieftains, Kaftziel and Chizkiel, SINCE GABRIEL CORRESPONDS TO DAN AND THE TWO CHIEFTAINS CORRESPOND TO ASHER AND NAFTALI, WHO ARE CONNECTED TO THE STANDARD OF DAN'S CAMP. This ox is from the left side. His horns rise from between his two eyes. He observes angrily, and the eyes glow like a burning fire. He rams and tramples with his feet and has no mercy.

119. כַּד גָּעֵי הַאי שׁוֹר, נָפְקִין מִנּוּקְבָּא דִתְהוֹמָא רַבָּא, כַּמָּה חֲבִילֵי שְׁרִיקִין, כֻּלְּהוּ גָּעָאן וְשָׁטָאן קַמֵּיהּ, וְחֵימָתָא, וְאַחְמְתָא דְּכָל חוֹבִין תַּלְיָיא קַמֵּיהּ, דְּהָא כָּל חוֹבֵי עָלְמָא, כֻּלְּהוּ בְּסִפְרָא סְלִיקִין וּכְתִיבִין.

119. When this ox bellows, many battalions of damaging demons emerge from the hole of that great deep. All bellow and wander in front of him, and wrath and the bag that contains all the sins hang in front of him, since all the sins of the world are written in the book.

120. שִׁבְעָה נַהֲרֵי דְּאֶשָׁא נַגְדִּין קַמֵּיהּ, כַּד צָחֵי אָזִיל לְגַבֵּי הַהוּא נְהַר

דִּינוּר, וְשָׁאִיב לֵיהּ בִּגְמִיעָא חֲדָא. וְהַהוּא נָהָר אִתְמְלֵי כְּדְבְקַדְמֵיתָא,
וְלָא כָּדִיב. כָּל אִינוּן חַיָּילִין, שָׁאֲבִין אֶשָׁא אַכְלָא אֶשָׁא. וְאִלְמָלֵא
דְּמִסְטְרָא דְּאַרְיֵה, נָפִיק חַד נַהֲרָא דְּמַיָּא, דִּמְכַבִּין גַּחֲלָתַיְיהוּ, לָא יָכִיל
עָלְמָא לְמִסְבַּל.

120. Seven fiery rivers flow in front of him. When he is thirsty, he goes to
the river Dinur (lit. 'of fire') and sucks it up in one draw. The river is
refilled AGAIN as originally, and it is not false, MEANING IT IS NOT LIKE A
FALSE SPRING WHOSE WATER CEASES FLOWING. All these legions OF
THIS OX, THE SECRET OF GABRIEL, draw up fire that consumes fire. If not
for the fact that from the lion's side another river of water emerges, WHICH
IS THE SECRET OF LIGHT OF CHASSADIM, which extinguishes their coals,
the world would not have been able to endure THEIR JUDGMENTS.

121. חֲשׁוֹכָא דְּשִׁמְשָׁא תַּמָּן אִשְׁתְּכַח, לָא אִשְׁתְּכַח נְהִירוּ. כַּמָה גַּרְדִּינֵי
נְמוּסִין אָזְלִין וְשָׁטָאן בְּחָשׁוֹכָא וְהַהוּא נָהָר דְּדָלִיק בְּסִטְרָא דָא, נוּרָא
אוּכָמָא חֲשׁוּךְ. וְאִי תֵּימָא, דְּלָא אִית אֶשָׁא חִוּוְרָא, אֶשָׁא אוּכָמָא, אֶשָׁא
סוּמָקָא, אֶשָׁא דִּתְרֵי גְוְונֵי. לָא תֵּימָא, דְּהָא וַדַּאי הָכִי הוּא, וְעכ״ד
לְעֵילָא לְעֵילָא הָכִי אִשְׁתְּכַח, וּמִתַּמָּן נָגִיד לְאִלֵּין תַּתָּאֵי.

121. The darkness of the sun, MEANING THE SHADOW, exists there IN THE
LEFT COLUMN. There is yet there is no light. Many Prosecutors wander and
loiter in the dark, and that river that is burning ON THE LEFT SIDE is a dark
black fire. You may think that here there is not a white fire, a black fire, a
red fire, and fire COMPOSED from two colors, MEANING GREEN. Do not
think SO, since it certainly is like that. THE BURNING RIVER IS BLACK, yet
high above, IN BINAH, it is also so – THAT THE FIRE IS COMPOSED FROM
FOUR FIRES. From there, it flows to the lower grades, BEFORE THE OX IN
ZEIR ANPIN AND THE ANGEL GABRIEL IN MALCHUT, SINCE IN THEM
ALSO THE FIRE OF GVURAH IS COMPOSED OF FOUR FIRES.

122. תָּנֵינָן אוֹרַיְיתָא בְּמָה אִשְׁתְּכַחַת. אֶשָׁא חִוּוְרָא, וְאֶשָׁא אוּכָמָא עַל
גַּבֵּי אֶשָׁא חִוּוְרָא. בִּתְרֵי אִשֵׁי אִשְׁתְּכַחַת אוֹרַיְיתָא. ת״ח, אֶשָׁא חֲדָא
הוּא, וְהַאי אִתְפְּלִיג לְאַרְבָּעָה. מַיָּא חֲדָא אִיהוּ, וְהַאי אִתְפְּלִיג לְאַרְבַּע.

רוּחָא חֲדָא אִיהוּ, וְהַאי אִתְפְּלִיג לְאַרְבַּע.

122. We learned in what manner the SUPERNAL Torah exists. It is white fire, AND IS WRITTEN in black fire on white fire. The Torah exists in the two fires. Come and behold: there is one fire, MEANING THE LEFT COLUMN THAT IS REFERRED TO AS 'FIRE', and this divides into four FIRES, BEING COMPRISED OF FOUR ASPECTS, AS MENTIONED. ALSO, there is one water, WHICH IS THE RIGHT COLUMN REFERRED TO AS 'WATER', and it divides into four, INCLUDING FOUR ASPECTS. AND ALSO, the wind is one, WHICH IS THE CENTRAL COLUMN, and divides into four, MEANING IT IS COMPOSED OF FOUR ASPECTS, WHICH ARE THE THREE COLUMNS AND MALCHUT THAT CONTAINS THEM.

123. תְּלַת רֵישִׁין אִשְׁתְּכָחוּ בְּמַשְׁרְיָין אִלֵּין. חוּשְׁבָּן דִּלְהוֹן, רֵישָׁא חֲדָא שִׁתִּין וּתְרֵי אֶלֶף וּשְׁבַע מְאָה. רֵישָׁא ב', אַרְבְּעִין וְחַד אֶלֶף וַחֲמֵשׁ מְאָה. רֵישָׁא תְּלִיתָאָה, תְּלַת וְחַמְשִׁין אֶלֶף וְאַרְבַּע מְאָה. בַּר כָּל אִינּוּן דַּרְגִּין אַחֲרָנִין דְּאִתְפָּרְשָׁן בְּסִטְרַיְיהוּ, וְלֵית לוֹן חוּשְׁבָּנָא. כֻּלְּהוּ דַּרְגִּין עַל דַּרְגִּין. בַּר כַּמָּה גַּרְדִּינֵי נְמוּסִין דְּאִינּוּן לְתַתָּא, חֲצִיפִין כְּכַלְבָּא, נַשְׁכִין כַּחֲמָרָא, וַוי מַאן דְּאִשְׁתְּכַח גַּבַּיְיהוּ, וְדִינָא דִּלְהוֹן בְּסִטְרָא רְבִיעָאָה.

123. Three heads exist in these camps, CORRESPONDING TO THE THREE TRIBES OF DAN'S CAMP. Their count is one head of 62,700, WHICH IS THE CENSUS OF DAN'S TRIBE, AS MENTIONED IN THE SCRIPTURES. The second head is 41,500, AND THAT IS THE CENSUS OF ASHER'S TRIBE. The third head is 53,400, AND THAT IS THE CENSUS OF NAFTALI'S TRIBE and all the other countless levels that are spread out on their sides – MEANING THE WOMEN AND CHILDREN OF THESE THREE TRIBES THAT ARE NOT INCLUDED IN THE MENTIONED CENSUS. All are grades upon grades, except for some Prosecutors THAT ARE DRAWN FROM THE LEFT COLUMN, and which are below IN THE KLIPOT and are impudent like dogs and bite like donkeys – THOSE THAT ARE NOT INCLUDED IN THESE CAMPS OF THE LEFT SIDE. Woe unto those who are with them and whose Judgment is on the fourth side, WHICH IS MALCHUT, MEANING THAT THEY GET THEIR SUSTENANCE FROM MALCHUT.

21. The fourth standard

A Synopsis
The fourth standard is the face of man under the domination of the angel Raphael, and it brings healing. We read of two silver trumpets that break the judgments and subdue them.

124. דִּגְלָא רְבִיעָאָה, אָדָ"ם רְפָא"ל. מַעֲרָב. בַּהֲדֵיהּ אַסְוָותָא. בְּסִטְרָא דְּאָדָם אִתְכְּלִיל דִּינָא עִלָּאָה עָלֵיהּ אַתְּסֵי. הַאי אָחִיד בְּקַרְנוֹי דְּשׁוֹר, כַּד מִבָּעֵי לְאַעֲלָא לוֹן לִתְהוֹמָא רַבָּא. וְכָפִית לוֹן, דְּלָא יוֹקִיד עָלְמָא. בָּתַר דָּא שַׁרְיָא קוֹל דְּמָמָה דַּקָּה. הָכָא מִלָּה בַּחֲשַׁאי, לָא מִשְׁתְּמַע מִלָּה דְּהַבָּרָה כְּלָל.

124. The fourth standard, WHICH IS THE STANDARD OF EPHRAIM'S CAMP, FROM THE ASPECT OF THE LIVING CREATURES IS THE FACE OF man. FROM THE FOUR ANGELS, IT IS Raphael, AND HE TRAVELS ON the west, SINCE ALL THESE ARE ASPECTS OF MALCHUT. With it is healing, SINCE on the side of man, the uppermost Judgment is contained in it and it is healed. He grasps the horns of the ox when it wishes to bring him to the great depth, and he binds them so they will not consume the world by fire. Following this, a thin small voice abides. Here the matter is very quiet, so that no syllable is heard.

125. בְּסִטְרָא דָּא, שַׁרְיָא מַאן דְּשַׁרְיָא, סָלִיק מַאן דְּסָלִיק, שִׁמְשָׁא אִתְכְּנִישׁ לְאַנְהָרָא לְהַאי אֲתָר. בְּגִין כָּךְ וּתְקַעְתֶּם תְּרוּעָה, בְּסִטַר דָּרוֹם. אֲבָל הָכָא, לָאו הַאי וְלָאו הַאי. אֲמַאי תְּרוּעָה. לְאַכְפַּיְיא סְטָר צָפוֹן, ובג"כ סְטָר צָפוֹן לַאֲחוֹרָא.

125. On that side, IN MALCHUT, something rests, MEANING CHASSADIM OF THE RIGHT COLUMN, and something rises, MEANING THE ILLUMINATION OF CHOCHMAH THAT IS IN THE LEFT COLUMN THAT SHINES WHEN RISING FROM BELOW UPWARD. The sun, ZEIR ANPIN, is gathered to illuminate this area, WHICH IS MALCHUT. Therefore, IT IS WRITTEN: "When you blow an alarm (Heb. *truah*)" (Bemidbar 10:5) on the south side. WHICH IS THE RIGHT COLUMN IN THE ILLUMINATION OF THE CENTRAL

COLUMN, AS MENTIONED. However, here IN MALCHUT, neither exist, NEITHER T'KIAH NOR T'RUAH. HE ASKS: WHY THE BLOWING OF THE *T'ruah*? HE RESPONDS: it subdues the north side, WHICH IS THE LEFT COLUMN, IN ORDER TO UNITE IT WITH THE RIGHT, SO IT WILL SHINE FROM NOW ON ONLY FROM BELOW UPWARD. Therefore, the north side is the rear OF ALL THE CAMPS, AS IS WRITTEN: "THE REARWARD OF ALL THE CAMPS" (IBID. 25). THAT IS BECAUSE IT IS ESTABLISHED THROUGH MALCHUT. THEREFORE, THE STANDARD OF EPHRAIM, WHICH IS MALCHUT, TRAVELS BEFORE THE LEFT COLUMN, WHICH IS THE CAMP OF DAN. AND THE CAMP OF DAN TRAVELS LAST.

126. ת״ח, שְׁתֵּי חֲצוֹצְרוֹת, בְּגִין דְּאִינּוּן מִסְטְרֵי תְּרֵי דְּקָאמְרֵי, מִמִּזְרָח וּמִדָּרוֹם. אִינְהוּ זְמִינִין לְתַבְּרָא דִּינִין, וּלְאַכְפְיָיא לוֹן. וע״ד אִינּוּן מִכֶּסֶף. ובג״כ וּבְיוֹם שִׂמְחַתְכֶם וּבְמוֹעֲדֵיכֶם וְגוֹ', וּתְקַעְתֶּם בַּחֲצוֹצְרוֹת, סְתָם, בֵּין לְעֵילָּא בֵּין לְתַתָּא. זַכָּאִין אִינּוּן יִשְׂרָאֵל, דְּקוּדְשָׁא בְּרִיךְ הוּא בָּעֵי בִּיקָרֵיהוֹן, וְיָהִיב לוֹן חוּלָקָא עִלָּאָה עַל כָּל שְׁאַר עַמִּין. וְקוּדְשָׁא בְּרִיךְ הוּא אִשְׁתְּבַּח בְּהוּ בְּתוּשְׁבַּחְתַּיְיהוּ, הה״ד וַיֹּאמֶר לִי עַבְדִּי אַתָּה יִשְׂרָאֵל וְגוֹ'.

126. Come and behold: there are two trumpets, since they are on the two sides we mentioned, from the east, WHICH IS THE CENTRAL COLUMN, and from the south, WHICH IS THE RIGHT COLUMN. They are prepared to break the Judgments and subdue them IN THE SECRET OF THE *TRUAH*, AS MENTIONED NEARBY. They are therefore from silver, WHICH IS CHESED, and hence, "also in the day of your gladness, and in your solemn days...you shall blow with the trumpets" (Bemidbar 10:10). This is not specific, which means both above and below IN THIS WORLD. Praised are Yisrael, whom the Holy One, blessed be He, wishes to have honor, and He gave them the highest part above all other nations. The Holy One, blessed be He, praises Himself for them with the praises WITH WHICH THEY PRAISE HIM. This is what is written: "and said to me, 'You are My servant, Yisrael'" (Yeshayah 49:3).

22. The Nuns

A Synopsis

Rabbi Elazar talks about the letter Nun that faces backwards in two places in the quoted verses. He says that when the Ark traveled the Shechinah traveled along and did not leave Yisrael; and just as She kept Her face turned back to the children of Yisrael the Nun that traveled with them turned back to them. Rabbi Shimon says that after the Ark came to rest and the people complained they caused Malchut to turn her back on them.

127. וַיְהִי בִּנְסֹעַ הָאָרוֹן וַיֹּאמֶר מֹשֶׁה וְגוֹ'. רִבִּי אֶלְעָזָר אָמַר, הָכָא אִית לְאִסְתַּכְּלָא, נ' דְּאִיהִי מְחַזְּרָא לַאֲחוֹרָא הָכָא בִּתְרֵי דוּכְתֵּי, אֲמַאי. וְאִי תֵּימָא נ' כְּפוּפָה, הָא יְדִיעָה נ' כְּפוּפָה נוּקְבָּא. נ' פְּשׁוּטָה, כְּלָלָא דִּדְכַר וְנוּקְבָּא. וְהָא אוֹקִימְנָא בַּאֲתַר דָּא, וַיְהִי בִּנְסֹעַ הָאָרוֹן. אֲמַאי אִתְהַדָּר לְבָתַר כִּגְווֹנָא דָּא.

127. "And it came to pass, when the Ark set forward, that Moses said..." (Bemidbar 10:35). Rabbi Elazar said: Here we must observe the letter *Nun* **נ** that is inverted, FACING backward here in two places, MEANING THE LETTER *NUN* THAT STANDS BEFORE THE PASSAGE, "AND IT CAME TO PASS, WHEN THE ARK SET FORWARD..." AND AFTER IT. Why? One may think THAT IT ALLUDES to a bent *Nun*, as it is known that a bent *Nun* is female, MEANING MALCHUT, and the straight *Nun* includes both male and female, WHICH ARE ZEIR ANPIN AND MALCHUT. We explained here THE BENT *NUN*, ABOUT WHICH IS SAID: "and it came to pass, when the Ark set forward, THAT MOSES SAID, 'RISE UP, HASHEM'"; THAT ON THE BENT *NUN* HE SAID, "RISE." YOU MAY SAY THAT THIS IS THE REASON, BOTH *NUN'S* WERE WRITTEN INVERTED, but IF SO, WHY WERE THEY turned again TO FACE FACING BACKWARD in this manner **נ**?

128. ת"ח, נ בְּאַשְׁרֵי יוֹשְׁבֵי בֵיתֶךָ לָא אִתְּמַר, בְּגִין דְּהִיא בְּגָלוּתָא. וְהָא אוֹקְמוּהָ חַבְרַיָּיא דִּכְתִיב נָפְלָה לֹא תוֹסִיף קוּם בְּתוּלַת יִשְׂרָאֵל וְגוֹ'. אֶלָּא מַה כְּתִיב לְעֵילָא, וַאֲרוֹן בְּרִית יְיָ' נוֹסֵעַ לִפְנֵיהֶם דֶּרֶךְ שְׁלֹשֶׁת יָמִים לָתוּר לָהֶם מְנוּחָה כֵּיוָן דַּהֲוָה נָטִיל אֲרוֹנָא, נו"ן נָטִיל עֲלֵיהּ, וְהָא

שְׁכִינְתָּא עַל גַּבֵּי אֲרוֹנָא יָתִיב. ת"ח, חֲבִיבוּתָא דְקוּדְשָׁא בְּרִיךְ הוּא
לְגַבַּיְיהוּ דְיִשְׂרָאֵל, דְּהָא אע"ג דְּאִינּוּן סָטָאן מֵאֹרַח מֵישָׁר, קוּדְשָׁא
בְּרִיךְ הוּא לָא בָּעֵי לְשַׁבְקָא לוֹן, וּבְכָל זִמְנָא אַהְדַּר אַנְפּוֹי לְקַבְלַיְיהוּ,
דְּאִי לָאו הָכִי לָא יְקוּמוּן בְּעָלְמָא.

128. Come and behold: no *Nun* is mentioned in THE ALPHABETICAL PRAISE, "happy are they who dwell in Your house" (Tehilim 84:5) because THE *NUN*, WHICH IS MALCHUT, is in exile. The friends have explained it, since it is written about her: "the virgin of Yisrael is fallen; she shall no more rise..." (Amos 5:2). However, it is written above: "and the Ark of the Covenant of Hashem went before them in the three days' journey, to search out a resting place for them" (Bemidbar 10:33). As soon as the Ark traveled, the *Nun* was traveling above it, THAT IS MALCHUT, since the Shechinah was residing on the Ark. Come and behold the love of the Holy One, blessed be He, for Yisrael. Even though they diverged from the straight path, the Holy One, blessed be He, did not wish to forsake them. He always turns His face back to them, for had it not been so, they would never have been able to survive in the world.

129. ת"ח, אֲרוֹנָא הֲוָה נָטַל קַמַּיְיהוּ אֹרַח תְּלָתָא יוֹמִין, נ לָא הֲוָה
מִתְפְּרַשׁ מִנֵּיהּ, וְנָטִיל עִמֵּיהּ. וּמִגּוֹ רְחִימוּ דִּלְהוֹן דְּיִשְׂרָאֵל, אַהְדַּר אַנְפּוֹי
וְאִסְתְּחַר מִלְּגַבֵּי אֲרוֹנָא, כְּהַאי אַיָּילָא דְּעָזָלְתָּא, כַּד אִיהוּ אָזִיל, אַהְדַּר
אַפּוֹי לַאֲתָר דְּנָפִיק. וע"ד בִּנְסוֹעַ הָאָרֹן, נו"ן אַסְחַר אַנְפִּין לְקַבְלַיְיהוּ
דְּיִשְׂרָאֵל, וְכַתְפֵי גוּפָא לְגַבֵּי אֲרוֹנָא.

129. Come and behold: the Ark was moving before of them on a three day journey. The *Nun*, INDICATING THE SHECHINAH, traveled along and did not leave it. Due to their love for Yisrael, He turned his face back TO YISRAEL, and She turned HERSELF around from the Ark – similar to a young deer that keeps turning her face back to the place she left when she goes forth. Therefore, when the Ark set forth, the *Nun* turned its face back towards Yisrael and the shoulders of its body towards the Ark.

130. וע"ד כַּד אֲרוֹנָא הֲוָה נָטִיל, מֹשֶׁה אָמַר קוּמָה יְיָ', לָא תִשְׁבּוֹק לוֹן,

אַהֲדַר אַנְפּוֹהּ לְגַבָּן, כְּדֵין נוּ"ן אִתְהַדַּר לְגַבַּיְיהוּ כְּגַוְונָא דָא כְּמַאן
דִּמְהַדַּר אַנְפֵּיהּ לְמַאן דִּרְחִים, וְכַד הֲוָה שָׁארֵי אֲרוֹנָא לְמִשְׁרֵי, כְּדֵין
אַהֲדַר נוּן אַנְפּוֹי מִיִּשְׂרָאֵל, וְאִתְהַדַּר לְגַבֵּי אֲרוֹנָא, וּבְכֹלָּא אִתְהַדַּר.

130. Therefore, when the Ark traveled, Moses said, "Rise up, Hashem," MEANING: 'Do not forsake us, but turn Your face toward us.' Then the *Nun* turned its front backward to us like this ꗄ, like one who turns his face to someone whom he loves. When the Ark began to rest, it turned back its face from Yisrael and turned ITS FACE toward the Ark. And it turned it completely.

131. אָמַר ר' שִׁמְעוֹן, אֶלְעָזָר, וַדַּאי הָכִי הוּא, אֲבָל הָכָא לָא אַהֲדַר
אַנְפּוֹי מִיִּשְׂרָאֵל, דְּאִי הָכִי בָּעֵי נוּן לְאִתְהַפְּכָא מִגַּוְונָא דְּאַחֲרָא עִלָּאָה,
הַאי מְנוּזַר לַאֲחוֹרָא, וְהַאי בְּאֹרַח מֵישָׁר לְגַבֵּי אֲרוֹנָא.

131. Rabbi Shimon said: Elazar, certainly it is like that, THAT THERE NEED TO BE TWO *NUN'S*, INVERTED, PRECEDING AND FOLLOWING, AS YOU SAID. However, FOLLOWING THE VERSE: "AND IT CAME TO PASS, WHEN THE ARK SET FORWARD," MALCHUT did not turn her face away from Yisrael, MEANING THAT SHE DID NOT CEASE TO PPOUR HER BOUNTY FROM YISRAEL, AS RABBI ELAZAR SAID. If it had been so, then the *Nun* THAT IS WRITTEN would have been inverted like another *NUN* above, WHICH IS THE SECRET OF MALCHUT. This *Nun* is kept backwards, TOWARD YISRAEL, and that SUPERNAL one, WHICH IS MALCHUT, is in a straight line with the Ark, MEANING THAT SHE IS UNITED WITH ZEIR ANPIN. SINCE SHE IS PAIRED WITH ZEIR ANPIN, THEN MOST CERTAINLY SHE FACES YISRAEL AND NOT LIKE RABBI ELAZAR SAID.

132. אֶלָּא וַדַּאי לָא אַהֲדַר אַנְפּוֹי מִנַּיְיהוּ, וּמַה עָבִיד בְּשַׁעֲתָא דְּשָׁארֵי
אֲרוֹנָא לְמִשְׁרֵי. אָמַר מֹשֶׁה שׁוּבָה יְיָ', כְּדֵין שָׁארֵי אֲרוֹנָא, וּשְׁכִינְתָּא
קָאֵים בְּסִטְרָא אַחֲרָא, וְאַנְפִּין לָקָבְלַיְיהוּ דְּיִשְׂרָאֵל, וְלָקָבְלֵיהּ דַּאֲרוֹנָא.
וּכְדֵין כֹּלָּא כָּלִיל לְגַוֵּוהּ, לַאֲרוֹנָא, וּלְיִשְׂרָאֵל. אֶלָּא דְּיִשְׂרָאֵל גַּרְמוּ
לְבָתַר, דִּכְתִיב וַיְהִי הָעָם כְּמִתְאוֹנְנִים.

132. It is definitely so THAT MALCHUT did not turn her face back FROM YISRAEL. What did she do when the Ark began to rest? Moses then said: "Return, Hashem" (Bemidbar 10:36), MEANING CEASE FROM THE ILLUMINATION OF CHOCHMAH AND RETURN TO THE ILLUMINATION OF CHASSADIM OF ZEIR ANPIN. Then the Ark stayed, MEANING IT RESTED, and the Shechinah stood on the other side, MEANING ON THE RIGHT SIDE. She turns THAT face toward Yisrael and to the Ark, MEANING THAT SHE FACES THE ARK TO RECEIVE CHASSADIM FROM IT, AND FACES YISRAEL TO BESTOW THEM WITH CHASSADIM THAT SHE RECEIVES FROM THE ARK OF THE COVENANT. Everything is then contained in Her, both the Ark and Yisrael. Only later, Yisrael caused MALCHUT TO TURN HER BACK ON THEM, as is written: "and when the people complained" (Bemidbar 11:1). THEREFORE, THE *NUN* ֆ IS INVERTED BETWEEN THE VERSES: "AND IT CAME TO PASS, WHEN THE ARK SET FORWARD," AND, "AND WHEN THE PEOPLE COMPLAINED."

133. אָמַר רִבִּי אֶלְעָזָר, אֲנָא דְּאָמָרָן מִסִּפְרָא דְּרַב יֵיבָא סָבָא, דְּאָמַר דְּבֵין בְּהַאי גִּיסָא, וּבֵין בְּהַאי גִּיסָא, אִתְהַדָּר. אָ״ל, שַׁפִּיר קָאָמַר, אֲבָל דָּא דַּאֲמֵינָא, הָכִי תִּשְׁכַּח בְּסִפְרָא דְּרַב הַמְנוּנָא סָבָא, וְהָכִי הוּא וַדַּאי.

133. Rabbi Elazar said: Whatever I said is derived from the book of Rabbi Yeba Saba (the elder), who said that THE *NUN* IS FACING backwards on both sides of the verse. PRECEDING, "AND IT CAME TO PASS, WHEN THE ARK SET FORWARD," THE FACE IS TURNED TO YISRAEL, AND FOLLOWING, "WHEN THE ARK..." IT REVERSES, TURNING ITS FACE TOWARDS THE ARK AND ITS BACK TOWARDS YISRAEL. He said to him that he said it properly, THAT THE WRITING OF THE *NUN'S* SHOULD BE SO. However, what I said, THAT IT TURNED ITS BACK TO YISRAEL, IS NOT DUE TO THE REASON OF REST BUT RATHER DUE TO THE REASON OF THE FOLLOWING VERSE: "AND WHEN THE PEOPLE COMPLAINED." You will find this in the book of Rav Hamnuna Saba (the elder), and it is most definitely so.

23. "Now the manna was like coriander seed"

A Synopsis

Rabbi Yosi gives two explanations of why the manna was like coriander seed.

134. וְהָמָן כִּזְרַע גַּד הוּא. אָמַר רִבִּי יוֹסֵי, לְקַיְּימָא זַרְעָא וְחֵילִין בְּאַרְעָא, כד"א גָּד גְּדוּד יְגוּדֶנּוּ. מַה זַרְעָא דְּגָד נַטְלֵי חוּלְקֵיהוֹן בְּאַרְעָא אַחֲרָא, כָּךְ מָן שַׁרְיָא עֲלַיְיהוּ דְּיִשְׂרָאֵל, לְבַר מֵאַרְעָא קַדִּישָׁא.

134. "Now the manna was like coriander (Heb. *gad*) seed" (Bemidbar 11:7). Rabbi Yosi said: "GAD SEED" HAS THE SAME MEANING AS, "RAIDERS (HEB. *GEDUD*)," NAMELY to establish seed and armies in the land, as it is written: "Gad, shall gather a regiment" (Beresheet 49:19). As the seed of Gad took their portion in another land, MEANING ACROSS THE JORDAN RIVER, the manna similarly descended to rest on Yisrael outside the Holy Land, NAMELY IN THE DESERT.

135. ד"א כִּזְרַע גַּד הוּא. כְּזַרְעָא דְּגָד חִוּוּרָא, וְאִקְפֵּי כַּד נָחִית לַאֲוִירָא, וְאִתְבְּלַע בְּגוּפָא, וְהָא אוּקְמוּהָ חַבְרַיָּיא. וְעֵינוֹ כְּעֵין הַבְּדוֹלַח, כְּהַהוּא בְּדוֹלְחָא דְּאִיהוּ חִוָּור, כְּגַוְונָא דִימִינָא דִּלְעֵילָּא.

135. Another explanation: "like coriander seed," means LIKE A TYPE OF coriander seed that is white and freezes when it comes down through the air, and is absorbed in the body. The friends have already explained this. "And its color was like the color of bdellium" (Bemidbar 11:7), which is like that crystal that is white, similar to the right above, WHICH IS CHESED AND IS REFERRED TO AS 'WHITE'.

24. "Kill me, I pray You, out of hand"

A Synopsis

Rabbi Shimon tells Rabbi Yitzchak that Moses was addressing the place where death prevails; he was speaking to the Tree of Death, thus he used the feminine form of "You." God granted him his wish to die by not letting him enter the Holy Land. It is therefore ill advised for a person to curse himself when he is angry because his curse will come true. Rabbi Shimon points to Moses' total humility, and that he ascended over all the elevated prophets.

136. אָמַר רִבִּי יִצְחָק, מַאי שְׁנָא דְּאָמַר מֹשֶׁה בְּמִלָּה דָּא לְעֵילָא כְּנוּקְבָא, דִּכְתִיב אִם כָּכָה אַתְּ עוֹשֶׂה לִי, אַתְּ, אַתָּה מִבְעֵי לֵיה. אֶלָּא לַאֲתָר דְּמוֹתָא שָׁארֵי בֵּיה קָאָמַר, וְהַהוּא אֲתָר דְּנוּקְבָא אִיהוּ. בְּגִין כָּךְ אָמַר הָרְגֵנִי נָא הָרוֹג, וְדָא אִילָנָא דְּמוֹתָא. וְהָא אוּקִימְנָא דְּבְאִילָנָא דְּחַיֵּי לָא שַׁרְיָיא בֵּיה מוֹתָא. וע"ד אִתְהַדָּר לְגַבֵּי אִילָנָא דְּמוֹתָא וְאָמַר אַתְּ, וְלָא אָמַר אַתָּה, וְהָכִי מִבְעֵי לֵיה.

136. Rabbi Yitzchak said: What is the difference here, why did Moses speak before, as if talking to a female, as written: "and if You (fem.) deal thus with me" (Bemidbar 11:15), USING THE FEMININE GENDER? He should have used the masculine term. HE RESPONDS: He was referring to the place where death prevails, and that area is of the female, MEANING MALCHUT. Therefore, he said: "kill me, I pray You, out of hand" (Ibid.) since this is the Tree of Death, and we have already explained that there is no death in the Tree of Life, ZEIR ANPIN. THEREFORE, HE COULD NOT POSSIBLY SAY TO IT, "KILL ME, I PRAY YOU, OUT OF HAND." He consequently turned HIMSELF AWAY FROM THE TREE OF LIFE and spoke to the Tree of Death, MALCHUT, saying, "You (fem.)," and did not use a masculine gender. That was how he was supposed to say it, SINCE MALCHUT IS A FEMALE.

137. מִיָּד וַיֹּאמֶר יְיָ' אֶל מֹשֶׁה אֶסְפָה לִי שִׁבְעִים אִישׁ וְגוֹ'. א"ל קוּדְשָׁא בְּרִיךְ הוּא, אַתְּ בָּעֵי מוֹתָא בְּכָל זִמְנָא, הֲרֵי לָךְ, וְאָצַלְתִּי מִן הָרוּחַ וְגוֹ'. ת"ח, דְּהָכָא יָדַע מֹשֶׁה דְּאִיהוּ יָמוּת, וְלָא יֵיעוּל לְאַרְעָא, דְּהָא אֶלְדָּד וּמֵידָד מִלָּה דָּא הֲווֹ אַמְרֵי.

137. Immediately, "Hashem said to Moses, 'Gather to Me seventy men...'" (Ibid. 16). The Holy One, blessed be He, said to him: 'You ask for death all the time, so here, have it.' "And I will take of the spirit..." (Ibid. 17). Come and behold: here, Moses became aware that he would die and would not be able to enter the Holy Land, since Eldad and Meidad prophesied this.

138. עַל דָּא, לָא לִבְעֵי לֵיהּ לֶאֱינָשׁ, בְּשַׁעֲתָא דְּרוּגְזָא שָׁארֵי בֵּיהּ, לְלַטְיָיא גַּרְמֵיהּ. דְּהָא כַּמָּה קַיְימֵי עֲלֵיהּ דִּמְקַבְּלֵי הַהִיא מִלָּה. בְּזִמְנָא אוֹחֲרָנָא דְּבָעָא מִיתָה, לָא קַבִּילוּ מִנֵּיהּ. בְּגִין דְּכֹלָּא לְתוֹעַלְתָּא דְּיִשְׂרָאֵל הֲוָה. הַשְׁתָּא לָאו אִיהוּ, אֶלָּא מִגּוֹ רוּגְזָא וְדוֹחֲקָא, וּבג״כ קַבִּילוּ מִנֵּיהּ. וע״ד אִשְׁתָּאֲרוּ לְבָתַר אֶלְדָּד וּמֵידָד, וְאָמְרוּ דָא, דְּמֹשֶׁה יִתְכְּנִישׁ, וִיהוֹשֻׁעַ יֵיעוּל לוֹן לְיִשְׂרָאֵל לְאַרְעָא.

138. Therefore, it is ill advised for a person to curse himself when he is angry, since many ADVERSARIES are standing by to accept such speeches, MEANING THAT HIS CURSE WILL COME TRUE. At another time, WHEN MOSES requested death AT THE EPISODE OF THE GOLDEN CALF, SAYING, "BLOT ME, I PRAY YOU, OUT OF YOUR BOOK WHICH YOU HAVE WRITTEN" (SHEMOT 32:32), they did not accept it from him because it was all for the benefit of Yisrael. This time, he said it out of pressure and anger, and therefore they accepted. Therefore, Eldad and Meidad remained IN THE CAMP and said that Moses would be gathered to his people and Joshua would usher Yisrael into the land.

139. ובג״כ אָתָא יְהוֹשֻׁעַ לְגַבֵּי מֹשֶׁה, וְקַנֵּי עֲלֵיהּ דְּמֹשֶׁה. וּמֹשֶׁה לָא אַשְׁגַּח בִּיקָרָא דִּילֵיהּ. וע״ד אָמַר, אֲדֹנִי מֹשֶׁה כְּלָאֵם. מַאי כְּלָאֵם. מְנַע מִנְּהוֹן אִינּוּן מִלִּין, כד״א וַיְכֻּלֵּא הָעָם מֵהָבִיא. וַיִּכָּלֵא הַגֶּשֶׁם מִן הַשָּׁמָיִם. מְנִיעוּתָא מַמָּשׁ. וּמֹשֶׁה לָא בָּעָא. פּוּק חָמֵי עַנְוְותָנוּתֵיהּ דְּמֹשֶׁה, מַה כְּתִיב הַמְקַנֵּא אַתָּה לִי וְגוֹ׳. זַכָּאָה חוּלָקֵיהּ דְּמֹשֶׁה, דְּאִיהוּ סָלִיק עַל כֻּלְּהוּ נְבִיאֵי עִלָּאֵי. אָמַר רִבִּי יְהוּדָה, כָּל שְׁאַר נְבִיאִין לְגַבֵּי מֹשֶׁה, כְּסִיהֲרָא לְגַבֵּי שִׁמְשָׁא.

139. Therefore, Joshua came to Moses and was zealous for Moses, but Moses was not concerned about his own honor. Consequently, JOSHUA said: "my master, Moses, restrain them" (Bemidbar 11:28). What is meant by, "restrain them"? It means to hold them from such speeches, SO THAT THEY WILL NOT COME TRUE, as it says, "so the people were restrained from bringing" (Shemot 36:6), and, "the rain from heaven was restrained" (Beresheet 8:2). THE MEANING OF, "WAS RESTRAINED," is actual restraining, but Moses did not wish to. Come and behold the humility Moses had. It is written: "envy you for my sake..." (Bemidbar 11:29). Praised is Moses's lot, in that he ascended above all the elevated prophets. Rabbi Yehuda said: All the other prophets in relation to Moses are like the moon in relation to the sun.

25. "Yet the Elohim does not give him power to eat of it"

A Synopsis

The rabbis discuss how hard-hearted people are in that they pay no attention to the matters of the higher world. Rabbi Shimon says that one eats in this world the fruits that he merits, and the capital, his soul, is kept for him in the higher world so that he can gain with it the higher life above. But for whoever contaminates himself and does not deprive his soul or body of anything, the Tree of Life is not available for him to eat from. Rabbi Aba says that when Moses saw that the people complained about the manna he saw that this blemished his own perfection and he could not bear to see his own wretchedness. It was considered that descending from a higher to a lower level was like death.

140. רִבִּי אַבָּא הֲוָה יָתִיב לֵילְיָא חַד, וְלָעֵי בְּאוֹרַיְיתָא. וַהֲווֹ עִמֵּיה ר' יוֹסֵי וְר' חִזְקָיָּה. א״ר יוֹסֵי, כַּמָה אִינּוּן בְּנֵי נָשָׁא תַּקִּיפוּ לִבָּא, דְּלָא מַשְׁגְּחֵי בְּמִלֵּי דְּהַהוּא עָלְמָא כְּלוּם. א״ר אַבָּא, בִּשְׁרָא דְּלִבָּא, דַּאֲחִידָא בְּכָל שַׁיְיפֵי גוּפָא, קָא עָבֵיד לוֹן. פָּתַח וְאָמַר, יֵשׁ רָעָה אֲשֶׁר רָאִיתִי תַּחַת הַשָּׁמֶשׁ וְרַבָּה הִיא עַל הָאָדָם. יֵשׁ רָעָה: דָּא אִיהִי תּוּקְפָּא בִּישָׁא דְּלִבָּא, דְּבָעֵי לְשַׁלְטָאָה בְּמִלֵּי דְּהַאי עָלְמָא, וְלָא אַשְׁגַּח בְּמִלֵּי דְּהַהוּא עָלְמָא מִדִי.

140. Rabbi Aba was sitting one night studying Torah. Rabbi Yosi and Rabbi Chizkiyah were present with him. Rabbi Yosi said: How hard-hearted are the people that they do not pay attention to that world's matters at all. Rabbi Aba said: It is the evil in the heart which infects all the organs of the body that does this to them. He opened the discussion saying, "there is an evil which I have seen under the sun, and it is heavy upon men" (Kohelet 6:1). "There is an evil"; that is the evil force in the heart that wishes to rule this world's matters and does not pay attention at all to the matters of that world.

141. אֲמַאי אִיהִי רָעָה. קְרָא דְּבַתְרֵיה אוֹכַח, דִּכְתִּיב אִישׁ אֲשֶׁר יִתֶּן לוֹ הָאֱלֹהִים עוֹשֶׁר וּנְכָסִים וְגוֹ'. הַאי קְרָא קְשִׁירָא, כֵּיוָן דִּכְתִּיב וְאֵינֶנּוּ חָסֵר לְנַפְשׁוֹ מִכָּל אֲשֶׁר יִתְאַוֶּה, אֲמַאי וְלֹא יַשְׁלִיטֶנּוּ הָאֱלֹהִים לֶאֱכוֹל מִמֶּנּוּ, דְּהָא אֵינוּ חָסֵר לְנַפְשׁוֹ כְּלוּם אֶלָּא. רָזָא אִיהוּ, וְכָל מִלּוֹי

-460-

דִּשְׁלֹמֹה מַלְכָּא, מִתְלַבְּשָׁן אִינּוּן בְּמִלִּין אַחֲרָנִין, כְּמִלֵּי דְאוֹרַיְיתָא, דְּאִינּוּן מִתְלַבְּשָׁן בְּסִפּוּרֵי עָלְמָא.

141. HE INQUIRES: Why is the heart evil? HE RESPONDS: The following verse proves this: "a man to whom the Elohim has given riches, wealth..." (Ibid. 2). This verse is difficult, since it says, "so that he lacks nothing for his soul of all that he desires" (Ibid.). Why then does it say, "yet Elohim does not give him power to eat of it" (Ibid.), seeing that he is not lacking for anything himself? HE RESPONDS: It is a secret and all of King Solomon's sayings are clothed with other words. They are like sayings of the Torah that are clothed with stories pertaining to THIS world.

142. ת"ח, אע"ג דְּבָעֵינָן לְאִסְתַּכְּלָא בִּלְבוּשָׁא, הַשְׁתָּא הַאי קְרָא הָכִי קָאָמַר, דב"נ אָזִיל בְּהַאי עָלְמָא, וְיָהִיב לֵיהּ קוּדְשָׁא בְּרִיךְ הוּא עוּתְרָא, בְּגִין דְּיִזְכֵּי בֵּיהּ לְעָלְמָא דְּאָתֵי, וְיִשְׁתְּאַר לְגַבֵּיהּ קֶרֶן. מַאי קֶרֶן. הַהוּא דְּאִיהוּ קַיָּים, דְּאִיהוּ אֲתָר לְאִתְצַרְרָא בֵּיהּ נִשְׁמָתָא. בג"כ בָּעֵי לְאַשְׁאָרָא אֲבַתְרֵיהּ לְהַאי קֶרֶן, וְהַאי קֶרֶן יְקַבֵּל לֵיהּ, בָּתַר דְּיִפּוֹק מֵהַאי עָלְמָא.

142. Come and behold: It is necessary to look at the garment, WHICH IS WORLDLY STORIES, MEANING THAT ALTHOUGH YOU CANNOT UNDERSTAND THE VERSE OUT OF ITS SIMPLE CONTEXT, this verse now says this. When a person goes about in this world, the Holy One, blessed be He, gives him riches in order to merit the World to Come, and he will have the capital OF HIS MONEY left over for himself. What is that capital? That MONEY that endures FOREVER. That is a place in which to store the soul. He therefore is required to leave behind him that capital, and this capital will be received by him after departing from this world.

143. בְּגִין דְּהַאי קֶרֶן, הוּא אִילָנָא דְּחַיֵּי דְּהַהוּא עָלְמָא, וְלָא קַיְּימָא בְּהַאי עָלְמָא, אֶלָּא הַהוּא אִיבָּא דְּנָפִיק מִנֵּיהּ, וע"ד אִיבָּא דִּילֵיהּ אָכִיל ב"נ, דְּזָכֵי בְּהַאי עָלְמָא, וְהַקֶּרֶן קַיְּימָא לֵיהּ לְהַהוּא עָלְמָא, לְמִזְכֵּי בֵּיהּ בַּחַיִּין עִלָּאִין דִּלְעֵילָא.

143. This capital is the Tree of Life of that world, WHICH IS ZEIR ANPIN, but is not present in this world, except for the fruits that come out of it. Therefore, one eats in this world the fruits that he merits, and the capital is kept for him in that world to gain with it the higher life above.

144. וּמַאן דְּסָאִיב גַּרְמֵיהּ, וְאִתְמְשַׁךְ בָּתַר גַּרְמֵיהּ, וְלֵיתֵיהּ חָסֵר לְנַפְשֵׁיהּ וּלְגַרְמֵיהּ כְּלוּם. וְהַהוּא אִילָנָא אִשְׁתְּאַר, וְלָא שַׁוְיֵה לְקַבְּלֵיהּ בִּדְחִילוּ, וּלְקַבְּלָא לֵיהּ לְעֵילָא. כְּדֵין וְלָא יַשְׁלִיטֶנּוּ הָאֱלֹהִים לֶאֱכֹל מִמֶּנּוּ, וּלְמִזְכֵּי בְּהַהוּא עוּתְרָא, וַדַּאי אִישׁ אַחֵר יֹאכְלֶנּוּ, כד"א יָכִין וְצַדִּיק יִלְבָּשׁ. בְּג"כ, בָּעֵי בַּר נָשׁ לְמִזְכֵּי, בְּמַה דְּיָהִיב לֵיהּ קוּדְשָׁא בְּרִיךְ הוּא לְהַהוּא עָלְמָא, וּכְדֵין אָכִיל מִינֵּיהּ בְּהַאי עָלְמָא, וְיִשְׁתְּאַר לְגַבֵּיהּ הַהוּא קֶרֶן לְעָלְמָא אַחֲרָא, לְמֶהֱוֵי צְרוּרָא בִּצְרוֹרָא דְּחַיֵּי. אָמַר רִבִּי יוֹסֵי וַדַּאי.

144. For he who contaminates himself and is carried away after his own GOOD, and does not deprive his soul and body of anything, that tree stays, WHICH IS ZEIR ANPIN. But he does not place it in front of him with awe, so as to receive it above. Then, "yet Elohim does not give him power to eat of it" (Kohelet 6:2), and gain this wealth. Certainly, "a stranger eats it" (Ibid.), as is written: "he may prepare it, but the just shall put it on" (Iyov 27:16). Therefore, a person needs to merit and gain in that world through that which the Holy One, blessed be He, gives him. Then he eats from it in this world, and the capital remains by him for the other world, so that he will be tied up in the bundle of life. Rabbi Yosi said: Most certainly, IT IS SO.

145. תּוּ אָמַר רִבִּי יוֹסֵי, כְּתִיב אִם כָּכָה אַתְּ עוֹשֶׂה לִי הָרְגֵנִי נָא וְגוֹ' וְכִי מֹשֶׁה דְּאִיהוּ עָנָו מִכָּל בְּנֵי עָלְמָא, בְּגִין דְּשָׁאִילוּ מִנֵּיהּ יִשְׂרָאֵל לְמֵיכַל, מָסַר גַּרְמֵיהּ לְמִיתָה, אֲמַאי. א"ר אַבָּא, הַאי מִלָּה אוֹלִיפְנָא, וְרָזָא עִלָּאָה אִיהוּ, מֹשֶׁה לָא אַבְאִישׁ קַמֵּיהּ, וְלָא שָׁאַל לְמִיתָה עַל דְּשָׁאִילוּ יִשְׂרָאֵל.

145. Rabbi Yosi also said that it is written: "and if You deal thus with me, kill me, I pray You, out of hand" (Bemidbar 11:15). HE INQUIRES: Did Moses, who was the most modest in the world, allow himself to get killed just because Yisrael were demanding from him food to eat? Why? Rabbi

Aba said: I have learned this matter and it is a great secret. Moses did not get angry for himself and did not ask to be killed on account of Yisrael's demand TO EAT MEAT.

146. ת"ח, מֹשֶׁה אִתְאֲחַד, וַהֲוָה סָלִיק בְּמַה דְּלָא אִתְאֲחַד נְבִיאָה אַחֲרָא. וּבְשַׁעְתָּא דְּאָ"ל קוּדְשָׁא בְּרִיךְ הוּא לְמֹשֶׁה, הִנְנִי מַמְטִיר לָכֶם לֶחֶם מִן הַשָּׁמַיִם. חַדִּי מֹשֶׁה וְאָמַר, וַדַּאי הַשְׁתָּא הַהוּא שְׁלִימוּ בִּי אִשְׁתְּכַח. דְּהָא בְּגִינִי אִשְׁתְּכַח מָן לְיִשְׂרָאֵל. כֵּיוָן דְּחָמָא מֹשֶׁה דְּאַהֲדְרוּ לְנַחְתָּא לְדַרְגָּא אַחֲרָא, וְשָׁאִילוּ בָּשָׂר, וְאָמְרֵי וְנַפְשֵׁנוּ קָצָה בַּלֶּחֶם הַקְּלוֹקֵל. אָמַר אִי הָכִי הוּא, הָא דַּרְגָּא דִּילִי פָּגִים. דְּהָא בְּגִינֵי יֵיכְלוּן יִשְׂרָאֵל מָן בְּמַדְבְּרָא, הָא אֲנָא פְּגִימָא, וְאַהֲרֹן פָּגִים, וְנַחְשׁוֹן בֶּן עֲמִינָדָב פָּגִים.

146. Come and behold: Moses was united above and he succeeded in matters to which no other prophet was connected. When the Holy One, blessed be He, told Moses: "Behold, I will rain bread from the heaven for you" (Shemot 16:4), Moses rejoiced and thought, 'I will now certainly acquire this perfection, since in my merit there will be manna for Yisrael.' As soon as Moses noticed that they again descended to another level and demanded meat, saying, "and our soul loathes this miserable bread" (Bemidbar 21:5), he thought, 'My level is deteriorated, since for my sake Yisrael ate manna in the desert. Now I am blemished, Aaron is blemished, and Nahshon the son of Amminadab is blemished,' SINCE AARON AND NAHSHON WERE ATTACHED TO THE RIGHT AND LEFT OF MOSES.

147. אָמַר וְאִם כָּכָה אַתְּ עֹשֶׂה לִי הָרְגֵנִי נָא הָרוֹג, דַּחֲשִׁיבְנָא נוּקְבָּא בְּמֵיכְלָא דִּילָה, וַאֲנָא נָחִית מִן שְׁמַיָּא דְּאִיהוּ דַּרְגָּא עִלָּאָה, לְנַחְתָּא לְדַרְגָּא דְּנוּקְבָּא, וַאֲנָא עָדִיף מִן שְׁאַר נְבִיאֵי עָלְמָא, וע"ד אָמַר וְאַל אֶרְאֶה בְּרָעָתִי כַּמֶּת וַדַּאי לְנַחְתָּא לְדַרְגָּא תַּתָּאָה.

147. Therefore, he said: "'And if You deal thus with me, kill me, I pray You, out of hand,'" since I have become as a female, WHICH IS MALCHUT, regarding her food, MEANING WITH THE MEAT THAT THEY WERE DEMANDING. I came down from the heaven that a the high degree,

MEANING ZEIR ANPIN, DUE TO THE FACT THAT THEY LOATHED THE
BREAD OF HEAVEN, to go down to the level of the female, TO THE
CONSUMPTION OF MEAT. YET I am superior to all prophets of the world' –
SINCE ALL PROPHETS USED 'COH' IN THEIR PROPHECY WHICH IS
FEMININE, AND MOSES USED THE TERM 'ZEH' WHICH IS ZEIR ANPIN,
REFERRED TO AS 'HEAVENS'. Therefore, he said, "and let me not see my
own wretchedness" (Bemidbar 11:15). IT WAS surely CONSIDERED like
death to descend to a lower level, SINCE DESCENDING FROM ONE LEVEL
TO THE OTHER LEVEL IS CONSIDERED FOR ONE LIKE DYING.

26. "Gather to Me seventy men"

A Synopsis

Moses was given the seventy men to assist him so that he should not become blemished and so that they would shine from his illumination. We are told that God loved Moses more than any other prophet in the world since his prophecy came without any intervention.

148. כְּדֵין וַיֹּאמֶר ה' אֶל מֹשֶׁה אֶסְפָה לִי שִׁבְעִים אִישׁ מִזִּקְנֵי יִשְׂרָאֵל. הָא אִינּוּן לְמֵיתַן לְהוּ מֵיכְלָא אַחֲרָא, וְלָא תְּהֵא פָּגִים בְּדַרְגָּא דִּילָךְ. וע"ד וְאָצַלְתִּי מִן הָרוּחַ אֲשֶׁר עָלֶיךָ וְשַׂמְתִּי עֲלֵיהֶם. מ"ט. בְּגִין דְּאִינּוּן אִתְאַחֲדוּ בְּסִיהֲרָא וּבָעֵי שִׁמְשָׁא לְאַנְהֲרָא לָהּ. וע"ד וְשַׂמְתִּי עֲלֵיהֶם, בְּגִין לְאַנְהֲרָא מִן שִׁמְשָׁא, כִּנְהוֹרָא דְּסִיהֲרָא. וּבְגִינֵי הַאי מֵיכְלָא דָּא, לָא אַתְיָיא עַל יְדָא דְּמֹשֶׁה, בְּגִין דְּלָא יִתְפְּגִים.

148. "And Hashem said to Moses, 'Gather to Me seventy men of the elders of Yisrael'" (Bemidbar 11:16). 'They are present here to be given other food,' THAT DOES NOT COME FROM HEAVEN, WHICH WAS THE LEVEL OF MOSES, 'and you will not be blemished in your level.' Therefore, "I will take of the spirit which is upon you, and will put it upon them" (Ibid. 17). What is the reason? Because they became united with the moon, WHICH IS FEMALE, and there was a need for the sun, WHICH IS THE DEGREE OF ZEIR ANPIN AND THE LEVEL OF MOSES, to illuminate upon her. Therefore, I "will put it upon them," so they will shine from the sun, BEING THE LEVEL OF MOSES, as the light of the moon THAT COMES FROM THE SUN. Hence, this food, MEAT, did not come through Moses, BUT RATHER THROUGH THE SEVENTY ELDERS, in order that he should not become blemished AND BE REQUIRED TO DECLINE FROM HIS LEVEL, AS MENTIONED.

149. זַכָּאָה חוּלָקָא דְּמֹשֶׁה, דְּקוּדְשָׁא בְּרִיךְ הוּא בָּעֵי בִּיקְרֵיהּ, עֲלֵיהּ כְּתִיב יִשְׂמַח אָבִיךָ וְאִמֶּךָ וְגוֹ'. יִשְׂמַח אָבִיךָ: דָּא קוּדְשָׁא בְּרִיךְ הוּא. וְאִמֶּךָ: דָּא כְּנֶסֶת יִשְׂרָאֵל. וְתָגֵל יוֹלַדְתֶּךָ: דָּא אִימָּא דְּמֹשֶׁה דִּלְתַתָּא. קוּדְשָׁא בְּרִיךְ הוּא רָחִים לֵיהּ יַתִּיר מִכָּל נְבִיאֵי עָלְמָא, בְּלָא, אֶמְצָעֵי כְּלָל. דִּכְתִיב פֶּה אֶל פֶּה אֲדַבֶּר בּוֹ, וְהָא אוֹקִימְנָא בְּכַמָּה אֲתָר.

149. Praised is the lot of Moses that the Holy One, blessed be He, wished his honor. About him, it is written: "let your father and your mother be glad..." (Mishlei 23:25). "...your father..." is the Holy One, blessed be He, and, "your mother," is the Congregation of Yisrael, WHICH IS MALCHUT. "And let her who bore you rejoice" (Ibid.), refers to Moses' mother below. The Holy One, blessed be He, loved him more than any other prophet in the world, SINCE HIS PROPHECY came without any intervention, as it is written: "with him I speak mouth to mouth" (Bemidbar 12:8). We have explained it in several places.

27. The Holy Name of eleven letters

A Synopsis

Rabbi Shimon tells us about the eleven letters in the Hebrew sentence, "Heal her now, El, I pray You," and says that Moses prayed such a short prayer so as not to burden God too much with his own family concerns. God wished for the glory of Moses because He always prefers the honor of the Just to His own honor. We are reminded that in the World to Come God will avenge the humiliation that was inflicted on the children of Yisrael, and he will make Yisrael happy with the gladness of Zion.

150. וַיִּצְעַק מֹשֶׁה אֶל יְיָ' לֵאמֹר אֵל נָא רְפָא נָא לָהּ. הָא אוּקְמוּהָ, וְהוּא רָזָא דִּשְׁמָא קַדִּישָׁא, מֵחַד סְרֵי אַתְוָון, וְלָא בָּעָא מֹשֶׁה לְצַלָּאָה יַתִּיר, בְּגִין דְּעַל דִּידֵיהּ לְמַלְכָּא לָא בָּעֵי לְאַטְרְחָא יַתִּיר. בְּג"כ קוּדְשָׁא בְּרִיךְ הוּא בָּעָא עַל יְקָרָא דְּמֹשֶׁה. וּבְכָל אֲתָר קוּדְשָׁא בְּרִיךְ הוּא בָּעָא עַל יְקָרֵיהוֹן דְּצַדִּיקַיָּיא, יַתִּיר עַל דִּילֵיהּ. וּלְזִמְנָא דְּאָתֵי, עָתִיד קוּדְשָׁא בְּרִיךְ הוּא לְמִתְבַּע עֶלְבּוֹנָא דְּיִשְׂרָאֵל מֵעַמִּין עכו"ם, וּלְמֶחֱדֵי לוֹן בְּחֶדְוָותָא דְּצִיּוֹן. דִּכְתִיב וּבָאוּ וְרִנְּנוּ בִמְרוֹם צִיּוֹן וְגוֹ'. וּכְדֵין וּבָא לְצִיּוֹן גּוֹאֵל וְגוֹ'.

150. "And Moses cried to Hashem, saying, 'Heal her now, El, I pray You'" (Bemidbar 12:13). This has already been explained. This is the secret meaning of the Holy Name of eleven letters, MEANING THE ELEVEN LETTERS THAT ARE IN THE WORDS "HEAL HER NOW, EL, I PRAY YOU." Moses did not wish to pray further because he did not wish to encumber the King too much with his own family. That is why the Holy One, blessed be He, delighted in the glory of Moses. The Holy One, blessed be He, always prefers the honor of the righteous to His own. In the World to Come, the Holy One, blessed be He, will avenge the humiliation that the idolatrous nations inflicted on Yisrael, and He will make Yisrael happy with the gladness of Zion, as is written: "therefore they shall come and sing in the height of Zion..." (Yirmeyah 31:11). Then, "to Zion a Redeemer shall come..." (Yeshayah 59:20).

NOTES